ENVIRONMENTAL LAW & POLICY IN INDIA

ENVIRONMENTAL LAW & POLICY IN INDIA

Cases and Materials

Third Edition

SHYAM DIVAN
ARMIN ROSENCRANZ

OXFORD
UNIVERSITY PRESS

OXFORD
UNIVERSITY PRESS

Great Clarendon Street, Oxford, OX2 6DP,
United Kingdom

Oxford University Press is a department of the University of Oxford.
It furthers the University's objective of excellence in research, scholarship,
and education by publishing worldwide. Oxford is a registered trade mark of
Oxford University Press in the UK and in certain other countries

Third Edition published in 2022

Published in the United States of America by Oxford University Press
198 Madison Avenue, New York, NY 10016, United States of America

British Library Cataloguing in Publication Data
Data available

Library of Congress Control Number: 2021951955

ISBN 978–0–19–286545–8 (hbk.)
ISBN 978–0–19–287183–1 (pbk.)

DOI: 10.1093/oso/9780192865458.001.0001

In memory of

Anil B Divan

1930 – 2017

Exemplary Lawyer and Father

PREFACE

In June 2006, I moved base from Mumbai to practice before the Supreme Court in New Delhi. I had hoped that the slack in practice during this transition would unlock the time required to complete the third edition. Not so. The unlearning required of a High Court practitioner adjusting to a 'green top' wicket allowed little room for academic pursuits. The writing, largely confined to court vacations, stretched over years. Fortuitously, the global pause imposed by the Covid -19 pandemic provided the chance to complete this volume. So here we are, a decade past the ETA.

The book is addressed to anyone with an interest in Indian law or the environment. This includes law faculty and students, the Indian judiciary, public interest lawyers undertaking to defend India's environment, government officials responsible for any of the subjects covered in this book, members of environmental organisations, and members of the public with an interest in environmental protection.

The flood of material now available at the tap of a touchscreen, demands deeper analysis and ruthless selectivity. Each chapter describes the legal framework for the topic, projects regulatory trends and inquires whether the law has helped attain the goals of government policy, assuming there is a discernible policy at all. To assist the reader, most chapters open with a snapshot of the regulatory contours. An interplay of cases and materials encourages critical thinking on the state of the law. The endeavour throughout is to stimulate the student of law to probe every topic and anticipate the controversies she will face in court.

The rapid proliferation of internet-based research tools has diminished the utility of textbooks in a practitioner's hunt for precedent. Nevertheless, alive to the litigator's needs, the usual student analysis is supplemented with an occasional dive into courtroom dynamics. We have sifted the coarser material from the previous editions and introduced several new chapters and topics of contemporary concern.

The authors attempt to address Indian environmental law, policy, problems and needs with the comprehensiveness and rigour of an American law casebook. The approach of this book may be unfamiliar to some readers. It relies on the case method, which has been the general method of instruction in American law and business courses for several decades. The premise of the case method is that by understanding the dynamics of current cases, one can understand both the state of the law in a given subject and the directions that courts are likely to take in the foreseeable future. Another benefit of the case approach is that students are encouraged, indeed expected, to think critically and analytically about the various strategic elements in a case and in the court's decision.

Each section of the book is interlaced with notes, comments and questions. The questions are designed to provoke further inquiry – and there are no easy answers. The questions are also intended to acquaint lawyers and future lawyers with the kinds of arguments that they will need to construct for themselves and rebut from their opponents in legal actions concerning the environment.

The book is both policy-oriented and practice-oriented. Environmental values are often assessed in relation to economic costs and benefits. The reader's attention may be directed to the political, social and economic circumstances that led to the adoption of a specific law or administrative ruling, as well as the political, social and economic circumstances that have often led to their non-implementation or circumvention.

Amongst the joys of practicing as a counsel, untethered from the rigidity of a law firm, is the bonhomie that develops amongst chamber colleagues. Since the last edition was published, what is known (discretely) as the Buttons and Trotsky chambers, has had dozens of denizens. Conversations with and research by my colleagues have enriched this volume in manifold ways. My thanks for friendship and mental ping pong over the years to Farzad Damania, Vicky Singh, Prashant Bhagwati, Vivek Menon and Kiran Desai at Mumbai and the Delhi complement of Dhruv Sanghvi, Vasuman Khandelwal, Rakesh Sinha, Ashish Giri, Nirman Sharma, Abhinav Malhotra, Avishkar Singhvi, Krishna Kedia, Aayush Agarwala, Udayaditya Banerjee, Akshay Puranik, Samiksha Godiyal, Govind Manoharan, Vinayak Bhandari, Sanam Tripathi, Ria Singh Sawhney, Sudipto Sircar, Anshula Laroiya Bakhru, Adith Deshmukh and Shreeyash Lalit.

My colleague Sugandha Yadav deserves special thanks. Her many talents sharpened the arguments and tightened the draft chapters as they emerged. She commenced her searching scrutiny as an intern and continued to deploy her exacting standards as a full member of our chambers.

My thanks to the many interns who helped with the research – you may discover traces of your contributions in this final offering.

My dear friend, co-author and the pioneer of this project Dr Armin Rosencranz would like to thank his colleagues at Jindal Global University: Kanika Jamwal, Prathik Kathikeyan, Shubham Janghu and Pratik Kumar.

My secretaries Farzana Shaikh at Mumbai and Naveen Rai at Delhi have been extraordinarily supportive in this venture for over a decade. My thanks to them and thank you Emma Slaughter and Caroline Quinnell for enhancing this work through your valuable editorial suggestions.

Madhavi, who cannot be out-worked, out-friended or out-lawyered is my model on how to balance academic pursuits, litigation and so much else. Thank you and especially our daughters, Avanti and Devaki, for all the encouragement and for lending so much joy to the journey.

While all these people, and most of all our supportive families, deserve our praise and thanks, the two co-authors are alone responsible for the book's failings.

The book profiles Indian environmental law as on 1 January 2022.

The inter-disciplinary nature of environmental law braids ecology, technology, ethics, community needs and legal principles in the search for justice in each individual case.

Enjoy the exploration.

Shyam Divan
New Delhi
July 2022

FROM THE PREFACE TO THE 2ND EDITION

Early in 1983, I received a letter from Professor P Leelakrishnan inviting me to an international weekend seminar on air and water pollution at the University of Cochin. I replied that 13,000 miles was a long way to go to take part in a seminar; but if he wanted me for a semester, I would certainly consider it. One thing led to another and I was granted a Fulbright award to teach environmental law at the University of Cochin, followed by a month of lectures at the University of Poona. My course in environmental law was one of the first such courses to be taught in India. Before I left India in 1984, the Ford Foundation asked me to submit a proposal for a book on Indian environmental law. Eventually I was awarded a grant from Ford, India to organize such a book. For several years I worked with R Sudarshan, the extraordinarily able assistant director of Ford, India during the 1980s.

I was very fortunate to find, through mutual colleagues, a recent LLM graduate of the law school at the University of California, Berkeley, Shyam Divan. The first edition of *Environmental Law and Policy in India* came out in 1991, and went through two supplementary printings. It seemed to fill a need within the community of law students, law teachers, practising lawyers and judges, as well as environmental activists.

After four years had passed, and after accepting another Fulbright professorship to teach the National Law School of India's first environmental law course in 1992, Shyam and I entered into discussions with Ford program officers Jeff Campbell and Maja Daruwala. This led to a new grant to prepare a thoroughly revised and updated second edition. We all agreed that the second edition would pay special attention to equity issues, and to the environmental problems of the urban and rural poor. This edition has been in preparation for five years.

ARMIN ROSENCRANZ
Stanford, California
January 2001

FROM THE PREFACE TO THE 2ND EDITION

ACKNOWLEDGEMENTS

The authors acknowledge the following publishers and authors for permissions to reprint excerpts from books and periodicals cited.

Academic Foundation and the Heritage and Environment Protection Association for Shyam Chainani, *Nhava & Sheva, Battling for the Environment: Oil, Ports and The Coastline* (2012).

Aleph Book Company for Valmik Thapar, Romila Thapar & Yusuf Ansari, *Exotic Aliens: The Lion and the Cheetah in India* (2013) and Valmik Thapar, *Saving Wild India: A Blueprint for Change* (2015).

Asienhaus for Hans Dembowski, *Taking the State to Court, Public Interest Litigation and The Public Sphere in Metropolitan India* (2001).

Basic Books, an imprint of Hachette Book Group, Inc. for Steven M Wise, *Rattling the Cage: Toward Legal Rights for Animals* (2000).

Bloomsbury Publishing Plc for Shibani Ghosh, *The Environment* in *Regulation in India: Design, Capacity, Performance* (Ed. Devesh Kapur & Madhav Khosla, 2019, Hart Publishing) and Patrick McCully, *Silenced Rivers: The Ecology and Politics of Large Dams* (1996, Zed Books).

Cambridge University Press for Anuj Bhuwania, *Courting the People – Public Interest Litigation in Post-Emergency India* (2017); D Dileep Kumar & C Jayakumar, *From Precautionary Principle to Nationwide Ban on Endosulfan in India* 4 Business and Human Rights Journal 343 (2019) and Gitanjali Nain Gill, *Mapping the Power Struggles of the National Green Tribunal of India: The Rise and Fall?* 7 Asian Journal of Law and Society 85 (2020).

The Centre for Science and Environment (CSE) for Banjot Kaur, *Namami Gange: 5 Reasons Why Ganga Will Not Be Clean by 2020*, Down to Earth, 15 October 2018; Shambhavi Shukla & Tanushree Ganguly, *Unacknowledged Health Risk* in *State of India's Environment* (2019); Anumita Roychowdhury, *Connecting the Dots in State of India's Environment* (2020) and Darryl D'Monte, *Temples or Tombs? Industry Versus Environment: Three Controversies* 57 (1985).

Cochin University for M K Prasad, *Silent Valley Case: An Ecological Assessment*, 8 Cochin University Law Review 128 (1984).

Edward Elgar Publishing Ltd for Nupur Chowdhury & Nidhi Srivastava, *The National Green Tribunal in India: Examining The Question of Jurisdiction*, 21 (2) Asia Pacific Journal of Environmental Law 190 (2018).

Elsevier for Dilnavaz S Variava, *The Saving of the Silent Valley: A Case Study of Environmental Education in Action* in *The Environment and Science and Technology Education* (Ed. A V Baez, *et al*, 1987).

Gautam Bhatia for *Natural Justice at the Bar of the Supreme Court* 5 November 2019.

Georgetown International Environmental Law Review for Kelly D Alley, *Legal Activism and River Pollution in India*, 21 Georgetown International Environmental Law Review 793 (2009).

HarperCollins Publishers India Private Limited for Kartik Shanker, *From Soup to Superstar: The Story of Sea Turtle Conservation Along the Indian Coast* (2015).

The Hindustan Times for Navroz Dubash & Sarath Guttikunda, *Delhi Has a Complex Air Pollution Problem*, 21 December 2018.

India International Centre for Darryl D'Monte, *Storm Over Silent Valley*, 9 India International Centre Quarterly 288 (1982).

The Indian Express for Medha Patkar, *Drowned by The Dam*, 7 October 2017.

Jairam Ramesh for his lecture, *The Two Cultures Revisited: Some Reflections on the Environment-Development Debate in India* (11th ISRO-JNCASR Satish Dhawan Memorial Lecture, 28 September 2010).

Japanese Association for South Asian Studies for Shinya Ishizaka, *The Anti Tehri Dam Movement as a New Social Movement and Gandhism* 18 Jr of The Japanese Assn for South Asian Studies 76 (2006).

Kunta Lahiri-Dutt for *Water, Women and Rights* in *Water and The Laws in India* (Ed. Ramawamy R Iyer, 2009).

Live Law for Ritwik Dutta, *How the Finance Act 2017 Cripples National Green Tribunal*, 7 July 2017.

National Academy of Sciences of the United States of America for Anne Guerry, *et al*, *Natural Capital and Ecosystem Services Informing Decisions: From Promise to Practice* (2015).

Oxford University Press for Madhu Sarin, *Undoing Historical Injustice: Reclaiming Citizenship Rights and Democratic Forest Governance through the Forest Rights Act* in *Democratizing Forest Governance in India* (Eds. Sharadchandra Lele & Ajit Menon, 2014); Shyam Divan, *Public Interest Litigation* in *Oxford Handbook of the Indian Constitution* (2016); Victor Mallet, *River of Life, River of Death: The Ganges and India's Future* (2017) and Lavanya Rajamani, *Public Interest Environmental Litigation in India: Exploring Issues of Access, Participation, Equity, Effectiveness and Sustainability* 19 Jr of Envir Law 1 (2007).

Penguin Random House India for Abhinav Chandrachud, *Supreme Whispers: Conversations with Judges of the Supreme Court of India: 1980–89* (2018); Sunita Narain, *Conflicts of Interest: My Journey Through India's Green Movement* (2017) and Pranay Lal, *Indica: A Deep Natural History of the Indian Subcontinent* (2016).

Permanent Black for Mahesh Rangarajan, *The Raj and the Natural World the Campaign against 'Dangerous Beasts' in Colonial India, 1875–1925* in *India's Environmental History: Colonialism, Modernity and the Nation* (Ed. M Rangarajan and K Sivaramakrishnan, 2014).

Phillippe Cullet for *Human Rights and Displacement: The Indian Supreme Court Decision on Sardar Sarovar in International Perspective*, 50 International and Comparative Law Quarterly 973 (2001).

Ramachandra Guha for *How Much Should a Person Consume?* (2006).

SAGE Publications for Usha Ramanathan, *A Word on Eminent Domain* in *Displaced by Development–Confronting Marginalisation and Gender Injustice* (Ed. Lyla Mehta, 2009).

The Sameeksha Trust for reproductions from the Economic and Political Weekly (EPW) from M V Nadkarni, *Poverty, Environment, Development – A Many Patterned Nexus*, 35 EPW 1184 (2000); Kanchi Kohli & Manju Menon, *The Nature of Green Justice*, 47 EPW 19 (2012); Bhagirath Behera & V Ratna Reddy, *Environment and Accountability: Impact of Industrial Pollution on Rural Communities*, 37 EPW 257 (2002); R B Bhagat, *Migration, Gender and Right to The City*, 52 EPW 35 (2017); E A S Sarma, *Saga of Sompeta: Public Deception, Private Gains*, 45 EPW 38 (2010); Vandana Asthana, *Forced Displacement: A Gendered Aanalysis of the Tehri Dam Project*, 47 EPW 96 (2012); Ramaswamy R Iyer, *Linking of Rivers: Judicial Activism or Error?* 37 EPW 4595 (2002); Ramaswamy R Iyer, *Interlinking of Rivers: A Plea to The Government*, 49 EPW 16 (2014); Hans Dembowski, *Courts, Civil Society and Public Sphere: Environmental Litigation in Calcutta*, 34 EPW 49 (1999); R Seenivasan, *Judiciary and The Destruction of Chennai's Wetlands*, 51 EPW 17 (2016) and Geetanjoy Sahu & Ritwick Dutta, *The Green Tribunal in India After 10 Years – From Ascendancy to Crisis*, 56 EPW 60 (2021).

University of Chicago Press for Amitav Ghosh, *The Great Derangement: Climate Change and the Unthinkable* (2016).

The Wire for Ria Singh Sawhney & Sugandha Yadav, *Of the Classes of Environmental Regulation, Grasslands are Poorest of the Poor*, 29 September 2019; Ritwick Dutta, *The Many Absurdities of the Supreme Court Judgment on Goa's New Airport,* 8 April 2020 and Hans Dembowski, *How an Unresolved Contempt Case Has Kept a Scholarly Book off the Shelves for 15 Years*, 21 February 2016.

SUMMARY CONTENTS

TABLE OF CONTENTS

COMMON ABBREVIATIONS

Air Act	Air (Prevention and Control of Pollution) Act of 1981
AQI	Air Quality Index
Bhopal Act/ Bhopal Gas Leak Disaster Act	The Bhopal Gas Leak Disaster (Processing of Claims) Act of 1985
C&D waste	construction and demolition waste
CAFA	Compensatory Afforestation Fund Act of 2016
CEC	Central Empowered Committee
CETP	common effluent treatment plant
CITES	Convention on International Trade in Endangered Species of Wild Fauna and Flora
CPCB	Central pollution control board
CRZ	Coastal Regulation Zone
CVCA	critical vulnerable coastal area
CZMP	coastal zone management plan
EAC	Expert Appraisal Committee
EC	environmental clearance
EIA	environmental impact assessment
EPA	Environment (Protection) Act of 1986
EPR	Environment (Protection) Rules of 1986
EPCA	Environment Pollution (Prevention and Control) Authority for the National Capital Region
ESA	Ecologically Sensitive Area
ETP	effluent treatment plant
FAR	floor area ratio
FCA	Forest (Conservation) Act of 1980
Forest Act	Indian Forest Act of 1927
FRA/Forest Rights Act	Scheduled Tribes and other Traditional Forest Dwellers (Recognition of Forests Rights) Act of 2006
FSI	floor space index
HTL	high-tide line
ICMR	Indian Council for Medical Research
ICRZ	Island Coastal Regulation Zone
IPZ	Island Protection Zone
IUCN	International Union for Conservation of Nature
JFM	joint forest management
JNPT	Jawaharlal Nehru Port Trust
KIADB	Karnataka Industrial Area Development Board
LTL	low-tide line
MMRDA	Mines and Minerals (Regulation and Development) Act of 1957
MoEF	Ministry of Environment, Forest and Climate Change
MSW	municipal solid waste
NBA	National Biodiversity Authority
NBWL	National Board for Wild Life
NCR	National Capital Region
NCS	National Conservation Strategy and Policy Statement on Environment and Development of 1992

NCT	National Capital Territory
NEERI	National Environmental Engineering Research Institute
NEP	National Environmental Policy of 2006
NGO	non-governmental organization
NGT	National Green Tribunal
NGT Act	National Green Tribunal Act of 2010
Noise Rules	Noise Pollution (Regulation and Control) Rules of 2000
NPV	Net Present Value
NTCA	National Tiger Conservation Authority
PCB	pollution control board
PIL	public interest litigation
PLIA	The Public Liability Insurance Act of 1991
PLP Act	Punjab Land Preservation Act of 1900
R&R	relief and rehabilitation
RFCA	Right to Fair Compensation and Transparency in Land Acquisition, Rehabilitation and Resettlement Act of 2013
R&R	resettlement and rehabilitation OR relief and rehabilitation
SEIAA	State Environmental Impact Assessment Authority
SPCB	state pollution control board
STP	sewage treatment plant
SWM	solid waste management
TDR	transferrable development rights
ToR	Terms of Reference
TTZ	Taj Trapezium Zone
UCC	Union Carbide Corporation
UCIL	Union Carbide of India Limited
UT	Union Territory
Water Act	Water (Prevention and Control of Pollution) Act of 1974
Wetlands Rules	Wetlands (Conservation and Management) Rules of 2017
Wild Life Act	Wild Life (Protection) Act of 1972

TABLE OF CASES

Page numbers in italics indicate excerpts

1

INTRODUCTION

A. ENVIRONMENTAL REGULATION SINCE 2000: AN OVERVIEW

I. THE PLASTIC COW

On a searing day at Karuna Society's animal hospital at Puttaparthi in Andhra Pradesh, Dr Narendra Reddy Mittapalli used his practised hands to conduct a rumenotomy. Slicing open the cow's stomach, his surgical team wielded scalpels to cut through a hard mass of foreign matter that sat in the cow's belly. The clumps were removed, the digestive juices that drained during the surgery were returned to the stomach and the vertical incision stitched before the animal was led away to rest. The rumenotomy yielded 61 kgs of plastic waste that had choked the digestive tract of the distressed animal.

By October 2011, Karuna's animal hospital documented 53 rumenotomies and in each case the cow had ingested huge quantities of plastic. Across India, plastic trash bags are used for disposing of kitchen waste in open garbage locations. To reach what is in the bags, cows and other animals chew and swallow the plastic. Cows that roam India are plastic cows.

Karuna's local lobbying succeeded in persuading the Anantpur municipal corporation to ban plastic bags and remove open garbage bins that attracted stray cattle. Teaming up with other animal rights activists, Karuna opened its animal shelter to the press, helped prepare a documentary film and then petitioned the Supreme Court.[1]

Marshalling material on the plastic pollution problem, the petitioners sought directions to prohibit the use, sale and disposal of plastic bags; require door-to-door collection of garbage in municipal areas; and phase out of the 'open garbage disposal system' in vogue. The petitioners demanded improved implementation of existing laws for municipal solid waste disposal.

Initially, the Supreme Court responded enthusiastically, permitting the petitioners to 'make an additional prayer for total ban on the use of plastic of all kinds or evolution of an appropriate mechanism for collection of plastic of all forms in different parts of the country'.[2] The case gained momentum when the court appointed an Expert Committee to report on the plastic waste problem in Rajasthan.[3] At a subsequent hearing a new bench of the Supreme Court reversed course. The court now appeared more intent on scoring a 'disposal' rather than grappling with the contentious issues raised by the proposed ban. Four years after it entertained the case and without considering the committee's report, the Supreme Court issued an insipid order, content to push the matter back to the executive:

---

1 *Karuna Society for Animals and Nature v Union of India*, Writ Petition (C) No. 154 of 2012, Supreme Court of India.

2 *Karuna Society for Animals and Nature v Union of India* MANU/SCOR/42215/2012, order dated 7 May 2012.

3 *Karuna Society for Animals and Nature v Union of India* (2015) 2 SCC 355.

Environmental Law & Policy in India. Shyam Divan and Armin Rosencranz, Oxford University Press.
 DOI: 1093/oso/9780192865458.003.0001

> After hearing the learned counsel for the parties and perusing the prayers made in the petition and the material evidence produced for our perusal, it is evident that the situation is very alarming but it is not for this Court to monitor the functioning of concerned authorities & local authorities to see that the areas of the local self government are not polluted. Accordingly, we direct the Union of India and the State Governments to consider the prayers in the petitions and take all necessary steps in the matter in accordance with law by constituting committees consisting of competent persons who have got sufficient knowledge on the subject matter.... The petitioners are at liberty to give their suggestions to the concerned authorities and approach concerned statutory authorities/Tribunal in case of violation of statutory provisions in accordance with law.[4]

Karuna's representations were ignored by the government. Plastic pollution continues. The unfulfilling journey of the *Plastic Cow* case provides a paradigm of India's unpredictable regulatory landscape.

II. THE REGULATORY STEW

On the surface, India's extensive environmental regulations comprise statutes that adopt command and control strategies backed by penal sanctions. What sets apart this legal regime from others is the distinctive and indeed, disproportionate role of judges and citizens in making the law work. For all the legislations and intricate rules, India's environmental laws are largely ineffective. The agencies responsible for implementing these laws have a feeble capacity to administer, a faint grasp of societal requirements and no resolve to match the performance of regulators elsewhere in the world. For over three decades, citizens have been compelled to petition the courts (and more recently, the National Green Tribunal) to secure enforcement of black letter laws and push the state to adopt global best practices. As a result, we have in India a regulatory stew of ample legislation, patchy enforcement and *ad hoc* judicial directions.

How does this work? Not predictably. When an entrepreneur seeks to establish a new industry or expand an existing facility, her concerns should be addressed by running down a check list: permissions required for the project, the processes involved in seeking these permissions and guidance on the time required to secure clearance. In addition, an environmental lawyer in India must advise on imponderables such as the course of public interest litigations (PILs) and the array of judicial pronouncements in the course of these cases. The enterprise may confront judicial orders passed in litigation concerning forests or mining, for instance. This regulatory uncertainty adds to the legal risk and discourages investments.

Throughout 2015, a slew of media reports despaired of Delhi's foul air quality, labelling India's capital as the most polluted city in the world. Despite an arsenal of legislation and empowered pollution control agencies, none in the government responded to combat the crisis. Yet again, three decades after the public-spirited lawyer, M C Mehta initiated a PIL to control vehicular emissions,[5] the judiciary was called in to fill the governance gap. Identifying diesel emissions as a probable culprit, the Supreme Court sealed off Delhi from trucks that transited through the metropolis, imposed an environment compensation charge on vehicles bringing in city supplies and issued assorted directions including a temporary ban on the sale of luxury diesel vehicles.[6] The Delhi High Court *suo motu* issued independent orders requiring the government to devise a time-bound action plan to clean the air.[7] The National Green Tribunal

---

[4] *Karuna Society for Animals and Nature v Union of India* (2016) 14 SCC 303.

[5] *M C Mehta v Union of India*, Writ Petition (C) No. 13029 of 1985.

[6] *M C Mehta v Union of India* (2016) 4 SCC 269, order dated 16 December 2015.

[7] *Court on its Own Motion (Air Pollution in Delhi) v Union of India*, Writ Petition (C) No. 1346 of 2015, order dated 3 December 2015.

(NGT) supplied a third prong of directions dealing with traffic congestion and construction activity dust.[8] This judicial litany was the best that the system could offer a choking citizenry.[9]

More generally, the judicial creep into aspects of governance is propelled by the asymmetry in knowledge, conviction and vision between the petitioning citizen and the dysfunctional state. To justify intervention, judgments of courts frequently lament the impaired formal apparatus. In the early days of PIL, what was considered as an exceptional judicial foray to stir into action a slothful government department, has now become a routine exercise. Where the official regulator fails, impatient citizens leverage their broadly interpreted 'right to life' by petitioning constitutional courts and the NGT.

In 2009, the Centre for Science and Environment published a report exposing the capacity constraints that plagued environmental regulators in India and prevented them from effectively discharging their functions.[10] Although there was considerable variation across the states, the report showed why India has failed to build effective institutions for implementing environmental laws.

Here are a few striking facts drawn from the report: (a) In some states, the chairpersons of the pollution control boards (PCBs) were changed so frequently that their effectiveness was curbed by a lack of experience on the job. Uttar Pradesh changed 24 chairpersons in as many years and Haryana changed the chairpersons 26 times between 1974 and 2009.[11] (b) In Karnataka, 60% of the sanctioned staff positions were not filled. The vacancies in the West Bengal PCB stood at 24%, while 32% of the positions remained vacant in Chhattisgarh.[12] (c) The functions of PCBs are technical in nature involving monitoring of pollution by industries. However, over half the staff employed in several industrialized states had no technical qualification. Consequently, with the spread of industrialization, the technical staff had to bear ever greater workloads.[13] (d) The low level of technical staff meant that the employees had very little time to monitor industries.[14] (e) The state PCBs did not collect a sufficient number of samples to assess compliance and effectiveness of treatment facilities installed.[15] (f) Most of the boards did not have the requisite staff to handle legal cases. The Chhattisgarh board operates without a single legal officer.[16] (g) Most of the boards had no training or capacity-building programmes to update the knowledge of employees and improve their skills.[17] (h) The civil society organizations surveyed found corruption to be a major problem in the boards.[18] The study found that the PCBs were generally perceived in poor light by the public and this lack of public confidence harmed institution building.[19]

---

8 *Vardhaman Kaushik v Union of India* MANU/GT/0238/2015. Original Application No. 21 of 2014, order dated 7 April 2015.

9 Though air pollution is severe across several Indian cities, the Supreme Court's benevolent eye has thus far focused on its immediate neighbourhood, leaving citizens beyond the National Capital Region to fend for their own health.

10 Centre for Science and Environment, *Turnaround: Reform Agenda for India's Environmental Regulators* (2009).

11 *Id.* at page 4.

12 *Id.*

13 *Id.* at page 6.

14 *Id.* at page 7. 'The average number of inspections per industry per year remains very small for almost all the boards. For example, the officials of Maharashtra PCB and Karnataka State PCB had not been able inspect all the industries within their jurisdiction even once during 2001–02 and 2005–06. The average number of inspections per industry for these boards is less than one for the entire duration mentioned above.' *Id.* at page 18.

15 *Id.* at page 20.

16 *Id.* at page 24.

17 *Id.* at page 27.

18 *Id.* at page 36. Himachal Pradesh was an exception and received a favourable assessment.

19 *Id.* at page 41.

III. THE JUDGE AS REGULATOR: TREND-LINES

As Indians work their Constitution with increasing confidence, the competition over the sub-continent's natural resources intensifies. Individuals, communities and groups using the tools of an open society—the media, the right to access official information, public demonstrations and the courts—strive to protect the environment. Arrayed against citizens and far more sophisticated in gaming the system are corporations, bureaucracies and political decision-makers. The contest to wrest control over land, forests, minerals, water and the commons is continuous and the nation's constitutional courts must chart the guiding principles to accommodate these competing interests.

Straddling the dispute resolution machinery is the Supreme Court and at a rung below, the High Courts in the states. The NGT, conceived with great promise under a law passed in 2010,[20] plays a supplementary role as adjudicator. The judges of these constitutional courts are the final arbiters of environmental disputes. But that is not all. Their role in spurring the evolution of Indian environmental law has been a journey without parallel in world environmental jurisprudence. Since the 1980s, these judges have not only resolved individual cases between citizen and the state, but have also shaped the contours of environmental policy. They refine judicial principles and infuse life into sterile statutes that were (and still are) assiduously ignored by an ineffectual bureaucracy.

The body of case law developed since the watershed tragedy of December 1984, at Bhopal, is testament to the judiciary's response to the massive ecological degradation that threatened and continues to threaten the quality of life across the nation. But this great surge of judicial energy directed at advancing environmental sensitivity in society may be dissipating. There is no immediate danger of the judges dropping the ball. But burdened by arrears and a faint self-realization that the judiciary cannot indefinitely administer the sub-continent's resources, there appears to be a drift towards judicial restraint. Judicial fatigue may have replaced the reformist zeal which once characterized the higher judiciary's approach in many sprawling public interest litigations that dominated the environmental docket. The courts continue to expound lofty principles but seldom apply them with a rigour that would tangibly benefit the affected communities. The final shape of judicial directions is frequently akin to a hedge-trimming exercise, snipping off a few stray vines here and there, whilst preserving intact the project clearance. The unwritten premise of judicial balancing dressed up as 'sustainable development' is that economic growth must continue unimpeded.

This 'hands off' approach is likely to strengthen. The emerging environmental challenges confronting India in the spheres of climate change, water management, energy and so on, are fraught with complex technical, economic, social and political choices. The Supreme Court was able to dictate the national environmental agenda throughout the 1990s because the executive was remiss in enforcing laws already on the statute book and slow to evolve environmental policies in matters requiring an urgent response. The most egregious instances of widespread air and water pollution by industry were sought to be contained. Although a lack of vision and resources continues to hobble the working of most enforcement agencies, the thicket of socio-economic and technical complexities that characterize emerging issues will likely deter judges from embarking on fresh and elaborate public interest litigations. The stimulus for the next generation of regulation and reform will come from India's international obligations as the global community works towards adapting to climate change and the growing national economy integrates with the world. These factors, together with the

---

[20] Section 3, The National Green Tribunal Act of 2010.

clout of business lobbies more than an activist judiciary, will decide the frame and content of new environmental laws.

There is clear evidence of warming on the Indian sub-continent in the twentieth century and this trend is expected to accelerate in the twenty-first century. While the complexity of climate issues and our partial understanding of factors that impact climate preclude any definite prognosis, there are some clearly discernible trends. All climate models indicate that in this century, surface air temperature in India will increase between 2° and 4° C; summer temperatures in the last two decades of the twenty-first century will be higher than the highest summer temperatures observed so far; precipitation patterns will alter; agricultural yields are expected to decrease and small glaciers in the Indian Himalayas may disappear in the next 50 years. Sea-level rise is a major concern and current global estimates project that a global mean temperature increase of 1° C translates into a sea-level rise of 2.5 metres. In India, the states of West Bengal and Gujarat are most vulnerable to rising sea levels. An increase of 1 metre in the sea level will inundate 6000 kms^2 of coastal lands. In the case of neighbouring Bangladesh, a 1-metre rise in sea level will cause 17% of the land to be inundated.[21]

What this review suggests is that improved environmental governance and future challenges appear well beyond the reach of *ad hoc* judge-crafted solutions. The vision and long-term adaptation strategies that must be quickly implemented require an effective national environmental regulator, not a role-playing judge. Perhaps the answer to this puzzle lies in India's ability to work a democratic constitution. The faith in constitutionalism has meant that over the decades high constitutional functionaries—the Comptroller and Auditor General of India,[22] the Finance Commission[23] and the Election Commission of India,[24] to name a few, have built institutions that deliver. India urgently needs an effective institutional machinery to regulate its natural resources and fulfil the promise of its laws. An independent constitutional functionary responsible for the quality of the national environment may be the best replacement for an over-extended judiciary.

This brings us to a counter current that may prolong judicial oversight. Since as far back as the 1970s, when the first environmental laws were written into the statute book, India has developed only one new institution, the NGT. Institution building is essential for good governance and to promote the Rule of Law in a democratic society. Institutions foster public confidence and fair play. They systemize decision-making and rein in capricious conduct. There is no government agency at the national or state levels that has earned a reputation for responsibly administering natural resources. During this period, certain other regulators such as the Securities and Exchange Board of India (SEBI) and the Telecommunication Regulatory Authority of India (TRAI), warts and all, have successfully created an institutional framework that responds to emerging challenges and commands respect. But no such authority exists for the environment. There is a drought of competence and institutional integrity when it comes to preserving and protecting the entitlements of indigenous people and their cultures, the national forests, wetlands, surface and groundwater, air quality, the coast, marine resources and several other facets of natural resource conservation. This is probably why there appears no immediate end to the disproportionate role of judges.

---

21 J Srinivasan, *Impacts of Climate Change on India* in HANDBOOK OF CLIMATE CHANGE AND INDIA: DEVELOPMENT, POLITICS AND GOVERNANCE 29, 35 (Ed. Navroz K Dubash, 2012).

22 Article 148, Constitution of India.

23 Article 280, Constitution of India.

24 Article 324, Constitution of India.

Who should the judges trust to oversee India's forests, for instance? Perhaps what is needed after several lost decades is a powerful, independent environmental protection agency or a constitutional functionary. Until such an institution emerges, judges by default will continue to oversee the protection of the country's natural resources.

IV. STATUTORY AND JUDICIAL DEVELOPMENTS SINCE 2000

The first two decades of this century have been a busy period for environmental lawmakers as well as judges and lawyers engaged in environmental cases. We examine the major statutes and cases later in this book. Here, we flag the key developments.

By 2000, India had in place the basic building blocks for environmental regulation. On the statutory front, the pollution control framework comprised the Water Act of 1974,[25] the Air Act of 1981[26] and the umbrella Environment (Protection) Act of 1986 (EPA). The EPA, passed in the wake of the Bhopal disaster of December 1984, is the primary workhorse for issuing rules and regulations on diverse aspects of the environment. Wildlife is protected under the Wild Life (Protection) Act of 1972, and the Forest (Conservation) Act of 1980 was passed to arrest the sharp decline in forest cover. Implementation of these statutes then (as now) was poor, inviting this lament from the Supreme Court:

> If the mere enactment of laws relating to the protection of environment was to ensure a clean and pollution free environment, then India would, perhaps, be the least polluted country in the world. But, this is not so. There are stated to be over 200 Central and State statutes which have at least some concern with environmental protection, either directly or indirectly. The plethora of such enactments has, unfortunately, not resulted in preventing environmental degradation which, on the contrary, has increased over the years.[27]

From the mid-1980s, the Supreme Court refused to remain a spectator to environmental deterioration and piloted efforts to improve statutory compliance. Amongst the sprawling PILs launched during this period (and some of which still continue) were actions to protect the Taj Mahal,[28] clean the River Ganga,[29] protect Doon Valley[30] and conserve forests.[31] In that period, the Supreme Court laid the groundwork for future developments in environmental law by setting out guiding principles such as the polluter pays principle, the precautionary principle, intergenerational equity and the public trust doctrine.

Since 2000, Parliament has enacted three major environmental laws: the Scheduled Tribes and Other Traditional Forest Dwellers (Recognition of Forest Rights) Act of 2006, the National Green Tribunal Act of 2010 and the Biodiversity Act of 2002.[32]

The Scheduled Tribes and Other Traditional Forest Dwellers (Recognition of Forest Rights) Act of 2006 is popularly called the 'Forest Rights Act' (FRA). The FRA seeks to right a

---

25 Water (Prevention and Control of Pollution) Act of 1974.

26 Air (Prevention and Control of Pollution) Act of 1981.

27 *Indian Council for Enviro-Legal Action v Union of India* (1996) 5 SCC 281, 293.

28 *M C Mehta v Union of India* (*Taj Trapezium*) AIR 1997 SC 734; 2010 (2) Scale 20; 2019 (17) Scale 344; (2018) 9 SCC 658; 2019 (17) Scale 332.

29 *M C Mehta v Union of India (Kanpur Tanneries)* AIR 1988 SC 1037; *M C Mehta v Union of India (Municipalities)* AIR 1988 SC 1115; *M C Mehta v Union of India (Calcutta Tanneries)* (1997) 2 SCC 411.

30 *Rural Litigation and Entitlement Kendra v State of Uttar Pradesh (Dehradun Quarrying)* AIR 1985 SC 652; AIR 1988 SC 2187.

31 *T N Godavarman Thirumulpad v Union of India* AIR 1997 SC 1228; AIR 1998 SC 769; (2006) 1 SCC 1; (2014) 6 SCC 150.

32 At the time of writing, a Presidential Ordinance was promulgated named the Commission for Air Quality Management in National Capital Region and Adjoining Areas Ordinance of 2021. As the title suggests, the Ordinance constitutes a commission to tackle the poor air quality in and around Delhi.

historical wrong by which tribal communities were alienated from their land by colonial laws which continued post Independence. The Act recognizes the entitlement of tribals and tribal communities over forest land on which they are traditionally dependent. The FRA also confers title on 'other forest dwellers' where a person can show that she or her ancestor has occupied the forest land for 75 years. While the benefits conferred by the Act are long overdue and far reaching, the legal sanction granted to permanent settlements ignores potentially devastating impacts on wildlife as well as the forests.

The second game changer is the National Green Tribunal Act of 2010. With this law, India entered a select band of nations that have established judicial fora for environmental adjudications. The NGT comprises judicial members as well as experts qualified in environmental sciences. It is chaired by a retired Justice of the Supreme Court. The NGT sits in benches in five cities across the country and is mandated to apply the principles of sustainable development, the precautionary principle and the polluter pays principle. The Tribunal may entertain applications for relief and compensation from victims of pollution including environmental accidents, it may award damages and require restoration of the damaged environment. It also exercises appellate jurisdiction with respect to statutory permissions and clearances granted to industry under pollution control laws as well as with respect to environmental impact assessment.

The NGT, unlike its predecessors, has been the most consistent and progressive environmental authority in India. It has been fairly successful in expanding the circle of environmental protection through liberal interpretations, taking *suo motu* cognizance of issues and being guided by expert panels to deal with scientific uncertainty. In many of its decisions, it has imposed large damages awards that are likely to curb pollution generally.

The third law is the Biodiversity Act of 2002, enacted to meet India's international obligations under the Convention on Biological Diversity (Rio de Janeiro, 1992). The law provides a framework for the use of biological resources and the sharing of benefits arising from their use.

Apart from these Parliamentary statutes, the MoEF has issued a vast number of rules and regulations under the Environment (Protection) Act of 1986. The rules chart new territory in fields such as noise pollution,[33] regulation of ozone-depleting substances,[34] and wetlands.[35] The rule-making power was also exercised to replace older rules with more evolved versions in the fields of solid waste management,[36] biomedical waste[37] and plastic waste.[38] The ministry also replaced the environmental impact assessment (EIA) regime in 2006[39] and issued fresh regulations in 2011 and 2019 to protect the coast.[40]

The Supreme Court's record since 2000 is a mixed bag. The first major environmental judgment rendered by the Supreme Court after 2000 was the split verdict clearing the decks for completion of the Sardar Sarovar Dam on the River Narmada.[41] This case has set the tone for other challenges to large projects. Indeed, in a judgment that could severely undermine

[33] Noise Pollution (Regulation and Control) Rules of 2000.
[34] Ozone Depleting Substances (Regulation and Control) Rules of 2000.
[35] Wetlands (Conservation and Management) Rules of 2017.
[36] Solid Waste Management Rules of 2016.
[37] Bio-Medical Waste Management Rules of 2016.
[38] Plastic Waste Management Rules of 2016.
[39] EIA notification of 14 September 2006.
[40] Coastal Regulation Zone (CRZ) notification of 6 January 2011 was replaced by CRZ notification of 18 January 2019.
[41] *Narmada Bachao Andolan v Union of India* (2000) 10 SCC 664.

ecological integrity of the sub-continent, destroy vast swathes of forests and uproot communities, the Supreme Court has mandated, *suo motu*, a grand nationwide river inter-linking scheme.[42]

On the positive side, the Supreme Court in 2002 required all buses in Delhi to be powered by compressed natural gas, a much cleaner fuel than diesel.[43] The court also helped to control rampant illegal mining activity that was destroying the environment and forests in Karnataka,[44] Odisha[45] and Goa.[46] Likewise, the Supreme Court was steadfast in recognizing the rights of the tribal community in the Niyamgiri Hills in western Odisha, despite enormous bauxite reserves awaiting exploitation.[47]

The social scientist Dr Geetanjoy Sahu surveyed the Supreme Court's environmental judgments between 1980 and 2010. He found that in a majority of the cases the weaker parties such as public interest environmental groups and citizens and environmental groups prevailed over organizationally strong parties such as the Central Government and state governments and industry. He attributes the success of the underdog to a proactive judiciary in the post-Emergency period, the pro-environment philosophy of several judges, the exceptional commitment of citizens' groups and lawyers who brought the cases and the indifference of government departments to implementing statutory mandates.[48]

B. ENVIRONMENT, DEVELOPMENT AND DEMOCRACY

This section carries two readings on the space that a democracy offers to officials and citizens keen on promoting development while protecting the environment. The first perspective is provided by Jairam Ramesh, the former Union Minister of Environment and Forests. The second piece is by the economist Dr M V Nadkarni.

In his lecture Ramesh notes the contribution of the economist Nitin Desai, whose compact definition of 'sustainable development' was adopted in the Brundtland Report:[49] 'Sustainable development is development that meets the needs of the present without compromising the ability of future generations to meet their own needs.' Building on this theme, he explains the dynamics of decision-making in a democracy.

JAIRAM RAMESH; THE TWO CULTURES REVISITED: SOME REFLECTIONS ON THE ENVIRONMENT-DEVELOPMENT DEBATE IN INDIA, 11th ISRO-JNCASR Satish Dhawan Memorial Lecture, 28 September 2010

Over half a century ago, while giving the Reith Lectures over the 122 BBC, the eminent British physicist-author C P Snow spoke of how the breakdown of communication between the 'two cultures' of modern society—the cultures of the science and that of the humanities—was becoming a hindrance to understanding and addressing pressing public issues.

---

42 *Networking of Rivers, In Re* (2012) 4 SCC 51.
43 *M C Mehta v Union of India* (2002) 4 SCC 356.
44 *Samaj Parivartan Samudaya v State of Karnataka* (*Bellary* case) (2013) 8 SCC 154.
45 *Common Cause v Union of India* (2017) 9 SCC 499.
46 *Goa Foundation v Union of India* (2014) 6 SCC 590.
47 *T N Godavarman Thirumulpad v Union of India* (2008) 2 SCC 222; *Orissa Mining Corporation Ltd v Ministry of Environment and Forests* (2013) 6 SCC 476.
48 Geetanjoy Sahu, *Why the Underdogs Came Out Ahead: An Analysis of the Supreme Court's Environmental Judgments, 1980–2010* 49 Economic & Political Weekly 52 (2014).
49 World Commission on Environment and Development, *Our Common Future* (1987). The report is widely known after the Norwegian Prime Minister who was chairperson of the Commission.

I wish to speak of a later-day facet of these 'two cultures' syndrome—the apparent gap between those espousing the case for faster economic growth and those calling for greater attention to protection of the environment. On the face of it, there should be no gap at all—who can argue against faster economic growth since that alone will generate more jobs and at the same time who can argue against the preservation of our rivers, lakes, mountains and wonderful biodiversity in its myriad forms, since that alone will make for sustainable development. But I am afraid that the two groups are not talking to each other—they are talking at each other and with every passing day, the gap seems to be widening....

The problem lies when you go beyond 'balance' as a general philosophical concept and try and give it some operational meaning. When hard choices need to be made about large projects that are considered central to economic growth, but are detrimental to the environment. Let us all accept the reality that there is undoubtedly a trade-off between growth and environment. In arriving at decisions to untangle the trade-off, three options present themselves—'yes', 'yes but' and 'no'. The real problem is that the growth constituency is used to 'yes' and can live with 'yes but'. It cries foul with 'no'. The environment constituency exults with a 'no', grudgingly accepts the 'yes but' cries foul with a 'yes'. Therefore, one clear lesson in this—maximize the 'yes, but', where this is possible.

The vast majority of environmental and forestry clearances are in the 'yes, but' category but they do not hit the headlines like the 'yes' or the 'no' decisions do. Of course, as we gain experience, we must refine the 'but' in the 'yes but' approach. The 'but' often takes the form of conditions that must be adhered to before, during the construction, and after the launch of the project. I believe that in laying down these conditions, we must strive for three things: First, the conditions must be objective and measurable, so that it is clear what is to be done and whether it has been complied with. Second, the conditions must be consistent and fair, so that similar projects are given similar conditions to adhere to. Finally, the conditions must not impose *inordinate* financial or time costs on the proponents (which would render them impractical)....

Economists all over the world have been at work for quite some time on developing a robust system of green national accounting but we are not there as yet. Ideally, if we can report both *Gross* Domestic Product and *Green* Domestic Product, we will get a better picture of the trade-offs involved in the process of economic growth. Alternatively, as some economist[s] have argued, we need alternative indicators to measure true welfare improvement, as Green GDP is not the best indicator of sustainability or future increases in consumption or welfare—indicators such as 'Genuine Savings/Investment', and 'Genuine Wealth Per Capita' are being developed as alternatives. We don't need precise numbers. Even a broad-brush estimate will be a huge step forward to give *practical* meaning to the concept of 'sustainable development' which all of us swear by in theory....

In one of his seminal pieces published along with others including the Nobel Laureate Kenneth Arrow, he has calculated that the 'genuine' domestic investment rate in India is around 2.3 percentage points lower than the normally reckoned domestic investment rate for the period 1970–2001 after taking into account environmental costs and both calculated as a proportion of GDP. He goes on to show that as against the estimated growth rate of India per capita GDP of 2.96% per year during this period, the growth rate of per capita genuine wealth after taking into account environmental costs works out to 0.31% per year. Such analyses help put a number to the environmental cost of our growth process, making our trade-offs more explicit, and hence must be mainstreamed.

Building on Professor Partha Dasgupta's work, the World Bank has institutionalised a metric called 'Adjusted Net Savings'. This measures the 'true' rate of savings in an economy after taking into account investments in human capital, depletion of natural resources and damage caused by pollution.... Just as an example—according to the World Bank data, India's Gross National savings as a percent of GDP was around 34.3% in 2008, but its Adjusted Net Saving in the same year was 24.2%, the difference arising due to the depletion of natural resources and pollution related damages, in addition to conventionally measured depreciation of the nation's capital assets....

There is no doubt in my mind that India desperately needs to sustain a high growth trajectory for at least two–three decades. This is absolutely essential for meeting our pressing social objectives and also our key strategic objectives. At the same time, the 'growth first at all costs and environment later' approach is clearly unacceptable. India needs to press into its development all that modern science and technology has to offer. At the same time, the notion that we can impose technological fixes without caring for their larger ecological consequences and without addressing larger social concerns is clearly untenable anywhere, but even more so in an open, argumentative society like ours.

And increasingly these concerns are of the poor and the traditionally disadvantaged sections of society.... Sunita Narain puts it well when she says that India's environmental movement is about managing contradictions and complexities—and to this I would add also conflicts. This environmentalism of the poor, as she calls it or livelihood environmentalism as I would term it as opposed to lifestyle environmentalism of the privileged sections, manifested itself on the national scene first in the mid-1970s with the birth and growth of the Chipko movement in the hills of Uttarakhand. The women were asserting the right of local communities over the use of local resources.

Such assertions are visible in different parts of the country today. We misread such assertions as the conflict between environment and development when they actually are about establishing a fundamental right to livelihood security that impacts their daily lives in a profoundly disturbing manner. Such assertions are also, I may add, a product of our boisterous democracy which the growth-fundamentalists are uncomfortable with and the empowerment it has engendered. Sustainable development, we need to remind ourselves every now and then, is as much of politics and involvement of local communities as it is of innovation and new technology....

Democracy means the need to explain, the need to justify, the need to convince, the need to get people on board, the need to compromise.... I would urge the scientific community and the larger community of growth-fetishists that they have a special role to play in this regard. They need to engage the larger public in a more collegial and in a less condescending manner....

NOTES AND QUESTIONS

1. The Ministry of Environment, Forest and Climate Change (MoEF) is responsible for granting environmental clearances under the environmental impact assessment (EIA) process. It is perceived by industry as anti-development while environmentalists frequently regard the ministry as a rubber-stamp. Consistent with Ramesh's prescriptions, the MoEF generally grants conditional clearances and these conditions typically add to the project cost.

Is this a good way to do business or, indeed, regulate the environment? At its present level of infrastructure and economic development, can India afford to reject new projects? What is the green alternative?

2. An estimated 4.5 million Indians enter the job market every year. With so many aspirations amongst young job seekers, are notions of a Green Domestic Product or environmental accounting in some other form realistic notions? Will social unrest that is caused by slowing economic growth result in a backlash against environmental regulators? How can sustainable development engage with such socio-economic needs?

3. Ramesh bemoans the lack of any meaningful dialogue between environmentalists and project proponents. Is this necessarily a bad thing? What might happen should a cosy relationship develop between NGOs and industry? Are existing fora such as the electronic and print media sufficient for dialogue or do we need new platforms to debate large projects?

4. Environmental decision-making is fraught with complexity. In most situations, the need to allocate natural resources or use them in a particular manner is driven by commercial interests or developmental needs. Frequently, both these factors are closely intertwined. Even where commercial pressures are disregarded, government agencies make tough calls on how best to secure economic benefits without irreversible harm to the environment. Invariably, there are trade-offs to be made. Policies permitting unrestricted groundwater extraction for irrigation or industry could deplete underground aquifers and deprive future generations of the resource. Removal of pollutants from industrial effluents or emissions could generate solid waste and attendant challenges for its disposal. These complexities frequently make for hard choices by officials and where their decisions are tested, by courts and tribunals.

Illustrative of this complexity is India's effort to reduce air pollution from thermal power stations. On 7 December 2015, the MoEF tightened emission norms, requiring power plants to install Flue Gas Desulphurization (FGD) systems to reduce sulphur dioxide emissions. There are two types of technologies for FGD: one employs ammonia and the other is based on wet limestone. Thermal power stations across the country faced real challenges. First, they required funds for the FGD system, but the electricity regulator resisted a tariff hike. Second, the choice of technology was fraught with environmental risks. Ammonia is a hazardous substance and any process that employs ammonia has attendant health risks to factory workers and transporters. Turning to limestone, there are over 400 thermal power plants in the country and if all of them were to adopt the wet limestone technology it would mean an annual requirement of nearly 22 million tonnes of limestone. Much of the limestone in India is found in forest areas or environmentally sensitive regions. The limestone would have to be mined or imported and thereafter transported across great distances, creating a new set of environmental concerns. The wet limestone process results in large-scale production of a by-product, gypsum. Disposing of massive quantities of gypsum at the power stations will create land pollution and solid waste disposal issues.

5. In the *Lafarge* case,[50] the Supreme Court provided a perspective on the abiding contest over natural resources:

> Universal human dependence on the use of environmental resources for the most basic needs renders it impossible to refrain from altering the environment. As a result, environmental conflicts are ineradicable and environmental protection is always a matter of degree, inescapably requiring choices as to the appropriate level of environmental protection and the risks which are to be regulated. This aspect is recognised by the concept of 'sustainable development'. It is equally well settled by the decision of this Court in *Narmada Bachao Andolan v Union of India*, (2000) 10 SCC 664 that environment has different facets and care of the environment is an ongoing process. These concepts rule out the formulation of an across-the-board principle as it would depend on the facts of each case whether diversion in a given case should be permitted or not, barring 'no go' areas (whose identification would again depend on undertaking of a due diligence exercise). In such cases, the margin of appreciation doctrine would apply.
>
> Making these choices necessitates decisions, not only about how risks should be regulated, how much protection is enough, and whether ends served by environmental protection could be pursued more effectively by diverting resources to other uses. Since the nature and degree of environmental risk posed by different activities varies, the implementation of environmental rights and duties requires proper decision-making based on informed reasons about the ends which may ultimately be pursued, as much as about the means for attaining them. Setting the standards of environmental protection involves mediating conflicting visions of what is of value in human life.

50 *Lafarge Umiam Mining (P) Ltd v Union of India* (2011) 7 SCC 338, 367.

6. Decisions to allocate natural resources are seldom easy. A range of commercial interests and social objects compete for supremacy through the political system. Eventually, ministers prioritize who gets how much of what and the goals to be attained. In this context, the 'margin of appreciation' doctrine limits the scope of judicial scrutiny. The doctrine requires that where government takes a call on natural resource use after considering relevant factors and based on correct principles, the court must give sufficient latitude to the decision-maker and endeavour to uphold the decision.

In the next reading, economist Dr M V Nadkarni writes about his travels to Ralegan Siddhi in the late 1990s to meet Anna Hazare, more than a decade before Hazare attained national fame for his anti-graft campaign. Nadkarni uses the Hazare model to illustrate how sensible natural resource conservation practices at the village level can dramatically improve economic conditions. This development model contrasts (and perhaps complements) the big project model referred to in the Ramesh piece.

M V NADKARNI; POVERTY, ENVIRONMENT, DEVELOPMENT – A MANY PATTERNED NEXUS, 35 Economic & Political Weekly 1184 (2000)

The relationship between poverty, environment and development is quite complex and not amenable to easy generalisation. Within a country like India, too, there is a big diversity of patterns and situations. To capture this diversity in terms of a single perception of 'vicious circle' (poverty—environmental degradation—more poverty) would be naïve....

There is a widely held view, particularly in the west, that poverty is the main cause of environmental deterioration, because the poor are not in a position to use natural resources sustainably. This degradation in turn, it is believed leads to aggravation of poverty, suggesting the completion of the 'vicious circle' or 'poverty trap' process....

G Hardin took the case of grazing pressure on pastures or common property resources to illustrate this conceptualisation of the vicious circle in terms of what he called the 'tragedy of the commons'. The pressure on the grazing lands led to their depletion and aggravation of poverty. Cultivation on fragile mountain slope leading to soil erosion and floods is another example. Shifting cultivation with shortened fallow cycles is often viewed as being ecologically destructive....

The existence of sacred groves and 'van panchayats', which have evolved over the years to restrain indiscriminate use of forests, and that of 'pani panchayats' for managing irrigation tanks and canals is proof that rural people of developing countries had the necessary vision and ingenuity to promote sustainable—and equitable—use of resources. Case studies of such institutions have been fairly well documented. Unfortunately, such traditional institutions came under tremendous pressure owing to their subjugation by state authority and market forces, person-oriented political patronage and political encouragement to encroachment....

A special case of the poor promoting the cause of the environment at a great cost to themselves needs attention. This is the case of urban ragpickers helping waste recovery and recycling. More than half the urban workers—sometimes even 75 % of them—eke out a meagre living in informal sectors. Women and children earn particularly low incomes. Waste-picking is one occupation where women and children dominate. As poor parents almost force their children to supplement their meagre earnings, children account for the bulk of the workers engaged in waste-picking. A survey in Bangalore showed that about 8.6 % of the total waste generated and 14.4 % of the waste received is taken care of by waste-pickers....

The waste-pickers hardly ever use gloves. They operate with bare hands. A survey in Delhi showed that children suffered from several cuts to their fingers exposing themselves to tetanus, hepatitis B and other infections. Long exposure to hot sun often induces nose-bleeding. Fumes in disposal sites cause respiratory problems. Since the children operate in unhygienic surroundings, they are exposed to various diseases. Containers of chemicals expose them to chemical poisoning risks. In addition, the children are harassed and exploited by municipal workers handling waste and by police. Sometimes they are forced to pay municipal workers' 'commission' for permission to pick waste.

The waste-picker children also bear costs other than health costs—mainly the costs of deprivation. Though primary schooling is compulsory up to 14 years of age, it is difficult to enforce it among the poor even though schooling is free....

A few non-government organisations (NGOs) like Wastewise in Bangalore have tried to organise ... street children, giving them gloves and pushcarts for collecting waste from household rather than from garbage dumps. Special schooling is provided in the evening so that the children can become literate and capable of acquiring skills. Recycling is thus sought to be promoted with least personal cost to the waste-picker children....

An improvement in the natural resource environment improves the resource base of the poor and can alleviate poverty, which in turn can strengthen the capability of the poor to enrich their environment. A vicious circle, to the extent that it operates, can be turned into a virtuous circle, with the poor becoming the protectors of the environment.

This is not just an imaginary possibility. There have been many instances of rural India's ingenuity turning a vicious circle into a virtuous one, particularly when they had the benefit of inspired leadership and guidance. This is illustrated by the case of Ralegan Siddhi village, in Ahmednagar district of Maharashtra.

Ralegan Siddhi was once perpetually drought-prone and poverty stricken. Only one industry thrived there—illicit distilleries, which helped the men to forget their miseries and frustrations in the evenings, but a great cost to themselves and their families. The villagers systematically overgrazed and exploited the surrounding forests and experienced shortage of fodder and water. Agriculture and animal industry husbandry were in a poor state in the village. Most of the families lived in absolute poverty. Anna Hazare, a native of Ralegan Siddhi who had joined the army, returned to the village in 1975. In a war with Pakistan, he had the mortifying experience of seeing all the other soldiers in his group being killed. He thought that God saved him with a purpose—the purpose of helping the people of his village to overcome backwardness and misery and live with dignity. Hazare won the confidence of the villagers by renovating an old village temple, using his retirement benefits, and turning it into a centre for intra-village discussions on developmental activities. Believing that moral reconstruction was a basic prerequisite to village development, he built a youth club and placed a ban on all the distilleries and liquor shops in the village. This helped people to save money, buy more and better food and work better.

The former servicemen mobilised local people to offer 'shramdan' (voluntary physical labour) for development schemes planned by them. To the extent that the schemes needed money, he sought loans from co-operative societies and banks. He and his people rejected the idea of donations from outside and relied on their own efforts and shramdan. They took a systematic inventory of Ralegan Siddhi's natural resources and devised plans for their sustainable use and enhancement of their productivity.

One of the first steps was to regulate grazing and regenerate uncultivated lands. Treating the village watershed as a unit for planning, the villagers took up civil works for conserving soils and water and storing rain water. They built check dams and developed agro-forestry themselves. Once the grazing lands and the water storage capacity were restored, they developed animal husbandry. Cowdung was used for generating biogas, the remaining sludge being used as a manure. The village could thus have clear drinking water and enough milk not only for home consumption but also for sale in nearby cities.

Attention was also devoted to other dimensions of development: the achievement of total literacy, full enrolment in schools and adequate health care. The villagers fought social evils like dowry and the exploitation of dalits and tribal people. The weaker sections of the population were integrated into the mainstream, the equality was promoted. It has thus become a model village and a centre of development tourism. What is more, by developing an institutional base, Hazare has tried to see that the villagers depend on themselves and not on constant guidance from him....

Probably the first victims of any environmental degradation are the women among the poor. A fuelwood crisis as a result of deforestation, for example, forces village women to travel for miles in search of wood. This involves waste of energy and time which the women could have devoted to more remunerative work. Sometimes poor families starve for want of fuelwood even when foodgrains are available. In such cases the husbands sometimes thrash their women accusing them of laziness. Shortage of drinking water imposes similar hardships on women. They have to bring water for cooking and washing from great distances. Fodder scarcity also affects women first: the care of livestock is their responsibility.

This burden on women in turn has an impact on girl children. When the mothers' time is spent on fetching fuelwood and drinking water, girl children are kept at home and discouraged from attending schools. They have to look after younger children, sweep the house and do other household chores....

Vulnerability to environmental degradation induces women to become agents of eco-restoration in organized efforts. Women have taken keen interest in planting fruit, fodder and fuelwood trees around their houses and on common lands. They have played an enthusiastic role in preventing over-exploitation of forests by commercial interests. There have been instances of women, undeterred by apathy and indifference on the part of their men folk, launching struggles for protecting grazing lands and forests from disruptive developments like mining. Women's participation is valuable for improving sanitation conditions in rural areas and urban slums. Since women are so closely linked with health and the environment, they represent a constructive and protective force for the environment. They can play a crucial role in turning vicious circles into virtuous ones....

NOTES AND QUESTIONS

1. In a section of his paper excluded from the excerpt, Dr Nadkarni observes that because the poor are dependent on nature for their livelihood, they are more vulnerable to natural calamities such as floods and droughts. They lose their productive assets in these disasters and it is a long time before normal economic activity is restored. Natural disasters accentuate the link between poverty and the environment.

2. Several government policies and programmes designed to protect the environment operate harshly on the poor. The poor are hit particularly hard when they are displaced by large development projects, the shifting of polluting industries away from cities, the translocation of villages from protected areas under the Wild Life Act and beautification campaigns to clear cities of slums.

C. SPECIAL FEATURES OF ENVIRONMENTAL LAW

Environmental law cannot easily be reduced to a coherent set of principles. This is because the subject covers diverse fields each of which has its own distinct legal framework, set of stakeholders, histories, science, and other peculiarities. For instance, the framework for regulating toxic substances is very different from wildlife protection or conserving our coastline. Nevertheless, as we shall examine in this book, there are a few core values and unifying principles that bind this field: sustainable development, the 'polluter pays principle' and the imperative that industry strictly comply with procedural and substantive environmental regulations.

To put our subject in perspective, let us first understand the fundamental notions of ecology and ecosystems. Ecology is the science of how living organisms interact with each other and the physical world. It involves the study of ecosystems. An ecosystem is a complex inter-related and inter-dependent web that supports different forms of life. The greater the number of inter-dependencies, the more stable the ecosystem. Every life form fights to survive, struggles to retain its place in the ecological niche and seeks to increase its numbers and range.

The human imprint on our planet from the start of agricultural practices and the laying out of urban settlements has disrupted natural ecosystems, substituting them with new ones. The success of our species draws on the prowess of sapiens to not just adjust and adapt to different regions on the planet but to invent and harness technologies that alter the environment. A paddy field, for example, is a valuable human-designed ecosystem. It is a monoculture and the least stable amongst ecosystems. It supports not just the farmer and her family but (with other grain fields) is the edifice of human civilization. Without tending, the rice will quickly yield to more rugged and resilient plants, forming a more stable ecosystem. While changes in ecosystems occur continuously and are felt down the chain of inter-connected species, human interventions have significant impacts:

> Dramatic examples of change (in ecosystems) can be seen where man has altered the course of nature. It is vividly evident in his well-intentioned but poorly thought out tampering with river and lake ecosystems. The Aswan Dam was primarily built to generate electric power. It produced power, but it also reduced the fish population in the Mediterranean, increased the numbers of disease-bearing aquatic snails, and markedly lowered the fertility of the Nile Valley.[51]

It is well to remember at the start of our exploration of Indian environmental law that human beings are as much a part of the ecosystem as other life forms. In protecting natural ecosystems, we protect ourselves. As the natural historian Pranay Lal reminds us in his sweeping study, *Indica*:

> The drama and violence of Earth's processes is central to the creation of life because every time Earth experiences big changes, new opportunities for life open up. Even small disturbances can cause extinctions of species and sometimes lead to the collapse of entire ecosystems. It is hard to believe that since life began nearly 3.8 billion years ago, 99% of all living things that have ever lived on Earth have become extinct. What we see today is just a miniscule 1% of all life that has ever lived on Earth.[52]

Physicist Carlo Rovelli suggests that our species will not last long. He argues that we do not:

> seem to be made of the stuff that has allowed the turtle, for example, to continue to exist more or less unchanged for hundreds of millions of years; for hundreds of times longer, that is, than we have even been in existence. We belong to a short-lived genus of species. All our cousins are already extinct.[53]

In considering how a legal system might respond to protect the environment against degradation, the gaps and uncertainties in our knowledge about environmental disruption must be stressed. For example, a substance may be known to cause cancer when its fibres or particles are inhaled by workers over several years. But what if the same substance is inhaled by a worker over a short period? Should the legal system compensate the worker, even though epidemiological and toxicological data may not exist or may be confusing and uncertain with regard to short-term exposures?

51 United States Council on Environmental Quality, *Environmental Quality: First Annual Report* 6 (1970).
52 Pranay Lal, *Indica: A Deep Natural History of the Indian Subcontinent* 77 (2016).
53 Carlo Rovelli, *Seven Brief Lesson on Physics* 76 (2016).

Uncertainty also exacerbates the difficulties of those who prescribe standards for the discharge of pollutants. Most scientists believe that it is not possible to identify health effect 'thresholds' for pollutants. (A threshold is the concentration at which sensitive individuals suffer adverse health effects.) Almost any non-zero concentration of a pollutant will adversely affect some sensitive individuals. And scientists are seldom unanimous on where to draw the line. Thus, decision-makers must simply pick a particular emission or discharge standard, amidst a cloud of ambiguous evidence. This makes standard-setting for pollutants seem unsystematic and baseless.

This 'number game' in standard-setting is exemplified by the national minimum standard in respect of a parameter for industrial effluent, namely, sodium. In view of the high incidence of sodium in the natural water in some regions, the effluent parameter published in this regard was deleted from the statute before the standard was brought into force.[54]

Environmental problems are complex, not only in their causes and effects, but also in how they relate to each other. Eliminating pollution from one medium often transfers it to another. For example, when we protect the air and human health by not burning toxic chemical wastes, our alternative is usually to bury the wastes, thereby risking eventual contamination of the soil and groundwater. Frequently, it is these complexities and inter-dependencies that make environmental problems so obstinate.

The uncertainty in our understanding of environmental issues is brought out in the debate about the causes of floods in the river basins of the Ganga and Brahmaputra. During the 1980s, a number of reports[55] strengthened the perception that the floods in the sub-Himalayan plains were caused primarily by poor land use practices and deforestation by the villagers dwelling in the Himalayan foothills. This notion was challenged with an alternative view which suggests that intense rain storms, seismic activity and silt-laden rivers are inherent to Himalayan ecology and are primarily responsible for flooding that has occurred for centuries. Deforestation in the past few decades may have exacerbated the problem of flooding but was not the only cause.[56]

NOTES AND QUESTIONS

1. At the current growth rates, world population will increase from 7.8 billion to an estimated 11.2 billion at the end of the twenty-first century. The great bulk of the increase will come in poorer nations whose natural resources are already under great pressure. Productive arable land, water, energy sources and biological diversity are all depleting. Already 800 million people are undernourished and as many as 2 billion people live in poverty.

Is conservation and sustainable development the answer to the world's environmental problems? Or are these efforts futile without effective population control? Is the population problem of the global South a ploy by the developed world to deflect attention from the resource-intensive lifestyles in the North? What about similar lifestyles of the elite in the South?

---

[54] The national minimum standard in respect of sodium was notified on 19 May 1993 and was to come into effect from 1 January 1994 vide the Environment (Protection) Second Amendment Rules of 1993. It was deleted by a further amendment on 31 December 1993.

[55] E.g., N Myers, *Environmental Repercussions of Deforestation in the Himalayas*, 2 Jr Of World Forest Res Mngm 63 (1986); World Resources Institute, *Tropical Forests: A Call for Action* (1985).

[56] Centre for Science and Environment, *Floods, Flood Plains and Environmental Myths: The Third Citizens' Report* 147 (1991).

2. There are other factors—political and technological—that contribute to environmental degradation. A democratic polity may be more responsive to environmental problems than an authoritarian regime. But a democratic system has its shortcomings: governments frequently adopt short-term, populist measures unmindful of their long-term impacts. Incremental decision-making that most closely approximates the status quo is usual for a government that must win a not-too-distant election. Consequently, short-term stability is prime, while long-term stability and welfare are discounted. In such a system it is difficult to persuade a government to take unpopular measures that would benefit future generations and strengthen the long-term stability of society.

3. Despite India's noisy politics and deteriorating environment, environmental issues such as clean air, groundwater stress and forest degradation are yet to enter popular political discourse. None of the major political parties or leaders seek votes on an environmental plank. Indeed, on the most important environmental issue of our time—climate change—politicians remain mute:

> The lack of a transitive connection between political mobilization, on the one hand, and global warming, on the other, is nowhere more evident than in the countries of South Asia, all of which are extraordinarily vulnerable to climate change. In the last few decades, India has become very highly politicized; great numbers take to the streets to express indignation and outrage over a wide range of issues; on television channels and social media, people speak their minds ever more stridently. Yet climate change has not resulted in an outpouring of passion in the country. This despite the fact that India has innumerable environmental organizations and grassroots movements. The voices of the country's many eminent climate scientists, environmental activists and reporters do not appear to have made much of a mark either.
>
> What is true of India is true also of Pakistan, Bangladesh, Sri Lanka and Nepal: climate change has not been a significant political issue in any of these countries even though the impacts are already being felt across the Indian subcontinent, not only in the increasing number of large-scale disasters but also in the form of a slow calamity that is quietly but inexorably destroying livelihoods and stoking social and political conflicts. Instead, political energy has increasingly come to be focussed on issues that relate, in one way or another, to questions of identity: religion, caste, ethnicity, language, gender rights and so on.[57]

4. What are the goals of environmental law, specifically having regard to global challenges of the day? Should the object and purpose of the law transcend constitutional goals? For instance, should India enact laws that prohibit the import and use of hardwood that is sourced from the rain forests of Borneo? The devastation of those forests is destroying the habitat of several critically endangered species including the orangutan. Is that permissible?

5. What incentives and disincentives would you propose to ensure that industries adopt appropriate technologies? What role can the legal system play in regulating private actors?

6. India's poor are the ones who suffer most from deterioration and loss of the nation's precious 'commons': water, air, soil and forest. They are the first victims of poor sanitation, bad air, contaminated water and scarce wood for fuel and fodder. For millions of Indians their only wealth is common property resources, and this is threatened by environmental degradation.

7. Can a village pond be allotted for private housing? Reversing the Allahabad High Court, the Supreme Court recognized the importance of common property resources:

---

[57] Amitav Ghosh, *The Great Derangement: Climate Change and the Unthinkable* 168 (2016).

There is concurrent finding that a pond exists and the area covered by it varies in the rainy season. In such a case no part of it could have been allotted to anybody for construction of house building or any allied purposes.... It is important to notice that the material resources of the community like forests, tanks, ponds, hillock, mountain etc. are nature's bounty. They maintain delicate ecological balance. They need to be protected for a proper and healthy environment which enables people to enjoy a quality life which is the essence of the guaranteed right under Article 21 of the Constitution. The Government ... having noticed that a pond is falling in disuse, should have bestowed their attention to develop the same which would, on one hand, have prevented ecological disaster and on the other provided better environment for the benefit of the public at large. Such vigil is the best protection against knavish attempts to seek allotment in non-abadi sites.... The State ... shall restore the pond, develop and maintain the same as a recreational spot which will undoubtedly be in the best interest of the villagers. Further it will also help in maintaining ecological balance and protecting the environment in regard to which this Court has repeatedly expressed its concern. Such measures must begin at the grass-root level if they were to become the nation's pride.[58]

Similarly, in a case arising from Andhra Pradesh, the Supreme Court held that community lands which were part of a tank or water body could not be alienated by the state even where the tank may have dried or fallen into disuse.[59]

In the next reading, Anne Guerry and colleagues elaborate on Gretchen Daily's 1997 exploration of ecosystem services.[60] Daily stressed the need for policy-makers to develop institutional frameworks to protect and sustain the earth's life-support systems.

ANNE GUERRY *ET AL.*, NATURAL CAPITAL AND ECOSYSTEM SERVICES INFORMING DECISIONS: FROM PROMISE TO PRACTICE (2015)*

Ecosystems sustain and fulfil human life through 'ecosystem services.' Forested riparian buffers hold soil in place and improve water quality for people downstream; aquatic habitats support populations of fish caught for food; mangroves stabilize shorelines and decrease damage to people and property from storms; forests and oceans store carbon that helps regulate climate; lakes and mountains provide aesthetic views, opportunities for recreation, and spiritual inspiration. Ecosystem services are the conditions and processes of ecosystems that generate—or help generate—benefits for people. These benefits result from the interactions among plants, animals, and microbes in the ecosystem, as well as biotic, abiotic, and human-engineered components of social-ecological systems. Ecosystem services are produced along the full spectrum of heavily managed ecosystems (e.g., agro-ecosystems) to ecosystems with low human imprint. Ecosystem services can be final (produce benefits directly, such as seafood) or intermediate (underpinning final services; e.g., the generation of habitats that support fish populations).

The pace of research on ecosystem services has increased greatly in the last decade. Rapid innovation and proliferation of approaches have been productive, but have resulted in inconsistent and confusing use of terms. For example, the terms 'environmental services' and 'ecosystem services' are used by different authors, but the intended meaning is similar. We use 'ecosystem services' for three pragmatic reasons: it is consistent with the considerable body of literature, ... the word 'ecosystem' connotes the integration of both biotic and abiotic components, and many people equate environmental services with waste and recycling services provided by local government.

---

58 *Hinch Lal Tiwari v Kamala Devi* (2001) 6 SCC 496, 501.

59 *Sarvepalli Ramaih v District Collector, Chittoor* (2019) 4 SCC 500, 506, 512.

60 Gretchen Daily, *What Are Ecosystem Services* in NATURE'S SERVICES (1997).

* https://www.pnas.org/content/pnas/112/24/7348.full.pdf, accessed 9 July 2021.

Understanding who affects the generation of ecosystem services (called providers or suppliers) and who benefits from ecosystem services (beneficiaries or consumers) allows assessments of the costs and benefits from a given policy, including the distributional consequences across affected parties. Institutions, such as property and access rights, together with the nature of the services in question, frame the policy context and influence the set of incentives for the private and public use and provision of ecosystem services. Understanding the institutional landscape and incentive structures can inform effective management and governance. For example, carefully designed policies, such as payments for eco-system services (PES), can motivate potential ecosystem service suppliers by using payments for action, access, or maintenance of a service. Similarly, rights-based fishery management can incentivize fishers to be better stewards of the ecosystems that produce the fish they catch.

Concerns about how ecosystems will respond to climate change and other gradual or abrupt changes have led to greater efforts to understand their resilience from local to planetary scales. Natural capital with enhanced resilience has a greater ability to persist and adapt in the face of change, to continue to provide ecosystem services, and to adapt and transform in beneficial ways. This capacity of social-ecological systems to sustain natural capital and ecosystem services in the face of disturbance and on-going changes is more likely to support development pathways in changing environments where uncertainty and surprise prevail. Robust solutions that generate desired outcomes for people and nature under a wide range of potential futures can be enhanced by adopting a more integrated dynamic systems approach to understanding complex social-ecological systems. Such thinking fosters more wide-ranging contemplation of potential future outcomes and places an emphasis on adaptive governance.

NOTES

1. Occasionally, Indian courts have recognized the importance of ecosystem services. The Supreme Court prohibited mining in the ancient Aravalli mountain range since destruction of the hills and the woodlands would allow the Thar desert to creep onto Delhi.[61] The Calcutta High Court has recognized the importance of wetlands in treating waste water discharged by the city and in preventing salt water intrusion.[62]

In *Regional Deputy Director v Zavaray S Poonawala*,[63] the Supreme Court emphasized the contributions of species and the value of biodiversity.

> The impacts of biodiversity loss [translate] into fewer new medicines, greater vulnerability to natural disasters and greater effects from global warming. In nature, everything is interconnected. Unfortunately, we often have very little idea of all the repercussions involved in the disappearance of a single animal population in a corner of a forest, swamp or river. Unrecognized benefits of maintaining biological diversity are those services we receive when ecosystems function normally. These ecosystem functions include energy fixation, chemical cycling (oxygen production by rainforests), soil generation and maintenance, ground water recharge, water purification, and flood protection. These services are provided to us at no cost. When we destroy the ability of ecosystems to function naturally, we not only lose these free services but all too often have to pay to replace them.
>
> Protecting these species contributes to a thriving, healthy planet for people's health and well-being. Wildlife nurtures a sense of wonder. It is integral to maintain the balance of nature. Ultimately, by protecting these species, we save this beautiful, vulnerable and utterly

61 *M C Mehta v Union of India* (2004) 12 SCC 188; (2004) 12 SCC 118; (2009) 6 SCC 142.
62 *People United for Better Living in Calcutta v State of West Bengal* AIR 1993 Cal 215.
63 (2015) 7 SCC 347.

irreplaceable planet we call home. By protecting species, we also protect the essential goods and services that make our lives possible and contribute enormously to human health and well-being — breathable air, clean water, food, fibres, building materials, medicines, energy, fertile soils, climate regulation, transport, and recreational and spiritual values.

2. The notion of ecosystem services received statutory recognition in section 2(e) of the Compensatory Afforestation Fund Act of 2016 (CAFA):

(e) 'environmental services' includes—

(i) provisions of goods such as wood, non-timber forest products, fuel, fodder, water and provisions of services such as grazing, tourism, wildlife protection and life support;

(ii) regulating services such as flood moderation carbon sequestration and health of soil, air and water regimes;

(iii) supporting such other services necessary for the production of ecosystem services, biodiversity, nutrient cycling and primary production including pollination and seed dispersal . . .

Project proponents who seek to divert forests for development are required to pay an amount towards the 'net present value' (NPV) of the forest area diverted for non-forestry uses. The NPV is defined as the money value of the environmental services provided by the diverted forest area and this quantification is made by an Expert Committee appointed by the Central Government.[64]

Net present value payments are a part of a general global trend to factor into decision-making the value of natural capital and the ecosystem services it provides. Payments for Ecosystem Services (PES) are mechanisms to protect vulnerable habitats and species. Where the PES is high, it may prompt relocation of the project or more typically channel funds towards an eco-renewal and rehabilitation programme.[65]

3. The Wetlands (Conservation and Management) Rules of 2017 framed under the Environment (Protection) Act of 1986 expressly recognize the ecosystem services provided by wetlands including 'water storage, water purification, flood mitigation, erosion control, aquifer recharge, microclimate regulation . . .'.[66]

D. COURTS, TRIBUNALS AND THE ENVIRONMENT

Throughout this book we will see how the courts, especially the High Courts and the Supreme Court of India, have seized opportunities presented by cases to protect the environment. The National Green Tribunal, created to assume the judicial mantle, has not yet acquired the stature of a powerful institution. Judicial action must however be only one of many tools to bring about environmental improvement. In many situations, lobbying, public education and political action by mobilizing people, are far more effective mechanisms than filing a petition.

---

[64] Section 2(j), Compensatory Afforestation Fund Act of 2016.

[65] See Anne D Guerry, *et al*, *Natural Capital and Ecosystem Services Informing Decisions: From Promise to Practice* (2015) https://www.pnas.org/content/pnas/112/24/7348.full.pdf, accessed 9 July 2021; James Salzman, *et al*, *The Global Status and Trends of Payments for Ecosystem Services* (2018) https://www.nature.com/articles/s41893-018-0033-0, accessed 9 July 2021.

[66] Preamble, Wetlands (Conservation and Management) Rules of 2017.

I. FEATURES OF THE JUDICIAL PROCESS

Before we examine individual cases, there are some features of the judicial process that should be recognized. First, judges are non-specialists, relatively insulated from the political process. This has its advantages. Generalist judges have a broader vision of national policies and interests than the parochial stand of specialist government agencies charged with establishing large, environmentally disruptive, industrial and developmental projects. Moreover, since judges are not involved in electoral politics, they may be more willing than the other wings of government to take unpopular decisions that are beneficial in the long run.

A second feature of the judicial process is that it frequently compels the defendant project authority to increase environment-related spending. For example, if the location of a project is challenged in court by an environmental group, the promoters frequently spend more funds on environmental impact appraisal and pollution abatement than they otherwise might.

Third, the courts can only respond to the cases that come before them. They can rarely effect systemic or society-wide changes in environmental conditions. Finally, unlike administrative decision-making, the judicial process is more structured. Parties who are not before the court are not able to project their perspective. In contrast, administrative agencies can visit the field, interact with communities and consult experts before arriving at a decision. This is why, in court, policy implications of a case are sometimes neglected. This possibility often persuades judges to defer to the supposed expertise of governmental agencies.

II. THE HIGH COURTS AND THE SUPREME COURT

The Indian Supreme Court has a full strength of 34 judges. While almost all of them are traditionally drawn from the pool of High Court justices, there is a recent trend to appoint distinguished members from the Bar.[67] Unlike the US Supreme Court where appointment is for life and many a judge lingers on the bench well into her eighties, an Indian Supreme Court judge retires at the age of 65 years and in the High Court the guillotine falls at 62. As a result, the composition of the courts is continuously in a flux with each judge stepping on the escalator at her appointment and then rising up the judicial hierarchy. The age bar requires the judge to step off the escalator, creating an opportunity for a replacement. The institutional strength of the higher judiciary in India is that it gains from the fresh directions and dynamism that the changing composition of courts imparts. A negative factor of this churning is that judges in the Supreme Court have short tenures of around 4 years on average, leaving little scope for individuals to develop a body of coherent environmental jurisprudence.

Finally, the mix of the men and women who constitute the higher judiciary in India—is not much of a mix. Most Supreme Court and High Court judges are male and are drawn from urban, middle-class settings. Unsurprisingly, they carry onto the Bench a value system and sensibilities characteristic of that slice of society.

III. THE NATIONAL GREEN TRIBUNAL

The National Green Tribunal has both judicial as well as technical members. The technical members have expertise in the natural sciences and their knowledge is intended to enhance the quality of environmental adjudications. There is very little to show from the orders of

[67] Besides High Court Judges and advocates, Article 124(3)(c) of the Constitution of India enables the President to appoint 'a distinguished jurist' to the Supreme Court. Thus far, the power has not been exercised, prompting Prof Upendra Baxi to lament: '[B]y now a custom of the Indian constitution [is], contrary to its original intention, that *no jurist may ever be elevated to the Supreme Court*.' U Baxi, *Prof P K Tripathi: A Tribute* (2001) 5 SCC (1(J) at 10).

the NGT that the Tribunal has a deep and nuanced understanding of the subject. This may change when the NGT engages in rigorous substantive review of the agency decisions and not just procedural review, which is the norm at present.[68] The NGT is unique amongst the family of tribunals with a *sui generis* role that extends beyond adjudication of disputes to an inquisitorial role.[69]

IV. THE BAR

Environmental law is practised mostly in the NGT, the High Courts and the Supreme Court. The subject has evolved through public interest litigations filed under the constitutional jurisdictions exercised by the High Courts and the Supreme Court. The tiers of the judiciary below the High Court have a marginal role in the overall regulatory design, most of their case load being criminal prosecutions against violators.

For several decades, the Bar has made important contributions to the development of environmental jurisprudence. Between the mid-1980s and the turn of the century, the leading environmental lawyer M C Mehta, through his petitions and interim applications, set the national agenda in the fields of water and air pollution, vehicular emission control, preservation of the coast and the translocation of heavy industry away from urban areas. His example inspired several lawyers in the High Courts to pursue polluting industry and negligent enforcement agencies. In a large number of such public interest litigations, the legal assistance is rendered *pro bono* or at a nominal fee. The Supreme Court has often appointed an *amicus curiae* to assist the court in tackling complex environmental and policy issues. The most important development from the perspective of the Bar is the establishment of the National Green Tribunal with benches in five cities. This has encouraged young lawyers to develop a specialization in environmental law and spurred the formation of a dedicated Bar.

We close this chapter with an excerpt from a March 2020 Supreme Court judgment upholding an order passed by the National Green Tribunal. In 2005, the Bengaluru Development Authority formulated plans for an eight-lane peripheral ring road (PRR) around Bengaluru. An environmental clearance was granted in November 2014 but was set aside in 2019 by the NGT. The project remained unimplemented for 15 years, including a four-year period when the case was pending before the NGT.

BENGALURU DEVELOPMENT AUTHORITY v SUDHAKAR HEGDE
(2020) 15 SCC 63

DR D Y CHANDRACHUD, J:

* * *

Courts today are faced with increasing environmental litigation. A development project that was conceptualised as early as in the year 2005 has surfaced before this Court over 15 years later. The period that has led up to the present litigation has involved a myriad of decisions and processes, each contributing to the delay of a project that was outlined to subserve a salient development policy of decongesting the city. Where project proponents and institutions envisaged under the 2006 [Environmental Impact Assessment] Notification abdicate their duty, it is not only the environment that suffers a serious setback, but also the development of the nation. In the eventual analysis, compliance with the deliberative and

---

[68] In *Hanuman Laxman Aroskar v Union of India* (2019) 15 SCC 401, the Supreme Court held that the NGT was itself an expert body and was required to conduct a merit review when exercising appellate jurisdiction.

[69] *Municipal Corporation of Greater Mumbai v Ankita Sinha* (2021) SCC Online SC 897. On the functioning of the NGT see Geetanjoy Sahu & Ritwick Dutta; *The Green Tribunal in India After 10 Years—From Ascendancy to Crisis*, 52 ECONOMIC & POLITICAL WEEKLY 60 (2021).

streamlined process envisaged for the protection of the environment ensures a symbiotic relationship between the development of the nation and the protection of the environment.

The adversarial system is, by its nature, rights based. In the quest for justice, it is not uncommon to postulate a winning side and a losing side. In matters of the environment and development however, there is no trade-off between the two. The protection of the environment is an inherent component of development and growth. Professor Charles E. Corker of the University of Washington School of Law said in a speech titled 'Litigating the Environment — are we overdoing it?':

> 'My answer is yes. We are overdoing our litigation of the environment. I do not mean that there are necessarily too many lawsuits being filed on environmental issues, and that we should somehow cut back—I would not know how, in any case—the number of those suits by ten per cent, twenty per cent, or fifty per cent. I do mean that a disproportionately large share of attention, effort and environmental concern is being focused on lawsuits. Lawsuits cannot accomplish, by themselves, solutions to the most pressing of our environmental problems. As a result, we are in some danger of leaving the most pressing environmental problems unsolved—or even made worse—because the commotion of litigation has persuaded us that something has been accomplished.'

Professor Corker draws attention to the idea that the environmental protection goes beyond lawsuits. Where the State and statutory bodies fail in their duty to comply with the regulatory framework for the protection of the environment, the courts, acting on actions brought by public-spirited individuals are called to invalidate such actions. Equally important however, is to be cautious that environmental litigation alone is not the panacea in the quest to ensure sustainable development.

The protection of the environment is premised not only on the active role of courts, but also on robust institutional frameworks within which every stakeholder complies with its duty to ensure sustainable development. A framework of environmental governance committed to the rule of law requires a regime which has effective, accountable and transparent institutions. Equally important is responsive, inclusive, participatory and representative decision-mmaking. Environmental governance is founded on the rule of law and emerges from the values of our Constitution. Where the health of the environment is key to preserving the right to life as a constitutionally recognised value under Article 21 of the Constitution, proper structures for environmental decision-making find expression in the guarantee against arbitrary action and the affirmative duty of fair treatment under Article 14 of the Constitution. Sustainable development is premised not merely on the redressal of the failure of democratic institutions in the protection of the environment, but ensuring that such failures do not take place.

2

ENVIRONMENTAL POLICY IN INDIA

A. INTRODUCTION

I. WHAT IS ENVIRONMENTAL POLICY

The state has certain environmental objectives. To attain them and steer societal conduct, it enacts laws. These laws give a fair sense of where a nation would like to be in terms of its environmental quality. In addition to these laws are constitutional goals, policy documents created by government and administrative directions issued by ministries. Together, they constitute national environmental policy.

The expression 'policy' covers the object or purpose of the law as well as the legislative and administrative strategy to achieve the goal. Law and policy are intertwined. When policies evolve and the object changes, the state replaces or amends the law. This also happens when the desired goals are not being attained and new strategies are needed for enforcement. For instance, India has a policy to regulate air pollution. This takes a legal form in the Air Act of 1981[1] which seeks to assure air quality to citizens through a permit system backed by penal sanctions. In the wake of the Bhopal disaster, amendments to the Air Act in 1987 conferred new administrative power on the pollution control boards to secure compliance.[2] Protecting wildlife and their habitat is another state policy. Its statutory avatar is the Wild Life Act of 1972.[3] The Wild Life Act has been repeatedly amended to engraft new policies, including an amendment in 2006 to address the sharp decline in the tiger population.[4]

Policies may be strong or weak. To attain policy goals in India, it is imperative for a policy to be backed by statute. Otherwise, implementation becomes mired in a bog of administrative and legal challenges. While a statutory foundation is necessary, it is not by itself enough. Implementation of a policy also depends on funding of the implementing agency, the zeal and imagination of officials and the political resolve of the Minister to attain the policy goal. Policies that do not have statutory support such as those contained in government reports, administrative circulars and policy statements are weak. India's groundwater regime, examined later in this chapter, exemplifies weak policy.

Why is it important to clearly identify the extant environmental policy? The obvious answer is that it enables us to assess whether the law is working. Having a clear idea of the policy objective helps society and government to bring about changes where the law fails to deliver. Second, in a complex and multi-disciplinary field like environment, sectoral policies may

---

[1] Air (Prevention and Control of Pollution) Act of 1981.

[2] Section 31A was introduced into the parent Act by the 1987 amendment and empowered the board to issue directions to close or prohibit any industry, operation or process and stop the supply of water or electricity to the polluter.

[3] Wild Life (Protection) Act of 1972.

[4] Chapters IV-B and IV-C containing provisions for the establishment of a National Tiger Conservation Authority and the constitution of a Tiger and Other Endangered Species Crime Control Bureau were inserted into the parent Act by the Wild Life (Protection) (Amendment) Act of 2006.

Environmental Law & Policy in India. Shyam Divan and Armin Rosencranz, Oxford University Press.
 DOI: 1093/oso/9780192865458.003.0002

come into conflict. A clear articulation of priorities helps resolve these conflicts before they reach a court. For instance, highways that slice through sanctuaries and national parks destroy the integrity of protected areas and disrupt corridors used by animals. Which policy prevails: road construction or wildlife conservation? Can both objectives be reconciled? Third, political and bureaucratic maneuvering can undermine the policy underlying a law. A clear idea of the legislative policy can help bring back on the rails a poorly administered statute. This is illustrated by the willful neglect (often connivance) by municipal officials in enforcing city building regulations and zoning plans. The ostensible state policy is orderly development in terms of the statutory city plan. On the ground, unauthorized constructions and impermissible land use are widespread:

> Invaders have pillaged Delhi for hundreds of years, but for the last couple of decades it is being ravaged by its own citizens and officials governing the capital city—we refer to unauthorized constructions and misuse of residential premises for industrial and other commercial purposes. This Court has focused on these illegal activities in several decisions and has issued directions from time to time to try and bring some sanity to urban living but to little or no effect.[5]

As noted by the Supreme Court, the Delhi Master Plan is routinely flouted, compelling the court to require 'sealing drives'[6] to restore the legislative policy.

II. THE COURTS AND POLICY

When judges decide environmental cases they are primarily concerned with applying the relevant provisions of the law to the facts before them. Policy considerations, as such, are peripheral to the judicial vision. Indeed, a familiar refrain from the bench when confronted with policy is to claim a lack of legislative authority and expertise. Judges like to believe that they have no role in policy-making. As we shall see, this is a myth: Judges do play a significant role in shaping and influencing environmental policy in India.

The reasons for the seeming judicial reticence are grounded in the Rule of Law and the doctrine of separation of powers. An essential feature of the Rule of Law is that the law must be certain and predictable. This is why judges generally interpret statutory provisions literally. A judge will apply the law as she finds it, presuming that the legislature has carefully chosen words to advance the policy that the law seeks to achieve. Moreover, framing policy is regarded as the domain of the executive and making laws to effect the policy, the domain of the legislature. Respectful of this separation, judges are reluctant to be seen as framing policy. From a judge's perspective, the environmental policy underlying the statute must be discovered from the language used by the legislature within the statute. Generally, there is no need for a judge to look beyond the statutory provisions to any other document.

A statutory provision may be ambiguous or, where interpreted literally, may result in absurdity. To avoid such situations, courts occasionally adopt a purposive interpretation. This rule requires the judge to advance the purpose of the law even though the interpretation departs from the plain language of a provision. To discern the purpose of a statute, a judge may refer to policy statements that are found in the Statement of Objects and Reasons accompanying the Bill or official policy documents such as the National Forest Policy of 1988.

---

5 *M C Mehta v Union of India* (2018) 2 SCC 144, 145.

6 A Monitoring Committee operating under court directions visits localities across Delhi and seals non-conforming premises. The premises are de-sealed where the occupant undertakes to comply with the Delhi Master Plan. See *M C Mehta v Union of India* (2020) SCC Online SC 648.

We anchor the readings in this chapter to a constitutional policy: the trust principle that is fundamental to democratic governance. After surveying environmental policy developments, we focus on the evolution of forest policy. The Scheduled Tribes and Other Forest Dwellers (Recognition of Forest Rights) Act of 2006 (FRA) is a transformative law that has upended forest governance structures. The final section on the FRA examines the contests over forest resources both before and after the law was passed.

B. NATURAL RESOURCES, POLICY AND PUBLIC TRUST

Before we examine policy prescriptions, the notion of public trust in relation to natural resources may be emphasized. All power under the Constitution is exercised in trust on behalf of the citizenry. The bedrock of every environmental policy is the principle that natural resources must be administered for the public good. The principle of public trust in the preservation of natural resources extends to all constitutional and statutory functionaries. This includes ministers, bureaucrats and judges including the personnel on the National Green Tribunal.

Centre for Public Interest Litigation v Union of India, popularly known as the *2G* case, is not an environmental case. Nevertheless, it lays down several important principles relating to the ownership and disposal of natural resources. In *2G*, the Supreme Court did what it seldom does: it overturned a government policy for the allocation of spectrum and voided licences issued to telecommunication companies. The procedure adopted by government to allocate spectrum was deeply flawed. The following excerpt relates to the first question framed by the Court at the opening of the judgment: does the government have the right to alienate, transfer or distribute national resources/national assets otherwise than by following a fair and transparent method consistent with the fundamentals of the equality clause enshrined in the Constitution?

CENTRE FOR PUBLIC INTEREST LITIGATION v UNION OF INDIA

(2012) 3 SCC 1

G S Singhvi, J:

* * *

At the outset, we consider it proper to observe that even though there is no universally accepted definition of natural resources, they are generally understood as elements having intrinsic utility to mankind. They may be renewable or non renewable. They are thought of as the individual elements of the natural environment that provide economic and social services to human society and are considered valuable in their relatively unmodified, natural, form. A natural resource's value rests in the amount of the material available and the demand for it. The latter is determined by its usefulness to production. Natural resources belong to the people but the State legally owns them on behalf of its people and from that point of view natural resources are considered as national assets, more so because the State benefits immensely from their value.

The State is empowered to distribute natural resources. However, as they constitute public property/national asset, while distributing natural resources, the State if bound to act in consonance with the principles of equality and public trust and ensure that no action is taken which may be detrimental to public interest. Like any other State action, constitutionalism must be reflected at every stage of the distribution of natural resources. In Article 39(b) of the Constitution it has been provided that the ownership and control of the material resources. In Article 39(b) of the Constitution it has been provided that the ownership and control of the material resources of the community should be so distributed so as to best sub-serve the common good, but no comprehensive legislation has been enacted to generally define natural resources and a framework for their protection. Of course, environment laws enacted by Parliament and State legislatures deal with specific natural resources. i.e., forest, air, water, coastal zones, etc.

The ownership regime relating to natural resources can also be ascertained from international conventions and customary international law, common law and national constitutions. In international law, it rests upon the concept of sovereignty and seeks to respect the principle of permanent sovereignty (of peoples and nations) over (their) natural resources as asserted in the 17th Session of the United Nations General Assembly and then affirmed as a customary international norm by the International Court of Justice in the case of *Democratic Republic of Congo v Uganda* (ICJ Reports 2005, pg.168) Common Law recognizes States as having the authority to protect natural resources insofar as the resources are within the interests of the general public. The State is deemed to have a proprietary interest in natural resources and must act as guardian and trustee in relation to the same. Constitutions across the world focus on establishing natural resources as owned by and for the benefit of, the country. In most instances where constitutions specifically address ownership of natural resources, the Sovereign State, or, as it is more commonly expressed, 'the People', is designated as the owner of the natural resource....

In India, the Courts have given an expansive interpretation to the concept of natural resources and have from time to time issued directions, by relying upon the provisions contained in Articles 38, 39, 48, 48A and 51A(g), for protection and proper allocation/distribution of natural resources and have repeatedly insisted on compliance of the constitutional principles in the process of distribution, transfer and alienation to private persons. The doctrine of public trust, which was evolved in *Illinois Central Railroad Co v People of the State of Illinois* 146 U S 387 (1892), has been held by this Court to be a part of the Indian jurisprudence.

In *Reliance Natural Resources Limited v Reliance Industries Limited* (2010) 7 SCC 1, P Sathasivam, J with whom Balakrishnan, C J, agreed, made the following observations:

> It must be noted that the constitutional mandate is that the natural resources belong to the people of this country. The nature of the word 'vest' must be seen in the context of the public trust doctrine (PTD). Even though this doctrine has been applied in cases dealing with environmental jurisprudence, it has its broader application.

Learned Judge then referred to the judgments, *In re Special Reference No. 1 of 2001* (2004) 4 SCC 489, *M C Mehta v Kamal Nath* (1997) 1 SCC 388 and observed:

> This doctrine is part of Indian law and finds application in the present case as well. It is thus the duty of the Government to provide complete protection to the natural resources as a trustee of the people at large.

The Court also held that natural resources are vested with the Government as a matter of trust in the name of the people of India, thus it is the solemn duty of the State to protect the national interest and natural resources must always be used in the interests of the country and not private interests.

As natural resources are public goods, the doctrine of equality, which emerges from the concepts of justice and fairness, must guide the State in determining the actual mechanism for distribution of natural resources. In this regard, the doctrine of equality has two aspects: *first,* it regulates the rights and obligations of the State *vis-à-vis* its people and demands that the people be granted equitable access to natural resources and/or its products and that they are adequately compensated for the transfer of the resource to the private domain; and *second,* it regulates the rights and obligations of the State *vis-à-vis* private parties seeking to acquire/use the resource and demands that the procedure adopted for distribution is just, non-arbitrary and transparent and that it does not discriminate between similarly placed private parties....

In conclusion, we hold that the State is the legal owner of the natural resources as a trustee of the people and although it is empowered to distribute the same, the process of distribution must be guided by the constitutional principles including the doctrine of equality and larger public good....

NOTES AND QUESTIONS

1. The Supreme Court declared that licences granted under the first-come first-served policy were subject to misuse, and the court proceeded to set aside the allocation of spectrum to the licensees. As a result, 122 licences for providing 2G services were quashed. Is this a case of the judicial cure being worse than the disease? Several companies had purchased the licences from the original allottees after investing very substantial amounts. How were the subsequent allottees at fault? They never participated in the flawed allocation process. Was the spectrum allotted akin to 'stolen goods' where the *bona fide* buyer does not get title? Should the disruptive effect of a judgment in public interest litigation impact innocent third parties?

2. Was the court under a duty to weigh the impact of its judgment on industry and consumers?

3. The court found that the government's policy had resulted in important national assets being gifted away at throw-away prices. Several licensees offloaded their licences to others and made staggering profits. The court held that where fiscal policies of the state or the implementation of such policies was contrary to public interest or violative of constitutional principles

> [i]t is the duty of the Court to exercise its jurisdiction in larger public interest and reject the stock plea of the State that the scope of judicial review should not be exceeded beyond the recognized parameters.

This principled approach is commendable but is seldom followed because the court usually prefers to issue prospective directions in PILs, rather than take on powerful entrenched economic interests.

4. Smarting from the defeat in the *2G* case, the Union Government sought a limited review of the judgment to the extent that it pronounced on allocation of natural resources *generally*. After the Supreme Court agreed to hear the review petition on this narrow aspect, the government changed track, filed a Presidential Reference under Article 143(1) of the Constitution of India and withdrew its review petition. The Presidential Reference sought the opinion of the Supreme Court on whether auctions were the *only* permissible method for disposal of natural resources across all sectors. The answer obviously is 'no'; and the Supreme Court said so in answer to the Reference.[7] From the government's perspective, the Reference served a political goal by diluting the rebuke in the *2G* case.

5. State governments in India receive royalties when minerals such as iron ore, bauxite and coal are mined. The royalty is treated as revenue and not a capital receipt. It is spent on ordinary government business. Since the state is a trustee for the people, including unborn generations, is there a need to change government accounting in respect of natural resources? Considering that mineral resources deplete, should these receipts be treated as a capital receipt instead and credited to a permanent fund to be used for public welfare? Will this green accounting practice better reflect the loss of mineral wealth? Will it sensitize the state and communities to the real value of the resource and encourage efficient use of non-renewable natural resources?

---

[7] *Natural Resources Allocation, In re: Special Reference No. 1 of 2012* (2012) 10 SCC 1, 99.

C. EARLY ENVIRONMENTAL LEGISLATION

A survey of early environmental legislation indicates the nature and extent of awareness of environmental issues in the government. Apart from forests,[8] nineteenth-century legislation also regulated two other aspects of India's environment: water and wildlife.[9] These laws had a narrow purpose and limited territorial reach, reflecting the policy of the time. Indeed, in the case of colonial forest statutes the object was to enrich Britain, not 'conservation', as we understand it today.

I. WATER POLLUTION

The Shore Nuisance (Bombay and Kolaba) Act of 1853, one of the earliest laws concerning water pollution, authorized the collector of land revenue in Bombay to order the removal of any object causing nuisance below the high-water mark in Bombay harbour. In 1857, an attempt was made to regulate the pollution produced by the Oriental Gas Company by imposing fines on the company and giving a right of compensation to anyone whose water was 'fouled' by the company's discharges.[10]

The Indian Penal Code, enacted in 1860, imposed a fine on anyone who voluntarily 'fouls the water of any public spring or reservoir'. In addition, the Code penalized negligent acts with poisonous substances that endangered life or caused injury and proscribed public nuisances. The Indian Easements Act of 1882 protected riparian owners against 'unreasonable' pollution by upstream users. The Indian Fisheries Act, passed in 1897, penalized those who kill fish by poisoning water and by using explosives. Legislative provisions regulating the discharge of oil into port waters[11] and prohibiting the poisoning of water in forests[12] were also enacted prior to Independence.

Two early post-Independence laws touched on water pollution. Section 12 of the Factories Act of 1948 required all factories to make 'effective arrangements' for waste disposal and empowered state governments to frame rules implementing this directive. Second, river boards, established under the River Boards Act of 1956 for the regulation and development of inter-state rivers and river valleys, were empowered to prevent water pollution. In both these laws, prevention of water pollution was only incidental to the principal objective of the enactment.

The earliest laws that aimed at controlling air pollution were the Bengal Smoke Nuisance Act of 1905 and the Bombay Smoke Nuisance Act of 1912.

II. WILDLIFE

In the field of wildlife protection, early legislation was limited to specific areas and particular species. In 1873, Madras enacted the first statute for the protection of wild elephants. The law introduced a general prohibition on the destruction of wild elephants and imposed a

[8] The Indian Forest Act of 1865 followed by a statute in 1878 constituted early attempts by Britain, the world leader in deforestation, to assert a state monopoly on India's forest resources. See Madhav Gadgil & Ramachandra Guha, *This Fissured Land: An Ecological History of India* 118 (1993).

[9] See generally, L N Mathur, *A Federal Legislative History of Control of Water Pollution in India* in Legal Control Of Environmental Pollution 86 (Ed. S L Agarwal, 1980); K Ramakrishna, *The Emergence of Environmental Laws in the Developing Countries: A Case Study of India* 12 Ecology L Q 907 (1985); and Ashish Kothari, Pratibha Pande, Shekhar Singh & Dilanavaz Variava, *Management of National Parks and Sanctuaries in India: A Status Report* 106–7 (1989).

[10] Sections 15–17, Oriental Gas Company Act of 1857.

[11] Section 21, Indian Ports Act of 1908.

[12] Section 26, Indian Forest Act of 1927.

penalty on those who violated the embargo. The first pan-India effort came six years later with the passing of the Elephants' Preservation Act of 1879. In 1887, the Legislative Council for India[13] enacted the Wild Birds Protection Act prohibiting the possession or sale of wild birds recently killed or taken, during notified breeding seasons.[14]

In 1912, the Legislative Council for India enacted a broader Wild Birds and Animals Protection Act. Extending to most of British India, this law specified closed hunting seasons and regulated the hunting of designated species through licenses. Indeed, all the statutes related primarily to the regulation of hunting and did not regulate trade in wildlife and wildlife products—both major factors in the decline of Indian wildlife. As a consequence, wildlife depredation continued, and many species became extinct.

This review suggests that early legislative efforts were inadequate or piecemeal at best. It was not until the 1970s that the Union Government began enacting comprehensive environmental laws.

D. SURVEY OF ENVIRONMENTAL POLICY SINCE THE 1970s

As we have seen, there are government policy statements and then there are statutes that seek to operationalize policy goals. In this section, we track some of the key policy statements. These developments took place alongside constitutional and statutory changes, examined in the next chapter.

In the summer of 1972, Stockholm staged the first UN Conference on the Human Environment. Attended by heads of state and high government officials from 113 participating countries, the Conference adopted a declaration and an action plan which served as an impetus for policy formation across the world. In a forerunner to the UN Conference, India established a National Committee on Environmental Planning and Co-ordination (NCEPC) in April 1972. The NCEPC, comprising both officials and specialists, was the first national body that worked to integrate environmental factors with development objectives.

At that time, India's developmental goals and policies were set out in five year plan documents. The 5th Five Year Plan (1974–79) stressed the role of the NCEPC in elevating environmental concerns when large industrial and development projects were undertaken. As awareness of environmental disruption due to development increased, subsequent plan documents contained specific chapters on 'Environment and Development'. The plans drew attention to aspects of degradation such as the loss of topsoil, forest cover and industrial pollution that were impairing economic and social progress. The 7th Five Year Plan (1985–86) emphasized the principle of sustainable development.[15]

The first national environmental statute that rode on the new environmental awareness of the 1970s was the Wild Life Act[16] followed soon after by the Water Act.[17] The Air Act[18] passed in

---

[13] The Legislative Council established under the Indian Council Act of 1861 could pass laws for the whole of India (British India as well as territories of any native prince or chief). M P Jain *Indian Legal and Constitutional History* 562 (7th Edition, 2014).

[14] E.g., rules published in the BOMBAY GOVERNMENT GAZETTE, 20 July 1951, page 1219 notifying the breeding season for the Talegaon Dabhade Municipality.

[15] O P Dwivedi, *India's Environmental Policies, Programmes and Stewardship* 54 (1997).

[16] Wild Life (Protection) Act of 1972.

[17] Water (Prevention and Control of Pollution) Act of 1974.

[18] Air (Prevention and Control of Pollution) Act of 1981.

1981 mirrored the structure and strategy of the Water Act by entrusting state pollution control boards with the responsibility to regulate industrial discharge through a permit system. To arrest the sharp decline in forest cover, Parliament enacted the Forest (Conservation) Act of 1980.[19]

A leak from Union Carbide's pesticide factory at Bhopal in December 1984 killed over 5,000 and injured several thousand others. This disaster spurred the Central Government to adopt stronger environmental policies; to enact fresh legislation; and to create, reorganize and expand regulatory agencies.

In December 1988, the Union Ministry of Environment and Forests (MoEF) constituted a committee to recommend a framework and an action plan for the conservation of resources. The committee, which was comprised of eminent scientists, journalists, environmentalists and senior bureaucrats, prepared a draft policy statement for a national conservation strategy and invited comments and suggestions on the draft from hundreds of respondents across the country. After assimilating the responses received from governmental and non-governmental organizations, the committee submitted a report to the Union Government in April 1990.[20] Based on the recommendations of the committee, the government of India adopted a National Conservation Strategy and Policy Statement on Environment and Development in June 1992 (NCS).[21] The preamble to the NCS adopts the policy of 'sustainable development' and declares the government's commitment to re-orient policies and action 'in unison with the environmental perspective'.[22] The NCS proceeds to recognize the enormous dimensions of the environmental problems facing India and declares strategies for action in various spheres such as agriculture, forestry, industrial development, mining and tourism. Special sections in the NCS deal with the rehabilitation of persons ousted by large development projects, the role of non-governmental organizations and the special relationship between women and the environment.

In February 1992, the Union Government published its policy for the abatement of pollution.[23] This statement declares the objective of the government to integrate environmental considerations into decision-making at all levels. To achieve this goal, the statement adopts fundamental guiding principles, namely, (i) prevention of pollution at source, (ii) the adoption of the best available technology, (iii) the polluter pays principle and (iv) public participation in decision-making.[24] The statement contained an early recognition of the citizen's role:

> The public must be aware in order to be able to make informed choices. A high government priority will be to educate citizens about environmental risks, the economic and health dangers of resource degradation and the real cost of natural resources. Information about the environment will be published periodically. Affected citizens and non-governmental organizations play a role in environmental monitoring and therefore allowing them to supplement the regulatory system and recognizing their expertise where such exists and their

---

19 Parliament drew on its recently expanded power to make laws pertaining to forests. The subject 'Forests' was moved from the State List to the Concurrent List pursuant to the Constitution (Forty-Second) Amendment Act of 1976. See Chapter 3.

20 Ministry of Environment & Forests, Government of India, *Report of the Core Committee for Recommending a National Strategy for Conservation and Sustainable Development* (April 1990).

21 Ministry of Environment & Forests, Government of India, *National Conservation Strategy and Policy Statement on Environment and Development* (June 1992).

22 *Id.* at paras 1.1 and 1.4.

23 Ministry of Environment & Forests, Government of India, *Policy Statement for Abatement of Pollution* (26 February 1992).

24 *Id.* at para 3.3.

> commitment and vigilance, will also be cost effective. Access to information to enable public monitoring of environmental concerns, will be provided for.
>
> Public interest litigation has successfully demonstrated that responsible non-governmental organizations and public-spirited individuals can bring about significant pressure on polluting units for adopting abatement measures. This commitment and expertise will be encouraged and their practical work supported.[25]

The policy statements, in themselves, are not enforceable in a court of law. However, these statements represent a broad political consensus and amplify the duties of government under the directive principles of state policy contained in Part IV of the Constitution. In the hands of a creative judge the policy documents may serve as an aid for interpreting environmental statutes or for spelling out the obligations of government agencies under environmental laws. For example, in *State of Himachal Pradesh v Ganesh Wood Products*,[26] the Supreme Court relied upon the National Forest Policy of 1988 and the State Forest Policy of Himachal Pradesh to invalidate a decision taken by the state industrial project authority. The authority approved the establishment of units which manufactured '*katha*' from the scarce *khair* tree without considering factors such as the availability of *khair* trees and the adverse impact on the forests in the state. The court held that the policy of economic liberalization has to be understood in light of the National Forest Policy and forest laws enacted by the government. The court cautioned government departments against ignoring forest policies and warned that disregard of these policies would imperil government decisions.

In many instances, judges are reluctant to adopt a pro-active approach by compelling government departments to take measures to improve the quality of the environment. In this situation, a clear statement of policy may persuade the judge to prefer an environment-friendly interpretation over a more conservative approach. The policy statements may also weigh with a court at the interlocutory stage when assessing the balance of convenience and the potential harm to the public interest. At the end of the day, unless government policy is backed by adequate budgetary allocations, changes to the statutory regime and bureaucratic will, the government's intentions are apt to remain on paper.

E. THE NATIONAL ENVIRONMENT POLICY OF 2006

On 18 May 2006 the Union Cabinet approved the National Environment Policy, 2006 (NEP). This policy was the outcome of deliberations between central ministries, the Union Government and the states as well as interactions with experts and non-governmental organizations. The policy document was the culmination of a public consultation process that commenced in August 2004. We carry a short excerpt from the policy statement.

> GOVERNMENT OF INDIA, NATIONAL ENVIRONMENT POLICY, 2006
>
> *Objectives of the National Environment policy*
>
> The principal objectives of this policy are enumerated below. These Objectives relate to current perceptions of key environmental challenges. They may, accordingly, evolve over time:
>
> i. Conservation of Critical Environmental Resources
>   To protect and conserve critical ecological systems and resources, and invaluable natural and man-made heritage, which are essential for life support, livelihoods, economic growth, and a broad conception of human well-being.
>
> ii. Intra-generational Equity: Livelihood Security for the poor

---

[25] *Id.* at para 11.1.

[26] AIR 1996 SC 149.

To ensure equitable access to environmental resources and quality for all sections of society, and in particular, to ensure that poor communities, which are most dependent on environmental resources for their livelihoods, are assured secure access to these resources.

iii. Inter-generational Equity
To ensure judicious use of environmental resources to meet the needs and aspirations of the present and future generations.

iv. Integration of Environmental Concerns in Economic and Social Development
To integrate environmental concerns into policies, plans, programmes, and projects for economic and social development.

v. Efficiency in Environmental Resource Use
To ensure efficient use of environmental resources in the sense of reduction in their use per unit of economic output, to minimize adverse environmental impacts.

vi. Environmental Governance
To apply the principles of good governance (transparency, rationality, accountability, reduction in time and costs, participation, and regulatory independence) to the management and regulation of use of environmental resources.

vii. Enhancement of Resources for Environmental Conservation
To ensure higher resource flows, comprising finance, technology, management skills, traditional knowledge, and social capital, for environmental conservation through mutually beneficial multi-stakeholder partnerships between local communities, public agencies, the academic and research community, investors, and multilateral and bilateral development partners.

Principles

This policy has evolved from the recognition that only such development is sustainable, which respects ecological constraints, and the imperatives of justice.... The following Principles may accordingly guide the activities of different actors in relation to this policy. Each of these Principles has an established genealogy in policy pronouncements, jurisprudence, international environmental law, or international State practice:

i. Human Beings are at the Centre of Sustainable Development Concerns
Human beings are at the centre of concerns for sustainable development. They are entitled to a healthy and productive life in harmony with nature.

ii. The Right to Development
The right to development must be fulfilled so as to equitably meet developmental and environmental needs of present and future generations.

iii. Environmental Protection is an Integral part of the Development Process
In order to achieve sustainable development, environmental protection shall constitute an integral part of the development process and cannot be considered in isolation from it.

iv. The Precautionary Approach
Where there are credible threats of serious or irreversible damage to key environmental resources, lack of full scientific certainty shall not be used as a reason for postponing cost-effective measures to prevent environmental degradation.

v. Economic Efficiency
In various public actions for environmental conservation, economic efficiency would be sought to be realized.
This Principle requires that the services of environmental resources be given economic value, and such value to count equally with the economic values of other goods and services, in analysis of alternative courses of action.
Further implications of this Principle are as follows:
(a) Polluter Pays
Impacts of acts of production and consumption of one party may be visited on third parties who do not have a direct economic nexus with the original act. Such impacts are termed 'externalities'. If the costs (or benefits) of the

externalities are not re-visited on the party responsible for the original act, the resulting level of the entire sequence of production or consumption, and externality, is inefficient. In such a situation, economic efficiency may be restored by making the perpetrator of the externality bear the cost (or benefit) of the same. The policy will, accordingly, promote the internalization of environmental costs, including through the use of incentives based policy instruments, taking into account the approach that the polluter should, in principle, bear the cost of pollution, with due regard to the public interest, and without distorting international trade and investment.

(b) Cost Minimization

Where the environmental benefits of a course of action cannot, for methodological or conceptual reasons, be imputed economic value (as in the case of 'Incomparable Entities' [see below]), in any event the economic costs of realizing the benefits should be minimized.

Efficiency of resource use may also be accomplished by the use of policy instruments that create incentives to minimize wasteful use and consumption of natural resources. The principle of efficiency also applies to issues of environmental governance by streamlining processes and procedures in order to minimize costs and delays.

vi. Entities with 'Incomparable' Values

Significant risks to human health, life, and environmental life-support systems, besides certain other unique natural and man-made entities, which may impact the well-being, broadly conceived, of large numbers of persons, may be considered as 'Incomparable' in that individuals or societies would not accept these risks for compensation in money or conventional goods and services. A conventional economic cost-benefit calculus would not, accordingly, apply in their case, and such entities would have priority in allocation of societal resources for their conservation without consideration of direct or immediate economic benefit.

vii. Equity

The cardinal principle of equity or justice requires that human beings cannot be treated differently based on irrelevant differences between them. Equity norms must be distinguished according to context, i.e. 'procedural equity', relating to fair rules for allocation of entitlements and obligations, and 'end-result equity', relating to fair outcomes in terms of distribution of entitlements and obligations. Each context, in addition, must be distinguished in terms of 'intra-generational equity', relating to justice within societies, and in particular, providing space for the participation of the underprivileged, and 'inter-generational equity', relating to justice between generations.

Equity, in the context of this policy refers to both equity in entitlements to, and participation of, the relevant publics, in processes of decision-making over use of environmental resources.

viii. Legal Liability

The present environmental redressal mechanism is predominantly based on doctrines of criminal liability, which have not proved sufficiently effective, and need to be supplemented.

Civil liability for environmental damage would deter environmentally harmful actions, and compensate the victims of environmental damage. Conceptually, the principle of legal liability may be viewed as an embodiment in legal doctrine of the 'polluter pays' approach, itself deriving from the principle of economic efficiency.

The following alternative approaches to civil liability may apply:

(a) Fault Based Liability

In a fault based liability regime a party is held liable if it breaches a pre-existing legal duty, for example, an environmental standard.

(b) Strict Liability

Strict liability imposes an obligation to compensate the victim for harm resulting from actions or failure to take action, which may not necessarily constitute a breach of any law or duty of care.

ix. Public Trust Doctrine
The State is not an absolute owner, but a trustee of all natural resources, which are by nature meant for public use and enjoyment, subject to reasonable conditions, necessary to protect the legitimate interest of a large number of people, or for matters of strategic national interest.

x. Decentralization
Decentralization involves ceding or transfer of power from a Central Authority to State and Local Authorities, in order to empower public authorities having jurisdiction at the spatial level at which particular environmental issues are salient, to address these issues.

xi. Integration
Integration refers to the inclusion of environmental considerations in sectoral policymaking, the integration of the social and natural sciences in environment related policy research, and the strengthening of relevant linkages among various agencies at the Central, State, and Local Self-Government levels, charged with the implementation of environmental policies.

xii. Environmental Standard Setting
Environmental standards must reflect the economic and social development situation in which they apply. Standards adopted in one society or context may have unacceptable economic and social costs if applied without discrimination in another society or context.
Setting environmental standards would involve several considerations, i.e. risks to human health, risks to other environmental entities, technical feasibility, costs of compliance, and strategic considerations.

xiii. Preventive Action
It is preferable to prevent environmental damage from occurring in the first place, rather than attempting to restore degraded environmental resources after the fact.

xiv. Environmental Offsetting
There is a general obligation to protect threatened or endangered species and natural systems that are of special importance to sustaining life, providing livelihoods, or general well-being. If for exceptional reasons of overriding public interest such protection cannot be provided in particular cases, cost-effective offsetting measures must be undertaken by the proponents of the activity, to restore as nearly as may be feasible, the lost environmental services to the same publics. . . .

NOTES AND QUESTIONS

1. The NEP was preceded by the National Forest Policy of 1988, the NCS of 1992 and the Policy Statement on Abatement of Pollution of 1992. In 2002, the Union Government declared a National Water Policy.

What is the utility of these policy statements in court? Should judges use them as interpretational aids? In the *Lafarge* case,[27] the Supreme Court conferred a statutory flavour on the National Forest Policy:

> The time has come for this Court to declare and we hereby declare that the National Forest Policy, 1988 which lays down far-reaching principles must necessarily govern the grant of permissions under section 2 of the Forest (Conservation) Act, 1980 as the same provides the

[27] *Lafarge Umium Mining Pvt Ltd v Union of India* (2011) 7 SCC 338, 381.

road map to ecological protection and improvement under the Environment (Protection) Act, 1986. The principles/guidelines mentioned in the National Forest Policy, 1988 should be read as part of the provisions of the Environment (Protection) Act, 1986 read together with the Forest (Conservation) Act, 1980. This direction is required to be given because there is no machinery even today established for implementation of the said National Forest Policy, 1988 read with the Forest (Conservation) Act, 1980. Section 3 of the Environment (Protection) Act, 1986 confers a power coupled with duty and, thus, it is incumbent on the Central Government, as hereinafter indicated, to appoint an appropriate authority, preferably in the form of regulator, at the State and at the Central level for ensuring implementation of the National Forest Policy, 1988.

Building on the *Lafarge* case, the Supreme Court in the *Asiatic Lion* case held: 'In our view, the integrated development of wildlife habitat under the Centrally Sponsored Scheme of 2009 and the National Wildlife Action Plan (2002–2016) have to be read along with the provisions of the Wild Life (Protection) Act. [Both schemes] have statutory status .... and have to be implemented in their letter and spirit.'[28]

Should the NEP similarly inform decision-making under the Environment (Protection) Act of 1986 as well as other environmental laws such as the Water Act and the Air Act?

2. Judges make environmental policy, albeit indirectly. The contribution of India's courts to the NEP is evident from the number of policy objectives and principles that may be traced to decisions of the Supreme Court. The principle of sustainable development,[29] the precautionary principle,[30] the polluter pays principle,[31] strict liability,[32] the public trust doctrine,[33] and intergenerational equity[34] were initially recognized by the Court and are now echoed in the NEP.

3. The NEP declares that human beings are at the centre of concerns for sustainable development. In articulating an eco-centric approach over an anthropocentric approach, has the Supreme Court moved beyond the NEP?[35] The eco-centric approach emphasizes the right of other species to exist, not just humans.

4. Persuading judges to rely on the NEP as a tool for interpretation or, indeed, to lean in favour of pro-environment outcomes, is exercised case by case. Far more potent would be legislative amendments to existing statutes so that bureaucrats and judges are required by law to implement the policy objectives and principles of the NEP whenever they take decisions. None of the principal environmental statutes were amended after 2006 to expressly articulate

---

[28] *Centre for Environmental Law, WWF-India v Union of India* (*Asiatic Lion* case) (2013) 8 SCC 234, 253, 255.

[29] *State of Himachal Pradesh v Ganesh Wood Products* AIR 1996 SC 149, 159, 163.

[30] *Vellore Citizens' Welfare Forum v Union of India* AIR 1996 SC 2715, 2721; *S Jagannath v Union of India* (*Shrimp Culture* case) AIR 1997 SC 811, 846; *A P Pollution Control v Prof M V Nayudu* AIR 1999 SC 812; *Glanrock Estate Pvt Ltd v State of Tamil Nadu* (2010) 10 SCC 96.

[31] *Indian Council for Enviro-Legal Action v Union of India* (*Bichhri* case) AIR 1996 SC 1446, 1466; *Vellore Citizens' Welfare Forum v Union of India* AIR 1996 SC 2715, 2721; *Glanrock Estate Pvt Ltd v State of Tamil Nadu* (2010) 10 SCC 96.

[32] *M C Mehta v Union of India* (*Shriram Gas Leak* case) AIR 1987 SC 1086.

[33] *M C Mehta v Kamal Nath* (*Span Motels* case) (1997) 1 SCC 388; *M I Builders v Radhey Shyam Sahu* AIR 1999 SC 2468, 2498; *Centre for Public Interest Litigation v Union of India* (2012) 3 SCC 1.

[34] *State of Himachal Pradesh v Ganesh Wood Products* AIR 1996 SC 149, 159, 163; *K Guruprasad Rao v State of Karnataka* (2013) 8 SCC 418.

[35] *Center for Environmental Law WWF-I v Union of India* (*Asiatic Lion* case) (2013) 8 SCC 234; *T N Godavarman Thirumulpad v Union of India* (*Sandalwood* case) (2012) 4 SCC 362.

the objectives and principles set out in the NEP.[36] This is why a policy statement that is not followed through by change in the law remains a weak, aspirational document.

F. THE FOREST RIGHTS ACT

British appetite for timber had destroyed the forests of Ireland, South Africa and north-eastern United States. The colonial period was devastating for India's forests and forest dwellers as well. Britain required wood for shipbuilding, iron smelting and farming. India's forests lay open for extracting teak and other valuable wood to feed imperial demands. The shipyards at Surat, Bombay and those along the Malabar coast built dozens of vessels from Indian hardwood for the British East India Company. Vast swathes of forests succumbed to the demand for railway sleepers as the network of rail tracks extended across the subcontinent.[37]

The British established the imperial forest department in 1864 and shortly thereafter enacted the Indian Forest Act of 1865 to create a state monopoly over forests. Succeeding forest laws tightened the grip of the state. The Indian Forest Act of 1878 turned the forests over to the forest department. The law ignored the community rights of forest dwellers and the customary entitlements of rural folk who for centuries had used forest resources for sustenance.

Post Independence, the forest regime hardly changed. The colonial era Indian Forest Act of 1927 continued to be implemented by a forest department that had an ingrained hostility to forest dwellers and their rights. From the perspective of the disenfranchised forest communities, the National Forest Policy of 1952 remained aligned to the forest policy of 1894. The imperial demands of two world wars were now replaced by large development projects along river valleys and the needs of the nascent industrial sector. There was scant regard for rural communities: '[T]he accident of a village being situated close to the forest does not prejudice the right of the country as a whole to receive benefits of a national asset.'[38]

The Wild Life Act of 1972 and the Forest (Conservation) Act of 1980, strengthened the 'exclusionary' model, further alienating forest-dependent communities. The legislative policy of these statutes was to strengthen the forest bureaucracy and exclude local citizens from any participatory role. Inevitably, these statutes deepened the cleavage between local communities demanding a say in the management of their surroundings and those advocating conservation through inviolate zones.[39]

Since the British period, local communities have protested unjust laws that expropriate forests. The most famous protest in recent times is the Chipko Andolan. In the 1970s, women in the Himalayan foothills of what is today Uttarakhand, hugged trees to prevent felling by the forest department's contractors.[40] The non-violent protest gained wide support across the country, inspired similar movements and underscored the close link between conservation and community.

---

36 Section 20 of the National Green Tribunal Act of 2010 requires the Tribunal to apply the principles of sustainable development, the precautionary principle and the polluter pays principle when the deciding cases.

37 Madhav Gadgil & Ramachandra Guha, *This Fissured Land: An Ecological History of India* 118 (1993).

38 Ministry of Food & Agriculture, Government of India, *National Forest Policy*, para 7 (12 May 1952).

39 Madhu Sarin, *Undoing Historical Injustice: Reclaiming Citizenship Rights and Democratic Forest Governance through the Forest Rights Act* in DEMOCRATIZING FOREST GOVERNANCE IN INDIA 100, 114 (Eds. Sharadchandra Lele & Ajit Menon, 2014).

40 Ramachandra Guha, *The Unquiet Woods: Ecological Change and Peasant Resistance in the Himalaya* (1991).

In a sharp departure from earlier policies, the National Forest Policy of 1988 stressed the importance of forests for ensuring environmental stability and maintaining the ecological balance.[41] Moreover, it prioritized 'meeting the requirements of fuel-wood, fodder, minor forest produce and small timber of the rural and tribal populations' and required associating 'the tribal people closely in the protection, regeneration and development of forests'. In June 1990, the Union Government issued guidelines for participatory forest management.[42] These guidelines required forest departments to work with village communities and voluntary agencies for afforestation. While community entitlement to a share in the forest produce was recognized, the guidelines specifically declared that no ownership or rights over forest land would be given to beneficiaries or voluntary agencies. Despite huge funding, joint forest management (JFM) programmes were only modestly successful in improving tree cover and meeting local needs.[43] The partial success of JFM is attributed by some scholars to the absence (until 2006) of any change in law that would operationalize the provisions of the 1988 policy.[44]

The Forest Rights Act of 2006 (FRA)[45] is a transformative piece of legislation that significantly altered the legal relationship between forest dwellers and the state. Madhu Sarin sets the backdrop for the passage of the FRA.[46]

> MADHU SARIN; UNDOING HISTORICAL INJUSTICE (2014)
>
> The last straw came with [Ministry of Environment and Forest's] MoEF's circular of 3 May 2002. This circular cited the Supreme Court's concern over growing forest encroachments in its 23 November 2001 order and asked all states and union territories (UTs) to summarily evict all forest 'encroachers' within five months. The Court order only directed the Union and state governments to report the steps they had taken to prevent encroachments and removal of post-1980 ones; the Court had refrained from ordering the removal of encroachments prayed for by the amicus as the petitioner. But the misguided circular led to a spate of brutal evictions across the country, including the use of elephants to destroy the huts and crops of impoverished tribals during a drought year, which in turn led to an uproar of protests. As the constitutional authority for [Scheduled Tribes] STs under Article 338 (9), the chairman of the ST Commission wrote to the prime minister objecting to not even being informed, leave aside being consulted by the MoEF and the [Central Empowered Committee] CEC (which had made draconian recommendations for eviction of forest 'encroachers' to the Court), in a matter drastically impacting an estimated 10 million tribals. The MoEF was compelled to issue a clarification order in October 2002 that the 1990 circulars remained valid and that not all forest-dwellers were 'encroachers'. Despite this, by the MoEF's own admission in Parliament on 16 August 2004, between May 2002 and August 2004, evictions were carried out from 1,52,000 ha of forest land. The Court itself has remained silent on the issue of an early resolution of disputed claims over forest land and the non-settlement of rights over vast areas classified as forest, while staying the regularization of even pre-1980 occupations without its permission.

---

[41] Ministry of Environment & Forests, Government of India, *National Forest Policy, 1988* (7 December 1988).

[42] Ministry of Environment & Forests, Government of India, *Guidelines for Participatory Forest Management* (1 June 1990).

[43] Sharadchandra Lele, *What is Wrong with Joint Forest Management?* in DEMOCRATIZING FOREST GOVERNANCE IN INDIA 25, 39–41 (Eds. Sharadchandra Lele & Ajit Menon, 2014).

[44] *Id.* at 45, 53.

[45] The Scheduled Tribes and other Traditional Forest Dwellers (Recognition of Forest Rights) Act of 2006.

[46] Madhu Sarin, *Undoing Historical Injustice: Reclaiming Citizenship Rights and Democratic Forest Governance through the Forest Rights Act* in DEMOCRATIZING FOREST GOVERNANCE IN INDIA 100 (Eds. Sharadchandra Lele & Ajit Menon, 2014).

In February 2004, just before the parliamentary elections, the MoEF issued two new circulars: one titled 'Regularisation of the rights of the tribals on the forest lands' that extended the cut-off date for regularization for tribals to December 1993 (instead of October 1980 under the first 1990 circular) and the other titled 'Stepping up of process for conversion of forest villages into revenue villages'. These were promptly stayed by the Supreme Court in response to an IA filed by the amicus that these were in violation of court orders staying both regularization and de-reservation of forest land. The Court's stay on the conversion of forest villages into revenue villages was particularly ironic as this has been the Government of India's stated policy since the 1970s. In its July 2004 affidavit to get the Court's stay vacated, the MoEF admitted that during the consolidation of state forests 'the rural people, especially tribals who have been living in the forests since time immemorial, were deprived of their traditional rights and livelihood and consequently, these tribals have become encroachers in the eyes of law' and that 'it should be understood clearly that the lands occupied by the tribals in forest areas do not have any forest vegetation'. It further asserted that its February 2004 circulars 'do not relate to encroachers, but to remedy a serious historical injustice' and that '(this) will also significantly lead to better forest conservation'. The Court has still not vacated the stay on the MoEF's 2004 February circulars.

With forest rights becoming a major national political issue due to the evictions, an informal alliance of grassroots movements, rights activists, and academics came together under the umbrella of the Campaign for Survival and Dignity (CSD). Together with left-wing political parties and other rights movements, the CSD undertook nationwide political mobilization with mass protests, rallies, public hearings, and conventions aimed at members of Parliament, state legislatures, and political parties. With a new central government in 2004 having made a commitment to stop forest evictions, the initial demand of the CSD and other mass movements was for the implementation of the 1990 circulars of the Ministry of Environment and Forests. However, this soon transformed into a demand for a comprehensive law for the statutory recognition of pre-existing rights, not only over cultivated lands but also over customary forest resources, and for the empowerment of village assemblies to protect, conserve, and manage such resources. The Scheduled Tribes and Other Traditional Forest Dwellers (Recognition of Forest Rights) Act, 2006, was an outcome of this prolonged struggle by grassroots movements for remedying a historical wrong through forest tenure reform.

NOTES AND QUESTIONS

1. In Sarin's telling, the strict enforcement of Supreme Court orders requiring the removal of encroachers snowballed into a formidable political movement. Notice the messy manner in which democracy works: court orders, lobbying, protests, unlikely alliances, campaigns, political rallies and eventually a statute recognizing the rights of forest dwellers.

2. The environmentalist Sunita Narain argues that Indian environmentalism differs in its roots from environmentalism in the West. In her view, the dominant theme in the Western world is 'protectionist conservationism' which involves maintaining natural environments in their pristine form, to the extent possible. In contrast, the Indian tradition builds mostly on 'utilitarian conservationism' since the movement sprang from the disruption caused to communities dependent on nature for their firewood, food, water, building materials, medicines and fodder.[47]

[47] Sunita Narain, *Changing Environmentalism*, SEMINAR 47 (August 2002).

The guiding concern for many environmentalists in India is—how does one protect the environment so that it continues to sustain dependent communities? The policy underlying the FRA exemplifies Indian environmentalism.

3. Dr Chhatrapati Singh faulted the pre-FRA regime on two counts. First, forest laws were premised on an abundance of forest resources where the forest department's primary task was to grant contracts to harvest timber for industry. This premise of plenty contrasted with the scarcity on the ground. Second, was the faulty assumption that only the forest department could grow forests and supply forest produce. Just as the department of agriculture was ill-suited to grow and supply food, Dr Singh argued that the forest department was incapable of increasing India's forest cover on its own. A viable strategy would involve village cooperatives and other local institutions engaged in growing forests and profiting from them. This strategy would strengthen local self-government and deepen democracy.[48]

In December 2005, the government introduced the Scheduled Tribes (Recognition of Forest Rights) Bill in the Lok Sabha. Seeking a deeper study of the Bill, Parliament requested a report from a Joint Parliamentary Committee (JPC) comprising members from both Houses. After 14 sittings the JPC recommended extending the benefits of the proposed law:

> The Committee note that the provisions of the Bill seek to recognize and vest rights only in respect of forest dwelling Scheduled Tribes. However, the Committee have been informed during evidence that a large number of traditional forest dwellers other than Scheduled Tribes have also been residing in the forest or in close proximity of the forest or forest land for generations and primarily depend on forest land or forest resources for their *bona fide* livelihood. These people have also been victims of historical injustice as they have lived on forest land from ancient times. Non-recognition of their rights would not only pose a threat to their livelihood but also could lead to their eviction from the forests. The Committee also note that these people have lived in forest in close harmony with the Scheduled Tribes community residing in the forest. The Committee also note that in many cases the non-Scheduled Tribes category of forest dwellers have been settled on forest land by Government to promote policy like Grow More Food or by way of rehabilitation due to displacement caused by development projects. The Committee also feel that classification of people into Scheduled Tribes and Non-Scheduled Tribes has come into being after Independence. Since the Bill seeks to undo historical injustice, the Non-Scheduled Tribes category people residing in forest should also be entitled for recognition and vesting of forest rights. The Committee have, therefore, decided to include a new definition in the Bill to cover 'other traditional forest dwellers' with specific conditions to become eligible for recognition and vesting of rights.[49]

The FRA came into force on 31 December 2007, ushering in a new era in forest regulation.

The preamble to the Act notes the historical injustice to forest dwellers and declares a lofty intention to right this wrong. Recognizing 'forest dwellers ... are integral to the very survival and sustainability of the forest system' and the need to address their insecurities, the preamble aims at conferring tenurial rights.

---

[48] Chhatrapati Singh, *India's Forest Policy and Forest Laws*, 177–8, 184 (2000).

[49] Lok Sabha Secretariat, *Report of the Joint Committee on the Scheduled Tribes (Recognition of Forest Rights) Bill, 2005* para 25 (2006).

The Act has 14 sections divided into six chapters. The first chapter describes the extent of the law which covers the whole of India except the State of Jammu and Kashmir.[50] Section 2 defines key expressions including:

> 2(o) 'other traditional forest dweller' means any member or community who has for at least three generations prior to the 13th day of December, 2005 primarily resided in and who depend on the forest or forests land for *bona fide* livelihood needs.
>
> *Explanation.*—For the purposes of this clause, 'generation' means a period comprising of twenty-five years.

Chapter II titled 'Forest Rights' contains a single section. Section 3(1) enumerates 13 sets of rights over 'forest lands'. These include the 'right to hold and live in the forest land' for habitation or agriculture; the right to own, collect, use and dispose of minor forest produce traditionally collected within or outside village boundaries; community rights to fish and graze; and the right of nomadic and pastoral communities to access seasonal resources. Section 3(2) requires the Central Government to allow the diversion of forests for schools, dispensaries, hospitals, shops, roads, community centres and other enumerated purposes.

Chapter III has two sections. Section 4 contains a potent statutory declaration that the Central Government 'recognises and vests forest rights' in forest dwelling Scheduled Tribes as well as other traditional forest dwellers. These rights are declared to be heritable but not transferable. Forest dwelling Scheduled Tribes or other forest dwellers are protected from eviction or removal from forest land. Section 4(8) reads:

> (8) The forest rights recognised and vested under this Act shall include the right of land to forest dwelling Schedule Tribes and other traditional forest dwellers who can establish that they were displaced from their dwelling and cultivation without land compensation due to State Government interventions, and where the land has not been used for the purpose for which it was acquired within five years of the said acquisition.

Two provisions in Chapter III relate to wildlife and other environmental issues. Section 4(2) provides the machinery for protecting 'critical wildlife habitats'. These habitats must be identified by the Central Government and are required to be kept inviolate for wildlife conservation. Forest dwellers may be resettled away from these zones through a consensual process where the State Government rules out coexistence between forest dwellers and the wildlife. The other provision is section 5 which carries a marginal note: 'Duties of holders of forest rights'. The language of the section appears to depart from the marginal note and instead of imposing duties, 'empowers' the holders of forest rights, village assemblies and village level institutions to:

> (a) protect the wildlife, forest and biodiversity;
> (b) ensure that adjoining catchments area, water sources and other ecological sensitive areas are adequately protected;
> (c) ensure that the habitat of forest dwelling Scheduled Tribes and other traditional forest dwellers is preserved from any form of destructive practices affecting their cultural and natural heritage;
> (d) ensure that the decisions taken in the Gram Sabha to regulate access to community forest resources and stop any activity which adversely affects the wild animals, forest and the biodiversity are complied with.

50 Section 1(2), The Scheduled Tribes and other Traditional Forest Dwellers (Recognition of Forest Rights) Act of 2006.

Chapter IV containing section 6 prescribes the procedure to be followed to vest forest rights. The process is initiated at the level of the Gram Sabha or village assembly which is charged with receiving, consolidating and verifying claims. The recommendation by the Gram Sabha is screened by two levels of committees constituted by the State Government. The decision of the District Level Committee on the existence and extent of the entitlement is termed as 'final and binding'. This is followed by the grant of a title document to the forest dweller recording a description of the forest land under occupation.[51]

Chapter V provides for offences and penalties while Chapter VI contains a clutch of miscellaneous provisions. Section 11 designates the Union Ministry of Tribal Affairs as the nodal agency to implement the FRA.

NOTES AND QUESTIONS

1. What political factors helped shape policy that led to the passage of the FRA? The FRA was piloted through the 14th Lok Sabha, constituted after the general election of 2004. Revisit the electoral result that led to the formation of a coalition government at the Centre. Recall the strong performance by the Left Front comprising communist parties and their political beliefs.

2. Is Parliament competent to pass the FRA? The answer turns on whether the Act is about 'forests' or 'land'.

Parliament has legislative competence to enact laws on 'forests' covered by Entry 17A of the Concurrent List.[52] It is the State legislatures alone that may enact laws on 'Land, that is to say, right in or over land, land tenures ....'[53] Moreover, the states have exclusive legislative authority to enact laws relating to 'the maintenance of land records, survey for revenue purposes and records of rights ....'[54]

Section 3(i) of the FRA specifically refers to securing 'individual or community tenure or both ... on all forest lands' and section 3(1)(h) specifically contemplates conversion of all forest villages into revenue villages. Since the procedure under the FRA culminates in the grant of a title document over land in favour of an individual or the community, the law in pith and substance appears to deal with land.

Moreover, the Union Government is not the owner of land in the territory of the states. Does Parliament have legislative competence to 'give away' forest land that does not belong to the Union and which vests in the states? These grounds render the FRA vulnerable to challenge.

3. Can Parliament's competence to legislate be traced to Article 253 of the Constitution? Article 253 empowers Parliament to enact law 'for implementing any treaty, agreement or convention with any other country or countries or any decision made at any international conference, association or other body'. Can the Act be justified based on the United Nations

---

[51] Rule 8(h) & Annexure II, The Scheduled Tribes and Other Traditional Forest Dwellers (Recognition of Forest Rights) Rules of 2008.

[52] Entry 17A, List III, Schedule VII, Constitution of India. Both Parliament as well as State legislatures may enact laws on the subjects enumerated in the Concurrent List. The division of legislative authority under the Constitution is discussed in the next chapter.

[53] Entry 18, List II, Schedule VII, Constitution of India.

[54] Entry 45, List II, Schedule VII, Constitution of India.

Convention concerning the Protection and Integration of Indigenous and Other Tribal and Semi-tribal Populations in Independent Countries (ILO Convention 107)?[55]

Can the legislative competence of Parliament to enact the FRA in 2006 be justified through a *subsequent* international convention? In 2007, India adopted the United Nations Declaration on the Rights of Indigenous Peoples (UNDRIP). The Declaration states:

> States, in consultation and cooperation with indigenous peoples, shall take the appropriate measures, including legislative measures, to achieve the ends of this Declaration[56]

Further, UNDRIP states:

> Indigenous peoples have the right to the recognition, observance and enforcement of treaties, agreements and other constructive arrangements concluded with States or their successors and to have States honour and respect such treaties, agreements and other constructive arrangements.[57]

Assume these conventions support Parliament's authority to make a law relating to indigenous and tribal peoples. Would this source of legislative authority enable Parliament to make laws relating to 'other traditional forest dwellers'? Remember, other traditional forest dwellers have neither indigenous nor tribal ancestry.

4. There is historical justification for recognizing the rights of forest dwelling Scheduled Tribes. Correcting the past injustice was the purpose of the Bill when it was introduced in the Lok Sabha. Does this rationale apply to 'other traditional forest dwellers'? In conferring title on persons (other than the Scheduled Tribes) who occupied forest lands before December 1935, is there a breach of the public trust doctrine? Can the state hand over public forest lands for free?

Will such a policy encourage or discourage encroachments in the future?

5. Examine the definition of 'other traditional forest dweller' excerpted earlier. Is occupying public forest lands for 75 years a tradition worthy of statutory protection?

6. The FRA has no provision for evicting encroachers. This includes every occupier who is not a forest-dwelling tribal or other traditional forest dweller. The notion of an encroacher would also cover persons who occupy forest lands beyond their entitlements as determined under the FRA.

By consciously excluding an eviction machinery, what is the state signalling? Is there a hidden forest policy underlying the FRA? What electoral pressures may come into play in the years ahead? Will there be a clamour to expand the definition of 'other traditional forest dwellers'?

7. Section 3(1)(e) recognizes 'rights including community tenures of habitat and habitation for *primitive* tribal groups and pre-agricultural communities'. Is the italicized expression constitutionally permissible? Does its use violate the dignity of those the legislature seeks to protect? Should a constitutional court excise the language?

---

55 Article 27 of ILO Convention 107 reads: '(1) The governmental authority responsible for the matters covered in this Convention shall create or develop agencies to administer the programmes involved. (2) These programmes shall include—(a) planning, co-ordination and execution of appropriate measures for the social, economic and cultural development of the populations concerned; (b) proposing of legislative and other measure to the competent authorities; (c) supervision of the application of these measures.'

56 Article 38, United Nations Declaration on the Rights of Indigenous Peoples (UNDRIP), https://www.un.org/development/desa/indigenouspeoples/declaration-on-the-rights-of-indigenous-peoples.html, accessed 10 July 2021.

57 *Id.* Article 37(1).

Does section 3(1)(e) seek to preserve the so-called 'primitive tribal groups and pre-agricultural communities' like fossils in a museum? Should the state be working to help these communities assimilate with the larger society?

8. According to the Ministry of Tribal Affairs 42,53,089 claims were lodged under the FRA and 19,85,911 titles distributed.[58] These titles covered 1,29,78,785.56 acres corresponding to 52,52,328 hectares. The area of forests over which titles have been distributed is approximately 52,523 sq kms, more than the entire State of Punjab.[59]

What is the value of the forests diverted under the FRA? In March 2008, the Supreme Court fixed a range of values for forests depending on the type of forest.[60] Applying the average value to the figure of diverted forests, the estimated forest cover loss is around Rs. 3,88,672 crores.

The Ministry of Tribal Affairs also acknowledges that 17,52,553 claims (constituting 41.22%) were rejected. Assume an average of 3.5 acres[61] for every rejected claim. Then, the total area under illegal occupation by persons whose claims were rejected works out to 24,82,315 hectares or 24,823 sq kms. This area is nearly two-thirds the size of Kerala.[62] The estimated value of the forests under illegal occupation works out to Rs. 1,83,691 crores.

9. The FRA envisages permanent settlements in forests with schools, hospitals, fair price shops, skill upgradation and vocational training centres, electric and telecommunication lines, community centres, etc. What will likely happen when the size of these forest communities increases?

10. Fourteen years after the enactment of FRA, not a single critical wildlife habitat was notified. Does the FRA reduce wildlife protection to a vanishing point? What happens to the national wildlife policy?

11. Wildlife First, a non-governmental organization, petitioned the Supreme Court challenging the constitutional validity of the FRA both on legislative competence as well as the violation of fundamental rights.[63] Acknowledging the historical injustice to Scheduled Tribes and their close bond to the forests, the petition impugned the validation of encroachments by other traditional forest dwellers. According to Wildlife First, the policies underlying the FRA and the Wild Life Act must be reconciled. This requires notifying critical wildlife habitats including (i) 'critical tiger habitats' in tiger reserves in terms of section 38V of the Wild Life Act; (ii) areas, habitats and ecosystems that support endangered species recognized by the MoEF in its National Wildlife Action Plan (2002–16) (e.g. snow leopard, wild buffalo, Bengal Florican, Great Indian Bustard, Asiatic Lion, Dugong, Manipur Brow Antlered Deer); and (iii) the habitats and forests of all species (flora and fauna) that are listed by the International Union for Conservation of Nature (IUCN) in the Red Data List.

---

[58] Ministry of Tribal Affairs, Government of India, *Status Report on the FRA for the period ending 31 August 2020*, https://tribal.nic.in/downloads/FRA/MPR/2020/(E)%20-MPR%20Aug%202020.pdf, accessed 10 July 2021. At this time a total of 36,51,414 constituting 87.15% claims were processed.

[59] The State of Punjab has an area of 50,362 sq kms.

[60] *T N Godavarman v Union of India* (2008) 7 SCC 126. The 'net present value' (NPV) ranged between Rs. 4,38,000 to Rs. 10,43,000 per hectare. The average NPV is Rs. 7,40,000 per hectare.

[61] This figure of 3.5 acres is based on the average occupation per claim as per the 21st Committee of Estimates (2012–2013) 21st Report presented to the 15th Lok Sabha on 23 April 2013.

[62] The State of Kerala has an area of 38,863 sq kms.

[63] *Wildlife First v Union of India*, Writ Petition (Civil) No. 109 of 2008 (the petition was pending at the time of writing).

12. Wildlife First also placed before the court pre and post-FRA satellite images of protected forests. These images showed pristine forest areas devastated by agriculture and encroachments after the passage of the FRA. What should the Supreme Court do?

13. Does the FRA represent a crisis of anthropocentrism? After the Forest Rights Act do we need a *Rights of the Forest* Act?

14. On 20 September 2014, the Chief Conservator of Forests, Maharashtra, wrote to the Secretary of the MoEF pointing out instances of misuse of the FRA. He asked the Ministry of Tribal Affairs to issue instructions to prevent abuse of the Act. The letter recorded:

> The confidential report submitted by Joint Commissioner, State Intelligence Department to Additional Chief Secretary ... mentions that [a certain NGO] led by Retd. Judge [. . .] is instigating Scheduled Castes, Scheduled Tribes and other communities to encroach on forest land in Pune District.[64]

15. On 10 March 2016, the State of Karnataka filed an affidavit before the Supreme Court providing an update on the implementation of the FRA. Karnataka received 2,97,639 applications out of which 1,64,329 applications were pending. Out of the 1,33,310 applications processed, 1,24,206 claims were rejected. Rights were conferred on 8,235 Scheduled Tribe families, 676 other traditional forest dwellers and 193 forest communities. The affidavit states that in terms of a decision by the Karnataka Cabinet on 20 June 2015, the government had:

> taken policy decision not to evict any of the encroachers who occupied forest land up to 3 acres (including the land already owned by them). Such encroachers if at all have to be evicted, it is decided to extend a rehabilitation package and only on implementation of such scheme eviction needs [to be] carried out.

In view of this policy, Karnataka stated that no steps had been taken to evict occupiers whose applications were rejected.[65]

16. M V Nadkarni and Khalil Shaha conclude their analysis of the FRA with a call for a humane resettlement policy that does not alienate the forest dwellers. They argue that the holdings under the FRA are 'intrinsically non-viable' for cultivation and forest dwellers must necessarily access forest resources outside their holdings. Unless resettlement is adopted, forest dwellers will be denied access to modern amenities, will suffer human–animal conflict and will continue to exert pressure on protected areas. In their view, generous resettlement packages are in the best interest of forest dwellers and forest conservation.[66]

---

64 Letter No. FLD-2013/CR-5/F-3 Revenue and Forest Department, Government of Maharashtra. The names of the non-governmental organization and Judge are redacted here.

65 Affidavit of Hari Kumar Jha, Additional Principal Chief Conservator of Forests dated 10 March 2016. Supreme Court of India, *Bombay Natural History Society v Union of India*, Writ Petition No. 514 of 2016.

66 M V Nadkarni & Khalil Shaha, *Reconciling Conservation of Forests with the Forests Rights Act 2006* 74 Indian Jr Of Agric Econ 527 (2019).

3

CONSTITUTIONAL PROVISIONS

The structure of environmental legislation and regulation is built on a constitutional edifice. The Constitution plays many roles in protecting India's environment. Apart from enabling the enactment of environmental laws by supplying the requisite authority to the legislature, it silently weighs in on every case. The Constitution provides the moral foundation for these laws, elevates environmental protection to a high state purpose, defines principles of environmental law through constitutional courts and gives an impetus for enforcement through the grant of constitutional writs.

In this chapter we examine the constitutional provisions that relate to the environment and the constitutional morality that infuses environmental ethics into governance.

A. CONSTITUTIONAL PROVISIONS AND THE ENVIRONMENT

I. FUNDAMENTAL NORMS

The Indian Constitution is amongst the few in the world that contains specific provisions on environmental protection. The chapters on Directive Principles of State Policy and the Fundamental Duties explicitly enunciate the national commitment to protect and improve the environment. Judicial interpretation has strengthened this constitutional mandate.

In a case where the Supreme Court intervened to protect the forest wealth and wildlife from the ravages of mining in and around Sariska sanctuary in the Alwar district of Rajasthan, the court viewed its own constitutional role thus:

> This litigation concerns environment. A great American Judge emphasizing the imperative issue of environment said that he placed Government above big business, individual liberty above Government and environment above all. The issues and concerns in this case far transcend the trivialities and inhibitions of an adversarial litigation. All the parties must be forthcoming in a concerted effort to find a satisfying solution to the problem which, in more ways than one, is typical of the Indian predicament. We are, therefore, entitled to expect that the State Government and the mining-entrepreneurs in their own enlightened self interest will discard the adversarial litigative stance. *The issues of environment must and shall receive the highest attention from this Court.*[1]

This approach has led the Supreme Court to derive, adopt and apply a range of principles to guide the development of environmental jurisprudence. Notable amongst the *fundamental norms* recognized by the court are:

---

[1] Emphasis supplied. *Tarun Bharat Sangh, Alwar v Union of India* (*Sariska* case), Writ Petition (Civil) No. 509 of 1991, Supreme Court, 14 May 1992 (M N Venkatachaliah and B P Jeevan Reddy, JJ).

Environmental Law & Policy in India. Shyam Divan and Armin Rosencranz, Oxford University Press.
 DOI: 1093/oso/9780192865458.003.0003

(1) Every person enjoys the right to a wholesome environment, which is a facet of the right to life guaranteed under Article 21 of the Constitution of India.[2]
(2) The 'polluter pays' principle requires that a polluter bear the remedial or clean-up costs and compensate the victims of pollution.[3]
(3) The 'precautionary principle' requires government authorities to anticipate, prevent and attack the causes of environmental pollution. It imposes the onus of proof on the developer or industrialist to show that his or her action is environmentally benign.[4]
(4) The doctrine of 'sustainable development' must inform the development strategy adopted by the state. This approach caters to the needs of the present without compromising the ability of future generations to satisfy their needs.[5]
(5) The principle of 'inter-generational equity' obliges the present generation to preserve natural resources and pass on to future generations an environment as intact as the one we inherited from the previous generation.[6]
(6) The public at large is the beneficiary of the sea-shore, running waters, air, forests and ecologically fragile lands. According to the 'public trust doctrine' the state is the trustee of all natural resources which are by nature meant for public use and enjoyment. These resources cannot be converted into private ownership.[7]
(7) Enforcement agencies are under an obligation to strictly enforce environmental laws.[8]

---

[2] *Subhash Kumar v State of Bihar* AIR 1991 SC 420, 424; *M C Mehta v Union of India* (*Delhi Stone Crushing* case) (1992) 3 SCC 256, 257; *Virender Gaur v State of Haryana* (1995) 2 SCC 577, 581; *State of Uttaranchal v Balwant Singh Chaufal* (2010) 3 SCC 402, 438–43; *Hinch Lal Tiwari v Kamala Devi* (2001) 6 SCC 496, 501; *T N Godavarman Thirumalpad v Union of India* (*Kudremukh Iron Ore Company* case) (2002) 10 SCC 606, 625; *State of M P v Kedia Leather & Liquor Ltd* (2003) 7 SCC 389, 394; and *Mantri Techzone Pvt Ltd v Forward Foundation* (2019) 18 SCC 494, 517.

[3] *Indian Council for Enviro-Legal Action v Union of India* (*Bichhri* case) AIR 1996 SC 1446, 1466; *Vellore Citizens' Welfare Forum v Union of India* AIR 1996 SC 2715, 2721; *S Jagannath v Union of India* (*Shrimp Culture* case) AIR 1997 SC 811, 846, 850; *Karnataka Industrial Area Development Board v C Kenchappa* (2006) 6 SCC 371, 387; *Bittu Sehgal v Union of India* (2001) 9 SCC 181, 193; *M C Mehta v Kamal Nath* (2002) 3 SCC 653, 660, 661; *Research Foundation for Science (18) v Union of India* (2005) 13 SCC 186, 200; *Lal Bahadur v State of UP* (2018) 15 SCC 407, 424–5; and *M C Mehta v Union of India* (*Kant Enclave* case) (2018) 18 SCC 397, 446.

[4] *Vellore Citizens Welfare Forum v Union of India* AIR 1996 SC 2715, 2721; *S Jagannath v Union of India* (*Shrimp Culture* case) AIR 1997 SC 811, 846; *A P Pollution Control Board v Prof M V Nayudu* AIR 1999 SC 812, 819; *Karnataka Industrial Area Development Board v C Kenchappa* (2006) 6 SCC 371, 386; *Bittu Sehgal v Union of India* (2001) 9 SCC 181, 193, 196; *Research Foundation for Science (18) v Union of India* (2005) 13 SCC 186, 200; *Amarnath Shrine, In Re* (2013) 3 SCC 247; *Arjun Gopal v Union of India* (2017) 16 SCC 267, 269 and *Hospitality Association of Mudumalai v In Defence of Environment and Animals* (*Elephant Corridor* case) (2020) 10 SCC 589, 607.

[5] *M C Mehta v Union of India* (2001) 4 SCC 577, 580; *N D Jayal v Union of India* (2004) 9 SCC 362, 381–3; *Amarnath Shrine, In Re* (2013) 3 SCC 247; *Alembic Pharmaceuticals Ltd v Rohit Prajapati* (2020) SCC Online SC 347; and *State of Meghalaya v All Dimasa Students Union* (2019) 8 SCC 177, 196.

[6] *State of Himachal Pradesh v Ganesh Wood Products* AIR 1996 SC 149, 159; *Glanrock Estate Pvt Ltd v State of Tamil Nadu* (2010) 10 SCC 96, 109; *Amarnath Shrine, In Re*, (2013) 3 SCC 247; *Alembic Pharmaceuticals Ltd v Rohit Prajapati* (2020) SCC Online SC 347; *State of Meghalaya v All Dimasa Students Union* (2019) 8 SCC 177, 196; and *Municipal Corporation of Greater Mumbai v Ankita Sinha* (2021) SCC Online SC 897.

[7] *M C Mehta v Kamal Nath* (*Span Motels* case) (1997) 1 SCC 388; *M I Builders v Radhey Shyam Sahu* AIR 1999 SC 2468, 2498; *Karnataka Industrial Area Development Board v C Kenchappa* (2006) 6 SCC 371, 388; *Intellectuals Forum v State of A P* (2006) 3 SCC 549, 574; *Fomento Resorts and Hotels Ltd v Minguel Martins* (2009) 3 SCC 571, 614; *Centre for Public Interest Litigation v Union of India* (2012) 3 SCC 1; *Association for Environment Protection v State of Kerala* (2013) 7 SCC 226, 229 and *Tata Housing Development Company Ltd v Aalok Jagga* (2020) 15 SCC 784.

[8] *Indian Council for Enviro-Legal Action v Union of India* (*CRZ Notification* case) (1996) 5 SCC 281, 294, 301; and *M C Mehta v Union of India* (2004) 6 SCC 588, 618.

(8) Government development agencies charged with decision-making ought to give due regard to ecological factors including the environmental policy of the Central and state governments.[9]

(9) Government agencies may not plead non-availability of funds, inadequacy of staff or other insufficiencies to justify the non-performance of their obligations under environmental laws.[10]

(10) The power conferred under an environmental statute may be exercised only to advance environmental protection and not for a purpose that would defeat the object of the law.[11]

(11) Stringent action ought to be taken against contumacious defaulters and persons who carry on industrial or development activity for profit without regard to environmental laws.[12]

(12) To protect endangered species, decision-makers ought to adopt an eco-centric approach over an anthropocentric approach. The eco-centric principle respects the intrinsic value, interdependence and integrity of all forms of life, not just humans. Where a species is endangered, the court may apply the 'species best interest standard' to test the validity of state action.[13]

(13) The principle of environmental Rule of Law requires that the process of environmental decision-making is transparent, responsive and inclusive.[14]

These norms were articulated by the Supreme Court by drawing on the core values protected by the fundamental right to life guaranteed by Article 21 of the Constitution.

Public Trust Doctrine

In the late 1970s Fomento Resorts & Hotels Ltd. commenced construction of Hotel Cidade de Goa. Designed by architect Charles Correa, the site evolved over several years on land abutting Vainguinim beach. The company owned several plots in the locale but the creation of a composite unit was impeded by privately held plots 803 and 804. Intending to set up health and recreational facilities, the company urged the state to acquire these two plots. The state government resorted to the Land Acquisition Act of 1894 and handed over the plots to the hotelier after signing an agreement on 26 October 1983. Clause 4 of the agreement which was made under section 41 of the Act, in pertinent part read:

---

[9] *State of Himachal Pradesh v Ganesh Wood Products* AIR 1996 SC 149, 163; and *N D Jayal v Union of India* (2004) 9 SCC 362, 382.

[10] *Dr B L Wadhera v Union of India* (*Delhi Garbage* case) AIR 1996 SC 2969, 2976; and *Almitra H Patel v Union of India* (2000) 2 SCC 679, 686–7.

[11] *Bangalore Medical Trust v B S Muddappa* AIR 1991 SC 1902, 1911, 1924; *Virender Gaur v State of Haryana* (1995) 2 SCC 577, 583; *Indian Council for Enviro-Legal Action v Union of India* (*CRZ Notification* case) (1996) 5 SCC 281, 299, 302; *Bombay Dyeing and Mfg Co Ltd v Bombay Environmental Action Group* (*Mill Lands* case) (2006) 3 SCC 434, 526; and *Lafarge Umium Mining (P) Ltd v Union of India* (2011) 7 SCC 338, 380.

[12] *Indian Council for Enviro-Legal Action v Union of India* (*Bichhri* case) AIR 1996 SC 1446, 1468; *Pratibha Co-operative Housing Society Ltd v State of Maharashtra* AIR 1991 SC 1453, 1456; *Pleasant Stay Hotel v Palani Hills Conservation Council* (1995) 6 SCC 127, 139; *M I Builders v Radhey Shyam Sahu* AIR 1999 SC 2468, 2505; and *Research Foundation for Science (18) v Union of India* (2005) 13 SCC 186, 201.

[13] *T N Godavarman Thirumulpad v Union of India* (*Sandalwood* case) (2012) 4 SCC 362, 374; *T N Godavarman Thirumulpad v Union of India* (*Asiatic Wild Buffalo* case) (2012) 3 SCC 277, 283; and *Centre for Environment Law, WWF-I v Union of India* (*Asiatic Lion* case) (2013) 8 SCC 234, 256.

[14] *Hanuman Laxman Aroskar v Union of India* (*Goa Airport* case) (2019) 15 SCC 401; *Bengaluru Development Authority v Sudhakar Hegde* (2020) 15 SCC 63; *Himachal Pradesh Bus Stand Management & Development Authority v Central Empowered Committee* (2021) SCC Online SC 15; and *Citizens for Green Doon v Union of India* (2021) SCC Online SC 1074.

4. (i) The Company shall not use the said land for any purpose other than that for which it is acquired.
   (ii) The Company shall undertake the work of creation of sports and other recreational facilities/amenities within one year from the date on which the possession of the said land is handed over to the Company and complete the same within three years from the aforesaid date. . . .
   (viii) The Company shall never construct any building or structures in the acquired land. Prior approval of Eco-Development Council of the Government of Goa, Daman and Diu will be obtained before undertaking activities for its development, besides other statutory requirements under the existing laws.
   (ix) The public access/road to the beach shall not be affected or obstructed in any manner.

After 1988 the hotelier commenced a new phase of expansion and secured permissions to extend the building over plot 803.

Several petitions were filed before the Goa Bench of the Bombay High Court to challenge the new construction on plot 803. According to the writ petitioners the construction blocked traditional access to the public beach and violated the construction embargo under clause 4 (viii). Impressed, the Bombay High Court directed demolition of the construction, ordered resumption by the state of the land acquired for the company, and restoration of public access through plot 803. In the hotelier's appeal, the Supreme Court largely maintained the directions issued by the High Court. We carry a short excerpt focusing on the public trust doctrine.

FOMENTO RESORTS AND HOTELS LIMITED v MINGUEL MARTINS

(2009) 3 SCC 571

***

G S Singhvi, J:

The matter deserves to be considered from another angle. The public trust doctrine which has been invoked [by the respondent's counsel] in support of her argument that the beach in question is a public beach and the appellants cannot privatise the same by blocking/obstructing traditional access available through Survey No. 803 is implicitly engrafted by the State Government in Clause 4(ix) of the agreement. That doctrine primarily rests on the principle that certain resources like air, sea, waters and the forests have such a great importance to the people as a whole that it would be wholly unjustified to make them a subject of private ownership. These resources are gift of nature, therefore, they should be freely available to everyone irrespective of one's status in life.

The public trust doctrine enjoins upon the Government to protect the resources for the enjoyment of the general public rather than to permit their use for private ownership or commercial purposes. This doctrine puts an implicit embargo on the right of the State to transfer public properties to private party if such transfer affects public interest, mandates affirmative State action for effective management of natural resources and empowers the citizens to question ineffective management thereof.

The heart of the public trust doctrine is that it imposes limits and obligations upon government agencies and their administrators on behalf of all the people and especially future generations. For example, renewable and non-renewable resources, associated uses, ecological values or objects in which the public has a special interest (i.e. public lands, waters, etc.) are held subject to the duty of the State not to impair such resources, uses or values, even if private interests are involved. The same obligations apply to managers of forests, monuments, parks, the public domain and other public assets. Professor Joseph L Sax in his classic article, 'The Public Trust Doctrine in Natural Resources Law: Effective Judicial Intervention' (1970), indicates that the public trust doctrine, of all concepts known to law, constitutes the best practical and philosophical premise and legal tool for protecting public rights and for protecting and managing resources, ecological values or objects held in trust. . . .

We reiterate that natural resources including forests, water bodies, rivers, seashores, etc. are held by the State as a trustee on behalf of the people and especially the future generations. These constitute common properties and people are entitled to uninterrupted use thereof. The State cannot transfer public trust properties to a private party, if such a transfer interferes with the right of the public and the court can invoke the public trust doctrine and take affirmative action for protecting the right of people to have access to light, air and water and also for protecting rivers, sea, tanks, trees, forests and associated natural ecosystems.

As a sequel to the above discussion, we hold that Clause 4(ix) of the agreement is binding on the appellants and Appellant 1 is under a statutory obligation to maintain access/road to the beach through Survey No. 803 without any obstruction of any kind and the High Court did not commit any error by issuing a mandamus in that regard....

In the result, the appeals are dismissed. Since execution of most of the directions given by the High Court remained stayed during the pendency of these appeals, we deem it proper to issue the following directions:

(i) The appellants are allowed three months' time to demolish the extended portion of the hotel building which was constructed on 1000 sq m of Survey No. 803 and, thereafter report the matter to the Development Authority which shall, in turn, submit a report to that effect to the Goa Bench of the Bombay High Court.

(ii) If the appellants fail to demolish the building and report the matter to the Development Authority within the time specified in Direction (i) above, the authority concerned shall take action in accordance with paras (a) and (b) of the operative part of the High Court's order.

(iii) The access shown in the plan, Ext. A attached to Writ Petition No. 141 of 1992 shall be kept open without any obstruction of any kind from Points A to B in order to come from Machado's Cove and then go to the beach beyond Point B. If during pendency of the litigation, Appellant 1 has put up any obstruction or made construction to block or hinder access to the beach through Survey No. 803, then the same shall be removed within one month from today....

NOTES AND QUESTIONS

1. Indian courts and the National Green Tribunal are yet to explain the rigour of the public trust doctrine. Scholars suggest that it imposes restrictions on the use of natural resources by imposing limits on state action while dealing with these resources and creating positive obligations for their preservation. According to this view, (a) certain natural resources are of immense ecological value and must be protected for the general public including future generations; (b) the state holds these natural resources only as a trustee of the public, and not as an owner; (c) therefore, the state cannot create private or commercial interests in these resources contrary to the rights of the general public; (d) the property must not be sold even for a fair value; and (e) the property must be maintained for a particular kind of use such as recreation or fishery.[15]

Is this understanding of the doctrine sufficient for it to be used as a jurisprudential tool? Can an undefined ecological value be relied on to stake out certain 'no-go' areas such as biodiversity hotspots and restrict development for ecological stability of the planet?

2. The hotelier claimed to have provided an alternative access to the beach by constructing a road, parking area and public footpath in terms of permissions granted by the village panchayat. It asked to be relieved of the obligation to maintain access through plot 803. In a

[15] Patricia Kameri-Mbote, *The Use of the Public Trust Doctrine in Environmental Law*, 3/2 Law, Envir & Devlop Jr 195, 199 (2007) <http://www.lead-journal.org/content/07195.pdf> accessed 10 July 2021.

portion of the judgment not excerpted, the Supreme Court rejected the request, holding that an age-old right of the public cannot be defeated by an alternative access arrangement. How convincing is this principle? What is wrong in providing alternative access if both the public and the hotelier stand to gain?

3. The Supreme Court judgment in *Fomento Resorts* was rendered on 20 January 2009. Within a few weeks the Goa Cabinet met on 24 February 2009 and noticed that the judgment would impact several other business groups and corporations, apart from Fomento. Goa promulgated an Ordinance on 20 February 2009, amending the Land Acquisition Act of 1894. The Ordinance was followed by a supplementary agreement on 6 March 2009 which deleted clause 4(viii) of the principal agreement of 1983 in the following manner:

> 1. That in the principal agreement, in Condition 4, clause (viii) shall be deemed to have been deleted with retrospective effect from 26-10-1983 and the principal agreement shall be so read and construed as if in Condition 4, clause (viii) never existed in the principal deed w.e.f. 26-10-1983.

As a consequence, according to both the state and the hotelier there was now no necessity to carry out the demolition on plot 803. The building was saved.

Goa Foundation and its secretary, Claude Alvares, would have none of this. As successful writ petitioners right up to the Supreme Court in *Fomento Resorts*, they filed for contempt and separately challenged the constitutional validity of the Amendment Act of 2009 (which replaced the Ordinance).

By the 2009 amendment, Goa inserted the following provisions into section 41 of the Land Acquisition Act of 1894:[16]

> 2. *Amendment of Section 41.*—In Section 41 of the Land Acquisition Act, 1894 (Central Act 1 of 1894), as in force in the State of Goa, after clause (5), the following shall be inserted, namely—
>
> (6) Notwithstanding anything contained in any judgment, decree or an order of any court, tribunal or any other authority, any development done or construction undertaken in pursuance of the agreement entered under this section between the Government and the Company on the basis of the statutory approvals like permissions granted by the Planning and Development Authority, Eco-Development Council, Goa Coastal Zone Management Authority, Municipal Council, Panchayat, including renewals and deviations thereof approved and regularised, and all permissions obtained by the company and all the buildings constructed by the Company and all the proceedings taken by the competent authorities to issue the licence or permission for undertaking construction, shall be deemed to have been validly done and have always been undertaken in accordance with the said agreement.
>
> (7) Notwithstanding anything contained in any judgment, decree, or order of any court, tribunal or any other authority the appropriate Government shall be at liberty to modify the agreement executed under this section between the Government and the Company on mutually agreed terms in furtherance of the purpose for which the land was acquired, by publication of the modified agreement in the Official Gazette, and any such modifications made in the agreement, shall come into force from the date on which the original agreement with the Company was executed under this section and any action taken or things done under the modified agreement, shall, for all purposes, be deemed and to have always been done or taken in accordance with the original agreement.

[16] The principal agreement of 26 October 1983 was executed under section 41.

(8) Notwithstanding anything contained in any judgment, decree or order of any court, tribunal or any other authority, if, in any agreement entered into between the Government and the Company, there be any clause prohibiting the Company to construct any building or structure in the acquired land, such clause shall [be] deemed to have been deleted with retrospective effect from 15-10-1964.

(9) No suit or other proceeding shall be instituted, maintained or continued in any court or before any tribunal or other authority for cancellation of such permission or for demolition of buildings which were constructed after obtaining the permissions from the statutory authorities and have been validated under this section, or for questioning the validity of any action taken or things done or permission granted in pursuance of the original agreement as modified and no court shall enforce or recognise any decree, judgment or order declaring any such action taken or things done under the original agreement as modified, as invalid or unlawful.

The Supreme Court repelled the challenge by Goa Foundation:[17]

> The principles on which first question would require to be answered are not in doubt. The power to invalidate a legislative or executive act lies with the court. A judicial pronouncement, either declaratory or conferring rights on the citizens cannot be set at naught by a subsequent legislative act for that would amount to an encroachment on the judicial powers. However, the legislature would be competent to pass an amending or a validating act, if deemed fit, with retrospective effect removing the basis of the decision of the court. Even in such a situation the courts may not approve a retrospective deprivation of accrued rights arising from a judgment by means of a subsequent legislation. However, where the court's judgment is purely declaratory, the courts will lean in support of the legislative power to remove the basis of a court judgment even retrospectively, paving the way for a restoration of the status quo ante. Though the consequence may appear to be an exercise to overcome the judicial pronouncement it is so only at first blush; a closer scrutiny would confer legitimacy on such an exercise as the same is a normal adjunct of the legislative power. The whole exercise is one of viewing the different spheres of jurisdiction exercised by the two bodies i.e. the judiciary and the legislature. The balancing act, delicate as it is, to the constitutional scheme is guided by the well-defined values which have found succinct manifestation in the views of this Court in *Bakhtawar Trust v M D Narayan* (2003) 5 SCC 298....
>
> If the above principles are to be applied to the present case what follows is that Sections 41(6) to (9) introduced in the principal Act by the Goa State Amendment renders ineffective Clause 4(viii) of the agreement executed by the parties under Section 41 of the principal Act. With Clause 4(viii) being deleted the embargo on constructions on the acquired land is removed. It is the aforesaid Clause 4(viii) and its legal effect, in view of section 42, that was the basis of the Court's decision dated 20-1-2009 holding the construction raised by the third respondent on the acquired land to be illegal and contrary to the principal Act. Once Clause 4(viii) is removed the basis of the earlier judgment stands extinguished. In fact, it may be possible to say that if Clause 4(viii) had not existed at all, the judgment of the Court dated 20-1-2009 [*Fomento Resorts*] would not have been forthcoming. It was, therefore, well within the domain of the legislature to bring about the Amendment Act with retrospective effect, the legislative field also being in the Concurrent List, namely, Entry 42 of List III (Acquisition and Requisition of Property) of the Seventh Schedule to the Constitution.

The net effect of this exercise was that the building extension over a part of plot 803 as well as the public access to the beach through another part of plot 803 survived.

[17] *Goa Foundation v State of Goa* (2016) 6 SCC 602.

4. Who do you think was the prime mover behind the legislation: the state executive, Fomento, other affected corporations? Would a legislative response with such alacrity have happened elsewhere in the country?

Eco-centrism

On 13 February 2012, Justice K S P Radhakrishnan delivered separate judgments in the *Asiatic Wild Buffalo* case[18] and the *Sandalwood* case (excerpted below). Read together, these judgments suggest that a fresh environmental ethic should inform decision-making. The Supreme Court urges a special respect for all species, regardless of their utility to humans. This eco-centric approach was necessary to protect two endangered species of sandalwood, and various other life forms that share our planet but are threatened with extinction.

T N GODAVARMAN THIRUMULPAD v UNION OF INDIA
(2012) 4 SCC 362

***

K S P Radhakrishnan, J:

The public trust doctrine developed in *M C Mehta v Kamal Nath* is also meant to ensure that all humans have equitable access to natural resources treating all natural resources as property and not life. That principle also has its roots in anthropocentric principle. Precautionary principle and polluter-pays principle affirmed by our Court in *Vellore Citizens' Welfare Forum v Union of India* are also based on anthropocentric principle since they also depend on harm to humans as a prerequisite for invoking those principles. The principle of sustainable development and intergenerational equity too presupposes the higher needs of humans and lays down that exploitation of natural resources must be equitably distributed between the present and future generations. Environmental ethics behind those principles were human need and exploitation, but such principles have no role to play when we are called upon to decide the fate of an endangered species or the need to protect the same irrespective of its instrumental value.

Anthropocentrism considers humans to be the most important factor and value in the universe and states that humans have greater intrinsic value than other species. Resultantly, any species that are of the potential use to humans can be a reserve to be exploited which leads to the point of extinction of biological reserves. Further, that principle highlights human obligations towards environment arising out of instrumental, educational, scientific, cultural, recreational and aesthetic values that forests have to offer to humans. Under this approach, environment is only protected as a consequence of and to the extent needed to protect human well-being.

On the other hand, economic approach to environment stresses the moral imperatives to respect intrinsic value, interdependence and integrity of all forms of life. Ecocentrism supports the protection of all life forms, not just those which are of value to humans or their needs and underlines the fact that humans are just one among the various life forms on earth. (See Environmental Ethics, *Standard Encyclopedia of Philosophy*, 2002; Revised Edn 2008.)

The same book also gives a clear distinction between instrumental value and intrinsic value which reads as follows:

> In the literature on environmental ethics the distinction between instrumental value and intrinsic value (meaning 'non-instrumental value') has been of considerable importance. The former is the value of things as means to further some other ends, whereas the latter is the value of things as ends in themselves regardless of whether they are also useful as means to other ends. For instance, certain fruits have instrumental value for bats who feed on them, since feeding on the fruits is a means of survival for the bats. However, it is not widely agreed that fruits have value as ends in themselves.

[18] *T N Godavarman Thirumulpad v Union of India* (2012) 3 SCC 277. This case is excerpted in the Wildlife Protection chapter.

We can likewise think of a person who teaches others as having instrumental value for those who want to acquire knowledge. Yet, in addition to any such value, it is normally said that a person, as a person, has intrinsic value i.e. value in his or her own right independently of his or her prospects for serving the ends of others. For another example, a certain wild plant may have instrumental value because it provides the ingredients for some medicine or as an aesthetic object for human observer. But if the plant also has some value in itself independently for its prospects for furthering some other ends such as human health, or the pleasure from aesthetic experience, then the plant also had intrinsic value. Because the intrinsically valuable is that which is good as an end in itself, it is commonly agreed that something's possession of intrinsic value generates a prima facie direct moral duty on the part of moral agents to protect it or at least refrain from damaging it.

The above principle had its roots in India, much before it was thought of in the western world. Isha Upanishad (as early as 1500–600 BC) taught us the following truth:

> The universe along with its creatures belongs to the Lord. No creature is superior to any other. Human beings should not be above nature. Let no one species encroach over the rights and privileges of other species....

NOTES AND QUESTIONS

1. Reviewing the development of environmental law, the Supreme Court found that the public trust doctrine, the precautionary principle and the polluter pays principle are all based on an anthropocentric world view that puts humans above all other species. Does the Supreme Court's arguably sentimental view of other species ignore thousands of years of building civilizations and the history of human development? Does the eco-centric approach provide a more reliable standard for judicial review? Will it be sustainable?

2. Is the eco-centric principle rigorously enforceable in a court of law or is it merely a convenient handle for judges to support their desired conclusion? If all species are entitled to live, what about vermin, harmful germs and a whole range of species that harm human health?

Sustainable Development

The notion of sustainable development provides a useful guideline for policy-makers and those responsible for executing projects. At the stage of conception and implementation, environmental factors should be considered in order to choose a suitable location, mitigate adverse impacts and temper decision-making otherwise premised exclusively on economic considerations.

When it comes to legal contests, 'sustainable development' is too vague and flexible a notion to promote certainty and predictability. It provides a poor foundation when made the sole support for a judicial verdict. Judges usually decide the dispute on the facts, independent of this vague construct and then hang their conclusion on this convenient peg. In practice, where there is no brazen violation of law and an element of judicial discretion is available with the judge, broad notions of sustainable development merely require some mitigation measures as palliative.

The Supreme Court judgment in *Karnataka Industrial Area Development Board v C Kenchappa*[19] collates developments in Indian environmental jurisprudence without contributing much of

[19] (2006) 6 SCC 371.

its own to the field. Gee India Technology Centre Pvt Ltd proposed a research and development laboratory that would employ 500 scientists and several other technical personnel. The company was allotted 20 acres of government land apart from tracts acquired by the KIADB from private citizens. Some agriculturists assailed the acquisition, claiming that these lands were necessary for grazing their cattle. The Karnataka High Court acknowledged the economic importance of the project and upheld the allotment in favour of the company. However, in seeking to strike a balance between industrial development and ecological preservation, the High Court directed the KIADB to maintain a buffer zone of 1 km from the outer periphery of villages for agriculture and cattle grazing. The buffer was intended to be a green area around land acquired for industrial or commercial purposes. KIADB assailed the judgment in the Supreme Court, submitting that the blanket directions issued by the High Court were tantamount to judicial legislation. The Supreme Court set aside the buffer zone directions, substituting them with these mild (and possibly unenforceable) directions:

> (1) We direct that, in future, before acquisition of lands for development, the consequence and adverse impact of development on environment must be properly comprehended and the lands be acquired for development that they do not gravely impair the ecology and environment.
>
> (2) We also direct the appellant to incorporate the condition of allotment to obtain clearance from the Karnataka State Pollution Control Board before the land is allotted for development. The said directory condition of allotment of lands be converted into a mandatory condition for all the projects to be sanctioned in future.[20]

As a judicial standard the notion of 'sustainable development' is vague and subjective, allowing the courts vast discretion in moulding relief. In the present case, the High Court and the Supreme Court solutions could well have been interchanged, with none being the wiser.

II. DIVISION OF LEGISLATIVE AUTHORITY

Under India's federal system, governmental power is shared between the Union or 'Central' Government and the 28 state governments. Part XI of the Constitution governs the legislative and administrative relations between the Union and the states.

Parliament has the power to legislate for the whole country, while the State legislatures are empowered to make laws for their respective states. Article 246 of the Constitution divides the subject areas of legislation between the Union and the states. The Union List (List I) in the Seventh Schedule to the Constitution contains 100 subjects over which Parliament has exclusive powers to legislate. These include defence, foreign affairs, atomic energy, interstate transportation, shipping, major ports, regulation of air traffic, regulation and development of oilfields, mines and mineral development and interstate rivers. The State legislatures have exclusive power to legislate with respect to 61 subjects in the State List (List II), such as public health and sanitation, agriculture, water supplies, irrigation and drainage and fisheries.

Under the Concurrent List (List III), both Parliament and the State legislatures have overlapping and shared jurisdiction over 52 subject areas including forests, the protection of wildlife, mines and mineral development not covered in the Union List, population control and family planning, minor ports and factories.

---

[20] *Id* at 391. The court succumbed to a bout of self-praise: 'This has been an interesting judicial pilgrimage for the last four decades. In our opinion, this is a significant contribution of the judiciary in making serious endeavour to preserve and protect ecology and environment, in consonance with the provisions of the Constitution.' *Id.*

Parliament has residual power to legislate on subjects not covered by the three Lists.[21] When a central law conflicts with a state law on a concurrent subject, the former prevails. However, a state law passed subsequent to the central law will prevail if it has received Presidential Assent under Article 254.

Parliament is also empowered to legislate in the 'national interest' on matters enumerated in the State List.[22] In addition, Parliament may enact laws on state subjects, for states whose legislatures have consented to central legislations. Thus, the Water (Prevention and Control of Pollution) Act of 1974 was enacted by Parliament pursuant to consent resolutions passed by 12 State legislatures.

From an environmental standpoint, the allocation of legislative authority is an important one: some environmental problems such as sanitation and waste disposal are best tackled at the local level. Others, like water pollution and wildlife protection, are better regulated by uniform national laws.

The Constituent Assembly that framed India's Constitution did not specifically consider the question whether Parliament or the State legislatures should regulate environmental matters. Instead, the distribution of environmental subjects within the three Lists was influenced by the Government of India Act of 1935 and by the conflict between those who wished to create a strong Centre and others who preferred to secure more powers for the states.[23] Understandably, there was a tussle for control over natural resources such as forests and fisheries which were important economic subjects. In July 1949 the Drafting Committee of the Constituent Assembly convened a meeting of the Premiers of the Indian states and provinces and the representatives of central ministers to discuss the division of legislative powers.[24]

At this meeting, proposals from the Ministry of Agriculture that 'Forests' and 'Fisheries' be transferred from the State List to the Concurrent List were strongly opposed by the provincial representatives.[25] The ministry argued that forests affect agricultural development and prosperity of the country: no province or state should, even inadvertently, follow a policy that could be detrimental to the rest of the country. 'For instance, floods which cause considerable havoc in the plains may be the result of indiscriminate felling in the catchment areas under the control and jurisdiction of an entirely different Province.'[26] But the arguments failed, the proposals were rejected and the topic 'Forests' was classified as a state subject.[27]

Another proposal, jointly sponsored by the Ministries of Health and Home Affairs, aimed at removing 'Public Health and Sanitation' from the State List and placing it with 'Vital Statistics including registration of births and deaths' in the Concurrent List. It was argued that central legislation would be necessary to prevent the spread of diseases from one province to another. Unconvinced, the Premiers of the United Provinces, Assam, Bombay and Bihar, successfully resisted the move. Only the second part, placing 'Vital Statistics' in the Concurrent List, was accepted at the meeting.[28]

---

21 Article 248 and Entry 97, List I, Seventh Schedule, Constitution of India.

22 Article 249.

23 See generally, H M Seervai, *Constitutional Law of India: A Critical Commentary* 164–71 (Vol I, 1991); Shiva Rao, *The Framing of India's Constitution: Select Documents* 315 (Vol IV, 1968); and Madhav Khosla, *India's Founding Moment: The Constitution of a Most Surprising Democracy* (2020).

24 Shiva Rao, *id.*

25 *Id.* At 635.

26 Shiva Rao, *The Framing of India's Constitution: A Study* 633 (Vol V, 1968).

27 The Constitution (Forty-Second Amendment) Act of 1976 moved 'Forests' to the Concurrent List.

28 Shiva Rao, *supra* note 26, at 634–5.

Elsewhere in these deliberations, the Ministry of Health successfully proposed an expansion of Parliament's power to regulate interstate rivers so that pollution of rivers by industrial wastes and sewage could be controlled. The ministry proposed that the draft Entry 74 in the Union List be widened to read: 'The development of *inter-State rivers* and inter-State waterways for purposes of flood control, irrigation, navigation and hydroelectric power *and for other purposes, where such development under the control of the Union is declared by Parliament by law to be expedient in the public interest.*'[29] This instance of environmental sensitivity was exceptional. The larger question of a decentralized versus a centralized federal structure prevailed over the issue of whether the Central or State legislatures were better situated to regulate environmental matters.

III. THE FORTY-SECOND CONSTITUTIONAL AMENDMENT

Environmental protection and improvement were explicitly incorporated into the Constitution by the Constitution (Forty-Second Amendment) Act of 1976. Article 48A was added to the Directive Principles of State Policy. It declares: 'The State shall endeavour to protect and improve the environment and to safeguard the forests and wild life of the country.' Article 51A(g) in a new chapter entitled 'Fundamental Duties' imposes a similar responsibility on every citizen 'to protect and improve the natural environment including forests, lakes, rivers and wild life, and to have compassion for living creatures'. Although the language in the two articles differs, the differences appear to relate to form rather than to substance. Together, the provisions highlight the national consensus on the importance of environmental protection and improvement and lay the foundation for a jurisprudence of environmental protection.[30]

There was considerable debate in Parliament over the wording of draft Article 48A. Several amendments were moved in the Lok Sabha. One of them required the state to 'conserve and develop the water, soil and other natural resources', while another proposed to ensure that the state's efforts to protect and improve the environment would not harm tribal forest dwellers. None of these amendments was accepted by the government, which took the position that the broad terms of a directive principle need not contain details.[31]

Welcoming the provision, members in the Rajya Sabha[32] proposed that the Article should also mention 'mineral wealth' and require the government to 'undertake adequate and effective measures to check environmental pollution'. Both amendments were rejected by the government as the existing wording was considered wide enough to cover the amendments' underlying concerns.[33]

IV. THE DIRECTIVE PRINCIPLES OF STATE POLICY

The directive principles are policy prescriptions that guide the government. Some of them are in the nature of economic rights that India could not guarantee when the Constitution was

---

29 Emphasis supplied. As finally adopted, Item 56 of the Union List (corresponding to draft Entry 74) reads: 'Regulation and development of inter-state rivers and river valleys to the extent to which such regulation and development under the control of the Union is declared by Parliament by law to be expedient in the public interest.'

30 *M C Mehta v State of Orissa* AIR 1992 Ori 225, 227; *Karnataka Industrial Areas Development Board v C Kenchappa* (2006) 6 SCC 371, 379, 380.

31 The Lok Sabha is the House of the People (Lower House of Parliament). *Lok Sabha Debates*, Eighteenth Session, Fifth Series, Vol LXV, No. 5, 29 October 1976, columns 94–116. The Constitution (Forty-Fourth Amendment) Bill of 1976 after passage became the Constitution (Forty-Second Amendment) Act of 1976.

32 House of the States (Upper House of Parliament).

33 *Parliamentary Debate: Rajya Sabha: Official Report*, Vol. XCVIII, No. 5, 9 November 1976, columns 158–71.

enacted, but that were expected to be realized in succeeding years. Although unenforceable by a court, the directive principles are increasingly being cited by judges as complementary to the fundamental rights.[34] In several environmental cases the courts have been guided by the language of Article 48A.[35]

Indeed, the Supreme Court has held:

> Whenever a problem of ecology is brought before the court, the court is bound to bear in mind Art. 48A of the Constitution ... and Art. 51 A(g).... When the court is called upon to give effect to the Directive Principle and the fundamental duty, the court is not to shrug its shoulders and say that priorities are a matter of policy and so it is a matter for the policy-making authority. The least that the court may do is to examine whether appropriate considerations are borne in mind and irrelevancies excluded. In appropriate cases, the court may go further, but how much further will depend on the circumstances of the case. The court may always give necessary directions. However, the court will not attempt to nicely balance relevant considerations. When the question involves the nice balancing of relevant considerations the court may feel justified in resigning itself to acceptance of the decision of the concerned authority.[36]

Since natural resources are national assets, it is the obligation of the Union Government and state governments 'to conserve and not waste these resources'.[37] Post Forty-Second Constitutional Amendment environmental laws seek to achieve the policy goals in Article 48A:

> [F]or understanding the real scope of Article 14, 19 and 21, the impact of Articles 48A and 51A must be taken into consideration. It is with this in mind, Parliament has enacted the Forest (Conservation) Act, 1980, the Wild Life (Protection) Act, 1972 as amended by Act 28 of 1986, the Environment (Protection) Act, 1986 and so on.[38]

India's rich cultural heritage is at times endangered by large development projects and short-sighted locational decisions. For example, emissions by industry which were permitted to operate in and around Agra threaten the Taj Mahal, a monument protected under the Ancient Monuments and Archeological Sites and Remains Act of 1958 and a World Heritage Site recognized by the 1972 UNESCO Convention for the Protection of the World Cultural and Natural Heritage. In such situations, a court may be guided by Article 49, which casts a duty on the state 'to protect every monument or place or object of artistic or historic interest declared by or under law made by Parliament to be of national importance, from spoliation, disfigurement, destruction, removal, disposal or export, as the case may be'. Moreover, in view of the range of international treaties on different aspects of environmental protection, the state's obligation to 'foster respect for international law and treaty obligations' in Article 51(c), read in conjunction with the specific treaty provisions, may also serve to strengthen the hands of a pro-conservation judge.

---

[34] E.g., *Som Prakash Rekhi v Union of India* AIR 1981 SC 212, 221–2; and *Ashoka Kumar Thakur v Union of India* (2008) 6 SCC 1, 515, 516.

[35] *Virender Gaur v State of Haryana* (1995) 2 SCC 571, 580; *Indian Council for Enviro-Legal Action v Union of India* (*Bichhri* case) AIR 1996 SC 1446, 1459; *M C Mehta v Union of India* AIR 1988 SC 1037, 1038; *Rural Litigation and Entitlement Kendra, Dehradun v State of Uttar Pradesh* AIR 1988 SC 2187, 2199; *Kinkeri Devi v State of Himachal Pradesh* AIR 1988 HP 4, 8; and *Arjun Gopal v Union of India* (2017) 16 SCC 267, 269.

[36] *Sachidanand Pandey v State of West Bengal* AIR 1987 SC 1109, 1114–15. See *T N Godavarman Thirumulpad v Union of India* (*Kudhremukh Iron Ore Company* case) (2002) 10 SCC 606, 621.

[37] *T N Godavarman Thirumulpad v Union of India* (*Net Present Value* case) (2006) 1 SCC 1, 11.

[38] *Glanrock Estate Pvt Ltd v State of Tamil Nadu* (2010) 10 SCC 96, 118. See also *Hospitality Association of Mudumalai v In Defence of Environment and Animals* (*Elephant Corridor* case) (2020) 10 SCC 589, 607.

Article 40 of the Constitution requires the State to organize village panchayats and endow them with necessary powers to function effectively. This directive principle was fortified by the Seventy-Third and Seventy-Fourth Amendments to the Constitution. The Constitution (Seventy-Third Amendment) Act of 1992 gave a boost to local self-government by inserting Part IX, titled 'The Panchayats'. Newly introduced Article 243G and the 11th Schedule to the Constitution lists 29 fields of administration where panchayats may exercise authority devolved on them by the State legislature. The list of subjects includes soil conservation, social forestry and farm forestry as well as minor forest produce. The twin Seventy-Fourth Constitutional Amendment of 1992 inserted Part IX-A into the Constitution titled, 'The Municipalities'. Article 243W read with the newly introduced 12th Schedule enables the states to devolve power and responsibilities on urban self-government institutions. The subjects included in the 12th Schedule include urban planning, 'urban forestry, protection of the environment and promotion of ecological aspects', slum improvement and amenities such as parks, gardens and playgrounds. These amendments have been operating since 1993. However, there is little real devolution of power on local governments in the environmental fields. The state governments appear reluctant to cede political control over local resources.

V. ARTICLE 253 AND ENVIRONMENTAL LEGISLATION

The Forty-Second Amendment also expanded the list of concurrent powers in the Constitution. The amendment introduced a new entry, 'Population Control and Family Planning', while 'Forests' and 'Protection of Wild Animals and Birds' were moved from the State List to the Concurrent List.

Article 253 of the Constitution empowers Parliament to make laws to implement India's international obligations and any decision made at an international conference, association or other such body. Article 253 states: 'Notwithstanding anything in the foregoing provisions of this Chapter, Parliament has power to make any law for the whole or any part of the territory of India for implementing any treaty, agreement or convention with any other country or countries or any decision made at any international conference, association or other body.' Entry 13 of the Union List covers: 'Participation in international conferences, associations and other bodies and implementing of decisions made thereat'. In view of the broad range of issues addressed by international conventions, conferences, treaties and agreements, Article 253 read with Entry 13 apparently gives Parliament the power to enact laws on virtually any entry contained in the State List.

Parliament has used its power under Article 253 read with Entry 13 of the Union List to enact the Air (Prevention and Control of Pollution) Act of 1981 and the Environment (Protection) Act of 1986.[39] The preambles to both laws state that these Acts were passed to implement the decisions reached at the United Nations Conference on the Human Environment held at Stockholm in 1972. At the conference, members of the United Nations agreed to work to preserve the world's natural resources and called on each country to pursue this goal.

The preamble to the Biological Diversity Act of 2002 refers to the United Nations Convention on Biological Diversity, signed at Rio de Janeiro on 5 June 1992. This reference is a clear pointer to Article 253 and the source of Parliament's legislative power. The preamble to the National Green Tribunal Act of 2010 reaches back to the Stockholm Conference of 1972 as well as the United Nations Conference on Environment and Development held at Rio de Janeiro in June 1992. The preamble cites the decisions at the Rio Conference 'calling upon the States to provide effective access to judicial and administrative proceedings, including

[39] *S Jagannath v Union of India* (*Shrimp Culture* case) AIR 1997 SC 811, 844, 846.

redress and remedy, and to develop national laws regarding liability and compensation for the victims of pollution and other environmental damage'.

The broad language of Article 253 suggests that in the wake of the Stockholm Conference in 1972 and the Rio Conference in 1992, Parliament has the power to legislate on all matters linked to the preservation of natural resources.[40] Parliament's use of Article 253 to enact four major laws confirms this view. It appears that the expansion of concurrent powers by the Forty-Second Amendment in 1976 only made explicit the powers that Parliament already possessed under Article 253.

VI. FEDERALISM: SOME ISSUES

Occasionally, the division of power under India's federal structure has led to tensions in matters concerning regional development and the preservation of natural resources. The areas of stress include coastal development and the commercial exploitation of mineral resources around federally protected areas. In some instances, such as development in the Dahanu Taluka of Maharashtra, the state government had, at one point, turned hostile to the imposition of central regulations.

Town planning, building regulations and local zoning are state subjects.[41] Consequently, provisions for development along the coast and foreshore are found in several municipal statutes and the land codes of the coastal states. These local laws, however, proved inadequate to protect the coastal ecology, prompting the Central Government to impose stringent national coastal development norms in 1991.[42] The norms severely restricted the nature of development in a 500 m wide strip along the entire Indian coast, adding up to more than 3,000 sq kms of land. Understandably, several state governments were upset at the sweeping assumption of power by the Centre,[43] particularly since the coastal norms are *delegated* legislation issued by the executive under the Environment (Protection) Rules of 1986 which, in turn, were framed under the Environment (Protection) Act of 1986 (EPA).

In the *Shrimp Culture* case,[44] the Supreme Court upheld the power of the Union Government to frame coastal regulations in view of Parliament's competence under Article 253 read with Entry 13, List I of the Seventh Schedule to the Constitution, to enact the EPA for implementing the decisions taken at the 1972 Stockholm Conference.[45] The court went further and recognized that the coastal regulations 'shall have overriding effect and shall prevail over the law made by the legislatures of the states'.[46] This decision settled the legal controversy but papered over the underlying claim of local authorities to regulate land use. The contest

---

40 In 1980 the Tiwari Committee recommended that a new entry on 'Environmental Protection' be introduced in the Concurrent List to enable the Central Government to legislate on environmental subjects. The Committee's recommendation was based on a note from the Indian Academy of Environmental Law which observed that there was no direct entry in the Seventh Schedule enabling Parliament to enact comprehensive environmental laws. The note, however, did not consider Parliament's power under Article 253. Department of Science and Technology, Government of India, *Report of the Committee for Recommending Legislative Measures and Administrative Machinery for Ensuring Environmental Protection* para 3.15 (1980).

41 These topics fall under the heads 'Land' and 'Local government' which are items 18 and 5 of List II (State List) in the Seventh Schedule to the Constitution.

42 The 1991 regulations were replaced in 2011 and these, in turn, were superseded in 2018.

43 *Coastal Zone Rules to be Amended Soon*, Economic Times, New Delhi, 13 November 1996. Maharashtra expressed strong reservations on the incursion by the Centre in its counter affidavit dated 10 August 1994 filed before the Supreme Court in *Bittu Sehgal v Union of India* (2001) 9 SCC 181.

44 *S Jagannath v Union of India* AIR 1997 SC 811, 846.

45 United Nations Conference on the Human Environment.

46 *Supra* note 44.

now plays out through the regulation-making process, where the states seek relaxation of norms to accommodate local interests such as tourism and real estate development.[47]

Another contentious issue relates to the quarrying of mineral deposits in areas close to forest lands and wildlife reserves. Central statutes designed to protect forests and prevent the destruction of wildlife habitat are viewed by some states as a needless fetter on industrial activity and mining. Several state governments, notably Rajasthan[48] and Gujarat,[49] were anxious to encourage the commercial exploitation of minerals and worked to neutralize federal protection in these areas.

The picturesque Dahanu Taluka, one of the richest horticultural districts in India, has strained Centre–state relations. In June 1991 the Union Ministry of Environment and Forests notified a scheme of restrictions under the EPA limiting industrial activity in this ecologically sensitive area. Maharashtra has decried the Central scheme,[50] claiming that it stifles legitimate development activity in a part of its territory and has lobbied hard for lifting the restrictions.[51]

The division of authority between the Centre and the states has also prompted some central agencies to resist compliance with state town planning regulations. In Maharashtra, for instance, until the 1981 decision of the Bombay High Court in the *Sassoon Harbour* case,[52] (implicitly settling the issue against the central agencies), several central authorities resisted regulation under the local town planning laws.

In the summer of 2018, Delhi blamed upstream Haryana for imperilling its drinking water supply. According to Delhi, its water treatment facilities could not cope with the high ammonia content in the water received through the Yamuna channel.[53] In another skirmish, Karnataka resisted Kerala's efforts to throw open a road to night traffic. Since the road passed through Bandipur National Park, night driving would disturb the wildlife. Besides, there were alternative routes open at night (which bypassed the National Park) that could be used by the transport companies behind Kerala's request.[54]

The *Asiatic Lion* case, excerpted below, is unique in many respects. First, it is perhaps the only case where a constitutional court judicially mandated the transfer of a large carnivore from one region to another, in order to improve the species' chances of survival. Second, it tackles

---

47 After states expressed dissatisfaction at the CRZ notification of 2011, a committee was set up in 2014 chaired by Dr Shailesh Nayak, former secretary in the Union Ministry of Earth Sciences. The committee recommended relaxing the notification, leading to a more flexible regime under the CRZ notification of 2019.

48 *Shekhawat Irritated by Centre's Move to Amend Forest Act*, Indian Express, Bombay, 1 February 1995; and *Tarun Bharat Sangh, Alwar v Union of India* (*Sariska* case) (1993) Supp 3 SCC 115, 128.

49 See *Consumer Education and Research Society v Union of India* (*Narayan Sarovar* case-I) AIR 1995 Guj 133.

50 Affidavit of the state government, *supra* note 43.

51 In 2019, the Union Government shifted its position and approached the Supreme Court to dissolve the special protection for Dahanu. Michelle C, *Future Tense for Ecologically Sensitive Dahanu*, Mongabay, 11 October 2019 <https://india.mongabay.com/2019/10/future-tense-for-ecologically-sensitive-dahanu/> accessed 10 July 2021.

52 *Shyam Chainani v The Board of Trustees of the Port of Bombay* Appeal No. 151 of 1980 in Miscellaneous Petition No. 58 of 1980, Bombay High Court, 30 April 1981.

53 The Supreme Court directed the parties to resolve matters by approaching the Upper Yamuna River Board, a statutory body that oversaw distribution of river water between states. *Comdr Sureshwar D Sinha v Union of India* Writ Petition (Civil) No. 537 of 1992, order dated 16 May 2018, MANU/SCOR/16879/2018.

54 *State of Kerala v L Srinivasa Babu* Special Leave Petition (C) No. 13838 of 2010, order dated 7 August 2019.

a sensitive federal issue between three constituents of the Union: the Central Government and Madhya Pradesh on one side and Gujarat on the other (even though none of these parties approached the court).[55] Third, the court issued operative directions for the transfer of lions, while recognizing the need for further technical assessment by an Expert Committee. Last, the Supreme Court barred the introduction of the African Cheetah into Kuno Wildlife Sanctuary (the intended destination for the lions) and torpedoed an arrangement between Namibia and India for re-introducing the cheetah to the Indian sub-continent.

CENTRE FOR ENVIRONMENT LAW, WWF-I v UNION OF INDIA

(2013) 8 SCC 234

K S P Radhakrishnan, J: We have been called upon to decide the necessity of a second home for Asiatic Lion (*Panthera leo persica*), an endangered species, for its long term survival and to protect the species from extinction as issue rooted on eco-centrism, which supports the protection of all wildlife forms, not just those which are of instrumental value to humans but those which have intrinsic worth.

The Wildlife Institute of India (for short 'WII'), an autonomous institution under the Ministry of Environment and Forests (for short 'MoEF'), Government of India, through its wildlife biologists had done considerable research at the Gir forest in the State of Gujarat since 1986. All those studies were geared to provide data which would help for the better management of the Gir forest and enhance the prospects for the long term conservation of lions at Gir, a single habitat of Asiatic lion in the world. The data collected by the wildlife biologists highlighted the necessity of a second natural habitat for its long term conservation. Few of the scientists had identified the Asiatic lions as a prime candidate for a re-introduction project to ensure its long term survival. In October 1993, a Population and Habitat Analysis Workshop was held at Baroda, Gujarat. Various issues came for consideration in that meeting and the necessity of a second home for Asiatic lions was one of the issues deliberated upon in that meeting. Three alternative sites for re-introduction of Asiatic lions were suggested for an intensive survey, the details of which are given below:

1. Darrah-Jawaharsagar Wildlife Sanctuary (Rajasthan)
2. Sitamata Wildlife Sanctuary (Rajasthan)
3. Kuno Wildlife Sanctuary (Madhya Pradesh)

The Research Advisory Committee of WII recognized the need for a prior survey to assess the potential of those sites. Accordingly, a field survey was conducted. Surveys of the three sites were made during winter as well as summer, to assess water availability during the summer and also to ascertain the changes in human impact on the habitat during the seasons. The surveyors concentrated on ascertaining the extent of forest area in and adjoining the chosen protected areas with the aim of establishing the contiguity of the forested habitat. Attempts were also made to establish the relative abundance of wild ungulate prey in the three sites based on direct sightings as well as on indirect evidence. An assessment of the impact on the people and their livestock on habitat quality in all three sites was also made. Of the three sites surveyed, Kuno Wildlife Sanctuary (for short 'Kuno') was found to be the most suitable site for re-introduction in establishing a free ranging population of Asiatic lions. A draft report to that effect was prepared by eminent scientists … on behalf of WII. The report revealed that the Kuno was a historical distribution range of Asiatic lions. Report also highlighted the necessity of a long term commitment of resources, personnel, the necessity of a comprehensive rehabilitation package, adequate staff and facilities. Committee did not consider the presence of tigers in Kuno to be a major limiting factor, especially since the tigers occur in such low numbers and density. Since lions live in stable social units, report highlighted that it is important to take lions for the translocation also from a single pride.

[55] The judgment was rendered on an application by a non-governmental organization, the Biodiversity Conservation Trust of India, which requested the transfer of lions to Kuno Wildlife Sanctuary, Madhya Pradesh.

Further, it was also pointed out that genetic consideration would not be a major factor, provided fresh male lions are moved from Gir to Kuno every three to five years and the resident males in Kuno selectively captured for zoos.

State of Madhya Pradesh then undertook a massive rehabilitation package for the villagers settled in and near Kuno so as to push forward the scheme of relocation of Asiatic lions in Kuno. It was noticed that about 1545 families of 24 revenue villages were living inside Kuno and they had to be rehabilitated outside the sanctuary. Since suitable and sufficient revenue land was not available in adjoining areas, it was decided to relocate those villages on degraded protected forests. Since proposed site of resettlement fell in various blocks of protected forest, the use as a rehabilitation purpose involved a legal obligation to obtain prior sanction from MoEF under Section 2 of the Forest (Conservation) Act, 1980.

The Secretary (Forests), Government of Madhya Pradesh, therefore, sent a letter dated 24.7.1996 to MoEF seeking final approval of the Central Government in accordance with the Forest (Conservation) Act, 1980. MoEF, after examining the request of the State of Madhya Pradesh, conveyed its approval under Section 2 of the Forest (Conservation) Act, 1980 for diversion of 3720.9 hectare of forest land for rehabilitation of 18 villages located inside the Kuno, subject to fulfillment of certain conditions.... The Government of India constituted a Monitoring Committee for the effective implementation of the Asiatic Lion Reintroduction Project at Kuno which met on 10.3.2004. The Survey report of WII was discussed in the meeting and it was noticed that Kuno Palpur Sanctuary of M P was identified as the project site/and a 20 year project was conceived in three phases as below:

a. Phase I (1995–2000) Village relocation and habitat development.
b. Phase II (2000–2005) Fencing at the side, translocation, research and monitoring.
c. Phase III (2005–2015) Eco-development.

It was pointed out in the meeting that, currently, the project was in Phase II and 18 villages had been rehabilitated from Kuno. Further, in the meeting, the Chief Wildlife Warden of Gujarat had, however, opined that there was no commitment on the part of the State of Gujarat for providing lions and the State Government had not agreed for the same. Based on the discussion, the Chairman summed up the consensus which emerged out of the deliberations as follows:

1. A letter from Minister of State, MoEF should be sent to the Chief Minister of Gujarat, highlighting the project justification with a request to provide lions for translocation to Kuno Palpur Sanctuary.
2. State of Gujarat should be provided with a set of project documents.
3. The Chief Wildlife Warden, MP should prepare a road map with a final detail for translocation of lions from Gir to Kuno.
4. An assessment of prey base in Kuno should be done by WII.
5. No further expenditure should be incurred with a focus on lion; however, funding support for habitat improvement/welfare initiatives for other wild animals can continue.

[The court narrated the events and set out counsels' arguments. Twenty-four villages were shifted outside Kuno involving relocation of 1,545 families. The Minister of MoEF wrote to the Gujarat Chief Minister on 20 July 2006 for translocating two lions to Kuno but no favourable response was received. On 30 November 2007, the Supreme Court directed that the matter be placed before the National Board for Wildlife (NBWL) to consider the views of the two states and to submit its recommendation to the court. The standing committee of the NBWL recommended translocation of lions from Gujarat to Kuno. On 22 April 2009, the court directed NBWL to have a fresh look at the subject after again hearing both the states. On 22 December 2009, the NBWL 'recommended that the translocation of lions from Gir area to an alternate area, presently to the Kuno-Palpur Sanctuary, is the necessity of the hour essential for conservation of lions for posterity'. Responding to a submission by Gujarat that the State Board of Wildlife (Gujarat) had not considered the issue, on 27 February 2012, the court directed the state board to submit its report. The state board took the view that there was no threat of Asiatic lions in the Gir forest from epidemic diseases or such factors;

the Asiatic lion population had risen; previous attempts for translocation had failed; the prey base at Kuno was inadequate; poaching in Madhya Pradesh was rampant; the peak summer temperatures were too high for survival of lions at Kuno and there was no need to create a second home for the Asiatic lion at Kuno.]

We reiterate that while examining the necessity of a second home for the Asiatic lions, our approach should be eco-centric and not anthropocentric and we must apply the 'species best interest standard', that is the best interest of the Asiatic lions. We must focus our attention to safeguard the interest of species, as species has equal rights to exist on this earth. Asiatic Lion has become critically endangered because of human intervention. The species originally existed in North Africa and South-West Asia formerly stretched across the coastal forests of northern Africa and from northern Greece across south-west Asia to eastern India. Today the only living representatives of the lions once found throughout much of South-West Asia occur in India's Gir Forest. Asiatic lion currently exists as a single sub-population and is thus vulnerable to extinction from unpredictable events, such as an epidemic or large forest fire etc. and we are committed to safeguard this endangered species because this species has a right to live on this earth, just like human beings....

We, as human beings, have a duty to prevent the species from going extinct and have to advocate for an effective species protection regime. NWAP 2002–2016 and the Centrally Sponsored Scheme 2009 indicate that there are many animal species which are close enough to extinction and some of the other species have already disappeared from this earth. No species can survive on the brink of extinction indefinitely and that the continued existence of any species depends upon various factors like human-animal conflict, epidemics, forest fire and other natural calamities etc.

The Wildlife Biologists of WII, after conducting a research on Gir Forests, noticed the necessity for long term conservation of Asiatic lion in Gir and also highlighted the necessity of a second natural habitat for its long term conservation. Population and Habitat Analysis Workshop held at Baroda in October, 1993 also highlighted that fact. NBWL, as already indicted, has taken a consistent view in all its meetings about the necessity of a second habitat for Asiatic lion, an endangered species. Asiatic lion, it has been noticed, has been restricted to only one single habitat, i.e. the Gir National Forest and its surrounding areas and an outbreak of possible epidemic or natural calamity might wipe off the entire species. A smaller population with limited genetic strength are more vulnerable to diseases and other catastrophes in comparison to large and widespread population. Threat, therefore, is real and has proved by the outbreak of canine distemper in the lions of Serengeti NP, Tanzania in 1994. 85% of the Serengeti lion population, it was noticed, had Canine Distemper Virus antibodies and at least 30% of the Serengeti and Mara lions died due to the infection. Compared with Gir, the lion population in the 40,000 sq km Serengeti-Mara ecosystem is large with about 2500 lions. It was felt that if an epidemic of this scale were to affect the lions in Gir, it would be very difficult to save them from extinction, given the much smaller area of the Gir forests and the smaller lion population. The possibility of the disease spreading to the pockets of habitat such as Girnar, Mityala, Rajula, Kodinar and the surrounding areas, cannot be ruled out.

We have already indicated that there is uniformity in the views expressed by the Bio-Scientists of WII, NBWL, MoEF and other experts that to have a second home for the endangered species like Asiatic lion is of vital importance. A detailed study has been conducted to find out the most suitable habitat for its re-introduction and Kuno Wildlife Sanctuary (for short 'Kuno') in Madhya Pradesh, as already indicated, has been found to be the most ideal habitat.

Ownership and Possession of Wild Animals

No state, organization or person can claim ownership or possession over wild animals in the forest. Wild Animal is defined under the Wild Life (Protection) Act, 1972 under Section 2(36) to mean any animal specified in schedules I to IV and found wild in nature. 'Wild Life' has been defined under Section 2(37) to include any animal, bees, butterflies, crustacean, fish and moths, and or land vegetation which forms part of any habitat. Section 9 prohibits hunting of wild animals, specified in Schedule I, II, III and IV except as provided under Section 11 and Section 12. Section 40 of the Act obliges a person to make a declaration and Section 41 enables the Chief Wild Life Warden to make an enquiry and preparation of inventories and Section 42 deals with the issue of certificates and confers no ownership of the wild animals to a particular state or others. Animals in the wild are properties of the nation for which no state can claim ownership and the state's duty is to protect the wild life and conserve it, for ensuring the ecological and environmental security of the country....

State of Gujarat has taken up the stand that it has got its own conservation programme in respect of Asiatic lion. Due the effective conservation programme carried out by the State of Gujarat at Gir, it was pointed out, that the number of Asiatic lions in the wildlife has increased, the range of these lions has increased, the statutorily protected habitat has increased, so also the area occupied by these lions has increased. The State has maintained the stand that there is no present or immediate danger to the Asiatic lions warranting any emergency measures.

State Board for Wildlife, Gujarat (SBWL, Gujarat), which has been constituted by the State Government under Section 6 of the Wildlife Protection Act, 1972, convened a meeting on 16.3.2012 to discuss the issue relating to translocation of Asiatic lion from Gujarat to Madhya Pradesh. SBWL, Gujarat took the view that the issue of giving or not giving lions to Kuno is not an issue of conflict between States, but it is a collective Indian cultural approach in the interest of long term conservation of lions as part of our family. SBWL further maintained the stand that Asiatic Lion being a 'family member' is beyond and higher than the 'scientific reasoning'. SBWL, therefore, did not agree with the proposal for translocation of lion from Gujarat to Kuno, a stand endorsed by the State of Gujarat.

Approach made by SBWL and the State of Gujarat is an anthropocentric approach, not eco-centric though the State of Gujarat can be justifiably proud of the fact that it has preserved an endangered species becoming extinct. We are, however, concerned with a fundamental issue whether the Asiatic lions should have a second home. The cardinal issue is not whether the Asiatic lion is a 'family member' or is part of the 'Indian culture and civilization', or the pride of a State but the preservation of an endangered species for which we have to apply the 'species best interest standard'. Our approach should not be human-centric or family-centric but eco-centric. 'Scientific reasoning' for its re-location has to supersede the family bond or pride of the people and we have to look at the species best interest especially in a situation where the specie is found to be a critically endangered one and the necessity of a second home has been keenly felt. We, therefore, find it difficult to agree with the reasoning of SBWL, Gujarat and the State of Gujarat that the Asiatic lion is a family member and hence be not parted with.

The views of NBWL constituted by the Central Government in exercise of its powers conferred under Section 5A of the Wild Life (Protection) Act, have to prevail over the views expressed by SBWL. The duties conferred on the National Board under Section 5C of the Act and on the State Board under Section 8 of the Act are entirely different. NBWL has a duty to promote conservation and development of wildlife and frame policies and advise the Central Government and the State Governments on the ways and importance of promoting wildlife conservation. It has to carry out/make assessment of various projects and activities on wildlife or its habitat. NBWL has also to review from time to time the progress in the field of wildlife conservation in the country and suggest measures for improving thereto. Those functions have not been conferred on the State Board. The State Board has been conferred with a duty to advise the State Government the selection and management of areas to be declared as protected areas and advise the State Government in formation of their policies for protection and conservation of the wildlife and specify plans etc. Statutorily, therefore, it is the duty of NBWL to promote conservation and development of wildlife with a view to ensuring ecological and environmental security in the country. We are, therefore, of the view that the various decisions taken by NBWL that Asiatic lion should have a second home to save it from extinction, due to catastrophes like epidemic, large forest fire etc, which could result in extinction, is justified. This Court, sitting in the jurisdiction, is not justified in taking a contrary view from that of NBWL.

[After an elaborate discussion the court struck down the MoEF's decision to introduce the African Cheetah into Kuno.]

MoEF's decision for re-introduction of Asiatic lion from Gir to Kuno is that of utmost importance so as to preserve the Asiatic lion, an endangered species which cannot be delayed. Re-introduction of Asiatic lion, needless to say, should be in accordance with the guidelines issued by IUCN and with the active participation of experts in the field of re-introduction of endangered species. MoEF is therefore directed to take urgent steps for re-introduction of Asiatic lion from Gir forests to Kuno.

Needless to say, the number of lions to be re-introduced would depend upon the density of prey base and other related factors, which the [Expert] Committee will assess.

The order be carried out in its letter and spirit and within a period of 6 months from today....

We are also inclined to highlight the necessity of an exclusive parliamentary legislation for the preservation and protection of endangered species so as to carry out the recovery programmes before many of the species become extinct and to give the following directions:

(a) NWAP (2002–2016) has already identified species like the Great Indian Bustard, Bengal Florican, Dugong, the Manipur Brow Antlered Deer, over and above Asiatic Lion and Wild Buffalo as endangered species and hence we are, therefore, inclined to give a direction to the government of India and the MoEF to take urgent steps for the preservation of those endangered species as well as to initiate recovery programmes.

(b) The government of India and the MoEF are directed to identify, as already highlighted by NWAP, all endangered species of flora and fauna, study their needs and survey their environs and habitats to establish the current level of security and the nature of threats. They should also conduct periodic reviews of flora and fauna species status, and correlate the same with the IUCN Red Data List every three years.

(c) Courts and environmentalists should pay more attention for implementing the recovery programmes and the same be carried out with imagination and commitment.

NOTES AND QUESTIONS

1. Justice K S P Radhakrishnan has gradually developed the principle of eco-centrism. He first articulated this principle in the *Asiatic Wild Buffalo*[56] and the *Sandalwood*[57] cases and then expanded this vision in the *Asiatic Lion* case. Eco-centrism, as the court explains, requires new application of the 'species best interest standard'. But the best interest of which species? While the transfer to Kuno may benefit the lion, would this move work to the advantage of the prey species at Kuno like the sambar and chinkara? In the end, is eco-centrism simply anthropocentrism in disguise?

2. Was Gujarat's stand reasonable? Surely, two populations of the Asiatic lion are better than one. Should Gujarat have deferred to the request made by the NBWL, MoEF and Madhya Pradesh? After all, Gujarat prided itself on a successful conservation programme, and permitting translocation of a pride of lions would not have seriously dented its ongoing effort. Were Gujarat's objections scientific or influenced by unstated political and economic considerations?

---

[56] *T N Godavarman Thirumulpad v Union of India* (2012) 3 SCC 277.
[57] *T N Godavarman Thirumulpad v Union of India* (2012) 4 SCC 362.

3. The Wild Life (Protection) Act of 1972 provides an elaborate statutory procedure for translocating wildlife. This procedure was not followed in the present case and approval of the Chief Wild Life Warden, Gujarat was not sought in order to translocate the lions. Should the Supreme Court have insisted upon Madhya Pradesh following the statutory procedure? Would this have been a tedious exercise with a foregone conclusion, considering that Gujarat had made its position well known on affidavits filed in the Supreme Court? What is more important from a judicial perspective: following statutory procedure or attaining the final object, regardless of the procedures?

4. The National Board of Wild Life (NBWL) is chaired by the Prime Minister and has representatives of various bureaucracies as well as experts on it. The State Board of Wild Life (SBWL) is chaired by the Chief Minister and also has a variety of bureaucrats and experts. Review the provisions of the Wild Life (Protection) Act and critically examine whether the Supreme Court was justified in holding that where there is a difference of opinion between the NBWL and the SBWL, it is the national board whose view must prevail.

5. The Supreme Court was concerned that a natural calamity such as the outbreak of a disease or a forest fire could endanger the lion population in Gujarat. Was this not reason enough to dismiss the objections of Gujarat and order translocation, even if there was some risk associated with this venture? Remember, very substantial funds had been invested in preparing Kuno and at great sacrifice by thousands of villagers who were shifted out of the park.

Twenty-three lions died in two weeks starting 12 September 2018. According to the Indian Council for Medical Research, in five of these cases the cause was canine distemper virus.[58]

6. Madhya Pradesh had a poor record in preventing poaching of tigers. The tiger population at the Panna Tiger Reserve was decimated from 25 tigers in 2002 to naught in 2009. The state took no serious action against any senior official and subsequently even promoted officers who were in charge during the carnage. A special investigation team report of 2009 pointed to collusion, incompetence and false reporting with respect to the tiger population at Panna. With this track record, was translocating big cats to Madhya Pradesh by a judicial direction consistent with the principle of eco-centrism? Does such a direction meet the 'species best interest standard'?

7. The premise of the judgment is that the Asiatic lion is a native species and the court must step in to ensure its survival. The court declares that Kuno was part of the historical habitat of the Asiatic lion and carefully uses the expression '*reintroduction*' to emphasize its intention to restore lions to a part of their original range.

Marshalling a range of historical material including pictorial records, Valmik Thapar, Romila Thapar and Yusuf Ansari, in their book *Exotic Aliens: the Lion and the Cheetah in India* published very shortly after the judgment,[59] debunk this premise. *Exotic Aliens* argues that lions and cheetahs were never native species but were imported from Africa by Indian royals. Historical accounts rarely speak of lions and it would have been impossible for the lion to survive in much of the Indian jungle dominated by the tiger. The Harappans of the Indus valley seemed ignorant of the lion and the present stock were descendants of captive animals bred in menageries and then propagated in private hunting parks. This is how the naturalist Valmik Thapar ends the book:

[58] Meena Venkataraman, *With 23 Asiatic Lions Dead in Gir, Here's What the Authorities Can Do To Preserve India's Pride*, SCROLL.IN (2018) <http://scroll.in/article/print/898643> accessed 10 July 2021.

[59] The judgment in the *Asiatic Lion* case was rendered on 15 April 2013 when *Exotic Aliens* was in press. Neither work had the advantage of the rival analysis.

As we come to the end of the book, I would like to leave the reader with a closing thought, one that has to do with the status of the lion and cheetah in the country today. Where the small pride of docile Junagadh lions is concerned, the rulers of present-day Gujarat are no different from the Nawab of Junagadh. The state government regards these animals as the property of the state, just as the nawab did, and has blocked all attempts by other states, like Madhya Pradesh, to propagate the lion. The lions of Junagadh still depend heavily on livestock and the farmers who lose their livestock are frequently compensated. They get medicare, and if injured, are treated and then released back into the forest. In a way, time stands still for them as history is repeated endlessly.

In the case of the cheetah, conservationists are calling for the Namibian sub-species to be introduced into India, either in Madhya Pradesh or Rajasthan, hence setting the stage for history to repeat itself in the case of the cheetah as well, with the animal being imported from Africa, just as it was for centuries. If imports had continued, I am sure the wealthy of today would have continued to have them as pets. Speaking for myself, I love both these animals and would rather watch them in their natural habitat—the wild open grasslands and bush country of Africa. They were never part of the Indian wild and, to my mind, will never be.[60]

8. Assuming the present stock of Asiatic lions are feral descendants of man-managed populations, does that weaken the court's reasoning? Would the judges be as enthusiastic in creating a second home for an exotic species, say a kangaroo? If the lions in Gujarat were of African descent, would the court's logic in barring the import of the Namibian cheetah then extend to the lion?

Alternatively, should Madhya Pradesh import both the lion and the cheetah from Africa?

On the basis of an eco-centric approach, does the exotic provenance of a species make any difference? After all, the lions in Gujarat have been around for more than a century and are now a part of the cultural and natural landscape.

9. The Supreme Court nominated senior scientist Dr Ravi Chellam, on an Expert Committee that was to be constituted by the MoEF to assess the number of lions to be reintroduced, density of prey base and other factors for a successful translocation programme. During the hearing of the case, Dr Chellam submitted a note dated 8 July 2012 to the Supreme Court where he found the Kuno prey data unreliable: 'Review of the most recent data (2011) presented by Madhya Pradesh reveals several flaws both with the data collection methods as well potentially with the analyses.... In summary, the prey density estimation seems to be inadequate in terms of design, data collection protocols and analytical methods when compared with internationally accepted standards. The current density of wild prey species in Kuno does not seem to have been reliably estimated.... Required Action: In my considered opinion commissioning of independent scientific studies to estimate wild ungulate and feral cattle populations in Kuno. Field studies have to be conducted at least over 12 months covering all seasons and habitats. Reliable results based on this fieldwork can be expected within 18 months.'

Should eco-centrism be founded on good science and reliable data? With this material on record, was the Supreme Court justified in directing immediate translocation of the lion without reliable prey data? Was it correct to order implementation within just six months when at least 18 months were required for prey studies? Suppose a reliable prey study revealed

[60] Valmik Thapar, Romila Thapar & Yusuf Ansari, *Exotic Aliens: The Lion and the Cheetah in India* 236 (2013).

an inadequate prey base? What might explain the anxiety of the court in ordering translocation before reliable data was available?

10. The judgment is important because it confers 'statutory status' on the National Wildlife Action Plan (2002–2016) and the Centrally Sponsored Scheme, 2009. This new status imposes enforceable duties on governments and bureaucrats whose decisions and priorities must now be guided by these policy statements.

11. When the Gujarat government was displaying its reluctance to allow translocation of lions, the Union Government and Madhya Pradesh agreed to receive the Namibian cheetah at Kuno. In 2011, an action plan was prepared by: (1) the Cheetah Task Force of the Madhya Pradesh Forest Department, (2) the Wildlife Institute of India, and (3) the National Tiger Conservation Authority. Home to the largest population of cheetahs in the world, Namibia engaged in wildlife diplomacy and agreed to donate several pairs of cheetahs to India. All arrangements for air-lifting the animals were in place, when the Supreme Court realized that this international experiment could jeopardize the proposal for the Asiatic lion's second home. Scientific opinion indicated that the cheetah must establish itself before the lion (a much stronger predator) is brought to the same area. Although three expert bodies had prepared this action plan, the Supreme Court found it flawed and stalled the cheetah project since initiating it would have meant deferring the lion transfer. When sailing in uncharted waters, the enormous discretion exercised by the judges of our superior courts frequently paves the path to a preferred outcome.

A green signal to move lions from Gujarat to Madhya Pradesh and a red light to halt the Namibian cheetah are an unusual investment of judicial resources. Is it the business of any court to direct big cat traffic?

12. In 2017 the National Tiger Conservation Authority (NTCA) applied before the Supreme Court to introduce the African Cheetah 'to suitable sites in India, based on detailed site specific action plan'. On 28 January 2020, the Supreme Court noted that the previous effort with respect to Kuno was struck down on the ground that detailed studies were not carried out. The court ordered:

> The instant application presumably seeks to remedy the defect that was noticed earlier. In that, it is submitted that African Cheetahs would be introduced on an experimental basis in a [carefully] chosen habitat and nurtured and watched to see whether it can adapt to the Indian conditions. In case there are some difficulties noticed about the location in which it is introduced, we are informed that the location would be changed to another forest which is more habitable for the animals. It is not desirable that this action of introducing the African Cheetahs into India be left to the sole discretion of the NTCA but we consider it appropriate that NTCA be guided and directed by the Committee of Experts in the field who would carry out the survey for the best location for introducing the African Cheetahs in India and take a careful decision about the viability of introducing this animal on a larger scale. The expert committee shall also supervise the entire process and NTCA shall be guided to act in co-ordination with the expert committee.[61]

The Expert Committee was directed to submit periodic reports every four months.

---

[61] *Centre for Environment Law, WWF-1 v Union of India*, order dated 28 January 2020 in IA No. 192/2017. MANU/SCOR/12052/2020.

B. ENVIRONMENTAL PROTECTION AND FUNDAMENTAL RIGHTS

I. THE RIGHT TO A WHOLESOME ENVIRONMENT

Encouraged by an atmosphere of freedom and articulation in the aftermath of the Emergency,[62] the Supreme Court entered one of its most creative periods. Specifically, the court fortified and expanded the fundamental rights enshrined in Part III of the Constitution. In the process, the boundaries of the fundamental right to life and personal liberty guaranteed in Article 21 were expanded to include environmental protection.[63]

The Supreme Court strengthened Article 21 in two ways. First, it required laws affecting personal liberty to also pass the tests of Article 14 and Article 19 of the Constitution,[64] thereby ensuring that the procedure depriving a person of his or her personal liberty be reasonable, fair and just.[65] Second, the court recognized several unarticulated liberties that were implied by Article 21. It is by this second method that the Supreme Court interpreted the right to life and personal liberty to include the right to a wholesome environment.

The first indication of the right to a wholesome environment may be traced to the *Dehradun Quarrying* case.[66] In July 1983, representatives of the Rural Litigation and Entitlement Kendra, Dehradun wrote to the Supreme Court alleging that illegal limestone mining in the Mussoorie-Dehradun region was devastating the fragile ecosystems in the area. On 14 July, the court directed its registry to treat the letter as a writ petition under Article 32 of the Constitution, with notice to the government of Uttar Pradesh and the collector of Dehradun. Over the years the litigation grew increasingly complex. By the time the court issued its final judgment in August 1988, it had heard lengthy arguments from the Central Government and state governments, government agencies and mine lessees; appointed several Expert Committees; and passed at least five comprehensive interim orders. None of these orders, however, articulates the fundamental right to a healthful environment.

Eight years after entertaining the *Dehradun Quarrying* case, the Supreme Court revealed the basis of its jurisdiction to entertain environmental cases. In *Subhash Kumar v State of Bihar*[67] the court held that the right to life includes the right to enjoy unpolluted air and water. If anything endangers or impairs the quality of life in derogation of law, a citizen has a right to

---

[62] On 25 June 1975 a Proclamation of Emergency was issued on the ground of 'internal disturbance' threatening the security of India. A widespread denial of civil and political rights followed. The proclamation was revoked in March 1977 shortly after the Indira Gandhi government was swept out of power in a national election.

[63] Article 21 states: 'No person shall be deprived of his life or personal liberty except according to procedure established by law.'

[64] *Maneka Gandhi v Union of India* AIR 1978 SC 597, 623–4. Article 14 enshrines the right to equality before law and protects a person against arbitrary or unreasonable state action. Article 19 enumerates certain fundamental rights, such as the right to freedom of speech and expression and the right to form associations or unions.

[65] *Francis Coralie Mullin v The Administrator, Union Territory of Delhi* AIR 1981 SC 746, 749–50; and *Common Cause (A Regd. Society) v Union of India* (2018) 5 SCC 1, 268.

[66] *Rural Litigation and Entitlement Kendra, Dehradun v State of Uttar Pradesh* AIR 1988 SC 2187.

[67] AIR 1991 SC 420, 424. Also see *M C Mehta v Union of India* (*Delhi Stone Crushing* case) (1992) 3 SCC 256, 257; and *Chameli Singh v State of Uttar Pradesh* AIR 1996 SC 1051, 1053. When deriving the right to shelter under Article 21 the Supreme Court held that this right would include 'the right to *decent environment* and a reasonable accommodation to live in'. *Shantistar Builders v Narayan K Totame* AIR 1990 SC 630. The right to a clean environment is also recognized in *A P Pollution Control Board II v Prof M V Nayudu* (2001) 2 SCC 62, 79; and *Arjun Gopal v Union of India* (2017) 16 SCC 280, 304, 305.

move the Supreme Court under Article 32 of the Constitution. Expanding upon this theme in a town planning case, *Virender Gaur v State of Haryana*,[68] the court observed:

> Article 21 protects the right to life as a fundamental right. Enjoyment of life ... including [the right to live] with human dignity encompasses within its ambit, the protection and preservation of environment, ecological balance free from pollution of air and water, sanitation, without which life cannot be enjoyed. Any contra acts or actions would cause environmental pollution. Environmental, ecological, air, water pollution, etc. should be regarded as amounting to violation of Article 21. Therefore, hygienic environment is an integral facet of right to healthy life and it would be impossible to live with human dignity without a humane and healthy environment.... [T]here is a constitutional imperative on the State Government and the municipalities, not only to ensure and safeguard proper environment but also an imperative duty to take adequate measures to promote, protect and improve both the man-made and the natural environment.[69]

Several High Courts explicitly recognized an environmental dimension to Article 21 before the Supreme Court did so. For example, while considering a writ petition to enjoin the Life Insurance Corporation and the Income-tax Department from building residential houses in a recreational zone, the Andhra Pradesh High Court held:

> [I]t would be reasonable to hold that the enjoyment of life and its attainment and fulfillment guaranteed by Article 21 of the Constitution embraces the protection and preservation of nature's gifts without [which] life cannot be enjoyed. There can be no reason why practice of violent extinguishment of life alone should be regarded as violative of Article 21 of the Constitution. The slow poisoning by the polluted atmosphere caused by environmental pollution and spoliation should also be regarded as amounting to violation of Article 21 of the Constitution....
>
> It, therefore, becomes the legitimate duty of Courts as the enforcing organs of Constitutional objectives to forbid all action of the State and the citizen from upsetting the environmental balance. In this case the very purpose of preparing and publishing the development plan is to maintain such an environmental balance. The object of reserving certain area as a recreational zone would be utterly defeated if private owners of the land in that area are permitted to build residential houses. It must, therefore, be held that the attempt of the Life Insurance Corporation of India and the Income tax Department to build houses in this area is contrary to law and also contrary to Article 21 of the Constitution.[70]

Judges of the High Courts of Rajasthan,[71] Kerala,[72] Himachal Pradesh,[73] Karnataka[74] and Madhya Pradesh[75] too, in early cases observed that environmental degradation violates the fundamental right to life.

The recognition of the right to a healthy environment as an aspect of the fundamental right to life under Article 21 of the Constitution of India has many advantages. First, this elevated status as a human right guaranteed under Part III of the Constitution of India locates environmental protection high in the hierarchy of values that courts and decision-makers must

---

[68] (1995) 2 SCC 577.

[69] *Id.* at 580–1.

[70] *T Damodar Rao v The Special Officer, Municipal Corporation of Hyderabad* AIR 1987 AP 171, 181.

[71] *L K Koolwal v State of Rajasthan* AIR 1988 Raj 2, 4; and *Arvind Textiles v State of Rajasthan* AIR 1994 Raj 195, 197.

[72] *Madhavi v Tilakan* 1988 (2) Ker L T 730, 731; and *Attakoya Thangal v Union of India* 1990 (1) Ker L T 580, 583.

[73] *Kinkeri Devi v State of Himachal Pradesh* AIR 1988 HP 4, 9.

[74] *V Lakshmipathy v State of Karnataka* AIR 1994 Kar 57, 67.

[75] *K C Malhotra v State of Madhya Pradesh* AIR 1994 MP 48, 52; and *Hamid Khan v State of Madhya Pradesh* AIR 1997 MP 191, 193.

pay heed to. Second, this articulation enables citizens to directly access the country's constitutional courts by recourse to the relatively inexpensive and straightforward writ remedy. Third, the human rights dimension serves as a rallying point for citizens' groups working in diverse areas of environmental protection and enables them to more effectively lobby for policy and regulatory changes. Fourth, the articulation as a fundamental right provides a platform for creative interpretation by the constitutional courts and the National Green Tribunal to respond to new challenges. Finally, were environmental protection to mature into a human right in customary international law, it might serve as a basis for non-discriminatory negotiations at a global level.[76]

II. THE RIGHT TO LIVELIHOOD

Another aspect of the right to life—the right to livelihood—can potentially check government actions with an environmental impact that threatens to dislocate poor people and disrupt their lifestyles. Conservative estimates place the figure of India's project-displaced people over five decades at 50 million,[77] no more than a quarter of whom were satisfactorily rehabilitated. The Morse Report to the World Bank which reviewed the Sardar Sarovar project on the Narmada notes that the 'record of resettlement and rehabilitation in India ... has been unsatisfactory in virtually every project with a large resettlement component'.[78]

The tenacious protests and agitations against the Sardar Sarovar project as well as the Supreme Court judgments in the *Narmada* case[79] have ensured improved relief and rehabilitation (R&R) measures by the state. Judicial monitoring of progress in R&R, a fresh pro-oustee judicial approach in land acquisition cases leading to a 2013 Act[80] have together worked to tilt the scales in favour of those whose land is taken. The new law provides better compensation packages as well as a stronger community consultation process with potential oustees.

The Supreme Court recognized the right to livelihood in the case of *Olga Tellis v Bombay Municipal Corporation*.[81] The petitioners, a journalist and two pavement dwellers, challenged a government scheme to deport pavement dwellers from Bombay to their places of origin. The main plank of the petitioners' argument was that the right to life includes the right to livelihood, and since the pavement dwellers would be deprived of their livelihood if they were evicted from their slum and pavement dwellings, their eviction would be tantamount to deprivation of their life, and was hence unconstitutional. Accepting the petitioners' argument, the court held:

---

[76] Michael R Anderson; *Human Rights Approaches to Environmental Protection: An Overview* in Human Rights Approaches To Environmental Protection 1, 21–2 (Eds. Alan Boyle & Michael Anderson, 2003); and Michael R Anderson; *Individual Rights to Environmental Protection in India* in *Id.*

[77] Indian Institute of Technology Roorkee, *Development Projects vs Internally Displaced Populations in India: A Literature Based Appraisal* 6 (2011); Lok Sabha Secretariat, Reference Note No. 30/RN/Ref./December/2013 *Displacement and Rehabilitation of People Due to Development Projects* 1 (2013) <http://164.100.47.193/Refinput/New_Reference_Notes/English/DisplacementandRehabilitation.pdf> accessed 10 July 2021; Sudesh Kumar & Anindya J Mishra, *Development-Induced Displacement in India: An Indigenous Perspective* 10 Jr Of Mngm & Public Policy 25 (2018) <https://www.researchgate.net/publication/330931432_Development-Induced_Displacement_in_India_An_Indigenous_Perspective> accessed 10 July 2021.

[78] *Sardar Sarovar: Report of the Independent Review* 351 (1992). The report was prepared by Bradford Morse, former Undp Director, and was commissioned by the World Bank.

[79] *Narmada Bachao Andolan v Union of India* (2000) 10 SCC 664; 2005 4 SCC 32; *State of Madhya Pradesh v Narmada Bachao Andolan* (2011) 7 SCC 639; and 2017 (3) Scale 268.

[80] The Right to Fair Compensation and Transparency in Land Acquisition, Rehabilitation and Resettlement Act of 2013 replaced the colonial Land Acquisition Act of 1894.

[81] AIR 1986 SC 180.

> Deprive a person of his right to livelihood and you shall have deprived him of his life.... The State may not by affirmative action, be compellable to provide adequate means of livelihood or work to the citizens. But, any person, who is deprived of his right to livelihood except according to just and fair procedure established by law, can challenge the deprivation as offending the right to life conferred by Art. 21.[82]

The court directed the municipal corporation to provide alternative sites or accommodation to the slum and pavement dwellers within a reasonable distance of their original sites, to earnestly pursue a proposed housing scheme for the poor and to provide basic amenities to slum dwellers.[83]

Thereafter, in *Banawasi Seva Ashram v State of Uttar Pradesh*,[84] the Supreme Court detailed safeguards to protect tribal forest dwellers who were being ousted from their forest land by the National Thermal Power Corporation Limited (NTPC) for the Rihand Super Thermal Power Project. The court permitted the acquisition of the land only after the NTPC agreed to provide certain court-approved facilities to the ousted forest dwellers.[85] In other Article 32 petitions, the court has passed interim orders requiring state agencies to resettle and rehabilitate tribals who were being displaced by dams.[86]

Can the right to livelihood be asserted to prevent environmentally disruptive projects that threaten to uproot villagers and, consequently, deprive them of their livelihood? Consider a case where the government sanctions the construction of a large dam without an adequate environmental impact analysis.[87] Does the procedure leading to the government decision—a decision that will jeopardize the livelihood of thousands of villagers—meet the *Olga Tellis* standard of being a just and fair procedure established by law? Many of these concerns are now addressed through the statutory environmental impact assessment procedure[88] and the beneficent provisions of the Right to Fair Compensation Act of 2013.[89] Should the state falter in implementing R&R, recourse may be had to the National Green Tribunal.

The search for a better livelihood draws rural folk to cities. Cities are a magnet to those displaced by large projects, marginalized due to the depletion of natural resources or in search of jobs and economic opportunity. Do Indians enjoy a 'right to the city'? Should courts recognize this dimension as part of the right to livelihood? Does the right to the city cover access to public housing, sanitation and city commons? What might happen if courts recognize such a right? The right to livelihood and its emanations (including, possibly the right to

---

82 *Id.* at 194.

83 *Id.* at 204.

84 AIR 1987 SC 374. In the course of its order the court observed that the tribals 'for generations had been using the jungles around for collecting the requirements for their livelihood—fruits, vegetables, fodder, flowers, timber, animals by way of sport and fuelwood'. Although not explicitly referred to in the order, Article 21 and the right to livelihood were impliedly relied on by the court. (Subsequent orders in the same case are reported at 1987 (1) SCALE 1149, (1992) 1 SCC 117, AIR 1992 SC 920 and (1993) 2 SCC 612.)

85 AIR 1987 SC 374, 378.

86 *Karanjan Jalasay Y A S A S Samiti v State of Gujarat* AIR 1987 SC 532 and *Gramin Sewa Sanstha v State of Uttar Pradesh* (1986) Supp SCC 578. Neither order explicitly refers to Article 21 or the right to livelihood. *N D Jayal v Union of India* (2004) 9 SCC 362, 417.

87 Environmental Impact Analysis (EIA) is an exercise to evaluate the probable changes in the various socio-economic and bio-physical characteristics in the environment which may result from a proposed project. It is undertaken to reduce to a minimum the possibility of an action causing unanticipated changes in the environment. It assists decision-makers in considering the environmental costs and benefits of the proposed project. Where the benefits sufficiently exceed the costs of the project, the project may be environmentally justified.

88 Environmental Impact Assessment notification of 2006.

89 *Supra* note 80.

the city) derive from the core constitutional value, dignity.[90] The state must treat its citizens with dignity.

III. THE RIGHT TO EQUALITY

Apart from Article 21, the right to equality guaranteed in Article 14 of the Constitution may also be infringed by government decisions that have an impact on the environment.[91] Article 14, among other things, strikes at arbitrariness 'because an action that is arbitrary must necessarily involve a negation of equality'.[92]

Thus, urban environmental groups frequently resort to Article 14 to quash 'arbitrary' municipal permissions for construction that are contrary to development regulations. Besides, Article 14 may also be invoked to challenge government sanctions for mining and other activities with high environmental impact, where the permissions are 'arbitrarily' granted without an adequate consideration of environmental impacts.[93] In *State of Himachal Pradesh v Ganesh Wood Products*,[94] the Supreme Court held that a decision-making authority must give due weight and regard to ecological factors such as the environmental policy of government and the sustainable use of natural resources. A government decision that fails to take into account relevant considerations affecting the environment is invalid.[95]

A right to intergenerational equity is derived from Articles 21 and 14. The central tenet of the theory of intergenerational equity is the right of each generation of human beings to benefit from the cultural and natural inheritance from past generations as well as the *obligation* to preserve such heritage for future generations. Intergenerational equity requires conserving the diversity and quality of biological resources, and of renewable resources such as forests, water and soils.[96]

In *Ganesh Wood Products*, the Supreme Court recognized the obligation of the present generation to preserve natural resources for the next and future generations.[97] Likewise, in the *CRZ Notification* case,[98] the Supreme Court observed that environmental statutes were enacted to ensure a good quality of life for unborn generations since it is they who must bear the brunt of ecological degradation.

The doctrine also obliges the present generation to use exhaustible resources such as iron ore in such a manner that resources remain available to the unborn generation. This concept has persuaded the Supreme Court to limit mining of iron ore in the Bellary region of Karnataka.[99]

Intergenerational equity requires the present generation to carefully weigh the impact of its decisions on future generations, particularly where the damage is irreparable. While

---

90 The importance of dignity as a high constitutional value is explained in *Justice K S Puttaswamy v Union of India* (*Privacy* case) (2017) 10 SCC 1.

91 Article 14 states: 'The State shall not deny to any person equality before the law or the equal protection of the laws within the territory of India.'

92 *Ajay Hasia v Khalid Mujib Shervardi* AIR 1981 SC 487, 499.

93 See generally, *Kinkeri Devi v State of Himachal Pradesh* AIR 1988 HP 4, 9.

94 AIR 1996 SC 149, 159, 163.

95 *Id.*; and *Pleasant Stay Hotel v Palani Hills Conservation Council* (1995) 6 SCC 127, 136, 139, 140.

96 See note on *Goa Guidelines on Intergenerational Equity*, 27 I L M 1108 (1988) and Chapter 17 on International Environmental Law and Global Issues.

97 *Supra* note 94.

98 *Indian Council for Enviro-Legal Action v Union of India* (*CRZ Notification* case) (1996) 5 SCC 281, 293.

99 *Samaj Parivartana Samudaya v State of Karnataka* (2013) 8 SCC 154. The Supreme Court by an interim order laid down parameters for reclamation and rehabilitation. These norms included a requirement capping the mining activity to a level where the mineral reserves would last 20 years.

discussing the duty of the National Green Tribunal to arrest irreversible harm, the Supreme Court adverted to the *'Seventh Generation' sustainability principle*, or the '*Great Law of the Iroquois*' which originates from the Iroquois Tribe. This philosophy requires decision-making to have positive benefits for at least seven generations into the future.[100]

IV. FREEDOM TO TRADE *VIS-À-VIS* ENVIRONMENTAL PROTECTION

As environmental regulation grows more stringent and its enforcement becomes vigorous, industry will challenge agency actions that disrupt business. Courts must balance environmental interests with the fundamental right to carry on any occupation, trade or business guaranteed in Article 19(1)(g).[101] For example, effluent discharge standards prescribed by the pollution control boards may be challenged under Article 19 for being excessive (too stringent to comply with, despite using the best available technology) or otherwise unreasonable. Likewise, unreasonable government decisions relating to the siting or translocation of industry may also be assailed under Article 19(1)(g).

The *Akhil Bharat Goseva Sangh* case, excerpted below, was the culmination of a long and keen contest that reached the Supreme Court on three occasions.[102] The project envisaged establishing a large slaughterhouse primarily for the export of buffalo meat. The government policy in the 1980s encouraged buffalo meat exports where a vet certified that the animal was not used for breeding or milching. The Sangh and others challenged the project on diverse grounds drawing on Article 48 of the Constitution which contains the following directive principle of state policy:

> 48. *Organisation of agriculture and animal husbandry* – The State shall endeavour to organise agriculture and animal husbandry on modern and scientific lines and shall, in particular, take steps for preserving and improving the breeds, and prohibiting the slaughter of cows and calves and other milch and draught cattle.

We carry a short excerpt from a lengthy judgment, focusing on the environmental issues.

AKHIL BHARAT GOSEVA SANGH v STATE OF ANDHRA PRADESH

(2006) 4 SCC 162

* * *

TARUN CHATTERJEE, J:

Al Kabeer Exports Limited (in short 'the Company') is a public company formed for the purpose of carrying on the business of processing meat, mainly for export purposes. The Company with a view to establish a slaughterhouse in Rudraram village, in the Medak district of the State of Andhra Pradesh applied to the Gram Panchayat, Rudraram for the requisite permission to construct a factory and other buildings connected therewith. On 24-3-1989, the Gram Panchayat concerned, issued a 'no-objection certificate' (in short 'NOC'). After obtaining opinion of the District Medical and Health Officer, Director of Town Planning and Director of Factories, State of Andhra Pradesh, permission was granted to the Company to run a slaughterhouse on the selected site on 29-6-1989.

Prior to this permission, the Andhra Pradesh Pollution Control Board (for short 'APPCB') also issued an 'NOC' on the application of the Company filed on 30-12-1988 subject to certain conditions concerning the treatment of effluents and air pollution. In the said NOC, it was *inter alia* stipulated that the Company shall obtain a second 'NOC' and a regular

---

100 *Municipal Corporation of Greater Mumbai v Ankita Sinha* (2021) SCC Online SC 897.

101 Article 19(1)(g) states: 'All citizens shall have the right . . . to practise any profession, or to carry on any occupation, trade or business.'

102 The earlier orders are reported at *Akhil Bharat Goseva Sangh (1) v State of A P* (1995) Supp 1 SCC 370; and *Akhil Bharat Goseva Sangh (2) v State of A P* (1997) 3 SCC 707.

consent under Sections 25 and 26 of the Water (Prevention and Control of Pollution) Act, 1974 from APPCB before commencing regular production. The Director, Animal Husbandry Department, Government of Andhra Pradesh also issued an NOC in favour of the Company by a letter dated 13-7-1989, subject to compliance with the provisions of Sections 5 and 6 of the Andhra Pradesh Prohibition of Cow Slaughter and Animal Preservation Act, 1977 (in short 'the A.P. Act') and the instructions issued thereunder. Subsequently, on 18-7-1989 the Central Government (Ministry of Industry) granted a letter of intent (in short 'LOI') under the provisions of the Industries (Development and Regulation) Act, 1951 (in short 'the IDR Act') for establishment of a new industrial undertaking to the Company at the selected site mentioned herein earlier for manufacturing of certain amount of frozen buffalo and mutton meat. LOI was granted, subject to the following conditions:

(a) Buffaloes to be slaughtered shall be subject to ante-mortem and post-mortem examination by the authorities concerned.
(b) Only old and useless buffaloes shall be slaughtered and for this purpose, their production and processing shall be subject to continuous inspection by the Municipal Authorities, Animal Husbandry and Health Department of the State Government or any other arrangement that the Central or the State Government may evolve for ensuring this.
(c) Slaughter of cows of all ages and calves of cows and buffaloes, male or female, shall be prohibited.
(d) The Company shall undertake measures for preserving and improving the breeds of the buffaloes by adoption of suitable animal husbandry practices in consultation with the State Government.
(e) At least 90% production of frozen buffalo meat would be exported for a period of ten years which may be extended by another five years at the discretion of the Government.
(f) Adequate steps shall be taken to the satisfaction of the Government to prevent air, water and soil pollution. Such anti-pollution measures to be installed should conform to the effluent and emission standards prescribed by the State Government in which the factory of the industrial undertaking is located.

[The court considered the claim by the appellant that the abattoir must be shut down because it was located 13 kms from Hyderabad, violating the locational parameters in the LOI.]

[W]e may keep it in mind that in pursuance of LOI granted by the Central Government and the various permissions granted by the State Government and other authorities, the Company commenced construction of its factory in 1989.... It also appears from the record that the industrial licence was granted by the Central Government on the strong recommendation of the State Government. The unit commenced production in April 1993 after dismissal of a batch of writ petitions challenging the permissions granted by various authorities to commence production, including that of APPCB. The unit achieved its full production in December 1993 and since then it is earning valuable and substantial foreign exchange for our country. Above all, the question on location, as noted herein earlier, was neither raised seriously before the High Court nor before us. It must also be noted that, in this regard various State authorities had granted permissions for the abattoir to be constructed and function at the selected site and production has been continuing for the last 10 to 15 years. That apart, the question on location requirement is always a question of fact which cannot be permitted to be raised at this stage before us. However, we keep it open to the Central Government and the State Government to consider the distance prohibition as indicated in LOI and the notification and general order of the State Government for the purpose of shifting the site to some other alternative place which would satisfy the location conditions. Subject to the above, this question is answered in favour of Al Kabeer (the Company).

The next question that was urged by the learned counsel for the appellant before us which needs to be decided is whether Al Kabeer (the Company) operates in violation of the Environmental Acts and Rules. According to the appellants, no study has been made of the prevailing environment and the impact of Al Kabeer on it. Therefore, it was contended that the precautionary principle has been ignored by the authority before granting permission to Al Kabeer to run the slaughterhouse.

The learned counsel appearing on behalf of [the appellant] contended that APPCB by its consent order dated 21-12-1993 allowed limit for BOD of 100 mg/lit whereas the maximum permissible limit specified in the Environment (Protection) Rules, 1986 was 30 mg/lit (Rule 3, Schedule I, Entry 50-B). According to the learned counsel ... the limit for suspended solids allowed by APPCB of 100 mg/lit was in excess of the limit of 50 mg/lit allowed in Rule 3, Schedule I, Entry 50-B of the Environment (Protection) Rules, 1986. Therefore, it was contended that the consent of APPCB was in violation of the Act and the Rules, and accordingly it must be quashed. It was also contended ... that since the samples collected on 6-8-1994 from Al Kabeer show that its BOD in fact reached 150 mg/lit which was much beyond the permitted limit of 30 mg/lit and its suspended solid discharge was recorded at 140 mg/lit which was much beyond the permitted 50 mg/lit, the question of giving consent to Al Kabeer by the authorities could not arise at all as it had clearly violated the maximum permissible limit specified in the Environment (Protection) Rules, 1986. Accordingly, permission granted should be withdrawn. These submissions were strongly disputed by the learned counsel for Al Kabeer (the Company).

From a careful consideration of the rival submissions of the parties on the question of environmental pollution, we find that this question was not seriously argued by the appellants during the course of hearing that the Company had violated the norms under the Environment (Protection) Rules, 1986. Thus we may not permit the appellant to raise this question before us. However, as environmental pollution has now become a public nuisance, we thought it fit to go into this question and decide the same.

From the record it appears that the recommendations regarding environment made by the Krishnan Committee so far as the abattoir is concerned, were accepted by the Central Government as would be evident from this Court's order dated 12-3-1997 [(1997) 3 SCC 707]. It also appears from the record that Al Kabeer Company had invested huge amount for installation of elaborate anti-pollution equipment, and operates the same with consent obtained from APPCB. It is true that the standards prescribed by APPCB for Al Kabeer while issuing its consent for slaughtering operation to begin, were indeed in violation of the Environment (Protection) Rules insofar as they prescribe a lower standard than was mandated by the aforesaid Rules. Under Rule 3 of the Rules, the State Boards are permitted to prescribe higher standards than those mentioned in the Rules but are not permitted to lower the standard. Considering the fact that the permission to operate the abattoir was granted by APPCB, the State Government and also by various authorities of the State 10 to 15 years back and considering the fact that Al Kabeer had installed elaborate anti-pollution equipment by investing huge amount, we are of the view that Al Kabeer must be directed to comply with the Environment (Protection) Rules by lowering down the pollution levels at the abattoir to permissible limits, rather than to direct closure of the abattoir of the Company. It also appears that the samples which were collected by the Department of Water and Waste Water Examination, Institute of Preventive Medicine, Narayanguda, Hyderabad from Al Kabeer's abattoir indicated violation of the standards prescribed under the Environment (Protection) Rules. Though Al Kabeer has installed elaborate anti-pollution equipment, it would be of no consequence if such equipment is in reality not bringing down the level of pollution below the permissible limits. However, it cannot be overlooked that Al Kabeer is continuing its operation for more than 10 years without any objection from APPCB. Therefore, considering all the circumstances, we are of the view that directly ordering closure of Al Kabeer abattoir is not called for; rather directions may be given to APPCB to rectify its consent order in accordance with the Environment (Protection) Rules and also to direct Al Kabeer to strictly comply with that rectified consent order and the Environment (Protection) Rules. In the event the abattoir fails to comply with such directions from APPCB, it would be open to the authorities to direct closure of the Al Kabeer unit. We are taking this view keeping in mind that the appellants had not seriously argued, during the course of hearing before this

Court, that the Company had in fact violated the standards laid down in the Environment (Protection) Act and the Rules.

It may also be noted that in the interim judgment dated 12-3-1997 this Court has noted the conclusions of the Central Government Committee in para 2, wherein it has recorded that the Committee had accepted the suggestions and recommendations made by the Krishnan Committee with regard to pollution of air and water. It has also been noted therein that the environmental audit report and the environmental management firm report along with the environmental management plan prepared by the Company are acceptable. As already noted herein earlier, the Company has installed elaborate anti-pollution equipment, imported as well as indigenous. The Company has been operating only after obtaining consent from APPCB which is regularly renewed. Insofar as standards for discharge of effluents from the slaughterhouse and meat processing are concerned, the same is prescribed under Rule 3 read with Entry 50-B of Schedule I of the Environment (Protection) Rules, 1986. In this connection Entry 50-B(*b*) of Schedule I of the Environment (Protection) Rules, 1986 is relevant as it prescribes the BOD, suspended solids and oil and grease limits. At this juncture it is also to be noted that the Ministry of Environment, Government of India, by its letter dated 29-5-1995 fixed the standards for Al Kabeer Exports Pvt. Ltd. at 100 BOD and 30 BOD for the slaughterhouse and meat processing respectively. As Al Kabeer has been operating on the basis of the norms specified by the Central Government and considering the fact that Al Kabeer unit has been operating for more than 10 years without any objection from APPCB and keeping in mind the economic policy of the Central Government, we are of the view that Al Kabeer may not be, at this stage, directed to stop their operation and close the unit. In view of our discussion made hereinbefore, and as APPCB reserves the right to take action against Al Kabeer for violation of the terms and conditions imposed in its permission, it would be open for APPCB to direct Al Kabeer to rectify the level of pollution below the prescribed limits and in the event that it is not done they may direct Al Kabeer to close down its abattoir. As noted hereinbefore, it is of course true that the prescribed limit of pollution by APPCB was in violation of the Environment (Protection) Rules, therefore in our view, directions must be given to APPCB to rectify its consent order and directions be given by them to the abattoir to comply with that rectified consent order in accordance with Rule 3 of the Environment (Protection) Rules....

NOTES AND QUESTIONS

1. The appellants challenged the constitution of the APPCB urging that the chairman and member secretary of the board did not possess the statutory qualifications. The Supreme Court agreed with this submission and found that merely because some of the other members of the board were scientific experts, the chairman and member secretary were not exempted from holding the prescribed qualifications. Nevertheless, the Supreme Court declined to set aside the statutory consent issued by the board in favour of the company in view of section 11 of the Water Act which provides that no act or proceeding of the board 'shall be called in question on the ground merely of the existence of any vacancy in, or defect in the constitution of the board....'

2. The Krishnan Committee referred to in the excerpt was appointed by the High Court at an interim stage. The committee recommended that the company must have an effective programme to raise cattle for at least half of the production capacity so as not to deplete the cattle wealth of the surrounding areas. Alternatively, it suggested that the government should take over the plant and move the operations of unhygienic private slaughterhouses in the state to the new facility. Eventually, the Krishnan Committee's recommendations were discarded.

3. The court finally directed strict monitoring of the pollution parameters and also asked the company to file annual reports before the state government on cattle populations in the surrounding areas. The Supreme Court asked the Central Government to review the meat export policy in the light of the directive principles of state policy under the Constitution and the potential harmful effects on the livestock population.

4. Reading the full judgment is instructive on the perils that confront new enterprises generally, and a mechanized slaughterhouse in particular. What are the cultural and religious sentiments simmering below the surface?

5. Organic titanates are used in the metal, plastic and glass industry. Polygel Industries started manufacturing organic titanates in 2002 at its plant located in the Union Territory of Dadra and Nagar Haveli. In 2011, the company sought to expand its capacity from 200 to 6,000 MT per year. These plans hit a road block since the factory was within 10 kms of the Dadra and Nagar Haveli Wildlife Sanctuary. On 4 September 2015, having regard to the scores of large industries in the region, the MoEF declared a buffer zone of 100 metres on all sides of the sanctuary. This relaxation deviated from the general rule of a 10 km buffer. After considerable delay, Polygel received all statutory permissions including consent to operate on 9 June 2016 for enhanced production. It began operations and, on 1 September 2016, withdrew its writ petition before the Bombay High Court for permission to manufacture at the enhanced capacity.

On 15 September 2017, the Supreme Court issued an order seeking an explanation from the MoEF with respect to the reduced eco-sensitive zone of just 100 metres.[103] Polygel explained how there were several large manufacturing units operating within a 10 km radius of the sanctuary and why the reduced limit was pragmatic. Due to business uncertainties, Polygel relocated its organic titanates manufacturing unit to Brunei. India lost jobs, economic activity and export income—all due to burdensome regulatory risks.

In the *Sushila Saw Mill* case, excerpted below, the Supreme Court was asked to invalidate section 4 of the Orissa Saw Mills and Saw Pits (Control) Act of 1991 which prohibited saw mills from operating in a forest or within a buffer of 10 kms from a forest. The law was enacted to preserve the state's forests and stop illegal felling of trees. When the 1991 Act came into force, Sushila mill which had been running for a decade in the Keonjhar district of Orissa, found that it fell within the prohibited zone. The mill challenged the ban in the Orissa High Court, contending that the complete bar violated its fundamental right under Article 19(1)(g). The High Court was not impressed and dismissed the writ petition. The mill carried the matter to the Supreme Court in a special leave petition under Article 136 of the Constitution.

SUSHILA SAW MILL v STATE OF ORISSA

AIR 1995 SC 2484

* * *

ORDER:

The right to carry on trade or business envisaged under Article 19(1)(g) is subject to statutory regulation. When the statute prescribes total prohibition to continue to operate even the existing saw mills situated within the prohibited area, the right to carry on trade or business

---

103 The case was pending in the Supreme Court in a petition against an interim order passed before the 2016 consent to operate. *Pollution Control Committee v Polygel Industries Pvt Ltd* Special Leave Petition (Civil) No. 2579-80/2014.

> is subject to the provisions of the Act. Proviso to Section 4(1) puts a total embargo on the right to carry on trade or business in saw milling operation or sawing operation within the prohibited area. It is settled law that in the public interest restriction under Article 19(1)(g) may in certain rare cases include total prohibition.
>
> This Court in *Narendra Kumar v Union of India* AIR 1960 SC 430, held that it is reasonable to think that makers of the Constitution considered the word 'restriction' to be sufficiently wide to save laws inconsistent with Article 19(1), or taking away the rights conferred by the Article, provided this inconsistency or taking away was reasonable in the interest of the different matters mentioned in the clause. There can be no doubt, therefore, that they intended the word 'restriction' to include cases of prohibition also in certain rare cases. The contention that a law prohibiting the exercise of a fundamental right is in no case saved cannot, therefore, be accepted. It is seen that the reserved forest is being denuded or depleted by illicit felling. Thereby denudation of the reserved forest was noticed by the legislature. The preservation of the forest is a matter of great public interest and one of the rare cases that demanded the total ban by the legislature. The Act came to be enacted to impose a total ban in prohibited area for the period during which the ban is in operation, to carry on saw mills business or sawing operation within the prohibited area. It is, therefore, clear that the statute intends to impose a total ban which is found to be in 'public interest'. The individual interest, therefore, must yield place to the public interest. Accordingly, it is neither arbitrary nor unreasonable.... It is true that by geographical contiguity, Keonjhar District appears to have been situated within the prohibited area but that in the legislative mandate that the entire area covered within the prohibited zone is treated as a class as against the other area. Therefore, when the limits of that district are within prohibited zone of the reserved or protected or forest area etc. or within 10 kms it is a legislative scheme to give effect to the legislative object in the public interest to preserve forest wealth and environment and to put an end to illicit felling of forest growth. Therefore, it is a class legislation; it is not discriminatory and does not offend Article 14 or Article 301 of the Constitution. It is a valid law. The special leave petition is accordingly dismissed.

NOTES AND QUESTIONS

1. Would the outcome of the case have been different if not one, but several saw mills employing hundreds of workers were involved?

2. The court was extremely deferential to the legislature in upholding the ban. Is this because India's forests are in a devastated condition? Or more generally, would all prohibitions in aid of environmental protection meet the court's standard, i.e., 'a matter of great public interest and one of the rare cases that demand a total ban by the legislature'?

Plastic pollution is devastating the planet. As we saw at the beginning of this book, stray cows in India are full of plastic trapped in the animals' stomachs. Plastic waste clogs drains, pollutes water bodies and channels and is littered across India's towns and cities. Polythene bags take centuries to decompose, resulting in persistent environmental pollution. In response, the Union Government and the states have enacted laws to curb the menace.

One of the strongest responses to rein in plastic use is a set of notifications issued under The Maharashtra Non-Biodegradable Garbage (Control) Act of 2006. Section 3 of the Act prohibits the throwing of non-biodegradable garbage (and biodegradable garbage in a non-biodegradable bag) in public drains, sewage lines, lakes and wetlands. Section 4 empowers the state government to prohibit the use of non-biodegradable material through a notification. In 2018, Maharashtra issued a series of notifications[104] that were sweeping in effect:

1) The ban in the whole State of Maharashtra for manufacture, usage, transport, distribution, wholesale & retail sale and storage, import of the plastic bags with handle and without handle, and the disposable products manufactured from plastic & thermocol (polystyrene) such as single use disposal dish, cups, plates, glasses, fork, bowl, container, disposable dish/bowl used for packaging food in hotels, spoon, straw, non-woven polypropylene bags, cups/pouches to store liquid, packaging with plastic to wrap or store the products, packaging of food items and food grain material etc.
2) These regulations are applicable to every person, body of person, government and non-government organization, educational institution, sport complex, clubs, cinema halls and theatres, marriage/celebration halls, industrial units, commercial institutions, offices, pilgrimage organisers, pilgrimages and religious places, hotels, dhabas, shopkeepers, malls, vendors or sellers, traders, manufacturers, caterer, wholesalers, retailers, stockist, businessmen, hawkers, salesmen, transporters, market, producers, stalls, tourist places, forest & reserved forest, eco-sensitive areas, all sea beaches, all public places, bus stands, railway stations in the State of Maharashtra.
3) There will be ban in whole state for use of plastic and thermocol for decoration purpose.[105]

The state government justified the ban in a challenge before the Bombay High Court through an affidavit:

> 24. I say that the use of plastic carry bag and disposable plastic items being part of our day-to-day life generated on disposal of such plastics tremendous quantity of plastic waste. In Maharashtra, near about 1200 Metric ton per day plastic waste is being generated and the disposal of such plastic waste in a scientific manner was not taking place. I say that there is a daily usage of above 1.25 crore of quantity of PET[106] bottles used for water and other aerated drinks and further same are not being recycled.
>
> 25. I say that as the plastic carry bags and other products made up of plastic are not bio-degradable. Plastic requires more than 100 years to degrade. Plastic waste are disrupting the natural balance of eco-system, thereby causing various environmental problems and harm to flora and fauna and also had harmful impacts on the biodiversity. Due to its non-biodegradable nature, the plastic bags obstruct the streams of all types of waters, resulting in clogging of drains and thereby giving rise to various health issues. Often the plastic bags, which are dumped carelessly on open spaces, are eaten up and swallowed by many animals and eventually results in animal death incidents. The use of plastic carry bags and articles had also endangered the aquatic life. The plastic waste and micro plastic causes danger to marine and freshwater bio-diversity and also hamper ecosystem services due to spreading of such waste in and around eco-system, on tourist places, beaches and on agriculture and forest areas.[107]

Do the notifications violate Article 19(1)(g) of the Constitution? According to the petitioners, the impugned notification would imperil 7,800 industrial units and 400,000 jobs in the state.

---

[104] The primary notification is dated 23 March 2018 and was followed by amendments on 11 April 2018 and 30 June 2018. The title of the primary notification is Maharashtra Plastic and Thermocol Products (Manufacture, Usage, Sale, Transport, Handling and Storage) notification of 2018.

[105] Clause 3(1) of the notification dated 23 March 2018.

[106] Polyethylene terephthalate.

[107] Affidavit quoted in Bombay High Court interim order dated 12 and 13 April 2018 in Writ Petition No. 4033 of 2018 *Maharashtra Plastic Manufacturers' Association v State of Maharashtra*.

4

LEGISLATIVE PROVISIONS

India's vast body of environmental law is mostly statutory. While private actions for compensation before the National Green Tribunal (NGT) may evolve into a regulatory tool, so far they remain a peripheral strategy. Pollution charges, fees or other economic approaches to discourage pollution are largely untested. Administrative initiatives such as the Namami Gange programme, aimed at rejuvenating the River Ganga, supplement the pollution control framework.

Federal statutes set out the essential legislative policy, leaving it to the Central Government to work out the nuts and bolts. The Central Government as the delegate of Parliament issues rules, regulations and other types of subordinate legislation that detail specific responsibilities. Environmental lawyers, judges and industry must grapple with the ever-expanding manual of regulations issued by the Union Ministry of Environment, Forest and Climate Change (MoEF).

The primary legislative strategy is a system of licensing backed by criminal sanctions. The criminal provisions are ineffective and mostly ornamental: there is little administrative or prosecutorial capacity to convict wrongdoers. The principal disciplinary tool with enforcement agencies is to withhold renewal of the licence or to cancel the permission in extreme cases. The pollution control laws also empower state agencies to shut down polluting industries or stop their supply of water and power. This last enforcement method is better suited to local conditions because it vests power in a single state agency—typically, the pollution control board. In contrast, successful prosecutions require coordination amongst board officials, technical witnesses, the prosecutor's office and their combined ability to persuade a court. This is a bridge too far for most of our environmental agencies.

As we shall see from a number of public interest litigations discussed in this book, the performance of most enforcement agencies is dismal—whether it be the pollution control boards, forest bureaucracies or local town planning authorities. Few bureaucrats effectively exercise their authority unless compelled to do so by judicial oversight. The judicial role in securing enforcement through public interest litigation lies outside the formal statutory framework and has been assumed by the higher judiciary in discharge of its constitutional obligations. In the years ahead, this judicial mantle may pass to the NGT as it secures greater traction. In practical terms this would reduce the role of the constitutional courts in favour of a more vibrant statutory jurisdiction of the NGT.

Reviewing implementation strategies across several countries, Kathuria and Haripriya argue that a fresh approach that departs from the traditional command and control model may help improve compliance. In their view, participation by community representatives and a negotiating process involving factory managers may be more effective in securing compliance than threat of harsh penalties and prosecutions.[1] What are the advantages and disadvantages of this approach?

[1] Vinish Kathuria & G S Haripriya; *Industrial Pollution Control: Choosing The Right Option*, 35 Economic & Political Weekly 3870 (2000).

Environmental Law & Policy in India. Shyam Divan and Armin Rosencranz, Oxford University Press.
 DOI: 1093/oso/9780192865458.003.0004

In this chapter we explain the principles for interpreting environmental statutes, digest the primary regulatory statutes and examine in some detail the Environment (Protection) Act of 1986. We analyse the National Green Tribunal Act of 2010 in the next chapter. India's international obligations under important multilateral treaties and conventions complement the municipal law. Quite a few international law norms have been assimilated into domestic law by judgments of the Supreme Court.[2]

A. INTERPRETATION OF ENVIRONMENTAL STATUTES

Frequently, judges must choose between two possible interpretations of an environmental statute, one that advances environmental protection, and the other favouring some other interest such as industry, jobs or the need for energy. In this situation a judge may be persuaded to a pro-environment construction on the basis of rules for the interpretation of statutes. A strong statement by the Supreme Court favouring a pro-environment interpretation was made in the *Sariska* case,[3] where the court held:

> This litigation concerns environment. A great American Judge emphasising the imperative issue of environment said that he placed Government above big business, individual liberty above Government and environment above all.... The issues of environment must and shall receive the highest attention from this Court.

Environment statutes are regarded as 'beneficent' legislation, enacted to advance the directive principle of state policy contained in Article 48A of the Constitution. Being beneficent legislation, it is the duty of the court to adopt an interpretation favouring ecological preservation.

Where the text of the provisions requires interpretation, the court must adopt a construction which advances the object and purpose of the legislation as a whole. In the context of the Environmental Impact Assessment (EIA) notification the Supreme Court held that where the size of the project increases, the magnitude of the environmental impact would also increase. Consequently, for a project expansion, a fresh environmental clearance (EC) must be applied for and obtained. A project proponent could not bypass the EIA procedure by claiming that the original EC was sufficient and that a marginal increase in project size would have no significant impact.[4]

When called on to explain the breadth of the powers of the Tribunal constituted under the National Green Tribunal Act of 2010, the Supreme Court drew on this rule:

> The NGT Act being a beneficial legislation, the power bestowed upon the Tribunal would not be read narrowly. An interpretation which furthers the interests of environment must be given a broader reading. The existence of the Tribunal without its broad restorative powers under Section 15(1)(c) read with Section 20 of the Act, would render it ineffective and toothless, and shall betray the legislative intent in setting up a specialized Tribunal specifically to address environmental concerns. The Tribunal, specially constituted with Judicial Members as well as with Experts in the field of environment, has a legal obligation to provide for preventive and restorative measures in the interest of the environment.[5]

---

[2] See Chapter 17 titled International Environmental Law and Global Issues.

[3] *Tarun Bharat Sangh, Alwar v Union of India*, Writ Petition (Civil) No. 509 of 1991, Supreme Court, 14 May 1992 (M N Venkatachaliah and B P Jeevan Reddy, JJ).

[4] *Keystone Realtors Pvt Ltd v Anil V Tharthare* (2020) 2 SCC 66.

[5] *Mantri Techzone Pvt Ltd v Forward Foundation* (2019) 18 SCC 494.

Another related rule requires courts to adopt a 'purposive' interpretation, or an approach that advances the purpose which the legislature had in mind when enacting the law.[6] When confronted with rival interpretations—one that would allow the sale of two-wheelers which were compliant on the date of manufacture but exceeded the emission norms when the vehicle was sold; and the other that barred all sales beyond the 1 April 2017 deadline—the Supreme Court adopted the latter construction. Applying the rule of purposive interpretation, the court held that public health considerations must prevail over an adverse impact on some vehicle manufacturers.[7] Tighter emission norms, like most pollution standards, are health-based and require strict enforcement.

In the *Goa Airport* case,[8] the Supreme Court adopted a purposive approach to explain disclosures that were required by the project proponent in Form 1 of the EIA notification of 2006. Since the purpose of Form 1 was to enable framing the Terms of Reference (ToR) by the Expert Appraisal Committee (EAC), the information in Form 1 must cover all ecological features such as wetlands, water sources, water bodies, mountains and forests falling within the impact zone. The court also adopted the rule of purposive interpretation to extend the understanding of forests to cover all forests as commonly understood and not just statutorily declared forests. This was because the underlying purpose of the EIA notification was that every effort be made not to 'overlook and destroy forests but to notice and protect them'.

To buttress its conclusion upholding confiscation of a tractor and trolley carrying illegally extracted sand, the Supreme Court supported a state amendment to the Indian Forest Act of 1927 thus:

> The Madhya Pradesh amendments to the Indian Forest Act 1927 are infused with a salutary public purpose. Protection of forests against depredation is a constitutionally mandated goal exemplified by Article 48A of the Directive Principles and the Fundamental Duty of every citizen incorporated in Article 51A(g). By isolating the confiscation of forest produce and the instruments utilised for the commission of an offence from criminal trials, the legislature intended to ensure that confiscation is an effective deterrent. The absence of effective deterrence was considered by the Legislature to be a deficiency in the legal regime. The state amendment has sought to overcome that deficiency by imposing stringent deterrents against activities which threaten the pristine existence of forests in Madhya Pradesh. As an effective tool for protecting and preserving environment, these provisions must receive a purposive interpretation. For, it is only when the interpretation of law keeps pace with the object of the Legislature that the grave evils which pose a danger to our natural environment can be suppressed. The avarice of humankind through the ages has resulted in an alarming depletion of the natural environment. The consequences of climate change are bearing down on every day of our existence. Statutory interpretation must remain eternally vigilant to the daily assaults on the environment.[9]

Another example is *V Shankar Reddy v State of Andhra Pradesh*,[10] where a division bench of the Andhra Pradesh High Court upheld the invalidation of a government order permitting a forest to be cleared, since the order was against the purpose of the legislation, which was forest conservation. Occasionally, powers delegated to enforcement agencies under environmental laws are exercised for a purpose that undermines the object of the law. This is impermissible. In the *Bangalore Medical Trust* case,[11] for instance, the Supreme Court held that

---

6 *State of Madhya Pradesh v Centre for Environment Protection Research & Development* (2020) 9 SCC 781.
7 *M C Mehta v Union of India* (2017) 7 SCC 243.
8 *Hanuman Laxman Aroskar v Union of India* (*Goa Airport* case) (2019) 15 SCC 401.
9 *State of Madhya Pradesh v Uday Singh* (2020) 12 SCC 733, 756.
10 1992 (2) Andh L T 514, 529.
11 *Bangalore Medical Trust v B S Muddappa* AIR 1991 SC 1902, 1911, 1924.

discretion vested in an authority must be exercised for the purpose of attaining the objects of the law. A plot reserved for a public park could not be allotted arbitrarily to a private hospital by altering the town planning scheme. The alteration did not improve the scheme and, therefore, was contrary to the *purpose* for which the power to alter the scheme was conferred.

Occasionally, the Supreme Court has relied upon policy documents to interpret statutory provisions or to fill gaps where the statute is silent. In *Lafarge*,[12] the Supreme Court held that the National Forest Policy of 1988 must govern the grant of permissions under section 2 of the Forest (Conservation) Act of 1980. The principles and guidelines set out in the 1988 policy are required to be read as part of the 1980 Act and the Environment (Protection) Act of 1986.

In the *Asiatic Lion* case,[13] the court followed the lead in *Lafarge*. To extend the reach of the Wild Life (Protection) Act of 1972, the court read the Act along with the National Wildlife Action Plan and the Centrally Sponsored Scheme for the integrated development of wildlife habitats.

B. DIGEST OF ENVIRONMENTAL LEGISLATION

Although there are over 200 central and state statutes that have some bearing on environmental protection,[14] in most cases the environmental concern is incidental to the law's principal object. For example, the Indian Fisheries Act of 1897 prohibited the destruction of fish by the use of explosives or by poisoning the water. Such scattered and piecemeal 'environmental' provisions held the field until the 1970s.[15]

In that decade, the evolution of national environmental policies resulted in Parliament enacting comprehensive laws in the fields of wildlife protection and water pollution. In the early 1980s, nationwide forest conservation and air pollution laws were passed. The Bhopal tragedy in December 1984 caused a surge in environmental legislation: An umbrella Environment (Protection) Act (EPA) was passed in 1986, followed by amendments tightening the laws relating to air and water pollution and to hazardous activities. The 1990s witnessed fresh legislation dealing with insurance cover for hazardous industries, new laws setting up an environmental tribunal and appellate authority, amendments to the wildlife regime and a spate of central regulations under the EPA.

The advent of the twenty-first century saw a succession of new statutes. The Biological Diversity Act of 2002 seeks to conserve India's rich biological resources for sustainable use and equitable sharing of benefits. Responding to a sharp decline in the tiger population, in 2006 Parliament engrafted a tiger protection mandate through extensive amendments to the Wild Life (Protection) Act. The Forest Rights Act of 2006[16] empowers genuine forest dwellers to live undisturbed in forests, but is potentially devastating for wildlife habitats.[17]

---

12 *Lafarge Umium Mining Pvt Ltd v Union of India* (2011) 7 SCC 338, 381.

13 *Centre for Environment Law, WWF-I v Union of India* (2013) 8 SCC 234, 253.

14 Department of Science and Technology, Government of India, *Report of the (Tiwari) Committee for Recommending Legislative Measures and Administrative Machinery for Ensuring Environmental Protection* para 3.1 (1980).

15 At the state level there are a few isolated instances of pre-1970 general environmental laws, e.g., the Orissa River Pollution Prevention Act of 1953 and the Maharashtra Prevention of Water Pollution Act of 1969.

16 The Scheduled Tribes and Other Traditional Forest Dwellers (Recognition of Forest Rights) Act of 2006.

17 See the discussion in Chapter 2 on Environmental Policy in India.

The failed experiments in the 1990s to set up effective environment tribunals led to the passage of the National Green Tribunal Act in 2010. The Compensatory Afforestation Fund Act of 2016 provides a permanent institutional mechanism for spending amounts collected against permissions to clear forests for development. On 28 October 2020, the President promulgated The Commission for Air Quality Management in National Capital Region and Adjoining Areas Ordinance. The Ordinance established a commission to address New Delhi's endemic air quality problems. The Ordinance was replaced (after its lapse) on 13 April 2021 as Ordinance No. 4 of 2021.[18]

I. THE AIR (PREVENTION AND CONTROL OF POLLUTION) ACT OF 1981

To implement the decisions taken at the United Nations Conference on the Human Environment held at Stockholm in June 1972, Parliament enacted the nationwide Air Act of 1981 under Article 253 of the Constitution. The Act's Statement of Objects and Reasons contains the government's explanation of the contents and the scope of the law, and its concern for the 'detrimental effect [of air-pollution] on the health of the people as also on animal life, vegetation and property'.

The Air Act's framework is similar to the one created by its predecessor, the Water Act of 1974. To enable an integrated approach to environmental problems, the Air Act expanded the authority of the Central and state boards established under the Water Act, to include air pollution control. States not having water pollution boards were required to set up air pollution boards.

Under the Air Act, all industries operating within designated air pollution control areas must obtain a 'consent' (permit) from the state boards. The states are required to prescribe emission standards for industry and automobiles after consulting the Central board and noting its ambient air quality standards.

Prior to its amendment in 1987, the Air Act was enforced through mild court-administered penalties on violators. The 1987 amendment strengthened the enforcement machinery and introduced stiffer penalties. Now, the boards may close down a defaulting industrial plant or may stop its supply of electricity or water. A board may also apply to a court to restrain emissions that exceed prescribed standards. Notably, the 1987 amendment introduced a citizens' initiative provision into the Air Act and extended the Act to include noise pollution.

In 2010, the Air Act was amended to provide an appeal to the NGT. Any person aggrieved by decisions of the board may first seek redress before the statutory appellate authority and if dissatisfied may approach the NGT.

The Rules issued under the Air Act focus on procedural matters.

II. THE WATER (PREVENTION AND CONTROL OF POLLUTION) ACT OF 1974

The Water Act of 1974 was the culmination of over a decade of discussion and deliberation between the Centre and the states. The history and the preamble of the Water Act suggest that only state governments can enact water pollution legislation. The Act, therefore, was passed by Parliament pursuant to enabling resolutions by 12 states, under Article 252(1) of the Constitution. Article 252 empowers Parliament to enact laws on state subjects for two or more states, where the State legislatures have consented to such legislation.

[18] At the time of writing Parliament had not passed an Act replacing the Ordinance.

The Act vests regulatory authority in state boards and empowers these boards to establish and enforce effluent standards for factories discharging pollutants into bodies of water. A Central board performs the same functions for Union territories and coordinates activities among the states.

The boards control sewage and industrial effluent discharges by approving, rejecting or conditioning applications for consent to discharge. The state boards also minimize water pollution by advising state governments on appropriate sites for new industry.

Prior to its amendment in 1988, enforcement under the Water Act was achieved through criminal prosecutions initiated by the boards, and through applications to magistrates for injunctions to restrain polluters. The 1988 amendment strengthened the Act's implementation provisions. Now, a board may close a defaulting industrial plant or withdraw its supply of power or water by an administrative order, the penalties are more stringent, and a citizens' initiative provision bolsters the enforcement machinery.

The National Green Tribunal Act of 2010 amended the Water Act to provide an appeal to the NGT against orders, decisions and directions made under the Water Act.

The Water (Prevention and Control of Pollution) Cess Act of 1977 was passed to help meet the expenses of the Central and state water boards. The Water Cess Act was repealed by section 18 of the Taxation Laws (Amendment) Act of 2017 as part of a wider tax reform exercise. During the four decades it remained in force, the Act required local authorities and industries to pay a cess (tax) for water consumption. The Act created economic incentives for pollution control: a differential tax structure (with higher rates applicable to defaulting units) and a rebate for industry which installed effluent treatment equipment.

III. THE WILD LIFE (PROTECTION) ACT OF 1972

In 1972, Parliament enacted the Wild Life Act pursuant to the enabling resolutions of 11 states under Article 252(1) of the Constitution. The Wild Life Act provides for state wildlife advisory boards, regulations for hunting wild animals and birds, establishment of sanctuaries and national parks, regulations for trade in wild animals, animal products and trophies, and judicially imposed penalties for violating the Act. Harming endangered species listed in Schedule I of the Act is prohibited throughout India. Hunting other species, like those requiring special protection (Schedule II), big game (Schedule III) and small game (Schedule IV) is regulated through licensing. A few species classified as vermin (Schedule V) may be hunted without restrictions. The Act is administered by wildlife wardens and their staff.

An amendment to the Act in 1982 introduced provisions permitting the capture and transportation of wild animals for the scientific management of animal populations. Comprehensive amendments to the parent Act in 1991 resulted in the insertion of special chapters dealing with the protection of specified plants and the regulation of zoos. The new provisions also recognized the needs of tribal and forest dwellers and introduced changes to advance their welfare.

In 2003, the Act was amended to allow conservation reserves and community reserves to be created. Conservation reserves are areas adjacent to national parks or sanctuaries and are intended as buffers to protect the landscape, seascape and habitat of fauna and flora. Community reserves comprise private or community lands where the community volunteers to conserve wildlife and its habitat. The purpose of these amendments was to reduce the alienation of local communities from conservation efforts.

A sharp fall in the tiger population prompted the amendment of 2006 which established the National Tiger Conservation Authority and a special wildlife crime control bureau to coordinate efforts to prevent poaching of tigers and other endangered species.

In December 2021, Bill No. 159 of 2021 was introduced in the Lok Sabha to amend the Wild Life Act. The object of this Bill was to rationalize and amend the schedules to the Act, insert a new chapter for regulating international trade in endangered species of wild fauna and flora and to provide for better management of protected areas.

IV. THE PUBLIC LIABILITY INSURANCE ACT OF 1991

This law (PLIA) was enacted to provide immediate relief to the victims of an accident involving a hazardous substance. To achieve this object, the Act imposes 'no-fault' liability upon the owner of the hazardous substance and requires the owner to compensate the victims irrespective of any neglect or default on her part. The PLIA stipulates the maximum compensation for injury or death at Rs. 25,000 and limits compensation in respect of damage to private property to Rs. 6,000. The right of a victim to claim additional relief under any other law is expressly reserved.

The Act requires every owner to take out an insurance policy covering potential liability from an accident. An 'accident' is defined to cover a sudden unintended occurrence while 'handling' any hazardous substance resulting in continuous, intermittent or repeated exposure leading to death or injury to any person, or damage to property or the environment. Accidents by reason of war or radioactivity are excluded from the scope of the Act. The expression 'handling' is defined widely to include manufacture, trade and transport of hazardous substances.

Along with the insurance premium, every owner must make a contribution to an Environmental Relief Fund established by the Central Government. The fund is designed to provide relief to the victims of an accident. The principal administrative authority under the PLIA is the collector, who is required to verify the occurrence of an industrial accident, give publicity to the event, invite applications for compensation and award relief.

The Act was amended in 1992 to introduce provisions relating to the relief fund. Rules framed in 1991 lay down the procedure for inviting and processing compensation applications and also cap the potential liability of an insurer at Rs. 450 million.

V. THE MINES AND MINERALS (REGULATION AND DEVELOPMENT) ACT OF 1957

As the short title suggests, the thrust of this law is to promote the prospecting of minerals and the development of mines. Recognizing the devastating environmental impact of mining activity in several regions across the country, Parliament amended the Act in 1986 to introduce provisions which would require greater environmental sensitivity whilst conducting mining operations.

Section 4A permits government to terminate a prospecting licence or mining lease in order to preserve the natural environment or prevent pollution or harm to public health, monuments, buildings and other structures. Sections 13 and 15 empower the Centre and the states to frame rules to restore vegetation destroyed by mining operations in any area.

VI. THE INDIAN FOREST ACT OF 1927

Although it embodies the colonial policies of the pre-Independence era, the Forest Act of 1927 remains in force. This Act consolidates, with minor changes, the provisions of the Indian Forest Act of 1878 and its amending Acts.

The 1927 Act deals with four categories of forests, namely, reserved forests, village forests, protected forests and non-government (private) forests. A state may declare forest lands or waste lands as reserved forests, and may sell the produce from these forests. Any unauthorized felling of trees, quarrying, grazing and hunting in reserved forests is punishable with a fine or imprisonment, or both. Reserved forests assigned to a village community are called village forests. The state governments are empowered to designate protected forests and may prohibit the felling of trees, quarrying and the removal of forest produce from these forests. The preservation of protected forests is enforced through rules, licences and criminal prosecutions.

The Forest Act is administered by forest officers who are authorized to compel the attendance of witnesses and the production of documents, to issue search warrants and to take evidence in an inquiry into forest offences. Such evidence is admissible in a magistrate's court.

VII. THE FOREST (CONSERVATION) ACT OF 1980

Alarmed at India's rapid deforestation and the resulting environmental degradation, the Central Government enacted the Forest (Conservation) Act in 1980. As amended in 1988, the Act requires the approval of the Central Government before a state 'de-reserves' a reserved forest, uses forest land for non-forest purposes, assigns forest land to a private person or corporation, or clears forest land for the purpose of reforestation. An Advisory Committee constituted under the Act advises the Centre on these approvals. The Act was amended in 2010 to allow an appeal to the NGT from any order or decision made under the Act.

VIII. THE SCHEDULED TRIBES AND OTHER TRADITIONAL FOREST DWELLERS (RECOGNITION OF FOREST RIGHTS) ACT OF 2006

The Forest Rights Act of 2006 is an unprecedented, transformative legislation empowering forest-dwelling Scheduled Tribes and other traditional forest dwellers. The Act seeks to correct historical injustice dating back to the colonial period. At that time, forest resources were nationalized, effectively expropriating forest communities who were residing in the forests for generations. These forest-dwelling communities were unable to have their individual and community rights recognized by the colonial forest department. This position continued post Independence, until the FRA came into effect.

The FRA recognizes 13 sets of rights on forest lands including the right to hold and live on the forest lands for habitation or for self-cultivation for livelihood. To enable forest communities to benefit from development, forest lands may be diverted for specified purposes such as schools, dispensaries, fair price shops, roads and the provision of water, electricity and telecommunication lines.

The FRA process of recognizing and recording rights culminates in the grant of title documents to individuals or the forest community. The grant is made after an evaluation by the Gram Sabha (the village assembly) and a three-tiered process of examination by statutory committees at the sub-divisional, district and state level. The FRA imposes a duty on holders of forest rights, the Gram Sabha and village-level institutions to protect wildlife, forests and biodiversity.

IX. THE COMPENSATORY AFFORESTATION FUND ACT OF 2016

The preamble of this Act narrates the events that led to its passage. In numerous cases, the Supreme Court had required users of forest lands to deposit amounts in a Compensatory Afforestation Fund. These amounts were collected towards compensatory afforestation, penalties, amount representing the net present value of diverted forest lands or catchment area treatment plans. The amounts received were lying unutilized with an *ad hoc* authority awaiting the establishment of a statutory authority. The preamble to the Act records that on 5 May 2006 over Rs. 38,000 crores were lying unspent with the *ad hoc* authority in nationalized banks.

The 2016 Act provides for the establishment of National and States Funds under the public accounts of India. These funds are now responsible for disbursing and utilizing the amounts collected towards reforestation, forest management, forest protection, wildlife protection and other allied activities.

X. THE INSECTICIDES ACT OF 1968

The Insecticides Act was designed to implement the recommendations of the Kerala and Madras Food-Poisoning Cases Inquiry Commission, which inquired into several deaths from insecticide-contaminated food in April and May 1958. The Act established a Central Insecticides Board to advise the Centre and the states on technical aspects of the Act. A committee of this board registers insecticides after examining their formulas and verifying claims regarding their safety and efficacy.

The manufacture and distribution of insecticides is regulated through licensing. A violation of the Act's registration and licensing provisions can lead to prosecution and penalties. The Central and state governments are vested with emergency powers to prohibit the sale, distribution and use of dangerous insecticides.

The following observations in the Tiwari Committee Report of September 1980 are still current:

> This Act, which regulates all aspects of the use of pesticides, has not encouraged strongly enough the move away from the use of organo-chlorine pesticides which are in disfavour all over the world for their proven detrimental effects on the various living natural resources of the environment. The use of biological and integrated pest control in India has hardly caught on in any significant measure. The implementation of the provisions of this Act for monitoring pesticide residues in the environment is totally inadequate. It is hence not surprising that increasing levels of pesticide residues are being recorded in foodstuffs, animal tissues and even human fat. Meanwhile, resistance of pests such as the malarial mosquito to chemical pesticides is on the rise.[19]

The Insecticides Rules of 1971 prescribe the procedures for licensing, packaging, labelling and transporting insecticides. They also provide for workers' safety during the manufacture and handling of insecticides through protective clothing, respiratory devices and medical facilities.

XI. THE BIOLOGICAL DIVERSITY ACT OF 2002

India is a party to the United Nations Convention on Biological Diversity signed at Rio de Janeiro on 5 June 1992. The Biological Diversity Act of 2002 seeks to conserve India's rich biological diversity, create a framework for its sustainable use and provide for the fair and equitable sharing of benefits from the use of biological resources. The Act also seeks to give effect to the Convention.

The Act establishes the National Biodiversity Authority (NBA). Its duties extend to approving proposals that seek to obtain any biological resource occurring in India or knowledge

---

[19] Department of Science and Technology, Government of India, *Report of the (Tiwari) Committee for Recommending Legislative Measures and Administrative Machinery for Ensuring Environmental Protection* (1980).

associated with such a resource for research, survey or utilization. The NBA also regulates transfers of the results of the research and the grant of intellectual property rights with respect to inventions based on the research. The NBA is empowered to lay down the terms for sharing benefits with local people while approving commercial utilization of research or the transfer of any biological resource or knowledge.

The Act imposes a statutory duty on the Central Government to develop national strategies, plans and programmes for conservation of biological resources and to take steps to prevent the extinction of threatened species.

XII. THE ATOMIC ENERGY ACT OF 1962

The regulation of nuclear energy and radioactive substances in India is governed by the Atomic Energy Act of 1962 and the Radiation Protection Rules of 1971. Under the Act, the Central Government is required to prevent radiation hazards, guarantee public safety and the safety of workers handling radioactive substances, and ensure the disposal of radioactive wastes. Nuclear research, the manufacture and transport of radioactive substances, and the production and supply of atomic energy and nuclear-generated electricity also fall within the Centre's authority.

The Centre's apparently unfettered power to withhold from the public what it deems to be 'restricted information', shrouds India's nuclear activities in secrecy. The government may classify as 'restricted information' any unpublished information regarding the location, quality, quantity, processing, acquisition and disposal of radioactive substances; the theory, design, construction and operation of nuclear reactors and of industrial plants that produce radioactive substances; and any information relating to nuclear research.

XIII. THE CIVIL LIABILITY FOR NUCLEAR DAMAGE ACT OF 2010

In international law, nuclear liability is governed by four instruments: the 1960 Paris Convention on Third Party Liability in the Field of Nuclear Energy, the 1963 Vienna Convention on Liability for Nuclear Damage, the 1997 Protocol to Amend the Vienna Convention and the 1997 Convention on Supplementary Compensation for Nuclear Damage. In 2010, India was not a party to any of these conventions and had developed its law within the context of the domestic framework under the Atomic Energy Act of 1962. Unlike the international conventions which dealt with trans-boundary liability, there was no corresponding provision under Indian law. To fill the gap in domestic law regarding nuclear liability generally and to make Indian law consistent with the international regime, the 2010 Act creates a civil liability regime for damage caused by nuclear incidents.[20]

The operator of the nuclear installation where the incident occurs is strictly liable on the principle of no-fault liability. The Act caps liability of an operator at Rs. 1,500 crores. However, a higher limit applies where the Central Government itself owns the nuclear installation or the compensation assessed is more than the maximum payable by an operator or where the nuclear incident is directly due to a grave natural disaster or is caused by armed conflict or terrorism. In such events, the Central Government is liable for a higher amount up to a maximum of the rupee equivalent of 300 million Special Drawings Rights (SDRs).[21] The Act provides for the appointment of a claims commissioner or the establishment of a Nuclear

[20] After enactment of the 2010 Act, India signed the Convention on Supplementary Compensation for Nuclear Damage and ratified the convention in 2016.

[21] SDRs as determined by the International Monetary Fund.

Damage Claims' Commission as alternative methods for the expeditious disposal of compensation claims arising from nuclear incidents.

XIV. THE FACTORIES ACT OF 1948

Passed shortly after the Bhopal tragedy and the Supreme Court's judgment in the *Shriram Gas Leak* case,[22] the 1987 amendment to the Factories Act introduced special provisions on hazardous industrial activities.

The 1987 amendment empowers the states to appoint site appraisal committees to advise on the initial location of factories using hazardous processes. The occupier of every hazardous unit must disclose to her workers, the Factory Inspector and the local authority all particulars regarding health hazards at the factory, and the preventive measures taken. These preventive measures must be publicized among the workers and nearby residents. Every occupier must also draw up an emergency disaster control plan, which must be approved by the Chief Inspector.

The occupier is required to maintain workers' medical records and must employ operations and maintenance personnel who are experienced in handling hazardous substances. The permissible limits of exposure to toxic substances are prescribed in the second schedule to the Act. Safety committees consisting of workers and managers are required periodically to review the factory's safety measures.

The Factories Act after its 1987 amendment, defines 'occupier' as a very senior level manager. Such a person is held responsible for compliance with the Act's provisions relating to hazardous processes. Non-compliance exposes the occupier to stiff penalties.

C. THE ENVIRONMENT (PROTECTION) ACT OF 1986

In the wake of the Bhopal disaster,[23] the government of India enacted the Environment (Protection) Act of 1986 (EPA) under Article 253 of the Constitution. The purpose of the Act is to implement the decisions of the United Nations Conference on the Human Environment of 1972, in so far as they relate to the protection and improvement of the human environment and the prevention of hazards to human beings, other living creatures, plants and property. The EPA is an 'umbrella' legislation designed to provide a framework for Central Government coordination of the activities of various Central and state authorities established under previous laws, such as the Water Act and Air Act. It is also an 'enabling' law, which articulates the essential legislative policy on environmental protection and delegates wide powers to the executive to enable bureaucrats to frame necessary rules and regulations. The EPA is the backbone of India's environmental law. Since the time it entered the statute book, the Act has served to back a vast body of subordinate environmental legislation in India.

I. THE SCOPE OF THE ACT

The scope of the EPA is broad, with 'environment' defined to include water, air and land and the inter-relationships which exist among water, air and land, and human beings and

[22] *M C Mehta v Union of India* AIR 1987 SC 965.

[23] On 3 December 1984, in the worst industrial accident in history, highly toxic methyl isocyanate leaked from Union Carbide's chemical plant at Bhopal. Over 5,200 people are estimated to have died. See the Bhopal section in Chapter 16 on the Regulation of Hazardous Substances.

other living creatures, plants, micro-organisms and property.[24] 'Environmental pollution' is the presence of any environmental pollutant, defined as any solid, liquid or gaseous substance present in such concentration as may be, or may tend to be, injurious to the environment.[25] 'Hazardous substances' include any substance or preparation which may cause harm to human beings, other living creatures, plants, micro-organisms, property or the environment.[26] To ensure sustainable development is one of the goals of the EPA. Further, sustainable development is one of the means to achieve the object and purpose of the Act.[27]

Section 3(1), of the Act empowers the Centre 'to take all such measures as it deems necessary or expedient for the purpose of protecting and improving the quality of the environment and preventing, controlling and abating environmental pollution'. Specifically, the Central Government is authorized to set new national standards for the quality of the environment (ambient standards) as well as standards for controlling emissions and effluent discharges, to regulate industrial locations, to prescribe procedures for managing hazardous substances, to establish safeguards for preventing accidents, and to collect and disseminate information regarding environmental pollution.

Section 3(3) permits the Central Government to constitute one or more authorities to implement the Act. Under section 5 of the Act such an authority may issue directions to close, prohibit or regulate any industry, operation or process as well as stop supply of energy, water or other service.

Section 23 of the Act empowers the Centre to delegate its powers and functions to any officer, state government or other authority. Section 24 of the EPA ensures that the provisions of this Act and subordinate rules or orders *override* any other law. A broad rule-making power is conferred on the Central Government under sections 6 and 25.

NOTES

1. The primary legislative responses to the Bhopal gas leak tragedy of December 1984 were the Bhopal Act of 1985[28] and the EPA. Consequently, the EPA bears the stamp of the legislature's immediate concern to strengthen the regulatory framework for hazardous industry and pollution control: one out of the four chapters in the Act (chapter 3) is devoted to environmental pollution; section 6 empowers the Centre to frame rules for pollution control;[29] and almost all the specific subjects of legislative concern enumerated in section 3 deal with industrial pollution.[30]

This legislative focus soon translated into a range of central rules and regulations laying down pollution norms and regulating toxic substances. Since the early 1990s, however, the breadth of government action under the EPA has extended to the protection of ecologically sensitive

24 Section 2(a).

25 Section 2(b) and (c).

26 Section 2(e). See *A P Pollution Control Board – II v Prof M V Nayudu* (2001) 2 SCC 62, 76.

27 *N D Jayal v Union of India* (2004) 9 SCC 362, 382–3.

28 The Bhopal Gas Leak Disaster (Processing of Claims) Act was passed to ensure that claims arising out of the disaster would be dealt with speedily, effectively and equitably. The Union Government was authorized to sue on behalf of claimants in foreign forums.

29 This provision is in addition to the general rule-making power under section 25.

30 This provision enables the Central Government to take all necessary measures to protect and improve the environment.

areas such as the coast, framing environmental impact assessment (EIA) regulations and the introduction of economic incentives through a product labelling scheme called 'Ecomark'.

2. The potentially broad sweep of the EPA is suggested by the range of issues mentioned in the Statement of Object and Reasons accompanying the Bill: 'The decline of environmental quality has been evidenced by increasing pollution, loss of vegetal cover and biological diversity, excessive concentrations of harmful chemicals in the ambient atmosphere and in food chains, growing risks of environmental accidents and threats to life support systems.'

3. Highlighting the necessity of strict compliance with the provisions of the EPA, the Supreme Court held:

> Thus the power under the Act cannot be treated as a power simpliciter, but it is a power coupled with duty. It is the duty of the State to make sure the fulfillment of conditions or direction under the Act. Without strict compliance, right to environment under Article 21 could not be guaranteed and the purpose of the Act will also be defeated.[31]

4. In the *Shrimp Culture* case,[32] the question arose whether provisions in state laws regulating coastal prawn farms were valid, despite a conflict with the EPA regulations. The Supreme Court clarified that the coastal regulations notified under the EPA would prevail over state legislation. This judgment bolsters section 24 of the EPA which declares the overriding effect of the Act and subordinate rules in relation to any other central or state law.

II. DELEGATED LEGISLATION

The mass of subordinate legislation framed under the EPA by the MoEF falls under six broad categories: (a) pollution control; (b) hazardous substance regulation; (c) environment impact assessment; (d) waste regulation; (e) the protection of the coast and other ecologically fragile areas; and (f) a residuary category. Most of these regulations are analysed in greater detail under the related chapters later in the book. Here, we summarize the broad features of these regulations.

Pollution Control

Section 7 of the EPA prohibits the discharge or emission of environmental pollutants in excess of the prescribed standards. To implement this mandate, the government has framed the Environment (Protection) Rules of 1986 (EPR). The standards are set out in the schedules appended to the EPR. Broadly, there are three types of standards: *source* standards which require the polluter to restrict at source the emission and discharge of environmental pollutants; *product* standards, which fix the pollution norms for new manufactured products such as cars and diesel engines for generators; and *ambient* standards to set maximum pollutant loads in the air, and to guide regulators on the environmental quality that ought to be maintained for healthy living.

Schedule I lays down industry-specific standards for effluent discharge and emissions in respect of 112 designated industries or activities. Every industrial unit must comply with the norms within one year of their publication[33] or such shorter period that may be ordered by the pollution control board.[34] In respect of any specific industry the Central Government may extend the lead time for compliance beyond one year.[35] In cases where the standards

[31] *N D Jayal v Union of India* (2004) 9 SCC 362, 383; *Milk Producers Assn v State of Orissa* (2006) 3 SCC 229, 240.

[32] *S Jagannath v Union of India* (*Shrimp Culture* case) AIR 1997 SC 811, 846.

[33] Rule 3(3).

[34] Rule 3(4).

[35] *Id.*

were prescribed prior to 16 January 1991 the industry was required to achieve compliance by the year end.[36]

Where the polluter is not covered by Schedule I, the unit must comply with the general standards for discharge of environmental pollutants prescribed in Schedule VI.[37] These general standards are also referred to as the 'minimum national standards' since they represent the parameters which every industry must meet until specific standards under Schedule I are prescribed. The pollution control boards in the states are empowered to specify stricter standards than those published in respect of any industry, operation or process, where necessary.[38]

Regarding product standards, new motor vehicles must meet emission[39] and noise limits.[40] Consumer durables such as air conditioners, refrigerators and air coolers and some types of construction equipment are required to meet prescribed noise levels.[41]

In addition to the source and product norms, Schedules III and VII of the EPR prescribe national ambient air quality standards in respect of noise and other air pollutants. The levels of ambient air quality have been fixed after providing an adequate margin of safety to protect public health, vegetation and property.

Supplementing the EPR are the Noise Pollution (Regulation and Control) Rules which were enforced on 14 February 2000. These Rules prescribe ambient air quality standards in respect of noise for industrial, commercial and residential areas as well as designated 'silence zones'. The state government is responsible for classifying localities into these zones. The Rules impose restrictions on the use of loudspeakers and public address systems and cast a duty on the local administration and police to ensure compliance. Bursting sound-emitting fire crackers in a silence zone or at night time (10 pm to 6 am) is prohibited and actionable.

Hazardous Substance Regulation

The Hazardous Wastes (Management and Handling) Rules framed under the EPA in 1989 introduced a permit system to regulate the handling and disposal of hazardous wastes. A public interest litigation initiated in the Supreme Court in 1995 exposed gaps in this regulatory regime with respect to the trans-boundary movement of hazardous wastes.[42] The case was monitored by the court for over one and half decades and prompted an altered regime in the shape of the Hazardous Wastes (Management, Handling and Transboundary Movement) Rules of 2008. In an offshoot of the same public interest litigation (PIL), the court set out detailed procedures for the anchoring, beaching and breaking of ships condemned to the scrapyard.[43]

---

36 Rule 3(5).

37 Rule 3(3A). Schedule VI has five parts. Apart from the general effluent and emission standards in Part A and Part D, the schedule also prescribes industry-specific standards for waste-water generation (Part B) and levels of pollution load, linked to manufacturing capacity (Part C).

38 Rule 3(2), (3A).

39 Schedule IV.

40 Schedule VI (Part E).

41 *Id.*

42 *Research Foundation for Science Technology and Natural Resource Policy v Union of India* (2012) 7 SCC 769. Several substantive interim orders were passed in this case, amongst them: (2005) 13 SCC 655 dated 5 May 1997; (1999) 1 SCC 223 dated 13 October 1997; (2000) 9 SCC 41 dated 10 December 1999; (2005) 13 SCC 657(2) dated 14 September 2001; (2005) 13 SCC 658 dated 3 December 2001; (2005) 13 SCC 659 dated 4 February 2002; (2005) 13 SCC 661 dated 24 September 2003; (2005) 10 SCC 510 dated 14 October 2003; (2005) 13 SCC 186 dated 5 January 2005; (2005) 13 SCC 671 dated 9 May 2005.

43 *Research Foundation for Science Technology and Natural Resource Policy v Union of India* 2007 (10) Scale 594; *Research Foundation for Science Technology and Natural Resource Policy v Union of India* 2007 (11) Scale 75; *Research Foundation for Science Technology and Natural Resource Policy v Union of India* (2012) 7 SCC 764.

The 2008 Rules were substituted in 2016 by a fresh set of rules having the same name. The 2016 Rules impose a duty on factories to prevent, minimize, reuse, recycle, recover and ensure safe disposal of hazardous wastes and other notified wastes. Handling and storage of hazardous wastes requires authorization from the state pollution control board. The Rules also prescribe the procedure for importing hazardous wastes, require statutory records to be maintained and periodic returns filed. The occupier, importer, exporter or operator of a disposal facility is liable for all damages caused to the environment or a third party due do improper handling or management of the hazardous waste.

The Manufacture, Storage and Import of Hazardous Chemicals Rules, 1989 spell out the responsibility of those handling hazardous substances (other than wastes). Hazardous industries are required to identify major accident hazards, take adequate preventive measures and submit a safety report to the designated authority. An importer of hazardous chemicals must furnish complete product safety information to the competent authority and must transport the imported chemicals in accordance with the road transport laws. The Rules impose a duty on every 'occupier who has control of an industrial activity' to ensure safe handling and prevent accidents at the site. The Rules also specify particular government agencies responsible for inspecting the industrial activity and preparation of on-site and off-site emergency plans.

Environmental Impact Assessment (EIA)

Until January 1994, EIA in India was carried out under a framework of administrative guidelines that required the proponent of major irrigation projects, river valley projects, power stations, ports and harbours to secure a clearance from the Ministry of Environment and Forests (MoEF). The project authority submitted information to the MoEF by filling out questionnaires or check lists. The environmental appraisal was carried out by the ministry's environmental appraisal committees. These committees discussed issues with project officials and on the basis of deliberations either approved or rejected the sites. When approved, the project clearance was generally made conditional on specified safeguards.

On 27 January 1994, the MoEF notified mandatory EIAs for 29 designated projects. The notification was issued under the EPA and required an EIA, an environment management plan (EMP) and a project report to be submitted to the impact assessment agency for clearance. The MoEF was designated as the impact assessment agency and was required to consult a multi-disciplinary committee of experts before taking a decision. The 1994 notification mandated public hearings and was India's first attempt at a comprehensive EIA regime.

Propelled by the corporate perception that EIA clearances took far too long and on the strength of its decade-long experience, a fresh EIA notification was issued in September 2006. The current regime for EIA is also framed under the EPA. The September 2006 notification covers 41 projects that must secure prior environmental clearance from the MoEF in respect of category A projects or from the State Environmental Impact Assessment Authority (SEIAA) for matters covered by category B of the schedule. An environmental clearance from one of these regulatory authorities must be obtained before commencing construction or preparing the land by the project proponent.

Both the MoEF and SEIAA are required to decide on whether to grant environmental clearance based upon the recommendation of an Expert Appraisal Committee (EAC). The EACs are entrusted with the task of screening, scoping and appraising projects. The EACs must determine detailed and comprehensive terms of reference addressing all environmental concerns and these must be conveyed to the applicant within 60 days of receiving the application.

The public consultation process is designed to address the concerns of local affected persons and others having a plausible stake in the environmental impact of the project. The public consultation involves a public hearing at the site and written responses from concerned stakeholders. The public hearing is organized by the state pollution control board within 45 days of a request being made in this behalf by the applicant. Once the public consultation process is complete, the project proponent is required to address all the material environmental concerns expressed during this process and to make appropriate changes in the draft EIA and EMP. The final EIA report is then submitted to the MoEF or the SEIAA.

The first stage of appraisal involves a detailed scrutiny by the EAC of the application and other documents such as the final EIA report and the outcome of public consultations. After interacting with the applicant and obtaining necessary clarifications, the EAC must make categorical recommendations to the MoEF or the SEIAA, either for the grant of environmental clearance or for rejection of the application. The EAC must furnish reasons in support of its recommendations. This appraisal exercise must be completed within 60 days of receiving the final EIA report.

The MoEF or SEIAA is required to convey its decision to the applicants within 45 days of receiving the recommendations of the EAC. Generally, the decision for grant of environmental clearance must be conveyed within 105 days of receiving the final EIA report. Normally, the recommendation of the EAC must be accepted and when the regulatory authority disagrees with its recommendations, it may request reconsideration by the EAC within a period of 45 days. The decision of the regulatory authority, after considering the recommendations of the EAC after the remand, is final and must be conveyed to the applicant.

It is mandatory for the project management to submit half-yearly compliance reports in respect of the conditions mentioned in the environmental clearance. All such compliance reports are available to the public and the latest compliance report must be displayed on the website of the concerned regulatory authority.

The EIA procedure draws on inputs from four sources. The primary burden is on the project proponent to choose the site, identify the technology and employ suitable mitigation measures. The second set of inputs comes from the affected community and environmentalists who can express their concerns through the public hearing process. The EIA notification creates an entitlement amongst the politically and economically weak to have their viewpoints heard in the course of decision-making. The third intervention is provided by the EAC tasked to advise the impact assessment agency. Finally, the impact assessment agency is required to assimilate the information placed before it and take an informed decision on whether to grant the environmental clearance. Orders granting or refusing an environmental clearance may be appealed to the NGT.[44]

Dissatisfied with a lack of objectivity in the EIA process, the Supreme Court directed the Central Government to establish a national regulator for appraising projects, enforcing environmental conditions contained in approvals and to impose penalties on polluters.[45] This direction was reiterated by the Supreme Court in January 2014 while granting further time to the Centre to appoint a regulator.[46]

---

44 Section 16(h), (i) National Green Tribunal Act of 2010.

45 *Lafarge Umiam Mining Pvt Ltd v Union of India* (2011) 7 SCC 338, 382.

46 *T N Godavarman Thirumulpad v Union of India* (2014) 4 SCC 61, 68. At the time of writing, there is no national regulator in place. However, the Centre has published a draft EIA notification seeking suggestions and objections from the public, in a move to replace the 2006 notification.

Waste Regulation

The collection and proper disposal of waste arising from large urban settlements is an essential municipal function. Despite local town planning and municipal laws imposing this duty on city administrators, the absence of effective garbage collection and disposal procedures compelled the Supreme Court to intervene and facilitate the framing of national regulations.[47] The MSW Rules imposed duties on municipal authorities to build infrastructure and put in place systems for the collection, segregation and disposal of municipal solid waste. The Rules envisaged the establishment of landfill sites and the operation of these landfills by licensed operators.

In 2016, the MSW Rules were replaced by two sets of rules: the Solid Waste Management (SWM) Rules and the Construction and Demolition (C&D) Waste Management Rules. Apart from mandating segregation and disposal obligations, the SWM Rules impose specific obligations on Union ministries, state governments, pollution control boards and municipalities. Illustratively, the Department of Fertilizers must develop markets for city compost and ensure co-marketing of compost with chemical fertilizers in prescribed ratios. The Ministry of Power is required to create appropriate mechanisms to ensure that tariffs are fixed for power generated from waste-to-energy plants based on solid waste and that such power is purchased by electricity distribution utilities.

The C&D Waste Management Rules impose new obligations on real estate developers. The Rules require the segregation of construction and demolition waste; the preparation and approval of waste management plans by large generators; and the creation of suitable sites by local authorities for storage, processing and recycling facilities. The Bureau of Indian Standards and Indian Roads Congress are required to prepare a code of practices for use of recycled materials and products made from C&D waste for construction of roads.

The Centre has also framed separate sets of rules to deal with bio-medical waste generated at hospitals, veterinary institutions, places where animals are kept for experiments or testing, research labs, pathological laboratories, etc.[48] The working of these Rules in the context of bio-medical waste management treatment facilities was explained by a division bench of the Andhra Pradesh High Court in *G J Multiclave (India) Pvt Ltd v State of Telangana*.[49]

The Central Government has framed rules under the EPA to curb the proliferation of plastic waste and discourage the use of plastic carry bags by shoppers.[50] Retailers and street vendors are prohibited from selling or providing commodities to consumers in carry bags which are not manufactured and labelled in the manner prescribed. Where plastic bags are provided, they must be priced—with a view to discourage use. Under the E-Waste (Management) Rules of 2016, producers including suppliers of electrical and electronic equipment are responsible for collecting e-waste and ensuring proper disposal.[51]

Coast, Wetlands and Protection of Ecologically Sensitive Areas

Comprehensive national regulations to protect the Indian coast were first issued on 19 February 1991 under the EPA. The 1991 regulations introduced the concept of a coastal regulation zone (CRZ) which comprised a strip of land falling between the high-tide line

---

47 The Municipal Solid Wastes (Management & Handling) Rules of 2000 (MSW Rules).

48 Bio-Medical Waste Management Rules of 2016 as amended in 2018. These rules superseded the Bio-Medical Waste (Management & Handling) Rules of 1998.

49 (2017) 6 ALT 461, (2017) SCC Online HYD 279.

50 Plastic Waste Management Rules of 2016. These rules replaced the Plastic Waste (Management & Handling) Rules of 2011.

51 The 2016 Rules superseded the E-Waste (Management & Handling) Rules of 2011.

and stretching to a distance of 500 metres on the landward side. The 1991 regulations were replaced on 6 January 2011 by two new regulations. The CRZ notification of 2011 applies generally to all coastal areas and it expands the regulatory zone to areas that were previously unregulated. Now, the CRZ includes the inter-tidal zone (land between the high-tide line and low-tide line) as well as the water and the bed area between the low-tide line up to the territorial water limit of 12 nautical miles. Separately, the Island Protection Zone notification of 2011, specific to the Andaman and Nicobar Islands in the Bay of Bengal and the Lakshadweep islands off the coast of Kerala, introduced a special framework for the integrated management of these island clusters.

In 2019, the MoEF replaced the 2011 regime with two fresh notifications: the CRZ notification for the mainland coast and an Island Coastal Regulation Zone notification.

Since the implementation of planning laws in India is weak, citizens at times lobby for protection through courts and the upper echelons of the MoEF. Citizens' initiatives have secured protective regimes in ecologically sensitive areas (ESAs). Typically, ESAs are small regions of aesthetic beauty and sufficient ecological significance to warrant special attention. The ESA notifications issued under the EPA generally impose a special set of town and country planning rules, limiting commercial and industrial development within the notified region.[52] Illustrative of the ESAs are the horticultural belt in the Dahanu region of Maharashtra,[53] the Himalayan foothills around Doon Valley,[54] the coastal Murud-Janjira area in the Raigarh District of Maharashtra,[55] the congested Antop Hill locality in Mumbai,[56] parts of the Aravali range in Rajasthan and Haryana,[57] the Mahableshwar Panchgani region in the Sahyadris,[58] Matheran and the surrounding region,[59] Mount Abu in Rajasthan[60]and the watershed of the river Bhagirathi from Gaumukh to Uttarkashi.[61] Most of these notifications were issued against the backdrop of specific environmental threats to each region brought into focus by a PIL.

Pursuant to a decision by the National Board for Wild Life on 17 March 2005 to declare ESAs around national parks and wildlife sanctuaries, numerous notifications have been issued to create a buffer zone and restrict development around protected areas.[62] To speed up

52 Meenakshi Kapoor, Kanchi Kohli & Manju Menon, *India's Notified Eco-logically Sensitive Areas: The Story So Far* (2009).

53 Notification dated 20 June 1991. The orchards of Dahanu were threatened by the possibility of rapid industrialization after a large thermal power plant was established in the area.

54 Notification dated 1 February 1989. Doon Valley was harmed by extensive limestone quarrying.

55 Notification dated 6 January 1989. A coastal strip of about 30 kms was threatened by several giant industrial projects. This notification encouraged environmentalists to press for national coastal norms which took shape in February 1991.

56 Notification dated 9 February 1990. The residents of Antop Hill lived under a continuous threat from vast quantities of hazardous chemicals stored in the neighbourhood.

57 Notification dated 7 May 1992. Limestone quarrying threatened the Project Tiger reserve in the Alwar District of Rajasthan.

58 Notification dated 17 January 2001. Mahableshwar and Panchgani are hill resorts in Satara District, Maharashtra.

59 Notification dated 4 February 2003 as amended on 16 January 2004. Matheran is a pedestrian-only hill resort in Maharashtra.

60 Notification dated 25 June 2009. Mount Abu is a forested region with significant man-made heritage including the Dilwara temples.

61 Notification dated 18 December 2012 as amended on 16 April 2018. This Himalayan watershed supports rich flora and fauna including migratory species and comprises a fragile mountain eco-system.

62 Illustratively, notification dated 26 June 2015 in respect of Pulicat Wildlife Sanctuary, Andhra Pradesh; and notification dated 7 June 2017 declaring an ESA around Amchang Wildlife Sanctuary, Assam.

this process, the MoEF framed guidelines in 2011 and urged the states and Union territories to submit site-specific proposals in respect of each national park and sanctuary.

To protect wetlands and preserve the ecological services they provide, the Central Government has framed rules restricting activities such as the reclamation and establishment of new industries within protected wetlands. An authority established under the rules is responsible for identifying wetlands and may issue directions necessary for the conservation, preservation and sustainable use of wetlands.[63] Before restrictions on development can apply to a wetland, it must be identified and finally notified. Construction by a property owner cannot be stopped by an executive order in anticipation of a wetland being notified in future.[64]

Other Delegated Legislation

In 1991, the Department of Environment, Forests and Wildlife announced a scheme for labelling environment friendly products. The objects of the scheme are to encourage manufacturers to introduce environment-friendly products, reward genuine initiatives to reduce adverse environmental impacts and assist consumers in making an informed, responsible choice while purchasing goods. The label known as 'Ecomark' may be used by the manufacturers of the consumer goods who meet the environment criteria notified by the Central Government for the purpose of the scheme. Though qualification criteria have long been published for a number of goods such as soaps, detergents, paper and paints the scheme has yet to gain popularity.

Consistent with India's obligations under the Montreal Protocol on Substances that Deplete the Ozone Layer, specific rules were introduced under the EPA in 2000.[65] These rules regulate the production, consumption, export and import of ozone-depleting substances. The rules also prohibit new investments in manufacturing facilities in relation to these substances and specifically prohibit the import of air-conditioning and refrigeration equipment containing specified substances from 1 July 2015.[66]

Since lead is toxic, two sets of rules regulate the use of this substance. The Batteries (Management and Handling) Rules of 2001 regulate the manufacture, import, assembly and reconditioning of lead acid batteries. The use of lead or lead compounds is prohibited in the manufacture of paints and a self-certification system of labelling assures consumers about the safety of the product.[67]

Responding to directions issued by the Supreme Court in the *Forest Conservation* case,[68] the MoEF issued guidelines for the establishment and regulation of wood-based industries such as saw mills, veneer mills and furniture units. The guidelines create a licensing system and are intended to prevent the illegal felling of trees and depletion of forests.[69]

---

63 Wetlands (Conservation & Management) Rules of 2017. These Rules replaced an earlier set of rules issued in 2010.

64 *Vardha Enterprises Pvt Ltd v Rajendra Kumar Rajdhan* (2015) 15 SCC 352, 362.

65 Ozone Depleting Substances (Regulation and Control) Rules of 2000.

66 Rule 11(1A), *id.*

67 The Regulation of Lead Contents in Household and Decorative Paints Rules of 2016.

68 *T N Godavarman Thirumulpad v Union of India* (2016) 13 SCC 586, 613, order dated 5 October 2015.

69 The Wood-Based Industry (Establishment & Regulation) Guidelines of 2016.

NOTES AND QUESTIONS

1. The statutory annexures to Schedule VI of the EPR lay down important guidelines for the state pollution control boards. While enforcing the standards, the boards should ensure use of the *best available technology*, *recycling* of waste-water and reuse of other materials, and the implementation of clean technologies by industry in order to increase *fuel efficiency*. While permitting discharge of effluents and emissions the assimilative capacity of the receiving bodies should also be kept in view so that the intended use of the receiving water body is not affected.

2. Section 7 of the EPA prohibits a person carrying on any industry, operation or process from discharging or emitting pollutants in excess of the prescribed standards. Although there is no express provision in the Act requiring the pollution control boards to enforce these standards, this scheme is implicit in the EPR. Sections 17(g) of the Water Act and Air Act empower the state boards to lay down standards for effluent discharge and emission and many state boards have notified norms under these two Acts. At times the pollution control board norms vary from the EPR standards. Which standards apply—those contained in the schedules to the EPR or the standards published by the state boards? Assuming the EPR standards prevail, should Parliament repeal sections 17(g) and should the boards reduce the confusion by annulling their own standards? One possible justification for retaining these provisions is that the state boards may specify *more stringent* standards than those in the EPR.

At least one leading pollution case affecting several hundred units was decided by the Gujarat High Court without regard to the EPR standards and on the basis of the state board norms.[70]

III. SECTIONS 3 AND 5 OF THE EPA

Section 3(1) confers very wide powers on the Central Government 'to take all such measures as it deems necessary or expedient for the purpose of protecting and improving the quality of the environment and preventing, controlling and abating environmental pollution'. Sub-section (2) illustrates the types of measures that the Centre may adopt under sub-section (1). Amongst those is the power to restrict areas in which industries may be set up, which enabled the Coastal Regulations, the EIA Regulations and the notifications to protect ecologically sensitive areas like Mount Abu, Mahableshwar and Panchgani, and the Bhagirath watershed. Commenting on the genesis of the Coastal Regulations in the *CRZ Notification* case,[71] the Supreme Court observed that the principal notification of 1991 was issued under section 3(1) and 3(2)(v) of the EPA 'presumably after a lot of study [was] undertaken by the government. Normally, such notifications are issued after a detailed study and examination of all relevant issues.'

Section 3(3) permits the Central Government to constitute one or more authorities to implement the Act. Under section 5 of the Act, such an authority may issue binding directions in writing to any person, officer or authority. Section 5 clarifies that the power to issue directions includes the power to close, prohibit or regulate any industry, operation or process as well as the power to stop supply of energy, water or other service.

In the *Bichhri* case,[72] chemical industries in an industrial complex in Bichhri, Rajasthan devastated the environment by discharging untreated toxic chemicals and sludge. All the

---

70 *Pravinbhai J Patel v State of Gujarat* 1995 (2) Guj L R 1210.
71 *Indian Council for Enviro-Legal Action v Union of India* (1996) 5 SCC 281, 296.
72 *Indian Council for Enviro-Legal Action v Union of India* AIR 1996 SC 1446.

regulatory agencies including the Central Government failed to perform their tasks. While considering whether a court in its writ jurisdiction was empowered to direct remedial measures and recover the clean-up costs from the polluter, the Supreme Court examined the scope of sections 3 and 5 of the EPA:

> Section 5 clothes the Central Government (or its delegates) with the power to issue directions for achieving the objects of the Act. Read with the wide definition of 'environment' in Section 2(a), Sections 3 and 5 clothe the Central Government with all such powers as are 'necessary or expedient for the purpose of protecting and improving the quality of the environment'. The Central Government is empowered to take all measures and issue all such directions as are called for the above purpose. In the present case, the said powers will include giving directions for the removal of sludge, for undertaking remedial measures and also the power to impose the cost of remedial measures on the offending industry and utilise the amount so recovered for carrying out remedial measures. This Court can certainly give directions to the Central Government/its delegates to take all such measures, if in a given case this Court finds that such directions are warranted.[73]

Environmentalists, non-governmental organizations and academics have long commended the idea of an autonomous agency along the lines of the US Environment Protection Agency, to oversee the enforcement of the EPA. Although the Central Government may create a specialist agency under section 3(3), thus far, the Centre has chosen to leave implementation of the EPA to the Union Ministry of Environment and Forests. The executive's reluctance, however, has not deterred the Supreme Court from directing the Centre to set up an authority under section 3(3) of the EPA when the court considered it necessary.

In *Vellore Citizens' Welfare Forum v Union of India*,[74] the court was dealing with the extensive damage caused by untreated effluent discharged by tanneries in Tamil Nadu. Turning to section 3(3) of the EPA, the court observed:

> The main purpose of the Act is to create an authority or authorities under section 3(3) of the Act with adequate powers to control pollution and protect the environment. It is a pity that till date no authority has been constituted by the Central Government. The work which is required to be done by the authority in terms of section 3(3) read with other provisions of the Act is being done by this court and other courts in the country. It is high time that the Central Government realises its responsibility and statutory duty to protect the degrading environment in the country.[75]

The Supreme Court directed the Centre to constitute an authority under section 3(3) with all necessary powers to deal with the situation created by the tanneries and other polluting industries in the state. A retired High Court judge was placed at the head of the new authority, which was to have persons with expertise in pollution control and environment protection as members. The authority was requested to identify the persons who had suffered because of the pollution, name the polluters liable to compensate the victims, assess the compensation to be paid and the costs of the remedial measures. The authority was asked to periodically review compliance by the tanneries and to direct relocation of any industry where necessary. On 30 September 1996, the MoEF constituted the Loss of Ecology (Prevention and Compensation) Authority for the State of Tamil Nadu with a term of two years. The authority's term was periodically extended. It eventually worked for two decades, awarding compensation in the range of Rs. 70 crores to over 90,000 farmers, apart from ordering

---

[73] *Id.* at 1464.
[74] AIR 1996 SC 2715.
[75] *Id.* at 2724.

clean-up and rehabilitation schemes worth Rs. 165 crores. The authority was wound up in 2016 and the applications pending before it transferred to the NGT.[76]

In the *Bayer* case,[77] the Supreme Court acknowledged its lack of expertise to resolve the complex issues arising from a demand to relocate hazardous industries away from urban areas. Bayer had petitioned the Bombay High Court to restrain the city of Thane from allowing residential buildings to come up to within a kilometre of its factory. Bayer asked for the safety zone since it used hazardous chemicals at its plant and was anxious to minimize the impact of an industrial accident. The High Court accepted the company's plea and restrained development.[78] Against this judgment, some of the affected builders appealed to the Supreme Court, where the case took a dramatic turn. One of the arguments that seemed to find favour with the apex court was that the industry shift away, and the residential buildings be allowed. After several hearings, the court directed the Union Government to constitute a special authority under section 3(3) of the EPA to resolve the relocation issues raised in the case.

In the *CRZ Notification* case,[79] the Supreme Court noted the poor enforcement of environmental laws and recognized the administrative burden on the pollution control boards which prevented them from effectively implementing the regulations. The court requested the Union Government to consider setting up state coastal management authorities in each state or zone and also a national coastal management authority under section 3(3) of the EPA to assume the responsibility for enforcing these regulations. The coastal authorities were established in November 1998.

The MoEF has established authorities under section 3(3) with regional mandates to tackle persistent environmental problems in the National Capital Region of Delhi,[80] Dahanu Taluka,[81] the Taj Trapezium Zone[82] and the Ganga River basin.[83] Typically, these authorities operate for the period specified in the statutory notification and upon the term expiring, a fresh notification for a new period is issued. The renewal notifications may, at times, alter the constitution of the authority.

The ambit of section 5 of the EPA was explained by the Gujarat High Court in a case concerning pollution of the Kharicut canal. *Pravinbhai J Patel v State of Gujarat*[84] was a mammoth PIL spanning several months and covering more than one thousand industrial units in Ahmedabad. After a prolonged hearing and several interim orders, a division bench of the court issued a range of final directions requiring the closure of polluting units, setting deadlines for compliance and levying a compensatory charge on polluters for the benefit of the

---

76 See *Vellore Citizens' Welfare Forums v Union of India* (2016) 3 Law Weekly 11; (2016) SCC Online Mad 1881.

77 *F B Taraporawala v Bayer India Ltd* AIR 1997 SC 1846.

78 *Bayer (India) Ltd v State of Maharashtra* 1994 (4) Bom C Rep 309.

79 *Indian Council for Enviro-Legal Action v Union of India* (1996) 5 SCC 281.

80 See notification dated 29 January 1998 and notification dated 3 October 2018. The authority has a broad mandate to improve the quality of the environment in the National Capital Region. Its powers include issuing directions under section 5 of the EPA.

81 Notification dated 19 December 1996. The authority was chaired by Justice C S Dharmadhikari (Retd) until his demise in January 2019.

82 Notification dated 17 May 1999 constituting an authority for a period of two years. The authority was responsible for monitoring schemes to protect the Taj Mahal and to improve the environment. The authority was empowered under section 5 of the EPA to issue suitable directions to any person or authority.

83 Notification dated 20 February 2009. The authority comprised the Prime Minister, several Union Ministers as well as Chief Ministers of Uttarakhand, Uttar Pradesh, Bihar, Jharkhand and West Bengal. The authority was required to evolve mechanisms for abating pollution of the River Ganga and for conservation of the river.

84 1995 (2) Guj L R 1210.

affected villagers. The court acknowledged that normally it was for the state government (as a delegate of the Centre) to issue appropriate closure directions under section 5 and that it was no part of a court's duty to do so.

> Where, however, there is a complete abdication of authority by the government and the court comes to the conclusion, like in the present case, that the government has failed to discharge its statutory duty, and which failure has resulted in the violation of the fundamental rights of the petitioners and lacs of other people guaranteed under Article 21 of the Constitution, then the court is left with no option but to issue appropriate direction to the government to pass the necessary orders under section 5 of the Environment Act.[85]

The court observed that under the EPA the government was the custodian of a clean environment and that its power under section 5 was coupled with a duty to exercise the power whenever the need arose.[86]

Section 5A was inserted into the parent act by the National Green Tribunal Act of 2010. This provision allows any person aggrieved by any directions issued under section 5 of the EPA to appeal to the NGT.

NOTES

1. In *Narula Dyeing*,[87] the industries argued that the power under section 5 of the EPA could be exercised by the Central Government alone and not the state. Even otherwise, the impugned directions suffered from the vice of excessive delegation since there were no guidelines to control administrative discretion. The High Court rejected these grounds since section 23 of the EPA empowered the Centre to delegate its functions and by a notification dated 10 February 1988 the Centre had conferred its power under section 5 on Gujarat.[88] The court also found sufficient guidance for the exercise of power under section 5 in section 3 of the EPA and the nature of functions required to be discharged by the Central Government under the Act.[89]

2. A division bench of the Orissa High Court refused to aid a soap factory which was asked to stop operations until it cleaned up its act and met the prescribed effluent standards. One of the grounds urged by the petitioner was that the section 5 direction was passed without giving a reasonable opportunity to be heard, since no personal hearing was granted. Reviewing the provisions of rule 4 of the EPR which lay down the procedure for directions issued under section 5, the High Court found that the requirement for granting an opportunity to be heard did not include a personal hearing and that it was sufficient if an opportunity for filing written objections was granted.[90]

---

85 *Id.* at 1253.

86 *Id.* at 1235.

87 *Narula Dyeing & Printing Works v Union of India* AIR 1995 Guj 185.

88 The Central Government delegated its power under section 5 to all the state governments (except Arunachal Pradesh and Nagaland) under six notifications issued between 1988 and 1991. The notification in respect of Arunachal Pradesh and Nagaland was issued on 15 July 1998.

89 In *Indian Council for Enviro-Legal Action v Union of India* (*CRZ Notification* case) (1996) 5 SCC 281, 302, the Supreme Court held that directions under section 5 'have necessarily to be in accordance with the provisions of law and to give protection to environment'.

90 *Mahabir Soap & Gudakhu Factory v Union of India* AIR 1995 Ori 218, 223.

3. Occasionally, a court may find that the government has overstepped its jurisdiction in ordering closure and may frame a less stringent compliance programme for the defaulting unit.[91]

4. The Telangana State Pollution Control Board (TSPCB) issued an order demarcating the operational areas around bio-medical waste treatment facilities. Through this process of demarcation, certain operators were prohibited from obtaining and treating the waste of health care establishments beyond their designated area of operation. Setting aside the order passed by TSPCB, the High Court of Andhra Pradesh held that the board could not derive authority to support such an order based on section 5 of the EPA.[92]

IV. VIOLATIONS AND PENALTIES UNDER THE ACT

The EPA was the first environmental statute to give the Central Government authority to issue direct written orders, including orders to close, prohibit or regulate any industry, operation or process or to stop or regulate the supply of electricity, water or any other service.[93] Other powers granted to the Central Government to ensure compliance with the Act include the power of entry for examination, testing of equipment and other purposes[94] and the power to take samples of air, water, soil or any other substance from any place for analysis.[95]

The Act explicitly prohibits discharges of environmental pollutants in excess of prescribed regulatory standards.[96] There is also a specific prohibition against handling hazardous substances except in compliance with regulatory procedures and standards.[97] Persons responsible for discharges of pollutants in excess of prescribed standards must prevent or mitigate the pollution and must report the discharge to governmental authorities.[98]

The Act provides for penalties. Any person who fails to comply with or contravenes any of the provisions of the Act, or the rules, orders or directions issued under the Act shall be punished, for each failure or contravention, with a prison term of up to five years or a fine of up to Rs. 1,00,000 or both. The Act imposes an additional fine of up to Rs. 5,000 for every day of continuing violation.[99] If a failure or contravention occurs for more than one year after the date of conviction an offender may be punished with a prison term which may extend to seven years.[100]

Corporate officials directly in charge of a company's business are liable for offences under the Act, unless the official can establish that the offence was committed without his or her knowledge or that he or she exercised all due diligence to prevent the commission of the offence.[101] In addition, if an offence is committed with the consent or connivance of, or is attributable to any neglect on the part of any director, manager, secretary or other officer, that person shall also be liable for the offence.[102] Similar provisions extend liability to the heads of departments of government and other department officers.[103]

91 *Rajiv Singh v State of Bihar* AIR 1992 PAT 86.
92 *G J Multiclave (India) Pvt Ltd v State of Telangana* (2017) 6 ALT 461, (2017) SCC Online HYD 279.
93 Section 5. Later, similar provisions were introduced in the Air Act and the Water Act.
94 Section 10.
95 Section 11.
96 Section 7.
97 Section 8.
98 Section 9(1).
99 Section 15(1).
100 Section 15(2).
101 Section 16(1).
102 Section 16(2).
103 Section 17.

Section 24 provides that if any act or omission constitutes an offence punishable under the EPA as well as any other law, the offender shall be liable to be punished under the other law and not under the EPA.

NOTES AND QUESTIONS

1. Section 24 of the Act is a curious and controversial provision. Generally, more recent legislation which conflicts with previous legislation supersedes the previous legislation. Standards established under the Environment (Protection) Act are also the subject of other statutes, such as the Water Act and Air Act. Until the amendment of the Air Act in 1987 and the Water Act in 1988, both these laws prescribed less stringent penalties than did the EPA. This situation led one commentator to describe the Environment (Protection) Act as a cobra that is seemingly fierce but has no venom in its fangs.[104]

2. Consider another serious problem with section 24. Suppose the Water Act allows discharge of a higher concentration of a particular pollutant than the concentration permissible under the EPA. If a factory discharges waste-water containing the pollutant at a level higher than allowed under the EPA but within the allowable limits of the Water Act, does the Water Act penalty provision apply? Are there other problems with having two statutes—with different standards and penalty provisions—regulating release of the same pollutants?

3. Will this legislative scheme lead to more, or less, effective enforcement of environmental laws? One of the basic purposes of law is to promote uniformity and predictability in the application of rules and regulations. Does a scheme of deferring to earlier overlapping statutes promote this purpose?

4. Section 5 gives the Centre broad powers to enforce the Act, including the power to order the closure of any industry. Do workers whose employers are ordered by the government to close or curtail operations have a constitutional right to be heard by a court concerning the government's action? Should the government weigh the costs to these workers in lost jobs against the benefits to society before ordering closure of a polluting operation?

V. ENFORCEMENT OF THE ACT

One of the recurring themes in the Supreme Court judgments is the poor implementation of environmental laws. In the *CRZ Notification* case, excerpted below, the court said that tolerating the infringement of an enacted law was worse than not enacting it at all. In this case, the petitioners challenged the 1994 amendment to the main notification of February 1991, introducing national Coastal Regulations.[105] The petitioners argued that the amendments were invalid since they relaxed the provisions of the parent notification and would lead to ecological degradation. Allowing the petition, the court struck down the amendments which were likely to cause environmental harm. We excerpt portions of this judgment where the court surveyed environmental law enforcement.

---

[104] Darryl D'Monte, *Environment Law Has No Teeth*, 1(4) Ecology 24–5 (1986).

[105] The 1991 Regulations were replaced by the CRZ notification of 2011. The CRZ notification of 2019 superseded the 2011 notification.

INDIAN COUNCIL FOR ENVIRO-LEGAL ACTION v UNION OF INDIA (1996) 5 SCC 281

***

Order:

If the mere enactment of the laws relating to the protection of environment was to ensure a clean and pollution free environment, then India would, perhaps, be the least polluted country in the world. But, this is not so. There are stated to be over 200 Central and state statutes which have at least some concern with environment protection, either directly or indirectly. The plethora of such enactments has, unfortunately, not resulted in preventing environmental degradation which on the contrary, has increased over the years....

It is with a view to protect and preserve the environment and save it for the future generations and to ensure good quality of life that the Parliament enacted the anti-pollution laws, namely, the Water Act, Air Act and the Environment (Protection) Act, 1986. These Acts and Rules framed and Notification issued thereunder contain provisions which prohibit and/or regulate certain activities with a view to protect and preserve the environment. When a law is enacted containing some provisions which prohibits certain types of activities, then, it is of utmost importance that such legal provisions are effectively enforced. If a law is enacted but is not being voluntarily obeyed, then it has to be enforced. Otherwise, infringement of law, which is actively or passively condoned for personal gain, will be encouraged which will in turn lead to a lawless society. Violation of anti-pollution laws not only adversely affects the existing quality of life but the non-enforcement of the legal provisions often results in ecological imbalance and degradation of environment, the adverse effect of which will have to be borne by the future generations.

The present case also shows that having issued the main Notification, no follow-up action was taken either by the coastal States and Union Territories or by the Central Government. The provisions of the main Notification appear to have been ignored and, possibly, violated with impunity. The coastal States and Union Territory Administrations were required to prepare Management Plans within a period of one year from the date of the Notification but this was not done. The Central Government was to approve the plans which were to be prepared but it did not appear to have reminded any of the coastal States or the Union Territory Administrations that the plans had not been received by it. Clause 4 of the main Notification required the Central Government and the State Governments as well as Union Territory Administrations to monitor and enforce the provisions of the main Notification, but no effective steps appear to have been taken and this is what led to the filing of the present Writ Petition.

There is no challenge to the validity of main Notification. Counsel for all the parties are agreed that the main Notification is valid and has to be enforced. Instances have been given by the petitioner as well as some of the intervenors where in different States, infringement of the main Notification is taking place but no action has been taken by the authorities concerned. The courts are ill-equipped and it is not their function to see day to day enforcement of law. This is an executive function which it is bound to discharge. A public interest litigation like the present, would not have been necessary if the authorities, as well as the people concerned, had voluntarily obeyed and/or complied with the main Notification or if the authorities who were entrusted with the responsibility, had enforced the main Notification. It is only the failure of enforcement of this Notification which has led to the filing of the present petition. The effort of this court while dealing with public interest litigation relating to environmental issues, is to see that the executive authorities take steps for implementation and enforcement of law. As such the court has to pass orders and give directions for the protection of the fundamental rights of the people. Passing of appropriate orders requiring the implementation of the law cannot be regarded as the Court having usurped the functions of the Legislature or the Executive. The orders are passed and directions are issued by the Court in discharge of its judicial functions, namely, to see that if there is a complaint by a petitioner regarding the infringement of any Constitutional or other legal right, as a result of any wrong action or inaction on the part of the State, then such wrong should not be permitted to continue....

NOTES AND QUESTIONS

1. Generally, most enforcement agencies have failed to discharge their obligations under environmental laws. What are the reasons for poor implementation?

2. Are the courts capable of transforming the enforcement culture? Does judicial intervention through public interest litigations strengthen the enforcement machinery or is it likely to further enfeeble administrators who may await court orders before taking action?

3. The EPA contains significant innovations for its enforcement, not contained in any other pollution abatement legislation at the time of the Act's adoption. For example, section 19 provides that *any person*, in addition to authorized government officials, may file a complaint with a court alleging an offence under the Act. This citizens' initiative provision requires that the person give notice of not less than 60 days of the alleged offence and the intent to file a complaint with the government official authorized to make such complaints.

The citizens' initiative provision appears to give the public significant powers to enforce the EPA. One commentator, however, has characterized the provision as an 'eye wash'. He notes that only government officials are given the power under the Act to collect samples needed as evidence of a violation of the Act. In addition, during the 60 days' notice period required for the government to decide whether to proceed against the alleged violator, the offending industry has time to clean up traces of the offence and prepare itself for the collection of samples.[106] What if the government decides to file a complaint against the alleged polluter but then does not diligently pursue prosecution? Should a citizen be allowed to file a separate action or intervene in the ongoing prosecution?

As a matter of practice, the citizens' initiative provision is seldom used. There are no significant reported decisions in cases arising from a citizen's complaint under section 19 of the EPA. Most environmental groups and concerned citizens prefer to obtain redress through the public interest litigation channel developed by the High Courts and the Supreme Court under their constitutional jurisdiction. Alternatively, the citizen may now approach the NGT.

4. The Act allows, but does not require, the Central Government to obtain reports, returns, statistics, accounts and other information in relation to its functions under the Act from any person, officer, state government or other authority.[107] Rule 14 of the EPR requires every polluter to file an annual environment statement containing the prescribed particulars. Could the citizens' initiative provision become an effective enforcement tool if industries were required to make mandatory public reports concerning their pollutant discharges? Severe penalties could be imposed for false reporting and the government could undertake random sampling to ensure that industries are complying with the reporting requirements. Mandatory reports submitted by industry under the Clean Water Act in the United States have been used by citizens' groups as evidence in suits filed against polluters.

5. In *Rural Litigation & Entitlement Kendra v State of Uttar Pradesh*,[108] the Supreme Court considered whether to order the closure of limestone mining operations that were affecting the water quality and degrading forest land in the Doon Valley. The defendant mining

---

[106] Agarwal, *Significance & Perspective Impact of India's Environment (Protection) Act, 1986*, 1(7) Ecology 28–9 (1986).
[107] Section 20.
[108] AIR 1988 SC 2187.

companies argued that because the issue of location of industries was one of the powers given to the Central Government under the EPA, the courts no longer have jurisdiction to consider the issue. The court summarily rejected this argument, noting that the Act does not purport to oust jurisdiction and that indeed the Act perhaps could not constitutionally oust the Supreme Court's jurisdiction.

5

NATIONAL GREEN TRIBUNAL

A. INTRODUCTION

Examining the state of India's environmental health, Shibani Ghosh writes:

> India is ranked 177th out of 180 countries on the 2018 Environment Performance Index; 275 rivers in the country are polluted; 6.3 crore people in rural India do not have access to potable water; 228 out of 280 cities in India do not comply with air quality standards for particulate emissions and 180 million people in these cities are exposed to levels that are twice the prescribed standards; and 6,407 sq km of dense forests were lost in just the last two years. Environmental health across indicators in India is rapidly declining and the Indian state's failure to regulate sources of, and causes for, environmental degradation has never been more apparent.[1]

Established under a Parliamentary Act passed in 2010, the National Green Tribunal (NGT) is the primary environmental dispute resolution forum in India. Potentially, the NGT can develop into a world class institution which improves environmental law enforcement and the quality of the environment enjoyed by citizens.

The provisions of the National Green Tribunal Act of 2010 create a Tribunal with immense jurisdiction that can wield this power to great effect to meet the daunting challenges that Ghosh summarizes. Several factors—political, administrative, budgetary and personality-related—impinge upon the growth of this forum into a dynamic agent of change. The record of the Tribunal thus far is mixed. However, with the necessary vision and leadership, the Tribunal could emerge as a forceful adjudicator that uses the cases before it to enhance 'green governance'.

With the advent of judicial activism in the 1980s, the doors of the Indian judiciary were thrown open. The Supreme Court, with path-breaking judgments, ushered in a new era of environmental jurisprudence. However, it was soon realized that constitutional courts[2] lacked the expertise to deal with complex matters relating to the environment. Similar concerns were raised regarding the appellate authorities that had been established under various environmental legislations such as the Water (Prevention and Control of Pollution) Act of 1974 and the Air (Prevention and Control of Pollution) Act of 1981.

The Supreme Court in the *Shriram Gas Leak* case,[3] the *Bichhri-1* case[4] and *A P Pollution Control Board v M V Nayudu*[5] acknowledged the shortcomings and recommended setting

---

[1] Shibani Ghosh, *The Environment* in REGULATION IN INDIA: DESIGN, CAPACITY, PERFORMANCE 203 (Eds. Devesh Kapur & Madhav Khosla, 2019).

[2] 'Constitutional courts' is shorthand for the Supreme Court and the High Courts in the states. They are established under the Constitution and exercise a constitutional writ jurisdiction under which most environmental litigations are entertained. See Chapter 6 on Judicial Remedies and Procedures.

[3] *M C Mehta v Union of India* AIR 1987 SC 965, 982.

[4] *Indian Council for Enviro-Legal Action v Union of India* AIR 1996 SC 1446, 1469.

[5] (1999) 2 SCC 718, 738–9.

Environmental Law & Policy in India. Shyam Divan and Armin Rosencranz, Oxford University Press.
 DOI: 1093/oso/9780192865458.003.0005

up specialized environmental courts. Parliament partially responded to such concerns by enacting the National Environment Tribunal Act of 1995 (NETA) and the National Environment Appellate Authority Act of 1997 (NEAA Act). However, the two tribunals were ineffective. NETA was never brought into force and consequently the National Environment Tribunal was never established. The NEAA barely functioned: it had little work having regard to its limited appellate jurisdiction and was disabled by the inordinate delay in appointing a chairperson.[6]

Justice M Jagannadha Rao, who delivered the first *A P Pollution Control Board* judgment as the junior judge,[7] was presiding when the case returned to the Supreme Court. On his last day before retirement, he reiterated the need for a specialized court:

> Inasmuch as most of the statutes dealing with environment are by Parliament, we would think that the Law Commission could kindly consider the question of review of the environmental laws and the need for constitution of Environmental Courts with experts in environmental law, in addition to judicial members, in the light of experience in other countries.[8]

After his retirement from the Supreme Court in December 2000, Justice M Jagannadha Rao was appointed chairperson of the Law Commission of India in 2003. His first task was to follow through on the recommendation he had made from the bench. In its 186th Report, the Law Commission of India recommended the establishment of environmental courts in every state, to be composed of judges and experts and empowered with original as well as appellate jurisdiction.[9]

B. OBJECTS OF THE NGT ACT

The Statement of Objects and Reasons (SOR) accompanying the National Green Tribunal Bill of 2009 referred to the dissatisfactory experience with earlier environmental tribunals (NET and NEAA) and the recommendations of the Law Commission of India. The SOR recognized that a large number of environmental cases were pending in higher courts involving multi-disciplinary issues. Against this backdrop, the SOR conveys the intention of the government to establish a specialized tribunal to handle civil cases relating to the environment.

The Constitution of India allows for the establishment of specialist tribunals to adjudicate disputes relating to public service[10] or other enumerated matters.[11] Environmental disputes are not covered by these provisions. Absent an express provision allowing establishment of environmental tribunals, Parliament reached out to Article 253 of the Constitution to back its legislative authority. Article 253 confers on Parliament the power to make a law for

---

6 Law Commission of India, *186th Report on Proposal to Constitute Environment Courts* 104 (2003), http://lawcommissionofindia.nic.in/reports/186th%20report.pdf, accessed 11 July 2021. See Armin Rosencranz & Geetanjoy Sahu, *Assessing the National Green Tribunal After Four Years* 5 JR OF INDIAN LAW & SOC 192 (2014).

7 *Supra* note 5.

8 *A P Pollution Control Board – II v M V Nayudu* (2001) 2 SCC 62, 84–5.

9 Law Commission of India, *supra* note 6.

10 Article 323-A of the Constitution of India allows the establishment of Administrative Tribunals.

11 Article 323-B (2) of the Constitution of India lists subjects where the appropriate legislature may establish tribunals, e.g., taxation, labour and industrial relations, and rent control.

implementing any international treaty, agreement or convention. Both the SOR as well as the preamble to the NGT Act record that the law intends implementation of the decisions taken at the United Nations Conference on the Human Environment held at Stockholm in June, 1972 and at the United Nations Conference on Environment and Development held at Rio de Janeiro in June, 1992. One of the decisions taken at the Rio Conference called on states 'to provide effective access to judicial and administrative proceedings including redress and remedy and to develop laws regarding liability and compensation for the victims of pollution and other environmental damage'.[12] The preamble also refers to judicial pronouncements which have interpreted the right to life under Article 21 of the Constitution to cover the right to a healthy environment.

Moreover, the long title of the NGT Act captures its purpose:

> An Act to provide for the establishment of a National Green Tribunal for the effective and expeditious disposal of cases relating to environmental protection and conservation of forests and other natural resources including enforcement of any legal right relating to environment and giving relief and compensation for damages to persons and property and for matters connected therewith or incidental thereto.

NOTES AND QUESTIONS

1. The contours of the NGT's jurisdiction are in the process of being delineated. The SOR, preamble and long title are useful tools for determining the scope of the NGT's powers.

2. What is the nature of the NGT's business? Does it substitute High Courts in the environmental PIL sphere? If so, are the NGT's inherent powers limited by statutory language or are they akin to plenary powers of constitutional courts?

3. Is the NGT a purely adjudicatory forum or does it have regulatory responsibilities as well?

4. Conventionally, tribunals are regarded as being 'creatures' of the statute under which they are established. Is the NGT similar to other adjudicatory tribunals or is there something different in the NGT having regard to the evolution of environmental litigation in India and the polycentric nature of environmental issues?

C. CONSTITUTION OF THE NGT

The Central Government notified establishment of the NGT on 18 October 2010. Despite the notification, the Tribunal was unable to work due to a lack of personnel and infrastructure. This required the Supreme Court of India to issue a series of directions to get the Tribunal functioning.[13] The directions covered the appointment of members of the Tribunal (including the chairperson), provision of office space to house the Tribunal at New Delhi as well as at its regional benches and arrangements for residential accommodation for members of the Tribunal. At one stage, the Supreme Court expressed its displeasure upon learning that

---

[12] Preamble, NGT Act.

[13] *Union of India v Vimal Bhai* Special Leave to Appeal (Civil) No. 12065 of 2009, Orders dated 12 May 2011, 11 July 2011, 19 September 2011, 14 October 2011, 28 November 2011, 14 December 2011, 16 March 2012, 19 March 2012, 9 April 2012, 3 May 2012, 13 July 2012, 26 September 2012, 10 October 2012, 6 December 2012, 4 April 2013, 2 August 2013, 27 August 2013 and 12 September 2013.

two judicial members of the NGT had tendered resignations since they were unable to function and had no residential accommodation.[14]

The Tribunal comprises: (a) a chairperson; (b) between 10 and 20 judicial members and (c) a minimum of 10 and a maximum of 20 expert members.[15] Where considered necessary, the chairperson is empowered to invite 'one or more person having specialized knowledge and experience in a particular case' to assist the Tribunal in that case.[16]

The NGT sits in benches across five cities: the principal bench is at New Delhi with regional benches at Pune, Bhopal, Chennai and Kolkata.[17]

A sitting or retired judge of the Supreme Court or Chief Justice of a High Court is qualified for appointment as chairperson of the NGT. Serving or retired judges of the High Court are qualified to be appointed as judicial members.[18] Expert members are drawn from two streams. To qualify, the expert member must hold advanced academic qualifications and experience in environmental sciences or have administrative experience of 15 years in dealing with environmental matters in the Central Government or state government or reputed national or state-level institutions.[19] During their term, members of the Tribunal are expected to serve full time and may not hold any other office during the tenure.[20] Moreover, the Act prescribes a two-year cooling off period and after completing her term, a member may not 'accept any employment in, or connected with the management or administration of, any person who has been a party to a proceeding before the Tribunal'.[21]

All members of the Tribunal including the chairperson are appointed by the Central Government. The chairperson is appointed after consulting the Chief Justice of India.[22] The judicial and expert members are appointed on the recommendations of a selection committee constituted under rules.[23] The selection committee is chaired by a sitting judge of the Supreme Court who is nominated by the Chief Justice of India in consultation with the Minister of Law and Justice. The selection committee also includes the chairperson of the NGT, the director of an Indian Institute of Technology, an expert in environment policy, an expert in forest policy and the Secretary to the government of India in the MoEF.[24] The salary and allowances of the chairperson are the same as those of a sitting judge of the Supreme Court. The judicial members are entitled to a monthly salary and allowances equivalent to those received by a High Court judge and the entitlements of an expert member correspond to those of a Secretary to the government of India.[25]

The chairperson and other members hold office for a term of five years and are not eligible for reappointment.[26] Different retirement ages are prescribed for the respective members, from

14 *Id.* at order dated 13 July 2012.
15 Section 4(1).
16 Section 4(2).
17 The Central Government is empowered to notify the ordinary place(s) of sitting of the Tribunal. Section 4(3).
18 Section 5(1).
19 Section 5(2).
20 Section 5(3).
21 Section 5(4).
22 Section 6(2).
23 Section 6(3).
24 Rule 3, National Green Tribunal (Manner of Appointment of Judicial and Expert Members, Salaries, Allowances and other Terms and Conditions of Service of Chairperson and other Members and Procedure for Inquiry) Rules of 2010.
25 Rule 7.
26 Section 7.

65 to 70 years: 70 years for a chairperson or judicial member who served on the Supreme Court, 67 years for a chairperson or judicial member who served as a High Court judge and 65 years for an expert member.[27]

D. CHANGES BROUGHT ABOUT BY THE FINANCE ACT OF 2017

The Finance Act, popularly known as the Budget, lays out the annual fiscal plan of the Union Government. Part XIV of the Finance Act of 2017 altered the tribunal landscape. It eliminated eight tribunals and transferred their jurisdictions to other existing tribunals. With respect to the NGT, the Tribunal survived the axe but its organization was impacted. First, the insertion of section 10A into the parent statute paved the way for the executive to frame rules that would cover the qualifications, selection and terms of service of the chairperson and members of the NGT. Second, generic rules applicable to 19 central tribunals including the NGT were brought in to introduce uniformity with respect to remuneration, conditions of service and removal of personnel.

The newly introduced Section 10A reads:

> 10A. *Qualifications, terms and conditions of service of Chairperson, Judicial member and Expert member* .—Notwithstanding anything contained in this Act, the qualifications, appointment, term of office, salaries and allowances, resignation, removal and other terms and conditions of service of the Chairperson, Judicial member and Expert member of the Tribunal appointed after the commencement of Part XIV of Chapter VI of the Finance Act, 2017, shall be governed by the provisions of section 184 of that Act:
>
> Provided that the Chairperson, Judicial member and Expert member appointed before the commencement of Part XIV of Chapter VI of the Finance Act, 2017, shall continue to be governed by the provisions of this Act, and the rules made thereunder as if the provisions of section 184 of the Finance Act, 2017 had not come into force.

Section 184 of the Finance Act of 2017 empowered the Central Government to notify rules for the Tribunals listed in the Eighth Schedule to that Act.[28] Consequently, from 1 June 2017 the NGT was covered by the Tribunal, Appellate Tribunal and other Authorities (Qualification, Experience and Other Condition of Service of Members) Rules of 2017. The Schedule to the 2017 Rules related to the qualifications for appointment, composition of the selection committee, term of office and the age of superannuation of the chairperson and members of the NGT.

The constitutional validity of the changes brought about by the Finance Act of 2017 was challenged in the Supreme Court. In *Rojer Mathew v South Indian Bank Ltd*,[29] the Supreme Court doubted whether such sweeping changes to tribunal structures could be brought through the Money Bill route[30] and referred the question to a larger panel of judges. While holding that section 184 of the Finance Act of 2017 'does not suffer from excessive delegation of legislative functions', the court held that the 2017 Rules 'suffer from various infirmities.... These Rules formulated by the Central Government under section 184 of the Finance Act of 2017 being contrary to the parent enactment and the principles envisaged in the Constitution as

27 Section 8.
28 The NGT was listed at Serial No. 19 of the Eighth Schedule.
29 (2020) 6 SCC 1.
30 Article 110, Constitution of India.

interpreted by this Court, are hereby struck down in entirety.'[31] The Supreme Court directed the Central Government to reformulate the rules and ordered that in the meanwhile the pre-2017 arrangement would continue. In the context of the NGT, the court observed:

> It is clear from the scheme contemplated under the Rules that the Government has significantly diluted the role of the judiciary in appointment of Judicial Members. Further, in many Tribunals like NGT, the role of the judiciary in appointment of non-Judicial Members has entirely been taken away. Such a practice violates the constitutional scheme and the dicta of this Court in various earlier decisions already referred to. It is also important to note that in many tribunals like the National Green Tribunal where earlier removal of members or Presiding Officer could only be after an enquiry by Supreme Court Judges and with necessary consultation with the Chief Justice of India, under the present Rules it is permissible for the Central Government to appoint an Enquiry Committee for removal of any Presiding Officer or member on its own. The Rules are not explicit on who would be part of such a Committee and what would be the role of the judiciary in the process. In doing so, it significantly weakens the independence of the Tribunal members. It is well understood across the world and also under our constitutional framework that allowing Judges to be removed by the executive is palpably unconstitutional and would make them amenable to the whims of the executive, hampering discharge of judicial functions.
>
> In *Madras Bar Assn v Union of India* (2014) 10 SCC 1, this Court held that:
>
> [It] was acknowledged that Parliament was not precluded from establishing a court under a new name to exercise the jurisdiction that was being exercised by members of the higher judiciary at the time when the Constitution came into force. But when that was done, it was critical to ensure that the persons appointed to be members of such a court/tribunal should be appointed in the same manner and should be entitled to the same security of tenure as the holder of the judicial office at the time when the Constitution came into force. Even in the treatise *Constitutional Law of Canada* by Peter W. Hogg, it was observed: if a province invested a tribunal with a jurisdiction of a kind, which ought to properly belong to a Superior, District or County Court, then that court/tribunal (created in its place), whatever is its official name, for constitutional purposes has to, while replacing a Superior, District or County Court, satisfy the requirements and standards of the substituted court. This would mean that the newly constituted court/tribunal will be deemed to be invalidly constituted, till its members are appointed in the same manner, and till its members are entitled to the same conditions of service as were available to the Judges of the court sought to be substituted.[32]

NOTES AND QUESTIONS

1. Once the NGT Act was brought into force in October 2010, High Courts began rejecting writ petitions since an alternative remedy was now available. For several months, the Union Government dragged its feet by not providing the necessary infrastructure and this prompted the Supreme Court to issue numerous directions:

> During the pendency of the special leave petition filed against order dated 11.2.2009 passed by the division bench of the Delhi High Court in Writ Petition No.17682 of 2005, this Court passed as many as 18 orders to facilitate the establishment of the National Green Tribunal, Principal Bench at Delhi and its four Benches at Chennai, Bhopal, Kolkata and Pune. These orders relate to appointment of Chairperson, Judicial and Expert members, sanction of posts in different cadres, creation of infrastructure and deputation of officers from Higher Judicial

31 *Rojer Mathew v South Indian Bank Ltd* (2020) 6 SCC 1, 173–4.

32 *Rojer Mathew v South Indian Bank Ltd* (2020) 6 SCC 1, 154.

> Services of Delhi, Madhya Pradesh and Maharashtra to work as Registrars of the Principal Bench as well as Bhopal and Pune Benches.
>
> The record of the case shows that at every stage the officers of the Ministry of Environment and Forests have created obstacle in the effective functioning of the Tribunal, Principal Bench at Delhi as well as its Benches at Bhopal and Pune and they had to be reminded time and again that it is the duty of the Central Government to provide infrastructure, man-power, etc. for effective functioning of the Tribunal.... [Learned senior counsel appearing for NGT] also pointed out that salary was not paid to the Registrar of the Principal Bench for many months and the amount was provisionally released on the intervention of the Chairman, NGT.
>
> These and other communications filed from time to time are clearly indicative of the attitude of total non-cooperation of the Department of Environment and Forests. It gives an impression that the department is making all out efforts to ensure that the NGT does not function effectively so that the Court may be compelled to pass an order for restoration of jurisdiction of the High Courts and other Courts in matters which are presently dealt with by NGT....[33]

2. Considering that the NGT was to replace the High Court as a forum, are five seats for the entire country adequate? Should the NGT have benches at every city where the High Courts have a permanent bench? Will more seats increase access to justice? Recall the recommendation of the Law Commission of India for environmental courts in every state.

3. The statute prescribes a minimum of 10 judicial members and a minimum of 10 expert members apart from the chairperson. The NGT is starved of personnel[34] and operates at a fraction of its mandated strength. Is the failure to make appointments caused by a lack of qualified individuals or due to a larger design on the part of government to limit access to justice and render the NGT a local tribunal for environmental issues around New Delhi? What can be done to ensure that the NGT operates at the minimum statutory strength? Would a mandamus lie against the government for failing in its duty to fill vacant posts?

On 23 July 2020, the Supreme Court noted that the strength of the Tribunal was just seven—a chairperson, three judicial and three technical members. The court ordered:

> This is an appalling situation concerning the premier institution such as National Green Tribunal, which is required to deal with environmental issues that cannot be countenanced.... Until the proposed selection process culminates with appointment order(s) of the concerned candidates against the existing vacancies, the members presently in office as on this date but are likely to retire shortly, shall continue to hold office in terms of this order and discharge their functions accordingly.[35]

On 5 January 2021, the Supreme Court closed the case observing:

> With regard to other existing vacancies and future vacancies, the Union of India is committed to abide by the directions given by this Court vide judgment dated 27.11.2020. Hence, nothing more need be said in that regard.[36]

4. Evaluating the first decade of the NGT's working, Dr Sairam Bhat and Lianne D'Souza conclude:

---

[33] *Union of India v Vimal Bhai* Special Leave to Appeal (Civil) No. 12065 of 2009, order dated 27 August 2013.

[34] On 26 May 2019, the NGT had four judicial members and two expert members, i.e., just six members plus a chairperson as against the minimum strength of 21.

[35] *NGT Bar Association (Western Zone) v Union of India* (2020) SCC Online SC 591.

[36] *NGT Bar Association (Western Zone) v Union of India*, Writ Petition (Civil) 1235 of 2017.

> It seems that just when the NGT has prepared to soar, its wings have been clipped. To address this predicament, first and foremost, it is incumbent on the responsible authorities to take active capacity building measures. Ensuring quality and integrity in appointments to the NGT, is the key to its success....[37]

5. Section 8 of the NGT Act prescribes different ages for retirement ranging between 65 and 70 years. Does this provision violate the equal protection guarantee under Article 14 of the Constitution? Is it discriminatory or *per se* arbitrary?

6. The executive appears unenthusiastic about the NGT. It was initially reluctant to operationalize the NGT, then to set up more than five benches and finally to appoint its minimum working strength. Do you see a deliberate design to contain or debilitate the NGT?

7. Justice Swatanter Kumar was the second chairperson of the NGT. He served on the Supreme Court for three years between December 2009 and December 2012. In September 2012, while he was serving on the court, Chief Justice S H Kapadia recommended Justice Kumar for the post.[38] Justice Swatanter Kumar was appointed as chairperson of the NGT on 20 December 2012, the day following his retirement from the Supreme Court. The third chairperson of the NGT was Justice Adarsh Kumar Goel. After serving a term of four years on the Supreme Court, he retired on 6 July 2018 and was appointed as chairperson on the same day.

Is this a healthy practice? Professor George H Gadbois Jr, author of *Judges of the Supreme Court of India: 1950–1989*, conducted over 116 interviews with more than 66 judges of the Supreme Court of India. Drawing on his papers, Abhinav Chandrachud published *Supreme Whispers*[39] which carries this passage:

> Several judges told Gadbois that post-retirement employment with the government was undermining the independence of the judiciary. Chandrachud said that some judges were looking for post-retirement positions and writing judgments with that in mind. Bhagwati added that most judges hanker after a good retirement job because it enables them to have a rent-free house, car and driver, and allowances, and also gives them some status. Pathak believed that judges with short tenures at the Supreme Court tended to be more pro-government in their approach since they were looking for a suitable position after retirement.[40]

Is it not likely that a Supreme Court judge, aware of his name being considered for a retirement position, may lean in favour of the government in sensitive cases before the Supreme Court? Is there a better way to constitute the NGT? Should there be a cooling-off period of say two years before a retired judge takes up such a post?

8. On 9 August 2012, the Supreme Court, while hearing a case filed by the victims of the Bhopal Gas Disaster, tucked in the following paragraphs:

> Keeping in view the provisions and scheme of the NGT Act, particularly Sections 14, 29, 30 and 38(5), it can safely be concluded that the environmental issues and matters covered under the NGT Act, Schedule I should be instituted and litigated before the National Green

---

[37] Dr Sairam Bhat & Lianne D'Souza, *NGT: A Tribunal in Trouble?* 7 Jr On Envir Law, Policy & Develop 1, 7 (2020).

[38] The first chairperson was Justice L S Panta who was earlier the chair of the Neaa. After Justice Panta resigned, Chief Justice Kapadia recommended Justice R V Raveendran as chairperson but Justice Raveendran declined the assignment. See Order of the Supreme Court dated 26 September 2012 in *Union of India v Vimal Bhai* (Special Leave to Appeal (Civil) No. 12065 of 2009).

[39] Abhinav Chandrachud, *Supreme Whispers: Conversations with Judges of the Supreme Court of India: 1980–89* 172 (2018).

[40] *Id.* At 172. The quotation refers to Chief Justices Y V Chandrachud, P N Bhagwati and R S Pathak.

> Tribunal. Such approach may be necessary to avoid likelihood of conflict of orders between the High Courts and NGT. Thus, in unambiguous terms, we direct that all the matters instituted after coming into force of the NGT Act and which are covered under the provisions of the NGT Act and/or in Schedule I to the NGT Act shall stand transferred and can be instituted only before NGT. This will help in rendering expeditious and specialised justice in the field of environment to all concerned.
>
> We find it imperative to place on record a caution for consideration of the courts of competent jurisdiction that the cases filed and pending prior to coming into force of the NGT Act, involving questions of environmental laws and/or relating to any of the seven statutes specified in Schedule I of the NGT Act, should also be dealt with by the specialised tribunal, that is, NGT, created under the provisions of the NGT Act. The courts may be well advised to direct transfer of such cases to NGT in its discretion, as it will be in the fitness of administration of justice.[41]

This judgment was authored by Justice Swatanter Kumar shortly before he retired from the Supreme Court and was appointed as chairperson of the NGT.

On what basis could the Supreme Court in the *Bhopal* case have issued such general directions?

9. On 10 March 2014, the Supreme Court in the *Adarsh* case issued the following directions:

> In our considered opinion, the directions in [the *Bhopal* case] that all matters instituted after coming into force of the National Green Tribunal Act, 2010 and which are covered under the said Act and/or [in Schedule I to] the said Act shall stand transferred and can be instituted only before the National Green Tribunal requires reconsideration by this Court.... Till we pass final orders on such reconsideration the direction for transferring the pending matters before the High Court to the Green Tribunal... will not be given effect to. A copy of this order be circulated to all High Courts in the country.[42]

The *Adarsh* case was withdrawn keeping the question of law open and without the Supreme Court re-examining the correctness of the directions in *Bhopal*.

On 7 May 2015, Justice Swatanter Kumar, now chairperson of the NGT, noticed the withdrawal of the *Adarsh* case and held that the directions issued in the *Bhopal* judgment are 'fully in force and operative'.[43]

In *Ratnagiri Nagar Parishad v Gangaram Narayan Ambekar*,[44] the Supreme Court followed the *Bhopal* decision without noting the doubt expressed in *Adarsh*.

10. The NGT Act contains specific provisions on qualifications, selection, tenure and removal of the chairperson and members. The 2017 Rules (since struck down) altered these provisions and were given overriding effect under section 10A. As a matter of constitutional law can subordinate legislation override and substitute plenary legislation (the substantive provisions in the NGT Act)?

11. Does section 10A suffer from the vice of excessive delegation? After having prescribed the qualifications of personnel and the manner of their selection in the NGT Act, could Parliament have delegated these key aspects to the executive? Could the executive use its rule-making power as delegate to dilute the standards prescribed by Parliament in the parent Act?

---

41 *Bhopal Gas Peedith Mahila Udyog Sangathan v Union of India* (2012) 8 SCC 326, 347.

42 *Adarsh Co-op Housing Society Ltd v Union of India* MANU/SC/0375/2014 (Special Leave Petition (C) Nos. 27327 and 28512 –13 of 2013).

43 *Aman Sethi v State of Rajasthan* Appeal No. 61 of 2013, (2015) SCC Online NGT 164.

44 (2020) 7 SCC 275.

12. The 2017 amendment and the 2017 Rules adversely impacted the independence and standing of the NGT. Consider this comment by Ritwick Dutta:

> Over the last 6 years, the National Green Tribunal has emerged, without doubt, as the most effective environmental court in the world. With hundreds of cases heard and decisions rendered, India's citizens have for the first time an institution which is independent, responsive, compassionate and able to deal, to some extent, with the environmental crisis facing the nation.... Most significantly the Rules fundamentally affect the independence, authority and capacity of the NGT to adjudicate on environmental issues. Once the [2017] Rules are implemented, the NGT will be manned by people who neither are qualified nor possess the experience, training, vision and outlook to deal with complex environmental problems. In addition to the above handicap, the members of the NGT will not have the administrative as well as functional autonomy and will be 'under' the control of the very Ministry whose decisions they are required to adjudicate upon. Public confidence is bound to be low on such an Institution.[45]

The illegal 2017 Rules, far from helping attract better personnel to serve on the NGT, would have transformed the NGT into a post-retirement pasture for favoured judges and bureaucrats.

E. JURISDICTION OF THE NGT

The National Green Tribunal has vast jurisdiction, original as well as appellate. Chapter III of the NGT Act comprising sections 14 to 25 is titled 'Jurisdiction, Powers and Proceedings of the Tribunal'. The discussion that follows is supplemented by the 'Statutory Remedies' section in the next chapter where we excerpt from the Supreme Court decision in *Mantri Techzone Pvt Ltd v Forward Foundation*.[46]

The original jurisdiction of the NGT is found in sections 14 and 15 of the Act. The Tribunal has jurisdiction over 'all civil cases where a substantial question relating to environment (including enforcement of any legal right relating to environment), is involved and such question arises out of the implementation of the enactments specified in Schedule I'.[47] Schedule I comprises seven statutes: the Water Act of 1974, the Water Cess Act of 1977,[48] the Forest (Conservation) Act of 1980, the Air Act of 1981, the Environment (Protection) Act of 1986, the Public Liability Insurance Act of 1991 and the Biological Diversity Act of 2002. Conspicuously absent from Schedule I are the Wild Life Act of 1972, the Indian Forest Act of 1927 and the Forest Rights Act of 2006.

The NGT is mandated to hear and settle disputes by passing appropriate orders.[49] An application for adjudication must be made within a period of six months 'from the date on which the cause of action for such dispute first arose'. However, the Tribunal is empowered to relax the period of limitation by up to 60 days where it is satisfied that the applicant was 'prevented by sufficient cause' from making the application within six months.[50]

45 Ritwick Dutta, *How the Finance Act 2017 Cripples National Green Tribunal* Live Law (7 July 2017), https://www.livelaw.in/finance-act-2017-cripples-national-green-tribunalngt/, accessed on 11 July 2021.

46 (2019) 18 SCC 494.

47 Section 14(1).

48 The Water Cess Act of 1977 was repealed by section 18 of the Taxation Laws (Amendment) Act of 2017.

49 Section 14(2).

50 Section 14(3).

The NGT may grant monetary relief to victims of pollution and other environmental damage including accidents while handling hazardous substance, may order restitution of damaged property and may issue directions to restore the environment.[51] A separate period of limitation of five years 'from the date on which the cause for such compensation or relief first arose'[52] applies to an application for compensation or restitution. The heads under which the Tribunal may grant compensation are specified in Schedule II to the Act.[53] The categories include death; permanent or temporary disability; loss of wages; medical expenses; damage to private property; expenses incurred by government or any local authority in providing relief and rehabilitation; harm or damage to fauna; harm or damage to flora including crops, vegetables, trees and orchards; and loss of business or employment. Where compensation is awarded or restitution granted by the NGT these reliefs are in addition to the relief paid under the Public Liability Insurance Act of 1991.[54] However, the claimant must inform the Tribunal about the compensation or relief received from any other court or authority.[55]

In the case of an environmental accident, the Tribunal is required to fix responsibility on the person liable to pay compensation and where the accident is a consequence of combined defaults, the NGT may apportion the liability on an equitable basis. While dealing with cases concerning loss from an accident, the Tribunal is required to apply the principle of no fault.[56]

Original applications under sections 14 or 15 may be filed by any person falling under the classes recognized in section 18(2), including a person who has sustained the injury, the owner of damaged property, legal representatives of the deceased and 'any person aggrieved, including any representative body or organization'. The Central Government or state government, pollution control board, local authority or any environmental authority established under the EPA also have standing to file original disputes.

Section 16 of the Act confers appellate jurisdiction on the NGT. Appeals must be filed within 30 days from the date of communication of the order with a grace period of 60 days (where there is good reason for the delay). An appeal to the NGT lies against orders passed by the appellate authority under section 28 of the Water Act, the state government under section 29 of the Water Act, a pollution control board under section 33A of the Water Act, the appellate authority under section 13 of the Water Cess Act, the state government or other authority under section 2 of the Forest (Conservation) Act, the appellate authority under section 31 of the Air Act; and National Bio-diversity Authority or State Bio-Diversity Board under the Biological Diversity Act. The appellate jurisdiction also covers appeals against any direction issued under section 5 of the Environment (Protection) Act (EPA) and orders granting or refusing to grant environmental clearance.

An appeal under section 16 may be preferred by 'any aggrieved person'. This expression would include a person with respect to whom the decision is materially adverse or who has suffered detriment from the order or decision.

Section 29 of the Act bars the jurisdiction of a civil court to entertain any appeal which the Tribunal is empowered to decide. Further, civil courts are also barred from entertaining any dispute or question relating to any claim that may be adjudicated upon by the NGT. The bar

---

[51] Section 15(1).
[52] Section 15(3).
[53] Section 15(4).
[54] Section 15(2).
[55] Section 15(5).
[56] Section 17.

also prevents an injunction from being granted by a civil court with respect to settlement of disputes or claims falling within the jurisdiction of the Tribunal.

The NGT is empowered to regulate its own procedure and is neither bound by the Code of Civil Procedure of 1908 nor the rules of evidence in the Indian Evidence Act of 1872. The Tribunal must be guided by the principles of natural justice.[57]

The NGT Act endorses principles evolved by the Supreme Court. Section 20 mandates:

> The Tribunal shall, when passing any order or decision or award, apply the principles of sustainable development, the precautionary principle and the polluter pays principle.

Decisions of the Tribunal may be appealed to the Supreme Court within 90 days on any substantial question of law.[58]

To preclude any conflict with provisions of any other law, section 33 provides that the NGT Act will have overriding effect 'notwithstanding anything inconsistent contained in any other law for the time being in force or in any instrument having effect by virtue of any law other than this Act.'

The NGT Act repealed the National Environment Tribunal Act of 1995 and the National Environment Appellate Authority Act of 1997.[59] The Act also amended several other environmental laws to align them with the NGT Act in respect of statutory appeals.

In *State of Madhya Pradesh v Centre for Environment Protection Research & Development*,[60] the Supreme Court outlined the original jurisdiction of the NGT. Reversing the Tribunal's order which directed petrol pumps in Madhya Pradesh to stop supplying fuel to vehicles that did not display a pollution under control (PUC) certificate, the court held that the NGT exceeded its jurisdiction. Summarizing the original jurisdiction limits, the court observed:

> The Tribunal constituted under the NGT Act has jurisdiction under Section 14 of the said Act to decide all civil cases where any substantial question relating to environment including enforcement of any right relating to environment is involved and such question arises out of the implementation of the enactments specified in Schedule I to the said Act, which includes the Air (Prevention and Control of Pollution) Act, 1981 and the Environment (Protection) Act, 1986.
>
> In view of the definition of 'substantial question relating to environment' in Section 2(1)(m) of the NGT Act, the learned Tribunal can examine and decide the question of violation of any specific statutory environmental obligation, which affects or is likely to affect a group of individuals, or the community at large.
>
> For exercise of power under Section 14 of the NGT Act, a substantial question of law should be involved including any legal right to environment and such question should arise out of implementation of the specified enactments.
>
> Violation of any specific statutory environmental obligation gives rise to a substantial question of law and not just statutory obligations under the enactments specified in Schedule I. However, the question must arise out of implementation of one or more of the enactments specified in Schedule I.

---

57 Section 19.
58 Section 22. See *Mantri Techzone Pvt Ltd v Forward Foundation* (2019) 18 SCC 494.
59 Section 38(1).
60 (2020) 9 SCC 781.

I. THE *TECHI TAGI TARA* CASE

When the National Green Tribunal found that persons with very little by way of qualification were appointed to the pollution control boards, it directed the state governments to reconsider the appointments and laid guidelines for selections. While sharing the anguish of the NGT, the Supreme Court set aside the directions, holding that the Tribunal lacked jurisdiction. Appointing professionally competent persons is essential for good governance and institution building.

TECHI TAGI TARA v RAJENDERA SINGH BHANDARI
(2018) 11 SCC 734

Madan B Lokur, J: [The court introduced the case and laid out the provisions of the Act.] On a combined reading of all these provisions, it is clear to us that there must be a substantial question relating to the environment and that question must arise in a dispute—it should not be an academic question. There must also be a claimant raising that dispute which dispute is capable of settlement by the NGT by the grant of some relief which could be in the nature of compensation or restitution of property damaged or restitution of the environment and any other incidental or ancillary relief connected therewith....

As far as we are concerned, in the context of the Act, a dispute would be the assertion of a right or an interest or a claim met by contrary claims on the other side. In other words, the dispute must be one of substance and not of form and it appears to us that the appointments that we are concerned with are not 'disputes' as such or even disputes for the purposes of the Act—they could be disputes for a constitutional court to resolve through a writ of quo warranto, but certainly not for the NGT to venture into. The failure of the State Government to appoint professional and experienced persons to key positions in the Spcbs or the failure to appoint any person at all might incidentally result in an ineffective implementation of the Water Act and the Air Act, but this cannot be classified as a primary dispute over which the NGT would have jurisdiction. Such a failure might be of a statutory obligation over which, in the present context and not universally, only a constitutional court would have jurisdiction and not a statutory body like the NGT. While we appreciate the anxiety of the NGT to preserve and protect the environment as a part of its statutory functions, we cannot extend these concepts to the extent of enabling the NGT to consider who should be appointed as a chairperson or a member of any Spcb or who should not be so appointed.

Additionally, no relief as postulated by section 15 of the Act could be granted to a claimant, assuming that a substantial question relating to the environment does arise and that a dispute does exist.

[The judgment reproduced the recommendations of several committees for strengthening the working of Spcbs.] All these suggestions and recommendations are more than enough for making expert and professional appointments to the Spcbs being geared towards establishing a professional body with multifarious tasks intended to preserve and protect the environment and consisting of experts. Any contrary view or compromise in the appointments would render the exercise undertaken by all these committees completely irrelevant and redundant. Surely, it cannot be said that the committees were not constituted for the purpose of putting their recommendations in the dustbin.

Unfortunately, notwithstanding all these suggestions, recommendations and guidelines the Spcbs continue to be manned by persons who do not necessarily have the necessary expertise or professional experience to address the issues for which the Spcbs were established by law. The Tata Institute of Social Sciences in a report published quite recently in 2013 titled '*Environmental Regulatory Authorities in India: An Assessment of State Pollution Control Boards*' had this to say about some of the appointments to the Spcbs:

> 'An analysis of data collected from State Pollution Control Boards, however, gives a contrasting picture. It has been observed that time and again across State Governments have not been able to choose a qualified, impartial, and politically neutral person of high

standing to this crucial regulatory post. The recent appointments of Chairpersons of various State Pollution Control Boards like Karnataka (*A*, a senior BJP leader), Himachal Pradesh (*B*, a Congress Party leader and former MLA), Uttar Pradesh (*C* appointed on the recommendation of SP leader *X*), Arunachal Pradesh (*D*, a sitting NCP Party MLA), Manipur Pollution Control Board (*E*, a sitting MLA), Maharashtra Pollution Control Board (*F*, a former bureaucrat) are in blatant violation of the Apex Court guidelines. The Apex Court has recommended that the appointees should be qualified in the field of environment or should have special knowledge of the subject. It is unfortunate that in a democratic set-up, key enterprises and boards are headed by bureaucrats for over a decade. In this connection, it is very important for State Governments to understand that filling a key regulatory post with the primary intention to reward an ex-official through his or her appointment upon retirement, to a position for which he or she may not possess the essential overall qualifications, does not do justice to the people of their own States and also staffs working in the State Pollution Control Boards. The primary lacuna with this kind of appointment was that it did not evoke any trust in the people that decisions taken by an ex-official of the State or a former political leader, appointed to this regulatory post through what appeared to be a totally non-transparent unilateral decision. Many senior environmental scientists and other officers of various State Pollution Control Boards have expressed their concern for appointing bureaucrats and political leaders as Chairpersons who they feel not able to create a favourable atmosphere and an effective work culture in the functioning of the Board. It has also been argued by various environmental groups that if the Government is unable to find a competent person, then it should advertise the post, as has been done recently by States like Odisha. However, the State Governments have been defending their decision to appoint bureaucrats to the post of Chairperson as they believe that the vast experience of IAS officers in handling responsibilities would be easy. Another major challenge has been appointing people without having any knowledge in this field. For example, the appointment of *G* with maximum qualification of Class X as Chairperson of the State Pollution Control Board of Sikkim was clear violation of the Water (Prevention and Control of Pollution) Act, 1974. [The names have been deliberately left out by us.]'

The concern really is not one of a lack of professional expertise—there is plenty of it available in the country—but the lack of dedication and willingness to take advantage of the resources available and instead benefit someone close to the powers that be. With this couldn't-care-less attitude, the environment and public trust are the immediate casualties. It is unlikely that with such an attitude, any substantive effort can be made to tackle the issues of environment degradation and issues of pollution. Since the NGT was faced with this situation, we can appreciate its frustration at the scant regard for the law by some State Governments, but it is still necessary in such situations to exercise restraint as cautioned in *State of U P v Jeet S Bisht* (2007) 6 SCC 586.

Keeping the above in mind, we are of the view that it would be appropriate, while setting aside the judgment and order of the NGT, to direct the Executive in all the States to frame appropriate guidelines or recruitment rules within six months, considering the institutional requirements of the SPCBs and the law laid down by statute, by this Court and as per the reports of various committees and authorities and ensure that suitable professionals and experts are appointed to the SPCBs....

NOTES AND QUESTIONS

1. The establishment of the National Green Tribunal is a positive development. Within a short time, the NGT has strongly influenced environmental litigation in India. Between 4 July 2011 and 30 April 2019, 29,939 cases/applications were instituted in the NGT. During this period, 27,022 cases were disposed of leaving less than 3,000 cases on the docket of

the Tribunal.[61] The Tribunal is progressing towards fulfilling the citizens' need for an independent and objective forum to resolve environmental disputes.

2. Although the NGT has both judicial as well as expert members, initially the Tribunal was unwilling to undertake a merits review when exercising appellate jurisdiction and was content to remand the matter back to the concerned authority. The Supreme Court held that the NGT with its expertise was obliged to conduct a merits review and could not abdicate that responsibility.[62]

3. There are several gains from the establishment of the NGT. Most important, the NGT Act strengthens access to justice.

The enactment of certain laws which establish dispute resolution fora are a step towards the constitutional goal of 'Justice, social, economic and political'.[63] Illustratively, the Consumer Protection Act of 1986 established three tiers of fora. Consumers who were previously without remedy were now able to seek redress through a simple inexpensive machinery. Similarly, the NGT Act has enabled thousands of complainants to petition a forum for environmental justice in disputes which would have otherwise festered.

4. There are other gains as well. First, by creating this Tribunal, Parliament has recognized the prevalence of environmental disputes and the need for a specialized forum to resolve them. Second, by creating independent machinery with reputed and high-ranking judicial members, the Tribunal is designed to foster independence, objectivity and fairness. Third, there is now a much greater amount of time available to aggrieved persons to explain their case to an objective adjudicator with more expertise. This is a significant improvement from the previous situation where busy constitutional courts were required to hear environmental PILs. Besides, environmental PILs entertained in the High Court and Supreme Court usually affect the larger community. Generally, individual grievances cannot be addressed through a PIL. Individual grievances in environmental cases are also heard and decided before the NGT. Fourth, with a large number of cases being heard and decided by the NGT, the administrative agencies receive periodic guidance through the orders of the NGT. Over time this improves the quality of regulatory decision-making.

5. In an early evaluation of the NGT, Kanchi Kohli and Manju Menon argue:

> *Tribunals as Regulators*
>
> Tribunals are considered to be different from courts and other judicial bodies. They are meant to play the role of the expert in an area where judicial remedy is being sought. It would, therefore, not be wrong to assume that this expert body 'adds' to the knowledge on the environmental impact produced in the regulatory process after the project has gone through all the basic regulatory filters. However, recent cases seem to indicate that the NGT is performing the role of the regulator simply because the MoEF and other state-level regulatory bodies set up under the EIA notification 2006 refuse to take their roles seriously. It is through this regulation that environmental impact of industrial and infrastructure projects is to be determined and they need to be either accorded approval or rejected.[64]

---

[61] See the case disposal statistics at the NGT website, http://www.greentribunal.gov.in/, accessed 11 July 2021.

[62] *Hanuman Laxman Aroskar v Union of India* (2019) 15 SCC 401.

[63] Preamble, Constitution of India.

[64] Kanchi Kohli & Manju Menon, *The Nature of Green Justice*, 47 Economic & Political Weekly 19 (2012).

Illustrative of its regulatory role, the NGT responded to a petition filed by Rajiv Dutta highlighting the devastation caused by forest fires in Uttarakhand and Himachal Pradesh. Noticing that fires had destroyed large swathes of forest land, the Tribunal directed the MoEF to prepare and implement forest fire management plans for each state;[65] to appoint a nodal officer to monitor and coordinate an improved response to fires;[66] and directed the establishment of a central Monitoring committee headed by the Secretary of the MoEF to strengthen implementation on the ground.[67]

6. The Parliamentary Standing Committee on Science and Technology, Environment and Forests in its 203rd report examined the NGT Bill of 2009 and observed:

> With regard to the addition of Wild Life (Protection) Act, 1972 in the Schedule I to the Bill, the Ministry stated that tribunal had been consciously provided with a jurisdiction limited to cases of civil nature because criminal adjudication requires a hierarchy of courts and the tribunal system does not fit into the architecture of criminal courts. Most of the violations of the Wild Life Act, 1972 are criminal offences. . . . That is why, Wild Life Act, 1972 has not been kept under the purview of this Bill. . . . The Committee [agrees with] the Ministry.[68]

Is this reason convincing? Consider some of the most pressing wildlife issues that have nothing to do with criminal offences: species extinction, encroachments into protected areas, translocation of animals, corridors allowing animal movement and human–animal conflicts.

7. Why exclude some environmental laws from Schedule I? Do you think a possible reason to exclude the Wild Life Act may be that the Prime Minister is the chairperson of the National Board for Wild Life (NBWL) and Parliament may not have desired NGT oversight with respect to action or inaction on the part of NBWL? What is the impact of exempting wildlife regulation from expert, judicial scrutiny? What about forest laws?

8. Section 34 of the Act empowers the Central Government to amend Schedule I by including or omitting any statute. The Schedule may be amended by merely issuing a notification and without having to go through the legislative process.

9. The general period available to file a civil suit is three years from the cause of action. Is the period of limitation at six months (plus 60 days with a satisfactory explanation for delay) too short for an environmental dispute? Where damage is caused to the environment, the impact is often diffused and it may be quite a while for the community to organize itself against the wrongdoer. Remember, the Tribunal sits in only five cities. It may take several weeks for a person living outside these five cities to locate a suitable lawyer to prepare and file the complaint.

10. What is the justification for two periods of limitation—six months under section 14; and five years under section 15? For a discussion on limitation under the NGT Act, see *Mantri Techzone Pvt Ltd v Forward Foundation*,[69] excerpted in the next chapter.

11. The Act expressly empowers the NGT to grant temporary injunctions.[70] There is also a power to issue final cease and desist orders or permanent injunctions.[71]

---

65 *Rajiv Dutta v Union of India* OA No. 216/2016 decided on 3 August 2017, (2018) SCC Online NGT 1561.

66 *Rajiv Dutta v Union of India* OA No. 60/2018 decided on 17 July 2018, (2017) SCC Online NGT 30.

67 *Rajiv Dutta v Union of India* MA No. 122/2019 in OA No. 60/2018 decided on 25 May 2019.

68 Parliamentary Standing Committee on Science and Technology, *Environment and Forests, 203rd Report on the National Green Tribunal Bill of 2009* (November 2009), https://prsindia.org/files/bills_acts/bills_parliament/2009/SCR_Green_Tribunal_Bill_2009.pdf, accessed 11 July 2021.

69 (2019) 18 SCC 494.

70 Section 19(4)(i).

71 Section 19(4)(j).

12. The expert members on the NGT played an important role in requiring the MoEF to examine cumulative environmental impacts.[72] Before this intervention, environmental clearances were routinely granted without assessing the impact of other projects in the vicinity or reasonably foreseeable future projects.

13. Section 29 of the NGT Act reads:

> 29. *Bar of jurisdiction.* — (1) With effect from the date of establishment of the Tribunal under this Act, no civil court shall have jurisdiction to entertain any appeal in respect of any matter, which the Tribunal is empowered to determine under its appellate jurisdiction.
>
> (2) No civil court shall have jurisdiction to settle dispute or entertain any question relating to any claim for granting any relief or compensation or restitution of property damaged or environment damaged which may be adjudicated upon by the Tribunal, and no injunction in respect of any action taken or to be taken by or before the Tribunal in respect of the settlement of such dispute or any such claim for granting any relief or compensation or restitution of property damaged or environment damaged shall be granted by the civil court.

In *Ratnagiri Nagar Parishad v Gangaram Narayan Ambekar*,[73] the Supreme Court held that a suit seeking to restrain the establishment of a solid waste disposal project on the ground that it was environmentally harmful and would pose a nuisance was hit by the embargo in section 29. The civil court where the suit was instituted in 2005 lost jurisdiction upon the NGT Act coming into force on 2 June 2010 'and in particular consequent to establishment of the Tribunal (NGT) on 18.10.2010'. The Supreme Court explained the correct course:

> Indeed, the dismissal of the suit would not come in the way of the plaintiffs or any other person affected by the proposed Project to make representation to the appropriate authority, considering the proposal for grant of statutory permissions under the environment laws concerned, and if that decision is not acceptable, to carry the matter further in appeal before NGT or any other forum, as may be permissible by law. We leave all questions open in that regard.

II. THE *ALL DIMASA STUDENTS UNION* CASE

The State of Meghalaya was plagued by unregulated coal mining. The practice of rat-hole mining involves digging small tunnels to extract coal from the thin coal seams in the hills. When the National Green Tribunal issued a range of directions prohibiting the unregulated mining, the decision was appealed to the Supreme Court. The lengthy judgment of the court covers several issues pertaining to the law of mineral development. We excerpt portions of the judgment that discuss the NGT's jurisdiction.

STATE OF MEGHALAYA v ALL DIMASA STUDENTS UNION
(2019) 8 SCC 177

Ashok Bhushan, J:

* * *

In order dated 25-3-2015 NGT noticed that the rampant, illegal, unscientific and life-threatening mining activity, particularly rat-hole mining is going on in the State of Meghalaya for years. NGT noticed the report of the Commissioner appointed by it and opined that in spite of the order dated 17-4-2014 [prohibiting rat-hole mining/illegal mining and illegal transport of coal] fresh mining was going on. The Tribunal also noticed that the State of Meghalaya has promulgated a Mining Policy of 2012 which does not deal with rat-hole

---

[72] Gitanjali Nain Gill, *Environmental Justice in India: The National Green Tribunal and Expert Members* 5 Transnational Envir Law 175 (2016), shorturl.at/nrvKX, accessed 11 July 2021.

[73] (2020) 7 SCC 275.

mining. The State Government was also directed to formulate and declare Mining Policy and Guidelines for the State of Meghalaya to deal with all aspects of mining, which Policy was yet to see the light of the day. The Tribunal also noticed that the order of the Tribunal has been violated by illegal mining despite complete prohibitory orders. It was noticed that the State Government has found as many as 73 cases of illegal transportation of coal in one district. Further, 15 more cases of specific violation of NGT orders had already been registered by the State Government. In all 11 districts of the State of Meghalaya, 308 cases of violation have been registered and a total number of 605 trucks and 2675.63 tonnes of coal has been seized. The stand of the State for non-compliance and its inability to comply with the direction was also noticed to the following effect:

(a) Lack of forces to carry out counter insurgency operations and implementation of NGT orders.
(b) The State Government proposes to approach the Central Government for claiming an exemption, in terms of Para 12-A(*b*) of the VIth Schedule of the Constitution of India and from the condition of previous approval of the Central Government under the Mines and Minerals (Development and Regulation) Act, 1957 in respect of reconnaissance, prospecting and mining of coal and from the operations of the Coal Mines Nationalisation Act. . . .

The learned *amicus curiae* have submitted a report in two volumes titled '*Curse of Unregulated Coal Mining in Meghalaya*', a Citizen's Report from Meghalaya, 1-12-2018. In Vol. I under the head 'Introduction' the Report states:

> 'Introduction
>
> Meghalaya has a resource curse. Although, we have been endowed with abundant forests and minerals, these resources have not contributed to the good of our society, because they have been extracted without any regulation or concern for the larger common good. This unregulated, narrow, self-interest based use of natural resources has exacerbated socio-economic inequality, destroyed the environment, heightened criminality, and torn asunder our egalitarian tribal social fabric.
>
> It also violates [Article] 39(b) of the Constitution which provides that the ownership and control of the material resources of the community should be so distributed so as to best subserve the common good and, therefore, the State cannot distribute the material resource of the community in any way it likes. The process of distribution must be guided by the constitutional principles including the doctrine of equality and larger public good.
>
> The National Green Tribunal's landmark order regarding unregulated and illegal coal mining in our State therefore came as a wake-up call for Meghalaya society at large. This order has been criticised and appealed against by a small section of locals most of who are coalmine owners, transporters, politicians and administrators who have 'illegally' benefited out of this unregulated mining and who want things to get back to business as usual. Coal miners and politicians who are miners, truck owners, weighbridge operators, etc. have filed appeals with the Honourable Supreme Court, asking the Hon'ble Court to rescind NGT orders so that mining can once again begin.'

[The court framed points for consideration:]

(1) Whether orders passed by the National Green Tribunal are without jurisdiction being beyond the purview of sections 14, 15 and 16 of the National Green Tribunal Act, 2010? . . .
(7) Whether the order of the National Green Tribunal dated 17-4-2014 directing for complete ban on mining is unsustainable?
(8) Whether the complete ban on mining of coal in the State of Meghalaya as directed by NGT deserved to be vacated/modified in the interest of the State and tribals?

(9) Whether NGT had any jurisdiction to constituted committees to submit reports, to implement the orders of NGT, to monitor storage/transportation; of minerals and to prepare action plan for restoration of environment?
(10) Whether NGT committed error in directing for constitution of fund, namely, Meghalaya Environment Protection and Restoration Fund? ...
(12) Whether direction to deposit Rs 100 crores by the State of Meghalaya by order dated 4-1-2019 of NGT impugned in CA No. 2968 of 2019 is sustainable?

[Point 1]

The present is not a case of mere allegation of applicant of environmental degradation by illegal and unregulated coal mining rather there were materials on the record including the report of the experts, the Meghalaya State Pollution Control Board published in the month of September 1992, the report of Katakey Committee appointed by the Tribunal where environmental degradation of water, air and surface of the land was proved.

Hence, there was sufficient allegation regarding substantial questions relating to environment and violation of enactments in Schedule I. We fail to see any substance in the submission of the learned counsel for the appellant that NGT has no jurisdiction to entertain the case and pass orders. During submission, the learned counsel for the appellant has not even referred to application which was filed by the applicant in OA No. 73 of 2014. There were reports of the Meghalaya State Pollution Control Board before the State Government pointing out environmental degradation and the Tribunal having taken up the issue, the submission on behalf of the State that the Tribunal has no jurisdiction, is not expected from the State Government which is under constitutional obligation to ensure clean environment to all its citizens....

In view of the foregoing discussion, we reject the submission of the learned counsel for the State that the Tribunal exceeded its jurisdiction under sections 14 and 15 in entertaining the application OA No. 73 of 2014. We also record our disapproval to the stand taken by the State in this regard....

[Points 7 & 8]

This Court in *State of T N v Hind Stone* (1981) 2 SCC 205, speaking through Chinnappa Reddy, J, has made the following weighty observations:

> 'Rivers, forests, minerals and such other resources constitute a nation's natural wealth. These resources are not to be frittered away and exhausted by any one generation. Every generation owes a duty to all succeeding generations to develop and conserve the natural resources of the nation in the best possible way. It is in the interest of mankind. It is in the interest of the nation. It is recognised by Parliament. Parliament has declared that it is expedient in the public interest that the Union should take under its control the regulation of mines and the development of minerals. It has enacted the Mines and Minerals (Regulation and Development) Act, 1957.'

* * *

The Tribunal after considering all pleas and materials including reports submitted by the committees affirmed the order dated 17-4-2014 and refused to withdraw the ban. We do not find any error in the order of NGT reaffirming its ban order in the facts of the present case. But the question which has been raised by the appellant before this Court is that whether the complete ban as imposed by NGT deserves to be vacated or modified in the interest of the State and tribals. The revenue earned by the State from coal mining plays substantial part in the economy of the State. It is also amply demonstrated from the record that tribals are the owners of the land who carry on mining of coal in their land by which they earn their substantial livelihood....

We thus clarify that in the event mining operations are undertaken by the tribals or other owners of Hills Districts of Meghalaya in accordance with mining lease obtained from the State of Meghalaya as per the 1957 Act and the Mineral Concession Rules, 1960, the ban order dated 17-4-2014 of the Tribunal shall not come in its way of carrying on mining operations. The ban order is for the illegal coal mining which was rampant in the State of Meghalaya and the ban order cannot be extended to valid and legal mining as per the 1957 Act and the 1960 Rules.

[Points 9 & 10]

The appellants contend that NGT has no jurisdiction to constitute any committee. NGT vide its different orders has constituted different committees for submitting reports for different purposes.... Similarly, order of the Tribunal directing for constituting a fund, namely, Meghalaya Environment Protection and Restoration Fund has been challenged on the ground that the Tribunal has no jurisdiction to constitute any fund....

Rule 24 [of the NGT (Practice and Procedure) Rules, 2011] which is relevant for the present case is as follows:

> 24. *Order and directions in certain cases*— The Tribunal may make such orders or give such directions as may be necessary or expedient to give effect to its order or to prevent abuse of its process or to secure the ends of justice.

Rule 24 empowers the Tribunal to make such orders or give such directions as may be necessary or expedient to give effect to its order or to secure the ends of justice. Rule 24 gives wide powers to the Tribunal to secure the ends of justice. Rule 24 vests special power to the Tribunal to pass orders and issue directions to secure the ends of justice. Use of words 'may', 'such orders', 'gives such directions', 'as may be necessary or expedient', 'to give effect to its orders', 'order to prevent abuse of process', are words which enable the Tribunal to pass orders and the above words confer wide discretion....

The enabling powers given to the Tribunal under rule 24 are for the purpose and object to decide the subjects which are to be examined, decided and an appropriate relief is to be granted by the Tribunal. Further, subjects contain wide range of subjects which require technical and scientific inputs. The Tribunal can pass such orders as it may think fit necessary or expedient to secure the ends of justice.

The object for which the said power is given is not far to seek. To fulfil the objective of the NGT Act, 2010, NGT has to exercise a wide range of jurisdiction and has to possess wide range of powers to do justice in a given case. The power is given to exercise for the benefit of those who have right for clean environment which right they have to establish before the Tribunal. The power given to the Tribunal is coupled with duty to exercise such powers for achieving the objects....

We, thus are of the considered opinion that there is no lack of jurisdiction in NGT to direct for appointment of a committee or to obtain a report from a committee in the given facts of the case. [The court set out reasons in the NGT order for establishing the Meghalaya Environment Protection and Restoration Fund (MEPRF) based on the polluter pays principle.] As noticed above, NGT could have passed any order or direction to secure ends of justice which power is especially conferred by rule 24 as noticed above, direction to constitute Fund is thus also saved under such power....

[Point 12]

We are of the view that the amount, which has been directed by NGT to be deposited by the State of Meghalaya is neither a penalty nor a fine imposed on the State. The amount has been directed to be deposited for carrying out steps regarding restoration of environment. We further agree with the submission of the learned counsel for the appellant that the said amount cannot be said to be amount of damages to be paid by the State. We further find force in the submission of the learned counsel for the appellant that the State of Meghalaya has very limited source of revenue and putting an extra burden on the State of Meghalaya to make payment of Rs 100 crores from its own financial resources and budgetary amount may cause great hardship to the State of Meghalaya. Ends of justice will be served in modifying the direction of NGT dated 4-1-2019 to the extent that the State is permitted to transfer an amount of Rs 100 crores from the amount lying in the MEPRF to the Central Pollution Control Board. The Central Pollution Control Board as directed by the Tribunal (NGT) shall utilise the aforesaid amount of Rs 100 crores only for restoration of the environment. The appeal is thus, partly allowed to the above extent....

NOTES AND QUESTIONS

1. The Supreme Court interprets the provisions of the NGT Act and NGT's procedural rules broadly, upholding the Tribunal's directions to prohibit unauthorized coal mining, establish Expert Committees and create funds for restoring damage caused to the environment. The recognition of these powers should help the NGT discharge its functions effectively.

2. The court relies on the doctrine of 'power coupled with duty' to exercise the power when circumstances warrant. Does this doctrine apply to administrative authorities alone or to quasi-judicial tribunals as well?

III. THE *SRIDEVI DATLA* CASE

Sridevi Datla objected to the EC granted for a new greenfield international airport at Bhogalpuram, Vishakhapatnam. The MoEF posted its decision on its website on 14 August 2017 and the project applicant published the approval in a newspaper on 13 September 2017. Datla approached the NGT on 13 November 2017, requesting condonation of the delay since the documents were voluminous, the matter required technical experts and she had to engage specialist lawyers at Delhi. The Tribunal declined to condone the delay and consequently the appeal failed. Datla carried her case to the Supreme Court.

SRIDEVI DATLA v UNION OF INDIA
(2021) SCC ONLINE SC 235

S RAVINDRA BHAT, J:

* * *

Environmental disputes are complicated and entail expertise in diverse fields (such as ecology, chemistry, biology, economics, administration, management, law etc.) for their determination in an effective and speedy fashion, that is not possible within the regular judicial and administrative set up in India. In other words, environmental disputes relating to forests, biodiversity, air and water are complicated in nature; resolving and expeditiously disposing of these cases is not possible without a separate special court.

[The court examined section 16 of the NGT Act, the relevant portion of which reads:

'16. *Tribunal to have appellate jurisdiction.* – Any person aggrieved by ...

(h) an order made, on or after the commencement of the National Green Tribunal Act, 2010, granting environmental clearance in the area in which any industries, operations or processes or class of industries, operations and processes shall not be carried out or shall be carried out subject to certain safeguards under the Environment (Protection) Act, 1986 (29 of 1986)... may, within a period of thirty days from the date on which the order or decision or direction or determination is communicated to him, prefer an appeal to the Tribunal;

Provided that the Tribunal may, if it is satisfied that the appellant was prevented by sufficient cause from filing the appeal within the said period, allow it to be filed under this section within a further period not exceeding sixty days.']

It is evident that the term *sufficient cause* is relative, fact dependent, and has many hues, largely deriving colour from the facts of each case, and the behaviour of the litigant who seeks condonation of delay (in approaching the court). However, what can broadly be said to be universally accepted is that in principle, the applicant must display *bona fides*, should not have been negligent, and the delay occasioned should not be such that condoning it would seriously prejudice the other party....

This court is of the opinion that there is merit in the appellant's argument. The respondents, especially, the project applicant, had urged that the appellant is an interested party, and cannot be called a public-spirited citizen, because she had opposed acquisition of land for the airport and therefore, was able to access legal advice at the High Court stage. There is, in our opinion, nothing in the NGT Act which excludes parties *who would be directly affected by a project*, that has environmental repercussions, from accessing the tribunal. Likewise, characterizing the nature of legal advice that can be accessed for challenging land acquisition, as similar to a challenge to environmental clearance which involves application of mind to technical issues in a detailed manner, would be unfair and simplistic. Scientific or technical support—apart from expert professional legal advice is necessary, if the NGT were to be approached. In these circumstances, this court is of the opinion that given the mandate of the NGT Act, the exercise of discretion, as was done in this case, to reject the appeal by dismissing the application for condonation of delay, on the ground that no sufficient cause was shown, was erroneous and based on a narrow reading of the law. An appeal to the NGT in such matters is no ordinary matter; it has the potential of irrevocably changing the environment with the possibility of likely injury. Application of judicial mind by an independent tribunal in such cases, at the first appellate stage, is almost a necessity....

NOTES

1. The court allowed the appeal, condoned the delay and required the NGT to decide the case on merits.

2. The court held that section 10 of the General Clauses Act of 1897 would apply to all appeals filed under the NGT Act. Section 10 stipulates that when the last date for doing something falls on a public holiday the act 'shall be considered as done' if it 'is done or taken on the next day afterwards on which the Court or office is open'.

F. *SUO MOTU* JURISDICTION AND JUDICIAL REVIEW

A contentious issue concerning the jurisdiction of the NGT is whether it can initiate cases on its own, that is, whether it has *suo motu* jurisdiction. Another moot point is with respect to the power of the Tribunal to set aside delegated legislation. The following excerpt focuses on the *suo motu* question.

NUPUR CHOWDHURY & NIDHI SRIVASTAVA; THE NATIONAL GREEN TRIBUNAL IN INDIA: EXAMINING THE QUESTION OF JURISDICTION, 21(2) Asia Pacific Journal of Environmental Law 190 (2018)

Over the past few years, the NGT has taken cognizance of reports, newspapers etc. and has initiated proceedings on its own in a number of instances. The Principal Bench and the South Zone bench have been particularly active in exercising *suo motu* jurisdiction. It must be noted that, until around 2012, the NGT was not initiating proceedings *suo motu*. In fact, the Tribunal itself noted that it was not conferred with *suo motu* powers in *Baijnath Prajapati v MoEF*.

While *suo motu* cognizance of matters was not taken by the NGT in the early years of its inception, it was clearly felt that the NGT needed *suo motu* powers. [The academic Gitanjali

Nain Gill] reports that judges of the Tribunal saw these powers as 'an integral part of the NGT for better and effective functioning of the institution'. The Tribunal even approached the MoEF seeking amendment to the NGT Act to grant *suo motu* powers. This demand was made repeatedly by the NGT, only to be rejected by MoEF. The Ministry stated that 'the government of India has not agreed to confer *suo motu* powers on the tribunal' and 'it is for the NGT, an adjudicatory body, to follow provisions of the NGT Act, 2010.'

A review of cases decided upon by the NGT shows that the approach of NGT has undergone a sea change since the *Baijnath Prajapati* days and the period when *suo motu* jurisdiction was 'sought' from the government. Recent instances where NGT has initiated proceedings on its own on a range of environmental matters such as pollution, groundwater contamination, protected areas, show that NGT is no longer discouraged by a lack of express provision allowing for *suo motu* jurisdiction. This could be seen as a reflection of 'NGT's self-proclaimed, expansionist power to review environmental issues on the grounds of environmental protection and human welfare'.

NOTES AND QUESTIONS

1. Can the NGT exercise *suo motu* jurisdiction? There are several reasons to support this view. First, having regard to environment as a subject with a multidimensional character, establishing a green tribunal strongly suggests that the legislature intended to confer inherent jurisdiction on the Tribunal to enable it to function effectively. To adjudicate complex environmental disputes and pass orders that meet the ends of justice it is essential for an environmental tribunal to have extensive inherent jurisdiction. Absent broad powers, the Tribunal may find that the grant of relief is limited to what is sought by the applicant and which may not be adequate to solve the real environmental problem. Second, situations arise where private litigants may compromise a case, allowing the environmental problem to persist. In such a situation, it is desirable for the NGT to be able to continue the case *suo motu* by appointing an *amicus curiae*, as is often the case before the Supreme Court. Third, if the NGT is to be regarded as a substitute for the constitutional courts then the inherent jurisdiction would enable the Tribunal to examine environmental issues that have come to its notice. Absent a *suo motu* power in the Tribunal, an incongruous situation may arise where the High Court under Article 226 would look into a particular issue *suo motu* but the NGT despite its expertise cannot. Fourth, there are many situations where, because the polluter is economically or politically influential or the impact of the pollution is diffuse, no complainant is willing to approach the NGT. A *suo motu* power addresses such gaps as you will see in the *Rohtang* case[74] at the end of this section. Fifth, the NGT is allowed to regulate its own procedure, guided by the principles of natural justice.[75] When this power is read along with section 18(2) that allows 'any person aggrieved, including any representative body or organization' to make an application 'for grant of relief or compensation or settlement of dispute' it suggests a liberal rule of *locus standi*. Since the NGT may regulate its own procedure there is no restriction on it to take up cases *suo motu*. Sixth, with its expert members and the requirement that the NGT conduct a merits review of decisions challenged before it, the functions of this Tribunal are more than merely adjudicatory. There is a regulatory dimension to the business of the NGT and this too suggests an inherent *suo motu* jurisdiction. Finally, a *suo motu* jurisdiction may be inferred having regard to the right to a healthy environment and Article 21 of the

[74] *Court on its Own Motion v State of Himachal Pradesh* Application No. 237(THC/2013) (CWPIL No. 15 of 2010 decided on 6 February 2014), (2014) SCC Online NGT 1.

[75] Section 19.

Constitution of India being mentioned in both in the Statement of Objects and Reasons as well as the preamble in relation to the NGT Act.

2. The arguments against reading into the statute a *suo motu* power are based on a narrow reading of the NGT Act. Had the legislature wished to confer such a power, it would have done so by using express language. A tribunal established under a statute cannot expand its own jurisdiction by conferring upon itself *suo motu* powers. The provisions for limitation in the Act point against a *suo motu* jurisdiction. Finally, as seen in the extract, the MoEF is against the NGT expanding its powers and jurisdiction *suo motu*.

Section 4 of the repealed National Environment Tribunal Act of 1995 empowered that tribunal to 'take up the cases for claims for compensation *suo motu*'.[76] Does the absence of a corresponding provision under the NGT Act suggest a legislative intention to exclude *suo motu* jurisdiction?

3. There are scores of executive orders, instructions, guidelines and delegated legislation that guide decision-making by environmental regulators. Occasionally, the impugned decision is based on instruments which are against the parent statute. In PILs filed before the High Court and in the Supreme Court, a defence that relied on such an illegal instrument posed little difficulty since the constitutional courts are empowered to strike down as *ultra vires* executive decisions and delegated legislation. Tribunals generally have no such inherent power and there is no express statutory provision empowering the NGT to declare subordinate legislation as invalid.

Unless the NGT Act is interpreted as conferring the power of judicial review on the NGT, it will mean that whenever some government instrument or delegated legislation stands in the way of a party obtaining relief, that party will have to move a constitutional court, not the NGT, since the Tribunal cannot grant full relief.

4. Apart from the statutory appeal to the Supreme Court on a substantial question of law,[77] the NGT is also subject to the supervisory jurisdiction of the High Courts under Article 227 of the Constitution of India. The High Court may interfere on narrow grounds, such as where a subordinate tribunal exceeds its jurisdiction or fails to follow principles of natural justice.

In October 2021, the Supreme Court resolved the issue regarding *suo motu* jurisdiction by holding that the NGT had power to self-activate cases. The court held that the NGT was a unique, one of its own kind forum and that the environmental watchdog should not be rendered toothless and ineffective.

MUNICIPAL CORPORATION v ANKITA SINHA
(2021) SCC ONLINE SC 897

* * *

Hrishikesh Roy, J:

> We have earlier discussed that the NGT is empowered to carry out restitutive exercise for compensating persons adversely affected by environmental events. The larger discourse which informs such functions is related to distributive and corrective justice.... Even in the absence of harm inflicted by human agency, in a situation of a natural calamity, the Tribunal will be required to devise a plan for alleviating damage. An inquisitorial function is also available for the Tribunal, within and without adversarial significance. Importantly, many of these functions do not require an active '*dispute*', but the formulation of *decisions*....

---

[76] Section 4(2), Neta.
[77] Section 22.

The above would show that from the very inception, the role of the NGT was not simply adjudicatory in the nature of a *lis* but to perform equally vital roles which are preventative, ameliorative or remedial in nature. The functional capacity of the NGT was intended to leverage wide powers to do full justice in its environmental mandate....

The NGT is a Tribunal with *sui generis* characteristic, with the special and all-encompassing jurisdiction to protect the environment. Besides its adjudicatory role as an appellate authority, it is also conferred with the responsibility to discharge role of supervisory body and to decide substantial questions relating to the environment. The necessity of having a specialized body, with the expertise to handle multidimensional environmental issues allows for an all-encompassing framework for environmental justice. The technical expertise that may be required to address evolving environmental concerns would definitely require a flexible institutional mechanism for its effective exercise....

The environmental impacts on climate change are gaining increasing visibility in the shape of uncertain rains, species extinction, loss of natural habitat and so on. These also have the propensity to diminish fresh water resources, reduce agricultural yields and impact public health, particularly in the cities. The flooding and erosion in riverine and coastal areas are matters of serious concern. Governmental assessment of India's increased vulnerability to such changes in the near future also exists with many countries declaring climate emergencies and many others being urged to follow suit.

Therefore, the nature of ecological imbalance which is visible even in our own times may cascade, and the unforeseen injustice of the future may not be capable of being handled within the frontiers set forth today. The long term and very often irreparable environmental damage which are expected to be arrested by the NGT, urge this Court to advert to what is termed as *the 'Seventh Generation' sustainability principle*, or the '*Great Law of the Iroquois*' (as it originates from the Iroquois Tribe) which requires all decision making to withstand for the benefit of seven generations down the line.

It is vital for the wellbeing of the nation and its people, to have a flexible mechanism to address all issues pertaining to environmental damage and resultant climate change so that we can leave behind a better environmental legacy, for our children, and the generations thereafter.

In circumstances where adverse environmental impact may be egregious, but the community affected is unable to effectively get the machinery into action, a forum created specifically to address such concerns should surely be expected to move with expediency, and of its own accord. The potentiality of disproportionate harm imposes a higher obligation on authorities to preserve rights which may be waylaid due to such restrictive access. It is also noteworthy that the '*global impacts of climate change will fall disproportionately on minority and low-income communities*'. Thus, an affirmative role, beyond mere adjudication at the instance of applicant, is certainly required for *serving the ends of environmental justice*, as the statute itself requires of the NGT. We cannot validate an argument which furthers uncertainty to justify the role of a spectator, if not inaction, and would most assuredly result in injustice.

G. ILLUSTRATIVE DECISIONS BY THE TRIBUNAL

I. THE *ROHTANG PASS* CASE

An example of the exercise of *suo motu* jurisdiction is the case pertaining to Rohtang Pass in Himachal Pradesh.[78] Noticing a huge influx of tourists and taxis at Rohtang Pass every day

[78] *Court on its Own Motion v State of Himachal Pradesh* Application No. 237(THC/2013) (CWPIL No. 15 of 2010 decided on 6 February 2014); (2014) SCC Online NGT 8.

during the months of May and June, the NGT issued a detailed judgment containing numerous directions to reduce congestion, air pollution and restore the aesthetics of the region. The extract that follows serially enumerates and consolidates from different paragraphs of the judgment some of the directions passed by the Tribunal.

National Green Tribunal

COURT ON ITS OWN MOTION v STATE OF HIMACHAL PRADESH

***

Swatanter Kumar, J:

1. The State Government shall also introduce and install computerized weigh-in-motion systems to check over-loading of the vehicles.
2. There should be regular pollution check of vehicles plying on that route.
3. If any vehicle is not adhering to the prescribed emission norms, it shall not be permitted to ply on that road. This will equally apply to Government and private vehicles.
4. No heavy vehicle—public or private—more particularly trucks will be permitted to cross the barrier to ply on that road if such vehicles or trucks exceed the prescribed permissible load. In other words, no over-loaded vehicle would be permitted to ply on that road, as recorded by the weigh-in-motion systems.
5. CNG or electricity operated buses or other vehicles of any kind, which would provide incentive to tourism are permitted to ply from Vashishta onwards ... No other vehicle—public or private or Government, including two wheelers—shall be permitted to ply between Vashishta and Rohtang Pass for tourism purposes.
6. The petrol driven vehicles plying in Manali and other surrounding areas of Rohtang Pass should have catalytic convertors in all types of vehicles. Preferably even the diesel driven vehicles should be provided with soot collector system to reduce carbon soot pollution. This could be checked at the time of issuing of PUC.
7. [T]he vehicles which are more than 10 years' old and plying on this route, shall be phased out and should not be permitted to operate or ply on the route to Rohtang Pass from Vashishta.
8. The State Government of Himachal Pradesh is further hereby directed to take appropriate steps in accordance with law to introduce BS-IV norms ...[79]
9. The Government of Himachal Pradesh should explore the possibility of providing ropeway from Vashishta to Rohtang Pass....
10. Carrying and/or use of any kind of plastic bags, packaging material of food or other items at Rohtang Pass is strictly prohibited. Littering of any kind in, around and also *en route* Rohtang Pass is also strictly prohibited.
11. The Government of Himachal Pradesh may develop a small market at Marhi, which will be entirely eco-friendly and would not be a permanent structure. This small market shall provide eatables, medicines or such other goods of necessities of day-to-day life for the tourists.
12. Collection of municipal solid wastes and other wastes shall be the responsibility of the State Government and it shall be ensured that these places and the toilets so provided are kept clean and hygienic. The wastes so collected shall be taken to the nearest Municipal Solid Waste (for short the 'MSW') plant and/or the prescribed dumping ground....
13. There shall be public toilets provided at Rohtang Pass which should be eco-friendly, the cleanliness of which is to be strictly maintained....
14. To ensure hygiene, cleanliness and natural beauty of the glacier, it is essential that no commercial activity of any kind is permitted at Rohtang Pass Glacier. Thus, we

[79] BS-IV refers to Bharat Stage-IV emission norms for motor vehicles. They are more stringent than the existing norms.

direct that no commercial activity of any kind would be carried on in, around and *en route* to Rohtang Pass without any exception.

15. Keeping in view the ecological and geological fragility of the area, it is directed that all forestry programmes must be preceded by soil and moisture conservation works including bio-engineering measures in steep hills ... the Government should take all precautionary measures and provide a scientific scheme for forecasting, controlling and preventing the forest fires.
16. The plantation programme must include at least 50% broad leaved species.... Joint forest management programme should be promoted by involving the local villagers by planting high conservation value medicinal plants like *atish, kutki, kuth,* etc.
17. We were informed by the State Government that it had created 'Green Tax Fund' in order to ensure proper development for protecting the environment in all its spheres. The persons who are travelling by public or private vehicles to the glacier of Rohtang Pass must pay a very reasonable sum of money as contribution on the principle of 'Polluter Pays'. Thus, we direct that every truck, bus and vehicle of any kind which passes through the route ahead of Vashishta and Rohtang Pass shall be liable to pay a sum of Rs.100 for heavy vehicles and Rs.50 for light vehicles. The passengers travelling through the CNG or electric buses to Rohtang Pass as tourists shall be liable to pay a sum of Rs.20 per head, which shall form part of the ticket for the bus.
18. The funds so collected shall be kept by the State Government under the existing head of Green Tax Fund. The amounts so collected shall be used exclusively for development of this area i.e. from Vashishta to Rohtang Pass and five kilometers ahead of Rohtang Pass.
19. To start with, the State Government shall provide all requisite funds for commencement and progress of the various projects that are to be commenced by it under these directions. These funds shall be provided on top priority basis.
20. The State Government and all its authorities, municipalities and all private organizations are directed to fully co-operate, co-ordinate and ensure that these directions are complied with, without default or demur.
21. We hereby constitute a Monitoring Committee consisting of Secretary (Environment), State Govt of Himachal Pradesh; Conservator of Forests concerned of Kullu Division; Director (Tourism), Govt. of Himachal Pradesh; Environmental Engineer, Himachal Pradesh Pollution Control Board; and an eminent environmentalist from G B Pant Institute of Himalayan Environment and Development, Kosi-Katarmal, Almora.
22. The above Monitoring Committee shall submit quarterly reports to the NGT, clearly stating non-compliances with the directions, if any, the persons responsible for such default(s) and also suggestions, if any, as it may consider appropriate in order to make further improvements and catalyze the prevention and control of pollution in that area more effectively.
23. The State Government of Himachal Pradesh has already taken a definite stand and made a statement that it shall follow the 'Madhya Pradesh Model' for prevention and control of forest fires. Thus, we direct that an extra effort should be made by the State Government of Himachal Pradesh, for ensuring prevention and control of forest fires, particularly in the Himalayan region, as they are the direct source of deposition of Black Carbon and suspended particulate matter on the glacier....

NOTES AND QUESTIONS

1. This case portrays an expansion of the polluter pays principle. One of the most important questions under the principle is: who is a 'polluter'? Traditionally, the definition was understood in a narrow sense to include industrial polluters and other entities, but not the ordinary

public and consumers of goods and services. The judgment portrays a partial implementation of the 'user pays' principle—expanding the polluter pays principle. The user pays principle directs the users of natural resources to bear the costs of the environmental harm.[80] As the tourists in Rohtang Pass are consuming petrol and diesel to ply their cars and consequently harming the environment, they must pay for it.

2. Can the NGT levy a general pollution charge/fee by judgment? Does this extension of the polluter pays principle exempt the state from following the basic rule that there must be a law to back the levy of every pollution charge or fee?

3. The Tribunal took up the case on its own motion (*suo motu*). Do you think that there is any statutory basis for invocation of such jurisdiction? Do you believe that a quasi-judicial body like the NGT must possess such wide-ranging powers?

4. Article 243W of the Constitution requires the State legislatures to enact legislations to confer powers on the municipalities so that they are able to carry out responsibilities laid down in the Twelfth Schedule of the Constitution. The Schedule specifies matters such as provision of public and urban amenities, public health, sanitation conservancy and solid waste management. In pursuance of this obligation, the State legislature of Himachal Pradesh enacted The Himachal Pradesh Municipal Corporation Act of 1994 and delegated such powers under it.[81] However, contrary to the above constitutional and legislative scheme, the Tribunal ruled that the state government will bear the responsibility of collecting municipal waste and other solids in the area in question. Have the courts and tribunals come to such distrust in the local governments that they have to go against the constitutional mandate? Is this move legitimate? If the obligation of waste collection and management were not to be displaced, could section 26 of the NGT Act (penalty for failure to comply with Tribunal's order) be helpful to ensure compliance from the municipality?

II. THE *MV RAK* CASE

The vessel *MV Rak* was carrying over 60,054 MT of coal on a voyage from Indonesia to Dahej in Gujarat for operationalizing a thermal power plant. The ship contained 290 tonnes of fuel oil and 50 tonnes of diesel. In the course of its voyage in August 2011, the ship sank just off the coast of Mumbai. The spilled oil spread beyond Mumbai to Raigad District, with traces of the oil seen on surrounding beaches. The oil spilled at the rate of 1–2 tonnes per hour on the day the ship sank, forming a thick oil slick across two nautical miles and oil trails longer than 12 nautical miles soon after.

Samir Mehta, an environmentalist, applied to the Tribunal seeking suitable directions to remedy the impact of the oil spill, which had seriously polluted the sea and the coast. The respondents included state instrumentalities, owners of the ship and their sister concerns. Mehta contended that the damage caused to the aquatic flora and fauna, the mangroves, the loss to fishermen and damage done to the surrounding eco-system—the soil, water and land—made the respondents jointly and severally liable to pay compensation.

The Tribunal found that the ship was not seaworthy at the time of the commencement of the voyage or during the journey. It suffered serious defects which were not dealt with, until the ship finally sank. The Tribunal concluded that the ship, the sunken cargo and the oil spill

---

80 The European Union has created a framework whereby it uses taxation and infrastructure charging to implement the user pays principle. See Directive 2011/76/EU of the European Parliament and of the Council of 27 September 2011 amending Directive 1999/62/EC on the charging of heavy goods vehicles for the use of certain infrastructures.

81 Section 42(1)(b)(iv).

polluted the marine environment. Amongst other directions extracted below, the Tribunal directed the respondents to pay environmental compensation of Rs. 100 crores for marine pollution, and for the ship to be removed from the seabed at the earliest.[82]

National Green Tribunal
SAMIR MEHTA v UNION OF INDIA

SWATANTER KUMAR, J: * * *

Issue No. 1: Whether the Applicant has no Locus standi to institute the present application with the prayers?

According to some of the Respondents who have taken the objection of locus standi, it is contended that Applicant is not a person as contemplated under section 18(2) of the Act of 2010 and locus standi under the provisions of the Act of 2010 cannot be expanded like in a public interest litigation before the higher courts. It is also contended that the Applicant is a resident of Mumbai and has no interest or involvement in the coastal area which is alleged to have been affected because of oil spill and other offending acts as alleged, thus, they pray for dismissal of this application on that ground alone....

Both these enactments [Environment (Protection) Act and NGT Act] have defined the expression 'environment' in very wide terms but in identical language. The above definition, therefore, provides an insight into the legislative intent of giving a very liberal construction to the Statute itself which would practically apply in all matters and events relating to environment. Section 2(j) of the Act of 2010 defines the word 'person' which would include an individual, a company, an association amongst others even every artificial juridical person, not falling within any of the proceedings of sub-clause 3 of section 25 of the Act of 2010. This again reflects that the definition of 'person' is to be given a liberal interpretation and it is an inclusive but not exhaustive definition and includes an individual, even a juridical person in any form....

The contention before the Tribunal is that a person filing an application has to be a person who has suffered personal injury otherwise he would have no right to file the application. This argument is misplaced. Under the provisions of the section 18(2) of the Act of 2010 which again have to be interpreted in light of the objects and reasons of the statute and the definition of 'environment' and scope and ambit of section 14 of the Act of 2010. The expression 'any person aggrieved' appearing in section 18(2)(e) of the Act of 2010 is to be given a wider meaning. This expression is not to be restricted only to a person who has suffered personal injury. It is to be interpreted and understood in contradistinction to section 18(2)(a) where the person who has suffered injury personally can invoke the jurisdiction of the Tribunal under section 14, 15 and 16 of the Act of 2010. Obviously, both these clauses are not meant for the same class of persons. A person who has not suffered any personal injury or does not have the personal grievance but his grievance is of general form of a larger public interest, such person can certainly invoke the jurisdiction of the Tribunal in terms of section 14 of the Act of 2010. If we were to accept the contention of the Respondents then the very object of the two enactments would stand defeated. In other words, a person would not be able to approach the tribunal if he is intending to protect the general environment, ecology and marine environment....

From the above judgments it is clear that locus standi of an Applicant cannot be given a strict construction under the environmental laws of our country. 'Environment' is not a subject which is person oriented but is society centric. The impact of environment is normally felt by a larger section of the society. Whenever environment is diluted or eroded the results are not person specific. If we were to adopt the reasoning given by the Respondents then it would lead to undesirable results....

[82] *Samir Mehta v Union of India* Original Application No. 24 of 2011 decided on 23 August 2016; (2016) SCC Online NGT 479; MANU/GT/0104/2016.

The Applicant admittedly is a resident of Mumbai and by the oil spills the coasts of various beaches in Mumbai including Juhu, Raigad, Uttan in Bhayandar and Gorai beach have been adversely impacted. The Applicant has raised a very substantial question of environment.... The question is the impact of oil spill on the marine ecology and environment, destruction of mangroves, its adverse impact on aquatic life, impact on fishermen ... would certainly be a question falling within the ambit and scope of section 14 of the Act of 2010 and would arise from implementation of the Acts, particularly, the Act of 1986 stated in Schedule I of the Act of 2010. To conclude the Applicant has the locus standi to file the present application, he has raised substantial question relating to environment arising in relation to the implementation of Scheduled Acts....

Issue No. 4: Whether the Tribunal has jurisdiction to entertain and decide the present case and whether or not the provisions of the Merchant Shipping Act, 1958 oust the jurisdiction of this Tribunal?

[The Tribunal discusses the meaning and implication of 'sovereignty' and the provisions of three conventions—International Convention on Civil Liability for Bunker Oil Pollution Damage-2001, International Convention for Prevention of Pollution from Ships, 1973 (MARPOL), International Convention on Civil Liability for Bunker Oil Pollution Damage-2001.]

Cumulative reading of the above Conventions, show that these Conventions are not intended to primarily interfere with or affect the sovereignty of the State but to take appropriate remedies and actions in relation to the territorial seas and even in respect of Exclusive Economic Zone. Furthermore, these Conventions show that protections, actions and remedies available including that of protection of marine environment, claim of damages and compensation are not restricted to the territorial waters of the State over which it exercises sovereignty. The Exclusive Economic Zone is also covered for specific purposes stated therein and protection of marine environment in that zone is specifically stated and covered.

Thus, it will not be appropriate to state that in relation to marine environment and pollution being caused in the exclusive economic zone the concerned State or contracting party is without remedy and has no control whatsoever. The laws of the State would come into play, except where their application is excluded or they are in conflict with the Convention....

Issue No. 7: What compensation, damages and which of the Respondents are liable to pay for causing pollution and degradation of marine environment in terms of sections 15 and 17 read with section 20 of the National Green Tribunal Act, 2010?

* * *

The present case has another feature that is, it is not a case of a particular claimant bringing his action before the Tribunal for compensation of the loss or injury that he has suffered. It is a case where the Applicant had approached the Tribunal in larger public interest and complaining of large scale pollution caused by oil spill and further pollution caused by sinking of the ship and its cargo. This is a continuing cause of action. The pollution persists.

Thus, the pollution is not limited to an individual or a singular item. It is a problem of multiple sources of pollution, resulting from oil spill, sinking of the ship and its cargo. It will affect the marine environment that includes sea water, aquatic life, shore, seabed, mangroves, tourism and public life of the people living at the shore. The adverse impacts were not seen only at a singular point but at multiple beaches as afore-stated....

The purpose of no fault or strict liability is not only to place the onus upon the Respondents in the application, but also to ensure that what is proved by the Applicant in relation to damage and degradation of marine environment is restored and restituted or in any case is prevented from further damage and re-occurring pollution....

Issue No. 10: The directions that are required to be issued in the present case?

Issue No. 11: Relief?

[W]e pass the following Order/Directions:–

1. On the true and purposive construction of the International Conventions and the statutory provisions afore-referred, no party from any country in the world has the right/privilege to sail an unseaworthy ship to the Contiguous and Exclusive Economic Zone of India and in any event to dump the same in such waters, causing marine pollution, damage or degradation thereof.
2. The Ship (*MV RAK* Carrier) and its cargo should be removed by Respondents No. 5, 6, 7 and 11[83] or they should cause it to be removed within a period of six months from the date of submission of the Report of the Committee before the Tribunal.
3. Respondents No. 5, 7 and 11 are held liable to pay environmental compensation of Rs. 100 crores to the Ministry of Shipping, Government of India in terms of Sections 15 and 17 read with Sections 14 and 20 of the Act of 2010, for causing marine environmental pollution by sinking of the ship in the Contiguous Zone of Indian waters (Arabian Sea) at 20 Nautical Miles offshore Mumbai coast.
4. The above Rs. 100 crores shall include the expenses incurred by the Coast Guard and other forces for the prevention and control of pollution in different ways, as stated above, caused by the oil spill and saving the crew etc. Out of this amount, a sum of Rs. 6,91,84,405 shall be adjusted and paid to the respective agencies.
5. Respondent No. 6 is held liable to pay a sum of Rs. 5 crores as environmental compensation in terms of sections 15 and 17 read with sections 14 and 20 of the Act of 2010 for dumping 60054 MT Coal in the seabed and causing pollution of marine environment, in different ways as stated above.
6. The liabilities to pay environmental compensation as afore directed are on account of and subject to adjustments, after the submission of the final report by the Committee. . . .
9. We hold Respondent No. 9[84] liable for claims awarded in this judgment, however, on the Principle of 'Pay to be Paid'. . . .

NOTES AND QUESTIONS

1. As of February 2019, the ship owners were yet to pay Rs. 3 crores spent by the government on cleaning up the spill.[85]

2. The Tribunal seems to have pursued the matter of imposing liability on parties aggressively. It lifted the corporate veil to prevent the companies from employing 'tools of manipulative management and business interests'. It reasoned that such an approach was necessitated by the larger interests of the public and environment. This case shows innovative thinking by the Tribunal and how one can use a principle from one area of law, here company law, to impose penalties and ensure that the costs of the environmental damage are not externalized. Do you agree with such an approach?

---

[83] Respondent Nos. 1, 2, 3 and 4 were the MoEF, State of Maharashtra, Maharashtra Pollution Control Board and Maharashtra Maritime Board. Respondent No. 5 was the owner of the ship. Respondent No. 6 was an Indian company who imported the coal. Respondent Nos. 7 and 11 were group concerns of Respondent No. 5.

[84] Respondent No. 9 was the insurance company.

[85] Chittaranjan Tembhekar, *Years after Oil Spills, Ship-Owners Yet To Pay For Scars They Left On Coastline*, The Times Of India, 27 February 2019, https://timesofindia.indiatimes.com/city/mumbai/years-after-oil-spills-ship-owners-yet-to-pay-for-scars-they-left-on-coastline/articleshow/68174352.cms, accessed 12 July 2021.

3. The Tribunal imposed a hefty fine/compensation of Rs. 100 crores. It further added that such a liability will be joint and several in nature. One of the components of the total amount payable is approximately Rs. 93 crores, i.e., environmental compensation for default, negligence and persistent pollution of the marine environment. However, the Tribunal failed to break down this cost and explain the reasons behind quantification. Is this arbitrary? Should the Tribunal have appointed an independent expert to determine the damage?

III. THE *JNPT* CASE

A project was initiated for widening and deepening the sea channel for a fourth additional berth at the port of Jawaharlal Nehru Port Trust (JNPT). Consequently, land was reclaimed for the expansion, mangroves in the area were removed and the mouth of the creek was narrowed, restricting movement of the boats of the fishermen. The construction impaired the free tidal current, disrupted spawning and substantially reduced breeding ground for the fish.

An application was filed before the Tribunal challenging the project. The applicants were fishermen from villages in the Raigad District who challenged the violation of their traditional fishing rights, sought compensation under section 15 of the NGT Act for loss of livelihood and the rehabilitation of their families displaced as a result of the project. According to the applicants, 1,630 families of traditional fishing communities were affected.

The Tribunal held that the JNPT proceeded with the project in utter disregard of the environmental consequences, in violation of the public trust doctrine and the principle of sustainable development. The project caused destruction of mangroves, degraded the environment in the area by reclaiming land, effecting tidal exchange and obstructing natural navigation routes of the traditional fishermen. The Tribunal directed payment of Rs. 50 lakhs as cost of environmental restoration and awarded compensation totaling Rs. 95,19,20,000 to the fishermen's families who lost their traditional source of livelihood.[86]

National Green Tribunal

RAMDAS JANARDAN KOLI v SECRETARY, MoEF

JUDGMENT:

* * *

(iv) Whether the width of entrance area for passage of the Boats of traditional fishermen inside the sea within Port area, near additional Berth No.4, of widening project, is likely to be reduced or substantially altered/bottlenecked due to reclamation activity/project activity of JNPT?

(v) Whether reclamation, cutting of Mangroves and other activities undertaken by JNPT and other respondents, did or would cause substantial environmental damage/degradation, which will result into loss of ecology, resulting into loss of natural spawning of fish species, breeding of fishes, availability of fish catch and species thereof?

A plain reading of section 19, quoted above, reveals that there are wide powers available with this Tribunal to regulate its own procedure for determination of environmental issues. We cannot and must not overlook the fact that substantial environmental dispute or question relating to environment, under the enactments under Schedule-I, of the NGT Act, 2010, need determination by taking pragmatic view. This kind of litigation is not adversarial in nature. The lis is not between the parties. The jurisdiction available to NGT, is, therefore inquisitive, investigative and if so required research oriented. The purpose of having Hon'ble Expert as Member of the Bench, is to render expert's conception to the judicial decision

86 *Ramdas Janardan Koli v Secretary, MoEF* Application No. 19 of 2013 decided on 27 February 2015; (2015) SCC Online NGT 4.

making process. Otherwise, for mere adversarial litigation perhaps, the Legislature might not have made such arrangement to establish the National level Green Tribunal....

The report received from three member committee of MCZMA,[87] is explicitly against counter claim of the Respondent No.8.[88] The report shows that there is Mangroves degradation at Gavhan–Nhava road. The reclamation was found ongoing process. Before reclamation, there were saltpan and Mangroves. The Committee made it very clear that clarification was required to be sought from JNPT on these issues. The photographs appended to the report also support reclamation on Mangroves patches, destruction of Mangroves, untreated effluent flowing into creek, obstruction caused to tidal exchange in the creek, bund without maintenance at Belpada, near parking terminal so on and so forth....

All said and done, perusal of the record shows that since very inception of the present matter, stand of JNPT, is obstinate, complete denial and even though there are various references, yet, non-halting of reclamation work and destruction of Mangroves by JNPT, continues reclamation of the land. Thus, JNPT without having regard to degradation of environment within the area, unabatedly attempted to go ahead with the project, is indicative of disregard to mandate of 'Public Trust Doctrine'. JNPT, no doubt, is entitled to seek development and the project is likely to cater the needs of cargo users, may give employment to several persons and would add some money in the account of exchequer. The project, however, ought to be carried out in keeping with principle of 'sustainable development'. The concept of 'sustainable development' has co-relation with eradication of poverty, which is offshoot of the project and project activity must be balanced against conservation of environment. The 'Sustainable Development' is development that meets the needs of the present without compromising the ability of the future generations to meet their own needs.

As a result of foregoing discussion, we have no hesitation in holding that JNPT, caused destruction of Mangroves and degraded the environment in the area of Port by reclamation of land as well as contemplated effect on tidal exchanges and obstruction in natural water navigation route available to the traditional fishermen....

(vii) Whether CIDCO through its land development activities have affected coastal system, in violation of CRZ Notification?

The Respondent No.7, (CIDCO),[89] no doubt, prepared plan for development of New Mumbai, and therefore acquired various parcel of lands. The owners of such acquired lands were paid due compensation. The fact finding Committee noted that soil/debris from the channel at the mouth and in the downstream portion of the creeklet had not been removed, so as to ensure free flow of tidal water through creeklet for dependent Mangrove vegetation. CIDCO was asked to ensure that debris be not dumped near Mangroves. A heap of soil was observed in the proximity of the Mangroves patches around site of Chhanje village by MCZMA team, which could probably cause destruction thereof. Thus, the activities of CIDCO also may have potential damage to Mangroves, as well as may cause destruction thereof, although some of the patches are still not fully destructed. In case of activities of CIDCO, we deem it proper to apply the 'Precautionary Principle' so as to protect Mangroves forest in the area. As stated before, as is explained in the instant case, the 'Precautionary Principle' is totally ignored by the MCZMA and the MoEF....

In the final analysis, we have come to the conclusion that JNPT degraded environment to much extent by destruction of Mangroves after and during commencement of the project activity, preparation of work at the site even prior to grant of EC and conducted the EIA report without proper R & R programme, as well as risks and benefits auditing due to implementation of the project. Loss of ecology, loss of livelihood to the Applicants, loss of spawning grounds, loss of species of fishes in the area and de-settlement of the Applicants,

---

[87] Maharashtra Coastal Zone Management Authority, a statutory authority under the Environment (Protection) Act of 1986.

[88] Chairperson, JNPT.

[89] CIDCO is the planning authority.

are significant issues, which require due payment of compensation to them, though it is difficult to relocate them with some kind of facilities, environment and culture. The Respondent No.9, (ONGC), also did not remove outer cover of the pipeline, in order to restore ecology and environment in the area. It appears that tidal exchanges of sea water are obstructed due to acts of the Respondent Nos.7,8 and 9. In addition to such a loss, mainly JNPT, admittedly, has undertaken the work of narrowing Nhava-Sheva creek, which will cause difficulty in ... passage of traditional boats of the Applicants. Under these circumstances, it is manifest that their main source of living is being taken away. We are inclined to hold, therefore, that they are entitled to recover compensation as stated below....

The issues of reasonable compensation, restitution, rehabilitation and restoration of environment to the extent it is practicable, are the facets with which now which we shall have to deal with. The Communication of Government dated 30-10-2012, reveals that amount of Rs.1,24,48,98,000 is legal and proper compensation. However, this report is not supported by any particular methodology adopted by the Authority. The communication goes to show that it is based upon conjunctures.

It is difficult to determine income derived by each fisherman with mathematical precision and the fishermen's family-wise income. Yet hypothetical exercise should have some rationale with normal period for which their family would suffer loss of earnings due to activities of the Respondent Nos.7, 8 and 9.[90] We hold that ordinarily such period will be at least that of three (3) years. The family may comprise four (4) members, including two (2) male and two (2) women. All the four may be earning about Rs.800 per day even if pro rata income is considered @ Rs.200 per day. This is normal income earned by any person of lower strata. Therefore, the yearly loss of income per family may be Rs.2,92,000. Considering the mere subsistence of 1/3rd of this amount, the gross loss per family per year turns out to be Rs.1,94,666 only. We may realistically assume that each of such family will need period of about three (3) years to switch over to some other vocation to earn livelihood. For example; some of them may be required to learn driving of transport vehicles, get due experience and jobs in such business. Some may go to sundry petty businesses so on and so forth. The gap of three (3) years is pragmatic having regard to sudden change over in their life's daily source of earning. Therefore, total loss of three (3) years for 1630 families, is Rs.95,19,20,000. That is why above period will be rather justifiable. The above is proper and reasonable compensation. In our view, each of the family is entitled to recover accordingly from the Respondent Nos.7, 8 and 9 i.e. CIDCO:JNPT:ONGC in ratio 10:70:20 as stated above....

NOTES AND QUESTIONS

1. The Regional NGT bench at Pune took a lenient approach towards the issue of limitation in *Koli's* case. It imported the concept of continuous cause of action in the NGT Act. This approach was disapproved by the Bombay High Court[91] in another matter where it noted:

> A bare perusal of the said section clearly discloses that period of limitation is six months from the date on which the cause of action first arose. *Prima facie*, therefore it cannot be interpreted by any stretch of imagination that it would arise from the date of knowledge of the original applicant of the alleged violation taking place or from the date on which the Environmental Authorities were informed about violation and inaction on their part. There appears to be a lot of confusion in the mind of NGT Bench, Pune on various aspects of continuous cause of action. Perusal of the said Section indicates that the concept of continuous

90 CIDCO, JNPT and ONGC.

91 *Windsor Realty Pvt Ltd v Secretary, Ministry of Environment and Forest*, order dated 9 June 2016: MANU/MH/2214/2016, Writ Petition Nos. 594, 589, 844 of 2015. See also *State of Telangana v Md Hayath Uddin*, order dated 8 November 2017: MANU/AP/0796/2017.

cause of action cannot apply to the complaints which are filed before the NGT because had it been so, the legislature would not have stated that the limitation would be six months from the date on which the cause of action for such dispute first arose. If the interpretation which is sought to be given to the provision by the NGT Bench, Pune in the impugned order is accepted, the complaint could be filed by the aggrieved person at any point of time, claiming that he came to know about the violation after 10 or 20 years. At the same time, if there is any violation of the provisions of the Environment (Protection) Act, 1986, the same have to be addressed and looked into. The only question is by which Authority.

Which approach do you agree with? In environmental matters is a strict limitation policy desirable?

2. On a comparison of this case to the *MV Rak* case, do you notice the difference in approach of the Tribunal towards the calculation of compensation? In the *MV Rak* case, the Tribunal did not give details on how it arrived at compensation of a whopping Rs. 100 crores. However, in the present case, the Tribunal attempts to calculate the loss of wages to the family, and thereafter, arrives at the compensation amount. The latter approach not only gives a clear reasoning behind the figure to the appellate court (potentially, reducing the chances of interference), but also limits excessive discretion in the determination of the amount.

IV. THE *ART OF LIVING* CASE

Art of Living organized a cultural jamboree between 11 and 13 March 2016. The event would host over three million people from all over the world. The venue chosen was on the river Yamuna flood plains. The flood plains and surrounding land were under the control of the Delhi Development Authority (DDA). Art of Living wrote to DDA seeking permission to proceed with construction and making requisite arrangements for the event. After flip-flopping, on 30 June 2015 DDA eventually granted conditional permission. The organizers were asked to maintain 'safe and sufficient distance' from the edge of the river; use eco-friendly material that could be removed immediately after the event; not concretize the area; make adequate sanitation arrangements (where there would be no discharge in the river); and were asked 'to obtain all the requisite approvals, sanctions from the various authorities for holding its function at the site.'

Shortly before the event, an application was filed on 8 February 2016 before the Principal Bench of NGT at New Delhi challenging the ongoing construction activities for the event in the flood plains. The applicant was a retired officer of the Indian Forest Service who had earlier initiated a public campaign to rejuvenate River Yamuna. The applicant asserted that the event and the preparation for it posed a serious threat to the river and its fragile eco-system. The applicant prayed for a prohibitory order to stop the event and ongoing construction work on the flood plains or the River Yamuna in Delhi. The applicant also sought an exemplary fine on DDA and Art of Living along with restoration of the damaged eco-system.

On 9 March 2016, the Tribunal declined the applicant's prayer for an injunction. While rejecting the prayer, the Tribunal noticed the delay in filing the application and the *fait accompli* situation with the event just two days away. The preferred course would be to direct restoration and restitution. The NGT directed Art of Living to comply with safety, construction stability and other requirements of the authorities as well as to secure permissions from the police department and the fire department. Art of Living was asked to deposit environmental compensation of Rs. 5 crores prior to commencement of the event on the understanding that the amount would be adjusted towards the final compensation determined to be paid for restoration work. They were also required to file an undertaking before the Tribunal that, if directed, they would pay the balance amount for restoration.

After the event a High Powered Expert Committee (HPEC) set out to examine the impact of the event. The report of the HPEC pointed out that the flood plain area used for the event was completely destroyed, construction debris dumped in the flood plain and severe ecological harm caused to the wetlands and marshy areas.

The Tribunal delivered its final judgment on 7 December 2017. Art of Living (respondent No. 3) was held responsible for causing environmental damage and liable for restitution/restoration of the flood plains in accordance with the reports of the HPEC. DDA was found liable in contributory negligence and for the failure to adhere to directions given in the prior judgments of the Tribunal and orders passed in the proceedings.[92]

National Green Tribunal

MANOJ MISRA v DELHI DEVELOPMENT AUTHORITY

SWATANTER KUMAR, J:

* * *

The reports submitted by the High Powered Committee examined in light of the orders of the Tribunal and the case pleaded by the official respondents leaves no scope for doubt that there has been damage to the flood plains. The undertaking furnished by Respondent No. 3 which was accepted by the Tribunal has to bear its consequences in law. It needs to be noticed that none of the [interim] orders passed by the Tribunal were taken up by any of the parties to the proceedings before the Hon'ble Supreme Court. They not only accepted the same but even acted thereupon. All the respondents including MoEF & CC, DDA and MoWR [Ministry of Water Resources] clearly admitted that the event was being held on the flood plains. Respondent No. 3 can hardly be permitted to raise the contention that event site does not fall in flood plains. The so called permission granted by DDA itself refers to the area as falling under active flood plains. In fact, it was on that ground that the DDA at one point of time declined the permission to hold the event at the site in question....

The Committee has specifically referred to the wetlands in their report and the steps that should be taken for conservation and protection of such wetlands. The contention that the wetlands have not been notified, would no way take the case of Respondent No. 3 any further. It is primarily for the reason that in large parts of the country the wetlands as of now have neither been identified nor notified in accordance with law. But that does not by itself establish the fact that the wetlands are not in existence. A wetland could be in existence *dehors* the fact that it has not been statutorily so notified. It is a part of natural process and is not a man made resource.... Wetlands are a water body that may be permanent and semi-permanent including lakes and channels generally quite shallow with wetland vegetation. In the Yamuna flood plains, the Expert Committee had reported presence of species of Typhaelephantine, other species of reeds, Catskill (Phragmites), grasses occurring in shallow marshes area on the flood plains. There was presence of a few species of trees also noticed which had been heavily pruned. While it may be true that September is a late monsoon period and would show higher presence of water bodies but that by itself cannot be a reason to suggest that there were no water bodies or wetlands as such. The reeds, Catskill and Typhasppand other grasses present in the floodplain at the site in question are a marker vegetation of the wetlands. Such wetlands generally very shallow are in dynamic equilibrium with the river stream close to the floodplain and are known to maintain over long periods even beyond monsoons. Also mere fact these are not formally notified wetlands under the wetland rules of 2010 cannot take away their ecological and hydrological status. The fact that they had wetland vegetation would imply that there were other species of flora, fauna and micro fauna which support the wetlands ecosystem. The mere fact that September being late monsoon month it was normal to find water bodies in the flood plains but the very presence of the vegetation which the Expert Committee has recorded would suggest that even beyond

92 *Manoj Misra v Delhi Development Authority* Original Application No. 65 of 2016 decided on 7 December 2017; (2017) SCC Online NGT 966.

the month of September these wetland and small water bodies would have continued to persist. In fact, the Expert Committee in its Report of 28th July, 2016 stated that the report is not merely based on the satellite images on 5th September, 2015 but the Committee on page No. 4 (internal) records that it visited both side of the river on 6th July 2016 having visual assessment and that the observations of the presence or otherwise of the wetlands, wet land vegetation and the assessment of damage to the flood plains. This is further substantiated in the report of 28th November 2016 that the damage was extensive.

The Committee has also referred to the status of flood plains even prior to the event as some of the Members of the Committee have been visiting over the 22 km of river stretch and its flood plains in connection with the preparation of the Reports to the NGT in Yamuna Judgement matter and had actually visited these areas during 2nd to 4th October, 2015 and noticed wet lands natural vegetation comprising trees, shrubs, reeds, etc., and other vegetation including water hyacinth. The Committee also noticed several species of aquatic vegetation including presence of shallow to deep water below them. The contention of Respondent No. 3 that the damage assessment of the flood plains and wetlands is only based on satellite imagery ... of September 5, 2015 is misplaced as [satellite] imagery has only supplemental value to the field inspection that was carried out by the Committee. [Satellite] images have only been used to support what the committee found during the field visits.

Respondent No. 3 has also contended that there is no way in which the flood plains, if damaged which they dispute, can be fully restituted or restored to their original presence. These can at best rehabilitated and, therefore, the argument advanced is that since rehabilitation is not envisaged under section 15 of the NGT Act, 2010 suggesting any such rehabilitation in terms of the Report of the Expert Committee will be not in accordance with the section 15 of the NGT Act, 2010. This contention is misplaced as the Expert Committee has discussed this aspect in detail and pointed out that since the flood plain is completely destroyed, levelled, compacted, water body flattened and depressions covered and in several places debris and soil dumped with crisscross paths through channels and water bodies, there is no way the original topography of the area including all the pre-existing water bodies streams channels and wetlands along with the vegetation can be restored to its original shape. In fact, complete restoration and restitution of any pre-existing land mass or natural ecosystem is neither practicable nor possible. The choices of the word restitution and restoration have to be understood and given meaningful construction with a view to achieving the objective of protecting the environment and the flora and fauna of the area that existed prior to the destruction. With such an interpretation as given to the word restitution and restoration the word rehabilitation has to be read as conveying identical meaning.

The Committee report of 22nd February, 2016 which was prior to holding of the event and at a time when the site preparation work was going on, had after field visit the Committee clearly mentioned that the entire flood plains between the river Yamuna and DND flyway is levelled flat, small water body that has been used have been filled up and all natural vegetation have been removed and the site has been compacted due to movement of heavy earth movement machines, trucks, vehicles. Beside this, ramps were constructed on the active flood plain close to the stage for providing access to the VIP's. This clearly shows that the entire morphological feature of the flood plains has been altered....

DDA in furtherance to the Yamuna judgement of the Tribunal dated 13th January, 2015 has already demarcated the flood plain of river Yamuna on 1 in 25 year's basis. Even as per that demarcation, the area in question falls within the flood plain.

According to Respondent No. 3, they have carried all the preparatory steps for the event. The event itself had caused serious pollution on the flood plain of the river as nearly 35 lacs people were gathered on the site. They have caused damage to the river and the flood plains. It is undisputable that flood plains of the rivers form an essential ecological continuum of healthy rivers. These provide essential space to the rivers to spread with ease and during their flood period flow to recharge their associated aquifers. These are also the lands that play an extremely important role in facilitating the self-cleansing ability of the river. The flood plains are not and cannot be equated to waste lands. They should not be treated as lands lying fallow and utilized in the manner which is unacceptable and would have adverse impacts. It is the duty of the statutory authority, Government and the people at large to protect and preserve the flood plains or river Yamuna. The riverbed and the flood plains should be protected and put to such use within the ambit of regulated activities which would not have any adverse effects and would also be in consonance with the Principle of Intergenerational Equity and Public Trust Doctrine. The utilization of the flood plain in a manner which would challenge the very basic characteristics of the flood plain would be impermissible. It is not an area that can be permitted for activities and particularly by making constructions of temporary or semi-permanent nature on the flood plain itself.

In our considered view, Respondent No. 3 has not been able to discharge his onerous burden in all aspects. Of course, in some areas justification has been provided particularly in the field of taking permission but in other areas the reports of the High Powered Committee on the contrary do not benefit Respondent No. 3 and in no uncertain terms places the fault on the said respondent. Principle of No Fault Liability is a tool for guiding the Tribunal in determining the liability of Respondent No. 3....

Order/Directions

Keeping in view the reports of the High Powered Expert Committee dated 22nd February, 2016, 28th July, 2016 and 28th November, 2016 which have been accepted by the Tribunal, the undertaking furnished by the Respondent No. 3 to the Tribunal and the orders of the Tribunal dated 9th March, 2016, 11th March, 2016 and 31st May, 2016, we pass the following order and directions:

1. In this judgement, we have not decided whether Respondent No. 3 and for that matter any person has a right to hold such cultural event or not, as it does not squarely lie within the jurisdiction of this Tribunal. However, the pollution resulting therefrom is a question that would be considered by the Tribunal in accordance with law.
2. We hold and declare that Respondent No. 3 is responsible for causing damage and environmental degradation of the flood plain of river Yamuna limited to the area that was awarded to it by DDA and the State of UP, in terms of the report of the High Powered Committee. We do not find any merit in the objections raised by Respondent No. 3 in relation to the reports of the High Powered Committee.
3. We hold Respondent No. 3 responsible for restoration and restitution of the flood plain limited to portion that was allotted to Respondent No. 3 in the original condition in which it was allotted to it prior to the event. However, the restoration/restitution and other works connected thereto are to be carried out by DDA as follows:
   a) The Delhi Development Authority shall assess the said quantum of damage caused to the flood plain and the costs of restoration thereof in line with the reports of the High Powered Expert Committee....
4. We further direct the Delhi Development Authority, under the guidance of the Expert Committee to carry out restoration/restitution/other necessary works and would also ensure construction/establishment of Bio-diversity park at the site which is part of Phase-II of the plan prepared by DDA for restitution/restoration and beautification of the flood plains of river Yamuna.
5. A sum of Rupees Five Crores deposited by Respondent No. 3 with DDA shall be utilised for restitution/restoration and other necessary works for the flood plains of river Yamuna in accordance with this judgement and under the supervision of the Expert Committee.
6. In the event, the expenditure for that purpose on the portion of the land forming part of Phase-II of the project of DDA is found to be in excess of Rupees Five Crores, the DDA would be at liberty to recover the said amount and Respondent No. 3 shall be liable to pay the said amount on demand. If finally the expenditure to be incurred on that amount is less than ₹5 Crores, the remaining amount would be refunded by DDA to Respondent No.3

7. We are of the considered view that the DDA has failed to exercise its statutory duty in consonance with the environmental laws in force. As evident, it is the duty of the DDA to maintain the natural features and ecology of the flood plain which they have failed to do, in the facts and circumstances of the present case. We would have imposed environmental compensation upon DDA as well but keeping in mind that it has already planned construction of bio-diversity park and improvement of flood plains from its funds, we do not impose any further environmental compensation upon DDA. However, we direct that in consonance with the directions of the Hon'ble Supreme Court and judgement of Delhi High Court that the flood plains of river Yamuna in NCT Delhi should not be permitted to be used to hold any activity of the present kind.
8. We grant liberty to Respondent No. 3, to move to Expert Committee and the DDA if it proposes to make any suggestions for restitution/restoration and other necessary works of the flood plains limited to the area that was allotted by the DDA to Respondent No. 3.
9. The DDA and the Irrigation Department of NCT Delhi shall be responsible for carrying out the directions contained in this order....

NOTES AND QUESTIONS

1. The Tribunal through its judgment describes how the event has caused enormous environmental damage to the flood plains of the river. However, during the initial stages of the proceedings before the NGT, it had ruled against the applicant who had prayed for an immediate prohibitory order and mandatory directions for removal of construction and restoration of the area in question. The Tribunal, relying on the doctrine of laches, held that for the reasons of *fait accompli* it could not accept the applicant's prayers. Do you think that the stand of the Tribunal is contradictory? Do you think that the Tribunal could have at least reduced and minimized the damage already caused if it had granted the injunction?

2. Praying for prohibitory orders, the applicant relied on the judgment of the Delhi High Court in *Anand Arya v Union Bank of India*. The case involved the 'Times Global Village Festival' planned for a period of ten years and to be held annually at a site on the western bank of the River Yamuna. The High Court relied on the recommendations of an Expert Committee report and the event was stopped.

In this case, NGT records the following contention made by Art of Living:

> The gravity of damage to the environment or property is substantial or not has to be adjudicated with reference to nature of event, kind of event, the type of area in which such events are held, the history of such kinds of event on such kind of area and the manner in which such events are held. The applicant virtually makes a prayer which would deny the citizens to carry on their traditional, cultural and religious rights as provided under the Constitution of India. The Tribunal has limited jurisdiction and such type of prayers of the applicant cannot be accepted.

In its interim order of 9 March 2016, the NGT held:

> This Tribunal is primarily dealing with the ecological, environmental and biodiversity damage done to the river and the flood plains by the activity of the Foundation and the environmental consequences of holding such an event. We are not strictly concerned with the cultural event that is proposed to be held from 11th to 13th March, 2016.

Do you think the consideration for cultural, traditional and religious practices may have been a factor to deny the applicant's prayer to prohibit the event? In a country steeped in religion, where religious practices contribute to environmental pollution, how long will decision-makers hesitate in curtailing these practices?

3. The Tribunal required a Rs. 5 crores deposit from Art of Living. The High-Powered Committee appointed by the Tribunal estimated that ecological rehabilitation would cost over Rs. 40 crores: a large quantity of debris had to be removed, the site had to be de-compacted, the natural topography and contours had to be restored, the temporary road had to be removed and the area had to be re-planted with natural vegetation, among many other remedial functions. Do you think, in case of such gross contravention, Art of Living got away lightly?

4. Recently, the Uttarakhand High Court in its landmark judgment, relying on its *parens patriae* jurisdiction, declared that the Ganga and Yamuna rivers, along with their 'streams, every natural water flowing with flow continuously or intermittently of these rivers' as juristic persons, possessing all corresponding rights, duties and liabilities of a living person. The court further declared the Director of Namami Gange, the Chief Secretary of the State of Uttarakhand and the Advocate General of the State of Uttarakhand as persons *in loco parentis* as the 'human face' to protect the Ganga, Yamuna, and their tributaries.[93] Do you think that this status is a positive step towards protection of the rivers? Should the NGT in this case also have adopted a similar reasoning and imposed the obligation on DDA to protect the river?

V. THE *GREAT INDIAN BUSTARD* CASE (NGT)

On 23 December 2020, the NGT decided an application concerning the critically endangered Great Indian Bustard (*Ardeotis nigriceps*). By some estimates, the population of the Great Indian Bustard has dwindled to less than 100. Wind turbine generators and overhead electricity transmission lines are responsible for bird fatalities caused by collision and electrocution. The species is one of the heaviest flying birds in India and has poor vision in its direct flight path. The order reviews several sets of recommendations made by Expert Committees and thereafter frames directions intended to save the species from extinction.[94]

National Green Tribunal

CENTRE FOR WILDLIFE AND ENVIRONMENT LITIGATION v UOI

> ORDER: The issue for consideration is the mitigation measures for protection of Great Indian Bustard (GIB)—rare bird and one of the critically endangered species, as per Schedule-I to the Wild Life (Protection) Act, 1972. Though the Ministry of Environment, Forest and Climate Change (MoEF) has taken up a project called 'Habitat Improvement of Great Indian Bustard—An Integrated Approach', wind projects are potential danger to the safety of the bird....
>
> According to the applicant, population of GIB has steadily declined by 75% in last thirty years. Main reason for such decline is fatal accidents with the power lines. This requires habitat improvement and conservation breeding. In the course of reviewing the project 'Habitat Improvement of Great Indian Bustard—An Integrated Approach' of the MoEF, in a review meeting on 19.07.2018 it was noted that the wind projects did not require any EIA studies. There was also no substitute mechanism to ensure safeguards for protection of such birds on 'Precautionary' principle of Environment. Forest Advisory Committee, Government of India considered the matter in its meeting on 10.11.2016 and recommended

[93] *Mohd Salim v State of Uttarakhand* (2017) SCC Online UTT 367. The judgment was challenged in Special Leave Petition (C) No. 016879/2017 where, by an order dated 7 July 2017, the operation of the judgment was stayed.

[94] *Centre for Wildlife and Environment Litigation v Union of India* Original Application No. 385 of 2019 decided on 23 December 2020; MANU/GT/0326/2020.

study of impact of such proposed project on wildlife as the GIBs face threat from high tension transmission lines....

The Wildlife Institute of India [WII] has made following recommendations:

'4. Recommendations:

4.1. Keeping the above scientifically established threats in mind, the following evidence based actions are recommended by WII that are required to be taken up in time bound manner to achieve the species recovery.

4.2. Mitigate all power transmission lines passing through priority bustard habitats identified by WII by undergrounding cables (where technically/technologically feasible) or installing bird diverters to make them prominent to birds....

4.3. Disallow new wind turbines, solar farms (photovoltaic power stations) from priority GIB habitats and remove existing ones that are in the critical areas....

4.4. Develop predator-proof enclosures of 5–10 sq km area in known breeding sites in and around DNP [Desert National Park] to improve GIB recruitment, and keep away nest predators by routinely translocating dogs, pigs, foxes, mongoose and other species outside the enclosures using professional trappers....

4.5. Create an inviolate area of 200 sq km (WII proposal—500 sq km) in northern DNP ... through voluntary and incentivized relocation of local people (if needed) with the mandate of conserving GIB....

4.9. Implement the conservation breeding programme by creating an offshore insurance population (if needed) by shipping a batch of about 10 GIB eggs to a state-of-the-art international breeding center ... at Abu Dhabi that produces up to 30,000 houbara chicks every year, and meanwhile, establish a national breeding center by training staff, developing a state-of the art center at Sarsen (main facility) and Ramdev (satellite facility), where eggs collected from wild can be artificially incubated, hatched, reared and captive bred to create an insurance population that can be reintroduced into the wild....'.

[On 4 September 2019, the Tribunal set up a committee of government officials and reviewing its work found that 'substantial progress has already been made' on the WII recommendations.]

We have duly considered the report and the deliberations of the six-member expert Committee, in consultation with the stake holders. The proposed action plan which has already been delayed needs to be finalised at the earliest, preferably within two months. Since the main reason for mortality of GIBs is the collisions with power lines laid by the Wind/Solar Energy projects, crisscrossing their paths and undergrounding of transmission lines is not viable for the projects already completed, installation of the bird diverters to prevent such fatalities needs to be undertaken on priority basis expeditiously, preferably within four months. Undergrounding of transmission lines needs to be ensured for all new projects henceforth, as recommended by the six-member expert Committee, by making it a mandatory condition for grant of consents under the Water/Air Acts by the concerned State PCBs which may be overseen by the CPCB and the MoEF. If consent is not required, even then undergrounding of transmission lines may be ensured. While granting such consents, impact of such projects on biodiversity of the area, specially in the context of GIBs, be undertaken. The MoEF/CPCB/State PCBs may take further action as per action plan suggested by the six-member Committee, appointed by this Tribunal....

NOTES AND QUESTIONS

1. Is the order without jurisdiction? How would you justify this exercise by the NGT, absent the Wild Life Act being enumerated in Schedule I?

2. Did the Tribunal go far enough? Considering that the survival of a species is at stake, should the NGT have directed the undergrounding of existing transmission lines and the dismantling of wind turbine generators installed in the GIB habitat? If so, who should bear the cost?[95]

3. Shortly after the NGT judgment, the Supreme Court issued directions for the removal and undergrounding of overhead electricity transmission lines in GIB habitats in Rajasthan and Gujarat.[96] This case is discussed in the Wildlife Protection chapter.

4. Reviewing the first decade of the NGT's working, the social scientist Geentanjoy Sahu and the environmental lawyer Ritwick Dutta offered these sharp observations:

> *Crises Phase*
>
> On 18 December 2017, Justice Swatanter Kumar retired, and the tenure of the majority of the non-judicial members also came to an end in December 2017. The NGT functioned without a full-time chairperson for close to seven months. Justice Adarsh Kumar Goel, judge of Supreme Court, assumed charge on 6 July 2018. It did not take long to witness how an institution that is to be feared and respected suddenly became inactive and defensive in its approach towards environmental problems. The functioning of the NGT and its exercise of power in post-December 2017 has raised concerns concerning the admission of appeals, access to benches, selective *suo motu* intervention, and dominance of bureaucrats as expert members....
>
> Disturbingly, since its inception, there has been no woman member in the tribunal. Similarly, environmental experts from diverse disciplinary backgrounds are missing in the NGT. All present expert members belong to the civil services—three from IFS and one from IAS background.[97]

---

95 See the discussion by the Supreme Court in *M K Ranjitsinh v Union of India* (2021) SCC Online SC 326 excerpted in Chapter 11, Section C on Wildlife Protection.

96 *M K Ranjitsinh v Union of India* (2021) SCC Online SC 326.

97 Geetanjoy Sahu & Ritwick Dutta, *The Green Tribunal in India After 10 Years—From Ascendancy to Crisis*, 52 ECONOMIC & POLITICAL WEEKLY 60 (2021). 'IFS' refers to the Indian Forest Service and 'IAS' refers to the Indian Administrative Service.

6

JUDICIAL REMEDIES AND PROCEDURES

The primary system of regulation under modern environmental law is provided by statutes. Administrative agencies created under environmental statutes are required to implement legislative mandates. Frequently, for lack of staff, money, capacity or will, these agencies fail to implement the laws under which they operate, and ecological degradation continues unabated. In this event, the citizen has a choice of three civil remedies to obtain redress: (1) an original application or appeal to the National Green Tribunal (NGT) under the National Green Tribunal Act of 2010; (2) a writ petition to compel the agency to enforce the law and to recover clean-up or remedial costs from the violator; or (3) a common law tort action against the polluter. Among the civil remedies, the NGT is now the most popular. The writ remedy, which was the primary workhorse for environmentalists for three decades, is now limited to cases that are *not* covered by the list in Schedule I to the NGT Act (such as wildlife) or where the constitutional validity of a provision is challenged. An action in tort is but rarely used and there is little prospect of a revival. Indeed, common law rights in the field of environment, by and large, stand subsumed in the statutory right to seek compensation and restitution through the NGT. The common law remedy has all but vanished.

In addition, if the pollution amounts to a 'public nuisance', a remedy under the Criminal Procedure Code of 1973 is also available. Finally, a citizen may make a criminal complaint under section 19 of the EPA[1] or the corresponding provisions under the Water Act and the Air Act to trigger the prosecution of polluters.

In this chapter we examine these judicial remedies. Historically, tort actions were the first to evolve. To contrast private nuisance cases with public nuisance cases, the opening section on torts is followed by the section on public nuisance. Next, we examine the writ procedure, followed by the procedure in the NGT. The next chapter contains two sections on more general topics: public interest litigation and the right to information. Taken together, these six sections comprise the environmental lawyer's procedural armory.

A. TORT LAW

We open with a caveat. A tort action in a civil court is likely to meet an insurmountable jurisdictional hurdle. This is because a range of environmental suits previously competent before a civil court are now barred in terms of section 29(2) of the NGT Act of 2010. The provision reads:

> 29. *Bar of jurisdiction*.... (2) No civil court shall have jurisdiction to settle dispute or entertain any question relating to any claim for granting any relief or compensation or restitution of property damaged or environment damaged which may be adjudicated upon by

[1] Environment (Protection) Act of 1986.

Environmental Law & Policy in India. Shyam Divan and Armin Rosencranz, Oxford University Press.
 DOI: 1093/oso/9780192865458.003.0006

the Tribunal, and no injunction in respect of any action taken or to be taken by or before the Tribunal in respect of the settlement of such dispute or any such claim for granting any relief or compensation or restitution of property damaged or environment damaged shall be granted by the civil court.

Principles of tort law underpin environmental law. The discussion that follows is best understood as providing the historical context for the subsequent evolution of environmental law.

Actions brought under tort law are among the oldest of the legal remedies to abate pollution. Most pollution cases in tort law fall under the categories of nuisance, negligence and strict liability. To these traditional categories, the Supreme Court has added a class based on the principle of 'absolute' liability. This norm was developed by the court in the post-Bhopal period in response to the spread of hazardous industries and was later adopted by the legislature.[2]

The rules of tort law were introduced into India under British rule. Initially, disputes arising within the Presidency towns of Calcutta, Madras and Bombay were subjected to common law rules.[3] Later, Indian courts outside the Presidency towns were required by Acts of British Parliament and Indian laws to reconcile disputes according to justice, equity and good conscience where there was no applicable statute.[4] Consequently, in suits for damages for torts (civil wrongs), courts followed the English common law in so far as it was consonant with these principles. By the eighteenth century, Indian courts had evolved a blend of tort law adapted to Indian conditions.[5] Common-law-based tort rules continue to operate under Article 372 of the Indian Constitution which ensured the continuance of existing laws.

In *Vellore Citizens' Welfare Forum v Union of India*,[6] the Supreme Court traced the source of the constitutional and statutory provisions that protect the environment to the 'inalienable common law right' of every person to a clean environment. Quoting from *Blackstone's Commentaries* on the English law of nuisance published in 1876, the court held that since the Indian legal system drew on English common law, the right to a pollution-free environment was a part of the basic jurisprudence of the land.[7]

I. DAMAGES AND INJUNCTION

A plaintiff in a tort action may sue for damages or an injunction, or both.

Damages

Damages are the pecuniary compensation payable for the commission of a tort. Damages may be either 'substantial' or 'exemplary'. Substantial damages are awarded to compensate the plaintiff for the wrong suffered. The purpose of such damages is restitution, that is, to restore the plaintiff to the position he or she would have been in if the tort had not been committed. Such damages, therefore, correspond to a fair and reasonable compensation for the injury.

---

2 The Public Liability Insurance Act of 1991, the repealed National Environment Tribunal Act of 1995 and the National Green Tribunal Act of 2010 adopt a 'no-fault' liability standard.

3 'Common law' refers to the customary law of England derived from judicial decisions, in contrast with legislative enactments.

4 Sharad Desai & Kumud Desai, *Ramaswamy Iyer's The Law of Torts* 21 (8th ed. 1987).

5 Motilal Setalvad, *The Common Law of India* 53 (1960).

6 AIR 1996 SC 2715.

7 *Id.* at 2722. For a general review of tort law principles see *Jay Laxmi Salt Works (P) Ltd v State of Gujarat* (1994) 4 SCC 1.

Exemplary damages are intended to punish the defendant for the outrageous nature of his or her conduct, as for instance, when he or she persists in causing a nuisance after being convicted and being fined for it.[8] The object of the court in such cases is to deter the wrong-doer.[9] The deterrence objective has prompted the Supreme Court to add a fresh category to the type of cases where exemplary damages may be awarded, viz, when harm results from an enterprise's hazardous or inherently dangerous activity. In the *Shriram Gas Leak* case,[10] oleum gas escaped from a unit of the Shriram Food and Fertilizer Industries and injured a few Delhi citizens. The court observed that in such cases, compensation 'must be correlated to the magnitude and capacity of the enterprise because such compensation must have a deterrent effect. The larger and more prosperous the enterprise, the greater must be the amount of compensation payable by it....'[11]

This dictum was followed by the Supreme Court in the *Sterlite* case when the company sought to reopen its copper smelter at Tuticorin:

> In the Annual Report 2011 of the appellant Company, at pp. 20 and 21, the performance of its copper project is given. We extract hereinbelow the paragraph titled 'Financial Performance':
>
> > PBDIT [Profit before deduction of income tax] for the financial year 2010–2011 was Rs 1043 crores, 40% higher than PBDIT of Rs 744 crores for the financial year 2009–2010. This was primarily due to higher LME prices and lower unit costs at Copper India and with the improved by-product realisation.
>
> Considering the magnitude, capacity and prosperity of the appellant Company, we are of the view that the appellant Company should be held liable for a compensation of Rs 100 crores for having polluted the environment in the vicinity of its plant and for having operated the plant without a renewal of the consents by the TNPCB for a fairly long period and according to us, any less amount, would not have the desired deterrent effect on the appellant Company. The aforesaid amount will be deposited with the Collector of Thoothukudi District, who will invest it in a fixed deposit with a nationalised bank for a period of five years. The interest there from will be spent for improving the environment, including water and soil, of the vicinity of the plant after consultation with TNPCB and approval of the Secretary, Environment, Government of Tamil Nadu.[12]

Damages awarded in tort actions in India are notoriously low, and pose no deterrent to the polluter. Lengthy delays in the adjudication of cases combined with chronic inflation dilute the value of any damages that a successful plaintiff may receive. Consequently, although in theory damages are the principal relief in a tort action, in practice injunctive relief is more effective in abating pollution. This may change with the arena shifting to the NGT which is statutorily empowered to grant compensation and restitution. The working of the NGT in its initial phase suggests a greater willingness to award substantial amounts as compensation.

Injunction

An injunction is a judicial process where a person who has infringed, or is about to infringe the rights of another, is restrained from pursuing such acts. An injunction may take either a

---

[8] *J C Galstaun v Dunia Lal Seal* (1905) 9 CWN 612, 617.

[9] *M C Mehta v Kamal Nath* (2000) 6 SCC 213.

[10] *M C Mehta v Union of India of India* AIR 1987 SC 1086.

[11] *Id.* at 1099.

[12] *Sterlite Industries (India) Ltd v Union of India* (2013) 4 SCC 575, 605. This case is discussed in the Environmental Impact Assessment chapter.

negative or a positive form. It may require a party to refrain from doing a particular thing or to do a particular thing. Injunctions are granted at the discretion of the court.

Injunctions are of a two kinds, temporary and perpetual. The purpose of a temporary injunction is to maintain the state of things at a given date until trial on the merits. It is regulated by sections 94 and 95 as well as Order 39 of the Code of Civil Procedure of 1908. It may be granted on an interlocutory application[13] at any stage of a suit. It remains in force until the disposal of the suit or until further orders of the court.

Rule 1 of Order 39 provides that temporary injunctions may be granted where it is provided:

(a) that any property in dispute in a suit is in danger of being wasted, damaged or alienated by any party to the suit, or wrongfully sold in execution, of a decree, or
(b) that the defendant threatens, or intends, to remove or dispose of his property with a view to defrauding his creditors, or
(c) that the defendant threatens to dispossess the plaintiff or otherwise cause injury to the plaintiff in relation to any property in dispute in the suit....

The Supreme Court has held that courts also have an inherent power to issue a temporary injunction in circumstances that are not covered by the provisions of Order 39 when the court is satisfied that the interests of justice so require.[14]

The grant or refusal of a temporary injunction is governed by three well-established principles: (1) the existence of a *prima facie* case (a showing on the facts that the plaintiff is likely to succeed in the suit); (2) the likelihood of irreparable injury (an injury that cannot be adequately compensated for in damages) if the injunction is refused; and (3) that the balance of convenience requires the issue of the injunction (a showing that the inconvenience to the plaintiff if the temporary injunction is withheld exceeds the inconvenience to the defendant if he or she is restrained).

Perpetual injunctions are regulated by sections 37 to 42 of the Specific Relief Act of 1963. A perpetual injunction permanently restrains the defendant from doing the act complained of. It is granted at a court's discretion after judging the merits of the suit. A perpetual injunction is intended to protect the plaintiff indefinitely (so that he or she need not resort to successive actions in respect of every infringement), assuming that the circumstances of the case remain essentially unchanged.

A court may permanently restrain the defendant where damages do not provide adequate relief or where the injunction would prevent a multiplicity of proceedings. Thus, where hazardous dust from a brick grinding machine polluted the air of a neighbouring medical practitioner's consulting room, the polluter was permanently restrained from operating the machine.[15] A court may grant an injunction even though the anticipated damage may not be very serious, as long as the damage is continuous or frequent. The 'balance of convenience' test also applies to the award of a permanent injunction: the court must be satisfied that the damage that the defendant would suffer by the grant of the injunction is outweighed by the damage the plaintiff would suffer if the injunction was refused. Finally, the court will consider the injunction's impact on third parties, for example, when the granting of an injunction would throw a large number of people out of work.

---

13 An application made between the commencement and end of a suit.

14 *Manohar Lal Chopra v Rai Baja Seth Hiralal* AIR 1962 SC 527, 532; *Vareeb Jacob v Sosamma Geevarghese* (2004) 6 SCC 378.

15 *Ram Baj Singh v Babulal* AIR 1982 All 285.

II. NUISANCE, NEGLIGENCE, STRICT LIABILITY AND ABSOLUTE LIABILITY

Nuisance

Modern environmental law has its roots in the common law relating to nuisance. A nuisance is an unlawful interference with the plaintiff's use or enjoyment of land. A plaintiff must, therefore, prove some injury to her enjoyment of property and her own interest in that property. An occupier of the property can sue for nuisance.

Ordinarily, a nuisance means anything that annoys, hurts or offends; but for an interference to be an *actionable nuisance*, the conduct of the defendant must be unreasonable. Further, a nuisance must not be momentary, but must continue for some time: a single, short inconvenience is not actionable. A nuisance would include offensive smells, noise, air pollution and water pollution.

There are two kinds of nuisance—public and private. A public nuisance injures, annoys or interferes with the quality of life of a class of persons who come within its neighbourhood. It is an unreasonable interference with a general right of the public. It is both a tort and a crime.

The remedies for a public nuisance are: (1) a criminal prosecution for the offence of causing nuisance;[16] (2) a criminal proceeding before a magistrate for removing a public nuisance;[17] (3) a civil action by the Advocate General or two or more members of the public with permission of the court, for a declaration, an injunction, or both.[18]

A private nuisance is a substantial and unreasonable interference with the use and enjoyment of land. Reasonableness of the defendant's conduct is the central question in nuisance cases. To determine 'reasonableness', courts will be guided by the ordinary standard of comfort prevailing in the neighbourhood. Minor discomforts that are common in crowded cities will not be viewed as a nuisance by the courts.

An action for private nuisance may seek injunctive relief as well as damages. In cases of a continuing cause of action, such as pollution of a stream by factory wastes or smoke emissions from a chimney, the proper course is to sue for an injunction. Repeated actions for damages may be brought to recover the loss sustained up to the date of the court's decree; but future losses, which are contingent on the continuance of the wrong, are not usually awarded. Damages offer poor relief since the plaintiff would be compelled to bring successive actions. Ordinarily, therefore, courts grant the plaintiff an injunction where a nuisance exists or is threatened, unless he or she is guilty of improper conduct or delay.

A two-decade journey through four tiers of courts culminated in the dismissal of an action to restrain a baking oven from being operated in a residential locality in *Kuldip Singh v Subhash Chander Jain*.[19] The plaintiff, Subhash Chander Jain, feared that the baking oven and 12-foot chimney built by his neighbour would cause a nuisance when the bakery commenced operations. The trial court restrained the defendant since operation of the oven 'would result in emitting smell and generating heat and smoke which taken together would amount to nuisance'. The Supreme Court drew a distinction between an existing nuisance and a future nuisance: 'In case of a future nuisance, a mere possibility of injury will not provide the plaintiff

[16] Section 268 of the Indian Penal Code of 1860.

[17] Sections 133–144 of the Code of Criminal Procedure of 1973.

[18] Section 91 of the Code of Civil Procedure of 1908. In the absence of special damage this is the only available civil remedy. A private action can be maintained against a public nuisance where the plaintiff has suffered particular damage beyond that suffered by all the other persons affected by the nuisance.

[19] AIR 2000 SC 1410.

with a cause of action unless the threat be so certain or imminent that an injury actionable in law will arise unless prevented by an injunction. The court may not require proof of absolute certainty or a proof beyond reasonable doubt before it may interfere; but a strong case of probability that the apprehended mischief will in fact arise must be shown by the plaintiff.' In a remarkable conclusion, the apex court found that the plaintiff's apprehension about a smoking oven next door causing a nuisance was not justified by the pleadings or the evidence and dismissed the suit.

In *B Venkatappa v B Lovis*,[20] the Andhra Pradesh High Court upheld the lower court's mandatory injunction directing the defendant to close the holes in a chimney facing the plaintiff's property. The court ensured enforcement of its order by authorizing the plaintiff to seal the holes at the defendant's cost if the defendant failed to do so. The High Court stated that the smoke and fumes that materially interfered with ordinary comfort were enough to constitute an actionable nuisance and that actual injury to health need not be proved. The court also observed that the existence of other sources of discomfort in the neighbourhood were no defence, provided that the source complained of materially added to the discomfort. The court rejected the defence that the plaintiff 'came to the nuisance': 'The fact that the nuisance existed long before the complainant occupied his premises, does not relieve the offender unless he can show that as against the complainant he has acquired a right to commit nuisance complained of.'[21]

The 1905 judgment of the Calcutta High Court in *J C Galstaun v Dunia Lal Seal*, excerpted below, may be the earliest reported pollution control case in India. Apart from its historical significance, the case is important because it shows how the common law regulatory system can check polluters in a pre-industrialized society. But would this system, unaided by statute, be sufficient today? While reading the judgment, notice: (a) the polluter's defences (rejected by this court at the beginning of the last century, but still raised today); and (b) the award of Rs. 1,000 in damages—a very large amount at that time.

J C GALSTAUN v DUNIA LAL SEAL
(1905) 9 CWN 612

Pargiter, J: This appeal arises out of a suit for a perpetual injunction to abate a nuisance and for damages on account of the same.

The Plaintiff has a garden-house in the Manicktollah Municipality in the suburbs of Calcutta and the Defendant has a shellac factory situated 200 or 300 yards to the north-west of it. The Defendant discharges the refuse-liquid of his manufactory into a Municipal drain that passes along the north of the Plaintiff's garden, and the Plaintiff alleges, first, that the liquid is foul-smelling and noxious to the health of the neighbourhood and specially to himself, and, secondly, that it has damaged him in health, comfort and the market value of his garden property. The Plaintiff has, therefore, asked for a perpetual injunction against the Defendant to restrain him from discharging the liquid refuse into the Municipal drain and for five thousand rupees as damages.

The Defendant admitted that the refuse-liquid from his shellac factory was discharged into the Municipal drain, but he denied that it was noxious or that it had injuriously affected the Plaintiff's property. He said he had been conducting the manufactory in a lawful and reasonable manner from the year 1896 and that it did not constitute a nuisance. He alleged that his

20 AIR 1986 AP 239.

21 The 'right to commit nuisance complained of' refers to a prescriptive right to emit smoke acquired under section 15 of the Indian Easements Act of 1882, or a right acquired by the authority of a statute. A right to cause a *public nuisance*, however, cannot be obtained by prescription.

factory had been licensed by the Municipality and that he had not caused the Plaintiff any damage and that the Plaintiff had no cause of action against him.

The Subordinate Judge decreed the suit, granted a perpetual injunction and awarded the Plaintiff a thousand rupees as damages. The Defendant has now appealed and has maintained the same pleas here as he did in the first court.

The first point is to ascertain the truth about the refuse-liquid and its character. [The court reviewed the evidence.]

Our conclusion on all the evidence adduced is that when the Defendant's factory was in full working, the refuse-liquid when first discharged into the Municipal drain was offensive, that is contained animal and vegetable matter, that decomposition cannot but have begun soon after it was discharged, that the liquid was subject to evaporation in the drain during the dry months which constituted the working season, that it became thick and sluggish in a very short time, and that the organic matter accumulated in the drain and gave off a stench which was highly offensive and noxious. That is, we find, that the refuse-liquid constituted a legal nuisance when discharged, and created a serious nuisance in its passage through the Municipal drain.

The Defendant made some attempt to prove that the stench arose not from his refuse but from the insanitary condition of the Plaintiff's garden. [This contention was rejected by the court.]

The Defendant has ... contended that the refuse-liquid is not noxious when it leaves the factory; that the refuse may become noxious if it stagnates; that the stagnation is really due to the faulty nature of the Municipal drain, which cannot carry the liquid off speedily and efficiently because of the partial block at the culvert; that if the Municipality would put the drain into good condition, there would be no nuisance; and that he cannot, therefore, be responsible for those injurious consequences.

Comparing these contentions with the findings which we have already expressed, it is clear that the essential question at issue in this suit is this: Whether the Defendant is at liberty to discharge into this Municipal drain such a refuse-liquid as we have described. We are of opinion that he can claim no such right.

In the first place, the Municipality did not admit that the Defendant had any such right, for it prosecuted him twice for allowing the refuse-liquid to flow into the drain, first, in the year 1897, and again, not long afterwards. The Defendant, it appears, gave a promise that he would not allow the liquid flow into the drain and the prosecution (apparently the first one) was withdrawn. For a few months, he turned the liquid into a pit which he dug, but afterwards he reverted to the old practice of discharging it into the drain. In the second prosecution, he was convicted and fined. The Municipality tried to prevent the discharge of the liquid into the drain first by blocking the mouth of the drain, and afterwards by putting up an iron plate with masonry, but both these preventions were broken and removed. From these facts it appears that the Municipality tried to enforce the Municipal law against the Defendant but succeeded only partially and ultimately gave up the contest....

[The Defendant] cannot shift the responsibility on to the Municipality by contending that, if the Municipality would improve the drain so as to carry off all the refuse quickly, there would be no nuisance. This contention rests on a serious misconception of the rights and duties created under the Municipal law. No private person can claim a right to foul an ordinary drain by discharging into it what it was not intended to carry off, and then throw on the Municipality an obligation to alter the drain in order to remedy the nuisance that he has produced; nor can he say that other persons must meanwhile put up with such nuisance.

The Defendant's action consists of two parts; first, he has discharged the refuse-liquid into the drain; and, secondly, he has done so knowing that it cannot be efficiently carried away. But must stagnate, decompose and give off an offensive and intolerable stench.

The first part of his action constitutes a legal nuisance which the Plaintiff is entitled to restrain. Carrying on an offensive trade so as to interfere with another's health and comfort or his occupation of property has been constantly held in England to be a legal nuisance against which the courts will give relief....

The second part of the Defendant's action also constitutes a legal nuisance. Defendant is responsible for the consequences that arise necessarily out of his action. The case of *Ogston v Aberdeen District Tramways Company* [LR (1897) App Cas 111 (1896)] has some points in resemblance with the present case. There a Tramway Company after heavy falls of snow used to clear the snow off its track and to heap it upon the side of the streets; then it scattered salt to make the snow melt in the grooves of its track in order to facilitate its own traffic, with the result that the fluid mixture of salt and snow permeated of heaps of snow and, forming a freezing compound, caused annoyance and injury to the other traffic in the streets. The Town Council did not take any immediate steps to remove the briny slush which was left upon the streets. It was held that the Tramway Company had committed a nuisance which was not sanctioned by either the general or the special Tramways Acts, and that the default of the Town Council did not affect the primary liability of the Tramway Company.

In that case, the Company put forward much the same propositions as have been put forward in this case. They contended that they were within their statutory rights, or that their action, if not expressly licensed by the statutes, was sanctioned by implication for the necessary purposes of the Tramway. But these pleas were disallowed. The statutes did not sanction what the Company did nor did they give the Company any right to create a nuisance. We have already pointed out that the Defendant's plea in the present case that he was entitled to discharge his refuse into the drain cannot prevail....

For these reasons, we think that the Plaintiff is entitled to restrain the Defendant from discharging the refuse-liquid of his factory into the Municipal drain. From the history of this case it appears that the Defendant has successfully resisted Municipal control, that he has enlarged his factory and that he has been discharging a greater volume of refuse-liquid into the drain. It is plain that if no injunction is issued, there will be nothing to prevent him from aggravating the present nuisance by further enlarging his factory and discharging still more refuse into the drain. An injunction for the permanent stoppage of the nuisance is the only effectual remedy, and we have abundance of authority for issuing an injunction in the cases decided in England.

With regard to the question of the damage caused to the Plaintiff, objections have been urged against the opinion formed by the Subordinate Judge. Persistence in a proved nuisance has been held in England to be a just cause for giving exemplary damages. The Defendant has certainly persisted in spite of Municipal warning. This, therefore, is not a case in which the damages awarded should be nominal. There can be no doubt that material injury has been caused to the Plaintiff and the damages should be substantial; and, while holding this view, we think that the Subordinate Judge's estimate is reasonable and not excessive. For these reasons, we affirm the decree of the court below and dismiss this appeal with costs.

QUESTIONS

Despite the plaintiffs' success in *Galstaun's* case, if a similar situation arose today, is a common law action advisable? What other options may the victim consider? What changes since 1905 might influence the choice of the remedy?

In *Ram Baj Singh's* case, excerpted below, the plaintiff successfully restrained the defendant from using a brick grinding machine that generated dust and polluted the air. Note in this case: (a) the court's recognition of a private right of action arising from a public nuisance; (b) the liberal test employed by the court to determine the existence of a nuisance; (c) the issue of an injunction apparently without examining the balance of convenience; and (d) the evidentiary problems faced by the plaintiff.

RAM BAJ SINGH v BABULAL
AIR 1982 ALL 285

JUDGMENT: The plaintiff-appellant has been denied the relief sought by him on the ground that [a] brick grinding machine of the defendant did not cause any substantial injury or special damage to the plaintiff. Learned Counsel appearing for the plaintiff has argued before me that the two courts below have not correctly appreciated the meaning of the expressions 'substantial injury' and 'special damage,' as used in law.

The plaintiff-appellant commenced the action giving rise to this second appeal for permanent injunction to restrain the defendant-respondent from running his brick-grinding machine.

It is not in controversy between the parties that the plaintiff is a Medical Practitioner. He has built a consulting chamber before the brick-grinding machine was erected by the defendant-respondent. There is a controversy between the parties as to whether the consulting chamber was established by the plaintiff in the year 1962 or in the year 1965.... It is also not disputed that the brick-grinding machine is electrically propelled and that it is situate at a distance of about 40 feet from the consulting chamber of the plaintiff-appellant in a north-eastern direction. There is a road which intervenes between the consulting chamber of the plaintiff-appellant and the brick-grinding machine.

The grievance of the plaintiff-appellant was that the brick-grinding machine was generating dust which polluted the atmosphere and entered the consulting chamber of the plaintiff-appellant and caused physical inconvenience to him and his patients who came to his chamber. It was further stated that the said machine had been set up by the defendant-respondent without any permission or licence from the Municipal Board.

The defendant-respondent contested the suit. He did not deny that the machine was erected by him in April, 1965. He contended that no dust emanated during the process of grinding bricks and there was no question of any pollution being caused in the atmosphere. He further stated that the bricks were moistened before being subjected to grinding process and no dust resulted therefrom. He further stated that his machine did not produce any noise and according to him, the erection and working of the machine did not cause any nuisance—whether public or private. He concluded by saying that the suit had been filed against him only on account of enmity and the same was not legally sustainable. The trial court came to the conclusion that the brick-grinding machine had been erected by the defendant-respondent in the year 1965 without obtaining any licence from the appropriate authority. It further held that the dust did emanate and pollute the atmosphere and that such dust was injurious to health. It also came to the conclusion that the dust produced by the machine entered the consulting chamber of the plaintiff-appellant depending on the direction of the wind. It further found that the defence taken up by the defendant-respondent was false and the evidence produced by him could not be relied upon. It, however, dismissed the suit of the plaintiff-appellant on the finding that the dust resulting from the machine did not cause any substantial injury either to the plaintiff or to his patients. The trial court also went into the question as to whether the machine belonging to the defendant-respondent caused any actionable nuisance to the plaintiff-appellant and decided that [issue] against him....

[A] person is ordinarily entitled to do anything on his own property provided that doing of such a thing is lawful. His conduct, however, becomes a private nuisance when the consequence of his acts no longer remain confined to his own property but spill over in a substantial manner to the property belonging to another person. However, anything done by a person on his property, repercussions of which are felt on the neighbour's land, may not always be a nuisance. The consequences of anything done by the owner of a land on his own land which are also felt over the neighbouring land may be of such a trivial nature that no reasonable person would object to the same. No precise or universal formula has been devised to determine the distinction between a trivial consequence of an act or a consequence which can be termed to be of substantial magnitude. The test which has always been found to be useful in distinguishing the two sets of cases is the test of ascertaining the reaction of a reasonable person according to the ordinary usage of mankind living in a particular society in respect of the thing complained of.

After a land had been built upon, the owner of the building cannot expect to have air of the same quality which existed before the building was erected. The freshness of the air is necessarily diminished by the erection of the building. If the whole locality in which a building is situated is built upon, the quality of freshness of air will be diminished further and the same may become tainted to a certain extent. But when something is done by the owner of a neighbouring land upon his own land which is not comfortable or is wholly uncomfortable with physical comfort and human existence, the person aggrieved gets a right to sue. The act of the neighbour of which he will complain will be an actionable nuisance. At this stage, a note of caution may be sounded. In order to judge whether the air has been polluted to an extent that it has ceased to be comfortable with human comfort and existence, the standard to be employed again is the standard of a sober and reasonable mind. Concepts of elegant and dainty living will be wholly out of place. Further in judging the question of this comfort or danger to human existence on account of the act complained of, the location of a property is also a relevant circumstance. A person living in an industrial locality cannot claim to have as much fresh air as a person living in a non-industrial area. . . .

[A]ccording to the findings of the two [lower] courts . . . the consulting chamber of the plaintiff-appellant started functioning before the machine was set up by the defendant-respondent.

The two [lower] courts . . . have been largely influenced by the fact that the plaintiff-appellant did not examine any of his patients to prove that any actual damage was caused to them on account of the dust emanating from the machine of the defendant-respondent. They have also referred to the statement of the plaintiff-appellant and have held that the plaintiff admitted that the damage caused to his patients was recorded in his register and the same had not been produced. From this omission on the part of the plaintiff, they have drawn an adverse inference against him and have come to the conclusion that the plaintiff-appellant has failed to establish that any special damage or substantial injury was caused to him.

The expression 'special damage' is used in law to indicate a damage caused to a party in contra-distinction to damage caused to the public at large. The damage caused to the public at large on account of a nuisance is referred in law as a public nuisance. [The court referred to the public nuisance provisions in the Indian Penal Code and the Code of Criminal Procedure.] However, there may be cases where a single act may amount to a public nuisance and also give rise to a cause of action to an individual to sue on the basis of private nuisance. For instance, if night soil is heaped by the side of a public highway, it may be a nuisance to the general public and the persons who pass along the said highway. At the same time it may be a private nuisance to a person who lives in a house which adjoins the place where night soil is collected. All that the law requires is that when an act amounts to public nuisance, an individual can sue in his own right only if he is able to prove special damage to himself, i.e. damage which is personal to him as opposed to the damage or inconvenience caused to the public at large or to a section of the public.

The expression 'special damage' was found by the text book writers to be somewhat inaccurate and confusing. In later editions of the text books such as 'Salmond on Torts', the expression which has been used is 'particular damage'. It actually follows from the findings recorded by the two courts below that the plaintiff had succeeded in establishing damage which was particular to himself. It has been held by the court of appeal that dust emanated from the crushing of bricks was a public hazard and was bound to cause injury to the health of the persons. It has further held that dust from bricks entered in sufficient quantity into the consulting chamber of the plaintiff-appellant so that a thin red coating was visible on the clothes of the persons sitting there. In view of these findings it is difficult to comprehend how it could be said that the plaintiff had failed to prove that special damage was not being caused to him on account of the offending brick-grinding machine.

Coming to the question of substantial injury, I have already indicated above that every injury is considered to be substantial which a reasonable person considers to be so. In assessing the nature of substantial injury, the test to be applied is again the appraisement made of the injury by a reasonable person belonging to the society. The expression does not take into account the susceptibilities of hypersensitive person or persons attuned to a dainty mode of living. No other meaning can be assigned or has been assigned to the expression 'substantial injury'. In view of the fact found by the two courts below concurrently, it was impossible to hold that no substantial injury was being caused to the plaintiff-appellant. Causing of actual damage by the act complained of as a nuisance is besides the point. If actual damage or actual injury were to be the criterion a person will have to wait before the injury becomes palpable or demonstrable before instituting a suit or its abatement. My opinion, in this point is fortified by the views of the text book writers and the decided cases. Any act would amount to a private nuisance which can reasonably said to cause injury, discomfort or annoyance to a person.

For reasons stated above, this appeal must succeed.

NOTES AND QUESTIONS

1. On the basis of the evidence adduced, the High Court concluded that the plaintiff's consulting rooms started functioning *before* the brick-grinding machine was set up by the defendant. The court, therefore, was not required to resolve the issue of the plaintiff having come to the nuisance. If the brick-grinding machine had been functioning before the plaintiff started his consultancy, would the case have had a different outcome? In his situation, might the court have preferred the softer relief of damages?

2. While judges in India routinely deal with cases involving a breach of a statute, tort cases involving subjective standards of 'reasonableness' are rare occurrences. In this situation, judges often seek a *statutory basis* to support their view of 'reasonableness'. The brick-grinding machine was being operated without an appropriate government licence. Did this factor weigh with the court while deciding that the machine was being used unreasonably? Would the court have been more circumspect in restraining the defendant if the machine had been properly licensed by the municipal authorities?

3. The court dispenses with the balance of convenience test before granting the mandatory injunction. Similarly, the injunction's impact on third parties is apparently not considered. What are some of the factors that the court could have considered before reaching its decision?

4. The court employs a liberal test for nuisance, holding that air pollution amounts to a nuisance where it causes injury, discomfort or annoyance to a 'reasonable person'. Significantly, the court rejects a health-based standard that would require the plaintiff to prove actual injury: 'Causing of actual damage by the act complained of as a nuisance is besides the point. If actual damage or actual injury were to be the criterion, a person will have to wait before the injury becomes palpable or demonstrable before instituting a suit....'

Apart from the problem of latent health effects, such a standard would also immeasurably increase the evidentiary burden on the plaintiff: medical evidence would need to be adduced and the causal link between the pollutant and the injury would have to be established. In contrast, the 'reasonable person' standard may easily be met by adducing non-technical evidence.

But does the common law standard of 'reasonableness' provide a satisfactory basis for regulating pollution? Should not pollution regulation be designed to protect the most vulnerable segments of the population and not merely the 'average' or 'reasonable person'?

5. For a discussion on the nuisance test for excessive noise, see *Noise Pollution (V), In Re*,[22] where the Supreme Court held:

> No one can claim a right to create noise even in his own premises which would travel beyond his precincts and cause nuisance to neighbours or others. Any noise which has the effect of materially interfering with the ordinary comforts of life, judged by the standard of a reasonable man is nuisance. How and when a nuisance created by noise becomes actionable has to be answered by reference to its degree and the surrounding circumstances, including the place and the time.... Quietness and freedom from noise are indispensable to the full and free enjoyment of a dwelling-house. No proprietor has an absolute right to create noises upon his own land, because any right which the law gives is qualified by the condition that it must not be exercised to the nuisance of his neighbours or of the public. Noise will create an actionable nuisance only if it materially interferes with the ordinary comfort of life, judged by ordinary, plain and simple notions, and having regard to the locality; the question being one of degree in each case.

6. Since 1989 the Environment (Protection) Rules prescribe ambient noise levels for industrial, commercial and residential areas as well as silence zones. In 1996, the Centre notified National Ambient Air Quality Standards (NAAQS) for several pollutants such as sulphur dioxide, suspended particulate matter, respirable particulate matter, carbon monoxide, etc. The NAAQS allow an adequate margin of safety to protect public health, vegetation and property[23] and may guide a civil court in assessing the reasonableness of a smoke nuisance or excessive noise.

7. Does the 'polluter pays' principle, adopted by the Supreme Court,[24] strengthen nuisance law? As explained by the Supreme Court, this principle not only requires the polluter to compensate the victims of the pollution but also requires her to foot the bill for remedial costs to restore the damaged ecology.

8. A plaintiff impacted by a local environmental nuisance (smoke, noise, offensive discharge into a municipal drain, etc.) could conveniently approach a local civil court for relief. Does the embargo under section 29(2) of the NGT Act apply to all such civil suits? If so, is such an embargo constitutional? Should the NGT supplement or replace existing civil remedies? In analysing these issues consider a local problem arising far away from one of the five benches of the NGT.

9. In the *Ratnagiri Nagar Parishad* case,[25] the Supreme Court gave an expansive interpretation to section 29 of the NGT Act. The embargo precluded a suit to restrain a local body from proceeding with a solid waste disposal project based on an apprehension of environmental harm. The remedy was not a suit but an action under the NGT Act.

Negligence

A common law action for negligence may be brought to prevent environmental pollution. In an action for negligence, the plaintiff must show that (1) the defendant was under a duty to take reasonable care to avoid the damage complained of; (2) there was breach of this duty; and (3) the breach of duty caused the damage. The degree of care required in a particular case

---

22 (2005) 5 SCC 733, 746 and 762.

23 Note 1, Schedule VII, Environment (Protection) Rules of 1986 as it stood between 1996 and 2009 read: 'National Ambient Air Quality Standard: The levels of air quality necessary with an adequate margin of safety, to protect the public health, vegetation and property.' With effect from 16 November 2009, Schedule VII was replaced with more stringent standards but the quoted note was dropped.

24 *Indian Council for Enviro-Legal Action v Union of India (Bichhri-1)* AIR 1996 SC 1446; and *Vellore Citizens' Welfare Forum v Union of India* AIR 1996 SC 2715.

25 *Ratnagiri Nagar Parishad v Gangaram Narayan Ambekar* (2020) 7 SCC 275.

depends on the surrounding circumstances and varies according to the risk involved and the magnitude of the prospective injury.

An act of negligence may also constitute a nuisance if it unlawfully interferes with the enjoyment of another's right in land. Similarly, it may also amount to a breach of the rule of strict liability in *Rylands v Fletcher*,[26] if the negligent act allows the escape of anything dangerous which the defendant has brought on the land.

The causal connection between the negligent act and the plaintiff's injury is often the most problematic link in pollution cases. Where the pollutant is highly toxic and its effect is immediate, as with the methyl isocynate that leaked from the Union Carbide plant is Bhopal, the connection is relatively straightforward. The causal link is more tenuous when the effect of the injury remains latent over long periods of time and can eventually be attributed to factors other than the pollutant, or to polluters other than the defendant.[27]

The *Mukesh Textile Mills* case, excerpted below, is one of the few reported pollution cases in which a judgment was rendered for damages. Note (a) the defences raised by the mill; (b) the witnesses examined by the parties to establish their respective contentions; (c) the discussion on the mitigation of damages; and (d) the manner in which the court quantified damages.

MUKESH TEXTILE MILLS (P) LTD v H R SUBRAMANYA SASTRY
AIR 1987 KANT 87

Venkatachaliah, J: Appellant-Mukesh Textile Mills (P) Ltd., the defendant in the court below, has a sugar-factory in Harige Village, Shimoga District. Adjacent to the sugar-factory, on the north, the respondents-plaintiffs own several extents of land irrigated by a distributory channel of the Badra Reservoir canal. The water channel runs West to East, in between the premises of the sugar-factory on the south and respondents' lands on the north.

Appellant stores molasses, a bye-product in the manufacture of sugar, in three tanks in the factory premises. Two of them are steel tanks and the third, a mud one with earthern embankment, is close to the respondents' land separated only by the said water channel. At the material point of time, some 8000 tonnes of molasses were stored in the earthern tank.

It would appear that the northern embankment of this earthern tank had become dilapidated having been dug into by rodents and as a result, on the night of 16th of April 1970, the northern embankment collapsed and a large quantity of molasses in the tank overflowed and emptied themselves into the water channel, inundated and spread over respondents' land. The inundation of water, fully laden with the molasses, damaged the standing paddy and sugarcane crop raised by the respondents.

Respondents brought the present suit O.S. 26 of 1972 on the file of the Civil Judge, Shimoga for damages of Rs. 35,000 contending that extensive cultivation of paddy and sugarcane had been damaged.

Originally the defence was one of denial that the molasses had so inundated respondents' land; but later the appellant sought, and was granted, leave to include by amendment the following defence:

> That in any event as the breach of the Tank wherein the molasses was stored was due to the burrowing activity of the rodents in the said tank precincts, this was an Act of God and the defendant is in no way liable to answer the suit claim even granting that the

[26] (1868) LR 3 HL 330.

[27] In numerous American suits brought against asbestos manufacturing by asbestos workers suffering from lung cancer, several courts reduced the damage award on the theory that a plaintiff's habit of smoking cigarettes had contributed, or could have contributed, to his condition. Some courts dismissed the suit entirely when the plaintiff had been a cigarette smoker.

plaintiff has suffered damages by reasons of his crops being destroyed. The defendant could not have seen this burrowing by rodents.

On these pleadings, the court below framed the necessary and relevant issues. On the plaintiff's side – P.W.1 – a Revenue Inspector; P.W. 2 – a Photographer, P.W. 3 – the Shanbogue and P.W.4 – the Patel of Harige Village were examined. The first plaintiff tendered evidence as P.W.5.

On the side of the appellant – defendant, D.W.1 – the Chief Chemist of the Factory; P.W.2 and P.W.3 – the Cane Superintendent and the Manager, respectively of the factory; were examined. A number of documents were marked on either side.

On an appreciation of the evidence on record, the court below held that as a result of a breach of the retaining-wall of the mud tank molasses overflowed contaminated the water channel resulting in the inundation of respondents' lands by molasses laden water and that the breach of the wall of the tank and the consequent damage suffered by respondents were attributable to actionable negligence on the part of the appellant. In regard to the quantum of damages the court below held that the claim as put forward by the respondents was somewhat exaggerated and that the loss of crops was only in respect of 14 acres of paddy and 3 acres of sugarcane. Rs.10,500 and 4,200 respectively, in all, Rs.14,700 was awarded as damages.

***

On the contentions urged at the hearing, the following points fall for determination in this appeal:

(a) Whether the breach of the molasses-tank and the inundation of the crops by molasses laden water was the direct consequence of appellant's omission to keep the said tank in a state of good repair?
(b) Even if the breach was attributable to appellant's neglect, whether the damage to the crop was too remote and the result of an independent cause?
(c) Whether, at all events, the respondents ought to have mitigated the damages and their omission in this behalf disentitles them to relief and,
(d) Whether the damages of Rs.14,700 awarded are supportable on the evidence on record?

Re: Point (a): [The appellant-defendant did not press the plea that the damage arose due to an 'Act of God']

The liability of the appellant rests at least on two principles. One is that the appellant, who had stored large quantities of molasses in a mud tank had the duty to take reasonable care in the matter of maintenance, in a state of good repair, of the embankments of the tank. The duty, no doubt, is not simply to act carefully but not to cause injury carelessly. The doctrine of legal causation, in reference both to the creation of liability and to measurement of damages is much discussed. So is the place of 'causation' and 'foreseeability' in the tort of 'negligence'.

But in this case it was virtually admitted that the rodents had burrowed holes into the earthen embankment of the tank rendering its walls weak. Both from the foreseeability test and of initial causation it must be held that the appellant is liable. Appellant could reasonably have foreseen that damage was likely to be caused if there was a breach of the tank. There was clearly a duty-situation and appellant had omitted to do what a reasonable man, in those circumstances, would have done or would not have omitted to do. The damage that was likely to occur to the neighbouring land by a breach of a tank in which were stored 8,000 tonnes of molasses was reasonably foreseeable, engendering a duty-situation. No defence was forthcoming that the tank had been inspected periodically and all reasonable steps taken to keep it in a state of good repair.

The second ground of liability is this: Appellant by storing a large quantity of molasses on the land had put the land to a non-natural user and if a person collects on his premises things which are intrinsically dangerous or might become dangerous, if they escape, he has a liability, if things so stored escape and cause damage. This is the rule in *Rylands v Fletcher* in which Blackburn, J enunciated the rule thus:

> We think that the true rule of law is that the person who for his own purposes brings on his lands and collects and keeps there anything likely to do mischief if it escapes, must keep it at his peril, and if he does not do so is prima facie answerable for all the damages which is the natural consequence of its escape.

On either of the two principles a duty-situation emerges and the appellant must be held liable for the consequence of the escape of the fluid from its tank....

Looked at from any side, the present one is a clear case of a duty-situation and also one of omission to discharge it on the part of the appellant. Point (a) is held against the appellant.

Re: Point (b): [Counsel for the appellant-defendant suggests] a defence of a 'novus actus interveniens.' If damage results from the intervention of acts of an independent third-party, it may be very difficult to discover the causal connection between such damage and the original wrongful act.

In this case, the plea of '*novus actus*' has absolutely no foundation. The chain of events set into motion by the negligence of the appellant, in improper maintenance of the tank which resulted in the breach of the tank and the damage caused to the crops, constitutes a direct and uninterrupted chain of events. It all happened in the night. The molasses contaminated the water in the channel and through it, the crops. The appeal to the principle of 'novus actus' appears to be somewhat misplaced. Point (b) is answered accordingly.

Re: Point (c): The contention of the [counsel for the appellant] pushed to its logical conclusions, is that though the respondents' land was infested with molasses, the respondents' remedy was simple enough—if fresh water had been allowed to further irrigate and inundate the lands, the contamination would have been washed out. Learned Counsel submitted that as the respondents had not shown that they had so taken the requisite care to mitigate the damages they are not entitled to any damages. This plea was not taken in the court below. There is no material to show that such a process would have been really effective and practicable. [Since the appellant had failed to discharge the onus of proof, the court held that the plea of mitigation fails.]

Re. Point (d): We have examined the evidence on record on this point. The Court below held that there was paddy crop on 14 acres and sugarcane crop on 3 acres. The court below estimated the probable yield at 15 pallas of paddy per acre. Valuing paddy at Rs.50 per palla, court below estimated the loss of paddy crop at Rs.10,500. The yield from 3 acres of sugarcane was estimated at 60 tonnes valued at Rs.70 per ton. That brought in a further sum of Rs.4200. D.W.2 himself admitted the existence of the paddy and sugarcane crop. There is other material also to support this finding apart from the evidence of the 1st plaintiff. (P.W.5).

However, there is some force in what [appellant's counsel] said about the gross value of the crops having been taken while the crops had not been ready for harvest and required some more expenditure for their maintenance for sometime more before harvest and that the expenses for its upkeep and maintenance of the crops and expenses of harvest having to be deducted. We think that it is appropriate to deduct some amount from the damages awarded towards such expenditure, which was reasonably expected to be incurred. Accordingly, we deduct a sum of Rs.2,500 on this score. The damages awarded would, therefore, have to be scaled down to Rs.12,200 from Rs.14,700. This is our finding on Point (d).

In the result, this appeal is allowed in part, only in relation to the quantum of damages. In modification of the judgment, and decree under appeal, the suit is decreed in a sum of Rs.12,200 on which respondent-plaintiff shall been entitled to interest at 6% from the date of suit till the date of realization. The respondents shall be entitled to their costs in the suit proportionate to their success. The appellant shall, however, bear and pay its own costs in the court below. Both the parties are left to bear and pay their own costs in the appeal.

NOTES AND QUESTIONS

1. In a suit for damages, a plaintiff may sue for every prospective loss that would naturally result from the defendant's conduct. Thus, if the molasses had harmed future cultivation, the plaintiff could have obtained prospective damages as well. In such a situation, the plaintiff's evidentiary burden would have been considerable. He or she would have had to adduce expert evidence to establish the type and extent of damage to the soil. Who might possess such expertise? Where can such expertise be obtained?

2. Damages for past as well as prospective loss resulting from the same cause must be recovered in a single suit as more than one suit will not lie on the same cause of action.[28] Assume that some future damage caused by the molasses remained latent for several years before being discovered. Is it fair that the suit for damages for the loss of the standing crops should preclude a suit for latent injuries discovered in the future? Should the principle of *res judicata* apply to such cases?

3. After 14 years of litigation, the High Court ordered damages of Rs. 12,200 with interest at 6% per year from the date of the suit. The High Court reduced the subordinate court's award by Rs. 2,500. Was this necessary? Does compensation afford fair relief when it ignores the high litigation costs of bringing a suit and battling it through multiple appeals? Should a court not be conscious of the fall in the value of the currency? Is the award of interest at 6% per year at all realistic?

4. In an appeal filed by the Rajkot Municipal Corporation contesting a decree for damages awarded to the widow and children of a pedestrian killed by a falling tree, the Supreme Court held:

> The conditions in India have not developed to such an extent that a corporation can keep constant vigil by testing the healthy conditions of the tree in the public places, roadsides, highways frequented by passers-by. There is no duty to maintain regular supervision thereof.... Consequently, there would be no common law right to file a suit for tort of negligence.[29]

Apparently, 'conditions in India' developed quite swiftly. Two years later, without reference to *Rajkot*, the Supreme Court upheld a decree against the Delhi Municipal Corporation where a scooterist was killed by a falling tree. The court agreed with the finding of the trial court that the municipal corporation had been negligent in discharging its duty of care to road users.[30]

---

[28] This is governed by the principle of *res judicata* enunciated in section 11 of the Code of the Civil Procedure of 1908.

[29] *Rajkot Municipal Corporation v Manjulaben Jayantilal Nakum* (1997) 9 SCC 552, 601.

[30] *Municipal Corporation of Delhi v Sushila Devi* AIR 1999 SC 1929, 1933.

Strict Liability

The rule in *Rylands v Fletcher*[31] holds a person *strictly liable* when he brings or accumulates on his land something likely to cause harm if it escapes, and damage arises as a natural consequence of its escape. But 'strict' liability is subject to a number of exceptions that considerably reduce the scope of its operation. Exceptions that have been recognized are: (1) an Act of god (natural disasters such as an earthquake or flood); (2) the act of a third party (e.g., sabotage); (3) the plaintiff's own fault; (4) the plaintiff's consent; (5) the natural use of land by the defendant (i.e., strict liability applies to a non-natural user of land); and (6) statutory authority.

Absolute Liability

With the expansion of chemical-based industries in India, increasing number of enterprises store and use hazardous substances. These activities are not banned because they have great social utility (e.g., the manufacture of fertilizers and pesticides). Traditionally, the doctrine of strict liability was considered adequate to regulate such hazardous enterprises. The doctrine allows for the growth of hazardous industries, while ensuring that such enterprises will bear the burden of the damage they cause when a hazardous substance escapes. Shortly after the Bhopal gas leak tragedy of 1984, the traditional doctrine was replaced by the rule of 'absolute' liability, a standard *stricter* than strict liability. Absolute liability or no-fault liability was first articulated by the Supreme Court and has since been adopted by Parliament.

The genesis of absolute liability was the *Shriram Gas Leak* case[32] which was decided by the Supreme Court in December 1986. The case originated in a writ petition filed in the Supreme Court by the environmentalist and lawyer M C Mehta as public interest litigation. The petition sought to close and relocate Shriram's caustic chlorine and sulphuric acid plants which were located in a thickly populated part of Delhi. Shortly after Mehta filed this petition, on 4 December 1985 oleum leaked from Shriram's sulphuric acid plant causing widespread panic in the surrounding community.

Chief Justice Bhagwati, who presided over the Supreme Court bench, was concerned for the safety of Delhi's citizens. Moreover, the Chief Justice saw in the oleum leak a way of influencing the pending and far more important *Bhopal Gas Leak* case. In the first reported order in *Shriram*, the Chief Justice observed that the principles and norms for determining the liability of large enterprises engaged in the manufacture and sale of hazardous products were 'questions of the greatest importance particularly since, following upon the leakage of MIC gas from the Union Carbide Plant in Bhopal, lawyers, judges and jurists are considerably exercised as to what controls, whether by way of relocation or by way of installation of adequate safety devices, need to be imposed upon [hazardous industries], what is the extent of liability of such corporations and what remedies can be devised for enforcing such liability with a view to securing payment of damages to the person affected by such leakage of liquid or gas'.[33]

Union Carbide hinted at a 'sabotage theory' to shield itself from the claims of the Bhopal victims. It was suggested that a disgruntled employee working in the pesticide factory owned by Carbide's Indian subsidiary may have triggered the escape of the gas. Such a theory afforded a defence under the rule of strict liability laid down in *Rylands v Fletcher*. But any faith Union Carbide may have reposed in the sabotage theory was soon shaken by Chief Justice

[31] (1868) LR 3 HL 330. For a discussion on 'strict liability' and the *Rylands* rule see *Jay Laxmi Salt Works (P) Ltd v State of Gujarat* (1994) 4 SCC 1.
[32] *M C Mehta v Union of India* AIR 1987 SC 1086.
[33] *M C Mehta v Union of India* AIR 1987 SC 965.

Bhagwati's rejection of the *Rylands* rule in situations involving hazardous industries. In his last judgment before retirement, Chief Justice Bhagwati spoke for the court:

> We are of the view that an enterprise which is engaged in a hazardous or inherently dangerous industry which poses a potential threat to the health and safety of the persons working in the factory and residing in the surrounding areas owes an absolute and non-delegable duty to the community to ensure that no harm results to anyone on account of hazardous or inherently dangerous nature of the activity which it has undertaken.... We would therefore hold that where an enterprise is engaged in a hazardous or inherently dangerous activity and harm results to anyone on account of an accident in the operation of such hazardous or inherently dangerous activity resulting, for example, in the escape of toxic gas the enterprise is strictly and absolutely liable to compensate all those who are affected by the accident and *such liability is not subject to any of the exceptions* which operate *vis-à-vis* the tortious principle of strict liability under the rule in *Rylands v Fletcher*.[34]

The absolute liability theory laid down by the Supreme Court in *Shriram* was first applied by the Madhya Pradesh High Court to support its award of interim compensation to the Bhopal victims.[35] In light of *Shriram*, Justice Seth of the High Court described the liability of the enterprise to be 'unquestionable'.

However, soon thereafter the wisdom of the theory was questioned by Chief Justice Ranganath Misra who presided over the proceedings before the Supreme Court for a review of the *Bhopal* case settlement.[36] Chief Justice Misra in his concurring judgment observed that the issue before the *Shriram* court was whether the delinquent company came within the ambit of 'state' under Article 12 of the Constitution so as to be subject to the discipline of Article 21 and to proceedings under Article 32 of the Constitution. Thus, according to the Chief Justice, what was said about the departure from the *Rylands v Fletcher* rule 'was essentially obiter'.[37]

Justice Venkatachaliah (speaking for Justices K N Singh, N D Ojha and himself) in the main judgment in the *Bhopal Review* also cast doubt on the absolute liability standard. He implicitly rejected the Madhya Pradesh High Court view that after the no-exception standard of *Shriram*, Carbide's liability was 'unquestionable'. The Supreme Court held that Carbide was entitled to its day in court when its defences, legal and factual, would have to be tested. In Justice Venkatachaliah's words:

> At the same time, it is necessary to remind ourselves that in bestowing a second thought whether the settlement is just, fair and adequate, we should *not* proceed on the premises that the liability of the UCC has been firmly established. It is *yet to be decided* if the matter goes to trial. Indeed, UCC has seriously contested the basis of its alleged liability.... Every effort should be made to protect the victims from the prospects of a protracted, exhausting and uncertain litigation. While we do not intend to comment on the merits of the claims and of the defenses, factual and legal, arising in the suit, it is fair to recognize that the suit involves complex questions as to the basis of UCC's liability and assessment of the quantum of compensation in a mass tort action.[38]

In recognizing Carbide's right to raise and urge defences the court stepped back from the 'without exception' absolute liability principle declared in *Shriram*.

---

34 Emphasis supplied. *Supra* note 32 at 1099.

35 *Union Carbide Corporation v Union of India* Civil Revision No. 26 of 1988, 4 April 1988. This judgment was never implemented in view of the final settlement between the parties.

36 *Union Carbide Corporation v Union of India (Bhopal Review)* AIR 1992 SC 248.

37 *Id.* at 261. *Obiter dicta* are words of a judgment unnecessary for the decision of the case.

38 Emphasis supplied. *Id.* at 306.

Meanwhile, in January 1991, Parliament enacted the Public Liability Insurance Act, giving statutory recognition to 'no-fault' liability in small measure. The victims of a hazardous industrial accident were now entitled to compensation at prescribed levels, without proof of negligence. The maximum compensation under the Act on a 'no-fault' basis however, is *limited* to Rs. 25,000; although the right of a victim to claim larger damages is expressly reserved. To safeguard the interest of victims, the law requires all hazardous enterprises to obtain sufficient insurance cover.

The application of absolute liability was extended *without limitation* by the National Environment Tribunal Act of 1995[39] to all cases where death or injury to a person (other than a workman) or damage to any property or the environment result from an accident involving a hazardous substance. The 'owner', who was defined to mean a person who owns or has control over the handling of any hazardous substance at the time of the accident, was liable to compensate the victims on a 'no-fault' basis. Applications for compensation could be made to the Tribunal established under the 1995 Act.

In the *Bichhri-1* case excerpted below, a Supreme Court bench of two judges grappled with the seemingly divergent views expressed by the five-judge constitution benches in the *Shriram* and *Bhopal Review* cases. While the judges may not be faulted for preferring the *Shriram* dictum, are there any errors that weaken the force of the reasoning?

INDIAN COUNCIL FOR ENVIRO-LEGAL ACTION v UNION OF INDIA
AIR 1996 SC 1446

B P Jeevan Reddy, J: * * *

Bichhri is a small village in Udaipur District of Rajasthan. To its north is a major industrial establishment, Hindustan Zinc Limited, a public sector concern. That did not affect Bichhri. Its woes began somewhere in 1987 when the fourth respondent herein, Hindustan Agro Chemicals Limited started producing certain chemicals like Oleum (said to be the concentrated form of sulphuric acid) and Single Super Phosphate. The real calamity occurred when a sister concern, Silver Chemicals (Respondent 5), commenced production of 'H' acid in a plant located within the same complex. 'H' acid was meant for export exclusively. Its manufacture gives rise to enormous quantities of highly toxic effluents—in particular, iron-based and gypsum-based sludge—which if not properly treated, pose grave threat to Mother Earth. It poisons the earth, the water and everything that comes in contact with it. Jyoti Chemicals (Respondent 8) is another unit established to produce 'H' acid, besides some other chemicals. Respondents 6 and 7 were established to produce fertilizers and a few other products.

All the units/factories of Respondents 4 to 8 are situated in the same complex and are controlled by the same group of individuals. All the units are what may be called 'chemical industries'. The complex is located within the limits of Bichhri village.

Because of the pernicious wastes emerging from the production of 'H' acid, its manufacture is stated to have been banned in the western countries. But the need of 'H' acid continues in the West. That need is catered to by the industries like the Silver Chemicals and Jyoti Chemicals in this part of the world. (A few other units producing 'H' acid have been established in Gujarat, as would be evident from the decision of the Gujarat High Court in *Pravinbhai Jashbhai Patel v State of Gujarat*, a decision rendered by one of us, B N Kirpal, J as the Chief Justice of that Court.) Silver Chemicals is stated to have produced 375 MT of 'H' acid. The quantity of 'H' acid produced by Jyoti Chemicals is not known. It says that it produced only 20 MT, as trial production, and no more. Whatever quantity these two units

[39] NETA was repealed and replaced by the National Green Tribunal Act of 2010 before it was brought into force.

may have produced, it has given birth to about 2400–2500 MT of highly toxic sludge (iron-based sludge and gypsum-based sludge) besides other pollutants. Since the toxic untreated waste waters were allowed to flow out freely and because the untreated toxic sludge was thrown in the open in and around the complex, the toxic substances have percolated deep into the bowels of the earth polluting the aquifers and the subterranean supply of water. The water in the wells and the streams has turned dark and dirty rendering it unfit for human consumption. It has become unfit for cattle to drink and for irrigating the land. The soil has become polluted rendering it unfit for cultivation, the mainstay of the villagers. The resulting misery to the villagers needs no emphasis. It spread disease, death and disaster in the village and the surrounding areas. This sudden degradation of earth and water had an echo in Parliament too. An Hon'ble Minister said, action was being taken, but nothing meaningful was done on the spot. The villagers then rose in virtual revolt leading to the imposition of Section 144 CrPC by the District Magistrate in the area and the closure of Silver Chemicals in January 1989. It is averred by the respondents that both the units, Silver Chemicals and Jyoti Chemicals have stopped manufacturing 'H' acid since January 1989 and are closed. We may assume it to be so. Yet the consequences of their action remain—the sludge, the long-lasting damage to earth, to underground water, to human beings, to cattle and the village economy. It is with these consequences that we are to contend with in this writ petition.

The present social action litigation was initiated in August 1989 complaining precisely of the above situation and requesting for appropriate remedial action. To the writ petition, the petitioner enclosed a number of photographs illustrating the enormous damage done to water, cattle, plants and to the area in general. A good amount of technical data and other material was also produced supporting the averments in the writ petition.

[The judgment considers the pleadings, interim orders passed by the court and the submission of the parties before turning to the applicable tort law principle.]

[W]e are of the opinion that any principle evolved in this behalf should be simple, practical and suited to the conditions obtaining in this country. We are convinced that the law stated by this court in *Oleum Gas Leak* case *(M C Mehta v Union of India*) AIR 1986 SC 1086) is by far the more appropriate one—apart from the fact that it is binding upon us. (We have disagreed with the view that the law stated in the said decision is *obiter*). According to this rule, once the activity carried on is hazardous or inherently dangerous, the person carrying on such activity is liable to make good the loss caused to any other person by his activity *irrespective* of the fact whether he took reasonable care while carrying on his activity. The rule is premised upon the very nature of the activity carried on. In the words of the Constitution Bench, such an activity:

> ... can be tolerated only on condition that the enterprise engaged in such hazardous or inherently dangerous activity indemnifies all those who suffer on account of the carrying on of such hazardous or inherently dangerous activity regardless of whether it is carried on carefully or not.

The Constitution Bench has also assigned the reason for stating the law in the said terms. It is that the enterprise (carrying on the hazardous or inherently dangerous activity) alone has the resource to discover and guard against hazards or dangers—and not the person affected *and* the practical difficulty (on the part of the affected person) in establishing the absence of reasonable care or that the damage to him was foreseeable by the enterprise.

Once the law in *Oleum Gas Leak* case is held to be the law applicable, it follows, in the light of our findings recorded here in before, that Respondents 4 to 8 are absolutely liable to compensate for the harm caused by them to the villagers in the affected area, to the soil and to the underground water and hence, they are bound to take all necessary measures to remove the sludge and other pollutants lying in the affected area.... and also to defray the cost of the remedial measures required to restore the soil and the underground water sources. Sections 3 and 4 of Environment (Protection) Act confers upon the Central Government the power to give directions of the above nature and to the above effect. Levy of costs required for carrying out remedial measures is implicit in Sections 3 and 4 which are couched in very wide and expansive language. Appropriate directions can be given by this court to the Central Government to invoke and exercise those powers with such modulations as are called for in the facts and circumstances of this case....

NOTES AND QUESTIONS

1. Although the Public Liability Insurance Act of 1991 and the National Environment Tribunal Act of 1995 (NETA) were on the statute book when the *Bichhri* case was decided, the court makes no reference to these laws. Is the judgment *per incuriam*? Do these provisions strengthen the Supreme Court's reasoning or do they militate against the opinion?

2. NETA was not in force on the date of judgment in *Bichhri-1*.[40] Possibly, in the assessment of the Central Government which was responsible for bringing the law into force, the time was not ripe for introducing the new standard. Should this have persuaded the court to reject the absolute liability standard?

3. Confronted by the strong language of Chief Justice Misra in the *Bhopal Review* case where he finds the *Shriram* 'absolute liability' standard to be in the nature of a passing observation and therefore not binding, the *Bichhri-1* court disagrees with the Misra opinion and notes 'the majority judgment delivered by M N Venkatachaliah, J.... has not expressed any opinion on the issue'.

4. Do the vacillations on the question of absolute liability—*Shriram, Bhopal Review, Bichhri-1*—suggest a preference for expediency over principle? Bear in mind the broad objective of the court in each case.

5. In its operative order, the court relegated the Bichhri villagers to the remedy of individual suits for compensation. Should not the court, in exercise of its expansive jurisdiction under Article 21, have awarded compensation in the writ proceedings? What are the pitfalls in adopting a summary procedure?

6. In a part of the judgment not excerpted earlier, the Supreme Court surveyed developments to the *Rylands* rule. In England, the rule continues to afford an independent head for claiming damages whereas in Australia the rule is absorbed in the tort of negligence.

7. In the *Vellore* case,[41] the Supreme Court bench presided over by Justice Kuldip Singh referred to the absolute liability principle in the context of pollution caused by the discharge of untreated effluent by industries in Tamil Nadu. This case did not involve an industrial accident nor did it concern the escape or discharge of a toxic substance—which constitute the class of cases to which 'absolute liability' is applied. The *Vellore* court, however, rolled together the 'polluter pays principle' (applicable to pollution cases) with the absolute liability standard (applicable to toxic torts). 'The "Polluter Pays Principle" as interpreted by this court [in *Bichhri-1*] means that the absolute liability for harm to the environment extends not only to compensate the victims of pollution but also the cost of restoring the environmental degradation.'[42] Is the extension of 'absolute liability' to pollution cases justified? On what principle?

[40] It was repealed in 2010 before being enforced.
[41] *Vellore Citizens Welfare Form v Union of India* AIR 1996 SC 2715.
[42] *Id.* at 2721. Also see *M C Mehta v Union of India (Taj Trapezium)* AIR 1997 SC 734.

8. The NGT Act of 2010 entered into force on 18 October 2010 and repealed NETA. With respect to no-fault liability, the applicable provision is section 17 which reads:

> 17. *Liability to pay relief or compensation in certain cases* — (1) Where death of, or injury to, any person (other than a workman) or damage to any property or environment has resulted from an accident or the adverse impact of an activity or operation or process, under any enactment specified in Schedule I, the person responsible shall be liable to pay such relief or compensation for such death, injury or damage, under all or any of the heads specified in Schedule II, as may be determined by the Tribunal.
> (2) If the death, injury or damage caused by an accident or the adverse impact of an activity or operation or process under any enactment specified in Schedule I cannot be attributed to any single activity or operation or process but is the combined or resultant effect of several such activities, operations and processes, the Tribunal may apportion the liability for relief compensation amongst those responsible for such activities, operations and processes on an equitable basis.
> (3) The Tribunal shall, in case of an accident, apply the principle of no fault.

Does the principle of no-fault liability apply to all situations of injury or damage caused by pollution or is this principle limited to cases where there is an accident?

9. In the *Art of Living* case,[43] the NGT was concerned with damage to the Yamuna flood plains from the erection of temporary structures for hosting an international cultural programme. Even though there was no accident, the Tribunal conflates two principles—polluter pays and no-fault liability:

> In India, the Tribunal is mandated under Section 17(3) of the National Green Tribunal Act, 2010 to apply the principles of no fault. Thus, application of this principle is inescapable. This doctrine imposes an obligation upon the project proponent or body intending to carry on an activity to bear the consequences of its actions. The consequences would obviously include amongst others such as cost of restoration/restitution. The onus lies upon the actor to satisfy that they took all the precautions that were required to be taken actually prior at the time and subsequent to the event and in fact there was neither any damage/degradation to the river or the flood plain nor was there any pollution after the event.

Do you agree with the NGT's reasoning on no-fault? Is it not consistent with *Vellore*?

B. PUBLIC NUISANCE

A public nuisance may be broadly defined as an unreasonable interference with a general right of the public. Because a public nuisance interferes with a public right, it is not tied to interference with the enjoyment and use of property; and remedies against a public nuisance are, therefore, available to every citizen.

Section 268 of the Indian Penal Code of 1860 defines the offence of a public nuisance:

> A person is guilty of a public nuisance who does any act or is guilty of an illegal omission which causes any common injury, danger or annoyance to the public or to the people in general who dwell or occupy property in the vicinity, or which must necessarily cause injury, obstruction, danger or annoyance to persons who may have occasion to use any public right.

The section also provides that '[a] common nuisance is not excused on the ground that it causes some convenience or advantage'.

43 *Manoj Misra v Delhi Development Authority* OA No. 65 of 2016, order dated 7 December 2017; (2017) SCC Online NGT 966.

Persons who conduct 'offensive' trades and thereby pollute the air, or cause loud and continuous noises that affect the health and comfort of those dwelling in the neighbourhood are liable to prosecution for causing a public nuisance. The penalty for this offence is merely Rs. 200,[44] which makes it pointless for a citizen to initiate a prosecution under section 268 by a complaint to a magistrate.[45]

A much better course would be to utilize the remedies provided in sections 133 to 144 of the Code of Criminal Procedure of 1973. Section 133 provides an independent, speedy and summary remedy against public nuisance.[46] The section empowers a magistrate to pass a 'conditional order' for the removal of a public nuisance within a fixed period of time.[47] The magistrate may act on information received from a police report or any other source including a complaint made by a citizen.[48] Although the magistrate's power to issue a conditional order under section 133 appears discretionary, the Supreme Court has interpreted the language to be mandatory.[49] Once a magistrate has before her evidence of a public nuisance, she must order removal of the nuisance, within a fixed time.[50]

The person directed to remove the nuisance (the opposite party) must either comply with the order or show cause against it. Where he or she opposes the order, the court must initiate an inquiry and call on the parties to adduce evidence. Moreover, to assist the inquiry, the magistrate may direct a local investigation to ascertain facts or summon expert witnesses. If measures are necessary to prevent imminent danger or serious injury to the public, the court may issue an injunction pending an inquiry. When a person fails to appear and show cause, or when the court is satisfied on the evidence adduced that the initial order was proper, the order is made final. Otherwise it is vacated.

Failure to comply with a final order within the specified time attracts the penalty provided by section 188 of the Indian Penal Code for disobedience of an order of a public servant. Further, the court may carry out the order and recover costs from the defaulter. A magistrate is also empowered to prohibit repetition or continuance of a public nuisance.

A magistrate, however, may not pass a final order that exceeds the conditional order in scope. For instance, in *Gobind Singh v Shanti Sarup*[51] the conditional order required a baker to demolish within 10 days an oven and chimney that emitted smoke 'injurious to the health and physical comfort of the people living or working in the proximity'. In the final order, the magistrate went beyond the conditional order and completely prohibited the baker from carrying on his trade. The Supreme Court found the final order far too broad and narrowed

---

[44] Section 290.

[45] A complaint may be made under section 190 of the Code of Criminal Procedure of 1973.

[46] A magistrate has no jurisdiction under section 133 to entertain private disputes between neighbours. For example, a flour mill that only disturbed a neighbouring family, but no other residents in the locality, constituted a private nuisance actionable in tort and not a public nuisance. *Dhareppa Ballapa Gondai v Sub-Divisional Magistrate* 1984 (2) Kar L J 444, 449–50.

[47] The order is 'conditional' because it is a preliminary order. The order may be made absolute (final) after giving the opposing party sufficient opportunity to be heard. The Kerala High Court has held that an order closing a polluting factory is illegal where no conditional order was first issued. *Vallikadar Assainar v P K Moideenkutty* 1999 Cri L J 4228.

[48] For example, in *K Ramachandra Mayya v District Magistrate* 1985 (2) Kar L J 289, the High Court approved of the magistrate's order shutting down a stone quarry, where the magistrate acted on complaints from neighbouring residents that the blasting of rocks at the quarry caused damage from flying stone chips.

[49] *Municipal Council, Ratlam v Vardhichand* AIR 1980 SC 1622.

[50] In urgent cases, a magistrate may direct the *immediate* removal of a nuisance. *Supra* note 48 at 295.

[51] AIR 1979 SC 143.

its scope to require the baker to demolish the offending oven and chimney within a month. The baker, however, was allowed to practice his trade.

Are the powers of a magistrate to deal with pollution under section 133 curtailed by the Air (Prevention and Control of Pollution) Act of 1981 or the Water (Prevention and Control of Pollution) Act of 1974? In *Nagarjuna Paper Mills Ltd v Sub-Divisional Magistrate and Divisional Officer, Sangareddy*,[52] the Andhra Pradesh High Court considered a petition from a magistrate's conditional order shutting down a paper mill that had failed to take adequate pollution control measures. The mill challenged the order, claiming that the state pollution control board had exclusive power to regulate air and water pollution. Rejecting this argument, the High Court upheld the magistrate's power to regulate pollution by restraining a public nuisance. This view was also adopted by a division bench of the Kerala High Court in *Krishna Panicker v Appukuttan Nair*,[53] overruling a contrary opinion expressed in *Tata Tea Ltd v State of Kerala*.[54]

In *Municipal Council, Ratlam v Vardhichand*, excerpted below, the Supreme Court for the first time treated an environmental problem differently from an ordinary tort or public nuisance. Environmental pollution in *Ratlam* affected a community of poor people and arose from a combination of diffuse causes: private polluters, slack and under-financed enforcement agencies, and haphazard town planning. In view of these peculiarities, the court tailored the existing public nuisance remedy to provide relief.

The judgment explicitly recognizes the impact of a deteriorating urban environment on the poor, and links the provision of basic public health facilities to both human rights and the directive principles in the Constitution. The court commends an activist judiciary to compel municipalities to provide proper sanitation and drainage, thereby enabling the poor to live with dignity.

Although the language of Justice Krishna Iyer is flowery in parts, the judgment is notable for the principles it enunciates. Notice the court's interpretation of the nature of a magistrate's power under section 133, the court's response to the municipality's plea of budgetary constraints, and the relief granted by the court.

MUNICIPAL COUNCIL, RATLAM v VARDHICHAND

AIR 1980 SC 1622

***

KRISHNA IYER, J:

The key question we have to answer is whether by affirmative action a court can compel a statutory body to carry out its duty to the community by constructing sanitation facilities at great cost and on a time-bound basis. At issue is the coming of age of that branch of public law bearing on community actions and the court's power to force public bodies under public duties to implement specific plans in response to public grievances.

[The court described conditions of fifth and stench resulting from the absence of public sanitation facilities or drains.]

The Sub-Divisional Magistrate, Ratlam, was moved to take action under S. 133 Cr PC to abate the nuisance by ordering the municipality to construct drain pipes with flow of water to wash the filth and stop the stench. The Magistrate found the facts proved, made the direction sought and scared by the prospect of prosecution under S. 188 IPC for violation of the order under S. 133 Cr PC, the municipality rushed from court to court till, at last, years

52 1987 CRI L J 2071. Also see *Harihar Polyfibers v The Sub-Divisional Magistrate* 1997 CRI L J 2731.

53 1993 (1) KER L T 771.

54 1984 KER L T 645.

after, it reached this court as the last refuge of lost causes. Had the municipal council and its executive officers spent half this litigative zeal on cleaning up the street and constructing the drains by rousing the people's sramdan resources and laying out the city's limited financial resources, the people's need might have been largely met long ago.

The Magistrate, whose activist application of S. 133 Cr PC, for the larger purpose of making the Ratlam municipal body do its duty and abate the nuisance by affirmative action, has our appreciation. [The court reproduced lengthy extracts from the Magistrate's order describing the extremely unhygienic and insanitary conditions in a locality of Ratlam and the unsuccessful efforts of tormented residents to activate the municipality.]

The Magistrate held in the end:

> 'Thus after perusing the evidence I come to this conclusion and after perusing the applications submitted by the persons residing on the New Road area from time to time to draw the attention of the non-applicants to remove all these public nuisances.'

He issued the following order which was wrongly found unjustified by the Sessions Court, but rightly upheld by the High Court:

> 'Therefore, for the health and convenience of the people residing in that particular area all the nuisance must be removed and for that the following order is hereby passed:
>
> (1) The Town Improvement Trust with the help of Municipal Council must prepare a permanent plan to make the proper flow in the said Nallah which is flowing in between Shastri Colony and New Road. Both the non-applicants must prepare the plan within six months and they must take proper action to give it a concrete form.
>
> (2) According to para 13 a few places are described which are either having the same drains and the other area is having no drain and due to this the water stinks there; so the Municipal Council and the Town Improvement Trust must construct the proper drainage system and within their own premises where there is no drain it must be constructed immediately and all work should be completed within six months.
>
> (3) The Municipal Council should construct drains from the jail to the bridge behind the southern side of the houses so that the water flowing from the septic tanks and the other water flowing outside the residential houses may be channelized and it may stop stinking and it should have a proper flow so that the water may go easily towards the main Nallah. All these drains should be constructed completely within six months by the Municipal Council.
>
> (4) The places where the pits are in existence the same should be covered with mud so that the water may not accumulate in those pits and it may not breed mosquitoes. The Municipal Council must complete this work within two months.
>
> A notice under S. 141 of the Criminal Procedure Code (Old Code) may be issued to the non-applicant Nos. 1 and 2 so that all the works may be carried out within the stipulated period. Case is hereby finalised.'

* * *

We proceed on the footing, as we indicated even when leave to appeal was sought, that the malignant facts of municipal callousness to public health and sanitation, held proved by the Magistrate, are true. What are the legal pleas to absolve the municipality from the court's directive under S. 133 Cr PC? [The court set out S. 133.]

So the guns of S. 133 go into action whenever there is public nuisance. The public power of the magistrate under the Code is a public duty to the members of the public who are victims of the nuisance, and so he shall exercise it when the jurisdictional facts are present as here.... Discretion becomes a duty when the beneficiary brings home the circumstances for its benign exercise.

There is no difficulty in locating who has the obligation to abate the public nuisance caused by the absence of primary sanitary facilities. [The court set out section 123 of the M P Municipalities Act of 1961.]

The statutory setting being thus plain, the municipality cannot extricate itself from its responsibility. Its plea is not that the facts are wrong but that the law is not right because the municipal funds being insufficient it cannot carry out the duties under S. 123 of the Act. This 'alibi' made us issue notice to the State which is now represented by counsel ... before us. The plea of the municipality that notwithstanding the public nuisance financial inability validly exonerates it from statutory liability has no juridical basis. The Criminal Procedure Code operates against statutory bodies and others regardless of the cash in their coffers, even as human rights under Part III of the Constitution have to be respected by the State regardless of budgetary provision. Likewise, S. 123 of the Act has no saving clause when the municipal council is penniless. Otherwise a profligate statutory body or pachydermic governmental agency may legally defy duties under the law by urging in self-defence a self-created bankruptcy or perverted expenditure budget. That cannot be.

Section 133 Cr PC is categoric, although reads discretionary. Judicial discretion when facts for its exercise are present, has a mandatory import. Therefore, when the Sub-Divisional Magistrate, Ratlam, has before him, information and evidence, which disclose the existence of a public nuisance and on the materials placed, he considers that such unlawful obstruction or nuisance should be removed from any public place which may be lawfully used by the public, he shall act. Thus, his judicial power shall, passing through the procedural barrel, fire upon the obstruction or nuisance, triggered by the jurisdictional facts....

A strange plea was put forward by the Municipal Council before the High Court which was justly repelled, viz., that the owners of houses had gone to that locality on their own choice with eyes open and, therefore, could not complain if human excreta was flowing, dirt was stinking, mosquitoes were multiplying and health was held hostage. A public body constituted for the principal statutory duty of ensuring sanitation and health cannot outrage the court by such an ugly plea. Luckily, no such contention was advanced before us. The request for further time for implementation of the Magistrate's order was turned down by the High Court since no specific time-limit was accepted by the Municipality for fulfilment of the directions. A doleful statement about the financial difficulties of the Municipality and the assurance that construction of drains would be taken up as soon as possible had no meaning....

In our view, what is important is to see that the worst aspects of the insanitary conditions are eliminated, not that a showy scheme beyond the means of the municipality must be undertaken and half done. From that angle we approve scheme 'C' which costs only around Rs.6 lakhs. We fix a time limit of one year for completing execution of the work according to that scheme. We further direct that the work shall begin within two months from today and the Magistrate shall inspect the progress of the work every three months broadly to be satisfied that the order is being implemented bona fide. Breaches will be visited with the penalty of S. 188, IPC.

We make the further supplementary directions which we specifically enjoin upon the municipal authority and the State Government to carry out.

1. We direct the Ratlam Municipal Council (RI) to take immediate action, within its statutory powers, to stop the effluents from the Alcohol Plant flowing into the street. The State Government also shall take action to stop the pollution. The Sub-Divisional Magistrate will also use his power under S. 133, IPC, to abate the nuisance so caused. Industries

cannot make profit at the expense of public health. Why has the Magistrate not pursued this aspect?

2. The Municipal Council shall, within six months from today, construct a sufficient number of public latrines for use by men and women separately, provide water supply and scavenging service morning and evening so as to ensure sanitation. The Health Officer of the Municipality will furnish a report, at the end of the six-monthly term, that the work has been completed. We need hardly say that the local people will be trained in using and keeping these toilets in clean condition. Conscious cooperation of the consumers is too important to be neglected by representative bodies.
3. The State Government will give special instructions to the Malaria Eradication Wing to stop mosquito breeding in Ward 12. The Sub-Divisional Magistrate will issue directions to the officer concerned to file a report before him to the effect that the work has been done in reasonable time.
4. The Municipality will not merely construct the drains but also fill up cesspools and other pits of filth and use its sanitary staff to keep the place free from accumulations of filth. After all, what it lays out on prophylactic sanitation is a gain on its hospital budget.
5. We have no hesitation in holding that if these directions are not complied with the Sub-Divisional Magistrate will prosecute the officers responsible. Indeed, this court will also consider action to punish for contempt in case of report by the Sub-Divisional Magistrate of wilful breach by any officer.

We are sure that the State Government will make available by way of loans or grants sufficient financial aid to the Ratlam Municipality to enable it to fulfil its obligations under this Order. The State will realize that Article 47 makes it a paramount principle of governance that steps are taken for the improvement of public health as amongst its primary duties. The Municipality also will slim its budget on low priority items and elitist projects to use the savings on sanitation and public health. It is not our intention that the ward which has woken up to its rights alone need be afforded these elementary facilities. We expect all the wards to be benefited without litigation. The pressure of the judicial process, expensive and dilatory, is neither necessary nor desirable if responsible bodies are responsive to duties....

NOTES AND QUESTIONS

1. The *Ratlam* judgment illustrates how an activist court can transform seemingly dull legislation into a powerful mandate to protect the environment. The judgment builds on two key interpretations. First, the court held that budgetary constraints did not absolve a municipality from performing its statutory obligation to provide sanitation facilities. Second, the court interpreted section 133 to impose a *mandatory* duty on a magistrate to remove a public nuisance *whenever* one exists. Reading these obligations together, the court supported the magistrate's order to compel the municipality to implement a sanitation scheme within a definite time frame.

Despite its vast potential, the *Ratlam* judgment remains under-used. Citizens' petitions to stir indolent municipalities into action are still rare. In another respect, however, the lead provided by *Ratlam* has been widely followed: judicial activism now characterizes the outcome of most environmental litigation.

2. In its judgment, the court condemned as an 'outrage' the municipality's plea that the affected persons came to the nuisance. Does the court's dictum also preclude a *private* respondent from raising this plea in a public nuisance case?

3. To ensure the implementation of its directions, the Supreme Court relied on a number of methods: judicial oversight, deadlines, the threat of prosecution under section 188 of the Indian Penal Code, and the threat to use its power to punish for contempt (the disobedience of a court order). But a critical weakness remained. Where were the funds to finance the sanitation scheme to come from? The judgment merely expressed the hope that the government would assist the municipality, and required the municipality to slim its budget on 'low priority items and elitist projects'. What could the court have done if the state government had declined to grant any financial aid? Could the court have ordered an appropriation of funds?

4. The primary duty of a municipality to provide sanitation may also be enforced through a writ petition and through an application to the NGT.

In *P C Cherian v State of Kerala*, excerpted below, the Kerala High Court considered whether carbon particles ('carbon black') emitted from two rubber factories amounted to an actionable public nuisance under section 133. Note the court's willingness to take judicial notice of the health effects of air pollution and the court's exercise in balancing the community interest against the interest of the workers keeping their jobs.

P C CHERIAN v STATE OF KERALA

1981 KER L T 113

Janaki Amma, J: Although the petitioners denied that their factories were responsible for the deposit of carbon black in the neighbourhood, there are documents produced which clearly make out a case of pollution at their instance. Ext. A3 in M.C. No. 4 of 1978 is a letter written by the Production Manager of the Padinjarekkara Factory to the Parish Priest, of the Veroor Catholic Church. In that letter the manager undertook to do all that was possible for the prevention of carbon black flying and invited from the priest suggestions other than those involving stoppage of work. Ext. A4 is the proceedings of a conference convened by the concerned Ministers which was attended by the representatives of the two factories meant for the stoppage of pollution due to black carbon. There is also evidence that the petitioners undertook to defray the expenses incurred by the St. Joseph's Church for removal of the carbon deposits on the walls of the Church. In the face of the above evidence the findings in the two cases that carbon black was emanating from the factories of the petitioners contaminating the atmosphere and was causing deposits of carbon in the neighbourhood do not call for interference. That the devices stated to have been adopted by the two factories to prevent black carbon from escaping into the atmosphere are grossly inadequate is also established beyond doubt.

The further question is whether there is weight in the contention that carbon has no toxic effect on human body and dissemination of carbon is not a public nuisance. It is sheer commonsense that if the atmosphere gets contaminated with carbon particles, visible or invisible there is every risk that they would get themselves deposited on the bodies, and get into the respiratory organs of the people residing in the neighbourhood. The evidence is that the particles get deposited on the wearing apparel of the people and the walls of buildings, not to mention the other umpteen articles which may get affected by the deposit. This is therefore an outstanding instance of air pollution which has become a menace to people in the industrial cities. The term air pollution according to the definition adopted by the WHO, is limited to the situations in which the outdoor ambient atmosphere contains materials in concentrations which are harmful to man and his environment. 'Air pollution has been shown to increase the incidences of emphysema, bronchitis, pneumonia and asthma. It is suspected of being an ancillary cause of lung cancer and arteriosclerosis. Air pollution obscures vision, damages buildings, destroys crops and alters weather' (See Environmental Legislation by Williams and Hurley page 34). The Supreme Court remarked in *Ratlam Municipality v Vardhichand* (AIR 1980 SC 1622):

> 'Public nuisance, because of pollutants being discharged by big factories to the detriment of the poorer sections, is a challenge to the social justice component of the rule of law.'

To hold that the deposit of carbon black in the instant cases is a public nuisance it need not necessarily be a hazard to the health of the people. The word public nuisance is not defined in the Code; but S. 2(y) of the Code states that words and expressions not defined therein but defined in the Indian Penal Code have meanings respectively assigned to them in that Code. [Section] 268 of the Indian Penal Code defines public nuisance as follows:

> 'Public nuisance: A person is guilty of a public nuisance, who does any act or is guilty of an illegal omission which causes any common injury, danger or annoyance to the public or to the people in general who dwell or occupy property in the vicinity, or which must necessarily cause injury, obstruction, danger or annoyance to persons who may have occasion to use any public right.'

Thus under the definition any act which causes annoyance to the public is a public nuisance. There is no scope for doubt that deposit of carbon black on the clothes of the residents which make them soiled, and their deposit on food articles would cause annoyance to their owners. The manner in which the work in the factories of the petitioners was being conducted amounted to a public nuisance and was also injurious to the health and physical comfort of the community.

An argument was advanced at the time of hearing that there is no evidence as to which of the two factories involved was responsible for the emanation of carbon and the court only proceeded on the footing that it was the carbon black from the two factories together that was causing nuisance. This does not appear to be correct. The court has entered separate findings in the two cases that the working of the concerned factory, viz., the service mixing in large quantities of carbon for supplying major tyre factories is injurious to the physical comfort of the community.

The argument based on the decision in *Ram Autar v State of UP* (AIR 1962 SC 1794), that the stoppage of work of the factories would deprive the workers there of their means of livelihood has no application in the cases before us because the danger that the general public has to face by the service mixing of carbon without adequate equipments to prevent dissemination of carbon outweighs the advantage in the form of jobs for a few persons and that too under threat of hazards to their own health.

We have no hesitation in holding that the Magistrate was justified in invoking his powers under S. 133 of the Code, in initiating action against the petitioners and in directing them to stop the service mixing of carbon in their factories. We, however, make it clear that it is open to the petitioners to restart the work of service mixing of carbon after introducing gadgets or equipments which would prevent dissemination of carbon black into the atmosphere. In order to avoid further trouble and a repetition of similar action against them they may choose the equipments in consultation with qualified experts in the field of environmental hygiene and to the satisfaction of the authorities concerned.

The Criminal Revision Petitions are dismissed with the above directions.

NOTES AND QUESTIONS

1. The court weighed the danger to the general public from the continued 'service mixing of carbon' against the loss of jobs for a few workers, and found that the former outweighs the latter. Is such balancing permissible under section 133? Does the Supreme Court's interpretation in *Ratlam* (that section 133 imposes a *mandatory* duty on the magistrate to abate a public nuisance), preclude such a balancing exercise?

2. Although the court held that it was not necessary to establish toxicity before restraining a public nuisance (mere annoyance to the public was enough), it went on to observe that carbon black was, indeed, injurious to public health. The court's conclusion on the toxicity of carbon black was supported, not by scientific proof, but by 'sheer common sense'. The court reasoned: (a) that carbon particles cause air pollution; (b) that air pollution has been shown to increase the incidences of emphysema, bronchitis, pneumonia and asthma and is suspected of being an ancillary cause of lung cancer and arteriosclerosis; and (c) therefore, carbon particles are hazardous to health. Is the court's reasoning flawed? It does not follow from (a) and (b) that *every* air pollutant harms health. Was judicial notice of the possible health effects of suspended carbon particles justifiable in this case?

C. THE WRIT JURISDICTION

I. SOURCE OF THE WRIT JURISDICTION

Articles 32 and 226 of the Constitution of India empower the Supreme Court and the High Courts, respectively, to issue directions or orders or writs, including writs of *habeas corpus*, *mandamus*, *prohibition*, *quo warranto* and *certiorari*. Writs of mandamus, certiorari and prohibition are generally resorted to in environmental matters.

The relative speed, simplicity and cheapness of the writ remedy have made it immensely popular with litigants. Ordinarily, the delay between the filing of a writ petition and the granting of a writ is far less than the time required to obtain a decree in a suit; and in writs there are fewer intervening proceedings between filing and judgment. The filing fee for a writ is nominal compared with the high *ad valorem* court fees[55] that must be paid in an ordinary civil suit. In addition, the expense of presenting oral evidence is eliminated as facts are set forth in the affidavits of the parties. Further, approaching the highest courts directly for a writ reduces the likelihood of prolonged litigation in subsequent appeals.

The power to issue writs has been borrowed in India from England, where the prerogative writs have been issued for centuries. Prior to the Constitution's adoption, the three High Courts at Calcutta, Madras and Bombay had the power to issue these writs under the Charter Act of 1861.[56] Other High Courts did not possess this power. The Constituent Assembly, which created India's Constitution, saw these writs as an effective means of enforcing fundamental rights, and consequently conferred on the Supreme Court and all the High Courts the power to issue these writs.[57]

The Supreme Court has interpreted Article 21, which guarantees the fundamental right to life and personal liberty, to include the right to a wholesome environment.[58] Accordingly, a litigant may assert his or her right to a healthful environment against the state, by a writ petition to either the Supreme Court or a High Court.

---

55 Fees related to the value of the suit.

56 The Indian High Courts Act of 1861 is popularly called the Charter Act. For a discussion on the source of the writ jurisdiction, see the judgment of Madon, J in *Prabodh Verma v State of Uttar Pradesh* AIR 1985 SC 167, 182.

57 H M Seervai, *Constitutional Law of India: A Critical Commentary* 1450 (Vol 2, 1993).

58 *Subhash Kumar v State of Bihar* AIR 1991 SC 420; and *Virender Gaur v State of Haryana* AIR 1995 SC 577.

II. WRITS OF MANDAMUS, PROHIBITION AND CERTIORARI

The writ powers of the Supreme Court and the High Courts under Articles 32 and 226 are not confined to the prerogative writs derived from English law but extend to 'directions or orders or *writs in the nature of* habeas corpus, mandamus, prohibition, quo warranto and certiorari'. The term 'writs in the nature of' widens the court's discretion in granting relief by releasing Indian courts from the procedural technicalities that govern the issue of these writs under English law.[59] A court may issue an order in the nature of these writs in all appropriate cases so long as it observes the broad and fundamental principles that govern such writs in English law.[60] The court may also issue directions and orders to vindicate the petitioner's rights. The court may grant declaratory relief,[61] issue an injunction or quash the impugned action without recourse to a specific writ. Indeed, a notable feature of the writ process is the court's flexibility is choosing an appropriate relief.

A court can issue a writ of mandamus to command action by a public authority when an authority is vested with power and wrongfully refuses to exercise it. A mandamus can also be issued to undo what has been done in contravention of a statute. This writ can issue against an administrative, quasi-judicial or judicial authority.[62]

An applicant seeking a mandamus must show that the duty sought to be enforced is a duty of a public nature (i.e. a duty created under the Constitution, a statute or some rule of common law) and that the duty is mandatory and not discretionary in nature. Normally a mandamus does not lie against a private individual, but it might be issued where it is proved that the individual was colluding with a public authority.[63] Before a mandamus is issued, the court must be satisfied that the petitioner had demanded justice and that the concerned authority had refused the demand.[64]

For instance, a mandamus would lie against a municipality that fails to construct sewers and drains, clean streets and clear garbage. Likewise, a state pollution control board may be compelled to take action against an industry discharging pollutants beyond the permissible level.

Rampal's case, excerpted below, illustrates the use of the writ process in securing government action to improve the urban environment. It also shows the simplicity of the writ procedure compared with the more cumbersome prosecution of a suit to enforce common law rights.

RAMPAL v STATE OF RAJASTHAN
AIR 1981 RAJ 121

ORDER: The petitioners are residents of Mundara Mohalla, situated in the town of Mandal in Bhilwara district. Their case is that in Mundara Mohalla, there is a blind lane and a common Chowk in the centre, which is surrounded by the house of the petitioners and others. The petitioner's grievance is that water of domestic use, including dirty water from the houses of the Mohalla, as also rain water has collected in the chowk and because there is no drain for the discharge of the accumulated water, there is growth of moss and insects and there is possibility of spread of epidemics. The petitioners have relied upon a letter written in

---

59 M Jain & S Jain, *Principles of Administrative Law* 513 (1986).

60 *T C Basappa v T Nagappa* AIR 1954 SC 440, 443.

61 *Kavalappara Kottarathil Kochuni v State of Madras* AIR 1959 SC 725, 732–3; *Ujjam Bai v State of Uttar Pradesh* [1963] 1 SCR 778.

62 M Jain & S Jain, *supra* note 59 at 520.

63 *Sohan Lal v Union of India* AIR 1957 SC 529, 532; *Shalini Shyam Shetty v Rajendra Shankar Patil* (2010) 8 SCC 329.

64 *Saraswati Industrial Syndicate Ltd v Union of India* AIR 1975 SC 460, 468; *D N Jeevraj v Chief Secretary, Government of Karnataka* (2016) 2 SCC 653.

this connection by the Medical and Health Officer, Government Hospital, Bhilwara, on 18 June 1979, to the Executive Officer of the Municipal Board, Mandal inviting his attention to the fact that stagnant water, which has collected in the common chowk of the Mundara Mohalla, has become the breeding place of mosquitoes and insects and may cause spread of diseases. The Medical and Health Officer in his aforesaid letter expressed the view that immediate steps should be taken for making a permanent arrangement for the disposal of such water as has collected in the chowk and which has caused a nuisance, for the residents of the area. As the Municipal Board has not cared to take any action in the matter, the petitioners have filed a writ . . . praying for a direction to the Municipal Board for removal and discharge of filthy and dirty water and the construction of proper drainage or sewers for the discharge of such water.

Section 98 of the Rajasthan Municipalities Act, 1959 . . . falls under Chapter VI which deals with the primary and secondary functions of the Municipal Boards. Amongst the primary duties enumerated in section 98 of the Act, it has been provided that the Municipal Board should make reasonable provisions for cleaning public streets, places and sewers and all spaces not being private property and removing noxious vegetation and removing filth, rubbish or other noxious and offensive matter and constructing drains, sewers, drainage works etc. [The court set out the relevant part of section 98.]

For the proper performance of the duties imposed upon the Municipal Boards under section 98 of the Act, all sewers, drains, privies, water closets, house-gullies and cesspools within the municipality have been placed under the survey and control of the Municipal Boards by the provisions of section 174 of the Act and under section 175 of the Act the Boards have been authorized to construct covered sewers and drains and make other constructions in order to carry out any drainage scheme. The Boards are also authorized to control the drainage system in respect of private houses under section 176 and the owners of houses and empty buildings and land within the municipality are enjoined to connect their sewers and drains with the municipal drains. Thus, under S. 174 to 187, extensive powers have been given to the Municipal Boards for the purpose of maintaining cleanliness within the municipal area by repairing the existing drains, directing the construction of new drains and controlling the drainage system. The Municipal Boards are thus primarily responsible for maintaining sanitation and for taking proper steps for creating and maintaining healthy conditions within the municipal area.

The Municipal Board, Mandal has not filed any reply and it has not been contended by its learned counsel that it is not the duty of the Municipal Board to remove or discharge the accumulated water and construct proper drainage system for the discharge of water accumulated in the chowk in Mundara Mohalla.

The only question, therefore, which arises for consideration in this writ petition is as to whether this Court should issue a Mandamus to the Municipal Board to construct the sewers and drains for the discharge of domestic including dirty water, as well as rain water. In *Municipal Corporation v Advance Builders (P) Ltd* (AIR 1972 SC 793) it was held by their Lordships of the Supreme Court that since development and planning is primarily for the benefit of the public, the local body was under an obligation to perform its duty in accordance with the provisions of the Act. In the present case, also, the statute imposes a duty upon the Municipal Boards and they are under a statutory obligation to perform such duties. . . . It may be pointed out that the Municipal Board has no discretion in the matter and it cannot refuse to discharge the obligations, duties and functions, which have been imposed upon it and are enumerated in section 98 as primary functions. When the statute imposes a duty, the performance and non-performance of which is not a matter of discretion, then this Court has a power to issue a Mandamus directing the local body to do what the statute requires to be done. The Municipal Board is under a statutory obligation to construct sewers and drains for the discharge of water, both domestic as well as rain, which is likely to cause public nuisance, if allowed to accumulate for a long time. There can be no doubt that if the water and filth is allowed to accumulate for a long time the place would became the breeding ground for mosquitoes, insects and is liable to become cause for spread of diseases. In these circumstances, it would be proper and reasonable in the present case if the Municipal Board is directed to perform its statutory duties in this respect.

The writ petition is, accordingly, allowed and the Municipal Board, Mandal is directed to remove the water and filth collected in the chowk in Mundara Mohalla, Mandal by the construction of proper sewers and drains, so as to remove the cause of possible nuisance in the locality, within a period three months. As the Municipal Board has not opposed the writ petition, the parties are left to bear their own costs.

NOTES AND QUESTIONS

1. Had the municipality pleaded an inability to construct the drain because of a lack of finances, should the court have refused relief?

2. Apart from a writ petition, what other legal remedies could Rampal have pursued to secure the same relief?

3. In *E Sampath Kumar v Government of Tamil Nadu*,[65] the Madras High Court held that a neighbour troubled by the excessive noise pollution and vibrations caused by electrical motors, diesel engines and generators used by a hotel could maintain a writ petition. The High Court rejected the hoteliers' plea that the proper remedy would be a civil suit. The court issued several directions to abate the nuisance and directed the authorities to periodically inspect the hotel.

The writs of certiorari and prohibition are designed to restrain public authorities from acting in excess of their authority. Certiorari is an order to an inferior court or quasi-judicial body to transmit the record of pending proceedings to the superior court for its review. Prohibition prevents a lower court or tribunal from assuming a jurisdiction which it does not possess. The expansion of the concept of natural justice and the emergence of the 'fairness' requirement, even in administrative functions, has blurred the distinction between quasi-judicial and administrative functions.[66] Certiorari and prohibition are now regarded as general remedies against an improper exercise of power by administrative as well as quasi-judicial authorities.[67]

The writs of certiorari and prohibition are issued where an authority (1) acts in excess of jurisdiction; (2) acts in violation of the rules of natural justice; (3) acts under a law which is unconstitutional; (4) commits an error apparent on the face the record; and (5) reaches factual findings that are not supported by the evidence.[68] The fundamental distinction between certiorari and prohibition is that they are issued at different stages of the proceedings. Prohibition is issued when the matter is pending before an authority. The writ prohibits the concerned authority from proceeding any further with the matter. Certiorari is issued only after the concerned authority has decided the question before it.

For example, a writ of certiorari will lie against a municipal authority that considers a builder's application and permits construction contrary to development rules such as a height restriction, or that disregards zoning requirements and wrongly sanctions an office building in an area reserved for a garden. Certiorari would also lie against a state pollution control board

---

[65] 1998 AIHC 4498.
[66] *A K Kraipak v Union of India* AIR 1970 SC 150, 154.
[67] M Jain & S Jain, *supra* note 59 at 525.
[68] *Id.*

that considers the application of an industry and wrongly permits it to discharge effluents beyond prescribed levels.

III. LIMITATIONS ON THE WRIT JURISDICTION

Although Articles 32 and 226 give the courts wide latitude to grant relief, the courts have imposed restraints on their own writ power. These pertain to the petitioner's standing to institute proceedings (*locus standi*), the exhaustion of alternative remedies, the principle of *res judicata*, and the time within which a writ may be sought (*laches*).

Neither Article 32 nor Article 226 describes who may seek redress from the courts. The rules of *locus standi* in relation to writs are judicial policies. Traditionally, *locus standi* was restrictive: only an 'aggrieved person' could petition the courts for a writ of certiorari, prohibition or mandamus. Until the early 1980s, only the person directly affected by the administrative action in question could challenge it.[69] According to this view, a person could assert a public right or interest only by showing that he or she had suffered an injury not suffered by others. During the 1980s, the Supreme Court recognized that where a public wrong or public injury is caused by the state, any member of the public acting in good faith can maintain an action for redress.[70] In particular, any member of the public may approach the court on behalf of a person or persons who have suffered a legal wrong and are unable themselves to petition the court by reason of poverty, disability, or their socially or economically disadvantaged position.[71] More than any other factor, the liberalization of the doctrine of standing in writ petitions has been responsible for the rapid growth in public interest litigation in India, and has provided easy access to the higher courts.

When a fundamental right, including the right to a wholesome environment, has been violated, relief through Articles 32 and 226 is fully appropriate. Where no fundamental right is involved, a High Court will decline to exercise its jurisdiction if an equally effective remedy is available and has not been used. The writ is an extraordinary remedy, and courts are reluctant to encourage petitioners who circumvent prescribed statutory procedure for correcting administrative action.[72] This rule of exhaustion of remedies can be waived by a court in a suitable case where, for instance, the impugned action violates the principles of natural justice, or where a government authority has exceeded its jurisdiction. The issue of an alternative remedy is very likely to arise in environment writs, since the National Green Tribunal Act of 2010 creates an alternative forum for dispute resolution.[73]

A petitioner must pursue her remedy within a reasonable time of the cause of action arising, and a writ petition may be rejected on the ground of inordinate delay. This doctrine of *laches* has even been applied to petitions asserting a breach of a fundamental right, although the courts may be more indulgent when a fundamental right is involved and where the impugned action is manifestly erroneous or unauthorized. Where no prejudice is caused to the other party from the petitioner's lack of diligence, the courts generally measure the delay by referring to the statutory limitation for the filing of similar suits prescribed by the Limitation Act of 1963.

---

69 *Calcutta Gas Company (Prop) Ltd v State of West Bengal* AIR 1962 SC 1044, 1047.

70 *People's Union for Democratic Rights v Union of India* AIR 1982 SC 1473, 1483.

71 *Id.*

72 E.g., the High Court are reluctant to entertain disputes arising under the Income Tax Act of 1961, as the statute creates a hierarchy of authorities from which a person may obtain redress.

73 By 'environment writs' we mean petitions to abate pollution or prevent environmental degradation. Note that there remain areas outside the NGT's jurisdiction, illustratively, wildlife, where a writ petition will not face the alternative remedy hurdle.

The doctrine of *laches* is often relaxed in environmental actions brought in the public interest. The court is usually indulgent, being aware of the financial constraints and obstacles that environmentalists face in obtaining authentic information and documentation.

The principle of *res judicata* has been applied to writ proceedings by judicial interpretation. Once a writ petition is rejected on its merits by the Supreme Court or a High Court, a subsequent writ petition cannot be moved in the same court on the same cause of action. Normally, *res judicata* also precludes a petition to the Supreme Court alleging the violation of a fundamental right once the same petition has been dismissed on its merits by a High Court.[74]

IV. ARTICLES 32 AND 226

The Supreme Court's jurisdiction under Article 32 is more limited than the jurisdiction of the High Court under Article 226. Article 32 guarantees the right to seek the Supreme Court's enforcement of fundamental rights. Moreover, Article 32 is itself a fundamental right and, therefore, cannot be abridged by legislation. An indispensable condition for invoking the Supreme Court's jurisdiction under Article 32 is the violation of a fundamental right conferred in Part III of the Constitution. Thus, an illegal government action that does not infringe a fundamental right cannot be challenged in writ proceedings under Article 32. In contrast, the writ jurisdiction of the High Courts under Article 226 may be invoked not only for the enforcement of a fundamental right but for 'any other purpose' as well. Ordinary legal rights may also be asserted through a writ petition in the High Court. For instance, although the freedom of trade, commerce and intercourse embodied in Article 301 is not a fundamental right and, therefore, cannot be enforced in a petition under Article 32,[75] such a right may be enforced in a High Court under Article 226. Invoking the High Court writ jurisdiction is the most popular method to obtain judicial review of administrative action. Article 226 cannot be curtailed by legislation, since it is a constitutional provision.

Thus, the Supreme Court and the High Courts have concurrent jurisdictions for the enforcement of fundamental rights. A person complaining of an infringement of fundamental rights may seek redress in either forum. As noted earlier, if the High Court is approached first, and the petition for relief is dismissed on its merits, the principle of *res judicata* will preclude a further petition to the Supreme Court under Article 32. The petitioner may, however, appeal to the Supreme Court under Article 133 or obtain special leave to appeal under Article 136.

Financial and tactical considerations influence the choice between the Supreme Court and a High Court for an environmental writ petition. Typically, litigating in the Supreme Court is more expensive because of higher lawyers' fees and travel costs. Nevertheless, a petition challenging a programme or project which affects more than one state, such as a dam over a long river, should be moved in the Supreme Court. Ordinarily, High Court judges are reluctant to pass orders which might disrupt planning and investment outside their jurisdiction.[76] Supreme Court judges are more likely to examine the issue from a national perspective and pass orders affecting several states. Similarly, the Supreme Court is more likely to examine a project involving large investments, or connected with important government policy, such as

---

74 *Daryao v State of UP* AIR 1961 SC 1457, 1465, 1466.

75 *Ram Chandra Palai v State of Orissa* AIR 1956 SC 298, 305.

76 Normally, a writ issued by a High Court cannot run beyond its territorial jurisdiction. Nevertheless, a writ issued in one state can indirectly affect neighbouring states. For example, an injunction restraining development plans on a river in one state could affect development activities in other states through which the river flows.

the location of a nuclear power station. High Court judges tend to be more deferential to the legislature and the executive in such matters.

The crowding of the Supreme Court docket by a spate of environmental public interest litigation prompted the court to issue a notice to bar associations across the country, seeking their response on how to check the tide of petitions filed under Article 32.[77] In the *CRZ Notification* case,[78] the Supreme Court offered a partial solution to the problem: since the High Courts were better placed to understand local conditions and the impact of environmental law violations, they ought to tackle issues which arise or pertain to the geographical areas within their respective states. Before the NGT was established, the Supreme Court continued to entertain fresh public interest litigation under Article 32 where the issue involved had national implications or required central monitoring such as the protection of forests[79] and the formulation of national guidelines for collection and management of municipal solid waste (garbage).[80]

Finally, the nature of court orders in public interest litigation depends on the personality of the judge. The decision whether to petition under Article 32 or 226 is sometimes made after comparing the inclinations of the judges of the Supreme Court and the High Court who are likely to consider the petition.

V. JUDICIAL REVIEW AND SPECIAL CONSIDERATIONS

The scope of judicial review in environmental writ petitions was explained by the Supreme Court in the *Calcutta Taj Hotel* case,[81] where a group of citizens challenged the location of a hotel on the ground that the construction would interfere with the flight path of migratory birds. After referring to the constitutional provisions relating to environment, the court outlined the scope of judicial review thus:

> The least that the court may do is to examine whether appropriate considerations are borne in mind and irrelevancies excluded. In appropriate cases the court may go further but how much further must depend on the circumstances of the case. The court may always give necessary directions. However, the court will not attempt to nicely balance relevant considerations. When the question involved the nice balancing of relevant considerations, the court may feel justified in resigning itself to acceptance of the decision of the concerned authorities.

Likewise, in a challenge directed against the location of a thermal power station in the horticulture-rich Dahanu region on the coast of Maharashtra, the Supreme Court declined to interfere after holding that the court's role was restricted to examining whether the government had taken into account all relevant aspects and was not influenced by extraneous material in reaching its final decision.[82]

The broad language of Articles 32 and 226 has enabled the courts to fashion relief and pass orders consistent with their own assessment of the public interest and principles of equity. In a petition under Article 226, the High Court has jurisdiction over issues of both fact and law; but ordinarily such a petition is based on facts established by affidavit. A High Court's

---

77 *Howrah Ganatantrik Nagarik Samity v State of West Bengal* 1995 (5) SCALE 224.

78 *Indian Council for Enviro-Legal Action v Union of India* (1996) 5 SCC 281, 301.

79 *T N Godavarman Thirumulpad v Union of India* AIR 1997 SC 1228; (2008) 2 SCC 222; (2016) 13 SCC 586; and *Samaj Parivartana Samudaya v State of Karnataka* (2013) 8 SCC 154.

80 *Almitra Patel v Union of India* AIR 1998 SC 993.

81 *Sachidanand Pandey v State of West Bengal* AIR 1987 SC 1109, 1115.

82 *Dahanu Taluka Environment Protection Group v Bombay Suburban Electricity Supply Company Ltd* (1991) 2 SCC 539, 541. Also see *Tehri Bandh Virodhi Sangarsh Samiti v State of Uttar Pradesh* (1992) Supp (1) SCC 44; and *Dr Shivrao Shantaram Wagle v Union of India* AIR 1988 SC 952.

reluctance to receive evidence in an Article 226 proceeding is a rule of practice and not of jurisdiction.

In environmental disputes that involve complicated questions of fact to be resolved after recording evidence, approaching the NGT is advisable. For example, if pollution injures health, a complaint to the NGT for damages is appropriate since medical evidence and evidence to establish causation would have to be adduced.[83]

The Supreme Court may not refuse to entertain a petition under Article 32 merely because it involves disputed questions of fact.[84] A writ court wishing to inquire into a disputed question of fact has the inherent power to appoint a commission to adduce evidence on its behalf. In several public interest cases, before the establishment of the NGT, the Supreme Court and the High Courts have appointed fact-finding commissions to investigate the petition's allegations. For example, in *L K Koolwal v State of Rajasthan*[85] a citizen of Jaipur petitioned the Rajasthan High Court for a mandamus, directing the Jaipur Municipal Council to clean certain areas of the city. The court appointed a commissioner to inspect the areas, and to report on the nature and extent of the problem. On the basis of the commissioner's report, the court issued directions to clean the designated areas.

There is a large backlog of cases in most High Courts. In environmental cases, such delays defeat the purpose of the writ petition unless appropriate interim orders are obtained at the admission stage. The interim order is usually an injunction against, or a direction to, an· authority. Long delays in obtaining judgment highlight the importance of effective argument at the admission stage, where the crucial interim orders are issued.

An innovation in public interest litigation that has helped overcome judicial delays is the notion of a continuing mandamus. This technique involves securing compliance through periodic 'interim' directions. Here, the court does not formally admit the petition, but prods the recalcitrant agency to perform its duty within a time frame. The case is posted every few months to monitor the agency's performance and for further 'interim' directions.

VI. WRIT JURISDICTION *VIS-À-VIS* THE NGT'S POWERS

Until the National Green Tribunal Act was brought into force on 18 October 2010, most major environmental disputes were adjudicated by the High Courts and the Supreme Court in their writ jurisdictions. Frequently, environmental cases involve policy choices where courts lack expertise. How should a writ court approach an environmental case with policy dimensions? In the following short excerpt from the *Lafarge* case,[86] the Supreme Court outlined the parameters of judicial review. Here, the court was considering whether to permit a cement manufacturer to resume operating its limestone mine although the mine had commenced working without permission to divert forest land in terms of the Forest (Conservation) Act of 1980.

LAFARGE UMIAM MINING (P) LTD v UNION OF INDIA
(2011) 7 SCC 338

S H Kapadia, C J:

* * *

The time has come for us to apply the constitutional 'doctrine of proportionality' to the matters concerning environment as a part of the process of judicial review in contradistinction

[83] A writ is also inappropriate in such a case because damages are not normally awarded under Articles 32 and 226.

[84] *Kavalappara Kottarathil Kochuni v State of Madras* AIR 1959 SC 725, 734.

[85] AIR 1988 Raj 2.

[86] The Forests chapter contains a longer excerpt and analysis of this judgment.

to merit review. It cannot be gainsaid that utilisation of the environment and its natural resources has to be in a way that is consistent with principles of sustainable development and intergenerational equity, but balancing of these equities may entail policy choices. In the circumstances, barring exceptions, decisions relating to utilisation of natural resources have to be tested on the anvil of the well-recognised principles of judicial review. Have all the relevant factors been taken into account? Have any extraneous factors influenced the decision? Is the decision strictly in accordance with the legislative policy underlying the law (if any) that governs the field? Is the decision consistent with the principles of sustainable development in the sense that has the decision-maker taken into account the said principle and, on the basis of relevant considerations, arrived at a balanced decision? Thus, the court should review the decision-making process to ensure that the decision of MoEF is fair and fully informed, based on the correct principles, and free from any bias or restraint. Once this is ensured, then the doctrine of 'margin of appreciation' in favour of the decision-maker would come into play. Our above view is further strengthened by the decision of the Court of Appeal in *R v Chester City Council* [(2011) 1 All ER 476, paras 14 to 16].

Accordingly, this matter stands disposed of keeping in mind various facets of the word 'environment', the inputs provided by the village durbar of Nongtrai (including their understanding of the word 'forest' and the balance between environment and economic sustainability), their participation in the decision-making process, the topography and connectivity of the site to Shillong, the letter dated 11-5-2007 of the Principal Chief Conservator of Forests and the report of Shri B N Jha dated 5-4-2010 (HPC) (each one of which refers to economic welfare of the tribals of Village Nongtrai), the polluter pays principle and the intergenerational equity (including the history of limestone mining in the area from 1858 and the prevalent social and customary rights of the natives and tribals). The word 'development' is a relative term. One cannot assume that the tribals are not aware of principles of conservation of forest. In the present case, we are satisfied that limestone mining has been going on for centuries in the area and that it is an activity which is intertwined with the culture and the unique landholding and tenure system of Nongtrai Village. On the facts of this case, we are satisfied with the due diligence exercise undertaken by MoEF in the matter of forest diversion. Thus, our order herein is confined to the facts of this case....

NOTES AND QUESTIONS

1. The National Green Tribunal (NGT) constituted under the National Green Tribunal Act of 2010 exercises original jurisdiction to hear environmental complaints[87] as well as appellate jurisdiction, *inter alia*, from orders granting environmental clearance.[88] What is the standard of review that the NGT should apply when hearing appeals? The NGT comprises judicial as well as technical members. Should they look into all issues of fact and law afresh as would an appellate court? Or should the standard of appellate review be closer to the formulation by the Supreme Court excerpted above?

2. In the *Goa Airport* case,[89] the Supreme Court considered *Lafarge* and held that the NGT with its expertise was equipped to carry out a merits review. The analysis by the NGT in that case was contained in a single paragraph where it deferred to the Expert Appraisal

[87] Sections 14 and 15.
[88] Section 16.
[89] *Hanuman Laxman Aroskar v Union of India* (2019) 15 SCC 401.

Committee (EAC)[90] and merely recorded its satisfaction that the EAC had looked into all issues. Reversing the order of the NGT, the court held:

> The failure of process in the present case has been compounded by the absence of a merits review by the NGT.... The NGT as an adjudicatory body failed to exercise the jurisdiction entrusted to it under section 16(h) read with section 20 of the NGT Act 2010 by merely deferring to the decision to recommend and grant an EC.

3. A project or activity may have diverse environmental impacts affecting different facets of the environment. For example, a proposed dam may impact forests, wildlife and fisheries. The impact assessment agency at the stage of granting environmental clearance receives inputs from technical experts in several environmental fields. However, the technical members serving on the NGT typically have specialized knowledge in one field. Illustratively, the technical member's expertise may lie in the study of fish. Is a bench of NGT with a generalist judicial member and a specialist in a single field equipped to evaluate and overturn an environmental clearance granted after a multidisciplinary assessment? Does this call for a larger panel of experts to sit on the NGT bench and not just one expert with one judicial member? Remember, section 4(2) of the NGT Act enables a chairperson to invite one or more specialists to assist the Tribunal in particular cases.

D. STATUTORY REMEDIES

Compared to tort actions and writs, recourse to statutory remedies in environmental cases is a recent development. As we saw in the last chapter, the establishment of the National Green Tribunal in 2010 has provided a specialized expert forum to adjudicate environmental disputes. Today, the NGT is by far the most popular option for securing access to environmental justice. Supplementing the previous chapter, we examine the procedures followed in the NGT. However, before doing so we carry a short excerpt from a comment by Gitanjali Gill. The author wonders if the Tribunal's early success in staking out its domain invited a blowback from entrenched interests including a pro-business, market-oriented government anxious to push economic growth.

GITANJALI NAIN GILL; MAPPING THE POWER STRUGGLES OF THE NATIONAL GREEN TRIBUNAL OF INDIA: THE RISE AND FALL?
7 Asian Journal of Law and Society 85 (2020)*

In addition, the NGT adopted an accountability-focused approach whereby a diverse set of actors including governmental and local authorities, companies, and multinational corporations were restrained in compromising human welfare and the ecology. Importantly, in its decisions, the NGT identified the MoEF and related regulatory agencies as demonstrating indifference, *ultra vires*, or negligence in the exercise of their responsibilities. In *Jai Singh v Union of India*, the NGT identified failure of government and regulatory authorities in preventing and controlling pollution arising from illegal and unauthorized mining, transportation, and running of screening plants and stone crushers. The tribunal stated:

> the activity must be brought within the control of legal and regulatory regime. The concerned authorities of the Government and Boards should not only realise their

[90] The EAC was constituted under the Environmental Impact Assessment notification of 2006.

* Gitanjali Nain Gill, *Mapping the Power Struggles of the National Green Tribunal of India: The Rise and Fall?* 7 Asian Jr Of Law And Society 85 (2020), https://www.cambridge.org/core/journals/asian-journal-of-law-and-society/article/mapping-the-power-struggles-of-the-national-green-tribunal-of-india-the-rise-and-fall/CB60FE6258D273938062A5898BD997B7, accessed 22 July 2021.

responsibility and statutory obligation but should ensure that there is no unregulated exploitation of the natural resources and degradation to the environment. Respondents, including the State Government, the Boards, MoEF and other concerned authorities have permitted such activity despite orders of the Hon'ble Supreme Court of India, the High Courts and the Tribunal. There is definite evidence on record to show that illegal mining has continued.... Merely denying the authenticity of the photos, videos and other documentary evidences on the pretext that they were doctored would not amount to discharge of the onus placed upon the respondents.

Frequently, the MoEF has been subjected to severe criticism by the NGT for failing to observe its own procedural rules, such as the improper granting of licences without prior environment impact assessments (EIAs) being completed or appropriately conducted. In India, there have been serious failures regarding cumulative environment impact assessment studies, rendering this crucial process meaningless. For example, in *Krishi Vigyan Arogya Sanstha v MoEF*, the tribunal cancelled the grant of environmental clearance for a coal-based thermal-power project in the absence of a proper cumulative environmental impact assessment (CEIA). No scientific assessments were done in relation to expected excess cardiovascular and respiratory mortality, children's asthma, and respiratory dysfunction attributable to the exposure to the air pollutants from the plant, the impact on the water bodies and its impact on aquatic life, and the effect of nuclear radiation in and around the plant....

The tribunal has been prepared to call senior civil servants to the court having heard often inappropriate or implausible explanations from the MoEF and related regulatory authorities' decisions including union and state governments. For example, the NGT stated:

Directions issued by us have not been complied. Though the counsel for MoEF submits that report has been filed which we notice, least we could say about that it is misleading and is not in terms of our direction. The affidavit as directed has not been filed. We direct presence of deponent in the affidavit, namely, ... Director, MoEF before the Tribunal on the next date of hearing.

On occasions, senior civil servants have been told that they face a term of 'state hospitality' (jail) for statements bordering on contempt. Indeed, in *Sudeip Shrivastava v State of Chhattisgarh*, the tribunal took the bold, provocative step of criticizing the Minister of State for Environment and Forest and the MoEF for acting arbitrarily and ignoring relevant material issues that would have contributed to a holistic appraisal of the environmental problem....

In addition, the recent development of non-filling bench membership, reluctance to authorize appropriate staff, infrastructure, and resource support by the MoEF bears testimony to the fact that the government wants to restrict the activities of the NGT. Seventy percent of the bench positions are currently vacant. This is a systematic way of dismantling the institution. The NGT Act 2010 states that the minimum number of full-time judicial and expert members will not be less than ten, with a maximum of 20. At present, the NGT has five bench members (three judicial and two technical experts) for the principal bench in Delhi. On 28 March 2018, the Supreme Court appointed Justice Jawad Rahim as the Acting Chairperson of the NGT because of the petition filed by the NGT Bar Association. The regional benches (Bhopal, Chennai, Pune and Kolkata) have no bench members and thus are dormant. The Supreme Court sought an explanation from the central government about the non-filling of vacancies in the NGT. Shocked by the crisis, the Delhi High Court recently asked the centre whether it 'planned to wind up the NGT?' Instead of filling the vacant positions, the MoEF on 1 December 2017 issued a notification empowering the NGT chairperson to constitute single-member benches. The Supreme Court, as a driving force, on 31 January 2018, held the ministry's notification approving the constitution of NGT single-judge benches to be *ultra vires* the NGT Act 2010. Nevertheless, there is evidence of strong 'restraining forces' seeking to destabilize the NGT....

> Speaking truth to power can be perilous, as the NGT judges, chairman, lawyers, and litigants have discovered. The creation of a tribunal that seeks to change the face of environmental jurisprudence by providing access to justice for all has created a powerful group of 'restraining forces.' The MoEF, state governments, and various environmental statutory bodies and their officers are unaccustomed to being questioned in a probing, informed, and systematic manner or have their decisions scathingly challenged or overturned in a public forum. Previously, these authorities enjoyed both an official and an unofficial decision- making licence power directly associated with various expert committees, boards, and officials, as well as the minister. The result was often arbitrary approval of projects without undertaking the proper environmental and social-impact assessments and disturbingly often in violation of pertinent laws and rules. Additionally, some High Courts along with the MoEF went so far as to challenge the authority of the tribunal to exercise *suo moto* and judicial review powers. The tribunal's constant position of decisions based on the principle of sustainable development and the enforcement of the rules upholding the protection of the environment has proven to be embarrassing to those committed to a fast-track economic development strategy.... Given the current and alarming number of vacancies on the NGT benches resulting in the *de facto* operational closure of the regional benches, could [this be the] fate planned for the NGT: death by 1000 cuts?

How does the National Green Tribunal do business? Every application to the NGT in its original or appellate jurisdiction is required to be made in a form prescribed under rules and must be accompanied by such documents and fees as are prescribed.[91] The Tribunal is required to provide an opportunity to the parties and deal with the case 'as expeditiously as possible and endeavour' to decide the matter finally within six months from the date of filing.[92]

The NGT regulates its own procedure,[93] guided by the principles of natural justice.[94] While not bound by strict rules of evidence in terms of the Indian Evidence Act of 1872,[95] the NGT may summon witnesses, require discovery and production of documents, receive evidence on affidavits and issue commissions for examining witnesses or documents.[96] The Tribunal is specifically empowered to issue temporary[97] and permanent injunctions[98] as well as to review its decisions.[99]

The Tribunal sits in benches or panels who decide by majority. Where the opinion of members is equally divided, the chairperson casts the deciding vote.[100] The Tribunal may 'make such order as to costs, as it may consider necessary'.[101] Where a claim is not maintainable, false or vexatious, the Tribunal may award costs against the complainant or appellant and factor in 'lost benefits due to any interim injunction'.[102] Where compensation or relief is ordered to be paid on the ground of any damage to the environment, such amount is require to be remitted to the Environmental Relief Fund established under section 7A of the Public

---

91 Section 18(1), National Green Tribunal Act of 2010.
92 Section 18(3).
93 Section 19(2).
94 Section 19(1).
95 Section 19(3).
96 Section 19(4).
97 Section 19(4)(i).
98 Section 19(4)(j).
99 Section 19(4)(f).
100 Section 21.
101 Section 23(1).
102 Section 23(2).

Liability Insurance Act of 1991.[103] The amount so credited is required to be utilized for the purposes relating to environment as a prescribed by the rules.[104]

An order of the NGT is executable by the Tribunal itself as if it were a decree of a civil court.[105] The failure to comply with any award or decision of the Tribunal is punishable with imprisonment for a term which may extend to three years or with a fine which may extend to Rs. 10 crores or with both. In aggravated circumstances where the failure or contravention continues, an additional fine of Rs. 25,000 for every day may be imposed on the person. In the case of companies, the fine may extend to Rs. 25 crores and the additional fine for default may go up to Rs. 1 lakh per day.

In exercise of its power to frame rules,[106] the Central Government has issued the National Green Tribunal (Practices and Procedure) Rules of 2011. The chairperson is empowered to constitute a bench of two or more members consisting of at least one judicial member and one expert member.[107] Statutory forms appended to the rules set out the format for original applications as well as appeals. Where an application or appeal seeks compensation, it must be accompanied by a fee equivalent to 1% of the amount of compensation claimed, subject to a minimum of Rs. 1,000.[108]

NOTES

1. The National Green Tribunal may be seen as part of a global trend to establish forums to advance governance and promote the environmental Rule of Law. The United Nations 2020 Agenda for Sustainable Development and the Sustainable Development Goals envisage building effective, accountable and inclusive institutions to provide access to justice. The twenty-first century has seen global proliferation of specialized courts and tribunals for adjudicating environmental disputes. By 2016 there were over 1,200 environmental courts and tribunals in at least 44 countries at the national, provincial and municipal levels.[109]

2. Underscoring the importance of institution building based on his experience as the Chief Judge of the Land and Environment Court of New South Wales, Justice Preston highlights several features of a credible environment tribunal: (a) the business of the Tribunal must promote the Rule of Law; (b) the Tribunal should be independent from other branches of government and impartial; (c) the adjudicative procedures adopted should be fair and open to the public; (d) to ensure conformity to the Rule of Law, the Tribunal should have supervisory jurisdiction to review both parliamentary and subordinate legislation as well as executive action; and (e) the Tribunal should be easily accessible to citizens.[110]

3. Apart from the NGT Act, there are certain rarely used statutory remedies. Until the enactment of the Environment (Protection) Act of 1986 (EPA), the power to prosecute under

---

103 Section 24(1).
104 Section 24(2).
105 Section 25.
106 Section 35.
107 Rules 3(1) & 5(1).
108 Rule 12(1).
109 George Pring & Catherine Pring, *Environmental Courts & Tribunals: A Guide for Policy Makers* United Nations Environment Programme (2016), https://wedocs.unep.org/handle/20.500.11822/10001, accessed 22 July 2021.
110 Brian J Preston, *The Role of Environmental Courts and Tribunals in Promoting the Rule of Law and Ensuring Equal Access to Justice for All*, 29 Envir Law & Mngm 72 (2017).

Indian environmental laws belonged exclusively to the government. Citizens had no direct statutory remedy against a polluter who, for example, discharged an effluent beyond the permissible limit. Section 19 of the EPA brought about a change. Under this section, a citizen may prosecute an offender by a complaint to a magistrate. Prior to complaining, however, he or she must give the government 60 days' notice of his or her intention to complain. This notice is intended to alert the government to the offence so that it may take appropriate remedial action on its own.

4. Similar provisions allowing citizen participation in the enforcement of pollution laws are now found in section 43 of the Air Act as amended in 1987 and in section 49 of the Water Act as amended in 1988. Significantly, both amended sections also require pollution control boards to disclose relevant internal reports to a citizen seeking to prosecute a polluter. The ease of the NGT procedure and the willingness of judges to entertain public interest litigation have led to the neglect of the private prosecution machinery. Private prosecutions entail adherence to strict rules of evidence. Besides, those seeking to launch a private prosecution are discouraged by the sampling requirements under the pollution control laws which confer the power to draw the effluent samples on government officials exclusively.

Bengaluru, an economic engine, is renowned for its information technology industry. Until its transformation into a metropolis, the city was a 'Garden city' with 262 water bodies in 1961. Apart from lakes, there were a large number of *rajakaluves* (storm water drains) which over time were encroached upon or filled up, altering the natural hydrology. Mantri Techzone and Core Mind Software (referred to as respondent Nos. 9 and 10 in the judgment excerpted shortly) secured permissions for establishing large software technology parks with ancillary facilities for commercial and residential buildings as well as a hotel and multi-level car parks.

Forward Foundation approached the NGT complaining that these projects involved encroaching upon two *rajakaluves* and would have a deleterious impact on Bellandur Lake and Agara Lake. According to the Foundation, the permissions secured were based on concealment of important information. The developers resisted the application on several counts. Amongst them, the Foundation had not challenged the planning permissions or the environmental clearance; in any case such a challenge was time barred on the date of the application, since it was beyond six months from the cause of action in terms of section 14(3); the projects were at a considerable distance from the lakes; the projects conformed to the city development plans; and there was no environmental damage suffered.

By an interim order, the Tribunal constituted a seven-member Expert Committee with a wide remit. The committee was asked to specifically report on whether the projects encroached upon or were constructed on wetlands and *rajakaluves* and if so to suggest remedial measures to restore the ecology of the area. Granting three months to the committee to submit its report, the NGT declined an interim injunction. Nevertheless, it required substantial deposits of Rs. 117.35 crores and Rs. 22.5 crores from Mantri and Core Mind. The Supreme Court declined to interfere in the interlocutory order but permitted the developers to go back to the NGT and seek recall of the interim order requiring payment of environmental compensation.

In its final judgment, the NGT declared no-development buffer zones around *rajakulaves*, water bodies and wetlands. Mantri and Core Mind were directed to remove all the offending constructions that were within the buffer area. As regards the environmental compensation, the amount required to be paid by Mantri was maintained and Core Mind's liability was reduced to Rs. 13.5 crores since it had not carried out construction activity and the remedial measures could be effected more easily.

The excerpt from the Supreme Court decision focuses on the appeals filed by the two developers. Notice the court's discussion on (a) the scope of a statutory appeal filed before the Supreme Court under section 22 of the NGT Act; (b) the interplay between sections 14, 15 and 18; (c) the distinct periods of limitation; and (d) the effect of section 33 of the Act.

MANTRI TECHZONE PVT LTD v FORWARD FOUNDATION

(2019) 18 SCC 494

S Abdul Nazeer, J:

***

It is settled that there is no vested right of appeal unless the statute so provides. Further, if a statute provides for a condition subject to which the appropriate Appellate Court can exercise jurisdiction, the Court is under an obligation to satisfy itself whether the condition prescribed is fulfilled. Exercise of appellate jurisdiction without the fulfilment of statutory mandate would be without jurisdiction. Therefore, the right of appeal provided under section 22 is to be read subject to the conditions provided therein.

Section 22 provides for an appeal to the Supreme Court on the grounds specified in section 100 of the Code of Civil Procedure, 1908 (CPC). Under section 100 CPC, an appeal can be filed only on the ground that the case involves a substantial question of law as may be framed by the Appellate Court. The scope of appeal under section 22, therefore, is restricted to substantial question of law arising from the judgment of the Tribunal. The test to determine whether the question is substantial question of law or not was laid down by a Constitution Bench of this Court in *Sir Chunilal V Mehta and Sons, Ltd v Century Spinning and Manufacturing Co Ltd* 1962 Supp (3) SCR 549. This Court has laid down the test as under:

> 'The proper test for determining whether a question of law raised in the case is substantial would, in our opinion, be whether it is of general public importance or whether it directly and substantially affects the rights of the parties and if so whether it is either an open question in the sense that it is not finally settled by this Court or by the Privy Council or by the Federal Court or is not free from difficulty or calls for discussion of alternative views. If the question is settled by the highest court or the general principles to be applied in determining the question are well settled and there is a mere question of applying those principles or that the plea raised is palpably absurd the question would not be a substantial question of law.'

It is equally settled that merely because the remedy of appeal is provided against the decision of the Tribunal on a substantial question of law alone, that does not *ipso facto* permit the appellants to agitate their appeal to seek re-appreciation of the factual matrix of the entire matter. The appellants cannot seek to re-argue their entire case to seek wholesale re-appreciation of evidence and the factual matrix that has been considered by the Tribunal is *ex facie* impermissible under section 22. There cannot be fresh appreciation or re-appreciation of facts and evidence in a statutory appeal under this provision....

[T]he Tribunal has special jurisdiction for enforcement of environmental rights. The jurisdiction of the Tribunal is provided under sections 14, 15 and 16 of the Act. Section 14 provides the jurisdiction over all civil cases where a substantial question relating to environment (including enforcement of any legal right relating to environment) is involved. However, such question should arise out of implementation of the enactments specified in Schedule I.

The Tribunal has also jurisdiction under section 15(1)(a) of the Act to provide relief and compensation to the victims of pollution and other environmental damage arising under the enactments specified in Schedule I. Further, under section 15(1)(b) and 15(1)(c) the Tribunal can provide for restitution of property damaged and for restitution of the environment for such area or areas as the Tribunal may think fit. It is noteworthy that section 15(1)(b) & (c) have not been made relatable to Schedule I enactments of the Act. Rightly so, this grants a glimpse into the wide range of powers that the Tribunal has been cloaked with respect to restoration of the environment.

Section 15(1)(c) of the Act is an entire island of power and jurisdiction read with section 20 of the Act. The principles of sustainable development, precautionary principle and polluter pays, propounded by this Court by way of multiple judicial pronouncements, have now been embedded as a bedrock of environmental jurisprudence under the NGT Act. Therefore, wherever the environment and ecology are being compromised and jeopardized, the Tribunal can apply section 20 for taking restorative measures in the interest of the environment....

Section 15 of the Act provides power & jurisdiction, independent of section 14 thereof. Further, section 14(3) juxtaposed with section 15(3) of the Act, are separate provisions for filing distinct applications before the Tribunal with distinct periods of limitation, thereby amply demonstrating that jurisdiction of the Tribunal flows from these Sections (i.e. sections 14 and 15 of the Act) independently. The limitation provided in section 14 is a period of 6 months from the date on which the cause of action first arose and whereas in section 15 it is 5 years. Therefore, the legislative intent is clear to keep section 14 and 15 as self contained jurisdictions.

Further, section 18 of the Act recognizes the right to file applications each under sections 14 as well as 15. Therefore, it cannot be argued that section 14 provides jurisdiction to the Tribunal while section 15 merely supplements the same with powers. As stated *supra*, the typical nature of the Tribunal, its breadth of powers as provided under the statutory provisions of the Act as well as the Scheduled enactments, cumulatively, leaves no manner of doubt that the only tenable interpretation to these provisions would be to read the provisions broadly in favour of cloaking the Tribunal with effective authority. An interpretation that is in favour of conferring jurisdiction should be preferred rather than one taking away jurisdiction.

Section 33 of the Act provides an overriding effect to the provisions of the Act over anything inconsistent contained in any other law or in any instrument having effect by virtue of law other than this Act. This gives the Tribunal overriding powers over anything inconsistent contained in the KIAD Act, Planning Act, Karnataka Municipal Corporations Act, 1976; and the Revised Master Plan of Bengaluru, 2015 (RMP). A Central legislation enacted under Entry 13 of List I Schedule VII of the Constitution of India will have the overriding effect over State legislations. The corollary is that the Tribunal while providing for restoration of environment in an area, can specify buffer zones around specific lakes & water bodies in contradiction with zoning regulations under these statutes or the RMP.

The second question raised ... is that the petition is barred by time. [E]nvironmental clearance was granted to the respondent No. 9 on 17.02.2012 for which notice was published in the leading newspaper on 12.03.2012 and 14.03.2012. Modified building plan was approved on 30.08.2012, which was followed up to 10.08.2014. Similar events had taken place in regard to the project of respondent No. 10 who had been granted environmental clearance on 30.09.2013. The application had to be filed within a period of six months from the date on which cause of action for such dispute has first arisen in terms of section 14 of the NGT Act. Admittedly, the present application has been filed in March, 2014 and according to them, it is much beyond the prescribed period of limitation. Also, there is no application for condonation of delay accompanying the main application. Therefore, the Tribunal will not have jurisdiction to condone the delay.

The OA No. 222 of 2014 was not an application *simpliciter* under section 14 of the Act. It was an application where a specific prayer has been made with reference to Lake Development Authority's Report dated 12.06.2013 and the Ministry of Environment,

Forest and Climate Change Monitoring Committee Report dated 14.08.2013 for restoration of ecologically sensitive land and for maintaining the sensitive [land] in its natural condition so that the ecological balance of the area is not disturbed. It is clear from the documentary evidence supported by data, that the project proponents have committed breaches and the implementation of the project is bound to have serious adverse impact on the ecology, hydrology and the environment in the catchment area of Bellandur Lake. The environmental degradation as established from the documents would give rise to an independent cause of action. Therefore, this was a petition under section 15 of the Act and thus it could be filed within 5 years from the date on which the cause for such compensation or relief first arose. [The court rejected the appeals filed by Mantri Techzone and Core Mind.]

NOTES AND QUESTIONS

1. Neither the NGT nor the Supreme Court set aside any of the planning and related permissions granted by various authorities such as the Karnataka Industrial Area Development Board, the State Level Environment Impact Assessment Authority and the Karnataka State Pollution Control Board. Indeed, there was no challenge to these permissions before the Tribunal. Moreover, both the projects had approvals from the electricity and water utilities. Is it fair and just to foist environmental liability on an enterprise creating economic assets where the enterprise has valid planning permissions?

2. The NGT noticed that in fixing buffer zones from water bodies, the Revised Master Plan of Bengaluru, 2015 (RMP) 'suffers from the inbuilt contradiction, legal infirmity and is without any scientific justification'. The NGT thereafter enlarged the buffer zone and ordered:

> 'Thus, we direct that the distance in the case of respondents Nos. 9 and 10 from Rajkulewas, waterbodies and wetlands shall be maintained as below:
>
> (i) In the case of Lakes, 75m from the periphery of water body to be maintained as green belt and buffer zone for all the existing water bodies i.e lakes/wetlands.
> (ii) 50m from the edge of the primary Rajkulewas.
> (iii) 35m from the edges in the case of secondary Rajkulewas.
> (iv) 25m from the edges in the case of tertiary Rajkulewas.
>
> This buffer/green zone would be treated as no construction zone for all intent and purposes. This is absolutely essential for the purposes of sustainable development particularly keeping in mind the ecology and environment of the areas in question.
>
> All the offending constructions raised by respondents Nos. 9 and 10 of any kind including boundary wall shall be demolished which falls within such areas. Wherever necessary dredging operations are required, the same should be carried out to restore the original capacity of the water spread area and/or wetlands. Not only the existing construction would be removed but also none of these respondents—Project Proponent would be permitted to raise any construction in this zone.
>
> All authorities particularly Lake Development Authority shall carry out this operation in respect of all the water bodies/lakes of Bangalore.'

By enlarging the buffer beyond what was laid down in the RMP, the Tribunal changed the goalposts and required the ongoing projects to comply. Is this consistent with the Rule of Law which requires that laws ordinarily need to be prospective, not retrospective; that they must be clear; that they should be certain and predictable and not require the impossible?[111]

[111] *Id.*

3. Apart from the appeals filed by the two project proponents, the state of Karnataka also appealed the general direction issued by the Tribunal requiring the authorities to implement the enlarged buffer areas around water bodies and lakes. The state argued that if the authorities were required to demolish all the offending constructions raised/built in the buffer zone it 'will result in demolition of 95% of the buildings in Bengaluru'. The Supreme Court allowed the state's appeal and set aside the general direction enlarging the buffer area. The consequence is that the expanded buffer areas were made applicable to Mantri and Core Mind alone. Is this fair?

4. The Supreme Court explained the contours of section 22 and held that an appeal to the Supreme Court lay only on a substantial question of law. The court answered two questions: the first with respect to maintainability of the Foundation's application before the NGT and the second on limitation. With respect to other matters, the court found that they involved a factual review and re-appreciation of evidence, which was impermissible under section 22.

5. Under most Indian statutes one appeal on fact and law is provided from trial courts and tribunals exercising original jurisdiction. The NGT is the first forum examining applications under sections 14 and 15 of the Act. The NGT is not bound by strict rules of evidence and may devise its own procedure. Given the complexity of factual issues in several environmental cases, should the NGT Act be amended to provide at least one appeal on facts? If so, should the appeal lie to the Supreme Court or the High Court?

6. Do you agree with the reasoning of the Supreme Court on section 33? While the provision clearly declares that the NGT Act would override other laws or instruments that are inconsistent, where is the mandate granting the Tribunal overriding powers? Is the Supreme Court correct in holding that the Tribunal can specify buffer zones 'in contradiction with zoning regulations' under Karnataka planning laws or the statutory RMP? What should a citizen follow: the Master Plan or NGT directions that contradict the Master Plan? Notice that while explaining the ambit of section 33, the Supreme Court appears to have conferred overriding authority in the NGT but when it came to upholding the general directions on the enlarged buffer, the Supreme Court set aside the Tribunal's order.

7. This case shows the tensions between different state authorities. On the one hand, several authorities wanted the projects to proceed while the Lake Development Authority and the MoEF were concerned about damage to the catchments of the lakes.

8. Environmental compensation was determined by following a rule of thumb: 5% of the project value for Mantri Techzone and 3% of the project cost for Core Mind. Is this a good measure to assess environmental damage? Though this point was raised in submissions, the Supreme Court did not consider the imposition of liability without any inquiry into the damage or injury as being a substantial question of law.

7

PUBLIC INTEREST LITIGATION

Public Interest Litigation (PIL) has played, and continues to play, a crucial role in the development of environmental law in India. Indeed, public discourse on the environment began in the 1980s when the Supreme Court responded to a series of PILs concerning river and air pollution. The constitutional courts have since used PILs to shine a harsh light on neglected environmental problems. They have worked to improve environmental governance, enhance the quality of the environment and protect forests and wildlife. Where legislative gaps persisted, PILs have even been used to nudge regulation into place. All this is in addition to the usual business of courts laying down legal principles applicable to environmental law. In this chapter, we explain how PILs differ from traditional cases and critique this branch of judicial business. Later in this chapter, we examine the right to access information as a facet of procedural environmental rights.

A. CHARACTERISTICS AND EVOLUTION

Our first reading tracks the journey of PIL jurisprudence from its inception in the 1970s. While the earliest full-blown PILs in the fields of government accountability[1] and environment[2] were initiated in the High Courts, the survey that follows focuses on Supreme Court cases.

SHYAM DIVAN; PUBLIC INTEREST LITIGATION IN OXFORD HANDBOOK OF THE INDIAN CONSTITUTION 662 (2016)*

Front and centre, PIL now occupies an unrivalled space in constitutional law that bridges the citizen, the court and the executive. It arose in response to citizens seeking to curb widespread human rights' violations or illegalities in government working that harmed public administration or the environment. Despair over an apathetic executive with no real possibility of near term improvements, spurred both litigant and judges to fix a broken system.

Characteristics

Public interest litigations are a type of judicial business carried out by the High Courts and the Supreme Court in the exercise of their constitutional writ jurisdictions. In contrast to private dispute adjudications affecting individual rights, PILs deal with public grievances over

---

[1] *Piloo Mody v State of Maharashtra* Bombay High Court; Miscellaneous Petition No. 519 of 1974 decided on 22 October 1975 (unreported). The case concerned the illegal allotment of plots at the Backbay Reclamation, Mumbai.

[2] *Society for Protection of Silent Valley v Union of India* Kerala High Court; Original Petition Nos. 2949 & 3025 of 1979 decided on 2 January 1980 (unreported). The petition challenged a hydroelectric project in Kerala's Palghat District.

* This excerpt is an edited version of the original chapter.

Environmental Law & Policy in India. Shyam Divan and Armin Rosencranz, Oxford University Press.
 DOI: 1093/oso/9780192865458.003.0007

flagrant human rights violations by the state or seek to vindicate public policies embodied in statutes or constitutional provisions. In the early evolution of PIL, the Supreme Court explained the scope of this nascent field: 'Public Interest Litigation, as we conceive it is essentially a co-operative or collaborative effort on the part of the petitioner, the State or public authority and the court, to secure observance of the constitutional or legal rights, benefits and privileges conferred upon the vulnerable sections of the community and to reach social justice to them.' (*People's Union for Democratic Rights v Union of India* (1982) 3 SCC 235). A PIL seeks to enhance general welfare of the community at large.

The advent of PIL in India transformed the litigation landscape. The orthodox bilateral dispute yielded space in the dockets of the constitutional courts to a polycentric, problem-solving exercise, often with a strong legislative flavour in terms of sweep, policy content and reformative focus.

Evolution

Looking back at three decades of PIL jurisprudence, the Supreme Court in 2010 classified the evolution of this field into three overlapping phases. In this view, the earliest phase was when the Supreme Court issued directions to protect the right to life for the benefit of marginalized groups and sections of society who could not access courts because of their poverty, illiteracy and ignorance. The second phase encompassed protection of environment, forests, natural resources, and cultural heritage such as historical monuments—for the benefit of society at large. This class of PILs concerns what may be termed as 'a collective right to a collective good'. The third phase comprised efforts by the court to maintain probity, transparency and integrity in governance. (*State of Uttaranchal v Balwant Singh Chaufal* (2010) 3 SCC 402).

The pivot in the development of PIL jurisprudence in India is Article 32 of the Constitution. Article 32 guarantees the remedy to petition the highest court for enforcement of any fundamental right assured in the Constitution. Not having to await initial adjudication at the High Court tier, the Supreme Court was able to script rapid developments in PIL jurisprudence in cases it directly received.

In what is possibly the most significant factor that spurred the growth of PIL, the Supreme Court lowered the standing barriers by enlarging the concept of 'person aggrieved'.

Traditionally, only a person whose own right was in jeopardy was entitled to seek a remedy. When extended to public actions, this meant that a person asserting a public right or interest had to show special circumstances, for example, that he or she had suffered some special injury over and above what members of the public had generally suffered.

Representative Standing

In the late 1970s and early 1980s, in cases involving the underprivileged, the Supreme Court began to override the procedural obstacles and technicalities that had until then obstructed redress. Rather than reject a petition for lack of standing, the court chose to expand standing so that it could decide the substantive issues affecting the rights of the underprivileged.

This modification of the traditional rule of standing which permits the poor and oppressed to be represented by volunteers may be described as *representative standing*.

Citizen Standing

The second modification of the classical standing doctrine, where a concerned citizen (or voluntary organization) may sue, not as a representative of others but in his or her own right as a member of the citizenry to whom a public duty is owed, may be termed 'citizen standing'. This liberalization stemmed from the need to check the abuse of executive authority in a modern welfare state.

Under increasing pressure to curb instances of official lawlessness, the Supreme Court expanded standing to enable a citizen to challenge such government actions in public interest, though the citizen had not suffered any individualized harm

Litigational Competence

The transformation in the law of standing in the PIL jurisdiction has seen the notion of a 'person aggrieved' replaced by a more accommodative concept of 'litigational competence'. Today, recognizing their constitutional obligation to protect fundamental rights and advance good governance, judges are primarily concerned about the issue raised in the PIL and will generally lower procedural barriers where the cause warrants judicial intervention. Affirmatively, the threshold for litigational competence requires the petitioner to act in utmost good faith. There is a high expectation of civic responsibility from a PIL petitioner. Where a petitioner's *bona fides* are in doubt but the cause of action is genuine and in the general public interest, the court may appoint an *amicus curiae* to deal with the matter keeping the original petitioner out. Negatively, the PIL jurisdiction cannot be invoked by a person pursuing a hidden agenda, acting as a surrogate for phantom lobbies, seeking to pursue commercial gain, using the court process merely for publicity, or similar oblique motivations. To preserve the sanctity of the PIL jurisdiction, a court will impose heavy costs where the petitioner lacks *bona fides*.

Procedural Innovations

A range of procedural innovations distinguish the PIL field from conventional litigation. Strict rules of pleading do not apply in PIL. Judges like to view PIL as a collaborative effort between the court, the citizen and the public official, where procedural safeguards have a diminished utility and may be relaxed to enable relief.

For instance, the Supreme Court and the High Court treat letters written to the court as writ petitions. An early case in point is the *Dehradun Quarrying Case*, (*Rural Litigation & Entitlement Kendra v State of Uttar Pradesh* (1989) Supp (1) SCC 504) where the Supreme Court directed a letter to be treated as a writ petition under Article 32 of the Constitution. The letter alleged that illegal limestone quarrying was devastating the fragile environment in the Himalayan foothills around Mussoorie. Satisfied that the matter merited inquiry, the court first issued notices to the State and the collector of Dehradun to appear before the court. Then, as a clearer picture of the facts, regulatory structures and policies emerged, other affected parties—the Union Government, concerned government agencies and the mine owners—were also impleaded. By August 1988, when the Supreme Court delivered its final order, five years after it had received the letter, the litigation had grown into a full-blown, complex environmental case. To streamline the procedure for letter petitions, the Supreme Court issued administrative guidelines indicating when letter petitions will be entertained and the procedure to be followed by its registry. As a PIL progresses, the court generally does not insist upon formal amendments to the petition so long as the parties have notice of the issues being considered. Akin to letter petitions, the *suo moto* PIL is occasionally resorted to where a High Court or Supreme Court bench learns about an emergent matter of public concern that troubles the judicial conscience. These cases are usually triggered by media reports.

In pollution cases in the 1990s, the Supreme Court relied on the National Environment Engineering Research Institute, Nagpur (NEERI) to visit the affected locality and submit its field report. Confronted with severe pollution caused by the chemical industry, the Supreme Court directed NEERI to study the situation around Bichhri village in Rajasthan and submit a report suggesting remedial measures. When tackling the pollution of the River Ganga by tannery clusters in Calcutta, the Supreme Court directed NEERI to report on the situation at the site and suggest solutions. NEERI's role as an expert has extended to assessing the damage caused by polluters or those who have caused other ecological harm.

The most notable expert body is the Central Empowered Committee (CEC) that assists the Supreme Court in forest cases and which has gained near institutional status over a decade of functioning. In December 1996, responding to a rapid decline in India's forests, the Supreme Court asserted jurisdiction over all matters pertaining to the diversion of forests to non-forest use. In discharging this role as custodian of national forests, the court relies heavily on the CEC for the purposes of assessing whether or not to permit forest clearance in individual cases and also to recommend measures to restore degraded areas.

Frequently, independent scientific expertise is essential to inform judicial decision-making. Judges in such cases usually appoint a committee of experts to probe scientific questions and advise the court on a course of action. Since eminent scientists drawn from leading institutions compose these committees, the court treats their opinion with great deference.

In the *Shriram Gas Leak* case (*M C Mehta v Union of India* (1986) 2 SCC 176), the Supreme Court solicited the help of several expert committees. For instance, the Nilay Choudhary committee was requested to advise the court on whether Shriram's hazardous chemical plant, which was located in Delhi, should be allowed to recommence operations in view of the danger to the neighbourhood. The committee was also asked to suggest measures to reduce the environmental threat that the plan posed.

In the *Dehradun Quarrying* case, the Supreme Court enlisted an expert committee to evaluate the environmental impact of limestone quarrying operations in the Mussoorie-Dehradun region. A 'monitoring committee' was formed to oversee the running of three limestone mines that had been allowed to continue operations, and to monitor reforestation measures in the region. A 'rehabilitation committee' was also set up to rehabilitate the mine owners whose mines had been closed by the court.

Justiciability

The growth of PIL shattered traditional notions of justiciability. With PIL reaching to areas of governance, notions of what could be decided by judges changed. The expanded reach of the right to life and the willingness of judges to declare policy based on technical and expert reports submitted to court blurred the boundaries circumscribing adjudication.

The courts have entertained lawyers, journalists, law teachers, academics, environmentalists, social activists, students, eminent citizens, affected residents, farmers and individuals with a special knowledge or concern on the subject of the petition.

Environmental protection has received special attention from the Supreme Court, possibly more than any other sphere of PIL activity. At a substantive level, the court has enunciated numerous principles that form the bedrock of environmental jurisprudence in India. These principles include the fundamental right of every person to a healthy environment, the principle of sustainable development, the precautionary principle, the polluter-pays principle, the public trust doctrine, and the principle of inter-generational equity. The tort liability regime was transformed in relation to accidents caused by hazardous industry with the articulation of the absolute liability principle. The Supreme Court has required strict compliance with environmental laws, set down policy when faced with an unresponsive administration and nudged the government to frame legislation. The most far reaching exercise by the Supreme Court is with respect to the national forests resources where the court acts as a custodian since 1996 permitting diversion of forests only where it is satisfied that the need is imperative. The Supreme Court through environmental PILs has elevated the importance of ecological issues in developmental decision-making, put a stop to some of the most egregious cases of pollution and illegal mining and worked to introduce a culture of compliance by insisting upon strict enforcement of environmental laws.

Critique

For close to four decades the constitutional courts have set apart judicial resources to foster PIL to a point where this jurisdiction defines public perception of the higher judiciary.

As Indians work towards realizing their constitutional goals and enforcing constitutional guarantees, they have secured to themselves a new manner of exerting pressure on the state to improve governance. It is heard in a high constitutional forum and is now a voice the state may not ignore. Although the PIL docket remains small, these cases are generally prioritized, having regard to the significant public interest element involved.

The electronic and print media increase the court's visibility by widely reporting judicial observations in PILs, a heady experience for members of a cloistered calling. Indeed, PILs in conjunction with the media have provided a platform to the Supreme Court and the High Courts to enhance their own prestige by catalyzing societal change in the face of moribund governance.

Inevitably, this has led to numerous criticisms. Judicial intervention has hobbled agencies which prefer to await court directions rather than perform their administrative functions. By wresting control over forests, monitoring pollution levels and overseeing relief after a natural disaster, the court acts as a super agency. The court's efforts to cleanse government by overturning natural resource allocations result in massive economic disruptions. Business rivals and racketeers abuse the PIL processes to stall projects. And on occasion, PILs have culminated in disastrous judgments depriving millions of Mumbai's citizens' access to green and recreational spaces and foisting on a nation a river inter-linking project that could severely undermine the sub-continent's ecological integrity. More modestly, the court's directions are at times unenforceable.

In contrast, the contribution of PILs in the fields of human rights and environment to pick two areas of activity, justify the activism. The fundamental principles of environmental law were all laid out in PILs, with the legislature catching up through subsequent legislation. It is the Supreme Court that raised public awareness about the importance of environmental protection, long before any sustained executive initiative. Parliament too has recognised the value of PILs by empowering the National Human Rights Commission as well as the National Legal Services Authority to petition the Supreme Court or the High Court in the discharge of their functions.

Nevertheless, in a nation that persistently scores low on the human development index, it will be a while before the governance deficit shrinks to justify judicial retreat. Until then, PIL remains the judiciary's most visible tool for marketing constitutionalism.

NOTES AND QUESTIONS

1. In some public interest cases, Supreme Court judges personally visited the site to make an assessment of the field conditions for themselves.[3] Justice V R Krishna Iyer visited Ratlam

[3] Geetanjoy Sahu, *Implications Of Indian Supreme Court's Innovations For Environmental Jurisprudence*, 4(1) Law, Envir & Development Jr 1, 9 (2008), http://www.lead-journal.org/content/08001.pdf, accessed 22 July 2021.

town before his judgment in *Ratlam Municipality v Vardhichand*,[4] and Justice P N Bhagwati was distressed by the devastation he saw on a visit to the Doon Valley which resulted in extensive directions in the *Dehradun Quarrying* case.[5] Although spot visits by judges of the Supreme Court remain rare occurrences in PILs, is this a practicable procedure? Does it weaken the objectivity of the process by the case becoming identified very closely with the personality of a particular judge? At least one study shows that an overwhelming 84% of the respondents felt that judges should visit the site of environmental degradation. Such visits would help judges make an assessment for themselves without having to rely on exaggerated claims or false denials in affidavits.[6]

What about the site visits by National Green Tribunal members? Do new technologies by which images can be streamed into the courtroom obviate such visits?

2. Prof Lavanya Rajamani closely examined two environmental cases in her analysis of public interest environmental litigation in India.[7] *Almitra Patel v Union of India*[8] was an effort by the Supreme Court to improve garbage collection in urban centres. The *Vehicular Pollution* case[9] comprised a massive effort by the court to clean up Delhi's air. Rajamani recognizes that a judge's social and value preferences influence the direction and outcome of the PIL. In *Almitra Patel*, the bench's strong middle-class moorings may have resulted in a neglect of the perspective of poor slum dwellers. Moreover, Rajamani notes:

> This is ironic given the origins of judicial activism and PIL in India. The court opened its doors and liberalised *locus standi* in the late 1970s to address the 'problems of the poor'. Yet today, three decades on, it is the problem of the middle-class, in particular the ones that affect them, that are most likely to be viewed sympathetically by the Courts. The petitioner in the *Municipal Solid Waste Management Case* noted, for instance, that the Judges tend to focus first on cleaning up Delhi where they live and only then on other cities.[10]

3. Analysing trends of the Supreme Court's approach to PIL after a decade of economic liberalization that commenced in the early 1990s, the public interest lawyer Prashant Bhushan observed that the court had bought the ideology underlying the economic reforms hook, line and sinker. According to him, this ideology venerates the virtues of the free market and undermines the role of the state in providing education, jobs and the basic amenities of life to its citizens. Such an ideology runs counter to the court's earlier expansive interpretation of Article 21.[11] Do you agree?

---

[4] AIR 1980 SC 1622.

[5] *Rural Litigation and Entitlement Kendra v State of Uttar Pradesh* AIR 1985 SC 652.

[6] P M Prasad, *Environmental Protection: The Role Of Liability System In India*, 39 Economic & Political Weekly 257, 267 (2004), https://www.jstor.org/stable/4414525, accessed 22 July 2021.

[7] Lavanya Rajamani, *Public Interest Environmental Litigation In India: Exploring Issues of Access, Participation Equity, Effectiveness And Sustainability*, 19 Jr Of Envir Law 293 (2007), https://academic.oup.com/jel/article-abstract/19/3/293/472422?redirectedFrom=fulltext, accessed 22 July 2021.

[8] The principal judgments in *Almitra Patel* are reported at AIR 1998 SC 993, (2000) 2 SCC 166 and 2000 (1) Scale 568.

[9] *M C Mehta v Union of India (Vehicular Pollution)*, Writ Petition No. 13029 of 1985. Several judgments and orders have been passed by the Supreme Court in this case, the principal reports being (1991) 2 SCC 137; (1991) 2 SCC 353; AIR 1998 SC 617; AIR 1998 SC 773; (1998) 6 SCC 60; (1998) 8 SCC 648 and (1999) 6 SCC 9.

[10] Lavanya Rajamani, *supra* note 7 at 304.

[11] Prashant Bhushan, *Supreme Court and PIL: Changing Perspective Under Liberalisation*, 39 Economic & Political Weekly 1770, 1774 (2004), https://www.jstor.org/stable/4414951, accessed 22 July 2021.

4. Since the principal relief in PIL is prospective and affirmative rather than compensatory, the tight linkage between right and remedy that characterizes traditional litigation is attenuated in these cases. Remedial orders are fashioned *ad hoc* to accommodate a range of interests and do not always flow from a narrow determination of rights and liabilities. Moreover, since there is wide discretion, the temperament of the judge, his or her compassion for the grievance and the nature of the grievance itself, invariably influence the outcome of a case. As a result, it is frequently impossible to identify a single clear-cut solution in PIL cases.

5. Relief in most of the PIL cases in the Supreme Court is obtained through interim orders. The judicial emphasis on the effective implementation of environmental laws has prompted judges to monitor compliance through periodic reports filed in court by the government agency. Generally, short interim directions in the nature of a 'continuing mandamus' are passed at frequent intervals. Non-compliance with court orders is met with judicial strictures, action in contempt of court or fines.

B. CRITIQUE OF PIL

Public interest litigation is now part of popular lore and feature in Bollywood films, Prof Anuj Bhuwania reminds us. He concludes his study with a caution: it would be improper to reject PIL jurisprudence merely because its Indian avatar is distinct and there are no similar cases on the dockets of leading courts elsewhere. Perhaps PILs are a form of postcolonial politics that is still to fully evolve. We carry a short excerpt from the book.

ANUJ BHUWANIA; COURTING THE PEOPLE – PUBLIC INTEREST LITIGATION IN POST-EMERGENCY INDIA 119 (2017)

The institutional critique of PIL

There has been a recent trend of legal scholars who diagnose the problem with PIL not just in its ideological transformation but in its judicial process as well. There is a realization that it is the process of PIL itself, which causes the outcomes that the ideological critics are singularly obsessed with, that needs to be at least partially reformed. In this vein, Krishnaswamy and Khosla have argued for the need to pay further attention to the judicial process in PIL, which this book tries to engage with seriously. There also seems to be a recognition that some clarity with regard to institutional norms regulating PIL procedure is necessary. This strand of criticism often relies on influential analyses of such litigation in other common law countries which would apparently bear comparison to PIL in India. While it is certainly a most useful exercise to contextualize and evaluate Indian PIL in a comparative manner, the difficulty is that such comparison ends up missing out on just how extreme the Indian experience of PIL really has been. Indeed, Krishnaswamy and Khosla take exception to India's PIL being seen as 'unique in the common law world'. Similarly, Thiruvengadam has suggested that Abram Chayes' influential theorization of 'Public Law Litigation' should be the reference point to think of the expanded role of a judge in PIL, as Clark Cunningham had also argued earlier. However, Indian PIL has gone much further than even Chayes' heterodox model. Thiruvengadam himself argued that the dilution of *locus standi* already makes Indian PIL different from Chayes' model. In fact, for all the procedural departures that Chayes theorized, he could not have envisaged litigation without the very existence of the petitioner or the complete absence of any affected parties. Indian PIL allows for a process which is *suo motu,* or entirely judge initiated, as well as enables the court petitioner herself to be removed and replaced with an *amicus curiae* appointed by it, as we have seen repeatedly in previous chapters. We have also seen how Indian PIL allows the judge to rely on rather low standards of evidence, which as Krishnaswamy has elsewhere argued, goes completely against Chayes's suggestion of a higher burden of proof in such cases. And

Indian PIL cases can culminate in clearly legislative remedies as well as decisions instructing the Executive to undertake specific construction projects costing enormous amounts of money. These are way beyond the imagination of any judicial process almost anywhere outside South Asia. Another astute recent critic of PIL has been Lavanya Rajamani, who has relied on Lon Fuller's famous argument that a judicial forum is ill-equipped to handle 'polycentric disputes', i.e. disputes that 'involve many affected parties and a somewhat fluid state of affairs.' She argues that intervention in such situations result in complex repercussions 'as not all affected parties are readily identifiable and therefore before the Court'. This is undoubtedly an important point to ponder over in such litigation. However, in Indian PIL cases, the situation is much more extreme. Even the 'necessary parties' who are directly affected by a PIL case are either not even made a party as we repeatedly saw in the slum demolition PILs [earlier], or are not heard even if they are allowed to intervene as we saw in the PIL relating to industrial closure.... However, this strand of criticism with its insightful procedural criticism of PIL offers a way forward if the pathologies of PIL are to be mitigated. Rajamani suggests that the court 'evolve a set of guidelines for restrained and responsible PIL; Thiruvengadam's suggestion is that the PIL judge should 'be encouraged to adopt a far more modest, facilitative role', while Khosla and Krishnaswamy argue for the need to clarify the question of *locus standi* in PIL cases.

The other institutional critique of PIL has come from within the Supreme Court itself. The close identification of PIL with Justice Bhagwati in the early 1980s meant that the famous 'epistolary jurisdiction', by which letters written to the court would be treated as petitions, often had letters being personally addressed to Justice Bhagwati. He would then ensure that the PIL was heard by him. As Upendra Baxi wrote in the early 1980s, this imprinted the early PILs 'with the insignia of an individual justice, whereas what is needed in days to come is a collective imprimatur of the Court for the new litigation.' An institutional response was attempted by the Bench of two judges (S M Fazal Ali and Venkataramiah, JJ) in the *Sudipt Mazumdar* case in 1983, when it formulated 10 questions regarding PIL and passed an order referring to a Constitutional Bench (of a minimum of five judges). These questions included, among others:

1. Should this court take notice of such letters addressed by individuals by post enclosing some paper cuttings and take action on them *suo motu* except where the complaint refers to deprivation of liberty of any individual? ...
6. Can this court take action on letters addressed to it where the facts disclosed are not sufficient to take action? Should these letters be treated differently from other regular petitions filed into this court in this regard and should the District Magistrate or the District Judge be asked to enquire and make a report to this court to ascertain whether there is any case for further action? ...
10. Would such informality not lead to greater identification of the court with the cause than it would be when a case involving the same type of cause is filed in the normal way?

After having kept this case pending for a long time, a constitution bench around 2000 decided that there was no need to order any such guidelines. Three decades after the 1983 order, these questions have still not been taken up and decided by any Bench of the Supreme Court. The *ad hoc* approach continues, and no attempt at tidying up PIL principles was ever successfully made. There have been a few judicial initiatives since then to lay down such principles, but all have met the fate of *Sudipt Mazumdar*. It is still worthwhile, in my opinion, to examine these attempts and the institutional inertia they were met with.

In a concurring judgment to Justice Bhagwati's in the *Bandhua Mukti Morcha* case of 1984, Justice Pathak tried to formulate an institutional response so that PIL could 'command broad acceptance'. He clarified that:

> All communications and petitions invoking the jurisdiction of the court must be addressed to the entire court, that is to say, the Chief Justice and his companion Judges. No such communication of petition can properly be addressed to a particular Judge.... Communications and petitions addressed to a particular Judge are improper and violate the institutional personality of the Court.

Feeling the need to place limits on the flexibility of procedure that can be adopted in a PIL, J Pathak laid down certain basic norms:

> Whatever the procedure adopted by the court it must be procedure known to judicial tenets and characteristic of a judicial proceeding.... The Court must ever remind itself that one of the indicia identifying it as a Court is the nature and character of the procedure adopted by it in determining a controversy. It is in that sense limited in the evolution of procedures pursued by it in the process of an adjudication and in the grant and execution of the relief.

His has been a lone voice in the wilderness.

In 1988, the Supreme Court did introduce a new streamlined procedure to deal with letter petitions: any letter petition received would first be screened by a new PIL cell and would then be placed before a judge nominated for this purpose by the Chief Justice. This was meant to make sure that letters, even if addressed to specific judges, would henceforth deal with in an institutional manner. But though their symbolic charge remains undiminished, letter petitions have come to form a negligible percentage of the PILs actually dealt with by the Supreme Court.

In one of the few academic writings to have expressed the need for an institutional approach to PIL, S K Agrawala proposed in 1985 that:

> The Court is not equipped in terms of the infrastructure to apply the non-adversarial procedure. If adversarial procedure is not to be applicable in PIL matters, the parties must know as to what the components of the alternative procedure(s) are. The laying down of guidelines for the non-adversarial procedure is, therefore, equally important.

Particularly important are his suggestions regarding the approach to questions of fact in PIL cases:

> If the court has to manage the collection of facts, data and evidence on its own, it seems to be obviously desirable that a permanent, trained and experienced fact-finding machinery is set up under the control and supervision of the Supreme Court.

In a prescient suggestion that anticipated Justice Vijender Jain's court commissioners in *Kalyan Sanstha,* Agrawala pointed out the problems that would emerge with Justice Bhagwati's blithe disregard for procedure:

> A judge who appoints commissioners would be inclined to appoint those, whom or about whom he knows personally. It is human nature. Such commissioners are likely to be at least as biased as the judges who have been enthusiastic about PIL litigation. Bias even for a good cause, is bias all the same. Secondly, they may not be adequately trained for the job that may be entrusted to them.... Fact finding, investigation and reporting are not something that everybody and anybody can be entrusted with.

NOTES AND QUESTIONS

1. Occasionally, the PIL process is misused. Business rivals discreetly fund NGOs to stymie or delay competitors, hoping that this may drive away projects from a state or even the country. Phony activists abound and are known to use the Right to Information machinery in tandem with the threat of a PIL to extort hush money from project proponents. Ever so rarely, a brazen effort is detected by the court, as in *Kalyaneshwari's* case.[12] Kalyaneshwari, a registered society, petitioned the Supreme Court under Article 32 of the Constitution seeking an immediate ban on the use of asbestos. The petitioner also asked for a scheme to compensate workers and victims suffering from asbestosis.

The Supreme Court found that the petition lacked merit since the court had already examined the issue in an earlier case.[13] Further, the petitioner had lost before the Gujarat High Court on the same issue.[14] In the principal judgment, the Supreme Court found that the Union Government and state governments were alive to the health impacts and that asbestos-related activities were being conducted in accordance with specified parameters and under due supervision. However, the court issued a *suo motu* contempt notice to B K Sharma, secretary of the petitioner, upon finding that the petition was an abuse of process sponsored by a business rival.[15]

In the contempt case, the Supreme Court found that the real object of the petition was to secure a ban in asbestos products and thereby increase the demand for cast and ductile iron products being manufactured by Electro Steel Castings Ltd (ESCL). The court was satisfied that Sharma was merely a front for ESCL. Rejecting the apology offered by the contemnor, the court issued the following directions:

(1) We order and award sentence of simple imprisonment till rising of this Court to the contemnor, Shri B.K. Sharma.
(2) We also impose a sentence of fine of Rs 2000 on the contemnors, to be paid within one week from today. In default, he shall undergo simple imprisonment for a period of one week.
(3) Lastly, we impose costs of Rs 1,00,000 upon the contemnors to be paid to the Supreme Court Legal Services Committee.
(4) We also hereby direct the Registrar of Societies, Government of NCT of Delhi to take action against the contemnor Society, namely, Kalyaneshwari, in accordance with law and submit its action-taken report, interim or final, to this Court within six weeks from today.[16]

The Supreme Court evidently wanted to make an example of B K Sharma to deter other misadventures. If so, was the sentence too light?

2. The efforts by the Supreme Court to sensitize society to the adverse impacts of ecological degradation extended to requiring environment studies to be included in the curricula of students at school and university.[17] Should judges decide syllabuses?

3. M C Mehta, advocate and environmentalist, petitioned the Supreme Court in 1991 to direct the exhibition and broadcast of environmental messages and information by the

12 *Kalyaneshwari v Union of India* (2011) 3 SCC 287 and (2012) 12 SCC 599.
13 *Consumer Education and Research Centre v Union of India* (1995) 3 SCC 842.
14 *B K Sharma v Union of India* AIR 2005 GUJ 203.
15 *Kalyaneshwari v Union of India* (2011) 3 SCC 287.
16 *Kalyaneshwari v Union of India* (2012) 12 SCC 599.
17 *M C Mehta v Union of India* (1992) 1 SCC 358; (2004) 1 SCC 571.

media.[18] The Supreme Court issued detailed directions regarding the compulsory screening of slides and documentaries in cinema halls and the broadcast of programmes on radio and television. Was the Supreme Court's order justified? Should judges decide what movie and television viewers should watch?

4. Professor Baxi describes the gradual judicial takeover of 'the direction of administration in a particular arena from the executive' as 'creeping jurisdiction'.[19] A good illustration of the Supreme Court's 'creeping jurisdiction' is the *Dehradun Quarrying* case where 'the Supreme Court considered, balanced and resolved competing policies—including the need for development, environmental conservation, preserving jobs, and protecting substantial business investments—in deciding to close a number of limestone quarries in the Mussoorie Hills and to allow others to continue operating under detailed conditions. In rendering this judgment the court reviewed the highly technical reports of various geological experts and gave varying weight to the expert opinions.'[20]

5. Has the recourse to constitutional remedies stifled alternative means of securing environmental justice? Consider this argument:

> The Supreme Court of India's obsessive pursuit of constitutional remedies has meant that other statutory remedies which are relatively easy to access like statutory remedies available under the Water Act and the Air Act have not been adequately explored or supported. Further, in most cases interventions have led to the creation of multiplicity of authorities which have lacked institutional support and therefore failed to deliver environmental justice to victims of environmental pollution. The continued emphasis on the polluter pay principle in the absence of robust methodologies for establishing causality for environmental damage or new evidentiary rules for establishing intention of the polluter to pollute has meant that in reality the approach facilitated payment of monies to pollute. This has thus impeded efforts to arrest environmental degradation through remediation and restoration.
>
> Institutionally the Supreme Court needs to build collaborations with other national regulators such as the National Human Rights Commission (NHRC) and the National Commission for Women in co-opting such bodies to monitor and report environmental violation. This is because it is well established that environmental degradation disproportionately affects the poor and the vulnerable. The Supreme Court also needs to allow for greater de-centralization and recognition of municipalities and panchayats in enforcing and monitoring of conditions for grant of environmental impact assessment. This would be a great first step towards strengthening the principle of subsidiarity in environmental governance, rather than in centralizing decision-making, monitoring and enforcement. It should direct its attention towards strengthening existing regulatory institutions like the pollution control boards and strengthen their mandate in devising new reliefs like injunctions and in pursuing more precautionary measures in intervening early enough in case of potential pollution. Finally it is critical for the Court to educate itself on the challenge of the anthropocene in abandoning the polluter pays principle and facile trade-offs between environment and development.[21]

---

18 *M C Mehta v Union of India* AIR 1992 SC 382: (1992) 1 SCC 358.

19 Upendra Baxi, *Taking Suffering Seriously: Social Action Litigation in the Supreme Court of India*, 4 THIRD WORLD LEGAL STUDIES 107 (1985), https://scholar.valpo.edu/cgi/viewcontent.cgi?article=1125&context=twls, accessed 22 July 2021.

20 *Id.*

21 Nupur Chowdhury, *Constitutionally Shackled: The Story of Environmental Jurisprudence in India* (2019), https://www.researchgate.net/publication/331063277_Constitutionally_Shackled_The_Story_of_Environmental_Jurisprudence_in_India, accessed 14 August 2021.

C. JUDICIAL THEORY AND PRACTICE

On 6 December 2007, the Supreme Court issued an order in the *Aravali Golf Club* case excerpted below. The order reversed a judgment of the Punjab and Haryana High Court which had directed the Haryana Tourism Corporation to create the post of a tractor driver since the plaintiff gardener complained that his primary task was driving a tractor to tend the golf course. The Supreme Court held that it was no part of the judiciary's business to create posts in an organization. The court thereafter embarked on a critique of judicial activism, commending judicial restraint. Justice Markandey Katju was the junior judge on the bench that passed the order and although the order does not attribute authorship to any judge, practitioners familiar with Justice Katju's writing style associate with him the passages that follow.

DIVISIONAL MANAGER, ARAVALI GOLF CLUB v CHANDER HASS

(2008) 1 SCC 683

ORDER:

***

Under our Constitution, the legislature, the executive and the judiciary all have their own broad spheres of operation. Ordinarily it is not proper for any of these three organs of the State to encroach upon the domain of another, otherwise the delicate balance in the Constitution will be upset, and there will be a reaction.

Judges must know their limits and must not try to run the Government. They must have modesty and humility, and not behave like emperors. There is broad separation of powers under the Constitution and each organ of the State—the legislature, the executive and the judiciary—must have respect for the other and must not encroach into each other's domains.

The theory of separation of powers first propounded by the French thinker Montesquieu (in his book *The Spirit of Laws*) broadly holds the field in India too. In Chapter XI of his book *The Spirit of Laws* Montesquieu writes:

> When the legislative and executive powers are united in the same person, or in the same body of Magistrates, there can be no liberty; because apprehensions may arise, lest the same monarch or senate should enact tyrannical laws, to execute them in a tyrannical manner.
>
> *Again, there is no liberty, if the judicial power be not separated from the legislative and executive. Were it joined with the legislative, the life and liberty of the subject would be exposed to arbitrary control; for the judge would be then the legislator. Were it joined to the executive power, the judge might behave with violence and oppression.*
>
> There would be an end of everything, were the same man or the same body, whether of the nobles or of the people, to exercise those three powers, that of enacting laws, that of executing the public resolutions, and of trying the causes of individuals. (emphasis supplied)

We fully agree with the view expressed above. Montesquieu's warning in the passage above quoted is particularly apt and timely for the Indian judiciary today, since very often it is rightly criticized for 'overreach' and encroachment into the domain of the other two organs.

[The court cited several authorities and text books to support the necessity for judicial restraint including *Tata Cellular v Union of India* (1994) 6 SCC 651; *Ram Jawaya Kapur v State of Punjab* AIR 1955 SC 549; *Asif Hameed v State of J&K* (1989) Supp (2) SCC 364 and the dissent of Frankfurter, J of the US Supreme Court in *Trop v Dulles* 356 US 86.]

Unfortunately, despite these observations in the abovementioned decisions of this court, some courts are still violating the high constitutional principle of separation of powers as laid down by Montesquieu. As pointed out by Hon'ble Mr Justice J S Verma, the former C J, in his Dr K L Dubey Lecture:

> ... Judiciary has intervened to question a 'mysterious car' racing down Tughlaq Road in Delhi, allotment of a particular bungalow to a judge, specific bungalows for the

judges' pool, monkeys capering in colonies, stray cattle on the streets, clearing public conveniences, levying congestion charges at peak hours at airports with heavy traffic, etc. under the threat of use of contempt power to enforce compliance with its orders. Misuse of the contempt power to force railway authorities to give reservation in a train is an extreme instance.

Recently, the courts have apparently, if not clearly, strayed into the executive domain or in matters of policy. For instance, the orders passed by the High Court of Delhi in recent times dealt with subjects ranging from age and other criteria for nursery admissions, unauthorized schools, criteria for free seats in schools, supply of drinking water in schools, number of free beds in hospitals on public land, use and misuse of ambulances, requirements for establishing a world class burns ward in the hospital, the kind of air Delhiites breathe, begging in public, the use of subways, the nature of buses we board, the legality of constructions in Delhi, identifying the buildings to be demolished, the size of speed-breakers on Delhi roads, auto rickshaw overcharging, growing frequency of road accidents and enhancing of road fines, etc. In our opinion these were matters pertaining exclusively to the executive or legislative domain. If there is a law, judges can certainly enforce it, but judges cannot create a law and seek to enforce it....

The justification often given for judicial encroachment into the domain of the executive or legislature is that the other two organs are not doing their jobs properly. Even assuming this is so, the same allegation can then be made against the judiciary too because there are cases pending in courts for half-a-century as pointed out by this Court in *Rajindra Singh v Prem Mai* (2007) 11 SCC 37.

If the legislature or the executive are not functioning properly it is for the people to correct the defects by exercising their franchise properly in the next elections and voting for candidates who will fulfil their expectations, or by other lawful methods e.g. peaceful demonstrations. The remedy is not in the judiciary taking over the legislative or executive functions, because that will not only violate the delicate balance of power enshrined in the constitution, but also the judiciary has neither the expertise nor the resources to perform these functions.

Of the three organs of the State, the legislature, the executive and the judiciary, only the judiciary has the power to declare the limits of jurisdiction of all the three organs. This is a great power and hence must never be abused or misused, but should be exercised by the judiciary with the utmost humility and self-restraint.

Judicial restraint is consistent with and complementary to the balance of power among the three independent branches of the State. It accomplishes this in two ways. First, judicial restraint not only recognizes the equality of the other two branches with the judiciary, it also fosters that equality by minimizing inter-branch interference by the judiciary. In this analysis, judicial restraint may also be called judicial respect, that is, respect by the judiciary for the other coequal branches. In contrast, judicial activism's unpredictable results make the judiciary a moving target and thus decreases the ability to maintain equality with the co-branches. Restraint stabilizes the judiciary so that it may better function in a system of inter-branch equality.

Second, judicial restraint tends to protect the independence of the judiciary. When courts encroach into the legislative or administrative fields almost inevitably voters, legislators and other elected officials will conclude that the activities of judges should be closely monitored. If judges act like legislators or administrators, it follows that judges should be elected like legislators or selected and trained like administrators. This would be counterproductive. The touchstone of an independent judiciary has been its removal from the political or administrative process. Even if this removal has sometimes been less than complete, it is an ideal worthy of support and one that has had valuable effects.

The constitutional trade-off for independence is that judges must restrain themselves from the areas reserved to the other separate branches. Thus, judicial restraint complements the twin, overarching values of the independence of the judiciary and the separation of powers.

***

> In this connection we may usefully refer to the well-known episode in the history of the US Supreme Court when it dealt with the New Deal legislation of President Franklin Roosevelt. When President Roosevelt took office in January 1933 the country was passing through a terrible economic crisis, the Great Depression. To overcome this, President Roosevelt initiated a series of legislation called the New Deal, which were mainly economic regulatory measures. When these were challenged in the US Supreme Court the Court began striking them down on the ground that they violated the due process clause in the US Constitution. As a reaction, President Roosevelt proposed to reconstitute the Court with six more Judges to be nominated by him. This threat was enough and it was not necessary to carry it out. The Court in 1937 suddenly changed its approach and began upholding the laws. 'Economic due process' met with a sudden demise.
>
> The moral of this story is that if the judiciary does not exercise restraint and overstretches its limits there is bound to be a reaction from politicians and others. The politicians will then step in and curtail the powers, or even the independence, of the judiciary (in fact the mere threat may do, as the above example demonstrates). The judiciary should, therefore, confine itself to its proper sphere, realizing that in a democracy many matters and controversies are best resolved in non-judicial setting....

On 6 February 2009, Justice Katju (still the junior judge) issued a concurring opinion in *State of Orissa v Government of India*,[22] a case where the Supreme Court directed the Central Government to constitute a Water Dispute Tribunal to resolve a contest between Orissa and Andhra Pradesh. Justice Katju's opinion contributes nothing to the issue before the court and instead bemoans the acute water scarcity confronting the country. The opinion concludes with a recommendation to the Central Government to immediately constitute a body of eminent scientists to conduct research on the problem and design solutions.

A month and a half later, on 26 March 2009, Justice Katju presided over the bench hearing *M K Balakrishnan's* case. Balakrishnan filed a writ petition in 2001 seeking measures to conserve wetlands and the bench, eight years on, seized the opportunity to *suo moto* expand the scope of the case to cover water scarcity.[23] Reproducing several paragraphs and observations from the Katju concurrence in *State of Orissa*, the court ordered:

> Let notice be issued to the Secretary, Ministry of Science and Technology, Union of India which will file its counter-affidavit within four weeks stating what measures are being taken to solve the water shortage problem in the country and for implementing the recommendation of Markandey Katju, J in the aforesaid decision, in *State of Orissa* v *Government of India*.[24]

On the 28 April 2009, the bench presided over by Justice Katju reproduced what had been said in the 6 February 2009 and 26 March 2009 orders and issued directions that we excerpt. The early part of this order refers to India's ancient scientific heritage, the global diaspora of Indian scientists whose talent may be tapped and the right to water being a part of the right to life under Article 21 of the Constitution.

---

22 (2009) 5 SCC 492.

23 *M K Balakrishnan v Union of India* (2009) 5 SCC 507.

24 *Id.* At 511.

M K BALAKRISHNAN (2) v UNION OF INDIA

(2009) 5 SCC 511

* * *

Order:

We, therefore, direct the Central Government to forthwith constitute a committee to address the problems referred to in our order dated 26-3-2009 which shall do scientific research on a war footing for solving the water shortage in most parts of our country because of which our people are suffering terribly. Without water there can be no life, as the Hindi poet Rahim wrote, and Article 21 of our Constitution guarantees the right to life to all persons living in India. The Central Government is, therefore, directed to form this committee to address the water shortage problem at the earliest, latest within two months from today. This committee shall have the Secretary, Union Ministry of Science and Technology as its Chairman. Amongst the members of the committee will be the Secretary, Union Ministry of Water Management. The other members of the committee will be scientists specialised in the field of solving water shortage problems nominated by the Chairman of the committee and they are requested to take help from foreign scientists specialised in this field. The members of the committee should regard this work as a patriotic duty, and the entire people of India including NRIs settled abroad should help this committee.

The committee is directed to do scientific research *on a war footing* to solve the water shortage in the country. In particular, the committee shall do the following:

(a) Scientific research on a war footing to find out inexpensive methods of converting saline water into fresh water. This will be very useful in the coastal States because the sea has almost an infinite amount of water reserves and the only problem is to find out inexpensive methods to convert it into fresh water. The present methods like distillation, reverse osmosis, etc. are very expensive methods and cannot be afforded by a poor country like India. Hence we have to find out inexpensive methods and this is only possible by scientific research.

(b) Scientific research to find out methods of harnessing and managing monsoon rainwater and also to manage the flood waters and also to do research in rainwater harvesting, and treatment of waste water so that it may be recycled and available as potable water.

(c) Any other methods or suggestions including for matters for protection and preservation of wetlands and matters connected thereto.

This committee should be given all the financial, technical and administrative help by the Central and State Governments for this purpose.

The committee is requested to do patriotic duty to the nation in this connection, and by scientific research to find out the ways of solving the water shortage problem in the country. The help and advice of foreign scientific experts and/or Indian scientists settled abroad who are specialized in this field may also be taken, since the solution to the problem will not only help India but also foreign countries which are facing the same problem, some of which may already have progressed significantly in this area.

In our opinion, this is absolutely essential now because the whole country is reeling under acute shortage of water as referred to in our order dated 26-3-2009, some details of which have been given in the said order.

We propose to monitor this case from time to time. For this purpose this matter will be listed on the second Tuesday possibly of every alternative month. List again on 11-8-2009, on which date a progress report will be submitted before us by the Chairman of the committee who is requested to be personally present before us. Thereafter the case will be listed on 20-10-2009 and so on. The Registry of this Court shall send a copy of this order to the members of the committee mentioned above.

NOTES AND QUESTIONS

1. Notice how Justice Katju's views evolved from commending judicial restraint, to recommending a committee of scientists and then mandating the establishment of a committee coupled with periodic judicial oversight to solve the nation's water scarcity problems. Can you reconcile the *Aravali Golf Club* approach with *M K Balakrishnan (2)*?

2. The committee submitted periodic reports to the Supreme Court which came to naught. What was achieved? Was this sheer waste of taxpayers' money? There is no effective order of the Supreme Court between 2009 and 2014 dealing with the water scarcity problem. In 2014, the focus of the case shifted back to wetland conservation.

D. PILs AND CRIMINAL LAW

In 2009, the Samaj Parivartan Samudaya petitioned the Supreme Court under Article 32 of the Constitution complaining about illegal iron ore mining in the Bellary District of Karnataka that was destroying forests and creating havoc. The state administration had collapsed. So pervasive was the connivance amongst the miners, transporters, officials and politicians that a mining mafia ruled the district and controlled the roads by which the ore was transported to sea ports for export to China. There was no hope for the region except judicial intervention at the highest level.

The main case is discussed in the Forests chapter. Here, we analyse a judgment which is unusual because while most environmental PILs are civil law oriented, so deep ran the administrative rot in Bellary that the Supreme Court directed a criminal investigation. When you review the case, examine the criticism of the Central Empowered Committee, a subject we explore more fully in the notes that follow the excerpt.

SAMAJ PARIVARTAN SAMUDAYA v STATE OF KARNATAKA

(2012) 7 SCC 407

SWATANTER KUMAR, J:

* * *

After examining the issues raised in the [interim application], the earlier orders of this Court and based on the meetings held by [the Central Empowered Committee (CEC)] on 20-3-2012 and 11-4-2012 respectively, CEC identified the issues as follows:

> 1. the alleged serious illegalities/irregularities and undue favour in respect of (a) the land purchased by the close relatives of the then Chief Minister, Karnataka for Rs 0.40 crore in the year 2006 and subsequently sold to South West Mining Limited in the year 2010 for Rs 20 crores, and (b) donation of Rs 20 crores received by Prerna Education Society from South West Mining Limited;
>
> 2. the alleged illegal export of iron ore from Belekeri Port and associated issues . . .

On Issue 1, after summarizing the facts and its observations during its enquiry, CEC pointed out illegalities, irregularities and instances of misuse of public office committed for the benefit of the close relatives of the then Chief Minister, State of Karnataka. It made the following recommendations:

> Keeping in view the above facts and circumstances CEC is of the considered view that the purchase of the abovesaid land notified for acquisition for public purpose, its denotification from acquisition, permission granted for conversion from agricultural to non-agricultural (residential) purpose and subsequent sale to South West Mining Limited *prima facie* involves serious violations of the relevant Acts and procedural lapses and *prima facie* misuse of office by the then Chief Minister, Karnataka thereby

enabling his close relatives to make windfall profits and raises grave issues relating to undue favour, ethics and morality. Considering the above and taking into consideration the massive illegalities and illegal mining which have been found to have taken place in Karnataka and the allegations made against the Jindal Group as being recipient of large quantities of illegally mined material and undue favour being shown to them in respect of the mining lease of M/s MML it is recommended that a detailed investigation may be directed to be carried out in the matter by an independent investigating agency such as the Central Bureau of Investigation (CBI) and to take follow-up action. This agency may be asked to delve into the matter in depth and in a time-bound manner. This agency may also be directed to investigate into other similar cases, if any, of lands denotified from acquisition by the Bangalore Development Authority and the illegalities/irregularities/procedural lapses, if any, and to take follow-up action.

Prerna Education Society set up by the close relatives of the then Chief Minister, Karnataka has during March 2010 vide two cheques of Rs 5 crores each received a donation of Rs 10 crores from South West Mining Limited, a Jindal Group company. In this context, it is of interest to note that during the year 2009–2010 the net profit (after tax) of the said company was only Rs 5.73 crores. Looking into the details of the other donations made by the said company or by the other Jindal Group companies to any other trust/society not owned, managed or controlled by the Jindal Group. After considering that a number of allegations, with supporting documents, have been made in the report dated 27-7-2011 of Karnataka Lokayukta regarding M/s JSW Steel Limited having received large quantities of illegal mineral and alleged undue favour shown to it in respect of the extraction/supply of iron ore by/to it from the mining lease of M/s MML, it is recommended that this Hon'ble Court may consider directing the investigating agency such as CBI to also look into the linkages, if any, between the abovesaid donation of Rs 10 crores made by South West Mining Limited and the alleged receipt of illegal mineral by M/s JSW Steel Limited and the alleged undue favour shown to it in respect of the mining lease of M/s MML.

CEC has filed its report dated 28-3-2012 wherein the representation filed by the petitioner against Mr R. Parveen Chandra (ML No. 2661) has been dealt with [refer Para 6(ii), pp. 11–13 of the CEC Report dated 28-3-2012]. In the said representation it has been alleged that Mr Parveen Chandra, the lessee of ML No. 2661 has made two payments, one of Rs 2.50 crores to M/s Bhagat Homes Private Ltd and the other of Rs 3.5 crores to M/s Dhavalagir Property Developers Private Ltd as a *quid pro quo* for allotment of the said mining lease. It is recommended that this Hon'ble Court may consider directing the investigating agency such as CBI to investigate the payments made by the abovesaid lessee to these two companies whose Directors/shareholders are the close relatives of the then Chief Minister, Karnataka and whether there was any link between such payments and grant of mining lease to Mr Parveen Chandra....

[Counsel appearing for the affected parties contended:

(a) CEC has submitted its report without providing them an opportunity of being heard.
(b) CEC has exceeded its jurisdiction and enlarged the scope of the enquiry beyond the reference made by the Court. Thus, the Court should not accept any of the recommendations made by CEC.
(c) In relation to the alleged irregularities and illegalities pointed out in the report of CEC, even where criminality is involved or criminal offences are suspected, the matters are *sub judice* before the court of competent jurisdiction. Thus, the Supreme Court should not pass any orders for transferring the investigation of such offences to the CBI as it would seriously prejudice their interests.]

The machinery of criminal investigation is set into motion by the registration of a first information report (FIR) by the specified police officer of a jurisdictional police station or otherwise. CBI, in terms of its manual has adopted a procedure of conducting limited pre-investigation inquiry as well. In both the cases, the registration of FIR is essential. A police investigation may start with the registration of FIR while in other cases (CBI, etc.), an inquiry may lead to the registration of an FIR and thereafter regular investigation may begin in accordance with the provisions of the Code of Criminal Procedure, 1973 (CrPC)....

Now, we shall proceed to examine the merit of the contentions raised before us. We may deal with Submissions (a) and (b), together, as they are intrinsically interrelated.

CEC had submitted the report dated 20-4-2012 and it has been stated in the report that opportunity of being heard had been granted to the affected parties. However, the contention before us is that while CEC heard other parties, it had not heard various companies like South West Mining Ltd and M/s JSW Steel Ltd.

Firstly, CEC is not vested with any investigative powers under the orders of this Court, or under the relevant notifications, in the manner as understood under CrPC. CEC is not conducting a regular inquiry or investigation with the object of filing charge-sheet as contemplated under Section 173 CrPC. Their primary function and responsibility is to report to the Court on various matters relating to collusion in illegal and irregular activities that are being carried on by various persons affecting the ecology, environment and reserved forests of the relevant areas. While submitting such reports in accordance with the directions of this Court, CEC is required to collect such facts. In other words, it has acted like a fact-finding authority.

CEC is not discharging quasi-judicial or even administrative functions, with a view to determine any rights of the parties. It was not expected of CEC to give notice to the companies involved in such illegalities or irregularities, as it was not determining any of their rights. It was *simpliciter* reporting matters to the Court as per the ground realities primarily with regard to environment and illegal mining for appropriate directions. It had made different recommendations with regard to prevention and prosecution of environmentally harmful and illegal activities carried on in collusion with government officers or otherwise.

We are of the considered view that no prejudice has been caused to the intervener/affected parties by non-grant of opportunity of hearing by CEC. In any case, this Court has heard them and is considering the issues independently.

As far as the challenge to the enlargement of jurisdiction by CEC beyond the reference made by the Court is concerned, the said contention is again without any substance. We have referred to the various orders of this Court. The ambit and scope of proceedings before this Court, pending in the above writ petition and civil appeal, clearly show that the Court is exercising a very wide jurisdiction in the national interest, to ensure that there is no further degradation of the environment or damage to the forests and so that illegal mining and exports are stopped. The orders are comprehensive enough to not only give leverage to CEC to examine any ancillary matters, but in fact, place an obligation on CEC to report to this Court without exception and correctly, all matters that can have a bearing on the issues involved in all these petitions in both the States of Karnataka and Andhra Pradesh. Thus, we reject this contention also.

Contention (c) is advanced on the premise that all matters stated by CEC are *sub judice* before one or the other competent court or investigating agency and thus, this Court has no jurisdiction to direct investigation by CBI. In any case, it is argued that such directions would cause them serious prejudice. This argument is misplaced in law and is misconceived on facts. Firstly, all the facts that had been brought on record by CEC are not directly *sub judice* in their entirety, before a competent forum or investigating agency.

In relation to Issue 1(a) raised by CEC which also but partially is the subject-matter of PCR No. 2 of 2011 pending before the Additional City Civil and Sessions Judge, Bangalore under the Prevention of Corruption Act, the Court took cognizance and summoned the accused to face the trial, writ petition against the same is pending in the High Court. It primarily relates to the improper de-notification of the land, which had been under acquisition but possession whereof was not taken. This land was purchased by the family members of the then Chief Minister for a consideration of Rs 40 lakhs and was sold after de-notification for a sum of Rs 20 crores to South West Mining Ltd. after de-notification. For this purpose, office of the Chief Minister and other higher government officials were used. While the earlier part of abovenoted violations is covered under PCR No. 2 of 2011, the transactions of purchase sale and other attendant circumstances are beyond the scope of the said pending case which refers only to the decision of de-notification. It appears that the entire gamut or the complete facts stated by CEC and supported by documents are not the matter *sub judice* before the trial court.

Similarly, Issue 1(b) relates to the donation of Rs 20 crores received by Prerna Education Society from South West Mining Ltd. The society is stated to be belonging to the members of the family of the Chief Minister Shri Yeddiyurappa.

The written submissions filed on behalf of South West Mining Ltd., do not reflect that Issues 1(a) and (b) of the CEC Report under consideration are directly and in their entirety the subject matter of any investigations in progress and proceedings pending before any competent forum. These are merely informatory facts, supported by relevant and authentic documents, highlighted by CEC in its report for consideration of the Court. A suspect has no indefeasible right of being heard prior to initiation of the investigation, particularly by the investigating agency. Even, in fact, the scheme of the Code of Criminal Procedure does not admit of grant of any such opportunity.

There is no provision in CrPC where an investigating agency must provide a hearing to the affected party before registering an FIR or even before carrying on investigation prior to registration of case against the suspect.

* * *

It is not for us to examine whether the stand taken by the intervener companies is correct or not. It requires to be investigated and an investigation *per se* would help them to clear their position, rather than subjecting them to face multifarious litigations, investigations and economic burden. Having heard them, we are unable to find any prejudice to the parties if further or wider investigation is directed by this Court. The direction of further investigation is based upon documents and facts brought to light by CEC as a result of examination conducted in the course of its primary function relating to inquiry into environmental violations and illegal mining activity. If the proceedings are permitted to continue and finally investigations reveal that a case which requires to be tried in accordance with law exists, then the interveners would have to face proceedings all over again. So, it is in their own interest that the specialized agency is permitted to investigate and bring out the true facts before the court of competent jurisdiction.

We must notice that the criminal offences are primarily offences against the State and secondarily against the victim. In this case, if the investigation by specialized agency finds that the suspect persons have committed offences with or without involvement of persons in power, still such violation undoubtedly would have been a great loss to the environmental and natural resources and would hurt both the State and national economy. We cannot expect an ordinary complainant to carry the burden of proving such complex offences before the court of competent jurisdiction by himself and at his own cost. Doing so would be a travesty of the criminal justice system....

The facts of the present case reveal an unfortunate state of affairs which has prevailed for a considerable time in the mentioned districts of both the States of Andhra Pradesh and Karnataka. CEC has recommended, and the complainant and the petitioners have also highlighted, a complete failure of the State machinery in relation to controlling and protecting the environment, forests and minerals from being illegally mined and exploited.

Wherever and whenever the State fails to perform its duties, the Court shall step in to ensure that the rule of law prevails over the abuse of process of law. Such abuse may result from inaction or even arbitrary action of protecting the true offenders or failure by different authorities in discharging statutory or legal obligations in consonance with the procedural and penal statutes. This Court expressed its concern about the rampant pilferage and illegal extraction of natural wealth and resources, particularly iron ore, as also the environmental degradation and disaster that may result from unchecked intrusion into the forest areas. This Court, vide its order dated 29-7-2011 [*Govt of A P v Obulapuram Mining Co (P) Ltd*

(2011) 12 SCC 491] invoked the precautionary principle, which is the essence of Article 21 of the Constitution of India as per the dictum of this Court in *M C Mehta v Union of India* [(2009) 6 SCC 142], and had consequently issued a ban on illegal mining. The Court also directed relief and rehabilitation programmes to be carried out in contiguous stages to promote intergenerational equity and the regeneration of the forest reserves. This is the ethos of the approach consistently taken by this Court, but this aspect primarily deals with the future concerns. In respect of the past actions, the only option is to examine in depth the huge monetary transactions which were effected at the cost of national wealth, natural resources, and to punish the offenders for their illegal, irregular activities. The protection of these resources was, and is the constitutional duty of the State and its instrumentalities and thus, the Court should adopt a holistic approach and direct comprehensive and specialized investigation into such events of the past.

Compelled by the above circumstances and keeping in mind the clear position of law *supra*, we thus direct:

(a) The issues specified at Points 1(a) and 1(b) of the CEC Report dated 20-4-2012 are hereby referred for investigation by the Central Bureau of Investigation.

(b) All the proceedings in relation to these items, if pending before any court, shall remain stayed till further orders of this Court. CBI shall complete its investigation and submit a report to the court of competent jurisdiction with a copy of the report to be placed on the file of this Court within three months....

NOTES AND QUESTIONS

1. The Central Empowered Committee (CEC) plays a crucial role in protecting national forests. The rigour of its analysis and the consistently high quality of CEC's reports have meant that the Supreme Court leans heavily on its factual findings and generally defers to its expertise.

The CEC was initially constituted by the Supreme Court on 9 May 2002 to examine and monitor various activities that infringed environmental laws and to guide the court on steps that may be required to protect the environment. At this time, the Supreme Court which had been hearing the *Forest Conservation* case since 1995 felt the need for a body that could make recommendations to the court with respect to diverse forest-related issues. Hundreds of interim applications from across the country seeking diversion of forests had piled up after the Supreme Court virtually froze development activity in forests by its orders of 12 December 1996,[25] 4 March 1997, 8 May 1997 and 15 January 1998.

On 9 September 2002, the Supreme Court noted violations of previous Supreme Court directions and recognized the need for a body to monitor implementation of court orders and place before the court unresolved cases of non-compliance and matters relating to encroachments, compensatory afforestation and other conservation issues. The court also approved a draft notification and placed before it by the Attorney General to give the CEC statutory status.[26]

On 17 September 2002, the Ministry of Environment and Forests (MoEF) constituted the CEC for a term of five years as a statutory committee under section 3(3) of the Environment (Protection) Act of 1986. A review of the Supreme Court decisions between 2002 and 2007 reveals that, by and large, the CEC mechanism worked smoothly with little friction between the MoEF and the notified committee. In September 2007, as the term of the CEC was

25 *T N Godavarman Thirumulpad v Union of India* AIR 1997 SC 1228.

26 *T N Godavarman Thirumulpad v Union of India* (2009) 17 SCC 755.

about to end, the tide turned and the MoEF adopted an aggressive posture, declining to renew the CEC's mandate. The Supreme Court, recognizing the vast amount of unfinished business, continued the CEC under its own orders.[27]

2. The CEC exists since May 2002, regularly filing reports before the Forest Bench of the Supreme Court. What is the legal status of the CEC? If it is neither quasi-judicial nor administrative, should it exist indefinitely? Should it exist at all? Should the Supreme Court disband the CEC? Who or what will take its place? Will terminating the CEC unspool the entire framework of stringent controls ordered by the court since 1995 and which have arrested depletion of India's forests?

Would dismantling the CEC help or hinder environmental protection generally and particularly the role of the Supreme Court as a trustee of natural resources? Were you a miner, highway authority, project proponent or hotelier in an environmentally sensitive zone, would you support the CEC structure or rather see it dismantled?

3. Apart from the suspected misuse of office by Chief Minister Yeddiyurappa, the CEC report dated 27 April 2012 (which was before the Supreme Court) highlighted the illegal export of iron ore from Belekeri port. The CEC found that during the four-month period between November 2009 and February 2010 more than 57 lakh metric tons (MT) of iron ore was brought for export to Belekeri and Karwar ports, of which more than 35 lakh MT was illegal. This illegal trafficking would have involved around 3,000 loaded trucks of iron ore plying *daily* to the ports. Moreover, so feeble was the law enforcement that over 7.57 lakh MT of iron ore, seized by the forest department at Belekeri port, disappeared under the watch of the customs and the port authorities. The illegal export of such large quantities of ore indicates criminal operations at an industrial scale. The collusion between the authorities and private parties, who were able to evacuate huge quantities of *seized* iron ore, beggars description.

4. Since the Supreme Court is at the summit of the judicial pyramid, any observation by it is bound to have a profound impact on the courts below. This is why the court when exercising jurisdiction in a PIL will not travel beyond ordering a proper criminal investigation. Were the court to make any observations regarding the guilt of the accused, it would severely undermine the Rule of Law and impact the valuable rights of the parties being investigated.

While the Supreme Court was endeavouring to protect the Taj Mahal in the *Taj Trapezium* case,[28] the government of Uttar Pradesh initiated a project known as 'Taj Heritage Corridor Project'. The project involved diverting the River Yamuna and reclaiming 75 acres of land between Agra Fort and the Taj Mahal for constructing food plazas, shops and amusement activities. An inquiry was carried out by the Central Bureau of Investigation (CBI) and the concerned Magistrate directed CBI to obtain sanction of the Governor of Uttar Pradesh. This is because Ms. Mayawati, the then Chief Minister and Mr. Naseemuddin Siddiqui, the then Minister of Environment as well as some officers of the state government were implicated. When the Governor refused to accord permission, the *amicus curiae* requested the Supreme Court to intervene and examine the validity of the Governor's order. The Supreme Court declined the request. It reasoned:

> In exercise of its jurisdiction under Article 32 of the Constitution of India and having regard to Article 49 and Clause (*g*) of Article 51-A of the Constitution of India, this Court while entertaining the public interest litigation at the instance of the writ petitioner had been taking all steps which have been thought necessary and proper in the matter. The question

[27] *T N Godavarman Thirumulpad v Union of India* (2013) 8 SCC 204.
[28] *M C Mehta v Union of India* AIR 1997 SC 734; AIR 1999 SC 3192.

which, however, has arisen for our consideration is, should we undertake such an exercise. No doubt, a first information report has been lodged at the instance of this Court. Yet again this Court thought it fit to issue requisite directions in its order dated 27-11-2006 [(2007) 1 SCC 110] directing the learned Special Judge to apply its mind on the materials collected during investigation by CBI and pass appropriate orders thereupon. This Court has been exercising its jurisdiction in public interest. It has been exercising its jurisdiction to issue a writ of continuous mandamus in the light of the decision of this Court in *Vineet Narain v Union of India* [(1998) 1 SCC 226].

We have no doubt in our mind that judiciary may step in where it finds the actions on the part of the legislature or the executive are illegal or unconstitutional but the same by itself would not mean that public interest litigation, in a case of this nature, should be converted into an adversarial litigation. The jurisdiction of the Court to issue a writ of continuous mandamus is only to see that proper investigation is carried out. Once the Court satisfies itself that a proper investigation has been carried out, it would not venture to take over the functions of the Magistrate or pass any order which would interfere with his judicial functions. Constitutional scheme of this country envisages dispute resolution mechanism by an independent and impartial tribunal. No authority, save and except a superior court in the hierarchy of judiciary, can issue any direction which otherwise takes away the discretionary jurisdiction of any court of law. Once a final report has been filed in terms of sub-section (1) of Section 173 of the Code of Criminal Procedure, it is the Magistrate and Magistrate alone who can take appropriate decision in the matter one way or the other. If he errs while passing a judicial order, the same may be a subject-matter of appeal or judicial review. There may be a possibility of the prosecuting agencies not approaching the higher forum against an order passed by the learned Magistrate, but the same by itself would not confer a jurisdiction on this Court to step in....

It is one thing to say that this Court will not refrain from exercising its jurisdiction from issuing any direction for protection of cultural heritage and the ecology and environment; but then in discharge of the said duty, this Court should not take upon itself the task of determining the guilt or otherwise of an individual involved in the criminal proceeding. It should not embark upon an enquiry in regard to the allegations of criminal misconduct so as to form an opinion one way or the other so as to prima facie determine guilt of a person or otherwise....

We may observe that while entertaining a public interest litigation in a given case, this Court may exercise a jurisdiction to set aside the decision of a constitutional authority, but we are not concerned with such a situation. We, therefore, are of the view that we need not go further than what we have already said in our order dated 27-11-2006 [(2007) 1 SCC 110] to go into the correctness or otherwise of the order of the Governor. If no sanction of the Governor was required or if he has committed an error in passing the said order, the appropriate court, in our opinion, would be entitled to deal therewith, but not this Bench.[29]

E. SHOULD RIVERS HAVE RIGHTS?

On 20 March 2017, a division bench of the Uttarakhand High Court pushed the envelope by declaring the Ganga and Yamuna rivers juristic persons having legal status. The bench presided over by Justice Rajiv Sharma was hearing a PIL where the Central Government had been asked to constitute the Ganga Management Board in terms of section 80 of the Uttar Pradesh Reorganization Act of 2000. The High Court expressed its displeasure at Uttar Pradesh and Uttarakhand failing to appoint members onto the board. The court thereafter observed that despite their religious and spiritual significance, both the rivers were facing an

[29] *M C Mehta v Union of India* (2008) 1 SCC 407, 411.

existential threat. Drawing on Supreme Court judgments that conferred juristic status on Hindu idols, the court concluded:

> A juristic person, like any other natural person is in law also conferred with rights and obligations and is dealt with in accordance with law. In other words, the entity acts like a natural person but only through a designated person.... For a bigger thrust of socio-political-scientific development, evolution of a fictional personality to be a juristic person becomes inevitable. This may be any entity, living inanimate, objects or things. It may be a religious institution or any such useful unit which may impel the Courts to recognize it. This recognition is for subserving the needs and faith of the society. *Corpus Juris Secundum*, Vol. 6, page 778 explains the concept of juristic persons/artificial persons thus: 'Artificial persons. Such as are created and devised by human laws for the purposes of society and government, which are called corporations or bodies politic.' A juristic person can be any subject matter other than a human being to which the law attributes personality for good and sufficient reasons. Juristic persons being the arbitrary creations of law, as many kinds of juristic persons have been created by law as the society require for its development. (See *Salmond on Jurisprudence* 12th edition, pages 305 and 306). Thus, to protect the recognition and the faith of society, Rivers Ganga and Yamuna are required to be declared as the legal persons/ living persons.
>
> All the Hindus have deep Astha in rivers Ganga and Yamuna and they collectively connect with these rivers. Rivers Ganga and Yamuna are central to the existence of half of Indian population and their health and well being. The rivers have provided both physical and spiritual sustenance to all of us from time immemorial. Rivers Ganga and Yamuna have spiritual and physical sustenance. They support and assist both the life and natural resources and health and well-being of the entire community. Rivers Ganga and Yamuna are breathing, living and sustaining the communities from mountains to sea.
>
> The constitution of Ganga Management Board is necessary for the purpose of irrigation, rural and urban water supply, hydro power generation, navigation, industries. There is utmost expediency to give legal status as a living person/legal entity to Rivers Ganga and Yamuna r/w Articles 48-A and 51A(g) of the Constitution of India.
>
> Accordingly, while exercising the *parens patriae* jurisdiction, the Rivers Ganga and Yamuna, all their tributaries, streams, every natural water flowing with flow continuously or intermittently of these rivers, are declared as juristic/legal persons/living entities having the status of a legal person with all corresponding rights, duties and liabilities of a living person in order to preserve and conserve river Ganga and Yamuna. The Director NAMAMI Gange, the Chief Secretary of the State of Uttarakhand and the Advocate General of the State of Uttarakhand are hereby declared *persons in loco parentis* as the human face to protect, conserve and preserve Rivers Ganga and Yamuna and their tributaries. These Officers are bound to uphold the status of Rivers Ganges and Yamuna and also to promote the health and well being of these rivers.
>
> The Advocate General shall represent at all legal proceedings to protect the interest of Rivers Ganges and Yamuna.[30]

Ten days later, the same division bench expanded the declaration issued in *Mohd Salim*. Here, the court was considering an application 'for declaring the Himalayas, Glaciers, Streams, Water Bodies etc. as legal entities as juristic persons at par with pious rivers Ganga and Yamuna'. The court noted with concern the retreat of the Gangotri and the Yamunotri glaciers from which the Ganga and Yamuna rivers originate. Since the glaciers were receding due to pollution and climate change, 'urgent remedial steps are required to be taken to ensure that the receding of these glaciers is stopped'. After an extensive survey of literature, international conventions, religious philosophies and precedent the court concluded:

30 *Mohd Salim v State of Uttarakhand* (2017) SCC Online UTT 367.

Rivers and Lakes have intrinsic right not to be polluted. Polluting and damaging the rivers, forests, lakes, water bodies, air and glaciers will be legally equivalent to harming, hurting and causing injury to person.

Rivers, Forests, Lakes, Water Bodies, Air, Glaciers and Springs have a right to exist, persist, maintain, sustain and regenerate their own vital ecology system. The rivers are not just water bodies. These are scientifically and biologically living.

The rivers, forests, lakes, water bodies, air, glaciers, human life are unified and are indivisible whole. The integrity of the rivers is required to be maintained from Glaciers to Ocean.

However, we would hasten to observe that the local inhabitants living on the banks of rivers, lakes and whose lives are linked with rivers and lakes must have their voice too....

A juristic person, like any other natural person is in law also conferred with rights and obligations and is dealt with in accordance with law. In other words, the entity acts like a natural person but only through a designated person. For a bigger thrust of socio-political-scientific development, evolution of a fictional personality to be a juristic person becomes inevitable.... Any person causing any injury and harm, intentionally or unintentionally to the Himalayas, Glaciers, rivers, streams, rivulets, lakes, air, meadows, dales, jungles and forests is liable to be proceeded against under the common law, penal laws, environmental laws and other statutory enactments governing the field....

[T]he Himalayan Mountain Ranges, Glaciers, rivers, streams, rivulets, lakes, jungles, air, forests, meadows, dales, wetlands, grasslands and springs are required to be declared as the legal entity/legal person/juristic person/juridicial person/moral person/artificial person for their survival, safety, sustenance and resurgence....

Accordingly, the following directions are issued: ...

2. We, by invoking our *parens patriae* jurisdiction, declare the Glaciers including Gangotri & Yamunotri, rivers, streams, rivulets, lakes, air, meadows, dales, jungles, forests wetlands, grasslands, springs and waterfalls, legal entity/legal person/juristic person/juridicial person/moral person/artificial person having the status of a legal person, with all corresponding rights, duties and liabilities of a living person, in order to preserve and conserve them. They are also accorded the rights akin to fundamental rights/legal rights.

3. The Chief Secretary, State of Uttarakhand, Director Namami Gange Project, Mr. Praveen Kumar, Director (NMCG), Mr. Ishwar Singh, Legal Advisor, Namami Gange Project, Advocate General, State of Uttarakhand, Dr Balram K Gupta, Director (Academics), Chandigarh Judicial Academy and Mr M C Mehta, Senior Advocate, Hon Supreme Court, are hereby declared the *persons in loco parentis* as the human face to protect, conserve and preserve all the Glaciers including Gangotri & Yamunotri, rivers, streams, rivulets, lakes, air, meadows, dales, jungles, forests wetlands, grasslands, springs and waterfalls in the State of Uttarakhand. These Officers are bound to uphold the status of these bodies and also to promote their health and well-being.

4. The Chief Secretary of the State of Uttarakhand is also permitted to co-opt as many as Seven public representatives from all the cities, towns and villages of the State of Uttarakhand to give representation to the communities living on the banks of rivers near lakes and glaciers.

5. The rights of these legal entities shall be equivalent to the rights of human beings and the injury/harm caused to these bodies shall be treated as harm/injury caused to the human beings....[31]

On 7 July 2017, the Supreme Court stayed the operation of the High Court order in *Mohd Salim* in a petition for special leave to appeal filed by Uttarakhand.[32] Similarly, the *Miglani* order was also stayed by the Supreme Court on the request of the Union Government.[33]

[31] *Lalit Miglani v State of Uttarakhand* (2017) SCC Online Utt 392.

[32] *State of Uttarakhand v Mohd Salim* (2017) SCC Online SC 903.

[33] Order dated 27 November 2017 in SLP (Civil) 33968 of 2017.

Undeterred, another bench of the Uttarakhand High Court (also presided over by Justice Rajiv Sharma) expanded the dimensions of the *parens patriae* doctrine in the context of animal welfare, specifically horse carts used for transport between Nepal and India.

> There is no check on the fare to be charged from the passengers and the luggage travelling from Nepal to India and India to Nepal. The horse dung is polluting the river water. The ailing, infirm and old horses are abandoned by the owners in the Indian Territory. The infected horses are hazardous to the human beings. The horse carts/tongas stay overnight and are being parked on the roadside. The tongas are overloaded. It causes cruelty to the horses. There is no record of the persons or their identity plying the horse carts/tongas with the Indian territory. The record of horse carts/tongas is required to be maintained. Pictures have also been placed on record showing the injured horses. It is in these circumstances, the present petition has been filed. . . .
>
> All the animals have honour and dignity. Every species has an inherent right to live and are required to be protected by law. The rights and privacy of animals are to be respected and protected from unlawful attacks. Their Lordships have evolved the term 'species' best interest.' The Corporations, Hindu idols, holy scriptures, rivers have been declared legal entities and thus, in order to protect and promote greater welfare of animals including avian and aquatic, animals are required to be conferred with the status of legal entity/legal person. The animals should be healthy, comfortable, well-nourished, safe, able to express innate behavior without pain, fear and distress. They are entitled to justice.
>
> Accordingly, the writ petition is disposed of by issuing the following mandatory directions:—
>
> A. The entire animal kingdom including avian and aquatic are declared as legal entities having a distinct persona with corresponding rights, duties and liabilities of a living person. All the citizens throughout the State of Uttarakhand are hereby declared persons in loco parentis as the human face for the welfare/protection of animals. . . .[34]

NOTES AND QUESTIONS

1. How persuasive are the judgments of the Uttarakhand High Court? What are the legal effects of granting rivers legal rights? What are the social, economic and political consequences of conferring rights on animals other than ourselves? Review the comment by Ashish Kothari and Shrishtee Bajpai[35] and the criticism of *Mohd Salim* by Bushra Quasmi.[36]

2. While the Uttarakhand High Court appears to be among the first judicial fora to bestow rights on rivers and glaciers,[37] legislatures have done so. In 2010, Bolivia passed the 'Law of Mother Earth' granting legal rights for nature.[38] In New Zealand, the Whanganui River and its catchment are recognized as a legal person under the Awa Tupua (Whanganui River Claims Settlement) Act of 2017.[39] In May 2017, the Madhya Pradesh legislature resolved to grant the river Narmada the status of a living entity.

34 *Narayan Dutt Bhatt v Union of India* (2018) SCC Online Utt 645.

35 Ashish Kothari & Shristee Bajpai, *Rivers and Human Rights: We Are the River, the River Is Us*, 52 Economic & Political Weekly 103 (2017).

36 Bushra Quasmi, *Rivers as Legal Persons: A Regressive Step*, 52 Economic & Political Weekly 25 (2017).

37 In May 2017, Columbia's constitutional court pronounced that the Atrato River basin (which was ravaged by illegal gold mining) had rights to protection, conservation, maintenance and restoration.

38 Ley de Derechos de la Madre Tierra 2010 (Bolivia).

39 Erin L O'Donnell, *At the Intersection of the Sacred and the Legal: Rights for Nature in Uttarakhand, India*, 30 Jr Of Envir Law 135 (2018).

3. Eventually, new principles and doctrine must yield practical benefits to society. Will the recognition conferred by the Uttarakhand High Court on rivers, glaciers and animals help achieve sustainable development goals? Is the High Court simply trying to give a voice to the unheard in an effort to curb over-exploitation of natural resources? Do we really know what rivers, glaciers and trees want?

4. Consider these explanations for India's generous standing doctrine:

> First, activist judges such as Bhagwati served as norm entrepreneurs, at times venturing 'far beyond the necessities of the particular case.' Second, India's Eastern philosophical roots predisposed the state and its judicial system to advance legal reasoning regarding issues of human rights and the environment. Third, certain threshold events such as the [Indira] Gandhi Emergency and the Bhopal disaster pushed the issue of human rights and environmental law to the extent that public pressure mandated some form of judicial action.[40]

Will they help sustain the Uttarakhand High Court's expansion of standing?

F. RIGHT TO INFORMATION AND OTHER PROCEDURAL RIGHTS

Public access to government information enables citizens to exercise their political choice meaningfully. Secrecy erodes the legitimacy of elected governments. A regime that conceals its actions and policies cannot be judged by the electorate and cannot be held accountable for its misdeeds. Moreover, governments in modern welfare states exercise vast powers that affect economic interests and impinge on a citizen's liberty. These powers are susceptible to misuse for private gain. The right to be informed of public acts helps check the abuse of executive power. Data that forms the basis of decision-making may at times be taken out of context, and bureaucrats may deliberately suppress certain viewpoints to favour others. Openness in government corrects these tendencies and raises the quality of decision-making. The right to know also strengthens participatory democracy. A peoples' right to influence government, other than through periodic elections, is widely recognized. Armed with information on government programmes, citizens may influence decision-making through representations, lobbying and public debate.

The right to know is especially critical in environmental matters. For example, government decisions to site dams may displace thousands of people and deprive them of their lifestyles and livelihoods. A responsible government, therefore, ought to widely publicize its river development plans and ought to be receptive to public feedback.

Information on the proposed location of nuclear power stations and hazardous industries directly affects the lives and health of neighbouring communities. As the Bhopal Gas Leak disaster grimly illustrates, pervasive ignorance to the dangers of methyl isocyanate contributed to the cause and the magnitude of the tragedy.[41] Moreover, access to government records helps litigants construct the necessary fact base for legal actions. It enhances access to justice.

Amongst the most important legislations enacted by Parliament is the Right to Information (RTI) Act of 2005. It has a constitutional flavor and it redefines the republic. The RTI Act

---

[40] Josh Gellers, *Righting Environmental Wrong: Assessing the Role of Legal Systems in Redressing Environmental Grievances*, 26 Jr Of Envir Law And Litigation 461, 479 (2011).

[41] Sheila Jasanoff, *The Bhopal Disaster and the Right to Know*, 27 Social Science & Medicine 1113 (1988).

deepens democracy by empowering citizens to secure government records. It has ushered in a new paradigm of transparency in government business.

The preamble of the law declares that 'democracy requires an informed citizenry and transparency of information which are vital to its functioning and also to contain corruption and to hold Governments and their instrumentalities accountable to the governed'. The law creates a regime where citizens can swiftly secure access to information lying with public authorities.

'Right to information' is defined as information accessible under the Act. Purposefully, it includes the right to inspect work, documents, records; take notes, extracts or copies of documents or records; take certified samples of material; obtain information in electronic formats or through print-outs.[42]

The RTI Act declares: 'Subject to the provisions of this Act, all citizens shall have the right to information.'[43] Public authorities are obliged to maintain all records duly catalogued and indexed and are also mandated to computerize records and make them accessible to the public.[44] The expression 'public authority' covers every constitutional or statutory authority and includes bodies which are owned, controlled or substantially financed by the state.[45]

Every public authority must appoint a public information officer (PIO) in all its administrative units or offices and the PIO is required to provide information to persons seeking it.[46] The Act contemplates submission of requests to the PIO. A request may be made in writing or through an electronic communication in English or Hindi or in the official language of the area.[47] The PIO is required to dispose of every request within 30 days[48] and the Act contemplates appeals where the applicant is dissatisfied by the response or the failure to comply with the requisition.[49]

The Act exempts certain broad classes of information from the disclosure obligation, including information that would prejudicially affect the sovereignty and integrity of India, relations with foreign states or lead to the incitement of an offence.[50] In addition to these exempted categories, the law expressly excludes from its purview certain organizations which are listed to the Second Schedule of the law.[51]

Pollution control boards, forest departments, the offices of the wildlife warden, municipal authorities, coastal zone management authorities, the MoEF, etc. are all covered by the RTI Act. The right to know also extends to other environmental regulators and authorities such as those constituted under section 3(3) of the Environment (Protection) Act of 1986. When effectively employed, the RTI Act will yield full facts that are on the record of the public authority, including environment regulators. Indeed, RTI activists routinely obtain the full government file dealing with a particular project. This allows the citizen to frame her challenge without facing the hurdle of opacity encountered during the pre-RTI era. The Act has also done away with recourse to discovery and inspection provisions against public authorities

42 Section 2(h).
43 Section 3.
44 Section 4(1)(a).
45 Section 2(h).
46 Section 5(1).
47 Section 6(1).
48 Section 7(1).
49 Section 19.
50 Section 8.
51 Section 24.

under the Civil Procedure Code, since documents are now available in response to a simple statutory application to the PIO.

The RTI Act codifies a facet of the fundamental right guaranteed under Article 19(1)(a) of the Constitution.[52] Before its passage, the Supreme Court had derived a right to know. Justice Mathew in *State of Uttar Pradesh v Raj Narain*[53] was the first to recognize the citizen's right to know:

> In a government of responsibility like ours, where all the agents of the public must be responsible for their conduct, there can be but few secrets. The people of this country have a right to know every public act, everything that is done in a public way, by their public functionaries. They are entitled to know the particulars of every public transaction in all its bearing. The right to know, which is derived from the concept of freedom of speech, though not absolute, is a factor which should make one wary, when secrecy is claimed for transactions which can, at any rate, have no repercussion on public security, see *New York Times Co v United States* (1971) 403 US 713. To cover with veil of secrecy, the common routine business, is not in the interest of the public. Such secrecy can seldom be legitimately desired. It is generally desired for the purpose of parties and politics or personal self-interest or bureaucratic routine. The responsibilities of officials to explain and to justify their acts is the chief safeguard against oppression and corruption.

Justice Bhagwati, too, in *S P Gupta v Union of India* (*Judges' Transfer* case),[54] recognized the right to know to be implicit in the right to free speech and expression. In *Dinesh Trivedi v Union of India*,[55] the Supreme Court once again acknowledged the vital importance of open government in a participative democracy.

Justice Mukharji in *Reliance Petrochemicals Ltd v Proprietors of Indian Express Newspapers Bombay Pvt Ltd*[56] recognized the right to know as emanating from the right to life: 'We must remember that the people at large have a right to know in order to be able to take part in a participatory development in the industrial life and democracy. Right to know is a basic right [to] which citizens of a free country aspire [in the broadening horizon of the right to life] under Article 21 of our Constitution. That right has reached new dimensions and urgency. The right puts greater responsibility upon those who take upon the responsibility to inform.' The strong link between Article 21 and the right to know is evident in environmental matters where secret government decisions may affect health, life and livelihood.

Forcefully applying the right to know (before the RTI Act), the Supreme Court held that a voter has a right to know the antecedents of a candidate in an election. Pegging this right to Article 19(1)(a), the Supreme Court struck down a statute that sought to curtail disclosures with respect to criminal antecedents, property and educational qualifications of electoral candidates.[57]

Procedural environmental rights extend beyond the right to access justice and the general right to information. There are specific provisions in environmental statutes that confer a right to obtain information. Both the Air Act and the Water Act as amended in 1987 and 1988 respectively, oblige pollution control boards to disclose relevant internal reports to a citizen seeking to prosecute a polluter.[58] As we

---

[52] 'All citizens shall have the right (a) to freedom of speech and expression ... '
[53] AIR 1975 SC 865, 884.
[54] AIR 1982 SC 149, 234.
[55] (1997) 4 SCC 306, 314.
[56] AIR 1989 SC 190, 202.
[57] *Peoples' Union for Civil Liberties v Union of India* AIR 2003 SC 2363; (2003) 4 SCC 399.
[58] Section 43(2), Air Act of 1981; and section 49(2), Water Act of 1974.

have seen, these provisions are largely unused since prosecutions are tedious and impractical.[59]

Of far greater utility are the procedural rights conferred under the Environmental Impact Assessment notification of 2006. The EIA regime requires that information about a proposed project be disclosed to the public. The disclosure includes access to the terms of reference issued by the regulatory authority, the draft EIA report and its summary prepared by the project proponent. Linked to this right to information is a further right to participate in a public hearing conducted before the decision on granting an environmental clearance is taken. The public participation process enables concerned citizens to project their viewpoints after studying the documents.

An indirect procedural dividend accrues from the establishment of the National Green Tribunal. Since the NGT exercises both original as well as appellate jurisdiction, decisions of environmental regulators are routinely examined by the Tribunal. Potential scrutiny by the NGT ensures that regulators record cogent reasons for their decisions. Otherwise, the decision may be overturned on review by the Tribunal.[60]

---

59 Provisos to section 43 of the Air Act and section 49 of the Water Act allow a board to withhold any report if it considers that disclosure would be against 'the public interest'. This qualification to the right of information seems unnecessary. It is difficult to envision a situation where the disclosure of reports on pollution could harm the public.

60 See generally, Shibani Ghosh, *Procedural Environmental Rights in Indian Law* in Indian Environmental Law: Key Concepts And Principles 55 (Ed. Shibani Ghosh, 2019).

8

WATER POLLUTION CONTROL

The Indian legal system provides four major sources of law for addressing water pollution problems: (1) a comprehensive scheme of administrative regulation through the permit system of the Water (Prevention and Control of Pollution) Act of 1974; (2) provisions of the Environment (Protection) Act of 1986 relating to water quality; (3) public nuisance actions against polluters, including municipalities charged with controlling water pollution; and (4) the common law right of riparian owners to unpolluted water. In addition, the Union Government has developed action plans for rejuvenating the Ganga and restoring the quality of her waters. The Supreme Court of India, the High Courts and the National Green Tribunal (NGT) have added to the force of these laws by hearing petitions that seek implementation of measures to prevent water pollution.

A. WATER RESOURCES AND PUBLIC TRUST

We open this chapter with a reading from the *Span Motels* case, where the Supreme Court lays down a frame of reference to guide natural resource managers. In borrowing the public trust doctrine from American case law, the court supplies a common property vision of water resources and a wellspring for future environmental jurisprudence.

In 1995, Span Motels built a resort on the bank of the Beas River between Kullu and Manali in Himachal Pradesh. Kamal Nath, formerly the Union Minister of Environment and Forests, had links to the hotelier, who had encroached a swathe of forest land. The encroachment was 'validated' in 1993–94, during Nath's tenure as Minister. During the 1995 monsoons, the river engulfed part of the land and threatened the resort. In an effort to protect its property, both before and after the 1995 floods, Span Motels carried out substantial work (dredging, construction of concrete barriers, wire crates, etc.) to deflect the flow of the river.

M C MEHTA v KAMAL NATH

(1997) 1 SCC 388

Kuldip Singh, J:

* * *

The forest lands which have been given on lease to the Motel by the State Government are situated at the bank of River Beas. Beas is a young and dynamic river. It runs through Kullu Valley between the mountain ranges of the Dhauladhar in the right bank and the Chandrakheni in the left. The river is fast-flowing, carrying large boulders, at the times of flood. When water velocity is not sufficient to carry the boulders, those are deposited in the channel often blocking the flow of water. Under such circumstances the river stream changes its course, remaining within the valley but swinging from one bank to the other. The right bank of the River Beas where the Motel is located mostly comes under forest, the left bank consists of plateaus, having steep bank facing the river, where fruit orchards and cereal cultivation are predominant. The area being ecologically fragile and full of scenic beauty should not have been permitted to be converted into private ownership and for commercial gains.

Environmental Law & Policy in India. Shyam Divan and Armin Rosencranz, Oxford University Press.
 DOI: 1093/oso/9780192865458.003.0008

The notion that the public has a right to expect certain lands and natural areas to retain their natural characteristic is finding its way into the law of the land.... The ancient Roman Empire developed a legal theory known as the 'Doctrine of the Public Trust.' It was founded on the ideas that certain common properties such as rivers, seashore, forests and the air were held by Government in trusteeship for the free and unimpeded use of the general public. Our contemporary concern about 'the environment' bear[s] a very close conceptual relationship to this legal doctrine. Under the Roman law these resources were either owned by no one (*res nullius*) or by everyone in common (*res communis*). Under the English common law, however, the Sovereign could own these resources but the ownership was limited in nature, the Crown could not grant these properties to private owners if the effect was to interfere with the public interests in navigation or fishing. Resources that were suitable for these uses were deemed to be held in trust by the Crown for the benefit of the public. Joseph L Sax, Professor of Law, University of Michigan—proponent of the Modern Public Trust Doctrine has given the historical background of the Public Trust Doctrine as under:

> The source of modern public trust law is found in a concept that received much attention in Roman and English Law—the nature of property rights in rivers, the sea, and the seashore. That history has been given considerable attention in the legal literature and need not be repeated in detail here. But two points should be emphasized. First, certain interests, such as navigation and fishing, were sought to be preserved for the benefit of the public; accordingly, property used for those purposes was distinguished from general public property which the sovereign could routinely grant to private owners. Second, while it was understood that in certain common properties—such as the seashore, highways, and running water—'perpetual use was dedicated to the public', it has never been clear whether the public had an enforceable right to prevent infringement of those interests. Although the State apparently did protect public uses, no evidence is available that the public rights could be legally asserted against a recalcitrant government.

The public trust doctrine primarily rests on the principle that certain resources like air, sea, waters and the forests have such a great importance to the people as a whole that it would be wholly unjustified to make them a subject of private ownership. The said resources being a gift of nature, they should be made freely available to everyone irrespective of the status in life. The doctrine enjoins upon the Government to protect the resources for the enjoyment of the general public rather than to permit their use for private ownership or commercial purposes. According to Professor Sax the Public Trust Doctrine imposes the following restrictions on governmental authority:

> Three types of restrictions on governmental authority are often thought to be imposed by the public trust: first, the property subject to the trust must not only be used for a public purpose, but it must be held available for use by the general public; second, the property may not be sold, even for a fair cash equivalent; and third the property must be maintained for particular types of uses.

[The court reviewed a number of U.S. Court decisions, particularly the judgment of the Supreme Court of California in the *Mono Lake Case (National Audubon Society v Superior Court of Alpine County,* 33 Cal 3d 419). In *Mono Lake*, the environmentalists filed a suit against the city of Los Angeles which was drawing water from streams that fed Mono Lake, a large saline lake rich in brine shrimps and bird life. As a result of the diversion, the lake level was falling, marring the scenic beauty and imperilling the birds. Upholding the plaintiff's claim that the public trust doctrine could be used to supersede Los Angeles' water diversion, the California Supreme Court held:

> Thus, the public trust is more than an affirmation of State power to use public property for public purposes. It is an affirmation of the duty of the State to protect the people's common heritage of streams, lakes, marshlands and tidelands, surrendering that right of protection only in rare cases when the abandonment of that right is consistent with

the purposes of the trust. The State has an affirmative duty to take the public trust into account in the planning and allocation of water resources, and to protect public trust use whenever feasible. Just as the history of this State shows that appropriation may be necessary for efficient use of water despite unavoidable harm to public trust values, it demonstrates that an appropriative water rights system administered without consideration of the public trust may cause unnecessary and unjustified harm to trust interest.]

It is no doubt correct that the public trust doctrine under the English common law extended only to certain traditional uses such as navigation, commerce and fishing. But the American Courts in recent cases have expanded the concept of the public trust doctrine. The observations of the Supreme Court of California in *Mono Lake* case clearly show the judicial concern in protecting all ecologically important lands, for example fresh water, wetlands or riparian forests. The observations of the Court in *Mono Lake* case to the effect that the protection of ecological values is among the purposes of public trust, may give rise to an argument that the ecology and the environment protection is relevant factor to determine which lands, waters or airs are protected by the public trust doctrine....

Our legal system—based on English common law—includes the public trust doctrine as part of its jurisprudence. The State is the trustee of all natural resources which are by nature meant for public use and enjoyment. Public at large is the beneficiary of the seashore, running waters, airs, forests and ecologically fragile lands. The State as a trustee is under a legal duty to protect the natural resources. These resources meant for public use cannot be converted into private ownership.

We are fully aware that the issues presented in this case illustrate the classic struggle between those members of the public who could preserve our rivers, forests, parks and open lands in their pristine purity and those charged with administrative responsibilities who, under the pressure of the changing needs of an increasingly complex society, find it necessary to encroach to some extent upon open lands heretofore considered inviolate to change. The resolution of this conflict in any given case is for the legislature and not the courts. If there is a law made by Parliament or the State Legislatures the courts can serve as an instrument of determining legislative intent in the exercise of its powers of judicial review under the Constitution. But in the absence of any legislation, the executive acting under the doctrine of public trust cannot abdicate the natural resources and convert them into private ownership, or for commercial use. The aesthetic use and the pristine glory of the natural resources, the environment and the ecosystem of our country cannot be permitted to be eroded for private, commercial or any other use unless the courts finds it necessary, in good faith, for the public good and in public interest to encroach upon the said resources.

Coming to the facts of the present case, large area of the bank of River Beas which is part of protected forest has been given on a lease purely for commercial purposes to the Motels. We have no hesitation in holding that the Himachal Pradesh Government committed patent breach of public trust by leasing the ecologically fragile land to the Motel management. Both the lease transactions are in patent breach of the trust held by the State Government. The second lease granted in the year 1994 was virtually of the land which is a part of the riverbed....

We therefore direct and order as under:

1. The public trust doctrine, as discussed by us in this judgment is a part of the law of the land.
2. The prior approval granted by the government of India, Ministry of Environment and Forest by the letter dated 24-11-1993 and the lease deed dated 11-4-1994 in favour of the Motel are quashed. The lease granted to the Motel by the said lease deed in respect of 27 bighas and 12 biswas of area, is cancelled and set aside. The Himachal Pradesh Government shall take over the area and restore it to its original-natural conditions.

3. The Motel shall pay compensation by way of cost for the restitution of the environment and ecology of the area. The pollution caused by various constructions made by the Motel in the riverbed and the banks of River Beas has to be removed and reversed....
4. The Motel through its management shall show cause why pollution fine in addition be not imposed on the Motel....

NOTES AND QUESTIONS

1. The public trust doctrine has vast potential and may serve as the touchstone to test executive action with a significant environmental impact. For example, it may extend to common property cases where officials permit development along the seashore or the non-recreational use of playgrounds. It may also apply to partially regulated areas such as the exploitation of groundwater.

2. In the United States, the public trust doctrine as an environmental protection theory developed over several years. The Indian Supreme Court, untroubled by the absence of any Indian precedent in this field, simply imported the doctrine and declared that it was a part of the law of the land. What are the implications of this approach on the Rule of Law, especially the tenets of predictability and certainty?

3. It was in December 1996 that the public trust doctrine was articulated for the first time in India in this case. When the doctrine was articulated in *Mono Lake*, it was used in that very case. Legal doctrines apply to the case at hand, as well as prospectively.

4. At the end of the day, Span Motels was trying to save its buildings from being washed away. Is that objectionable? Was the judicial response an over-reaction? Or was the court seeking to emphasize ecological values by making an example of a powerful government functionary?

5. Does the public trust doctrine apply only to the allocation of pristine natural resources or does it extend to pollution cases as well? Are not river polluters 'allocating' to themselves clean water at the cost of downstream users? What are the implications of this doctrine on pollution control boards (PCBs) charged with issuing consents or permits to water and air polluters?

6. In addition to the orders excerpted earlier in the chapter, the court issued a direction to the Himachal Pradesh PCB to prevent all hotels, institutions and factories from discharging untreated waste-water into the Beas. Is it good judicial practice to issue general directions which travel beyond the scope of the petition? Are they justified because they strengthen the hands of the board officials?

7. In *M I Builders v Radhey Shyam Sahu*,[1] the Supreme Court held that allowing an underground shopping complex to be built below a public park violated the public trust doctrine. The court directed the demolition of the structures and restoration of the park. The public trust doctrine was also applied in *Fomento Resorts*[2] discussed in the Constitutional Provisions chapter.

---

[1] AIR 1999 SC 2468.
[2] *Fomento Resorts and Hotels Ltd v Minguel Martins* (2009) 3 SCC 571.

The principal judgment in the *Span Motel* case was rendered on 13 December 1996 by Justice Kuldip Singh.[3] By the time the further judgment was rendered on 12 May 2000, Justice Singh had retired and Justice S Saghir Ahmad presided on the bench.

M C MEHTA v KAMAL NATH

(2000) 6 SCC 213

S Saghir Ahmad, J: [The court summarized the operative directions passed on 13 December 1996.]

Pursuant to the above order, notice was issued requiring the Motel to show cause on two points: (*i*) why the Motel be not asked to pay compensation to reverse the degraded environment, and (*ii*) why pollution fine, in addition, be not imposed.

[L]earned Senior Counsel appearing for M/s Span Motel Private Ltd, has contended that though it is open to the Court, in proceedings under Article 32 of the Constitution, to grant compensation to the victims whose fundamental rights might have been violated or who are the victims of an arbitrary executive action or victims of atrocious behaviour of public authorities in violation of public duties cast upon them, it cannot impose any fine on those who are guilty of that action. He contended that the fine is a component of criminal jurisprudence and cannot be utilised in civil proceedings specially under Article 32 or 226 of the Constitution either by this Court or the High Court as imposition of fine would be contrary to the provisions contained in Articles 20 and 21 of the Constitution. It is contended that fine can be imposed upon a person only if it is provided by a statute and gives jurisdiction to the court to inflict or impose that fine after giving a fair trial to that person but in the absence of any statutory provision, a person cannot be penalised and no fine can be imposed upon him.

[The court recorded the submissions of the petitioner and highlighted the importance of protecting the environment. It referred to various environmental statutes as well as the Constitution. It then explained the polluter pays principle and specifically turned to the provisions dealing with penalties under the Water Act, 1974, the Air Act, 1981 and the EPA, 1986.]

All the three Acts, referred to above, also contemplate the taking of the cognizance of the offences by the court. Thus, a person guilty of contravention of provisions of any of the three Acts which constitutes an offence has to be prosecuted for such offence and in case the offence is found proved then alone can he be punished with imprisonment and fine or both. The *sine qua non* for punishment of imprisonment and fine is a fair trial in a competent court. The punishment of imprisonment or fine can be imposed only after the person is found guilty.

* * *

The contention that the notice should be treated to have been issued in exercise of power under Article 142 of the Constitution cannot be accepted as this article cannot be pressed into aid in a situation where action under that article would amount to contravention of the specific provisions of the Act itself. A fine is to be imposed upon the person who is found guilty of having contravened any of the provisions of the Act. He has to be tried for the specific offence and then on being found guilty, he may be punished either by sentencing him to undergo imprisonment for the period contemplated by the Act or with fine or with both. But recourse cannot be taken to Article 142 to inflict upon him this punishment.

Thus, in addition to the damages which have to be paid by M/s Span Motel, as directed in the main judgment, it cannot be punished with fine unless the entire procedure prescribed under the Act is followed and M/s Span Motel is tried for any of the offences contemplated by the Act and is found guilty.

[3] On the bench with Justice Singh was Justice S Saghir Ahmad.

The notice issued to M/s Span Motel why pollution fine be not imposed upon it is, therefore, withdrawn. But the matter does not end here.

Pollution is a civil wrong. By its very nature, it is a tort committed against the community as a whole. A person, therefore, who is guilty of causing pollution has to pay damages (compensation) for restoration of the environment and ecology. He has also to pay damages to those who have suffered loss on account of the act of the offender. The powers of this Court under Article 32 are not restricted and it can award damages in a PIL or a writ petition as has been held in a series of decisions. In addition to damages aforesaid, the person guilty of causing pollution can also be held liable to pay exemplary damages so that it may act as a deterrent for others not to cause pollution in any manner. Unfortunately, notice for exemplary damages was not issued to M/s Span Motel although it ought to have been issued. The considerations for which 'fine' can be imposed upon a person guilty of committing an offence are different from those on the basis of which exemplary damages can be awarded. While withdrawing the notice for payment of pollution fine, we direct that a fresh notice be issued to M/s Span Motel to show cause why in addition to damages, exemplary damages be not awarded for having committed the acts set out and detailed in the main judgment. This notice shall be returnable within six weeks. This question shall be heard at the time of quantification of damages under the main judgment.

On 15 March 2002, Justice Doraiswamy Raju authored the final judgment in this series[4] from which we carry a short excerpt:

M C MEHTA v KAMAL NATH

(2002) 3 SCC 653

* * *

RAJU, J:

Having regard to what has been stated supra, the question as to the imposition of exemplary damages and the liability of Span Motels Pvt. Ltd. in this regard has to necessarily depend upon the earlier findings of this Court that the Motel by constructing walls and bunds on the river banks and in the river bed as detailed in the judgment has interfered with the flow of the river and their liability to pay the damages on the principle of 'polluter pays' and also as an inevitable consequence thereof. The specification in the NEERI report regarding details of the activities of Span Motels Pvt Ltd and the nature of constructions made in 1993 in Figure 2 that (a) 'in 1993, to protect the newly acquired land as also the main resort land, SMPL constructed concrete studs, stepped wall and concrete bars as depicted in Figure 2'; (b) 'blocked the mouth of the natural relief/spill channel by dumping of boulders' resulting in the levelling of the leased area; and (c) 'at the downstream of M/s SMPL, a private property-owner has blocked the relief/spill channel by constructing a stonewall across the channel (E and F)' also confirms and only reinforces the need and justification for the indictment already made. The basis for their liability to be saddled with the exemplary costs has been firmly and irreversibly already laid down in the main judgment itself and there is no escape for Span Motels Pvt Ltd in this regard. We have to necessarily proceed further only on those ... facts and position of law, found and declared.

The question remaining for further consideration relating to the award of exemplary damages is only as to the quantum. The various laws in force to prevent and control pollution and protect the environment and ecology provide for different categories of punishment in the nature of imposition of fine as well as of imprisonment or either of them, depending upon the nature and extent of violation. The fine that may be imposed alone may extend

---

4 By this time, Justice S Saghir Ahmad had retired. Justice Raju was the junior judge on the bench that delivered the previous judgment on 12 May 2000.

even to one lakh of rupees. Keeping in view all these and the very object underlying the imposition of imprisonment and fine under the relevant laws to be not only to punish the individual concerned but also to serve as a deterrent to others to desist from indulging in such wrongs which we consider to be almost similar to the purpose and aim of awarding exemplary damages, it would be both in public interest as well as in the interests of justice to fix the quantum of exemplary damages payable by Span Motels Pvt Ltd at rupees ten lakhs only. This amount we are fixing keeping in view the undertaking given by them to bear a fair share of the project cost of ecological restoration which would be quite separate and apart from their liability for the exemplary damages. The question relating to the said quantum of liability for damages on the principle of 'polluter pays', as held by this Court against Span Motels Pvt Ltd and undertaken by them, will be determined separately and is left open for the time being. The amount of special damages of ten lakhs of rupees, shall be remitted to the State Government in the Department of Irrigation and Public Health to the Commissioner/Secretary for being utilized only for the flood protection works in the area of Beas river affected by the action of Span Motels Pvt Ltd.

NOTES AND QUESTIONS

1. The court was correct in holding that a fine is penal and can only be imposed in the manner contemplated by a statute after a fair trial. The court was also correct in rejecting recourse to Article 142 of the Constitution which empowers the Supreme Court to pass 'such decree or make such order as is necessary for doing complete justice in any cause or matter pending before it'. The notion of doing 'complete justice' would certainly not extend to bypassing the protection of a fair trial.

2. The court in its final judgment imposed exemplary damages of Rs. 10 lakhs. Was this not a relabelled 'fine'? Notice that the court has no additional material beyond the findings recorded in the main judgment.

3. Usually, exemplary or special damages are awarded over and above general damages and not where general damages remain to be quantified. Was it correct for the court to impose exemplary damages before assessing general damages?

B. WATER POLLUTION: SCOPE OF THE PROBLEM

The following readings provide descriptions of the nature and scope of the water pollution problem in India. The first article draws on a field study on the environmental impact of water pollution in rural Andhra Pradesh. The 'externality' referred to by the authors comprises impacts that are suffered by rural folk and economic costs borne by them, in contrast to the industry which failed to 'internalise' the cost by investing in technologies that would eliminate the pollution. By neglecting to invest in cleaner manufacturing practices, industry boosted its profits and competitiveness.

BHAGIRATH BEHERA, V RATNA REDDY; ENVIRONMENT AND ACCOUNTABILITY: IMPACT OF INDUSTRIAL POLLUTION ON RURAL COMMUNITIES, 37 Economic & Political Weekly 257 (2002)

For the purpose of the present study, a village under the Patancheru industrial belt Medak district of Andhra Pradesh has been selected. The village has been badly affected by the industrial pollution, an environmental externality....

There are four major industrial areas in Ranga Reddy and Medak districts of Andhra Pradesh. These are Patancheru, Pashamylaram, Bollarum and Kazipally. Among these, Patancheru is one of the oldest and most environmentally degraded. The Patancheru region houses some 80 firms, nearly half of which are chemical units, including those making life-saving drugs. Major chemical and bulk drugs manufacturing units are located here which generate significant quantities of hazardous waste. These wastes are not controlled effectively and are dumped along with municipal solid waste on vacant lands close to the factories or along roadsides. These hazardous waste dump sites result in contamination of soil, surface and ground-water. A drive from Patancheru to Sangareddy in Medak district is a nauseating experience, due to visible and invisible sources. It is a health hazard for cattle roaming in and around the industrial waste. In fact, the burden of pollution on the environment has already crossed its assimilative capacity. The negligence on the part of policy-makers can only be described as environment forfeited for the sake of industrialisation, chemical consumption, and competitiveness in global chemical product markets.

Patancheru is among the most unplanned industrial estates in Hyderabad, with no specific plan for establishing industrial units, which are established in a very unsystematic, haphazard and scattered manner. As a result, it is increasingly difficult to assess the environmental impact of a particular unit. For instance, if all the chemical industries are located in a particular area, then the impact assessment of the chemical industries could be easier, and accordingly, measures can be taken to reduce or prevent the environmental damage. However, the situation in Patancheru is different because it is a cluster of less and more polluting industries....

Irrigation systems are the worst affected due to the industrial pollution in Patancheru region. In Patancheru, there are at least 15 irrigation tanks, and according to unofficial sources, all of them have been completely polluted. However, officially (Sangareddy pollution control board) it is claimed that five irrigation tanks have been completely spoiled and rest are partially affected. Among these, the Krishtareddy pet and Gandigudem tanks are highly polluted. But the farmers have no option but to irrigate with polluted water. As a result, productive lands are turning unproductive. The entire water body of both ground and surface water is contaminated. The biological oxygen demand (BOD) level in the polluted water has already crossed the limit for drinking. The pollution control board of Sangareddy has tested samples of polluted water of the Patancheru industrial belt and found that dissolved oxygen in the water body is zero, indicating that it is no longer suitable for consumption....

Air or water pollution or both have affected around 15 villages in this region. The most serious problem is of drinking water. As mentioned earlier, in the Patancheru mandal both surface and groundwater are totally polluted. People depend entirely on the municipal drinking water supply. But the meagre municipal water supplies force the villagers to depend on the contaminated water for purposes other than drinking. Livestock is also forced to drink the polluted water and hence suffer from various diseases. A number of deaths has also been reported in the village, apart from declining milk yields and fertility rates. This adds to the woes of the households.

The situation in Patancheru is alarming. Due to the use of contaminated water, people are suffering from various water-borne diseases like skin infections, fever and joint pain. As there is no in-depth study on the impact of pollution on the health of the people, it is difficult to estimate the exact costs of the problem. Adding these costs (health) will bring out the real costs borne by the households. Besides, these costs need to be added to the cost-benefit analysis of the polluting industries.

After major protest by the villagers, a common effluent treatment plant (CETP) has been established in the Patancheru industrial belt. The entire liquid waste of Patancheru industrial belt now comes to the CETP for treatment. After treating the wastes it releases the water into the nearby streams, which join the Manjira river. The villages that are located on the streams and the river are severely affected. For the CETP is not effective, as we see later. The fish population is the streams and Manjira river has been affected badly....

The entire village has been suffering from various diseases arising out of water pollution. However, it was observed that most of the diseases are water-borne, such as skin infections, teeth corrosion, joint pains, loss of appetite, defective vision, fever, abdominal pain, respiratory diseases, and diarrhoea. Also, general muscular weakness, stunted growth, chronic cold and cough among the middle-aged and children are noticed in the village. A majority of complaints are about the problems regarding lung diseases and extreme weakness. It is found that seven people in the village have been paralysed due to drinking contaminated water. This had lead to severe psychological and economic pressure on the families concerned. People get exposed to the toxic chemical water while working in the farm, taking bath and washing clothes. This causes serious health problems including loss of hair for women.

The most important feature of the health problem due to pollution is that women are the worst affected. The percentage of affected women in each household is higher. This is because women do the entire household work with contaminated water. The average number of days sick and unable to work per household is about 50 a year. This indicates loss of income and expenditure on health care. Across the size classes, the incidence of sickness is higher in the case of large farmers, while the number of working days lost due to sickness is higher among small cultivators. Similarly, the number of visits to doctors and expenditure on health before and after pollution reveal substantial increases. The expenditure on health depends on two factors: the severity of the diseases and the economic condition of the family. The marginal farmer's average visits to doctors 30 per annum and their medical expenditure is Rs.4,476. In case of small farmers, the average visits to doctors numbers 26 and their medical expenditure is Rs.6,733. Small farmers are spending more money per visit to the doctor, which is perhaps due to their better ability to pay. When expenditure is directly related to quality of treatment, frequency of visits to the doctor would naturally come down....

Livestock is one of the main sources of income in rural areas. Since all the local water sources are polluted, livestock in the village are also facing serious health problems. In the absence of sufficient municipal water supplies, livestock are forced to depend on polluted water and graze on contaminated grasses. It was reported by the villagers that 338 cattle have died after drinking polluted water during the past six-year. A majority of the cattle have fallen sick over the years. Another serious problem is that some cows have lost their reproductive capacity. Reduction in milk productivity of buffaloes and cows is also reported. As a result of grazing on contaminated grasses the quality of dung has been reduced to an unuseable level. Due to fear of further deaths, people have started selling their cattle very cheap.... In fact, farmers now depend more on tractors to plough their land rather than keeping/buying bullocks, because of the huge risks of death....

Apart from the decline in agricultural productivity, the polluted water has imposed enormous costs due to corrosion of agricultural equipment, damage to pump sets, and repairing costs of machines. The damage to pump sets has become a serious concern for the villagers, as most of the pump sets were bought with loans from banks. This has lead to farmers' indebtedness. Irrigation water containing detergents wash out lubricants from oscillates and pumps. And an excessive amount of suspended solids in the water requires frequent cleaning of filters and nozzles....

Pollution from the industries that produce life-saving drugs has turned the surrounding villages into virtual killing fields. The way in which the environmental externalities have occurred can mainly be attributed to three important failures: market failure, policy failure and institutional failure.

NOTES AND QUESTIONS

1. The authors found that the average loss per household per year worked out to Rs. 36,085 comprising losses due to impacts on health, livestock and agriculture. Industrialization in the areas started in the mid-1980s and according to the villagers they first became aware of the pollution impacts in the early 1990s. Initially, the villagers felt that the chemical-laden water would increase fertility of the land but by 1991–92, the colour of the tank water changed, fish in the tanks began to die and soon thereafter crop yields plummeted.

2. The authors argue that the unacceptable level of water pollution arose from a 'market failure' in that the costs for producing the industrial products were borne by the rural communities, not the industry. The markets failed to 'internalize the externalities'. The village community was in no bargaining position to force industry to pay for polluting the tanks which were a common property resource. While economists speak of externalities, the legal principle to prevent such distortions is the 'polluter pays' principle. Internalizing economic costs results in economic efficiency apart from being equitable and just. Moreover, the CETP, rather than providing relief, was a principal culprit in contamination of groundwater.

The policy failure arose when the Andhra Pradesh PCB failed to exercise its powers to discipline polluters. The complaints by the villagers resulted in routine inspections by the board raising a strong suspicion of a nexus between industry and board officials. The judicial system too failed to abate the pollution.

In terms of the institutional failure, the authors noticed that the rural community lacked committed leadership and each separate village was isolated in its frustration.

3. Notice how the CETP resulted in severely impacting downstream villages on the River Manjira. Poorly planned and executed pollution control strategies can cause great harm. The object of environmental impact assessment is to eliminate such collateral damage by anticipating potential impacts which here the CETP designers failed to do.

4. The Patancheru study was conducted in the late 1990s underscoring the ineffectiveness of the Water Act which by then had been on the statute book for a quarter century.

Next, we carry two water stories from the environmentalist Sunita Narain's memoir.

SUNITA NARAIN; CONFLICTS OF INTEREST: MY JOURNEY THROUGH INDIA'S GREEN MOVEMENT, 166, 176 (2017)

Visited the village of Laporiya in Rajasthan. I got there when people had seen five years of successive, backbreaking, debilitating drought. I expected dry lands, desolation and nearly abandoned villages. But instead I could see greenery, irrigated agriculture, people tending to vegetable crops and livestock. The village dairy—a one-room shop with an electronic machine to detect fat content in the milk—was lined with people bringing their product for sale. I asked to check the records and found that they had sold Rs.34 lakh worth of milk in the previous year. I asked about water and was told that there were 103 wells in the village. People could use the wells for one hour each day to irrigate their fields. I saw that water visible from the naked eye—some 50 feet below the surface.

After five years of crippling drought, how could there be water in the wells? My hosts were the Gram Vikas Yuvak Mandal and its head Laxman Singh. He took me to see a map—displayed in the village centre. The green painted area was the village common land—grazing land vested with the government. This, explained Singh, was the land we had to fight to regain control over as it was encroached and degraded. On the map, squares had been painted. There were the *chaukas*—a unique water harvesting system designed by Singh and his colleagues—to retain every drop of rainwater and to recharge the ground. All over the common land, villagers had dug rectangular trenches—less than one foot step—so that the rainwater would 'jump' across the land till it flowed into the village tanks.

With this system in place, the village common land had become a grand water collection area. Painstakingly, every drop of water was captured and channelled and stored in the three connected village tanks, deepened by voluntary labour. Downstream lay 1000-odd hectares of agricultural land, of which roughly 600 hectares were irrigated. There was a gleam in Singh's eye as he told me about the good rain years when the tanks had overflowed with water. But for the past some years the tanks had barely filled. Today, these were bone dry. But still the wells have water. Laporiya practices the conjunctive use of irrigation structures—surface and ground—that engineers love to boast about, but have no clue how to build.

* * *

A few years ago, the Supreme Court had asked the committee I work with to monitor a state government's effort to clean city drains, which lead to the Yamuna river and pollute it to hell. The government presented an action plan to the court. They would build sewage treatment plants, upgrade existing plants, lay sewage drains in housing colonies and repair conveyance systems to pump the waste to sewage plants. It fit all the prescriptions.

I presumed our task was to check if the sewage plants had been built and if they were working. How ignorant of me.

My first lesson came when we visited the sewage treatment plant. The plant's management had records of the quality of waste received and the treated effluent. They showed us samples as well. It seemed to be in order. The only, small, problem was that the sewerage plant remained underutilized—it received only 40% of the waste that it could treat. Officials told us that this was because the sewerage systems and drains were laid but had not been connected to households, because of high costs. They said it was only a matter of time before the infrastructure would be completed and sewerage would flow into the plant. Their emphasis was to add to the infrastructure of the sewage plant itself. They needed more capacity in anticipation of this additional sewage that would be generated. Once done, the river, they assured us, would be clean.

Made perfect sense. Then, by chance, I asked how they disposed the treated effluent. Pat came the reply: we have a treatment effluent disposal drain, which meets the river at some distance. This is what happens in most cities, I was reassured. My colleague, a senior and respected bureaucrat, and I then wanted to see the disposal point.

The disposal point was in the drain in front of the sewage plant. From where we stood, it was clear that the treated effluent—meeting all pollution parameters and costing money and electricity to clean—was discharging into a drain already putrid and full of sewage. The treated effluent did little to dilute the floating filth. In fact, the stuff in the drain negated the pollution control efforts. The plant had been built where land was available. The officials had never considered how the treated effluent would be disposed of and if it could be reused.

Then we asked about the drain. It was a storm-water drain and the official told us that it should not have any waste (we were visiting in peak summer). The problem was that the adjoining colonies did not yet have sewage drains but once they did, the situation would be under control.

Then we opened another can of worms. We learnt that roughly half the population residing in this part of the city were not connected to the sewage system. They lived in illegal, unauthorized or slum areas. So their waste was also 'illegal', not to be accounted for. This is not unusual. In most large Indian cities, 20–50% of the people live in similar settlements. Since official drainage does not effectively connect the entire population, only a part of the sewage is trapped, pumped and taken to the conveyance system. Their sewage gets carried by gravity to the open drains, which in the official books only transport storm water, not excreta. The pieces fit together when we understand that this 'legal' and 'illegal' sewage gets mixed in the same drain, which by the time it meets the river is grossly polluted. No wonder the river never gets cleaned.

The next sewage treatment plant is located downstream of the first. It retreats the effluents discharged from the first plant, which has turned dirt to dirt. The treatment effluents of this plant then meet another drain, which collects more sewage on its way to the river. The river is tapped at the barrage upstream of the city, for drinking water. Then, in its journey, it picks up sewage from my city. By the time it exits, it has only sewage, no water. The cities downstream of my city do the same. The river had no water to dilute our excreta. It is even losing its assimilative capacity—to turn sewage to soil and water. To bring it to life would require us to take water and to return water to the river.

I began to then understand the economics of the excreta business. Put out a tender and build drains, pumps and sewage treatment plants. The problem is we don't know our maths. The more water we use, the more waste is discharged. The state does not charge for the water it supplies, forget for the waste it collects or treats. The relatively rich—or call them 'legal' settlers with 'legal' excreta—cost the state. It does not have the money or the wherewithal to pay to build, run or repair the system for all. There is no way the river cannot get polluted.

This is not a parody. This water-excreta tale is not unique to Yamuna or Delhi. This is the political economy of defecation where the rich are subsidized in the name of the poor, where the environment is discounted in the name of progress.

The next excerpt points out the gender asymmetry in water management decisions and water scarcity impacts in rural communities.

KUNTALA LAHIRI-DUTT; WATER, WOMEN AND RIGHTS IN WATER AND THE LAWS IN INDIA 275 (Ed. RAMASWAMY R IYER 2009)

The Indian Constitution ensures equality for women and men before the law, and prohibits discrimination against any citizen. Yet women's exclusion from domains of decision-making permeates through every section of Indian society and remains an everyday reality in spite of the positive response of the policymakers in amending the Constitution to ensure the participation of women in the public sphere. The near invisibility and exclusion of women is most apparent in water management in India. The view of water, as a physical resource and national good, to be planned and managed by the State, often overlooks the fact that women are the primary water managers and educators, and play important roles in the national economy as small-scale farmers and irrigators. The constitutional provisions have not yet translated into real empowerment for women in India....

Women are important as irrigators in terms of their numbers although they continue to remain concentrated in traditional or small-scale irrigation systems. In India, nearly one-third of agricultural workers are women; in addition, rural women in general are well-known for producing some crops for the household as a measure of food security. Altogether, this requires managing of a large amount of water. However, the crops produced by women or waters managed by them tend to receive very low or zero priority from irrigation analysts.

The single biggest impediment in making water a means of empowering women lies in the lack of recognition of women as irrigators and water users. Even when the responsibility of water management is devolved on the local level, it is often seen that women are not part of new bodies such as Water Users' Association (WUAs). The various formal and informal membership criteria and the process through which new water user organisations are formed in management transfer programmes and gender-biased as a result of planners' preconceptions about the definition of 'user' itself....

A study undertaken by Upadhaya in Gujarat that examines gender roles of men and women as both domestic activities and productive water users to show these roles help the latter to improve their socio-economic status. She found that costs of labour hours for women are not considered as 'real' costs since women are not paid for their contributions. Also, although women are significantly involved in irrigated agriculture, the revenues earned are entirely controlled by men. Women also bear the brunt of all ill-effects of deteriorating water quality and of excesses or scarcities, such as those during floods and droughts.

NOTES AND QUESTIONS

1. Narain argues that establishing sewage treatment plants alone will not clean our rivers. Effective plants must trap and treat all the sewage generated in the city. Otherwise, the investment in the STPs is wasted with the treated effluent again mixing with untreated sewage. She also advocates the reuse of treated effluent and a reduction in the overall water consumption by our cities.

2. Despite huge investments under various river cleaning schemes, our rivers remain polluted. According to one study, the five states with the most polluted stretches are Maharashtra, Assam, Madhya Pradesh, Gujarat and West Bengal. The polluted stretches add up to over 12,000 kms which is nearly five times the length of the Ganga.[5]

An evaluation of water bodies monitored by the Central PCB in 2018 showed that 17% were critically polluted. Karnataka, Telangana and Kerala had the most critically polluted rivers and water bodies.[6]

3. Will empowering rural women in water management decisions help in better and more equitable use of water resources?

C. THE WATER ACT

The Water (Prevention and Control of Pollution) Act of 1974 is a complex statute which has been in effect for nearly five decades. Many features of the Act have been challenged in the courts. In this section we discuss the framework of the Water Act and analyse major issues including the scope of judicial relief authorized by the Act, constitutional challenges to the Act, liability of corporate officers and funding of the administration of the Act.

I. FRAMEWORK OF THE WATER ACT

The Water Act of 1974 represented one of India's first attempts to deal comprehensively with an environmental issue. Parliament adopted minor amendments to the Act in 1978 and revised the Act in 1988 to more closely conform to the provisions of the Environment (Protection) Act of 1986. In 2010 the Water Act was amended again to provide for appeal to the National Green Tribunal.

Water is a subject in the State List under the Constitution.[7] Consequently, the Water Act, a central law, was enacted under Article 252(1) of the Constitution, which empowers the Union Government to legislate in a field reserved for the states, where two or more State legislatures consent to a central law. All the states have approved implementation of the Water Act as enacted in 1974.

---

[5] Sushmita Sengupta, *Cleaning India's Polluted Rivers* in *State of India's Environment 2018* 52 (Ed. Sunita Narain, *et al*, 2018).

[6] *State of Water Pollution* in *State of India's Environment 2019* 42–3 (Ed. Sunita Narain, *et al*, 2019).

[7] Entry 17, List II, Seventh Schedule.

The Water Act establishes a Central and state pollution control boards. The Central board may advise the Central Government on water pollution issues, coordinate the activities of state PCBs, sponsor investigation and research relating to water pollution, and develop a comprehensive plan for the control and prevention of water pollution.[8] The Central board also performs the functions of a state board for the union territories. In conflicts between a state board and the Central board, the Central board prevails. Since 1982, the Central board has been attached to the Union Government's Department of Environment, Forests, and Wildlife.

The Water Act is comprehensive in its coverage, applying to streams, inland waters, subterranean waters and sea or tidal waters. Standards for the discharge of effluents or the quality of the receiving waters are not specified in the Act itself. Instead, the Act enables state boards to prescribe these standards.[9]

The Act provides for a permit system or 'consent' procedure to prevent and control water pollution. The Act generally prohibits disposal of polluting matter in streams, wells and sewers or on land in excess of the standards established by the state boards.[10] A person must obtain consent from the state board before taking steps to establish any industry, operation or process, any treatment and disposal system or any extension or addition to such a system which might result in the discharge of sewage or trade effluent into a stream, well or sewer or onto land.[11] The state board may specify the location, construction and use of the outlet as well as the nature and composition of new discharges. The state board must maintain and make public a register containing the particulars of the consent orders. The Act empowers a state board, upon 30 days' notice to a polluter, to execute any work required under a consent order which has not been executed. The board may recover the expenses for such work from the polluter.

Other functions of the state boards specified by the Water Act include: (1) planning a comprehensive programme for prevention, control and abatement of water pollution in the state; (2) encouraging, conducting and participating in investigations and research of water pollution problems; (3) inspecting facilities for sewage and trade effluent treatment; and (4) developing economical and reliable methods of treatment of sewage and trade effluents.[12] The Act gives the state boards the power of entry and inspection to carry out their functions.[13] Moreover, a state board may take emergency measures if it determines that an accident or other unforeseen event has polluted a stream or well. These measures include removing the pollutants, mitigating the damage and issuing orders to the polluter prohibiting effluent discharges.

The 1988 amendment introduced a new provision, section 33A, which empowers state boards to issue directions to any person, officer or authority, including orders to close, prohibit or regulate any industry, operation or process and to stop or regulate the supply of water, electricity or any other service. Prior to the adoption of section 33A, a state board could issue direct orders to polluters under section 32 of the Act. A state board, however, could only exercise this power if the pollution arose from 'any accident or other unforeseen

[8] Section 16.

[9] Section 17(g). The Environment (Protection) Act of 1986 gives the Central Government similar authority to establish water quality and effluent standards throughout India.

[10] Section 24.

[11] Section 25. Section 26 requires that persons releasing water pollutants prior to the adoption of the Water Act must also meet the consent requirements of section 25.

[12] Section 17.

[13] Section 23.

act or event'. Moreover, a state board's authority to issue orders under section 32 was limited to orders directed to the polluter, not to government officials or other parties. The state boards can also apply to courts for injunctions to prevent water pollution under section 33 of the Act. Under section 41, the penalty for failure to comply with a court order under section 33 or a direction from the board under section 33A is punishable by fines and imprisonment.

The amendments also increased the power of the Central board relative to the state boards. Under section 18 of the Act, the Central Government may determine that a state board has failed to comply with Central board directions and that because of this failure an emergency has arisen. The Central Government may then direct the Central board to perform the functions of the state board.

The 1988 amendments modified section 49 to allow citizens to bring actions under the Water Act. Now a state board must make relevant reports available to complaining citizens, unless the board determines that the disclosures would harm 'public interest'. Previously, the Act allowed courts to recognize only those actions brought by a board, or with a previous written sanction of a board. The 2010 amendment inserted section 33B into the parent Act. This new provision provides for an appeal to the NGT from decisions relating to the grant or refusal to grant consent as well as directions by the board issued under section 33A.

Five years after it petitioned the Supreme Court to curb industrial pollution across the country, the Paryavaran Suraksha Samiti was left holding a set of general directions that lack bite. Notice how, even after four decades, the Water Act remains poorly implemented, not just with respect to private industry but also organs of the state—municipalities.

PARYAVARAN SURAKSHA SAMITI v UNION OF INDIA

(2017) 5 SCC 326

Jagdish Singh Khehar, C J: * * *

It is ... apparent that all running industrial units, which require 'consent to operate' from the Pollution Control Board concerned, have a functional primary effluent treatment plant, in place.

The question that arises for our consideration is, whether the same is maintained in good order, after the industry itself has become functional. The industry requiring 'consent to operate', can be permitted to run, only if its primary effluent treatment plant is functional. We, therefore, consider it just and appropriate, to direct the State Pollution Control Boards concerned, to issue notices to all industrial units, which require 'consent to operate', by way of a common advertisement, requiring them to make their primary effluent treatment plants fully operational, within three months from today. On the expiry of the notice period of three months, the State Pollution Control Board(s) concerned are mandated to carry out inspections, to verify, whether or not, each industrial unit requiring 'consent to operate', has a functional primary effluent treatment plant. Such of the industrial units, which have not been able to make their primary effluent treatment plant fully operational, within the notice period, shall be restrained from any further industrial activity. This direction may be implemented by requiring the electricity supply and distribution agency concerned, to disconnect the electricity connection of the defaulting industry. We, therefore, hereby further direct that in case the State Pollution Control Boards concerned make a recommendation to the electrical supply and distribution agency/company concerned, to disconnect electricity supply to an industry, for the reason that its primary effluent treatment plant is not functional, it shall honour such recommendation, and shall disconnect the electricity supply to such defaulting industrial concern, forthwith....

Having effectuated the directions recorded in the foregoing paragraphs, the next step would be, to set up common effluent treatment plants. We are informed, that for the aforesaid purpose, the financial contribution of the Central Government is to the extent of 50%, that of the State Government concerned (including the Union Territory concerned) is 25%. The balance 25%, is to be arranged by way of loans from banks. The above loans, are to be repaid, by the industrial areas, and/or industrial clusters. We are also informed that the setting up of a common effluent treatment plant, would ordinarily take approximately two years (in cases where the process has yet to be commenced). The reason for the above prolonged period, for setting up 'common effluent treatment plants', according to the learned counsel, is not only financial, but also, the requirement of land acquisition, for the same.

In view of the fact that the financial position has been taken care of, as has been expressed above, we are of the view, that the setting up of 'common effluent treatment plants', should be taken up as an urgent mission. With reference to common effluent treatment plants, which are already under implementation, we hope and expect that they would be completed within the timelines already postulated. With reference to common effluent treatment plants, which are yet to be set up, we consider it just and appropriate to direct the State Governments concerned (including the Union Territories concerned) to complete the same within a period of three years, from today. We are also of the view that while acquiring land for the 'common effluent treatment plants', the State Governments concerned (including the Union Territories concerned) will acquire such additional land, as may be required for setting up 'zero liquid discharge plants', if and when required in the future....

Given the responsibility vested in municipalities under Article 243-W of the Constitution, as also, in Item 6 of Schedule XII, wherein the aforesaid obligation, pointedly extends to 'public health, sanitation conservancy and solid waste management', we are of the view that the onus to operate the existing common effluent treatment plants, rests on municipalities (and/or local bodies). Given the aforesaid responsibility, the municipalities (and/or local bodies) concerned, cannot be permitted to shy away from discharging this onerous duty. In case there are further financial constraints, the remedy lies in Articles 243-X and 243-Y of the Constitution. It will be open to the municipalities (and/or local bodies) concerned, to evolve norms to recover funds, for the purpose of generating finances to install and run all the 'common effluent treatment plants', within the purview of the provisions referred to hereinabove. Needless to mention that such norms as may be evolved for generating financial resources, may include all or any of the commercial, industrial and domestic beneficiaries, of the facility. The process of evolving the above norms, shall be supervised by the State Government (Union Territory) concerned, through the Secretaries, Urban Development and Local Bodies, respectively (depending on the location of the respective common effluent treatment plant). The norms for generating funds for setting up and/or operating the 'common effluent treatment plant' shall be finalised, on or before 31-3-2017, so as to be implemented with effect from the next financial year. In case, such norms are not in place, before the commencement of the next financial year, the State Governments (or the Union Territories) concerned, shall cater to the financial requirements, of running the 'common effluent treatment plants', which are presently dysfunctional, from their own financial resources.

Just in the manner suggested hereinabove, for the purpose of setting up of 'common effluent treatment plants', the State Governments concerned (including, the Union Territories concerned) will prioritise such cities, towns and villages, which discharge industrial pollutants and sewer, directly into rivers and water bodies.

We are of the view that in the manner suggested above, the malady of sewer treatment, should also be dealt with simultaneously. We, therefore, hereby direct that 'sewage treatment plants' shall also be set up and made functional, within the timelines and the format, expressed hereinabove....

NOTES AND QUESTIONS

1. In *Paryavaran Suraksha Samiti*, the Supreme Court drops any pretence of adjudicating a dispute. The judgment does not record any facts. It neither makes reference to pleadings nor to counsels' submissions. What is styled as a 'judgment' is simply a set of administrative directions with minimal reasoning. The decision props up long neglected statutory obligations under the Water Act. To what end?

2. Was this a lost opportunity? Should the Supreme Court have retained the case and forced the states and municipalities to instal sewage treatment plants in a time frame? Remember, the judgment rendered in February 2017 was passed more than four decades after the enactment of the Water Act and over 37 years after the Supreme Court judgment in *Ratlam*.[14] Strategically, should the court have made an example of half a dozen major metropolises and summoned the municipal commissioners to ensure full treatment of the sewage generated by those cities?

3. To ensure that its directions are obeyed, the Supreme Court placed the onus of compliance on the member secretaries of the PCBs and the secretaries of the Department of Environment in the states. It also directed benches of the NGT to supervise implementation of the directions. In order that compliance improves, the Supreme Court directed the states to establish within six months an 'online, real time, continuous monitoring system' that would display emission levels to the public.

4. Article 243-W of the Constitution empowers the legislature of a state to devolve responsibilities on municipalities in matters listed in the 12th Schedule. Item 6 of the 12th Schedule covers 'public health, sanitation conservancy and solid waste management'. Article 243-X of the Constitution provides for the funding of municipalities through taxes and grants. Article 243-Y imposes a duty on the Finance Commission to make recommendations for strengthening the financial position of municipalities. The Supreme Court notices these provisions and leaves it to the states to allocate resources. Without budgets, how will the municipalities treat the sewage? What did the Supreme Court mean when it said: 'In case there are further financial constraints, the remedy lies in Articles 243-X and 243-Y of the Constitution'?

5. The Supreme Court judgment is a bleak reminder of how dysfunctional the pollution regulatory system is.

6. Highlighting the poor implementation of the Water Act, Kerban Anklesaria describes the law as a set of 'rules without regulation'.[15] Her critique of the Act begins at the composition of the state water boards which are packed with state government nominees and representatives of government companies.[16] There is hardly an independent voice on the board representing the affected citizen or environmentalist. According to Anklesaria, the penalties are too low to deter defaulters. She would like to see them raised. She would also spur citizen prosecutions under section 49 by offering compensatory costs to concerned citizens who successfully prosecute a violator.

7. The Water Act allows diversion of water resources for industrial use based on a licence called 'consent' which is issued by the PCB to capture or appropriate a specified quantity of

[14] *Municipal Council, Ratlam v Vardhichand* AIR 1980 SC 1622.

[15] Kerban Anklesaria, *A Judicial Regime of Environment Protection: The Case of the Indian Water Act* (unpublished manuscript, 1998).

[16] Section 4.

water from a river or other source. The Water Act by itself contains no explicit requirement to maintain a minimum flow in the river to maintain fish populations and the health of riverine eco-systems. This aspect is required to be addressed by the *ad hoc* environmental impact assessment (EIA) procedure. Does the Water Act require 'greening'?[17] Should Parliament mandate minimum flow levels to protect riparian life or is this an unrealistic idea in a monsoon dependent region with few perennial rivers? How would a minimum flow law be enforced?

8. To encourage efficient use of water, should water tariffs be scaled to incentivize conservation? When water is drawn from a river by industry, the eco-system services provided by the flowing river are impaired. Apart from supporting river life, flowing rivers purify the water and detoxify waste. Should industry pay for this impairment?

9. Section 25 of the Water Act obliges municipal bodies to obtain the consent of the state board before discharging sewage from new outlets. Section 26 requires municipal bodies to secure consent in respect of the sewers which were existing at the time when the Act was brought into force. Despite these provisions having long been in the statute book, most local bodies have neglected their obligation, prompting the Supreme Court to direct the Central board and the state boards to ensure compliance by municipalities.[18] Two decades after the *Almitra Patel* order, the position was unchanged in *Paryavaran Suraksha Samiti*.[19]

10. Section 21 of the Act provides detailed procedures for sampling effluents. The analysis of a sample is not admissible into evidence in any legal proceeding under the Act, unless the sample is taken in accordance with that section. In *Delhi Bottling Co Pvt Ltd v Central Board for the Prevention and Control of Pollution*,[20] the Central board took a sample of trade effluent from a bottling company's discharge stream. The board analysed the sample and determined that the trade effluent did not conform to the requirements of the consent order granted to the company. The board sued under section 33 and the magistrate's court issued an injunction requiring the company to establish a treatment plant. The company challenged the injunction, claiming that a representative of the company, present at the sampling, had requested that a sample be analysed by the Delhi administration laboratory as provided under section 21(e) of the Act. This analysis was not carried out.

Based on the pleadings, the court ruled in favour of the company, holding that samples not taken in strict compliance with section 21 are inadmissible as evidence and, therefore, the board had not proved that the company was violating its consent orders. Given the clear language of the statute and the court's determination of the facts, the ruling was correct. Note, however, that the company did not challenge the results of the analysis itself, the integrity of the sampling method or the method of analysis. In addition, the requirement that polluters be given notice before a board may take a sample gives the polluters the opportunity to temporarily reduce or cease releasing pollutants during the period the sample is taken.

In *Delhi Bottling*, the court set aside the magistrate's order. The board must now commence a new action against the company to obtain judicial relief, resulting in a long delay. Consider whether the court could have issued an alternative order. For example, could the court have ordered the magistrate to retain jurisdiction of the case until samples could be taken in

---

17 Stefano Burchi, *Balancing Development and Environmental Conservation and Protection of the Water Resource Base – The 'Greening' of Water Laws*, 66 FAO Legal Papers Online (2007), https://www.fao.org/3/bb099e/bb099e.pdf, accessed 10 May 2021.

18 *Almitra Patel v Union of India* 1997 (6) Scale 12 (SP). The failure of the Cuttack Municipality to apply for consent was noted by the Orissa High Court in *M C Mehta v State of Orissa* AIR 1992 Ori 225.

19 (2017) 5 SCC 326.

20 AIR 1986 Del 152.

compliance with the Water Act? Could the court require that such samples be taken while the company was carrying on normal operations at the plant?

The Gujarat High Court also shares the view that the provisions of section 21 relating to sampling are mandatory and must be substantially complied with by the prosecuting board. However, where the polluter does not make a request for part of the sample drawn after due notice, the magistrate ought to frame the charge and she would not be justified in discharging the accused.[21]

11. Ordinarily, judges are reluctant to exercise their discretionary jurisdiction in favour of polluters, particularly where the industry fails to invest in effluent treatment facilities. In a rare departure, the Patna High Court indulged Shiv Shankar Chemical Industries Pvt Ltd, an ethyl alcohol manufacturer located close to Rajpura village near Bhagalpur.[22] In breach of its consent, Shiv Shankar failed to establish an effluent treatment plant (ETP). When the consent lapsed, the board refused to extend it, compelling the company to shut down its distillery. The distillery challenged the refusal under Article 226 before the High Court, where its case was heard along with a public interest litigation complaining against the harmful discharges from the factory.

On a balance of the rival contentions, the High Court permitted Shiv Shankar to restart its production on the condition that it adopted various interim measures until the ETP became operational. In effect, the High Court directed the board to extend its consent on the terms imposed on the polluter in the judgment.

The Patna High Court was apparently persuaded by the recommendations of a court-appointed Expert Committee. Though the committee found the distillery's effluent 'highly polluting', it noted that the waters in the wells of Rajpura village were clean and did not show any evidence of pollution. To safeguard the villagers, the court directed the company to bear the medical expenses of any person suffering due to the effluent.

12. *Narula Dyeing and Printing Works v Union of India*[23] is a strong pro-environment judgment where Justice Abhichandani of the Gujarat High Court repelled the challenge to closure orders issued by the state government under section 5 of the Environment (Protection) Act of 1986. Narula Dyeing was releasing untreated effluents into the Kharicut Canal for over a decade, though its 12-year-old consent required the firm to set up a treatment plant within six months. Stressing the importance of the conditions in the consent relating to the nature, composition, temperature, volume, rate of discharge, etc. of the industrial effluent, the court held:

> [A] mere consent order issued by the State Board under Section 25(2) did not entitle the applicants to discharge trade effluents and it was incumbent upon the applicants to comply with the conditions mentioned in the consent order, as also to put up the effluent treatment plants within the time prescribed in the consent order. Failure of complying with the requirement of putting up effluent treatment plant resulted in lapse of the consent. Therefore, mere fact that consent orders were obtained by the Petitioners cannot insulate them against the requirement of putting up the effluent treatment plants and complying with the standards of tolerance limits prescribed.[24]

---

[21] *Dahyabhai K Solanki v Kashiram Textiles Mills Pvt Ltd* 1994 (2) Guj L R 1166.
[22] *Rajiv Singh v State of Bihar* AIR 1992 Pat 86.
[23] AIR 1995 Guj 185.
[24] *Id.* at 189.

One of the conditions in the consent letter was that the consent would lapse unless the treatment plants were set up within six months.

13. The Water Act regulates water pollution through a system of 'command and control'. Effluent discharge standards are established and persons whose discharges exceed the standards are subject to fines and imprisonment. Other means of regulation are possible. For example, the government could establish an upper limit of allowable pollutant release based on public health standards and charge fees based on the amount of the pollutant released within those limits. Under this system, polluters would have an economic incentive to reduce pollution if the fees were higher than the costs of reducing pollution. Would a fee system be any less burdensome to administer than a command and control system? How should the government use revenues obtained through a fee system?

14. Historically, Parliament had enacted a positive economic incentive for controlling water pollution. The Water (Prevention and Control of Pollution) Cess Act of 1977 levied a cess on water consumed by industries and local authorities. A rebate of 25% of the cess was given for the installation of a water treatment plant and compliance with section 25 of the Water Act and standards set under the Environment (Protection) Act of 1986. The Cess Act was repealed in 2017.

15. Difficulties faced by Surana Oils and Derivatives (India) Ltd (SODL) in establishing a factory to manufacture castor oil derivatives illustrate the uncertainties in an environmental case. Since the factory was located close to Himayat Sagar Lake which supplied water to Hyderabad, the Andhra Pradesh PCB rejected SODL's application for consent. SODL challenged the refusal before the appellate authority and adduced evidence to show that it had adopted the latest eco-friendly technology with all safeguards. The appellate authority reviewed the material and, on being satisfied that the factory 'is not a polluting industry', asked the board to grant consent. The decision of the appellate authority was challenged in public interest litigations filed before the High Court. The High Court declined to interfere since the matter was highly technical and it was inappropriate for a court exercising its writ jurisdiction to sit in appeal over the order of the appellate authority. The Supreme Court used the opportunity presented by the special leave petition filed by the board and an environmental group, to explain the precautionary principle and the special principle of burden of proof in environmental cases. The apex court remitted the matter to the National Environment Appellate Authority for an expert opinion on whether SODL should be allowed to operate at the controversial site.[25] The Supreme Court eventually allowed the appeals and upheld the decision of the board rejecting consent.[26]

II. CONSTITUTIONAL CHALLENGES TO SECTION 33 RESTRAINING ORDERS

A tactic of polluters to avoid restraining orders under section 33 is a motion to quash the order on the grounds that the Water Act violates the fundamental right to carry on a trade or business guaranteed by Article 19(l)(g) of the Constitution of India.

The Rajasthan High Court balanced the interests protected by the Water Act against the competing interests protected by Article 19(l)(g) in the following case. A lower court had issued a restraining order against textile companies that were discharging effluents after the

[25] *A P Pollution Control Board v Prof M V Nayudu* AIR 1999 SC 812. The High Court judgment is reported at *Society for Preservation of Environment and Quality of Life v Industries Department* 1998 (3) ANDH L T 516.

[26] *A P Pollution Control Board II v Prof M V Nayudu* (2001) 2 SCC 62.

expiration of consent orders from the state and Central boards. The companies filed writ petitions in the Rajasthan High Court challenging the validity of the restraining order.

AGGRAWAL TEXTILE INDUSTRIES v STATE OF RAJASTHAN
S B C Writ Petition No. 1375/80
2 March 1981

ORDER: [Petitioners' counsel] has vehemently argued that the problem of prevention of water pollution is a problem of vast magnitude and that it would be beyond the means of an individual to prevent or control the pollution resulting from an industry set up by him and that the prohibition contained in Section 24 of the Act would result in complete closure of the business of the petitioners and that it would thus result in imposing unreasonable restrictions to carry on their trade and business. I am unable to accept the aforesaid contention.... It is true that the prevention and control of pollution of water may involve expenditure beyond the means of a particular individual carrying on any particular industry and it may require co-operation amongst various units and ... the local authorities to effectively prevent and control such pollution. The Act also envisages that one of the functions of the State Board is to plan a comprehensive programme for the prevention, control abatement of pollution of steams and wells in the State and to secure the execution thereof and to evolve economical and reliable methods of treatment of sewage and trade effluent, having regard to the peculiar conditions of soils, climate and water resources of different regions. But, this does not mean that an individual, while exercising his right to carry on his trade or business, is free to pollute the source of supply of water to other citizens, and thereby cause harm to the interest of the general public. It cannot be disputed that pollution of water is a very serious hazard for the health of the general public, and the provisions of the Act which seek to provide for the prevention and control of water pollution and maintaining or restoring the wholesomeness of water are enacted in the interest of the general public....

The question which next arises for consideration is, whether the aforesaid restriction that has been placed by Section 24 of the Act is an unreasonable restriction.... [S]ub-section (2) of Section 24 enables a person to cause or permit a trade effluent to enter into a stream provided the consent of the State Government is obtained. Sections 25 and 26 of the Act make provisions for the grant of consent by the State Board for discharging any sewage or trade effluent into a stream or well. Section 28 provides for an appeal against an order made by the State Board under Sections 25 and 26, and a further right of revision is conferred under Section 29 of the Act. This shows that the Act contains adequate provisions for grant of consent by the State Board as well as provisions for appeal and revision against the orders passed by the State Board so as to enable a person to carry on his trade or business after obtaining the consent of the State Board. It is, therefore, not possible to hold that Section 24(1) imposes unreasonable restrictions on the right of the petitioners to carry on their trade or business....

NOTES AND QUESTIONS

1. Since the decision in *Aggrawal Textile Industries*, the Supreme Court has explicitly recognized the right to a wholesome environment as being an aspect of the fundamental right to life guaranteed by Article 21 of the Constitution.[27] How will this development affect challenges to section 33 injunctions based on the fundamental right to carry on a trade or business guaranteed by the Article (19)(1)(g)? Would it be more difficult for a court to find

[27] *Subhash Kumar v State of Bihar* AIR 1991 SC 420.

that a restriction on effluent discharge was unreasonable? What balance should the courts strike between these rights?

2. Another major challenge to section 33 restraining orders is the contention that *ex parte* restraining orders issued against polluters violate principles of natural justice embodied in the Constitution.[28] A pre-decisional hearing must be granted to the polluter before a court issues a section 33 restraining order.[29] This rule of fair play may be relaxed, however, in the case of an emergency, such as where the effluent discharged poses an imminent threat to public health.

3. The Gujarat High Court has suggested a number of measures to ensure that pollution-related cases are disposed of expeditiously.[30] Board officials should take effective steps for the service of the summons upon the accused, prepare cases thoroughly, resist adjournments, seek exemplary costs to deter the accused from adopting dilatory tactics and vigorously pursue appeals in the superior court. The High Court also directed the subordinate judiciary not to adjourn cases, to record the plea of the accused without delay, to ensure that all necessary witnesses are examined at the earliest and to adopt a pro-active approach so that the objects of the Water Act are attained.

III. CRIMINAL LIABILITY

The Water Act establishes criminal penalties of fines and imprisonment for non-compliance with section 33 orders, section 20 directions concerning information, section 32 emergency orders and section 33A directions issued by a state board.[31] Polluters violating the Act are also subject to criminal penalties.[32] The 1988 amendments to the Water Act increased the penalties for these offences, bringing them into line with the 1987 amendments to the Air Act.

Section 47 of the Water Act extends liability for violations committed by companies to certain corporate employees and officials. The Act also extends liability for violations to heads of government departments when a department has committed a violation, unless the department head can prove that the offence was committed without his knowledge or that he exercised all due diligence to prevent the commission of the offence.[33]

NOTES AND QUESTIONS

1. Criminal sanctions are intended to deter potential violators from committing crimes, to increase public safety and to promote respect for the law. Typically, environmental statutes use the following boilerplate clause to impose liability on individuals:

> *Offences by companies.* – (1) Where an offence under this Act has been committed by a company, every person who at the time the offence was committed was in charge of, and was responsible to the company for the conduct of, the business of the company, as well as the company, shall be deemed to be guilty of the offence and shall be liable to be proceeded against and punished accordingly.

---

28 *Ex parte* orders are issued before the alleged polluter has an opportunity to be heard by the court.

29 *Megh Shyam Sharma v State of Uttar Pradesh* 1985 All L J 1195.

30 *Gujarat Water Pollution Control Board II v Kohinoor Dyeing and Printing Works* 1993 (2) Guj L R 1368, 1392, 1393.

31 Section 41.

32 Sections 43 and 44.

33 Section 48.

Provided that nothing contained in this sub-section shall render any such person liable to any punishment provided in this Act if he proves that the offence was committed without his knowledge or that he exercised all due diligence to prevent the commission of such offence.

(2) Notwithstanding anything contained in sub-section (1), where an offence under this Act has been committed by a company and it is proved that the offence has been committed with the consent or connivance of, or is attributable to any neglect on the part of, any director, manager, secretary or other officer of the company, such director, manager, secretary or other officer shall also be deemed to be guilty of that offence and shall be liable to be proceeded against and punished accordingly.

Explanation. – For the purposes of this section –

(a) 'company' means anybody corporate and includes a firm or other association of individuals; and

(b) 'director' in relation to a firm means a partner in the firm.'

To improve enforcement, should Parliament adopt an additional strategy requiring every company that pollutes to designate a high-level manager as the 'Responsible Corporate Officer' (RCO)? Such a provision may require the company to specify and make public the name of a senior officer who is responsible for environmental compliance and who would face criminal penalties should a breach be established in court.[34] The RCO responsibility principle would reduce the evidentiary burden on prosecutors, build internal pressure within an organization for complying with environmental standards and prevent offenders from ducking jail terms because of the inability (or incompetence) of prosecutors to establish exactly who in the company was responsible.[35]

2. The Karnataka PCB initiated prosecutions against two public servants under section 48 of the Water Act. According to sections 48 and 60 of the Water Act:

> 48. *Offences by Government Department.* – Where an offence under this Act has been committed by any Department of Government, the Head of the Department shall be deemed to be guilty of the offence and shall be liable to be proceeded against and punished accordingly:
>
> Provided that nothing contained in this section shall render such Head of the Department liable to any punishment if he proves that the offence was committed without his knowledge or that he exercised all due diligence to prevent the commission of such offence.
>
> 60. *Overriding effect.* – The provisions of this Act shall have effect notwithstanding anything inconsistent therewith contained in any enactment other than this Act.

Additionally, sections 5 and 197(1)(b) of the Code of Criminal Procedure, 1973 read:

> 5. *Savings* – Nothing contained in this Code shall, in the absence of a specific provision to the contrary, affect any special or local law for the time being in force, or any special jurisdiction or power conferred, or any special form of procedure prescribed, by any other law for the time being in force.
>
> 197. *Prosecution of Judges and public servants.* – (1) When any person who is or was ... public servant not removable from his office save by or with the sanction of the Government is accused of any offence alleged to have been committed by him while

34 Under the Factories Act of 1948, it is necessary to specify an 'occupier' who is a senior-level manager. The occupier is required to ensure compliance with the safety provisions in that Act.

35 See generally, Nancy Mullikin, *Holding The 'Responsible Corporate Officer' Responsible: Addressing The Need for Expansion of Criminal Liability for Corporate Environmental Violators*, 3 Golden Gate Univ Envir Law Jr 395 (2010).

acting or purporting to act in the discharge of his official duty, no Court shall take cognisance of such offence except with the previous sanction. – * * *

(b) in the case of a person who is employed or, as the case may be, was at the time of commission of the alleged offence employed, in connection with the affairs of a State, of the State Government.

The aggrieved public servants petitioned the High Court to quash the complaints, claiming that sanction of the state under section 197 is necessary before prosecutions are launched. The High Court and the Supreme Court rejected the challenge. The Supreme Court reasoned that under section 48, the head of the department is deemed to be guilty of the offence under the Water Act. However, this is a rebuttable presumption and the accused would get an opportunity to demonstrate that the offence was committed without her knowledge or despite the exercise of due diligence on her part. If prior sanction under section 197 were required '[it] would virtually negate the deeming fiction provided under section 48'.[36] The court found that the Water Act was a special law in terms of section 5 of the Code and that the effect of section 60 of the Water Act was to override the requirement of section 197 of the Code.

3. The City Municipal Council, Krishnarajapuram, Bangalore failed to instal sewage treatment plants and persisted in discharging untreated sewage into water bodies like ponds, lakes and onto low-lying areas. Fed up with the council's obstinacy, the Karnataka PCB refused to renew the council's consent to discharge. Then the board launched prosecutions against the commissioner of the council and former commissioners for having breached the Water Act. The Karnataka High Court came to the aid of the officials, quashing the criminal complaint since the commissioner and chief officer were not 'head of any Department of Government' under section 48. The Supreme Court reversed the High Court decision and directed the magistrate to proceed with the complaints. The Supreme Court acknowledged that the council was not a department of government, but held that it did not enjoy immunity from prosecution. The municipal council was a body corporate and having regard to the object of the Water Act, the PCB was justified in prosecuting the officers and the Council under section 47 of the Water Act.[37]

The excerpt that follows illustrates how dysfunctional the criminal justice system is in certain parts of the country with respect to Water Act prosecutions. The Supreme Court judgment rendered on 12 December 2008 revived a prosecution relating to breaches committed a quarter century earlier.

U P POLLUTION CONTROL BOARD v DR B K MODI
(2009) 2 SCC 147

* * *

P Sathasivam, J:

Background facts, in a nutshell, are as follows:

The State Board for Prevention and Control of Water Pollution was constituted on 3-2-1975 by the Government of U.P. and it has been named as U.P. Pollution Control Board (hereinafter referred to as 'the Board') which is the appellant herein vide Notification No. 2179/9-2-100-74 dated 13-7-1982. On the application submitted by M/s Modi Carpets Ltd, Raebareli, seeking consent to discharge the effluent, the appellant Board granted conditional consent to discharge their trade effluent in River Sai. Since the conditions of consent were not being

36 *V C Chinnappa Goudar v Karnataka State Pollution Control Board* (2015) 14 SCC 535.
37 *Karnataka State Pollution Control Board v B Heera Naik* (2020) 16 SCC 298.

complied with by M/s Modi Carpets Ltd, a letter dated 30-4-1983 was sent by the appellant Board to M/s Modi Carpets Ltd, Raebareli informing that non-compliance with the consent conditions is an offence under section 44 of the Act.

On 7-6-1983, the inspection of unit of M/s Modi Carpets Ltd was done by the officers of the Board wherein it was found that polluted trade effluent was being discharged into River Sai through a drain without any treatment and construction of the effluent treatment plant was yet to be started. On 19-1-1984 the Board again sent a letter to M/s Modi Carpets Ltd that conditions of the consent order dated 22-1-1983 were not complied with. Again it was reiterated that non-compliance with the conditions of consent would be an offence under section 44 of the Act.

On 13-9-1984, the unit was again inspected by the officers of the Board and it was found that the effluent was being discharged without any treatment. For this, Modi Carpets Ltd sent a reply dated 18-10-1984 to the appellant Board giving clarifications for not complying with the consent conditions and the same was considered and rejected by the Board on 31-10-1984 on the ground that the unit was not complying with the prescribed standards, consent conditions and also the application was incomplete in various aspects.

Since M/s Modi Carpets Ltd was not complying with the provisions of the Act and there was violation of sections 25 and 26 of the Act, a complaint under section 44 was filed by the Board through its Assistant Environmental Engineer against Respondent 1 as well as other persons, namely, Chairman, Vice-Chairman, Managing Director, Joint Managing Director, Directors, General Manager, Commercial Manager and Company Secretary of M/s Modi Carpets Ltd before the CJM, Raebareli. It was specifically mentioned in the complaint that the aforesaid persons are responsible for the conduct of the business of the Company and for their monetary benefits continued to discharge noxious and polluting trade effluent of the Company without complying with the conditions of consent and mandatory provisions of law.

A petition under section 482 of the Criminal Procedure Code was filed before the High Court of Judicature at Allahabad being Criminal Misc. Petition No. 14119 of 1985 by M/s Modi Carpets Ltd and others for quashing the aforesaid complaint and also for other reliefs. Vide order dated 5-11-1985, the High Court stayed further proceedings in the complaint case.

On the objection of the Board that the Principal Bench at Allahabad had no territorial jurisdiction to decide the petition, the first respondent herein filed a petition under section 482 of the Criminal Procedure Code before the Lucknow Bench of the High Court being Criminal Misc. Case No. 1347 of 2001. In the said petition, it was alleged that the first respondent, Dr. Bhupendra Kumar Modi, Joint Managing Director was not concerned with day-to-day business of the Company and cannot be prosecuted for the offence committed by the Company, hence, it was prayed that Complaint Case No. 44 of 1988 filed by the appellant Board be quashed.

The appellant Board filed a counter-affidavit before the High Court wherein it was stated that the complaint could not be quashed at the initial stage and whether a person is responsible for conduct of day-to-day business of the Company or not, is a question which has to be decided by evidence. In any event, it was stated that the complaint discloses materials to proceed further.

By impugned order dated 29-11-2004, the High Court quashed the complaint so far as it related to Respondent 1 on the main ground that there was no material on record to show that Respondent 1 was, at the relevant time, in charge of and responsible to the Company for conduct of its business. Aggrieved by the said judgment of the Lucknow Bench, the appellant Board has filed the present appeal by way of special leave.

* * *

Among the various provisions of the Act, we are more concerned about section 47 which speaks about offences by companies. [The judgment reproduced section 47 which is identical to the provision quoted under Note 1 in the Criminal Liability section, *supra.*]

Section 25 speaks about restrictions on new outlets and new discharges and section 26 relates to provision regarding existing discharge of sewage or trade effluent. Section 44 speaks about penalty for contravention of section 25 or section 26.

It is not in dispute that the first respondent before letting out trade effluent into a stream or a river has to satisfy certain conditions in terms of the provisions of the Act and the order of the authorities concerned. It is also not in dispute that without a consent order by the Board the Company cannot let out untreated effluent into a land or stream or river. Though a consent order was issued by the Board, it has been specifically stated in the complaint that those conditions have not been fulfilled by the Company. In those circumstances, in the interest of the public health, the appellant Board through its officers laid a complaint against the persons who were in charge of the day-to-day affairs and in the decision-making process. There is no need to place all the materials at the threshold. However, on perusal of the complaint and the relevant materials in the form of documents, the learned Special Judicial Magistrate (Pollution) entertained the same and issued summons to the named persons in the complaint.

Inasmuch as the High Court quashed the complaint against the first respondent herein who is a Joint Managing Director of the Company, we are concerned about the averments/allegations against him in respect of his concern in the day-to-day affairs and in the decision-making process. We have already referred to the relevant averments/materials adverted to in the complaint. Before going into the reasoning and conclusion of the High Court for quashing the complaint against the first respondent herein, let us consider various decisions of this Court with reference to the very same provisions, namely, sections 44 and 47 of the Act as well as the jurisdiction of the High Court under section 482 CrPC.

***

It is useful to refer to the facts and other details stated in the complaint as noted by this Court. Thomas, J … observed [in] *Mohan Meakins* case, (2000) 3 SCC 745:

> … In the complaint filed by the appellant before the Chief Judicial Magistrate, the Company (M/s Mohan Meakins Ltd) has been arrayed as the first accused and the other persons who were arrayed as Accused 2 to 10 were described as the Directors of the said Company. The eleventh person arrayed in the complaint as accused is described as the Manager of the Company. The averments in the complaint show that the Distillery Unit of the Company at Daliganj, Lucknow, has been discharging noxious trade effluents into River Gomti and causing continuous pollution of the river. It was further averred in the complaint that on 19-9-1982, samples of trade effluents were collected by the officers empowered in this behalf, from the drain 'just outside the plant inside the factory', and from the irrigation plant out of which the effluents were pumped into the river. When the samples were analysed in the Industrial Toxicology Research Centre, Lucknow, it was revealed that the quality of effluents was beyond the standard laid down for the purpose. Therefore, it is alleged that the Company has violated section 24 of the Act and thereby the Company is guilty of the offence under section 43 of the Act.
>
> Where an offence under the Act has been committed by a company every person who was in charge of and was responsible to the company for the conduct of the business of the company is also made guilty of the offence by the statutory creation. Any director, manager or other officer of the company, who has consented to or connived in the commission of the said offence, is made liable for the punishment of the offence.

This Court [in *Mohan Meakins*] has also noted further allegations in the complaint against the Managers or Directors of the Company which are as under:

> In the above context what is to be looked at during the stage of issuing process is whether there are allegations in the complaint by which the Managers or Directors of the Company can also be proceeded against, when the Company is alleged to be guilty of the offence. Para 12 of the complaint reads thus:

> That the accused persons from 2 to 11 are Directors/Managers/Partners of M/s Mohan Meakins Distillery, Daliganj, Lucknow, as mentioned in this complaint are responsible for constructing the proper works and plant for the treatment of their highly polluting trade effluent so as to conform to the standard laid down by the Board. Aforesaid accused persons are deliberately avoiding to abide by the provisions of sections 24 and 26 of the aforesaid Act which are punishable respectively under sections 43 and 44 of the aforesaid Act, for which not only the Company but its Directors, Managers, Secretary and all other responsible officers of the accused Company, responsible for the conduct of its business are also liable in accordance with the provision of section 47 of the Act.
>
> The appellant has further stated in Para 23 of the complaint that 'the Chairman, Managing Directors and Directors of the Company are the persons responsible for the act and therefore, they are liable to be proceeded against according to the law.

Taking note of the averments in the complaint against the Directors, Managers and the ingredients of section 47 of the Act, this Court declined to accept the reasoning of the High Court and the Sessions Court for quashing the complaint and thereby set aside both the orders and directed the trial court to proceed with the case in accordance with law.

In the case on hand which is also similar to *Mohan Meakins Ltd* had commenced its journey in the year 1985, nonetheless lapse of such a long period cannot be a reason to absolve the respondents from the trial. In a matter of this nature, particularly, when it affects public health if it is ultimately proved, courts cannot afford to deal lightly with cases involving pollution of air and water. The message must go to all persons concerned whether small or big that the courts will share the parliamentary concern and legislative intent of the Act to check the escalating pollution level and restore the balance of our environment. Those who discharge noxious polluting effluents into streams, rivers or any other water bodies which inflicts (*sic* harm) on the public health at large, should be dealt with strictly dehors the technical objections. Since escalating pollution level of our environment affects the life and health of human beings as well as animals, the courts should not deal with the prosecution for offences under the pollution and environmental Acts in a casual or routine manner. . . .

In the light of the above discussion and in view of the specific averments in the complaint as referred to by us in the earlier paragraphs coupled with the statutory provisions, namely, sections 25, 26, 44 and 47 of the Act, we are unable to share the view expressed by the High Court in quashing the complaint insofar as the first respondent herein is concerned. Accordingly, we set aside the same. The Special Judicial Magistrate (Pollution) is directed to proceed with the complaint and dispose of the same in accordance with law. If the first respondent herein applies for dispensing with his personal presence in the court, after making the first appearance, the Special Court can exempt him from continuing to appear in the court by imposing any condition which the court deems fit.

NOTES AND QUESTIONS

1. Not surprisingly, given the threat of imprisonment and fines, the liability of individual corporate officials has been the subject of extensive litigation. Challenges to actions against corporate officials generally are in the form of motions to quash the action, brought under section 482 of the Code of Criminal Procedure which recognizes the inherent powers of a High Court to prevent an abuse of the judicial process or to secure the ends of justice.

Many courts have refused to grant these motions when they are based on technical defects in pleadings. In *Uttar Pradesh Pollution Control Board v Modi Distillery*,[38] the Supreme Court reversed an order quashing a prosecution under section 44 of the Water Act. The state board initiated the prosecution under section 47 against a company and its corporate officials. The board's complaint erroneously designated corporate officials as officials of Modi Distillery, instead of Modi Industries Limited. The corporate officials sought to quash the prosecution on the grounds that under section 47 corporate officials could not be prosecuted if the company was not also prosecuted.

The Supreme Court was particularly hostile to the claims of the corporate officials because, in this case, the officials had failed to respond to the board's request for information concerning the corporation. The Supreme Court also found that the technical flaw in the complaint could be easily removed by having the matter remitted to the chief judicial magistrate with a direction to call upon the state board to make the formal amendment in the averments of the complaint by simply substituting the proper name of the company. The court's attitude is clearly expressed in the following statement from the opinion:

> It would be a travesty of justice if the big business house of Messrs Modi Industries Limited is allowed to defeat the prosecution launched and avoid facing the trial on a technical flaw which is not incurable for their alleged deliberate and wilful breach of the provisions contained in Sections 25(1) and 26. . . .

Twelve years after *Modi Distillery* the farce continued. In *U P Pollution Control Board v Mohan Meakins Ltd*,[39] the Supreme Court revived a prosecution launched in 1983 against the company and its directors, that had been erroneously quashed by the sessions court. The case had languished in the lower courts for 16 years. 'Those who discharge noxious polluting effluents into streams may be unconcerned about the enormity of the injury which it inflicts on the public health at large, the irreparable impairment it causes on the aquatic organisms, the deleteriousness it imposes on the life and health of animals. So the courts should not deal with the prosecution for offences under the Act in a casual or routine manner.' Who is to blame for the abject delays? Who gains—and who pays?

2. One of the few reported decisions in a case where the board successfully prosecuted the polluter is the Punjab and Haryana High Court judgment in *Haryana State Board v Jai Bharat Woollen Finishing Works*.[40] Jai Bharat discharged untreated effluent into an open drain in Panipat city without obtaining the consent of the board. A number of notices issued by the board were ignored by the firm and eventually on the basis of a test sample, the board prosecuted the firm, one of its partners and its manager. The trial court acquitted the accused on the ground that the discharge was onto vacant land and did not constitute an offence. Partly allowing the board's appeal, the High Court held that the discharge of a trade effluent, without the consent of the board, did constitute an offence. It made no difference whether the trade effluent was discharged into a municipal drain or flowed directly onto land. However, the court held that in the absence of proof that the concerned partner was in charge of or was responsible to the firm for the conduct of business, it would not be possible to convict the partner. On this interpretation, the court upheld the acquittal of a sleeping partner who did not participate in the business of the firm, while imposing a nominal fine of Rs. 3,000 on the firm and Rs. 2,500 on its manager.

[38] AIR 1988 SC 1128.
[39] (2000) 3 SCC 745.
[40] 1993 For L T 101.

3. Most state PCBs have enjoyed little success in bringing to book violators under pollution control laws. Does the fault lie with the boards, the laws, the courts or some other factor? What systemic changes might improve the conviction rate?

IV. THE REPEALED WATER CESS ACT

Parliament adopted the Water Cess (Prevention and Control of Pollution) Act of 1977 to provide funds for the Central and state PCBs. The Act was *repealed* in 2017 as part of a broad tax reform exercise where a single Goods and Services Tax (GST) replaced several taxes and disparate levies.[41] We retain a short discussion on the repealed statute since economic incentives to alter polluter behaviour may be revived by Parliament in a new form.

The Act empowered the Central Government to impose a cess on water consumed. Industries and local authorities were subject to the cess if they used water for purposes listed in Schedule II of the Act, which included: (1) industrial cooling, spraying in mine pits or 'boiler feed'; (2) domestic purposes; (3) processing which results in water pollution by biodegradable water pollutants; or (4) processing which results in water pollution by water pollutants which were not easily biodegradable or were toxic. A rebate of 25% of the cess was given to complying industries and authorities.

The Central Government adopted the Water Cess Act without the approval of the state governments. Water is a subject in the State List under the Constitution. Many industries claimed that the Water Cess Act violated the constitutional separation of state and central powers. Most courts concluded that the water cess was a tax which Parliament is authorized to impose under Entry 97, List I of Schedule VII of the Constitution.[42] The ruling in *Agra Engineering Industries v Union of India*[43] is typical of the reasoning applied by the courts in resolving this issue. In *Tata Iron & Steel Co Ltd (Tisco) v State of Bihar*,[44] a division bench of the Patna High Court also concluded that the cess imposed under the Act was within the legislative competence of Parliament.

In 1991 the Cess Act was amended. The charging section and the provisions relating to rebate as they stood at the time of their repeal in 2017 are reproduced below:[45]

3. *Levy and collection of cess*

(1) There shall be levied and collected a cess for the purposes of the Water (Prevention and Control of Pollution) Act, 1974 (6 of 1974) and utilisation thereunder.
(2) The cess under sub-section (1) shall be payable by –
(a) every person carrying on any industry; and
(b) every local authority,
and shall be calculated on the basis of the water consumed by such person or local authority, as the case may be, for any of the purposes specified in column (1) of Schedule II, at such rate, not exceeding the rate specified in the corresponding entry in column (2) thereof, as the Central Government may by notification in the Official Gazette, from time to time, specify.
(2A) *Where any person carrying on any industry or any local authority consuming water for domestic purpose liable to pay cess fails to comply with any of the provisions of Section 25 of the*

[41] Repealed by section 18, Taxation Laws Amendment Act of 2017.
[42] Entry 97 is a residuary entry enabling Parliament to make laws on matters that are not enumerated in the State List and Concurrent List. The entry specifically covers any tax not mentioned in either of those Lists.
[43] 1987 All L J 41.
[44] AIR 1991 Pat 75.
[45] The italicized clauses were introduced by the 1991 amendment.

Water (Prevention and Control of Pollution) Act, 1974 (6 of 1974) or any of the standards laid down by the Central Government under the Environment (Protection) Act, 1986, cess shall be, notwithstanding anything contained in sub-section (2) of this section, calculated and payable at such rate, not exceeding the rate specified in column (3) of Schedule II, as the Central Government may, by notification in the Official Gazette, from time to time, specify.

(3) Where any local authority supplies water to any person carrying on any, industry or to any other local authority is liable to pay cess [under sub-section (2) or sub-section (2A)][46] so supplied, then, notwithstanding anything contained [in those sub-sections],[47] the local authority first mentioned shall not be liable to pay such cess in respect of such water.

Explanation: For the purposes of this section and Section 4, consumption of water includes supply of water.

* * *

7. *Rebate*

Where any person or local authority, liable to pay the cess under this Act, installs any plant for the treatment of sewage or trade effluent, such person or local authority shall, from such date as may be prescribed, be entitled to a rebate of *[twenty five per cent]*[48] of the cess payable by such person or as the case may be, local authority.

Provided that a person or local authority shall not be entitled to a rebate, if he or it –

(a) consumes water in excess of the maximum quantity as may be prescribed in this behalf for any industry or local authority; or

(b) fails to comply with any of the provisions of Section 25 of the Water (Prevention and Control of Pollution) Act, 1974 (6 of 1974) or any of the standards laid down by the Central Government under the Environment (Protection) Act, 1986 (29 of 1986).

In *Tisco's* case,[49] the High Court was concerned with the provisions of section 7 as they stood prior to the 1991 amendment. Tisco claimed rebate though its water treatment plant could treat only a part of the industrial effluent generated by the company. In its assessment order, the Bihar PCB refused to grant rebate due to the limited facilities. Accepting the company's claim, the court held that an assessee was entitled to rebate even where it was not in a position to treat the entire trade effluent or sewage in the water treatment plant. In reaching this conclusion, the High Court applied a liberal interpretation, holding that the rebate provisions were for the benefit of industry. Was this approach justified?

The Madras High Court followed *Tisco* in *Seshasayee Paper and Board Ltd v The Appellate Committee.*[50] The High Court permitted rebate, finding that the company had installed a 'relatively successful' effluent treatment plant. The assessing authority had declined to grant the rebate since the treated effluent did not meet the norm for bio-chemical oxygen demand. Interpreting the provisions of section 7 (pre-1991 amendment), the court held: 'It will be most unreasonable in my view to say that a person can claim rebate only when the treatment by the plant installed by him is successful, in the sense that no further treatment of the effluent is required at all....' The court held that once an assessee contributed towards the treatment of the effluent, the revenue ought to allow rebate. Since the 1990s there has been a

46 Substituted for 'under sub-section (2)' and 'in that sub-section' respectively by Act No. 53 of 1991.
47 *Id.*
48 Substituted for the words 'seventy percent' by Act No. 53 of 1991.
49 AIR 1991 Pat 75.
50 1994 (2) Mad L J Rep 394.

shift in the judicial approach. Today, had the Cess Act been in force, most courts would insist on strict compliance with all pollution control parameters before allowing rebates.

A fertile field of dispute prior to 2003 was whether a particular industry was covered by the list of specified industries in Schedule I of the Cess Act. An amendment in 2003 eliminated these contests by extending coverage of the Act to all industries. The 2003 amendment is an example of progressive legislation that improves tax administration by simplifying the law.

Since the Water Cess Act was a taxing statute the entries in Schedule I were construed strictly to determine whether liability is fastened on a particular industry.[51]

In *Saraswati Sugar Mills v Haryana, State Board*,[52] the Supreme Court strictly construed the entry covering 'processing of animal or vegetable products industry' to *exclude* the manufacture of sugar from sugar cane. Following the *Andhra Pradesh Rayons* case, the court preferred the common parlance meaning of 'vegetable' covering edible plants over the botanical definition which was applied by the High Court. The High Court held that the expression 'vegetable' was used in distinction to the word 'animal' and extended beyond common kitchen vegetables to include sugar cane. Despite the judgment in *Saraswati Sugar Mills*, the state board refused to refund the cess collected from the industry. This prompted another round of litigation, starting in the Allahabad High Court, which culminated in the Supreme Court nearly a decade later.[53] The Supreme Court upheld the High Court decision which directed the board to refund the amounts collected from the sugar units.

In *Britannia Industries Ltd*,[54] the Supreme Court followed *Saraswati Sugar Mills*. Britannia manufactured biscuits, bread and cake from wheat flour, milk powder, sugar and vanaspati. The High Court found that wheat, sugar and vanaspati (hydrogenated vegetable oil) were agricultural products while milk powder was an animal product. According to the High Court, the company was liable to pay cess under Entry 15 of Schedule I to the Water Cess Act. The Supreme Court reversed the High Court, drawing a distinction between vegetable products and agricultural products. Entry 15 was limited to 'vegetable products' and the expression would not cover wheat or sugar. Further, milk powder, although the result of processing an animal product, was not by itself an animal product. Besides, manufacturing biscuits through a series of processes was not covered by the language of Entry 15. Parliament sensibly amended the Water Cess Act in 2003, omitting Schedule I and extending the levy to all industries other than hydel power units. As discussed, in 2017 the Water Cess Act was removed from the statute book.

Besides industry, section 3 of the Cess Act required every local authority to pay cess on water consumed or supplied. Regrettably, municipal bodies neither obtained consent under section 25 of the Water Act nor paid cess under the Cess Act. In this regard, until the repeal of the Cess Act, almost every municipality and local authority in India was a tax dodger, liable to the penalties imposed under section 14 of the Cess Act.

The Delhi Electric Supply Undertaking (DESU) has a thermal power plant on the banks of the River Yamuna. The plant draws water from the river to cool its turbines and discharges the water used back into the river. DESU challenged the assessment orders passed under the

[51] *Andhra Pradesh State Board for Prevention and Control of Water Pollution v Andhra Pradesh Rayons Ltd* AIR 1989 SC 611.

[52] AIR 1992 SC 224. The strict construction test was reiterated by the Supreme Court in a 1995 decision reported at *Bihar State Pollution Control Board v Tata Engineering & Locomotive Co Ltd* (1998) 8 SCC 720.

[53] *U P Pollution Control Board v Kanoria Industrial Ltd* (2001) 2 SCC 549.

[54] *Britannia Industries Ltd v T N Pollution Control Board* (2000) 9 SCC 68.

Cess Act on the ground that there was no 'consumption' of water and consequently the taxable event for the levy of cess had not occurred. In a brief order the Supreme Court declined to interfere with the reasoning and conclusions of the cess appellate authority. The authority held that the water drawn by the utility was 'consumed'.[55]

In *Arvind Textiles* case,[56] the Rajasthan High Court upheld the levy of an additional octroi on grey cloth brought into Balotara town. The octroi was imposed to finance the municipal board's scheme to put up a common effluent treatment plant to treat discharges from 200 textile processing units in the area.

D. THE ENVIRONMENT (PROTECTION) ACT

The Environment (Protection) Act of 1986 (EPA) clearly extends to water quality and the control of water pollution. Section 2(a) of the Act defines the environment to include water and the interrelationship which exists among and between water and human beings, other living creatures, plants, micro-organisms and property. The Act authorizes the Central Government to establish standards for the quality of the environment[57] and for emission or discharge of environmental pollutants from any source.[58] The Ministry of Environment and Forests has published Environment (Protection) Rules establishing general standards and industry-based standards for certain types of effluent discharge.[59] The ministry has not yet promulgated rules establishing ambient inland water quality standards, though state boards must have regard to the assimilative capacity of receiving bodies.[60] In 1997, the Maharashtra PCB pioneered the development of ambient norms for freshwater bodies.[61] However, these norms do not have statutory sanction and serve only to guide industry in selecting a suitable location.

The EPA includes a provision authorizing the Central Government to issue direct orders to protect the environment.[62] The Central Government may delegate specified duties and powers under the EPA to any officer, state government or other authority.[63] For example, the power to issue directions under section 5 has been delegated to the state governments and the power of entry and the right to take samples under sections 10 and 11 has been delegated to various officers.

55 *Delhi Electric Supply Undertaking v Central Board* (1995) Supp (3) SCC 385. Whether recycled water returned to a stream is a 'trade effluent' is a mixed question of law and fact. *Rajasthan State Electricity Board v Cess Appellate Committee* (1991) 1 SCC 93.

56 *Arvind Textiles v State of Rajasthan* AIR 1994 Raj 195.

57 Section 3(2)(iii).

58 Section 3(2)(iv).

59 Schedule I and Schedule VI, Environment (Protection) Rules. Industry-based standards override general standards.

60 Annexure I, Schedule VI, Environment (Protection) Rules. In December 1998, the ministry issued water quality standards for coastal waters. Entry 86, Schedule I. Environment (Protection) Rules.

61 Maharashtra Pollution Control Board, *Classification of River Water & Guidelines for Location of Industrial Activity* (1997).

62 Section 5.

63 Section 23.

E. NUISANCE LAW AND WATER POLLUTION

I. PUBLIC NUISANCE ACTIONS UNDER THE CODE OF CRIMINAL PROCEDURE

In the landmark *Ratlam Municipality* case,[64] discussed in the Judicial Remedies and Procedures chapter, the Supreme Court did not consider the effect of the Water Act on the availability of injunctive relief under section 133. There is a divergence of judicial opinion on this issue. Initially, the Kerala High Court in *Tata Tea* ruled that a court could not entertain a section 133 action to abate water pollution, even where the state board was remiss. According to this view, the Water Act was a complete code to prevent water pollution and impliedly repealed the provisions of section 133 of the Criminal Procedure Code in so far as they relate to the prevention and control of water pollution.[65]

In *Nagarjuna Paper Mills Ltd v Sub-Divisional Magistrate*,[66] the Andhra Pradesh High Court established a less stringent rule, taking the position that section 133 injunctive relief was available as long as it did not interfere with an order of a state PCB issued under the Water Act. The court noted that the magistrate's decision to issue an order for injunctive relief was based on a report submitted by the superintendent engineer of the PCB itself, which stated that water pollution from the paper mills was harming people and cattle. This view was also adopted by a division bench of the Kerala High Court in *Krishna Panicker v Appukuttan Nair*,[67] overruling the contrary opinion expressed earlier in *Tata Tea*. However, without considering *Panicker's* case, the Karnataka High Court in 1997 followed *Tata Tea*,[68] then quickly retreated,[69] preferring the approach of the Andhra Pradesh High Court.

II. INJUNCTIVE RELIEF UNDER COMMON LAW

A private party who suffers an unreasonable interference with the enjoyment of his or her property may bring a common law action to restrain the polluter. The following case considers whether section 58 of the Water Act bars the jurisdiction of the civil courts to entertain private nuisance suits.

SREENIVASA DISTILLERIES v THYAGARAJAN

AIR 1986 AP 328

ORDER:

* * *

Section 58 enacts two prohibitions. Firstly, not to entertain any suit or proceedings in respect of any matter which the appellate authority constituted under the Act is empowered to determine. Secondly, no injunction shall be granted in respect of any action taken by any authority under the Act in pursuance of the provisions of the Act. This is the only provision barring the jurisdiction of a Civil Court. The section is intended to preserve the statutory protection given to the Boards untouched by civil actions. Now, the present action is only preventing the defendant from polluting water. But this section is not directed to annul any orders passed by the authority constituted under this Act. Now it is admitted that no orders are passed under the Act, and, therefore, any order passed by the Civil Court will not take away the jurisdiction of authorities constituted under the Act. Hence, I am of the view that

64 *Supra* note 14.
65 *Tata Tea Ltd v State of Kerala* 1984 KER L T 645.
66 1987 CRI L J 2071.
67 1993 (1) KER L T 771.
68 *Executive Apparel Processors v The Taluka Executive Magistrate* 1997 (4) KAR L J 181.
69 *Harihar Polyfibres v Sub-Divisional Magistrate* ILR 1997 KAR 1139.

S. 58 does not prohibit the jurisdiction of the Civil Court to entertain any suit or proceeding restraining the defendant to cause pollution.

NOTES AND QUESTIONS

1. Do you find an intent of Parliament in the Water Act to bar private remedies for water pollution or is the Act intended to supplement other remedies for the control of water pollution?

2. A private litigant can seek damages rather than injunctive relief in a civil lawsuit. In view of section 58 of the Water Act can a court hearing a private lawsuit order the polluter to pay damages?

3. Does a statutory provision, such as section 58, bar the jurisdiction of a High Court to entertain a petition under Article 226 of the Constitution or the jurisdiction of the Supreme Court to entertain petitions under Article 32? Citizens have a fundamental duty to protect and improve the natural environment under Article 51 A(g) of the Constitution: should a statutory provision curtail availability of legal remedies which enable a citizen to discharge this fundamental duty?

4. Examine section 29 of the National Green Tribunal Act of 2010 extracted at the end of this note. Having regard to the breadth of sub-section (2), is a common law action seeking to abate a nuisance barred? Does the NGT Act oust the jurisdiction of every local civil court and compel citizens troubled by pollution to travel to New Delhi or one of the other four regional seats of the NGT to secure redress? Is there an interpretation that saves common law actions? Is it constitutionally permissible for Parliament to bar a common law remedy without providing for an effective, alternative locally available remedy?

> 29. *Bar of jurisdiction.* (1) With effect from the date of establishment of the Tribunal under this Act, no civil court shall have jurisdiction to entertain any appeal in respect of any matter, which the Tribunal is empowered to determine under its appellate jurisdiction
> (2) No civil court shall have jurisdiction to settle dispute or entertain any question relating to any claim for granting any relief or compensation or restitution of property damaged or environment damaged which may be adjudicated upon by the Tribunal, and no injunction in respect of any action taken or to be taken by or before the Tribunal in respect of the settlement of such dispute or any such claim for granting any relief or compensation or restitution of property damaged or environment shall be granted by the civil court.

F. RIPARIAN RIGHTS AND WATER POLLUTION

A riparian owner is one who has title to land adjacent to a natural stream. The Indian legal system has recognized the right of riparian owners to unpolluted waters at least since the adoption of the Indian Easements Act of 1882. Under section 7 of that Act every riparian owner has the right to the continued flow of the waters of a natural stream in its natural condition without obstruction or unreasonable pollution.

The legal system also recognizes a common law riparian right to unpolluted water. This common law right is rarely invoked in contemporary litigation concerning water pollution. The Supreme Court, however, revived this doctrine in *M C Mehta v Union of India (Municipalities)* by stating:

In common law the Municipal Corporation can be restrained by an injunction in an action brought by a riparian owner who has suffered on account of the pollution of the water in a river caused by the Corporation by discharging into the river insufficiently treated sewage from discharging such sewage into the river.[70]

NOTES AND QUESTIONS

1. The Supreme Court in *Mehta (Municipalities)* noted that the Central and state water boards and the municipality that was releasing sewage effluent had failed to implement or enforce the law for controlling water pollution. Suppose an industrial manufacturer or municipality is releasing effluent in compliance with the consent orders of a state board. The effluent causes harm to a riparian landowner who uses the water for domestic purposes or irrigation. How should a court rule on the riparian landowner's request for an injunction restraining the polluter from releasing effluent?

2. Assume a court decides to issue a restraining order to protect a plaintiff's riparian rights. What should the order require of the polluter—primary treatment of the effluent, no discharge whatsoever of effluents, or removal only of those substances which interfere with the actual riparian uses of the water? Assume the riparian landowner requires water of very high quality for aquaculture. Assume also that the water in the stream in its natural condition—that is, not subject to any other use—is suitable for aquaculture. Must all users of water on the stream return the water in its natural condition? Should small farmers be exempt from this requirement? Should large industrial concerns be exempt if they apply the best available technology for treating the water?

3. Do actions to enforce riparian rights survive section 29(2) of the NGT Act?

4. Excessive exploitation of riparian resources can destroy the river. In *Deepak Kumar v State of Haryana*,[71] the Supreme Court found that uncontrolled sand mining in river beds was damaging the eco-system of rivers and threatening biodiversity. Real estate development and infrastructure projects such as highways had fuelled a ferocious surge in riparian mining activity. The existing framework of laws was too feeble to contain the onslaught. The court made it mandatory for all sand miners to secure an environmental clearance by following the EIA process and also directed the states as well as the Union Government to frame suitable subordinate legislation that would protect river beds from uncontrolled mining of minor minerals such as sand, boulders and gravel.

G. ADMINISTRATIVE ACTION TO CLEAN THE GANGA

Cleaning the Ganga has been a priority of the Union Government for several decades. Amidst great fanfare in 1985, the government of India announced an ambitious plan for cleaning up the river. Periodically, this initiative has transmuted, the latest avatar being Namami Gange, an ambitious mission to clean and rejuvenate the river. After nearly four decades of efforts to clean the river, the Central PCB acknowledges that the water in the river was fit for drinking at just five out of over 70 monitoring stations and was suitable for bathing at seven stations. Despite thousands of crores spent, the pollution problem remains obstinate. Review the

[70] AIR 1988 SC 1115.
[71] (2012) 4 SCC 629.

following readings which provide a backdrop to the *Ganga Pollution* cases discussed later in this chapter.

VICTOR MALLET; RIVER OF LIFE, RIVER OF DEATH: THE GANGES AND INDIA'S FUTURE, Oxford University Press 230 (2017)

Mission Impossible? How to Clean the Ganges

The successful clean-ups of the Thames in England and the Rhine in Continental Europe are the projects most often mentioned by Indians concerned about the Ganges. In 1957, the Natural History Museum in London is said to have declared that the River Thames in the city was biologically dead (although the actual findings were more nuanced—scientists found that there were essentially no *fish* other than eels in the tidal Thames in greater London). As a child I recall being told that close contact with the toxic Thames was something to be avoided at all costs.

Fifty years later, the Thames in London is so clean that numerous types of fish have returned to the river, sea-horses have been found in the estuary, and financial traders can see seals at Canary Wharf. A lost whale even swam past the Houses of Parliament. I have seen kingfishers and herons along the canals of central London and cormorants fishing in the Thames under Southwark Bridge.

The fate of the Thames is instructive—there are many parallels in the way people have used and abused the Thames and the Ganges—because it was in Britain that the industrial revolution first took hold in the eighteenth century, which meant that London's river was among the first to undergo the cycle of fluvial death and eventual rebirth. Just as the tanneries of Kanpur pour their filthy waste into the Ganges today; so potteries in Fulham, porcelain factories in Chelsea, glassmakers in Vauxhall, the sugar refineries of Whitechapel, and the tanneries of Bermondsey did the same to the Thames for a canal and construction on the banks in London narrowed the river to a third of its natural breadth....

Indian state governments crippled by corruption; venal industrialists; the terrifying inertia of India's bureaucracy: all these will make restoring the Ganges to health an extraordinarily challenging task. But that task is not impossible. Rivers have been sullied for millennia, and they have been turned black and pungent by manufacturing industries for centuries, in England, in Germany, in the United States, in Japan, in China, in Southeast Asia, and in India. And they have—like the Thames, the Rhine, and the Chicago River—recovered....

Necessary measures to restore a river—any river—can be separated into three broad categories: first, collecting data about water quality and quantity; second, preparing policies and projects to deal with the problems revealed by the analysis of that data; and, third, implementing those policies and projects. When it comes to the Ganges and its tributaries, Indian governments have been slow to collect reliable data, although they have organized some monitoring of water quality and flow; they have been prolific formulators of policies and plans for more than three decades; and they have failed dismally on implementation. This pattern is not confined to rivers—students of modern India will notice the similarities with, say, the shockingly poor state of public education and health care—and it reflects the dysfunctional nature of government at the centre and in the states of north India and the Gangetic plain.

To understand the first failure—data collection—it helps to visit the gloomy offices of the Central Pollution Control Board in east Delhi, on the other side of the Yamuna from the rest of the city. The CPCB is the central government body for collating data on the Ganges, while states have their own State Pollution Control Boards (SPCBs), which vary widely in effectiveness. After months of trying and failing to obtain an appointment with the CPCB, I simply showed up unannounced at the offices with a colleague in an attempt to obtain better information on Ganges pollution than the outdated and incomplete information on their website. The anti-pollution bureaucrats were friendly but did not reveal much that was new. In an office in which five-year-old reports on the river's water quality and 'guidelines for idol immersion' lay on dusty shelves, an environmental engineer told us of the World Bank project and the 113 locations along the river that had been identified for real-time water monitoring. He also confirmed that the CPCB had little data on heavy metals because 'we are not equipped for that.'....

The Congress administration of Manmohan Singh established the National Ganga River Basin Authority in 2009, and the National Mission for Clean Ganga two years later; the five Ganges Basin states each have a State Ganga River Conservation Authority. Modi re-energized the institutional focus on saving the Ganges after he took office in 2014, putting the name of the river in the relevant ministry so that it became the Ministry of Water Resources, River Development and Ganga Rejuvenation. He launched 'Namani Gange' (Obeisance to the Ganges), a national campaign under which the central government took control of the river clean-up, quadrupled its budget, and promised to spend 200 billion rupees (about $3 billion) in the five financial years to 2019–20. The programme has been sensibly split into three parts, starting with 'quick wins' for immediate, visible impact, including the collection of plastic waste, rural sanitation, to cut sewage flow, the construction of crematoria to reduce the number of unburnt or partly burnt corpses in the river and the beautification of river *ghats*.

Then, in the medium term (over five years), the government will build additional municipal sewage treatment plants with a capacity of 2.5 billion litres a day, enforce industrial effluent controls, protect wildlife, plant 30,000 hectares of forest in the watershed to reduce erosion and install the 113 water monitoring stations. In the long term, a ten-year period that would extend into the mandate of the next government, the government will ensure adequate water flow (environmental flow or 'e-flow') in the river and improve the efficiency of irrigation....

What should give optimists pause for thoughts is the record of previous clean-up projects. It is not just that the river evidently remains filthy after they were supposedly implemented. No one is even sure how much money was spent or where it went.... [I learned] that anywhere between 30% and 100% of project money is stolen. 'All the money disappears, and they check it off on the list: "Project completed". And there is no project.' ...

At the tanneries in Kanpur, for example, they pointed out that in almost all cases the effluent monitoring devices did no more than measure the quantity of liquid and made no measurement of chromium or any other pollutant. 'I've lost hope and surrendered', said Rakesh Jaiswal, the Kanpur environmental activist. Expressing his view that pollution by the tanneries had not been cut, he stated: 'There is no reduction in wastewater generation by the tanneries. Ganga is more polluted than ever before.' Jaiswal went on, describing his experiences in Kanpur: 'PM Modi has rekindled the hope. He's allocated 20,000 crore rupees ($3 billion) towards the Ganga cleaning and keeps talking about Ganga cleaning but nothing is visible on the ground.' According to Jaiswal, there has been no material change in the flow of sewage or industrial effluent and no efforts have been made to augment the flow of the river....

Indian governments have spent hundreds of millions of dollars on projects to clean the Ganges since the 1980s, but most of the money was diverted by corrupt officials or simply wasted. Yet cleaning the Ganges is far more important to India—religiously, economically, and socially—than the restorations of the Rhine or the Thames were to Germany, the Netherlands, or England. For Sanskrit scholar Diana Eck, we are watching a cultural and theological crisis as well as an environmental one: there is arguably nowhere in the world that should have a higher standard of river quality than India, 'for there is no other culture in which rivers have such a central role in the daily rituals lives of countless millions'. Indians bathe in river water, drink it, and make offerings of it to the departed, yet the 'rivers that are said to have descended to earth as sources of salvation are now, in their earthly form, in need of salvation themselves.'

BANJOT KAUR; NAMAMI GANGE: 5 REASONS WHY GANGA WILL NOT BE CLEAN BY 2020, Down to Earth, 15 October 2018*

Challenge I: Sewage treatment

Sewage treatment plants (STPs) have been at the centre of Ganga pollution abatement. As per Namami Gange targets, STPs with over 2000 million litres a day (MLD) capacity had to be rehabilitated of which only 328 MLD have been done. A look at the status of all the projects undertaken makes one doubt whether the government would even achieve its revised deadline. As far as sewage infrastructure projects are concerned, 68 projects were sanctioned after the Namami Gange was approved by the cabinet and only six were completed till August. Till August 31, 2018 a total of 236 projects, including STPs, had been sanctioned out of which only 63 had been completed....

Not sensing any progress in controlling pollution, NGT in July last year gave more than 100 specific directions related to 86 drains going into the Ganga, Ramganga, Kali and the Pandu rivers. 'The government agencies have submitted compliance reports regarding most of the directions. But what I gather from the field is that most of the submissions are coloured,' says M C Mehta, who has been fighting cases on the Ganga in the Supreme Court and NGT.

Besides cleaning the Ganga, the Namami Gange also talks about afforestation as an important activity as it helps groundwater recharge. According to NMCG, it has already spent Rs 114 crore on afforestation but to no avail. Showing the plants being planted, assistant professor in Allahabad University Pramod Sharma says, 'They have planted kachnaar and gulmohar plants. They can only be used for decorative purposes. What is required for the Ganga is bargad, peepal, gular and neem as they help in better conservation of water.'

Challenge II: Restoring the flow

There is another fundamental problem that will ensure the holy river remains dirty. A river is a self-purifying system only when water flows through it. The Ganga fails this basic test except during monsoons. So it's not just about unclean Ganga, it is about the existence of Ganga.... [T]hese surmises get credence in the paper published by IIT-Kharagpur's Abhijit Mukherjee and others in August 2018 which says that according to their estimates the baseflow amount of the river has decreased by 56% in 2016 as compared to the 1970s. The decrease in flow has led to an increase in groundwater extraction for various uses.

According to a report published by Wildlife Institute of India in May 2018, 16 existing, 14 ongoing and 14 proposed hydroelectric projects on the Bhagirathi and Alaknanda river basins have turned the upper stretch of the Ganga [into] 'ecological deserts'. To deal with these projects, A K Gosain, professor at IIT-Delhi and a member of the panel that has drafted the Ganga protection law, says, 'The designs of hydroelectric projects can be tweaked in such a manner that they consume less water. It may raise the cost of the projects but should be done for long-term preservation of the Ganga. It is now for the government to decide whether it comes out with such a mandatory policy or not.'

---

* https://www.downtoearth.org.in/coverage/pollution/namami-gange-5-reasons-why-ganga-will-not-be-clean-by-2020-61891, accessed 10 May 2021.

Challenge III: Sludge control

The river has another persistent problem that is going to be more pronounced. 'I have a toilet in my home but the two pits under are overflowing with waste. How do I use it?' Says Rashid Ali of Chhapri village in Allahabad District. He and his family are back to defecating in the open near the Ganga. Other villages also narrate similar issues and say the construction of toilets has compounded their problem because the overflowing toilets have also made their homes dirty. The damning indictment is supported by many people living in cities along the banks of the Ganga.

A staggering 99.93% villages lying on the banks of Ganga, also known as Ganga Grams, have been declared open defecation free (ODF) by the government under the Swachh Bharat Mission (SBM). As per SBM data, more than 2.7 million toilets have been constructed in over 4,000 villages till September 17, 2018. Not surprisingly, CAG in its December 2017 report casts aspersions on the claim. The report said the state government was to verify the ODF status through its own teams or through a third party but 1,144 villages of UP and Bihar didn't get it done. The whole objective of making villages lying in the Ganga basin to be ODF was to reduce the faecal coliform levels in the Ganga. Against the standard of 2,500 per 100 ml, the faecal coliform ranged from 2,500 to 2,40,000 per 100 ml in the Ganga basin cities in May 2018, as per data provided by pollution control boards of five states along the Ganga basin.

Experts say that while toilets were constructed, hardly a thought was given to management of sludge. According to a study conducted by CSE, most of the cities surveyed had twin-pit technology which is not recommended in low-lying areas. The National Policy on Faecal Sludge and Septage Management (FSSM) 2017 also anticipated the challenge as more and more toilets are constructed. As urban households without toilets obtain facilities under SBM, it is likely that many will acquire on-site arrangements like pit latrines and septic tanks in cities at locations where sewerage systems are not available. Thus, while the containment of human waste will be largely achieved, its safe disposal still poses a huge challenge.

Challenge IV: Cost overruns

Many of the projects sanctioned as early as 2011 could not meet their deadlines even after they came under the ambit of Namami Gange. Sample the case of STPs to be built in Varanasi with the assistance of Japan International Cooperation Agency (JICA). A close look at the development of the project has quite a story to narrate. It was sanctioned on July 14, 2010 at a cost of Rs.496 crore with a deadline for completion in 2017–18, with some parts to be completed in 2016. Documents accessed by DTE reveal that there was absolutely no physical progress of the plan at the end of December 2014, the year in which the Modi government took over, with JICA concurrence for technical bid awaited. The situation was exactly the same by December 2015. STP construction was completed by 34% in December 2016. Then the government issued a revised sanction of the project and pegged the cost at Rs.641.19 crore with a revised deadline of June 2018. That is not one sample in UP. Bihar has similar cases. A 17 MLD STP was sanctioned in the state's Begusarai district on March 8, 2010 at a cost of Rs.65 crore. The project is aided by the World Bank. The NMCG documents reveal no progress took place till December 2016, the original deadline. In December 2017, the tender was cancelled. Revision sanctioned was issued in March 2018 with escalated cost of Rs.230 crore and a deadline of January 2020 and it has now become a project of the Central government.

Besides, CAG also pointed out poor financial management for the programme in its December 2017 report. It said, 'Only eight to 63% of the funds were utilized during 2014–15 to 2016–17 for the river clean-up programme.' A corpus of Rs.198.14 crore (as of March

31, 2017) was available in the Clean Ganga Fund. It is a fund under which entities or a commoner can contribute for the Ganga clean-up. However, NMCG could not utilize any amount out of the Clean Ganga Fund and the entire amount was lying in banks due to non-finalisation of action plan.

Challenge V: Governance glitches

The cleaning of the Ganga requires seamless coordination between the agencies responsible for carrying out different tasks. This calls for vision and a clear-cut governance strategy. The water resources ministry signed MOUs with 10 ministries for better implementation of Namami Gange. However, till date no detail is available as to how these ministries are functioning for better convergence. Vinod Tare of IIT-Kanpur who helmed the consortium says, 'The Ganga Actions Plans lacked the coordination of ministries. It is still lacking in Namami Gange. If the departments do not coordinate well, the programme will not achieve desired objectives.' Ganga Mahasabha's head Swami Jitendranand Saraswati says, 'After the memoranda were signed, nobody knows what they did. I tried enquiring often, but to no avail.'

The draft Ganga protection law is with the government but experts question its utility. 'It is immaterial whether you come up with a new law or not. What is required is an autonomous body for the rejuvenation of Ganga which is independent of the government when it comes to its functioning. Instead of bureaucrats, it should consist of experts well-versed with the river,' says environmentalist G D Agrawal, the 86-year-old former IIT-Kanpur professor who is on an indefinite fast to save the Ganga from June 22, 2018....

'Namami Gange' is the name of the administrative programme launched in 2014 to clean the Ganga. The legal framework to execute the project was provided on 7 October 2016 when the Union Ministry of Water Resources, River Development and Ganga Rejuvenation issued a statutory notification called the River Ganga (Rejuvenation, Protection and Management) Order, 2016. The order applies to ten states comprising the River Ganga Basin and the National Capital Territory of Delhi. The order recognizes the unique importance of the River Ganga as well as the pollution threats faced by the river. The order constitutes a set of authorities under the Environment (Protection) Act of 1986 with powers to undertake measures to abate pollution and restore the river.

The order sets out ten principles to guide the mission. These principles require the River Ganga and all its tributaries to be managed as a single system, the water quality to be restored 'in a time bound manner', use of the river 'in an ecologically sustainable manner' and maintenance of the 'continuity of flow' in the river.[72]

Every state government is mandated to ensure uninterrupted 'ecological flow of water' in the River Ganga.[73] The direct or indirect discharge of untreated or treated sewage or sludge into the river is prohibited.[74] However, local authorities which do not have sewage schemes or infrastructure are required to meet targets within the period specified by the National Mission for Clean Ganga (NMCG).[75]

---

72 Paragraph 4(1).
73 Paragraph 5(1).
74 Paragraph 6(1).
75 Paragraph 6(1), proviso.

The NMCG is a statutory authority comprising officials drawn from the Union Government and state governments. It has a two-tier management structure with a Governing Council and an Executive Committee, both of which are chaired by the Director General of the NMCG.[76]

To curb pollution, the order prohibits discharge of trade effluent and industrial waste into the river or on the banks of the Ganga and its tributaries. Here too, where on the date of commencement of the order the requisite infrastructure is not functional, the NMCG may specify a period for 'connection, storage, transportation and disposal of trade effluent and industrial waste, bio-medical waste or other hazardous substance'.[77] The NMCG and other authorities under the order are in the local language required to disseminate and publicize information about measures to clean the river.[78]

The NMCG is empowered to issue directions 'necessary for abatement of pollution and rejuvenation, protection and management of the River Ganga' to any authority and the person receiving these directions is obliged to comply with them.[79] The NMCG is obliged to monitor pollution using physical stations as well as satellite imagery and remote sensing technologies.

The National Ganga Council is chaired by the Prime Minister and consists of ten Union Ministers, as well as Chief Ministers of the five riparian states and three bureaucrats including the Director General of NMCG.[80] Apart from the Council, the order constitutes an Empowered Tasked Force,[81] State Ganga Rejuvenation, Protection and Management Committees,[82] and District Ganga Protection Committees.[83]

The core of the 2016 order is paragraph 39 which enumerates the functions and duties of the NMCG:

> 39. *Functions of National Mission for Clean Ganga.*– (1) Without prejudice to the provisions of this Order, the National Mission for Clean Ganga shall identify or cause to be identified –
>
> (a) the specific threats to the River Ganga in areas in each village and town of such specified District abutting River Ganga and its tributaries, including sewerage and industrial waste, cremation and burial of corpses and disposal of animal carcasses, and threats from commercial, recreational and religious activities;
>
> (b) the type of measures required to address such threat in each village and town of all districts abutting River Ganga and its tributaries;
>
> (c) the specific areas where such remedial actions are required to be taken for rejuvenation and protection of River Ganga and its tributaries.
>
> (d) the measures which may be necessary for reuse of treated water and enter in to Memorandum of Understanding in this regard with the Ministries of the Central Government like Railways, Power, Petroleum and Natural Gas etc., State Governments, autonomous bodies at the Central and State level, recognized Institutes and organizations which the National Mission for Clean Ganga may deem fit.
>
> (2) The National Mission for Clean Ganga shall make or cause to make the River Ganga Basin Management Plan along with cost, timelines and allocation of responsibilities,

---

76 Paragraphs 31, 35.
77 Paragraph 6(2).
78 Paragraph 6(5).
79 Paragraph 8.
80 Paragraph 12.
81 Paragraph 17.
82 Paragraph 20.
83 Paragraph 53.

among other things, for rejuvenation and protection of River Ganga and its tributaries in each village and town of specified District abutting River Ganga and its tributaries and execute projects there for.

(3) The National Mission for Clean Ganga shall –

(a) cause to be determined the magnitude of ecological flows in the River Ganga and its tributaries required to be maintained at different points in different areas at all times with the aim of ensuring water quality and environmentally sustainable rejuvenation, protection and management of River Ganga and its tributaries and notifying the same and take or direct all such measures necessary to maintain adequate ecological flows;

(b) cause to be identified places where the environmental flow of water of River Ganga has been modified and take measures for correction thereof to maintain the continuous flow of water for rejuvenation, protection and management of River Ganga and its tributaries;

(c) identify places of discontinuity of water in River Ganga and its tributaries due to engineered diversion of water or storage of water or by any other means and execute plans in respect thereof or take remedial action therefor;

(d) devise a system to be put in place for continuous monitoring of flow of water and pollution levels in River Ganga and its tributaries;

(e) take all such measures which may be necessary to give effect to the decisions of the National Ganga Council so as to maintain adequate ecological flows in the River Ganga and tributaries;

(f) render assistance or cause them to be rendered by any agency for preparation of detailed project reports or execution of projects for abatement of pollution and rejuvenation, protection and management of the River Ganga and its tributaries to the State Governments, the State Ganga Committees, District Ganga Committees or local authorities or any person or body, any authority, Board or Corporation;

(g) set up or facilitate setting up or designate and direct one or more existing centers to research, develop and disseminate knowledge base and analytical tools on abatement of pollution and rejuvenation, protection and management of River Ganga and its tributaries;

(h) take any other measures which may be necessary for continuous flow of water and abatement of pollution in River Ganga and its tributaries

(4) The National Mission for Clean Ganga shall take all such other emergency measures as outlined in paragraph 7.

NOTES AND QUESTIONS

1. Is the National Mission any different from its predecessors? The dissolved and ineffective National Ganga River Basin Authority was headed by the Prime Minister and had a full crew of Union Ministers, Chief Ministers and bureaucrats.

2. The 2016 order constitutes a surfeit of committees. For good measure and as if the abundance of statutory committees was not enough, the NMCG may 'constitute one or more River Ganga Management Committees from amongst its members and such experts in the field of rivers or water as it may consider appropriate'.[84] Are committees an effective tool for administration? Will loading the busy officials who serve on these committees with an additional responsibility spur efficiency?

[84] Paragraph 51.

3. Paragraph 23 of the order reads:

> The decision taken at the meetings of the State Ganga Committee shall, *notwithstanding anything contained in this Order*, be binding upon every District Ganga Committee and every local authority or other authority or Board or person referred in such decision and they shall comply with the decisions of the State Ganga Committee.

As a matter of administrative law, can a statutory order create a statutory committee and then empower that committee to decide matters in conflict with the parent order? Focus on the italicized portion of the quote.

4. The District Ganga Committees are required to prepare plans to protect the river and tributaries. Do these committees have the technical, administrative, financial capacity or vision to prepare effective plans? Will they fail, much as the pollution control boards have for half a century?

5. Is India's federal structure a boon or bane for projects to clean up interstate rivers?

H. THE *GANGA POLLUTION* CASES

The *Ganga Pollution* cases are the most significant water pollution cases to date. In 1985, M C Mehta, an activist Supreme Court advocate, filed a writ petition under Article 32 of the Constitution. Among other things, the petition was directed at the Kanpur Municipality's failure to prevent waste-water from polluting the Ganga. Mehta asked the court to order governmental authorities and tanneries at Jajmau near Kanpur to stop polluting the Ganga with sewage and trade effluents. (As we shall see later in this section, the case was transferred to the National Green Tribunal in 2017.)

The ensuing litigation involved hundreds of polluters and the Supreme Court noticed the action as a representative action under Order 1, Rule 8 of the Code of Civil Procedure. We excerpt from three major opinions in the case, where the court ruled against the Kanpur tanneries, the municipalities on the Ganga and the Calcutta tanneries.[85]

While reading the following excerpts, consider particularly these issues: (a) the polluted condition of the River Ganga more than two decades after the enactment of the Water Act; (b) the basis for the court's jurisdiction under Article 32; and (c) the specific actions ordered by the court in each case.

M C MEHTA v UNION OF INDIA (KANPUR TANNERIES)
AIR 1988 SC 1037

VENKATARAMIAH, J: This is a public interest litigation. The petitioner who is an active social worker has filed this petition, *inter alia*, for the issue of a writ/order/direction in the nature of mandamus to the respondents other than Respondents 1 and 7 to 9 restraining them from letting out the trade effluents into the river Ganga till such time they put up necessary treatment plants for treating the trade effluents in order to arrest the pollution of water in the said river. Respondent 1 is the Union of India, Respondent 7 is the Chairman of the Central Board for Prevention and Control of Pollution, Respondent 8 is the Chairman, Uttar Pradesh Pollution Control Board and Respondent 9 is the Indian Standards Institute.

Water is the most important of the elements of nature. River valleys have been the cradles of civilization from the beginning of the world. Aryan civilization grew around the towns and

[85] For convenience, these opinions are referred to as *Kanpur Tanneries*, *Municipalities* and *Calcutta Tanneries*.

villages on the banks of the river Ganga. Varanasi which is one of the cities on the banks of the river Ganga is considered to be one of the oldest human settlements in the world. It is the popular belief that the river Ganga is the purifier of all but we are now led to the situation that action has to be taken to prevent the pollution of the water of the river Ganga since we have reached a stage that any further pollution of the river water is likely to lead to a catastrophe. There are today large towns inhabited by millions of people on the banks of the river Ganga. There are also large industries on its banks. Sewage of the towns and cities on the banks of the river and the trade effluents of the factories and other industries are continuously being discharged into the river. It is the complaint of the petitioner that neither the government nor the people are giving adequate attention to stop the pollution of the river Ganga. Steps have, therefore, to be taken for the purpose of protecting the cleanliness of the stream in the river Ganga, which is in fact the life sustainer of a large part of northern India.

When this petition came up for preliminary hearing, the court directed the issue of notice under Order 1 Rule 8 of the Code of Civil Procedure treating this case as a representative action by publishing the gist of the petition in the newspapers in circulation in northern India and calling upon all the industrialists and the municipal corporations and the town municipal councils having jurisdiction over the areas through which the river Ganga flows to appear before the Court and to show cause as to why directions should not be issued to them as prayed by the petitioner asking them not to allow the trade effluents and the sewage into the river Ganga without appropriately, treating them before discharging them into the river. Pursuant to the said notice a large number of industrialists and local bodies have entered appearance before the Court. Some of them have filed counter-affidavits explaining the steps taken by them for treating the trade effluents before discharging them into the river. When the above case came up for consideration before the Court on the last date of hearing we directed that the case against the tanneries at Jajmau area near Kanpur would be taken up for hearing first. [The court noted that only 47 of the 75 tanneries designated as parties to the lawsuit were represented before the court by counsel. The remaining tanneries did not appear before the court at the time of the hearing nor were they represented by any counsel. The court invoked the Water Act and the Environment (Protection) Act as an indication of the importance of the prevention and control of water pollution. The court emphasized that notwithstanding the comprehensive provisions contained in the Water Act the state boards had not taken effective steps to prevent the discharge of effluents into the river Ganga. The court ruled that the fact that effluents are first discharged into municipal sewers did not absolve the tanneries from being proceeded against under the provisions of the law in force, since ultimately the effluents reach the river Ganga from municipal sewers.]

There is not much dispute on the question that the discharge of the trade effluents from these tanneries into the river Ganga has been causing considerable damage to the life of the people who use the water of the river Ganga and also to the aquatic life in the river. The tanneries at Jajmau in Kanpur have themselves formed an association called Jajmau Tanners Pollution Control Association with the objects among others:

(1) To establish, equip and maintain laboratories, workshops, institutes, organisations and factories for conducting and carrying on experiments and to provide funds for the main objects of the Company.

(2) To procure and import wherever necessary the chemicals etc. for the purpose of pollution control in tanning industries.

(3) To set up and maintain common effluent treatment plant for member tanners in and around Jajmau.

(4) To make periodical charges on members for the effluent treatment based on the benefit it derives from time to time to meet the common expenses for maintenance, replacement incurred towards effluent treatment.

* * *

A study of the conditions prevailing at Jajmau, Kanpur was made by the Sub-Committee on Effluent Disposal constituted by the Development Council for Leather and Leather Goods Industries along with the various tanneries situated in some of the other parts of India and in its report submitted in April 1984, the Sub-Committee has observed in the case of the tanneries at Jajmau, Kanpur thus:

> In the case of Jajmau, Kanpur, the committee visited few tanneries where the effort has been made to have primary treatment of the effluent before it is discharged to the common drain/the river Ganges. There are 60 tanneries in Jajmau which will be covered under joint effluent disposal. The total production is to the tune of 12,000 hides with a total discharge of 5 million litres per day. The State Government has taken appropriate steps in preparation of the feasibility report under the guidance of the UP Pollution Control Board. This proposal was also supported by Central Pollution Control Board, Delhi by sharing the total fee of Rs.80,000 to be paid to the Public Health Engineering Consultancy, Bombay....
>
> The report suggests that each tannery should make arrangement for the primary treatment of their effluent and then it will be discharged into common treatment plant.

There is a reference to the Jajmau tanneries in An Action Plan for Prevention of Pollution of the Ganga prepared by the Department of Environment, Government of India in the year 1985 which is as under:

* * *

> 4.4.12 Effluent from industries: Under the laws of the land the responsibility for treatment of the industrial effluents is that of the industry. While the concept of 'Strict Liability' should be adhered to in some cases, circumstances may require that plans for sewerage and treatment systems should consider industrial effluents as well. Clusters of small industries located in a contiguous area near the river bank and causing direct pollution to the river *such as the tanneries in Jajmau in Kanpur* is a case in point. In some cases, waste waters from some industrial units may have already been connected to the city sewer and, therefore, merit treatment along with the sewage in the sewage treatment plant. It may also be necessary in some crowded areas to accept waste waters of industries in a city sewer to be fed to the treatment plant, provided the industrial waste is free from heavy metals, toxic chemicals and is not abnormally acidic or alkaline. In such circumstances, scheme proposals have to carefully examine the case of integrating or segregating industrial wastes for purposes of conveyance and treatment as also the possibilities for apportionment of capital and operating costs between the city authorities and the industries concerned.' (Emphasis added)

* * *

In the counter-affidavit filed on behalf of Hindustan Chambers of Commerce, of which 43 respondents are members, it is admitted that the tanneries discharge their trade effluents into the sewage nullah which leads to the municipal sewage plant before they are thrown into the river Ganga. It is not disputed by any of the respondents that the water in the river Ganga is being polluted grossly by the effluents discharged by the tanneries. We are informed that six of the tanneries have already set up the primary treatment plants for carrying out the pre-treatment of the effluent before it is discharged into the municipal sewers which ultimately leads to the river Ganga. About 14 of the tanneries are stated to be engaged in the construction of the primary treatment plants. It is pleaded on behalf of the rest of the tanneries who are the members of the Hindustan Chambers of Commerce and three other tanneries represented by [counsel] that if some time is given to them to establish the pre-treatment plants they would do so. It is, however, submitted by all of them that it would not be possible for them to have the secondary system for treating waste water as that would involve enormous expenditure, which the tanneries themselves would not be able to meet....

The financial capacity of the tanneries should be considered as irrelevant while requiring them to establish primary treatment plants. Just like an industry which cannot pay minimum wages to its workers cannot be allowed to exist, a tannery which cannot set up a primary treatment plant cannot be permitted to continue to be in existence for the adverse effect on the public at large which is likely to ensue by the discharging of the trade effluents from the tannery to the river Ganga would be immense and it will outweigh any inconvenience that may be caused to the management and the labour employed by it on account of its closure. Moreover, the tanneries involved in these cases are not taken by surprise. For several years they are being asked to take necessary steps to prevent the flow of untreated waste water from their factories into the river. Some of them have already complied with the demand. It should be remembered that the effluent discharged from a tannery is ten times as noxious when compared with the domestic sewage water which flows into the river from any urban area on its banks. We feel that the tanneries at Jajmau, Kanpur cannot be allowed to continue to carry on the industrial activity unless they take steps to establish primary treatment plants. In cases of this nature this Court may issue appropriate directions if it finds that the public nuisance or other wrongful act affecting or likely to affect the public is being committed and the statutory authorities who are charged with the duty to prevent it are not taking adequate steps to rectify the grievance.

[The court then ordered the tanneries which did not appear before the court to stop running their tanneries and releasing trade effluents into the river Ganga without subjecting the trade effluents to a pre-treatment process by setting up primary treatment plants as approved by the state board. The court made its order effective from 1 October 1987. The court also ordered that tanneries with primary treatment plants may continue production as long as the primary treatment plants are in sound working order.]

[Counsel] for the other tanneries who are members of the Hindustan Chambers of Commerce and the other tanneries who have entered appearance ... submits that they will establish primary treatment plants within six months and he further submits that in the event of their not completing the construction of the primary treatment plants as approved by the State Board (respondent 8) and bringing them into operation within the period of six months the said tanneries will stop carrying on their business. We record the statement made by the learned counsel and grant them time till 31 March 1988 to set up the primary treatment plants. If any of these tanneries does not set up a primary treatment plant within 31 March 1988 it is directed to stop its business from 1 April 1988.

We issue a direction to the Central Government, the Uttar Pradesh Board established under the provisions of the Water (Prevention and Control of Pollution) Act, 1974 and the District Magistrate, Kanpur to enforce our order faithfully. Copies of this order shall be sent to them for information....

NOTES AND QUESTIONS

1. Part III of the Constitution, which includes Article 32, contains the fundamental rights. The fundamental right to petition the Supreme Court is guaranteed in Article 32(1) which reads:

> The right to move the Supreme Court by appropriate proceedings for the enforcement of the rights conferred by this Part is guaranteed.

In *Kanpur Tanneries*, the court does not explicitly invoke a fundamental right found in Part III of the Constitution as the basis for its jurisdiction to hear the writ petition. Is concern over this issue of constitutional authority mere quibbling? Is the Supreme Court's failure to expressly invoke a fundamental right under Part III bad jurisprudence?

2. Normally, an order issued in an Article 32 petition is directed at public officials or authorities who are instrumentalities of the 'State' under Article 12. In *Kanpur Tanneries*, the court issued direct orders to private tanneries, including orders to cease operations. Are private enterprises subject to the discipline of Part III of the Constitution? Should the court have moulded the relief differently?

M C MEHTA v UNION OF INDIA (MUNICIPALITIES)

AIR 1988 SC 1115

VENKATARAMIAH, J:

* * *

Since it was found that Kanpur was one of the biggest cities on the banks of the river Ganga, we took up for consideration the case in respect of the Kanpur Nagar Mahapalika. . . .

Shri M C Mehta, the petitioner herein, drew our attention to the Progress Report of the Ganga Action Plan (July 1986–January 1987) prepared by the Industrial Toxicology Research Centre, Council of Scientific and Industrial Research. At page twenty of the said report the details of the analysis of the Ganga water samples collected during August 1986 to January 1987 from Uttar Pradesh region are furnished. That report shows that the pollution of the water in the river Ganga is of the highest degree at Kanpur. [Data from the report on biological oxygen demand, chemical oxygen demand and bacterial contamination indicate that water is not fit for drinking, bathing and fishing purpose. The report recommended that all nullahs be trapped immediately and raw water be treated conventionally at water works and disinfected with chlorination.]

In the concluding part of the said Progress Report it is stated thus:

> The Ganga is grossly polluted at Kanpur. All nullahs are discharging the polluted waste water into river Ganga. But Jajmau by-pass channel, Sismau, Muir Mill, Golf Club and Gupta Ghat nullahs are discharging huge quantities of polluted waste water. To improve the quality of the Ganga all major nullahs should be diverted and treated. Combined treatment should be provided for Jajmau tanneries. Effluent treatment plants should be installed by all polluting industries.

It is needless to say that in the tropical developing countries a large amount of misery, sickness and death due to infectious diseases arises out of water supplies.

[The court discussed common law riparian rights to unpolluted water.] The petitioner in the case before us is no doubt not a riparian owner. He is a person interested in protecting the lives of the people who make use of the water flowing in the river Ganga and his right to maintain the petition cannot be disputed. The nuisance caused by the pollution of the river Ganga is a public nuisance, which is widespread in range and indiscriminate in its effect and it would not be reasonable to expect any particular person to take proceedings to stop it as distinct from the community at large. The petition has been entertained as a Public Interest Litigation. On the facts and in the circumstances of the case we are of the view that the petitioner is entitled to move this court in order to enforce the statutory provisions which impose duties on the municipal authorities and the Board constituted under the Water Act. We have already set out the relevant provisions of the statute which imposes those duties on the authorities concerned. On account of their failure to obey the statutory duties for several years the water in the river Ganga at Kanpur has become so polluted that it can no longer be used by the people either for drinking or for bathing. The Nagar Mahapalika of Kanpur has to bear the major responsibility for the pollution of the river near Kanpur.

It is no doubt true that the construction of certain works has been undertaken under the Ganga Action Plan at Kanpur in order to improve the sewerage system and to prevent pollution of the water in the river Ganga. But as we see from the affidavit filed on behalf of the authorities concerned in this case the works are going on at a snail's pace. . . .

It is seen that there [are] a large number of dairies in Kanpur in which there are about 80,000 cattle. The Kanpur Nagar Mahapalika should take action under the provisions of the Adhiniyam or the relevant bye-laws made thereunder to prevent the pollution of water in the Ganga on account of the waste accumulated at the dairies. The Kanpur Nagar Mahapalika may either direct the dairies to be shifted to a place outside the city so that the waste accumulated does not ultimately reach the river Ganga or in the alternative it may arrange for the removal of such waste by employing motor vehicles to transport such waste from the existing dairies in which event the owners of the dairy cannot claim any compensation. The Kanpur

Nagar Mahapalika should immediately take action to prevent the collection of manure at private manure pits outside the city.

The Kanpur Nagar Mahapalika should take immediate steps to increase the size of the sewers in the labour colonies so that the sewage may be carried smoothly through the sewerage system. Whenever sewerage line is not yet constructed steps should be taken to lay it.

Immediate action should also be taken by the Kanpur Mahapalika to construct sufficient number of public latrines and urinals for the use of the poor people in order to prevent defecation by them on open land. The proposal to levy any charge for the making use of such latrines and urinals shall be dropped as that would be a reason for the poor people not using the public latrines and urinals. The cost of maintenance of cleanliness of those latrines and urinals has to be borne by the Kanpur Nagar Mahapalika.

It is submitted before us that whenever the Board constituted under the Water Act initiates any proceeding to prosecute industrialists or other persons who pollute the water in the river Ganga, the persons accused of the offences immediately institute petitions under section 482 of the Code of Criminal Procedure, 1973 in the High Court and obtain stay orders thus frustrating the attempt of the Board to enforce the provisions of the Water Act. They have not placed before us the facts of any particular case. We are, however, of the view that since the problem of the pollution of the water in the river Ganga has become very acute the High Courts should not ordinarily grant orders of stay of criminal proceedings in such cases and even if such an order of stay is made in an extraordinary case the High Courts should dispose of the case within a short period, say about two months, from the date of the institution of such orders have been issued under section 482 of the Code of Criminal Procedure, 1973 staying prosecutions under the Water Act within two months. The counsel for the Board constituted under the Water Act shall furnish a list of such cases to the Registrar of the concerned High Court for appropriate action being taken thereon. One other aspect to which our attention is drawn is the practice of throwing corpses and semi-burnt corpses into the river Ganga. This practice should be immediately brought to an end. The cooperation of the people and police should be sought in enforcing this restriction. Steps shall be taken by the Kanpur Nagar Mahapalika and the Police authorities to ensure that dead bodies are not thrown into the river Ganga.

Whenever applications for licences to establish new industries are made in future, such applications shall be refused unless adequate provision has been made for the treatment of trade effluents flowing out of the factories. Immediate action should be taken against the existing industries if they are found responsible for the pollution of water.

Having regard to the grave consequences of the pollution of water and air and the need for protecting and improving the natural environment which is considered to be one of the fundamental duties under the Constitution (vide clause (g) of Article 51-A of the Constitution) we are of the view that it is the duty of the Central Government to direct all the educational institutions throughout India to teach for one hour in a week lessons relating to the protection and improvement of the natural environment including forests, lakes, rivers and wild life in the first ten classes. The Central Government shall get text books written for the said purpose and distribute them to the educational institutions free of cost.... This should be done throughout India.

***

What we have stated above applies mutatis mutandis to all other Mahapalikas and Municipalities which have jurisdiction over the area through which the Ganga flows. Copies of this judgment shall be sent to all such Nagar Mahapalikas and Municipalities. The case against the Nagar Mahapalikas and Municipalities in the State of Uttar Pradesh shall stand adjourned by six months. Within that time all the Nagar Mahapalikas and Municipalities in the State of Uttar Pradesh through whose areas the river Ganga flows shall file affidavits in this Court explaining the various steps they have taken for the prevention of pollution of the water in the river Ganga in the light of the above judgment.

NOTES AND QUESTIONS

1. The court relied on expert evidence to show the extent and consequences of the pollution of the Ganga. The evidence in *Municipalities* included affidavits from engineers employed by the Uttar Pradesh water pollution control board and the progress reports of the Ganga Action Plan. The court also gave judicial recognition to textbooks. Compare this evidence with the requirements of the Water Act for taking and analysing samples admissible as evidence. Is it not more difficult to establish that pollutants are being released under the Water Act? Does the Water Act require that the government or citizen proceeding against a polluter show harm from the pollution?

2. Note that in this case there appears to be no dispute that the pollution of the Ganga has harmed the public health and welfare. Has the court acted in this case because of the overwhelming and admitted degradation of the Ganga? The Water Act empowers the state boards and the courts to issue orders if pollution appears likely. Can the Supreme Court, under Article 32, order measures to prevent pollution before harm has actually occurred, or is the court's power only remedial?

3. In *Municipalities*, the Supreme Court found that the nagar mahapalika of Kanpur had to bear the major responsibility for the pollution of the Ganga near Kanpur. The court ordered all municipalities and all nagar mahapalikas in Uttar Pradesh along the river to take steps to prevent the polluting of the Ganga. The court specifically addressed the problems in Kanpur by ordering the city to fulfil statutory duties including: removal of dairies, or the wastes from dairies, at the city's expense; increase of the capacity of the sewers in labour colonies; provision of public latrines and urinals at the city's expense; stricter enforcement to prevent the placing of dead bodies in the Ganga; and submission of sewer proposals to the state within six months. Why has the city failed to take these steps in the past?

4. The Supreme Court describes in great detail the laws, plans and administrative authorities at all levels of government—all directed towards restoring the water quality of the Ganga. Note, however, the court's observation that the sewers of Kanpur have not had adequate cleaning in almost 20 years. How can one explain this administrative failure to implement obvious and basic measures to prevent water pollution?

5. The Supreme Court retained jurisdiction in *Municipalities* to review the steps taken by all the mahapalikas and municipalities along the Ganga in Uttar Pradesh to control water pollution. Does the Supreme Court have the resources to undertake this review? Should the courts become involved in such massive administrative tasks?

M C MEHTA v UNION OF INDIA (CALCUTTA TANNERIES)
(1997) 2 SCC 411

Kuldip Singh, J: This petition—public interest—under Article 32 of the Constitution of India was initially directed against the tanneries located in the city of Kanpur. This Court by the order dated 22-9-1987 (*M C Mehta v Union of India* AIR 1988 SC 1037) issued various directions in relation to Kanpur tanneries. While monitoring the said directions, the scope of the petition was enlarged and the industries located in various cities on the banks of River Ganga were called upon to stop discharging untreated effluent into the river. In this judgment we are concerned with the tanneries located at Tangra, Tiljala, Topsia and Pagla Danga the four adjoining areas in the eastern fringe of the city of Calcutta (the Calcutta tanneries).

These areas accommodate about 550 tanneries. According to the examination report dated 30-9-1995 by the National Environmental Engineering Research Institute (NEERI), ninety per cent of the Calcutta tanneries use chrome-based tanning process, while the remaining utilise vegetable tanning process. The present status of the four tannery clusters in Calcutta, according to the NEERI Report, is as under:

> It was observed by the inspection team that no appropriate waste water drainage and collection systems are available in any of the tannery clusters. The untreated waste water flows through open drains causing serious environmental, health and hygiene problems. Also, no waste water treatment facilities exist in any of the four tannery clusters.

The observations by the NEERI team, regarding the Calcutta tanneries in the report are as under:

> Tannery units are located in highly congested habitations, offering little or no scope for future expansion, modernisation or installation of effluent treatment plants (ETPs). Tannery units are located in thickly populated residential areas.
>
> Surroundings of the tanneries are extremely unhygienic due to discharge of untreated effluents in open drains, stagnation of wastewater in low-lying areas around the tannery units, and accumulation of solid waste in tanneries.

It is thus obvious that the Calcutta tanneries have all along been operating in extremely unhygienic conditions and are discharging highly toxic effluents all over the areas.

This Court on the basis of the material on the record in Kanpur tanneries' order observed as under regarding the noxious nature of the tannery effluent:

> It should be remembered that the effluent discharged from a tannery is ten times more noxious when compared with the domestic sewage water which flows into the river from any urban area on its banks.

Needless to say that the State of West Bengal and the West Bengal Pollution Control Board (the Board) are wholly remiss in the performance of their statutory obligations to control pollution and stop environmental degradation.

[The judgment refers to the principal interlocutory orders passed by the court: the response of the state government and the board to various solutions mooted during the hearings; and the steps taken for relocating the tanneries to a new site.]

This Court has been monitoring this petition for a long time primarily with a view to control pollution and save the environment. In the process the Calcutta tanneries have been extended all possible help to relocate themselves to the new complex. Despite repeated reports by the Board that the Calcutta tanneries were/are discharging highly noxious effluents and are polluting the land and the river, this Court did not order the closure of the tanneries because they agreed before this Court and had given clear undertaking that they would relocate to the new complex. In spite of all the efforts made by this Court to provide every possible facility to the Calcutta tanneries to shift to the new complex they remained wholly non-cooperative....

In view of categoric findings of the NEERI and also several reports by the Board there is no possibility of setting up of common effluent treatment plants at the existing locations of the Calcutta tanneries. In the facts and circumstances discussed in this judgment, we have no hesitation in holding that the Calcutta tanneries shall have to be relocated from their present locations.

[The court considered and rejected the tanneries' contention that the designated new site would damage an ecologically fragile wetland. The court summarised the steps taken under judicial supervision to facilitate relocation; set out the provisions of the Water Act that were being breached by the tanneries and after referring to the 'precautionary principle' and 'polluter pays principle' concluded:] It is thus settled by this Court that one who pollutes the environment must pay to reverse the damage caused by his acts.

We, therefore, order and direct as under:

1. The Calcutta tanneries . . . shall relocate themselves from their present location and shift to the new leather complex set up by the West Bengal Government. The tanneries which decline to relocate shall not be permitted to function at the present sites.
2. The Calcutta tanneries shall deposit 25% of the price of the land before 28-2-1997 with the authority concerned. The subsequent installments shall be paid in accordance with the terms of the allotment letters issued by the State Government.
3. The tanneries who fail to deposit 25% of the price of the land as directed by us above shall be closed on 15-4-1997. . . .

* * *

8. The State Government shall render all assistance to the tanneries in the process of relocation. The construction of the tannery buildings, issuance of any licenses/permissions etc. shall be expedited and granted on priority basis.
9. In order to facilitate shifting of the tanneries the State Government shall set up unified single agency consisting of all the departments concerned to act as a nodal agency to sort out all the problems. The single window facility shall be set up by 31-1-1997. We make it clear that no further time shall be allowed to the State Government to set up the single window facility.
10. The use of the land which would become available on account of shifting/relocation/closure of the tanneries shall be permitted for green purposes. While framing the scheme the State Government may keep in view for its guidance the order of this Court in *M C Mehta v Union of India* (1996) 4 SCC 351, relating to the shifting of Delhi industries. The shifting tanneries on their relocation in the new leather complex shall be given incentives which are normally extended to new industries in new industrial estates.
11. The tanneries which are not closed on 15-4-1997 must relocate and shift to the new leather complex on or before 30-9-1997.
12. All the Calcutta tanneries shall stop functioning at the present sites on 30-9-1997. The closure order with effect from 30-9-1997 shall be unconditional. Even if the relocation of tanneries is not complete they shall stop functioning at the present sites with effect from 30-9-1997.
13. We direct the Deputy Commissioner/Superintendent of Police of the area concerned to close all the tanneries operating in Tangra, Tiljala, Topsia and Pagla Danga areas of the city of Calcutta by 30-9-1997.
14. The State Government shall appoint an Authority/Commissioner who with the help of Board and other expert opinion and after giving opportunity to the polluting tanneries concerned assess the loss to the ecology/environment in the affected areas.
15. The said authority shall further determine the compensation to be recovered from the polluter-tanneries as cost of reversing the damaged environment. The authority shall lay down just and fair procedure for completing the exercise.
16. The amount of compensation shall be deposited with the Collector/District Magistrate of the area concerned. In the event of non-deposit the Collector/District Magistrate shall recover the amount from the polluter-tanneries, if necessary, as arrears of land revenue. A tannery may have set up the necessary pollution control device at present, but it shall be liable to pay for the past pollution generated by the said tannery which has resulted in the environmental degradation and suffering to the residents of the area.
17. We impose pollution fine of Rs. 10,000 each on all the tanneries in the four areas of Tangra, Tiljala, Topsia and Pagla Danga. The fine shall be paid before 28-2-1997 in the office of the Collector/District Magistrate concerned.

18. We direct the Collector/District Magistrate of the area concerned to recover the fines from the tanneries.
19. The compensation amount recovered from the polluting tanneries and the amount of fine recovered from the tanneries shall be deposited under a separate head called 'Environmental Protection Fund' and shall be utilised for restoring the damaged environment and ecology. The pollution fine is also liable to be recovered as arrears of land revenue. The tanneries which failed to deposit the amount of Rs.10,000 by 15-3-1997 shall be closed forthwith and shall also be liable under the Contempt of Courts Act.
20. The State Government in consultation with the expert bodies like NEERI, Central Pollution Control Board and the Board shall frame scheme/schemes for reversing the damage caused to the ecology and environment by pollution. The scheme/schemes so framed shall be executed by the State Government. The expenditure shall be met from the 'Environment Protection Fund' and from other sources provided by the State Government.
21. The workmen employed in the Calcutta tanneries shall be entitled to the rights and benefits as indicated hereunder;
    (a) The workmen shall have continuity of employment at the new place where the tannery is shifted. The terms and conditions of their employment shall not be altered to their detriment.
    (b) The period between the closure of the tannery at the present site and its restart at the place of relocation shall be treated as active employment and the workmen shall be paid their full wages with continuity of service.
    (c) All those workmen who agree to shift with the tanneries shall be given one year's wages as 'shifting bonus' to help them settle at the new location.
    (d) The workmen employed in the tanneries which fail to relocate shall be deemed to have been retrenched with effect from 15-4-1997 and 3-9-1997 respectively keeping in view the closure dates of the respective tanneries provided they were in continuous service for a period of one year as defined in section 25-B of the Industrial Disputes Act, 1947. These workmen shall also be paid in addition six years' wages as additional compensation.
    (e) The workmen who are not willing to shift along with the relocated industries shall be deemed to have been retrenched under similar circumstances as the workmen in (d) above but they shall be paid only one year's wages as additional compensation.
    (f) The shifting bonus and the compensation payable to the workmen in terms of this judgment shall be paid by 31-5-1997 by the tanneries which close on 15-4-1997 and by 15-11-1997 by the other tanneries closing on 3-9-1997.
    (g) The gratuity amount payable to any workman shall be in addition.

We have issued comprehensive directions for achieving the end result in this case. It is not necessary for this Court to monitor these matters any further. We are of the view that the Calcutta High Court would be in a better position to monitor these matters hereinafter. The 'Green Bench' is already functioning in the Calcutta High Court. We direct the Registry of this Court to send the relevant records, orders, documents, etc., pertaining to the Calcutta tanneries to the Calcutta High Court before 1-1-1997. The High Court shall treat this matter as a petition under Article 226 of the Constitution of India and deal with it in accordance with law and also in terms of the directions issued by us. We make it clear that it will be open to the High Court to pass any appropriate order/orders keeping in view the directions issued by us. We give liberty to the parties to approach the High Court as and when necessary. The matter pertaining to Calcutta tanneries is disposed of with costs which we quantify as Rs. 25,000.

NOTES AND QUESTIONS

1. A decade after the Supreme Court's rebuke to the Kanpur tanneries, the Calcutta tanneries were discharging untreated effluents into the Ganga. What does this say about the pollution control board, the polluters, the West Bengal government, the city of Calcutta and, more generally, public interest litigation as a vehicle for environment protection?

2. In many ways the acute and complicated problems of Calcutta are typical of the milieu in other cities. Environmental pollution continues unchecked because of negligent officials, a weak city administration, the absence of budgetary support and political will at the state level and persistent refusal on the part of polluters to clean up their act. Once the problem attains huge proportions, there is no single agency capable of tackling all the aspects: land acquisition, translocation, displacement, workers' compensation and the financial outlay. Does this mean that the Supreme Court, the High Courts and the NGT must continue playing the role of a superagency to tackle urban India's environmental woes? Is there an alternative?

3. Note the shifting stand of the tanneries. Initially, they bought time through a cooperative posture. When the alternative site was identified and relocation seemed imminent, resistance set in: initially, on the ground that a CETP could be accommodated at the existing site and then an ironic plea that the new site would damage an ecologically fragile wetland.

4. The Supreme Court judgment attempts to sensitize many layers of the bureaucracy and the judiciary to the importance of environment protection. For example, apart from the officials directly involved in the case, the order casts implementation and oversight responsibilities on the Collector/District Magistrate, the Deputy Commissioner/Superintendent of Police and the 'Green bench' of the Calcutta High Court.

5. Review the directions issued by the court, especially the workers' entitlements crafted by the court. Were you a tannery operator, would you comply? Would you prefer to file for bankruptcy/dissolution? Is the fiscal burden imposed by the court disproportionately high?

6. Justice Kuldip Singh delivered the *Calcutta Tanneries* judgment on the eve of his retirement. What strategic considerations might have prompted the transfer of the case to the Calcutta High Court?

7. Is industrial relocation policy the province of the court? Should the court have shut down the violating units and issued time-bound directions to the state government to frame and implement a suitable relocation scheme? What are the pitfalls in this approach?

8. In *Vellore Citizens' Welfare Forum v Union of India*,[86] the Supreme Court issued a range of directions to bring to book the leather tanneries of Tamil Nadu.

---

[86] AIR 1996 SC 2715.

9. Where the chairman and secretary of the Uttar Pradesh PCB permitted Mohan Meakins' brewery to discharge its untreated effluent into the Gomti beyond the deadline imposed by the Supreme Court, contempt proceedings were initiated against the board officials. Finding the officials guilty of violation of the court's order, the judges administered a severe warning to both officers.[87]

10. On 24 January 2017, 32 years after M C Mehta filed his writ petition to clean the Ganga, the Supreme Court disposed of the case by transferring it to the NGT. What was achieved in three decades? For how much longer will the case linger in the NGT? Remember, the poor water quality in the Ganga has required launching of the National Mission for Clean Ganga in 2016.

11. The pace of a PIL is driven by the personality of the presiding judge. During the hiatus after Justice Kuldip Singh's retirement, Justice Malaviya of the Allahabad High Court moved matters along in the High Court. Upon Justice Malaviya's retirement, the High Court case went into hibernation.

KELLY D ALLEY; LEGAL ACTIVISM AND RIVER POLLUTION IN INDIA, 21 Georgetown International Environmental Law Review 793 (2009)

In *Rakesh Jaiswal v State of UP*, Justice Malaviya also assumed an activist and charismatic position. During hearings in the High Court of Judicature in Allahabad, the courtroom was packed with lawyers and observers. The case drew quite a bit of media attention and this may have motivated the petitioner to persevere and the justice to take a special interest in the issue so close to the end of his career. In this case, Justice Malaviya issued long and poetic orders while the other two justices on the bench yielded the limelight to him.

Rakesh Jaiswal v the State of UP was initiated by a letter written directly to Justice Malaviya, son of the freedom fighter for Indian independence, Madan Mohan Malaviya. In this letter, an environmental activist from Kanpur alleged that police officers were throwing unclaimed bodies into the river Ganga to dispose of them and pocketing the money allocated by the police department for cremation. The activist wrote:

> 'Hon'ble Sir,
>
> Almost after a fortnight since we cleaned river Ganges of Kanpur by removing 127 dead bodies (117 human and 10 animal carcasses), more than 100 dead-bodies could be counted in the same stretch of the river. Hon'ble Supreme Court had defined the duties of Kanpur Municipality in 1988. It is the duty of Kanpur Nagar Nigam to ensure that no dead-bodies are thrown into Ganga, but KNN [Kanpur Nagar Nigam] seems to be in a slumber. Our efforts have failed to awaken the government machinery, be it police department (biggest culprit), KNN or Pollution Control Boards (State and Central). Instead, a strange rivalry is going on between Eco-Friends and police department. Were removing the pollutants and police personnel are all out to thwart our efforts and other concerned departments are looking the other way.
>
> Sir, please you do something.'

Invoking the relaxed doctrine of standing and treating the letter as a writ petition submitted in the public interest, Justice Malaviya ordered that notices be issued to several respondents. In fact, the Justice broadened the reading of the letter to identify a wide range of the accused. In his memo to the court clerk, he wrote:

> 'This letter from Rakesh Jaiswal is treated as a writ petition by way of public interest litigation as it involves not only pollution of river Ganges but also of the entire

[87] *Vineet Kumar Mathur v Union of India* (1996) 1 SCC 119.

atmosphere at Kanpur. It is further obvious that this position may not only be true for Kanpur but may be equally true as regards the other places wherever there is a city falling on the banks of river Ganges. Accordingly, let the notice be issued to State of U.P., respondent no. 1, State Pollution Control Board, U.P. Lucknow as respondent no. 2, Central Pollution Control Board, Delhi as respondent no. 3 and the concerned authority of Ganga Action Plan as respondent no. 4. The notices shall also be issued to Director General of Police, U.P. Lucknow treating him to be respondent no. 5 as the letter under reference states that even when eco-friendly people or society try to clean Ganga by taking out the dead bodies and carcasses the police, instead of appreciating them, thwart their efforts. At this stage, notice is not being issued to the municipal authority as it may not be a matter concerning only one Municipal Corporation but may involve Municipal bodies throughout the state or even outside this state.'

Saldanha, a Judge in the High Court of Karnataka, has noted that a petitioner must ultimately woo a Justice's activism for any concerted public interest litigation to proceed. Justice Malaviya was aware of the precedents set in *M C Mehta v the Union of India*. By broadening the reading of the original writ, he drew in a range of groups whose special interests resided not only in Kanpur but also in other riparian cities in the river basin. Yet in the reports and orders that followed, there was very little mention made of fundamental rights. Early on, the Justice appointed a Muslim advocate of Allahabad to act as *amicus curiae* for the petitioner. This High Court advocate had no prior experience with environmental cases or with public interest litigation.

After the case opened in September 1997, the petitioner began a long period of commuting back and forth from Kanpur to Allahabad to argue the matter. Before the first hearing in the case, the petitioner met several times with his *amicus curiae* to plan the argument. However, it was immediately evident that the advocate had no real interest in the matter. In a public interest capacity, he had no chance of collecting fees from the petitioner to pay for his expenses in time and office supplies. This meant that the case took a back seat to his other work. In the first court hearing, the *amicus curiae* was responsible for presenting an outline of the problem, and he did so after much coaching from the petitioner before and during the hearing. Eventually wooed by the newsworthiness of the case, he continued over the next year in an uncommitted manner.

During the year, the petitioner became well versed in the procedures and practices of law in the High Court and took many opportunities to argue the matters himself. However, the petitioner was soon drawn into the operations of his respondents, operations that eventually co-opted his *amicus curiae*. We find that the loose working relationship evolving between the petitioner, the *amicus curiae* and the respondents came to exemplify the non-adversarial nature of public interest litigation. Additionally, the Court had to decide what outside committees could be called upon to provide scientific opinion and assist in an investigation of government offices and industrial units. The Justice organized a conference to encourage full cooperation by all departments to formulate measures to deal with this problem. This meant including in the resolution process the government agencies he was sanctioning.

In the first year, the Court closed 150 tanneries in Kanpur, 50 saree printing units in Varanasi, and 10 carpet dyeing units in Mirzapur for failing to set up primary effluent treatment plants. The Court stopped seven stone crushing units at Hardwar and ordered the constitution of a river police in twenty-two towns of the state to prevent defecation on the riverbank and ensure that corpses and pollutants are not thrown in the river. Justices ordered an uninterrupted supply of power to waste treatment plants, pumping stations, and crematoria created under the first phase of the Ganga Action Plan. They also directed officials to clean the Lower Ganga Canal, a channel that brings a raw water source to residents of Kanpur. The petitioner was also able to include a demand that the municipality remove 500 trucks of sludge laced with chrome from the industrial area and ensure safe disposal. However, while sounding ambitious and interventionist on paper, these orders were not completely implemented or were implemented in a way unintended by the petitioner and the Justices.

The Allahabad High Court also nominated a team of senior retired officers of the Indian Audit and Accounts Services to investigate how money under Ganga Action Plan Phase-I had been spent. The audit team submitted a report to the court indicating many improprieties in spending and many inefficiencies in service activities executed by all agencies involved with Ganga Action Plan projects.

Many observers have pointed out that court orders may become boons for government agencies. For instance, the *Jal Nigam* (the state water and engineering board) benefitted from an order the High Court Justice passed in this case. The court set up a monitoring committee to check the work of government agencies under GAP. The committee submitted a recommendation that work be done to halt discharge of wastewater from a particular drain feeding the river Ganga. This drain had been running wastewater from the city of Banaras into the river for years. The Justice issued an order that money be cleared by the city administrator of Banaras to fix the problem. But all players knew that without an overhaul of the entire sewer system, the problem could not be fixed with a one-time allocation. The *Jal Nigam* profited from the order because money was dispersed to solve the problem, but the drain was not, in actuality, 'tapped' or diverted. Critics have also alleged that orders requiring Pollution Control Board officials to permit and monitor industrial effluent plants also generate a good deal of monetary exchange.

While M C Mehta's *Ganga Pollution* case lay dormant before the Supreme Court, beginning in 2013 several applications were moved before the NGT seeking remedial directions against Ganga polluters (including the Kanpur tanneries). Since the NGT was hearing these applications on a daily basis, on 24 January 2017, the Supreme Court transferred the *M C Mehta* case to the Tribunal.

On 13 July 2017, a six-member bench of the Tribunal comprising three judicial and three expert members rendered a 543-page judgment. Authored by the chairperson, Justice Swatanter Kumar, the judgment acknowledges the failure of past efforts to reduce the pollution. Despite Supreme Court directions and two phases of the Ganga Action Plan, the river remained one of the most polluted in the country. According to the Tribunal, the past failures were in large part due to delays in implementing projects and the partial coverage for collection, transport and treatment of sewage from across cities. Moreover, even where treatment plans were established, there was inadequate maintenance and the financial models were unviable. The judgment traces the efforts made by the Tribunal to build a consensus on the way forward, including securing recommendations from a consortium of eminent professors from seven Indian Institutes of Technology. Eventually, the Tribunal issued general as well as specific directions designed to trap major drains and treat the waste-water from these drains before discharge into the river. The Tribunal also prohibited the disposal of municipal solid waste, electronic waste and bio-medical waste on the flood plain; prevented landfill sites along the river and required the tanneries as well as other industries to comply with pollution standards. Pending further studies, the Tribunal ordered 20% of the average monthly lean season flow at Haridwar (before the river waters are diverted) as the minimum environment flow in the main stem of the river.

Will the NGT succeed in reducing the pollution where the Supreme Court failed? What factors might contribute to its success?

I. RIVER POLLUTION

I. THE NOYYAL

The Noyyal River rises in the Vellingiri Hills in the Westerns Ghats and flows over 160 kms before joining the Cauvery. On the banks of the river is Tirupur, a major industrial hub with a flourishing textile industry. The bleaching and dyeing units of Tirupur discharge untreated effluent into the river, turning the water toxic and unsuitable for irrigation or any other use. In some stretches the river runs red. Downstream, the river waters flow into Orathapalayam Dam, built in 1992 for irrigation. Within a few years of its construction, the dam became a storage tank of effluent and its sullied waters could not be used for irrigation.

In 1996, the first attempt to curtail the pollution was made when the Karur Taluk Noyyal Canal Agriculturists Association filed a petition before the Madras High Court seeking directions against the state PCB to act against the dyeing and bleaching units. This writ petition was disposed of by a joint memo of understanding in 1998 which envisaged implementation of pollution control measures and the payment of amounts by the polluters to clean up Orathapalayam Dam. Despite this order, a study carried out by the state government revealed that there was no improvement in the quality of water. This compelled the Noyyal River Ayucutdars Protection Association (NRAPA) to file a second public interest litigation in the High Court seeking suitable directions to preserve the river. The High Court issued detailed directions in its interim judgment dated 22 December, 2006, a part of which is quoted below:

(a) The [Common Effluent Treatment Plants] (CETPs) are given time up to 31-7-2007 to achieve the zero liquid discharge (ZLD) of trade effluents subject to the following conditions:

(i) The CETPs concerned are directed to pay a fine on pro rata basis at the rate of six paise per litre from 1-1-2007 to 31-3-2007; at the rate of eight paise per litre from 1-4-2007 to 31-5-2007; and at the rate of ten paise per litre from 1-6-2007 to 31-7-2007. The fine amount payable by the respective CETPs shall be arrived at by multiplying the fine amount i.e. six, eight or ten paise, as the case may be, by the total quantity of discharge of each member unit of CETP as per the consent certificate or as the quantity found in the application for consent and also by the total number of working days in a month. The fine amount thus calculated shall be paid by the respective CETPs on the last date of every month. In case the CETPs or any of them commit any default in payment of fine, the Pollution Control Board shall direct closure of such defaulting CETP and the member units and also disconnect the power supply to such defaulting CETP and the member units.

(ii) The CETPs or any of them on achieving zero liquid discharge shall satisfy the Pollution Control Board about their ZLD status and the Pollution Control Board upon verification shall issue appropriate certificate from which date, such CETP shall not be liable to pay the fine. In any event, if the CETPs or any of them fail to achieve the ZLD on or before 31-7-2007 the Pollution Control Board shall forthwith direct closure of such CETPs and the member units and also disconnect the power supply to such defaulting CETP and the member units.

(b) Respondents 4 to 7 [representative associations of owners of the factories] herein are directed to deposit the balance sum of Rs 8.50 crores out of Rs 12.50 crores estimated by PWD towards the cleaning and desilting operations of the Orathapalayam Dam to be carried out by the Public Works Department in two equal instalments, the first of such instalments being payable on or before 28-2-2007 and the second instalment to be paid on or before 30-4-2007.

(c) Respondents 4 to 7 are directed to deposit a sum of Rs 22,99,98,548 being the remaining of the total compensation of Rs 24,79,98,548 awarded by the Loss of Ecology Authority in its award dated 17-12-2004. This amount shall also be payable in two equal instalments, the first of such instalments being payable on or before 28-2-2007 and the second instalment to be paid on or before 30-4-2007.

(d) Respondents 4 to 7 are further directed to deposit a sum of Rs 12 crores as an *ad hoc* compensation towards the estimated loss for the years 2005, 2006 and 2007. This amount shall be payable in two equal instalments, the first of such instalments being payable on or before 15-6-2007, and the second instalment to be paid on or before 31-7-2007....

(q) The Public Works Department is directed to continue with the cleaning and desilting operations of Orathapalayam Dam and the cleaning of Noyyal River shall be carried out through the petitioner Association as per the orders of this Court. The District Collector, Coimbatore is directed to release a sum of Rs 25 lakhs directly to the petitioner Agriculturists Association towards the charges for cleaning of Noyyal River and the works to be carried out up to the confluence point of the river with River Cauvery.

(r) Respondents 1 to 3 are directed to finalise the site for dumping the solid waste from the Orathapalayam Dam as well as from Noyyal River which has been kept in bags and in open spaces. The Pollution Control Board is directed to provide the infrastructure and technical expertise for removal of the solid waste from the units as well as the dam to the notified site. The above exercise shall be done within a period of three months.

(s) Both the Expert Committee as well as the Monitoring Committee shall submit periodical reports before this Court every two months.

(t) The Monitoring Committee shall be paid a sum of Rs 15,000 per day/per visit as charges.

After a review application in the High Court failed, the factory owners moved the Supreme Court where they primarily contended that the very heavy fine imposed for water discharge from each unit was wrong. According to the factory owners, there was no justification for the fine since 17 CETPs had been established at a very large investment of around Rs. 700 crores and that the fine would cripple operations and impact more than 40,000 families who earned their livelihood from the dyeing and bleaching industry, quite apart from several lakh persons employed in ancillary industries. This is how the Supreme Court responded.

TIRUPUR DYEING FACTORY OWNERS ASSOCIATION v NOYYAL RIVER AYUCUTDARS PROTECTION ASSN

(2009) 9 SCC 737

DR B S CHAUHAN, J:

* * *

So far as imposition of fine @ 6 paise per litre and then enhancing to 8 paise and subsequently to 10 paise per litre periodically is concerned, the High Court imposed it on the basis of award/report dated 17-12-2004 by the Expert Committee under the heading 'Loss of Ecology (Prevention and Payments of Compensation) by the Authority'. The Expert Committee consisted of Hon'ble Mr Justice P Bhaskaran, a retired Judge of the Madras High Court, the Secretary of the Department of Environment, Government of Tamil Nadu and Member-Secretary, Central Pollution Control Board, New Delhi as its Member and Dr K R Ranganathan, former Member-Secretary of the Central Pollution Control Board. The Committee had taken note of all the previous developments and assessed the loss to ecology and environment in the affected area. It also identified the individuals and families who suffered because of pollution and further determined the amount of compensation to be paid to each affected individual or family. It also fixed the liability for making the payment of compensation.

The award mainly provided as under:

(a) The Authority assessed loss to the ecology and environment in terms of use value of the groundwater resources polluted with excessive total dissolved solids (inorganic) utilised for irrigation as a result of the pollutional impact of effluents discharged by textile industries located in and around Tirupur and its vicinity falling in Noyyal River basin. Extent of the so irrigated land is arrived at 28,449.816 hectares in 68 villages comprised in seven taluks or Coimbatore, Erode and Karur Districts.

(b) The Authority identifies 28,596 individuals, affected because of the pollution as eligible for compensation.

(c) The Authority assesses the compensation to be paid to the aforesaid individuals as in (*b*) supra, at a total sum of Rs 24,79,98,548 for the period from 28-8-1996 to 31-12-2004.

* * *

It is pertinent to point out that thrust of the work for reversal is preventing further pollution of the groundwater which requires a number of cleaning technology and treatment measures to be undertaken by the industries with their own funds.

[The High Court constituted a Monitoring Committee.]

It was, in fact, the Monitoring Committee in its memo dated 12-7-2005 which made various suggestions before the High Court regarding establishment of CETPs and gave costs for various operations and one of the recommendations read as under:

> 'Apart from the earlier recommendation of the Committee that no CETP which had not achieved financial closure and deposited monies should be permitted to reopen till financial closure is achieved and monies deposited, the Committee further recommends that all CETPs deposit the entire project cost within a period of 2 weeks (after adjusting the money spent by them towards the works in progress). If the units do not so deposit, the Committee recommends that they be shut down. The Committee reiterates the fact that all CETPs ought to have commissioned their RO system by today, if not much earlier, if their earlier undertakings were taken into account.
>
> Apart from the condition on deposit of the entire project cost (minus the monies actually spent), the member units of all CETPs should be subject to a fine of at least 10 paise per litre of effluent generated (subjected to a minimum of Rs 10,000 per lakh litres of effluent as *reflected in the consent*) at least from 1-8-2006.' (emphasis added)

[The court referred to various decisions establishing the precautionary principle, polluter pays principle and the notions of the intergenerational equity and sustainable development.]

In case in spite of stringent conditions, degradation of environment continues and reaches a stage of no return, the court may consider the closure of industrial activities in areas where there is such a risk. The authorities also have to take into consideration the macro effect of wide-scale land and environmental degradation caused by absence of remedial measures. The right to information and community participation for protection of environment and human health is also a right which flows from Article 21....

The correctness of the impugned order is to be tested on the basis of the aforesaid settled legal propositions. This court vide order dated 18-5-2007 stayed the impugned order of the High Court only to the extent that the directions to close down the industries would not be given effect to from 31-7-2007. This order has been extended from time to time. On 10-8-2007 this court directed the members of the petitioners' Association to deposit a sum of Rs 25 crores within a period of six weeks before the High Court and further to file an affidavit as to what progress has been made in respect of the CETPs and treatment plants. This court vide order dated 12-5-2009 directed the Board to inspect Noyyal River and find out whether any pollution is caused by the factories owned by the members of the appellant Association and file a report on or before 27-7-2009.

The Inspection Committee constituted by the Board made the following observations during inspections on 8-7-2009 and 9-7-2009: ...

(C) Along with the primary treated effluent from existing bleaching and dyeing units, domestic effluent from Tirupur Corporation (formerly Tirupur Municipality), Nallur Municipality and other villages located along the banks of Noyyal River is discharged into Noyyal River, which also contributes to the flow in the river and organic pollution load.

(D) In the entire stretch of Noyyal River falling in the jurisdiction of Tirupur Corporation and Nallur Municipality, municipal solid wastes are being dumped along the river itself, which also contributes to the pollution load in Noyyal.

The impact of industrial pollution on the river is revealed by the presence of high pH (alkalinity), very high total dissolved solids (TDS), excess chloride (C1) and per cent sodium (%Na). Also biochemical oxygen demand (BOD) and chemical oxygen demand (COD) are not at an acceptable level. Moreover, the dark red colour of the water in River Noyyal was seen during inspection.

In pursuance of the order of this Court dated 27-7-2009 the said Inspection Committee again inspected the 17 CETPs in Tirupur during 3-8-2009 and 4-8-2009 and submitted the report. The 17 CETPs had paid only Rs 17,22,46,031 as against Rs 55,60,96,848. This total sum has been arrived at on the basis of number of working days multiplied by the daily consented quantity/applied quantity of effluent of member units, leaving a balance to be remitted as Rs 38,38,50,817. The appellant has deposited a sum of Rs 25 crores in the High Court of Madras as per the direction of this Court dated 10-8-2007.

* * *

A large number of farmers have suffered because of the pollution caused by [the factories]. They could not cultivate any crop in the said land. The Committee had made a complete survey and assessed the loss and identified the families which are entitled to compensation. This Court only stayed the operation of the direction of the High Court to the extent that the units of the members of the appellant Association would be closed on 31-7-2007. The said interim order has been extended from time to time. None of the other directions have been interfered with. A period of more than two-and-a-half years has ... passed.

Many steps have been taken but the Association has to ensure the compliance with the orders passed by the High Court fully and in order to do so, it is desirable that the Association be given three months' time to ensure compliance with the directions to make the CETPs functional and pay the balance amount for cleaning the dam and river and meet the compensation to the adversely affected persons within a period of three months from today. The Pollution Control Board is directed to ensure that no pollution is caused, giving strict adherence to the statutory provisions.

NOTES AND QUESTIONS

1. The Supreme Court exercised commendable restraint, upholding the High Court's directions and limiting its appellate oversight to extending the period granted to the units for compliance. Given the massive problem posed by the Tirupur factories and their persistent refusal to meet environmental standards, the Supreme Court was correct in allowing the High Court to deal with the aggravated situation in the state.

The strategy employed by the High Court was to increase non-compliance costs for the defaulting units to a level where the financial disincentive was so great that the factories collectively abated the pollution. This was the job of the Tamil Nadu PCB (TNPCB), which the board failed to perform despite prodding in *Vellore*. Should the TNPCB be disbanded for its masterly inactivity and collusion? Who takes its place?

2. Should a High Court impose a 'fine', absent statutory sanction? Is the recommendation for a fine made by the court-appointed Monitoring Committee sufficient legal justification? Or was the 'fine' really a compensatory charge imposed on non-compliant units that wished to operate during the grace period granted by the High Court?

3. Since the units failed to comply within the period extended by the Supreme Court, NRAPA moved contempt petitions before the High Court. A division bench of the High Court in a detailed judgment rendered on 28 January 2011[88] found that the units continued to pollute the Noyyal River. The court ordered the CETPs and the bleaching and dyeing units in Tirupur to immediately close down and directed the PCB to ensure disconnection of power supply. This order hit the industry hard. The units eventually reopened under temporary authorizations granted by the PCB for the purpose of trial runs meant for testing the efficiency of the pollution control equipment.

4. On 1 November 2012, a division bench of the Madras High Court[89] held that the compensation amounts collected were intended for all 28,596 farmers recognized in the earlier judgments and not just the 360 members of the NRAPA. Consequently, the High Court set aside government orders that sanctioned the distribution of Rs.75 crores to NRAPA members alone and directed each of them to repay the amounts received.

5. The Loss of Ecology (Prevention and Payment of Compensation) Authority was constituted under section 3(3) of the Environment (Protection) Act, 1986 pursuant to the directions of the Supreme Court in the *Vellore* case.[90] The Authority did commendable work for nearly two decades, processing claims from affected farmers in the Vellore region as well as those impacted by the Tirupur pollution. After the establishment of the NGT, the Central Government declined to extend the term of the Authority, since the NGT was competent to handle the claims. On 7 April 2016, a division bench of the Madras High Court accepted the contention of the Central Government and transferred claims that were pending investigation before the Authority to the NGT. Having regard to the increased case load, the High Court directed the Central Government to constitute at least one additional bench for the NGT, Chennai.[91]

Until the Authority was disbanded, Tamil Nadu had a special regime where mass tort compensation claims arising from pollution could be filed before the Authority.

6. The Supreme Court judgment recognizes that the Tirupur textile exporters were earning several thousand crores in foreign exchange and were in stiff competition with Bangladesh and China. What is more important—exports or environmental compliance? Will the added costs consequent upon judicial intervention render Tirupur uncompetitive in the global market?

II. THE KHARI

In early 1995, under the stewardship of Chief Justice B N Kirpal the Gujarat High Court embarked on a campaign against industrial pollution. The court learnt that Gujarat's large chemical and textile industries had thrived at the cost of the environment. Untreated effluent had blighted agricultural fields around Ahmedabad city. Describing the pollution as a 'Chemical War' launched by some industries, the court issued extensive directions in a public interest litigation filed by two farmers. The petitioners complained that industrial units were

88 *M Y Eqbal v S Ramasundaram* MANU/TN/0156/2011.
89 *M Ramasamy v The Chief Secretary, Government of Tamil Nadu* (2012) 8 MAD L J 628.
90 *Vellore Citizens' Welfare Forum v Union of India* (1996) 5 SCC 647.
91 *Vellore Citizens' Welfare Forum v Union of India* (2016) 4 MAD L J 25.

discharging untreated effluents into Kharicut canal which joined the Khari River. Eleven villages in Kheda district which depended on the Khari found the water unsuitable for agriculture. Apart from lands losing their fertility, groundwater up to a depth of 300 ft was reddish in colour and was affecting the livestock.

The main judgment of the Gujarat High Court[92] recognized the economic impact of shutting down several hundred units that employed around 25,000 workers. Nevertheless, absent primary and secondary effluent treatment and the prolonged failure on the part of the Gujarat Pollution Control Board (GPCB) to enforce the Water Act and EPA, the court issued these directions:

> We accordingly:
>
> A.I. Issue a writ of mandamus to the state of Gujarat to direct the closure forthwith of the manufacturing operations of [highly polluting units enumerated in the order].
>
> II. In order to ensure that production is suspended by those units, to whom the directions have been issued, the state will issue, where necessary, directions for the stoppage of supply of electricity and/or water in order to ensure compliance. These units, however, will be given the connection, if they require, for the purposes of satisfying the GPCB that the units are in a position to meet the GPCB norms. Electricity and water are required for sufficiently long time to enable the checking of the claim but till No Objection Certificate/Consent is obtained, no permission should be given for commercial production.
>
> III. Furthermore, the units ordered to suspend or close their operations, as aforesaid, may start them only after obtaining the consent letter of the GPCB....
>
> B.(II)The state of Gujarat, [Gujarat Industrial Development Corporation (GIDC) and Ahmedabad Municipal Corporation] are directed to lay separate/necessary pipes and/or drains to carry the treated industrial effluent to Pirana for mixing the same with the treated sewage before discharge into the river. The expense for this shall be borne entirely by the polluting units, who shall contribute pro-rata as and when demanded by the Government. The work on this should start immediately and be completed by 31st December, 1995, or within such extended time as the Court may allow on the proper application being made....
>
> C. (XII) Since for the last number of years pollution has adversely affected the 11 Kalambandi villages of Kheda, as also villages of Lali, Navagam, Bidaj, Sarsa, Aslali, Jetalpur, Bareja, Vinzol and Vatva comprised in Dascroi and Mahemedabad Talukas, a lump sum payment should be made by the 756 industrial units, calculated at the rate of 1% of their one year's gross turnover for the year 1993–94 or 1995–96, whichever is more and that amount should be kept apart by the Ministry of Environment and should be utilised for the works of socio-economic uplift of the aforesaid villages and for the betterment of educational, medical and veterinary facilities and the betterment of the agriculture and livestock in the said villages. Payment should be quantified by the GIDC within three months and the collections made within two months thereafter.

NOTES AND QUESTIONS

1. In a further order in *Pravinbhai Patel's* case passed on 10 May 1996 the High Court extended by six months the compliance deadline of 31 December 1995. While doing so, the court required units availing the extension to abide by stringent compliance conditions. In view of the authorities' inability to maintain round-the-clock vigil, the court introduced a self-regulatory mechanism by which industry associations were directed to monitor the

[92] *Pravinbhai J Patel v State of Gujarat* 1995 (36) GUJ L R 1210.

discharges by member units. Further, the May 1996 order established a coordinating committee under the chairmanship of M D Pandya, an advocate, to monitor compliance, coordinate action between industry and the authorities, and assist the court in matters relating to the implementation and enforcement of its orders.

2. What is the nature of the 1% levy? Is it a fee, a tax, a fine, a penalty, a charge or compensation by way of damages? What is the legal significance of the character of the levy?

3. The 1% levy was imposed on all 756 polluting units, irrespective of the facts in each case. Some of the units were wilful defaulters, others deviated from the norms very slightly. Had the executive or legislature imposed such a levy without regard to the extent of compliance by individual units or the extent of pollution caused, what might have been the judicial response? Would an across the board levy on all polluting units be termed discriminatory, arbitrary or violative of the equal protection guarantee under Article 14? On the other hand, is such a levy akin to a case of 'mass-copying' or a mass tort where even some honest students suffer because of the misconduct of their peers?

4. The Gujarat High Court supplied a rationale for the 1% payment in *Deepak Nitrite Limited v Ajit B Padiwal*.[93] While considering a PIL alleging large-scale industrial pollution at an industrial estate at Nandesari, Baroda, the High Court impleaded 252 units and appointed an Expert Committee. A common effluent treatment plant (CETP), funded by industry, failed to achieve the prescribed parameters necessitating an upgrade. Guided by its previous decision in *Pravinbhai Patel* the High Court directed all the industries to pay 1% of the maximum annual turnover of any of the preceding three years towards compensation and betterment of the environment. The High Court held:

> Looking to the large number of industries in large industrial estates and also at other places where industries are established, the affected people and those concerned for the environment would find it difficult, if not impossible, to point out the exact nature of damage being caused by an individual unit. Once an industrial unit is found to be violating the GPCB norms, it would follow that damage has been caused to the environment. Now, if an individual inquiry were to be made in respect of each industrial unit as to which particular area of soil was damaged or which particular sub-stratum of underground water level was affected on account of the discharge of untreated or improperly treated industrial effluent not meeting with the GPCB norms, either on account of percolation or on account of such effluent going on to the agricultural fields or into the water sources of the community, such inquiry would not lend itself to easy quantification in a civil suit for damages which would take years, if not decades, for final decision. On the other hand, in last two years, this Court has in a number of decisions applied the aforesaid formula of 1% of the turnover as compensation for the betterment of the environment and allied purposes in various industrial areas of Ahmedabad, Nandesari (where the present unit is situated), Vapi and Ankleshwar and 1% of the highest turnover has been found to be the lowest common denominator as the figure for compensation. If such inquiry is held, we are sure that the extent of damage would be more than 1% as assessed. At this stage, we would also like to place on record that after the decision of this Court in the case of *Pravinbhai* covering industrial units of Ahmedabad, the formula of quantifying 1% of the highest turnover as compensation for damage caused to the environment on account of violation of pollution control laws during the period prior to judicial cognizance has come to be widely accepted even by the industries in Baroda, Bharuch, Surat and other districts of Gujarat.

[93] 1997 (1) GUJ L HER 1062.

Do you agree with the justification? Is not establishing liability *after* applying rules of evidence and procedure the quintessential judicial function? Would every deviation from a pollution norm necessarily imply 'damage to the environment', as the court suggests?

5. In 2004 the Supreme Court considered a set of appeals arising from orders passed by the Gujarat High Court in *Deepak Nitrite* in 1997. The Supreme Court held:

> The fact that the industrial units in question have not conformed with the standards prescribed by GPCB, cannot be seriously disputed in these cases. But the question is whether that circumstance by itself can lead to the conclusion that such lapse has caused damage to environment. No finding is given on that aspect which is necessary to be ascertained because compensation to be awarded must have some broad correlation not only with the magnitude and capacity of the enterprise but also with the harm caused by it. Maybe, in a given case the percentage of the turnover itself may be a proper measure because the method to be adopted in awarding damages on the basis of 'polluter-to-pay' principle has got to be practical, simple and easy in application. The appellants also do not contest the legal position that if there is a finding that there has been degradation of environment or any damage caused to any of the victims by the activities of the industrial units certainly damages have to be paid. However, to say that mere violation of the law in not observing the norms would result in degradation of environment would not be correct.
>
> Therefore, we direct the High Court to further investigate in each of these cases and find out broadly whether there has been any damage caused by any of the industrial units by their activities in not observing the norms prescribed by GPCB as reported by the Modi Committee appointed by the High Court or by an expert body like NEERI and that exercise need not be undertaken by the High Court as if the present proceeding is an action in tort but an action in public law. A broad conclusion in this regard by the High Court would be sufficient. We, therefore, direct the High Court to re-examine this aspect of the matter as to whether there is degradation of environment and as a result thereof any damage is caused to any victim, and what norms should be adopted in the matter of awarding compensation in that regard. In this process it is open to the High Court to consider whether 1% of the turnover itself would be an appropriate formula or not as applicable to the present cases.[94]

6. On 30 December 2008 a division bench of the Gujarat High Court finally disposed of the public interest litigation initiated by Ajit Padiwal. Based on the remand order by the Supreme Court, the High Court constituted a three-members committee to ascertain the degradation and damage caused by individual industrial units. Although this committee recommended maintaining the levy based on the turnover of the polluter, the High Court found this methodology inadequate:

> But it is not discernible from the Report as to the extent of damage caused by the units to the environment. It has been specifically stated in … the judgment of the Supreme Court that the compensation must have broad correlation not only with the magnitude and capacity of the enterprises but also with the harm caused by it. What is the extent of harm caused by each industrial unit is not clearly discernible from the Report.
>
> Under such circumstances, one of the options available is to give direction to undertake a fresh exercise for ascertainment of degradation of environment but, due to long lapse of time, it may not be possible to assess the damage caused by these units in the year 1994 onwards.[95]

The court secured the consent of the parties and arrived at a workable solution to put an end to the litigation: '[I]t is agreed on either side that an amount of Rs.10 lacs be paid

94 *Deepak Nitrite Ltd. v State of Gujarat* (2004) 6 SCC 402, 407.
95 *Ajit D Padiwal v State of Gujarat*, Spl Civ Application No. 2922 of 1995, order dated 30 December 2008.

as compensation for the damage caused to the environment which may be utilized by the Department of Forests and Environment, State of Gujarat for preventing further degradation of the environment and also for the work of socio economic upliftment of various villages in which the units are situated and also for related activities.'[96]

III. THE YAMUNA

Rising from the slopes of the Bandarpunch massif of the Garhwal Himalayas, the Yamuna flows over 1,300 kms before merging into the River Ganga at Allahabad. Along this journey, it passes several large cities including Delhi, Mathura and Agra. Untreated sewage and industrial effluents combine to render the Yamuna amongst the most polluted rivers in India. Despite her religious significance in Hinduism, which regards Yamuna as a sacred river, administrative and judicial efforts have failed to clean her waters.

There are several cases before the NGT that deal with aspects of Yamuna pollution.[97] We carry a short excerpt from an order in the leading case that reviews two decades of futile efforts to make a dent in this stubborn problem.

National Green Tribunal

MANOJ MISHRA v UNION OF INDIA

11 September 2019

ORDER: The matter has been taken up to review the progress in execution of directions in the judgment of this Tribunal dated 13.01.2015. In the said judgment, the Tribunal dealt with the issue of control of pollution and rejuvenation of River Yamuna in Delhi. The matter of enforcement of the said directions has been taken up from time to time in the last four years but the progress has been found to be far from satisfactory. Even today the situation is same.

It is necessary to give a brief background of the case before issuing further directions. The issue of control of pollution and rejuvenation of river Yamuna was taken up by way of Writ Petition No. 725/1994 by the Hon'ble Supreme Court based on a news item published in Hindustan Times titled 'And Quiet Flows the *Maily* Yamuna'. Grim situation of pollution and failure of authorities to take appropriate action was noted by Hon'ble Supreme Court in various orders.[98] Vide order dated 10.12.2012, the Hon'ble Supreme Court noted 'despite heavy expenditure, in thousands of crores, having been incurred by the Central Government, Government of the States of Haryana and Uttar Pradesh and the local authorities in the National Capital Territory of Delhi, the pollution of river Yamuna has increased by the day'. It was further observed that the water quality of river Yamuna at the Nizammudin Bridge as shown from the analysis of the samples by the Central Pollution Control Board (CPCB) to be: BOD 37 mg/l (against permissible limit of 3 mg/l), faecal coliform 17,00,00,00,000 (against permissible limit of 500 MPN/100 ml). The situation was found to be similar at Kalindi Kunj, Okhla and even Palwal. The Hon'ble Supreme Court directed preparation of action plans and after continuing to monitor it for 23 years, on 24.04.2017, the proceedings were transferred to this Tribunal. In the meanwhile, O.A. No. 6/2012 was filed before this Tribunal on which response was sought from Govt. of NCT of Delhi, DJB, DDA, DPCC and the States of Haryana and Uttar Pradesh. In the light of material furnished, vide order

---

96 *Id.*

97 See *Tapesh Bharadwaj v UP State Pollution Board* OA 596/2016 decided on 13 April 2017 MANU/GT/0034/2017; *Akash Vashishtha v Union of India* OA 594/2016 decided on 31 January 2018 (2018) SCC Online NGT 591; *News Item Published in 'The Hindu' Authored by Shri Jacob Koshy Titled 'More River Stretches are now Critically Polluted'*, OA 673/2018; *Madhumangal Shukla v Nagar Palika Parishad, Vrindavan* OA 136/2015.

98 (1999) 1 SCC 161; (2000) 10 SCC 587; (2000) 9 SCC 440; (2004) 8 SCC 638; (2009) 17 SCC 708, 716, 718; (2012) 13 SCC 736, 786.

dated 13.01.2015, this Tribunal issued directions to take remedial steps to control the pollution and to rejuvenate the river Yamuna. Further directions were also issued in the light of order of the Hon'ble Supreme Court dated 24.04.2017. The said orders required time bound actions. Orders dated 13.01.2015 and 08.05.2015 divided the project of cleaning and rejuvenation into 2 phases. First Phase related to Nazafgarh, Delhi and supplementary drains. Second phase related to all other drains. Order dated 08.05.2015, accepted 'Maily Se Nirmal Yamuna' Revitalization Plan, 2017 in principle subject to specific directions. It was further directed that environmental compensation will be recovered from every household generating sewage on polluter pays principle irrespective whether the household was sewered or not.

Finally, on 25.07.2018, after noticing the earlier proceedings, it was again noted that there was no meaningful progress in the last three years. The work for 14 STPs had not even begun for which no justification was furnished. The Tribunal directed that the said work must commence positively by 01.12.2018. Coronation Pillar was to be completed by 11.04.2019. Work of Najafgarh drain was to be completed by 31.12.2018. 11 drains were said to have been trapped and work for trapping of 5 drains was to be awarded and completed by December 2020, except the one for which the work was to be completed by 2018. The State of Haryana was directed to file an affidavit showing the steps taken to ensure that no untreated pollutants are discharged into Najafgarh drain and no untreated sewage flows from DD2 drain at Panipat.

In continuation of the said order, on 26.07.2018, a status report on sewage management was noted and it was found that at most of the places, BOD/SS levels were not meeting the required parameters. The Tribunal constituted a two Member Committee for time bound action plan and framework for implementation. The Committee was to draw up comprehensive, integrated and inclusive strategy with clear measurable indicators of progress and success. The action plans were also to include creation of biodiversity parks. The DDA was required to make the entire flood plains available to the Forest Department after demarcation. The Monitoring Committee was also required to lay down a plan for collection of funds on the 'Polluter Pays' principle and to deal with the problems of idol immersion in the river Yamuna. The States of Uttar Pradesh and Haryana were directed to constitute their own Monitoring Committees. The existing Committees were to function in tandem with the Committees so constituted. The Committee was to give interim report by 31.12.2018.

***

Having noticed the status of compliance of directions of this Tribunal in NCT Delhi, State of Haryana and Uttar Pradesh, we may now consider further directions to be issued in respect of each of the identified action points. As already noted in the order dated 23.08.2019, in view of repeated failure of the timelines earlier, fresh timelines have to be laid down with accountability for failure in the interest of protection of environment and public health and for rejuvenation of the river Yamuna, which is a major tributary of river Ganga and has its unique significance. This is also necessary to comply with the mandate of directions of the Hon'ble Supreme Court referred to earlier. It may be noted that there are 351 polluted river stretches in the country identified as such by CPCB which include all major rivers and their tributaries. This Tribunal is also dealing with the pollution of River Ganga and several directions have been issued including that no untreated sewage or effluents are discharged in the river and floodplains are protected. Yamuna flows through the National Capital and its rejuvenation can be a model to be followed for all other polluted river stretches. Restoration of the river is a matter of grave environmental urgency that also concerns the prestige of the country.

One of the major concerns of this Tribunal is that repeated directions remain un-complied and in spite of large scale failures, no accountability is fixed. There is huge loss to public exchequer for which no action is taken. Timelines are conveniently and unilaterally changed. Officers indulge in blame game in shifting responsibility from one to another. There is failure at higher levels in monitoring and taking actions. If this continues, it is difficult to expect any positive change for long. This requires paradigm shift in approach adopted so far. The approach to be adopted is to have clear time-bound plan with flexibility and due to accountability for failure by way of departmental action and monetary compensation. The rescheduled timelines have to be compressed so as to complete every action by December, 2020 except where shorter timelines are specified in this order or are otherwise possible. If any contract permits longer timeline, it is clearly in violation of binding orders of the Tribunal which has attained finality. Violation thereof is per se criminal offence. Such longer timeline has to be consistent with orders of the Tribunal and compressed within 31.12. 2020. Failing to do so may invite criminal prosecution. NMCG may also monitor the compliance. The Chief Secretaries of Delhi, Haryana and U.P. have to personally see the compliance and have to set up Monitoring Cell directly under them. Vice Chairman, DDA can also monitor and coordinate with Chief Secretary, Delhi. All other departments can monitor subject to overall directions of the Chief Secretaries. This can avoid shifting of responsibilities once ownership is with highest authorities in the State. Monthly review reports may be shared with the Monitoring Committee and also placed on websites of concerned States. Failure and successes of the individual involved may be specifically recorded and reflected in service record of the concerned officer. Stock taking may be done by the Chief Secretaries of the failure and successes so far and appropriate actions be initiated against those who have been responsible for the failure. Nodal Officers may be identified in respect of different projects clearly defining the responsibilities. Wherever there is misappropriation of funds, criminal case has to be registered. Posting of Officers entrusted with the responsibility may be reviewed from time to time depending on their responsibility. Procedure for giving of contracts may be shortened and standardized at State level and if possible at National level by NMCG and CPCB. Giving of contracts should be based on successful credentials instead of mere lowest rates. Pollution load at entry and exit point of each concerned State may or at entry points of each drains need to be recorded periodically. The Chief Secretaries of Delhi, Haryana and U.P. may furnish action taken reports in this regard at the time of their personal appearance before this Tribunal in O.A. 606/2018.

Priorities need to be planned. The first step is to ensure that no pollutant is discharged into the river or drains connected thereto. Projects of setting up and upgradation of STPs including setting up of interceptors, laying of sewerage line network etc. have to be completed within strict timelines. Pending such action, immediate bioremediation and/or phytoremediation or any other alternative remediation measure may be undertaken as an interim measure. Pollution of river or water bodies is a criminal offence which needs to be checked by setting up ETPs/CETPs/STPs. The Hon'ble Supreme Court has directed[99] that establishment and proper functioning of ETPs/CETPs/STPs in the country be ensured. This is to enforce the right of access to water. It has been noted by the Hon'ble Supreme Court that water pollution is the cause of various diseases and also affects food safety apart from affecting the environment as such. Following the said judgment, this Tribunal has directed[100] that 'All the local bodies have to ensure 100% treatment of the generated sewage and in default to pay compensation which is to be recovered by the States/UTs, with effect from 01.04.2020. In default of such collection, the States/UTs are liable to pay such compensation. The CPCB is to collect the same and utilize for restoration of the environment.' While dealing with the pollution of river Ganga, this Tribunal directed:

> 'Bioremediation and/or phytoremediation or any other remediation measures may start as an interim measure positively from 01.11.2019, failing which the State may be liable to pay compensation of Rs. 5 Lakhs per month per drain to be deposited with the CPCB. This however, is not to be taken as an excuse to delay the installation of STPs. For delay of the work, the Chief Secretary must identify the officers responsible and assign specific responsibilities. Wherever there are violations, adverse entries in the ACRs must be made in respect of such identified officers. For delay in setting up of STPs and

---

[99] (2017) 5 SCC 326.

[100] Order dated 28 August 2019 in *Paryavaran Suraksha Samiti v Union of India* OA 593/2017, (2019) SCC Online NGT 2834.

sewerage network beyond prescribed timelines, State may be liable to pay Rs. 10 Lakhs per month per STP and its network. It will be open to the State to recover the said amount from the erring officers/contractors.

With regard to works under construction, after 01.07.2020, direction for payment of environmental compensation of Rs. 10 lakhs per month to CPCB for discharging untreated sewage in any drain connected to river Ganga or its tributaries and Rs. 10 lakhs per month to CPCB per incomplete STP and its sewerage network will apply. Further with regard to the sectors where STP and sewerage network works have not yet started, the State has to pay an Environmental Compensation of Rs. 10 lakhs per month after 31.12.2020. The NMCG will also be equally liable for its failure to the extent of 50% of the amount to be paid. Till such compliance, bioremediation or any other appropriate interim measure may start from 01.11.2019.' . . .

NOTES AND QUESTIONS

1. The Supreme Court tried and failed. Thousands of crores of rupees spent on the Yamuna action plan were wasted with no improvement in the river water. Should we give up? Is there any reason why the NGT may succeed where others failed?

2. As the excerpt shows, the NGT periodically extended the timelines fixed for completing projects. Will the new deadlines be met? Is the strategy of fixing responsibility on the chief secretaries likely to improve compliance? What is the guarantee that the water quality will improve even where the works are executed?

3. Is extending judicial timelines a sign of strength or weakness? Do such extensions weaken respect for court orders?

4. The Tribunal was acting as a coordinating agency, goading various authorities after securing expert inputs. Was this the purpose of establishing the NGT? There is nothing in the NGT's orders which elevates environmental jurisprudence or indeed our understanding of the environmental challenges that confront the clean-up exercise. The case remained before the Supreme Court for 18 years. Was it wise to transfer the case to an inferior forum? What (apart from time) does the NGT offer that the Supreme Court could not?

5. On 13 January 2021, when hearing a petition by the Delhi Jal Board complaining about increased ammonia levels in the Yamuna due to pollutants, the Supreme Court registered a *suo moto* petition titled '*Remediation of polluted rivers*'. Observing '[o]ne of the major causes of water pollution is discharge of non-treated/partially treated municipal waste including sewage effluent of cities into rivers', the court decided to examine the nationwide problem, initially focusing on municipalities along the River Yamuna.[101]

J. LAKES

Many of India's freshwater lakes are imperilled by civic and development pressures. In this section we track judicial interventions over two decades. In an early case, the Supreme Court attempts to stem the rot by framing *ad hoc* regulations to preserve two lakes in Haryana. Is

[101] *Delhi Jal Board v State of Haryana* MANU/SCOR/01884/2021.

this a worthy regulatory model? Do we need national freshwater regulations (similar to the coastal regulations) to preserve our water bodies? Or is this field best left to local planning authorities?

M C MEHTA v UNION OF INDIA (BADKHAL & SURAJKUND LAKES) (1997) 3 SCC 715

Order: This Court by the order dated 10-5-1996 dealt with the question whether—to preserve environment and control pollution—mining operations should be stopped within the radius of 5 kms from the tourist resorts of Badkhal Lake and Surajkund in the State of Haryana. The Court gave five directions in the said order. Direction 4 is in the following terms:

> We further direct that no construction of any type shall be permitted now onwards within 5 km radius of the Badkhal Lake and Surajkund. All open areas shall be converted into green belts.

* * *

The Municipal Corporation, Faridabad, Haryana Urban Development Authority and builders having interest in the area have approached this Court for modification/clarification of the above-quoted direction. It is contended by learned counsel appearing for the parties that in the said area of 5 kms buildings are under construction, plots have been allotted/sold under various development schemes and the plot-holders have even started construction. According to the learned counsel vested rights of several persons are likely to be adversely affected causing huge financial loss to them. [The court observed that the direction was not intended to apply to plots under construction. It also took on record two plans showing the proposed green belts around Badkhal lake (Ex. 'A') and Surajkund (Ex. 'B').]

This court by the order dated 13-9-1996 in IA No. 18 [WP (C) No. 4677 of 1985] has directed the Central Government to constitute an authority (the Authority) under Section 3(3) of the Environment (Protection) Act, 1986. The said Authority shall have the jurisdiction over the National Capital Region as defined under the National Capital Region Planning Act, 1955. It is . . . obvious that the area of Badkhal and Surajkund, with which we are concerned, comes within the jurisdiction of the said authority.

[Counsel] appearing for some of the builders had vehemently contended that banning construction within one km radius from Badkhal and Surajkund is arbitrary. According to him it is not based on technical reasons. He has referred to the directions issued by the Government of India under the Environment (Protection) Act, 1986 and has contended that the construction can at the most be banned within 200 to 500 metres as was done by the Government of India in the coastal areas. He has also contended that restriction on construction only in the areas surrounding Surajkund and Badhkal lakes is hit by Article 14 of the Constitution of India as it is not being extended to other lakes in the country. We do not agree with [Counsel]. The functioning of ecosystems and the status of environment cannot be the same in the country. Preventive measures have to be taken keeping in view the carrying capacity of the ecosystems operating in the environmental surrounding under consideration. Badkhal and Surajkund lakes are popular tourist resorts almost next door to the capital city of Delhi. We have on record the inspection Report in respect of these lakes by the National Environmental Engineering Research Institute (Neeri) dated 20-4-1996 indicating the surroundings, geological features, land use and soil types and archaeological significance of the areas surrounding the lakes. According to the report Surajkund Lake impounds water from rain and natural springs. Badhkal Lake is an impoundment formed due to the construction of an earthen dam. The catchment areas of these lakes are shown in a figure attached with the report. The land use and soil types as explained in the report show that the Badhkal Lake and Surajkund are monsoon-fed water bodies. The natural drainage pattern of the surrounding hill areas feed these water bodies during rainy season. Large-scale construction in the vicinity of these tourist resorts may disturb the rain water drains which in turn may badly affect the water level as well as the aquifers which are the source of ground water. It may also cause disturbance to the aquifers which are the source of ground water. The hydrology of the area may also be disturbed.

The two expert opinions on the record—by the Central Pollution Control Board and by the NEERI—leave no doubt on our mind that the large-scale construction activity in the close vicinity of the two lakes is bound to cause adverse impact on the local ecology. NEERI has recommended green belt at one km radius all around the two lakes. Annexures A and B, however, show that the area within the green belt is much lesser than one km radius as suggested by the NEERI.

[The court refers to the 'precautionary principle' and concludes: 'We have no hesitation in holding that in order to protect the two lakes from environmental degradation it is necessary to limit the construction activity in the close vicinity of the lakes.' The court limited the no-development zone to a distance of 1 km. from the lakes and excluded plots that were sold from the embargo.]

NOTES AND QUESTIONS

1. Most lakes in the sub-continent are fed by monsoon streams, springs and aquifers and extensive construction in the catchments could disturb the water systems. Should the precautionary principle be applied across the board to all riparian developments and lake-front properties or only to those like Badhkal and Surajkund which are tourist spots?

2. The judgment is significant because it recognizes a key environmental concept, namely, the 'carrying capacity' of an eco-system. This notion is central to the sustainable use of resources as well as the proper management of wildlife. Loading a river with excessive pollutants beyond its regenerative or carrying capacity may cause long-term damage. To prevent such harm, source-specific effluent and emission norms are supplemented by general ambient water and air quality standards. The carrying capacity of a forest determines the size of its animal population. Reducing the size of a national park or permitting logging operations in a forest may reduce the carrying capacity of the eco-system.

3. The builders' argument under Article 14 of the Constitution: 'Why pick on us – look at all the others'—is a refrain heard in many environmental cases. The court had little trouble rejecting the contention, holding that each eco-system is unique and every case must be dealt with having regard to the specific facts and circumstances.

4. The Madras High Court, in *Palani Hills Conservation Council v Union of India*,[102] considered a challenge to a holiday resort which threatened Kodaikanal lake and its environs. The court directed the state government to constitute an Expert Committee. Recognizing the lake as a priceless and unique feature of the hill station, the committee recommended several measures specific to the hotelier, Sterling Resorts, and more general steps including setting up a common sewage treatment plant. The court directed the state government to take appropriate measures on the lines recommended by the committee.[103]

102 Writ Petition No. 4257 of 1988, Madras High Court, 20 December 1991, MANU/TN/0795/1991.

103 The same citizens' group thwarted another hotelier in Kodaikanal in *Pleasant Stay Hotel v Palani Hills Conservation Council* (1995) 6 SCC 127.

5. Troubled by 'Nainital, a beautiful butterfly ... turning into an ugly caterpillar',[104] the Supreme Court stepped in to save the hill station's lake from degradation. Responding to a public interest litigation filed by a member of the Nainital Bachao Samiti, the court appointed a commissioner to inspect the town and report on the grievances. The September 1994 report supported the petitioner's case:

> A perusal of that report shows that on local inspection it was found that the lake has turned dark green with an oily surface and is now full of dirt, human faeces, horse dung, paper-polythene bags and all sorts of other waste. Most of the sewer lines which leak, open into it. The Commissioner also found that wherever the drains open at the shores of the lake, big heaps of rubble used in construction of the buildings are collected and these materials ultimately settle down on the shores of the lake thereby reducing the length, depth and width of the lake, besides polluting the water to a great extent. It has been mentioned in the report that ecologists feel that if nothing was done to prevent this siltation then the lake will dry up.[105]

Accepting the recommendations made by the commissioner, the court urged the authorities to constitute a monitoring committee to implement remedial measures such as preventing sewage from entering the lake, maintaining the drains and restricting lakeshore construction.

Mansagar Lake is a manmade lake on the northern fringe of Jaipur. Within the lake is a pleasure pavilion, Jal Mahal, constructed by the former rulers of Jaipur in the eighteenth century. Around 1962, two main sewerage drains of the city were diverted into the lake, sullying the water. The monument too was neglected and became a dilapidated ruin. In 1999, the state government prepared a Detailed Feasibility Report ('DFR') which covered conservation measures to restore the monument, revive the lake and encourage integrated tourism development and recreational facilities. In November 2000, the Jaipur Municipal Corporation approved the DFR. Thereafter, the MoEF approved a Detailed Project Report (DPR) under the National Lake Conservation Programme (NLCP). Pursuant to a global tender to restore the lake and its environs through a public–private partnership, the state awarded the work to Jal Mahal Resorts Pvt Ltd (JMRPL) and entered into a 99-year lease for a project area of around 100 acres.

Jal Mahal Resorts secured various approvals and thereafter, in the first phase of the project, restored the Jal Mahal monument under the supervision of conservation architects. A public promenade was constructed around the lake along with jetties enabling public access to the restored monument and its gardens. Simultaneously, under expert supervision, the Central Government and state governments as well as JMRPL expended substantial funds to restore the water quality in the lake by realigning the drains and taking measures to prevent sedimentation.

In 2010–11, several years into the project, a set of public interest petitions were filed before the Rajasthan High Court. The petitions assailed the project on environmental and other grounds. On 17 May 2012, a division bench of the Rajasthan High Court allowed the petitions. The High Court cancelled the lease, set aside various statutory approvals and even directed dismantling and removal of all works including the diversion of the two drains that were polluting the water body.

---

[104] *Ajay Singh Rawat v Union of India* (1995) 3 SCC 266, 267.
[105] *Id.* at 268.

Jal Mahal Resorts as well as the state of Rajasthan assailed the judgment and the Attorney General pressed the case on behalf of the state. Curiously, a change in the state administration pursuant to an election during the hearing of the appeal, prompted the state government to reverse course. Not only did the new counsel withdraw the state's special leave petitions but he also sought to argue contrary to the submissions made by the Attorney General before the Supreme Court and the stand of the state before the High Court.[106] The Supreme Court partly allowed the appeal filed by JMRPL, but, as you will see, that was not the end. We carry a short excerpt from the judgment:

JAL MAHAL RESORTS P LTD v K P SHARMA
(2014) 8 SCC 804

GYAN SUDHA MISRA, J: Leave granted. These appeals by way of special leave have been preferred against the common judgment and final order dated 17-5-2012 passed by the High Court of Judicature of Rajasthan at Jaipur Bench, Jaipur in three public interest litigation petitions filed by the petitioners, K.P. Sharma, Dharohar Bachao Samiti, Rajasthan and Heritage Preservation Society, respectively against the State of Rajasthan and the beneficiary of the project who was Respondent 7 in the High Court and is now the appellant-petitioner in the civil appeal. The three petitions were DB Civil Writ (PIL) Petition No. 6039 of 2011, DB Civil Writ (PIL) Petition No. 5039 of 2010 and DB Civil Writ (PIL) Petition No. 4860 of 2010 whereby the division bench of the High Court was pleased to cancel an Environment and Monument Improvement/Preservation and Tourism Development Project at Jaipur by declaring it as illegal which was awarded to the appellant-petitioner, Jal Mahal Resorts (P) Ltd. via global tender floated in 2003 and finally granted in 2005 after all requisite approvals as per the appellant-petitioner under the environmental law including environment impact assessment under the Environment Protection Act and the notifications issued thereunder of the Rajasthan Pollution Control Board. However, in view of the cancellation of the Project, the High Court has directed immediate dismantling and removal of the entire project and diversion of the two drains which was done to purify waters of a manmade artificial water body and detritus....

As a consequence of the same, the appellant Jal Mahal Resorts (P) Ltd. has been directed to bear costs to be incurred in restoration of the original position of 100 ac of land in removing the soil filled in by it and to restore back the possession of land to Rajasthan Tourism Development Corporation ('RTDC', for short) which in turn will hand over the land to Jaipur Development Authority ('JDA', for short), Jaipur Municipal Corporation ('JMC', for short) and the State of Rajasthan. The appellant has further been directed to immediately remove all sedimentation and settling tanks from Mansagar Lake Basin and to realise costs from M/s Jal Mahal Resorts (P) Ltd. and to examine restoring position of Nagtalai and Brahampuri Nallah (drains) to their original position as redesigned ... under Mansagar Lake Restoration Plan in consultation with the Ministry of Environment and Forests ('MoEF', for short) of the Central Government.

The respondent authorities of the State of Rajasthan have been further directed to monitor, maintain and refix boundaries of Mansagar Lake in its full original length, breadth and depth in consultation with MoEF of the Central Government and not to reduce normal water level. All encroachments made in the ... area of Mansagar Lake have been ordered to be removed immediately and the control erected by appellant M/s Jal Mahal Resorts (P) Ltd. into the Lake is ordered to be dismantled and costs have been ordered to be realised from the appellant M/s Jal Mahal Resorts (P) Ltd. All the three writ petitions were thus disposed of by the High Court....

It is no doubt urged on behalf of the respondent-PIL petitioner and taken note of by the High Court that the National Lake Conservation Plan did not contemplate any commercial

[106] *Jal Mahal Resorts Pvt Ltd v K P Sharma* (2014) 8 SCC 866.

venture upon the Lake to be restored under the plan. But it cannot be overlooked that the State Government had full authority to carve out a plan for development of the Lake and the Lake area considering the fact that way back in 1962 the Lake's glory as a pristine water body lasted only until the former rulers had their control over the city and unpleasant history of the Lake began when the new administration of Jaipur diverted walled city sewage in 1962 through two main waste water drains, namely, Brahmapuri and Nagtalai. It is borne out from the factual history of the Lake that most notorious aquatic weed water hyacinth entered into the Lake in 1975 and the waterfowl population started affecting the resident and migratory species. It is in this background that the Government of Rajasthan submitted project for restoration of Mansagar Lake to the Central Government.

* * *

On perusal of the background and other materials on record, it could be noticed that the genesis of restoration and conservation of Mansagar Lake goes back to 1984 whereby the efforts of the State from 1984 onwards have been directed towards restoring and developing the largest water body in Jaipur (that was lying disused with sewage, filth, stench and effluent) into an attractive public interest destination with a pleasing environmental ambience for attracting tourists from all over the world.

The figures and conclusions in the impugned order itself indicate the enormous difficulty and repetitive failures of the State Government to either implement the restoration itself or to get any private entity to do so over a period of approximately 20 years from 1984 to year 2003. Indeed, the attempts immediately preceding the present tender from year 2000 to 2002 have also admittedly failed. Had the figures found in the impugned order or the conclusion of the impugned order that the project proposal constituted a squandering of State largesse had been correct, the applicants would have been falling over themselves to bid for the project not only in the present tender but also in the preceding unsuccessful attempts. Even in the present case, despite the attendance of as many as 20 major participants (including corporate names like Oberoi, Taj, Ansal, Neemrana to mention a few) who admittedly attended the pre-bid meeting, no one except the SLP appellant-petitioner and three others ultimately came forward. Obviously, the proposal was *ex facie* not an attractive one for potential investors, and the inescapable conclusion is that all attempts to restore the Lake and develop the area as a tourism hub had failed when the SLP appellant-petitioner was nowhere in the picture.

We have further taken note of the reasons for the clear reluctance of potential investors which have been stated as follows:

> The pre-existing state of the entire area of approximately 310 ac of Lake and more than 100 ac of land seemed physically irreparable which has been demonstrated by the photographs submitted. There was no water body; the so-called Lake consisted of an empty large hollow filled with sewerage stench, filth and huge sedimentation; two major nallahs of the city were emptying all their sewerage and effluents into the Lake; the monument was completely dilapidated, there was overgrowth of shrubbery, and was not visited by anyone for decades; the nearby land was barren, filled with mud and dirt and therefore not in use.

The impugned order further appears to have ignored that the whole structure of the tender was conceptually different and had been thus in all previous attempts failed as:

(i) It sought huge investment by the successful bidder to restore the entire area which, at conservative estimates, would cost approximately Rs 100 crores (in the year 2003), and now with the gross delay occasioned by the PIL petitioner, involves an investment of (approximately) Rs 500 crores.

(ii) No commercial exploitation either of the monument or of the Lake was involved and indeed was not permitted.

(iii) Approximately 10.5 ac out of 14 ac would be utilised for a walk-way around the Lake involving no commercial return.

(iv) The successful bidder would pay the State Government/RTDC Rs 2.52 crores per year which would be escalated by 10% every 3 years, which, if calculated in the 99th year of the lease would amount to Rs 27 crores approximately, and if calculated in the 50th year of the lease would amount to Rs 12 crores approximately.

(v) The accommodation/resort could only be constructed within an FAR of 0.1362. Relevantly, the normal FAR permitted is 2 while the FAR permitted for the SLP petitioner's project is only 0.1362.

(vi) No structure in the entire project could exceed the height of 9 m and also could not exceed more than a total of two floors viz. ground and first.

(vii) Almost 12 ac of land would be devoted to a handicrafts village showcasing the cultural heritage of Rajasthan where the commercial return to the bidder would be only in the form of lease rent, and the sales occurring due to footfalls would accrue to the sub-lessee who sells the craft and not to the SLP petitioner.

(viii) The project has a long gestation period not only in terms of restoration and development costs but also construction of infrastructure, and the footfalls would increase only over time after the project has fully established its credentials.

(ix) In a nutshell, therefore, huge investments, sure, certain and unavoidable, were front ended; possible returns, unsure and uncertain, were back ended.

(x) All the foregoing admitted points have been completely ignored in the impugned order, or not noticed or cursorily mentioned and not decided, and in any event not given adequate probative weight.

(xi) Equally ignored has been the very raison d'être of the project actuated by the fundamental object by the State Government to restore heritage site and to create a sustainable and pleasing environmental ambience. The lease rent model, increasing as time goes on had always been the consistent approach of the State since 1999 when restoration was first envisaged. It is inconceivable that this model could be created to assist or benefit the bidder like the SLP petitioner who came into the picture for the first time only in year 2003.

[The court held that since so many expert bodies had examined the project, the High Court ought to have exercised restraint and deference:

> 'In our considered view unless the detailed project report, Master Plan of Jaipur, revenue record indicating the nature of land that the Project was fraught with risk of environmental degradation which could establish with facts and figures that the decision is not in public interest, interference by the Court adopting an overall view smelling foul play at every level of administration is bound to make the governance an impossibility.'

The court found that having regard to the transparent process employed by the State involving high government officials and experts, the genuine purpose behind the project could not be doubted. The Supreme Court however pared the term of the lease to 30 years, consistent with extant rules and also reduced the leased area. An area of 8.65 acres claimed as part of the lake bed was ordered to be handed back to the state and excluded from the leased area. Around 14.15 acres were directed to remain a construction-free zone for the exclusive use by the public as a promenade.]

NOTES AND QUESTIONS

1. In its final judgment dated 25 April 2014, the Supreme Court issued the following directions, expecting rapid completion of the stalled project:

   (a) 'We are informed that the first phase of the Project has been completed since February 2011. It is, therefore, directed that the completion certificate and the lease agreement for the first phase be issued expeditiously but not later than a period of 30 days from the date of receipt of this order. Accordingly, the State Government shall issue the restoration completion certificate for Phase I to enable the Project along with the Jal Mahal monument as per the lease deed, to open for entry and visit of the members of the public. Upon issuance of the Phase I certificate, the project developer/lessee/

appellant shall be allowed to undertake the construction as per the approved plan in terms of the lease deed.'

(b) 'It is further clear by now that the project comprising the leasehold land is not in conflict with the development of Lake area or Jal Mahal monument so as to raise issues or concern regarding the Lake area or environment degradation as restoration and maintenance of Jal Mahal cannot possibly disturb the monument or lead to environmental degradation. In any view, the dispute being confined to the leasehold area for development of the project which we have now resolved, we direct that the appellant lessee shall be entitled to restart the project forthwith subject to what we have recorded hereinbefore.'

The State refused to issue a Phase I completion certificate, stalling public entry. It also refused to allow construction of the resort. Instead, it filed applications for review which were dismissed by the Supreme Court and also applications for modification/clarification that too were unsuccessful. Despite these setbacks, officials of the RTDC resisted issuing a restoration completion certificate for Phase I, compelling JMRPL to initiate contempt of court proceedings in November 2014. On 22 January 2015, the Supreme Court issued notice to the officers in the contempt petition.

2. On 25 January 2015, three days after the contempt notice, Rajasthan promulgated an Ordinance which was eventually replaced by the Rajasthan Lakes (Protection and Development) Authority Act of 2015.

On 1 July 2015, the State notified Mansagar Lake under the Act and declared an area of 97.21 acres (including the land leased to JMRPL) as a 'protected' zone. Separately, the State prohibited construction within the protected area, in effect rendering JMRPL's tourist resort a non-starter. This compelled JMRPL to challenge the 2015 Act before the Supreme Court under Article 32.[107]

3. What might have prompted the state government to reverse its position after having stoutly defended the project before the High Court (unsuccessfully) and the Supreme Court? Is the state of Rajasthan simply a sore loser or are there other factors that might have induced the state to resort to administrative and legislative manoeuvres to undermine Supreme Court directions?

4. This case shows how environmental factors may be used by the government of the day to stall a partially implemented project. Before the High Court the pleadings and reports relied by the state strongly endorsed the project and underscored how it will improve Mansagar Lake. After the change of government in Rajasthan in December 2013, the state applied to the Supreme Court to alter its stand by seeking to identify the leased area as a protected wetland under the Central Wetlands Rules of 2010. This ploy failed when the Supreme Court rejected the state's application to change its stand.

This case also illustrates the enormous difficulties entrepreneurs face in India. Here, the High Court quashed the project in a grossly delayed set of public interest petitions even though the project had secured permissions from the authorities including environmental clearance. The absence of any finality and consequential investment risk due to environmental considerations is evident from the refusal of the state to accept the Supreme Court judgment. The lesson appears to be that unless the project proponent is continuously aligned to decision-makers, even a partially implemented project that envisages a restored monument, a revived lake and the creation of a lake-front public promenade can be indefinitely thwarted. The case

[107] At the time of writing the contempt petition and the Article 32 petition were pending.

is indicative of a weak Rule of Law regime in India where success of an enterprise is often dependent on patronage.

The Rajasthan High Court has made significant contributions to restore the state's water bodies, critical for every arid region. The Supreme Court judgment in *NIMS v State of Rajasthan* is in two parts: the first part (which we excerpt) summarizes the efforts made by the Rajasthan High Court in its public interest jurisdiction. The second part deals with the construction put up by the university.

NATIONAL INSTITUTE OF MEDICAL SCIENCES UNIVERSITY v STATE OF RAJASTHAN

(2018) 13 SCC 390

Madan B Lokur, J: These petitions are illustrative of how some interests can frustrate the rule of law and get away with it. What the petitioners are responsible for, apparently along with several others, is creating a water shortage in Jaipur City and also ensuring that Ramgarh Lake which was made famous in the Asian Games held in 1982 is now completely dry and the catchment areas of Ramgarh Dam are rendered completely useless. This is a tragedy of enormous proportions and rather unfortunately neither the State of Rajasthan nor the Jaipur Development Authority has thought it fit to take stern remedial action. They are thereby compounding the woes of the residents of the city of Jaipur. It is often said that power comes with responsibility—and so should it be with the State and the authorities and the petitioner, particularly when it concerns the interests of the people.

The origin of these petitions can be traced back to the decision of the Rajasthan High Court in *Abdul Rahman v. State of Rajasthan* (2004) SCC Online Raj 676. In this decision, the High Court attempted, through a series of directions, to ensure free flow of water in the catchment areas of Ramgarh Dam (near Jaipur) and through Tala River and Banganga River. The directions were the conclusion of a public interest litigation in which a public-spirited person approached the Rajasthan High Court and highlighted the necessity of protecting tanks and ponds in Rajasthan for a proper and healthy environment to enable the people to enjoy quality life, the essence of the right of a citizen guaranteed by Article 21 of the Constitution.

What is the significance of Ramgarh Dam? The dam was constructed in 1903 having a catchment area of about 769.20 sq km spread over four tehsils, namely, Jamvaramgarh, Amer, Shahpura and Viratnagar. The water harnessed by the dam was, till 1978, a source of irrigation. Thereafter, it became a source of drinking water for Jaipur City. During the Asian Games held in India in 1982, Ramgarh Lake was one of the highlights of the Games and events relating to water sports were held in the lake. Unfortunately, today the lake is dry and apparently heavily encroached upon due to the omissions and commissions of various departments of the Government of Rajasthan. What is worse is that with the lake drying up and the catchment areas without any water, Jaipur city is faced with a scarcity of water.

With these ground realities in mind and while entertaining the public interest litigation (PIL) initiated by Abdul Rahman, the High Court passed an order on 18-7-2003 requiring the State Government to undertake a general survey to identify the catchment areas of Ramgarh Dam that were misused for construction and mining purposes. This was in the context of what appeared to the High Court as indiscriminate misutilization of the catchment areas for construction and mining purposes which prevented lakes, reservoirs, rivers, ponds, etc., from receiving water even during the monsoon season. The survey was also intended to study the effect of utilization of the catchment areas for construction, mining and other purposes. The State Government was also required to suggest measures for restoring the catchment areas to their original shape and use.

Pursuant to the directions given by the High Court on 18-7-2003, the State Government constituted an Expert Committee which gave a report that makes for some very sad reading.

However, the Expert Committee also gave as many as 15 valuable suggestions for restoring the catchment areas to their original shape and use. These suggestions were accepted by the High Court and directions issued to the State Government to consider the recommendations of the Expert Committee and chalk out a plan to take effective steps to restore the catchment areas. Three months' time was granted to the State Government to give concrete and positive shape to the suggestions.

Not surprisingly, no seriousness was attached to the decision and directions of the High Court in *Abdul Rahman* and matters were allowed to drift.

Under these circumstances, due to the lack of any positive and visible action by the State Government in preserving and protecting the catchment areas of Ramgarh Dam, a learned Single Judge of the Rajasthan High Court was persuaded to initiate suo motu proceedings titled as *State of Rajasthan, In re* (2012) SCC Online RAJ 1732.

On 23-8-2011, the learned Single Judge noted that the catchment areas of Ramgarh Dam were not being given the deserved importance due to a lack of coordination between various departments of the Government of Rajasthan. The learned Judge also noted that no effective steps had been taken for implementing the directions issued in *Abdul Rahman*, particularly with reference to Ramgarh Dam and that there was a lack of willingness on the part of the State Government to take required measures. Accordingly, the learned Judge felt that some monitoring action was necessary for saving the water resources in Rajasthan and initially with reference to Ramgarh Dam. In view of this, the learned Judge appointed a two-member Monitoring Committee for implementing the directions relating to Ramgarh Dam in terms of the judgment in *Abdul Rahman*. The learned Single Judge also gave certain directions on 23-8-2011 some of which included the following:

> '(*i*) All the Departments involved in the present matter like revenue, forest, irrigation, PHED, environment, mining, Panchayati raj are directed to cooperate with each other to stop encroachment and illegal construction in the drainages, channels, nalas, river, etc. in the four tehsils named above.
>
> (*ii*) The State Government will ensure stoppage of encroachment and construction in the catchment area of Ramgarh Dam....
>
> (*iv*) The State Government will come out with the plan for removal of encroachments so as to restore the position as was existing on 15-8-1947.'

A perusal of the proceedings in the suo motu petition indicates that the Monitoring Committee put in considerable efforts and gave valuable inputs through its reports. In its written submissions, filed before the learned Single Judge, it was noted that there is a problem of scarcity of water and even Ramgarh Dam, which was considered the only reservoir of water supply to Jaipur City had become dry due to encroachments and obstructions. The dam was unable to get water due to land grabbers, property dealers, constructions and farmhouses, club houses, resorts, etc.

In its written submissions, the Monitoring Committee noted that the petitioners before us had made massive encroachments in the catchment areas of Ramgarh Dam. The learned Single Judge took note of the reports and submissions of the Monitoring Committee and passed a final order on 29-5-2012 [*State of Rajasthan, In re* (2012) SCC Online RAJ 1732] giving a series of directions with the expectation and hope that the directions would not remain only on paper but would be implemented in reality.

The sequence of events over the last 15 years indicates that the effort made by the division bench of the High Court in *Abdul Rahman* as well as the effort made by the learned Single Judge in the suo motu proceedings hardly yielded any positive results at least insofar as they relate to the petitioner the National Institute of Medical Sciences University or NIMS.

However, before detailing the steps concerning NIMS, it must be stated that the Government of Rajasthan prepared an initial action plan in July 2012 followed by a report prepared by a

Technical Committee on 9-1-2013 on less/no inflow in Ramgarh Dam (District Jaipur) despite average and above average rainfall and remedial measures to restore inflow.

During the hearing of these petitions, we had enquired from the learned counsel whether there is any water in Ramgarh Lake but were told that it is still bone dry. It appears to us, therefore, that the initial action plan and the report of the Technical Committee as well as expectations and hope of the learned Single Judge that the directions, plans of action and remedial measures would not remain only on paper but would be implemented in reality have been completely belied. This is a pity....

NOTES AND QUESTIONS

1. Notice how ineffective the executive is in reining in rampant unauthorized construction in the catchment areas of lakes. This is despite judicial oversight by the Rajasthan High Court. What is the solution for protecting our lakes and water bodies? Considering the failure of local planning statutes in regulating development, is the answer a central regulation similar to the CRZ notification? But will new laws help when the enforcement machinery is so slack?

2. NIMS University put up massive constructions on plot No. 526 in village Jugalpur, district Jaipur. The buildings were erected on land owned by the Jaipur Development Authority (JDA). NIMS requested the authorities to allot the plot, now that it had buildings on JDA land. The Supreme Court upheld the decisions of the single judge as well as the division bench of the Rajasthan High Court rejecting the university's plea for allotment and regularisation. Recognizing that NIMS was a powerful and influential entity, the court directed immediate demolition and eviction from the encroached plot: '[W]e are of the opinion that the possibility of water being now made available to Jaipur City in due course of time takes far greater precedence over the interests of NIMS and those associated with it.'

Two lakes, Himayat Sagar and Osmam Sagar, supply drinking water to the twin cities of Hyderabad and Secunderabad. To protect water quality in these reservoirs in March 1994, the state government prohibited various types of development activity within a radius of 10 kms of the lakes. Surana Oils purchased 12 acres of land on 26 September 1995 and applied for consent to establish its factory to manufacture BSS castor oil and byproducts like glycerine. The problem with the site was that it fell within the prohibited zone around Himayat Sagar. The Supreme Court considered this case twice: first, the court called for the expert opinion of the National Environment Appellate Authority (NEAA)[108] regarding the risks posed by Surana Oils;[109] and upon receiving expert evidence adjudicated on the merits of the appeal.[110]

Earlier, the Andhra Pradesh PCB dug its heels in and rejected Surana Oil's application to establish an industry under section 25 of the Water Act. However, armed with a government order that exempted its factory from the 10 kms prohibitory zone, Surana Oil appealed to the appellate authority constituted under section 28 of the Water Act. Before the appellate authority, the company relied on expert evidence to show that the latest eco-friendly technology was used with all safeguards against pollution. Based on this material, the appellate

---

[108] The National Environment Appellate Authority was established under National Environment Appellate Authority Act of 1997 and was the predecessor to the National Green Tribunal.

[109] *A P Pollution Control Board v Prof M V Nayudu* (1999) 2 SCC 718.

[110] *A P Pollution Control Board-II v Prof M V Nayudu* (2001) 2 SCC 62.

authority allowed the appeal and directed the board to give consent in terms of the exemption granted by the state.

The stage shifted to the Andhra Pradesh High Court where the appellate authority decision was challenged in public interest writ petitions. Surana Oil also petitioned the High Court seeking a direction against the board to give its consent. The High Court found the matter highly technical and deferred to the expertise of the appellate authority. It directed the board to grant consent on such terms as the board considered appropriate.

The board petitioned the Supreme Court for special leave to appeal. On 27 January 1999, the Supreme Court recorded the consent of the parties and sought the expert opinion of the NEAA on the risks posed by the industry to the drinking water supply. The Supreme Court founded the reference to NEAA on this groundwork:

(i) 'The basic insight of ecology is that all living things exist in interrelated systems; nothing exists in isolation. The world system is weblike; to pluck one strand is to cause all to vibrate; whatever happens to one part has ramifications for all the rest. Our actions are not individual but social; they reverberate throughout the whole ecosystem.' [*Science Action Coalition* by A Fritsch, *Environmental Ethics: Choices for Concerned Citizens*, 3–4 (1980)] (1988, Vol. 12, Harv Env L Rev at p 313).[111]

(ii) The 'uncertainty' of scientific proof and its changing frontiers from time to time has led to great changes in environmental concepts during the period between the Stockholm Conference of 1972 and the Rio Conference of 1992. In *Vellore Citizens' Welfare Forum v Union of India* (1996) 5 SCC 647 a three-Judge Bench of this Court referred to these changes, to the 'precautionary principle' and the new concept of 'burden of proof' in environmental matters.[112]

(iii) A basic shift in the approach to environmental protection occurred initially between 1972 and 1982. Earlier, the concept was based on the 'assimilative capacity' rule as revealed from Principle 6 of the Stockholm Declaration of the UN Conference on Human Environment, 1972. The said principle *assumed* that science could provide policy-makers with the information and means necessary to avoid encroaching upon the capacity of the environment to assimilate impacts and it *presumed* that relevant technical expertise would be available when environmental harm was predicted and there would be sufficient time to act in order to avoid such harm. But in the 11th Principle of the UN General Assembly Resolution on World Charter for Nature, 1982, the emphasis shifted to the 'precautionary principle', and this was reiterated in the Rio Conference of 1992 in its Principle 15 which reads as follows:

'Principle 15 – In order to protect the environment, the *precautionary approach* shall be widely applied by States according to their capabilities. Where there are threats of serious or irreversible damage, lack of full *scientific certainty* shall not be used as a reason for proposing cost-effective measures to prevent environmental degradation.'[113]

(iv) The principle of precaution involves the anticipation of environmental harm and taking measures to avoid it or to choose the least environmentally harmful activity. It is *based* on scientific uncertainty. Environmental protection should not only aim at protecting health, property and economic interest but also protect the environment for its own sake. Precautionary duties must not only be triggered by the suspicion of concrete danger but also by (justified) concern or risk potential.[114]

---

111 *A P Pollution Control Board v Prof M V Nayudu* (1999) 2 SCC 718, 724.
112 *Id.* at 732.
113 *Id.* at 733.
114 *Id.* at 734.

The NEAA Report was against Surana Oils and so were two further reports sought by the Supreme Court on certain technical aspects. The Supreme Court eventually allowed the appeals filed by the board and upheld its decision rejecting the grant of consent. Surana Oils would have to shift away. Justice M Jagannadha Rao's second judgment in the case is also rich in principles:

(i) Drinking water is of primary importance in any country. In fact, India is a party to the resolution of the UNO passed during the United Nations Water Conference in 1977 as under:

'All people, whatever their stage of development and their social and economic conditions, have the right to have access to *drinking water* in quantum and of a quality equal to their basic needs.'

Thus, the right to access to drinking water is fundamental to life and there is a duty on the State under Article 21 to provide clean drinking water to its citizens.[115]

(ii) There is, therefore, a need to take into account the right to a healthy environment along with the right to sustainable development and balance them.[116]

(iii) In today's emerging jurisprudence, environmental rights which encompass a group of collective rights are described as 'third-generation' rights. The 'first-generation' rights are generally political rights such as those found in the International Convention on Civil & Political Rights while 'second-generation' rights are social and economic rights as found in the International Covenant on Economic, Social and Cultural Rights. 'Right to Healthy Environment', (See Vol 25) 2000 *Columbia Journal of Environment Law* by John Lee p. 283, at pp. 293–294, fn. 29).[117]

(iv) Thus, the concept of a healthy environment as a part of the fundamental right to life, developed by our Supreme Court, is finding acceptance in various countries side by side with the right to development.[118]

(v) In our earlier judgment in *A P Pollution Control Board (I) v Prof M V Nayudu* (1999) 2 SCC 718 this court had occasion to refer to the basis of the precautionary principle and to explain the basis and content of the very principle. This court also explained the new principle of burden of proof.

Therefore, it was for [Surana Oils] to establish that there would be no danger of pollution to the two reservoirs even if the industry was established within 10 km radius of the said reservoirs. In the present proceedings, [Surana Oils] has failed to discharge the said onus.[119]

(vi) It is no doubt stated by [Surana Oils] that it is prepared to adopt the safety measures suggested by the appellant Board on 1-7-1997 and also those suggested by Dr Bhowmick, by trying to see that during storage of raw materials and after release of the hazardous liquids, they are put in containers and removed.

In respect of these drinking water reservoirs which cater to the needs of about 70 or 80 lakhs population, we cannot rely upon a bare assurance that care will be taken in the storage of serious hazardous materials. Nor can we rely on an assurance that these hazardous substances would be effectively removed without spillage. It is, in our view, not humanly possible for any department to keep track whether the pollutants are not spilled over. This is exactly where the 'precautionary principle' comes into play. The chance of an accident, within such close proximity of the reservoirs cannot be ruled out, as pointed out in the reports. Thus, we are led to the inference that there is a very great risk that these highly hazardous materials could seep into the earth and reach the tanks, after passing through the dolerite dykes, as pointed [out] by the National Geophysical Research Institute. Our inference from facts

115 *A P Pollution Control Board-II v Prof M V Nayudu* (2001) 2 SCC 62, 69.
116 *Id.*
117 *Id.* at 70.
118 *Id.* at 71.
119 *Id.* at 79.

and the reports is that of a reasonable person, as pointed out in the main judgment in *A P Pollution Board v Prof M V Nayudu*.[120]

The next case resolves a contest between villagers seeking to preserve a pond and the development authorities which had leased the tract to Sharp Enterprises. The villagers were first alerted to the potential destruction when excavators began levelling the area. Since the District Collector and police failed to respond to complaints, the villagers petitioned the National Green Tribunal. The NGT accepted the plea of the development authority that it was developing a larger water body as an alternative to the seasonal pond. The villagers appealed.

JITENDRA SINGH v MINISTRY OF ENVIRONMENT

2019 (17) SCALE 29[121]

SURYA KANT, J:

* * *

Given that Section 22 of the NGT Act, 2010 specifies that the nature of the appeal shall be akin to a second appeal as specified under Section 100 of the Code of Civil Procedure, 1908, we would restrict our deliberation to a singular substantive question of law. That is, whether it is permissible for the State to alienate common water-bodies for industrial activities, under the guise of providing alternatives?

* * *

This Court reiterated in *Jagpal Singh v State of Punjab* (2011) 11 SCC 396, and noted that since time immemorial, certain common lands had vested in village communities for collective benefit. Except in exceptional circumstances when used exclusively for the downtrodden, these lands were inalienable. It was observed that such protections, however, remained on paper, and since Independence powerful people and a corrupt system had appropriated these lands for personal aggrandisement. Pointing out the harms in allowing such misappropriation, the Court noted an urgent public interest in stopping such misdeeds. Further, various directions were issued for eviction of illegal occupants and restoration of the common land to villagers. It was explicitly specified that 'long duration of such illegal occupation or huge expenditure in making constructions thereon' cannot be a 'justification for condoning this illegal act or for regularising the illegal possession'.

It is uncontroverted, in the present case, that the Government Order dated 03.06.2016 was a consequence of the afore-cited judgment in *Jagpal Singh*. Curiously, however, Clause 5 of the Government Order carves an exception of 'huge projects/works' (albeit in extraordinary circumstances) to *Jagpal Singh's* strict principle of non-alienation of common water-bodies. It is clear that such ground of exception doesn't fall under the limited class of grants to 'landless labourers or members of the Scheduled Castes/Scheduled Tribes, or where there is already a school, dispensary or other public utility on the land'. Such industrial activities without any rational classification, unlike the narrow class exempted, do not serve a social public purpose or benefit the local people, and thus will be hit by the inalienability bar....

There remains therefore no doubt that it is the responsibility of the respondents to ensure the protection and integrity of the environment, especially one which is a source for livelihood for rural population and life for local flora and fauna.

Protection of such village-commons is essential to safeguard the fundamental right guaranteed by Article 21 of our Constitution. These common areas are the lifeline of village communities, and often sustain various chores and provide resources necessary for life. Waterbodies, specifically, are an important source of fishery and much needed potable water.

---

120 *Id.* at 83.
121 (2019) SCC Online SC 1510.

Many areas of this country perennially face a water crisis and access to drinking water is woefully inadequate for most Indians. Allowing such invaluable community resources to be taken over by a few is hence grossly illegal.

The respondents' scheme of allowing destruction of existing water bodies and providing for replacements, exhibits a mechanical application of environmental protection. Although it might be possible to superficially replicate a waterbody elsewhere, however, there is no guarantee that the adverse effect of destroying the earlier one would be offset. Destroying the lake at Khasra Nos. 552 and 490, for example, would kill the vegetation around it and would prevent seepage of groundwater which would affect the already low water-table in the area. The people living around the lake would be compelled to travel all the way to the alternative site, in this case allegedly almost 3 kms away. Many animals and marine organisms present in the earlier site would perish, and wouldn't resuscitate by merely filling a hole with water elsewhere. Further, the soil quality and other factors at the alternate site might not be conducive to growth of the same flora, and the local environment would be altered permanently. The respondents' reduction of the complex and cascading effects of extinguishing natural water-bodies into mere numbers and their attempt to justify the same through replacement by geographically larger artificial water-bodies, fails to capture the spirit of the Constitutional scheme and is, therefore, impermissible.

Hence, it is clear that schemes which extinguish local water bodies albeit with alternatives, as provided in the 2016 Government Order by the State of UP, are violative of Constitutional principles and are liable to be struck down....

NOTES AND QUESTIONS

1. Is the proposition regarding inalienability of common lands overbroad? Should exceptions extend beyond the narrow carve-outs recognized in *Jagpal Singh*?

2. In balancing development and the genuine local requirements (including environmental protection), is a winner-takes-all resolution satisfactory or should environmental dispute resolution be more nuanced? Here, should the Supreme Court have remitted the matter back to the NGT to devise a scheme that would have preserved the pond and allowed Sharp (which had paid Rs. 25 crores for the land) to pursue its enterprise?

K. GROUNDWATER

The National Environment Policy which was adopted by the Union Cabinet on 18 May 2006 outlines the problem of groundwater depletion.

GOVERNMENT OF INDIA, NATIONAL ENVIRONMENT POLICY 2006

Groundwater is present in underground aquifers in many parts of the country. Aquifers near the surface are subject to annual recharge from precipitation, but the rate of recharge is impacted by human interference. Deep aquifers, on the other hand, occur below a substratum of hard rock. The deep aquifers generally contain very pure water, but since they are recharged only over many millennia, must be conserved for use only in periods of calamitous drought, such as may happen only once in several hundred years. The boundaries of groundwater aquifers do not generally correspond to the spatial jurisdiction of any local public authorities or private holdings, nor are they easily discernable, nor can withdrawals be easily monitored, leading to the unavoidable situation of groundwater being an open access resource.

The water table has been falling rapidly in many areas of the country in recent decades. This is largely due to withdrawal for agricultural, industrial, and urban use, in excess of annual recharge. In urban areas, apart from withdrawals for domestic and industrial use, housing and infrastructure such as roads, prevent sufficient recharge. In addition, some pollution of groundwater occurs due to leaching of stored hazardous waste and use of agricultural chemicals, in particular, pesticides. Contamination of groundwater is also due to geogenic causes, such as leaching of arsenic and fluoride from natural deposits. Since groundwater is frequently a source of drinking water, its pollution and contamination leads to serious health impacts.

The direct causes of groundwater depletion have their origin in the pricing policies for electricity and diesel. In the case of electricity, wherever individual metering is not practiced, a flat charge for electricity connections makes the marginal cost of electricity effectively zero. Subsidies for diesel also reduce the marginal cost of extraction to well below the efficient level. Given the fact that groundwater is an open access resource, the user then 'rationally' (i.e. in terms of his individual perspective), extracts groundwater until the marginal value to him equals his now very low marginal cost of extraction. The result is inefficient withdrawals of groundwater by all users, leading to the situation of falling water tables. Support prices for several water intensive crops with implicit price subsidies aggravate this outcome by strengthening incentives to take up these crops rather than less water intensive ones. In coastal areas this overexploitation and inadequate recharge of ground water may also cause serious problem of saline ingress, leading to adverse health impacts and loss of land productivity.

Falling water tables have several perverse social impacts, apart from the likelihood of mining of deep aquifers, 'the drinking water source of last resort'. The capital costs of pump sets and bore wells for groundwater extraction when water tables are very deep may be relatively high, with no assurance that water would actually be found. In such a situation, a user who may be a marginal farmer able to borrow the money only at usurious rates of interest, may, in case water is not found, find it impossible to repay his debts. This may lead to destitution, or worse. Even if the impacts were not so dire, there would be excessive use of electricity and diesel.

The efficient use of groundwater would, accordingly, require that the practice of non-metering of electric supply to farmers be discontinued in their own enlightened self-interest. It would also be essential to progressively ensure that the environmental impacts are taken into account in setting electricity tariffs, and diesel pricing.

Increased run-off of precipitation in urban areas due to impermeable structures and infrastructure prevents natural groundwater recharge. This is an additional cause of falling water tables in urban areas as large quantities of ground water are pumped out for urban use. In rural areas several cost-effective rainwater harvesting and artificial recharge techniques have been proven to enhance groundwater recharge. A number of effective traditional water management techniques to recharge groundwater have been discontinued by the local communities due to the onset of pump sets extraction, and need to be revived. Finally, increase in tree cover is also effective in enhancing soil moisture retention and preventing soil erosion.

Pollution of groundwater from agricultural chemicals is also linked to their improper use, once again due to pricing policies, especially for chemical pesticides, as well as agronomic practices, which do not take the potential environmental impacts into account. While transiting through soil layers may considerably eliminate organic pollution loads in groundwater, this is not true of several chemical pesticides. The pesticides themselves may become a source of pollution when it leaches into the ground water.

The following actions will be taken:

(a) Take explicit account of impacts on groundwater tables of electricity tariffs and pricing of diesel.

(b) Promote efficient water use techniques, such as sprinkler or drip irrigation, among farmers. Provide necessary pricing, inputs, and extension support to feasible and remunerative alternative crops which may be raised by efficient water use.
(c) Ensure availability of ground water potential maps through a designated institution.
(d) Support practices of rain water harvesting and artificial recharge and revival of traditional methods for enhancing groundwater recharge.
(e) Mandate water harvesting and artificial recharge in all new constructions in relevant urban areas, as well as design techniques for road surfaces and infrastructure to enhance groundwater recharge. Promote capacity development of relevant stakeholders and provide web based information on water harvesting techniques.
(f) Prepare and implement a comprehensive strategy for regulating use of ground water by large industrial and commercial establishments on the basis of a careful evaluation of aquifer capacity and annual recharge.
(g) Support R&D in cost effective techniques suitable for rural drinking water projects for remedial measures and removal of arsenic[,] fluoride, and other toxic substances and mainstream their adoption in rural drinking water schemes in relevant areas.
(h) Improve productivity per unit of water consumed in industrial processes, by making water assessments and water audits mandatory in identified industries and utilities.
(i) Suitable sites for dumping the toxic waste material may be identified and remedial measures may be taken to prevent the movement of the toxic waste in the ground water.
(j) Excessive use of fertilizers, pesticides and insecticides are the main non point source of the pollution. These pollutants contribute to the pollution of the ground water as well as surface water. The optional utilization of fertilizers, pesticides and insecticides should be encouraged for improving the water quality....

NOTES AND QUESTIONS

1. Conspicuously absent in the actions proposed under the 2006 Policy is a statute to regulate groundwater extraction. What factors—constitutional, political, geological, practical—hinder the framing of a national groundwater law?

2. Notice the adverse impact of poor economic policies, here the electricity and diesel tariffs, on depletion of a vital natural resource. How are electricity and diesel prices determined? Is groundwater depletion at all a factor when deciding the price of electricity and diesel?

3. Should electricity tariff regulators fix the tariff in accordance with the 2006 Policy? Who might bring this policy statement to the attention of these regulators: the power and water utilities, electricity consumers, environmental NGOs?

4. In many parts of India, industry, agriculturists and municipalities are increasing their dependence on groundwater resources.[122] For the user this is an attractive option since the source is continuous (unlike monsoon-fed rivers and streams), the water is generally clean and the user need not depend on an external agency for the supply. The rights to the groundwater attach to the land and hence landowners may draw on the groundwater and use it as if it were their own private property.[123] According to Chhatrapati Singh, this private ownership regime is inequitable because it leaves out all the landless and tribals who do not enjoy private ownership.[124]

---

122 Chhatrapati Singh, *Water Rights and Principles of Water Resources Management* 39 (1991).
123 *Id.*
124 *Id.*

Since the exploitation of groundwater has a bearing on the user's fundamental right to life under Article 21 of the Constitution, her right to dig bore wells cannot be restricted by an executive fiat. This right may be restricted or regulated only by an Act of the legislature.[125]

There is no national *statute* regulating groundwater resources.[126] However, on 24 September 2020, the Central Government issued 'Guidelines to regulate and control groundwater extraction in India' under section 3(3) read with section 5 of the Environment (Protection) Act of 1986 (EPA).[127]

Until the Supreme Court judgment in *M C Mehta v Union of India*,[128] the Union Government was of the view that central legislation may not be permissible since 'Water' was a state subject under Schedule VII of the Constitution. Each state would need to introduce separate legislation to regulate and control groundwater resources and to assist the states, a model bill was circulated in 1970. The Supreme Court, however, expressed a *prima facie* view that Article 253 of the Constitution and the provisions of the EPA empowered the Centre to regulate groundwater exploitation. The court's observations were made on an application filed by M C Mehta urging the Central Government to constitute a national authority under section 3(3) of the EPA to ensure that groundwater resources are managed sustainably. The Supreme Court directed the Union Ministry of Environment and Forests to constitute the Central Ground Water Board as an authority under section 3(3) of the EPA to regulate the indiscriminate exploitation of underground water in the country. The authority was constituted on 14 January 1997 by a statutory notification and was empowered to exercise powers under section 5 of the EPA for groundwater management.

5. The current groundwater regulatory regime in India comprises a mix of national guidelines issued in September 2020 and state laws. The 2020 Guidelines were issued pursuant to periodic directions issued by the National Green Tribunal requiring a more robust regulatory regime to address the rapid depletion of groundwater resources across the country. The 2020 Guidelines open with a preamble explaining their scope:

> To have sustainable management of water resources in the country groundwater abstraction guidelines have been prepared to regulate groundwater extraction and conserve the scarce groundwater resources in the country.
>
> These guidelines will come into force with immediate effect from the date of Gazette Notification and will supersede all earlier guidelines issued by the Central Ground Water Authority (CGWA).
>
> Further, wherever States/UTs have come out with their own groundwater abstraction guidelines, which are inconsistent with the CGWA guidelines, the provisions of CGWA guidelines will prevail. However, in case the guidelines followed by such State/UTs contain some more stringent provisions than CGWA guidelines, such provisions may also be given effect to by the States/UTs Authorities in addition to those contained in the CGWA guidelines. States may be at liberty to suggest additional conditions/criteria based on the local hydro-geological situations which shall be reviewed by CGWA /Ministry of Jal Shakti, Government of India before acceptance.
>
> All new/existing industries, industries seeking expansion, infrastructure projects and mining projects abstracting ground water, unless specifically exempted under Para 1.0 below, will be required to seek No Objection Certificate from Central Ground Water Authority or, the concerned State/UT Ground Water Authority as the case may be. The entire process of grant of No Objection Certificate shall be online through a web based application system.

125 *Puttappa H Talavar v Deputy Commissioner* AIR 1998 KAR 10.
126 Philippe Cullet & Sujith Koonan, *Water Law in India: An Introduction to Legal Instruments* 342 (2017).
127 Ministry of Jal Shakti, Government of India, SO 3289(E) dated 24 September 2020.
128 (1997) 11 SCC 312.

> Water management plans shall be prepared by all the State Ground Water Authorities/ Organizations for all Over-exploited, Critical and Semi-critical assessment units starting with Over-exploited units. Water management plans shall be reviewed and updated periodically. Water management plans, data on water availability and scarcity and policy framed in this regard shall be placed on the websites of Central Ground Water Authority/State Ground Water Authority.[129]

The Guidelines are styled differently from statutory rules and regulations framed under the EPA. Do the Guidelines have lesser efficacy than other subordinate legislation? Clause 15 of the Guidelines provides for environmental compensation where industrial units extract groundwater without a valid 'No Objection Certificate' (NOC) and clause 16 prescribes penalties for breach of the NOC. Can monetary impositions and penalties be imposed by 'Guidelines', absent express statutory sanction?

6. At the state level, a number of states have enacted laws drawing on a model bill mooted by the Union Government. These state laws establish a permit system where groundwater users are required to obtain a licence from a designated authority and must comply with the conditions in the permit. Among the states that have enacted groundwater regulatory statutes are Andhra Pradesh,[130] Kerala,[131] Goa,[132] Himachal Pradesh,[133] Karnataka[134] and West Bengal.[135] In the National Capital Territory, directions have been issued under section 5 of the EPA with regard to groundwater extraction through bore wells and tube wells. A new framework legislation or model legislation was proposed by the Union Government in 2016.[136]

7. The need for good management of groundwater resources was recognized earlier by the Kerala High Court in a public interest litigation filed by local islanders seeking to protect freshwater resources on the Lakshadweep Islands. The petitioners apprehended that the government scheme to pump out groundwater on the island would cause saline intrusions in the freshwater table which would, in turn, imperil the potable water supply on the islands. The Kerala High Court commissioned an expert report which opposed the government scheme. Recognizing the importance of fresh water to the islanders and holding that the right to fresh water was an aspect of the fundamental right to life, the High Court prohibited the government from implementing the scheme until it was reviewed and modified by the Union Ministry of Environment and the Ministry of Science and Technology.[137]

8. The citizens of Karaikudi town in Tamil Nadu challenged a government scheme which would carry away waters from an ancient spring named Sambai Uthu which was the principal source of water for the town from time immemorial. In 1987, the municipality of Karaikudi unanimously opposed the scheme which was intended to benefit Tirupattur. In the face of this opposition the state government suspended the scheme. Seven years later the government revived the project, leading to a public outcry and allegations that the project was being hurried through to benefit a mineral water factory at Tirupattur, where a government minister had an interest. Though the High Court rejected the allegations against the

---

129 Ministry of Jal Shakti, Government of India, SO 3289(E) dated 24 September 2020.

130 Andhra Pradesh Water, Land and Trees Act of 2002.

131 Kerala Groundwater (Control and Regulation) Act of 2002.

132 Goa Groundwater Regulation Act of 2002.

133 Himachal Pradesh Groundwater (Regulation and Control of Development and Management) Act of 2005.

134 Karnataka Groundwater (Regulation for Protection of Sources of Drinking Water) Act of 1999.

135 West Bengal Groundwater Resources (Management, Control and Regulation) Act of 2005.

136 Philippe Cullet & Sujith Koonan, *Water Law in India: An Introduction to Legal Instruments* 359–60 (2017).

137 *Attakoya Thangal v Union of India* 1990 (1) Ker L T 580.

Minister in the absence of evidence, it directed the state government to review the scheme after taking into consideration the availability of groundwater and also the views of the residents of Karaikudi.[138]

9. Responding to a public interest litigation alleging failure and neglect by the state in providing safe drinking water to villagers in Mandla district, a division bench of the Madhya Pradesh High Court directed the state to extend free medical treatment and compensation to the affected persons. Water drawn from hand pumps sunk by the state contained excessive fluoride which caused bone diseases, deformities and dental fluorosis.[139]

10. In January 1996, an Expert Committee appointed by the Gujarat High Court submitted its report on pollution caused by Gujarat Fluorochemicals Ltd (GFL) in the Panchmahals district. Several residents of the villages neighbouring GFL complained of crop failures, health problems and a loss of milk production. The report (a model of sound methodology and clear analysis) records that most water samples drawn from tube wells indicated fluoride and chloride concentrations exceeding potable water limits. *Prima facie*, GFL appeared to be responsible for the adverse environmental impact.[140]

11. Binani Zinc Ltd was directed by the Kerala High Court to supply drinking water to the affected villagers after test samples drawn from neighbouring wells were found to contain 'acidic' water unfit for drinking. The water contained very high concentrations of zinc, cadmium and total dissolved solids which may have been caused by seepages from the factory.[141]

12. In March 2000, Coca Cola commissioned a plant at Plachimada village in the Pallakkad District of Kerala. In 2003, local protests complaining against the exploitation of groundwater culminated in the panchayat refusing to renew the company's licence to draw groundwater. The campaign against the beverage plant and the journey of the case through the courts is tracked by Sujith Koonan in *Ground Water—Legal Aspects of the Plachimada Dispute*[142] and a report by Aathira Konikkara.[143]

---

138 *Pazha Karuppiah v State of Tamil Nadu* AIR 1997 Mad 144.

139 *Hamid Khan v State of Madhya Pradesh* AIR 1997 MP 191. There is no indication in the judgment whether the excessive fluoride was a natural occurrence or caused by pollution.

140 Gupta, Pandya, Rao & Shukla, *Report of the Expert Committee* (1996) submitted in *Andarsingh Parmar v State of Gujarat* Spl Civ Application No. 5280 of 1995.

141 *Edayar Environment Protection Council v Government of India* Orig Petn 4419/96, Kerala High Court, 10 April 1997.

142 The chapter appears in *Water Governance in Motion: Towards Socially and Environmentally Sustainable Water Laws* 159 (Ed. P Cullet, *et al*, 2010).

143 *Nearly 15 Years After Coca Cola Plant Shut Down, Plachimada's Fight for Rs 216 crore in Compensation Continues*, The Caravan (16 March 2019), https://caravanmagazine.in/communities/coca-cola-plachimada, accessed 10 May 2021.

9

AIR POLLUTION CONTROL

A. SCOPE OF THE PROBLEM

This chapter casts a net over issues that impair the quality of the air we breathe—dust, vehicular emissions, industrial pollution and crackers during the Diwali festival. The chapter closes with a section on noise. Responding to the familiar story of pollution control board failure, the judiciary after numerous attempts to goad executive action has assumed a near-permanent seat at the regulatory table. Citizens and regulators expect little by way of progress without judicial intervention. Nevertheless, despite court directions spanning over two decades, there is little to show by way of tangible improvements in the air quality. The magnitude of the challenges faced across urban India and a strategy for the way forward are outlined in the opening set of readings.

SHAMBHAVI SHUKLA & TANUSHREE GANGULY; UNACKNOWLEDGED HEALTH RISK IN STATE OF INDIA'S ENVIRONMENT (2019)

India's ascent up the ease-of-doing-business ranking ladder is commendable. Unfortunately, not the same can be said about its struggle with air pollution. With burgeoning motorisation levels, increasing industrial activity, widespread construction activities to assist the growth of sprawling cities, the number of cities grappling with air pollution is on the rise.

Sources of air pollution, India's most severe environmental problem, come in several forms, including vehicular emissions, untreated industrial smoke, smoke from abandoned untreated piles of garbage and unchecked emissions emanating from construction sites. Besides rapid industrialisation, urbanisation has led to the emergence of industrial centres without a corresponding growth in civic amenities and pollution control mechanisms.

In 2015, the Central Pollution Control Board (CPCB) identified 102 non-attainment cities across the country. Cities that fail to meet the national ambient air quality standards are classified as non-attainment cities. World Health Organization's air quality database, updated in 2018, lists cities on the basis of their annual average particulate matter (PM) 2.5 concentration. According to this list, 14 of the world's 20 most polluted cities are in India and five of these feature above Delhi on the list.

The increased level of air pollution is manifesting itself in the form of health impacts on vulnerable as well as healthy individuals. Industrialisation and urbanisation have resulted in profound deterioration of India's air quality. Of the millions of premature deaths in the world that occur each year due to outdoor air pollution, the highest number is assessed to occur in India. A report published in *The Lancet* in December 2018 reveals that in 2017 alone, close to 1.24 million people in India lost their lives due to air pollution-related health ailments. As per the report, 0.67 million deaths were due to ambient air pollution, and rest because of household air pollution. The burden due to household air pollution is highest in the states of Bihar, Chhattisgarh, Jharkhand, Madhya Pradesh, Odisha, Rajasthan, Uttarakhand and Uttar Pradesh, where its improvement since 1990 has also been the slowest. On the other hand, the burden due to outdoor air pollution is highest in a mix of northern states, including Haryana, Uttar Pradesh, Punjab, Rajasthan, Bihar and West Bengal....

Majority cities in the country are in the grip of critical particulate pollution. CPCB maintains an air quality database for all the cities on its Environmental Information System (ENVIS) centre. Data is available from 2007 to 2017. The annual average concentration for pollutants

Environmental Law & Policy in India. Shyam Divan and Armin Rosencranz, Oxford University Press.
 DOI: 1093/oso/9780192865458.003.0009

for 46 cities, of which data is available for 44 cities, with a million-plus population is analysed. CPCB classifies annual average pollution levels in terms of low (50% less than the standard), moderate (meeting the standards), high (1.5 times the standards) and critical (more than 1.5 times the standards). Accordingly, the number of cities with PM_{10} levels in critical category has increased from 56% in 2007 to 79% in 2017. It is, however, evident that out of 255 cities nearly 78% cities exceeded the standard in 2016.

The share of cities with good annual air quality years has also reduced drastically. There is a drastic fall in the number of cities with particulate levels below the standard. It has reduced from 13% in 2007 to 2% in 2017. There are no cities which are in low category between 2007 and 2017.

ANUMITA ROYCHOWDHURY; CONNECTING THE DOTS IN STATE OF INDIA'S ENVIRONMENT (2020)

The National Clean Air Programme (NCAP), launched in January 2019 is a step towards creating a national framework for air quality management and compliance. Under this programme, 122 cities that do not meet the National Ambient Air Quality Standards (NAAQS) in PM_{10} and $PM_{2.5}$ have been identified as 'non-attainment' cities. About 60% of these towns and cities are in the Indo-Gangetic Plain. The rest are in other six major climatic zones.

While the list of non-attainment cities includes megacities like Bengaluru, Delhi, Kolkata, and Mumbai, it also contains a large number of tiny urban centres with very small populations. About 70% of these cities and towns have less than 1 million populations each. Anpara, Gajraula and Rae Bareilley, all in Uttar Pradesh, have populations of 18,000; 55,045 and 190,000 respectively. Similarly, Gaya and Muzaffarpur in Bihar each have less than 500,000 populations. In such urban centres, localised action can certainly reduce local exposure to air pollution, but if their larger influence area is neglected, their air cannot be cleaned up beyond a point.

On the other hand, non-attainment cities in industrial zones impact quality of down-wind cities and regions. Pollution sources in these urban centres will require stricter emissions control looking beyond localised action and air quality indices. City-based approach under NCAP also does not help address the sources of air pollution and the quality of air in rural areas.

For these and other reasons, there is a need to shift the focus to larger airsheds. But this is easier said than done. Airsheds are a complex mix of multiple state jurisdictions and governance systems. There is no clear mechanism for delineating regional airsheds and creating a common and harmonised framework of action, monitoring and compliance across states.

There is a growing interest among scientists to assess regional build up and profile of pollution by using high resolution satellite data and utilising methods like aerosol optical depth. For instance, scientists at the Indian Institute of Technology, Delhi and the Indian Institute of Tropical Meteorology (IITM) are tracking the nature and shifts in the buildup of pollution peaks in the Indo-Gangetic Plain. Moreover, with incidents of winter smog becoming a serious concern, interest has grown in the episodic pollution caused by the movement of smoke from crop stubble burning across the region. Dr. Gufran Beig of IITM's System of Air Quality and Weather Forecasting tracks the speed and direction of wind and intensity of crop stubble burning in Haryana and Punjab on a daily basis to assess its contribution to the regional buildup of pollution. This science needs to be developed further to allow us a better understanding of the up-wind and down-wind movement and effects of pollution in the region to help inform a regional framework for air pollution control....

As this decade comes to an end and India gets closer to an air pollution road map for the next decade, it is important to integrate this emerging landscape of learning with integrated planning and action on a regional basis. Given the magnitude of the regional air pollution crisis in India, time is ripe for a framework of regional co-operation and obligations based on mutually agreed action plans that include targets with adequate resource support.

India's NCAP has recognised the idea of a regional approach and inter-state co-ordination. It mentions that a comprehensive regional plan needs to be formulated, incorporating inputs from regional source apportionment studies. It has listed a series of majors that cut across multiple jurisdictions and are regional in nature. These include stringent norms for fuels, shift from road to railways and waterways, fleet modernisation, policies for electric vehicles and relevant and precise taxation policies. In the industrial sector, it recommends stringent industrial standards, and clean fuels and technologies. Continuous emission monitoring systems are preferred. In addition, NCAP calls for increasing the penetration of liquefied petroleum gas as domestic fuel for cooking and heating, and similar measures at the household level. Interventions in episodic matters like crop stubble burning are also on the agenda. These measures must be immersed into regional paradigms and not seen in isolation and localised.

NOTES AND QUESTIONS

1. In the *Delhi Vehicular Pollution* case,[1] the Supreme Court noticed the health impacts of air pollution and listed major air pollution-related diseases in India: acute respiratory disease, chronic obstructive pulmonary disease, lung cancer, asthma, tuberculosis and cardiovascular disease. These diseases contribute to early mortality and add enormously to health costs in India, burdening both the citizen and state.

2. The solutions suggested by several commentators are fairly obvious: employ a regional approach rather than a city-specific approach; eliminate dirty fuels such as coal for power plants and diesel for vehicles; shift polluting industries away from cities, and employ abatement technologies to reduce construction dust. Nevertheless, year upon year, come November the air across the entire Indo-Gangetic Plain turns into a toxic soup. Why is the political and regulatory system paralysed? Why is India unable to improve the lot of millions of citizens? Remember, as far back as 2002, the Supreme Court in the *Delhi Vehicular Pollution* case drew attention to the ill-effects of extreme air pollution.

3. Why is air pollution not a political issue in India?

4. Responding to a petition seeking directions to curb smoking in public places, the Supreme Court recognized the adverse health impacts on passive smokers. 'Tobacco smoking also adds to the air pollution.'[2] Unwilling to wait until a statute was framed and implemented, the court prohibited smoking in auditoriums, hospitals, educational institutions, courts and public conveyances including railways. Seven years after the judgment, the Central Government issued the Prohibition of Smoking in Public Places Rules of 2008.

B. THE STATUTES

Unlike the Water Act, which was enacted by Parliament under Article 252(1) of the Constitution after securing enabling resolutions from 12 states, the Air (Prevention and Control of Pollution) Act of 1981 was enacted by invoking the Central Government's power under Article 253 to make laws implementing decisions taken at international conferences. The preamble to the Air Act states that the Act represents an implementation of the decisions made at the United Nations Conference on the Human Environment held at Stockholm in

[1] *M C Mehta v Union of India* (2002) 4 SCC 356.
[2] *Murli S Deora v Union of India* (2001) 8 SCC 765, 767.

1972. Although a central statute, executive functions under the Air Act are carried out in the states by state pollution control boards. This delegation of executive functions is permitted by Article 258(2) of the Constitution. Article 258(3) requires the Central Government to compensate the states for the cost of carrying out these delegated functions.

The Air Act of 1981, as amended in 1987, contains several interesting features. First, the Act grants discretion to each state government to designate particular areas as 'air pollution control areas'.[3] Within a declared air pollution control area, neither the board nor the state government may exempt a polluter from the purview of the Act.[4] Polluters located outside such air pollution control areas cannot be prosecuted by the state board, but every industrial operator within an air pollution control area must obtain a permit (consent order) from the state board.[5] Second, the Act enables a magistrate to restrain an air polluter from discharging emissions,[6] and empowers both the Central and state boards to give directions to industries which, if not followed, can be enforced by the board closing down the industry or withdrawing its supply of power and water.[7] Third, citizens can not only sue to enforce the Act to gain compliance by the industries, but can also require the board to provide the emissions data needed to build a citizens' case.[8]

Procedurally, the Air Act follows the basic structure of the Water Act—with a Central board and state boards administering a system of consent orders, monitoring activities, and enforcement through fines and criminal prosecutions. The Air Act specifies that Central and state air pollution control authority is to be exercised by the Central and state water boards. (These boards have generally dropped the term 'Water' from their title and are usually known as 'State Pollution Control Board' [PCB].) It is mandatory for industry to obtain consents under the Water Act and the Air Act and secure renewals when the term of the consents expires.[9]

The state board is required to carefully examine all relevant facts, including the measures taken to prevent pollution, when processing a consent application.[10] Although there is no express mandate in the Air or Water Acts requiring community consultation or transparency at this stage, the Supreme Court has intervened to review the board's decision where the consent issued affected the community at large. The court termed 'incongruous' certain conditions in the consent requiring deferred compliance, despite the immediate impact of the pollution on the public.[11]

Consent may be revoked only after granting an opportunity of hearing to the holder.[12] Where action is proposed against a polluter under both the Water Act as well as the Air Act, the PCB must specify the violation under each law and provide separate and independent reasons.[13] Adverse decisions by the PCB may be appealed to the appellate authority. However, the

---

[3] Section 19.

[4] *K Muniswamy Gowda v State of Karnataka* 1998 (3) Kar L J 594.

[5] Section 21.

[6] Section 22A.

[7] Section 31A.

[8] Section 43.

[9] *Oil Country Tubular Limited v A P Pollution Control Board* 2005 (3) Andh L T 715.

[10] *Mahabir Coke Industry v Pollution Control Board* AIR 1998 Gau 10.

[11] *Sugarcane, G & S S Association v Tamil Nadu Pollution Control Board* AIR 1998 SC 2614. This case was a water pollution case.

[12] *Biswaranjan Sahoo v Regional Officer* 110 (2010) Cuttack L T 859; *DLF Power Ltd v State of Jharkhand* AIR 2004 Jhar 85.

[13] *Shivram Minerals v Maharashtra Pollution Control Board* (2018) SCC Online Bom 18259.

appellate authority constituted under section 31 of the Air Act has no power to review its own orders.[14]

The Air Act, as a matter of practice, operates in tandem with the Environment (Protection) Act of 1986 (EPA). Being a self-contained statute, the Air Act empowers the state boards to independently notify standards under section 17(g). There is an overlap, however. The EPA enables the Central Government to lay down emission standards[15] which are found in the schedules appended to the Environment (Protection) Rules of 1986 (EPR). By operation of section 24 of the EPA, the EPR norms take precedence and hence in practice the state boards generally re-notify the EPR standards under the Air Act. Broadly, there are three types of standards: source standards which require the polluter to restrict at source the emission and discharge of environmental pollutants; product standards which fix the pollution norms for new manufactured products such as cars; and ambient standards that set maximum pollutant loads in the air, and to guide regulators on the environmental quality that ought to be maintained for healthy living.

The rules framed under the EPA prescribe emission norms for over 110 designated specific industries[16] and general emission standards which are 'concentration based', 'equipment based' and 'load/mass-based'.[17] The general standards apply in the absence of industry-specific norms.[18] These general standards are also referred to as 'minimum national standards' since they represent the parameters which every industry must meet until specific standards under Schedule I are prescribed. The pollution control boards in the states are empowered to specify stricter standards than those published in respect of any industry, operation or process, where necessary. In addition to emission norms, National Ambient Air Quality Standards (NAAQS) are notified for industrial, residential and rural areas, and ecologically sensitive regions.[19] The NAAQS are levels of air quality intended to protect public health, vegetation and property with an adequate margin of safety. Two other major areas where standards have been issued under the EPR are ambient air quality standards in respect of noise[20] and emission standards for motor vehicles.[21]

Rule 3(2) of the EPR enables a state board to prescribe standards that are more stringent than those specified in the rules. To do so, the state board must provide good reasons. With a view to improving air quality in Kolkata, the West Bengal PCB relied on this provision to direct a steel mill to switch to a cleaner fuel. The High Court repelled a challenge by the mill asserting that its emissions were within the scheduled limits. The board's policy decision was based upon the recommendations of an Expert Committee. To reduce particulate matter emissions, the experts felt that coal-fired furnaces in steel mills must shift to using oil or natural gas as fuel.[22]

The Delhi High Court rejected a petition brought by a diesel generator manufacturer challenging new noise limits. The technology-forcing standards introduced by amendment to the EPR were in the broader public interest and fell within the ambit of the parent Act. The

---

14 *Manoj Kumar Roy v Appellate Authority* AIR 2002 CAL 216.
15 Sections 3 and 6.
16 Schedule I, Environment (Protection) Rules of 1986.
17 Part D, Schedule VI.
18 Rule 3.
19 Schedule VII.
20 Schedule III. Noise standards are also prescribed under the Noise Pollution (Regulation and Control) Rules of 2000 framed under the EPA.
21 Schedule IV.
22 *Alloy Steel Rolling Mills v West Bengal Pollution Control Board* AIR 2006 CAL 75.

manufacturer had no legitimate grievance since its freedom to carry on business was subject to reasonable restrictions under Article 19(6) of the Constitution of India.[23]

In the National Capital Region, the Air Act is buttressed by a statutory commission created to dodge a Supreme Court order. On 16 October 2020, dismayed by the persistent air quality problem in Delhi and the surrounding areas, the court constituted an oversight body headed by a retired judge. In doing so, the court brushed aside the objection of the Central Government:

> Accordingly, we find that the suggestion … that a former Judge of this Court who is aware of the problem be appointed to monitor the situation in the States of Punjab, Haryana, Uttar Pradesh and NCR of Delhi, is acceptable.
>
> We, accordingly, accept the suggestion and appoint Hon'ble Mr. Justice Madan Lokur, a former Judge of this Court to act as the one-man Monitoring Committee to monitor the measures taken by the States to prevent stubble burning. For this purpose, we consider it appropriate to direct that the Chief Secretaries of the States of Punjab, Haryana and Uttar Pradesh and NCR of Delhi shall assist where stubble is likely to be burnt and devise additional means and methods for preventing the burning of stubble. We find that it would be fitting, if services of National Cadet Corps, NSS and Bharat Scouts and Guides, wherever available, are deployed for assisting in the monitoring of stubble burning in the agricultural fields in these States. We trust that the authorities in-charge of these forces shall enlist their services to the extent possible, to assist the one-man Justice Lokur Committee for this purpose.[24]

Opposed to the Justice Lokur Committee taking charge, on 26 October 2020 the Union Government informed the court that fresh legislation was proposed to tackle the issue and consequently, the court put its earlier order 'in abeyance until further orders'.[25] On 28 October 2020, the Commission for Air Quality Management in National Capital Region and Adjoining Areas Ordinance of 2020 was promulgated by the President. After this Ordinance lapsed in March 2021, it was reissued (with a few modifications) on 13 April 2021 as Ordinance No. 4 of 2021. The Ordinance establishes an unwieldy body of 21 persons and confers upon them:

> the power to take all such measures, issue directions and entertain complaints, as it deems necessary or expedient for the purpose of protecting and improving the quality of the air in the National Capital Region and Adjoining Areas and shall also have the duty to take all such measures as may become necessary for protecting and improving the quality of the air in the National Capital Region and Adjoining Areas.[26]

C. AIR ACT CASES

In this section we digest air pollution cases, including prosecutions, briefly dwelling on the role of the pollution control boards. As you read the opening excerpt of the Gujarat High Court judgment, critically review Justice Vaidya's opinion on the responsibilities of corporate management in pollution cases.

---

[23] *Jackson & Company v Union of India* 2005 (82) DRJ 298.

[24] *Aditya Dube (minor) v Union of India*, Writ Petition (Civil) 1135/2020.

[25] *Id.*

[26] Clause 12 (1), the Commission for Air Quality Management in National Capital Region and Adjoining Areas Ordinance of 2021.

DWARKA CEMENT WORKS LIMITED v STATE OF GUJARAT
1992 (1) GUJ LAW HERALD 9

K J Vaidya, J: The Dwarka Cement Works, a limited company and five others who are its Chairman, Directors and General Manager respectively, have by this Misc. Criminal Application, under section 482 of the Code of Criminal Procedure, 1973, moved this court for quashing and setting aside the impugned order issuing process against them in Criminal Case No. 162/89, by the learned [Magistrate], Dwarka, for their alleged offences under sections 21 (4), 21 (5), 31-A, 39 and 40 of the Air (Prevention and Control of Pollution) Act, 1981 (for short the Pollution Act).

[Counsel for the petitioners argued that the process deserved to be quashed since there were no specific averments in the complaint regarding the way the petitioner Nos. 2 to 6 were directly in charge of and responsible to the company.] Now it true that in what manner each of the petitioner Nos. 2 to 6 were directly in charge and responsible to the conduct of the company, is not deftly and exhaustively stated in the complaint, but then at the same time, such minute details of evidence are not necessary while filing the complaint for putting the criminal law in motion. The matter and material details are always subject matter of the evidence to be led at the time of the trial while recording the evidence. At the initial stage of issuing the process, the court has to mainly find out whether the facts disclosed in the complaint contain a 'germ' of the alleged offence—the 'ingredient', to put the criminal law in motion or not. If that 'germ' or the 'ingredient' is found to be present in the complaint, there is no scope for any grievance that because the detailed description about the manner was absent in the complaint, the learned Magistrate was not justified in issuing the process.... The averment 'accused Nos. 2 to 6 are *responsible* for the management of the accused No. 1-company' is sufficient enough for any court to take cognizance of the offence and order issuance of process on the basis of the same. Thus taking into consideration the contents of the complaint, at this stage, it cannot be said that the averments made therein lack any vital ingredient showing no ground made out that the process could not be issued. In fact, to accept the first contention raised by the petitioners at this stage, would be simply prejudging the issue without affording a reasonable opportunity to the prosecution to substantiate allegations as held by the Supreme Court in the case of *State of Bihar v Raj Narayan Singh* AIR 1991 SC 1308. Such an unwarranted interference at a preliminary stage, according to this Court would be nothing less than miscarriage of justice....

[T]here is yet one more important angle or perspective from which the point is required to be looked at, viz., that of the social welfare jurisprudence. This perspective and angle none of us can ever afford [to lose sight of].... [E]xamining the point raised from that angle of social welfare jurisprudence, it is obviously clear— (i) That the offences alleged against the petitioner Nos. 2 to 6 are under an important social legislation, viz. the Pollution Act; (ii) That such proceedings under the Pollution Act, be it civil or criminal, the same needs to be attended to and disposed of as expeditiously as possible to make the provisions of the Act effective and meaningful enough to bring about the social justice; (iii) That the petitioner No. 1-company unlike an ordinary accused is a *limited company*; (iv) That the petitioner Nos. 4 to 6 are sought to be prosecuted and tried for the alleged vicarious liability of the petitioner No. 1-company; (v) That the prosecution of the petitioner Nos. 2 to 6 by way of their vicarious liability under the Pollution Act stand distinctly apart and on different footings than that of the prosecution of the other accused under the ordinary criminal law; (vi) That unlike the accused in ordinary criminal cases, the petitioner No. 1-company and its Directors who are to be prosecuted and tried, maintain the record of their day-to-day business and names of persons concerned with the management in their ordinary course of the business. In this view of the matter, as to who in fact were the real persons at the relevant time of the alleged offences committed by the company concerned with the management of the company to be prosecuted for their vicarious liabilities is a *fact within the special knowledge of the company and so far as its Directors are concerned, they have at least access to that special knowledge.* Under such circumstances, the vague assertions of the petitioner No. 2 to 4 by merely saying that there is nothing in the complaint to indicate as to how they were concerned with the management of the company and that they were prosecuted on mere assumptions, cannot be straightway accepted. In such type of criminal cases, both the offending company and its Directors owe a foremost duty to the court and to the cause of justice to place on record full and true disclosures of the facts and particulars (on the basis of the relevant notings, entries, etc. pertaining to the duty assignments and/or some other material) pointing out there from as to whether the particular Director or such other persons were or were not concerned with the management of the company at the relevant time when the alleged offence came to take place.... Instead of coming to this court praying for quashing the process, the petitioners Nos. 2 to 6 ought to have gone first before the concerned learned Magistrate who had issued the process and requested him for reasonable adjournment and exemption to appear before the court in order to point out as to if they were not concerned with the affairs of the management of the company, who else as per the record were the persons concerned with the same, so that they can be brought on the record for prosecuting them for their vicarious liabilities. The oft quoted dictum that the accused need not open his mouth in defence can be a good principle of criminal jurisprudence in the matter of ordinary prosecution and trials, but as stated earlier, in such types of cases under special statutes in the direction of social welfare, the petitioner No. 1- company which is a Public Limited Company and its Directors have got to open their mouth and point out who are the real persons concerned with the management and affairs of the company who can be held vicariously liable.

***

To lightly invoke the inherent powers of this Court under section 482 of the Code, is itself abusing the discretion of the court and doing injustice to the society, which is allegedly the victim of the air pollution. The power under section 482 of the Code is a discretionary power which has to be sparingly exercised 'to prevent the abuse of the process of law' or otherwise 'to secure the ends of justice'. The exercise of such powers, in the opinion of this court, under such types of prosecutions, would frustrate the ends of justice.... In the result, this Misc. Criminal Application having no substance fails and is dismissed summarily....

NOTES AND QUESTIONS

1. Do you agree with the court's conclusion that under the scheme of the Air Act an accused company and its directors are obliged to disclose the identity of the managers who could be held liable? Are the six factors listed in the judgment sufficient to cast this burden on the accused?

2. In a part of the judgment which is not excerpted, the High Court applied 'common sense' to repel the company's contention that there was no provision under the Act that cast a duty to disclose the responsible manager. According to the court, a common-sense interpretation of the Act casts such a duty on the management. Is this strained reasoning or sage jurisprudence?

3. The environmental duties of company directors have expanded. In a case concerning the protection of the critically endangered Great Indian Bustard, the Supreme Court drew attention to provisions in the Companies Act of 2013 which broaden the duties of companies and their directors in relation to environmental protection. This discussion was in the context of raising finance for the undergrounding of overhead electricity transmission lines that pose a mortal threat to the Great Indian Bustard:

> In fact, a few suggestions were made in the course of arguments, as to how financial resources can be mobilised. One of the options that could be explored, is to invite the attention of each electricity utility engaged in the generation of power, to Section 135 of the Companies Act, 2013, which imposes corporate social responsibility upon companies having a specified net worth or turnover or net profit. Section 166(2) of the Companies Act, 2013 ordains the

Director of a Company to act in good faith, not only in the best interest of the Company, its employees, the shareholders and the community, but also for the protection of environment. The word 'environment', though not defined in the Companies Act, has to be given the meaning assigned to it under the Environment (Protection) Act, 1986. Section 2(a) of the Environment (Protection) Act, 1986, defines the word 'environment' to include the 'inter-relationship which exists among and between water, air and land, and human beings, other living creatures, plants, micro-organisms and property'.[27]

4. In *S M Dubash v V M Bhosale*,[28] the Bombay High Court quashed the prosecution of directors and officers of a company since there was no specific sanction against them. In this case, the state board had approved the prosecution of the company alone. The court held: 'The authority and power of the Board cannot be delegated to an officer to pick and choose the accused against whom the prosecution can be launched.'[29]

5. The Karnataka PCB initiated prosecutions against iron ore dealers who illegally established stack yards in the district of Uttara Kannada without implementing pollution control measures. The criminal complaints filed before the judicial magistrate were challenged as incompetent. According to the dealers, the complaints were not by the 'Board or any officer authorised in this behalf by it', as required under section 43(1)(a) of the Air Act. The Regional Officer, Karwar, who had initiated the criminal process was not directly authorized by the board.

The Supreme Court allowed the appeal by the accused on this technical ground. The court found that although the Karnataka PCB had resolved to empower its chairman to initiate legal action, the chairman in turn could not entrust this work to regional officers on the principle that the delegate could not further delegate the authority vested in her, except by clear mandate of law. There was no statutory mandate. Realizing that the suspected Air Act violators might escape scot-free, the Supreme Court directed the board to reinitiate proceedings within two months of the judgment.[30]

6. The Orient Paper Mills found itself in a pickle when samples of emission collected from its boilers exceeded the limits prescribed for suspended particulate matter (SPM). When the magistrate framed charges against the company and its officers on 11 October 1995, the company filed a revision before the Sessions Court on the ground that there was no evidence to show that its plant was in an air pollution control area. According to the company, this was because the rules framed under the Air Act did not prescribe the manner for declaring an air pollution control area.[31] The additional sessions judge was impressed by this clever argument and the High Court found no illegality or irregularity in the order allowing the revision.

The company's luck ran out in the Supreme Court which noticed a series of notifications published by the state government in the Official Gazette that declared the company's premises as an air pollution control area. The relevant parts of sections 19 and 22 of the Air Act read:

> 19. *Power to declare air pollution control areas.* — (1) The State Government may, after consultation with the State Board, by notification in the Official Gazette, declare in such manner as may be prescribed, any area or areas within the State as air pollution control area or areas for the purposes of this Act.

---

27 *M K Ranjitsinh v Union of India* (2021) SCC Online SC 326 (IA 85618 of 2020 in Writ Petition (Civil) 838 of 2019, order dated 19 April 2021).

28 1996 (2) Mah L J 312.

29 *Id.* at 315.

30 *P Pramila v State of Karnataka* (2015) 17 SCC 651.

31 Section 2(n) of the Air Act reads: ' "prescribed" means prescribed by rules made under this Act by the Central Government or, as the case may be, the State Government.'

(2) The State Government may, after consultation with the State Board, by notification in the Official Gazette, —

(*a*) alter any air pollution control area whether by way of extension or reduction;

(*b*) declare a new air pollution control area in which may be merged one or more existing air pollution control areas or any part or parts thereof.

22. *Persons carrying on industry etc. not to allow emission of air pollutants in excess of the standards laid down by State Board.* — No person operating any industrial plant in any air pollution control area shall discharge or cause or permit to be discharged the emission of any air pollutant in excess of the standards laid down by the State Board under clause (*g*) of sub-section (1) of section 17.

The Supreme Court held:

> In view of the discussion held above, in our view it would not be correct to say that simply because the rules have not been framed prescribing the manner it would render the Act inoperative. The area was notified as an air pollution control area by the State Government as authorized and provided by virtue of the powers conferred under section 19 of the Act. The declaration is provided to be made by means of a notification published in the Official Gazette. No other manner is prescribed nor exists. The relevant notifications issued by the Government cannot be said to be contrary to any rules in existence as framed by the Government. The respondent had knowledge of the notification and had also applied for consent of the Board which was granted to the respondent. But it may be clarified that this is not the reason for taking the view that we have taken, it is mentioned only by way of an additional fact and nothing more. The whole working and functioning of the Act which is meant for controlling the air pollution cannot be withheld and rendered nugatory only for the reason of absence of the rules prescribing the manner declaring an air pollution control area which otherwise is provided to be notified by publication in an Official Gazette which has been done in this case.[32]

7. Belmaks manufactures bicycle and automobile parts across the country. To service southern India, it obtained a no-objection certificate from the local pollution control committee and established a manufacturing unit at Pondicherry. Despite several representations, the PCC refused to grant consent under the Air Act and the Water Act, compelling Belmaks to petition the High Court. The PCC claimed that electroplating operations at the unit discharged heavy metals like chromium and nickel and this was against the policy to encourage non-polluting, environment-friendly industry. Remitting the case to the PCC for considering Belmaks' representations, the Madras High Court underscored the importance of economic development:

> We are of the further opinion that in deciding such applications for grant of Air and Water Consent Orders, the authorities concerned must have a positive approach towards business and industry and should not reject such applications on hyper-technical or minor grounds.... Unless authorities like Pollution Control Board, etc. have a positive approach in encouraging the expansion of industries, the country will not achieve the goal of rapid industrialization which is the main aim of the nation today.... Power and strength comes from a high degree of industrialization. As long as our country remains poor, we cannot command respect in the comity of nations and it is for this reason that we must keep the national object always in mind and never lose track of it.[33]

The Supreme Court followed the public interest litigation route pioneered in the *Ganga Pollution* cases[34] to discipline kiln operators in Uttar Pradesh who were breaching emission

[32] *Orissa State (Prevention of Pollution Control) Board v Orient Paper Mills* (2003) 10 SCC 421, 433.

[33] *Belmaks Metal Works v The Member Secretary* 2005 (1) Law Weekly 429.

[34] *M C Mehta v Union of India* AIR 1988 SC 1037; AIR 1988 SC 1115; and (1997) 2 SCC 411.

norms. Responding to a petition filed by a citizens' group under the banner World Saviors, the court directed the state board to check whether scores of industries operating kilns had installed abatement equipment and achieved the required standards. Show cause notices issued to units that met the norms were discharged by the court, though the board was directed to periodically inspect the units and act should a lapse occur. Industries operating kilns that had not installed air-pollution control equipment or were not attaining the standards were ordered to shut down. Units that had invested in equipment but were unable to operate it due to the unavailability of energy, were permitted to resume operations only after the power was restored and the new equipment proven.[35]

Justice Sankaran Nair of the Kerala High Court expounds the dangers of air pollution in *Mathew Lukose v Kerala State Pollution Control Board*,[36] where the residents of Chingavanam organized themselves to confront Travancore Electro Chemicals Industries. The company manufactured calcium carbide and acetylene black in large quantities. In addition to the complaints about the slurry, which was polluting streams in the neighbourhood, the petitioners claimed that the intense atmospheric pollution was causing pulmonary diseases and ailments. Though seven chimneys spewed carbon dioxide and sulphur dioxide into the air the authorities did little to control the emissions. The state board conceded violations by the polluter but pleaded that it was doing its best in the circumstances. The company drew attention to its earnest efforts and claimed that raising the chimney heights and installing a Rs. 35 lakhs 'multiple cyclone guided inlet dust collector' had reduced the problem. Holding that the sweep of Article 21 of the Constitution includes the right to a healthy environment, the court granted the company three months to attain the limits prescribed by the board. The board was directed to close the plant if the company failed to achieve these norms. In prescribing the time frame, the court recognized that the company had already had over two years since the filing of the petition to eliminate the deficiencies.

Justice Nair's judgment is notable for introducing several features that came to be accepted by the Supreme Court in later judgments. Among these are the express articulation of the right to a wholesome environment as a facet of the right to life under Article 21, securing assistance from an *amicus curiae* and reference to the emergent norm of inter-generational equity. The judge also urged the government to prescribe ambient air quality standards, ambient noise levels and environmental impact assessment regulations, all of which now appear in the statute book.

For years, the residents of the Bombay suburb Ghatkopar suffered extremely poor air quality due to the burning of garbage at the city's garbage dumping ground at Deonar, located a few kilometres up-wind from the suburb. Thick clouds of smoke rose from Deonar and drifted over the residential localities in Ghatkopar, posing a nuisance and health hazard to the residents. The state board confirmed the very poor air quality. Considering the provisions of the Air Act, the ambient air quality norms and the statutory obligations of the municipal corporation, the High Court issued comprehensive directions to the respondents to abate the nuisance. The directions included proper management of the solid waste disposal site.[37]

The issue whether the provisions of the Air Act operate to impliedly repeal the application of section 133 of the Criminal Procedure Code (dealing with public nuisance) arose before the

---

35 *World Saviors v Union of India* 1996 (3) SCALE 32 (SP); and 1996 (4) SCALE 22 (SP). The same order is reported twice.

36 1990 (2) KER L T 686.

37 *Shanti Park 'Sorento' Co-op Hsg Soc Ltd v Municipal Corporation*, Writ Petition No. 1138 of 1996, Bombay High Court, 6 August 1996.

Rajasthan High Court in *Lakshmi Cement v State.*[38] Having rejected the consent application, the board by its letter dated 19 September 1984 directed the company to stop operations[39] and endorsed a copy of the letter to the District Collector with a request to take administrative action against the factory. The collector forwarded the letter to the magistrate, Mount Abu, who issued an order on 19 November 1984 under section 133 of the Code requiring Lakshmi Cement to abate the nuisance. By the time the High Court decided the company's petition challenging the magistrate's order, the petition was rendered infructuous by subsequent events. The board issued a provisional consent to the company shortly after the magistrate's order and the company installed air pollution control equipment which brought the emissions within the limits. Allowing the petition to 'secure the ends of justice' since the public nuisance had long abated, the High Court nevertheless rejected Lakshmi Cement's plea that section 133 stood impliedly repealed by passage of the Air Act.[40]

Throughout this book are cases where the statutory agency abdicates its responsibility, compelling judges to fill the regulatory vacuum. Several reasons contribute towards the ineffective functioning of the PCBs: corruption, a lack of independence and diffuse responsibilities among regulators are some of the reasons for the administrative sloth. The lack of funding and staff cripples effective administration.

The laxity in implementing the Air Act is illustrated in the division bench judgment of the Gauhati High Court in *Mahabir Coke Industry v Pollution Control Board.*[41] Mahabir Coke operated its coke factory with a consent issued under the Water Act by the Assam board. On 12 May 1993, 12 years after the passage of the Air Act, the state government declared the whole state as an 'air pollution control area' under section 19 and thus extended application of the Act to Assam. Initially, the firm failed to apply for consent under the Air Act and submitted its application in August 1995, after receiving a show cause notice from the board. In September 1995, the board refused consent on the ground that the factory was emitting 'black smoke' and no preventive measures were being taken to control the emissions. The board alleged that the firm had failed to control emissions for the past two years and directed the unit to shut down until anti-pollution measures were adopted. The firm informed the board that two out of three ovens had the necessary anti-pollution devices and in respect of the third unit, orders were placed, and the equipment would be installed in six months. In the first week of November 1995, the board monitored the air quality in the locality and thereafter issued an order under section 31A of the Air Act, directing Mahabir Coke to close its manufacturing units. The single judge of the Gauhati High Court rejected the writ petition which was carried on appeal to the division bench.

Reviewing the provisions of the Air Act, the division bench held that the appellant ought to have applied for consent and that its failure to do so clearly amounted to a breach of

---

[38] 1994 (2) RAJ L W 308. The Patna High Court followed *Laxmi Cement* in *Ganesh v State of Bihar* 1997 CR L J 928.

[39] This direction was issued prior to the introduction of section 31A which was brought into effect from 1 April 1988.

[40] The Karnataka High Court has disapproved the execution of closure orders passed by the state board under the Water Act through the magistrate. *Executive Apparel Processors v Taluka Executive Magistrate* 1997 (4) KAR L J 181. The judgments discussing section 133 of the Code of Criminal Procedure in relation to the Water Act are discussed in the Water Pollution Control chapter.

[41] AIR 1998 GAU 10. The court found that emission standards had not been issued under the Air Act; the state board did not have a recognized laboratory to analyse emissions and lacked the equipment to measure emissions.

the provisions of the Act. Nevertheless, the division bench allowed the appeal, permitting Mahabir Coke to run its factory. The appellate court found that the state board had failed to prescribe emission standards under section 17(1)(g).[42] In the absence of standards and a chemical examination of the composition of the smoke emitted by the firm, it was not open to the board to issue a closure notice merely because a thick black smoke was spewing out from the factory chimney.

The judgment appears flawed. The division bench failed to notice the provisions of the Environment (Protection) Act of 1986 (EPA) and the national standards prescribed in the schedules to the Environment (Protection) Rules of 1986 (EPR). Section 24 of the EPA gives overriding force to all rules framed under the Act. Rule 3(3A) requires every industry, operation or process to comply with the minimum national standards set out in Schedule VI to the EPR from 1 January 1994. Schedule VI, Part D contains general emission standards which would apply to coke ovens. Once these standards are notified by the Central Government, they apply nation-wide, without need for the state PCBs to re-issue these standards under the Air Act or the Water Act. If the EPR standards applied, could the Assam board have issued a closure direction under section 31A of the *Air Act* based on *EPR norms*? While the court may have looked to the EPR to fill the gap in the Air Act standards, this may not have changed the outcome of the appeal: It is difficult to justify a section 31A closure direction in the absence of measuring equipment to analyse the composition of the emissions released by the firm.

The judgment is also marred by a misconstruction of section 31A. The division bench observes that a direction by the board under section 31A may be issued only where the Central Government has first issued a direction in that behalf. This appears incorrect. A Central Government direction is not a condition precedent for the issue of a direction by the state board; but where the board issues a direction, any such direction is 'subject to' overriding Central Government orders.

No less remarkable is the restrictive interpretation placed on section 31A by the Delhi High Court in *Gopi Nath Pvt Ltd v Department of Environment*.[43] The petitioner ran an iron casting business in a residential premises without obtaining consent under the Air Act. Relying on its power to issue 'any directions in writing to any person, officer or authority' in the performance of its functions under the Air Act, the respondent directed the magistrate to seal the offending unit. Quashing the direction, the High Court held that though section 31A enabled the board to direct '*closure*' or discontinuance of the objectionable activity, *sealing* the unit and preventing access was unauthorized.

In *Suma Traders v Chairman, Karnataka State Pollution Control Board*,[44] the High Court came down heavily on the KPCB. The petitioner challenged a closure order passed by the chairperson under section 31A of the Air Act. The impugned order was issued after residents complained against the air pollution caused by the firm's food grain processing plant. The firm challenged the order on the sole ground that the chairperson was incompetent to issue orders under section 31A in the absence of the proper delegation of authority by the board under section 15 of the Air Act. On the board conceding that there was no delegation in favour of the chairperson, the court held that the impugned order was passed in violation of

---

42 When the board relied on a notification dated 11 July 1996 which declared that the Assam board would follow the CPCB standards issued from time to time, the High Court held that the notification could not be relied upon since it was issued after the closure noticed dated 15 November 1995. Moreover, it appears that the notification was not published in accordance with law. The court also rejected the board's attempt to support its order on the basis of National Ambient Air Quality Standards.

43 1998 (72) DEL L T 536.

44 AIR 1998 KAR 8.

the provisions and amounted to a misuse of statutory power. The judge wondered whether the incumbent was suitable for the post of chairperson and imposed personal costs on her, assessed at Rs. 2,500.[45]

In equally galling circumstances, the Gujarat High Court was more restrained in its approach. N J Industries was acquitted in an Air Act prosecution because the Gujarat PCB failed to produce before the magistrate the Official Gazette declaring Ahmedabad as an 'air pollution control area' and was also unable to produce any local newspaper where the declaration was notified.[46]

In 2011, Ramco Industries established its factory to manufacture asbestos fibre cement sheets, having secured an environmental clearance and a consent to establish the unit. The industry operated for five years but, in 2016, the chairperson of the Bihar PCB rejected the consent renewal application. While Ramco appealed the refusal, the chairperson ordered the unit to shut down operations by issuing directions under section 31A of the Air Act. The High Court set aside the closure order holding that such a drastic direction could not have been made without first granting an opportunity and a hearing to the company. Moreover, absent express delegation by the PCB of its power under section 31A to the chairperson, she could not exercise such power.[47]

D. THE ARAVALLI HILLS, STONE QUARRYING, STUBBLE BURNING, FIREWORKS

I. ARAVALLI HILLS

The Supreme Court has made several efforts to reduce pollution and improve the quality of Delhi's environment. These efforts have extended to relocating industries away from the city,[48] reducing vehicular emissions,[49] controlling construction dust[50] and banning the burning of garbage, leaves, and crop and agricultural waste.[51] Likewise, the court has endeavoured to control mining activity at the ancient Aravalli Hills. Apart from quarry dust sullying Delhi's air, mining the hills was dismantling a natural bulwark that prevents expansion of the desert into Delhi. On 18 March 2004, the Supreme Court sketched the geological and natural features of this range:

> The Aravallis, the most distinctive and ancient mountain chain of peninsular India, mark the site of one of the oldest geological formations in the world. Heavily eroded and with exposed outcrops of slate rock and granite, it has summits reaching 4950 feet above sea level. Due to its geological location, the Aravalli range harbours a mix of Saharan, Ethiopian, peninsular, oriental and even Malayan elements of flora and fauna. In the early part of [the last] century, the Aravallis were well wooded. There were dense forests with waterfalls and one could encounter a large number of wild animals. Today, the changes in the environment at Aravalli

---

[45] Under the Water Act, the Gujarat High Court has upheld the chairperson's right to accord sanction to prosecute a polluter where the state board delegates its function to her. *Gujarat Pollution Control Board v Indian Chemicals Manufacturer* 1990 (2) Guj L R 1306.

[46] *Dayalbhai Solanki v N J Industries* 1996 (1) Guj L Her 466.

[47] *Ramco Industries Ltd v The Bihar State Pollution Control Board* MANU/BH/0163/2017. On the requirement of natural justice see *Gunavathi v The Chairman, Tamil Nadu Pollution Control Board* 2006 (4) Law Weekly 302.

[48] *M C Mehta v Union of India* AIR 1996 SC 2231.

[49] *M C Mehta v Union of India* (1998) 6 SCC 63.

[50] *M C Mehta v Union of India* (2016) 4 SCC 269, 294, 295.

[51] *M C Mehta v Union of India* (2016) 4 SCC 269, 294, 296.

are severe. Though one finds a number of tree species in the hills, timber-quality trees have almost disappeared.[52]

Recognizing the harm that stone mining was causing the environment, on 7 May 1992 the Ministry of Environment and Forests (MoEF) issued a notification restricting operations in the Aravallis:

> Now, therefore, in exercise of the powers conferred by sub-section (1) and clause (v) of sub-section (2) of section 3 of the Environment (Protection) Act, 1986 (29 of 1986), read with rule 5 of the Environment (Protection) Rules, 1986 the Central Government hereby prohibits the carrying on of the following process and operations, except with its prior permission, in the areas specified in the table appended to this notification: ...
>
> (ii) (a) all new mining operations including renewals of mining leases;
> (b) existing mining leases in sanctuaries/national parks and areas covered under Project Tiger; and/or
> (c) mining is being done without permission of the competent authority;
>
> (iii) cutting of trees; ...
>
> 2. Any person who desires to undertake any of the abovementioned processes or operations in the said areas, shall submit an application to the [MoEF] specifying, *inter alia*, details of the area and proposed process or operation. He shall also furnish an environment impact statement and an environmental management plan along with the application and such other information as may be required by the Central Government for considering the application.
> 3. [MoEF] shall, having regard to the guidelines issued by it from time to time for giving effect to the provisions of the said Act, grant permission within a period of three months from the date of receipt of the application or where further information has been asked for from the applicant, within a period of three months from the date of the receipt of such information, or refuse permission within the said time on the basis of the impact of the proposed process or operation on the environment in the said area....

This notification covered the Gurgaon District near Delhi where a part of the Aravalli range is located.

On 27 January 1994, the MoEF issued a statutory notification under the EPA, introducing for the first time in India a statutory environmental impact assessment (EIA) regime. This notification (as amended 4 May 1994) mandated EIA for mining projects in respect of major minerals with leases of more than 5 hectares.[53]

On 29 December 1999, the MoEF delegated its powers under the 7 May 1992 notification to the states of Haryana and Rajasthan. Each of the states was required to constitute an Expert Committee (to advise the state on EIA) as well as a monitoring committee (to ensure compliance with the conditions in the environmental clearance). The states were also directed to prepare suitable master plans integrating these environmental concerns. On 28 February 2003, the Central Government withdrew the delegation in favour of the state governments because most of the mines in the states were found to be operating in violation of the approved plans.

---

52 *M C Mehta v Union of India* (2004) 12 SCC 118, 172.

53 The distinction between major minerals and minor minerals may be traced to Entry 54, List 1, Schedule VII read with Article 246 of the Constitution of India and the Mines and Minerals (Development and Regulation) Act, 1957. While the 1994 notification was limited to mining major minerals, the 7 May 1992 notification, specific to Aravallis, covered all mining.

> [M]ining operations were carried out unscientifically with the sole aim of maximizing profits which resulted in indiscriminate scattering of the overburden, wasteful manner of mining with complete disregard to mineral conservation aspect, rendering reclamation of the mined area impossible.[54]

On 6 May 2002, the Supreme Court responded to an application made by the Delhi Ridge Management Board seeking an embargo on mining activities and pumping of groundwater in the belt falling within 5 kms from the Delhi–Haryana border on the Haryana side of the ridge. The court issued an ad-interim order:

> [W]ithin 48 hours from today the Chief Secretary, Government of Haryana is directed to stop all mining activities and pumping of groundwater in and from an area up to 5 km from the Delhi-Haryana border in the Haryana side of the ridge and also in the Aravalli hills.[55]

On 29 and 30 October 2002, in the *Forest Conservation* case,[56] the court ordered:

> ***Illegal mining in Aravallis***
>
> ... We, prohibit and ban all mining activity in the entire Aravalli hills. This ban is not limited only to the hills encircling Kote and Alampur Villages but extends to the entire hill range of Aravalli from Dholpur to Rajasthan. The Chief Secretary, State of Haryana and Chief Secretary, State of Rajasthan are directed to ensure that no mining activity in the Aravalli hills is carried out, especially, in that part which has been regarded as forest area or protected under the Environment (Protection) Act.

The reasons for this ban were supplied by the court more than six years later:

> The question to be answered at the outset is why did this Court impose a complete ban on mining in the Aravalli range falling in the State of Haryana which broadly falls in District Gurgaon and District Faridabad, including Mewat?
>
> The statistical data placed before this Court indicated that, in October 2002 twenty-six mines were inspected which indicated wide-scale non-compliance with statutory rules and regulations applicable to mines. Broadly stated, most of these mines failed to obtain environmental clearances. Most of these mines failed to submit the environmental management plan. In some cases, the status of mining indicated below groundwater table. Mining pits were turned into huge groundwater lakes. No efforts were made to create plantation. Broadly, these were silica sand mines. In some cases, even groundwater stood extracted. Deep mining pits with large water bodies were detected. Huge amounts of overburden were also seen in the area. These are some of the defects which were highlighted by EPCA[57] in various reports as far back as October 2002. These non-compliances have also been highlighted with the names of the mines meticulously [in *M C Mehta*].[58]
>
> It is important to note that by the Notification dated 7-5-1992 issued by MoEF under section 3(2)(*v*) of the Environment (Protection) Act, 1986 ('the EP Act', for short), as amended, all new mining operations including renewal leases stood banned. The notification further laid down the procedure for taking prior permission before undertaking mining activity.
>
> At this stage it may be noted that by the notification dated 27-1-1994 as amended on 4-5-1994 issued by MoEF under section 3(2) of the EP Act, 1986 read with rule 6, environment

---

[54] *M C Mehta v Union of India* (2009) 6 SCC 142, 150.
[55] *M C Mehta v Union of India* (2004) 12 SCC 188.
[56] *T N Godavarman Thirumulpad (57) v Union of India* (2008) 16 SCC 337.
[57] EPCA is an abbreviation for the Environment Pollution (Prevention and Control) Authority for the National Capital Region constituted on 29 January 1998 under the EPA. EPCA was dissolved by clause 26 of the Commission for Air Quality Management in National Capital Region and Adjoining Areas Ordinance of 2020. Upon the 2020 Ordinance lapsing, it was replaced by Ordinance No. 4 of 2021 which had a similar repealing provision in clause 29.
[58] *M C Mehta v Union of India* (2004) 12 SCC 118, 143.

impact assessment (EIA) before commencement of any mining operation became mandatory. Therefore, by order dated 29-10-2002/30-10-2002,[59] when this Court found large-scale mining without approved plans, it decided to ban all mining activities in the Aravalli range.[60]

On 16 December 2002, the court considered applications by Rajasthan, Haryana and mine owners seeking a modification of the embargo imposed on 29 and 30 October 2002. The court ordered:

> On consideration of the report of the Central Empowered Committee dated 14-12-2002, we issue the following further directions:
>
> (1) Mining may be permitted in forest areas where specific prior approval under section 2 of the Forest (Conservation) Act, 1980 has been accorded by the Ministry of Environment and Forests, Government of India. However, in view of this Court's order dated 14-2-2000 passed in IA No. 548 no mining activity is permitted within areas which are notified as sanctuary, national park under sections 18, 35 of the Wild Life (Protection) Act, 1972 or any sanctuary, national park or game reserve declared under any other Act or the Rules made thereunder even if prior approval have been obtained from the MoEF under the FC Act in such an area.
>
> (2) Under the Notification dated 29-11-1999 issued under section 23 of the Environment (Protection) Act for certain districts including Gurgaon District in the State of Haryana, the Ministry has delegated power to grant approval for mining purposes to the State. The mining activities are being regulated under the Notification dated 7-5-1992 issued by the Ministry of Environment and Forest. We direct that, for the time being, no mining shall be permitted within the areas of Gurgaon District in the State of Haryana where mining is regulated under the Notification dated 7-5-1992 issued under section 3 of the Environment (Protection) Act, pursuant to the permission granted after 29-11-1999.
>
> Meanwhile, the Central Empowered Committee which is examining the matter will give its suggestions within a period of six weeks. On the receipt of those suggestions, the prayers made by the applicants for modification of the order dated 29-10-2002/30-10-2002 insofar as Gurgaon District is concerned will be considered.
>
> (3) No mining activity would be permitted in respect of areas where there is a dispute of applicability of the FC Act,[61] till such time the dispute is resolved or approval under the FC Act is accorded, in addition to order already passed in Writ Petition No. 4677 of 1985.
>
> For the present, no mining will be permitted in the areas for which notification under sections 4 and 5 of the Punjab Land Preservation Act, 1900 have been issued for regulating the breaking up of the land, etc. and such lands are or were recorded as 'forest' in government records even if the notification period has expired, unless there is approval under the FC Act....

The 6 May 2002 interim prohibitory order was sustained by the Supreme Court in a lengthy judgment rendered on 18 March 2004. We carry a short excerpt.

M C MEHTA v UNION OF INDIA

(2004) 12 SCC 188

Y K Sabharwal, J: The main question to be examined in these matters is whether the mining activity in area up to 5 kilometres from the Delhi-Haryana border on the Haryana side of the ridge and also in the Aravalli hills causes environment degradation and what

59 *T N Godavarman Thirumulpad v Union of India* (2008) 16 SCC 337.
60 (2009) 6 SCC 142, 149.
61 Forest (Conservation) Act of 1980.

directions are required to be issued. The background in which the question has come up for consideration may first be noticed....

IA No. 1785 of 2001 has been filed by the Delhi Ridge Management Board praying that the Government of Haryana be directed to stop all mining activities and pumping of groundwater in and from the area up to 5 km from Delhi-Haryana border on the Haryana side of the ridge, *inter alia*, stating that in the larger interest of maintaining the ecological balance of the environment and protecting Asola Bhatti Wildlife Sanctuary and the ridge located in Delhi and adjoining Haryana, it was necessary to stop mining. In the application, it has been averred that Asola Bhatti Wildlife Sanctuary is located on the southern ridge which is one of the oldest mountain ranges of the world and represents the biogeographical outer layer of the Aravalli mountain range which is one of the most protected areas in the country. The sanctuary is significant as it is instrumental in protecting the green lungs of the National Capital of Delhi and acts as a carbon sink for the industrial and vehicular emissions of the country's capital which is witnessing rapid growth in its pollution level each year. The ridge, it is averred, is a potential shelter belt against advancing desertification and has been notified as a wildlife sanctuary and reserve forest by the Government of the National Capital Territory of Delhi. Regarding the mining activities, it is averred that for extraction of *badarpur* (silica sand), there is large-scale mining activity on the Haryana side just adjacent to the wildlife sanctuary of the ridge which activities threaten the sanctuary's habitat and also pumping of large quantity of groundwater from mining pits. It was also stated that the groundwater level was being depleted as a result of the mining activity. Further, the quarry dust that comes out of mining pits is a serious health hazard for the human population living nearby and also the wild animals inhabiting the sanctuary pointing out that the mining and extraction of groundwater had been banned in the National Capital Territory of Delhi and the ridge being protected as per the order of this Court, it was necessary, that the ridge on the Haryana side was also protected—that being the extension of the range and, therefore, mining, withdrawal of groundwater and destruction of flora, etc. should also be restricted outside Delhi or at least up to 5 km from Delhi-Haryana border towards Haryana.

On 6-5-2002, this Court directed the Chief Secretary, Government of Haryana to stop, within 48 hours, all mining activities and pumping of groundwater in and from an area up to 5 km from the Delhi-Haryana border on the Haryana side of the ridge and also in the Aravalli hills. The question to be considered is whether the order should be made absolute or vacated or modified.

Our examination of the issues is confined to the effect on the ecology of the mining activity carried on within an area of 5 km of Delhi-Haryana border on the Haryana side in areas falling within the districts of Faridabad and Gurgaon and in the Aravalli hills within Gurgaon district. The question is whether the mining activity deserves to be absolutely banned or permitted on compliance of stringent conditions and by monitoring it to prevent the environmental pollution.

[The court set out the recommendations made by the EPCA in its reports made after site visits and inspection of 26 mines. The mines extracted diverse minerals including silica sand, china clay, ordinary sand and masonry stone. The court noted the suggestions of the CEC. The judgment sets out provisions of the Constitution, various statutes and refers to an assessment by the Central Mine Planning and Design Institute Ltd (CMPDI).]

The [EIA] notification has been reproduced in the earlier part of the judgment. It, *inter alia*, applies to mining projects (major minerals) with leases of more than 5 hectares. It can neither be disputed nor has been disputed that the notification is mandatory. It, *inter alia*, provides that on and from the date of its publication in the Official Gazette expansion or modernisation of any activity (if pollution load is to exceed the existing one) or a new project listed in Schedule I of this notification shall not be undertaken in any part of India unless it has been accorded environmental clearance by the Central Government in accordance with the procedure specified therein. The contention urged on behalf of the leaseholders is that the leases in question do not relate to expansion or modernisation of any activity as postulated by the notification. Further, it is contended, that the notification applies to 'a new project' which means that it will apply to mining lease granted after issue of notification. It has been strenuously contended that the renewal of existing mining lease is neither 'an expansion' nor 'modernisation' nor is it a 'new project' and, therefore, the notification will have no applicability at the time of consideration of the renewal of the lease. Reliance has been placed on a decision of this Court in *Narmada Bachao Andolan v Union of India*, (2000) 10 SCC 664 holding that the notification is clearly prospective and, *inter alia*, prohibits the undertaking of a new project listed in Schedule I without prior environmental clearance from the Central Government. The contention urged was that since in *Narmada* case, where construction had commenced nearly 8 years prior to the notification, the very same notification was not held applicable. On the same analogy, it cannot have any applicability to the leases granted prior to the issue of notification.

* * *

In *Rural Litigation and Entitlement Kendra v State of U P*, (1989) Supp (1) SCC 504 agreeing with views expressed in *Ambica Quarry Works v State of Gujarat*, (1987) 1 SCC 213, it was held that the FC Act applies to renewals as well and even if there was a provision for renewal in the lease agreement on exercise of the lessee's option, the requirement of the Act had to be satisfied before such renewal could be granted. In *State of M P v Krishnadas Tikaram*, (1995) Supp (1) SCC 587, these two decisions were relied upon and it was held that even the renewal of lease cannot be granted without the prior concurrence of the Central Government. It is settled law that the grant of renewal is a fresh grant and must be consistent with law.

We are unable to accept the contention that the notification dated 27-1-1994 would not apply to leases which come up for consideration for renewal after issue of the notification. The notification mandates that the mining operation shall not be undertaken in any part of India unless environmental clearance by the Central Government has been accorded. The clearance under the notification is valid for a period of five years. In none of the leases the requirements of the notification were complied with either at the stage of initial grant of the mining lease or at the stage of renewal. Some of the leases were fresh leases granted after issue of the notification. Some were cases of renewal. No mining operation can commence without obtaining environmental impact assessment in terms of the notification.

[The court constituted a monitoring committee comprising government officials as well as noted environmentalist. The monitoring committee was directed to inspect the mines and to file a report containing suggestions for the recommencement of mining in individual cases.]

Though notification dated 27-1-1994 is not applicable to minor minerals, but having regard to what we have discussed above in regard to degradation of environment and the required standard about the risk of harm to the environment or to human health to be decided in public interest according to 'reasonable person's test', and the report of CMPDI, we direct the Monitoring Committee to examine the leases granted for extraction of minor minerals in light thereof and file its report. The Committee would, however, bear in mind that the notification dated 27-1-1994 as such is not applicable to these leases.

* * *

1. The order dated 6-5-2002 as clarified hereinbefore cannot be vacated or varied before consideration of the report of the Monitoring Committee constituted by this judgment.
2. The notification of environment assessment clearance dated 27-1-1994 is applicable also when renewal of mining lease is considered after issue of the notification.
3. On the facts of the case, the mining activity in areas covered under sections 4 and/or 5 of the Punjab Land Preservation Act, 1900 cannot be undertaken without approval under the Forest (Conservation) Act, 1980.
4. No mining activity can be carried out on area over which plantation has been undertaken under the Aravalli Project by utilisation of foreign funds.
5. The mining activity can be permitted only on the basis of sustainable development and on compliance of stringent conditions.
6. The Aravalli hill range has to be protected at any cost. In case despite stringent conditions, there is an adverse irreversible effect on the ecology in the Aravalli hill range

area, at a later date, the total stoppage of mining activity in the area may have to be considered. For similar reasons such step may have to be considered in respect of mining in Faridabad district as well.

7. MoEF is directed to prepare a short-term and long-term action plan for the restoration of environmental quality of Aravalli hills in Gurgaon district having regard to what is stated in final report of CMPDI within four months.
8. Violation of any of the conditions would entail the risk of cancellation of mining lease. The mining activity shall continue only on strict compliance of the stipulated conditions.

Five years after the judgment excerpted above, the court revisited the prohibition on mining in the Aravalli range. The *M C Mehta* case referred to in the next judgment is a reference to the 18 March 2004 decision.

M C MEHTA v UNION OF INDIA
with
T N GODAVARMAN THIRUMULPAD v UNION OF INDIA
(2009) 6 SCC 142

S H KAPADIA, J: Has the situation (optimisation of land and ecological degradation in an area admeasuring approximately 448 sq km in the Aravalli hill range falling in the districts of Faridabad and Gurgaon, including Mewat) predicted in … the judgment in *M C Mehta case* come about so as to warrant total stoppage of mining activity as stated in [concluding paragraph (6) of the said judgment]; and if so, what should be the duration of such ban/stoppage?

In this connection, at the very outset, we quote [the relevant portions] of the said judgment, which read as follows:

> 'It may be reiterated that if, despite stringent conditions, the degradation of environment continues and reaches a stage of no-return, this Court may have to consider, at a later date, the closure of mining activity in areas where there is such a risk….
>
> 6. The Aravalli hill range has to be protected at any cost. In case despite stringent conditions, there is an adverse irreversible effect on the ecology in the Aravalli hill range area, at a later date, the total stoppage of mining activity in the area may have to be considered. For similar reasons such step may have to be considered in respect of mining in Faridabad District as well….'

Consequences of continuous violation of the Rules

As stated above, the Notification dated 7-5-1992 was passed with a view to strictly implement the measures to protect the ecology of the Aravalli range. It was followed more in its breach.

The Aravallis, the most distinctive and ancient mountain chain of Peninsular India, mark the site of one of the oldest geological formations in the world. Due to its geological location, desertification is stopped and it prevents expansion of the desert into Delhi. On account of extensive mining on a disproportionate scale, without taking remedial measures has resulted in irreversible changes in the environment at Aravallis. It is in the aforestated background that any mining activity came to be banned under the order dated 29-10-2002/30-10-2002.

Even as far back as 2002, the environmental problems in the Aravalli range in Gurgaon District came to be identified. Remedial measures including pollution control guidelines and action plan for various stakeholders came to be suggested by CMPDI. Though guidelines for mining operations came to be issued by the State Government, the compliance was not there. Moreover, there was no mechanism to upgrade the mining technologies to minimise the impact due to mining in the eco-sensitive zones.

CMPDI also noticed that in the Aravalli hills a large number of activities, operations of stone-crushers and deforestation had caused environmental degradation even in 2002 which is clear from ... the above judgment in *M C Mehta case* and the tragedy is that despite all warnings, the mines continued their operations without any environment management plan. That, right from 18-3-2004, when this Court pronounced the judgment in *M C Mehta case*, till date, a number of reports came to be submitted as the Court tried to balance mining activity on the one hand with protection of environment on the other hand. In fact, in ... the said judgment, this Court stated that so long as it is possible to undertake mining operations on the sustainable development principle, the Court should not impose complete ban on mining as it generates revenue for the State. However, ... a warning was given that if despite imposition of stringent conditions, the degradation of environment continues and reaches a stage of no return, then this Court may have to consider at a later date the closure of mining activity. This prediction has come true. The consequence is that the State now has decided to close the mining activity.

[This warning] is also important from another angle. The judgment in *M C Mehta case* has left it to this Court to consider at a later date the closure of mining activity. Even in [concluding paragraph (6)], this Court observed that mining activity can be permitted only on the basis of sustainable development and on compliance with stringent conditions as the Aravalli hill range has to be protected at any cost and in case despite stringent conditions, mining results in an irreversible consequence on the ecology in the said area then at a later date the total stoppage of mining activity may have to be considered. In other words, in the judgment of this Court in *M C Mehta case*, a window was left open for this Court to impose a complete ban on mining operations if an emergent situation arises.

The decision to ban/suspend mining in the above area has been taken by the State of Haryana. In the said meeting held on 7-1-2009, a consensus has been reached between CEC and the State of Haryana to declare the entire Aravalli hill range falling in the districts of Faridabad and Gurgaon, including Mewat as a 'Prohibited Zone' so far as mining of major minerals is concerned. The decision of the State of Haryana is also supported by MoEF....

Breaches

As stated above, as far back as 18-3-2004 this Court noticed that in large number of cases no requisite clearances for mining operations were obtained. No environmental management plan was prepared. In some cases, mining operations were carried out below groundwater table. Groundwater was even extracted without obtaining clearances (see *M C Mehta case*). The paradox is that there is no dearth of enactments, the problem lies in non-compliance and as a result, mining on extensive scale without approved plans and without taking remedial measures has led to land and ecological degradation.

At this stage, one point needs to be highlighted. Over the years, the focus was on individual mining leases. Over the years, this Court tried to balance mining operations vis-à-vis environmental protection. Even after noticing non-compliance with the above Rules, as far back as 2004, this Court, after sounding a warning to the existing mines to comply with the Rules, did not suggest a complete ban on mining operations so long as it was possible to undertake such operations on the principles of sustainable development. However, the position did not improve. The position worsened. In the circumstances, the Court has now decided not to focus only on individual sites but to take a macro view of the matter, particularly while deciding the question of suspending mining operations. The Court is required to take a holistic view.

It is important to note that most of the applicants who are seeking to mine today in the virgin areas have mined-out areas in the past without taking remedial measures. They have abandoned the sites after mining without rehabilitation of the degraded lands and the consequence is devastation.

As stated above, in 2004 this Court detected many cases where operations were done without proper environment management plan, mining plan, etc. In this order we are not examining faults of individual user agencies. Suffice it to state that when these mines operated without proper clearances in the past they have left pits/quarries without reclamation and without compliance with the provisions of the mining plan. Today, it is too late in the day to say that leases granted subsequently complied with various clearances because these lessees which operated mines earlier have left the pits/quarries open to the sky without taking remedial measures including reclamation.

In this order what we are emphasising is extensive mining and not individual unauthorised mining because even in the case of former no steps to rehabilitate were ever taken. The result is that mining operations have been carried out on a disproportionate scale in the Aravalli hills mainly in Gurgaon and Faridabad, including Mewat in the State of Haryana. The satellite images indicate the devastation caused to the area by the extensive mining operations. Extraordinary situations demand extraordinary remedies. In the circumstances, we are of the view that mining operations should be immediately suspended in the above area.

[The court recorded submissions on behalf of individual mines but declined to accept these submissions and preferred to take 'a macro view based on the satellite images'. The miners contended that termination of mining leases ought to be carried out in accordance with section 4A of the Mines and Minerals (Development and Regulation) Act, 1957 and that the court could not bypass the statutory procedure.]

We find no merit in the above arguments. As stated above, in the past when mining leases were granted, requisite clearances for carrying out mining operations were not obtained which have resulted in land and environmental degradation. Despite such breaches, approvals had been granted for subsequent slots because in the past the authorities have not taken into account the macro effect of such wide-scale land and environmental degradation caused by the absence of remedial measures (including rehabilitation plan). Time has now come, therefore, to suspend mining in the above area till statutory provisions for restoration and reclamation are duly complied with, particularly in cases where pits/quarries have been left abandoned.

Environment and ecology are national assets. They are subject to intergenerational equity. Time has now come to suspend all mining in the above area on sustainable development principle which is part of Articles 21, 48-A and 51-A(*g*) of the Constitution of India. In fact, these articles have been extensively discussed in the judgment in *M C Mehta case* which keeps the option of imposing a ban in future open.

Mining within the principle of sustainable development comes within the concept of 'balancing' whereas mining beyond the principle of sustainable development comes within the concept of 'banning'. It is a matter of degree. Balancing of the mining activity with environment protection and banning such activity are two sides of the same principle of sustainable development. They are parts of precautionary principle.

At this stage, we may also note that under section 13(2)(qq) of the 1957 Act, rules have been framed for rehabilitation of flora and other vegetation destroyed by reason of any prospecting or mining operations. Under section 18 of the 1957 Act, rules have been framed for conservation and systematic development of minerals in India and for the protection of environment by preventing or controlling pollution caused by prospecting or mining operations which also form part of the Mineral Concession Rules, 1960 and the Mineral Conservation and Development Rules, 1988.

Under rule 27(1)(s)(i) of the Mineral Concession Rules, 1960 every lessee is required to take measures for planting of trees not less than twice the number destroyed by mining operations. *Under the Mineral Conservation and Development Rules, 1988, vide rule 34, mandatory provisions for reclamation and rehabilitation of lands are made for every holder of prospecting licence or mining lease to be undertaken and that work has to be completed by the lessee/licensee before abandoning the mine or prospect.*

Similarly, under rule 37 of the Mineral Conservation and Development Rules, 1988 the lessee/licensee has to calibrate the air pollution within permissible limits specified under the EP Act, 1986 as well as the Air (Prevention and Control of Pollution) Act, 1981. Under the said Rules of 1988, the most important guidelines are Guidelines 25.26.3, 25.26.4, 25.26.5 and 25.26.6. These guidelines deal with reclamation, planning and implementation, restoration strategy, principles of rehabilitation, rehabilitation of mined-out sites and methods of reclamations.... It may be noted that there are two steps to be taken in the method of reclamation, namely, technical reclamation and biological reclamation. *The most important aspect of the above guidelines is making of a rehabilitation plan.*

Conclusion

None of the above provisions have been complied with. In the circumstance, by the present order, we hereby suspend all mining operations in the Aravalli hill range falling in the State of Haryana within the area of approximately 448 sq km in the districts of Faridabad and Gurgaon, including Mewat till the reclamation plan duly certified by the State of Haryana, MoEF and CEC is prepared in accordance with the above statutory provisions contained in various enactments enumerated above as well as in terms of the rules framed thereunder and the guidelines. The said plan shall state what steps are needed to be taken to rehabilitate (including reclamation) followed by status reports on steps taken by the authorities pursuant to the said plan....

NOTES AND QUESTIONS

1. This case brings out how dysfunctional the regulatory system is. Though the Union Government, states of Haryana and Rajasthan, the CPCB, EPCA are all anxious to protect the Aravalli range, they appear incapable of effectively implementing protective measures without intervention by the Supreme Court. The initial injunction passed on 6 May 2002 was issued at the request of the Delhi Ridge Management Board. The Delhi Ridge is an elevated geological feature at the tail end of the Aravallis and the board is a non-statutory agency responsible for protecting it. Despite its official status, the board was unable to persuade other government agencies and consequently applied to the Supreme Court.

Is the problem a design fault, a personnel issue or something else? How would you redesign the regulatory framework to make it more responsive and effective? Can you remodel the agencies to make them self-reliant and potent without as ever leaning on a judicial crutch?

2. The Supreme Court judgments are unclear with respect to the application of the EIA notification of 1994. Despite holding that this notification applies only to major minerals and without expressly holding how this notification applies to ordinary sand, building stones, ordinary clay and other minor minerals,[62] the court directs the monitoring committee to keep

[62] '"Minor minerals" means building stones, gravel, ordinary clay, ordinary sand other than sand used for prescribed purposes, and any other mineral which the Central Government may, by notification, in

in view the notification. Is the court indirectly amending a statute? How is the monitoring committee to apply the EIA notification when the notification itself excludes minor minerals from its scope?

3. Does the Supreme Court have power to place a complete embargo on a lawful activity such as mining, absent any law to that effect? Is the court riding roughshod over the fundamental right to carry on business guaranteed under Article 19(1)(g)?

While the court would be entirely within its powers to issue directions for strict enforcement of laws enacted, can it travel beyond the rules and regulations and impose a complete ban on mining over an area of 448 sq kms? For the Supreme Court, is the only rule: 'There are no rules'?

4. Notice how the state governments were lax in implementing the 1992 notification, compelling the MoEF to reclaim the delegated power. This is an example of how a generally desirable policy of devolving power and responsibility to the states and local governments may fail because of poor state-level institutions or the disproportionate influence of local economic interests.

5. The court declares: 'Extraordinary situation demands extraordinary remedies'. It then applies a 'holistic' approach to trump the submissions of individual miners. Are there any discernible principles supporting the judgment of the court?

II. STONE QUARRYING

Limestone quarrying in the Dehradun Valley triggered the first major public interest environmental case in the Supreme Court.[63] The primary ecological concerns of the court were the devastation of forests, landslides and the impact of quarrying on the hydrological system in the Mussoorie Hill Range. In this section, we focus on air pollution problems caused by unregulated quarrying.

Over six months in 1993, a division bench of Himachal Pradesh High Court guided a public interest litigation to prevent stone crushing in the hills around Shimla. Assisted by a team of *amici curiae*, the court framed a scheme that would protect Shimla's environs while cushioning the economic impact on the quarry owners.

COURT ON ITS OWN MOTION v STATE OF HIMACHAL PRADESH
1994 For L T 103

> Kamlesh Sharma, J: By way of this writ petition, this Court took *suo motu* cognizance of the reports appearing in the daily edition of the Tribune on 31 December 1992 and Indian Express on 10 January 1993, that illegal mining and installation of stone crushers have caused havoc at twelve places in the suburbs of Shimla, including Kamla Nagar, Tara Devi, Dhalli Nal Dehra and Choora Chowki. Kamala Nagar is also known as Bhatha Kuffar.
>
> [The court traced the stages through which the case developed. Interim injunctions prohibiting quarrying were issued against the mine lessees but were partially modified. The Himachal Pradesh PCB was repeatedly directed to file detailed affidavits, the first two efforts by the board being 'deficient'. The court recorded the opinion of the Controller of Mines that the air pollution was 'caused mainly due to mechanical operation of stone crushers and not from manual extraction of stones, in which case the emission of dust remains within the standards of Ambient Air Quality.' In a development parallel to the case, the state government

the Official Gazette, declare to be a minor mineral.' Section 3(e), Mines and Minerals (Development and Regulation) Act of 1957.

[63] *Rural Litigation and Entitlement Kendra, Dehradun v State of Uttar Pradesh* AIR 1985 SC 652.

constituted a high level committee headed by the Chief Secretary to look into environmental degradation caused by mining operations and polluting industries in the state. The committee recommended that Shimla and its suburbs be declared an Environment Protection Zone by the Central Government under rule 5 of the Environment (Protection) Rules of 1986. The High Court impleaded the committee and sought its recommendations in relation to the quarries around Shimla. In light of the deliberations of the committee, the state government urged the High Court to confirm the interim injunction in the interest of local residents, tourists and the environment. 'The lessees may apply for suitable sites outside the Zone for mining and establishment of crushers which will be considered on priority.' The respondent lessees (Nos. 9 to 27) resisted the injunction claiming that they had the requisite permits and were operating the mines manually.]

[T]he, next question [is] whether respondents No. 9 to 27 should be permitted to work their mines/quarries and to operate their stone crushers till the Shimla Environment Protection Zone is created. From the proceedings of the third meeting of the High Level Committee held on 11 May 1993, it appears that while it accepted the recommendations of the Sub-Committee headed by Sh. H.C. Sharma, Additional Chief Conservator of Forests, it did not keep in view that creation of Shimla Environment Protection Zone by the Central Government will take minimum six months' time and what will happen during the interregnum to the business of respondents No. 9 to 27 and how the needs of common man as well as the Government will be met who are consumers for their produce, that is, stones, grit and sand for the construction of buildings, roads, bridges and other development projects....

It is correct that for the larger public interest of protection of environment and ecological balance, the interests of a group of individuals should be sacrificed but eyes cannot be closed to the hard realities that mines and industries, even if hazardous to the environment and the health of the people, are required to be worked and set up since they are essential for economic development and advancement of the well being of the people. All efforts are required to be made, to minimise the element of hazards or risk to the environment and people by taking all necessary steps by locating such industries and mines at such places and adopting such safety measures which will pose least risk and hazard to environment and people. [The High Court noted the stands of the state government and the state board as well as the latter's recommendations for controlling air pollution.]

The result of the above discussion is that writ petition is disposed of with the following directions:

(1) The state government will approach the Central Government for creation of Shimla Environment Protection Zone by issuing notification under clause (v), sub-section (2) of section 3 of the Environment (Protection) Act, 1986 read with clause (a), sub-rule (3) of rule 5 of the Environment (Protection) Rules, 1986 within a period of fifteen days from the date of this order. The state government will depute a responsible officer not below the rank of Deputy Secretary to pursue the matter with the Central Government and supply all necessary documents and material required by it without any delay.

(2) The Government of India will finally decide and issue the notification, if it deems necessary, for creating Shimla Environment Protection Zone, within a period of six months from the date of receipt of the request of the state government. Since the Central Government is not a party to this writ petition, we direct that it be impleaded as party respondent No. 29 and a copy of this judgment be sent to it through the Secretary, Ministry of Environment, Government of India, New Delhi.

(3) Respondent No. 10 and 13 to 27 are permitted to work their mines and operate their stone crushers for a period of six months from the date of this judgment or till the notification creating Shimla Environment Protection Zone is issued by the Central Government, whichever is earlier. For working their mines and operating their stone crushers, they will strictly follow all laws, rules, instructions issued/to be issued by the state government for mining soil and forest conservation and other purposes and also the H P State Pollution Control Board for the prevention of environmental

degradation. The period of six months will not be extended even if the notification creating Shimla Environment Protection Zone is not issued by the Central Government and mining lessees and stone crusher owners are not rehabilitated on alternative site(s) within the period of six months. There will be no mines/quarries and stone crushers in the proposed Shimla Environment Protection Zone on the expiry of the period of six months from the date of the judgment and the mines/quarries and Stone Crushers of respondents No. 10 and 13 to 27 will be wound up.

(4) The state government is directed to rehabilitate respondents No. 10 and 13 to 27 on alternative site(s) by granting all necessary permissions within a period of six months....

NOTES AND QUESTIONS

1. In addition to the directions excerpted above, the High Court directed the lessees and stone crusher operators to contribute 20% of their gross profit to a fund to be used for restoring the scarred hills and afforestation.

2. The Shimla Environment Protection Zone was not notified. What factors might have stalled the move?

3. Several hill stations and mountain holiday destinations have been robbed of their charm by deforestation, poor town planning and sanitation, excessive tourist pressure and burgeoning hotels in response to the tourist influx. Among the earliest judicial efforts to stem the rot was the attempt to restore the Mussoorie Hills and Doon Valley in the *Dehradun Valley* case.[64] Other cases seeking to preserve hill station ecology are *M C Mehta v Kamal Nath*,[65] *Ajay Singh Rawat v Union of India*,[66] *Bombay Environmental Action Group v State of Maharashtra*[67] and *Bombay Environmental Action Group v State of Maharashtra*.[68]

4. Stone crushing operations around Delhi caught the attention of the Supreme Court on an application under Article 32 of the Constitution. MC Mehta objected to the quarrying because the dust particles polluted the air and the quarries violated town planning regulations.[69] The court directed the CPCB to inspect the plants and verify the allegations.[70] On 15 May 1992, the court issued a detailed order 'for the reasons to be recorded and pronounced at a later stage'.[71] Quarries in Delhi and in the surrounding areas of Haryana were told to close down in three months. Quarry owners operating without licences from the town planning authorities or who were issued closure orders under section 31A of the Air Act or section 5 of the Environment (Protection) Act of 1986 were directed to forthwith cease operations. The Haryana authorities were asked to allot alternative sites in a new 'crushing zone' located at a suitable distance from the capital. (It is unclear whether the court considered what might

---

64 *Rural Litigation and Entitlement Kendra v State of Uttar Pradesh* AIR 1985 SC 652.

65 (1997) 1 SCC 388, 415. Directions to the Himachal Pradesh PCB to inspect all hotels, institutions and factories in the Kullu-Manali areas and ensure that none of them discharged untreated effluents in the Beas River.

66 (1995) 3 SCC 266. Directions to preserve Nainital.

67 (1999) 2 BOM C R 243. Directions to preserve Mahabaleshwar.

68 (1999) 1 BOM C R 455. Quashing a letter of intent issued by the state to Sahara India Housing Ltd in respect of the proposed Sahara Lake City in Pune District.

69 *M C Mehta v Union of India (Stone Crushing)* (1992) Supp (2) SCC 85 and 86.

70 *Id.* at 87.

71 *M C Mehta v Union of India (Stone Crushing)* (1992) 3 SCC 256, 257. It is unclear whether any reasons followed. If so, the law reports appear to have missed them.

happen to the persons residing in and around the new 'crushing zone'). The Supreme Court prefaced its directions with this observation:

> We are conscious that environmental changes are the inevitable consequences of industrial development in our country, but at the same time the quality of environment cannot be permitted to be damaged by polluting air, water and land to such an extent that it becomes a health hazard for the residents of the area. We are constrained to record that Delhi Development Authority, Municipal Corporation of Delhi, Central Pollution Control Board and Delhi Pollution Control Committee have been wholly remiss in the performance of their statutory duties and have failed to protect the environment and control air pollution in the union territory of Delhi. Utter disregard to environment has placed Delhi in an unenviable position of being the world's third grubbiest, most polluted and unhealthy city as per the study conducted by the World Health Organisation. Needless to say that every citizen has a right to fresh air and live in pollution-free environment.[72]

Pushing the quarry operators away from Delhi and further into Haryana was fraught with danger. Haryana has an abysmal record for protecting bonded labourers working in stone quarries in the Faridabad District of the state. A few months earlier, the Supreme Court in *Bandhua Mukti Morcha v Union of India*[73] urged the state to ensure that 2,000 quarry workers received better health care, education and other facilities. Anticipating the orders in the *Stone Crushing* case, the court observed:

> The State of Haryana must come forward to play its role in a better way. As already pointed out these are quarries near about the industrial belt of Haryana and not far away from Delhi. Ecology is not only a local problem but must be taken to be a problem of Delhi also. Dust emanating from the working area in Haryana is bound to affect adversely the Delhi atmosphere. In fact, if adequate importance is given to the angle of pollution the industry itself has to be regulated or may have to be stopped.

The Haryana government permitted the quarry operators to relocate their operations in the new 'crushing zones' around Pall and Mohabatabad. Predictably, the operators were quick to despoil the environment around the new sites, forcing M C Mehta to revive the case in the Supreme Court in late 1995. On 20 November 1995, the court directed a team of scientists and environmental engineers from the CPCB to inspect the new locations. The report submitted to the court projected a dismal picture. The air pollution was intense, chiefly because the dust containment systems, although installed, were not being operated by any of the quarry owners and a water shortage prevented the sprinklers from being used. The report revealed that the mining operations were being conducted haphazardly and warned of an imminent ecological disaster. The Supreme Court directed the parties to arrange for the sprinkler water supply. The quarry owners were granted two months in which to install necessary pollution control devices and the state government was asked to lay a road to the quarrying zone besides implementing the suggestions and directions given by the CPCB.[74]

As a separate issue, one may wonder whether the Supreme Court of India can have the time and resources for the sort of micro-management described above.

5. Hiranand Stone Works ran a small stone crushing unit at village Pakartalla. Since 1990, the firm had operated under a consent issued by the Bihar PCB. In July 2000, the board required a 12 ft high wind-breaking wall to be built around the works and also laid conditions for housing the stone crusher, spraying water to suppress the dust and tree plantation. When

---

[72] *Id.*
[73] (1991) 4 SCC 177, 193, 195.
[74] *M C Mehta v Union of India (Delhi Stone Crushing)* 1996 (1) SCALE 29 (SP).

the board threatened to close the unit, Hiranand moved the High Court claiming that the conditions stood fulfilled. The single judge accepted the petition. He found that the refusal to grant consent was based on a misreading of the PCB's location policy. The policy which required industrial units to be located 200 metres from a highway was applicable to new units or existing units that sought expansion. This was clear from the opening words of the policy: 'Any person, who proposes to establish or expand or modernize or diversify any industrial unit or project in any part of the State of Bihar ...'

The PCB appealed to the division bench which reversed the single judge, relying on section 31A of the Air Act. The court reasoned:

> If the Board has the authority to issue directions for closure, prohibition or regulation of any industry, operation or process then it certainly has the power to direct shifting of the unit. The Board has simply asked the petitioner that it should close its operation and shift. If the petitioner is not agreeable to shift then the direction to close the unit would be a direction issued under section 31A of the Act and the petitioner would be bound to observe the said direction and close the unit for all times to come. In our opinion small technicalities should not defeat the public interest. If autonomy to some extent is not given to the Board, for every small thing it would be required to look at State Government. In fact in matters of pollution, the Board must be held to hold sufficient powers.... When the activity of the industries are dangerous or threat to public health then either it has to be closed or it has to be relocated or shifted from the existing operation area.
>
> In the present matter we are of the considered opinion that the appellants are absolutely justified and acted within their jurisdiction in issuing the guidelines. If the petitioner is of the opinion that he is not required to shift the existing unit then he must feel content to close the operations. The submission of the petitioner that he has spent a good fortune in observing the conditions earlier imposed against him should not detain the Court unnecessarily. The expenditure for earning profits by running industry would not be sufficient to allow the petitioner to play with the health of the public at large. The distance of two or five metres from the highway in fact is too close a distance to a hazardous activity or to the pollution. The public of this country is entitled to breathe in fresh air and have freedom of movement without fear of anything.[75]

How persuasive is this reasoning? What about the proprietor's fundamental right under Article 19(1)(g) of the Constitution? What happens to scores of large existing industries across Bihar that operate next to highways? Must they all move? Are they entitled to compensation? Why has the Bihar PCB singled out one small stone crushing unit operating in a village? Do you sense a subterranean current?

6. The failure of the Karnataka government and the state board to frame a suitable zoning policy for stone quarrying and crushing compelled the High Court to issue general directions in *Obayya Pujari v Karnataka State Pollution Control Board*.[76] The petition challenged the board's consent permitting stone crushing. The petitioners feared that the new unit would damage their crops and adversely affect the health of residents in the locality. Extending the scope of the petition to cover stone crushing operations across the state, the High Court directed the government to immediately formulate a policy regulating the business and to identify 'safer zones' for such operations. The Karnataka High Court drew upon the Punjab and Haryana High Court decision in *Ishwar Singh v State of Haryana*[77] to highlight the

[75] *Bihar State Pollution Control Board v Hiranand Stone Works* AIR 2005 Pat 62.
[76] AIR 1999 Kar 157.
[77] AIR 1996 P&H 30.

environmental damage caused by unregulated stone quarrying. Over a decade after the judgment, the state policy took shape in the Karnataka Regulation of Stone Crushers Act of 2011.

7. In *Kennedy Valley Welfare Association v Ceylon R L W & S Society*,[78] the Supreme Court restored a ban imposed by the single judge of the Madras High Court, prohibiting stone crushing operations within 500 metres of residential colonies. Earlier, a division bench of the High Court on appeal had restricted the ban to 50 metres.

8. Since dusting and cleaning old and used gunny bags was creating dust pollution, the Gunny Bags Merchants Association was asked to shift business away from densely populated Maharajgunj, Hyderabad. Dismissing the challenge to the relocation direction, the High Court held that the fundamental right to carry on trade or business under Article 19(1)(g) of the Constitution did not permit public nuisance.[79]

III. STUBBLE BURNING

The piece below explains why Delhi's infamous air pollution problem is so obstinate. Several other north Indian cities such as Faridabad, Patna, Kanpur, Lucknow and Varanasi also have very poor air quality. Indeed, in 2020, South Asia had 37 out of the 40 most polluted cities in the world.[80] Air pollution has severe health impacts and causes premature death due to pneumonia, lung cancer and by triggering strokes and heart disease.

> NAVROZ DUBASH & SARATH GUTTIKUNDA; DELHI HAS A COMPLEX AIR POLLUTION PROBLEM, Hindustan Times, 21 December 2018
>
> In this article, we focus on $PM_{2.5}$ or very small particles that experts agree are a major health hazard in India. There are at least four discrete sectors that each substantially contribute to Delhi's pollution: industry; transport; biomass and waste burning; and dust. Delhi's air problem is so hard to solve in part because it is not a single problem; it is a 4x25% (+/-10%) problem, with at least four implications.
>
> First, because Delhi's air is already about 13 times the World Health Organisation safe levels, we have to make progress on all these sources if Delhi's air is to be made safe. Even completely removing one or two of these sources will not achieve the objective. Second, because all sources have to be addressed, it is pointless to debate which source is more or less at fault. At different times different sources predominate—crop burning in October, dust in the summer, transport year around—but on an annual basis, all are important. As a result, for Delhi's citizens to point accusing fingers at farmers, or transport interests to point fingers to industry, and vice versa, ignores the data - all sources have to be reduced.
>
> Third, a positive feedback loop—successful actions leading to public support for more action—is extremely hard to build. For example, a heroic effort to limit truck traffic may lead to reduced emissions, but this may not be perceptible; trucks are only a portion of all transport, which is only a quarter of all pollution. Wind and other atmospheric conditions further complicate matters. As a result, painful and disruptive measures may be successful but not appear so, and arouse a backlash. To counter this requires public patience and clear management of public expectations.
>
> Finally, a sector-by-sector approach to solving Delhi's air has the greatest chance of success—each distinct sector and sub-sector has different technical, regulatory and political characteristics. For example, power plants require high-level regulatory and enforcement solutions, while transport needs attention to behaviour and public procurement to enable a shift to

[78] 2000 (2) Scale 143.
[79] *The A P Gunnies Merchants Association v The Government of A P* AIR 2001 AP 453.
[80] IQAir, 2020 World Air Quality Report 21 (2021), https://www.iqair.com/world-most-polluted-cities/world-air-quality-report-2020-en.pdf, accessed 12 May 2021.

public transport. The political context will also vary: crop burning is linked to agrarian politics, while construction dust involves powerful contractors and poor construction labour. The institutional scale will also differ: industries are regulated by pollution control boards, while Resident Welfare Associations can play a role in managing local waste burning. Air pollution solutions need to be based on understanding source sectors, even while keeping the larger picture in mind.

NOTES AND QUESTIONS

1. To be meaningful and enforceable, every right must have a remedy. How should a citizen of Delhi enforce her right to a clean environment? Would you advise filing a public interest litigation, an action before the National Green Tribunal, a class action suit, a criminal prosecution or a combination of these strategies?

2. Will an action lie to sue political and bureaucratic decision-makers who have failed to exercise their power to clean Delhi's air? Would any of them personally be liable for damages? Would an action lie to personally sue members of the PCBs or EPCA,[81] who failed to recommend and adopt vigorous measures despite wielding enormous power?

At the peak of the winter smog the Supreme Court passed an order on 4 November 2019. A short excerpt from this order is followed by Gautam Bhatia's critique.

M C MEHTA v UNION OF INDIA
(2020) 7 SCC 573

ORDER: We have heard Mr Bhurelal, who has pointed out about irrigation.

We have also heard some experts from the Ministry and the IIT and learned senior counsel for the parties and *amicus curiae.*

Today everyone is concerned about level of pollution in Delhi and NCR region. This is not something new, every year this kind of piquant situation arises for a substantial period. It is compounded by the fact that year to year in spite of various directions issued by High Court, other authorities including this Court, the State Governments, Government of NCT of Delhi and the corporations of Delhi and nearby States are not performing their duties as enjoined upon them. This is a shocking state of affairs in which we are put as on today. This is blatant and grave violation of right to life of the sizeable population by all these actions and the scientific data which has been pointed out indicates that life span of the people is being reduced by this kind of pollution which is being created and that people are being advised not to come back to Delhi or to leave the Delhi due to severe pollution condition which has been created. There cannot be large scale exodus. People have to perform their duty in Delhi also and people cannot be evacuated from Delhi being a capital city. We are at a loss to understand why we are not able to create a situation in which this kind of pollution does not take place, that too in a routine manner every year. Obviously, it is writ large that the State Governments, Government of NCT of Delhi and civic bodies have miserably failed to discharge their liability as per the Directive Principles of State Policy which have found statutory expression, they are being made statutory mockery and also the directions of this Court and High Courts in this regard are being violated with impunity.

Time has come when we have to fix the accountability for this kind of situation which has arisen and is destroying right to life itself in gross violation of Article 21 of the Constitution of India. No farmer can be said to be having a right under the guise that he is not having sufficient time to use the stubble for the purpose of manure, since they have less time between

---

[81] See *supra* note 57.

two crops, cutting and sowing of next crop. As such, they cannot by burning it in their fields, put life of sizeable population in jeopardy.

It is apparent from the satellite images which has been produced before us for the period 30.10.2019 to 04.11.2019. The satellite image clearly indicates that in Punjab there is widespread stubble burning which has taken place as compared to Haryana, in which only in four districts it has taken place. There is some burning in Western U P also. It could not have taken place even in a singular district or gram panchayat area as we live in a civilized country in which such kind of activities which create such menacing pollution not only in the area concerned but to the neighbouring States also, by ill-effects of that people cannot be left to die or to suffer various ailments.

Everybody has to be answerable including the top state machinery percolating down to the level of gram panchayat. The very purpose of giving administration power up to the panchayat level is that there has to be proper administration and there is no room for such activities. The action is clearly tortuous one and is clearly punishable under statutory provisions, besides the violation of the Court's order. In the circumstances, as widespread stubble burning has taken place, we direct the States of Punjab and Haryana and adjoining State of Uttar Pradesh where there is blatant violation which has taken place, to halt it. We direct the Chief Secretaries of the States of Punjab, Haryana and Uttar Pradesh to be present in this Court on 06.11.2019 including Chief Secretary of Government of NCT of Delhi.

We direct the Chief Secretaries of the State Governments, District Collectors, Tehsildars, Director General, IG/SP and other police officers of the area of concerned police station and the entire police machinery to ensure that not even a single incident takes place of stubble burning henceforth. If it is found that any stubble burning has been made not only that person doing it will be hauled up for the violation of the order passed by this Court but the entire administration, right from the Chief Secretary, Commissioner, Collector and all other concerned functionaries and Panchayats. Gram Pradhan/Sarpanch Panchayat are also directed to ensure that no such stubble burning takes place.

* * *

We direct that construction, demolition and activities be stopped forthwith as well as garbage burning. In case, any person is found in construction and demolition activity and garbage burning in Delhi and NCR region, he/she shall be penalized. Any person is doing construction and demolition activity in violation of this order, shall be penalized with Rs.1 Lac for such activity. For garbage burning he/she shall be penalized with Rs.5,000/- and besides liable for violation of the order passed by this Court to be dealt with in accordance with law.

With respect to open dumping of waste and garbage, we direct the Government of NCT of Delhi as well as the concerned Municipal Corporation to chalk out immediate plan and to ensure that waste and garbage to be removed to safe places forthwith and also to ensure that no open dumping takes place. We direct Zonal Deputy Commissioner to be responsible with other officers in this regard. Let road-maps be prepared so as to provide proper amenities in order to prevent open dumping of waste and garbage, and be placed before this Court within four weeks.

For taking care of the road dust let water sprinklers/dust suppressors be used on the roads. An IIT expert suggested about the appropriate water pressure for the sprinklers. At what pressure water should be sprinkled so as to reduce the pollution and dust so that it does not add to the pollution. Let the Corporations act on advice of the expert of the IIT. Such roads where traffic congestion is more, let traffic plan be also prepared in such a manner so that there is no extra burden on a particular road so that traffic congestion is taken care of. It is for the concerned traffic authorities to take immediate steps in this regard....

GAUTAM BHATIA; NATURAL JUSTICE AT THE BAR OF THE SUPREME COURT 5 November 2019[82]

M C Mehta v Union of India is numbered Writ Petition No. 13029/1985. In other words, this public interest litigation has been pending in the Supreme Court for the last thirty-four years. Every once in a while, the Supreme Court Registry unfreezes it from its cryostat, dusts it down, and posts it for hearing. One of those occasions was yesterday, when the city of New Delhi was suffering from extremely high air pollution. A bench was constituted, and a slew of directions were passed to ostensibly address the situation.

The Supreme Court's seventeen-page order, authored by Justice Arun Mishra, is difficult to read, and even more difficult to comprehend: it is rambling, and at times borders on the incoherent. For example, the opening line is: '*We have heard Mr Bhurelal, who has pointed out about irrigation.*' Who is Mr Bhurelal?[83] But more importantly, *what* is it that he has pointed out 'about irrigation'? We do not know, and the Court does not tell us. Two paras down, the order says: '*Today everyone is concerned about level of pollution in Delhi and NCR region. This is not something new, every year this kind of piquant situation arises for a substantial period.*' The word 'piquant', according to the Merriam-Webster Dictionary, means 'engagingly provocative' or 'agreeable stimulating to the taste.' The Thesaurus lists some of its synonyms as 'peppery', 'poignant', 'pungent', 'racy', and 'savoury'. Pollution is 'piquant'? What on earth is the Court talking about? Later on, the Court appears to confuse 'tortious action' (i.e., a tort) with 'tortuous action' (i.e., convoluted or meandering acts). The Court asks why state governments of Punjab, Uttar Pradesh and Haryana 'should not be held liable to compensate [for allowing stubble burning]', but refuses to complete the thought and explain who it is that will be compensated. There is repeated reference to statutory obligations (at one point, the odd phrase 'statutory mockery' is used), but the Court refuses to tell us what statute it is invoking, what the obligations are, and what (statutory) consequences exist. And some of the directions simply boggle the mind: on the advice of an unnamed 'expert of the IIT', the Municipal Corporation is told to use water sprinklers on roads (the 'pressure' at which they will be used is to be determined on the basis of the aforementioned unnamed IIT expert); because generators cause pollutions, the state governments are told that electricity is not to be cut, so that there will be no need for generators. And so on.

There is a lot to be said here about the use of PILs to resolve complex poly-centric problems, and how this order represents a textbook examples of all the perils underlying that approach. But for the moment, I want to focus on something else. In particular, I want to focus on this paragraph in Justice Mishra's order:

> *No farmer can be said to be having a right under the guise that he is not having sufficient time to use the stubble for the purpose of manure, since they have less time between two crops, cutting and sowing of next crop. As such, they cannot by burning it in their fields, put life of sizeable population in jeopardy.*

Reading this paragraph, it would seem that the farmers of Punjab and Haryana are a bunch of perverse individuals who literally want to watch the world burn. Naturally, nothing could be further from the truth. As environmental journalist Aruna Chandrasekhar explains, the roots of stubble burning go back to the Green Revolution, and are linked to patterns of agriculture, water usage, and laxity on part of the State to implement available policy solutions. In other words, stubble-burning does not happen because farmers just love being surrounded by all that smoke and fire—but rather, it is an economic compulsion closely linked to structural questions of livelihood.

---

[82] Gautam Bhatia, *Natural Justice at the Bar of the Supreme Court*, Indian Constitutional Law And Philosophy (2019), https://indconlawphil.wordpress.com/2019/11/05/natural-justice-at-the-bar-of-the-supreme-court/, accessed 12 May 2021.

[83] He was the chairperson of Epca. See *supra* note 57.

This could have been explained to the Court. It could have been explained if the farmers were effectively represented at the hearing.[84] But the order makes no mention of any arguments advanced on behalf of the farmers....

And here is the problem: these are undoubtedly coercive orders passed against the farmers. They undoubtedly affect their livelihood (notwithstanding the Court's bizarre use of the words 'in the guise of'). In other words, they affect their Article 21 rights—the same Article 21 that the Court is so quick to invoke in order to justify its jurisdiction in this very case. *How can the Court possibly pass these orders without hearing the affected farmers—and hearing them at length, recording their arguments, and addressing them?* The Supreme Court is not Emperor Jahangir, dispensing 'swift and brutal justice' whenever someone rings his golden bell, however much that vision might appeal to public imagination. It must follow certain basic rules and principles that underpin its adjudication, and one of the most important of those principles is that if you are going to deprive people of livelihood, you have to give them a fair hearing....

In other words, the Court passes orders on stubble burning (a) without considering the structural reasons underlying the activity, (b) determining in advance that any justification that might be proffered will *ipso facto* be fake and a sham ('under the guise of'), and (c) without effectively hearing the people whose rights will be directly affected. Needless to say, this is light years away from how a constitutional court is supposed to conduct itself.

The procedural injustice of the order is reflected in the final paragraph of Chandrasekhar's report. She points out that '*the unions have even suggested that while the government gets its act in order, farmers are ready to reduce the burning to 25 percent*' but, as noted by representatives of the farmers' Unions, completely stopping the burning is not economically feasible. Such issues should not—and indeed, cannot—be resolved by gunboat-style judicial orders threatening to 'haul up' anyone found burning stubble, and the preparation of 'inventories' of people who have (previously) burnt stubble (under what law?)—*without even according a substantive hearing to the people involved.* I say this at the cost of repetition, because above all it is important to push back against the creeping normalisation of the manner in which the fundamental principles of judicial adjudication are being eroded by the Court; it becomes necessary, therefore, to record the proliferation of such violations, even when they occur at such a basic and an obvious level, that it hardly seems worthwhile to dignify them with analysis.

NOTES AND QUESTIONS

1. Do you agree with Bhatia's critique? Does the 4 November 2019 order lack in tone, care, language, fairness and dignity—what citizens reasonably expect from India's highest court? Or is this pettifogging—considering the emergent situation and the court's purpose?

2. Does the Central Government have any responsibility with regard to air quality in the capital of India? Could it issue appropriate directions under section 5 of the Environment (Protection) Act of 1986? Is the power of the Central Government under section 5 coupled with a duty to exercise that power when circumstances warrant? Having regard to the multi-state dimensions of the problem and the larger issue of hazardous air quality across the entire Indo-Gangetic Plain, is the Centre primarily guilty of neglect?

[84] It is impossible to tell from the order whether the farmers were formally represented at the hearing. However, as the order makes no reference whatsoever to arguments advanced on their behalf—or any attempt to address them—the point that it is an order without an effective hearing of the affected parties remains.

3. The Supreme Court blames everyone but the Centre. Why?

4. Is toxic air affecting millions of citizens across north India a public health emergency comparable to the one triggered by the Covid-19 virus in 2020?

5. In the following week the Supreme Court heard counsel for the farmers. The court learned about various schemes disbursing compensation to farmers and mechanical options to remove the stubble. The state governments were directed to disburse compensation to farmers as an incentive to stop the burning of crop residue.[85]

6. On 13 January 2020, the court issued a range of directions including:

> With respect to preventing stubble burning, let a comprehensive plan be prepared and be placed before this Court including the action taken. Let Crop Residuary Management be prepared, its use *inter alia* as fertilizer, cattle food and biofuel be also worked out. Let the final decision be taken with respect to incentive and disincentive of Rs 100 per quintal and the in situ farming.
>
> Let the Central Government, State Governments of Punjab, Haryana and U P prepare a scheme for making available Combine Harvesters, Happy Seeders, Hydraulically Reversible MB Plough, Paddy Straw Chopper, Mulcher, Rotary Slasher, Zero Till Seed Drill and Rotavators and balers especially dedicated to small and marginal farmers to be made available either free of charge or on nominal rental basis.
>
> Let the Government of NCT of Delhi/NCR Region and Governments of Haryana and U P concerned file reports with respect to various identified hotspots and steps taken for their management and to clear the environmental hazards created by such hotspots....
>
> As proposed in the reply of the Delhi Government, let the Smog Tower at Connaught Place be completed by Delhi Government as proposed in their reply-affidavit. Let the Smog Tower be completed within three months....
>
> Let anti-smog guns be used in Delhi and NCR region for the following:
>
> (a) Large construction sites;
>
> (b) Road construction stretches, particularly during earthwork and compacting;
>
> (c) Mining activities;
>
> (d) Large parking sites on unpaved areas and during large public gatherings;
>
> (e) Demolition activities;
>
> (f) Sprinkling on dust-prone traffic corridors.
>
> (g) It be made compulsory to make use of anti-smog guns in Delhi-NCR in the projects that require environmental clearance from the State/Central level on site having built-up area of more than 20,000 sq m including excavation, material handling and other dust generating activities. Let an appropriate policy decision be also taken with respect to cost of installation, duly considering the principle 'polluters pay' evolved by this Court....
>
> Let the Government of NCT of Delhi work out the details with respect to 45% deficit capacity to lift the garbage and waste as there is only 55% capacity available with respect to garbage and waste generated in Delhi. Let it work out a comprehensive plan within three months to have full (100%) capacity to deal with garbage and wastes and place it before this Court, including the implements, tools, manpower and the expenditure required in that connection.[86]

7. These directions, in part, were based upon the report of a high-level committee constituted by the MoEF on 27 November 2019 and reports filed by Epca. What happens to these

[85] *M C Mehta v Union of India* (2020) 7 SCC 581.
[86] *M C Mehta v Union of India* (2020) 7 SCC 530.

directions with the constitution of the Commission for Air Quality Management in National Capital Region and Adjoining Areas in October 2020?[87]

IV. FIREWORKS

In late 2015, the Supreme Court clamped down on diesel-powered commercial trucks transiting through Delhi.[88] In November 2016, the court turned its attention to fireworks which wreck the Air Quality Index (AQI) in the wake of the Diwali festival and what the Supreme Court termed 'the wedding season'. As you examine the excerpt, focus on the competing fundamental rights at play.[89]

ARJUN GOPAL v UNION OF INDIA

(2017) 10 SCC 701

ORDER:

* * *

Reports indicate that AQI in Delhi was much above the severe standard, shooting off the AQI 500 mark on many days this November. On the day after Diwali, it was more than 14 times the safe limits. The adverse health effects of these hazardous levels of pollution are only too evident.... We do not intend to refer to the multiplicity of reports and data on this front.

The hazardous levels of air pollution in the last few weeks has spared very few from its ill effects. The life of the citizens of National Capital Region (NCR) was brought to a virtual standstill, not to speak about the plight of the thousands of mute flora and fauna in NCR. Schools were declared shut, denizens of the city advised to stay indoors, construction activities stopped, power stations shut and ban imposed on burning of garbage and agricultural waste. The fall in air quality has had a significant impact on people's lifestyle as well. The rising costs to protect against air pollution are substantial. It has come to our notice that people are queuing up to purchase protective masks and air purification systems in the wake of dense smog all over the NCR. In short, the capital was 'smogged' into an environmental emergency of unseen proportions.

The adverse effects of these extreme levels of air pollution spare no one—the young, the old, the infirm and even the future generations. A study of the data of the Global Health Depository of the World Health Organisation reveals that India has the *world's highest death rate* from chronic *respiratory diseases* and that about 1.5 million people in India die annually due to indoor and outdoor pollution. The Kolkata-based Chittaranjan National Cancer Institute, in a study commissioned and handed over to the Central Pollution Control Board, found that key indicators of respiratory health, lung function to palpitation, vision to blood pressure, of children in Delhi, between four and 17 years of age, were worse off than their counterparts elsewhere. It also found that more than 40% of the school children suffer from lung damage. We note with apprehension that there are nascent studies that suggest that pollution can *lower children's IQ*, hurt their *test scores* and increase the risks of *autism, epilepsy, diabetes* and even adult-onset diseases like *multiple sclerosis*....

Grievance was made before us about the thousands, even a lakh of crackers on one string going off at night; and several such strings going off in the neighbourhood, totally unmindful of the aged, the tender and the ill. All this firework, even that which is not noisy, leaves the ambient air thick with noxious particles. Marriage processions, *barats*, passing through an area generated the same kind of noise and leave behind the same kind of air, by the use of fire crackers. It is not necessary to speculate if those who suffer send their good wishes for the event, or to those 'celebrating' Diwali in this way.

We are conscious that we are dealing with time honoured ways of celebrating certain occasions. The petitioners and every member of the Bench and the Bar also celebrate in the same

[87] See *supra* note 57.

[88] *M C Mehta v Union of India* (2016) 2 SCC 33; (2016) 4 SCC 269.

[89] The excerpt excludes references to media reports mentioned in the judgment in support of the pollution levels and adverse health impacts.

way. But does that justify the continuance of this manner of celebration, when the quality of air in the region is so poor and injurious to health and well-being and is destroying essential components of the freedom to live a healthy life? In any case till the quality of air improves we do not pronounce finally on this question at this stage.

It is however certain that, now, when the AQI in the NCR is abysmally and threateningly severe, allowing free trade in fireworks which is a major source of noise and air pollution and is causing immense harm to the lives and health of citizens, and allowing availability of such fireworks or explosives constitutes a serious invasion of the Freedoms and Rights conferred on citizens by Part III of the Constitution of India. Such an invasion is all the more deleterious towards the rights and freedom of the poor and the underprivileged who must breathe such air without any means of protecting themselves....

We thus consider it inappropriate that explosives which are used as fireworks should be available in the market in the NCR till further orders. The mechanism of the law in this regard is clear. [Rule 118 of the Explosive Rules, 2008 framed under the Explosives Act, 1884 reads:

118. *Suspension and revocation or cancellation of licence.*—(1) Every licence granted under these Rules shall—

(I) stand cancelled, if—

(*a*) the licensee has ceased to have any right for the lawful possession over the licensed premises;

(*b*) the licensee is convicted and sentenced under any criminal offences or ordered to execute under Chapter VIII of the Code of Criminal Procedure, 1973 (2 of 1974), a bond for keeping peace for good behaviour.

(II) stand cancelled, if the no-objection certificate is cancelled by the authority issuing the same or District Magistrate or the State Government in accordance with Rule 115.

(III) be liable to be suspended or cancelled by an order of the licensing authority for any contravention of the Act or these Rules or of any condition contained in such licence, or by order of the Central Government, if it is satisfied that there are sufficient grounds for doing so:

Provided that before suspending or cancelling a licence under this rule, the holder of the licence shall be given an opportunity of being heard.

(2) The suspension or cancellation shall take effect from the date specified therein.

(3) An order of suspension or revocation of a licence shall be deemed to have been served if sent by post to the address of the licensee entered in the licence.

(4) The suspension of a licence shall not debar the holder of the licence from applying for the renewal.

(5) Notwithstanding anything contained in sub-rule (1), an opportunity of being heard may not be given to the holder of the licence before his licence is suspended or cancelled in cases—

(*i*) where the licence is suspended by a licensing authority as an interim measure for violation of any of the provisions of the Act or these Rules or of any conditions contained in such licence and in his opinion such violation is likely to cause imminent danger to the public: Provided that where a licence is so suspended, the licensing authority shall give the holder of the licence an opportunity of being heard before the order of suspension is confirmed; or

(*ii*) where the licence is suspended or cancelled by the Central Government, if that Government considers that in the public interest or in the interest of the security of the State, such opportunity should not be given.

(6) A licensing authority or the Central Government suspending or cancelling a licence shall record its reason for so doing in writing.]

Sub-rule (5) [of Rule 118] specifically confers on the Central Government a power to suspend or cancel a licence if it considers that it is in public interest. This provision also makes it clear that an opportunity to hear the licensee could be dispensed with if the Central Government considers that it is in public interest. This Court finds that the grave air quality situation in NCR is one such case, where this Court can intervene and suspend the licences to store and sell fireworks in the NCR. We direct the Central Government to:

(i) Suspend all such licences as permit sale of fireworks, wholesale and retail, within the territory of NCR.
(ii) The suspension shall remain in force till further orders of this Court.
(iii) No such licences shall be granted or renewed till further orders....

NOTES AND QUESTIONS

1. Year after year, the Supreme Court stretches its resources and the limits of its jurisdiction to combat Delhi's poor air quality. The AQI in several other cities is just as bad as Delhi. Should the Supreme Court look beyond the NCR in its ameliorative jurisdiction?

2. The AQI was launched in India in October 2014 by the MoEF. It is an index of eight pollutants (PM_{10}, $PM_{2.5}$, NO_2, SO_2, CO, O_3, NH_3 and Pb). Based on the levels of concentrations, the air quality is graded between 'good' (indicating minimal health impacts) and 'severe' (indicating serious health impacts). As the Supreme Court notes, the air quality on several days after Diwali in November 2016 was far in excess of the safe limits.

In May 2021, the CPCB issued a report on the impact of Diwali celebrations on air quality:

> City wise increase/decrease in PM_{10} and $PM_{2.5}$ on Diwali day compared to Pre-Diwali period (in %). Highest increment in PM_{10} on Deepawali day was reported in Lucknow (114%) followed by Bhopal (86.2%), Delhi (67.1%), Shillong (53.7) and Kolkata (22.6%). $PM_{2.5}$ was increased by 26 – 82.9% compared to Pre-Deepawali period among the various cities monitored. Highest increment was recorded in Delhi (82.9%), followed by Bhopal (81.3%), Lucknow (67.6%), Kolkata (53.6%), Shillong (30.5%) and Vadodara (26%).... Year-wise comparison (2017 – 2020) of $PM_{2.5}$ and elements in $PM_{2.5}$ in Delhi during Deepawali has been made. Reduction in Aluminium and Barium concentrations were observed in 2020 compared to 2019. Gradual betterment in ambient air metal concentrations in $PM_{2.5}$ was observed every year since 2017 after the implementations of regulatory mechanisms as suggested by Hon'ble Courts for either restricting/banning of firecrackers or development of 'Green Crackers' was initiated in 2018.[90]

3. The court justified its directions in light of the health emergency in Delhi. It observed that the temporary nature of its order and the suspension of trade would impact only 'a miniscule section of the population'. On balance, the court found that its duty to present and future generations outweighed the commercial interest of manufacturers and traders of fireworks.

4. Do you agree with the court's interpretation of rule 118(5)?

5. The record of appearances in the case suggests that the Central Government (to whom the directions were issued) was not represented through a counsel before the court. However, the judgment records: 'In fairness, we must say that there was no serious opposition to the impact

---

[90] Central Pollution Control Board, *Report on Ambient Noise Levels & Ambient Air Quality during Deepawali Festival 2020* 2, 3 (2021).

of fireworks on the ambient air quality and the unhealthy effects of fireworks on it. The opposition was mainly about the total banning of fireworks in all circumstances.'

6. Despite the health emergency none of the executive organs of the State responded with suitable measures. The Supreme Court was once again left to bell the cat.

E. PRESERVING THE TAJ MAHAL

On the eve of his retirement, Justice Kuldip Singh delivered the Supreme Court judgment in the *Taj Trapezium* case, culminating a long and arduous battle fought by M C Mehta for over a decade. In the winter of 1984, M C Mehta, a conscientious advocate practising at the Bar of the Supreme Court, placed before the court the material he had gathered, and warned of damage to the Taj Mahal from air pollutants, The *Taj* case was Mehta's first tentative step in the nascent field of environmental litigation.[91] In the following year, he filed Article 32 petitions to clean up the Ganga;[92] rid Delhi of hazardous and heavy industry;[93] close down and relocate Shriram's industrial complex in the heart of the capital[94] and regulate air pollution caused by automobiles, thermal power stations and industries.[95] Over time, each of these cases grew into full-blown class actions involving scores of parties.

Mehta's cases rode on the passion of the presiding judge. The *Shriram Gas Leak* case was the first to kick off under the stewardship of Chief Justice Bhagwati, who was anxious to help the Bhopal victims by articulating the principles of mass tort liability.[96] The next of Mehta's cases to gain momentum was the *Ganga Pollution* case, where Justice Venkataramiah issued a series of opinions to discipline the Kanpur tanneries and riparian municipalities.[97] Troubled by the deteriorating air quality in Delhi and the soot on his shirt collar, Chief Justice Ranganath Misra pulled the *Motor Vehicles* case off the back burner in 1991.[98] Although first among Mehta's cases, the *Taj* case was the last to evoke interest. It was propelled to the fore in 1993 by a series of orders issued by Justice Kuldip Singh. We carry excerpts from the judgment delivered almost four years after the periodic hearings commenced in January 1993. The 'Taj Trapezium Zone' referred to by the court is a 10,400 sq km trapezium-shaped area covering five districts in Uttar Pradesh and Bharatpur District in Rajasthan.

M C MEHTA v UNION OF INDIA (TAJ TRAPEZIUM CASE)
AIR 1997 SC 734

KULDIP SINGH, J: Taj Mahal—The Taj—is the 'King Emperor' amongst the World Wonders. The Taj is the final achievement and acme of the Moghul Art. It represents the most refined aesthetic values. It is a fantasy-like grandeur. It is the perfect culmination and artistic interplay of the architects' skill and the jewellers' inspiration. The marble in-lay walls of the Taj are amongst the most outstanding examples of decorative workmanship. The elegant symmetry of its exterior and the aerial grace of its domes and minarets impress the beholder in

---

91 *M C Mehta v Union of India*, Writ Petition (Civil) No. 13381 of 1984.

92 *M C Mehta v Union of India*, Writ Petition (Civil) No. 3727 of 1985.

93 *M C Mehta v Union of India*, Writ Petition (Civil) No. 4677 of 1985.

94 *M C Mehta v Union of India*, Writ Petition (Civil) No. 12739 of 1985.

95 *M C Mehta v Union of India*, Writ Petition (Civil) No. 13029 of 1985.

96 See the judgments of Chief Justice Bhagwati in *M C Mehta v Union of India* AIR 1987 SC 965 and AIR 1987 SC 1086.

97 See the judgments of Justice Venkataramiah in *M C Mehta v Union of India* AIR 1988 SC 1037 and AIR 1988 SC 1115.

98 See the next section on vehicular pollution and Chief Justice Misra's judgment in *M C Mehta v Union of India* 1991 (2) SCC 353.

a manner never to be forgotten. It stands out as one of the most priceless national monuments, of surprising beauty and worth, a glorious tribute to man's achievement in architecture and engineering....

The Taj is threatened with deterioration and damage not only by the traditional causes of decay, but also by changing social and economic conditions which aggravate the situation with even more formidable phenomena of damage or destruction. A private sector preservation organisation called 'World Monuments Fund' (American Express Company) has published a list of 100 most endangered sites (1996) in the World. The Taj has been included in the list by stating as under:

> The Taj Mahal, marble tomb for Mumtaz Mahal, wife of Emperor Shah Jahan, is considered the epitome of Mughal monumental domed tombs set in a garden. The environment of Agra is today beset with problems relating to the inadequacy of its urban infrastructure for transportation, water and electricity. The densest pollution near the Taj Mahal is caused by residential fuel combustion, diesel trains and buses, and back-up generators. Construction of the proposed Agra Ring Road and Bypass that would divert the estimated daily 6,50,000 tons of trans-India truck traffic awaits financing. Strict controls on industrial pollution established in 1982 are being intensively enforced following a 1993 Supreme Court Order. The Asian Development Bank's proposed $300 million loan to the Indian Government to finance infrastructure improvements would provide the opportunity to solve the chronic problems. Agra contains three World Heritage Sites, including the Taj Mahal.

According to the petitioner, the foundries, chemical/hazardous industries and the refinery at Mathura are the major sources of damage to the Taj. The Sulphur Dioxide emitted by the Mathura Refinery and the industries when combined with Oxygen—with the aid of moisture—in the atmosphere forms sulphuric acid called 'Acid rain' which has a corroding effect on the gleaming white marble. Industrial/Refinery emissions, brick-kilns, vehicular traffic and generator-sets are primarily responsible for polluting the ambient air around Taj Trapezium (TTZ). The petition states that the white marble has yellowed and blackened in places. It is inside the Taj that the decay is more apparent. Yellow pallor pervades the entire monument. In places the yellow hue is magnified by ugly brown and black spots. Fungal deterioration is worst in the inner chamber where the original graves of Shah Jahan and Mumtaz Mahal lie. According to the petitioner the Taj—a monument of international repute—is on its way to degradation due to atmosphere pollution and it is imperative that preventive steps are taken and soon. The petitioner has finally sought appropriate directions to the authorities concerned to take immediate steps to stop air pollution in the TTZ and save the Taj.

* * *

[This Court considered the affidavit filed by the Board and directed the board to issue a public notice.] Pursuant to this Court's order ... the Board filed affidavit dated 5-8-1993 wherein it is stated that public notice was published in two local newspapers of Agra on 17-5-1993 and two national newspapers on 18-5-1993 calling upon the industries to file their replies during the extended time. The affidavit states that all the listed industries were polluting industries and 507 out of them had not even installed any air pollution control device. The 212 industries who did not respond to the notice and failed to take any step towards installing the pollution control devices were closed by the order dated 27-8-1993 with immediate effect. The closure order was to operate till the time necessary pollution control devices were to be set up by the industries concerned.

[The judgment records subsequent developments in the case between 1993 and 1996. The court was assisted in its efforts to improve air quality in the TTZ by the reports prepared by the National Environment Engineering Research Institute (NEERI); inputs from the Gas Authority of India Ltd. (GAIL) on the supply of fuel gas to industries in the area; and the study conducted by the Vardharajan Committee which was constituted in May, 1994 by the Union Ministry of Environment and Forests at the prompting of the court. On 3 August

1995 the court formed a tentative view that polluting industries in the TTZ would have to be relocated and sought the assistance of the Union Government to devise an appropriate solution. However, in the words of the judgment: 'There being no helpful response from the Government of India, we finally heard the matter at length for several days and are disposing of the issues raised before us by this judgment.']

The Taj, apart from being a cultural heritage, is an industry by itself. More than two million tourists visit the Taj every year. It is a source of revenue for the country. This Court has monitored this petition for over three years with the sole object of preventing and protecting the Taj from deterioration and damage due to atmosphere and environmental pollution. It cannot be disputed that the use of coke/coal by the industries emits pollution in the ambient air. The objective behind this litigation is to stop the pollution while encouraging development of industry. The old concept that development and ecology cannot go together is no longer acceptable. Sustainable development is the answer. The development of industry is essential for the economy of the country, but at the same time the environment and the ecosystem have to be protected. The pollution created as a consequence of development must be commensurate with the carrying capacity of our ecosystems.

Various orders passed by this Court from time to time ... clearly indicate that the relocation of the industries from TTZ is to be resorted to only if the Natural Gas which has been brought at the doorstep of TTZ is not acceptable/available by/to the industries as a substitute for coke/coal. The GAIL has already invited the industries in TTZ to apply for gas connections. Before us ... learned counsel for the industries have clearly stated that all the industries would accept gas as an industrial fuel. The industries operating in TTZ which are given gas connections to run the industries need not relocate. The whole purpose is to stop air pollution by banishing coke/coal from TTZ....

Based on the reports of various technical authorities mentioned in this judgment, we have already reached the finding that the emissions generated by the coke/coal consuming industries are air pollutants and have damaging effect on the Taj and the people living in the TTZ. The atmospheric pollution in TTZ has to be eliminated at any cost. Not even one per cent chance can be taken when—human life apart—the preservation of a prestigious monument like the Taj is involved. In any case, in view of the precautionary principle as defined by this Court, the environmental measure must anticipate, prevent and attack the cause of environmental degradation. The 'onus of proof' is on an industry to show that its operation with the aid of coke/coal is environmentally benign. It is, rather, proved beyond doubt that the emissions generated by the use of coke/coal by the industries in TTZ are the main polluters of the ambient air.

We, therefore, hold that ... 292 industries (out of 511) shall as per the schedule indicated hereunder change over to the natural gas as an industrial fuel. The industries which are not in a position to obtain gas connections for any reason—shall stop functioning with the aid of coke/coal in the TTZ and may relocate themselves as per the directions given by us hereunder.

We order and direct as under:

(1) The industries (292 listed in the order]) shall approach/apply to the GAIL before 15-2-1997 for grant of industrial gas connection.

(2) The industries which are not in a position to obtain gas connections and also industries which do not wish to obtain gas connection may approach/apply to the UP State Industrial Development Corporation (UPSIDC)/Government before 28-2-1997 for allotment of alternative plots in the industrial estates outside TTZ.

(3) The GAIL shall take final decision in respect of all the applications for grant of gas connections by 31-3-1997 and communicate the allotment letters to the individual industries.

(4) Those industries which neither apply for gas connection nor for alternative industrial plot shall stop functioning with the aid of coke/coal in the TTZ with effect from 3-4-1997. Supply of coke/coal to these industries shall be stopped forthwith.

The District Magistrate and the Superintendent of Police shall have this order complied with.

(5) The GAIL shall commence supply of gas to the industries by 30-6-1997. As soon as the gas supply to an industry commences, the supply [of] coke/coal to the said industry shall be stopped with immediate effect.

(6) UPSIDC Government shall finally decide and allot alternative plots, before 31-3-1997, to the industries which are seeking relocation.

(7) The relocating industries shall set up their respective units in the new industrial estates outside TTZ. The relocating industries shall not function and operate in TTZ beyond 31-12-1997. The closure by 31-12-1997 is unconditional and irrespective of the fact whether the new unit outside TTZ is completely set up or not.

(8) The Deputy Commissioner, Agra and the Superintendent (Police), Agra shall effect the closure of all the industries on 31-12-1997 which are to be relocated by that date as directed by us.

(9) The UP state government/Corporation, shall render all assistance to the industries in the process of relocation. The allotment of plots, construction of factory buildings, etc., and issuance of any licence/permission, etc., shall be expedited and granted on priority basis.

(10) In order to facilitate shifting of industries from TTZ, the State Government and all other authorities shall set up unified single agency consisting of all the departments concerned to act as a nodal agency to sort out all the problems of such industries. The single window facility shall be set up by the UP State Government within one month from today.... We make clear that no further time shall be allowed to set up the single window facility.

(11) The state government shall frame a scheme for the use of the land which would become available on account of shifting/relocation of the industries before 30-6-1997. The state government may seek guidance in this respect from the order of this Court in *M C Mehta v Union of India* [(1996) 4 SCC 351. In this case the court issued directions to shift industries from Delhi.]

(12) The shifting industries on the relocation in the new industrial estates shall be given incentives in terms of the provisions of the Agra Master Plan and also the incentives which are normally extended to new industries in new industrial estates.

(13) The workmen employed in the above-mentioned 292 industries shall be entitled to the rights and benefits as indicated hereunder:

(a) The workmen shall have continuity of employment at the new town and place where the industry is shifted. The terms and conditions of their employment shall not be altered to their detriment.

(b) The period between the closure of the industry in Agra and its restart at the place of relocation shall be treated as active employment and the workmen shall be paid their full wages with continuity of service.

(c) All those workmen who agree to shift with the industry shall be given one year's wages as 'shifting bonus' to help them settle at the new location. The said bonus shall be paid before 31-1-1998.

(d) The workmen employed in the industries who do not intend to relocate/obtain Natural Gas and opt for closure, shall be deemed to have been retrenched by 31-5-1997, provided they have been in continuous service (as defined in Section 25-B of the Industrial Disputes Act, 1947) for not less than one year in the industries concerned before the said date. They shall be paid compensation in terms of Section 25-F(b) of the Industrial Disputes Act. These workmen shall also be paid, in addition, six years' wages as additional compensation.

(e) The compensation payable to the workmen in terms of this judgment shall be paid by the management within two months of the retrenchment.

(f) The gratuity amount payable to any workmen shall be paid in addition. Before the parting with this judgment, we may indicate that the industries in the TTZ other than 292 industries shall be dealt with separately. We direct the Board to issue individual notices and also public notice to the remaining industries in the TTZ to apply for gas connection/relocation within one month of the notice by the Board. The Board shall issue notice within one month from today. The matter to come up for further monitoring in this respect before this Court on 4-4-1997.

We may also indicate that this Court by order dated 10-5-1996 has stopped the operation of all the brick kilns in the TTZ with effect from 15-8-1996. This Court by order dated 4-9-1996 has directed that the fly-ash produced in the process of the functioning of thermal plants may be supplied to the brick kilns for the construction of bricks. This would be a useful step to eliminate the pollution caused by fly-ash.

The Court is separately monitoring the following issues for controlling air pollution in TTZ:

(a) The setting up of hydro-cracker unit and various other devices by the Mathura Refinery.

(b) The setting up of a 50-bed hospital and two mobile dispensaries by the Mathura Refinery to provide medical aid to the people living in the surrounding areas (Court order dated 7-8-1996).

(c) Construction of Agra bypass to divert all the traffic which passed through the city. Under directions of this Court, 23 kms stretch of the bypass shall be completed by the end of December 1996 (Court order dated 10-4-1996).

(d) Additional amount of Rs.99.54 crores sanctioned by the Planning Commission to be utilized by the State Government for the construction of electricity supply projects to ensure 100% uninterrupted electricity to the TTZ. This is necessary to stop the operation of generating sets which are major source of air pollution in the TTZ (Court orders dated 10-4-1996, 10-5-1996, 30-8-1996, 4-9-1996 and 10-9-1996).

(e) The construction of Gokul Barrage, water supply work of Gokul Barrage, roads around Gokul Barrage, Agra Barrage and water supply of Agra Barrage, have also been undertaken on a time-schedule basis to supply drinking water to the residents of Agra and to bring life into River Yamuna which is next to the Taj (Court order dated 10-5-1996 and 30-8-1996).

(f) Green belt as recommended by NEERI has been set up around Taj. Pursuant to continuous monitoring of this Court, the Green belt has become a reality.

(g) This Court suggested to the Planning Commission by order dated 4-9-1996 to consider sanctioning separate allocation for the city of Agra and the creation of separate cell under the control of Central Government to safeguard and preserve the Taj, the city of Agra and other national heritage monuments in the TTZ.

(h) All emporia and shops functioning within the Taj premises have been directed to be closed.

(i) Directions have been issued to the Government of India to decide the issue, pertaining to declaration of Agra as heritage city within two months.

We are mentioning these issues dealt with by this Court because it may be necessary to monitor some of these matters to take them to a logical extent. This Court may look into these matters on 4-4-1997.

The issue relating to 292 industries is thus disposed of.

NOTES AND QUESTIONS

1. Having survived the threat of Governor General William Bentinck to demolish the Mughal monuments at Agra and ship the marble to London, as well as outdoor balls, picnic parties, revellers and brigands,[99] the Taj may pull through its present ordeal. Environmentalists argue

[99] Darryl D'Monte, *Temples or Tombs? Industry versus Environment: Three Controversies* 91–2 (1985).

that the air problem could have been avoided had the authorities heeded warnings not to build the Mathura Refinery in the 1970s. The debate over the suitability of the site is tracked by Darryl D'Monte in his study *Temples or Tombs?*[100] Within two years of commissioning the refinery in 1982, sulphur dioxide around the Taj increased three-fold.[101]

2. Would environmental impact assessment (EIA) procedures have prevented the establishment of the Mathura Refinery? Are the current EIA regulations strong enough to prevent recurrence of the folly? Was it a folly? In the wake of the controversy, several experts cleared the project in the 1970s.

3. The Supreme Court relied heavily on the NEERI Report to support its relocation directives. But NEERI's methods, analysis and conclusions are questioned by experts and Agra's small industry owners. They refer to the Vardharajan Committee Report of 1994 which found no evidence of pollution-related damage to the monument and attributed deteriorating air quality mainly to non-industrial sources such as traffic and diesel generator sets. Some experts doubt the veracity of NEERI's air quality data, point to several archaeological errors, question why the Mathura Refinery was ignored by the report and criticize the over-estimates of emissions from Agra's foundries.[102]

4. Would you regard the court's approach as too 'monument-oriented' and insensitive to economic realities? One study feared that shifting the small industrial units would render them financially unviable and might jeopardize the employment of over 50,000 people.[103]

5. The breadth of judicial activity in the *Taj Trapezium* case is unmatched. The court supervised the installation of pollution abatement equipment, shut down violators, cajoled GAIL to pipe gas to the industries, urged development of a green belt around the monument, relocated industries, fashioned a labour compensation and entitlement scheme, expedited the construction of a highway to direct traffic away from Agra, prodded the government to speed up work on barrages that would revive the flow in the Yamuna and generally monitored development activity in the Trapezium.

Was this a legitimate response to 'the felt necessities of the times'[104] or a manifestation of the 'natural, self-aggrandizing instinct of altogether too many lawyers and judges ... to stand up and do something—anything at all—when any aspect of life seems less than perfect'?[105]

6. The judgment vigorously applied the 'precautionary principle'; casting the burden on industry to show that operating with the aid of coke/coal was environmentally benign.

7. The ringing tone of the judgment had little effect on the parochial approach of the UP State Electricity Board. Raising several technical quibbles, the board declined to supply power to the air quality monitoring station at the Taj Mahal. The objections were brushed aside by the court in January 1998.[106]

---

100 *Id.*

101 N Raghuram, *The Trouble with the Trapezium*, DOWN TO EARTH, 15 April 1996, https://www.downtoearth.org.in/coverage/the-trouble-with-the-trapezmium-25709, accessed 13 May 2021.

102 *Id.*

103 Report of the Tripathi Committee set up by the Uttar Pradesh government in 1994 to study the impact of pollution on the Taj. *Id.*

104 Sriram Panchu, *Environmental Law in India: Key Environmental Issues; Legislation; Case Law; Enforcement; Lessons to be Learnt* 14 November 1997 (unpublished manuscript).

105 Peter Huber, *Safety and Second Best: The Hazard of Public Risk Management in the Courts*, 85 COLUMBIA LAW REVIEW 277 (1985).

106 *M C Mehta v Union of India* (*Taj Trapezium* case) 1998 (2) SCALE 7 (SP).

8. In February 1998 the Central Government informed the court that Agra did not qualify for declaration as a World Heritage City because of its polluted atmosphere and haphazard growth.

9. A key feature of the Supreme Court scheme to clean the air in the Taj Trapezium was the introduction of natural gas to replace dirtier fuels such as coke and coal. On 31 August 1999, the court reviewed the progress in respect of gas supply to the Trapezium and directed 53 iron foundries which had not agreed to accept the gas to close down. Seventy-eight iron foundries that used cupola-based technology submitted that despite their best efforts no reliable technology was available to convert their units to gas. These foundries claimed that the new technology was in the last stages of development and that they would switch over to natural gas as soon as the technology became available. The Supreme Court declined to accept the plea for an indefinite extension. The court directed the District Magistrate to ensure that no coal or coke was supplied to the cupola-based foundries after 15 September 1999. The foundries were permitted to operate after they converted to natural gas.[107]

10. In May 1999, the Centre constituted the Taj Trapezium Pollution (Prevention and Control) Authority under section 3 of the Environment (Protection) Act of 1986. The Authority, initially comprising eight government officials, is headed by the Commissioner, Agra Division. It has the wide powers to implement schemes for protecting the Taj Mahal and improving the environment, including necessary measures to ensure compliance with emission standards by motor vehicles. The Authority is empowered to issue statutory directions under section 5 of the Act and initiate prosecutions under section 19.[108] The record of the Authority is poor, compelling the Supreme Court to monitor pollution in the region.

11. Retaining hold over the case, the Supreme Court has spent considerable time examining individual cases of tree felling in the TTZ, particularly where a large number of trees are required to be cleared for projects such as highways[109] and a railway corridor.[110] The court has critically reviewed reafforestation claims by the state government[111] and has also examined alternatives with respect to a crematorium located close to the Taj Mahal.[112] What is the use of a statutory authority if the Supreme Court is required to monitor ground-level activities? Is this a wise use of judicial time?

12. Despite having been established in May 1999 the Authority does little to assist the court or implement initiatives in the field. Should the Authority be disbanded?

13. The court has also overseen improvements to the Taj complex for having better facilities for visitors[113] and has helped to create a Vision document for the entire TTZ region.[114] How long should the Supreme Court continue with this 1984 case?

---

[107] *M C Mehta v Union of India* AIR 1999 SC 3192.

[108] S O 350 (E) dated 17 May 1999.

[109] *M C Mehta v Union of India* (*Taj Trapezium* case) 2011 (5) Scale 135; 2011(5) Scale 136; 2016 (3) Scale 645; 2016 (3) Scale 655.

[110] *M C Mehta v Union of India* (*Taj Trapezium* case) 2016 (3) Scale 644.

[111] *M C Mehta v Union of India* (*Taj Trapezium* case) 2016 (3) Scale 648; 2016 (3) Scale 659.

[112] *M C Mehta v Union of India* (*Taj Trapezium* case) 2016 (3) Scale 653; 2016 (3) Scale 659.

[113] *M C Mehta v Union of India* (*Taj Trapezium* case) 2010 (2) Scale 20.

[114] *M C Mehta v Union of India* (*Taj Trapezium* case) 2019 (17) Scale 344; (2018) 9 SCC 658; 2019 (17) Scale 332.

F. VEHICULAR POLLUTION

I. STATUTORY PROVISIONS

The principal statutes governing vehicular emissions are the Motor Vehicles Act of 1988 (MVA) and the Central Motor Vehicles Rules of 1989 (MVR) framed under the MVA. The Environment (Protection) Rules of 1986 (EPR) and the Air Act supplement the primary regulations.

Section 110 of the MVA empowers the Central Government to prescribe emission standards for vehicles and to frame rules regulating the construction, equipment and maintenance of motor vehicles in relation to the emission of smoke, visible vapour, sparks, ashes, grit or oil. Any person committing a breach of the prescribed air pollution standards is liable to be punished with a Rs. 1,000 fine for a first offence and a Rs. 2,000 fine for subsequent offences.[115]

Rule 115 of the MVR prescribes nationwide emission levels for both diesel and petrol engine vehicles. Every motor vehicle is required to be maintained and driven so as to comply with the standards prescribed. No distinction is made between old and new vehicles. Rule 115(6) obliges the manufacturer to certify that every new vehicle conforms to the prescribed standards and that the vehicles are designed and constructed to meet these emission levels.

Rule 115(7) specifies that year-old vehicles must have a 'pollution under control' (PUC) certificate issued by the state government's authorized agency. The PUC certificate is required to be produced on demand to the officers referred to in rule 116(1). Each certificate is generally valid for a period of six months or for a year where the vehicle is manufactured to comply with Bharat Stage IV for Bharat Stage VI norms.

Rule 115(9) of the MVR lays down 'mass emission standards' for diesel and petrol-driven vehicles. This sub-rule is amended periodically to introduce stricter standards with a lead time provided to manufacturers to upgrade their vehicles and reduce emissions. The Bharat Stage VI standards are effective from 1 April 2020. Mass emission standards are prescribed separately for vehicles operating on compressed natural gas (CNG),[116] liquefied petroleum gas (LPG),[117] hybrid electric systems,[118] ethanol or ethanol blends[119] and bio-diesel.[120] Manufacturers must also meet the average fuel consumption standards notified under the Energy Conservation Act of 2001.[121]

Rule 116 provides that a sub-inspector of police or inspector of motor vehicles (or their superiors) may require the driver of a vehicle to get the automobile emissions tested. Where the vehicle does not meet the emission standards, the driver is required to rectify the defect within seven days. The failure to rectify the defects attracts penalties under section 190(2) of the MVA. The primary agency for enforcement of vehicular emission norms is the state/regional transport authority appointed under the MVA. The EPA adopts a consistent regulatory model. In exercise of its powers under section 10 of the EPA, the Central Government has empowered the state/regional transport authority to inspect motor vehicles and collect samples for the purposes of analysis under the EPA.

---

115 Section 190(2).
116 Rule 115B.
117 Rule 115C.
118 Rule 115D.
119 Rule 115E.
120 Rule 115F titled 'Mass emission standards for bio-diesel (B-100)'.
121 Rule 115F titled 'Fuel consumption standard'. (There are two rules with the same number.)

Section 17(1)(g) of the Air Act empowers the state boards to lay down standards of air pollutants released by automobiles in consultation with the Central board. Under section 20 of the Act, the state government is required to give necessary instructions to the vehicle registration authority under the MVA to ensure that automobile emission norms are complied with.

II. VEHICULAR POLLUTION CASES

M C Mehta (Motor Vehicles case)

The *Motor Vehicles* case was filed by M C Mehta in 1985.[122] In early 1998, the case took an abrupt turn with the Supreme Court welcoming the Central Government's proposal to constitute an authority under section 3 of the Environment (Protection) Act of 1986, to be called the Environment Pollution (Protection and Control) Authority for the National Capital Region (EPCA). Acknowledging this step as appropriate and timely, the Supreme Court clarified that the jurisdiction of the new authority would extend to the entire sphere of environmental pollution problems faced by the National Capital Region, not just vehicular emissions.[123]

The constitution of the EPCA seemed to have come as a relief to the court. Despite numerous orders since early 1991 exerting pressure on the authorities to introduce ameliorative measures, the air pollution problem persisted. The *Motor Vehicles* case is a stage for judicial experimentation when the legislature and executive fail to respond to deteriorating air quality. There are few tangible gains in improved air quality and a perusal of the orders reveals a colossal waste of judicial time and effort. In shifting responsibility to the EPCA, the court tacitly recognized that Delhi's dirty air cannot be banished by judicial decree.

The petition when originally filed sought directions to close hazardous industries located in the densely populated areas in Delhi, to regulate air pollution caused by automobiles operating in the capital and to reduce pollution from the thermal power stations generating energy for the Delhi Electricity Supply Undertaking.[124] However, most of the orders sought in the petition relate to vehicular pollution.

On 14 November 1990, the MoEF acknowledged on affidavit that air pollution in Delhi was chiefly caused by vehicular emissions. The court directed the city administration to place before it a complete list of prosecutions launched against defaulting vehicles and noted that heavy vehicles such as buses and trucks were the main contributing factor to pollution and ought to receive more attention from the authorities. The ministry was also asked to carry out appropriate experiments to test whether a pollution reduction device suggested by the petitioner could be adopted.[125] On 16 January 1991, the Supreme Court permitted the Association of Indian Automobile Manufacturers to intervene in the proceedings.[126] On 12 February 1991, the Additional Solicitor General assured the court that on the next date of hearing he would be able to 'demonstrate with reference to documentary evidence that the Delhi administration and the Union of India are taking effective steps to control pollution in Delhi'.[127] On 19 February 1991, a bench comprising Chief Justice Ranganath Misra and Justice Kania adjourned the case after a protracted hearing to enable the Attorney General to file a scheme which would lead to setting up a committee for the purpose of controlling air pollution in Delhi.[128]

---

122 *M C Mehta v Union of India*, Writ Petition (Civil) No. 13029 of 1985.

123 *M C Mehta v Union of India* AIR 1998 SC 617 and 773. EPCA was dissolved in 2020. See *supra* note 57.

124 *M C Mehta v Union of India* (*Vehicular Pollution* case) (1991) 2 SCC 353.

125 Writ Petition (Civil) No. 13029 of 1985, order dated 14 November 1990.

126 *Id.*, order dated 16 January 1991.

127 *Id.*, order dated 12 February 1991.

128 *Id.*, order dated 19 February 1991.

On 22 February 1991, the case came up before a bench of the Chief Justice and Justice K N Saikia. The record of proceedings states that an order adjourning the matter was passed by the court.[129] Justice Saikia retired in the following week, on 1 March 1991.[130]

On 14 March 1991, a bench presided over by the Chief Justice passed an interim order describing the problems of vehicular pollution in Delhi. Confronted by various technical issues that came up during the deliberations at the bar, the court directed the Union Government to set up a high-level committee.[131] The terms of reference required the committee:

(a) to make an assessment of the technologies available for vehicular pollution control in the world;
(b) to make an assessment of the current status of technology available in India for controlling vehicular pollution;
(c) to look at the low-cost alternatives for operating vehicles at reduced pollution levels in the metropolitan cities of India;
(d) to examine the feasibility of measures to reduce/eliminate pollution from motor vehicles both on short-term and long-term basis and make appropriate recommendations in this regard;
(e) to make specific recommendations on the administrative/legal resolution required for implementing the recommendations in (iii) above.

Recently retired Justice K N Saikia (who in the previous week sat on the bench which heard this case) was appointed as chairman of the committee and the court ordered: 'Shri Justice K N Saikia shall be entitled to all the benefits to which a retired judge of this court *while called back to duty is entitled.*'[132] The committee was directed to submit bi-monthly reports in the matter. On 27 March 1991, the Union Government constituted the high power committee.

Over the next several years, the Justice Saikia Committee produced mounds of reports running into thousands of pages. The reports are prolix, lack analysis and are frequently little more than a string of quotations interspersed with platitudes. Some of the reports deal with subjects which appear unrelated to the task before the committee. For example, the Sixth Bi-monthly Report contains a tract on the absolute liability principle laid down in the *Shriram Gas Leak* case,[133] a discussion on the Bhopal gas leak disaster[134] and a dissertation on water pollution.[135] It would appear that the committee found time to deliberate on limestone quarrying in the Doon Valley[136] and on why 'Personal Interest Petition cannot be masqueraded as Public Interest Petition by abusing the process of the court'.[137] The reports also speak of cycling in German towns,[138] the traffic and transport structure in the Netherlands,[139] Mexico's efforts to control pollution,[140] the energy tax controversy in USA[141]

---

129 *Id.*, order dated 22 February 1991.

130 Ministry of Law and Justice, Government of India, *Judges of the Supreme Court and the High Courts* 131 (1996).

131 *M C Mehta v Union of India* (*Vehicular Pollution* case) (1991) 2 SCC 353. The judgment records that the Union Government agreed to the constitution of the committee for devising methods to solve the air pollution problems in Delhi.

132 *Id.* at 359 [emphasis supplied].

133 Sixth Bi-monthly Report, paras 4.61–4.67; pages 487–530.

134 *Id.*, para 4.65; page 498.

135 *Id.*, paras 5.3–5.28; pages 508–51.

136 *Id.*, para 5.22; pages 538–9.

137 *Id.*, para 5.50; pages 571–6.

138 Ninth Bi-monthly Report, para 8.12; pages 779–82.

139 *Id.*, para 8.23; pages 790–1.

140 Eighth Bi-monthly Report, para 7.33; pages 685–9.

141 Fifteenth Bi-monthly Report, para 15.45; pages 1048–9.

and hi-tech parking garages in Japan.[142] The committee also suggested the best ways to prevent illegal parking in Indian cities.[143] The Supreme Court refers to the committee's junket to Canada,[144] doubtless 'to make an assessment of available world technologies ... by visiting selected countries'.[145]

The Supreme Court hardly ever relied on the Saikia Committee Reports and references to the reports in the court's orders are rare. Did the committee serve any purpose? Should it have been disbanded within a few months? Is this an instance of wasted public money?

During the litigation, the Supreme Court shifted focus from one scheme to another. In 1990, the emphasis was on the prosecution of defaulters.[146] In 1991, the court was anxious to have buses of the Delhi Transport Corporation converted from diesel to gas operation.[147] In early 1992, the court's attention shifted to bringing down emissions from public buses.[148] Throughout 1994, the court exerted pressure on the government to ensure that new vehicles are fitted with catalytic converters and that lead-free petrol is introduced in the four metros by April 1995.[149] Thereafter the court monitored the extension of the unleaded petrol distribution network and obtained assurances from the Centre in respect of reductions in the lead content of petrol and the notification of year 2000 emission norms.[150] In late 1996 and 1997, the Supreme Court pressed the Central Government to convert its vehicles to operate on a cleaner fuel—compressed natural gas (CNG)[151]—and also sought technical solutions to reduce harmful emissions from two and three-wheelers[152] and diesel trucks and buses.[153]

Shortly after the Supreme Court endorsed the Central Government's decision to set up the EPCA,[154] the authority headed by Mr Bhure Lal was constituted on 29 January 1998. There was little progress in the next few months, prompting the Supreme Court to censure the administration:

> We are not satisfied with the performance of the concerned authorities in tackling the acute problem of vehicular pollution and traffic regulations in Delhi. Environmental protection appears to have taken a back seat. In fact, we are distressed to find that the directions given by this Court, from time to time, have not evoked the response they were expected to evoke.... The directions issued by this Court were aimed at making the state to effectively discharge their obligations. In their response the Delhi Administration and the Union of India have pleaded, among other factors, lack of manpower to deal with the growing menace of chaotic traffic and decline in the environmental quality.[155]

The tone of the order conveys the judges' despair. The bench even considered appointing court officers to assist the administration and had to remind the respondents of their obligation to

---

142 Sixteenth B-monthly Report, para 16.18; pages 1071–2.
143 *Id.*, para 16.19; pages 1071–2.
144 1997 (3) SCALE 24 (SP), 25.
145 First Bi-monthly Report, page 5.
146 (1991) 2 SCC 137.
147 Writ Petition (Civil) No. 13029 of 1985, orders dated 3 October 1991 and 25 October 1991.
148 *Id.*, order dated 8 January 1992.
149 Orders dated 12 August 1994; 21 October 1994 and 28 March 1995 reported at 1997 (4) SCALE 4 (SP), 1997 (4) SCALE 5 (SP) and 1997 (4) SCALE 6 (SP).
150 Order dated 14 February 1996 reported at (1998) 8 SCC 648.
151 Order dated 26 April 1996 reported at 1997 (4) SCALE 7 (SP).
152 Orders dated 23 September 1996; 7 October 1996 and 9 December 1996 reported at 1997 (4) SCALE 9 (SP), 1997 (4) SCALE 10 (SP) and 1997 (4) SCALE 11 (SP).
153 1997 (3) SCALE 24 (SP), 25.
154 *M C Mehta v Union of India* AIR 1998 SC 617 and 773.
155 Order dated 12 May 1998 reported at (1998) 6 SCC 60.

'act in aid of the Supreme Court', under Article 144 of the Constitution. EPCA was directed to submit in ten weeks a report and action plan to curb vehicular pollution.

On 28 July 1998, the court yet again expressed distress at the apathy of the state, but this time followed the litany with sweeping directions to axe New Delhi's obsolete commercial fleet. All commercial vehicles including taxis which were 15 years old were ordered off the road by 2 October 1998. The court also endorsed a time frame fixed by EPCA for eliminating leaded petrol; converting autorickshaws, taxis and buses to clean fuels; reducing the age of the commercial fleet and strengthening the clean-fuel distribution network.[156] It is unclear from the court order whether the age-related embargo had a statutory basis, though section 59 of the MVA does empower the Centre to notify age limits for different classes or different types of motor vehicles.

On 16 April 1999, the Supreme Court targeted diesel vehicles, which EPCA blamed for more than 90% of the nitrogen oxide and respirable particulate matter (RSPM) in Delhi's air. Noting that the California Air Resource Board had on 27 August 1998 formally designated diesel particulate as a toxic air contaminant, and the *amicus curiae*'s request to suspend the registration of diesel vehicles in Delhi, the court adjourned the case to 29 April 1999 to consider submissions on the issue.[157]

On the adjourned date a bench headed by Chief Justice A S Anand imposed super norms for vehicles registered in the National Capital Region (NCR), which 'appeared appropriate' to the bench.[158] The court required all private vehicles registered after 1 June 1999 to conform to Euro I norms and those registered after 1 April 2000 to meet the Euro II norms. Diesel taxis were prohibited in NCR unless they conformed to Euro II norms. The Euro norms are European standards enforced across Europe. On 13 May 1999,[159] the court clarified that what it meant by 'Euro I norms' were the India 2000 norms, notified by the Central Government on 28 August 1997. In other words, the court advanced the statutory emission norms that were to come into effect on 1 April 2000 to 1 June 1999; and introduced more stringent emission standards (Euro II) with effect from 1 April 2000. The Euro II norms were re-christened 'Bharat Stage II' standards by the Central Government and were notified through the Central Motor Vehicles (Third Amendment) Rules of 2000.

What was gained in the first decade and half of the case? Should the court have been more focused? Should the court have restricted the new emission regime to the NCR or extended it to all polluted metropolitan regions?

Institutionally, each bench of the Supreme Court over a period of several years is likely to have different members with different degrees of interest in a particular environmental problem. The *Motor Vehicles* case indicates the difficulty of the court's intermittent attempts to oversee a complex problem fraught with political, economic and technological considerations.

During this period, the Kerala High Court achieved a more modest agenda in requiring the Kerala government to strictly implement vehicular emission regulations framed under the MVA. The court directed the state to provide a smoke meter and gas analyser in every major town.[160] Similar directions were issued by the Gwalior bench of the Madhya Pradesh High Court.[161]

---

156 (1998) 6 SCC 63. On 29 September 1998, the court modified the ban order by setting a time frame for a more gradual phase out of old commercial vehicles, AIR 1999 SC 291.

157 (1999) 6 SCC 9.

158 (1999) 6 SCC 12.

159 (1999) 6 SCC 14.

160 *Murali Purushothaman v Union of India* AIR 1993 KER 297.

161 *Santosh Kumar Gupta v Secy., Ministry of Environment* AIR 1998 MP 43.

In April 2002, the Union Government applied to the Supreme Court requesting a variation of previous court directions regarding converting the public transport fleet of diesel buses into CNG vehicles. The government applied a three-pronged strategy: first, it tried to discredit CNG as a proper fuel. Second, it claimed that there was a shortage of CNG and finally, that the deadlines prescribed by the court needed to be extended since there was a delay in setting up adequate dispensing stations. We carry a short excerpt where the Supreme Court underscores the health impact of air pollution and lays out the progress of the case. The court found that the grounds urged by the government were mere excuses to avoid implementing orders.

M C MEHTA v UNION OF INDIA

(2002) 4 SCC 356

ORDER:

* * *

The concern of this Court in passing various orders since 1986 has only been one, namely, to protect the health of the people of Delhi. It is only with this objective in mind that directions had been issued in an effort to persuade the governmental authorities to take such steps as would reduce the air pollution. It is as a result of intervention by this Court that the following measures were taken in controlling pollution to some extent:

(a) lowering of sulphur content in diesel, first to 0.50% and then to 0.05%;
(b) ensuring supply of only lead-free petrol;
(c) requiring the fitting of catalytic converters;
(d) directing the supply of pre-mix 2T oil for lubrication of engines of two-wheelers and three-wheelers;
(e) directing the phasing out of grossly polluting old vehicles;
(f) directing the lowering of the benzene content in petrol; and
(g) ensuring that new vehicles, petrol and diesel, meet Euro II standards by September 2000.

It was during the course of these proceedings that the Bhure Lal Committee was established under Section 3 of the Environment (Protection) Act, 1986.

The Environment Pollution (Prevention and Control) Authority is a statutory authority constituted under Section 3 of the Environment (Protection) Act, 1986, and its directions are final and binding on all persons and organisations concerned. This position has been reiterated by this Court in *Sector 14 Residents' Welfare Assn v State of Delhi* (1999) 1 SCC 161. It is this authority which had directed the phasing out of non-CNG buses. It is the Bhure Lal Committee which had also recommended the conversion to CNG mode and issued directions that non-CNG buses should be phased out.

It is the report of the Bhure Lal Committee which was accepted and orders were passed by this Court on 28-7-1998 [*M C Mehta v Union of India* (1998) 6 SCC 63], fixing the time-limit within which the switchover to CNG was to take place. It may be mentioned here that the need for finding an alternative fuel to diesel had been drawing the attention of this Court for quite some time. This is evident from the order dated 21-10-1994, in which it was observed as follows:

> 'On an earlier occasion when these matters came up before this Court it was suggested that to begin with, government vehicles and public undertaking vehicles including public transport vehicles could be equipped with CNG cylinders with necessary modification in the vehicles to avoid pollution which is hazardous to the health of the people living in highly polluted cities like Delhi and the other metros in the country.' … [The court recorded how the timeframe was extended by the court even though the authorities appeared lax in obeying court directions. The court found that the reluctance by the government was 'baffling' and 'which leaves us with no doubt that its intention,

clearly, is to frustrate the orders passed by this court with regard to conversion of commercial vehicles to CNG.']

The plea of the Government that CNG is in short supply, and that it is unable to supply adequate quantity is incorrect, and this is clearly a deliberate attempt to frustrate the orders passed by this Court. Particulars filed in the Court show that as of today no CNG is being imported. The indigenous produce is far in excess of what is supplied to the transport sector. It is only a small fraction of CNG produced in India which is earmarked for non-industrial use. Overwhelming quantity is allocated to industries, including the power sector....

If there is a short supply of an essential commodity, then the priority must be of public health, as opposed to the health of the balance sheet of a private company. To enable industries to cut their losses, or make more profit at the cost of public health, is not a sign of good governance, and this is contrary to the constitutional mandate of Articles 39(e), 47 and 48-A....

The statistics show that the continuing air pollution is having a more devastating effect on the people, than what was caused by the Bhopal gas tragedy. In that case, the nation, including the Union of India, was rightly agitated and sought action and compensation from the multinational company, who was held to be responsible for the same. Here, in the case of CNG, the shoe is on the other foot because the Government is not facilitating measures for clean air and water including the supply of CNG or any other clean unadulterated fuel. It is due to the lack of proper concern on the part of the governmental authorities that people are suffering from respiratory and other diseases. The Bhopal gas tragedy was a one-time event which, hopefully, will not be repeated, but here, with not enough concern or action being undertaken by the Union of India, far greater tragedies in the form of degradation of public health are taking place every day.

Under these circumstances, it becomes the duty of this Court to direct such steps being taken as are necessary for cleaning the air so that the future generations do not suffer from ill health....

Even though the time for phasing out diesel buses had expired but in view of the situation created by the Government of not cooperating or complying with the Court's order, a different formula has to be worked out so as to cause as little inconvenience to the travelling public as possible, while at the same time punishing the wrongdoer. Directions are, therefore, to be issued regarding the lifting of 1500 buses plus phasing out of 800 buses per month. The permits to be given are to be time-bound and the continued operation of the diesel buses till they are replaced would require them to pay Rs 500 per bus per day for 30 days of operation and thereafter Rs 1000 per day and the same is to be deposited with the Director of Transport, Delhi....

[Amongst the directions issued while rejecting the Government's request for extension were:]

1. The Union of India will give priority to the transport sector including private vehicles all over India with regard to the allocation of CNG. This means that first the transport sector in Delhi, and in the other air polluted cities of India, CNG will be allocated and made available and it is only thereafter, if any CNG is available, that the same can be allocated to the industries, preference being shown to public sector undertakings and power projects....
6. For implementing these directions, the Union of India and all governmental authorities, including IGL shall:
   (a) allocate and make available 16.1 lakh kg per day (2 mmscmd) of CNG in NCT of Delhi by 30-6-2002 for use by the transport sector;
   (b) increase the above supply of CNG whenever the need arises;

(c) prepare a scheme containing a time schedule for supply of CNG to the other polluted cities of India and furnish the same to this Court by 9-5-2002 for its consideration; and

(d) it will be open to the Union of India to supply LPG in addition to CNG as an alternate fuel or to supply any other clean non-adulterable fuel as the Bhure Lal Committee may recommend ...

NOTES AND QUESTIONS

1. The decision with respect to the type of fuel to be used by motor vehicles in Delhi, the allocation of CNG amongst competing claimants and the period for implementing new fuel norms are all essentially policy decisions. Ordinarily, in a democracy they fall within the purview of elected representatives who must be voted out if they fail to deliver. In India, courts have assumed the responsibility of intervening where public health is at stake and the executive was remiss in discharging its responsibility.

2. Why are mobile sources of pollution more difficult to regulate than stationary sources?

3. The *Motor Vehicles* case raised important issues of equity, argues Prof. Lavanya Rajamani. The court-driven conversion of the commercial bus and passenger car fleets meant great hardship to passengers who were stranded by the Delhi Transport Corporation's (DTC) decision to take diesel buses off the roads in deference to the court deadlines. CNG buses that plied were crippled by the non-availability of CNG in the initial weeks. Moreover, DTC's requirement for 2,000 CNG buses in just 14 months disrupted its finances.[162]

The CNG conversion reduced one important pollutant—suspended particulate matter (SPM)—but increased greenhouse gases that may be considered a harmful option from a global warming perspective.

While CNG is a high-cost, environmentally friendly fuel—a conversion of the commercial fleet is only a partial answer to Delhi's vehicular emissions problem:

> This is evident, in part, from the fact that notwithstanding the introduction of the CNG programme in Delhi, there is a 21.3% increase in cases of lung disease, and more than 20% increase in asthma attacks. A complete solution would address all the relevant pollutants, choose a range of clean fuels and institutionalise inspection and maintenance facilities. CNG only addresses the problem of suspended particulate matter (in this CNG has the clear advantage over other fuels). According to the Mashelkar Committee Report although a CNG vehicle emits 80% less particulate matter, 25% less nitrous oxides and 35% less hydrocarbons, the output of carbon monoxide (CO), a precursor to greenhouse gases (GHGs), is over five times greater than that for diesel. And, a CNG vehicle driven for a mile emits 20% more GHGs than driving a comparable diesel vehicle for a mile. It concludes that 'from the perspective of global warming, the decision to move from diesel to CNG is a harmful one.'[163]

After a prolonged spell of dormancy and three decades after M C Mehta filed his 1985 petition to control vehicular pollution in Delhi, the case dramatically revived in October 2015. Troubled at Delhi's dubious distinction of being the city with the world's most noxious air,

---

[162] Lavanya Rajamani; *Public Interest Environmental Litigation In India: Exploring Issues Of Access, Participation, Equity, Effectiveness and Sustainability* 19 Jr Of Envir Law 293 (2007).

[163] *Id.* The Mashelkar Committee Report was an Expert Committee report on automobile fuel policy issued in 2002. The Committee was appointed by Central Government and was headed by R A Mashelkar, The Director General of the Council for Scientific and Industrial Research with the mandate to draft an automobile fuel policy for India.

the court embarked on a remarkable enterprise to scrub clean the capital's murky atmosphere. The court's efforts spanned several hearings over several months. We excerpt the principal orders with connecting notes. The big question in this case is whether there are any constitutional limits to the Supreme Court's jurisdiction and if so, whether these limits were transgressed? As you review this material reflect on the role and responsibility of the Supreme Court and whether this phase of the case involved any element of adjudication. Attempt to reconstruct what played out in the Chief Justice of India's court, what pulls and pressures might have operated on the governments—Union and states, the vehicle manufacturers, the taxi owners and other persons impacted by these orders.

M C MEHTA v UNION OF INDIA

(2016) 2 SCC 33

ORDER: The issue relates to steps to be taken to check pollution by commercial traffic travelling from North India towards Jaipur and onwards via Delhi.

It has been pointed out that even though alternative routes are available for such traffic, the only reason for such traffic entering into Delhi is to save higher rate of toll tax in taking such alternative routes. In the process, pollution caused by such traffic inflicts heavy cost on the health of the residents of Delhi. To tackle this situation an 'Environment Compensation Charge' (ECC) may be required to be imposed on all light and heavy duty commercial vehicles and the amount so collected ought to be exclusively used for augmenting public transport and improving roads, particularly for most vulnerable users, that is, cyclists and pedestrians in Delhi.

Reference has been made to a report prepared by the Environment Pollution (Prevention and Control) Authority (EPCA) [constituted under the provisions of Environment (Protection) Act, 1986] on 'strategies to reduce air pollution from trucks entering and leaving Delhi'. According to the said report, a study was commissioned by the Centre for Science and Environment to M/s V R Techniche Consultants Pvt Ltd. According to the study, the commercial vehicles entering Delhi spew close to 30% of the total particulate load and 22% of the total nitrogen oxide load from the transport sector. About 23% of the commercial vehicles and 40–60% of the heavy trucks entering Delhi were not destined for Delhi. NH 71 and NH 71-A are toll roads connecting Rewari to Panipat via Jhajjar and Rohtak and this alternative route obviates the need to travel through Delhi. Thus, apart from MCD toll, it was necessary to impose ECC to equalise the difference in cost in travelling through alternative routes.

The learned *amicus curiae* . . . , learned Solicitor General . . . , and . . . learned Senior Counsel appearing for the Government of NCT Delhi have jointly suggested that ECC ought to be imposed by the Delhi Government at the following rates:

(*i*)	Category 2 (light duty vehicles, etc.) and Category 3 (2 axle trucks)	Rs 700
(*ii*)	Category 4 (3 axle trucks) and Category 5 (4 axle trucks and above)	Rs 1300

The above charge shall not be imposed on

(a) Passenger vehicles and ambulances
(b) On vehicles carrying essential commodities, that is, foodstuffs and oil tankers.

The charge will be collected by the toll operators without any deduction and handed over to the Delhi Government on every Friday. The Delhi Government shall furnish accounts of the receipts and the expenditure incurred to EPCA and to this Court each quarter.

The Governments of UP, Haryana and Rajasthan will provide large size billboards at the exit points towards the alternative highways to inform commercial traffic of the diversions. The said Governments will take steps to ensure that commercial traffic having destination other than Delhi use alternative routes. The said Governments will ensure that in the course of implementation of this order, traffic jams and other inconvenience to the public is avoided. The Government of NCT Delhi will issue advertisements to inform commercial traffic of the bypass routes and the information about the imposition of ECC required to be paid for entry into Delhi. The toll collectors will put in place Radio Frequency Identification (RFID) system at their own cost at nine main entry points in the city by 30-11-2015 and by 31-1-2016 at all the remaining 118 entry points to the city, failing which the contractors will be treated as being in breach of their obligation. The RFID data will be supplied to MCD and Transport Department of the Government of NCT Delhi.

The NCT Government will install its own CCTV cameras at nine entry points and also organise surprise visits to oversee the collection of ECC and other necessary arrangements.

On due consideration, we do not see any reason not to accept the above suggestion. Accordingly, we approve the suggested arrangements.

The Government of NCT Delhi may issue an appropriate notification to levy the aforesaid charge forthwith which will be operative for a period of four months starting from 1-11-2015 to 29-2-2016 on an experimental basis. This order will override any order to the contrary by any authority.

To review the above mechanism, the matter may be posted for further consideration in the third week of February, 2016.

NOTES AND QUESTIONS

1. This order was passed by the Supreme Court on 9 October 2015. What does the court do? First, it frames the issue, that is, steps to be taken to check pollution by commercial vehicles travelling from North India towards Jaipur and onwards through Delhi. Second, it recognizes that although alternative routes that bypass Delhi are available, the passage through Delhi is preferred by the trucks to save the high toll payable on the alternative roads. Third, the court records that the vehicular emissions impact the health of Delhi residents. Fourth, the court refers to a report prepared by EPCA which in turn referred to a study indicating that commercial vehicles entering Delhi contribute substantially to its pollution load and that between 40 and 60% of the heavy trucks entering Delhi are not destined for Delhi. Fifth, the court records the joint suggestion of counsel appearing in the case to impose an Environment Compensation Charge (ECC), 'to equalise the difference in costs in travelling through alternative routes'. Sixth, the court records counsel's suggestions with respect to the role and responsibilities of the state governments in diverting commercial traffic onto the alternative routes. Seventh, the court records suggestions with respect to what is required to be done by the toll collectors to upgrade their systems and to collect the ECC on behalf of the Delhi government. Eighth, the court provides its reasoning in two crisp sentences: 'On due consideration, we do not see any reason not to accept the above suggestion. Accordingly, we approve the suggested arrangements.' Finally, the court directs the arrangements to commence from 1 November 2015 for a period of four months ending 29 February 2016 'on an experimental basis'.

2. The ECC is a compulsory exaction in the nature of a charge or toll imposed upon commercial vehicles entering Delhi. Does the judiciary have any authority under the Constitution to impose such a charge or toll? Is the power to levy such a charge or toll the realm of the legislature?

The entries pertaining to taxation are specifically enumerated in List I (Union List) as well as List II (State List) of Schedule VII of the Constitution of India. Entry 59 of List II specifically covers 'tolls' and Article 248 of the Constitution reads:

248. *Residuary powers of legislation.* —

(1) Parliament has exclusive power to make any law with respect to any matter not enumerated in the Concurrent List or State List.
(2) Such power shall include the power of making any law imposing a tax not mentioned in either of those Lists.

Under the Constitution who may properly impose an ECC? The Parliament, state legislatures or the Supreme Court?

3. Under the constitutional scheme, the High Courts and the Supreme Court are conferred with the power of judicial review and may strike down as *ultra vires*, executive actions or legislative enactments that are found to be unconstitutional. But where can the citizen challenge an imposition such as ECC by a court? Is this levy, when imposed by the highest court, immune from scrutiny? Does this mean that while a constitutional amendment in India may be assailed before a court,[164] the act of placing a law in Schedule IX of the Constitution may be tested in court,[165] and an environmental charge imposed by a competent legislature may be questioned before a court, but a Supreme Court-imposed ECC is completely insulated from scrutiny? Since a judicial order in India cannot be challenged on the ground that it violates fundamental rights[166] and because there is no court above the Supreme Court, the ECC is ring-fenced against any assault.

4. Apart from judicial review, a compulsory exaction in the form of a tax, fee, toll or charge is subject to other constitutional safeguards. Article 265 provides: 'No tax shall be levied or collected except by authority of law.' Every compulsory exaction in India must be backed by a valid law. This article builds on the American experience. A significant pre-Independence milestone in US constitutional history was the protest against taxes imposed by the British Parliament on American colonies. The call 'no taxation without representation' demanded that, to tax citizens, the citizenry must have representation in the legislature—a condition that was absent under colonial rule.

At fair distance from basic constitutional tenets, the ECC may be described as 'taxation by suggestion'—a court-imposed tax on the suggestion of eminent counsel appearing before it. How safe is the citizen when courts begin to tax in this manner? Can High Courts do the same? What about the National Green Tribunal? At what rate should the ECC be fixed? Can it be doubled? Who is to say?

On 20 October 2015, the Delhi government issued a notification imposing the ECC. The notification is silent on a statutory source of power to justify the charge—it only refers to the Supreme Court order. The levy continued and soon the Supreme Court was issuing directions with respect to utilization of ECC.[167]

5. Article 19(1)(d) sets out the fundamental right by which all citizens have a right to move freely throughout the territory of India. Article 19(5) of the Constitution provides that the freedom guaranteed under Article 19(1)(d) is subject to the state 'making any law' imposing reasonable restrictions on the exercise of this right in the interest of the public. Does the

---

164 *Supreme Court Advocates-on-Record Association v Union of India* (2016) 5 SCC 1.

165 *I R Coelho v State of Tamil Nadu* (2007) 2 SCC 1. Certain laws set out in Schedule IX of the Constitution are immune from challenge on the ground that the law violates fundamental rights. However, judicial review does extend to examining the placement of the law into Schedule IX.

166 *Naresh Shridhar Mirajkar v State of Maharashtra* AIR 1967 SC 1.

167 See *M C Mehta v Union of India* MANU/SCOR/07452/2019, order dated 6 March 2019.

embargo on commercial vehicles entering Delhi through a judicial direction violate constitutional norms? Is the Supreme Court order '*law*' within the meaning of Article 19(5)?

6. Part XIII of the Constitution covers trade, commerce and intercourse within the territory of India. Article 301 specifically provides that trade, commerce and intercourse 'throughout the territory of India shall be free', subject to the provisions of Part XIII. Parliament 'may by law' impose restrictions on the freedom of trade, commerce or intercourse between one state and another or within any part of the territory of India as may be required in the public interest. In the absence of any law enacted by Parliament, is it constitutionally permissible for a court to restrict the movement of goods carried by trucks that pass through Delhi?

7. Consider the issue framed by the court in the opening lines of the order. Is the business of regulating and redirecting commercial vehicular traffic entering Delhi an administrative function or judicial function?

8. Revisit the reasons offered by the court. Are they reasons at all? Is there anything to show that the judges applied their mind to constitutional limitations?

9. The penultimate sentence in the order reads: 'This order will override any order to the contrary by any authority.' Why was this inserted?

The next effective order, excerpted below, was passed by the Supreme Court on 16 December 2015.

M C MEHTA v UNION OF INDIA

(2016) 4 SCC 269, 277

ORDER: [L]earned Senior Counsel appearing as Amicus, argued that imposition of ECC and the directions issued by this Court regarding diversion of commercial vehicles/trucks to alternative routes has made some difference but the pollution levels continue to remain high despite such measures. He submitted by reference to the material placed on record that the level of pollution detected on or before 9-10-2015 [*M C Mehta v Union of India* (2016) 2 SCC 33] was in fact lower than the levels recorded on subsequent dates. [Amicus] further submitted that although diversion of vehicles to alternative routes in terms of the order passed by this Court was given effect to belatedly on 6-11-2015, yet the said direction has not been effectively enforced inasmuch as vehicles not bound for Delhi are being allowed to enter Delhi on payment of the prescribed ECC. It was submitted that the true spirit of the order passed by this Court was that vehicles that were bound for Delhi alone were to enter Delhi and other vehicles bound for other destinations/cities were supposed to bypass Delhi by using alternative routes. He drew our attention to a similar direction issued by this Court in *M C Mehta v Union of India* (2003) 10 SCC 561. It was in that view urged that the order passed by this Court on 9-10-2015, (2016) 2 SCC 33 could be modified/clarified to make it clear that the State Governments shall take steps to divert vehicles that are not bound for Delhi through alternative routes especially those using National Highway 8 and National Highway 1 for entering the national capital. It was also contended ... that in order to effectively discourage vehicles from entering Delhi, ECC could be revised upwards especially when the Government of NCT of Delhi, MCD and the Union of India were all agreeable to the same.

[L]earned Solicitor General appearing for the Union of India, submitted that diversion of traffic away from Delhi by use of alternative routes as also by way of enhancement of ECC has been thoroughly discussed with the learned *amicus curiae* and that the Union of India and so also the Government of NCT have no objection to such a direction being issued. He submitted that as a matter of fact discussions held between the representatives of the two

Governments, namely, the Union of India and the Government of NCT of Delhi as also the MCD had led to a consensus on five other points also on which this Court could issue suitable directions to help reduce the pollution levels in Delhi. It was submitted that the revision of ECC could be up to 100% of the amount already stipulated for vehicles that are Delhi bound while other vehicles which are not bound for Delhi could be directed to bypass Delhi by using alternative routes which the two Governments could be directed to specify.

By our order dated 6-12-2001, passed in *M C Mehta v Union of India* (2003) 10 SCC 561, we had, *inter alia*, directed:

> 'It appears that vehicles which transit through Delhi do not adhere to the vehicular standards which are applicable in Delhi, namely, they are not Euro II-compliant nor are they using low sulphur and low benzene fuel. *There is no reason why very large number of goods vehicles should transit through Delhi thereby adding to the pollution level and the traffic on the road.*
>
> It is, therefore, proposed that with effect from 15-1-2002 no heavy medium or light goods vehicles will ply on inter-State routes by passing through Delhi or New Delhi. It is only those goods vehicles which on payment of octroi/toll tax carry goods to or from Delhi which would be allowed to ply. The Commissioner of Police is directed to formulate a scheme in this behalf and give due publicity to all concerned and implement the same.' (emphasis supplied)

Our order dated 9-10-2015 was in the same spirit intended to act as a restraint against vehicles not bound for Delhi entering Delhi. The said direction appears to have been understood to mean as though vehicles not bound for Delhi could also enter Delhi provided they pay ECC. The true intention, however, was that the vehicles that are not bound for Delhi are diverted to alternative routes to bypass Delhi. The levy of ECC has no doubt resulted in some diversion of such vehicles but a very large number of vehicles not bound for Delhi still appear to be entering Delhi on payment of ECC, stipulated by us. In the circumstances, we consider it necessary to make it clear that no vehicle which is not bound for Delhi will be allowed to enter from NH 8 which connects Jaipur to Delhi and NH 1 that connects the States of Punjab, Haryana and other northern States to Delhi via Kundli border. We are limiting the restraint order to these two entry points for the present because from the figures given to us the largest number of vehicles that are entering into Delhi are from these two entry points. We, accordingly, direct that traffic from these two entry points viz. Kundli border on NH 1 and Rajokri on NH 8, shall be diverted to bypass Delhi through such alternative routes as the transport/traffic departments of the Governments concerned may stipulate.

We are further of the view that empty/unladen vehicles bound for Delhi, can enter Delhi on payment of ECC earlier stipulated by us @ Rs700 and Rs1300 per vehicle depending upon the category to which the vehicle belongs. We, however, direct that for Delhi bound vehicles loaded with goods, ECC will be twice the charge stipulated by us by our order dated 9-10-2015 [*M C Mehta v Union of India* (2016) 2 SCC 33]. This measure shall, in our opinion, discourage any vehicle trying to enter Delhi on a false pretext of the goods loaded on it being Delhi bound.

[Amicus] next argued that the transport vehicles registered on or before 2005 which are non-compliant with the current pollution control standards also need to be disallowed from entering Delhi even if the same are Delhi bound with goods loaded for consumption in the city. There was a consensus among the learned counsel for the parties even on this issue who submitted that the Union of India or Government of NCT of Delhi have no real objection if a direction to that effect is issued. We, accordingly, direct that while vehicles 'bound for Delhi' may enter on payment of ECC at the rates stipulated hereinabove, those registered in the year 2005 or earlier shall not qualify for such entry. The State Governments and Union Territories concerned shall ensure that vehicles bearing registration numbers of the year 2005 or earlier do not enter Delhi. The Governments will evolve a suitable system for implementation of this direction.

It was contended by [Amicus] that since diesel vehicles are the most polluting vehicles contributing to the current state of affairs in Delhi, it is time to issue directions banning registration of any new private and commercial light duty diesel vehicles in the National Capital Region. This submission was opposed by [the Solicitor General] who submitted that banning of commercial light duty diesel vehicles is likely to affect trade and commerce within Delhi and supply of essential commodities to the people living in the National Capital Region especially because such vehicles are used in large numbers for ferrying goods from one place to the other in the region.

[L]earned Senior Counsel appearing for the automobile dealers selling diesel vehicles, also opposed any ban on registration of new private vehicles and commercial light duty diesel vehicles as proposed.... Having given our anxious consideration to the submissions made at the Bar, we are of the view that the new commercial light duty diesel vehicles can for the present continue being registered in Delhi on account of the dependence of the public on such vehicles for supply of essentials. There is, however, no reason why registration of private cars and SUVs using diesel with an engine capacity of 2000 cc and above should not be banned up to 31-3-2016. It is noteworthy that diesel vehicles of 2000 cc and above and SUVs are generally used by more affluent sections of our society and because of the higher engine capacity are more prone to cause higher levels of pollution. A ban on registration of such vehicles will not, therefore, affect the common man or the average citizen in the city of Delhi. We, accordingly, direct that registration of SUVs and private cars of the capacity of 2000 cc and above using diesel as fuel shall stand banned in the NCR up to 31-3-2016.

It was then argued by [Amicus] that all taxis including aggregators like OLA and Uber plying in the National Capital Region may be moved to CNG fuel within a reasonable time but not later than 31-3-2016. There was a general consensus on this subject also primarily because it is hoped by all concerned that it will contribute substantially to the reduction of the pollution. We, therefore, direct that all taxis including those operating under aggregators like OLA and Uber in the NCR of Delhi, plying under city permits shall move to CNG not later than 31-3-2016.

* * *

We, accordingly, direct the Government of NCT of Delhi to take immediate steps for repair of pavements and make pavements wherever the same are missing and also to take immediate steps for procurement of the requisite vacuum cleaning vehicles for use on Delhi roads expeditiously but not later than 1-4-2016.

It was argued by the learned counsel for the parties that one of the major contributors to the current pollution levels is the construction activities going on in the National Capital Region. It was submitted that the Union of India and the State Governments concerned must be directed to take steps to enforce the Cpcb rules and norms against those engaged in such construction activities to prevent further rise of pollution levels. We see no reason to decline a direction to that effect. Cpcb norms regarding prevention of pollution by putting curtains and other devices at construction sites must be strictly enforced by the enforcement agencies concerned. We direct accordingly.

It is also contended by the learned counsel for the parties that one of the contributors to the pollution is burning of solid waste by local bodies like MCD, Ndmc and institutions that generate such waste. It was submitted that burning of solid waste was impermissible under the relevant rules and that lapses on the part of the authorities concerned in the matter of enforcing the said rules is contributing to the deteriorating situation. It was, therefore, prayed that authorities including the local bodies and institutions within the National Capital Region be directed to refrain from disposing of solid waste by burning such waste and to take steps for proper management/disposal of such waste in a scientific manner following the norms and the requirements of the relevant rules in that regard. We see no reason to decline that prayer either. We, accordingly, direct that the State Government and the local bodies concerned including MCD, NDMC and all other institutions that are generating solid waste shall take steps to ensure that no part of such waste is burnt and that proper arrangements are made for disposal of such waste in a scientific way without causing any hazard to environment. . . .

NOTES AND QUESTIONS

1. The Supreme Court quotes from its order passed 14 years earlier on 6 December 2001. In that order, the court directed the Commissioner of Police to formulate a scheme to prevent vehicles carrying goods from using Delhi as a transit point. It appears that no scheme was framed.

Keeping in mind Articles 19(1)(d) and 301 of the Constitution referred to in the previous set of notes, was the court justified in directing: '[W]e consider it necessary to make it clear that no vehicle which is not bound for Delhi will be allowed to enter from NH8 which connects Jaipur to Delhi and NH1 which connects the State of Punjab, Haryana and other Northern States to Delhi via Kundli border.' Absent a specific law, can a state government or the Union Government or any constitutional functionary such as the Chief Minister or the Prime Minister issue a diktat restricting the movement of vehicles or goods into or through a city or impose a mandatory charge like the ECC? Would a constitutional court countenance such a diktat? Considering that the exercises being conducted by the court in redirecting traffic, banning vehicles, reducing construction dust, etc. are purely administrative and not adjudicatory, how is the judicial direction any different from a similar executive diktat?

2. Notice how the court simply doubles the ECC levy: 'We, however, direct that for Delhi bound vehicles loaded with goods, the ECC will be twice the charge stipulated by us by our order dated 9th October 2015.' Why not treble it? Are we in the realm of the Rule of Law?

3. The court's order reflects a broad consensus amongst the counsel appearing before it, including law officers representing the Union Government and state governments. Notice the absence of any resistance against the court extending its reach into areas of taxation, interstate commerce and the freedom of movement of citizens. Why is counsel representing government apparently willing to allow the judiciary to make inroads into the executive and legislative sphere? Is there any mechanism to correct Supreme Court orders that may be excessive? What are the features of a Supreme Court hearing that make it difficult to rein in a bench that has discarded self-restraint?

4. The Supreme Court banned the registration of private cars using diesel with an engine capacity of 2000 cc and above in the National Capital Region. Impossible to predict and devastating in its impact, the order hit manufacturers, dealers and thousands of their employees. Manufacturing such vehicles, buying, selling and registering them is perfectly lawful. Corporations and individuals invest huge resources to build and run businesses which employ persons whose families earn a living from these enterprises. Considering that it was imposed without warning and without assessing the impact the ban would have on improving Delhi's air, was the ban justified? Was it fair?

The ban on registration was conditionally lifted by the Supreme Court on 12 August 2016. The court recorded offers made by manufacturers that they were 'willing without demur to deposit environment protection charge ... equivalent to 1% of the ex-show room price of the diesel vehicles manufactured by that company as a condition precedent for registration of such vehicles by the jurisdictional Registration Officers'. Latching on to the offer, the court ordered:

> We accordingly direct that the CPCB shall open a separate account in a Scheduled public sector bank to receive the amount representing 1% of the Ex-show room price of every diesel car that is sold by any manufacturer/dealer in Delhi and NCR region. The deposit of the amount alone shall entitle the manufacturer/dealer or the purchaser of the car to have the car registered within Delhi or NCR region.[168]

Is there any principle that might support such an order?

5. The National Capital Region admeasures over 46,000 sq kms and extends deep into the neighbouring states of Haryana, Uttar Pradesh and Rajasthan. The effect of this ban was to prohibit the sale of some popular diesel vehicles and several top-end luxury vehicles. Dealers in the luxury car segment found their business at a standstill while vehicle manufacturers found the manufacturing process disrupted. These dealers and manufacturers were engaged in lawful businesses protected by the fundamental right to carry on trade and business guaranteed under Article 19(1)(g) of the Constitution. But what is the worth of this fundamental right or any fundamental right for that matter if the Supreme Court, which is constitutionally obliged to protect these rights, issues directives that disrupt legitimate businesses?

6. Does this order lend legal certainty, or does it further add to the risk of doing business in India? How does this order square with the Indian government's ambitious plan to make the country a manufacturing hub for motor cars? If you were to make investment decisions for an automobile maker, would you set up a manufacturing plant in India or would you rather invest in a country where the investment was not likely to be jeopardized by a court directive?

7. The Supreme Court directed all taxis plying under city permits to move to CNG by 31 March 2016. This direction of the court was understood to cover taxis operating on diesel fuel. At the time, unlike petrol engines there were no commercially available kits to convert diesel engines into engines that run on CNG. How does a taxicab owner comply with this order? Must she scrap her cab? Who bears the cost of her wasted investment? Remember, there was *no* statutory prohibition that prevented the registration and running of diesel taxis in NCR and until this order was passed, taxi owners were running lawful businesses.

8. *Lex non cogit ad impossibilia*—the law does not compel the doing of impossibilities. Does this maxim apply to the Supreme Court? How does one convert a diesel cab into a CNG vehicle, absent the technology? What does this say about the quality of assistance available to the court?

M C MEHTA v UNION OF INDIA
(2016) 4 SCC 269, 282

> ORDER: [Amicus] also points out that there is typographical mistake in our order dated 16-12-2015 inasmuch as instead of 'NCR' the expression 'NCT' and instead of '31-3-2016' expression '1-3-2016' have been used in para 11 (above) of that order. We had in the said paragraph directed all taxis including those operating under aggregators like OLA and UBER to be converted to CNG not later than 31-3-2016. We make it clear that the said direction will apply to all such taxis as are operating in the NCR and to be converted to CNG but not later than 31-3-2016. The expressions 'NCT' and '1-3-2016' shall, accordingly, stand replaced by 'NCR' and '31-3-2016'....

[168] (2018) 18 SCC 752.

NOTES AND QUESTIONS

1. This order was passed on 5 January 2016. The court simply substitutes the expression 'NCT' with 'NCR' accepting the *amicus*' submission about the typographical error. The result of this substitution was that the order which originally covered taxis operating in the National Capital *Territory* admeasuring around 1483 sq kms, expanded to cover all taxis in the National Capital *Region* which spreads over 46,000 sq kms, over 30 times the area that constitutes NCT. Considering that this case has to do with vehicular air pollution in Delhi, was it reasonable, fair or just to require taxi operators working at great distances from Delhi to also convert their diesel vehicles into CNG vehicles (assuming that were even possible)? The NCR covers distant towns such as Panipat, Sonepat and Rohtak in Haryana, the cities of Meerut and Muzaffarnagar in Uttar Pradesh and the districts of Alwar and Bharatpur in Rajasthan. How does plying a diesel taxicab in Alwar or Meerut affect air quality in Delhi? Do you think the authorities or cab owners in these distant towns and districts were even aware of the Supreme Court deadline for conversion of vehicles?

2. The Supreme Court extended the deadline for conversion of diesel taxis from 31 March 2016 to 30 April 2016, but not beyond. Since conversion was impossible, hundreds of cab drivers weary of police harassment went off the road, upsetting the rhythms of citizens who depended on Delhi's taxi fleet. Moreover, the order disrupted economic activity by curtailing available public transport. Amongst those most deeply impacted were business process outsourcing (BPO) companies based in the NCT employing thousands of young persons and providing support services to multinational corporations for overseas customers in the fields of banking, medicine, automobile support, information technology, etc. These companies engaged fleets of diesel taxis to ferry their employees to and from their offices and were concerned about their employees' safety upon the ban coming into force.

Post ban, who would safely transport the employees working in night shifts? NASSCOM[169] members feared that with decreased staff attendance, the quality of services provided to customers would be impaired and dissatisfied customers would shift their business to the Philippines or other rival locations.

3. On 10 May 2016,[170] the court relented and diluted the embargo by permitting diesel taxis to operate until their existing permits lapsed. This modification brought immediate relief as most permits had a balance term of two to four years. In this order, the court also directed: 'Registration of new city taxis shall be permitted only if the vehicles operate on dual fuel or petrol or CNG. We make it clear that no vehicle shall be registered as a city taxi if it runs on diesel fuel. The competent authorities shall faithfully comply with this direction.'

Should a court prohibit registration of diesel taxis used across the world and across India when there is no *statutory* embargo? Can every High Court issue such a direction in respect of cities within its territorial jurisdiction? Can the NGT do so? Is the lead provided by the Supreme Court a recipe for economic disruption and the destruction of honest livelihoods? Does this series of orders suggest a pattern of boundless enthusiasm leading to great economic uncertainty with respect to activities that are perfectly legal under statute? Should the court have abided by its own advice: 'the doctrine of sustainable development although [not an empty slogan] is required to be implemented taking a pragmatic view and not on *ipse dixit* of the court.'[171]

---

[169] National Association of Software and Services Companies (NASSCOM) is the trade association of Information Technology (IT) and BPO firms.

[170] *M C Mehta v Union of India* MANU/SC/0739/2016.

[171] *Susetha v Tamil Nadu* (2006) 6 SCC 543, 547.

4. The first order passed on 9 October 2015, refers to a report prepared by EPCA. How was EPCA formed?

On 7 January 1998,[172] the Supreme Court examined a draft order proposed to be made under section 3(1) and (3) of the Environment (Protection) Act, 1986 to constitute an authority with respect to pollution in the NCR. The order records:

> We are satisfied that this step being taken by the Government is appropriate and timely. We would, however, like to add that except for the Chairman Central Pollution Control Board being the *ex officio* member of the authority, the remaining four persons named above are to be in the committee not merely by virtue of their office but because of their personal qualification on account of which they are included in the committee.... It is also necessary to take note of the fact that the constitution of a Committee as above with the comprehensive authority to deal with the entire matter relating to environmental pollution in the National Capital Region the continuance of any other authority with concurrent jurisdiction in any area within the entire sphere of environmental pollution in the National Capital Region is bound to create an embarrassing situation because of conflict of jurisdiction of the two authorities within the common sphere. Such a result would not be conducive to proper administration and implementation of the programme of preventing and controlling environmental pollution in the National Capital Region. It is, therefore, necessary to make an appropriate order which would avoid any conflict of jurisdiction between the two authorities....[173]

On 29 January 1998, the Central Government constituted EPCA for the National Capital Region for a term of two years. The chairman of the EPCA was Bhure Lal, then the Secretary to the Central Vigilance Commission. The notification defined the functions of EPCA in broad terms:

> '2. The Authority shall exercise the following powers and perform the following functions for protecting and improving the quality of the environment and preventing, controlling and abating environmental pollution, namely:–
>
> (1) exercise the powers under section 5 of the said Act for issuing directions in respect of complaints relating to the violation of an order by any authority or measure specified pertaining to –
>
> (i) standards for the quality of the environment in its various aspects,
>
> (ii) standards for omission or discharge of environmental pollutants from various sources,
>
> (iii) restriction of areas in which any industries, operations or processes or class of industries or processes shall not be carried out or shall be carried out subject to certain safeguards,
>
> (iv) procedures and safeguards for the prevention of accidents which may cause environmental pollution and remedial measures for such accidents,
>
> (v) procedures and safeguards for the handling of hazardous substances.
>
> (2) The Authority shall have the power to take up matters as mentioned above, suo-moto, or on the basis of complaints made by any individual, representative body or organization functioning in the field of environment. Such complaints may be against any individual, association, company, public undertaking or local body carrying on any industry, operation or process.
>
> 3. The Authority shall, for controlling vehicular pollution, take all necessary steps to ensure compliance of specified emission standards by vehicles including proper calibration of

[172] *M C Mehta v Union of India* AIR 1998 SC 617.

[173] The Supreme Court disbanded an earlier committee under Justice R K Shukla and by a subsequent order dated 13 January 1998 clarified: 'In case there are certain matters which are outside the scope of the authority of Bhure Lal Committee constituted under section 3(3) of the Environment Protection Act, the same shall be dealt with by the concerned statutory authorities....' *M C Mehta v Union of India* AIR 1998 SC 773.

the equipment for testing vehicular pollution, ensuring compliance of fuel quality standards, monitoring and coordinating action for traffic planning and management.

4. The Authority shall, for ensuring maintenance of the specified ambient noise standards, have the power to issue directions under section 5 of the said Act, including banning or restricting any industry, process or operation emitting noise.
5. The Authority shall deal with environmental issues pertaining to the National Capital Region which may be referred to it by the Central Government.
6. The Authority shall monitor the progress of the action plan drawn up by the Ministry of Environment and Forests on pollution in Delhi as contained in the 'White Paper on Pollution in Delhi with an Action Plan', issued by the Central Government on 3rd December, 1997.
7. The Authority shall exercise the powers of entry, inspection, search and seizure under section 10 of the said Act, in respect of any action to be taken under sub-paragraph (1) of the paragraph 2 of this Order.
8. The Authority shall exercise the power to take samples under section 11 of the said Act, in respect of any action to be taken under sub-paragraph (1) of paragraph 2 of this Order.
9. The Authority shall exercise the powers under section 19 of the said Act, for making complaints against offences under the said Act and for non-compliance of directions issued by it under sub-paragraph (1) of paragraph 2 of this Order.
10. The Authority shall have jurisdiction over the National Capital Region as defined in clause (f) of section 2 of the National Capital Region Planning Board Act, 1985 (2 of 1985).
11. The foregoing powers and functions of the Authority shall be subject to the supervision and control of the Central Government.
12. The Authority shall furnish a progress report about its activities at least once in two months to the Central Government.
13. The Authority shall have its headquarters in the National Capital Region.
14. (1) Notification of the Government of India in Ministry of Environment and Forests number S.O.704(E), dated the 9th October, 1996 consisting the Environmental Impact Assessment Authority for the National Capital Region shall stand superseded (expect in respect of things done or omitted to be done before such supersession) from the date of publication of this Order.
    (2) Any matter which relates to the powers and functions enumerated in this Order, and pending with the Environmental Impact Assessment Authority shall stand transferred to the Environment Pollution (Prevention and Control) Authority for the National Capital Region constituted under this Order.
    (3) Any matter specifically not falling within the scope and jurisdiction of the Authority as so constituted shall be dealt with by the statutory authorities concerned.'

On 25 January 2000, when the term of EPCA was about to expire the government amended the original notification and substituted the original two-year term with the words 'for a period of four years'. On 25 January 2002, the words, 'for a period of 5 years' were inserted to extend the term. On 28 January 2003, the words, 'for a period of 5 years' were substituted with the words 'for a period of 8 years'. This process continued with periodic statutory notifications extending the tenure of EPCA by additional terms ranging between three months and a year.[174] The notification issued on 22 July 2014 extended the term of EPCA by just three months and the notification issued on 24 February 2015 provided: 'In the said order [dated 29 January 1998], in the opening paragraph, for the words "for a period of sixteen years and nine months", the words "for a period up to 30th June, 2015" shall be substituted.' EPCA lost its statutory status on 30 June 2015 until the status was re-conferred on 4 July 2016. After

174 The amending notifications were issued on 25 January 2006, 27 July 2006, 27 April 2007, 26 July 2007, 18 July 2008, 27 July 2009, 25 January 2010, 19 January 2011, 27 January 2012, 24 January 2013, 30 January 2014, 2 July 2014 and 23 February 2015.

periodic extensions, on 3 October 2018, EPCA was reconstituted with 20 members with a tenure 'of six months or until further orders . . . whichever is earlier'.[175]

For over 20 years, Bhure Lal continued at the helm of EPCA as its chairman and for two decades the composition of EPCA too hardly underwent any change. The environmentalist Sunita Narain served on EPCA and was its driving force.

5. The Environment Pollution (Prevention and Control) Authority was constituted in 1998 with extensive powers including the power to issue statutory directions in terms of section 5 of the EPA. The deteriorating air quality in the NCR is a clear indicator that EPCA failed in its primary duty. But, if EPCA was ineffective, why was government continuously extending its term? Should EPCA have been wound up? Should the composition of EPCA have been changed? In a democracy, should personnel (however eminent) serve on statutory authorities for virtually indefinite tenures? Repeated extensions of term without any change in personnel undermine institution-building and result in individual-centric organizations. Similarly, short-term extensions prevent authorities from implementing medium- and long-term projects, policies and programmes.

Had EPCA resorted to its wide powers and issued directives prohibiting entry of vehicles into Delhi, banning registration of diesel taxis or imposing an ECC, its initiatives might well have been thwarted by judicial injunctions on constitutional principles. Instead, EPCA persuaded the Supreme Court through the *amicus* to issue directions in a PIL, thereby insulating the directives from judicial oversight. Curious 'constitutionalism'?

6. The Authority was dissolved on 28 October 2020 by a Presidential Ordinance promulgated to constitute the Commission for Air Quality Management in National Capital Region and Adjoining Areas.[176] This Ordinance was issued to avoid a Supreme Court order passed on 16 October 2020 constituting the Justice Madan Lokur Monitoring Committee to monitor the measures taken by the states to prevent stubble burning.[177]

Examine the statutory provisions. Will the Commission succeed where the PCBs, EPCA and judicial intervention failed? Why?

7. In an environmental emergency, one might expect the responsible environmental protection agencies to step in and combat the crisis. Despite media reports over several months commenting on the foul quality of Delhi's air and the grave threat to its residents, none of the state agencies or the MoEF came up with any meaningful plan. Unsurprisingly, the system responded through its judges. First off the mark was the National Green Tribunal in the case entitled *Vardhaman Kaushik v Union of India*.[178] Next was the Delhi High Court in a *suo motu* action titled *Court on its Own Motion (Air Pollution in Delhi) v Union of India*.[179] Finally, the Supreme Court of India reactivated the *M C Mehta* case filed in 1985.

The emerging picture is one of deeply concerned judges unwilling to tolerate administrative sub-competence and sloth. It is also bizarre that three sets of judicial proceedings were running simultaneously on the same subject in the same city.

[175] Notification dated 3 October 2018.
[176] *Supra* note 57.
[177] See *supra* notes 24–26 and the accompanying text.
[178] Original Application No. 21 of 2014, Principal Bench, New Delhi, NGT. (The case was renumbered Original Application No. 44 of 2018.)
[179] Writ Petition (C) No. 1346/2015.

8. When the Supreme Court imposed the ECC, its purpose was to discourage trucks laden with goods meant for destinations other than Delhi to use Delhi's roads for transit. The court supplemented the ECC with directions to redirect commercial traffic onto alternative routes that bypassed Delhi. These directions had enormous consequences, both negative and positive, on the private toll collectors working on these roads. The scheme for toll collection was that the government auctioned the routes to the party assuring the government of the highest return during the contractual term. Because of these directions the anticipated toll collection at Delhi's entry points dropped, compelling the toll collector to move the Supreme Court. However, the court declined to examine the legal challenge to the imposition of ECC, and instead granted the alternative request of releasing the collector from its contractual obligations.[180]

An unnoticed impact of these traffic diversion directions of the Supreme Court was a bonanza for the toll collectors on the alternative routes that trucks were now compelled to take.

9. Vehicular emissions depend on a combination of the fuel quality and the technology employed. In 2003, the government announced a National Auto Fuel Policy providing a road map for reducing vehicular emissions. The policy envisaged cleaner fuels through investments in refineries and required vehicle manufacturers to upgrade their engines so that progressively strict emission norms are met by the target dates. The emission norms are prescribed by amending the Central Motor Vehicle Rules of 1989. In 2014, while the Bharat Stage—III (BS-III) norms were in vogue, the Rules were amended to prescribe that new models of two-wheelers manufactured on and after 1 April 2016 comply with the more stringent BS-IV emission norms; and a further horizon of 1 April 2017 was provided for existing models of two-wheelers.

Bajaj Auto Limited, one of the manufacturers of two-wheelers, upgraded its models and to steal a march on the competition asked the Supreme Court to prohibit the sale of any BS-III two-wheeler after 1 April 2017. The rival manufacturers as well as the government protested, claiming a window after 1 April 2017 to dispose [of] unsold BS-III vehicles manufactured before that date. The Supreme Court found that BS-IV compliant vehicles reduced pollution by about 80% in particulate matter as compared to BS-III vehicles. Besides, government refineries had invested Rs. 30,000 crores to make BS-IV fuel available across the country. The court preferred a purposive interpretation over a literal reading of the provisions:

> The learned counsel for the interveners sought to impress upon us that we should interpret the various notifications issued from time to time only in a literal manner. When the health of millions of people in our country is involved, notifications relating to commercial activities ought not to be interpreted in a literal manner. The only option in such eventualities is to give a purposive interpretation to notifications that directly concern public health issues which have an impact not only in the present but also in the future. We were informed that the life of vehicles is in the range of 10 and 15 years. While the development versus environment paradigm could be debated upon, there cannot be any debate in the development versus public health paradigm....
>
> Additionally, if the entire scheme laid out by the Government—of discouraging the manufacture of polluting vehicles and gradually phasing them out coupled with their gradual replacement with fuel efficient vehicles, availability of cleaner and greener fuel and compliance with fuel emission norms is appreciated in a much larger context rather than on a notification by notification basis—the objective behind the scheme would be apparent. The Government could very well have issued one single notification way back in 2010 that with effect from 1-4-2017 the manufacture, sale and registration of vehicles that do not comply

180 (2016) 4 SCC 269, 287.

> with BS-IV emission norms would be prohibited. It did not do so to enable all concerned, particularly the auto industry and marketing strategists to gradually manage their affairs rather than subject them to a sudden future shock. The scheme of a gradual phase-out is now sought to be perverted through a literal interpretation of each notification, unfortunately, for a commercial benefit rather than being appreciated in a larger canvas for the benefit of society as a whole.[181]

Was the Supreme Court justified in adopting an interpretation that was at odds with past practice where manufacturers could clear accumulated stock? Or was the Supreme Court correct in its approach considering that the BS-III vehicles sold after 1 April 2017 would continue to pollute for the life of such vehicles estimated at nearly 10–15 years? What could the manufacturers do with their stocks?

Vardhaman Kaushik's Case (NGT)

Nearly one year before the Supreme Court imposed the ECC, the NGT in *Vardhaman Kaushik's* case on 27 October 2014 constituted a committee under the Secretary, MoEF to urgently report on steps that would prevent air pollution in Delhi.

Disappointed by the committee's report since it suggested 'nothing substantive' while the air quality continued to deteriorate, the NGT issued the following interim directions on 26 November 2014:

> All vehicles, diesel or petrol, which are more than 15 years old shall not be permitted to ply on the road and wherever such vehicles of this age are noticed, the concerned authorities shall take appropriate steps in accordance with law including seizure of the vehicles in accordance with the provisions of the Motor Vehicle Act, 1988.
>
> The vehicles which are more than 15 years old, will not be permitted to be parked in any public area and they shall be towed away and challaned by the police in accordance with law. This direction would be applicable to all vehicles without exception i.e. two wheelers, three wheelers, four wheelers, light vehicles and heavy vehicles irrespective of whether commercial or otherwise....
>
> The Commissioner of Police of Delhi, NCT of Delhi, Municipal Authorities and DPCC shall ensure that tarred reads for regular traffic are not permitted to be used for parking thus causing avoidable congestion of traffic.
>
> Once there is a congestion of traffic and vehicles are forced to keep their engines on for considerable long period, it results in extra emissions causing serious air pollution....
>
> RTO shall not issue/renew registration of the vehicles or fitness certificate to any vehicle which is more than 15 years old.
>
> We direct the Ministries, NCT of Delhi and DPCC to examine the possibility of installation of air-purifiers in all the markets and crowded places or where the traffic load is heavier. Air purifier be installed and Report to the Tribunal be placed on the next date of hearing.[182]

The directions also covered a bypass route for traffic entering Delhi, burning of plastic waste, creation of 'a special force' to process and respond to complaints in respect of burning of plastic or other material including leaves, the parking of vehicles and the need to ensure that trucks are not overloaded.

On 28 November 2014, the NGT issued further directions including:

> Air filter should be installed in terms of our order dated 26 November, 2016 particularly in the markets places which are highly crowded in terms of human beings and vehicles

[181] *M C Mehta v Union of India* (2017) 7 SCC 243.
[182] *Vardhaman Kaushik v Union of India* (2014) SCC Online NGT 2365.

and places and garden where the residents go for morning and evening walks, as the case may be.[183]

On 4 December 2014, the NGT identified three primary sources of pollution with respect to PM_{10}—dust, burning of plastic and other materials in open areas and vehicular pollution. The Tribunal issued diverse directions, including:

> An argument has been advanced before us to say that banning of 15 years old vehicles in Delhi would be unfair to the owners of the case and consequently if cars are sent outside Delhi, it would mean that they will cause pollution in other cities and hence, it would shift the pollution. This submission is not only misconceived but void of reasoning as well. Foremost, it pre-supposes that the vehicles of more than 15 years age are not causing pollution. The direction for not permitting the 15 years old vehicles to ply in Delhi may cause some hardship but certainly that hardship on individual or group of individuals must give way to the public cause of better environment and public health, which as per constitution mandate is the fundamental right of the public at large. Individual rights must conceal in favour of public rights. [The tribunal also suggested that sending 15 year old vehicles to less congested areas outside Delhi may enable dispersion of the pollutants.] ...
>
> Thus, we direct the Governments and all public and other Authorities to immediately install air filters in the colleges, schools and gardens and other public places which are visited by a greater number of people in the day.' ...
>
> We direct that the DPCC and the transport department shall immediately ensure installation of appropriate 'catalytic converters', particularly for diesel vehicles, if not already fitted which would ensure reduction of pollutants entering the atmosphere in Delhi. The Government of NCT will take steps to introduce and enforce BS-V vehicles in NCR, Delhi. All other neighbouring states would ensure that they also take effective steps to have BS-IV compliant vehicles only. The progress report should be submitted before the next date of hearing of the Tribunal....
>
> [I]f any person is found to be causing such pollution [burning of waste material, garbage and leaves in an open area] then decides the action that can be taken against him, we make it clear that such person shall be liable to pay compensation in terms of Section 15 of the National Green Tribunal Act, 2010 under the principle of 'polluter pays'. This compensation may vary depending on facts and circumstances of the case from Rs.20,000 to Rs.1,00,000 per incident....
>
> Crop ruminant burning in agricultural field falling in NCR shall be strictly prohibited.

On 19 January 2015, the NGT found that the deteriorating air quality justified further 'drastic measures' including the following:

> It will be ensured that stagnation of vehicle and traffic congestion are avoided particularly by prohibiting parking on the main roads or any parking area on the metalled roads. We direct all the SHOs concerned, the Traffic Police and the Concerned Corporation to ensure compliance of these directions without any default. There will be complete prohibition of parking of any cars on the metalled roads and the corporation would take strict action against the persons who violate it. This shall include payment of Rs.1000 per car on account of compensation for degradation of environment and its restoration. This would also be charged on the cars, which are parked on the metalled roads....
>
> All the vehicles which are more than 15 years will not be permitted to ply in Delhi. Transport commissioner shall ensure that such vehicles are not registered in NCR Delhi.

183 *Vardhaman Kaushik v Union of India* (2014) SCC Online NGT 6818.

On 10 April 2015, the NGT focused its attention on construction dust and adherence to MoEF Guidelines, 2010 pertaining to building activity. The NGT ordered:

> If any person, owner and/or builder is found to be violating any of the conditions stated in this order and/or for their non-compliance, such person, owner, builder shall be liable to pay compensation of Rs.50,000 per default in relation to construction activity at its site and Rs.5000 for each violation during carriage and transportation of construction material, debris, through trucks and other materials in terms of Section 15 of the NGT Act on the principle of Polluter Pay.

On 13 April 2015, the NGT noted that the prohibitory orders issued by it 'in relation to 10-year-old diesel vehicles are causing serious concern and practical difficulties to the Government and Authorities'. The Tribunal directed that there would be no impounding of vehicles on account of age during a period of two weeks.[184]

On 28 April 2015, the NGT focused on the burning of garbage and crop residues and micro-managed composting arrangements:

> We direct that for every incident of burning of any such above stated material, the person who is found actually burning such material and/or responsible for or abetting such burning would be liable to pay compensation in terms of Section 15 of the National Green Tribunal Act, 2010 for polluting the environment and would be liable to pay a sum of Rs.5000, to be paid instantaneously....
>
> The composting sites should be provided nearer to the places where there are a large number of trees, gardens and the compost which can be used as manure should be used for horti-culture purposes to ensure that the burden on the site does not increase beyond its capacity.

On 30 July 2015, the NGT issued directions to expedite the completion of peripheral expressways so that heavy traffic would not have to enter Delhi.

On 14 August 2015, the Tribunal declared the case closed for judgment with respect to dust pollution and smoke from burning materials. The matter relating to vehicular pollution including commercial vehicles plying in Delhi and transiting through Delhi was adjourned for further consideration.

On 11 December 2015, the NGT directed:

> As an interim measure till next date of posting subject to hearing of all the concerned parties, we direct that Diesel Vehicles of more than 10 years of age as already directed, as well as new diesel vehicle would not be registered in NCT, Delhi.[185]

On 6 January 2016, the Tribunal observed that since the air pollution issues concerning Delhi were being looked at by the Supreme Court, it 'should not pass any direction in this regard at this stage'. The Tribunal decided to hear applications concerning other polluted cities like Mumbai, Kolkata, Bengaluru, Patna, Lucknow, Allahabad, Kanpur, Varanasi, Pune, Nagpur, Chennai, Hyderabad, Ludhiana and Amritsar.

On 18 July 2016, the NGT rejected an application seeking recall of the 7 April 2015 order by which diesel vehicles which were more than 10 years old were prohibited from plying on Delhi roads. The Tribunal reasoned that a statutory appeal to the Supreme Court from the order was dismissed and consequently the issue had attained finality. The NGT directed the

---

[184] *Vardhaman Kaushik v Union of India* MANU/GT/0110/2015. The NGT issued prohibitory directions in respect of *10-year-old* vehicles on 7 April 2015. Previous orders of the NGT dated 14 December 2014 and 19 January 2015 refer to *15-year-old* vehicles.

[185] *Vardhaman Kaushik v Union of India* (2015) SCC Online NGT 837.

transport authorities in the NCR (covering parts of Haryana, Uttar Pradesh, Punjab and Rajasthan) to cancel the registration of all diesel vehicles which were more than 10 years old.[186] The directions to deregister diesel vehicles that were more than 10 years old were re-iterated on 20 July 2016.[187]

With the air quality declining to levels 'which are unimaginable, unacceptable and are a clear indication of negligence on the part of the concerned authority to the disadvantage of the human health of the citizens' on 10 November 2016, the NGT issued a set of directions including constituting monitoring committees at the central and state levels. Describing the situation in Delhi as an 'environmental emergency', the Tribunal directed the state to 'ensure that the water is sprinkled through helicopters all over the city and other areas where the values are found to be in excess of the above standards'.[188]

On 9 November 2017, the Tribunal lamented the poor enforcement of directions issued a year earlier on 10 November 2016: 'The judgment has been complied with only in default.' The NGT prohibited 'construction (structural) activity of any kind in the entire NCR'.[189]

On 11 November 2017, the NGT permitted the Delhi government to implement the 'Odd and Even' scheme[190] but emphasized:

> There shall be no exemption to any person, officer and individual and the two wheelers from the ambit and scope of odd and even scheme. They will be applied with equal rigour to all cases and all vehicles.[191]

On 15 December 2017, the Tribunal rejected a review application by the NCT of Delhi in respect of the 11 November 2017 order. Delhi sought an exemption for two-wheeler vehicles from the Odd and Even scheme, but the Tribunal declined, holding that such a carve-out was discriminatory and unjustified.

On 18 December 2017,[192] the NGT noted that all states in the NCR had submitted action plans prepared with reference to the Graded Response Action Plan (GRAP). The GRAP had formulated five categories, that is, emergency, severe, very poor, moderate to poor, and moderate with reference to air quality parameters. The NGT preferred the following categorization with clear parameters:

(1) Category I (Average): When PM_{10} is more than 100 μg/m^3 but below 300 μg/m^3 and $PM_{2.5}$ is more than 60 μg/m^3 but below 180 μg/m^3.
(2) Category II (Severe): When PM_{10} is more than 300 μg/m^3 but below 700 μg/m^3 and $PM_{2.5}$ is more than 180 μg/m^3 but below 400 μg/m^3.
(3) Category III (Critical): When PM_{10} is more than 700 μg/m^3 but below 1000 μg/m^3 and $PM_{2.5}$ is more than 400 μg/m^3 but less than 600 μg/m^3.
(4) Category IV (Environmental Emergency): When PM_{10} is above 1000 μg/m^3 and $PM_{2.5}$ is above 600 μg/m^3.

Then the NGT issued these directions with respect to each category:

(1) *Action/Steps to be taken when the pollution levels fall in Category I:*
(a) All concerned should make every effort to increase the green/forest cover.

186 *Vardhaman Kaushik v Union of India* (2016) SCC Online NGT 3987.
187 *Vardhaman Kaushik v Union of India* (2016) SCC Online NGT 3812.
188 *Vardhaman Kaushik v Union of India* (2016) SCC Online NGT 4176.
189 *Vardhaman Kaushik v Union of India* (2017) SCC Online NGT 758.
190 This scheme is discussed in the Notes and Questions later in this section.
191 *Vardhaman Kaushik v Union of India* MANU/GT/0108/2017.
192 *Vardhaman Kaushik v Union of India* (2017) SCC Online NGT 983.

There shall be complete prohibition of burning of garbage, biomass and/or any kind of waste anywhere. Violation thereof would invite the penalty of Rs. 5000 for each default (order dated 28th April 2015).

The respective Corporations, Local Authorities, Pollution Control Boards and police authorities would be responsible for ensuring this compliance.

(b) The Pollution Control Boards, Local Authorities and the State Governments should ensure stringent enforcement of all pollution laws, particularly, in relation to the industries or activities which cause emissions into the air for carrying on their activity. There should be regular inspection of Thermal Power Plants through the respective Pollution Control Boards and the Local Authorities to ensure that the Thermal Power Plants are not emitting any gases or substances in excess of prescribed limit.

(c) The States and its instrumentalities shall encourage composting of biomass.

(d) Mechanized sweeping of roads.

...

(h) All State Governments and their instrumentalities including public authorities shall ensure that there is no crop residue burning in the agricultural fields or anywhere else. Due incentives and even machines like happy seeder, etc. should be provided to the farmers wherever necessary and recourse to punitive provisions should be taken. The State Government, its instrumentalities and the monitoring Committees shall take effective steps through publicity (print or electronic media) to inform the farmers at large the adverse impacts of burning of crop residue upon the environment, public health and the soil on the one hand. While on the other, utilising crop residue for providing them some income for productive and beneficial purposes like fuel in plants, bio-mass or thermal, manufacturing of boards, compact wood and such other useful items.

...

(m) The State Government and the concerned departments should take effective steps to enhance public transport facilities and provide due infrastructure in that behalf. It will be ensured that public transport become more user-friendly. Due prevention should be taken to ensure that empty buses do not ply on the roads, proper time table relatable to the passenger peak load should be prepared by DTC and all other stakeholders. The State Governments, transport authorities and all other concerned agencies particularly NCT of Delhi, shall provide destination buses which will have not more than three bus stops within the colony of its origin and then would go non-stop to its point of termination. The destination buses could be ordinary buses but preferably should be air conditioner buses. This direction must be complied with now, without delay and default (order dated 20th April 2017)....

(o) The Government and all its concerned departments shall put a cap on the number of vehicles of all kinds that can ply in NCT of Delhi. Government should formulate policy of putting higher registration fee and road tax on purchase of second vehicle by the same person, body, company, society or trust....

(q) All builders involved in construction of buildings, howsoever, small or big would ensure compliance to the laws in force and the directions of the Tribunal. No dust should be emitted during demolition. No construction material should be kept on the roads. The construction material inside the plot should also be kept in covered conditions and labour should be provided with all anti-pollution gears during the course of construction. The State Governments, Pollution Control Boards and local authorities shall maintain due vigil in this regard (order dated 4th December 2014).

(r) Regulation of hours and vehicles for loading and unloading of vehicles particularly in the congested area (order dated 16th March 2015).

(s) All steps shall be taken by the State Governments, Horticulture Department, Corporation, Directorate of Education and all the private schools that to ensure increase of green belt in their respective schools within a period of one month from the date of pronouncement of this order. Large number of trees should be planted.

(2) *Category II (Severe)–Action and measures to be taken and penalties to be imposed*:

1. All the steps directed under category I shall continue to be strictly enforced in relation to this category as well.
2. All the brick kilns, thermal plants and heavy industries which are causing emissions would be instantaneously stopped and inspected by Pollution Control Board and all other concerned authorities and if their emissions are found to be beyond the prescribed standards, such plants shall be directed to be shut down.

...

5. There shall be complete prohibition on burning of any material, waste or biomass. The Government shall issue warning to the public at large requiring them to take appropriate precautionary steps and not to expose themselves to the high pollutants during particular hours of the day.
6. The Government shall immediately take steps for segregating the office time for various offices including the Government Departments. The Government shall provide destination buses and make every effort to discourage the use of private vehicles, including two-wheelers, cars and heavy vehicles.
7. All necessary steps should be taken to ensure that the construction activity is carried on strictly as per prescribed guidelines and the directions of the Tribunal. The transportation of the construction material should also be strictly in accordance with the directions issued earlier such as ensuring that carrying of construction material of any kind, particularly sand, cement, etc., is done after properly covering the transportation vehicle. In default, the concerned Government, Board and the local authority shall invoke the penal directions in regard to payment of environmental compensation at the rate of Rs. 5,000 per event for transporting material in violation of directions and Rs. 50,000 in relation to storage of construction material of any kind (order dated 11th December 2015)....

(3) *Category III Critical (Measures required to be taken)*:

Category III would relate to pollution of ambient air quality, i.e., severe and high and without exception have serious adverse impacts on public health and environment. Thus, the measures that are required to be taken under this category have to be preventive and punitive both.

1. All the directions contained under category I and II shall be enforced without default and delay. All those directions shall *mutatis mutandis* apply under this category as well.
2. The construction shall be stopped immediately and no construction would be permitted during the duration when the PM_{10} is falling under this category, particularly, towards the higher value i.e. 1000 $\mu g/m^3$ or $PM_{2.5}$ is towards higher value of 600 $\mu g/m^3$.
3. There shall be complete prohibition on burning of crop residue and all the departments concerned, particularly, the Pollution Control Board and the Government Department would take recourse to the punitive provisions for payment of environmental compensation in terms of the judgement of this Tribunal in the case of *Vikrant Tongad v EPCA* dated 10th December 2015. Officers who are found to be avoiding performance of their statutory duties in consonance with these directions would be liable to departmental action in accordance with law.
4. There shall be complete prohibition on transportation of construction material during the relevant period.
5. To avoid traffic congestion and consequential air pollution, the scheme of odd and even shall be implemented by the respective State Governments/ Departments of the State.

(4) *Category IV (Environmental Emergency)*:

The directions and steps directed hereinafter shall be carried out by the State Governments, concerned Departments, Local Authorities and all the stakeholders, when PM_{10} exceeds 1000μg/m^3 and $PM_{2.5}$ exceeds 600μg/m^3, respectively.

1. All the directions under category I, II and III, respectively shall apply *mutatis mutandis* even to this category. All State Governments would comply with all such directions.
2. Besides, we also issue the following directions.
   (i) There would be a complete prohibition on all kind of construction activity and transportation of construction material. The default or violation of directions would incur penalty/environmental compensation to the extent of Rs. 1 Lakh for every default. . . .
   (iii) There will be complete and absolute prohibition on burning of all agricultural residues. . . .
   (iv) All the Thermal Power Plants in NCT of Delhi shall not operate.
   (v) There shall be complete prohibition and ban on lifting, transportation and generation of fly ash. The concerned State Government and Authorities shall sprinkle water from the high rising buildings or through helicopters to ensure that excessive parameters are immediately brought down to reasonable limits.
   (vi) There shall be complete prohibition on use of [Diesel Generator] sets. The trucks and heavy vehicles carrying material including trailers shall be prohibited from entering NCT of Delhi. Only the heavy vehicles carrying essential goods like medicine, food etc. would be permitted, while all other heavy vehicles will not be permitted to enter NCT of Delhi for the duration of Environmental Emergency.
   (vii) Whenever there is environmental emergency, i.e., PM_{10} exceeds 1000 μg/m^3 and $PM_{2.5}$ exceeds 600 μg/m^3 then the NCT of Delhi shall consider and pass appropriate orders in regard to closure of the schools for that period. . . .
   (viii) . . . There shall be complete prohibition on bursting of crackers. . . .[193]

NOTES AND QUESTIONS

1. The NGT was hearing *Vardhaman Kaushik's* case pertaining to Delhi's air quality since 2014 and had passed a series of orders since 27 October 2014. Notice that both the Supreme Court and the NGT passed orders on several issues—traffic transiting through Delhi, the need for peripheral roads around the city, banning of vehicle registration, construction dust, burning of leaves, etc. Considering that an expert statutory forum was looking into the issue, was it correct for the Supreme Court to wade in and revive the *M C Mehta* case? Does the Supreme Court's intervention undermine the authority and stature of the NGT and disregard the legislative intent behind the 2010 Act that established the Tribunal?

2. Keeping in view section 22 of the National Green Tribunal Act of 2010 which confers appellate jurisdiction on the Supreme Court from orders passed by the NGT, was it correct for the Supreme Court to have exercised its original jurisdiction when *Vardhaman Kaushik's* case was pending before the Tribunal? Are these merely technical quibbles or substantive issues? Do rules of self-restraint and self-discipline apply to the Supreme Court as an institution or is it a matter of discretion of the individual judges hearing a case?

[193] *Id.* These directions were ordered to be 'fully implemented and action taken in terms thereof' when the Tribunal disposed of the case on 27 July 2018. *Vardhaman Kaushik v Union of India* (2018) SCC Online NGT 292.

3. Does the NGT have jurisdiction to ban vehicles of a certain age or impose penalties (thinly disguised as compensatory charges on the polluter pays principle)? Locate the source of the NGT's power.

4. Can you make sense of the directions passed by the NGT with respect to car parking? Is parking prohibited on every tarred road? Does the direction with respect to 'metalled' roads cover every paved road? Where can one park in Delhi?

5. Can you comprehend what the Tribunal intended by repeatedly insisting upon installation of air filters in crowded areas, marketplaces and gardens? What do you think about the helicopters with sprinkler systems?

6. The Delhi High Court initiated its *suo motu* action in early 2015[194] before the Supreme Court revived *M C Mehta*. The High Court in a series of orders issued directions to restore Delhi's tree cover, reduce the dust from road repairs, improve the movement of vehicular traffic and other assorted issues.

7. On 28 December 2015, the NCT of Delhi introduced a scheme on an experimental basis for 15 days beginning 1 January 2016. The thrust of the scheme was to permit vehicles to ply either on odd or even days based on the vehicle's registration number. The statutory notification provided a list of 25 categories of vehicles exempt from the rigour of the scheme comprising senior state officials, from the President of India downwards and including judges of the Supreme Court as well as the Delhi High Court. In matters of improving Delhi's air, is there any legal or moral justification for excluding high state officials? Should not each of these officials set an example for the common citizen by adjusting to the scheme? Or do the remnants of a feudal order still cast a shadow across the egalitarian ethos of the Constitution?[195]

8. The Howrah Ganatantrik Nagarik Samiti petitioned the Calcutta High Court to preserve the Victoria Memorial, Kolkata, a grand marble building and museum that stands amidst vast public greens. The thrust of the petition was to reduce vehicular pollution and harm to the marble exterior. The High Court accepted a suggestion made by the National Environmental Engineering Research Institute (NEERI) and ordered shifting of a bus terminus located at 2 kms from the building. The state appealed, drawing attention to the potential disruption of public transport and inconvenience to thousands of commuters. Allowing the appeal, the Supreme Court struck a pragmatic note. Since NEERI's recommendation was a 'long term measure', it held that the High Court was not justified in directing shifting of the bus terminus within six months. The Supreme Court asked the state to 'consider and take appropriate action on the NEERI report recommending relocation of the bus terminus away from the Esplanade'.[196] It set no deadline.

9. A group of morning walkers were less successful in persuading the Supreme Court. The Calcutta High Court imposed a ban on parking vehicles around the Memorial and refused to relent when the walkers requested a two-hour respite in the early morning. The Supreme Court agreed with the High Court which guided the enthusiasts to alternative sites including the Maidan and areas along the Hooghly River.[197]

10. Reviewing the regulatory framework to control vehicular pollution, the Calcutta High Court repelled a challenge to the authority of the West Bengal PCB to inspect the automobile

---

194 *Court on its Own Motion (Air Pollution in Delhi) v Union of India*, Writ Petition (C) No. 1346/2015.
195 The NGT struck down the exception in its order dated 11 November 2017. *Supra* notes 190, 191.
196 *State of West Bengal v Howrah Ganatantrik Nagarik Samiti* 2011 (10) SCALE 310.
197 *Friends of Victoria Memorial v Howrah Ganatantrik Nagarik Samiti* 2011 (10) SCALE 313.

emission testing centres. The court held that the PCB's power could be traced to the Motor Vehicle Rules and the Air Act.[198]

11. The National Green Tribunal exceeded its jurisdiction when directing petrol pumps to withhold fuel supply to vehicles that did not have a valid pollution under control (PUC) certificate:

> It is well settled that when a statute or statutory rules prescribed a penalty for any act or omission, no other penalty not contemplated in the statute or statutory rules can be imposed. It is well settled that when statute requires a thing to be done in a particular manner, it is to be done only in that manner.
>
> There can be no doubt that strong measures must be taken to protect the environment and improve the air quality whenever there is contravention of statutory rules causing environmental pollution. Stringent action has to be taken, but in accordance with law.
>
> Stoppage of supply of fuel to vehicles not complying with the requirement to have and/or display a valid PUC certificate is not contemplated either in the 1989 Rules or in the NGT Act. Motor vehicles not complying with the requirement of possessing and/or displaying a valid PUC certificate cannot be debarred from being supplied fuel.
>
> In passing blanket direction, directing the appellant State Government to ensure that no dealer and/or outlet and/or petrol pump should supply fuel to vehicles without PUC certificate, *dehors* the Central Motor Vehicles Rules, the learned Tribunal overlooked the fact that no vehicle can either be repaired to comply with pollution norms, nor tested for compliance with the [pollution] norms upon repair, without fuel.[199]

G. NOISE POLLUTION

I. STATUTES

Acute exposure to high noise levels and prolonged exposure at lower levels are known to adversely affect the health and social development of exposed persons. The direct physiological effects include a loss of hearing, either temporary or permanent. The non-auditory effects include cardiac ailments, stress and fatigue, and sleep disturbances. Among the physiological effects documented by experts are lack of concentration, loss of memory and an adverse impact on the education of children. Noise is also suspected of aggravating nausea, headache, insomnia and a loss of appetite.[200]

The Environment (Protection) Act of 1986 (EPA) recognizes noise as an environmental pollutant and empowers the Central Government to frame rules prescribing the maximum permissible limits for noise in different areas.[201] On 14 February 2000, the Centre framed the Noise Pollution (Regulation and Control) Rules. Two types of noise standards are prescribed: ambient air quality standards in respect of noise[202] and emission limits for designated types of machinery, automobiles,[203] appliances[204] and fire crackers.[205]

---

198 *Ashim Kumar Banerjee v The State of West Bengal* (2012) 2 CHN 1.

199 *State of Madhya Pradesh v Centre for Environment Protection Research & Development* (2020) 9 SCC 781.

200 *Report of the Expert Committee on Noise Pollution*, paras 4.1–4.2.4 (1986). The committee was constituted by the Bombay High Court in Writ Petition No. 1879 of 1985 (*Dr Y T Oke v State of Maharashtra*).

201 Section 6(2)(b).

202 Rule 3 of the Noise Rules read with the Schedule to these Rules. Earlier ambient noise levels were prescribed in Schedule III, Environment (Protection) Rules of 1986. This Schedule appears to have been impliedly repealed by the Noise Rules of 2000. For airports ambient standards are prescribed in Entry 112, Schedule I, Environment (Protection) Rules of 1986.

203 Entry 47, Schedule I, Environment (Protection) Rules of 1986.

204 Schedule VI, Part E.

205 Entry 89, Schedule I, Environment (Protection) Rules of 1986.

Separate ambient levels are fixed for industrial, commercial and residential areas and silence zones. The state governments must categorize areas into these zones. The prescribed day-time levels (6 am to 10 pm) are typically 10 decibels higher than the corresponding levels for night time. The Noise Rules require the states to designate an authority or officer responsible for maintaining the ambient standards. The designated authority could be the District Magistrate or Police Commissioner or any other official. Rule 3 requires the states to take measures to ensure that ambient air quality standards are met and imposes a duty on local bodies to have regard to noise pollution as a parameter of quality of life while planning development activity. Rule 5 prohibits the use of loudspeakers at night except in closed premises like auditoria, community halls and banquet halls. Day-time use of loudspeakers is allowed after obtaining permission of the authority. Rule 5 was amended in 2002, 2010 and 2017 to supply flexibility in the night-time ban on loudspeakers. The state governments may now permit loudspeakers till midnight during cultural, religious or other festivals up to 15 days in a year. The authority has jurisdiction to entertain complaints about excess noise and may issue directions under rule 8 to abate the nuisance.

Rule 5A prohibits the blowing of horns or the bursting of fire crackers in silence zones or during the night in residential areas. Sound-emitting construction equipment may not be operated during the night time in residential areas and silence zones.

The emission equipment standards prescribed in Schedule VI of the Environment (Protection) Rules of 1986 relate to motor vehicles, air conditioners, refrigerators, diesel generators for domestic use and certain types of construction equipment.

The 1987 amendments to the Air Act specifically extended the provisions of the Air Act, including increased penalties and the issuance of injunctions by magistrates, to noise pollution. The definition of 'air pollutant' was expanded to include noise. Besides these central statues, local municipal legislation and the Police Acts also regulate certain types of activity which generates noise. For example, in several states regulations governing the use of loudspeakers are framed under the local Police Act.

II. NOISE POLLUTION CASES

Anil Mittal, an engineer, petitioned the Supreme Court to strictly implement the Noise Pollution (Regulation and Control) Rules of 2000 in relation to loudspeakers and other high-volume audio and video systems. The tragic story of a 13-year-old victim of rape, whose cries for help were drowned by loudspeakers, was the immediate provocation for filing the petition.[206] More generally, Mittal complained that the indiscriminate use of loudspeakers during religious festivals, marriages and social events caused tremendous disturbance to neighbours, particularly students. The Supreme Court expanded Mittal's petition and re-labelled the cause title as shown below. In a separate case, a forum named Prevention of Environmental and Sound Pollution (PESP) challenged an amendment to the Noise Rules that allowed the use of loudspeakers between 10.00 pm and midnight during cultural and religious occasions up to 15 days in a year. The Supreme Court clubbed both these cases and rendered a comprehensive judgment from which we carry a short excerpt. As you review the judgment rendered on 18 July 2005 consider how effective the court's directions have been in abating the noise nuisance in your city or neighbourhood. Has this judgment made a difference?

206 The victim later set herself ablaze and died of burn injuries.

NOISE POLLUTION (V), IN RE
(2005) 5 SCC 733

R C Lahoti, C J: These two matters before us raise certain issues of far-reaching implications in day-to-day life of the people in India relatable to noise pollution *vis-à-vis* right to life enshrined in Article 21 of the Constitution as interpreted in its wide sweep by the constitutional courts of the country. Though a limited grievance was raised to begin with but several intervenors and interlocutory applications enhanced the scope of hearing and the cases were heard in a very wide perspective centring around Article 21 of the Constitution. Several associated and incidental issues have also been gone into....

Article 21 of the Constitution guarantees life and personal liberty to all persons. It is well settled by repeated pronouncements of this Court as also the High Courts that the right to life enshrined in Article 21 is not of mere survival or existence. It guarantees a right of persons to life with human dignity. Therein are included, all the aspects of life which go to make a person's life meaningful, complete and worth living. Human life has its charm and there is no reason why life should not be enjoyed along with all permissible pleasures. Anyone who wishes to live in peace, comfort and quiet within his house has a right to prevent noise as pollutant reaching him. None can claim a right to create noise even in his own premises which would travel beyond his precincts and cause nuisance to neighbours or others. Any noise which has the effect of materially interfering with the ordinary comforts of life judged by the standard of a reasonable man is nuisance. How and when a nuisance created by noise becomes actionable has to be answered by reference to its degree and the surrounding circumstances, the place and the time.

Those who make noise often take shelter behind Article 19(1)(a) pleading freedom of speech and right to expression. Undoubtedly, the freedom of speech and right to expression are fundamental rights but the rights are not absolute. Nobody can claim a fundamental right to create noise by amplifying the sound of his speech with the help of loudspeakers. While one has a right to speech, others have a right to listen or decline to listen. Nobody can be compelled to listen and nobody can claim that he has a right to make his voice trespass into the ears or mind of others. Nobody can indulge in aural aggression. If anyone increases his volume of speech and that too with the assistance of artificial devices so as to compulsorily expose unwilling persons to hear a noise raised to unpleasant or obnoxious levels, then the person speaking is violating the right of others to a peaceful, comfortable and pollution-free life guaranteed by Article 21. Article 19(1)(a) cannot be pressed into service for defeating the fundamental right guaranteed by Article 21. We need not further dwell on this aspect. Two decisions in this regard delivered by the High Courts have been brought to our notice wherein the right to live in an atmosphere free from noise pollution has been upheld as the one guaranteed by Article 21 of the Constitution. These decisions are *Free Legal Aid Cell Shri Sugan Chand Aggarwal v Govt of NCT of Delhi* AIR 2001 Del 455 and *P A Jacob v Supdt of Police* AIR 1993 Ker 1. We have carefully gone through the reasoning adopted in the two decisions and the principle of law laid down therein, in particular, the exposition of Article 21 of the Constitution. We find ourselves in entire agreement therewith.

The present cases provide an opportunity for examining several questions, such as what is noise? What are its adverse effects? Whether noise pollution runs in conflict with the fundamental rights of the people? And what relief can be allowed by way of directions issued in public interest?

[The court drew on various definitions of noise to conclude 'the disturbance produced in our environment by undesirable sound of various kinds is called "noise pollution".' The court traced the harmful effects of noise including hearing loss, interference with communication, disturbance in sleep, annoyance, decrease in performance, physiological effects on the human body, impacts on foetuses, effects on children, etc. After enumerating different sources of noise, the court turned to a particularly vexed issue—fireworks.]

Noise pollution in the special context of fireworks

Fireworks are used all over the world to celebrate special occasions. In India, fireworks are burst on festivals like Dussehra, Diwali and on special occasions like social gatherings, marriages, Independence day, Republic day, New year day, etc. In other countries of the world, fireworks are generally burst either on the New Year day or on the birthday of their respective countries. However, bursting of firecrackers is a health hazard since it is responsible for both air pollution and noise pollution....

The use of fireworks has led to air pollution in the form of noise and smoke. Their excessive use has started to be a public hazard and violation of their fundamental rights as enshrined in the Constitution.

It has been held in the case of *Om Birangana Religious Society v State* (1996) 100 CWN 617 that the

> 'Freedom of speech and expression guaranteed under Article 19(1)(*a*) of the Constitution of India includes, by necessary implication, freedom not to listen and/or to remain silent. A citizen has a right to leisure, right to sleep, right not to hear and right to remain silent. He also has the right to read and speak with others.'

Because of the tremendous sound and noise, the citizens cannot exercise all these fundamental rights.

It has been seen that firecracker noise is an impulsive noise and is hazardous. Bursting of a firecracker near the ear can lead sometimes to non-recoverable hearing loss.

Diwali is the most important festival of India. The bursting of firecrackers during this period is a widespread practice. The unpredictable, intermittent and impulsive noise produced by bursting of crackers all around, turns the festival of lights into a cacophony of noise. [Ambient noise-level and Air-quality status in Delhi during Diwali Festival days 1999–2002, published by Central Pollution Control Board, October 2003.] People are unable to even sleep due to this excessive noise pollution. Several people are injured due to the noise produced by firecrackers every year.

Firecrackers not only increase the ambient noise level but also contribute significantly in increasing the air pollution by means of toxic gases and particles due to their blast wave resulting from a rapid release of energy.

In order to assess the situation of noise pollution caused by firecrackers at the time of Diwali the Central Pollution Control Board (CPCB) has been conducting ambient noise level monitoring during Diwali festival regularly at various locations in Delhi since 1993, to find increased ambient noise level caused by intensive burning of crackers. As in the past, the noise and air-quality monitoring have been carried out in the years 1999, 2000, 2001, and 2002. The noise monitoring locations have been selected to cover almost all areas of Delhi.

An analysis of the reports prepared in the years 1999, 2000, 2001, and 2002 reveals that the ambient noise level on Diwali day exceeded the limit at almost all the places during these years. The noise level was higher during Diwali-2000 as compared to the values recorded during Diwali festival in the years 1999, 2001, and 2002.

The percentage of violation in Leq. noise level varied from 2 to 49% in the year 2002, 12 to 55% in the year 2001, 11 to 58% in the year 2000 and 22 to 47% in the year 1999 with respect to the daytime standards at all the areas. [Leq is the level of that steady sound which over the same interval of time, contains the same total energy (or dose) as the fluctuating sound. Equivalent continuous sound-level has gained widespread acceptance as a scale for the measurement of long-term noise exposure.]

The ambient noise level during the years 1999 to 2002 on Diwali festival, exceeded the limit at all places in every year and the percentage of violation varies from 2% to 58%. Thus, the study does reveal that the noise levels that have been measured on all these occasions have been more than the prescribed norms. This is a point of worry as it has been discussed that noise pollution does tend to have adverse effects on a person. Thus immediate steps in this direction need to be taken.

[The court surveyed laws in other countries. Apart from the usual suspects—UK, USA and Australia, the court examined noise regulations in Japan and China and finally ended the exercise by delving into the Noise Control Ordinance of Montgomery County in the State of Maryland, USA. The judgment then sets out statutory provisions in India, specifically the Noise Rules, 2000; sections 268, 290 and 291 of the Penal Code, 1860; section 133 of the Criminal Procedure Code, 1973 as well as provisions in Motor Vehicles Act, 1988, the Air Act, 1981 and the Explosives Act, 1884 with respect to fireworks. Thereafter, the court refers to several High Court and the Supreme Court judgments to conclude that Indian judicial opinion is uniform in recognizing the right to live free from noise pollution as a fundamental right protected under Article 21.]

Interim orders

During the course of the hearing of this case the Court had passed several interim orders keeping in mind the importance of the issue.

The interim order dated 27-9-2001 [*Noise Pollution (II), In re*, (2005) 5 SCC 728] deserves to be mentioned in particular, which directed as under:

'(1) The Union Government, the Union Territories as well as all the State Governments shall take steps to strictly comply with Notification No. GSR 682(E) dated 5-10-1999 whereby the Environment (Protection) Rules, 1986 framed under the Environment (Protection) Act, 1986 were amended. They shall in particular comply with amended Rule 89 of Schedule I to the said Rules, which reads as follows:

89. *Noise standards for firecrackers*

A. (i) The manufacture, sale or use of firecrackers generating noise level exceeding 125 dB(AI) or 145 $dB(C)_{pk}$ at 4 metres distance from the point of bursting shall be prohibited.

(ii) For individual firecracker constituting the series (joined firecrackers), the abovementioned limit be reduced by 5 $\log_{10}(N)$ dB, where N = number of crackers joined together.

(2) The use of fireworks or firecrackers shall not be permitted except between 6.00 am and 10.00 pm No fireworks or firecrackers shall be allowed between 10.00 pm and 6.00 am.

(3) Firecrackers shall not be used at any time in silence zones, as defined in S.O. No. 1046(E) issued on 22-11-2000 by the Ministry of Environment and Forests. In the said notification, silence zone has been defined as:

'Silence zone is an area comprising not less than 100 metres around hospitals, educational institutions, courts, religious places or any other area which is declared as such by the competent authority.'

(4) The State Education Resource Centres in all the States and the Union Territories as well as the management/principals of schools in all the States and Union Territories shall take appropriate steps to educate students about the ill-effects of air and noise pollution and apprise them of Directions (1) to (3) above.'

These interim directions were also directed to be given wide publicity both by electronic and print media. It was said that Doordarshan and other television channels shall give publicity to these directions, at least once every day during prime time, during the fortnight before

Dussehra and Diwali. The Ministry of Information and Broadcasting was asked to bring these directions to the notice of the general public through appropriate advertisements, issued in the newspapers. All-India Radio was asked to broadcast these directions on prime time on FM and other frequencies for information of the general public.

Due to the imposition of the restrictions on the bursting of firecrackers, several interim applications came to be filed before the Court. The Court vide its interim order dated 10-9-2003 [*Noise Pollution (III), In re*, (2005) 5 SCC 730] stated:

> '5. Through the IAs filed in this Court the following two suggestions deserve notice. Firstly, it is submitted that certain local festivals and celebrations are accompanied customarily by bursting of firecrackers which is at times at such hours as is not permissible under the order of this Court dated 27-9-2001 [*Noise Pollution (II), In re*, (2005) 5 SCC 728]. Secondly, it is pointed out that the industry of fireworks may face serious difficulty, even partial closure, on account of the directions made by this Court.
>
> 6. We have grave doubts if the abovesaid considerations can come in the way of the enforcement of fundamental rights guaranteed by the Constitution for the citizens and people of India to live in peace and comfort and in an atmosphere free from pollution of any kind, such as one caused by noise and foul/poisonous gases. However still, without expressing any final opinion on the pleas advanced, we allow the parties adversely affected, the liberty to make representation to the respective State Governments and the State Governments may, in their turn, if satisfied of the genuineness of the representation made, invite the attention of the Government of India to the suggestions made.'

We are happy to note that the initial reluctance to abide by the interim directions made by this Court as displayed by the subsequent interlocutory applications soon gave way to compliance. By and large the interim directions made by the Court were observed in compliance. Police and civil administration remained alert during the Diwali festival to see that the directions made by the Court were complied with. Resident Welfare Associations and school children gave a very encouraging response, who voluntarily desisted from bursting firecrackers during prohibited hours of the night and also bursting such firecrackers as produce high-level noise.

[The court examined the legal regime with respect to firecrackers in great detail and considered whether there was justification for supplementing existing regulations with stricter rules as sought by the *amicus curiae* or whether a dilution was necessary as requested by the fireworks manufacturers. After balancing the equities, the court issued the following directions.]

Directions

It is hereby directed as under:

(i) Firecrackers

1. On a comparison of the two systems i.e. the present system of evaluating firecrackers on the basis of noise levels, and the other where the firecrackers shall be evaluated on the basis of chemical composition, we feel that the latter method is more practical and workable in Indian circumstances. It shall be followed unless and until replaced by a better system.
2. The Department of Explosives (DOE) shall undertake necessary research activity for the purpose and come out with the chemical formulae for each type or category or class of firecrackers. DOE shall specify the proportion/composition as well as the maximum permissible weight of every chemical used in manufacturing firecrackers.
3. The Department of Explosives may divide the firecrackers into two categories — (i) sound-emitting firecrackers, and (ii) colour/light-emitting firecrackers.

4. There shall be a complete ban on bursting sound-emitting firecrackers between 10 pm and 6 am. It is not necessary to impose restrictions as to time on bursting of colour/light-emitting firecrackers.
5. Every manufacturer shall on the box of each firecracker mention details of its chemical contents and that it satisfies the requirement as laid down by DOE. In case of a failure on the part of the manufacturer to mention the details or in cases where the contents of the box do not match the chemical formulae as stated on the box, the manufacturer may be held liable.
6. Firecrackers for the purpose of export may be manufactured bearing higher noise levels subject to the following conditions: (i) the manufacturer should be permitted to do so only when he has an export order with him and not otherwise; (ii) the noise levels for these firecrackers should conform to the noise standards prescribed in the country to which they are intended to be exported as per the export order; (iii) these firecrackers should have a different colour packing, from those intended to be sold in India; (iv) they must carry a declaration printed thereon something like 'not for sale in India' or 'only for export to country AB' and so on.

(ii) Loudspeakers

1. The noise level at the boundary of the public place, where loudspeaker or public address system or any other noise source is being used shall not exceed 10 dB(A) above the ambient noise standards for the area or 75 dB(A) whichever is lower.
2. No one shall beat a drum or tom-tom or blow a trumpet or beat or sound any instrument or use any sound amplifier at night (between 10 pm and 6 am) except in public emergencies.
3. The peripheral noise level of privately-owned sound system shall not exceed by more than 5 dB(A) than the ambient air-quality standard specified for the area in which it is used, at the boundary of the private place.

(iii) Vehicular noise

No horn should be allowed to be used at night (between 10 pm and 6 am) in residential area except in exceptional circumstances.

(iv) Awareness

1. There is a need for creating general awareness towards the hazardous effects of noise pollution. Suitable chapters may be added in the textbooks which teach civic sense to the children and youth at the initial/early-level of education. Special talks and lectures be organised in the schools to highlight the menace of noise pollution and the role of the children and younger generation in preventing it. Police and civil administration should be trained to understand the various methods to curb the problem and also the laws on the subject.
2. The State must play an active role in this process. Resident Welfare Associations, service clubs and societies engaged in preventing noise pollution as a part of their projects need to be encouraged and actively involved by the local administration.
3. Special public awareness campaigns in anticipation of festivals, events and ceremonial occasions whereat firecrackers are likely to be used, need to be carried out.

The abovesaid guidelines are issued in exercise of power conferred on this Court under Articles 141 and 142 of the Constitution. These would remain in force until modified by this Court or superseded by an appropriate legislation.

(v) Generally

1. The States shall make provision for seizure and confiscation of loudspeakers, amplifiers and such other equipment as are found to be creating noise beyond the permissible limits.
2. Rule 3 of the Noise Pollution (Regulation and Control) Rules, 2000 makes provision for specifying ambient air-quality standards in respect of noise for different areas/zones, categorisation of the areas for the purpose of implementation of noise standards, authorising

the authorities for enforcement and achievement of laid down standards. The Central Government/State Governments shall take steps for laying down such standards and notifying the authorities where it has not already been done.

Though, the matters are closed consistently with the directions as issued above in public interest, there will be liberty of seeking further directions as and when required and in particular in the event of any difficulty arising in implementing the directions.

NOTES AND QUESTIONS

1. The Supreme Court issued sweeping directions under Articles 141 and 142 of the Constitution[207] in relation to firecrackers. Should the court have looked at the primary problem caused by firecrackers during the Diwali festival: air pollution? Did the Supreme Court miss the wood for the trees and an opportunity to reduce air pollution from firecrackers? What is the point of allowing noise-compliant firecrackers that cause respiratory diseases?

2. While the court and those assisting the judges should be commended for their extensive research on global noise control practices, to what end was the analysis of the Montgomery County Noise Control Ordinance?

3. The court found that there were three primary problems in controlling noise pollution: (a) the absence of a comprehensive statute; (b) the absence of a competent enforcement agency with qualified personnel; and (c) the lack of proper equipment to measure sound. Do you agree? Are the Noise Rules of 2000 not comprehensive enough? Is the real problem legal and technical as the court suggests, or is it a social and cultural problem peculiar to South Asia?

4. Was the court's direction with respect to vehicular noise counter-productive? With effect from 11 January 2010, the Central Government amended the Noise Rules by inserting rule 5A(1) which reads:

> No horn shall be used in silence zones or during night time in residential areas except during a public emergency.

The purpose of this rule was to give statutory backing to the Supreme Court direction. The rule as framed suggests that it is all right to honk in residential areas during the day.

Consistent with global norms, the court ought to have banned the use of vehicular horns completely at all times and at all places, except in emergencies. Instead, the effect of the Supreme Court direction is to dilute the global norm.

5. In its interim order passed on 27 September 2001, the Supreme Court imposed a complete ban on fireworks and firecrackers between 10 pm and 6 am. It also prohibited firecrackers at any time in silence zones. In its final judgment, the court refused to relax these embargoes. Are these directions of the Supreme Court being effectively implemented? If they are, all Indian cities should be firecracker free. Remember, a 'silence zone', as statutorily defined, extends to an area of at least 100 metres around hospitals, educational institutions, courts, religious places or other designated areas. In effect, most parts of a city are covered by the definition of silence zone.

207 Article 141: 'The law declared by the Supreme Court shall be binding on all Courts within the territory of India.' Article 142: '(1) The Supreme Court in the exercise of its jurisdiction may pass such decree or make such order as is necessary for doing complete justice in any cause or matter pending before it ...'

6. In *Church of God (Full Gospel) in India v K K R Majestic Colony Welfare Assn*,[208] the Church assailed a judgment of the Madras High Court. The respondent complained to the Tamil Nadu PCB that prayers in the Church were accompanied by the use of loudspeakers, drums and other instruments which disturbed the neighbourhood. When the authorities failed to take action, the respondent moved the High Court. The Church claimed that the petition was filed with an oblique motive to prevent a religious minority from pursuing its religious activity and the court ought not to issue an injunction when most of the noise was due to vehicular traffic and not the loudspeakers. The Madras High Court directed the authorities to bring down noise levels by requiring the Church to reduce the amplification of its speakers.

The Supreme Court dismissed the appeal holding:

> Undisputedly, no religion prescribes that prayers should be performed by disturbing the peace of others nor does it preach that they should be through voice amplifiers or beating of drums. In our view, in a civilised society in the name of religion, activities which disturb old or infirm persons, students or children having their sleep in the early hours or during day-time or other persons carrying on other activities cannot be permitted. It should not be forgotten that young babies in the neighbourhood are also entitled to enjoy their natural right of sleeping in a peaceful atmosphere. A student preparing for his examination is entitled to concentrate on his studies without there being any unnecessary disturbance by the neighbours. Similarly, the old and the infirm are entitled to enjoy reasonable quietness during their leisure hours without there being any nuisance of noise pollution.... Their rights are also required to be honoured.

The Supreme Court in *Noise Pollution (V), In Re*,[209] applied this reasoning to reject a claim by the Tamil Nadu Fireworks and Amorces Manufacturers' Association that a restriction on bursting firecrackers infringed the freedom of religion guaranteed under Article 25 of the Constitution:

> The Court by restricting the time of bursting the firecrackers has not in any way violated the religious rights of any person as enshrined under Article 25 of the Constitution. The festival of Diwali is mainly associated with pooja performed on the auspicious day and not with firecrackers. Diwali is considered as a festival of lights, not of noises.

7. The Supreme Court judgment is silent on the validity of the amendment to the Noise Rules that was assailed by the PESP as being *ultra vires*. For the present, states may permit the use of loudspeakers post 10 pm until midnight during 'cultural, religious or festive' occasions for up to 15 days a year.[210]

8. The travails of a private citizen residing close to the State legislature are captured in the case of *Balwant Singh*.[211] A retired director general of police, Singh found his dream of a quiet retirement shattered by frequent protests outside his home. The demonstrators would 'make use of the compound walls of nearby houses (including that of Balwant Singh's) to ease themselves at any time'. Singh initially complained to the National Human Rights Commission which forwarded the complaint to the State Commission for suitable action. When the administration failed to comply with the directions of the State Commission and miscreants attacked Singh's house, he decided to move the courts to protect his property and restore quiet in the neighbourhood. The Supreme Court relied on principles of nuisance, its previous

[208] (2000) 7 SCC 282.
[209] (2005) 5 SCC 733.
[210] Rule 5(3).
[211] *Balwant Singh v Commissioner of Police* (2015) 4 SCC 801.

judgment on noise pollution[212] and pinned down the administration to the following assurances made by the state:

(a) The Deputy Commissioner of Police has been put in charge of the area in order to ensure law and order in and around the residence of the petitioner.
(b) Barricading at appropriate distance from the residence of the petitioner so that the movement of the residents as well as of the petitioner is not restricted.... When the legislative assembly is in session barricading is done at least 60 ft away from the residence of the petitioner.
(c) Mobile public toilets (two vehicles) have been placed by Rajasthan Municipal Corporation in the area concerned so that hygiene is maintained in and around the area which has been affected by regular demonstration. Further all cautions have been taken that the public uses such facilities and neither police personnel on duty nor the demonstrator may spoil the walls of the petitioner by urinating.
(d) Prior permission as per the Rules are being given by the Office of Deputy Commissioner of Police, Jaipur (South) to the demonstrators and District Collector is directed to ensure that while giving permission for demonstration it may also check that no instruments are allowed which may violate the Rules or cause noise pollution.

How far can judicial orders alter social conduct? If a person of Balwant Singh's status found the administrative machinery so slack, how responsive will the administration be to an ordinary citizen's complaint about noise and other nuisances?

9. The Patna High Court recorded its displeasure at the failure of the Bihar PCB to respond to a complaint by a school against a noisy printing press established without statutory permission under the Air Act. The court berated the casual approach by the board, specifically its reluctance to inspect the premises and its failure to direct closure of the press despite the absence of any permission. The Chief Secretary, State of Bihar was asked to enquire why officers of the board were refusing to perform their statutory duties and the board was required to pass appropriate orders and take action on the school's complaint within two months.[213]

10. The Madras High Court restrained 'employing the driven pile system for foundation work' with respect to a multistoried building in a residential locality. The equipment comprised a hammer made from heavy iron weights that dropped from a considerable height onto a concrete pile. The hammering drove the pile into the ground but the vibrations and noise were far beyond the ambient standards for a residential area. Despite complaints to the authorities and the police, none helped, forcing the residents to approach the High Court under Article 226. The High Court permitted the foundation work by other (less noisy) methods.[214]

11. In a PIL decided before the Noise Rules of 2000, the Orissa High Court relied on the Orissa Fire Works and Loudspeaker (Regulation) Act of 1958, in an early attempt to prevent noise pollution. The division bench noticed the adverse health impacts of noise and relied on a Calcutta High Court decision holding that money could not afford adequate relief against noise nuisance and an injunction was justified.[215] The Orissa High Court issued a set of general directions and suggested the establishment of separate courts for noise pollution.[216] Is establishing special courts a solution?

---

212 *Noise Pollution (V), In re* (2005) 5 SCC 733.
213 *New Era High School v The State of Bihar* AIR 2013 Pat 70.
214 *Shobana Ramasubramanyam v Member Secretary, CMDA* 2002 (1) CTC 449.
215 *Gotham Construction Co v Amulya Krishna Ghose* AIR 1968 Cal 91.
216 *Bijayananda Patra v District Magistrate* AIR 2000 Ori 70.

12. The High Courts have responded energetically to citizens' complaints about noise. On 30 September 1985, Justice Sujata Manohar of the Bombay High Court constituted an Expert Committee to report on the extent of noise pollution in the city and to recommend steps to improve regulations.[217] The petition was filed by doctors, including Dr Oke, who were concerned about the adverse health impact on the citizens of Bombay from exposure to high noise levels. The report prepared by the Expert Committee provides an excellent survey of the problems faced by the citizens in the Greater Bombay area. Noting the recommendations of the Expert Committee, the High Court disposed of the petition by recording the decision of government to suitably amend existing legislation and to address the concerns expressed by the committee.

Despite these assurances, the Maharashtra government did little to regulate noise, prompting Dr Oke to file another petition before the High Court in 1995. This time he challenged the loudspeaker rules framed under the Bombay Police Act which permitted the use of loudspeakers contrary to the national ambient air quality levels and the EPA. On 18 December 1995, the High Court ordered:

> The potential of adverse effects on the human system resulting from prolonged exposure to noise and acute exposure to high noise levels has been established by studies of general population exposed to different levels of noise. Noise is especially troublesome in urban areas. People in or near cities are exposed to loud noise much of the time. Noise causes discomfort in people. It can cause several harmful effects which can be both physiological and psychological. Noise pollution can also cause some adverse sociological and psychological effects. Parliament has, therefore, while enacting the Environment Act, specifically dealt with the aspect of the noise pollution....
>
> Considering the [Expert Committee Report of 1986] and the provisions of the Environment Act and Rules framed thereunder for restricting the noise pollutant as provided in Schedule III quoted above, it is the duty of the state government to frame the Rules under the various Acts including the Bombay Police Act in conformity with the said Rules. Section 15 provides for punishment to person or companies for contravention of the provisions of the Environment Act and the Rules. Section 17 provides for punishment of Government department for contravention of the provisions of the Environment Act and the Rules thereunder. It *inter alia*, provides that where an offence under the Environment Act has been committed by any department of Government, the head of the department shall be deemed to be guilty of the offence and shall be liable to be proceeded against and punished accordingly. Therefore, prima facie it appears that permission for use of loud speakers which results in noise pollution in violation of Rule 3 cannot be granted. Hence, it would be just and proper to direct the respondent to find out and report to this court what actions can be taken under the provisions of the Environment Act and the Rules framed thereunder with regard to noise pollution in conformity with the Environment Act and the Rule by taking into consideration the Report submitted by the committee appointed by Mrs Justice Sujata Manohar on Noise Pollution as the said Report has taken into consideration various aspects in various areas on noise pollution of the Bombay city.[218]

The Bombay High Court declined to permit loudspeaker use beyond 11:30 pm during the Ganesh festival and Navratri celebrations. Quoting from an earlier judgment in *State of Bombay v Narasu Appa Mali*,[219] where the court drew a distinction between religious faith

[217] *Dr Y T Oke v State of Maharashtra*, Writ Petition No. 1879 of 1985.

[218] *Dr Y T Oke v State of Maharashtra*, Writ Petition No. 1732 of 1995, Bombay High Court, 18 December 1995.

[219] AIR 1952 Bom 82. 'A sharp distinction must between drawn between religious faith and belief and religious practices. What the state protects is religious faith and belief. If religious practices run counter to public

and belief and religious practices, as well as the Report on the National Commission on Urbanisation,[220] the court held:

> While dealing with a similar application during the Ganesh festival, we have rejected it by our order dated 10th September, 1996 by observing that religious ceremony nowhere provides that on religious festival days loudspeaker is a must without which festivals cannot be observed. For us, it would be difficult to distinguish Ganesh festival from Navratri festival. We note that during Ganesh festival the respondents had taken proper steps for controlling the noise pollution. Therefore, we do not find any justifiable reason to grant permission to use loudspeakers as prayed for during Navratri festival which would result in increase in noise pollution. In any case, there is no question of granting any permission by us or putting an imprint or seal to do something which is in violation of the Environment Act and the Rules. It is for the State Government to implement the said Act and the Rules and prohibit certain activities which adversely affect the lives of persons who cannot oppose the noise pollution for various restraints. It is the duty of the State Government not to encourage the activities which will lead to violation of law. Nobody can object to Navratri festival or any festival for that matter. These festivals can be enjoyed even without loudspeakers. Garba or Dandiya during the Navratri festival without noise pollution by the loudspeaker were played in the recent past and can be played without use of loudspeaker.
>
> Hence, the State Government would take appropriate steps to control noise pollution created by loudspeakers during these festivals and protect the silent sufferers [who] may be students, old, infirm or others not interested. It is for the State to implement the law as it is.[221]

13. The Kerala High Court in *P A Jacob v Superintendent of Police*[222] grappled with loudspeakers. The court held that the fundamental right to freedom of speech guaranteed under Article 19(1)(a) of the Constitution did not include the right to use a loudspeaker. The petitioner sought permission to use loudspeakers at a public meeting where he proposed to denounce the practice of an orthodox Christian sect which barred its members from marrying outside their denomination. When the sub-inspector of police withdrew loudspeaker permission, apprehending that the petitioner's view may cause public disorder, the petitioner moved the Kerala High Court. Justice Sankaran Nair's judgment reviewed in depth the authorities on freedom of speech and then discussed the right of the unwilling listener:

> Apart from the right to be let alone—freedom from aural aggression—Article 21 guarantees freedom from tormenting sounds. What is negatively the right to be left alone, is positively the right to be free from noise. Exposure to high noise, is a known risk and it is proved to cause bio-chemical changes in man, elevating levels of blood catecholamine, cholesterol, white cell counts and lymphocytes. Laboratory studies made by monitoring electroencephalographic (EEG) responses changes in neurovegetative reactions during sleep, show that disturbance of sleep becomes increasingly apparent as ambient noise levels exceed about 35 db (A).... Sound levels generally caused by loudspeakers transgress safe limits by a wide margin. Loudspeakers have become part of political, social, religious and cultural life of this country. To allow advocates of various persuasions to commit unlimited aural aggression on unwilling listeners, would be to allow them to subjugate the right of life of unwilling listeners, to their aggressions. Protests made by sufferers like the student community or sick, generally fall on heedless ears.

order, morality or health or a policy of social welfare upon which the state has embarked, then the religious practice must give way before the good of the people of the state as a whole.'

[220] *Report of the National Commission on Urbanisation*, Vol II, para 14.4.3 (1988).

[221] *Dr Y T Oke v State of Maharashtra*, Writ Petition No. 1732 of 1995, Bombay High Court, order dated 11 October 1996.

[222] AIR 1993 Ker 1.

Finding that the authority had acted arbitrarily in refusing permission, the court held that the petitioner would be permitted to avail of loudspeakers in a reasonable manner so long as the output from the loudspeakers was modulated and reasonable. In an earlier case, Justice Nair declined to issue a mandamus to compel the respondents to grant loudspeaker permission, recognizing that noise pollution was an accepted danger and the indiscriminate use of loudspeakers could not be permitted.[223]

The approach of the Kerala High Court to loudspeakers has varied from case to case, with permission being granted to the Guruvayur temple management to use loudspeakers,[224] but a prohibition being imposed in respect of loudspeaker use at a congested junction.[225]

14. The Calcutta High Court was among the first to tackle public interest issues relating to noise. In *Rabin Mukherjee v State of West Bengal*,[226] the High Court recognized the nuisance created by noisy electric and air horns used in buses and trucks. The court directed the transport authorities to strictly enforce the provisions of the Motor Vehicles Act and the Bengal Motor Vehicle Rules which restricted the use of loud and shrill horns.

In 1996, the Calcutta High Court clamped down on the indiscriminate use of microphones and loudspeakers. In *Om Birangana Religious Society v The State*,[227] Justice Bhagabati Prosad Banerjee considered an application by a religious organization which was aggrieved by the respondents' refusal to permit microphones and loudspeakers during the daily poojas and other religious activities. The petitioners prayed for a mandamus directing the District Magistrate to accord the necessary permission under the Police Act. Justice Banerjee used the case to frame detailed guidelines for the issue of loudspeaker permits and asked the authorities to accord permissions in accordance with the guidelines. The court directed the West Bengal PCB to maintain noise level registers, prohibited the use of loudspeakers between 9 pm and 7 am, and required the authorities to calibrate and seal the apparatus amplifying the sound so that the noise did not exceed the prescribed limit. In the course of his judgment, Justice Banerjee recognized that every citizen has a right to leisure, a right to sleep and a right *not* to hear. Noise generated from loudspeakers and microphones posed a serious threat to public health. Building on the principal order, the High Court proceeded to tone up the administration. In July 1996, Justice Banerjee urged the West Bengal government to sanction more posts so that the PCB had adequate personnel to effectively discharge their functions under the court order. The court also urged the police to be vigilant in the discharge of its duties and directed All India Radio and Doordarshan to disseminate information and create awareness on the harmful effects of noise pollution.[228]

Thereafter, taking judicial notice of complaints from the districts outside Calcutta, the court directed the district police authorities to strictly administer the judicial norms. The PCB was asked to devise suitable measures to regulate the noise from electric and air horns of public vehicles, fireworks and other sources of noise pollution.[229] When organizers of Durga Pooja festivities and hotels were found to have breached court orders, contempt proceedings were initiated against them. Generally, the contempt proceedings were dropped after securing an

---

[223] *Venu v Director General of Police* 1992 (2) Ker L T 86.

[224] *Chairman, Guruvayur D M C v Superintendent of Police* AIR 1998 Ker 122.

[225] *New Road Brothers v Commissioner of Police* AIR 1999 Ker 262.

[226] AIR 1985 Cal 222.

[227] (1996) 100 CWN 617. C O No. 4303 (W) of 1995, 1 April 1996.

[228] *Id.*, order dated 23 July 1996. In a subsequent order passed in February 1997, the court urged all media and newspapers to publish information regarding the method of lodging complaints with the PCB.

[229] *Id.*, order dated 30 September 1997.

undertaking of future good behaviour and a goodwill contribution in favour of the West Bengal PCB.[230]

The Calcutta High Court quelled the clamour raised by the organizers of religious gatherings thus:

> It is made clear that the effect of the judgment and order passed by this Court is to be followed by all sections of people including people of all communities irrespective of caste, creed and religion. In the parent order it was provided that the right to propagate one's religion means the right to communicate a person's belief to another or to expose the tenets of that faith. But, the right to propagate religion [that] includes the right to use the loudspeakers and microphones for the purpose of granting religious texts also implies the duties not to indiscriminately use the microphone or loudspeakers during religious performance in the society by any religion. One can practice, profess and propagate religion as granted under Article 25 (1) of the Constitution, but that is not an absolute right, it cannot be said that a citizen should be coerced to hear anything which he does not like or which he does not require.
>
> Accordingly, the Pollution Control Board is directed to issue notices to the District Magistrate, Superintendent of Police in the districts and the Commissioner of Police at Calcutta to take steps for controlling noise levels and/or restricting the noise level in the temples, mosques and churches, gurudwaras and/or other religious place at the time of religious functions which is a rising phenomenon and is creating sound pollution violating the permissible noise level. It is made clear that India being a secular State, the order passed by this Court should be complied with by all irrespective of caste, creed and religion and not by any particular community, otherwise it will be a discriminatory treatment which is not the intention of this Court. Steps should be taken in this regard so that the sound generated in the temples, mosques, churches or gurudwaras, etc. does not flow beyond the vicinity of such religious place.[231]

Referring to the national ambient noise levels prescribed under the Environment (Protection) Rules of 1986, the court directed the PCB to monitor noise levels at different parts of the city and directed the police to strictly enforce the provisions relating to silence zones.

On 3 March 1997, the High Court banned the use of microphones and loudspeakers around schools and colleges in Kolkata and any district in the state of West Bengal during the school board examinations. Moreover, during this period, the use of microphones in the entire state was prohibited between 6 pm and 7 am.

Meanwhile, spurred by the directions issued on 30 September 1997,[232] the police prevented the sale of firecrackers which emanated noise exceeding 65 decibels. In a petition filed by the fireworks dealers, the High Court declined relief since no person had a right to manufacture or sell fireworks that created sound beyond the ambient noise levels prescribed under the Environment (Protection) Act of 1986.[233] The Supreme Court approved the view taken by the High Court while dismissing a special leave filed by an aggrieved fireworks dealer.[234] But the fireworks dealers were quick to strike back. They successfully lobbied the Union Ministry of Environment and Forests to amend Schedule I to the Environment (Protection) Rules of

---

230 *Id.*, orders dated 9 January 1997 and 16 January 1997. The contribution ranged between Rs. 5,000 and Rs. 25,000.

231 *Id.*, order dated 29 November 1996.

232 *Birangana Religious Society v The State* C O No. 4303 (W) of 1995.

233 *Burrabazar Fire Works Dealers v Commissioner of Police* AIR 1998 Cal 121.

234 Order dated 12 January 1998 in a petition filed by Mohan Fire Works. The order is reproduced in *Maulalana Mufti Syed Barkati v State of West Bengal* AIR 1999 Cal 15, 26.

1986 by introducing statutory noise standards for firecrackers that allow noise levels up to 125 decibels.[235]

A division bench headed by Justice Banerjee in *Maulana Mufti Syed Barkati v State of West Bengal*[236] repelled a challenge to the restrictions on loudspeakers imposed by the state between 9 pm and 7 am. The petitioners assailed the restrictions on the ground that they violated their fundamental right to freedom of religion guaranteed under Article 25 of the Constitution. The petitioners claimed that Azan, which was integral to Islam, was required to be called five times a day through loudspeakers. Without loudspeakers, it was not possible to for the voice of Azan to reach the believers of Islam. The High Court dismissed the petition, holding that the use of loudspeakers was a technological development and was not a part of Islam.

[235] Entry 89, Schedule I was inserted vide the Environment (Protection) (Second Amendment) Rules of 1999. The Kerala High Court considered these standards in *Ananda Parthasarthy v State of Kerala* OP Nos 11016 of 1998, 1 December 1999. The division bench directed strict implementation of the norms and suggested that special courts to tackle noise pollution be established.

[236] AIR 1999 Cal 15.

10

FORESTS

Despite recent efforts to increase forest cover through reforestation, India's forests are in poor condition, with less than 22% of India under forest cover in 2019.[1] To ensure ecological stability, 30% of the nation should be under adequate forest cover. Some of the domestic consequences of deforestation are disrupted river flows, flooding, drought, wildlife extinction, displacement of forest dwellers and scarcity of forest products on which the survival of many depends. Deforestation also has global impacts on climate change and desertification.

All sectors of the economy make demands on forest resources. Forest land is sacrificed for massive development projects, such as the Narmada Valley Project and the Tehri Project discussed in a later chapter.[2] Large industrial interests use forests as the source of raw material for paper, pulp and rayon mills. India's mineral reserves of iron ore, bauxite and manganese are located under forests requiring the destruction of those forests to reach the mineral. Small businesses depend on forests as the source of wood for myriad products. Firewood brought in from the forests remains a source of cooking fuel. Forests are crucial to many, particularly tribal communities, as a source of fuel, fodder, building materials and minor forest products. In addition, some communities traditionally use the forests as their homes, either permanently or seasonally. Forests and wildlife parks also generate tourist income. Finally, forests serve as a source of emotional and spiritual renewal for visitors from India and all over the world.

That some uses are incompatible with others is exemplified by both commercial logging and industrial strip mining on forested land. Such logging or mining destroys the integrity of the forest eco-system upon which both endangered wildlife and forest dwellers depend. Soil stability is lost. The resulting erosion and runoff lead to flooding and siltation of water courses, reservoirs and irrigation channels. Given the breadth of demands on India's forests, it is not surprising that the problem of deforestation has gained significant public attention, and that implementation of conservation and afforestation programmes has sparked intense controversy.

The most decisive and influential judicial intervention in the environmental field is the on-going *Forest Conservation* case.[3] The orders in this case form a separate section in this chapter. Before turning to this case, we outline the forest statutes. We also examine the legal controversy of mining and other industrial uses on forest land beginning with the *Dehradun Quarrying* litigation.[4] The rights of forest dwellers in India who have historically received

---

[1] The Forest Survey of India undertakes an assessment of the county's forest resources every two years. '[F]orest cover includes all patches of land with a tree canopy density of more than 10% and more than 1 ha in area, irrespective of land use, ownership and species of trees.' The total forest cover is 21.67% of the geographical area. Forest Survey of India, *India State of Forest Report: 2019* xi, xii (2019).

[2] Large Projects, Chapter 14.

[3] *T N Godavarman Thirumulpad v Union of India* AIR 1997 SC 1228; AIR 1998 SC 769 and AIR 1999 SC 97.

[4] *Rural Litigation and Entitlement Kendra, Dehradun v State of Uttar Pradesh* AIR 1985 SC 652.

Environmental Law & Policy in India. Shyam Divan and Armin Rosencranz, Oxford University Press.
 DOI: 1093/oso/9780192865458.003.0010

scant legal protection are explored in the Environmental Policy in India chapter.[5] The *Vedanta* case[6] and the *Lafarge* case,[7] discussed later in this chapter, bring out facets of the rights of tribal communities. Notes and questions to more fully flesh out the issues and prompt further reflection are interspersed throughout the chapter.

A. FOREST LAWS

When India gained Independence, forests were placed on the State List of the Constitution. Forest departments of individual states continued to regulate forests in accord with the Indian Forest Act of 1927, as implemented by state regulations. The Indian Forest Act gives the states jurisdiction over both public and private forests and facilitates the extraction of timber for profit. Public forests, those in which state governments have a proprietary interest, are divided into three categories: reserve forests, village forests and protected forests.

Forest land or wasteland may be notified as a reserve forest by a state government's declaration in the Official Gazette.[8] Previously recognized individual and community rights over the forest are extinguished upon such a notification[9] and access to the forest and forest products becomes a matter of privilege, subject to permission of forest officials acting under governing laws and regulations.[10] The Act includes procedures for making claims against the government for the loss of legal rights over the forest.

Village forests are established when a state assigns to a village community the rights over any land which has been constituted a reserve forest.[11] State governments make rules for managing the village forest and prescribe conditions under which the village community is provided with timber, other forest products or pasture. The rules may also assign duties to the village for the protection and improvement of the forest.[12]

State governments may designate as a protected forest any forest or wasteland in which the government has a proprietary right or rights to any part of the forest's products.[13] Protected forests cannot be created from reserve forests.[14] The government must survey the rights and claims of private persons in forests being considered for protection but may declare the forest area a protected forest pending completion of the survey.[15] The Act authorizes state governments to close portions of the forests as long as the remainder of the forest is sufficient for individuals and communities to exercise their existing legal rights to use the forest.[16] State governments may prohibit certain activities such as grazing, cultivation, charcoal burning and stone quarrying.[17] The state government may also regulate all rights and privileges for use of the protected forest.[18]

---

5 Chapter 2, Section F.
6 *Orissa Mining Corporation Ltd v Ministry of Environment and Forest* (2013) 6 SCC 476.
7 *Lafarge Umiam Mining (P) Ltd v Union of India* (2011) 7 SCC 338.
8 Section 4.
9 Section 9.
10 Section 15.
11 Section 28.
12 *Id.*
13 Section 29.
14 *Id.*
15 *Id.*
16 Section 30.
17 *Id.*
18 Section 31.

In extending to forest lands which are not the property of the government,[19] the Indian Forest Act represents strong governmental intrusion into private rights. State governments may regulate timber cutting, cultivation, grazing and burning or clearing of vegetation on private forest land.[20] The Act also authorizes state governments to acquire private land for public purposes under the Land Acquisition Act of 1894.[21]

Countering governmental powers under the Act, the Indian Forest Act also provides protection and compensation for legally recognized individual or community rights to forest land or forest products. However, for most forest dwellers, particularly tribal people,[22] the crucial issue is not the *protection* of recognized legal rights but rather the threshold issue of *recognition* of legal rights over forests.

The debate over how to balance the various demands of the nation on the forests intensified in the 1970s. The Constitution (Forty-Second Amendment) Act of 1976 transferred forests from the State List to the Concurrent List of the Constitution. This transfer empowered the Central Government to act directly in managing India's forests. The Ministry of Environment and Forests now has administrative jurisdiction over national forest policy, forestry development and the Indian Forest Service. Since 1976, the Central Government has taken four major actions with regard to forests: the Forest (Conservation) Act of 1980, an amendment in 1988 of this Act, the adoption of a revised National Forest Policy in 1988[23] and the passage of a Forest Rights Act of 2006.[24]

The 1980 Act was Parliament's response to the rapid decline in forest cover. Until then, deforestation averaged 1 million hectares a year.[25] The Act prohibits the deletion of a reserved forest, or the diversion of forest land for any 'non-forest' purpose, and prevents the cutting of trees in a forest without the prior approval of the Central Government.[26] Contravention of the Act attracts up to 15 days in prison.[27]

Despite the National Forest Policy of 1988 emphasizing environmental protection and participatory management of forests involving the local community, the position in the field did not change. Continuing to be governed by the Indian Forest Act of 1927, the forest

[19] Chapter V.

[20] Section 35.

[21] Section 37. The 1894 Act was replaced on 1 January 2014 by the Right to Fair Compensation and Transparency in Land Acquisition, Rehabilitation and Resettlement Act of 2013.

[22] Because of the diversity of racial origins, languages and economic conditions, the exact description of 'tribal' people is impossible. Scholars have suggested numerous functional definitions of tribal people, most of which include cultural or racial distinctions and a lack of integration into the nation's predominant economic and political institutions. Legally, the Constitution incorporates the recognition of tribal people through the notion of 'Scheduled Tribes'. Under Article 342, the President of India, subject to review and modification by Parliament, may designate any tribe or tribal community or group within any tribe or tribal community as a Scheduled Tribe for purposes of the Constitution. Over 104 million people constituting 8.6% of the total population in India are classified as tribal people according to the 2011 census. Ministry of Tribal Affairs, Government of India, *Statistical Profile of Scheduled Tribes in India: 2013* (2013).

[23] At the time of writing, the Draft National Forest Policy of 2020 'is under consideration for adoption'. Ministry of Environment, Forest and Climate Change, Government of India, *Annual Report 2020–21*, 54 (2021). Earlier, the MoEF had circulated for discussion a Draft National Forest Policy of 2018 which was revised in 2019.

[24] The full form of the FRA is the Scheduled Tribes and other Traditional Forest Dwellers (Recognition of Forests Rights) Act of 2006. See the discussion on the FRA in Chapter 2, Section F.

[25] World Bank, *India: Forest Sector Review* (1993). Between 1987 and 1989, a quarter million hectares of forests were lost. Society for the Promotion of Wasteland Development, *Need for Increased Funding for Forests* (1991).

[26] Section 2.

[27] Section 39.

department held firm to the conventional governmental view of timber production for the national interest. The local community remained alienated, with tension continuously festering across India between forest dwellers and forest guards.

The historian Ramachandra Guha explains the policy debates and tensions that set the stage for the passage of the path-breaking Forest Rights Act in 2006.

RAMACHANDRA GUHA; HOW MUCH SHOULD A PERSON CONSUME? 151 (2006)

The forestry debate of the 1970s and 1980s drew at times on the heritage or earlier movements and critiques. The peasants of Garhwal and Kumaon, as I found out while doing fieldwork there, were acutely conscious of how Chipko had drawn on a long and honorable history of peasant resistance to state forestry.... [I]n the villages of the Deccan social workers [agreed] that proper access to forests and pasture was vital to survival, and that it was the 'great superstructure' of the Forest Department which continued to deny herders and farmers this access.

As tempers cooled and the polemic exhausted itself, there came a second phase which we might call the 'politics of negotiation.' In villages and state capitals, forest officers and their critics found themselves at the same table, talking and beginning to appreciate, if not fully understand, the other's point of view. Concessions were made by each side, protests suspended by one and leases of forest produce to industry cancelled by the other. One product of the growing dialogue between activists and bureaucrats was the approval by India's Parliament in 1988 of a new National Forest Policy. Where the ruling Forest Policy of 1952 had stressed state control and industrial exploitation, the new document instead emphasized the imperatives of ecological stability and peoples' needs.

Then, slowly and hesitatingly, began the third phase which we can term 'the politics of collaboration'. In the state of West Bengal, for example, the Forest Department initiated remedial action on its own, abandoning its traditional custodial approach by inviting peasants to co-operate with it. Thousands of village forest protection committees (VFPCs) were constituted, each of which agreed to protect nearby forests in collaboration with the state. These VFPCs signed individual agreements with the Forest Department, pledging to protect forests from outsiders and smugglers, not to graze their cattle in areas undergoing reproduction, and not to lop tree branches. In exchange they were allowed to enter the forests on foot to take away firewood and collect non-timber forest produce such as honey, fruit, and rope-making material. Each village was also granted 25% of the final timber harvest undertaken by the Forest Department—this is an unprecedented concession because over the past century all such monies had been credited directly into the state treasury.

In this manner, previously authoritarian government officials joined with previously suspicious villages to jointly manage forests. As time went by, the scheme was refined to make the division of rights and responsibilities more precise. The incentive for village participants was also increased by making their share 40% of the timber harvest. In some parts of Bengal, the new programs have been spectacularly successful. Badly degraded sal forest have been regenerated so successfully in fact that they now attract migratory elephants in search of food. A steady stream of benefit has ensued to the local economy and the conflict between state and peasant has come down to very manageable levels.

The success of joint forest management (JFM) in West Bengal has encouraged scholars, activists, and sympathetic civil servants to demand its replication in other parts of India. Outside its original home, however, the progress of JFM has been slow. Administrative styles and cultures of governance vary widely among the states and regions of India. So do individual orientations, with some forest officials still loath to relinquish control; while others have been inspired to start village protection committees on their own.

A mapping of the forestry debate in contemporary India would therefore show significant regional variation. In some states it is still stuck in the politics of blame; in others, it has moved tentatively on to the politics of negotiations. In West Bengal and parts of Andhra Pradesh,

Madhya Pradesh, and Himachal Pradesh it has gone further, embracing the politics of collaboration through the creation of JFM regimes. In this last scenario, too, there is abundant room for improvement. For the JFM model promoted by the Government of India reflects and sometimes reinforces inequities within rural society. Gender and caste are two axes of discrimination, with women and low-caste members of the village community not having adequate representation or voice in the decision-making process (this is also true, to a great extent, of van panchayats in Kumaon.) Likewise, pastoral groups and artisans who have legitimate claims on forest resources are sometimes given short shrift. Moreover, forest officials still claim a monopoly of 'scientific expertise,' refusing to entertain villagers' own ideas on species choice, spacing, and harvesting techniques.

* * *

One can thus envision a fourth, possibly final, phase for the Indian forestry debate, the 'politics of partnership.' For collaboration, even where it does exist, takes places on terms set down by the state, through officials of the Forest Department. We need to move to a more inclusively democratic structure where the state listens and learn from the community, and where the community recognizes and deals fairly with the inequities within its own ranks.

The enactment of the Forest Rights Act in 2006 altered the equation between the community and the bureaucracy. The FRA grants individual as well as community rights to forest dwelling Scheduled Tribes and other traditional forest dwellers. These rights take shape in the form of title documents that record the nature of the rights with a description of the land where the forest dweller engages in self-cultivation or some other similar activity to secure her livelihood. With the passage of the FRA, tenure holders and forest communities are now secure in their traditional forest range.

B. THE *FOREST CONSERVATION* CASE

Beginning in December 1996, the Supreme Court issued sweeping directives to oversee the enforcement of forest laws across the nation. Assisted by an *amicus curiae*, the court froze all wood-based industrial activity, reinforced the scope of the embargo on forest exploitation, issued detailed directions for the sustainable use of forests and created its own monitoring and implementation machinery through regional and state-level committees. The case has no parallel, even by the expansive standards of India's proactive judiciary. As we shall see, the court assumes the role of a super-administrator, regulating the felling, use and movement of timber across the country in the hope of preserving the nation's forests. There are a number of orders in the case and we excerpt from five principal orders dated 12 December 1996, 4 March 1997, 8 May 1997, 15 January 1998 and 26 September 2005. The analysis that follows these excerpts focuses on the issues impacting the North-East region where the wood-based industry contributes substantially to the region's economy.

T N GODAVARMAN THIRUMULPAD v UNION OF INDIA

AIR 1997 SC 1228

* * *

ORDER:

After hearing all the learned counsel, who have rendered very able assistance to the Court, we have formed the opinion that the matters require a further indepth hearing to examine all the aspects relating to the National Forest Policy.

It has emerged at the hearing that there is a misconception in certain quarters about the true scope of the Forest (Conservation) Act, 1980 (for short the Act) and the meaning of the word 'forest' used therein. There is also a resulting misconception about the need of prior approval of the Central Government, as required by section 2 of the Act, in respect of certain activities in the forest area which are more often of a commercial nature. It is necessary to clarify that position.

The Forest (Conservation) Act, 1980 was enacted with a view to check further deforestation which ultimately results in ecological imbalance; and therefore, the provisions made therein for the conservation of forests and for matters connected therewith, must apply to all forest irrespective of the nature of ownership or classification thereof. The word 'forest' must be understood according to its dictionary meaning. This description covers all statutorily recognised forests, whether designated as reserved, protected or otherwise for the purpose of section 2(i) of the Forest (Conservation) Act. The term 'forest land', occurring in section 2, will not only include 'forest' as understood in the dictionary sense, but also any area recorded as forest in the Government record irrespective of the ownership. This is how it has to be understood for the purpose of section 2 of the Act. The provisions enacted in the Forest (Conservation) Act, 1980 for the conservation of forests and the matters concerned therewith must apply clearly to all forests so understood irrespective of the ownership or classification thereof.... This has become necessary also because of the stand taken on behalf of the State of Rajasthan, even at this late stage, relating to permissions granted for mining in such area which is clearly contrary to the decisions of this Court. It is reasonable to assume that any state government which had failed to appreciate the correct position in law so far, will forthwith correct its stance and take necessary remedial measures without any further delay. We further direct as under:

I. General:

1. In view of the meaning of the word 'forest' in the Act, it is obvious that prior approval of the Central Government is required for any non-forest activity within the area of any 'forest'. In accordance with section 2 of the Act, all on-going activity within any forest in any State throughout the country, without the prior approval of the Central Government, must cease forthwith. It is, therefore, clear that the running of saw mills of any kind including veneer or ply-wood mills, and mining of any mineral are non-forest purposes and are, therefore, not permissible without prior approval of the Central Government. Accordingly, any such activity is *prima facie* violation of the provisions of the Forest (Conservation) Act, 1980. Every state government must promptly ensure total cessation of all such activities forthwith.
2. In addition to the above, in the tropical wet ever-green forests of Tirap and Changlang in the State of Arunachal Pradesh, there would be a complete ban on felling of any kind of trees therein because of their particular significance to maintain ecological balance needed to preserve bio-diversity. All saw mills, veneer mills and ply-wood mills in Tirap and Changlang in Arunachal Pradesh and within a distance of 100 kms from its border, in Assam, should also be closed immediately. The state governments of Arunachal Pradesh and Assam must ensure compliance of this direction.
3. The felling of trees in all forests is to remain suspended except in accordance with the Working Plans of the state governments, as approved by the Central Government. In the absence of any Working Plan in any particular state, such as Arunachal Pradesh, where the permit system exists, the felling under the permits can be done only by the Forest Department of the state government or the State Forest Corporation.
4. There shall be a complete ban on the movement of cut trees and timber from any of the seven north-eastern states to any other state of the country either by rail, road or water-ways. The Indian Railways and the state governments are directed to take all measures necessary to ensure strict compliance of this direction. This ban will not apply to the movement of certified timber required for defence or other Government purposes. This ban will also not affect felling in any private plantation

comprising of trees planted in any area which is not a forest. [Directions specific to the States of Jammu and Kashmir, Himachal Pradesh, Uttar Pradesh, and West Bengal and Tamil Nadu are omitted.]

We also direct that notwithstanding the closure of any saw mills or other wood-based industry pursuant to this order, the workers employed in such units will continue to be paid their full emoluments due and shall not be retrenched or removed from service for this reason.

We are informed that the Railway authorities are still using wooden sleepers for laying tracks. The Ministry of Railways will file an affidavit giving full particulars in this regard including the extent of wood, and the steps taken by them to find alternatives to the use of wood....

T N GODAVARMAN THIRUMULPAD v UNION OF INDIA
AIR 1997 SC 1233

* * *

ORDER:

We are satisfied that there is need to constitute a High Power Committee to oversee the strict and faithful implementation of the orders of this Court in the North-Eastern region and for certain ancillary purposes. Accordingly, we direct as under. [The Court constituted the High Power Committee (HPC) and directed it to prepare an inventory of timber and timber products lying in the forests, transport depots and mills in the region. The HPC was empowered to permit the use or sale of timber products if it considered appropriate through the State Forest Corporation. Pending the final hearing, the expenses relating to the HPC were to be borne by the Central and State Governments.]

All unlicensed saw mills, veneer and plywood industries in the State of Maharashtra and the State of Uttar Pradesh are to be closed forthwith and the state governments would not remove or relax the condition for grant of permission/licence for the opening of any such saw mill, veneer and plywood industry and it shall also not grant any fresh permission/licence for this purpose. The Chief Secretary of the State will ensure strict compliance of this direction and file a compliance report within two weeks....

It is made clear that the orders passed by this Court in these matters, including the order dated 12-12-1996 [AIR 1997 SC 1228] and the present order shall be obeyed and carried out by the Union Government as well as the State Government notwithstanding any order of direction passed by a Court, including a High Court or Tribunal, to the contrary.

We further direct the Registrar General to communicate the order dated 12-12-1996 as well as the present order to the Registrars of all the High Courts to ensure strict compliance. It is also clarified that the orders passed by this Court including the order dated 12-12-1996 and this order will apply to all Autonomous Hill Councils in the north-eastern states as well as the union territories.

It is made clear that all the concerned authorities would, in the meantime, continue to examine the various aspects of the problems requiring solution and try to solve these problems in collaboration with the Central Government and the state governments. An efficacious exercise of this kind would enable reduction of the area which may require judicial scrutiny and adjudication in these matters.

[The court clarified/modified its previous order. The directions were not to apply to minor forest produce, including bamboo; plantations were permitted to fell fuel trees; and the golf courses at Kodaikanal and Udagamandalam were allowed to function until permission from the Union Government was received.]

T N GODAVARMAN THIRUMULPAD v UNION OF INDIA
(1997) 7 SCC 440

Order:

***

In relation to the seven north-eastern states, it is further directed as under:

(a) The ban on felling and transportation of trees and timber as already imposed shall continue.

(b) As directed by the High-Powered Committee (HPC), the State Government shall take all measures necessary to bring the felled timber lying in the forest to the depots/storage points, and have it stacked.

(c) After the process of inventorisation is over, the HPC may permit saw mills and other wood-based industry to utilise their own legitimate stocks of timber for conversion into finished produce. Such finished produce may then be disposed of by these mills under supervision of the HPC and the State Forest Department. The permission granted by the HPC to these mills shall be on suitable terms to ensure that no malpractice occurs in the future, and the mills shall be required to file an undertaking to comply with such terms, any breach thereof having the same consequence as a breach of the order of this Court.

(d) After the inventory of the felled timber gathered at the depots/storage points is complete, the HPC may permit sale of such rounded timber for utilization within the state to the extent it is from a lawful source. The movement of rounded timber within the state as well as the movement of rounded timber within and outside the state shall be under transit passes —the issuance and disposal of which will be under the overall supervision of the HPC.

(e) No person other than a local inhabitant, a Forest Officer or Police Officer or any other personnel on official duty shall be permitted to enter the reserved forests except in accordance with permission in writing issued by the Principal Chief Conservator of Forests. The ban on movement of cut trees, timber or veneer from any of the seven northeastern states to any other state in the country in any manner applies also to the growth and/or felled timber from any private plantation....

T N GODAVARMAN THIRUMULPAD v UNION OF INDIA
AIR 1998 SC 769

Order:

***

Learned Attorney General submits that the perception of the Ministry of Environment and Forests (MoEF) is as under:

1. It has been estimated by the HPC that about 1.20 lakhs cubic metres of illicitly felled seized timber, belonging to the state governments is lying in the forests and depots for varying periods of time between 1 to 2 years and is thereby getting degraded on account of decay and rotting of the wood. It is necessary to dispose it off at the earliest to minimise any further loss in its monetary value. There is, in addition, considerable quantity of timber claimed by the private industry and local people. In view of the approaching monsoon season (April 98) all such timber needs to be disposed of with urgency to save further loss in quality, as also in value, albeit with proper checks and balances.

2. Given the weak infrastructure in the north-eastern region, it does not seem feasible to transport such huge quantities of timber for auction in markets outside the region in a short time. Moreover, there would be uncertainty of the response in timber markets far away from the source of timber which has been subject to elements of degradation in varying degrees. There is also the likelihood of local resentment, in an otherwise sensitive area, if all such material is removed from the region without processing and value addition, which could be conceived as creating an adverse effect on the region's economy.

3. Even though the proliferation of wood based industries has been the main cause of degradation of forests in the north-eastern states, considering the extent of forests (64% of the geographical area) and the dependence of the local people on the forest resources in the region it is neither feasible, nor desirable, to ban completely either the timber trade or running of the wood based industries. However, their numbers and capacities need to be regulated qua the sustainable availability of forest produce and they are also required to be relocated in specified industrial zones. Moreover, the industrial requirements have to be subordinated to the maintenance of environment and ecology as well as *bona fide* local needs.

4. There shall be no fresh felling in the forests belonging to the Government, District and Regional Councils till the disposal of their existing stocks of legal and illegal timber.

5. In view of the multi-dimensional issues impinging upon forest protection, foolproof institutional arrangements need to be put in place, and made functional under the strict supervision of the North-East Council (NEC), Technical backstopping in the forestry matter will be provided by MoEF by opening a separate cell in the Ministry under an officer of the rank of Chief Conservator of Forests (CCF) and starting a satellite office of the Forest Survey of India at Shillong....

We have heard the *amicus curiae*, the learned Attorney General and learned counsel for north-eastern states. In view of the report of the High Power Committee and taking into account the factors which require an order to be made by the Court for disposal of the felled timber and ancillary matters which are lying in the north-eastern states, we consider it appropriate to make the following order:

1. Disposal of timber shall commence only after the concerned Principal Chief Conservator of Forests irrevocably certifies that inventorisation of all felled timber in the state has been completed.
2. As a first measure all inventorised timber, including seized timber lying in the forests should be immediately transported to specified forest depots.
3. All illegal/illicit timber found in possession of an offender or abandoned in the forest shall be confiscated to the state government and shall be disposed of in accordance with the procedure to be adopted for disposal of Government timber.
4. Out of the seized timber, logs found suitable for manufacture of veneer and plywood shall be processed by the state governments within their own factories and by hiring such facilities. The finished product can be marketed freely.
5. The remaining timber belonging to Government and District Councils shall be offered for sale to Government Departments for their *bona fide* official use and the rest shall be sold in public auction or through sealed tender after fixing floor price by an Expert Committee with a representative from the MoEF. Private timber owners whose stocks have been cleared by HPC shall have the option of selling the timber either in the auctions organized by the State Forests Departments/Forests Development Corporation or directly.
6. The state government shall formally notify industrial estates for locating the wood based industrial units in consultation with the Ministry of Environment and Forests.
7. Timber as per inventory cleared by HPC may be allowed to:
   (a) be converted/utilized if the unit is located within the notified industrial estate. As the relocation in proposed industrial estates may take some time, existing units with only legal stocks may convert this timber, as one-time exception, notwithstanding anything contained in para 12 hereunder, till such stocks last subject to the maximum period as per the norms prescribed by the High Power Committee (vide their III report) or six months whichever is less. Any stock remaining thereafter shall vest in the state government. However, fresh trees/timber will be allotted to these units only when they start functioning within the designated industrial estates. The territory Deputy Conservator of Forests/Divisional Forest Officer shall be responsible for ensuring that such units process the legal stocks only and will closely monitor the various transit permits (inward and outward) and maintenance of the prescribed records. All such record shall be countersigned (with date) by an officer not less than the rank of an Assistant Conservator of Forests.

(b) allowed to be sold to other units which are located in these industrial estates subject to the condition that such transactions are routed through an authority notified/constituted by the Principal Chief Conservator of Forests.

(c) The state governments shall ensure disposal of illegal timber before permitting the conversion/disposal of legal/authorized timber available with the wood based industries.

8. Transportation of auctioned timber (as well as legal timber) including sawn timber outside the North-Eastern Region shall only be done through railways under the strict supervision of the Forest Department. The Railway Board shall give priority for providing rakes/wagons for such transportation.
9. Modalities for transportation of timber/timber products and alternative modes in case of difficulties in transportation by Railways, will be worked out by the state government in concurrence of the Ministry of Environment and Forests.
10. Existing inventorized stock of timber originating from plantations in private and community holdings in the States of Meghalaya, Mizoram, Tripura, Manipur and Nagaland may be disposed of by their owners under the relevant state laws and rules. In states where such laws and rules do not exist, the necessary laws and rules may be framed within six months.

Pricing of Timber

11. The state governments shall ensure that timber/forest produce is supplied to industries, including Government Undertakings, at full market rate. The existing royalty shall be reviewed and revised upwardly by a Committee constituted under the Chairmanship of Principal Chief Conservator of Forests with representatives from the concerned Departments and shall also include a representative of the Ministry of Environment and Forests. The price of timber for which royalty has not been realized in full shall also be reviewed by this Committee and the concerned industry shall be required to pay the revised price or the royalty (including surcharge, fee etc.), whichever is higher after deducting the part of royalty already paid.

Licensing

12. Licences given to all wood based industries shall stand suspended.
13. Wood based industries which have been cleared by the High Power Committee without any penalty shall have the option to shift to industrial estates which shall be identified by the states within 45 days and developed within six months thereafter.
14. Units which have been penalized because they were found to exceed normal recovery norms, but were within 15% of the said norms, will have a right to approach the High Power Committee on or before 9 February 1998. The High Power Committee shall examine all relevant material, in particular the income tax and excise records for the preceding three years. The High Power Committee shall dispose of all such applications within 45 days thereafter and such mills may be granted licence if the High Power Committee finds that it is not against public interest so to do.
15. Units which have not furnished details/information to the High Power Committee so far or which have not been cleared by the High Power Committee, shall not be granted any licence and the stocks in their custody if any, shall be confiscated to the state government. In case of leased mills belonging to corporation/trusts/co-operative societies owned/controlled/managed by the state government and where the lessees have been penalized by the High Power Committee, the lease shall stand revoked. Such mills shall, however, be eligible for relicensing subject to the condition that these mills are not leased out in future except to an entity fully owned by the Government.
16. Units who do not want to shift to the designated industrial estates shall be allowed to wind up as per law.
17. Henceforth, licences of units shall be renewed annually only in those cases where no irregularity is detected.
18. There shall be a complete moratorium on the issue of a new licences by the state governments or any other authority for the establishment of any new wood based

industry for the next five years after which the situation shall be reviewed with the concurrence of Ministry of Environment and Forests.

19. Number of wood based industries shall be determined strictly within the quantity of timber which can be felled annually on sustainable basis as determined by the approved working plans from time to time. If it is found that units after relocation in industrial estate have excess capacity, then their capacities shall be reduced *pro rata* to remain within the sustainable levels.

Forest Protection

20. An action plan shall be prepared by the Principal Chief Conservator of Forests/ Chief Forest Officer for intensive patrolling and other necessary protective measures to be undertaken in identified vulnerable areas and quarterly report shall be submitted to the Central Government for approval. The approved plan together with the modifications, if any, shall be acted upon.
21. To ensure protection of the forest wealth the forest officers in the northeastern states may be empowered with authority to investigate, prosecute and confiscate on the lines of the powers conferred on the forest officers in many other states in the country.
22. The state government shall be responsible for providing all facilities including security and police force to strictly enforce forest protection measures to stop illicit felling, removal and utilization of such timber. The Chief Secretary shall review the various matters concerning from protection and development in his state at least once every six months with senior forest officers up to the rank of Conservator of Forests. Regional Chief Conservator of Forests of MoEF shall be invited to all such meetings.

Scientific Management of Forest

23. Working Plans for all forest divisions shall be prepared by the state governments and approved from the Government of India. Forest working shall be carried out strictly in accordance with the approved prescriptions of the working plans. The working plans should be prepared within a period of two years. During the interregnum the forests shall be worked according to an annual felling programme approved by the MoEF which shall be incorporated in the concerned working plan. In case a working plan is not prepared within this time frame, further felling will remain suspended till the regular working plan is prepared and got approved.
24. The forests under the District, Regional and Village Councils shall be worked in accordance with working schemes which shall specify both the programme for regeneration and harvesting and whose period shall not be less than 5 years.
25. The maximum permissibly annual yield in the ad interim measures suggested above, shall not exceed the annual harvestable yield determined by Ministry of Environment and Forests. The plantation schemes raised on private and community holdings shall be excluded from these requirements but shall be regulated under respective state rules and regulations.
26. The states shall identify ecologically sensitive areas in consultation with leading institutions like the Indian Council of Forests Research and Education, Wildlife Institute of India, North Eastern Hill University, North Eastern Regional Institute of Science and Technology, leading NGOs, etc. and ensure that such areas are totally excluded from any kind of exploitation. The minimum extent of such areas shall be 10% of the total forest area in the state.

Action against Officials

27. The state government shall identify within 45 days all those forest divisions where significant illegal fellings have taken place and initiate disciplinary/criminal proceedings against those found responsible. The first action taken report (ATR) in this regard shall be submitted to the Central Government within three months which shall be followed by quarterly reports (QRs) till culmination of the matter.

General

28. Timber extraction in forests irrespective of ownership, except in private plantations, shall be carried out by a state agency only. The states shall endeavour to adopt pattern obtaining in the State of Himachal Pradesh as described in para 25.3 of the Rajamani Committee Report.

    If there be any local laws/customs relating to the forest in any state, the concerned state government may apply to this Court for the needed modifications, if any, with alternative proposal.
29. The penalties levied on the wood based industries as ordered by the High Power Committee shall constitute the revolving fund to meet the expenses involved in collection and transportation of seized illegal timber. These can be augmented by utilizing the funds generated by the initial sales of illegal timber already available in the forest depots.
30. Each state shall constitute a State Level Expert Committee for matters concerning the preparation of working plans, their implementation, development of industrial estates, shifting of industrial units to these estates, rules and regulations regarding the grant and renewal of licences to wood based industry and other ancillary matters, under the chairmanship of Principal Chief Conservator of Forests and with a nominee of Ministry of Environment and Forests as one of its members. Any decision of this Committee which is not acceptable to the state government shall be referred to the Central Government.
31. The existing permit system in Arunachal Pradesh shall stand abolished. The state government may provide financial assistance in cash or kind in the form of timber only for the *bona fide* use of the local tribals alone. Such concessional timber shall not be bartered or sold. Felling of trees for such purpose shall be carried out only by a Government agency.
32. The total sale proceeds from the sale of seized timber, as well as timber products manufactured and disposed by the state government (vide para 4) and penalties would be credited to the state revenues. Out of this, the state shall utilize one half of the amount for raising forest plantations by local tribal population and as assistance to the tribals. The remaining one half of the total sale proceeds, after deduction of the expenses there from, would go to the state coffers for other developmental activities in the state.
33. The state shall ensure that sufficient budgetary provisions are made for the preservation of biodiversity and protection of wildlife.
34. To ensure that timber/forest produce smuggled across the border may not be used as cover for trade in illegal timber, it is directed that all such timber seized by Customs/Border Security Force should not be redeemed in favour of individuals who are smuggling it but should be confiscated and handed over to the concerned State Forest Department along with offenders, vehicles, tools and implements for prosecution under the relevant Acts.
35. For the proper and effective implementation of these orders, Ministry of Environment and Forests will have the liberty to issue suitable directions consistent with this order.
36. Action taken report be filed by each state government and the Ministry of Environment and Forests every two months.
37. Liberty to apply for modification/clarification in case of need.

(Note: In this order the term 'state government' would include District Council also except where the context implies otherwise.)

On 17 September 1998, the MoEF constituted the Arunachal Pradesh Forest Protection Authority under section 3(3) of the Environment (Protection) Act of 1986 with powers to protect the environment and forests in the state. The Authority was asked to monitor and implement the directions of the Supreme Court in the *Forest Conservation* case, in which the above orders were issued. The responsibilities of the Authority included issuing necessary directions for disposing felled timber, determining the sustainable number of wood-based industries, approving industrial estates, managing the forests scientifically, pricing timber and fixing the royalty payable to the state.

On the same day, the Supreme Court referred all pending applications in respect of Arunachal Pradesh to the Authority. The Authority was empowered to consider these applications and issue appropriate directions consistent with the orders of the Supreme Court.

NOTES AND QUESTIONS

1. In its order dated 23 February 1998, the Supreme Court noted the contents of the *State of Forests Report 1997* which was placed before the court by the *amicus curiae*. He submitted that between 1995 and 1997, 17,777 sq kms of dense forest were lost to the country. The court observed: 'This presents a rather dismal picture and is an alarming situation depicting deforestation on a large scale. We find from a perusal of the report that major defaulters appear to be the states of Andhra Pradesh, Madhya Pradesh, Assam, Manipur, Nagaland, Orissa and Meghalaya.'[28]

2. In a case of this complexity the role of the *amicus curiae* is extremely challenging. Whose interests should he protect? The forest dwellers? The forest? Persons whose livelihood depends on timber-related economic activity?

3. The court's interpretation of the expressions 'forest' and 'forest land' was timely. To overcome the FCA, some state governments regarded section 2(i) of the Act as covering only those forests that were designated as 'reserved' forests and not forests classified as village forests or protected forests. This narrow interpretation enabled some states to de-reserve or reclassify forests. As a first step, these governments declared protected forest lands as 'non forest' and then allocated them to industries or other agencies. The court's clarification prevents such misuse. No forest, by whatever name designated, can now be re-classified and diverted to a non-forest purpose without prior Central Government permission.

4. Apart from the interpretation of the expressions 'forest' and 'forest land', the Supreme Court opinions take the form of detailed administrative directions. There is hardly a mention of the arguments advanced before the court by the *amicus curiae* or other parties appearing in the case. There is no weighing of rival contentions or analysis of the issues and the arguments made before the court. The court's directions are not supported by any reasons. Is this summary approach justified by the urgent need to prevent deforestation and degradation? Considering the finality of Supreme Court orders and their far-reaching impact, should not the court have supplied reasons to support the directions issued?

In *Sabia Khan v State of UP*,[29] the petitioner claimed that the directions issued in the *Forest Conservation* case were not 'judicial verdicts' but were '*ad hoc* orders.' The petitioner submitted that these orders breached the citizen's fundamental right under Article 19(1)(g) to operate saw mills. The Supreme Court rejected the petition with costs assessed at Rs. 10,000, holding that the petition was an abuse of process.

5. The orders issued by the Supreme Court cover a wide range of forest issues: felling trees, transport of timber, timber pricing, licensing of wood-based industries, forest protection,

[28] AIR 1999 SC 43.
[29] AIR 1999 SC 2284.

scientific management of forests, action against errant officials and the spending of forest revenue. Is this a legitimate extension of the judge's role? Can the directions issued by the court be reasonably derived from the provisions of the FCA or any other statutory or constitutional provision?

6. In its order of 12 December 1996 (AIR 1997 SC 1228), the Supreme Court observed that the matter required an in-depth hearing to examine all aspects relating to the National Forest Policy. Do the comprehensive directions issued more than a year later on 15 January 1998 (AIR 1998 SC 769) conform to the National Forest Policy resolution of 1988? Do they advance the policy objectives of promoting tribal welfare and encouraging joint forest management programmes between forest officers and local communities? Do the court's orders strengthen the policing and centralized decision-making features of the forest laws, to the exclusion of local people? Is such a regime of 'fencing' the forests equitable and sustainable?

7. On 12 December 1996, the court ordered the closure of all saw mills, veneer mills and plywood mills that were operating within any forest without prior Central Government approval. Several of these mills were operating openly for several years to the knowledge of government and revenue authorities. Likewise, mining within any forest was ordered to cease forthwith. On 15 January 1998, the court suspended all licences given to wood-based industries in the north-east region. Were the drastic directions fair to the mill operators? Keep in view that the closure and the suspension orders were passed without issuing show cause notices or granting a hearing to the affected mills. Contrast this approach with the *Ganga Pollution* case,[30] where the Supreme Court directed closure only after granting an opportunity to the industries to explain whether they were functioning under a statutory 'consent' and whether they were complying with the norms. Which is a higher value—natural justice or ecological integrity? Can they be reconciled?

8. Were a zealous administrator to issue closure orders and suspend licences in a like manner, would her action withstand judicial review? Should not the standards of fairness expected from an administrator apply with greater rigour to a 'super-administrator'?

The role of the Supreme Court as a super-administrator continues, as seen from its 29 November 2021 decision allowing applications by the Delhi Metro for construction of tunnels and other works [*T N Godavarman v Union of India* (2021) SCC Online SC 1147].

9. The Supreme Court orders dated 8 May 1997, 14 July 1997 and 15 January 1998 refer to and rely upon reports submitted by the HPC. The content of the reports was not disclosed by the court. Moreover, copies of these reports were not released by the HPC and scores of affected mills and industries had no access to the material in the reports. Nevertheless, in its 15 January 1998 order the court issued numerous important directions relating to the licensing of mills, the resumption of operations and the conversion of timber stock, on the basis of the HPC reports. Is it a fair procedure to pass orders on the basis of material that is not made available to the affected parties? Can you suggest a better procedure to overcome the problem?

10. The task before the HPC was to prepare an inventory of timber lying in the north-east region and to perform certain ancillary functions specified in the order dated 4 March 1997. After preparing an inventory, the HPC appears to have fixed 'norms' for plywood and veneer production from timber. Where the mill exceeded the norms, the HPC surmised that they used illegally felled timber and directed the state government to recover penalties running into several lakhs of rupees from individual units.

[30] *M C Mehta v Union of India* 1992 Supp (2) SCC 633 and 1992 Supp (2) SCC 637.

Was the imposition of penalty lawful? There does not appear to be any such power under the FCA or the Indian Forest Act. No power to impose penalties or fix norms was conferred on the HPC by the Supreme Court while constituting the committee on 12 December 1996. The norms were not disclosed to the mills. The method of arriving at these norms was not explained to the affected parties. The units were neither given notice nor granted an opportunity to explain their case before the penalty was imposed. Is a penalty imposed without notice, without grant of an effective opportunity and hearing and without disclosing the norms, fair to the affected parties?

11. The procedure adopted by the Supreme Court and the HPC appears to fall far short of recognized rules of fair play. While forest conservation is a laudable end, has the court strayed from its primary function—to do justice in *accordance with law*?

12. Contempt of court proceedings were initiated against officials of the Jammu and Kashmir government who circumvented the court's orders. The officials permitted a private company to fell *khair* trees on the basis of the court's clarification that minor forest produce was not covered by the directions issued in the case. The court observed that '*katha*' which was extracted from *khair* wood was minor forest produce but not *khair* which was timber. *Prima facie*, the permission to fell *khair* trees was a deliberate attempt to circumvent the order of the court.[31] Where under the garb of removing infected *saal* trees, healthy trees were being cut in the regions around Kanha National Park in Madhya Pradesh, the court restrained the state government from cutting any of the trees (whether considered diseased or not) until appropriate material was furnished to satisfy the court that its orders were not violated.[32]

13. In the course of this vast exercise, the Supreme Court responded to several administrative challenges. The court investigated complaints of illegal mining activity in the Doon Valley that were brought to its notice by an advocate.[33] It did so by constituting a fact-finding committee, summoning the Chief Secretary of Uttar Pradesh to court and censuring the Director of Geology and Mining, whose casual approach to the problem was 'evident from his demeanour in court, before us'. In situations where local villagers and activists had been threatened with violence or were beaten up, the court directed the state to provide protection and security.[34] The Supreme Court asked the Karnataka government to prevent new encroachments and retrieve encroached forests in the Chickmagalur District.[35] A wide range of directions were issued to regulate saw mills in Jammu and Kashmir[36] and ban the felling of rare tree species in the state.[37] To reduce its administrative burden, the court required the Union Government to consider constituting authorities (similar to the Arunachal Pradesh Forest Protection Authority) under section 3(3) of the EPA for other states, and a national supervisory and appellate authority.[38] In the case of Madhya Pradesh, the court asked the Central Bureau of Investigation (CBI) to investigate a case where files in the office of the District Forest Officer, Damoh, were destroyed to cover up the illegal smuggling of teak wood.[39]

14. Applying the principles laid down by the court in the *Forest Conservation* case, a division bench of the Bombay High Court, in *Goa Foundation v Conservator of Forest*,[40] quashed the

31 1998 (2) SCALE 5 (SP) and (1999) 1 SCC 210.
32 AIR 1999 SC 43.
33 AIR 1999 SC 97; 1998 (5) SCALE 8, 10, 11, 13 (SP).
34 1998 (5) SCALE 8 (SP); 1999 (5) SCALE 189.
35 1998 (5) SCALE 4 (SP).
36 1998 (5) SCALE 21 (SP).
37 1998 (6) SCALE 21 (SP).
38 1998 (6) SCALE 17 (SP).
39 1999 (5) SCALE 187, 189, 422.
40 AIR 1999 BOM 177.

permissions granted to the Tata Housing Development Company to construct a residential complex on a hill to the north of Mandovi River. The High Court directed Tata to remove all development work and restore the hill to its original vegetation. While so directing, the court rejected the developer's plea that 28 units in the residential complex had already been sold for Rs. 45 million and that more than Rs. 55 million had been spent on the project.

15. In *Sriram Sah v State of West Bengal*,[41] a division bench of the Calcutta High Court held that the directions issued in the *Forest Conservation* case did not apply to private plantations. Here, the petitioner confronted police and revenue officials who claimed that the Supreme Court order prevented him from cutting 14 old mango trees that had lost their fruit-bearing ability and were infected by parasites.

Dissatisfied with implementation of the National Forest Policy of 1988, the Supreme Court boosted finances available for reafforestation in a notable judgment rendered on 26 September 2005. The thrust of the court's exercise was to ensure that project proponents factor realistic economic costs for the forest loss and contribute to a fund administered for implementing compensatory afforestation. Earlier, on 9 August 2002, the Central Empowered Committee (CEC) recommended that the project proponent be required to pay amounts representing the Net Present Value (NPV) to a 'Compensatory Afforestation Fund'. Since there was a broad consensus amongst the states and the MoEF with respect to the CEC's recommendations, the court directed the Union Government to frame comprehensive rules. On 23 April 2004, the MoEF constituted an authority known as the Compensatory Afforesation Fund Management and Planning Authority ('CAMPA'), under section 3(3) of the EPA. In its 26 September 2005 judgment, the Supreme Court suggested certain amendments for the better operation of CAMPA along with the inclusion of two more environmentalists with expertise in forest and forest economy development. It also required an audit of the fund by the Comptroller and Auditor General.

T N GODAVARMAN THIRUMULPAD v UNION OF INDIA

(2006) 1 SCC 1

Y K SABHARWAL, J:

* * *

Forests are a vital component to sustain the life support system on the earth. Forests in India have been dwindling over the years for a number of reasons, one of it being the need to use forest area for development activities including economic development. Undoubtedly, in any nation development is also necessary but it has to be consistent with protection of environments and not at the cost of degradation of environments. Any programme, policy or vision for overall development has to evolve a systemic approach so as to balance economic development and environmental protection. Both have to go hand in hand. In the ultimate analysis, economic development at the cost of degradation of environments and depletion of forest cover would not be long-lasting. Such development would be counterproductive. Therefore, there is an absolute need to take all precautionary measures when forest lands are sought to be directed for non-forest use.

The point in issue is whether before diversion of forest land for non-forest purposes and consequential loss of benefits accruing from the forests should not the user agency of such land be required to compensate for the diversion. If so, should not the user agency be required to make payment of net present value (NPV) of such diverted land so as to utilise the amounts so received for getting back in the long run the benefits which are lost by such diversion? What guidelines should be issued for determination of NPV? Should guidelines

---

[41] AIR 1999 CAL 10.

apply uniformly to all? How to calculate NPV? Should some projects be exempted from payment of NPV? These are the main aspects which require examination and determination in the backdrop of various legislations which we would presently notice....

First, we may consider the meaning of NPV and determine what is NPV.

The NPV is the present value (PV) of net cash flow from a project, discounted by the cost of capital. Forestry is a public project. It is important to bear in mind that a benefit received today is worth more than that received later. The benefit received today is in fact 'cost-incurred' today. Time value of the cash inflow/outflow is important in investment appraisal. NPV is a method by which future expenditures (costs) and benefit are levelised in order to account for the time value of money. The object behind NPV is to levelise costs. What is the value of rupee today would not be the value of rupee say 50 years later. For example, let us have the starting point of value of rupee in India in the year 2005 and analyse it with the value of rupee that may be in the year 2050. Costs incurred or to be incurred in 2050 have to be discounted by using appropriate parameters like rate of discount, gestation period, ratio of deflators to GDP. Therefore, expenses incurred in each year between say 2005 and 2050 have to be brought down to their present values by using appropriate discount rate in the NPV....

How does one value the intangibles? There are several methods, viz., opportunity cost, replacement cost, travel cost, contingent value method (CVM) and social benefit cost analysis (SBCA).

SBCA can be applied to the evaluation of environmental impacts of forestry projects. Here, one must appreciate that the environmental outputs from forests appear as public goods for which there is no market. Various environmental outputs can be classified into this category, namely, flood control benefits, water production, soil conservation, outdoor recreation, biodiversity and conservation, habitat [and] air purification.

* * *

The basic objectives leading to the laying down of the National Forest Policy, 1988 may also be noted and also the need and requirement for its enforcement. This policy was framed on realising that the 1952 Forest Policy for the management of State forest in the country had not halted the depletion of forests. It was, therefore, considered necessary to evolve a fresh policy for the future to lay down new strategies of forest conservation which had become imperative. Conservation includes preservation, maintenance, sustainable utilisation, restoration and enhancement of the natural environment. The principal aim of the Forest Policy is to ensure environmental stability and maintenance of ecological balance including atmospheric equilibrium which are vital for sustenance of all life forms, human, animal and plant. The derivation of direct economic benefit must be subordinated to this principal aim.

The Forest Policy has a statutory flavour. The non-fulfilment of the aforesaid principal aim would be violative of Articles 14 and 21 of the Constitution. The basic objectives of the Forest Policy, 1988 are:

'2.1. The basic objectives that should govern the National Forest Policy are the following:

— Maintenance of environmental stability through preservation and, where necessary, restoration of the ecological balance that has been adversely disturbed by serious depletion of the forests of the country.
— Conserving the natural heritage of the country by preserving the remaining natural forests with the vast variety of flora and fauna, which represent the remarkable biological diversity and genetic resources of the country.
— Checking soil erosion and denudation in the catchment areas of rivers, lakes and reservoirs in the interest of soil and water conservation, for mitigating floods and droughts and for the retardation of siltation of reservoirs.
— Checking the extension of sand dunes in the desert areas of Rajasthan and along the coastal tracts.

— Increasing substantially the forest/tree cover in the country through massive afforestation and social forestry programmes, especially on all denuded, degraded and unproductive lands.
— Meeting the requirements of fuelwood, fodder, minor forest produce and small timber of the rural and tribal populations.
— Increasing the productivity of forests to meet essential national needs.
— Encouraging efficient utilisation of forest produce and maximum substitution of wood.
— Creating a massive people's movement with the involvement of women, for achieving these objectives and to minimise pressure on existing forests.

2.2. The principal aim of the Forest Policy must be to ensure environmental stability and maintenance of ecological balance including atmospheric equilibrium which are vital for sustenance of all life forms, human, animal and plant. The derivation of direct economic benefit must be subordinated to this principal aim.'

It has been recognised that one of the essentials for forest management is the conservation of total biological diversity, the network of national parks, sanctuaries, biosphere reserves and other protected areas to be strengthened and extended adequately.

The strategy under the Forest Policy is to have a minimum of one-third of the total land area of the country under forest or tree cover. In the hills and in mountainous regions, the aim should be to maintain two-thirds of the area under such cover in order to prevent erosion and land degradation and to ensure the stability of the fragile ecosystem. [The court again quoted from the policy:]

'4.8.1. Encroachment on forest lands has been on the increase. This trend has to be arrested and effective action taken to prevent its continuance. There should be no regularisation of existing encroachments....

4.16. The objective of this revised policy cannot be achieved without the investment of financial and other resources on a substantial scale. Such investment is indeed fully justified considering the contribution of forests in maintaining essential ecological processes and life support systems and in preserving genetic diversity. Forest should not be looked upon as a source of revenue. Forests are a renewable natural resource. They are a national asset to be protected and enhanced for the well-being of the people and the nation.'

It is clearly a constitutional imperative to preserve and enhance forest cover as a natural gene pool reserve.

As opposed to the above, the ground reality has been depletion of forest.

* * *

Having regard to the above, amounts under CAMPA have to be used for regeneration of the ecosystem and the same cannot be handed over to any State Government on the premise that the ecology is not the property of any State but belongs to all, being a gift of nature for the entire nation. The object of the FC Act and the EP Act is protection of environments. These Acts do not deal with any proprietary rights of anyone.

As already stated the question as to what amount of NPV is required to be paid to achieve these objects is a matter to be gone into by the experts. However, the amounts shall have to be updated from time to time after every three years. For grant of approval under section 2 of the FC Act, besides payment of NPV as being presently calculated by MoEF, the user agencies shall have to give undertakings to pay the remaining amount, if any, pending finalisation of determination by the experts....

We are clear that if let loose, the benefits achieved as indicated in the State Forest Report of 2001 would be lost and we may be again where we were in the 1990s or 1980s and earlier period during which there was immense depletion of forest and insignificant regeneration....

NOTES AND QUESTIONS

1. The NPV is a compulsory exaction. Was it proper for the Supreme Court to levy a charge? Is imposing NPV a purely legislative function, beyond the ken of the Supreme Court? Notice that the court itself acknowledges a lack of expertise in determining how NPV should be computed and appoints an Expert Committee.

2. The state of Kerala submitted that while NPV may be levied, the funds received should come to the state, not CAMPA. According to Kerala, the notification dated 23 April 2004 constituting CAMPA lacked Parliamentary or legislative sanction and was unconstitutional. The bulk of the judgment is devoted to repelling the state's claim to the money. The Supreme Court justified its conclusion on a number of grounds: (i) the NPV amount was in the nature of a fee that was deployed in a special fund and did not merge in general revenue but was ear-marked for the protection of natural resources; (ii) the imposition of the fee was competent in terms of Entry 20 and Entry 47 of List III of the Seventh Schedule to the Constitution;[42] (iii) '[N]atural resources are not the ownership of any one State or individual, the public at large is its beneficiary and, therefore, the contention of [counsel for Kerala] that the amount of NPV shall be made over to the State Government cannot be accepted.'; (iv) Since the notification of 23 April 2004 'does not deprive any State of any land, timber or mineral and, therefore, there is no question of disbursement of any amount to the State. The damage to the environment is a damage to the country's assets as a whole. Ecology knows no boundaries.'; and (v) Since the 12th Finance Commission Report recommended a grant of Rs. 1,000 crores over the period 2005–10 to the states for maintenance of forests, it was not open for the states to claim that the NPV paid by the user agency be handed over to the states.

How convincing are these reasons?

3. Based on the report of the Expert Committee as well as inputs from the CEC, on 28 March 2008,[43] the Supreme Court classified India's forests into six categories: illustratively, tropical wet evergreen forests, dry deciduous forests and swamp forests. The court thereafter fixed specific rates of NPV for each of the categories, depending on the forest density. It also granted exemption to certain projects such as schools and hospitals.

4. On 12 March 2014,[44] the court noted that the money collected towards NPV together with the accrued interest was around Rs. 30,000 crores. The court permitted release of additional funds to the states up to an annual amount equal to 10% of the principal lying to credit of the state. The disbursal of funds was ordered from the interest that the principal generated.

5. The 12 March 2014 order traces the steps through which the *Forest Conservation* case evolved from a PIL to conserve the tropical rain forest and wildlife in the Nilgiris into a full-blown regulatory exercise by the court. During this passage, the court found that the 23 April 2004 notification establishing CAMPA 'only remained on paper and it has not been made functional till date by the MoEF'. Consequently, the court set up an *ad hoc* body (*ad hoc* CAMPA) for administering the funds.

---

[42] The Constitutional entries read: '20. Economic and social planning'; '47. Fees in respect of any of the matters in this List, but not including fees taken in any court'.
[43] *T N Godavarman Thirumulpad v Union of India* (2008) 7 SCC 126.
[44] (2014) 6 SCC 150.

6. The Compensatory Afforestation Fund Act of 2016 (CAFA) has a lengthy preamble explaining its purpose. The primary object of this law is to provide a statutory framework to bring the amounts collected under the *Forest Conservation* case for compensatory afforestation, NPV, etc. 'under the public accounts of India and the public accounts of each State'. The preamble also recognizes that, in compliance with the direction of the Supreme Court, over Rs. 38,000 crores have been placed under CAMPA and deposited in nationalized banks.

The Compensatory Afforestation Fund Act requires the Central Government to establish the National Compensatory Afforestation Fund[45] and also mandates that each state government establish a state fund.[46] The amounts lying in these funds are required to be utilized for compensatory afforestation, catchment area treatment plans and for site-specific schemes. The scope of the disbursals covers forest management, forest protection, forest and wildlife-related infrastructure development, wildlife protection and management, supply of wood and allied activities.[47]

The responsibility for administering the funds through appropriate schemes is the responsibility of the national authority constituted under section 8 and the state authorities constituted under section 10. These authorities were constituted on 14 September 2018 by the Central Government.

On 28 January 2019 the Supreme Court allowed the transfer of funds from CAMPA to the National Fund and permitted transfers to the state funds upon these funds being established.[48]

7. In September 2018, the Supreme Court closed a case filed in 2005 by Bhupesh Baghel, a Member of the Legislative Assembly of Chhattisgarh. Baghel sought criminal prosecution of state officials and an industrialist, Anil Lunia. The application claimed that Lunia had applied for a prospecting licence to mine iron ore in Bastar and had cut down thousands of trees in violation of the FCA as well as the approved mining plan. The CEC submitted its report to the Supreme Court in September 2008, cataloguing massive violations and recommending prosecution. While the case was pending before the Supreme Court, the state took disciplinary actions against its officials and attempted to recover the unlawful gain made by Lunia. Since the state was alive to the violations, the court closed the matter.[49] Lunia's foray into the forests of Bastar began in 1998 and two decades later he was still contesting the recovery before a local court. Had it not been for the Supreme Court oversight, do you think the government would have moved against its officials? Notice how slowly the wheels of justice grind.

8. In *Muneer Enterprises v Ramgad Mineral and Mining Ltd*,[50] the Supreme Court reiterated the position that for the diversion of any forest land and its use for some other purpose, prior approval is necessary under the FCA.

---

45 Section 3.

46 Section 4.

47 Section 6.

48 *T N Godavarman Thirumulpad v Union of India* IA No. 5891 of 2020 in Writ Petition (C) No. 202 of 1995, order dated 28 January 2019.

49 *T N Godavarman Thirumulpad v Union of India* (2018) 9 SCC 760.

50 (2015) 5 SCC 366.

C. THE *DEHRADUN QUARRYING* LITIGATION

The *Dehradun Quarrying* litigation[51] is significant as the first case requiring the Supreme Court to balance environmental and ecological integrity against industrial demands on forest resources. The case arose from haphazard and dangerous limestone quarrying practices in the Mussoorie Hill Range of the Himalayas. Miners blasted out the hills with dynamite, extracting limestone from thousands of acres. The miners also dug deep into the hillsides, an illegal practice which resulted in cave-ins and slumping. As a result, the hillsides were stripped of vegetation. Landslides killed villagers and destroyed their homes, cattle and agricultural lands. Mining operations upset the hydrological system of the Doon Valley. Springs dried up and severe water shortages occurred in the Valley, an area formerly blessed with abundant water supplies. At the same time, mining debris clogged river channels and during the monsoon season severe flooding occurred. Dehradun is the principal city in Doon Valley.

The State of Uttar Pradesh failed to regulate the mining as required by existing mining laws. In 1961 the state minister of mines did sharply curtail mining in the area. In less than a year, however, quarry operators successfully lobbied with the Chief Minister of the state to reopen mining operations. Mining leases were granted for 20 years. Illegal and destructive practices continued and existing mining safety rules were flouted with no enforcement by corrupt and ineffective state officials.

In 1982, 18 leases came up for renewal. The state, finally recognizing the dimensions of the ecological devastation in the Valley, rejected all the renewal applications. The Allahabad High Court, however, issued an injunction allowing the applicants to continue mining, presumably in the belief that economic considerations outweighed ecological factors. At this point, in 1983, the Supreme Court treated a letter received from the Rural Litigation and Entitlement Kendra, complaining against the environmental degradation, as an Article 32 petition. The case developed into complex litigation as lessees of more than 100 mines joined the action, engaging an impressive array of the nation's top lawyers to argue for continued mining in the region.

The Supreme Court played an activist role in this litigation, essentially conducting a comprehensive environmental review and analysis of the national need for mining operations located in the Doon Valley. In addition, the court provided for funding and administrative oversight of reforestation of the region. The following synopsis highlights the major rulings in the case.

(1) In 1983, the court prohibited blasting operations pending a review to determine if the mines were being operated in compliance with the safety standards laid down in the Mines Act of 1952 and the relevant mining regulations. The court appointed an Expert Committee (the Bhargava committee) to assess the mines.

(2) In March 1985, the court, upon the recommendations of the Bhargava committee, ordered that the most dangerous mines and those falling within the Mussoorie city board limits be denied leases and that their operations cease immediately. Operations of a second group of mines were restricted, pending review by another committee. This second committee (the Bandopadhyay committee) was empowered to consider plans submitted by the

[51] *Rural Litigation and Entitlement Kendra, Dehradun v State of Uttar Pradesh*. The Supreme Court has issued numerous opinions and orders in this case, of which the principal orders are 12 March 1985, AIR 1985 SC 652; 13 May 1985, AIR 1985 SC 1259; 30 September 1985, 1985 (2) SCALE 906; 18 December 1986, AIR 1987 SC 359; 19 October 1987, AIR 1987 SC 2426; 30 August 1988, AIR 1988 SC 2187; 16 December 1988, JT 1988 (4) SC 710; 4 May 1990, JT 1990 (2) SC 391; 30 April 1991, AIR 1991 SC 2216; 1 August 1991, (1993) Supp (1) SCC 57 and 20 November 1991, (1993) Supp (1) SCC 426.

miners to safeguard the environment and to hear the claims of people adversely affected by the mining. The Uttar Pradesh government was directed to provide the necessary funds for the Bandopadhyay committee as well as 'transport and other facilities for the purpose of enabling them to discharge their functions'.[52] The court determined that a third group of mines, including a major operation owned by the state of Uttar Pradesh, could remain open because the environmental damage was less clear.

(3) In 1987, the court concluded after review of the Bandopadhyay committee's report that, based on ecological considerations alone, mining in the Valley should cease. The court, however, was concerned about the effect of closure on other national interests and made the following request for information from the Central Government:

> While we reiterate our conclusion that mining in this area has to be stopped as far as practicable, we also make it clear that mining activity has to be permitted to the extent necessary in the interests of the defence of the country as also for the safeguarding of the foreign exchange position. We call upon the Union of India in the relevant ministry or ministries to place before the Court on affidavit the minimum total requirement of this grade of limestone for manufacture of quality steel and defence armaments. The affidavit should also specify as to how much of high grade ore is being imported into the country and as to whether other indigenous sources are available to meet such requirements. This Court would also require an affidavit from responsible authorities of the Union of India as to whether keeping the principles of ecology, environmental protection and safeguards and anti-pollution measures, it is in the interests of the Society that the requirements should be met by import or by tapping other alternate indigenous sources or mining activity in this area should be permitted to the limited extent. The Court expects the Union of India to balance these two aspects and place on record its stand not as a party to the litigation but as a protector of the environment in discharge of its statutory and social obligation for the purpose of consideration of the Court by way of assisting the Court in disposing of the matters in issue. If the Court comes to the conclusion that the minimum requirement of limestone will be permitted to be lifted from some of the quarries, it shall be for the Court to indicate as to which of the quarries shall be operated for that limited purpose. We make it clear that whichever quarries may be permitted to be worked out the same shall be subject to strict control and regulations and would have to undertake acceptance of the obligation to maintain the green cover of the area by diverting a major portion of its profits.[53]

(4) The court rejected as unresponsive the first affidavit from the central government, submitted by the Director of Environment, Forests and Wildlife in the MoEF. The rejected affidavit detailed uses of limestone for industrial operations within Uttar Pradesh, but did not provide a satisfactory evaluation of other sources of the limestone within India and the extent to which national defence industries relied on the limestone. A second affidavit, submitted by the Secretary of the MoEF, contained the required evaluation and concluded that the requirements of the defence industries did not justify continuing operations of any mine in the Dehradun-Mussoorie region.[54]

(5) In 1988, the court concluded that all mines in the Doon Valley remain closed, except three operations. The court directed that the leases of the three remaining mines should not be renewed and that upon expiration of the existing leases the three remaining operations should close.

---

52 AIR 1985 SC 652, 656.
53 AIR 1987 SC 2426, 2428.
54 AIR 1988 SC 2187, 2204.

Although the Doon Valley mining operations occupied 800 hectares of reserved forests and the Forest (Conservation) Act of 1980 was in effect in 1982, when the lessees applied to the state government for renewal of their leases, the state did not seek Central Government approval for the mining operations. This failure may have reflected confusion as to whether the requirement of the Act applied to renewal of leases which had originally been granted before the Act came into force. The Supreme Court resolved this question in *Ambica Quarry Works v State of Gujarat*.[55] The court held that state governments may renew pre-existing mining leases only with the review and approval of the Centre, as required under the Forest (Conservation) Act.

In the *Dehradun Quarrying* litigation, the court concluded in 1988 that continued mining in the Valley violated the Forest (Conservation) Act. Moreover, the court went beyond the requirements of the Act to merely conserve forest and issued orders to ensure that the Valley be reforested. The court noted that although the state of Uttar Pradesh had a reforestation programme, the record of reforestation was not encouraging. The court established a Monitoring committee comprised of Central, state, and local officials and two 'public-spirited' citizens to oversee reforestation, mining activities and 'all other aspects necessary to bring about normalcy in the Doon Valley'. The court also provided the Monitoring committee with funding by ordering that 25% of the gross profit of the remaining mines be deposited in a fund controlled by the committee.

(6) Vijay Shree Mines, one of the lessees permitted by the court to operate until the expiry of its lease in 1990, misused the permission. The lessee continued to quarry limestone in an unscientific manner and in disregard of the directions issued by the Monitoring committee. In an application filed by the committee, the court held that the mining activity surreptitiously carried on by Vijay Shree Mines had caused immense damage to the area and directed the firm to pay Rs. 3 lakhs to the fund of the Monitoring committee.[56]

(7) An offshoot of the *Dehradun Quarrying* litigation was the *ARC Cement* case. ARC Cement operated a cement factory in the Valley since November 1982 until restrained by an order of the court. The company employed about 400 persons. In 1987 the Supreme Court declined permission to ARC to open its polluting cement factory and encouraged the company to shift it elsewhere. When the matter came up four years later, the Supreme Court was dismayed by the lack of progress, primarily because the company had failed to propose an alternative site. The court held:

> We cannot go back upon our earlier order that the cement factory shall not be permitted to run at the site. Shifting from this place has, therefore, got to be done. We permit the petitioner to indicate some alternative site so that there would be an option available to the State Government as also to the Pollution Board to consider which of the sites offered may be acceptable to them for the purpose of shifting the cement factory from the present location.[57]

The court granted the petitioner two weeks' time to come up with alternatives. On 20 November 1991 the Supreme Court recorded some of the terms of a general understanding between the company and the UP State Mineral Development Corporation for the supply of limestone and other related issues. However, no consensus was reached on a new site and while disposing the case the court acknowledged that certain aspects of the arrangement remained to be negotiated between the parties.[58] The efforts to relocate the cement factory

[55] AIR 1987 SC 1037.
[56] (1991) 3 SCC 347.
[57] *ARC Cement Ltd v State of UP* (1993) Supp (1) SCC 57.
[58] (1993) Supp (1) SCC 426.

apparently failed and the company was declared 'sick'. On 13 February 1995 ARC Cement was ordered to be wound up by the Board for Industrial and Financial Reconstruction.[59]

NOTES AND QUESTIONS

1. The Central Government became concerned about the destructive mining operations in the Valley at the same time that the Supreme Court took up the issue. In 1983, the government of India appointed a Working Group to inspect the limestone quarries in the Dehradun-Mussoorie area. The same individual, D N Bhargava, headed both the government's Working Group and the court's first Expert Committee. Not surprisingly, the Working Group and the court's committee came to similar conclusions as to the harmful effect of the mines on the environment. The Working Group also prepared reports for the court on the few mining operations which were allowed to remain open.

2. During the course of the litigation, in 1986, Parliament enacted the Environment (Protection) Act. The mining operators contended that because the Act provides procedures to deal with the situation at issue, the court should dismiss the case and leave the issue to administrative authorities under the Environment (Protection) Act. Counsel for the miners relied on the following statement from a 1986 opinion issued in the case:

> It is for the Government and the Nation—and not for the Court—to decide whether the deposits should be exploited at the cost of ecology and environmental consideration or the industrial requirement should be otherwise satisfied.[60]

In rejecting the miners' arguments for dismissal, the court relied on the fact that the litigation commenced and significant orders were issued before the adoption of the Environment (Protection) Act. The court also addressed the potential effect of the Act in ousting the court's jurisdiction over Article 32 public interest writ petitions as follows:

> The Act does not purport to—and perhaps could not—take away the jurisdiction of this Court to deal with a case of this type. In consideration of these facts, we do not think there is any justification to decline the exercise of jurisdiction at this stage. Ordinarily the Court would not entertain a dispute for the adjudication of which a special provision has been made by law but that rule is not attracted in the present situation in these cases. Besides it is a rule of practice and prudence and not one of jurisdiction. The contention against exercise of jurisdiction ... must stand overruled.[61]

3. In the *Dehradun Quarrying* case, the opinions of the court and the Central Government did not conflict. Since the court's ruling, the Centre has designated the Valley as an ecologically fragile area under the Environment (Protection) Act. The Centre has also appointed a Doon Valley Board, under the chairmanship of the Minister for Environment and Forests, which is charged with conserving and restoring degraded areas of the Valley.

4. In addition to ecological integrity and national interests, the Supreme Court was also concerned with the welfare of mine operators and labour left unemployed by closure of the Doon Valley operations. The court issued the following directions to try to mitigate the effects of closing the mines:

---

59 *ARC Cement Limited v Appellate Authority for Industrial and Financial Reconstruction* 1998 (71) Del L T 213.

60 AIR 1987 SC 359, 363.

61 AIR 1988 SC 2187, 2195.

(a) orders that mine lessees whose operations were terminated by the court be given priority for leases in new areas open to limestone mining; and
(b) orders that the Eco-Task Force of the Central Department of Environment reclaim and reforest the area damaged by mining and that workers displaced by mine closure be given priority for jobs with the Eco-Task Force operations in the region.

5. In the *ARC Cement* case, the logic of the court seems to be: 'we cannot change our previous orders so the factory must move.' What kind of reasoning is that? Is it more important to preserve the integrity of court orders and consequent faith in the judicial system than to re-evaluate the merits of a case?

The court gave two weeks to ARC Cement to suggest alternative sites and four weeks to pick one: is this adequate time for a comprehensive environmental impact assessment? Where did the court find those numbers? Are those even feasible deadlines? What expertise does the court have in assessing various environmental impacts of a cement factory?

Who is to blame for the commercial bankruptcy of ARC Cement: the entrepreneur for poor site selection, the management for failing to promptly suggest alternative sites or the court for closing down operations without regard to the impact on the company and its employees?

6. Building on the principles laid down in the *Dehradun Quarrying* litigation and the *Ambica Quarry Works* case, the Supreme Court has clarified that the renewal of a lease should be in accordance with the law in operation on the date of renewal. Renewal was not a vested right and unless *prior* concurrence of the Central Government was obtained, mining in a forest area was completely prohibited.[62] The prior approval of the Central Government is a condition precedent and the grant of a lease or renewal without such approval renders the lease void.[63]

7. To protect the Saproon Valley from degradation, the Himachal Pradesh High Court followed the lead provided by the Supreme Court in the *Dehradun Quarrying* litigation. The mountains in Saproon Valley are rich in limestone deposits that have been quarried for over a century. The expansion of unscientific and unsystematic mining operations in the 1980s caused severe water pollution and erosion of the top soil. In a public interest litigation filed by the residents of Saproon Valley, the High Court abided by the recommendations of an Expert Committee and ordered those mines where scientific mining was not economically viable or technically possible to shut down. Other mines where further mining was possible subject to safeguards and precautions, were permitted to continue under the supervision of a Monitoring committee.[64]

8. The guidelines for bureaucrats assessing an application to mine in a forest were set out by the Supreme Court in *Samatha v State of Andhra Pradesh*:

> Mining operations, though detrimental to forest growth, are part of layout of the industry; provision should be made for investment or infrastructural planning to reforest the area; and to protect environment and regenerate forest. The Ministry of Environment and Forests and all Secretaries of all the State Governments holding charge of Forest Departments have a duty to prevent mining operations affecting the forest. It is significant to note that, whether mining operations are carried on within the reserved forest or other forest area, it is their duty to ensure that the industry or enterprise does not denude the forest to become a menace to human [existence] nor a source to destroy flora and fauna and biodiversity. [In *State of*

[62] *Divisional Forest Officer v S Nageswaramma* (1996) 6 SCC 442.
[63] *Samatha v State of Andhra Pradesh* AIR 1997 SC 3297, 3346, 3348.
[64] *General Public of Saproon Valley v State of Himachal Pradesh* AIR 1993 HP 52.

Himachal Pradesh v Ganesh Wood Products (1995) 6 SCC 363, this court] held that the application of sustainable development requires that the application of sustainable development requires that appropriate assessment should be made of the forest wealth and the establishment of industries based on forest produce; other working should also be monitored closely to maintain the required ecological balance. No distinction can be made between the Government forest and private forests in the matter of forest wealth of the nation and in the matter of environment and ecology.[65]

D. MINERAL EXTRACTION IN FORESTS

I. VEDANTA

In the late 1970s, the Silent Valley project stirred up a hornet's nest in India's first major 'environment versus development' controversy. While a great number of environmentalists, scientists and non-governmental organizations campaigned to prevent the valley from being dammed, it was perhaps the personal preference of Prime Minister Indira Gandhi that eventually tilted the outcome in favour of the Kuntipuzha River flowing in Kerala's Palghat District.[66] Four decades later, her grandson Rahul Gandhi, holding no ministerial office in 2008 although perceived by some as heir apparent, played a decisive role in preserving the Niyamgiri Hills in Western Odisha's Kalahandi District.

The Niyamgiri contest arose from a bauxite mining project that threatened to destroy the home range of the Dongaria Kondhs, indigenous tribals. This case was examined by the Supreme Court on three occasions. We carry excerpts from the judgments, dated 23 November 2007 and 18 April 2013. The intervening order of the court passed on 8 August 2008 is summarized in the connecting notes. The judgments, true to judicial rigour, reveal nothing about the backstage politics that influenced the MoEF's changing posture. Here are a few of the political factors that affected the overall dynamics of this case:

(a) Throughout its gestation, the state government backed the project, anxious to bring development to a neglected region. The Congress party that led the government at the Centre was the main political rival to the Biju Janata Dal government in Odisha state.
(b) In March 2008, Rahul Gandhi visited the Niyamgiri Hills and assured the protesting tribals that he would act as their representative in Delhi.
(c) The tribals' plea was well received when Jairam Ramesh, the Union Minister of Environment and Forests and a member of the Congress party rejected the stage II forest clearance for mining the Niyamgiri Hills. Ramesh, in his order of 24 August 2010, decisively declared that the environmental clearance for the mine was inoperable.
(d) Alongside these developments two major issues occupied public and political discourse. The first was the armed resistance against the state by Maoist cadres which affected several districts across eight states including Odisha: how should the Indian state respond to this dangerous insurgence and win back its alienated citizens? The second was the debate regarding the taking of private land by the state from small land holders under the antiquated Land Acquisition Act of 1894.[67] Was it fair to impoverish rural folk by snatching away their lands for private projects?

---

[65] AIR 1997 SC 3297, 3347.

[66] Darryl D'Monte, *Temples or Tombs? Industry versus Environment: Three Controversies* 57–8 (1985).

[67] This Act was replaced by the Right to Fair Compensation and Transparency in Land Acquisition, Rehabilitation and Resettlement Act of 2013.

By any measure, the *Vedanta* case is a remarkable triumph of constitutional governance. It demonstrates how a fusion of politics and law can unlock the promise of life and liberty in the Indian Constitution for Indians living on the margins. Notice the shift in the judicial approach between the first Supreme Court judgment of 2007 and the final decision in 2013.

T N GODAVARMAN THIRUMULPAD v UNION OF INDIA
(2008) 2 SCC 222

ORDER: M/s Vedanta Aluminium Ltd has filed an application before this Court seeking clearance of the proposal for use of 723.343 ha of land (including 58.943 ha of reserve forest land) in Lanjigarh Tehsil of Kalahandi District for setting up alumina refinery. The matter has been pending since 6-3-2004. The project consists of setting up of a large integrated aluminium complex in Orissa by M/s Vedanta Aluminium Ltd ('M/s VAL', for short).

The short question which needs to be answered is: whether M/s VAL should be allowed to set up its refinery/project known as 'Alumina Refinery Project'? As stated above the Project involves the proposal for diversion of 58.943 ha of forest land.

As a matter of preface, we may state that adherence to the principle of sustainable development is now a constitutional requirement. How much damage to the environment and ecology has got to be decided on the facts of each case. While applying the principle of sustainable development one must bear in mind that development which meets the needs of the present without compromising the ability of the future generations to meet their own needs is sustainable development. Therefore, courts are required to balance development needs with the protection of the environment and ecology. It is the duty of the State under our Constitution to devise and implement a coherent and coordinated programme to meet its obligation of sustainable development based on inter-generational equity. Mining is an important revenue-generating industry. However, we cannot allow our national assets to be placed into the hands of companies without a proper mechanism in place and without ascertaining the credibility of the user agency.

It is not in dispute that in this case mining of bauxite deposits is required to take place on the top of Niyamgiri Hills. MoEF has given an environmental clearance for Alumina Refinery Project. All requisite permissions have been obtained by the said applicant. The refinery to be constructed by M/s VAL is one-million-ton alumina refinery at Lanjigarh at an estimated cost of Rs 4000 crores. The mining lease shall stand in the name of OMC Ltd (State undertaking). The agreement between OMC Ltd and M/s VAL indicates that it is a joint venture in which M/s VAL is a contractor. The agreement further indicates that the material will be sold by the lessee to M/s VAL.

CEC has objected to the grant of clearance as sought by M/s VAL on the ground *inter alia* that the refinery is totally dependent on mining of bauxite from Niyamgiri Hills, Lanjigarh, which is the only vital wildlife habitat, part of which constitutes elephant corridor and also on the ground that the said Project, including the mining area, would obstruct the proposed wildlife sanctuary and the residence of tribes like Dongaria Kondh. According to CEC, Niyamgiri Hills would be vitally affected if mining is allowed in the above area as Niyamgiri Hills is an important water source for two rivers. According to CEC, the Project would also destroy flora and fauna of the entire region and it would result in soil erosion. According to CEC, use of forest land in an ecologically sensitive area like Niyamgiri Hills should not be permitted.

On the other side, we have a picture of abject poverty in which the local people are living in Lanjigarh Tehsil including the tribal people. There is no proper housing. There are no hospitals. There are no schools and people are living in extremely poor conditions which is not in dispute.

Indian economy for the last couple of years has been growing at the rate of 8 to 9% of GDP. It is a remarkable achievement. However, accelerated growth rate of GDP does not provide *inclusive growth*. Keeping in mind the two extremes, this Court thought of balancing development *vis-à-vis* protection of wildlife ecology and environment in view of the principle of sustainable development.

At this stage, we may observe that M/s VAL has obtained all necessary clearances. It now seeks clearance of the Project from this Court before it is placed before the Central Government.

[The court noted that M/sVAL was a subsidiary of Sterlite Industries (India) Ltd. ('SIIL') and that the project was funded by Vedanta Resources, a UK-based company. The court quoted a newspaper report on the Norwegian government's decision to stop its pension fund investments in Vedanta Resources due to the company's record of causing severe environmental damage and human rights violations.]

We do not wish to express any opinion on the correctness of the said report. However, we cannot take the risk of handing over an important asset into the hands of the company unless we are satisfied about its credibility . . .

Liberty is, however, given to M/s SIIL to move this Court if they agree to comply with the following modalities as suggested by this Court. It is made clear that such an application will not be entertained if made by M/s VAL or by Vedanta Resources.

(i) State of Orissa shall float a Special Purpose Vehicle (SPV) for scheduled area development of Lanjigarh Project in which the stakeholders shall be State of Orissa, OMC Ltd and M/s SIIL. Such SPV shall be incorporated under the Companies Act, 1956. The accounts of SPV will be prepared by the statutory auditors of OMC Ltd and they shall be audited by the Auditor General for State of Orissa every year. M/s SIIL will deposit, every year commencing from 1-4-2007, 5% of its annual profits before tax and interest from Lanjigarh Project or Rs 10 crores whichever is higher for Scheduled Area Development with the said SPV and it shall be the duty of the said SPV to account for the expenses each year. The annual report of SPV shall be submitted to CEC every year. If CEC finds non-utilisation or misutilisation of funds the same shall be brought to the notice of this Court. While calculating annual profits before tax and interest M/s SIIL shall do so on the basis of the market value of the material which is sold by OMC Ltd to M/s SIIL or its nominee.

(ii) In addition to what is stated above, M/s SIIL shall pay NPV of Rs 55 crores and Rs 50.53 crores towards Wildlife Management Plan for Conservation and Management of Wildlife around Lanjigarh bauxite mine and Rs 12.20 crores towards tribal development. In addition, M/s SIIL shall also bear expenses towards compensatory afforestation.

(iii) A statement shall be filed by M/s SIIL with CEC within eight weeks from today stating number of persons who shall be absorbed on permanent basis in M/s SIIL including land-losers. They shall give categories in which they would be permanently absorbed. The list would also show particulars of persons who would be employed by the contractors of M/s SIIL and the period for which they would be employed.

(iv) [The court set out 16 points suggested by the state for rehabilitation, resettlement and conservation. These issues included undertakings by the project proponent to take up compensatory afforestation, rehabilitate project affected families, phased reclamation of the mined areas and the preparation of a comprehensive plan for the development of tribals in the project impact area.]

If M/s SIIL is agreeable to the aforestated rehabilitation package then they shall be at liberty to move this court by initiating a proper application. This court is not against the Project in principle. It only seeks safeguards by which we are able to protect nature and subserve development. IAs are disposed of accordingly. However, we once again reiterate that the applications filed by M/s VAL stand dismissed. . . .

NOTES AND QUESTIONS

1. The court notes that the matter was pending before it for more than three years. Are such delays in securing a project clearance acceptable from a business and investment standpoint? Why should an investor block her funds for such a lengthy period? Does this cumbersome procedure require overhauling in order to attract investment and encourage economic growth?

2. The CEC objected to the clearance by raising important issues concerning the destruction of the home range of the Dongaria Kondh and the wildlife habitat. The Supreme Court was impressed by the growth in the national GDP but wanted to ensure that the benefits of a growing economy were enjoyed by the local people. The court set out an elaborate template for sustainable development and virtually invited the project proponent to return back with a suitably re-tailored application. For reasons difficult to discern, the court's invitation to return was restricted to SIIL and not its associates VAL or Vedanta Resources which was funding the project.

3. The judges reproduced a damaging story by an economic daily under the caption '*Norway Dumps Vedanta from Oil Fund*' and then refrained from expressing any opinion on the report. If the news report was unworthy of reliance, was the court justified in quoting it?

Justifying reference to the news report, the court asserts that it would not hand over important national assets to a company unless it was satisfied about its credibility. Considering that Vedanta Resources, a UK-based mining conglomerate, was funding the project and the Norwegian government had reservations about its business ethics, should the Supreme Court have allowed its associate, SIIL to reapply? In the real world, how likely is it that an associate entity operates in a different ethical milieu?

4. The court sets about the task of applying the principle of sustainable development. Why is the court engaging in this balancing? Is this the province of the judiciary or the executive? Is the Supreme Court equipped to undertake such an exercise for every mining project?

5. Sterlite Industries returned to the Supreme Court, unconditionally accepting the terms suggested by the court. In its decision rendered on 8 August 2008 reported at *T N Godavarman Thirumulpad v Union of India* (2008) 9 SCC 711 the court ordered:

> For the above reasons and in the light of the affidavits filed by SIIL, OMCL and the State of Orissa, accepting the rehabilitation package, suggested in our order dated 23-11-2007 [(2008) 2 SCC 222], we hereby grant clearance to the forest diversion proposal for diversion of 660.749 ha of forest land to undertake bauxite mining on Niyamgiri Hills in Lanjigarh. The next step would be for MoEF to grant its approval in accordance with law.

6. A project involving the diversion of forests must pass through several hoops. Administratively, the MoEF adopts a two-stage approach when evaluating an application for forest diversion. Stage I of the procedure involves an approval 'in principle' where the Forest Advisory Committee (FAC) in the MoEF forms a *prima facie* view to either accept or reject the project. Where stage I clearance is issued by the MoEF, the project authority must deposit an amount of compensation for mitigating the environmental harm. Following the deposit, a stage II clearance is issued after the project authority has secured all other requisite clearances. These clearances include permissions from the pollution control board and an environmental clearance under the EIA notification, where required.

Overlaying this administrative process is the judicial clearance introduced in the *Forest Conservation* case.[68] The project proponent must also get a go-ahead from the Supreme Court. Before allowing the project, the Supreme Court is generally guided by the opinion of the Central Empowered Committee (CEC) which independently evaluates the justification for forest diversion and submits a report to the Forest Bench.[69]

7. On 24 August 2010, the MoEF rejected the stage II forest clearance. This order, passed by the Congress Minister, Jairam Ramesh was in harmony with Rahul Gandhi's assurance to the tribals of Niyamgiri in March 2008. Was this happy congruence mere happenstance or a display of fealty? Recall the disruptive impact of the rejection and the changing political tides as you review the project milestones.

8. The Vedanta group filed an application to the MoEF on 19 March 2003 for its Alumina Refinery Project (ARP) in Lanjigarh, Kalahandi District. On 22 September 2004, the MoEF granted environmental clearance to the ARP, delinking it from the mining project that envisaged exploiting the rich bauxite deposits from the Niyamgiri Hills. (The refinery was dependent on mining bauxite from the Niyamgiri Hills.) On 27 October 2006, the FAC, after examining reports of the Wildlife Institute of India and the Central Mining Planning and Design Institute, approved the proposal for diverting 660.749 ha of forest land for mining bauxite. This clearance stipulated various conditions. On 11 December 2008, the MoEF informed the state government that it had, in principle, agreed to diversion of the forest land for mining bauxite subject to fulfilment of specified conditions. On 10 August 2009, the state government confirmed that these conditions stood fulfilled and that since the Supreme Court had cleared the project, there was no further impediment in respect of the Scheduled Tribes and other Traditional Forest Dwellers (Recognition of Rights) Act of 2006 (FRA). The state government claimed that since the issue of violations in respect of the FRA was raised before the Supreme Court and the project was allowed to proceed by the orders dated 23 November 2007 and 8 August 2008, 'no further action' was called for.

On 1 January 2010, the MoEF constituted a three-member team headed by Dr Usha Ramanathan which, after site inspections, suggested an in-depth study on the application of the FRA. The MoEF then constituted a four-member committee headed by Dr Naresh Saxena to make a detailed investigation. On 23 August 2010, reviewing the Saxena Committee Report, the FAC found that the tribal groups were not consulted and that there was a violation of the provisions of the Forest Rights Act and other statutes. The FAC suggested applying the precautionary principle to prevent irreparable harm to the tribals and now supported withdrawing the stage I forest clearance which it had commended earlier. This was followed by the Minister's order dated 24 August 2010, rejecting the stage II clearance.

In substance, the MoEF disabled the ARP by refusing to allow bauxite mining in the Niyamgiri Hills. The MoEF also undermined the Supreme Court's vision of sustainable development by rendering naught the elaborate rehabilitation package suggested by the court in its order dated 23 November 2007.

9. The project proponents and the state officials bristled at this about-turn. OMC, a state government undertaking, petitioned the Supreme Court seeking a writ of certiorari to quash the MoEF order dated 24 August 2010. OMC appealed to the Supreme Court's lofty position in the constitutional scheme and attacked the MoEF for effectively neutralizing the

[68] *T N Godavarman Thirumulpad v Union of India* discussed earlier in this chapter.

[69] The 'Forest Bench' is a three-judge bench of the Supreme Court that hears cases linked to the diversion of forests. This bench is specially constituted by the Chief Justice and assembles periodically to pare its exploding docket.

Supreme Court's directions issued on 23 November 2007 and 8 August 2008. The Supreme Court's third judgment on this project is excerpted below.

ORISSA MINING CORPORATION LTD v MoEF
(2013) 6 SCC 476

K S Radhakrishnan, J: Orissa Mining Corporation (OMC), a State of Orissa Undertaking, has approached this Court seeking a Writ of Certiorari to quash the order passed by the Ministry of Environment and Forests (MoEF) dated 24.8.2010 rejecting the Stage-II forest clearance for diversion of 660.749 hectares of forest land for mining of bauxite ore in Lanjigarh Bauxite Mines in Kalahandi and Rayagada Districts of Orissa and also for other consequential reliefs....

Petitioner's assertion that the Alumina Refinery Project and the Bauxite Mining Project are two separate and independent projects, cannot be accepted as such, since there are sufficient materials on record to show that the two projects make an integrated unit. In the two earlier orders of this Court (in the *Vedanta* case and the *Sterlite* case) also the two Projects are seen as comprising a single unit. Quite contrary to the case of the petitioner, it can be strongly argued that the Alumina Refinery Project and Bauxite Mining Project (BMP) are interdependent and inseparably linked together and, hence, any wrong doing by Alumina Refinery Project may cast a reflection on the Bauxite Mining Project and may be a relevant consideration for denial of Stage II clearance to the Bauxite Mining Project.

In this judgment, however, we do not propose to make any final pronouncement on that issue but we would keep the focus mainly on the rights of the Scheduled Tribes [STs] and the 'Traditional Forest Dwellers' [TFDs] under the Forest Rights Act.

STs and TFDs

Scheduled Tribe, as such, is not defined in the Forest Rights Act, but the word 'Traditional Forest Dweller' has been defined under Section 2(o) as any member or community who has at least three generations prior to the 13th day of December, 2005 primarily resided in and who depend on the forest or forests land for *bona fide* livelihood needs. Article 366(25) of the Constitution states that STs means such tribes or tribal communities or parts of or groups within such tribes or tribal communities as are defined under Article 342 to be the Scheduled Tribes. The President of India, in exercise of the powers conferred by Clause (1) of Article 342 of the Constitution, has made the Constitution (Schedule Tribes) Order, 1950. Part XII of the Order refers to the State of Orissa. Serial No. 31 refers to Dongaria Kondh, Kutia Kandha etc....

Constitutional Rights and Conventions

Article 244(1) of the Constitution of India which appears in Part X provides that the administration of the Scheduled Areas and Scheduled Tribes in States (other than Assam, Meghalaya and Tripura) shall be according to the provisions of the Fifth Schedule and Clause (2) states that Sixth Schedule applies to the tribal areas in Assam, Meghalaya, Tripura and Mizoram. Evidently, the object of the Fifth Schedule and the Regulations made thereunder is to preserve tribal autonomy, their cultures and economic empowerment to ensure social, economic and political justice for the preservation of peace and good Governance in the Scheduled Area. This Court in *Samatha v Arunachal Pradesh* (1997) 8 SCC 191 ruled that all relevant clauses in the Schedule and the Regulations should be harmoniously and widely be read as to elongate the Constitutional objectives and dignity of person to the Scheduled Tribes and ensuring distributive justice as an integral scheme thereof. The Court noticed that agriculture is the only source of livelihood for the Scheduled Tribes apart from collection and sale of minor forest produce to supplement their income. Land is their most important natural and valuable asset and imperishable endowment from which the tribal derive their sustenance, social status, economic and social equality, permanent place of abode, work and living. Consequently, tribes have great emotional attachments to their lands.

Part B of the Fifth Schedule [Article 244(1)] speaks of the administration and control of Schedules Areas and Scheduled Tribes. Para 4 thereof speaks of Tribes Advisory Council.

Tribes Advisory Council used to exercise the powers for those Scheduled Areas where Panchayat Raj system had not been extended. By way of the Constitution (73rd Amendment) Act, 1992, Part IX was inserted in the Constitution of India. Article 243-B of Part IX of the Constitution mandated that there shall be panchayats at village, intermediate and district levels in accordance with the provisions of that Part. Article 243-C of Chapter IX refers to the composition of Panchayats. Article 243-M (4)(b) states that Parliament may, by law, extend the provisions of Part IX to the Scheduled Areas and the Tribal areas and to work out the modalities for the same. The Central Government appointed Bhuria Committee to undertake a detailed study and make recommendations as to whether the Panchayat Raj system could be extended to Scheduled Areas. The Committee submitted its report on 17.01.1995 and favoured democratic, decentralization in Scheduled Areas. Based on the recommendations, the Panchayat (Extension to Scheduled Areas) Act, 1996 (for short 'PESA Act') was enacted by the Parliament in the year 1996, extending the provisions of Part IX of the Constitution relating to Panchayats to the Scheduled Areas....

This court had occasion to consider the scope of PESA Act when the constitutional validity of the proviso to section 4(g) of the PESA Act and few sections of the Jharkhand Panchayat Raj Act, 2001 were challenged in *Union of India v Rakesh Kumar* (2010) 4 SCC 50 and this Court upheld the Constitutional validity.

Section 4 of the PESA Act stipulates that the State legislation on Panchayats shall be made in consonance with the customary law, social and religious practices and traditional management practices of community resources. Clause (d) of Section states that every Gram Sabha shall be competent to safeguard and preserve the traditions and customs of the people, their cultural identity, community resources and the customary mode of dispute resolution. Further it also states in clause (i) of Section 4 that the Gram Sabha or the Panchayats at the appropriate level shall be consulted before making the acquisition of land in the Scheduled Areas for development projects and before re-settling or rehabilitating persons affected by such projects in the Scheduled Areas and that the actual planning and implementation of the projects in the Scheduled Areas, shall be coordinated at the State level. Sub-clause (k) of Section 4 states that the recommendations of the Gram Sabha or the Panchayats at the appropriate level shall be made mandatory prior to grant of prospective licence or mining lease for minor minerals in the Scheduled Areas. Panchayat has also endowed with the powers and authority necessary to function as institutions of Self-Government.

The customary and cultural rights of indigenous people have also been the subject matter of various international conventions. International Labour Organization (ILO) Convention on Indigenous and Tribal Populations Convention, 1957 (No. 107) was the first comprehensive international instrument setting forth the rights of indigenous and tribal populations which emphasized the necessity for the protection of social, political and cultural rights of indigenous people. Following that there were two other conventions ILO Convention (No. 169) and Indigenous and Tribal Peoples Convention, 1989 and United Nations Declaration on the rights of Indigenous Peoples (UNDRIP), 2007, India is a signatory only to the ILO Convention (No. 107).

Apart from giving legitimacy to the cultural rights by 1957 Convention, the Convention on the Biological Diversity (CBA) adopted at the Earth Summit (1992) highlighted necessity to preserve and maintain knowledge, innovation and practices of the local communities relevant for conservation and sustainable use of bio-diversity, India is a signatory to CBA. Rio Declaration on Environment and Development Agenda 21 and Forestry principle also encourage the promotion of customary practices conducive to conservation. The necessity to respect and promote the inherent rights of indigenous peoples which derive from their political, economic and social structures and from their cultures, spiritual traditions, histories and philosophies, especially their rights to their lands, territories and resources have also been recognized by United Nations in the United Nations Declaration on Rights of Indigenous Peoples. STs and other TFDs residing in the Scheduled Areas have a right to maintain their distinctive spiritual relationship with their traditionally owned or otherwise occupied and used lands.

Many of the STs and other TFDs are totally unaware of their rights. They also experience [a] lot of difficulties in obtaining effective access to justice because of their distinct culture and limited contact with mainstream society. Many a times, they do not have the financial resources to engage in any legal actions against development projects undertaken in their abode or the forest in which they stay. They have a vital role to play in the environmental management and development because of their knowledge and traditional practices. State has got a duty to recognize and duly support their identity, culture and interest so that they can effectively participate in achieving sustainable development.

We notice, bearing in mind the above objects, the Forest Rights Act has been enacted conferring powers on the Gram Sabha constituted under the Act to protect the community resources, individual rights, cultural and religious rights.

The Forest Rights Act

... The Statement of Objects and Reasons of the Act states that forest dwelling tribal people and forests are inseparable and that the simplicity of tribals and their general ignorance of modern regulatory framework precluded them from asserting their genuine claims to resources in areas where they belong and depended upon and that only recently that forest management regimes have initiated action to recognize the occupation and other right of the forest dwellers. Of late, we have realized that forests have the best chance to survive if communities participate in their conservation and regeneration measures. The Legislature also has addressed the long standing and genuine felt need of granting a secure and inalienable right to those communities whose right to life depends on right to forests and thereby strengthening the entire conservation regime by giving a permanent stake to the STs dwelling in the forests for generations in symbiotic relationship with the entire ecosystem.

We have to bear in mind the above objects and reasons, while interpreting various provisions of the Forest Rights Act, which is a social welfare or remedial statute. The Act protects a wide range of rights of forest dwellers and STs including the customary rights to use forest land as a community forest resource and not restricted merely to property rights or to areas of habitation.

Forest rights of forest dwelling STs and other TFDs are dealt with in Chapter II of the Act. Section 3 of that chapter lists out what are the forest rights for the purpose of the Act....

Forest Rights Act and MMRDA[70]

... The Forest Rights Act, neither expressly nor impliedly, has taken away or interfered with the right of the State over mines or minerals lying underneath the forest land, which stand vested in the State. State holds the natural resources as a trustee for the people. Section 3 of the Forest Rights Act does not vest such rights on the STs or other TFDs. PESA Act speaks only of minor minerals, which says that the recommendation of Gram Sabha shall be made mandatory prior to grant of prospecting licence or mining lease for minor minerals in the Scheduled Areas. Therefore, as held by this Court in *Amritlal Athubhai Shah v Union Government of India* (1976) 4 SCC 108, the State Government has the power to reserve any particular area for Bauxite mining for a public sector corporation.

Gram Sabha and other Authorities

[The court summarized the multitier system under the FRA for recognizing rights with reference to the FRA and the rules framed under the Act.]

Individual/Community Rights

Forest Rights Act prescribed various rights to tribals/forest dwellers as per Section 3 of the Act. As per Section 6 of the Act, power is conferred on the Gram Sabha to process for determining the nature and the extent of individual or community forests read with or both that may be given to forest dwelling STs and other TFDs, by receiving claims, consolidate it, and verifying them and preparing a map, delineating area of each recommended claim in such

70 Mines and Minerals (Regulation and Development) Act of 1957.

a manner as may be prescribed. The Gram Sabha has received a large number of individual claims and community claims from the Rayagada District as well as the Kalahandi District. From Rayagada District Gram Sabha received 185 individual claims, of which 145 claims have been considered and settled by granting alternate rights over 263.5 acres of land. Forty individual claims pending before the Gram Sabha pertain to areas which fall outside the mining lease area. In respect of Kalahandi District 31 individual claims have been considered and settled by granting alternate rights over an area of 61 acres.

Gram Sabha has not received any community claim from the District of Rayagada. However, in respect of Kalahandi District 6 community claims had been received by the Gram Sabha of which 3 had been considered and settled by granting an alternate area of 160.55 acres. The balance 3 claims are pending consideration.

Customary and Religious Rights (Sacred Rights)

Religious freedom guaranteed to STs and the TFDs under Articles 25 and 26 of the Constitution is intended to be a guide to a community of life and social demands. The above mentioned Articles guarantee them the right to practice and propagate not only matters of faith or belief, but all those rituals and observations which are regarded as integral part of their religion. Their right to worship the deity Niyam-Raja has, therefore, to be protected and preserved.

Gram Sabha has a role to play in safeguarding the customary and religious rights of the STs and other TFDs under the Forest Rights Act. Section 6 of the Act confers powers on the Gram Sabha to determine the nature and extent of 'individual' or 'community rights'. In this connection, reference may also be made to Section 13 of the Act coupled with the provisions of PESA Act, which deal with the powers of Gram Sabha. Section 13 of the Forest Rights Act reads as under:

> 13. *Act not in derogation of any other law.* — Save as otherwise provided in this Act and the provisions of the Panchayats (Extension of the Scheduled Areas) Act, 1996 (40 of 1996), the provisions of this Act shall be in addition to and not in derogation of the provisions of any other law for the time being in force.

PESA Act has been enacted, as already stated, to provide for the extension of the provisions of Part IX of the Constitution relating to Panchayats to the Scheduled Areas. Section 4(d) of the Act says that every Gram Sabha shall be competent to safeguard and preserve the traditions, customs of the people, their cultural identity, community resources and community mode of dispute resolution. Therefore, Grama Sabha functioning under the Forest Rights Act read with Section 4(d) of PESA Act has an obligation to safeguard and preserve the traditions and customs of the STs and other forest dwellers, their cultural identity, community resources etc., which they have to discharge following the guidelines issued by the Ministry of Tribal Affairs vide its letter dated 12.7.2012.

We are, therefore, of the view that the question whether STs and other TFDs, like Dongaria Kondh, Kutia Kandha and others, have got any religious rights i.e. rights of worship over the Niyamgiri hills, known as Nimagiri, near Hundaljali, which is the hill top known as Niyam-Raja, have to be considered by the Gram Sabha. Gram Sabha can also examine whether the proposed mining area Niyama Danger, 10 km away from the peak, would in any way affect the abode of Niyam-Raja. Needless to say, if the BMP, in any way, affects their religious rights, especially their right to worship their deity, known as Niyam Raja, in the hills top of the Niyamgiri range of hills, that right has to be preserved and protected. We find that this aspect of the matter has not been placed before the Gram Sabha for their active consideration, but only the individual claims and community claims received from Rayagada and Kalahandi Districts, most of which the Gram Sabha has dealt with and settled.

The Gram Sabha is also free to consider all the community, individual as well as cultural and religious claims, over and above the claims which have already been received from Rayagada and Kalahandi Districts. Any such fresh claims be filed before the Gram Sabha within six weeks from the date of this Judgment. State Government as well as the Ministry of Tribal

Affairs, Government of India, would assist the Gram Sabha for settling of individual as well as community claims.

We are, therefore, inclined to give a direction to the State of Orissa to place these issues before the Gram Sabha with notice to the Ministry of Tribal Affairs, Government of India and the Gram Sabha would take a decision on them within three months and communicate the same to the MoEF, through the State Government. On the conclusion of the proceeding before the Gram Sabha determining the claims submitted before it, the MoEF shall take a final decision on the grant of Stage II clearance for the Bauxite Mining Project in the light of the decisions of the Gram Sabha within two months thereafter.

The Alumina Refinery Project is well advised to take steps to correct and rectify the alleged violations by it of the terms of the environmental clearance granted by MoEF. Needless to say that while taking the final decision, the MoEF shall take into consideration any corrective measures that might have been taken by the Alumina Refinery Project for rectifying the alleged violations of the terms of the environmental clearance granted in its favour by the MoEF.

The proceedings of the Gram Sabha shall be attended as an observer by a judicial officer of the rank of the District Judge, nominated by the Chief Justice of the High Court of Orissa who shall sign the minutes of the proceedings, certifying that the proceedings of the Gram Sabha took place independently and completely uninfluenced either by the Project proponents or the Central Government or the State Government.

The Writ Petition is disposed of with the above directions. Communicate this order to the Ministry of Tribal Affairs, Gram Sabhas of Kalahandi and Rayagada Districts of Orissa and the Chief Justice of High Court of Orissa, for further follow up action.

NOTES AND QUESTIONS

1. The *OMC* case tested the Supreme Court's capacity to correct course. After the *Siil* judgment rendered on 8 August 2008, it was expected that the MoEF (which had already granted stage I forest clearance after examining the reports of Wildlife Institute of India and the Central Mining Planning and Design Institute) would swiftly issue the stage II clearance. In the first two rounds before the Supreme Court, the MoEF supported the project and gave no hint of a shift in position.

The volte-face by the MoEF, before round three, severely undermined the credibility of the court process and exposed the hollowness of the first two orders. The Supreme Court may well have responded to the MoEF's order of 24 August 2010 by holding that the executive could not undermine its judgments by this type of manoeuvring. The court may have hauled up the ministry for derailing the carefully crafted rehabilitation package articulated by the Supreme Court in its November 2007 order and which was subsequently endorsed in the *Siil* case in 2008 after hearing counsel for the Union Government. The court's prestige and the Rule of Law depend on the finality of Supreme Court judgments. Here, rather humbly, the court overlooked these factors and chose to examine the tribal rights issues that had escaped its attention at the previous stages.

Was the Supreme Court's willingness to revisit the project and depart from its previous judgments a good decision or an unhealthy precedent? What reasons—legal, political and societal—may have impelled the court to do so? The Forest Bench that heard the case in 2013 had a different constitution from the bench that heard the first two rounds. Could this have made a difference?

2. One of the criticisms levelled against the Supreme Court was that in the first two rounds it failed to address the concerns of the tribal community. Is this criticism valid? After all,

the thrust of the first two court orders was effective 'rehabilitation'. Was the court's initial approach unduly growth-centric or simply patronizing? How is a court to determine the sentiment of a distant tribal community?

3. The *OMC* judgment is a powerful articulation of the rights of traditional forest dwellers. Drawing on the provisions in the Constitution and international conventions, the Supreme Court recognized the inherent right of indigenous people 'to maintain their distinctive spiritual relationship with their traditionally owned or other occupied and used lands'. Appreciating the role of traditional forest dwellers in environmental management and their limitation in accessing mainstream institutions, the court held: 'State has got a duty to recognise and duly support their identity, culture and interest so that they can effectively participate in achieving sustainable development.' Moreover, the court recognized the religious rights of the Dongaria Kondh to worship their deity who was believed to reside at the top of the Niyamgiri range of hills.

4. The Saxena committee found that Vedanta had increased its capacity six-fold from 1 mtpa to 6 mtpa without obtaining environmental clearance under the EIA notification of 2006. According to the committee, '[t]his expansion, its extensive scale and advanced nature, is in complete violation of the EPA and is an expression of the contempt with which this company treats the laws of the land.' In hindsight, was the Norwegian government's assessment of the company's ethics better than the Supreme Court's more trusting approach?

Apart from illegal expansion, the MoEF found that the ARP was sourcing bauxite from a large number of mines in Jharkhand, though most of these mines did not have an environmental clearance. (Most had not even been granted a mining licence). What factors may have encouraged such conduct on the part of Vedanta's management? Lengthy delays? Cost overruns? A 'too big to fail' bravado? The Supreme Court's 'growth oriented' prescription in previous orders and its record of waiving through big ticket projects like *Lafarge*?[71]

5. In the *Lafarge* case,[72] the Supreme Court held that general principles of judicial review apply to environmental decisions by government. If this standard had been applied by the Supreme Court in *OMC*, it would have merely examined whether the decision-making process was procedurally fair (with all affected parties heard) and whether the Minister was alive to the relevant factors. The court frequently reminds us that judicial review is concerned with the decision-making process, *not* the final decision. Do you see an application of the *Lafarge* standard of review here?

If the Minister's decision of 24 August 2010 met the test of judicial review, should the court have rejected OMC's request for certiorari and closed the case? The court did not find any defect in the impugned decision but nevertheless required an elaborate exercise for ascertaining religious rights before the Gram Sabha. It then required the MoEF to 'take a final decision on the grant of stage II clearance' for the mining project.

Is it possible to reconcile the *Lafarge* standard of review with the exercise embarked upon by the *OMC* court?

6. Pursuant to the Supreme Court's directions, 12 Gram Sabhas convened meetings to vote on the project. All of them rejected the project.

71 *Lafarge Umiam Mining (P) Ltd v Union of India* (2011) 7 SCC 338.
72 *Id.*

II. IRON ORE MINING

Karnataka

In 2009, Samaj Parivartana Samudaya (SPS), a non-governmental organization, approached the Supreme Court under Article 32 of the Constitution complaining about indiscriminate mining in the District of Bellary, Karnataka. Bellary and its neighbouring districts Tumkur and Chitradurga hold rich iron ore deposits, much of it lying under forest. SPS complained that illegal mining operations were being carried out with impunity in collusion with government officials at every level. A mining mafia reigned. So complete was its hold that the region was known in jest as the 'Republic of Bellary'—beyond the reach of Indian law. Despite a report made by the Lokayukta[73] in December 2008, no effective action was taken by any authority to regulate the mining and stop the ecological devastation.

'What followed thereafter is unprecedented in the history of Indian environmental jurisprudence' is how the Supreme Court described the progression of the case between 2010 and 2013. The court directed the CEC to inspect the region and assess the extent of the environmental harm. When the CEC reported massive environmental degradation, in a drastic step the court shut down all mining operations. It appointed a Joint Team to carry out a detailed survey of the region to ascertain the extent of illegal encroachments by miners. The Joint Team conducted a detailed survey using the best available technology known as 'total station', fixed the lease boundaries and confirmed the encroachments. Meanwhile, with mining operations at a standstill, the iron and steel industry based in Karnataka faced an acute shortage of ore and urged the court to lift the ban. The court held firm, insisting that the miners first implement Reclamation and Rehabilitation (R&R) measures to restore the devastated region.

After the R&R activity progressed, the court turned its attention to the CEC's recommendations regarding the 166 leases surveyed. The CEC classified the mines into three categories: Category 'A' comprised leases where there was no encroachment; Category 'B' comprised leases where the illegal mining by way of mining pits was up to 10% of the lease area, or the overburden/waste dumps outside the sanctioned leased area was up to 15% of the lease area; Category 'C' comprised 49 leases that were gross violators, having encroached more than the percentages indicated or where there was flagrant violation of the Forest (Conservation) Act of 1980. The CEC recommended reopening of Category 'A' mines provided they undertook R&R measures. Category 'B' leases were also recommended for reopening after R&R measures were implemented and the lessees made compensatory payments.[74] In respect of Category 'C' mines, the CEC recommended cancellation of the leases.

The Category 'C' lessees strongly resisted cancellation, claiming that such action was unprecedented and harsh. The following excerpt captures the essence of the Supreme Court's analysis.

SAMAJ PARIVARTANA SAMUDAYA v STATE OF KARNATAKA
(2013) 8 SCC 154

Ranjan Gogoi, J: What should be the appropriate contours of this Court's jurisdiction while dealing with allegations of systematic plunder of natural resources by a handful of opportunists seeking to achieve immediate gains? This is the core question that arises in the present proceeding in the context of mining of Iron Ore and allied minerals in the State of Karnataka. . . .

We may now proceed to deal with the issues arising in proper sequential order.

73 The Lokayukta, Karnataka is a statutory watchdog constituted by the state government under law.

74 The compensatory payments were directed at the rate of Rs. 5 crores per encroached hectare of land in respect of mining pits and Rs. 1 crore per encroached hectare in respect of other encroachments.

Issue No. 1

Credibility of the CEC A scathing attack has been made against the CEC on behalf of one of the lessees.... It is contended that the said authority has virtually become a law unto itself making recommendations which is in defiance of both law and logic. Assumption of unguided, unbridled and absolute powers has been attributed to the CEC. The implicit trust of this Court in the said body has been misutilised requiring a review by this Court with regard to the continuance of the said body or at least in respect of a change in its present composition, it is argued.

The CEC was first constituted by the Court by its order dated 9.5.2002 as an interim body until creation of the statutory agency contemplated under the provisions of section 3(3) of the EP Act. Thereafter by a Notification dated 17.9.2002 published in the Gazette of India the constitution of the Central Empowered Committee (CEC) for a period of 5 years was notified indicating its composition together with the extent of its powers and duties. It transpires from the Court's order dated 7.9.2007 that an issue with regard to the correctness of the extent of empowerment of the said body made by Notification dated 17.9.2002 was raised on behalf of the Union of India, whereafter, on the suggestions of the Attorney General for India, this Court by its order dated 14.12.2007 had determined the extent of powers of the CEC in the following terms:

1. In supersession of all the previous orders regarding constitutions and functioning of the Central Empowered Committee (hereinafter called the 'Empowered Committee') is constituted for the purpose of monitoring and ensuring compliance with the orders of this Court covering the subject matter of forest and wild life and related issues arising out of the said orders.
2. The Committee shall exercise the following powers and perform the following functions:
   (i) to monitor the implementation of this Court's orders and place reports of non-compliance before the Court and Central Government for appropriate action.
   (ii) to examine pending Interlocutory Applications in the said Writ petitions (as may be referred to it by the Court) as well as the reports and affidavits filed by the States in response to the orders passed by the Hon'ble Court and place its recommendations before the Court for orders
   (iii) to deal with any applications made to it by any aggrieved person and wherever necessary, to make a report to this Court in that behalf;
   (iv) for the purposes of effective discharge of powers conferred upon the Committee under this order; the Committee can:–
      (a) call for any documents from any persons or the government of the Union or the State or any other official;
      (b) undertake site inspection of forest area involved;
      (c) seek assistance or presence of any person(s) or official(s) required by it in relation to its work;
      (d) co-opt one or more persons as its members or as special invitees for dealing with specific issues;
      (e) co-opt, wherever feasible, the Chief Secretary or his representative and Principal Chief Conservator of Forests of the State as special invitees while dealing with issues pertaining to a particular state;
      (f) suggest measures generally to the State, as well as Central Government, for the more effective implementation of the Act and other orders of this Court.
   (v) to examine and advise/recommend on any issue referred to the Committee.'

As the period of five years mentioned in the Notification dated 17.9.2002 had expired and the terms of reference to the body had been re-determined by this Court, perhaps, a fresh notification should have been issued which was not forthcoming. It is in such a situation that the CEC had continued to function under orders of the Court submitting its reports from time to time in various environmental issues pending before this Court. It is on consideration of such Reports that the Court has been passing its orders from time to time.

In the circumstances enumerated above, questions concerning the credibility of the CEC are absolutely unfounded, particularly in the absence of any materials to substantiate the apprehensions, if not allegations, that have been leveled. The said body has been performing such tasks as had been assigned by this Court by its orders passed from time to time. The directions on the basis of which the CEC had proceeded and had submitted its Reports are within the framework of the terms of reference of the CEC as determined by this Court by order dated 14.12.2007. Needless to say, acceptance of the recommendations made by the CEC on the basis of which orders of the Court are formulated is upon the satisfaction of the Court. We, therefore, close the issue by holding the contentions made to be wholly untenable.

Issue No. 2

Exercise of jurisdiction under Article 32/142 of the Constitution on the basis of the facts revealed by Reports of the CEC i.e. large scale damage to the forest wealth of the country due to illegal mining on an unprecedented scale *vis-à-vis* resort to remedies under the provisions of Mines and Minerals (Development and Regulation) Act, 1957, Forest (Conservation) Act, 1980 and Environment (Protection) Act, 1986.

On the above issue the short and precise argument on behalf of the leaseholders is that the provisions of each of the statutory enactments, i.e., the MMDR Act, FC Act and EP Act prescribe a distinct statutory scheme for regulation of mining activities and the corrective as well as punitive steps that may be taken in the event mining activities are carried out in a manner contrary to the terms of the lease or the provisions of any of the statutes, as may be. The argument advanced is that as the statutes in question contemplate a particular scheme to deal with instances of illegal mining or carrying on mining operations which is hazardous to the environment, the CEC could not have recommended the taking of any step or measure beyond what is contemplated by the statutory scheme(s) in force. It is argued that it will not be proper for this Court to act under Article 32 and to accept any of the said recommendations which are beyond the scheme(s) contemplated by the Statute(s). In other words, what is sought to be advanced on behalf of the leaseholders is that no step should be taken or direction issued by this Court which will be contrary to or in conflict with the provisions of the relevant statutes. Several judgments of this Court, which are perceived to be precedents in support of the proposition advanced, have been cited in the course of the arguments made.

On the other hand, the learned *amicus curiae* has submitted that the present is a case of mass destruction of the forest wealth of this country resulting not only in a plunder of scarce natural resources but also causing irreparable ecological and environmental damage and degradation. The learned *amicus curiae* has submitted that the extent of illegal mining that had happened in the three districts of the State of Karnataka is unprecedented. The relevant data compiled by different bodies has been placed by the learned *amicus curiae* to indicate that in the Bellary-Hospet region the annual production of Iron Ore had increased from 12.4 MMT in the year 2001–02 to 44.39 MMT in the year 2008–09. The then Chief Minister of the State had made a statement on the floor of the legislative assembly on 9.7.2010 that 30.49 MMT of illegal Iron Ore has been exported from the State of Karnataka between 2003–04 to 2009–10 valued at approximately Rs. 15,245 crores. In the year 2009–10 alone the total quantity of illegal Iron Ore exported stood at 12.9 MMT. During the inspection carried out by the Indian Bureau of Mines in December, 2009 it was found that not a single mining lease was operating without violating the provisions of the MMDR Act and the FC Act. In an affidavit filed by the official Respondents in a writ petition registered and numbered as W.P. No. 14551/2010 before the Karnataka High Court it was stated that between November, 2009 and February, 2010 (i.e., within a period of four months) 35.319 lakh MT of illegal Iron Ore was received at Belekeri and Karwar ports, for movement of which for a period of about 4 months 2986 trucks were required to undertake the journey every day in both directions i.e., to the ports and thereafter back.

According to [the *amicus curiae*], the present is a case of mass tort resulting in the abridgment of the fundamental rights of a large number of citizens for enforcement of which the writ petition has been filed under Article 32. He has submitted, by relying on several decisions of this Court, that in a situation where the Court is called upon to enforce the fundamental rights and that too of an indeterminate number of citizens there can be no limitations on the power of Court. It is the satisfaction of the Court that alone would be material. Once such satisfaction is reached, the Court will be free to devise its own procedure and issue whatever directions are considered necessary to effectuate the Fundamental Rights. The only restriction that the Court will bear in mind is that its orders or directions will not be in conflict with the provisions of any Statute. However, if the statute does not forbid a particular course of action it will be certainly open for the Court under Article 32 to issue appropriate directions. According to the learned *amicus curiae* in the present case none of the recommendations of the CEC is inconsistent or contrary to any statutory provision. They are at best supplemental to the existing provisions seeking to achieve the same end through a procedure which may be somewhat different. The justification for this, according to the learned *amicus curiae*, lies in the extraordinary situation that had occurred in the present case.

At this stage, very briefly, the statutory scheme under the three enactments in question may be taken note of. Under the provisions of the MMDR Act the State Government has been provided with the power of termination of licenses or mining leases in the interest of regulation of mines and minerals (section 4A) whereas under section 5, power has been conferred not to grant mining leases in certain specified situations. The rule making power under section 23C extends to framing of rules by the State Government to prevent illegal mining, transportation and storage of minerals and to provide for checking and inspection of the mining lease area. The Karnataka (Prevention of Illegal Mining, Transportation and Storage of Minerals) Rules, 2011 has been notified on 5th February, 2011. Under the Mineral Concession Rules, 1960, the expression 'illegal mining' has been explained in rule 2(iia). The aforesaid Rules also contemplate that while determining the extent of illegal mining the area granted under the lease will be deemed to have been held by the holder of the license under lawful authority. Under the provisions of the EP Act, closure, prohibition or regulation of industry, operation or process is contemplated, whereas under the provisions of the FC Act prior approval of the Central Government for use of forest land for non forest purpose is mandatory. The question that has been raised on behalf of the leaseholders is whether the aforesaid provisions under the different statutes should be resorted to and the recommendations made by the CEC including closure of Category-'C' mines should not commend for acceptance of this Court.

* * *

We may now take up the decisions cited on behalf of the leaseholders to contend that the power under Articles 32 and 142 ought not to be exercised in the present case and instead remedies should be sought within the relevant statutes. The sheet anchor is the case of *Supreme Court Bar Association v Union of India* reported in (1998) 4 SCC 409. We do not see how or why we should lie entrapped within the confines of any of the relevant Statutes on the strength of the views expressed in *Supreme Court Bar Association* (supra). The observations made in para 48 of the judgment and the use of words 'ordinarily' and 'are directly in conflict' as appearing in the said paragraph (underlined by us) directly militates against the view that the lease holders would like us to adopt in the present case.

> 48. The Supreme Court in exercise of its jurisdiction under Article 142 has the power to make such order as is necessary for doing complete justice 'between the parties in any cause or matter pending before it'. The very nature of the power must lead the Court to set limits for itself within which to exercise those powers and ordinarily it cannot disregard a statutory provision governing a subject, except perhaps to balance the equities between the conflicting claims of the litigating parties by 'ironing out the creases' in a cause or matter before it. Indeed, this Court is not a court of restricted jurisdiction of only dispute-settling. It is well recognised and established that this Court has always been a law-maker and its role travels beyond merely dispute-settling. It is a 'problem-solver in the nebulous areas' [see *K Veeraswami v Union of India* (1991) 3 SCC 655)] but the substantive statutory provisions dealing with the subject-matter of a given case cannot be altogether ignored by this Court, while making an order under Article 142. Indeed, these constitutional powers cannot, in any way, be controlled by any statutory provisions but at the same time these powers are not meant to be exercised when their exercise may come directly in conflict with what has been expressly provided for in a statute dealing expressly with the subject.

Even if the above observations are understood to be laying down a note of caution, the same would be a qualified one and can have no application in a case of mass tort as has been occasioned in the present case. The mechanism provided by any of the statutes in question would neither be effective nor efficacious to deal with the extraordinary situation that has arisen on account of the large scale illegalities committed in the operation of the mines in question resulting in grave and irreparable loss to the forest wealth of the country besides the colossal loss caused to the national exchequer. The situation being extraordinary the remedy, indeed, must also be extraordinary. Considered against the backdrop of the statutory schemes in question, we do not see how any of the recommendations of the CEC, if accepted, would come into conflict with any law enacted by the legislature. It is only in the above situation that the Court may consider the necessity of placing the recommendations made by the CEC on a finer balancing scale before accepting the same. We, therefore, feel uninhibited to proceed to exercise our constitutional jurisdiction to remedy the enormous wrong that has happened and to provide adequate protection for the future, as may be required.

Issue No. 3

Sanctity of the process of survey undertaken by the Joint Team constituted by this Court's order dated 6th May, 2011 and the determination of the boundaries of the leases on the basis of the said survey.

The above issue will require examination from two perspectives. The first is the fairness of the procedure adopted in carrying out the survey and the second is with regard to acceptability of the technical part of the survey process. In so far as the fairness of the procedure adopted is concerned it is on record that notice of the dates proposed for survey of a particular lease was intimated to the lease holder well in advance to enable the lease holder or his representative to be present at the site while the survey is conducted. The field survey was done by 7 teams consisting of one surveyor each from the Karnataka Forest Department, Karnataka Mines and Geological Department, Karnataka Revenue Department and a representative of the National Institute of Technology, Surathkal. The field survey undertaken by each team was supervised by the Joint Team constituted by this Court. During the field survey, the representative of the concerned lessees was present and the Mahazars (Panchnamas) for each day's survey were prepared incorporating the details of the survey carried out. The said Panchnamas were signed by, apart from the Government representatives and the representative of the National Institute of Technology, Surathkal, also by the concerned lessee or their representatives. The readings recorded during the field survey were shared with the concerned lessees or their representatives and before finalizing the survey sketches the concerned lessees or their representatives were given a personal hearing. After the field survey was completed, in terms of the order of the Court dated 23.9.2011, the representations filed by the leaseholders against the findings of the Joint Team were reconsidered by the Joint Team and personal hearing was afforded to 122 lease holders. On the basis of the said hearings, necessary corrections were made in respect of 33 number of leases. Thereafter, the final Report of the CEC dated 3.2.2012 was submitted to the Court. In terms of the Court's order dated 10.2.2012, the CEC again considered the representations filed by as many as 66 lease holders. The findings of the Joint Team in respect of 4 leases were modified by the CEC though the said modification did not result into any change of categorization. Two representations, one filed by M/s V S Lad & Sons and another by M/s Hothur Traders have been placed before the Court for appropriate orders [issue is being dealt with separately] whereas the rest of the representations were rejected by the CEC. In the above facts, procedural fairness in the process of survey carried out by the Joint Team is writ large and there can be no room for any doubt so as to question the sanctity of the survey process on the above stated ground.

This will require the Court to go into the details of the technical aspect of the survey which was conducted by the Joint Team. The consideration of the details of the survey undertaken, naturally, has to be in the backdrop of the multifold complaints that have been raised on behalf of the leaseholders in the several IAs filed. As already noted, on a very broad plane, the complaints in this regard are that the Joint Team has ignored judicial orders passed in respect of boundaries between neighbouring/adjacent leases; reduction of the area of the lease provided in the lease deed/lease sketch; shifting of the lease area to a new location as a result of the survey. Specifically, objections have been raised to the effect that overburden dumps in different areas have been taken into account to come to the finding that mining had been carried out in such areas without necessary clearances under the FC Act (in case of forest areas) or in the absence of mining leases in respect of such areas (non forest areas) though the activity in question i.e. dumping does not amount to mining operations under the MMDR Act.

* * *

The participation of the lessee or his representative throughout the process of survey by the Joint Team; the details of the manner of conduct of the actual process of survey delineated above; the use of the state of the art technology; the composition of the Joint Team entrusted with the responsibility of the survey and the constitution of the 7 teams that conducted the field survey under the supervision of the Joint Team; the two stages of re-verification of the findings of the survey in the light of the objections raised by the lease holders under orders of this Court dated 26.9.2011 and 10.2.2012 and the corrections made on the basis thereof can leave no doubt as to the credibility of the findings of the survey conducted under the orders of the Court. True it is that we cannot claim to be experts; but we need not be to see what is *ex facie* evident. Therefore, notwithstanding the protracted arguments advanced on behalf of lease holders and the large scale reference to sketches, maps and drawings filed before this Court by the said lease holders, we are satisfied that all complaints and grievances must fade away in the light of the survey undertaken by the Joint Team and the events subsequent thereto. It would also be significant to take note of the fact that in the written submission on behalf of the Federation of Indian Mineral Industries (FIMI), in the opening paragraph it has been stated as under.

> The applicant submits that FIMI has full faith in the integrity and fairness of the survey done by the Joint Team and recommended by CEC. FIMI is in full agreement with the recommendations made by CEC with regard to Categories A and B and the directions issued by this Hon'ble Court. FIMI is simultaneously of the view that instead of cancellation of Category 'C' mining leases, these may be directed to make appropriate compensatory afforestation payment, undertake R&R work as per R&R Plan prepared by ICFRE and approved by CEC and after successful completion and implementation of R&R Plan, they should be allowed to recommence mining operations in such leases.

We make it clear that we have not understood the above statement as an admission on the part of the Federation and it is on a consideration of the totality of the facts placed before us that we accept the findings of the survey conducted by the Joint Team constituted by the orders of this Court and the boundaries of each of the leases determined on that basis. We further direct that in supersession of all orders either of the authorities of the State or Courts, as may be, the boundaries of leases fixed by the Joint Team will henceforth be the boundaries of each of the leases who will have the benefit of the lease area as determined by the Joint Team. All proceedings pending in any court with regard to boundaries of the leases involved in the present proceeding shall stand adjudicated by means of present order and no such question would be open for re-examination by any body or authority.

Before proceeding to the next issue we would like to observe that the contention urged on behalf of some of the lessees that dumping of mining waste (overburden dumps) do not constitute operations under section 2(d) of the MMDR Act is too naive for acceptance. The wide terms of the definition contained in section 2(d) of the MMDR Act encompasses all such activity within the meaning of expression 'mining operations'. Use of forest land for such activity would require clearance under the FC Act. In case the land used for such purpose is not forest land the mining lease must cover the land used for any such activity.

ISSUE NO. 4

Acceptability of the Recommendations of the CEC with regard to (i) categorization, (ii) Reclamation and Rehabilitation (R&R) Plans, (iii) Reopening of Category 'A' and 'B' mines subject to conditions, (iv) Closure/reopening of Category 'C' mines and (v) future course of action in respect of Category 'C' mines if closure thereof is to be ordered by the Court

In the light of the discussions that have preceded sanctity of the procedure of laying information and materials before the Court with regard to the extent of illegal mining and other specific details in this regard by means of the Reports of the CEC cannot be in doubt. Inter-generational equity and sustainable development have come to be firmly embedded in our constitutional jurisprudence as an integral part of the fundamental rights conferred by Article 21 of the Constitution. In enforcing such rights of a large number of citizens who are bound to be adversely affected by environmental degradation, this Court cannot be constrained by the restraints of procedure. The CEC which has been assisting the Court in various environment related matters for over a decade now was assigned certain specified tasks which have been performed by the said body giving sufficient justification for the decisions arrived and the recommendations made. If the said recommendations can withstand the test of logic and reason which issue is being examined hereinafter we will have no reason not to accept the said recommendations and embody the same as a part of the order that we will be required to make in the present case.

(i) Categorization The issue is whether categorization on the basis of percentage of the encroached area qua the total lease area is an arbitrary decision. Arbitrariness in the adoption of a criteria for classification has to be tested on the anvil of Article 14 and not on the subjective notions of availability of a better basis of classification. The basis suggested i.e. total encroached area has the potential of raising questions similar to the ones now raised on behalf of the lease holders. This is on account of the lack of uniformity in the areas covered by the different leases in question. The test, therefore, ought not to be what would be a 'better' basis for the categorization for that would introduce subjectivity in the process; the test is whether categorization on the basis adopted results in hostile discrimination and adoption of the criteria of percentage has no reasonable nexus with the object sought to be achieved, namely, to identify the lessees who have committed the maximum violations and damage to environment. Viewed from the aforesaid perspective, the categorization made does not fail the test of reasonableness and would commend for our acceptance.

In this regard, we may take note of two IAs (IA. No. 74 of 2012 and IA. No. 4 of 2012) filed by Federation of Indian Mineral Industries which body claims membership of a vast number of the lessees involved in the present proceedings. In the aforesaid IAs, as already noticed in a different context, the Federation has unequivocally accepted the findings of the survey conducted by the Joint Team and the recommendation of the CEC in so far as categorization of the leases and the actions suggested for reopening of Category 'A' and 'B' mines along with other pre-conditions stipulated including the preparation of the R & R plans. The only caveat in this regard is in respect of category 'C' mines. The Federation had suggested that the said mines be also allowed to reopen subject to similar or even more stringent conditions and, alternatively, for reopening of 39 total out of the total of 49 category 'C' mines by adoption of certain more liberal criteria than those recommended by the CEC. In the totality of the circumstances, we are of the view that the categorization suggested by the CEC in its Report dated 3.2.2012 should be accepted by us.

(ii) Conditions which have been suggested for opening of Category 'A' mines and additionally the R & R Plans for Category 'B' mines

* * *

The precise extent of illegal mining that took place in the three districts of Karnataka have been noted in detail in an earlier part of this order. The same, therefore, will not require any repetition. Illegal mining apart from playing havoc on the national economy had, in fact, cast an ominous cloud on the credibility of the system of governance by laws in force. It has had a chilling and crippling effect on ecology and environment. It is evident from the compilation submitted to the Court by the CEC that several of the Category 'C' mines were operating without requisite clearances under FC Act or even in the absence of a mining lease for a part of the area used for mining operations. The satellite imageries placed before the Court with regard to environmental damage and destruction has shocked judicial conscience. It is in the light of the above facts and circumstances that the future course of action in respect of the maximum violators/polluters, i.e., Category 'C' mines has to be judged. While doing so, the Court also has to keep in mind the requirement of Iron Ore to ensure adequate supply of manufactured steel and other allied products.

Once the result of the survey undertaken and the boundaries of the leases determined by the Joint Team has been accepted by the Court and the basis of categorization of the mines has been found to be rational and constitutionally permissible it will be difficult for this Court to visualize as to how the Category 'C' mines can be allowed to reopen. There is no room for compassion; fervent pleas for clemency cannot have even a persuasive value. As against the individual interest of the 49 Category 'C' leaseholders, public interest at large would require the Court to lean in favour of demonstrating the efficacy and effectiveness of the long arm of the law. We, therefore, order for the complete closure of the Category 'C' mines and for necessary follow up action in terms of the recommendations of the CEC in this regard, details of which have already been extracted in an earlier part of this order.

* * *

In the result, we summarize our conclusions in the matter as follows:–

1) The findings of the survey conducted by the Joint Team constituted by this Court by order dated 6.5.2011 and boundaries of the leases in question as determined on the basis of the said survey is hereby approved and accepted.
2) The categorization of the mines ('A', 'B' and 'C') on the basis of the parameters adopted by the CEC as indicated in its Report dated 3.2.2012 is approved and accepted.

...

6) The recommendations of the CEC contained in the Report dated 15.2.2013 for reopening of remaining Category 'A' mines and Category 'B' mines (63 in number) and sale of sub-grade iron ore subject to the conditions mentioned in the said Report are approved.
7) The recommendations contained in paragraphs VI and VII of the CEC Report dated 3.2.2012 are accepted, meaning thereby, the leases in respect of 'C' Category mines will stand cancelled and the recommendations of the CEC of Report dated 3.2.2012 with regard to the grant of fresh leases are accepted....

NOTES AND QUESTIONS

1. As recorded in the judgment, the plunder in Bellary continued for several years in full view of the authorities. Until the Supreme Court stepped in and issued drastic orders, a state of lawlessness prevailed. Iron ore was illegally mined in violation of the MMDRA and the ore was transported to ports from where it was exported to China. Much of the ore was mined from forests outside the leased areas, royalty payments to the state were evaded and a parallel administration of politically influential goons controlled operations. What does this say about the checks and balances in government? What does it say about the Forest Bench of the Supreme Court that picked up the case, steered it over several years and put in place a framework for restoration of the region? Did SPS have any option under the Indian system, except to approach the Supreme Court? What might be the limitations of such an approach?

2. The 'C' Category lessees put forward individual objections to the proposed cancellation. Some of the lessees claimed that they had genuine boundary disputes with their neighbours; others asserted that they were mining where they were asked to by government officials; most faulted the methodology applied in conducting the survey. The Supreme Court declined to deal with individual objections once it was satisfied about the integrity of the process adopted by the Joint Team and the CEC. Should the Supreme Court have dealt with each individual case or is this norm inapplicable to mass tort situations? Could a High Court have adopted a similar approach under Article 226?

3. Each 'C' Category lessee was operating its mine under a registered lease. A mining lease is an extremely valuable contract and in this case neither contracting party desired cancellation. In what circumstances can a court order cancellation of a registered lease? What about the property rights of the lessee?

4. Supreme Court judgments are a source of law and its judges lay down suitable principles for dispute resolution in response to new challenges. These principles serve to guide the High Courts and subordinate courts and tribunals. To support its ground-breaking directions, the Bellary Court drew on Article 142 of the Constitution and declared: 'The situation being extraordinary the remedy, indeed, must also be extraordinary.' Article 142 (1) reads:

> The Supreme Court in the exercise of its jurisdiction may pass such decree or make such order as is necessary for doing complete justice in any court or matter pending before it ...

While the court was justified in cancelling the category 'C' leases 'for doing complete justice', this constitutional power under Article 142 is not available to the High Courts or the National Green Tribunal (NGT). How should they deal with mass tort cases? Would the High Courts and the NGT be justified in dealing with mass torts in the same manner as the Supreme Court? If so, what might be the source of their power?

5. The Supreme Court overhauled the administration of Bellary, Tumkur and Chitradurga. The extent of judicial intervention is evident from the principal milestones in the case. On 19 November 2010, when issuing notice on SPS's writ petition, the Supreme Court sought a report from the CEC with respect to six mining leases. On 7 January 2011, the CEC reported widespread violations regarding encroachments and mining in reserved forests. The report recognized the need for proper demarcation of boundaries between lessees including the inter-state boundary between Karnataka and Andhra Pradesh.[75] The CEC found evidence of active connivance of officers and the absence of government monitoring of mining operations.

On 25 February 2011, the Supreme Court directed the CEC to report with respect to all mining in Bellary. The CEC filed five comprehensive reports on different aspects of the illegalities. The Supreme Court by its order dated 29 April 2011 suspended mining operations in 19 leases. Thereafter, on 6 May 2011, the Supreme Court constituted a Joint Team for carrying out a survey and demarcation of 99 mines in Bellary. The court ordered that where the Joint Team found any encroachment, mining operations were to shut down immediately. On 28 July 2011, the CEC filed a report highlighting the degradation in Bellary and recommending suspension of operations as well as the need for R&R. On 29 July 2011, taking a holistic view of the problem and invoking the precautionary principle, the Supreme Court suspended mining operations on all 8,868 hectares of Bellary District where mining was being undertaken. The Supreme Court directed the MoEF to indicate the requirements of the steel industry and requested the CEC to submit reports on the neighbouring districts of Tumkur and Chitradurga.

On 5 August 2011, the Supreme Court directed a macro-level EIA study by the Indian Council of Forestry Research and Education (ICFRE) and the state government was asked to submit an R&R plan. A central public sector undertaking, the National Mineral Development Corporation was allowed to operate its mine with a view to provide some iron ore to domestic industry. On 26 August 2011, the Supreme Court extended its order suspending mining operations in Bellary, to the districts of Tumkur and Chitradurga. It also expanded the scope of ICFRE's remit to cover the macro-level EIA study and R&R, to all three districts. In September 2011, the Supreme Court accepted the recommendations of the CEC and permitted ore mined before the ban to be sold by new transparent system of online auction (E-auction).

Between June 2011 and January 2012, the Joint Team submitted its work with respect to 166 leases surveyed. The survey revealed that more than 1,700 hectares of land were illegally encroached upon by miners. The Supreme Court accepted the recommendations of CEC with regard to broad guidelines regarding R&R. ICFRE was asked to prepare the macro-level R&R plan as well as individual lease-specific R&R plans on the basis that the annual ceiling for all mining activity in Bellary was 25 MMT and 5 MMT for Chitradurga and Tumkur. Each individual lessee would have to scale down operations to fall within these limits. On 17 August 2012, the Supreme Court directed CEC to file a report on resumption of mining operations in Category A. Accepting the progress made in R&R, on 3 September 2012, the

[75] To avoid accounting for the ore mined and paying royalties to the state, some of the miners exploited their proximity to the inter-state boundary by falsely claiming that the ore was mined across the border, thereby escaping regulatory oversight—such as it was—in both the states.

Supreme Court permitted resumption of mining in respect of 18 Category 'A' mines. On 7 September 2012, the Supreme Court directed the CBI to investigate the export of 50.79 lakh MT of iron ore which was illegally extracted during the period 1 January 2009 to 31 May 2010 and exported out of the country through Belekeri port. On 28 September 2012, the court issued directions for R&R of Category 'B' mines and directed payment of compensation by Category 'B' lessees.

6. To overcome numerous boundary disputes between neighbouring lessees, the Supreme Court issued a sweeping direction:

> We further direct that in supersession of all orders either of the authorities of the State or Courts, as may be, the boundaries of leases fixed by the Joint Team will henceforth be the boundaries of each of the leases who will have the benefit of the leased area as determined by the Joint Team. All proceedings pending in any court with regard to boundaries of the leases involved in the present proceeding shall stand adjudicated by means of present order and no such question would be open for re-examination by anybody or authority.

Without this clarity, the edifice on which the judgment rests would crumble. Remember, clear demarcated boundaries were essential for implementing the remedial measures ordered and the categorization adopted by the court. Under what jurisdiction could the Supreme Court have issued such directions? Is this an instance of judicial overreach?

7. One of the impacts of the Supreme Court's interim orders was that economic activity in the three districts dwindled to a standstill. Thousands of persons whose employment depended on the mining of iron ore were thrown out of jobs. The transport business stalled. Manufacturers of iron and steel were forced to shut down their furnaces. Was this scale of economic disruption justified? Does it give the judiciary a bad name?

8. As a result of the transparent e-auction process, the state government's royalty earnings soared and the price realized per metric tonne of ore sold was much higher than that which was previously obtained. What do you infer from the improved recoveries?

9. The impact of the Supreme Court judgment was dramatic. The new discipline introduced by the Supreme Court orders along with inspection and oversight by the court-appointed Monitoring committee resulted in improvements to the air quality, restoration of forested areas and well-regulated transportation of iron ore. Apart from the improvements to the environment, an important gain from this case was the restoration of environmental Rule of Law.

10. The environmental depredation caused by illegal mining and the arbitrary allocation of mining blocks resulted in a major overhaul of the MMDRA in 2015 and in the subordinate legislation framed under the Act. The new regime mandates the establishment of a district mineral foundation in every district.[76] The foundations, required to be established by the state governments, receive contributions from the lessee and these funds are used for local community welfare on projects such as providing drinking water, sanitation and health. Chapter V of the Mineral Conservation and Development Rules of 2017 obliges the lessee to undertake sustainable mining and specifically to adhere to the prescribed standards in respect of air pollution, discharge of effluents and noise pollution.

11. On 30 March 2009, Janthakal Enterprises filed a writ petition before the Karnataka High Court seeking a direction to the authorities to allow the petitioner to lift dumped material lying in its mining yard. The petitioner claimed that between 1965 and 1980 it had dumped

[76] Section 9B.

117,800 MT of low-grade iron ore that had no commercial value at that time. Due to a surge in global demand, the dumped material now had buyers and the petitioner offered to pay the requisite fee and royalty against permission to sell the ore.

A division bench of the Karnataka High Court responded with alacrity. On 24 April 2009, it issued interim directions to the forest department seeking a report on the quantity of the dumped material, the financial liability of writ petitioner to pay the fee, royalty, etc. as well as the cost to repair damage to the flora and fauna and for afforestation. On receiving the report, the High Court rendered a final judgment on 2 July 2009 permitting the petitioner to remove the dumped iron ore upon payment of various amounts that were set out in the report of the forest department.

The Supreme Court reversed the High Court in an appeal filed by the state. The Supreme Court found that the petition was delayed by at least 24 years, Janthakal's lease having expired in 1985. Moreover, the petitioner had taken contradictory stands with respect to the origin of the material: at one point it claimed that the material was natural eroded soil and waste from neighbouring mines, while in the petition the material was labelled as low-grade ore. What tipped the scale against the petitioner was the unusual dispatch in disposing the case in just three months without the concerned government departments filing pleadings:

> The courts should share the legislative concern to conserve the forests and the mineral wealth of the country. Courts should be vigilant in issuing final or interim orders in forest/mining/environment matters so that unscrupulous operators do not abuse the process of courts to indulge in large-scale violations or rob the country of its mineral wealth or secure orders by misrepresentation to circumvent the procedural safeguards under the relevant statutes. The court should also realise that the Central Government and the State Governments are huge and complex organisations and many a time require considerable time to secure information and provide them to the court, in matters requiring enquiry, investigation or probe. Where writ petitions involving disputed questions of fact in regard to forest/mining/environment matters, come up for consideration, courts should give sufficient time and latitude to the Ministries/departments concerned to file their objections/counter-affidavits after thoroughly verifying the facts. If there is undue hurry, the Ministries/departments concerned will not be able to make proper or thorough verifications and place the correct facts. Instances are not wanting where the public interest will be sabotaged, by the officers of the State/Central Government who are supposed to safeguard the public interest, by colluding with the unscrupulous operators. A wrong decision in such matters may lead to disastrous results—in regard to public interest—financially and ecologically. Therefore, writ petitions involving mineral wealth, forest conservation or environmental protection should not be disposed of without giving due opportunity to the departments concerned to verify the facts and file their counter-affidavits/objections in writing.[77]

An unseen factor may have affected this case. The Karnataka High Court division bench that decided the petition was presided over by Chief Justice P D Dinakaran. In August 2009, the Supreme Court collegium recommended Justice Dinakaran's elevation to the Supreme Court. The Forum for Judicial Accountability, Chennai protested the elevation and accused Justice Dinakaran of corruption and serious irregularities. The storm that ensued blocked Justice Dinakaran's elevation to the Supreme Court. Might this public controversy including an impeachment motion against Justice Dinakaran have influenced the outcome of the appeal?

[77] *State of Karnataka v Janthakal Enterprises* (2011) 6 SCC 695, 703.

Goa

Goa produces low-grade iron ore which is mostly exported to Japan and China. Responding to widespread complaints about illegal iron ore and manganese ore mining in several states, the Central Government appointed the Justice M B Shah Commission under the Commissions of Inquiry Act of 1952. The Commission's remit was extensive:

(i) to inquire into and determine the nature and extent of mining and trade and transportation, done illegally or without lawful authority, of iron ore and manganese ore, and the losses therefrom; and to identify, as far as possible, the persons, firms, companies and others that are engaged in such mining, trade and transportation of iron ore and manganese ore, done illegally or without lawful authority;

(ii) to inquire into and determine the extent to which the management, regulatory and monitoring systems have failed to deter, prevent, detect and punish offences relating to mining, storage, transportation, trade and export of such ore, done illegally or without lawful authority, and the persons responsible for the same;

(iii) to inquire into the tampering of official records, including records relating to land and boundaries, to facilitate illegal mining and identify, as far as possible, the persons responsible for such tampering; and

(iv) to inquire into the overall impact of such mining, trade transportation and export done illegally or without lawful authority, in terms of destruction of forest wealth, damage to the environment, prejudice to the livelihood and other rights of tribal people, forest dwellers and other persons in the mined areas, and the financial losses caused to the Central and State Governments.

The Commission submitted an interim report on 15 March 2012. It uncovered and investigated the widespread disregard for mining and environmental laws. As a result, Goa suspended all mining operations on 11 September 2012. Subsequently, District Magistrates issued orders also banning transport of iron ore. On 14 September 2012, the MoEF suspended all environmental clearances granted to mines in the state.

The Goa Foundation petitioned the Supreme Court. It sought termination of the mining leases since the mines had violated the mining laws as well as the Forest (Conservation) Act of 1980, the Water Act of 1974, the Air Act of 1981 and the Wild Life (Protection) Act of 1972. The foundation also sought prosecution of offenders including officials who had abetted the illegal mining activity. Several mining lessees moved the Goa Bench of the Bombay High Court challenging the Shah Commission Report and the consequential government action. These petitions were transferred to the Supreme Court and were decided along with Goa Foundation's writ petition on 21 April 2014. We carry a short excerpt.

GOA FOUNDATION v UNION OF INDIA

(2014) 6 SCC 590

A K Patnaik, J:

* * *

We, therefore, find that the Expert Committee as well as Indian School of Mines (ISM), Dhanbad, after considering the available data and after considering the adverse impact on environment and the limited carrying capacity of the transport system in Goa, are of the opinion that a cap between 20 to 27.5 million tons per annum should be fixed for excavation of iron ore in the State of Goa. In its recommendations, however, the Expert Committee has suggested that till the scientific study by the Expert Committee is completed in about 12 months or so, and more of data including impacts on different ecological environmental parameters is available through monitoring of the impacts by different agencies including the Goa State Pollution Control Board, 20 million tons per annum should be fixed as the annual excavation of iron ore in Goa. Even this mining of 20 million tons per annum in the State of Goa, according to the Expert Committee, has to be strictly monitored and regulated by the Department of Mines and Geology, Government of Goa and the Goa State Pollution

Control Board in consultation with other statutory bodies such as the Indian Bureau of Mines, the Ministry of Environment and Forests (Government of India) and others. It was the responsibility of the Government of Goa, Department of Mines, to enforce the provisions of the MMDR Act, the MC Rules and the MCD Rules, but as we have already noticed, this responsibility was not properly discharged. We hope that in future, it will enforce the provisions of the MMDR Act, the MC Rules, the MCD Rules and the Goa (Prevention of Illegal Mining, Storage and Transportation of Minerals) Rules, 2013....

It will be clear from the aforesaid provisions of section 33-A of the [Water Act, 1974] and section 31-A of the [Air Act, 1981] that the Goa State Pollution Control Board had powers to issue any direction including the power to close, prohibit or regulate mining operations or even to stop or regulate supply of electricity, water or any other service with a view to prevent water pollution or air pollution. Yet, from the report of the Expert Committee as well as the reports of ISM, Dhanbad and NEERI, it is clear that iron ore production in Goa has led to massive negative impacts on all ecosystems leading to enhanced air, water and soil pollution affecting quality of life across Goa....

We do not agree with ... learned Senior Counsel for the Goa State Pollution Control Board, that sincere efforts were made by the Pollution Control Board to monitor the water quality and air quality in the mining areas. Rather, it appears that the Goa State Pollution Control Board, though conferred with immense statutory powers, has failed to discharge its statutory functions and duties. We hope that in future the Goa State Pollution Control Board exercises strict vigil and monitors the water quality and air quality in accordance with the provisions of the two Acts and if necessary, exercises the powers conferred on it to close down mining operation of a lessee, if the lessee does not conform to the air emission and water discharge standards while carrying on mining operations and does not take other preventive measures as directed by the State Pollution Control Board....

The regulatory and monitoring measures enforced by the Departments of Mines and Geology, the Goa State Pollution Control Board and the Regulator appointed by the Central Government under sub-section (3) of section 3 of the Environment (Protection) Act, 1986 cannot, however, restore entirely the environment that is damaged in course of mining operations. The Expert Committee has, therefore, recommended that a permanent fund for intergenerational equity and sustainability of mining for all times to come named as 'Goan Iron Ore Permanent Fund' be created and an expert group may be constituted by the State for working out the details of this fund. [L]earned *amicus curiae*, submitted that as the lessees of mining leases earn out of the sale proceeds of the iron ore excavated by them, they should be directed to contribute 10% of the sale proceeds of all iron ore excavated in the State of Goa and sold by them towards the Goan Iron Ore Permanent Fund. He cited the judgment of this Court in *Samaj Parivartana Samudaya v State of Karnataka* (2013) 8 SCC 154 in which this Court has similarly directed for creation of a Special Purpose Vehicle out of 10% of the sale proceeds of the ore sold by e-auction. There is a lot of force in the aforesaid submission....

We find from the report of the Expert Committee that the State of Goa heavily depends on iron ore mining for revenue as well as employment. The legislative policy behind the MMDR Act made by Parliament is mineral development through mining. The State Government of Goa has also adopted the executive policy to encourage mining of minerals in Goa. Moreover, as ... learned Senior Counsel appearing for 33 Panchayats, has submitted about 1.5 lakh people are directly employed in mining in Goa and large number of persons have taken bank loans and purchased trucks for transportation of iron ore. Hence, people who earn their livelihood through work in connection with mining will be seriously affected if mining is totally banned to protect the environment. We cannot, therefore, prohibit mining altogether, but if mining has to continue, the lessees who benefit the most from mining, must contribute from their sale proceeds to the Goan Iron Ore Permanent Fund for sustainable mining. Accordingly, in exercise of our powers under Article 32 read with Article 21 of the Constitution, we direct that henceforth 10% of the sale proceeds of iron ore excavated in the State of Goa and sold by the lessees must be appropriated towards the Goan Iron Ore

Permanent Fund for the purpose of sustainable development and intergenerational equity and the State of Goa in consultation with CEC will frame a comprehensive scheme in this regard and submit the same to this Court within six months....

In the result, we declare that:

The deemed mining leases of the lessees in Goa expired on 22-11-1987 and the maximum of 20 years' renewal period of the deemed mining leases in Goa expired on 22-11-2007 and consequently mining by the lessees after 22-11-2007 was illegal and hence the impugned Order dated 10-9-2012 of Government of Goa and the impugned Order dated 14-9-2012 of MoEF, Government of India are not liable to be quashed.

Dumping of minerals outside the leased area of the mining lessees is not permissible under the MMDR Act and the Rules made thereunder.

Until the order dated 4-8-2006 [*T N Godavarman Thirumulpad v Union of India* (2010) 13 SCC 740] of this Court is modified by this Court in IA No. 1000 in *T N Godavarman Thirumulpad v Union of India*, there can be no mining activities within one kilometre from the boundaries of national parks and sanctuaries in Goa.

By the order dated 4-12-2006 in *Goa Foundation v Union of India*, (2011) 15 SCC 791, this Court has not prohibited mining activities within 10 kilometres' distance from the boundaries of the national parks or wildlife sanctuaries.

It is for the State Government to decide as a matter of policy in what manner mining leases are to be granted in future but the constitutionality or legality of the decision of the State Government can be examined by the Court in exercise of its power of judicial review.

And we direct that:

MoEF will issue the notification of eco-sensitive zones around the national park and wildlife sanctuaries of Goa after following the procedure discussed in this judgment within a period of six months from today.

The State Government will initiate action against those mining lessees who violate rules 37 and 38 of the MC Rules.

The State Government will strictly enforce the Goa (Prevention of Illegal Mining, Storage and Transportation of Minerals) Rules, 2013.

The State Government may grant mining leases of iron ore and other ores in Goa in accordance with its policy decision and in accordance with the MMDR Act and the Rules made thereunder in consonance with the constitutional provisions.

Until the final report is submitted by the Expert Committee, the State Government will, in the interests of sustainable development and intergenerational equity, permit a maximum annual excavation of 20 million MT from the mining leases in the State of Goa other than from dumps.

The Goa Pollution Control Board will strictly monitor the air and water pollution in the mining areas and exercise powers available to it under the 1974 Act and the 1981 Act including the powers under section 33-A of the 1974 Act and section 31-A of the 1981 Act and furnish all relevant data to the Expert Committee.

The entire sale value of the e-auction of the inventoried ores will be forthwith realised and out of the total sale value, the Director of Mines and Geology, Government of Goa, under the supervision of the Monitoring Committee will make the following payments:

(a) Average cost of excavation of iron ores to the mining lessees;

(b) 50% of the wages and dearness allowance to the workers in the muster rolls of the mining leases who have not been paid their wages during the period of suspension of mining operations;

(c) 50% of the claim towards storage charges of Marmagao Port Trust.

Out of the balance, 10% will be appropriated towards the Goan Iron Ore Permanent Fund and the remaining amount will be appropriated by the State Government as the owner of the ores.

The Monitoring Committee will submit its final report on the utilisation and appropriation of the sale proceeds of the inventoried ores in the manner directed in this judgment within six months from today.

Henceforth, the mining lessees of iron ore will have to pay 10% of the sale price of the iron ore sold by them to the Goan Iron Ore Permanent Fund.

The State Government will within six months from today frame a comprehensive scheme with regard to the Goan Iron Ore Permanent Fund in consultation with CEC for sustainable development and intergenerational equity and submit the same to this Court within six months from today; and

The Expert Committee will submit its report within six months from today on how the mining dumps in the State of Goa should be dealt with and will submit its final report within twelve months from today on the cap to be put on the annual excavation of iron ore in Goa. . . .

NOTES AND QUESTIONS

1. As it did in the *Bellary* case,[78] the Supreme Court in *Goa Foundation* passed an interim order to verify the inventory and conduct e-auctions of iron ore lying in Goa.[79] In addition, the court acknowledged the immediate need to eliminate continued pressure on the state's transport infrastructure. Importantly, it recognized the urgency of conserving iron for future generations and limiting the environmental degradation that its production involves. Considering these objectives, the court constituted an Expert Committee to conduct a macro EIA study and explore the possibility of fixing a cap on the annual iron ore excavation in the state.

2. The Supreme Court found that the state machinery in Goa was compromised and unable to stand up against the miners. Until the Shah Commission submitted its interim report, government departments were incapable of taking tough regulatory action against the lessees. Even after the Shah Commission Report, the Supreme Court was compelled to intervene at the request of the Goa Foundation, reflecting a lack of confidence in Goa's ability to turn over a new leaf.

3. The issue of cancelling leases did not arise here (unlike *Bellary*) since the court held that all the mining leases in Goa expired on 22 November 2007. Consequently, the state was directed to frame a policy for granting future leases.

4. The lessees asked the Supreme Court to ignore the Shah Commission Report. They argued that the Commission had failed to follow the statutory procedure and grant an adequate opportunity to the lessees to put forward their explanations. Consequently, the Supreme Court relied upon the report of the Central Empowered Committee (CEC) and the report of the court-appointed Expert Committee to conclude that there were pervasive violations of mining and environmental laws.

5. The magnitude of illegal mining was brought home by the massive disparity in the iron ore export figures and the total production as disclosed to the Indian Bureau of Mines. For a period of five years commencing 2006–07, the exports from Goa exceeded production by around 396 lakh metric tonnes. According to the CEC, this was illegally mined ore.

---

[78] *Samaj Parivartana Samudaya v State of Karnataka* (2013) 8 SCC 154.

[79] *Goa Foundation v Union of India* (2014) 6 SCC 738.

6. While courts decide cases based on pleadings, the evidence and an application of the law, a wide chasm often separates the ground reality and the set of facts before a court. The backstory and political economy behind this case is explored from the perspective of an environmentalist by Hartman De Souza in his compelling tract *Eat Dust: Mining and Greed in Goa* (2015). The book recognizes the role played by Dr Claude Alvares of the Goa Foundation and U V Singh, the former Chief Conservator of Forests, Karnataka who unearthed the illegalities at Bellary and Goa.

In *A Chowgule & Co*, the Supreme Court followed a string of judgments to reaffirm the principle that a lease executed in violation of the Forest (Conservation) Act of 1980 is void. The Central Government's prior approval is imperative before diverting any forest land. Chowgule was engaged in mining and exporting iron ore. It executed a lease on 1 November 1989 for an area of 12 hectares in Sanguem Taluka, Goa, tied up an export contract with a Japanese corporation and secured permissions from various state agencies including the pollution control board. The company installed machinery worth Rs. 12 crores for processing the iron ore.

In 1992, the Goa Foundation filed a public interest petition before the High Court challenging the lease, since forest land was being diverted without statutory permission under the FCA. While the petition was pending, the MoEF issued an approval for diverting 4.44 hectares of forest land (being part of the lease) on conditions which Chowgule claimed were fulfilled.

The High Court allowed the petition and cancelled the lease. A division bench of the Bombay High Court concluded that prior approval was the *sine qua non* for execution of the lease and the *ex post facto* decision would not save the lease. In addition, establishing a beneficiation plant would generate dust and water pollution that would adversely impact the adjoining forest and ecology. Consequently, the lease was held to be 'still born'.

The Supreme Court concurred, emphasizing the procedure prescribed in the rules under the FCA. The following excerpt makes the distinction between reforestation and afforestation and draws attention to the shrinking space for birds and reptiles as the human footprint expands.

A CHOWGULE AND COMPANY LTD v GOA FOUNDATION
(2008) 12 SCC 646

***

Harjit Singh Bedi, J:

The basic question is as to what is implied by the terms afforestation or reforestation. Is it merely the replacement of one tree with another or does it imply something a little more complex? 'Reforestation is the restocking of existing forests and woodlands which have been depleted, with *native tree stock*, whereas afforestation is the process of restoring and recreating areas of woodlands or forest that once existed but were deforested or otherwise removed or destroyed at some point in the past.'

In the present case, we are concerned with afforestation and the promise of the appellant to plant trees in an equivalent area. We, however, find from experience and observation that the reforestation or afforestation that is being carried out in India does not meet the fundamentals and the planting of new trees to match the numbers removed is too simplistic and archaic a solution, as in the guise of compensatory replantation, local varieties of trees are being replaced by alien and non-indigenous but fast growing varieties such as poplar and eucalyptus which make up the numbers but cannot satisfy the needs of our environmental system. It must be borne in mind that both reforestation and afforestation envisage a resurrection and replantation of trees and other flora similar to those which have been removed and which are suitable to the area in question.

> There is yet another circumstance which is even more disturbing inasmuch as the removal of existing forest or trees suited to the local environment has destroyed the ecosystem dependent on them. This is evident from the huge depletion of wildlife on account of the disturbance of the habitat arising out of the destruction of the existing forest cover. A small but significant example is the destruction of plantations alongside the arterial roads in India. 30 years ago all arterial roads had huge peripheral forest cover which not only provided shade and shelter to the travellers but were a haven to a large variety and number of birds and other wildlife peculiar to that area.
>
> With the removal of these plantations to widen the roads to meet the ever-growing needs of the traffic, and their replacement by trees of non-indigenous varieties (which are often not eco or bird friendly) in the restricted and remaining areas bordering the widened roads, the shelter for birds has been destroyed and where thousands of birds once nested and bred, there has been a virtual annihilation of the bird life as well.
>
> Those who live in North India would do well to remember that a drive along the Grand Trunk Road, National Highway No. 1, northwards of Delhi, particularly during the hours of dawn or dusk, was as if through an aviary with thousands of birds representing a myriad of species with their distinctive calls reaching a crescendo during early evening and gradually fading into silence as darkness set in. Sadly, all that can now be seen are crows feeding on the decaying and mutilated carcasses of dogs and other animals killed by speeding vehicles. Equally disturbing is the decrease in the reptilian population as the undergrowth in which it lived and prospered has been destroyed, and with the concomitant increase in the rodent population, colossal losses and damage to the farmer and in the storage of foodgrains....

NOTES AND QUESTIONS

1. The judgment makes a case for sharing the planet with its other inhabitants and adopting a suitable development model for doing so. Should animals have rights?

2. Despite the financial investment and the potential disruption of export revenue, the courts stood firm. They were unimpressed by Chowgule's plea that cancellation was excessive since MoEF's conditions were complied with and they were willing to afforest an equivalent area of land.

3. In the High Court, the forest department filed two affidavits. In the first affidavit, the Conservator of Forests stated that the leased land was classified as Revenue Land meant for 'Dry Crops' and was not a forest area. Later, the Deputy Conservator of Forests filed another affidavit displaying keener vision. In the Supreme Court's telling:

> The plea of the appellant that the area concerned was not a forest was also repelled with the observations that an average of 250 trees per hectare were growing on the land, as was clear from the affidavit filed by the Deputy Conservator of Forests, R Nagbhushan Rao and that the entire area was heavily forested with 3000 trees and was in addition contiguous to the government forests.

Since the courts eventually accepted the existence of the forest, should action have been taken against the Conservator for conveying incorrect information?

Odisha

In 2009, Ravi Das, the editor of a newspaper, *Ama Rajdhani*, filed an interim application in the *Forest Conservation* case[80] drawing attention to illegal mining in Odisha. Das asked for the

[80] *T N Godavarman v Union of India*, Writ Petition (Civil) No. 202 of 1995.

CEC to carry out a fact-finding exercise. He sought directions to shut down mines, restore the damaged environment and prosecute and punish those found guilty of illegal mining.

Between November 2009 and January 2014, the Supreme Court issued a series of procedural directions but the case remained dormant. This was despite an interim report by the CEC, filed on 26 April 2010, that made general recommendations for mines working in the region.

Meanwhile, on 22 November 2010, the Central Government constituted the Justice M B Shah Commission under the Commissions of Inquiry Act of 1952. The Commission's remit extended to enquiring about illegal mining in iron and manganese ore. On 1 July 2013, the Commission made its first report on illegal mining in Odisha and noticed 'all modes of illegal mining' as well as 'the complete disregard and contempt for law and lawful authorities on the part of many of the emerging breed of entrepreneurs'. In its second report pertaining to Odisha, the Commission dealt with specific lease holders and the violations committed by them.

Armed with the Commission's reports, Common Cause filed an Article 32 petition before the Supreme Court in seeking a stop to the illegal mining, termination of the leases of violators and an investigation into crimes that appeared to have been committed. The petition also sought directions to disgorge 'the illegally accumulated wealth through illegal mining and related activity' and to use these amounts for the welfare of local communities, tribals and villagers.

On 16 May 2014, the Supreme Court passed a detailed interim order[81] based on CEC's final report dated 25 April 2014. The Supreme Court found that out of 187 leases granted in three districts of Odisha, 102 lease holders did not have the requisite statutory permissions under environmental laws.

After a lengthy hearing spanning several weeks, the Supreme Court rendered its final judgment on 2 August 2017. While the judgment examines the mining activity from several perspectives such as compliance with the mining laws and the Forest (Conservation) Act, the excerpt below focuses on the environment impact assessment regime.

COMMON CAUSE v UNION OF INDIA
(2017) 9 SCC 499

MADAN B LOKUR, J:

* * *

The facts revealed during the hearing of these writ petitions filed under Article 32 of the Constitution suggest a mining scandal of enormous proportions and one involving megabucks. The lessees in the districts of Keonjhar, Sundergarh and Mayurbhanj in Odisha have rapaciously mined iron ore and manganese ore, apparently destroyed the environment and forests and perhaps caused untold misery to the tribals in the area. However, to be fair to the lessees, they did detail the steps taken to ameliorate the hardships of the tribals, but it appears to us that their contribution is perhaps not more than a drop in the ocean—also too little, too late....

EIA Notification of 27.1.1994

As can be seen from the statutory scheme adverted to above, protection and preservation of the environment is a significant and integral component of a mining plan, a mining lease and mining operations—and rightly so.

Keeping this in mind, an Environment Impact Assessment Notification dated 27-1-1994 was issued by the Central Government. The Environment Impact Assessment Notification dated

[81] *Common Cause v Union of India* (2014) 14 SCC 155.

27-1-1994 (for short 'EIA 1994') is a prohibitory notification and directs that on and from the date of its publication in the Official Gazette:

(i) expansion or modernisation of any activity (if pollution load is to exceed the existing one); and
(ii) a new project listed in Schedule I to the notification;

shall not be undertaken unless it has been accorded environmental clearance (for short EC) by the Central Government in accordance with the procedure specified in the Notification.

The Notification provides, among other things, that in case of mining operations, site clearance shall be granted for a sanctioned capacity and shall be valid for a period of five years from commencing mining operations. What this means is that on receipt of an EC a mining leaseholder can extract a mineral only from a specified site, up to the sanctioned capacity and only for a period of five years from the date of the grant of an EC. This is regardless of the quantum of extraction permissible in the mining plan or the mining lease and regardless of the duration of the mining lease. Consequently, a mining leaseholder would necessarily have to obtain a fresh EC every five years and can also apply for an increase in the sanctioned capacity. There is no concept of a retrospective EC and its validity effectively starts only from the day it is granted. Thus, the EC takes precedence over the mining lease or to put it conversely, the mining operations under a mining lease are dependent on and 'subordinate' to the EC.

On 4-5-1994 an Explanatory Note was added to EIA 1994. We are concerned with the 1st Note which deals with the expansion and modernisation on of existing projects. This reads as follows:

> '1. *Expansion and modernisation of existing projects* — A project proponent is required to seek environmental clearance for a proposed expansion/modernisation activity if the resultant pollution load is to exceed the existing levels. The words 'pollution load' will in this context cover emissions, liquid effluents and solid or semi-solid wastes generated. A project proponent may approach the State Pollution Control Board (SPCB) concerned for certifying whether the proposed modernisation/expansion activity as listed in Schedule I to the notification is likely to exceed the existing pollution load or not. If it is certified that no increase is likely to occur in the existing pollution load due to the proposed expansion or modernisation, the project proponent will not be required to seek environmental clearance, but a copy of such certificate issued by the SPCB will have to be submitted to the Impact Assessment Agency (IAA) for information. The IAA will however, reserve the right to review such cases in the public interest if material facts justifying the need for such review come to light.'

The Note is significant and from its bare reading it is clear that if any proposed expansion or modernisation activity results in an increase in the pollution load, then a prior EC is required. The project proponent should approach the State Pollution Control Board concerned (for short 'SPCB') for certifying whether the proposed expansion or modernisation is likely to exceed the existing pollution load or not. If the pollution load is not likely to be exceeded, the project proponent will not be required to seek an EC but a copy of such a certificate from SPCB will require to be submitted to the Impact Assessment Agency which can review the certificate.

What is the requirement, if any, under EIA 1994 with regard to an existing mining lease where there is no proposal for expansion or modernisation? Does such a mining leaseholder require an EC to continue mining operations? This is answered in the 8th Note which is also of some importance and this reads as follows:

> '8. *Exemption for projects already initiated* — For projects listed in Schedule I to the notification in respect of which required land has been acquired and all relevant clearances of the State Government including NOC from the respective State Pollution Control Boards have been obtained before 27-1-1994, a project proponent will not

be required to seek environmental clearance from the IAA. However, those units who have not as yet commenced production will inform the IAA.'

The above Note makes it clear that existing mining projects that have a no-objection certificate from SPCB before 27-1-1994 will not be required to obtain an EC from the Impact Assessment Agency. Of course, this is subject to the substantive portion of EIA 1994 and the 1st Note. However, if the existing mining project does not have a no-objection certificate from SPCB, then an EC will be required under EIA 1994.

Two questions immediately arise from a reading of the 1st and the 8th Note. The first question is: What is the base year for considering the pollution load while proposing any expansion activity? The second question is: What is the duration for which an EC is not necessary for an ongoing project which does not propose any expansion, or to put it differently, what is the validity period for a no-objection certificate from SPCB?

In our opinion, as far as the first question is concerned, a reading of EIA 1994 read with the 1st Note implies that the base year would need to be the immediately preceding year, that is, 1993–94. This is obvious from the opening sentence of the 1st Note, that is,

> 'A project proponent is required to seek environmental clearance for a proposed expansion/modernisation activity if the resultant pollution load is to exceed the *existing levels*.'

In its report, CEC has taken 1993–94 as the base year and we see no error in this. Even the MoEF in its Circular dated 28-10-2004 stated with regard to the expansion in production:

> 'If the annual production of any year from 1994–95 onwards exceeds the annual production of 1993–94 or its preceding years (even if approved by IBM), it would constitute expansion.'

If that expansion results in an increase in the pollution load over the existing levels, then an EC is mandated....

It is clear from the decision rendered by this Court that EIA 1994 is mandatory in character; that it is applicable to all mining operations—expansion of production or even increase in lease area, modernisation of the extraction process, new mining projects and renewal of mining leases. A mining leaseholder is obliged to adhere to the terms and conditions of a mining lease and the applicable laws and the mere fact that a mining plan has been approved does not entitle a mining leaseholder to commence mining operations. In *M C Mehta v Union of India* (2004) 12 SCC 118 this Court concluded that EIA 1994 is clearly applicable to the renewal of a mining lease.

Subsequent to the decision in *M C Mehta* two clarificatory Circulars were issued by MoEF on 28-10-2004 and 25-4-2005. These were adverted to by the learned counsel for the mining leaseholders but in our opinion they are not relevant except to the extent that they make it explicit that following the decision of this Court in *M C Mehta*, an EC is required to be obtained before the renewal of a mining lease and that the term 'expansion' would include an increase in production or the lease area or both.

It was submitted on behalf of the mining leaseholders that the possibility of getting an *ex post facto* EC was a signal to the mining leaseholders that obtaining an EC was not mandatory or that if it was not obtained, the default was retrospectively condonable. We do not agree. We have referred to various provisions of the MMDR Act and the Rules framed thereunder to indicate the statutory importance given to the protection and preservation of the environment. This was also emphasized in *M C Mehta* in which it was also stated that:

> 'It does not appear that MoEF intended to legalise the commencement or continuance of mining activity without compliance of stipulations of the notification.'

It appears to us that the MoEF was, in a sense, cajoling the mining leaseholders to comply with the law and EIA 1994 rather than use the stick. That the mining leaseholders chose to misconstrue the soft implementation as a licence to not abide by the requirements of the law is unfortunate and was an act of omission or commission by them at their own peril. We cannot attribute insensitivity to the MoEF or even to the mining leaseholders to environment protection and preservation, but at the same time we cannot overlook the obligation of everyone to abide by the law. That the MoEF took a soft approach cannot be an escapist excuse for non-compliance with the law or EIA 1994.

EIA Notification of 14-9-2006

On 14-9-2006 another EIA Notification was issued by the MoEF. This notification (for short EIA 2006) required prior EC for projects or activities mentioned in the Schedule to it both for major as well as minor minerals if the leased area is 5 ha or more. We were informed that several mining leaseholders, in compliance with EIA 2006, applied for and were granted an EC....

All that we need to say on this subject is that there is no confusion, vagueness or uncertainty in the application of EIA 1994 and EIA 2006 insofar as mining operations were commenced on mining leases before 27-1-1994 (or even thereafter). Post EIA 2006, every mining leaseholder having a lease area of 5 ha or more and undertaking mining operations in respect of major minerals (with which we are concerned) was obliged to get an EC in terms of EIA 2006....

Finally, it was submitted that whenever an EC is granted, it would have retrospective effect from the date of the application for grant of an EC. In this context, it was pointed out that there were enormous delays in granting an EC and that the Hoda Committee had noted with reference to EIA 2006 that if all goes well, the grant of an EC takes about 232 days whereas the international norm is that an EC is granted within six months or 180 days. According to the additional affidavit filed by some mining leaseholders, the period of 232 days mentioned by the Hoda Committee was actually a conservative estimate and that in fact it takes anything up to 390 days for the grant of an EC. It was submitted that the position was even worse under EIA 1994 since the MoEF rarely showed any urgency in the grant of an EC. Examples were cited before us to show that in some instances the grant of an EC took more than two years. Taking all this into consideration it was submitted that it would be more appropriate that the EC is given retrospective effect from the date of the application.

We are not in agreement with the learned counsel for the mining leaseholders. There is no doubt that the grant of an EC cannot be taken as a mechanical exercise. It can only be granted after due diligence and reasonable care since damage to the environment can have a long-term impact. EIA 1994 is therefore very clear that if expansion or modernisation of any mining activity exceeds the existing pollution load, a prior EC is necessary and as already held by this Court in *M C Mehta* even for the renewal of a mining lease where there is no expansion or modernisation of any activity, a prior EC is necessary. Such importance having been given to an EC, the grant of an *ex post facto* environmental clearance would be detrimental to the environment and could lead to irreparable degradation of the environment. The concept of an *ex post facto* or a retrospective EC is completely alien to environmental jurisprudence including EIA 1994 and EIA 2006. We make it clear that an EC will come into force not earlier than the date of its grant....

NOTES AND QUESTIONS

1. This judgment is important for explaining the EIA regime and insisting on prior environmental clearance. Far too many projects across the country discount the importance of an EC by commencing work and presenting the authorities with a *fait accompli*. This judgment should strengthen the EIA law.

2. The judgment is also important in defining what constitutes 'illegal mining'. The court held that the holder of a mining lease must adhere to all mining as well as environmental

laws. 'If any mining operation is conducted in violation of any of these requirements, then that mining operation is illegal or unlawful. Any extraction of a mineral through an illegal or unlawful mining operation would become illegally or unlawfully extracted mineral.'[82]

3. Having given a broad interpretation to the notion of illegal mining, the Supreme Court proceeded to determine the quantum of disgorgement. The court reached out to section 21(5) of the MMDRA which provides that the state government may recover the price of the mineral from a person who has extracted mineral without lawful authority.

Rejecting the recommendation of the CEC and the Attorney General that 30% of the value of the illegally mined ore should be recovered, the Supreme Court directed recovery of 100% of the price of the mineral from every defaulting lessee.

4. The judgment appears incorrect in one respect. An EC by its very nature is a clearance that operates *for the life of the project*. This is the consistent global understanding. Once granted, the project may proceed and there is a system of reporting to the impact assessment agency to ensure that the conditions prescribed in the EC are followed. The court incorrectly holds that a mining lessee has to obtain a fresh EC every five years. The five years' period granted by the EIA notification is for commencing operations: the lessee must begin work within five years of the EC and should the lessee fail to do so, the EC lapses and the party must apply afresh. The Supreme Court's interpretation of a five-year EC is illogical. If extended to other large projects such as an industrial plant or a township or a dam it will mean that even though an EC is initially granted, midway through the project, the fresh EC may not be granted. What then is to happen to the investment?

Moreover, obtaining an EC is a one-time exercise involving a detailed impact assessment study, public hearing, etc. If such an exercise is to be repeated every few years, it will be impossible to get any project off the ground.

5. The petitioners urged the Supreme Court to lay down a cap on mining in Odisha on the principle of intergenerational equity. The court held that it was no part of its business to lay down limits on the extent of mining activities. Nevertheless, recognizing the importance of this submission, the court directed the Union Government to revisit the National Mineral Policy 2008 and devise a 'more effective, meaningful and implementable policy' so that 'rapacious mining' is controlled.

6. Having regard to the environmental devastation from iron ore mining and breakdown of the regulatory machinery in Karnataka, Goa and Odisha, would you regard India as a strong or weak Rule of Law state? Are strong, principled judgments like this one indicative of a robust regard for the Rule of Law or a symptom of how feeble the legal regime really is?

E. FORESTS AND DEVELOPMENT

I. THE *LAFARGE* CASE

The *Lafarge* case severely tested the judicial process. Here are the facts, cut to the bone. Lafarge, a multinational corporation, had established a cement factory in the northern plains of Bangladesh, close to the international boundary with India. The project was a symbol of Indo-Bangladesh cooperation and was supported by the Asian Development Bank and the International Finance Corporation. The manufacture of cement requires limestone,

[82] *Common Cause v Union of India* (2017) 9 SCC 499, 554.

but Bangladesh has none. In terms of an agreement between the governments of India and Bangladesh, Lafarge mined limestone in the East Khasi Hills District in the state of Meghalaya and transferred the limestone by a conveyor belt (7.2 km long within India) to its Bangladesh plant. In India, Lafarge had a captive limestone mine of 100 ha that provided the vital raw material without which the Bangladesh plant could not operate. Lafarge obtained an environmental clearance on 9 August 2001 on the basis that no diversion of forest land was involved. Mining commenced, limestone crushed in India was transported to Bangladesh and the cement factory hummed.

The mine site on the southern fringe of the Meghalaya plateau is characterized by limestone caverns and is technically described as karst topography. When Lafarge applied for environmental clearance, it described this land as 'barren' and supported its claim that there was no forest with a certificate dated 27 August 1997 issued by the Khasi Hills Autonomous District Council, Shillong (KHADC), a constitutional authority under the Sixth Schedule to the Constitution. The council certified that the area did not fall within a forest. Meanwhile, on 12 December 1996,[83] the Supreme Court clarified that a 'forest' for the purposes of the Forest (Conservation) Act of 1980 (FCA) must be understood in terms of the dictionary meaning apart from the description in the land records. To address this issue, Lafarge submitted a certificate dated 13 June 2000 from the District Forest Officer (DFO) asserting that there was no forest at the mining site and the tree density was 0.0009 per ha (i.e. 1 tree for every 10 sq kms). Since the 100 ha site corresponds to 1 sq km, the certificate declared there were no trees—consistent with Lafarge's description of the land being 'barren' or a near wasteland.

The Chief Conservator of Forests visited the limestone mine and was startled by what he saw. On 1 June 2006, he wrote to the Ministry of Environment and Forests (MoEF) that the area opened for mining was 'surrounded by thick natural vegetation cover with sizable number of tall trees'. On 9 April 2007, another Chief Conservator of Forests complained that the DFO's certificate of 13 June 2000 was misleading and that the mining lease area 'lies in the midst of virgin and natural forest'.

On 30 April 2007, the MoEF directed complete closure of mining activities by Lafarge. On 3 May 2007, Lafarge applied for forest clearance under the FCA 'without prejudice' to its claim that there was no forest. Lafarge then moved the Supreme Court for permission to operate its mine until the forest clearance application was decided. The Supreme Court initially permitted Lafarge to temporarily mine but later stopped mining on 5 February 2010.[84]

In response to a direction by the Supreme Court, the CEC submitted a report on 6 September 2007. The CEC stated that Lafarge should have sought permission under the FCA before starting operations. However, since a *fait accompli* obtained, it had no option but to recommend the case for grant of permission for use of the forest land for the mining lease, the conveyor belt system and associated activities.

A committee appointed by the MoEF (High Power Committee [HPC]) made a report on 5 April 2010 after a site inspection. The HPC found that there were 9,345 trees on the mining site, out of which 1,200 were already felled. Thereafter, on 19 April 2010, the MoEF granted a fresh environmental clearance followed by a forest clearance on 22 April 2010 (*ex post facto* clearance).

Before the Supreme Court, Lafarge was anxious to resume operations, and the Union Government supported this request. The *amicus curiae* submitted that the project was

---

[83] *T N Godavarman Thirumulpad v Union of India* (1997) 2 SCC 267.

[84] *T N Godavarman Thirumulpad v Union of India* (2010) 12 SCC 376.

established in brazen violation of the FCA and ought not to be regularized by grant of permission *ex post facto*. The Shella Action Committee (SAC), a registered society of local villagers, resisted resumption of mining since Lafarge's conduct was less than honourable. Lafarge had obtained its initial environmental clearance by representing the lease area to be barren, which was simply untrue. According to SAC, neither the MoEF nor the court ought to sanctify such conduct by allowing the project proponent to operate. The Supreme Court after an elaborate analysis thought otherwise. We carry a short excerpt from the judgment.

LAFARGE UMIAM MINING (P) LTD v UNION OF INDIA

(2011) 7 SCC 338

S H Kapadia, C J: * * *

Issues

(*i*) Nature of land;

(*ii*) Whether *ex post facto* environmental and forest clearances dated 19-4-2010 and 22-4-2010 respectively stood vitiated by alleged suppression by Lafarge regarding the nature of the land. In this connection it was contended by the learned *amicus* and by the learned counsel appearing on behalf of SAC that the EIA clearance under section 3 of the 1986 Act dated 9-8-2001 (being a parent clearance) was obtained by Lafarge on the basis of 'absence of forest' with full knowledge that the project site was located on forest land....

Nature of the land

In the Nehu Report of June 1997 (Rapid EIA Report of Proposed Limestone Mining Project at Nongtrai, Meghalaya), a brief history of limestone mining in Khasi Hills of Meghalaya is spelt out. It indicates that mining of limestone in Khasi Hills dates back to 10-7-1763 when an agreement was signed between the East India Company and the Nawab of Bengal for preparation of chunam. Regular trade of limestone from Khasi Hills of Bengal started on and from 1858. Substantial revenue was earned by the British Government from these limestone quarries as rentals, which was Rs.23,000 in 1858 and which subsequently stood increased to Rs.67,000 in 1878. The first historical account of exploitation of Nongtrai limestone dates back to 1885 when Don Rai of Shella obtained permits from the Wahadars (Heads of Confederacy) of Shella to quarry limestone in Nongtrai Village. There are historical records about continuance of limestone trade between Khasi Hills and Bengal up to 1947. The business declined after partition. Limestone mining and trade slipped into the hands of unorganised sector. According to the Nehu Report of 1997, today a number of private parties quarry limestone using unscientific methods and export it to counterparts in Bangladesh, often illegally. These private parties sell the product at a very low price....

One more aspect needs to be highlighted. According to the State of Forest Report, 2001, the north-eastern hill State of Meghalaya is predominantly tribal with 86% population being tribal. According to the Nehu Report of 1997, approximately 60 settlements consisting of 50–200 inhabitants each with a total estimated population of 16,500 persons exist within 10 km radius of the proposed mining site. Under an agreement dated 29-9-1993 (lease agreement), the village durbar represented by a Special Committee headed by the Headman as the lessor granted lease of the limestone quarry in Nongtrai to [Lafarge]. Thus, an area of 100 ha stood acquired on lease basis for mining whose lessor was the village durbar of Nongtrai.

Coming to the topography of the area, one finds that the limestone bearing area around Nongtrai and Shella Villages falls under karst topography. This area falls on the southern fringe of the Meghalaya plateau. Karst topography is characterised by limestone caverns/caves. The factum of limestone bearing area around Nongtrai and Shella falling under karst topography is also borne out by the certificate dated 27-8-1997 issued by Khadc, Shillong. This Council is a constitutional authority under the Sixth Schedule to the Constitution....

The site was selected after thorough consultation with the village durbar concerned who is the custodian of the land. The land was left unused covered with degraded forests and this was the reason for the Durbar to lease out the said land to the project proponent for mining.

The village durbar also felt that in the area unscientific limestone quarrying was going on resulting in loss of revenue both to the State as well as the inhabitants of the village particularly because the said mining was undertaken by unorganised sectors and, thus, it was decided to enter into the lease with the project proponent so that mining could be done on scientific basis. The site was also selected because of easy accessibility by road and less vegetation clearance stood involved. According to the NEHU Report, the site is located in the area on the outskirts of the forest.

Validity of ex post facto clearance An important argument has been advanced on behalf of SAC that the site clearance dated 18-6-1999 and EIA clearance dated 9-8-2001 were based on misrepresentation by Lafarge. They proceeded on the basis that there was no forest. That, both the said clearances stood vitiated by suppression of material fact of existence of forest by Lafarge and as a sequel the subsequent revised environmental clearance dated 19-4-2010 and forest clearance (Stage I) dated 22-4-2010 stood vitiated. In this connection, it was submitted that having regard to Para 4.3.1 of the National Forest Policy, 1988 tropical rain/moist forest is required to be totally safeguarded; that, the project is located in a tropical moist forest and no forest clearance ought to have been granted by MoEF because of the special ecological significance recognised by the 1988 Policy.

According to SAC, the fact that tropical moist forest existed in the area and continues to exist was known to Lafarge at all material times as can be seen from the NEHU Report of 1997 in which it has been categorically stated that the vegetation at the study site is a mixed moist deciduous forest composed of deciduous and evergreen tree elements; that, in the same report it has been further stated that the vegetation of the area is a tropical semi-evergreen forest composed of deciduous and evergreen elements which is further corroborated by the assessment of floral diversity prepared by NEHU dated June 2010 in which it has been stated that the forest in the study area is tropical moist deciduous forest, tropical semi-evergreen forest, savannah, subtropical broad-leaved forest, forest garden, orchards and riparian forest; that, the vegetation in the unbroken area is tropical moist deciduous type with variable canopy cover mostly sparse. Thus, according to SAC and CEC, the undisputed position emerging from the record that the subject area is covered by a tropical moist forest deserving highest degree of ecological protection ought to have been taken into account by MoEF which was not done at the time of initial clearances dated 18-6-1999 and 9-8-2001.

[L]earned Senior Counsel appearing for SAC submitted before us that the case in hand essentially deals with the decision-making process in relation to the grant of environmental clearance and to test whether the decision-making process stood up to judicial review. According to the learned counsel, the following basic points regarding the legal framework must be kept in view. From the environmental perspective, in relation to a mining project, there are three main sets of permissions that are required to be obtained:

(i) The first set of permissions is at the State level. This set of permissions primarily has to do with pollution. In each State or a group of States, a Pollution Control Board issues consent/permit. These consents or permits are granted from a pollution perspective. The scope of enquiry is limited to pollution impacts. Obtaining such consents and permits are essential but they are not a substitute for compliance with other environmental laws.

(ii) The second set of permissions, according to the learned counsel, is with regard to environmental clearance. The scope of environmental clearance is wider than a pollution control clearance. The authority granting environmental clearance will look at broader impacts beyond pollution and will examine the effect of the project on the community, forests, wildlife, ground water, etc. which are beyond the scope of the Pollution Control Board examination. The exercise of granting environmental clearance with regard to a limestone mining project of the present magnitude requires MoEF clearance.

(iii) A clearance for diversion of forest under the 1980 Act which is granted by MoEF on the recommendation of the FAC should logically precede the grant of environmental clearance as the environmental clearance is broader in scope and deals with all aspects, one of which may be forest diversion.

Applying the said legal framework to the facts of the present case, the learned counsel appearing for SAC submitted that MoEF, as the authority which decides on diversion of forests and which grants environmental clearances, is duty-bound to examine the diversion application in the context of the 1988 Policy, particularly, where tropical moist forests are sought to be cleared by the project proponent. According to the learned counsel, where MoEF grants environmental clearance in ignorance of the existence of a forest due to misdeclaration, it is duty-bound to take severest possible action against the party that made the false declaration for profit.

According to the learned counsel, since impact assessment and EIA clearances are processes based on self-declarations by the project proponent(s), the decision-making by MoEF depends upon honest and cogent material supplied by the project proponent and since the said process is premised on a full and fair disclosure of relevant facts by the project proponent, in cases where material facts are not disclosed, MoEF should withdraw both the site as well as the environmental clearances. According to the learned counsel, the most important input in this regard must be received by MoEF in the course of its decision-making from the public which is an essential check for a failure to disclose correct facts or to have regard to environmental issues that may have escaped the attention of the project proponent. According to the learned counsel, the requirement of public hearing is, thus, mandatory both under the 1994 Notification and the 2006 Notification. That, the requirement for payment of NPV does not automatically mean that environmental clearance is to be granted.

We are in full agreement with the legal framework suggested by the learned counsel for SAC. There is no dispute on that point. The question is confined to the application of the legal framework to the facts of the present case. Can it be said on the above facts that a misdeclaration was wilfully made by Lafarge or its predecessor (project proponent) while seeking site and environmental clearances? Was there non-application of mind by MoEF in granting such clearances? Was the decision of MoEF based solely on the declarations made by the project proponent(s)?

At the outset, one needs to take note of section 2 of the 1980 Act which stipulates prior approval. That section refers to restriction on the dereservation of forests or use of forest land for non-forest purpose. It begins with non obstante clause. It states that:

> '2. *Restriction on the dereservation of forests or use of forest land for non-forest purpose.* — Notwithstanding anything contained in any other law for the time being in force in a State, no State Government or other authority shall make, except with the prior approval of the Central Government, any order directing—
>
> (i) ...
>
> (ii) that any forest land or any portion thereof may be used for any non-forest purpose;'

This is how the concept of prior approval by the Central Government comes into picture. Thus, prior determination of what constitutes 'forest land' is required to be done.

* * *

While granting environmental clearance dated 9-8-2001 there was an express finding to the effect that 'no diversion of forest land was involved'. In terms of the order of this Court dated 12-12-1996 [*T N Godavarman Thirumulpad v Union of India* (1997) 2 SCC 267], an Expert Committee was in fact formed by the State of Meghalaya vide Notification dated 8-1-1997 with the Principal Chief Conservator of Forests as its Chairman. On 10-2-1997, the State of Meghalaya had addressed a specific letter to the Khasi Hills Autonomous District Council, which as stated above is a constitutional authority, stating that the land in question was reckoned as non-forest land and the Council was asked to clarify whether the area in question under the mining lease fell in the forest as per the records of the Council.

The Council by its letter dated 28-4-1997 had informed the State Government that the area in question did not fall in the forest. Apart from the said letter, the Chairperson of the Expert Committee appointed by the State of Meghalaya being the Principal Chief Conservator of Forests also submitted his report in which it was expressly stated that the mining lease granted by the State Government did not fall in the forest. Since the mining lease granted by the State did not fall in the forest, the State Government did not submit any proposal to the Central Government under section 2 of the 1980 Act as it treated the site in question as falling on the outskirts of the forests. It is almost after nine years that there was a change of view on the part of MoEF under which the report of the Expert Committee headed by the Principal Chief Conservator of Forests was given a go-by. Between 1997 and 2007, the view which prevailed was that the project site stood located on the outskirts of the forests.

In this connection, it needs to be stated that on 1-6-2006 for the first time the Chief Conservator of Forests (C), Shri Khazan Singh came out with the change of view which was ultimately accepted in 2007 by MoEF. According to the Chief Conservator of Forests (C), he had visited the limestone mining project of Lafarge on 24-5-2006 when he found that the mining lease area stood surrounded by thick natural vegetation covered with sizeable number of tall trees and in the circumstances he recommended that the project proponent should be directed to obtain clearance under the 1980 Act and not to carry on the mining activities till such clearance is obtained.

The most important fact is that subsequent to the letter dated 1-6-2006, addressed by the Chief Conservator of Forests (C), Shri Khazan Singh, the Principal Chief Conservator of Forests agreed with the opinion of the Chief Conservator of Forests (C). This was by letter dated 11-5-2007. However, even according to the Principal Chief Conservator of Forests, who was the Chairperson of the Expert Committee appointed by the State Government, Lafarge was not at fault because the certificate indicating absence of forests was given by the Khasi Hills Autonomous District Council. In fact, the letter dated 11-5-2007 further goes to state that the activities of Lafarge will provide employment to a large number of local tribals and rural people and consequently the application for forest clearance made by Lafarge without prejudice to their rights and contentions dated 3-5-2007 be considered by MoEF.

At this stage one more argument advanced on behalf of SAC needs to be addressed. According to SAC, in this case a decisive factor which clearly shows that there is 'forest' on the core area is the statutory definition of forest contained in the United Khasi and Jaintia Hills Autonomous District (Management and Control of Forests) Act, 1958. Section 2(f) defines the expression 'forest' and the tree count emerging from the High-Powered Committee (HPC) Report which establishes that the area answers the statutory definition. According to SAC, in terms of the said definition of forest, if there exist more than 25 trees per acre then it is a forest. This argument has no merit.

According to . . . learned Senior Counsel appearing on behalf of the village durbar of Nongtrai Village (Respondent 5), SAC has not stated the full facts in this regard. We find merit in this contention. Section 5 of the 1958 Act *inter alia* provides that no timber or forest produce shall be removed for the purpose of sale, trade and *business* without prior permission. Section 7 of the said Act deals with restrictions on felling of trees and further provides that no tree below 1.37 m in girth at the breast level shall be felled. Thus, it is the trees of a particular girth and breast height and not every tree should be counted while computing whether a particular area is a forest area or not. In fact, in the year 2007, a survey of the unbroken area was conducted by the Forest Department of the State of Meghalaya wherein an inventory of the existing trees was prepared based on their nature and girth. The said record confirms that the unbroken area has less than 25 trees per acre having girth of more than 120 cm per acre.

It is in view of the existence of the 1958 Act, which is a local legislation, that the native people as also the State officials like the DFO understood the area in the light of the said Act. It is important to note once again that this understanding of the natives and tribals about the Local Act is an important input in the decision-making process of granting environmental clearance. It is deeply engrained in the local customary law and usage. It is so understood by the Expert Committee headed by the then Principal Chief Conservator of Forests on the basis of which the State granted the mining lease saying that there was no forest. This certificate was granted by the State in terms of the order of this Court dated 12-12-1996 [*T N Godavarman Thirumulpad v Union of India* (1997) 2 SCC 267].

This understanding also existed in the mind of KHADC when it gave certificates on 28-4-1997, 10-7-1997 and 27-8-1997. In fact, this has been the understanding of the Council as is apparent even from its letter dated 18-1-2011 (see p. 126 of the affidavit dated 9-3-2011 filed by the State of Meghalaya). As stated above, this view prevailed with MoEF between 1997 and 2007. The word 'environment' has different facets (see SCC para 127 of the judgment of this Court in *Narmada Bachao Andolan* [(2000) 10 SCC 664]). On the above facts, it is not possible for us to hold that the decision to grant *ex post facto* clearances stood vitiated on account of non-application of mind or on account of suppression of material facts by Lafarge as alleged by SAC.

Similarly, it is not possible for us to hold on the above facts that *ex post facto* clearances have been granted by MoEF in ignorance of the existence of forests due to misdeclaration....

NOTES AND QUESTIONS

1. The Supreme Court rejected the submission that the project proponent wilfully misstated the facts while seeking environmental clearance. Was this conclusion justified? In its application, the limestone mine area was described as 'barren' and Lafarge relied on a DFO's certificate which specified the tree density at around 1 tree for every 10 sq kms. The HPC on an inspection of the 1 sq km leased area found that there were 9,345 trees out of which 1,200 were felled. Is it conceivable that a project proponent could honestly miss 9,345 trees? Does a landscape with 9,345 trees strike you as 'barren'? How were the trees invisible to the DFO? Do you think he visited the site? Remember, two Chief Conservators of Forests found thick natural vegetation at the mine site.

Were the Supreme Court judges simply gullible or is there a more compelling explanation to justify this conclusion and the outcome of the case?

2. Although the analysis in the judgment is entirely within the frame of Indian law, the court was aware of the diplomatic repercussions if Lafarge's limestone mine in Meghalaya was shut down. The cement factory put up in Bangladesh at great expense was an important economic asset. The manufacturing operations depended on India honouring its cross-border commitment to permit limestone mining and transport of limestone to Bangladesh. Bangladesh was entitled to assume that all permissions required were validly issued in India. Should a court in these circumstances issue an order that may jeopardize friendly relations with a neighbouring country? Or is this an irrelevant consideration when interpreting and applying municipal environmental laws?

3. As societies develop and economies grow, it is physically impossible for government agencies to independently verify every fact contained in an application seeking an environmental clearance. This reality extends to other fields of regulation as well. Generally, government departments require the applicant to make an honest disclosure of all facts and the department then proceeds on the basis that the statements are true. This honour system is premised on stern action should any material statement be found false. The efficacy of an honour system is eroded where a party caught out is allowed to retain the fruit of its misstatement. Is the *Lafarge* judgment consistent with this basic norm in modern administration? Will it tempt project proponents to cast an invisibility cloak over forest lands and charm local authorities to issue unreal certificates?

4. When it comes to enforcing section 2 of the FCA, the Supreme Court is generally strict. Indeed, the saga of the *Forest Conservation* case is testimony to this commitment. Where a project proponent requires forest land and approaches the Supreme Court, the court usually refers the matter to the CEC and is guided by its recommendation. While prior permission

for diversion of forest land to a non-forest purpose is the rule, on occasion the Supreme Court is confronted with a *fait accompli* where the project stands commissioned at great cost, but is found to lack forest clearance. The judicial dilemma is how to protect the environment without jeopardizing the enterprise. The resolution frequently takes the shape of a 'pay and play' formula: Put down some extra money for environmental restoration and community uplift, and then continue business.

In *Lafarge*, the court stipulated several conditions beyond the usual conditions imposed by the MoEF when granting environmental clearance and forest clearance. These conditions included: (a) Lafarge depositing Rs. 55 crores towards five times of the normal NPV[85] (as recommended by the CEC) with interest at 9% per annum from 1 April 2007; (b) formation of an SPV[86] under the chairmanship of the Chief Secretary, Meghalaya, which would receive Rs. 90 per tonne of the limestone mined from the date on which mining commenced;[87] (c) preparation of detailed plans by Lafarge with respect to catchment area treatment, air quality monitoring, forest rehabilitation and conservation, biodiversity management, etc.

5. The north-eastern states are a politically sensitive region with a special constitutional status conferred on autonomous councils that have tribal populations. The Supreme Court gives great weight to the certificate by the Khasi Hills Autonomous District Council (KHADC), a constitutional council exercising powers under the Sixth Schedule to the Constitution. The powers of KHADC include the power to allot land (other than land which is a reserved forest). The KHADC issued a certificate on 22 August 1997 that there was no forest at the site of the proposed mining lease. What is the worth of the KHADC certificate when every site inspection showed an abundance of natural growth and trees? Should the constitutional status of KHADC make a difference to the court's approach? Or was the *Lafarge* court being suitably sensitive to local sentiment?

The Supreme Court also accorded due respect to the understanding of the local tribal community regarding the definition of 'forest' under the local Forest Act of 1958 (i.e. more than 25 trees per acre constituted a forest).[88] According to the court, the local understanding of this law required measurement of the girth of every tree, and trees with a narrow girth were excluded from the tree count for the purpose of the definition. Is this a sage interpretation or impractical humbug? How would you work such a statute?

6. The Supreme Court found no blameworthy conduct. It attributed the change of view on the part of the MoEF to a difference in perception. The local understanding of what constituted a forest (that guided Lafarge when it sought environmental clearance) was at odds with what the Chief Conservators of Forests saw for themselves many years later when they visited the site. The NEHU Rapid EIA Report of June 1997, referred to in the judgment and available to Lafarge when it sought environmental clearance, undercuts the court's conclusion. The NEHU Report records: (a) 'The vegetation at the study site is a mixed moist deciduous forest composed of deciduous and evergreen tree elements'; and (b) 'The vegetation of the area is a tropical semi-evergreen forest composed of deciduous and evergreen tree elements.'

---

[85] NPV denotes Net Present Value which is the monetary value of the forest being destroyed.

[86] SPV stands for Special Purpose Vehicle and is a corporation formed for a particular purpose.

[87] The SPV was charged with using its funds for development, health, education, irrigation and agriculture for the benefit of the local community and for the welfare of tribals.

[88] '2(f) "Forest" means and shall be deemed to be a forest, if in the area, there are reasonable number of trees, say, not less than 25 trees per acre, reserved or any other forest produce growing on such area, which have been or are capable of being exploited for purposes of business or trade.' Section 2(f) of the United Khasi Jaintia Hills Autonomous District (Management and Control of Forests) Act of 1958.

7. In a portion of the judgment that is not excerpted, the Supreme Court declared that the National Forest Policy of 1988 must necessarily govern the grant of permissions under section 2 of the FCA as the policy provides the road map to ecological protection and improvement. The principles and guidelines mentioned in the 1988 policy must be read as part of the Environment (Protection) Act of 1986 and the FCA. With this declaration, the Supreme Court reinforced its earlier determination[89] that the National Forest Policy 1988 has a statutory flavour. The Supreme Court also directed the Central Government to appoint a national regulator to ensure implementation of the forest policy.

8. Paragraph 4.3.1 of the National Forest Policy, 1988 in pertinent part reads:

> Tropical rain/moist forest, particularly in areas like Arunachal Pradesh, Kerala, Andaman and Nicobar islands, should be totally safeguarded.

Now that the Supreme Court has declared the 1988 policy as being statutory, does it render tropical rain/moist forest regions in the country as 'no-go' areas for industrial projects?

II. THE *OKHLA BIRD SANCTUARY* CASE

In January 2008, the Chief Minister of Uttar Pradesh commenced one of her favourite projects to set up a memorial park near New Delhi to honour Dalit leaders. The park was budgeted at Rs. 685 crores and covered an area previously used for five parks on the Yamuna front, including a children's park. The Chief Minister ensured that the iconography included her own statue.

The Forest Bench decision authored by Justice Aftab Alam is a dexterous exercise, navigating past three principal objections. The following excerpt covers the challenge with respect to the lack of a forest clearance and the park's proximity to a bird sanctuary. In the chapter on Environmental Impact Assessment, we carry another excerpt from this judgment focusing on the EIA issue. How persuasive is the Supreme Court's reasoning?

IN RE: CONSTRUCTION OF PARK AT NOIDA NEAR OKHLA BIRD SANCTUARY
(2011) 1 SCC 744

Aftab Alam, J: At the centre of the controversy is a very large project of the Uttar Pradesh Government at Noida. Objecting to the project are the two applicants who are residents of Sector 15-A, Noida, U.P. They claim to be public-spirited people, committed to the cause of environment. According to them, the project, undertaken at the instance of the Uttar Pradesh Government is a 'huge unauthorised construction'.

The applicants state that a very large number of trees were cut down for clearing the ground for the project. The trees that were felled down for the project formed a 'forest' as the term was construed by this Court in its order dated 12-12-1996 in *T N Godavarman Thirumulpad v Union of India* (1997) 2 SCC 267 and the action of the Uttar Pradesh Government in cutting down a veritable forest without the prior permission of the Central Government *and* this Court, was in gross violation of section 2(ii) of the Forest (Conservation) Act, 1980 (hereafter 'the FC Act'). The project involved massive constructions that were made without any prior environmental clearance from the Central Government based on environment impact assessment. The constructions were, therefore, in complete breach of the provisions of the Environment (Protection) Act, 1986 (hereafter 'the EP Act') and the notification issued under the Act. More importantly, the project was causing great harm, and was bound to further devastate the delicate and sensitive ecological balance of the Okhla Bird Sanctuary

[89] See *T N Godavarman Thirumulpad v Union of India* (2006) 1 SCC 1 excerpted earlier in this chapter.

to which the site of the project lay adjacent. The project was, thus, in complete disregard of this Court's directions concerning 'buffer zones'.

The State of Uttar Pradesh, of course denies, equally strongly, all the allegations made by the applicants. According to the State, it was setting up a park that would develop and beautify the area in a unique way. The park was conceived as a fine blend of hard and soft landscaping with memorial structures and commemoration pieces....

Section 2 of the FC Act, insofar as relevant for the present, provides as follows:

> '2. *Restriction on the de-reservation of forests or use of forest land for non-forest purpose* — Notwithstanding anything contained in any other law for the time being in force in a State, no State Government or other authority shall make, except with the prior approval of the Central Government, any order directing—
>
> (i) ...
>
> (ii) that any forest land or any portion thereof may be used for any non-forest purpose;
>
> (iii)–(iv) ...
>
> *Explanation* — For the purposes of this section 'non-forest purpose' means the breaking up or clearing of any forest land or portion thereof for—
>
> (a) the cultivation of tea, coffee, spices, rubber, palms, oil-bearing plants, horticultural crops or medicinal plants;
>
> (b) any purpose other than re-afforestation,
>
> but does not include any work relating or ancillary to conservation, development and management of forests and wildlife, namely, the establishment of checkposts, fire lines, wireless communications and construction of fencing, bridges and culverts, dams, waterholes, trench marks, boundary marks, pipelines or other like purposes.'

The restriction imposed by section 2(ii) is in respect of forest land. It, therefore, needs to be ascertained whether the project area can be said to be forest land where there was a forest that was cut to make the site clear for the project.

In support of the contention that the trees that were cleared for the construction of the project comprised a forest, the applicants rely heavily on the order passed by this Court on 12-12-1996 in *T N Godavarman Thirumulpad*, being the first in a series of landmark orders passed by this Court in an effort to save the fast diminishing forest cover of the country against the greedy and wanton plundering of its natural resources. In that order the Court gave a number of directions. One such direction, at Serial No. 5 to each of the State Governments, is as under:

> '5. (5) Each State Government should constitute within one month an Expert Committee to:
>
> (i) identify areas which are 'forests', irrespective of whether they are so notified, recognised or classified under any law, and irrespective of the ownership of the land of such forest;
>
> (ii) identify areas which were earlier forests but stand degraded, denuded or cleared; and
>
> (iii) dentify areas covered by plantation trees belonging to the Government and those belonging to private persons.'

In pursuance of the direction of the Court in *T N Godavarman Thirumulpad*, the Uttar Pradesh Government constituted the State Level Expert Committee for identifying forests and forest-like areas. The Committee in its report dated 12-12-2007 framed certain parameters for identification of forest-like areas according to which, in the plains, any stretch of land over 2 ha in area with the minimum density of 50 trees per hectare would be considered as 'forest'. On 11-1-2008 (as taken note of in the order of that date) it was reported to this Court that the guidelines were issued for identification of forest-like areas and steps would be taken to identify 'forest-like areas' in all the districts in the State of Uttar Pradesh within four months and such areas would be handed over to the Forest Department, excepting the private areas, if any.

As the process of search and identification of forest-like areas in the districts of Uttar Pradesh proceeded, the District Level Committee headed by the District Collector, Gautam Buddha Nagar, by its letter dated 26-2-2008 addressed to the Conservator of Forests and Regional Director intimated that there was no forest-like area in the district and consequently the project site was not identified as a forest or forest-like area by the State Level Expert Committee constituted in pursuance of this Court's order dated 12-12-1996. It was in this background that the project started, according to the State Government, in January 2008. When the work on the project became noticeable from the outside the applicants filed their complaint before the Central Empowered Committee (CEC) on 5-3-2009.

As the controversy erupted with regards to 'large-scale construction near the Okhla Bird Sanctuary by the State Government' the Ministry of Environment and Forests (hereafter 'MoEF') asked the Chief Conservator of Forests (CCF), Central Region, Lucknow, to make a site inspection of the project and to give his report. The CCF in his report dated 10-7-2009 did not accept the stand of the State Government that there was no forest on the project site. He stated that 6000 trees were 'sacrificed' in an area of 32.5 ha and that showed that the area had sufficiently dense forest cover and would qualify as 'forest' according to the dictionary meaning of the word and as directed by the Supreme Court. He, however, suggested that before taking a final view on the matter a report may be called for from the Forest Survey of India (hereafter 'FSI') in order to verify the vegetation cover over the area before the construction work started there.

In the light of the report by the CCF, the MoEF noted that the number of cut trees, in ratio to the project area, was apparently more than three times in excess of the criterion fixed by the State Level Expert Committee for identification of forest like areas (i.e. minimum of 50 trees per hectare). As suggested by the CCF, therefore, the MoEF called for a report from the FSI based on satellite imagery and properly analysed by GSI application from the year 2001 onwards (vide Letter dated 17-7-2009 from the Deputy Conservator of Forests (C) to the Director, Forest Survey of India). The FSI gave its report on 7-8-2009 which we shall examine presently. In light of the report of the CCF and the report from the FSI, MoEF in its first response to the applicants' complaint before the CEC (under covering letter that is undated, received at the CEC on 12-8-2009) stated that at the project site 'there was a good patch of forests and which *could* be treated as deemed forest'. It further said that the report of the FSI showed that the forest cover existed there up to 2006 and the felling of trees might have taken place after that only.

In the meeting convened by the CEC on the applicants' complaint on 12-8-2009, the Chief Conservator of Forests (CCF), MoEF, Lucknow stated that the plantation done in the project area was naturalised and having regard to the number of trees that existed in the area, the project area should be seen as 'deemed forest' and, therefore, it attracted the provisions of the FC Act, and any non-forest use of the land required prior approval of the Central Government. In view of the stand taken by the CCF, the CEC by its letter of 13-8-2009 requested the MoEF to give its response on the issue.

Here it may be noted that till that stage the stand of the MoEF, based on the reports of the CCF and the FSI, though tentative, seemed to be definitely inclined towards holding that the trees that were felled for clearing the site comprised a forest/deemed forest and the construction at the project site was hit by the provisions of the FC Act. But now in a perceptible shift in its stand the MoEF informed the CEC by its Letter of 22-8-2009/24-8-2009 that in its view, the project site did not attract the provisions of the FC Act. It referred to the order of this Court dated 12-12-1996 and pointed out that the project site did not appear in the list of deemed forest land identified by the State Level Expert Committee in pursuance of the order of the Court. It concluded by saying as follows:

> 'In view of the above, it is informed that the area under discussion is neither recorded as forest nor deemed forest and is actually an urban tree park. Therefore, construction work in this area does not attract the provisions of the Forest (Conservation) Act, 1980.'

The letter dated 22-8-2009/24-8-2009 from the MoEF was followed by another Letter of 2-9-2009. This was purportedly to put the observation in the previous letter that '... [C]onstruction work in this area does not attract the provisions of the Forest (Conservation) Act, 1980' in context. This letter referred to the satellite images provided by the FSI and the reports submitted by the CCF but in the end, 'given the sensitivity of the matter and the high degree of public interest' left it to the CEC to draw appropriate conclusions from the materials furnished to it.

The CEC on a consideration of all the materials made available to it, including the report of the FSI (on which the applicants heavily rely), came to hold and find that the project site was not a forest or a deemed forest or a forest-like area in terms of the order of this Court dated 12-12-1996. In its report to this Court dated 4-9-2009 it observed in this regard as follows:

> '28. ... In the present case, even though as per the report of the Forest Survey of India, the area was having good forest/tree cover and the project area had more than 6000 trees, it does not fall in the category of 'forest' for the purpose of Section 2 of the Forest (Conservation) Act and therefore does not require any approval under the Forest (Conservation) Act. *The project area does not have naturally grown trees but planted trees. The area has neither been notified as 'forest' nor recorded as 'forest' in the government record. In the exercise carried out by the State of Uttar Pradesh, after detailed guidelines for identification of deemed forest were laid down, the project area was not identified to be deemed forest.* The CEC does not agree with the Regional Chief Conservator of Forests, MoEF, Lucknow that the plantation done in the area has naturalised because of natural regeneration and therefore now falls in the category of deemed forest. Most of the trees are of species such as subabul, bottle brush, bottle palm, morepankhi, *Ficus benjamina*, *Cassia siamea*, eucalyptus, fishtail palm, rubber plant, silver oak, etc. *which are not of natural regeneration. As such hardly any tree of natural regeneration exists.*
>
> 29. As per the definition of 'forest' as held by the Hon'ble Supreme Court in its order dated 12-12-1996, the project area therefore cannot be treated as 'forest' for the purpose of the Forest (Conservation) Act.'

* * *

The satellite images tell us how things stand at the time the images were taken. We are not aware whether or not the satellite images can ascertain the different species of trees, their age and the girth of their trunks, etc. But what is on record does not give us all that information. What the satellite images tell us is that in October 2006 there was thin to moderately dense tree cover over about half of the project site. But this fact is all but admitted; the State Government admits felling of over 6000 trees in 2008. How and when the trees came up there we have just seen with reference to the revenue and land acquisition proceedings records. Now, we find it inconceivable that trees planted with the intent to set up an urban park would turn into forest within a span of 10 to 12 years and the land that was forever agricultural, would be converted into forest land. One may feel strongly about cutting trees in such large numbers and question the wisdom behind replacing a patch of trees by large stone columns and statues but that would not change the trees into a forest or the land over which those trees were standing into forest land.

* * *

The order dated 12-12-1996 indeed gives a very wide definition of 'forest'. But any definition howsoever wide relates to a context. There can hardly be a legal definition, in terms absolute, and totally independent of the context. The context may or may not find any articulation in the judgment or the order but it is always there and it is discernible by a careful analysis of the facts and circumstances in which the definition was rendered. [The court distinguished several decisions with respect to 'forest' and 'forest land' stating that those decisions were rendered in the context of mining or illegal felling of trees for timber or within protected areas such as national parks and wildlife sanctuaries.]

In the light of the discussion made above, it must be held that the project site is not forest land and the construction of the project without the prior permission from the Central Government does not in any way contravene section 2 of the FC Act.

[Next, the court turned to the issue of the project's impact on the Okhla Bird Sanctuary.]

The CEC in its report to the Court dated 4-9-2009 put the blame on the State Government of U.P. for its omission to identify the eco-sensitive zones but like the MoEF seemed to accept that in the absence of a decision/notification there was no legal bar against the construction of the project on the ground that it was sited adjacent to the bird sanctuary. In its report to the Court, the CEC observed as follows:

> 'The issue regarding identification/notification of eco-sensitive zones around the national park and sanctuaries is presently pending for consideration before this Hon'ble Court. The National Board of Wildlife (NBWL) had earlier decided that area within 10 km around national parks/sanctuaries should be the eco-sensitive zone. Later on, it was decided by NBWL that eco-sensitive zone should be specific to each national park/sanctuary. The CEC had recommended that 500 m around national park/sanctuary should be declared as eco-sensitive zone. The recommendation of the CEC has not so far been accepted by the Hon'ble Supreme Court after the learned *amicus curiae* took a view that 500 m may not be adequate. Pursuant to this Hon'ble Supreme Court's order dated 4-8-2006 [*T N Godavarman Thirumulpad v Union of India* (2010) 13 SCC 740], mining is presently prohibited up to a distance of one kilometre from the boundary of national parks/sanctuaries. For other projects, no restriction has so far been imposed. The MoEF has time and again requested the States/UTs to identify the eco-sensitive zones around the national parks/sanctuaries. However, the State of Uttar Pradesh has so far not prepared any proposal in this regard. *The CEC is of the view that in the absence of a decision/notification, presently there is no legal restriction against the implementation of the project on the ground that the project is adjacent to the Okhla Bird Sanctuary.*'

However, it has to be borne in mind that the project area is hardly at a distance of 50 m from the Okhla Bird Sanctuary and that in all probability the project site would have fallen in the eco-sensitive zone, had a timely decision in this regard been taken by the State Government/MoEF.

The report of the CEC succinctly sums up the situation. Though everyone, excepting the project proponents, view the construction of the project practically adjoining the bird sanctuary as a potential hazard to the sensitive and fragile ecological balance of the sanctuary there is no law to stop it. This unhappy and anomalous situation has arisen simply because despite directions by this Court the authorities in the Central and the State Governments have so far not been able to evolve a principle to notify the buffer zones around sanctuaries and national parks to protect the sensitive and delicate ecological balance required for the sanctuaries. But the absence of a statute will not preclude this Court from examining the project's effects on the environment with particular reference to the Okhla Bird Sanctuary. For, in the jurisprudence developed by this Court environment is not merely a statutory issue. Environment is one of the facets of the right to life guaranteed under Article 21 of the Constitution. [Citations omitted.] Environment is, therefore, a matter directly under the Constitution and if the Court perceives any project or activity as harmful or injurious to the environment it would feel obliged to step in. The question of the likelihood of the project causing any adverse effects on the Okhla Bird Sanctuary must, therefore, be examined from this angle.

[The court examined the recommendations of the Salim Ali Centre for Ornithology and Natural History, the Wildlife Institute of India and the Expert Appraisal Committee (EAC) of the MoEF.]

It is significant to note that none of the expert bodies has taken the view that the project is so calamitous or ruinous for the bird sanctuary that it needs to be altogether scrapped in order to save the sanctuary. The expert bodies have given recommendations which allow the completion of the project subject to certain conditions. On behalf of the State of U.P. it is unequivocally stated that all the conditions laid in the reports of the expert bodies are acceptable to the State Government/Noida in their entirety. In the light of the two study reports and the report submitted by the EAC, we see no justification for directing the demolition of the constructions made in the project, as prayed for on behalf of the applicants. We would rather allow the project to be completed, subject, of course to the conditions suggested by the three expert bodies and further subject to the directions contained hereinbelow. [The court proceeded to set out conditions.]

NOTES AND QUESTIONS

1. The judgment records (in a portion not excerpted) that two of the 302 species of birds that visited or lived in the sanctuary were *critically endangered.* What is more important—protecting a species from extinction or permitting a memorial park with statues of political leaders? Should the court have applied a more meaningful standard of judicial review considering that the project may have further threatened two critically endangered species?

2. Is there a constitutional morality that proscribes a Chief Minister from using public funds to fell 6,000 trees and erect a statue of herself and political leaders? Which provisions of the Constitution permit or proscribe such an exercise?

3. Reforestation is one of the primary strategies to replenish the loss of forest cover. Is it not counterproductive or ignorant to permit the large-scale felling of trees planted as part of a reforestation effort?

4. Was the Supreme Court overwhelmed by the political profile of the memorial project? Or, are such factors entirely irrelevant before high calibre Supreme Court justices trained to decide cases ignoring the status of the parties before them?

5. Does the court's reasoning on the forest issue hold water? The 12 December 1996 order of the Supreme Court (repeatedly referred to in the judgment) defined the expression 'forest' as used in the FCA to include the dictionary definition of the term. Elsewhere in the judgment, the Supreme Court uses the expression 'urban forest', recognizing that such forests are part of the urban landscape in several cities across the world. A standard dictionary defines a forest as a wooded area. Would not 6,000 trees (which in the CCF's assessment constituted a forest), qualify as an 'urban forest' and therefore require a forest clearance under the FCA? Applying the precautionary principle, should the court have erred on the side of protecting the urban forest?

6. The CEC stated that the tree species felled were 'not of natural regeneration'. How is this relevant? Urban forests on urban tree parks provide improved air quality, moderate local climate, cool cities, and provide several other eco-system services. With India urbanizing rapidly should the CEC and the court have included urban forests within the scope of the FCA? And what about the principle of intergenerational equity? Within a decade, the 6,000 trees would have provided a thick canopy to the denizens of Noida. Did the Supreme Court fail in its duty to protect the quality of urban life for future generations?

7. Is this then a case of towering hypocrisy on the part of the court? On the one hand, the court projects itself as a guardian of national forest wealth and retains control over any

diversion of forests through the *Forest Conservation* case. On the other hand, when a reforestation exercise that used public funds to nurture 6,000 trees is set at naught, the court adopts an ostrich-like approach and cannot see a forest. So much for judicial consistency.

8. How is India's forest acreage to increase unless young forests are accorded a high level of legal protection? What may happen to other reforestation projects if, as in the Supreme Court's assessment, they are not covered by the FCA until they cross a fuzzy threshold of being 'naturalised'?

9.'Lawful but awful'[90] suggests the Supreme Court, letting the project proceed. Does this approach square with the larger role of the court in protecting the environment as a facet of Article 21 of the Constitution?

10. Where the CEC Report and other material establish how part of a bus stand complex including a hotel with a restaurant had been built on forest land at Mcleod Ganj in Himachal Pradesh, the Supreme Court upheld the NGT order directing demolition of the structure and payment of compensation for the environmental harm.[91]

III. THE *GODREJ* CASE

Godrej is a lengthy judgment full of statutory intricacies and interplay between the Forest Act of 1927, the Maharashtra Private Forests (Acquisition) Act of 1975 (Private Forests Act) and protective orders issued by the Supreme Court and the Bombay High Court to save forests. The facts have a surreal Alice in Wonderland quality—the forest department's bizarre dream being eventually interrupted by the Supreme Court judgment.

The case was of immense importance to real estate developers and numerous citizens of Mumbai who had invested in homes. Over decades, several buildings were erected on extensive tracts until the state, rising from its prolonged slumber, claimed these tracts to be 'forests'. When the Bombay High Court dismissed a batch of petitions assailing 'stop work notices' issued by the municipal corporation, hundreds of families stared at imminent demolition of their homes. The corporation, until then acting on the city development plans (approved after a public hearing process and which showed *no* forests) had permitted construction on the very lands where the forest department now laid claim. How did this happen?

In response to extensive deforestation in Maharashtra, the state enacted the Private Forests Act to extinguish private holdings and vest the forests under state control to enable better preservation. Despite the rigour of this law, official inaction (possibly in collusion with some private holders) nullified the law's purpose and the take-over of private forests was simply not recorded in official registers. In 2002, the Bombay Environmental Action Group (BEAG) filed a public interest litigation complaining that across Maharashtra forest officials were grossly negligent in updating land records and, as a result, the diversion of forest lands continued. The Bombay High Court accepted BEAG's submissions and issued a direction on 26 June 2005 requiring the state to complete the exercise of updating the records by 31 May 2006. After dragging their feet for decades, the forest officials on 8 May 2006 informed the municipal corporation that Godrej's lands were 'affected' by the reservation of a private forest and no construction could be permitted on these lands without permission of the Central

---

[90] The expression is borrowed from Nikos Passas, *Lawful But Awful: 'Legal Corporate Crimes'* 34 JR OF SOCIO-ECONOMICS 771 (2005).

[91] *Himachal Pradesh Bus Stand Management & Development Authority v Central Empowered Committee* (2021) SCC Online SC 15.

Government in terms of the FCA. Numerous other developers received notices similar to the ones served on Godrej and these notices were challenged in writ petitions before the High Court.

The Supreme Court allowed Godrej's appeal, reversing the Bombay High Court ruling. To appreciate the issues in the excerpt, this additional material is relevant:

(a) Section 35(1) of the Forest Act of 1927 empowered the government by a notification in the Official Gazette to regulate or prohibit activities in any forest with a view to protect forests and encourage conservation. Section 35(2) enabled the government to carry out works at its expense in any forest for the purposes enumerated in section 35(1). Section 35(3) reads:

> 35. *Protection of forests for special purposes.* —...
>
> (3) No notification shall be made under sub-section (1) nor shall any work be begun under sub-section (2), until after the issue by an officer authorised by the State Government in that behalf of a notice to the owner of such forest calling on him to show cause, within a reasonable period to be specified in such notice, why such notification should not be made or work constructed, as the case may be, and until his objections, if any, and any evidence he may produce in support of the same, have been heard by an officer duly appointed in that behalf and have been considered by the State Government.

(b) On 6 September 1956, the following notice under section 35(3) of the Forest Act of 1927 was published in the Bombay government gazette which according to Godrej was not served upon the company. In pertinent part, the notice read:

> *Notice No. WT/53*
>
> In pursuance of sub-section (3) of section 35 of the Indian Forest Act, 1927 (16 of 1927), read with rule 2 of the Rules published in Government Notification, Agriculture and Forests Department, No. 5133/48513-J, dated the 19th day of September, 1950, I, J V Karamchandani, the Conservator of Forests, Western Circle, hereby give notice to—
>
> 1. The Manager, Godrej Boyce and Manufacture Factory, at and Post Vikhroli, B S D calling on him to appear within two months from the date of receipt of this notice before the Divisional Forest Officer, West Thana, to show cause why the accompanying notification (hereinafter referred to as 'the notification') should not be made by the Government of Bombay under sub-section (1) of the said section 35 in respect of the forest specified in the Schedule hereto appended and belonging to him.
> 2. If the said Manager, Godrej Boyce and Manufacture Factory, at and Post Vikhroli, B S D, fails to comply with this notice, it shall be assumed that the said Manager, Godrej Boyce and Manufacture Factory, at and Post Vikhroli, B S D, has no objection to the making of the notification....

(c) Section 3(f)(iii) of the Private Forests Act enacted in 1975 (two decades after the section 35(3) notice) reads:

> (f) 'private forest' means any forest which is not the property of Government and includes—
>
> ...
>
> (iii) any land in respect of which a notice has been issued under sub-section (3) of section 35 of the Forest Act, but excluding an area not exceeding two hectares in extent as the Collector may specify in this behalf;

(d) Sections 3(1) and 3(3) of the Private Forests Act read:

3. *Vesting of private forests in State Government.* – (1) Notwithstanding anything contained in any law for the time being in force or in any settlement, grant, agreement, usage, custom or any decree or order of any court, tribunal or authority or any other document, with effect on and from the appointed day, all private forests in the State shall stand acquired from the appointed day, all private forests in the State shall stand acquired and vest, free from encumbrances, in, and shall be deemed to be, with all rights in or over the same or appertaining thereto, the property of the State Government, and all rights, title and interest of the owner or any person other than Government subsisting in any such forest on the said day shall be deemed to have been extinguished.

…

(3) All private forests vested in the State Government under sub-section (1) shall be deemed to be reserved forests within the meaning of the Forest Act.

The 'appointed day' when the Private Forests Act came into force was 30 August 1975.

(e) The constitutional validity of the Private Forests Act was upheld by a Bench of five judges of the Bombay High Court in *J C Waghmare v State of Maharashtra*.[92]

(f) Having succeeded before the Bombay High Court in repelling Godrej's challenge, the state government backpedaled in the Supreme Court and filed an application before the Forest Bench in *T N Godavarman v Union of India* asking the court to sanctify the constructions. The state government stated:

> As stated earlier since the records did not reveal that these are acquired private forests the erstwhile owners went on selling these lands to several persons who also in turn went on selling them to the strangers without there being any fault on their part. Subsequently developers purchased these lands and after getting requisite permissions from the Planning Authority carried on constructions thereon. Thereafter individuals and members of the public who wanted accommodation for housing probably invested their lifetime savings and/or raising loans entered into transactions of purchasing the flats constructed on these lands without their fault. In some of these areas commercial activities have also come up with due permission from the government authorities. In such cases, injustice is being alleged by the subsequent purchasers who claimed to be bona fide purchasers. This has necessitated the State of Maharashtra to come out with the present application. Abstract of constructions made on private forest lands in Mumbai Suburban and Thane City makes it very clear that the problem is more severe for the common man. Errors were also committed while declaring the lands as having been acquired by the Government under the Maharashtra Private Forests (Acquisition) Act, 1975. Some of the lands/properties owned by the Government like Bhabha Atomic Energy Complex and Employees State Insurance Scheme Hospital also came to be declared as acquired under the Maharashtra Private Forests (Acquisition) Act, 1975.

(g) The Forest Bench referred the case to the CEC which made the following recommendations in a report dated 13 July 2009:

> It is thus clear that after the issue of notices under section 35(3) or the notification under section 35(1) of the Indian Forest Act, no follow-up action was taken by the State Government. Even after the Private Forests Act came into force, neither physical possession of the land was taken nor were the areas recorded as 'forest'. A substantial part of such area falls in urban conglomerations and have been used for various non-forest purpose including construction of buildings for which permissions have been granted by the State Government authorities concerned. Sale/Purchase and resale have taken place and third-party interests

[92] AIR 1978 Bom 119.

have been generated. People are residing for last 30–40 years in hundreds of buildings constructed with the then valid approvals. It was only after the order dated 26-5-2005 of the Hon'ble Bombay High Court, that these areas are now being treated as falling in the category of 'forest'. Many of such areas are surrounded all around by other buildings and within metropolitan areas and are no longer suitable for afforestation or to be managed as 'forest'.

In the above complex background, at this belated stage, it is neither feasible nor in public interest to demolish the existing buildings/structures, relocate the existing occupants/owners and physically convert such area into forest. CEC in these circumstances considers that the balance of convenience lies in granting permission under the Forest (Conservation) Act for dereservation and non-forest use of such area on a graded scale of payment depending upon the category/sub-category in which such land falls.

(h) Godrej paid Rs. 14.7 crores towards NPV upon which the Forest Bench dissolved an interim order of *status quo* and permitted construction on the subject lands.

GODREJ AND BOYCE MFG CO LTD v STATE OF MAHARASHTRA
(2014) 3 SCC 430

Madan B Lokur, J: Leave granted. The principal question for consideration is whether the mere issuance of a notice under the provisions of section 35(3) of the Forest Act, 1927 is sufficient for any land being declared a 'private forest' within the meaning of that expression as defined in Section 2(f)(iii) of the Maharashtra Private Forests (Acquisition) Act, 1975. In our opinion, the question must be answered in the negative. Connected therewith is the question whether the word 'issued' in section 2(f)(iii) of the Maharashtra Private Forests Acquisition Act, 1975 read with section 35 of the Forest Act, 1927 must be given a literal interpretation or a broad meaning. In our opinion the word must be given a broad meaning in the surrounding context in which it is used. A tertiary question that arises is, assuming the disputed lands are forest lands, can the State be allowed to demolish the massive constructions made thereon over the last half a century? Given the facts and circumstances of these appeals, our answer to this question is also in the negative....

In our opinion, the failure of the State to take any decision on the show-cause notice for several decades (assuming it was served on Godrej) is indicative of its desire not to act on it. This opinion is fortified by a series of events that have taken place between 1957 and 2006, beginning with the consent decree of 8-1-1962 in Suit No. 413 of 1953 whereby the disputed land was recognised as not being forest land; permission to construct a large number of buildings (both residential and otherwise) as per the Development Plans of 1967 and then of 1991; exemptions granted by the competent authority under the Urban Land (Ceiling and Regulation) Act, 1976 leading to Godrej making unhindered but permissible constructions; and finally, the absence of any attempt by the State to take possession of the 'forest land' under section 5 of the Private Forests Act for a couple of decades. The subsequent event of the State moving an application in *Godavarman* virtually denying the existence of a private forest on the disputed land also indicates that the State had come to terms with reality and was grudgingly prepared to accept that, even if the law permitted, it was now too late to remedy the situation. This view was emphatically reiterated by the Central Empowered Committee in its Report dated 13-7-2009....

The next question is whether at all the unstated decision of the State to take over the so-called forest land can be successfully implemented. What the decision implies is the demolition, amongst others, of a large number of residential buildings, industrial buildings, commercial buildings, Bhabha Atomic Energy Complex and Employees State Insurance Scheme Hospital and compulsorily rendering homeless thousands of families, some of whom may have invested considerable savings in the disputed lands. What it also implies is demolition of the municipal and other public infrastructure works already undertaken and in use, clearing away the rubble and then planting trees and shrubs to 'restore' the 'forest' to an acceptable condition. According to the learned counsel for the State, this is easily achievable. But it is easier said than done....

The broad principle laid down by this Court is not in doubt. An unauthorised construction, unless compoundable in law, must be razed. In question are the circumstances leading to the application of the principle and the practical application of the principle. More often than not, the municipal authorities and builders conspiratorially join hands in violating the law but the victim is an innocent purchaser or investor who pays for the maladministration. In such a case, how is the victim to be compensated or is he or she expected to be the only loser? If the victim is to be compensated, who will do so?

* * *

The application of the principle laid down by this Court, therefore, depends on the independent facts found in a case. The remedy of demolition cannot be applied per se with a broad brush to all cases. The State also seems to have realised this and that is perhaps the reason why it moved the application that it did in *Godavarman*.

Looking at the issue from the point of view of the citizen and not only from the point of view of the State or a well-meaning pressure group, it does appear that even though the basic principle is that the buyer should beware and therefore if the appellants and the purchasers of tenements or commercial establishments from the appellants ought to bear the consequences of unauthorised construction, the well-settled principle of *caveat emptor* would be applicable in normal circumstances and not in extraordinary circumstances as these appeals present, when a citizen is effectively led up the garden path for several decades by the State itself. The present appeals do not relate to a stray or a few instances of unauthorised constructions and, therefore, fall in a class of their own. In a case such as the present, if a citizen cannot trust the State which has given statutory permissions and provided municipal facilities, whom should he or she trust?

Assuming the disputed land was a private forest, the State remained completely inactive when construction was going on over acres and acres of land and of a very large number of buildings thereon and for a few decades. The State permitted the construction through the development plans and by granting exemption under the Urban Land (Ceiling and Regulation) Act, 1976 and providing necessary infrastructure such as roads and sanitation on the disputed land and the surrounding area. When such a large-scale activity involving the State is being carried on over vast stretches of land exceeding a hundred acres, it is natural for a reasonable citizen to assume that whatever actions are being taken are in accordance with law otherwise the State would certainly step in to prevent such a massive and prolonged breach of the law. The silence of the State in all the appeals before us led the appellants and a large number of citizens to believe that there was no patent illegality in the constructions on the disputed land nor was there any legal risk in investing on the disputed land. Under these circumstances, for the State or Bombay Environment Action Group to contend that only the citizen must bear the consequences of the unauthorised construction may not be appropriate. It is the complete inaction of the State, rather its active consent that has resulted in several citizens being placed in a precarious position where they are now told that their investment is actually in unauthorised constructions which are liable to be demolished any time even after several decades. There is no reason why these citizens should be the only victims of such a fate and the State be held not responsible for this state of affairs; nor is there any reason why under such circumstances this Court should not come to the aid of victims of the culpable failure of the State to implement and enforce the law for several decades.

In none of these cases is there an allegation that the State has acted arbitrarily or irrationally so as to voluntarily benefit any of the appellants. On the contrary, the facts show that the appellants followed the due legal process in making the constructions that they did and all that can be said of the State is that its Rip Van Winkleism enabled the appellants to obtain valid permissions from various authorities, from time to time, to make constructions over a long duration. The appellants and individual citizens cannot be faulted or punished for that.

These appeals raise larger issues of good administration and governance and the State has, regrettably, come out in poor light in this regard. It is not necessary for us to say anything more on the subject except to conclude that even if the State were to succeed on the legal issues before us, there is no way, on the facts and circumstances of these appeals, that it can reasonably put the clock back and ensure that none of the persons concerned in these appeals is prejudiced in any manner whatsoever.

Accordingly, for the reasons given, all these appeals are allowed and the impugned judgment and order [*Oberoi Constructions (P) Ltd v State of Maharashtra* (2008) 3 Bom CR 408] of the Bombay High Court is set aside in all of them and the notices impugned in the writ petitions in the High Court are quashed....

NOTES AND QUESTIONS

1. In 1975, five years prior to the central Forest (Conservation) Act, the Maharashtra legislature responded to the crisis of vanishing forests in the state by taking over private forests. The Forest Act of 1927, in vogue for nearly half a century had failed to arrest the depletion of forests. Confronting a bleak situation, the state passed a law that expressly defined 'private forests' to include 'any land in respect of which a notice has been issued' under section 35(3) of the Forest Act. The clear intent of the legislature appears to be to include in the fold of 'private forest' any land (whether or not a forest in the dictionary sense) where a section 35(3) notice was issued.

Here, the statutory notice was published in the Official Gazette leaving little room for Godrej to argue that the notice had not been 'issued'. Almost always, the plain language of the law ought to be given effect, and 'issued' must mean 'issued' and not 'served' as held by the Supreme Court in a part of the judgment not excerpted. Discussing use of the expression 'issue', the Supreme Court said Against this backdrop, does the Supreme Court judgment advance the legislative intent of protecting every remaining private forest in the state?

Assuming you agree with this reasoning, it may still not alter the outcome. The Supreme Court is on firm footing when it holds that a notice under section 35(3) issued 19 years before the Private Forests Act came into force is stale and deadwood since it was not acted upon. When in law does a notice become a dead letter—three, five or seven years after issuance? Is there a bright line to guide citizens?

2. The forest jurisprudence developed by the Supreme Court is generally pro-forest. Is *Godrej* an aberration or a turn in the court's approach? Is this an instance of the adage: hard cases make bad law?

3. Was not the Supreme Court fully justified in quashing the forest department's absurd action? Here was a fully developed part of Mumbai with extensive urban infrastructure and which for decades was zoned in the city development plan for residential or commercial purposes. It was not demarcated as a forest in the city land-use maps. The forest department failed to adduce any evidence to show a forest on these tracts (howsoever degraded) on the appointed day of 30 August 1975. Absent any evidence, was it responsible on the part of the forest department to trigger massive economic and social disruptions by laying claim over developed lands more than three decades after the Private Forests Act was enacted? What was the forest department hoping to achieve? What were individual forest officers seeking to gain?

4. Should the municipal corporation have resisted the forest department by defending its own permissions? Was it under a statutory or constitutional duty to protect citizens who *bona fide* acted on the strength of its permissions? Imagine the homeowner's nightmare suffered solely due to the callous conduct of the state.

5. What eventually may have tipped the balance in favour of the developers was the inability of the state to show forests on the contested terrain. Absent any evidence of forests on 30 August 1975, the Supreme Court refused to allow the expropriatory Private Forests Act to override private rights over property.

6. Had *no* construction been erected on the land would the result of the appeal have been different? Why?

The reality of judicial adjudications is that judges deciding issues of law are invariably influenced by the impact of their verdict. Indeed, outcomes vary with the personality of the judge and a more timorous bench in Godrej may well have agreed with the High Court, leaving it to the state government to untangle a problem of its own making.

7. Was there a simpler way around this knotty issue? Could the court have simply held that in metropolitan areas the development plan, a public document fashioned after public inputs and the DNA of city growth—trumps all contesting claims? Since the development plan did not show forests, that was that. Would such an approach promote certainty?

8. Notice how the state which staunchly resisted the writ petitions in the High Court diluted its stand in the Supreme Court. The state government virtually implored the Supreme Court to bell the cat. Why?

9. The judgment tiptoes around a minefield of precedent, statutory language and some inconvenient facts relating to the issuance of section 35(3) notices, to arrive at a fair resolution. Every so often, rising above the clash of arguments comes a creative judgment that is subtle, humane and, at the end of the day, just.

10. In seeking demolition of several buildings, was BEAG being reasonable? How probable was its hunch that the forest department's amnesia may have been induced by some of the private forest owners?

11. Godrej voluntarily paid Rs. 14.7 crores towards NPV and assured the court it would not seek a refund. This was a carrot to dissolve the interim injunction that had prevented Godrej from completing housing projects it had begun. The rest of the builders got away scot-free.

IV. PUNJAB LAND PRESERVATION ACT

The Punjab and Haryana High Court responded to a newspaper article published on 22 January 2004 by registering a *suo moto* petition. The article claimed that the Forest Hill Golf and Country Club in Karoran village near Chandigarh was illegally operating a golf course on forest land. According to the news report, the Punjab government had turned a blind eye to the illegalities because a large number of high-ranking government officers were given honorary membership of the club or were allowed to use the facilities for private events.[93] Colonel B S Sandhu, proprietor and managing director of the club, claimed that it stood on private land acquired from different owners. The High Court rejected the submission. The High Court held that the whole of Karoran village was a forest area because the land was notified under the Punjab Land Preservation Act of 1900 (PLP Act); the land was shown as forest area in the annual reports and register of the forest department; and an Expert Committee had included the whole of Karoran village as forest area in its report made to the state government in March 1997 following Supreme Court orders in the *Forest Conservation* case.[94] The High Court directed that the club be closed down, all buildings constructed be

[93] This *suo moto* petition was joined by a private petition under Article 226 assailing the project, and both cases were decided together.

[94] Order dated 12 December 1996 in *T N Godavarman Thirumulpad v Union of India* (1997) 2 SCC 267.

demolished within three months and the land be handed over to the state forest department. The High Court also cancelled licences issued to the club, instructed that the power supply be disconnected and required the Central Bureau of Investigation to probe into whether senior government officials had engaged in any wrongful conduct. Aggrieved, Col B S Sandhu, a few home owners and shopkeepers at Karoran, along with a union of farmers petitioned the Supreme Court. Their case was directed against the finding that the entire village was forest land and in view of the Forest (Conservation) Act of 1980 could not be used for any non-forest purpose, without prior permission from the Central Government.

B S SANDHU v GOVERNMENT OF INDIA
(2014) 12 SCC 172

A K Patnaik, J: * * *

The High Court has also taken a view in the impugned order that as the entire land of Village Karoran, District Ropar, was closed in the PLP Act, 1900, it was 'forest land' for the purpose of section 2 of the Forest (Conservation) Act, 1980. Para 53 of the impugned order of the High Court is quoted hereinbelow:

> '53. For the reasons aforementioned and relying upon the expression "forest" and "forest lands" as defined by Their Lordships in *T N Godavarman* case and the principles laid down in *M C Mehta* case (2004) 12 SCC 118, we hold that the entire land of Village Karoran which has been notified under section 3 of the PLP Act, 1900 and is regulated by the prohibitory directions notified under sections 4 and 5 thereof, is a "forest land" and attract the provisions of section 2 of the Forest (Conservation) Act, 1980, if sought to be used for "non-forest purposes".'

Hence, the first question that we have to decide is whether the conclusion of the High Court that the land which is notified under section 3 of the PLP Act, 1900 and is regulated by the prohibitory directions notified under sections 4 and 5 of the aforesaid Act is 'forest land' is correct in law. Sections 3, 4 and 5 of the PLP Act, 1900 as it was originally enacted are extracted hereinbelow:

> '3. Whenever it appears to the local Government that it is desirable to provide for the better preservation and protection of any local area, situated within or adjacent to the Sivalik mountain range or affected or liable to be affected by the deboisement of forest in that range or by the action of chos, such Government may, by notification, make a direction accordingly.
>
> 4. In respect of areas notified under section 3 generally or the whole or any part of any such area, the local Government may by general or special order temporarily or permanently, regulate, restrict or prohibit—
>   (a) the clearing or breaking up or cultivating of land not ordinarily under cultivation prior to the publication of the notification under section 3;
>   (b) the quarrying of stone or the burning of lime at places where such stone or lime had not ordinarily been so quarried or burnt prior to the publication of the notification under section 3;
>   (c) the cutting of trees or timber, or the collection or removal or subjection to any manufacturing process, otherwise than as described in clause (b) of this subsection of any forest produce other than grass, save for bona fide domestic or agricultural purposes;
>   (d) the setting on fire of trees, timber or forest produce;
>   (e) the admission, herding, pasturing or retention of sheep or goats or camels;
>   (f) the examination of forest-produce passing out of any such area; and
>   (g) the granting of permits to the inhabitants of towns and villages situate within the limits or in the vicinity of any such area, to take any tree, timber or forest produce for their own use therefrom, or to pasture sheep or goats or to cultivate

or erect buildings therein and the production and return of such permits by such persons.

5. In respect of any specified village or villages, or part or parts thereof, comprised within the limits of any area notified under section 3, the local Government may, by special order, temporarily regulate, restrict or prohibit—
   (a) the cultivating of any land ordinarily under cultivation prior to the publication of the notification under section 3;
   (b) the quarrying of any stone or the burning of any lime at places where such stone or lime had ordinarily been so quarried or burnt prior to the publication of the notification under section 3;
   (c) the cutting of trees or timber or the collection or removal or subjection to any manufacturing process, otherwise than as described in clause (b) of this sub-section, of any forest produce for bona fide domestic or agricultural purposes; and
   (d) the admission, herding, pasturing or retention of cattle generally other than sheep and goats, or of any class or description of such cattle.'

It will be clear from the language of section 3 of the PLP Act, 1900 extracted above that for the better preservation and protection of any local area, situated within or adjacent to Shivalik mountain range which is liable to be affected by deboisement of forests in that range or by the action of 'cho', such Government may by notification make a direction accordingly. The expression 'local area' has not been defined in the PLP Act, 1900 and may include not only 'forest land' but also other land. In section 4 of the PLP Act, 1900 extracted above, the local Government was empowered by general or special order, temporarily or permanently to regulate, restrict or prohibit various activities mentioned in clauses (a), (b), (c), (d), (e), (f) and (g) thereof. A reading of these clauses would show that activities such as cultivation, pasturing of sheep and goats and erection of buildings by the inhabitants of towns and villages situated within the limits of the area notified under section 3 can be regulated, restricted or prohibited by a general or special order of the local Government. All these activities are not normally carried on in forests. Similarly, under section 5 of the PLP Act, 1900, the local Government was empowered by special order, temporarily or permanently to regulate, restrict or prohibit the cultivating of any land or to admit, herd, pasture or retain cattle generally other than sheep and goats. These activities are also not normally carried on in forests.

In our view, therefore, land which is notified under section 3 of the PLP Act, 1900 and regulated by orders of the local Government under sections 4 and 5 of the PLP Act, 1900 may or may not be 'forest land'. Therefore, the conclusion of the High Court in the impugned order that the entire land of Village Karoran, District Ropar, which has been notified under section 3 of the PLP Act, 1900 and is regulated by the prohibitory directions notified under sections 4 and 5 thereof is 'forest land' is not at all correct in law. The basis for inclusion of the entire area in Village Karoran, District Ropar, in the list of forest areas in the State of Punjab pursuant to the order dated 12-12-1996 of this Court in *T N Godavarman Thirumulpad v Union of India* is legally not correct. Similarly, the conclusion of the High Court in the impugned order that the entire land in Village Karoran, District Ropar, having been notified under section 3 of the PLP Act, 1900 and being under the regulatory regime of sections 4 and 5 of the said Act is 'forest land' is also legally not correct....

We, therefore, set aside the finding of the High Court that the entire land in Village Karoran, District Ropar, is 'forest land' for the purpose of section 2 of the Forest (Conservation) Act, 1980 and remand the matter to the High Court for fresh hearing and fresh order in accordance with law. Consequently, all directions in the impugned order which flow out of the aforesaid finding of the High Court that the land was 'forest land' for the purpose of section 2 of the Forest (Conservation) Act, 1980 are set aside. We, however, make it clear that we have not set aside the directions for investigation by CBI in the impugned order.

NOTES AND QUESTIONS

1. In setting aside the order of the High Court, the Supreme Court found that the land in Karoran village was recorded as land under the control of the forest department as the area was closed under the PLP Act. It was for this reason alone that the area was recorded as a forest area. However, this classification of the land under the PLP Act did not make it 'forest land' for the purposes of section 2 of the FCA. A notification under the PLP Act does not by itself convert land to a 'forest'. In other words, what was not a forest in fact could not have been made a forest in law.

2. An important consideration that weighed with the Supreme Court was that several villagers, agriculturists, farmers and others were carrying out their occupation on the land prior to the enactment of the FCA. The court concluded that the High Court's findings were in violation of the right to property of the concerned landowners under Article 300-A of the Constitution.

3. The High Court was perhaps overwhelmed by the forest department's records, the acknowledged position that the department exercised administrative control over Karoran village and the murky allegations involving *quid pro quo* between the club and senior government officials.

4. The Supreme Court must be commended for examining the case under Article 136 despite the strong findings of wrongdoing by the High Court. Frequently, the Supreme Court dismisses such cases at the admission stage itself. It may have helped the lead appellant, Col B S Sandhu, that other affected parties such as a farmers' union, house owners and shopkeepers also approached the Supreme Court.

5. Do you agree with the Supreme Court's direction upholding the investigation by the CBI? If the appellants succeeded in setting aside the High Court judgment where was the need for a CBI investigation?

V. THE *KANT ENCLAVE* CASE

R Kant & Co entered into an agreement with the state of Haryana to set up a film studio and a residential township. The project was supported by the town planning authorities who issued building permissions and through its Director confirmed that the provision of residential plots in Kant Enclave is permissible. A tussle ensued between the planning authorities and the state's forest department which claimed that the lands were 'forest', based on a 1992 notification under the PLP Act which curbed listed activities for a period of 30 years. R Kant & Co relied on *B S Sandhu*,[95] urging that a PLP Act notification did not by itself convert a tract of land into forest land. Directing demolition of buildings and ordering compensatory payments for environmental damage, the court shored up its conclusion by drawing on general issues—the depletion of groundwater, quarrying in the Aravalli Hills and drying up of the Badkal Lake. We carry a short excerpt from the judgment:

M C MEHTA v UNION OF INDIA

(2018) 18 SCC 397

Madan B Lokur, J: The principal question that arises in this batch of substantive applications is whether, in the State of Haryana, land notified under the provisions of the Punjab Land Preservation Act, 1900 (for short the PLP Act) is forest land or is required to be treated

[95] *B S Sandhu v Government of India* (2014) 12 SCC 172.

as forest land. If so, whether construction carried out by the applicant R Kant & Co on this land is in contravention of the notification dated 18 August 1992 issued under the provisions of the PLP Act, the Forest (Conservation) Act, 1980 and decisions of this Court.

Our answer to both the questions is in the affirmative. We have no doubt that land notified by the State of Haryana under the provisions of the PLP Act must be treated as 'forest' and 'forest land' and has in fact been so treated for several decades by the State of Haryana. There is no reason to change or alter the factual or legal position. The construction activity carried out by the applicant R Kant & Co is clearly in violation of the notification dated 18 August 1992 and in blatant defiance of orders passed by this Court from time to time. Unfortunately, the Town & Country Planning Department of the State of Haryana has been supporting the illegalities of the applicant despite strong resistance from the Forest Department of the State of Haryana. There is no doubt that at the end of the day, the State of Haryana comes out in very poor light and must be held accountable for its conflicting and self-destructive stand taken in spite of affidavits filed by the Chief Secretary of the State of Haryana from time to time supporting the Forest Department.

The unfortunate and distressing consequence of this is that because of a complete lack of any concern for the environmental and ecological degradation carried out in the Aravalli hills by influential colonizers like the applicant and what appears to be a very strong mining lobby in Haryana, the damage caused to the Aravalli hills is irreversible. It is not only the future generations that have to pay a heavy price for this environmental degradation, but even the present generation is paying a heavy price for the environmental and ecological degradation inasmuch as there is an acute water shortage in the area as prophesied by the Central Ground Water Board. In addition, what was once a popular tourist destination, namely, Badkal Lake has now vanished and the entire water body has become bone dry. What are the more severe consequences that will be felt in the years to come, only time and nature will tell....

The notification dated 18 August 1992 (which included the land of the applicant and there is no dispute about this) reads as follows:

No. S.O.104/P A-2/1900 S 3/92 – Whereas the Governor of Haryana is satisfied after the due enquiry that the prohibitions hereinafter contained are necessary for the purpose of giving effect to the provisions of the Punjab Land Prevention Act, 1900;

Now, therefore in exercise of the powers conferred by section 4 of the said Act, the Governor of Haryana hereby prohibits the following acts for a period of thirty years (30 years) with effect from the date of publication of this order in the official Gazette in the areas specified in the schedule annexed hereto, the said area forming part of the village Anangpur in Ballabhgarh, Tehsil Faridabad District specified in the schedule annexed Haryana Government Forest Department Notification No. S.O.59/P A -2/1900 S 3/92, dated 10 April 1992.

'1. The clearing or breaking up of the land not ordinarily under cultivation prior to the publication of Haryana Government Forest Department Notification No. S.O.59/ P A-2/1900 S 3/92 dated 10 April 1992 provided that the breaking in the land for cultivation may be permitted by the Divisional Forest Officer, Faridabad Forest Division.

2. The quarrying of stones or the burnings of lime at place where such stone or lime had not ordinarily been as quarried or burnt prior to the publication of the said notification except with the permission of the Collector of Faridabad District who will consult the Divisional Forest Officer, Faridabad Forest Division before according such permission.

3. The cutting of trees or timber or the collection or removal or subjection to any manufacturing process of any forest produce other than grass, flower, fruit and honey save for the bona fide domestic or agricultural purpose of right holders in the land provided that owners of the land may sell trees or timber after first obtaining a permit to do so from the Divisional Forest Officer, Faridabad Forest Division. Such permit will prescribe such conditions for sale as may from time to time appear necessary in the interest of forest conservancy.

4. The setting on fire of trees, timber of forest produce.
5. The admission, herding or pasturing, retention of sheep, goats or camels provided that in case where sickness necessitates for the keeping of goats, for milk, Divisional Forest Officer, Faridabad Division may issue a permit at his discretion for the retention of a limited number of stall-fed goat, to be specified for a specified period.'

[When Haryana sought to change its stand regarding the character of the land, the Supreme Court by an earlier order dated 18 March 2004, *M C Mehta v Union of India* (2004) 12 SCC 118 declined the request.]

'In the instant case, it is not necessary to decide the legal effect of issue of the notification under Sections 4 and/or 5 of the PLP Act. Not only in their record has the area been shown as forest but affidavits have been filed in this Court stating the area to be "forest". In *T N Godavarman Thirumulpad v Union of India* (1997) 2 SCC 267 this Court held that the term "forest" is to be understood in the dictionary sense and also that any area regarded as a forest in government records, irrespective of ownership, would be a forest. The State of Haryana, besides having filed affidavits in the forest matters treating such areas as forest for the purposes of the Forest (Conservation) Act has been seeking prior approval from the Central Government for diversion of such land for non-forestry purpose. Reference in this connection may also be made to the affidavit dated 8-12-1996 filed by Banarsi Das, Principal Chief Conservator of Forests, Chandigarh, Haryana in *Environmental Awareness Forum v State of J&K* [Civil Writ No. 171 of 1996]. Our attention has also been drawn to letter dated 26-11-2002 addressed by the Divisional Forest Officer, Faridabad to the Mining Officer, Faridabad forwarding to him a list of blocked forest areas of Faridabad district and requesting him to ensure that the said forest areas are not affected by any mining operations as also to a letter dated 17-9-2001 sent by the Principal Chief Conservator of Forests, Haryana (Panchkula) to the Director of Environment, Haryana stating therein that no mining activity can be permitted in the area. On the facts and circumstances of the case, we cannot permit the State Government to take a complete somersault in these proceedings and contend that the earlier stand that the area is forest was under some erroneous impressions. In the present case, for the purposes of the FC Act, these areas shall be treated as forest and for use of it for non-forestry purpose, it would be necessary to comply with the provisions of the FC Act.'

* * *

[The court distinguished the decision in *B S Sandhu*.] We may mention, without comment, that the purpose of issuing a notification under the PLP Act is to ensure that in the closed area there is no activity such as cultivation, pasturing of sheep and goats, erection of buildings, herding, pasturing or retaining cattle etc. Therefore, the notification is a clear indication that such closed areas must be forest land or treated as forest land so that such objectionable non-forest activities are not carried out therein and that activities that are not normally carried out in forests are prohibited in forest land, so as to preserve and protect such forest land. A notification under the PLP Act does not convert land into forest land but recognizes it as such or at least requires it to be treated as such.

We may also mention, *en passant*, the provisions of section 35(1) of the Indian Forest Act, 1927. This refers to breaking up or clearing of land for cultivation, pasturing of cattle etc. and reads as follows:

35. *Protection of forests for special purposes.* — (1) The State Government may, by notification in the Official Gazette, regulate or prohibit in any forest or waste-land—
   (a) the breaking up or clearing of land for cultivation;
   (b) the pasturing of cattle; or
   (c) the firing or clearing of the vegetation;
   when such regulation or prohibition appears necessary for any of the following purposes:
   (i) for protection against storms, winds, rolling stones, floods and avalanches;

(ii) for the preservation of the soil on the ridges and slopes and in the valleys of hilly tracts, the prevention of landslips or of the formation of ravines, and torrents, or the protection of land against erosion, or the deposit thereon of sand, stones or gravel;

(iii) for the maintenance of a water-supply in springs, rivers and tanks;

(iv) for the protection of roads, bridges, railways and other lines of communication;

(v) for the preservation of the public health.

(2) …
(3) …

We leave it at that because of the distinguishing features in the *M C Mehta* set of orders as contrasted and recognized with the facts in *Sandhu*....

The Polluter Pays Principle is a wholesome principle that has been universally accepted and also adopted and applied in our country through several decisions of this Court.... The law having been settled for more than two decades, we are of the view that it must be applied in a case such as the present. The damage caused to the Aravalli hills, as already noted, is irreversible. However, perhaps some of the damage could be remedied—at least we hope so. According to R Kant & Co it has expended Rs. 50 crore in developing Kant Enclave. We do not know the exact or accurate figure but proceed on the basis as stated. In our opinion, it would be reasonable to require R Kant & Co to deposit 10% of this amount (that is, Rs.5 crore) for rehabilitation of the damaged areas. This amount should be deposited by R Kant & Co in the Aravalli Rehabilitation Fund within one month and in any case on or before 31 October 2018.

NOTES AND QUESTIONS

1. The judgment dismissed Kant Enclave's reliance on *B S Sandhu* since *Sandhu* 'cannot, by any stretch of imagination, come to the aid of the applicants' and '[t]here is absolutely no doubt that *Sandhu* is distinguishable on both facts and in law'. Do you agree? Should the two-judge bench in *Kant Enclave* have followed the *Sandhu* judgment which was delivered by a bench of equal strength? How persuasive is the court's reference to the chess move, *en passant*, in order to side-step binding precedent?

2. Revisit the *B S Sandhu* judgment. Did the Supreme Court in *Kant Enclave* adopt the very reasoning which the High Court used in *B S Sandhu* and which the Supreme Court disapproved?

3. Although the *Kant Enclave* judgment extensively refers to illegal mining in the Aravalli Hills, groundwater depletion and the drying up of the Badkal Lake, there is nothing in the judgment to suggest that R Kant & Co contributed to these problems. Should a private developer be blamed where two departments of government hold opposite views whether the land is 'forest' or not?

4. Was the Supreme Court correct in refusing to allow the state government to alter its position regarding the character of the land? Remember, the judgment in *B S Sandhu's* case validated the state's new position that land notified under the PLP Act may or may not be 'forest land'.

5. Although the Supreme Court holds that 'forest land' was developed, there was no evidence to show that the land was forested, recorded as forest area or notified as a forest under forest laws. The Supreme Court overcame this hurdle by holding that while the PLP Act does not convert the land into forest it 'at least requires it to be treated as such'. Does land become

'forest' merely because it was *administered* by the forest department with a view to 'preserve' it for 30 years under the PLP Act?

6. The notification dated 18 August 1992 issued under the PLP Act did not prohibit 'erection of buildings'. Nevertheless, the Supreme Court construed the notification as imposing an embargo. Was the court justified in inferring a ban?

VI. KERALA

The *Nature Lovers* case portrays the tussle between those who want to preserve forests, and the displaced and impoverished eking out a living by cultivating erstwhile forest lands. Contests over forests are likely to heighten over the next few decades as the sub-continent confronts a burgeoning population and mass migrations triggered by climate change. As you examine this case, visualize the popular pressures that will build on elected representatives to dilute the rigour of the FCA. Will the judiciary be able to withstand this onslaught?

NATURE LOVERS MOVEMENT v STATE OF KERALA

(2009) 5 SCC 373

G S Singhvi, J: Whether section 2 of the Forest (Conservation) Act, 1980 (for short 'the 1980 Act') is prospective in operation and whether the Government of Kerala could, without obtaining prior approval of the Central Government grant pattas/leasehold rights to the unauthorised occupants/encroachers of forest land are the questions which arise for determination in this appeal filed against the order of the Full Bench of the Kerala High Court.

The Indian society has, for many centuries, been aware and conscious of the necessity of protecting environment and ecology. Sages and saints of India lived in forests. Their preachings contained in Vedas, Upanishads, Smritis, etc. are ample evidence of the society's respect for plants, trees, earth, sky, air, water and every form of life. The main motto of social life is to live in harmony with nature. It was regarded as a sacred duty of everyone to protect them. In those days, people worshipped trees, rivers and sea which were treated as belonging to all living creatures. The children were educated by elders of the society about the necessity of keeping the environment clean and protecting earth, rivers, sea, forests, trees, flora, fauna and every species of life.

[The court traced the history of forest laws in Kerala beginning with the pre-Independence regulations framed by the Maharaja of Travancore and recognized the relentless pressure on the forests despite efforts to deter encroachments.]

The appellant, which is a society formed for protection of environment and ecology in the State of Kerala, challenged the decision of the Government to regularise unauthorised occupation/encroachment of forest lands by filing a writ petition under Article 226 of the Constitution. It prayed for grant of a declaration that the Government of Kerala is not entitled to dereserve the reserved forest or permit use of forest land for any non-forest purpose without obtaining approval of the Central Government in terms of section 2(iii) of the 1980 Act. The appellant further prayed that pattayams (title deeds) issued in respect of forest land without obtaining approval of the Central Government should be quashed. In the affidavit filed on behalf of the appellant before the High Court, it was claimed that regularisation of unauthorised occupation/encroachments of forest land will adversely affect the environment and wildlife and ultimately the population of the State.

In the counter-affidavit filed on behalf of the State Government, it was averred that due to pressure of population and due to implementation of colonisation scheme, arable land assignment scheme, grow more food programme, hydroelectric irrigation projects, plantations, etc. considerable extent of forest lands in the State had been exposed to human habitation and such forest lands had been actually used for non-forest purposes and converted into populated areas with structures and improvements; that in those days people were not conscious of the fact that the maintenance of forest was required for ecological balance and substantial extent of forest lands had been transformed into agricultural holdings and human settlements and there is no scope for reverting them into forests; that because of high density of population any scheme for evicting the occupants of those converted forest lands and providing them with rehabilitation facilities is unworkable; that because of the pressing need for production of more foodgrains, the Governments had in the past allowed cultivation in the forest lands; that the decision to regularise the encroachments made prior to 1-1-1977 was taken because it was impossible to rehabilitate all the occupants if they were evicted; that the Government of India has already clarified that no sanction under section 2 of the 1980 Act is necessary for utilising the forest lands dereserved for non-forest purposes prior to the promulgation of the Act and that eligibility of persons to whom the holdings are to be assigned has been decided after a field verification of the entire area by a joint team of officials of the Forest and Revenue Departments.

[The judgment sets out the state's pleadings regarding compensatory afforestation and the government policy to evict persons who had encroached *after* a cut-off date of 1 January 1977.]

Learned counsel for the appellant submitted that his client is not serious in pressing the challenge to the Central Government's decision to approve the use of forest land for non-forest purpose, namely, assignment of forest land to pre-1-1-1977 unauthorised occupants/encroachers because the said decision was taken for solving the problem being faced by 50,000 families which are settled in forest areas for last more than five decades, but argued that the declaration made by the Full Bench of the High Court that the 1980 Act is prospective and is not applicable to the cases involving use of forest land for non-forest purpose prior to 25-10-1980 is *ex facie* erroneous and is liable to be set aside, else the same is likely to be misused by the State Governments for regularising the encroachments of forest land made prior to 25-10-1980 without seeking prior approval of the Central Government.

[The court set out the relevant provisions of the Kerala Forests Act of 1961.] An analysis of the above-reproduced provisions of the 1961 Act makes it clear that once a land was declared as reserved forest, no right could be acquired by anyone after issue of notification under section 4 except under a grant or contract in writing made or entered into by or on behalf of the Government, or by or on behalf of some person in whom such right or power to create the same was vested or by succession from such person and no activity of clearing such land or collection of forest produce could be made. Sub-section (2) of section 7 of the 1961 Act also imposes prohibition against grant of patta in such land without previous sanction of the Government . . .

We shall now consider whether section 2 of the 1980 Act is prospective in operation and the State Government, etc. are not required to obtain prior approval of the Central Government before regularising use of any forest land for any non-forest purpose or issue patta or grant lease to unauthorised occupants/encroachers of forest land, or the provision contained in section 2 is applicable qua any action which the State Government or other authority may take with reference to activity undertaken in any reserved forest or any forest land prior to 25-10-1980. [The court reviewed a long line of cases.]

The ratio of the abovenoted judgments is that the 1980 Act is applicable to all forests irrespective of the ownership or classification thereof and after 25-10-1980 i.e. the date of enforcement of the 1980 Act, no State Government or other authority can pass an order or give a direction for dereservation of reserved forest or any portion thereof or permit use of any forest land or any portion thereof for any non-forest purpose or grant any lease, etc. in respect of forest land to any private person or any authority, corporation, agency or organisation which is not owned, managed or controlled by the Government.

Another principle which emerges from these judgments is that even if any forest land or any portion thereof has been used for non-forest purpose, like undertaking of mining activity for a particular length of time, prior to the enforcement of the 1980 Act, the tenure of such activity cannot be extended by way of renewal of lease or otherwise after 25-10-1980 without obtaining prior approval of the Central Government.

We may now revert to the facts of the case in hand. It is not in dispute that before the enactment of the 1980 Act, the Government of Kerala had taken a policy decision to regularise the illegal/unauthorised occupation and encroachments of forest land made prior to 1-1-1977 and also to remove all unauthorised occupation/encroachments made on and after 1-1-1977. For implementation of that decision, the State Government approached and succeeded in persuading the Central Government to grant approval for diversion of 28,588.159 ha of land by way of assignment to the unauthorised occupants/encroachers.

The approval granted by the Central Government was in consonance with the guidelines framed by it for Regularisation of Encroachments on Forest Land. Therefore, we do not find any valid reason to interfere with the High Court's refusal to nullify the action taken by the State Government to regularise the unauthorised occupation/encroachment of 28,588.159 ha of forest land in five districts.

As regards 10,000 ha of forest land, the State Government has not taken any decision for assignment thereof to unauthorised occupants/encroachers. This has been made clear in the additional affidavit dated 13-1-2009 of Shri B R Mohan Kumar (Law Officer to the Government of Kerala), Para 7 whereof reads as under:

> 'It is submitted that the State Government has initiated steps to move the Government of India with suitable proposal for obtaining clearance under the Forest (Conservation) Act, 1980 for assignment of about 10,000 ha of forest land to the occupants prior to 1-1-1977. Alternate non-forest lands are being identified for compensatory afforestation in various districts. For regularisation of these forest lands encroached prior to 1-1-1977, prior approval of the Government of India is necessary. The respondent will submit an additional proposal to the Government of India for grant of approval for diversion of forest land, as and when joint verification is completed. It may be pointed out that instructions have been issued in unequivocal terms to take stern action to evict the encroachments after 1-1-1977.'

In view of the stand taken by the State Government, the grievance made by the appellant in that regard will have to be treated as premature. However, we deem it necessary to clarify that as and when the State Government takes a decision to assign 10,000 ha of forest land or permit use thereof for any non-forest purpose and approaches the Central Government for grant of approval in terms of sections 2(ii) and (iii), the latter shall be duty-bound to examine the proposal keeping in view the object of the 1980 Act and the guidelines framed in the light of the National Forest Policy and then take appropriate decision. Needless to say that the appellant or any other person who may feel aggrieved by the decision of the State Government to assign 10,000 ha of forest land or any portion thereof or permit use of forest land for any non-forest purpose shall be free to avail appropriate legal remedy.

In the result, the appeal is disposed of in the following terms:

(1) The policy decision taken by the Government of Kerala to assign 28,588.159 ha of forest land to unauthorised occupants/encroachers after seeking approval from the Central Government does not suffer from any legal infirmity and the High Court rightly declined to interfere with the said decision.

(2) After the enforcement of the 1980 Act, neither the State Government nor any other authority can make an order or issue direction for dereservation of reserved forest or any portion thereof or permit use of any forest land or any portion thereof for any non-forest purpose or assign any forest land or any portion thereof by way of lease or otherwise to any private person or to any authority, corporation, agency or organisation not owned, managed or controlled by the Government except after obtaining prior approval of the Central Government.

(3) Conclusion D recorded by the High Court in para 103 of the impugned judgment is legally unsustainable and is set aside.

(4) As and when the State Government decides to assign 10,000 ha of forest land to unauthorised occupants/encroachers, it shall do so only after obtaining prior approval of the Central Government and the latter shall take appropriate decision keeping in view the object of the 1980 Act and the guidelines framed for regularisation of encroachments on forest land.

NOTES AND QUESTIONS

1. Is the second paragraph of the judgment an accurate reference to a bygone idyll or sanctimonious humbug? In ages past, life was likely hard, brutal and short.

2. The PIL petitioner adopted a fair and balanced approach in seeking a suitable declaration to curb forest loss in the future, rather than displace 50,000 families who had settled in forest areas for over half a century. The PIL jurisdiction is not intended to foist additional hardships on displaced individuals forced to settle in forests.

3. Then again, why should this approach not apply to encroachers after the cut-off date, 1 January 1977? Does this imply that, on humanitarian grounds, a PIL court ought not to remove trespassers from common property resources such as forests, public parks, recreational grounds, village commons and beaches?

4. What did the appellants gain in the Supreme Court? Were the Nature Lovers better off with the declarations issued in the final paragraph of the judgment including setting aside conclusion 'D' of the High Court?[96]

5. In a democracy, how stable are *ad hoc* cut-off dates intended to curb encroachments on public lands? With constitutional guarantees protecting the right to life, the right to move across the country and the right to secure a livelihood, coupled with the statutory right to vote, is it not inevitable that electoral mathematics will compel the cut-off date to slide forward and accommodate more voters? This is the experience in Maharashtra with respect to controlling the proliferation of slums where the cut-off to tolerate encroachers was brought forward progressively through legislative amendments.

6. The Supreme Court decision traced the gradual strengthening of the Travancore/Kerala laws to curb unauthorized occupation of forest lands. Despite the prohibitions and criminal sanctions under the 1961 Act, the state adopted a policy to validate encroachers prior to 1 January 1977. Is this evidence of a soft state incapable of enforcing its own law, or a liberal, progressive and humane state that seeks redistribution of resources to disadvantaged segments of society?

7. Notice the raft of justifications put forward by the state to support regularizing the encroachments prior to the cut-off date. Will not most of these reasons apply to post-1 January 1977 encroachments as well? What then will a court do? Uphold the fresh cut-off date?

---

[96] The full bench in conclusion 'D' held that the provisions of the FCA 'have no retrospective operation and they operate prospectively'.

11

WILDLIFE PROTECTION

A. INTRODUCTION

The geological record suggests that in five previous ages, within a short span of time, millions of life forms perished. After each such age new species that were better adapted to the changed environment flourished. There is consensus among scientists that the present epoch is comparable to the great extinctions of the past.[1]

The difference between the previous extinctions and the present one is the role of humans. As our technological civilization progresses, our appetite for natural resources and our spread across the globe crowd out other species. Climate change is upon us. The stress experienced by other life forms will exacerbate as climate change forces eco-systems and species to shift.

Wildlife law is about accommodating other species, protecting their habitats and preserving biodiversity. Valmik Thapar writes:

> The biodiversity of wild India is still rich and varied and within sixteen types of different forests live 15,000 species of flowering plants, more than 410 species of mammals (9% of the world's species), 1,250 species of birds (12% of the world's species), more than 408 species of reptiles (6% of the world's species), 197 species of amphibians (4.4% of the world's species), 2,546 species of fish (11% of the world's species), and so far, nearly 60,000 species of insects (nearly 6% of the world's species). Therefore, the need to safeguard wild India is unquestionable. Today, there are about 2,00,000 forest staff, including daily wagers, whose job it is safeguard these parts of the country, including 668 protected areas or 4.83% of our geographical area.[2]

For over a century, Indian wildlife has received sporadic protection through numerous species-specific statutes. The primary intent of the earliest statutes was to preserve game animals for hunting. The Indian Forest Act of 1927 included provisions for hunting restrictions in reserved or protected forests and authorized the establishment of sanctuaries. In 1972, India adopted a comprehensive national law, the Wild Life (Protection) Act of 1972, intended solely to protect wildlife. The Forty-Second Constitutional Amendment in 1976 moved 'Protection of wild animals and birds' and 'Forests' from the State List of the Constitution to the Concurrent List.[3] Subsequently, the Central Government has increased its role in developing national wildlife policy. The Supreme Court has recognized that the National Wildlife Action Plan (NWAP) and the Centrally Sponsored Integrated Development

---

[1] Elizabeth Kolbert, *The Sixth Extinction* (2014).

[2] Valmik Thapar, Saving Wild India: A Blueprint for Change xii (2015).

[3] Articles 48A and 51A(g), introduced into the Constitution on 3 January 1977, use the expression 'wild life' as two words. The legislative lists in the Constitution use the expression 'wild animals and birds'. The use of 'Wild Life' as two words in the 1972 Act over the more common single word usage may be traced to the Constitution.

Environmental Law & Policy in India. Shyam Divan and Armin Rosencranz, Oxford University Press.
 DOI: 1093/oso/9780192865458.003.0011

of Wildlife Habitat Scheme of 2009 have a statutory flavour.[4] The most recent statutory initiatives are the 2002 and 2006 amendments to the Wild Life Act.

The Forty-Second Amendment engrafted into the Constitution provisions covering the state policy with respect to wildlife and the responsibility of citizens. The directive principle in Article 48A mandates: 'The State shall endeavour ... to safeguard the forests and wild life of the country'. Part IVA of the Constitution casts a fundamental duty on every citizen 'to protect and improve the natural environment including forests, lakes, rivers and wild life, and to have compassion for living creatures'.[5]

We open this chapter with readings on wildlife depredation during the colonial period and a contemporary campaign to protect sea turtles. This is followed by a survey of the statutory law. Next we examine the notion of eco-centrism and the issue of poaching. Some of the current debates among conservationists are reflected in the cases discussed in this chapter. The people-park controversy, for example, raises core issues relating to the rights and livelihood of forest dwellers and villagers who live in and around protected areas. How should courts balance their immediate and acute community needs against the national agenda of minimizing human intervention in the national parks and sanctuaries? Another theme is the conflict between environmentalists and commercial interests in exploiting mineral resources in the protected regions. Straddling the rival claimants are the state governments, many of which depend on mineral royalties or are keen to encourage industry in remote regions of the state.

For five decades during the colonial period a policy of branding certain species as vermin devastated the population of large carnivores. As you will discover in the course of this chapter, the policy today is the opposite with great effort and resources expended to protect the very species that were consciously hunted down a century ago.

M RANGARAJAN; THE RAJ AND THE NATURAL WORLD: THE CAMPAIGN AGAINST 'DANGEROUS BEASTS' IN COLONIAL INDIA, 1875–1925[6]

The relationship with large predators was a multifaceted one. Animals like the lion and tiger were often metaphors for power even as they were a source of danger. The importance of the lion in the Asokan pillar (third century BCE) is well known. The Valmiki Ramayana, possibly dating to the fourth to sixth century CE, refers to Dasratha as a 'lion among kings', and describes Rama and Lakshmana as 'tigers among men'. The former 'moves with the boldness of a lion, a lion-like man, a lion among men'. Evidently the tiger was also a powerful symbol, though much more work is needed on the history of such emblems. Yet, power and danger often emanated from the same source. Even at a much later date, the killing of large mammals was a sign of the prowess of a warrior. Farid's slaying of a tiger earned him the name Sher Khan (1540–5) and the fact that it was killed with a spear while he was on foot, was a mark of bravery. Rulers or landed groups often legitimized their power by defending subjects against wild animals. Akbar (1556–1605) was on a pilgrimage to the Chishti shrine at Ajmer (in July 1572) when he hunted down a man-eating tiger.

---

[4] *Centre for Environment Law, WWF-1 v Union of India* (2013) 8 SCC 234. The judgment refers to the NWAP 2002–16 which is replaced by NWAP 2017–31.

[5] Article 51A(g).

[6] This extract is from *India's Environmental History: Colonialism, Modernity and the Nation* 95 (Ed. M Rangarajan and K Sivaramakrishnan, 2014).

The religious dimensions of perceptions of the natural world were often significant. Mughal chroniclers cited evidence of the divine nature of the Badshah by referring to an incident between Akbar and a tiger that threatened his hunting companion. When Akbar stared at the tiger, it 'cowered down from that divine glance, and turned right about trembling over.' Even the beasts of the forest 'recognized' the divine gaze of the Badshah. An early European account in 1670 in the mangrove swamps of eastern Bengal, an area notorious for man-eaters, refers to a place where 'every Thursday night a tiger comes out and salaams to *fakir's*[7] tomb there.' Islam had clearly co-opted and assimilated older traditions of tiger worship into a new framework. Holy men and deities like Bon Bibi helped control beasts of the forests just as they repelled evil spirits that could harm the faithful....

A War Against Vermin

Provincial-level schemes were sought to be extended after a debate on the ravages of wild beasts. Effective control of rural India hinged on the elimination of both human and animal rebels against the Raj. The wider context of the debate was the disarming of the Indians after the Rebellion of 1857–8. There were fears that the denial of modern firearms to people in rural areas was indirectly contributing to 'serious depredations' of cattle and crops. In Madras Presidency, there were frequent complaints of increased damage by tigers, wolves, and other animals.... European leadership was seen as crucial to a successful battle against wild beasts. In each district, the local shikaris were to be organised into a corps under the command of a civil, or preferably, military officer. Their sole task would be to eliminate large carnivores.... Parallels were also drawn between the work of vermin control in the home country and the tasks at hand in India. Major Tweedie wanted to employ tiger killers 'just like' the mole catchers and rabbit killers in England.... In October 1873, a police officer, Col Caulfield, was paid an extra stipend to kill tigers in Coimbatore district. He killed seven tigers using traps made by Toda tribals and was then dispatched to the Vizag region in the Eastern Ghats, an area known for tigers....

Some princes had already initiated or were willing to follow through with a scheme of rewards for killing vermin. It is necessary to ask why these rulers had such programmes while many of the neighbouring states did not. It is possible that the predators were a threat to livestock in certain areas. In Ajmer Mhairwara, which was under direct imperial rule, leopards and tigers claimed the lives of large numbers of cattle and rewards were given to kill the carnivores. Elsewhere in India, Mysore and Hyderabad were prominent in their extensive system of bounties for wild animals and snakes. Religious beliefs may have been crucial in resisting such measures though this was only so in the case of Marwar where the Raja refused to help in 'any organised attempt' to get rid of venomous reptiles. In Jhalawar, the Raj Rana was already giving out rewards for tigers and Bundi was ready to follow suit. Kotah had a comprehensive system of bounties, with Rs.10 for a tiger and Rs.5 for bears, wolves and leopards. The state was unusual as it appears to be the only princely house that still rewarded the killing of lions which were already very rare. The bounty was as high as Rs.25, compared to only Rs.10 for a tiger....

The shift in attitudes by the 1920s was in part a consequence of the success of vermin extermination operations. Although the number of lives lost and beasts killed for rewards were still high in the mid-1920s, a decision was taken to stop collating any information at the all-India level. Provinces were free to peruse their own line of action. By this time, there was a visible though not universal softening of attitudes to many key carnivores. If the tiger found breathing space, the wolf did not. The former won admirers who saw it as an embodiment of gentlemanly virtue. Others acknowledged the positive role of predators in controlling herbivores in forests and on the fringes of cultivated arable land. But such views were still held by a minority. Programmes to wipe out vermin continued for much longer. Even those

[7] *Fakir* is a religious ascetic or holy person.

who wanted tigers spared, urged more vigorous campaigns against other target species. But the era of branding a species as vermin was drawing to a close.

NOTES

1. The Asiatic Lion was the subject of extensive litigation before the Supreme Court, where the court directed translocation of lions from Gujarat to the Kuno Wildlife Sanctuary, Madhya Pradesh. The court reasoned that despite Gujarat's success in increasing the population of lions the species would be more secure if it had a second home on the sub-continent. This case is discussed in the section on federalism in the Constitutional Provisions chapter.[8]

2. While conservation efforts in India have focused on the tiger, wild canids (dholes, wolves, foxes, jackals) and hyenas continue to be ignored by conservation initiatives.[9] Though no longer labelled vermin, without concerted efforts to restore populations, these species will remain endangered and are unlikely to recover from the colonial policy of exterminating carnivores.

3. The success of our species and our appetite for energy extending to subterranean reserves is changing the composition of the atmosphere. Indeed, the chemistry of both the air and the oceans is being altered. Some plants and animals may adjust by moving. But a great many, eventually thousands of species, will find themselves marooned. No creature has ever altered life on the planet as we have in our pursuit of food, energy and the city. Our responses to climate change, enormously challenging as they are, may have to be interwoven with preserving biodiversity and in turn discharging a fiduciary duty to others on the ark.

Successful conservation initiatives involve good science, field work and endless toil against development initiatives that could harm habitat and species. These challenges are particularly acute in marine wildlife conservation where species migrate in and out of designated protected areas. Kartik Shanker's survey of sea turtle conservation in India blends science, personal history and the work of dedicated environmentalists over several decades. Five species of sea turtle are found in Indian waters: olive ridley, green, hawksbill, loggerhead and leatherback.

KARTIK SHANKER; FROM SOUP TO SUPERSTAR: THE STORY OF SEA TURTLE CONSERVATION ALONG THE INDIAN COAST 151, 188 (2015)

CIRCA 2005, Raphael, Michelangelo, Donatello and Leonardo made an impromptu appearance in front of Bombay House, the head office of the Tata Group, in Mumbai. The four teenage mutant ninja turtles were on a new adventure, unauthorized, of course, by their creators. This was a crusade to save their brethren, the olive ridley turtles of Odisha, by preventing the Tatas from building a port at Dhamra, which would ostensibly spell doom for the olive ridleys that nest at Gahirmatha. Led by campaigners such as Sanjiv Gopal and Shailendra Yashwant, the turtles held up banners that said 'Don't say Tata to turtles.' The campaign led by Greenpeace India did not end here.

---

[8] *Centre for Environment Law WWF-1 v Union of India* (2013) 8 SCC 234.

[9] Arjun Srivathsa, *et al*, *Opportunities for Prioritising and Expanding Conservation Enterprise in India using a Guild of Carnivores as Flagships* 15 Envir Res Lett (2020), https://iopscience.iop.org/article/10.1088/1748-9326/ab7e50, accessed 28 May 2021.

Greenpeace put out advertisements in newspapers in 2009 comparing the Nano small car manufactured by the Tatas (cheap) and the olive ridley (priceless). A while later, Greenpeace launched a Pacman-like online video game, called 'Turtle vs Tata,' where little yellow (olive?) turtles had to eat white dots (=healthy food) while avoiding Ratty, Matty, Natty or Tinku (the bad guys). In response, the Tatas launched a trademark infringement and defamation lawsuit against Greenpeace India.

But this was hardly the first time that Greenpeace had courted trouble. When they started their campaign in Odisha in early 2004, there was already tension between fishers, conservationists and the forest department. Though some of my colleagues and I warned them that their entry might exacerbate the situation, Greenpeace decided that it should address the problem of boundary demarcation for the Gahirmatha National Park. When fishermen were caught fishing illegally inside the park, they often claimed that they didn't know where the boundaries lay, and the forest department claimed that this made enforcement difficult. Greenpeace decided that if they performed public service by demarcating the boundaries with buoys, both the fishermen and the forest department would be grateful.

Greenpeace consulted with the local forest department as well as fishers and received what they thought was support for this activity. Organized as a big media event, Greenpeace invited one of their key supporters, film actress, Amala Akkneni, and sailed out to Gahirmatha from Paradip along with fishworkers and several observers. I met Amala at a sea turtle workshop in Visakhapatnam in April 2015, and we talked about the Gahirmatha trip and conservation in general. An avid diver and a turtle enthusiast from the time she rescued a sea turtle hatchling as a child, Amala had supported Greenpeace programmes for many years. She helped raise funds for the buoys and was later involved in a stray-dog sterilization programme along the central Odisha coast, aimed at reducing predation of turtle eggs.

Once they reached the park boundary, a group of dashing young activists threw their shirts off and themselves into the water. Amala recalled that it was really hot and they were all happy to be in the water for a while. Buoys were installed using GPS coordinates, and the crew retuned, dare I say, buoyed by their success. But sadly, the fishermen were not in the least happy that they could no longer profess ignorance about the boundaries and mumbled their discontent. And the forest department, the supposed beneficiaries, pulled Greenpeace up for entering a protected area without permission.

As a final episode in this saga, Greenpeace campaigners ran afoul of the law again when they brought dead olive ridley turtles to the capital, New Delhi, to get the attention of Odisha Chief Minister Naveen Patnaik. They were then arrested on grounds of illegally handling and hunting a Schedule I animal, and spent two days in Tihar jail. As absurd as accusations against Greenpeace might have been, it is quite clear that the environmental NGO's intent was to create publicity around the issue. When I queried Amala about the fact that the issues that get the biggest publicity may not be the ones most important for conservation, she said: 'You hear the shout, but not the whisper.' There is little doubt that the individuals concerned are deeply passionate and committed to conservation. But the question is: does the shouting help conservation or does it just help the NGOs? At heart, are environmental organizations any different from the corporations they claim to battle? . . .

Additionally, in numerous negotiations with NGOs, the Tatas repeatedly assured NGOs of their commitment to environmental conservation and sea turtles. At a meeting, one executive said something like, 'The Tatas do not want to be responsible for the extinction of the olive ridleys in Orissa'. But their promises of a long-term commitment to sea turtles in Odisha proved empty as they have sold their share and moved out, and are no longer 'responsible.' . . .

[I] had pointed out that Dhamra port might not even be the biggest problem in Odisha for marine turtles. The state government was already planning many other ports, and other major constructions (Posco at Jatadhar) and expansions (Paradip Port) were in the pipeline. We needed to be working to counter the large-scale uncontrolled economic growth model—with little concern about environmental and social impacts—that the government was proposing. Certainly, the subsequent trajectory of development in Odisha has shown this to be true. Conservation in Odisha has been driven more by rhetoric than action. Conservation organizations have a lot more in common with corporations than they would like to believe, in the way they function and make decisions, but particularly in the way they like to use information selectively. If nothing has indeed changed in the thirty-odd years of sea turtle conservation in Odisha, could it be possibly because all the players (the state, conservationists, corporations, academics, fishers) intentionally or institutionally continue to pursue agendas and strategies that are geared to help mainly themselves, regardless of whether it helps sea turtles in the long run or not?

NOTE

The Supreme Court of India[10] and several High Courts[11] frequently quote a reply attributed to 'The wise Indian Chief of Seattle' to the President of the United States in 1854. The reply evokes environmental ethics and values but, as Shanker explains, has a doubtful provenance:

> The Indian chief's speech was made in response to an offer to buy their land. Chief Seattle (Seathl, to be accurate) made his speech to the Commissioner for Indian Affairs in his native language, and it was translated by Dr Henry Smith, a physician. Smith visited the chief many times to get the translation right and published it thirty-odd years later in the *Seattle Sunday Star*. Eighty years later, Prof William Arrowsmith of the University of Texas discovered the speech, edited it to a more 'authentic' style and published it in 1969. When Arrowsmith read the speech out to a large student gathering on the first Earth Day in 1970, a young film professor, Ted Perry, was in the audience. Perry adapted the speech to write a script about pollution and the state of the planet, borrowing the spirit of the speech and applying to contemporary issues. But the speech acquired a life of its own. A couple of year later, *Environmental Action* magazine published it as a letter from Chief Seattle to President Franklin Pierce. The speech became (further) immortalized in a children's story which sold hundreds of thousands of copies. Eventually the story of the fabrication of the speech emerged in the 1990s. Many people still do not believe that the speech is fake and think that Perry was trying to take credit for monetary benefit. But what is probably more ironic is that the fake speech is far more famous than the story of the origins. The story of the speech and an interview with Ted Perry is published in *The New Earth Reader: The Best of Terra Nova*, 1999.[12]

B. THE WILD LIFE ACT: SCOPE AND IMPLEMENTATION

The Wild Life (Protection) Act of 1972 provides the statutory framework for protecting wild animals, plants and their habitats. The Act adopts a two-pronged conservation strategy: *specified* endangered species are protected regardless of location, and *all* species are protected in

[10] *Sachidanand Pandey v State of West Bengal* (1987) 2 SCC 295, 302; *T N Godavarman Thirumulpad v Union of India (Kudremukh Iron Ore Company* case*)* (2002) 10 SCC 606, 618.

[11] *Kholamuhana Primary Fishermen Coop Society v State of Orissa* AIR 1994 Ori 191; *Centre for Environmental Law World Wide Fund for Nature v State of Orissa* AIR 1999 Ori 15; *Thilakan v Circle Inspector of Police* AIR 2008 Ker 48; *Rakesh v State of Rajasthan* (2012) 2 RLW 1200; *Kondiba v Spl Dy Collector* (2013) 6 ALT 1; *Govinda Prasad Ladia v WBHIDC Ltd* (2015) 3 Cal L T 142; *Court on its Own Motion v State of Maharashtra* 2012 (1) MH L J 232; *Naveen Chandra Pant v State of Uttarakhand* (2017) SCC Online Utt 389.

[12] Kartik Shanker, *From Soup to Superstar: The Story of Sea Turtle Conservation along the Indian Coast* 191 (2015).

designated protected areas called national parks, sanctuaries, conservation reserves or community reserves.

The Wild Life Act was enacted by Parliament under Article 252, after 11 State legislatures passed the required resolutions.[13] After the subject wildlife was moved to the Concurrent List by the Forty-Second Constitutional Amendment in 1976, Parliament was empowered to enact laws relating to wildlife without recourse to Article 252(1). By the 1991 amendment to the Wild Life Act, Parliament extended the Act to the whole of India except Jammu and Kashmir, which has its own Wild Life Protection Act similar to the national law.[14]

The Wild Life Act provides for the appointment of wildlife wardens and other staff to implement the Act.[15] In several states, the office of the Chief Wild Life Warden and the Chief Conservator of Forests is united in a single post and the responsibilities under both statutes are discharged by the same person.

Except under specified conditions,[16] the Act prohibits hunting the animals listed in Schedules I, II, III and IV.[17] Generally, a species listed in Schedule I and Part II of Schedule II receives the highest degree of protection. Offences committed with respect to species in these lists attract the maximum punishment. Under the Act, the state government may declare any area of adequate 'ecological, faunal, floral, geomorphological, natural or zoological significance' a sanctuary[18] or a national park.[19] In both sanctuaries and national parks, public entry is restricted[20] and the destruction of any wildlife or habitat is prohibited.[21] In theory, national parks enjoy a higher degree of protection than sanctuaries. For example, the grazing of livestock is prohibited within a national park,[22] but permissible in a sanctuary.[23]

By the 1991 amendment, specified plants were brought under the protective umbrella of the Act.[24] The amendments also envisaged establishment of a Central Zoo Authority to regulate the management and functioning of zoos.[25]

In 2003, several key provisions were inserted by amendment. The Central Government was required to constitute the National Board for Wild Life with the Prime Minister as chairperson and with over 40 other members.[26] The National Board promotes conservation of wildlife and forests by framing policies, advising the government, making recommendations and reviewing the progress of conservation initiatives.[27] The National Board is required to publish a status report every two years on wildlife in the country.[28] Unsurprisingly, in view

[13] *Pradeep Krishen v Union of India* AIR 1966 SC 2040. Article 253 (relied on to enact the Air Act in 1981 and the Environment (Protection) Act in 1986) was not invoked by Parliament to introduce national wildlife legislation.

[14] A. Kothari, P. Pandey, S. Singh & D. Variava, *Management of National Parks and Sanctuaries in India: A Status Report* 107 (1989).

[15] Sections 3 and 4.

[16] Sections 11 and 12.

[17] Section 9.

[18] Section 18.

[19] Section 35.

[20] Sections 27 and 35(8). In *Bombay Burmah Trading Corporation v Field Director (Project Tiger)* AIR 2000 Mad 163, the High Court upheld restrictions on plying vehicles in the sanctuary.

[21] Sections 29 and 35(6).

[22] Section 35(7).

[23] Sections 29 and 33(d).

[24] Chapter IIIA.

[25] Chapter IVA.

[26] Section 5A.

[27] Section 5C.

[28] Section 5C(2)(e).

of its unwieldy size, the National Board seldom convenes and mostly operates through its standing committee. A State Board for Wild Life[29] under the Chief Minister of the State must advise the state government on selecting and managing protected areas, formulating conservation policies and adopting measures to harmonize the needs of tribals and other forest dwellers with a view to improving conservation.[30]

The 2003 amendment introduced two additional categories of protected areas: conservation reserves and community reserves. A conservation reserve may be declared by a state after consulting local communities in respect of state land adjacent to national parks and sanctuaries which link one protected area with another.[31] The purposes of creating a conservation reserve are to provide corridors and buffers and to protect landscapes, seascapes, flora and fauna and their habitat. A community reserve may be declared by a state government where a community or individual has volunteered to conserve wildlife and its habitat on any private or community land.[32]

After the 2003 amendment, the boundaries of sanctuaries and national parks may not be altered by the state government except on a recommendation of the National Board.[33] The 2003 amendment also inserted chapter VI-A into the parent statute. This chapter contains a set of provisions covering the forfeiture of property derived from illegal hunting and trade.

A steep decline in the national tiger count attributed to poaching prompted the 2006 amendment. Chapters IV-B and IV-C were introduced, providing for the constitution of the National Tiger Conservation Authority[34] (NTCA) and a specialist Wildlife Crime Control Bureau.[35] The NTCA, headed by the Minister of Environment and Forests, is tasked with approving the Tiger Conservation Plan prepared by each state government[36] and submitting an annual report of its activities to Parliament.[37] The responsibilities of the Wildlife Crime Control Bureau extend to collecting and collating intelligence relating to organized wildlife crime, implementing national obligations under international conventions and protocols and developing capacities to investigate and prosecute wildlife crimes.[38]

The Act regulates trade and commerce in wild animals, animal articles, trophies[39] and derivatives from certain animals.[40] Any violations of the provisions in the Act attract imprisonment and fines which have progressively increased with amendments to the parent Act. Patterned on similar provisions in the Air and Water Acts, citizen prosecutions are permitted after giving 60 days' notice of intent to the government.[41]

In December 2021, Bill No. 159 of 2021 was tabled in the Lok Sabha to amend the Wild Life Act. The Bill sought to rationalize the statutory schedules and introduce a new chapter for the better implementation of the Convention on International Trade in Endangered Species of

29 Section 6.
30 Section 8.
31 Section 36A.
32 Section 36C.
33 Sections 26A(3) and 35(5).
34 Section 38L.
35 Section 38Y.
36 Section 38O.
37 Sections 38S and 38T.
38 Section 38Z.
39 Chapter V.
40 Chapter VA.
41 Section 35.

Wild Fauna and Flora (CITES). The Bill also envisioned empowering the state board to constitute a standing committee and to delegate its powers to the committee.

On 27 August 2003, the Supreme Court rendered two judgments relating to the ban on ivory trade in terms of section 49C of the Wild Life Act. In *Indian Handicrafts Emporium v Union of India*,[42] the appellant manufactured objects of art made from ivory. Between 1971 and 1986, the emporium imported from Africa around 755 kgs of ivory articles and another 10 kgs of ivory with metal. At the time of import, there were no restrictions. In 1977, the government accorded the Indian elephant the highest degree of protection by including it in Schedule A of the Act and in the same year it also banned the export of ivory. In 1986, the Wild Life Act was amended to impose restrictions on trade in wild animals, animal articles and trophies. In 1991, section 49C was amended to completely ban the trade of imported ivory and a period of six months was provided for the disposal of imported ivory stocks.[43]

The emporium petitioned the Delhi High Court challenging the constitutionality of the 1991 Act and enjoyed a brief temporary injunction against operation of the Act. Eventually, the High Court rejected the challenge. The emporium did not sell its stock of imported ivory during the six-month window provided by the statute or during the term of the High Court injunction. Instead, it carried the case to the Supreme Court claiming that the legally imported ivory did not vest in government, that it be allowed to retain the ivory and in any case it could not be deprived of property without due compensation.

The focus of the case was section 49C which reads:

> 49-C. *Declaration by dealers* – (1) Every person carrying on the business or occupation referred to in sub-section (1) of section 49-B shall, within thirty days from the specified date, declare to the Chief Wild Life Warden or the authorised officer, —
> (a) his stocks, if any, as at the end of the specified date of—
> (i) scheduled animal articles;
> (ii) scheduled animals and parts thereof;
> (iii) trophies and uncured trophies derived from scheduled animals;
> (iv) captive animals, being scheduled animals;
> (v) ivory imported into India or articles made therefrom;
> (b) the place or places at which the stocks mentioned in the declaration are kept; and
> (c) the description of such items, if any, of the stocks mentioned in the declaration which he desires to retain with himself for his bona fide personal use.
> (2) On receipt of a declaration under sub-section (1), the Chief Wild Life Warden or the authorised officer may take all or any of the measures specified in section 41 and for this purpose, the provisions of section 41 shall, so far as may be, apply.
> (3) Where, in a declaration made under sub-section (1), the person making the declaration expresses his desire to retain with himself any of the items of the stocks specified in the declaration for his bona fide personal use, the Chief Wild Life Warden, with the prior approval of the Director, may, if he is satisfied that the person is in lawful possession of such items, issue certificates of ownership in favour of such person with respect to all, or as the case may be, such of the items as in the opinion of the Chief Wild Life Warden, are required for the bona fide personal use of such person and affix upon such items identification marks in such manner as may be prescribed:

---

42 (2003) 7 SCC 589.

43 Section 49A(a) read with section 49C allowed traders a lead time of six months before the embargo set in.

Provided that no such item shall be kept in any commercial premises.

(4) No person shall obliterate or counterfeit any identification mark referred to in sub-section (3).

(5) An appeal shall lie against any refusal to grant certificate of ownership under sub-section (3) and the provisions of sub-sections (2), (3) and (4) of section 46 shall, so far as may be, apply in relation to appeals under this sub-section.

(6) Where a person who has been issued a certificate of ownership under sub-section (3) in respect of any item, –

(a) transfers such item to any person, whether by way of gift, sale or otherwise, or

(b) transfers or transports from the State in which he resides to another State any such item,

he shall, within thirty days of such transfer or transport, report the transfer or transport to the Chief Wild Life Warden or the authorised officer within whose jurisdiction the transfer or transport is effected.

(7) No person, other than a person who has been issued a certificate of ownership under sub-section (3) shall, on and after the specified date, keep under his control, sell or offer for sale or transfer to any person any scheduled animal, a scheduled animal article or ivory imported into India or any article made therefrom.

The Supreme Court recognized the importance of preserving wildlife and that the 1991 Amendment Act was to give effect to the prohibition of internal and trans-border trade in ivory in terms of CITES. The Supreme Court held:

(a) Dealing in imported ivory so long the law permits may be a fundamental right but if the statute prohibits it, it must be held to be a law within the meaning of clause (6) of Article 19 of the Constitution of India in terms whereof reasonable restriction is imposed.[44] A trade which is dangerous to ecology may be regulated or totally prohibited. For the aforementioned purpose, regulation would include prohibition.[45]

(b) The primal object for which dealing in ivory imported from Africa had been prohibited was to see that while holding the stock, the people may not deal in Indian ivory which may be procured from illegal killings of the Indian elephant. The amending Act indirectly seeks to protect the Indian elephant and to arrest their further depletion.[46]

(c) Wildlife forms part of our cultural heritage. Animals play a vital role in maintaining ecological balance. The amendments have been brought for the purpose of saving the endangered species from extinction as also from arresting depletion in their number caused by callous exploitation thereof.'[47]

(d) Experience shows that poaching may be difficult to be completely checked. Preventive measures as regards poaching leading to killing of elephants for the purpose of extraction of their tusks is a difficult task to achieve and, thus, Parliament must have thought it expedient to put a complete ban on trade in ivory to meet the requirement of the country.[48]

The court rejected the appeal, holding that the impugned amendment imposed reasonable restrictions. The following excerpt examines the court's construction of section 49C (which appears correct) and its casual treatment of the compensation issue. Can you supply a better reason (than the one furnished by the court) to deny compensation?

---

[44] Article 19(6) permits the state to make 'any law imposing, in the interest of the general public, reasonable restrictions' on the practice of any trade or business.

[45] (2003) 7 SCC 589, 603.

[46] *Id.* at 606.

[47] *Id.* at 608.

[48] *Id.* at 609.

INDIAN HANDICRAFTS EMPORIUM v UNION OF INDIA

(2003) 7 SCC 589

S B Sinha, J:

* * *

Section 49-C provides that every person carrying on the business or occupation referred to in sub-section (1) of section 49-B, within thirty days from the specified date, declare to the Chief Wild Life Warden or the authorised officer, his stocks, if any, as at the end of the specified date of ivory imported into India or articles made therefrom, the place or places at which the stocks mentioned in the declaration are kept and the description of such items, if any, of the stocks mentioned in the declaration which he desires to retain with himself for his *bona fide* personal use. Sub-section (3) of section 49-C further provides that where, in a declaration made under sub-section (1), the person making the declaration expresses his desire to retain with himself any of the items of the stocks specified in the declaration for his *bona fide* personal use, the Chief Wild Life Warden, with the prior approval of the Director, may, if he is satisfied that the person is in lawful possession of such items, issue certificate of ownership in favour of such person with respect to all, or as the case may be, such of the items as in the opinion of the Chief Wild Life Warden, are required for the *bona fide* personal use of such person and affix upon such items identification marks in such manner, as may be prescribed. Sub-section (6) of section 49-C further provides that where a person who has been issued a certificate of ownership under sub-section (3) in respect of any item, it is permissible for him to transfer any such item to any such person, whether by way of gift, sale or otherwise, or transfer or transport from the State in which he resides to another State any such item and he shall within thirty days from such transfer or transport, report the transfer or transport to the Chief Wild Life Warden or the authorised officer within whose jurisdiction the transfer or transport is affected.

On coming into force of Act 28 of 1986 or Act 44 of 1991, however, it may be true that the property does not automatically vest in the Government. It is not in dispute that in terms of clause (c) of section 39 of the Act which was inserted by Act 44 of 1991 only ivory imported into India and articles made from such ivory in respect of which any offence against this Act or any rule or order made thereunder has been committed, would be the property of the State Government and not otherwise. But the issue is required to be considered from a different angle.

On or from the specified date, however, carrying on any trade or commerce, *inter alia*, in relation to ivory imported into India or any article made therefrom is completely prohibited. Despite such provision, however, a person carrying on a business or occupation or dealing in trophies, animal articles etc. derived from scheduled animals would be, in terms of sub-section (1) of section 49-C of the Act, entitled to file a declaration disclosing his stocks of ivory imported into India or articles made therefrom. Once such a declaration is made and in the event such person makes a declaration expressing his desire to retain with himself any of the items specified therein for his *bona fide* use, a certificate of ownership may be granted for such item or items which in the opinion of the Chief Wild Life Warden are required therefor. Only in relation to items for which such certificate of ownership has been granted, a transfer thereof is permissible subject to the restrictions imposed under sub-section (6) of section 49-C. Sub-section (7) of section 49-C, however, provides for prohibition of such ivory imported into India or any article made therefrom from being kept under the control of the trader for sale or offer for sale or transfer to any person whatsoever.

The upshot of the aforesaid provisions is that any trader who has imported ivory legally into India prior to coming into force of Act 44 of 1991, although would not be entitled to carry on any business or trade in respect thereof, but having regard to the provisions referred to hereinbefore, unless he commits an offence in relation thereto, the same would not vest in the Government. He would, however, not be entitled to keep possession thereof except in the mode and manner provided for in section 49-C of the Act.

On a conjoint reading of the aforesaid provisions, there cannot be any doubt whatsoever that any person who has obtained such a certificate under sub-section (3) of section 49-C only may keep possession of the property i.e. subject to grant of ownership certificate. In the event he complies with the aforesaid provisions, he would be entitled to transfer or transport such item as provided for in sub-section (6) of section 49-C. There cannot further be any doubt that in the event no certificate of ownership is granted in favour of a trader in terms of sub-section (3) of section 49-C, the question of his becoming entitled to transfer or transport the property would not arise, in which event, in terms of sub-section (7) of section 49-C, he would be disentitled not only from selling or offering for sale or transfer the said items but also from keeping the said items under his control....

The legislature has deliberately used the words '*bona fide* personal use' in section 49-C and has placed the onus on the traders to prove the same so as to be entitled to retain the articles out of the stocks declared by it. This requirement is due to the fact that the acquisition of an animal article by an individual non-trader at the time of purchase would be presumed to be one for his own personal *bona fide* use, while on the other hand in the case of the traders the acquisition of animal articles as reflected in the stocks of a trader would solely be for the purpose of sale. Hence, the imposition of the requirement of personal *bona fide* use in the case of traders cannot be said to be discriminatory or arbitrary or irrational or perverse entitling the appellants to continue to have control thereover....

A trader in terms of a statute is prohibited from carrying on trade. He also cannot remain in control over the animal article, the logical consequence where for would be that he must be deprived of the possession thereof. The possession of the animal article including imported ivory must, therefore, be handed over to the competent authority. In a case of this nature where a statute has been enacted in public interest, restriction in the matter of possession of the property must be held to be implicit. If section 49(7) is not so construed, it cannot be given effect to.

We, therefore, are of the opinion that the appellants have no right to possess the articles in question. Keeping in view the fact that the provisions of the statute have been held to be *intra vires* the question of compensating the appellants would not arise as vesting of possession thereof in the State must be inferred by necessary implication....

The second judgment concerned mammoth ivory. M/s Unigems, a trader, imported mammoth fossils in 1987. The case bears the name of another appellant, Balram Kumawat, a skilled carver. The appellants claimed that mammoth fossil ivory was distinct because it belonged to an extinct species and could not be the subject of a ban relatable to the elephant, a living species. The appellant submitted that the Delhi High Court erred in extending the ivory ban to mammoth ivory since these distinct items were distinguishable by visual and non-destructive means.

BALRAM KUMAWAT v UNION OF INDIA
(2003) 7 SCC 628

S B Sinha, J:

***

What has been banned is ivory. There is complete prohibition of trade in ivory. Such a complete prohibition is a reasonable restriction within the meaning of clause (6) of Article 19 of the Constitution of India. The impugned Act being not unreasonable does not also attract the wrath of Article 14 of the Constitution of India.

For the purpose of determination of the question, we need to consider only the dictionary meaning of the term 'ivory'. Commercial meaning or technical meaning of an object or article is required to be taken recourse to when the same is necessary for the purpose of meeting the requirements of law. The law in no uncertain terms says that no person shall trade in ivory. It does not say that what is prohibited is trade in elephant ivory or other types of ivory. The purport and object of the Act, as noticed in the judgment in *Indian Handicrafts Emporium* is that nobody can carry on business activity in imported ivory so that while doing so, trade in ivory procured by way of poaching of elephants may be facilitated. Parliament, therefore, advisedly used the word 'ivory' instead of elephant ivory. The intention of Parliament in this behalf, in our opinion, is absolutely clear and unambiguous. We cannot assume that Parliament was not aware of the existence of different types of ivory. If the intention of Parliament was to confine the subject-matter of ban under Act 44 of 1991 to elephant ivory, it would have said so explicitly.

As noticed hereinbefore, the object of Parliament was not only to ban trade in imported elephant ivory but ivory of every description so that poaching of elephants can be effectively restricted....

The courts will therefore reject that construction which will defeat the plain intention of the legislature even though there may be some inexactitude in the language used. Reducing the legislation [to] futility shall be avoided and in a case where the intention of the legislature cannot be given effect to, the courts would accept the bolder construction for the purpose of bringing about an effective result. The courts, when rule of purposive construction is gaining momentum, should be very reluctant to hold that Parliament has achieved nothing by the language it used when it is tolerably plain what it seeks to achieve....

NOTES AND QUESTIONS

1. In *State of Bihar v Murad Ali Khan*,[49] the Supreme Court allowed the state government's appeals and restored the orders of the magistrate taking cognizance of the offence under the Wild Life Act. The accusation against the respondents was that they had shot and killed an elephant in the Kundurugutu Range Forest and had removed its ivory tusks. In its judgment, the Supreme Court explained the object of the Wild Life Act:

> The policy and object of the Wild Life Laws have a long history and are the result of an increasing awareness of the compelling need to restore the serious ecological imbalances introduced the depredations inflicted on nature by man. The state to which the ecological imbalances and the consequent environmental damage have reached is so alarming that unless immediate, determined and effective steps were taken, the damage might become irreversible. The preservation of the fauna and flora, some species of which are getting extinct at an alarming rate, has been a great and urgent necessity for the survival of humanity and these laws reflect ... a grave situation emerging from a long history of callous insensitiveness to the enormity of the risks to mankind that go with the deterioration of environment.... Environmentalists' conception of the ecological balance in nature is based on the fundamental concept that nature is 'a series of complex biotic communities of which a man is an inter-dependent part' and that it should not be given a part to trespass and diminish the whole. The largest single factor in the depletion of the wealth of animal life in nature has been the 'civilized man' operating directly through excessive commercial hunting or more disastrously, indirectly through invading or destroying natural habitats.[50]

2. Concerned by the lax enforcement of the Wild Life Act in several states, the Centre for Environmental Law, WWF, petitioned the Supreme Court under Article 32 seeking diverse directions to improve implementation. In an interim order dated 14 August 1997, the Supreme Court directed the states which had either not constituted wildlife advisory boards or where the term of the board had expired, to constitute boards within two months. State governments which had failed to appoint wildlife wardens were asked to appoint wardens for all the areas within the states. The court noticed several instances where despite notifications intending to establish sanctuaries and national parks, the concerned government had failed to take further steps to finally notify the protected areas. The states were directed to complete

[49] AIR 1989 SC 1.
[50] *Id.* at 3, 4.

the process of determining the rights and acquisition of lands as contemplated by the Act, within a period of one year. To guard protected areas from 'de-notification' or 'de-reservation' the state governments were directed to refer the proposal to the Indian Board for Wild Life (IBWL) for its opinion and place the proposal and the opinion of the IBWL before the Legislative Assembly.[51]

The 2003 amendments substituted section 6 in the parent Act and replaced the wildlife advisory board with the State Board for Wildlife. Moreover, after the 2003 amendment, boundaries of a sanctuary or national park may be altered only upon a recommendation by the National Board for Wild Life.

3. Earlier, the WWF approached the Delhi High Court seeking directions against the Union Government and the states to take effective steps to protect wild animals, tigers in particular, from being poached or illegally hunted. The petitioners also sought directions to curb the illegal trade in animal articles. The division bench judgment delivered by Justice Dalveer Bhandari refers to the Parliamentary debates that preceded enactment of the Wild Life Act, reviews India's international obligations under CITES and records the grim statistics and trends regarding seizures of animal skins by the Wild Life Department.

The judgment looked closely at the problems confronting the tiger. Incidents of poaching were on the rise, and census figures of the tiger population suggested that the gains made by the 'Project Tiger' initiative launched by the Union Government in 1972 might soon dissipate because of the tremendous demand for tiger skins and bones in China and elsewhere. In an effort to improve implementation, the High Court directed the respondents to provide adequate staff and to equip the forest guards with modern weapons. The court urged the staff to enlist the aid of villagers living in the neighbourhood of sanctuaries. The postal and customs authorities as well as local police and revenue intelligence were told to strengthen the enforcement machinery to prevent the illegal traffic in animal articles. Finally, the High Court constituted a high-level committee to implement the directions and to make recommendations for the preservation and protection of wild animals in national parks with particular reference to the tiger.[52]

So long as there remains an unbridled international demand for tiger products, will any of these well-intentioned policing measures help? Is a well-enforced international ban on tiger articles (similar to the ivory ban, which may have reduced the slaughter of African elephants for their tusks) the answer? If so, should WWF focus its energy to that end? Do lawyers and judges have a role in this effort?

4. I R Coelho and other landowners living in the hilly tracts of Tamil Nadu wanted a free hand to protect their property. Animals listed in Schedule I to the Act were damaging their property, including standing crops.[53] Despite the threat to property, according to Coelho the Act unreasonably prevented the hunting of these animals. The High Court rejected this plea, holding that the Act did not deprive the owner from holding, enjoying and protecting her property. The right claimed by the petitioners to hunt wild animals when they proved dangerous to property was without basis.

5. Sukh Dev Singh Roy brought an unusual complaint to the Delhi High Court in 1992. Singh was a farmer in Ghaziabad, Uttar Pradesh. His crops were frequently damaged by wild

---

51 *Centre for Environmental Law, WWF v Union of India* 1997 (6) SCALE 8 (SP). 'WWF', the World Wide Fund for Nature, is a leading non-governmental organization working in the field of wildlife conservation.

52 *World Wide Fund for Nature v Union of India* 1994 (54) DEL L T 286.

53 *I R Coelho v State of Tamil Nadu* 1992 (1) MAD L REP 355.

boars and 'blue bulls' (Nilgai). Section 62, prior to its amendment in 1991, allowed the state government to declare any wild animals to be 'vermin' for an area. (Vermin may be hunted without restriction.) However, the 1991 amendment divested the state of this power and now the Centre alone was empowered to declare vermin. Singh considered the impugned provisions illegal since they divested the state government of lawful authority. The High Court dismissed the petition since the subject of wildlife was in the Concurrent List and Parliament had the power to legislate in this regard. Applying the doctrine of pith and substance, the court held that the impugned provision related principally to the protection of animals and birds and not agriculture (a state subject).[54]

6. In *Chief Forest Conservator (Wild Life) v Nisar Khan*,[55] the respondent held a licence for dealing in several species of birds specified in Schedule IV of the Act. He mainly sold munias, parakeets, mainas and buntings. When he sought renewal of his licence, it was not granted by the authority, which prompted Khan to approach the Allahabad High Court for a direction to the authorities to issue the licence. He claimed that his fundamental right to carry on the trade or business was being infringed by the state. The High Court allowed the writ petition. It quashed a notice that required Khan to dispose of all the birds in his possession, restrained the conservator from interfering in the business and required a licence to be issued to Khan. The Supreme Court reversed the High Court decision. The Supreme Court held that trapping birds was prohibited and unless the licensing authority was satisfied that the source of the birds was by reason of captive breeding, the authority was justified in rejecting the application. The court held that the provisions of the Act and Rules must be construed strictly in order to serve the purpose of the statute. A licence to deal in birds in captivity could not be granted where the birds were sourced illegally. Khan was permitted to apply afresh and the authority was directed to issue a licence upon being satisfied that the provisions of the Act and the Rules would not be violated.

Madhukar Rao's case decided by the Supreme Court in January 2008 brought to a close Madhya Pradesh's spirited effort to retain custody of a vehicle seized 11 years earlier under section 50(1)(c) of the Wild Life Act.

STATE OF M P v MADHUKAR RAO

(2008) 14 SCC 624

Aftab Alam, J: This judgment will dispose of four appeals in all of which the same question arises for consideration. The question is: whether a vehicle or vessel, etc. seized under section 50(1)(c) of the Wild Life (Protection) Act, 1972 (hereinafter referred to as 'the Act') is put beyond the power of the Magistrate to direct its release during the pendency of trial in exercise of powers under section 451 of the Code of Criminal Procedure, 1973 (hereinafter referred to as 'the Code')?

On behalf of the appellant, the State of Madhya Pradesh, it is strongly contended that the answer to the question would be only in the affirmative. The contention appears to us to be *ex facie* untenable but in order to examine the stand of the State Government it would be necessary to state the facts and circumstances in which the question arises and to take note of the relevant provisions of law in light of which it is to be answered.

The facts of the case are taken from Civil Appeal No. 5196 of 2001, *State of M P v Madhukar Rao*, which was the leading case before the High Court. On 12-3-1997 at about 3.30 a.m. in course of checking a Sub-Inspector of Excise found a Tata Sumo vehicle, bearing Registration No. MH 31 H 6919, carrying 206 kg of antlers. The vehicle was owned by Madhukar Rao, the

---

[54] *Sukh Dev Singh Roy v Union of India* 1993 (60) Del L T 319.
[55] (2003) 4 SCC 595.

respondent, but he was not in it at the time of checking. The Excise Sub-Inspector informed the officers of the Forest Department who registered a case being Offence No. 6527/97 under sections 39, 42, 43, 44, 49 and 51 of the Act. The four persons occupying the vehicle were arrested and the vehicle and the antlers were seized under section 50(1)(c) of the Act. The Judicial Magistrate, Raipur, was duly informed about the institution of the case on 13-3-1997. [The magistrate directed release of the vehicle; the Sessions Judge in revision reversed the magistrate's order declaring the seized vehicle as government property in terms of section 39(1)(d); and eventually a Full Bench of the High Court restored the magistrate's order.]

On behalf of the State, it is contended that after the amendments made in section 50 and section 39(1)(d) of the Act w.e.f. 2-10-1991 by Act 44 of 1991 there was no way that a vehicle seized for violation of the Act could be released. The amendments in section 50 took away the power from the Assistant Director of Wild Life Preservation or Wild Life Warden (or an officer superior to them) and the Magistrate under the Code, in any event, had no such power. Moreover, the amendment of section 39(1)(d) of the Act made any interim release of the vehicle further impossible.

In order to appreciate the submissions made on behalf of the State it would be necessary to examine the relevant provisions of law. Chapter VI of the Act contains provisions dealing with the prevention and detection of offences. The chapter begins with section 50 that gives to the specified officers the powers of entry, search, arrest and detention. It is a long section having as many as nine sub-sections. Sub-section (1) which is sub-divided into three clauses is as follows:

> 50. *Power of entry, search, arrest and detention* – (1) Notwithstanding anything contained in any other law for the time being in force, the Director or any other officer authorised by him in this behalf or the Chief Wild Life Warden or the authorised officer or any Forest Officer or any police officer not below the rank of a sub-inspector, may, if he has reasonable grounds for believing that any person has committed an offence against this Act, –
>
> (a) require any person to produce for inspection any captive animal, wild animal, animal article, meat, trophy, uncured trophy, specified plant or part or derivative thereof in his control, custody or possession, or any licence, permit or other document granted to him or required to be kept by him under the provisions of this Act;
>
> (b) stop any vehicle or vessel in order to conduct search or inquiry or enter upon and search any premises, land, vehicle or vessel, in the occupation of such person, and open and search any baggage or other things in the possession;
>
> (c) *seize any* captive animal, wild animal, animal article, meat, trophy or uncured trophy, or any specified plant or part or derivative thereof, in respect of which an offence against this Act appears to have been committed, in the possession of any person *together with any trap, tool, vehicle, vessel or weapon used for committing any such offence* and, unless he is satisfied that such person will appear and answer any charge which may be preferred against him, arrest him without warrant, and detain him:
>
> Provided that where a fisherman, residing within ten kilometres of a sanctuary or National Park, inadvertently enters on a boat, not used for commercial fishing, in the territorial waters in that sanctuary or National Park, a fishing tackle or net on such boat shall not be seized. (emphasis supplied)

Before the Act was subjected to a large number of amendments with effect from 2-10-1991, section 50 had sub-section (2) which was as follows:

> 50.(2) Any officer of a rank not inferior to that of an Assistant Director of Wild Life preservation or Wild Life Warden, who, or whose subordinate *has seized any trap, tool, vehicle, vessel or weapon* under clause (c) of sub-section (1), *may release the same on* the execution by the owner thereof of a bond for the production of the property so released, if and when so required, before the Magistrate having jurisdiction to try the offence on account of which the seizure has been made.

The Amendment Act 44 of 1991 deleted sub-section (2) and inserted in its place sub-section (3-A) which is as follows:

> 50.(3-A) Any officer of a rank not inferior to that of an Assistant Director of Wild Life Preservation or as Assistant Conservator of Forests, who, or whose subordinate, has seized any captive animal or wild animal under clause (c) of sub-section (1) may give the same for custody on the execution by any person of a bond for the production of such animal if and when so required, before the Magistrate having jurisdiction to try the offence on account of which the seizure has been made.

At the same time, amendments were made in section 39(1)(d) after which it reads as follows:

> 39. *Wild animals, etc., to be government property* — (1) Every –
>
> (d) vehicle, vessel, weapon, trap or tool that has been used for committing an offence and has been seized under the provisions of this Act, shall be the property of the State Government, and, where such animal is hunted in a sanctuary or National Park declared by the Central Government, such animal or any animal article, trophy, uncured trophy or meat derived from such animal, or any vehicle, vessel, weapon, trap or tool used in such hunting shall be the property of the Central Government.

* * *

We are unable to accept the submissions [of the state]. To contend that the use of a vehicle in the commission of an offence under the Act, without anything else would bar its interim release appears to us to be quite unreasonable. There may be a case where a vehicle was undeniably used for commission of an offence under the Act but the vehicle owner is in a position to show that it was used for committing the offence only after it was stolen from his possession. In that situation, we are unable to see why the vehicle should not be released in the owner's favour during the pendency of the trial.

We are also unable to accept the submission that section 50 and the other provisions in Chapter VI of the Act exclude the application of any provisions of the Code. It is indeed true that section 50 of the Act has several provisions especially aimed at prevention and detection of offences under the Act. For example, it confers powers of entry, search, arrest and detention on Wild Life and Forest Officers besides police officers who are normally entrusted with the responsibility of investigation and detection of offences; further sub-section (4) of section 51 expressly excludes application of section 360 of the Code and the provisions of the Probation of Offenders Act to persons eighteen years or above in age. But it does not mean that section 50 in itself or taken along with the other provisions under Chapter VI constitutes a self-contained mechanism so as to exclude every other provision of the Code. This position becomes further clear from sub-section (4) of section 50 that requires that any person detained, or things seized should forthwith be taken before a Magistrate.

Sub-section (4) of section 50 reads as follows:

> 50.(4) Any person detained, or things seized under the foregoing power, shall forthwith be taken before a Magistrate to be dealt with according to law under intimation to the Chief Wild Life Warden or the officer authorised by him in this regard.

It has to be noted here that the expression used in the sub-section is 'according to law' and not 'according to the provisions of the Act'. The expression 'according to law' undoubtedly widens the scope and plainly indicates the application of the provisions of the Code.

We find that the Full Bench of the High Court has correctly taken the view that the deletion of sub-section (2) and its replacement by sub-section (3-A) in section 50 of the Act had no effect on the powers of the Magistrate to release the seized vehicle during the pendency of trial under the provisions of the Code. The effect of deletion of sub-section (2) and its replacement by sub-section (3-A) may be summed up thus: as long as sub-section (2) of section 50 was on the statute book the Magistrate would not entertain a prayer for interim release of a seized vehicle, etc. until an application for release was made before the departmental authorities as provided in that sub-section. Further, in case the prayer for interim release was rejected by the departmental authority the findings or observations made in its order would receive due consideration and would carry a lot of weight before the Magistrate while considering the prayer for interim release of the vehicle. But now that sub-section (2) of section 50 stands deleted, an aggrieved person has no option but to approach the Magistrate directly for interim release of the seized vehicle....

The decision of this Court closer to the issue under consideration may be found in *Moti Lal v CBI* (2002) 4 SCC 713. In that case an offence committed under the Act was handed over for investigation to the Central Bureau of Investigation and the action was assailed exactly on the plea that the Wild Life (Protection) Act is a special law and it contained comprehensive provisions for investigation, inquiry, search, seizure, trial and imposition of punishment and, therefore, the police force establishment under the Delhi Special Police Establishment Act was not empowered to investigate the case. This Court rejected the contention and after examining in detail the various provisions of the Act particularly the provisions of section 50 came to find and hold as follows:

> 'The scheme of section 50 of the Wild Life Act makes it abundantly clear that a police officer is also empowered to investigate the offences and search and seize the offending articles. For trial of offences, the Code of Criminal Procedure is required to be followed and for that there is no other specific provision to the contrary. The special procedure prescribed is limited for taking cognizance of the offence as well as powers are given to other officers mentioned in section 50 for inspection, arrest, search and seizure as well as of recording statement. The power to compound offences is also conferred under section 54. Section 51 provides for penalties which would indicate that certain offences are cognizable offences meaning thereby a police officer can arrest without warrant. Sub-section (5) of section 51 provides that nothing contained in Section 360 of the Code of Criminal Procedure or in the Probation of Offenders Act, 1958 shall apply to a person convicted of an offence with respect to hunting in a sanctuary or a national park or of an offence against any provision of Chapter 5-A unless such person is under 18 years of age. The aforesaid specific provisions are contrary to the provisions contained in the Code of Criminal Procedure and that would prevail during the trial. However, from this, it cannot be said that operation of rest of the provisions of the Code of Criminal Procedure are excluded.
>
> *In this view of the matter, there is no substance in the contention raised by the learned counsel for the appellant that section 50 of the Wild Life Act is a complete code and, therefore, CBI would have no jurisdiction to investigate the offences under the said Act.* Hence, it cannot be said that the judgment and order passed by the High Court rejecting the petition filed by the appellant is in any way illegal or erroneous.'

We have, therefore, no doubt that the provisions of section 50 of the Act and the amendments made there under do not in any way affect the Magistrate's power to make an order of interim release of the vehicle under section 451 of the Code.

Learned counsel submitted that section 39(1)(d) of the Act made the articles seized under section 50(1)(c) of the Act as government property and, therefore, there was no question of their release. The submission was carefully considered by the Full Bench of the High Court and on an examination of the various provisions of the Act it was held that the provision of section 39(1)(d) would come into play only after a court of competent jurisdiction found the accusation and the allegations made against the accused as true and recorded the finding that the seized article was, as a matter of fact, used in the commission of offence. Any attempt to operationalise section 39(1)(d) of the Act merely on the basis of seizure and accusations/ allegations levelled by the departmental authorities would bring it into conflict with the constitutional provisions and would render it unconstitutional and invalid. In our opinion, the High Court has taken a perfectly correct view and the provisions of section 39(1)(d) cannot be used against exercise of the magisterial power to release the vehicle during pendency of the trial....

NOTES AND QUESTIONS

1. In *Principal Chief Conservator of Forests v J K Johnson*,[56] the Supreme Court reached a conclusion similar to the last paragraph of the excerpt, holding that forfeiture of a vehicle used for committing an offence must await conviction by a competent court. Otherwise, the forfeiture would transgress constitutional guarantees with regard to property.

2. Why was the state so keen to hold on to the vehicle? Was it because it lacked the confidence to successfully prosecute the owner and retaining the vehicle was its best hope of inflicting some cost on the suspected deer hunters?

3. The application to have the vehicle released took 11 years in court. Is the process the punishment?

4. The state of Madhya Pradesh had better luck in persuading the Supreme Court in *Uday Singh's* case.[57] Finding that the state amendments to the Indian Forest Act of 1927 create special machinery for confiscation of vehicles used to commit forest offences, the court distinguished *Madhukar Rao*. This leads to an incongruent situation where the deterrence for a forest offence is considerably greater than for a wildlife offence.

5. Viewed from the perspective of the wildlife and forest officers, an effective manner of dealing with timber smugglers is to confiscate the wood and the vehicle used. When the Forest Department seized teakwood, a tractor and a trolley since the driver did not have documents to transport the teak, they thought they were on firm ground until the Sessions Judge quashed the confiscation and directed return of the vehicle.[58] The Madhya Pradesh High Court upheld the judgment, reasoning that there could not be confiscation unless the guilt of the accused is first established.

The state successfully appealed to the Supreme Court. The Supreme Court found that under the statutory scheme applicable in Madhya Pradesh, departmental confiscation proceedings were distinct from the criminal proceedings and were independent of whether or not the guilt of the accused was established in the prosecution. The power of confiscation extended to 'specified forest produce so seized together with all tools, vehicles, boats, ropes, chairs or other articles used in committing such offence'.[59]

Suppose no offence is eventually established, what happens to the vehicle and teakwood? Does it remain with the state? Is a provision depriving an innocent person of her vehicle and timber constitutionally valid?

6. Ineptitude cost the state dear when it failed to confiscate a car under section 61A of the Kerala Forest Act of 1961. According to the prosecution, the car carried several poachers to the Vazhachal forest range where they shot dead two wild tuskers. Later, the car was used to transport the tusks. The Supreme Court found that 'forest offences' under the 1961 Act did not cover illicit ivory and the vehicle could not be seized or confiscated. Offences committed under the Wild Life (Protection) Act of 1972 may have exposed offenders to prosecutions under that Act, but absent a specific charge under that law, recourse to the 1961 Act was unjustified.[60]

---

56 (2011) 10 SCC 794. This case is also discussed in the section dealing with poaching.
57 *The State of Madhya Pradesh v Uday Singh* (2020) 12 SCC 733.
58 *State of Madhya Pradesh v Kallo Bai* (2017) 14 SCC 502.
59 Section 15(4), Madhya Pradesh Van Upaj (Vyapar Viniyam) Adhiniyan of 1969.
60 *State of Kerala v P V Mathew (Dead) by Lrs* (2012) 4 SCC 457.

Find provisions in the 1972 Act that would have enabled the prosecution to sustain the confiscation.

7. Detecting a wildlife crime, collecting the evidence and successfully prosecuting a case are often beyond the capacity of wildlife officials in the field. To enhance their capacities wildlife activists train and guide government departments. A fine example of such an effort is Praveen Bhargav's *Wildlife Law for Rangers* (2019, Wildlife First).

C. ECO-CENTRISM, ENDANGERED SPECIES AND POACHING

I. THE *ASIATIC WILD BUFFALO* CASE

Since the colonial period, the wild buffalo has suffered decimation. Mahesh Rangarajan writes:

> The extension of cultivation often entailed sharper conflict not only with carnivores but even with herbivores. In Assam, for instance, the plains regions were the home of a large ungulate, the wild buffalo (*Bubalus Bubalis*). It was disliked by cultivators due to its ferocity and by herders because it mingled with domestic water buffalo. In 1876 alone as many as 164 wild buffalos were killed for rewards in the province, mainly in the plains regions of Lakhimpur and Nowgong.[61]

In the *Asiatic Wild Buffalo* case, the Supreme Court enriched environmental jurisprudence in three significant ways: it suggested the need for an eco-centric vision to resolve human–wildlife conflicts, it relied on a respected international conservation body's assessment of the threat to the survival of a species and it planted the seed for the incipient notion of animal rights. When reviewing the case, consider what the court might have done differently to better the buffalos' survival prospects.

T N GODAVARMAN THIRUMULPAD v UNION OF INDIA

(2012) 3 SCC 277

> K S P Radhakrishnan, J: Asiatic Wild Buffalo is reported to be the most impressive and magnificent animal in the world. Often it is found in the Western and Eastern Ghats of the country. The learned *amicus curiae* have moved this Court seeking a direction to the Union of India and the State of Chhattisgarh to prepare a rescue plan to save wild buffalo, an endangered species from extinction and to make available necessary funds and resources required for the said purpose and also for a direction to take immediate steps to ensure that interbreeding between the wild and domestic buffalo does not take place and the genetic purity of the wild species is maintained. Direction was also sought for to prepare a scheme in consultation with the villagers for relocation of villagers from the Udanti Wildlife Sanctuary to ensure the survival of the endangered wild buffalo. Direction was also sought for that all research and monitoring inputs including scientific management of the wild buffalo and its habitat be made available on long term basis by involving institutes such as the Wildlife Institute of India, the Bombay Natural History Society, etc.
>
> The State of Chhattisgarh filed its reply-affidavit on 30-1-2006 explaining the steps taken to conserve and preserve the endangered species which was declared as a State Animal. Along with the affidavit, a comprehensive operational Management Plan for Udanti Wildlife

[61] M Rangarajan, *The Raj and the Natural World The Campaign against 'Dangerous Beasts' in Colonial India, 1875–1925* in India's Environmental History: Colonialism, Modernity And The Nation 95 (Ed. M Rangarajan and K Sivaramakrishnan, 2014).

Sanctuary was also enclosed stating that the execution of the said management plan had suffered setbacks due to acute financial shortage for its implementation. Further, it was stated that the funds allotted under Central assistance from the Government of India, Ministry of Environment and Forests was not in tune with the budget requirement for development of the sanctuary and the conservation of the endangered species....

Steps taken by the State of Chhattisgarh to preserve and conserve the wild buffalo which was declared as a State animal is far from satisfactory. When the matter came up for final hearing, the counsel appearing for the MoEF made available a copy of the Centrally Sponsored Integrated Development of Wildlife Habitats Scheme, 2009 (the 2009 Scheme). The Scheme was formulated during the Eleventh Five Year Plan. The Scheme has also incorporated additional components and activities for implementing the provisions of the Wild Life (Protection) Act, 1972 (for short 'the Act'), National Wildlife Action Plan (2002–2016), Recommendations of the Tiger Task Force, 2005, and the National Forest Commission, 2006 and the necessities felt from time to time for the conservation of wildlife and biodiversity in the country.

Before coming into force of the Act, the scheme which was in force was 'Assistance for the Development of National Parks and Sanctuaries' which used to support only national parks and wildlife sanctuaries. However, following the amendment to the Act, in 2003, two more categories of protected areas (PAs) i.e. the conservation reserves and community reserves have been recognised. Conservation reserves, which are government land, but do not require acquisition of rights, nor the curtailment of activities as envisaged in national parks and wildlife sanctuaries are stated to be the most appropriate strategy for connecting protected areas, by providing corridors. Community reserves are entirely based on efforts of the local people on privately-owned lands which require financial and technical assistance for their future management....

Section 36-A of the Act empowers the State Government, after consultations with the local communities, to declare any area owned by the Government, particularly the areas adjacent to national parks and sanctuaries and those areas which link one protected area with another, as a conservation reserve for protecting landscapes, seascapes, flora and fauna and their habitat. The Act also empowers the State Government, where the community or an individual has volunteered to conserve wildlife and its habitat, to declare any private or community land not comprised within a national park, sanctuary or a conservation reserve, as a community reserve, for protecting fauna, flora and traditional or cultural conservation values and practice. The management of community reserves shall primarily be done by the communities/individuals themselves. The Centrally Sponsored Integrated Development of Wildlife Habitats Scheme, 2009, therefore, intended to bring these two categories of PAs also under the ambit of the Scheme along with the existing national parks and wildlife sanctuaries....

Human–wildlife conflict

Human–wildlife conflict is fast becoming a critical threat to the survival of many endangered species, like wild buffalo, elephants, tiger, lion, etc. Such conflicts affect not only its population but also has broadened environmental impacts on ecosystem equilibrium and biodiversity conservation. Laws are man-made, hence there is likelihood of anthropocentric bias towards man, and rights of wild animals often tend to be of secondary importance but in the universe man and animal are equally placed, but human rights approach to environmental protection in case of conflict, is often based on anthropocentricity.

Man–animal conflict often results not because animals encroach human territories but vice versa. Often, man thinks otherwise, because man's thinking is rooted in anthropocentrism. Remember, we are talking about the conflict between man and endangered species, endangered not because of natural causes alone but because man failed to preserve and protect them, the attitude was destructive, for pleasure and gain. Often, it is said that such conflicts are due to human population growth, land use transformation, species' habitat loss, degradation and fragmentation, increase in eco-tourism, access to natural reserves, increase in livestock population, etc.

Proper management practices have to be accepted, like conservation education for local population, resettlement of villages, curbing grazing by livestock and domestic animals in forest, etc., including prey-preservation for the wild animals. Provision for availability of natural water, less or no disturbance from the tourists has to be assured. The State also has to take steps to remove encroachments and, if necessary, can also cancel the patta already granted and initiate acquisition proceedings to preserve and protect wildlife and its corridors. Areas outside PAs is reported to have the maximum number of man-animal conflict, they fall prey to poachers easily, and often invite ire of the cultivators when they cause damage to their crops. These issues have to be scientifically managed so as to preserve and protect the endangered species, like wild buffalo and other species included in Schedule I Part I of the Wild Life (Protection) Act, as well as other species which face extinction....

Environmental justice could be achieved only if we drift away from the principle of anthropocentric to eco-centric. Many of our principles like sustainable development, polluter-pays principle, intergenerational equity have their roots in anthropocentric principles. Anthropocentrism is always human interest focussed and that non-human has only instrumental value to humans. In other words, humans take precedence and human responsibilities to non-human based benefits to humans. Eco-centrism is nature-centred where humans are part of nature and non-humans have intrinsic value. In other words, human interest does not take automatic precedence and humans have obligations to non-humans independently of human interest. Eco-centrism is therefore life-centred, nature-centred where nature includes both humans and non-humans. The National Wildlife Action Plan 2002–2012 and the Centrally Sponsored Integrated Development of Wildlife Habitats Scheme, 2009 are centred on the principle of eco-centrism....

The Centrally Sponsored Integrated Development of Wildlife Habitats Scheme, 2009 specifically highlighted the necessity to preserve and conserve the habitat of wild buffalo. The 2009 Scheme states as follows:

> 'Wild buffalo is one of the worst affected mammalian species in the recent times. Domestication of the species and continuous interbreeding with domestic buffalo has led to inbreeding, genetic disorders, competition and mortality due to disease. Apart from this, habitat fragmentation, degradation, and poaching are the main threats to the conservation of this globally threatened species. Urgent and concerted efforts are needed to recover this species from the brink of extinction.'

* * *

The State of Chhattisgarh, in the instant case, has pointed out that they could not effectively give effect to some of the programmes for preservation and conservation of wild buffalo due to lack of funds. The Scheme envisages 100% assistance.

The State of Chhattisgarh has maintained the stand that they do not have sufficient funds to undertake various programmes for protection of wild buffalo within the national parks, sanctuaries and also at conservation reserves and community reserves. This stand cannot be countenanced now, especially after the introduction of the Scheme....

The International Union for Conservation of Nature (IUCN) has calculated the percentage of endangered species as 40% of all organisms. IUCN red list refers to specific categories of endangered species and includes critically endangered species. IUCN red list of threatened species uses the term 'endangered species' as a specific category of imperilment, rather than as a general term.

Under the IUCN categories and criteria, endangered species is between critically endangered and vulnerable. Wild water buffalo is included in the category of endangered species. Apart from the human-animal conflict, the most important threat to wild buffalo is inbreeding with feral and domestic buffalo, habitat loss/degradation and hunting. Diseases and parasites (transmitted by domestic livestock) and competition for food and water between wild buffalo and domestic stock are also serious threats. Habitat loss is also a major concern for species endangerment. When wild buffaloes' eco-system is not maintained, they lose their home and are either forced to adopt new surroundings or human habitat. Eminent ecologists have proposed biological corridors, biosphere reserves, ecosystem management and eco-regional planning as approaches to integrate biodiversity conservation and socio-economic development at increasingly larger spatial scales....

We are, therefore, inclined to dispose of this application with the direction to the State of Chhattisgarh to give effect fully to the Centrally Sponsored Integrated Development of Wildlife Habitats Scheme, 2009, so as to save wild buffalo from extinction. The State also would take immediate steps to ensure that interbreeding between wild and domestic buffaloes does not take place and genetic purity of the wild species is maintained. The State is also directed to take immediate steps to undertake intensive research and monitor the wild buffalo population in Udanti Wildlife Sanctuary and other areas, where the wild buffalo may still be found, including preparing their genetic profile for future reference.

The State is also directed to take appropriate steps to initiate wildlife training programmes for the officials of the State Forest Department, especially for managing the above sanctuary and other areas where the wild buffaloes are found. The State is also directed to submit Annual Plan of Operations to the Central Government detailing the proposed course of action, if not already done, as per the 'Integrated Development of Wildlife Habitats' Scheme, within a period of three months from today. All effective steps should be taken by the State to protect the Asian wild buffalo (*Bubalus Bubalis*), which is declared as a State animal by the State of Chhattisgarh.

NOTES AND QUESTIONS

1. In the final analysis what did the court do? It merely asked the state of Chhattisgarh to take 'effective steps' to protect the Asiatic wild buffalo. Was the state bureaucracy likely to do much beyond filing away a copy of the Supreme Court judgment?

Would it have helped to retain hold over the case by requiring the state to file periodic compliance reports on measures taken in the field? A continuing mandamus might have ensured brisk implementation of conservation measures.

2. The Asiatic wild buffalo is a charismatic species. Large animals or mega fauna are the celebrities of the wild. They engender awe and are the focus of the global tourism industry. However, ecologically, all species are equal. Would the Supreme Court have devoted as much effort in preserving a humbler species? Is the court then applying an anthropocentric approach in selecting which species to protect, while commending to others an eco-centric approach? Alternatively, in working to protect mega fauna, is not the court preserving all species, great and small, that live in the zones inhabited by the wild buffalo?

3.'Man-animal conflict often results not because animals encroach human territories but *vice versa*.' Is this a recognition of collective animal rights? While the law may not recognize a territorial entitlement of an individual animal, does the law now recognize a species' right to survive in the wild and therefore a right to be left undisturbed in its natural ecosystem?

4. In working through this dilemma, consider Steven Wise's analysis from *Rattling the Cage*:

> For four thousand years, a thick and impenetrable legal wall has separated all human from all nonhuman animals. On one side, even the most trivial interests of a single species—ours—are jealously guarded. We have assigned ourselves, alone among the million animal species, the status of 'legal persons.' On the other side of that wall lies the legal refuse of an entire kingdom, not just chimpanzees and bonobos but also gorillas, orangutans, and monkeys,

dogs, elephants, and dolphins. They are 'legal things.' Their most basic and fundamental interests—their pains, their lives, their freedoms—are intentionally ignored, often maliciously trampled, and routinely abused. Ancient philosophers claimed that all nonhuman animals had been designed and placed on this earth just for human beings. Ancient jurists declared that law had been created just for human beings. Although philosophy and science have long since recanted, the law has not.[62]

5. Will the recognition and growth of animal rights subvert social order? Consider what changes we must bring in our attitudes towards temple elephants, pets, dairy animals, and our approach to animal products that surround us and are a part of our diet.

6. The influential American ecologist Aldo Leopold in his book *A Sand County Almanac*[63] proposed: 'A thing is right when it tends to preserve the integrity, stability, and beauty of the biotic community. It is wrong when it tends otherwise.' The ethical underpinning of Leopold's thesis is that humans are but one amongst other species and the ecological niche occupied by other species must be protected. Justice Radhakrishnan builds on this idea and commends an eco-centric approach to inform decision-making. Does eco-centrism oblige humans to protect *every* other species? Is the state obliged to demarcate 'no go' protected areas where *all* human activity is proscribed?

7. The Supreme Court correctly rejected the state government's plea that it lacked funds to protect wild buffaloes. A similar argument was rejected by the Supreme Court in the *Ratlam Municipality* case[64] more than three decades earlier when the local body pleaded an absence of resources to clean up the municipal waste and provide adequate sanitation.

8. What is the monetary value of a species? Can the value be monetized? How much should governments spend to prevent the extinction of a species?

9. Ria Singh Sawhney and Sugandha Yadav argue that to save the Great Indian Bustard from extinction it is imperative to protect grasslands, their primary habitat:

> Grasslands are not managed as an ecosystem in their own right by the Forest Department whose interest lies mainly in trees, not by the Agriculture Department who are interested in agriculture crops, nor the Veterinary Department who are concerned with livestock, but not the grass on which the livestock depends. Grasslands are the 'common' lands of the community and while there have been robust traditional institutions ensuring their sustainable management in the past, today due to take-over by government or breakdown of traditional institutions they are the responsibility of none. They are the most productive ecosystems in the Indian Subcontinent, but they belong to all, are controlled by none, and they have no godfathers. Indeed, they are often looked at as 'wastelands' on which tree plantations have to be done, or which can be easily diverted for other uses.
>
> [M K Ranjitsinh] a retired IAS officer recently filed a petition in the Supreme Court alerting the judiciary to this prejudice and its dangers. The officer wants to protect the last living members of two endemic grassland species: the great Indian bustard and the lesser florican. Both birds have been protected under the Wild Life (Protection) Act, 1972, for over two decades and both birds suffered a decline of over 80%. Today, only 100–150 great Indian bustards and fewer than 700 lessor floricans survive.
>
> One of the greatest challenges these birds face is the loss of their habitat. The anthropocentric and exclusive idea of green growth means that the Centre has rooted for rapid afforestation and green energy projects, such as windmills and solar power plants—projects that have proved fatal for the bustards, whose eyes evolved to navigate rolling grasslands, not

62 Steven M Wise, *Rattling the Cage: Toward Legal Rights for Animals* 4 (2000).
63 Aldo Leopold, *A Sand County Almanac: And Sketches Here and There* (1949).
64 *Municipal Council, Ratlam v Vardhichand* AIR 1980 SC 1622.

objects right in front of them. Many of these birds have died after head-on collisions with power lines.[65]

II. THE *SANDALWOOD* CASE

The *Sandalwood* case approaches the challenge to protect two endangered species of sandalwood through the lens of eco-centrism. Since the discussion on eco-centrism from this case is in the Constitutional Provisions chapter, this excerpt connects India's international obligations with municipal law.

Here, the court noticed the absence of uniform regulations. Karnataka and Tamil Nadu acknowledged that there were no mature sandalwood trees available for felling in these states. Kerala claimed that it had shut down 24 unlicensed sandalwood oil factories in implementation of a closure order passed by the Supreme Court on 10 February 2006. The Central Empowered Committee (CEC) filed several reports in the court recommending shutting down private sandalwood industries if sandalwood 'so unique and a special gift of nature to India [was not to] become extinct in the not too distant future'. The Indian Sandalwood Association, whose members were engaged in extracting sandalwood oil, resisted any judicial directions that would harm oil manufacturers, big and small cultivators, farmers and vendors of sandalwood products. Noting that sandalwood is mentioned in the *Ramayana* and was part of India's cultural heritage, the court found the existing statutory protection inadequate.

T N GODAVARMAN THIRUMULPAD v UNION OF INDIA
(2012) 4 SCC 362

K S P Radhakrishnan, J: We are in this case concerned with the question whether sandalwood (*Santalum album linn*) stated to be an endangered species, be declared as a 'specified plant' within the meaning of section 2(27), and be included in Schedule VI of the Wild Life (Protection) Act, 1972 (for short 'the Act'). On going through the various international conventions, we thought it appropriate to examine the repeated requests made by the State of Andhra Pradesh to the Central Government to notify red sanders (*Pterocarpus santalinus*) as a 'specified plant' and be included in Schedule VI of the Act.

A non-governmental organisation moved the Central Empowered Committee (CEC) to initiate steps for closure of all unlicensed sandalwood oil industries, particularly in the State of Kerala. CEC after conducting a detailed enquiry and hearing the State officials, representatives of the sandalwood industries and various other interested persons, submitted its report dated 24-2-2005 before this Court praying that all unlicensed sandalwood oil industries be also brought within the purview of this Court's order dated 30-12-2002 by which this Court had ordered the closure of all unlicensed sawmills, veneer and plywood industries in the country. Various other decisions were also sought for....

The Biological Diversity Act, 2002 was also enacted by Parliament with the object of conserving biological diversity, sustainable use of its components and for fair and equitable sharing of the benefits arising out of utilisation of genetic resources. Biological diversity includes all the organisms found on our planet viz. the plants, animals and microorganisms. The Environment (Protection) Act, 1986 enacted by Parliament empowers the Central Government under section 3 to take such measures for the purpose of protecting and improving the quality of environment.

When we examine all those legislations in the light of the constitutional provisions and various international conventions like the Convention on International Trade in Endangered

[65] Ria Singh Sawhney & Sugandha Yadav, *Of the Classes of Environmental Regulation, Grasslands are Poorest of the Poor*, The Wire, 29 September 2019, https://thewire.in/environment/grasslands-afforestation-bustard-biodiversity-unccd, accessed 28 May 2021.

Species of Wild Fauna and Flora, 1973 (CITES), and the Convention on Biological Diversity, 1992 (CBD) evidently, there is a shift from environmental rights to ecological rights, though gradual but sustainable. Earlier, the Rio Declaration on Earth Summit asserted the claim 'human beings are the centre of concern.' The UN Conference on Environment and Development (UNCED 1992), was also based on anthropocentric ethics, same was the situation in respect of many such international conventions that followed....

CITES and CBD highlight the following principles:

(a) The State is bound to initiate measures to identify threatened species.
(b) The State is obliged to initiate measures to conserve and protect such threatened species.
(c) The State is also required to formulate policies, legislation and appropriate laws to curb those practices (including trade) that result in extinction of species.
(d) The State is obliged to undertake in situ conservation of biological diversity as it is not sufficient that a species is cultivated elsewhere. It ought to be protected in its natural habitat.

Indian sandalwood (*Santalum album linn*) is not seen included in the species listed in Appendix II of CITES, however, red sandalwood (*Pterocarpus santalinus*) is seen included in Appendix II. At the same time International Union for Conservation of Nature (IUCN) which is an international organisation dedicated to finding pragmatic solutions for our most pressing environmental and development challenges has included *Santalum album linn* in its Red List of Threatened Species as 'vulnerable' and red sandalwood (*Pterocarpus santalinus*) in the Red List of as 'endangered'. Therefore, both in CITES and in the IUCN Red List of Threatened Species red sandalwood is described as 'threatened with extinction', 'endangered'.

A taxon is *critically endangered* when the available evidence indicates that it meets with the criterion of extremely high risk of extinction. It is *endangered* when it meets with the criterion of facing a *very high risk of extinction.* A taxon is *vulnerable* when it is considered to be facing *a high risk of extinction. Near threatened* means a taxon is likely to qualify for a threatened category in the near future.

Red sandalwood is a species of *Pterocarpus* native of India seen nowhere else in the world. It is reported that the same is found only in South India, especially in Cuddapah and Chittoor in the States of Tamil Nadu and Andhra Pradesh border which is also known as Lal Chandan/ Rakta Chandan in Hindi which is an endemic and endangered species. Red sandalwood possesses medicinal properties viz. an anticoagulant, improves local circulation and used on traumatic wounds, aberrations and bruises. Since the trading is mostly in South India, especially in Andhra Pradesh (AP), it is stated that AP Forest Corporation has been appointed as an agent to the Government of AP for disposal of red sandalwood available with the Forest Department.

Red sanders are an endemic and endangered species as already mentioned, found only in the State of AP. The AP Government has banned the sale of red sanders even by private parties, the wood is of huge demand in Japan, China and the western world and is very costly and it is included in the negative list of plant species for export purposes, implemented by the Directorate General of Foreign Trade, Ministry of Commerce, placing restrictions on international trade of red sanders. Large-scale smuggling of red sanders is however reported from various quarters. In order to protect the species, a proposal was made by the State of AP to the Government of India for its inclusion in Schedule VI of the Act which, in our view, is justified.

CITES as well as IUCN has acknowledged that red sandalwood is an endangered species. It is settled law that the provisions of the treaties/conventions which are not contrary to municipal laws, be deemed to have been incorporated in the domestic law. [Citations omitted.] *Under the abovementioned circumstances, following the eco-centric principle, we are inclined to give a direction to the Central Government to take appropriate steps under section 61 of the Act to include red sanders in Schedule VI of the Act as required by the State of AP, within a period of six months from the date of this judgment.* We are giving this direction, since, it is reported that nowhere in the world, this species is seen, except in India and we owe an obligation to the world, to safeguard this endangered species, for posterity. Power is also vested with the Central Government to delete from the Schedule if the situation improves, and a species is later found to be not endangered.

Sandalwood as such as have already indicated finds no place in CITES but it is included in the Red List of IUCN as 'vulnerable' and hence calls for serious attention by the Central Government, considering the fact that all the sandalwood growing States have stated that it faces extinction. Section 61 of the Act empowers the Central Government to add or delete any entry to or from any schedule if it is known that it is expedient so to do. Section 5 deals with the constitution of National Board for Wildlife (NBWL) which is headed by the Prime Minister as Chairman. Section 5-C deals with the function of NBWL which states that it shall be the duty of the National Board to promote the conservation and development of wildlife and forests by such measures as it thinks fit. Section 5-C(ii)(a) states that the measures may provide for promoting policies and advising the Central Government and the State Governments on the ways and means of promoting wildlife conservation and effectively controlling poaching and illegal trade of wildlife and its products and also for reviving from time to time the progress in the field of wildlife conservation in the country and suggesting measures for improvement thereto. Various other powers have also been conferred on the National Board which consists of experts in the field of environment. *In such circumstances, rather than giving a positive direction to include sandalwood in Schedule VI, we are inclined to give a direction to the Central Government to examine the issue at length in consultation with NBWL and take a decision within a period of six months from today as to whether it is to be notified as a specific plant and be included in Schedule VI of the Act.*

We are also inclined to give a direction to the Central Government to formulate a policy for conservation of sandalwood including provision for financial reserves for such conservation and scientific research for sustainable use of biological diversity in sandalwood. The Central Government would also formulate rules and regulations under sections 3 and 5 of the Environment (Protection) Act, 1986 for effective monitoring, control and regulation of sandalwood industries and factories and it should also formulate rules to ensure that no imported sandalwood is sold under the name of Indian sandalwood and adequate labelling to this effect be mandated for products manufactured from or of import of sandalwood. The States are directed to immediately close down all unlicensed sandalwood oil factories, if functioning and take effective measures for proper supervision and control of the existing licensed sandalwood oil factories in the States.

We are also of the view that time has also come to think of a legislation similar to the Endangered Species Act, enacted in the United States which protects both endangered species defined as those 'in danger of extinction throughout all or a significant portion of their range' and 'threatened species', those likely to become endangered 'within a foreseeable time.' The term 'species' includes species and sub-species of fish, wildlife and plants as well as geographically distinct populations of vertebrate wildlife even though the species as a whole may not be endangered. We hope Parliament would bestow serious attention in this regard. [The court disposed of all applications.]

NOTES AND QUESTIONS

1. Section 61 of the Wild Life (Protection) Act of 1972 empowers the Central Government 'if it is of opinion that it is expedient so to do' to add or delete any entry in any of the schedules to the Act. The Central Government exercises this power by publishing an appropriate notification in the Official Gazette. What is the nature of the Central Government's power? Is it administrative or legislative? If it were legislative, did the Supreme Court exceed its jurisdiction in requiring the government to legislate?

If it were administrative, was the power discretionary? Should the Supreme Court then have overridden the government's apprehension that including sandalwood in Schedule VI would alienate people from growing the species? The MoEF felt that 'all India sandalwood legislation' was a better solution, but offered no time frame for such legislation.

Where a statute is expressed in discretionary language, courts may take recourse to a doctrine of 'power coupled with duty'. This doctrine requires that an authority conferred with a discretionary power is duty bound to exercise that power when the circumstances warrant. A failure to exercise power would invite judicial intervention. Here, since the Supreme Court found that red sanders demanded urgent protection, it could have invoked this doctrine to require amendment of Schedule VI in addition to the eco-centric principle on which the judgment rests. (But will this line of argument be sustainable should the power under section 61 be legislative in character?)

2. The effect of inserting red sanders in Schedule VI was that chapter IIIA titled 'Protection of Specified Plants' would apply to this species of sandalwood. The provisions of this chapter are very stringent. There is a prohibition on picking, uprooting or damaging any specified plant or possessing selling or transferring a specified plant.[66] Cultivation,[67] dealing[68] and purchase[69] of specified plants are regulated. Violation of these provisions invites prosecution and penalties.[70]

3. With regard to *Santalum album linn*, the Supreme Court left the matter to the NBWL, headed by the Prime Minister. Was this a good idea considering that the NBWL hardly ever meets? The object of having the Prime Minister at the helm of the NBWL is to elevate the importance of wildlife protection in the broader scheme of governance. Is there a downside to this mandate?

4. Should the Supreme Court have retained the case by monitoring the effect of its directions? For example, should the Supreme Court have asked for periodic reports from the CEC about the situation in the field?

III. THE *GREAT INDIAN BUSTARD* CASE (SC)

In 2019, the conservationist M K Ranjitsinh approached the Supreme Court seeking directions to save the Great Indian Bustard (GIB) and the Lesser Florican from extinction. Both species had dwindled due to a loss of habitat and other contributing factors. In 2021, the bench headed by Chief Justice Sharad Bobde responded to an interim application that highlighted the threat posed by overhead electricity transmission lines.

M K RANJITSINH v UNION OF INDIA
(2021) SCC ONLINE SC 326

ORDER:

* * *

It is contended that GIB is one of the heaviest flying birds in the world, about a meter in height and wing span of around seven feet. It has disappeared from 90% of habitat except parts of Rajasthan and Gujarat which is to be protected. According to the petitioners, overhead power lines are the biggest threat to the survival of the GIBs. The Wildlife Institute of India (WII) in its Report 'Power Line Mitigation, 2018' has stated that every year 1 lakh

66 Section 17A.
67 Section 17C.
68 Section 17D.
69 Section 17G.
70 Section 51.

birds die due to collision with power lines. The Report concluded that unless power line mortality is mitigated urgently, extinction of GIBs is certain. Surveys conducted by WII in Thar covering 80 km of power lines repeated 7 times over a year found 289 carcasses of around 30 species, including the Great Indian Bustard (GIB). The study estimated 3 bird mortalities/km/month for low-tension lines, 6 bird mortalities/km/month for high-tension lines, and about 1 lakh birds/per year within a 4200 sq km area in/around Desert National Park, Rajasthan. In terms of GIB, 6 mortalities have been recorded in Thar during 2017–20, all due to high-tension transmission lines—some of them connected to wind turbine. Therefore, petitioner seeks undergrounding all future overhead power lines; selected power lines in priority GIB habitat and installation of divertors in potential habitat.

In fact, it is admitted by the Ministry of Power, Union of India in their affidavit dated 15.03.2021 as follows: –

> 'The Great Indian Bustard … lacks frontal vision. Due to this, they cannot detect powerlines ahead of them, from far. As they are heavy birds, they are unable to manoeuvre across power lines within close distances. Thus, they are vulnerable to collision with power lines. In case of low voltage lines, electrocution is often the cause of death due to smaller phase to phase separation distance. High voltage lines do not cause death due to electrocution but cause death due to collision.'

* * *

In the above background, there cannot be disagreement whatsoever that appropriate steps are required to be taken to protect the said species of birds. In that view, insofar as the existing overhead powerlines are concerned the respondents shall take steps forthwith to install divertors and in respect of existing overhead powerlines all future cases of installing the transmission lines a study shall be conducted with regard to the feasibility for the lines to be laid underground. In all such cases where it is feasible, steps shall be taken to lay the transmission line underground. For the lines to be laid in future if as per the technical report the overhead line alone is feasible and the same is ratified by the Committee, in such event the installation of the divertors shall also be a condition attached in the contract to be entered with generating companies. Insofar as, the cost incurred in the said process, the [the states of Rajasthan and Gujarat] shall work out and provide for the same.… Irrespective of the cost factor the priority shall be to save the near extinct birds.…

In the light of the contentions urged on this aspect of the matter, we are conscious that the laying of the underground power line more particularly of high-voltage though not impossible, would require technical evaluation on case-to-case basis and an omnibus conclusion cannot be reached laying down a uniform method and directions cannot be issued unmindful of the fact situation. Though that be the position the consensus shall be that all low voltage powerlines to be laid in the priority and potential habitats of GIB shall in all cases be laid underground in future. In respect of low voltage overhead powerlines existing presently in the priority and potential habitats of GIB, the same shall be converted into underground powerlines. In respect of high-voltage powerlines in the priority and potential habitats of GIB … and indicated in the operative portion of this order shall be converted into underground power line.

[The court constituted a committee of three experts; specified the powerlines that were to be taken underground; identified the lines where bird divertors were to be installed and set a timeline.] While considering the laying of underground power line the said habitats shall be kept in perspective and steps be taken for the safety of the GIB in the said habitat.…

The respondents … while arranging to lay the powerlines underground in respect of the powerlines, the feasibility of which is not in doubt shall proceed with the work right away. However, in cases where the respondents find that there are issues relating to feasibility, the matter shall be referred to the committee with all relevant material and particulars. The committee shall assess the matter and arrive at a conclusion as to whether the underground powerline is feasible or not. Based on the report to be rendered by the committee the further action shall be taken by the respondent.

In all cases where the overhead powerlines exist as on today in the priority and potential GIB area the respondents shall take steps forthwith to install divertors pending consideration of the conversion of the overhead cables into underground powerlines. In all such cases where it is found feasible to convert the overhead cables into underground powerlines the same shall be undertaken and completed within a period of one year and till such time the divertors shall be hung from the existing powerlines. Ordered accordingly.

NOTES AND QUESTIONS

1. Despite the affidavit of the Ministry of Power which acknowledged the mortal threat overhead power lines posed to GIB, the government balked. Why?

2. The Supreme Court recognized that where species such as the GIB and the Lessor Florican are on the brink of extinction:

> The State as well as the Central Government therefore, have a duty cast to preserve the endangered species and as such the expenses incurred will have to be provided by them either under the schemes available or by earmarking the same in such manner.

In reaching this conclusion, the court drew on the *Asiatic Wild Buffalo* case[71] and the *Asiatic Lion* case.[72]

3. Efforts by the National Green Tribunal to protect the Great Indian Bustard are discussed in the NGT chapter.

IV. POACHING

Poaching syndicates operate extensively in India and Africa, feeding the demand for ivory, rhinoceros horn, big cat pelage and tiger bones. The Indian criminal justice system, weak and ineffective in routine cases, is severely tested when it seeks to bring poachers to book. In the case excerpted below, the police arrested Balwan on 5 January 2003 when he was travelling in a train with a carton containing leopard skins. During investigations, Balwan disclosed that two leopard skins were to be handed over to Sansar Chand, the appellant. Mostly on the strength of Balwan's statement, the police charged Sansar Chand and secured his conviction. Sansar Chand petitioned the Supreme Court for special leave to appeal under Article 136 of the Constitution of India.

SANSAR CHAND v STATE OF RAJASTHAN
(2010) 10 SCC 604

***

MARKANDEY KATJU, J:

The appellant herein has been convicted under the Wild Life (Protection) Act, 1972 by all the three courts below and now he is in appeal before us.

Before dealing with the facts of this case, we would like to comment upon the background. India, at one time, had one of the richest and most varied fauna in the world. However, over the last several decades there has been rapid decline of India's wild animals and birds which is a cause of grave concern. Some wild animals and birds have already become extinct e.g. the cheetah and others are on the brink of extinction. Areas which were once teeming with wildlife have become devoid of it, and many sanctuaries and parks are empty or almost empty of

71 *T N Godavarman Thirumulpad v Union of India* (2012) 3 SCC 277.
72 *Centre for Environmental Law WWF-I v Union of India* (2013) 8 SCC 234.

animals and birds. Thus, the Sariska Tiger Reserve in Rajasthan and the Panna Tiger Reserve in Madhya Pradesh today have no tigers.

One of the main causes for this depredation of the wildlife is organised poaching which yields enormous profits by exports to China and other countries....

Preservation of wildlife is important for maintaining the ecological balance in the environment and sustaining the ecological chain. It must be understood that there is interlinking in nature. To give an example, snakes eat frogs, frogs eat insects and insects eat other insects and vegetation. If we kill all the snakes, the result will be that the number of frogs will increase and this will result in the frogs eating more of the insects and when more insects are eaten, then the insects which are the prey of other insects will increase in number to a disproportionate extent, or the vegetation will increase to a disproportionate extent. This will upset the delicate ecological balance in nature. If we kill the frogs the insects will increase and this will require more insecticides. Use of much insecticide may create health problems. To give another example, destruction of dholes (wild dogs) in Bhutan was intended to protect livestock, but this led to a greater number of wild boar and to resultant crop devastation causing several cases of abandonment by humans of agricultural fields. Destruction of carnivorous animals will result in increase of herbivorous animals, and this can result in serious loss of agricultural crops and other vegetation....

Interpol says that trade in illegal wildlife products is worth about US $20 billion a year, and India is now a major source market for this trade. Most of the demand for wildlife products comes from outside the country. While at one time there were hundreds of thousands of tigers in India, today according to the survey made by the Wildlife Institute of India (an autonomous body under the Ministry of Environment and Forests), there were only 1411 tigers left in India in 2008. There are no reliable estimates of leopards as no proper census has been carried out, but the rough estimates show that the leopard too is a critically endangered species.

There is virtually no market for the skins or bones of tigers and leopards within India. The evidence available points out that tigers and leopards, poached in the Indian wilderness, are then smuggled across the border to meet the demand for their products in neighbouring countries such as China. When dealing with tiger and leopard poachers and traders, it is therefore important to bear in mind that one is dealing with transnational organised crime. The accused in these cases represents a link in the larger criminal network that stretches across borders. This network starts with a poacher who in most cases is a poor tribal and a skilled hunter. Poachers kill tigers and leopards so as to supply the orders placed by a trader in a larger city centre such as Delhi. These traders are very wealthy and influential men. Once the goods reach the trader, he then arranges for them to be smuggled across the border to his counterpart in another country and so on till it reaches the end consumer. It is impossible for such a network to sustain itself without large profits and intelligent management.

Under the Wild Life (Protection) Act, 1972, trading in tiger, leopard and other animal skins and parts is a serious offence. Apart from that, India is a signatory to both the UN Convention on International Trade in Endangered Species (CITES) and the UN Convention against Transnational Organised Crime (CTOC). However, despite these national and international laws many species of wildlife, e.g. tigers, leopards, bison, etc. are under threat of extinction, mainly due to the poaching organised by international criminal traders and destruction of the habitats.

Sansar Chand, the appellant before us has a long history of such criminal activities, starting with a 1974 arrest for 680 skins including tigers, leopards and others. In the subsequent years the appellant and his gang has established a complex, interlinking smuggling network to satisfy the demand for tiger and leopard parts and skins outside India's borders, particularly to China. It is alleged that the appellant and his gang are accused in 57 wildlife cases between 1974 and 2005....

As already stated above, in such cases it is not easy to get direct evidence, particularly against the leader of the gang (like the appellant herein). The appellant, Sansar Chand has been doing this illegal trade for more than 30 years. He is habitual of doing this illegal business of

> trade in skins and parts of panthers and tigers. He has, as far back as in 1974, committed his first crime when he was barely 16 years of age and the conviction was upheld by the Supreme Court in Criminal Case No. 15 of 2001. A large number of cases are pending against him in Delhi, Uttar Pradesh and Rajasthan. Taking all these materials into account there is no doubt that the appellant is guilty of the offence charged.
>
> There is no absolute rule that an extra-judicial confession can never be the basis of a conviction, although ordinarily an extra-judicial confession should be corroborated by some other material. [Citations omitted.]
>
> In the present case, the extra-judicial confession by Balwan has been referred to in the judgments of the learned Magistrate and the Special Judge, and it has been corroborated by the other material on record. We are satisfied that the confession was voluntary and was not the result of inducement, threat or promise as contemplated by section 24 of the Evidence Act, 1872....

NOTES AND QUESTIONS

1. In a part of the judgment not excerpted, the court catalogues Sansar Chand's previous entanglements with the law. Some of these cases resulted in convictions and others were pending in different courts. According to the prosecution, other members of Sansar Chand's family were also involved in the racket.

Considering that Article 136 is a discretionary jurisdiction, why did the Supreme Court entertain Sansar Chand's petition? Did the judges want to fairly examine Sansar Chand's pleas or did the case simply provide them an opportunity to write an essay on poaching and illegal trafficking in animal parts?

2. How convincing is the Supreme Court's reasoning? Since there was no direct evidence against Sansar Chand, the court held that direct evidence is difficult to obtain; Sansar Chand is a habitual offender; a large number of cases are pending against him and therefore 'there is no doubt that the appellant is guilty of the offence charged'. Is this a case of a conviction based on suspicion? Where is the hard evidence?

Rather than adopt such a feeble line of reasoning, if the judges were satisfied about Sansar Chand's guilt, should they have simply dismissed his special leave petition summarily?

3. In *Principal Chief Conservator of Forests v J K Johnson*,[73] the Supreme Court decided an important jurisdictional question: whether a wildlife officer could order forfeiture of seized items when allowing composition[74] of an offence. While inspecting a jeep in the early hours of 25 July 2004, the police found gunny bags containing a hunted wild boar and three rabbits. They seized the dead animals together with the jeep and two rifles fitted with telescopes. The respondents who were in the vehicle claimed that their actions were in ignorance of the law and they offered to pay money by way of composition of the offence. The empowered wildlife officer ordered composition under section 54 of the Wild Life (Protection) Act of 1972 and directed that the vehicle and weapons used in committing the offence stood forfeited to the state. The respondents challenged the forfeiture and succeeded before the Andhra Pradesh High Court which directed release of the vehicle and rifles.

---

[73] (2011) 10 SCC 794.

[74] Certain statutes permit a person suspected of committing an offence to tender payment and save herself from facing criminal prosecution. This is termed 'composition' or 'compounding'.

Rejecting the conservator's submission, the Supreme Court construed the provisions of the 1972 Act (as amended in 2003) to hold that departmental officers have no authority to order forfeiture. Vehicles, weapons, traps and tools 'that had been used for committing an offence' are indeed liable to vest in the state, but such forfeiture can take place only upon conviction by a competent court. Where the statute allows an offender to apply for composition by payment of a sum of money, the suspect stands discharged on making the payment and is saved from criminal prosecution. Absent a conviction, the seized property was *not* used 'for committing an offence' but was merely '*suspected* to have been used for committing an offence'. In view of constitutional guarantees with regard to property rights, there cannot be a deprivation of property on suspicion alone.

The Supreme Court judgment was rendered on 17 October 2011, more than seven years after the seizure. Even at this distance of time when the seized property had diminished in value, the court required the respondents to again approach the magistrate and apply for return of the seized items. Was the court being needlessly technical and parsimonious when reversing the High Court's direction ordering release?

4. When checking a vehicle on the night of 18 December 1999, sales tax officers of the Uttar Pradesh government found a bundle of cloth containing 50 skins of leopard, three skins of tiger and five skins of jungle fox. When the Forest Department was informed, its officers seized the skins under section 50 of the Act and the driver and the conductor of the truck were detained. On 21 March 2000, the Central Government issued a notification transferring investigation of the case to the Central Bureau of Investigation (CBI).[75] The appellant, Motilal, was arrested in the course of investigations. He challenged the transfer of investigation claiming that the CBI had no authority. The Supreme Court rejected Motilal's contention. It found that the appropriate notifications specifying the classes of offences which were to be investigated by the CBI had been issued by the Central Government and the state government too had consented in the exercise of jurisdiction. The provisions of section 50 of the Wildlife Act empowered a police officer to investigate the offences apart from the forest and wildlife officers.[76]

V. ANIMAL TROPHIES

Zavaray Poonawala's passion for hunting drew him to Zambia, where he secured permissions from the government in June 2000. In order to bring the trophies to India (including a leopard) Poonawala secured permissions from the Director General of Foreign Trade (DGFT) and the Chief Wildlife Warden. When the Deputy Director, CITES[77] refused permission, Poonawala petitioned the High Court to quash the refusal and allow import of the stuffed leopard.[78] The High Court allowed the petition which was then appealed by the CITES authority in the Supreme Court.

REGIONAL DEPUTY DIRECTOR v ZAVARAY S POONAWALA
(2015) 7 SCC 347

A K SIKRI, J: * * *

The leopard, *Panthera pardus*, is a member of the felidae family. This secretive and elusive large cat was once distributed across eastern and southern Asia and Africa. Now at the centre

[75] The CBI is established under the Delhi Special Police Establishment Act of 1946.
[76] *Moti Lal v Central Bureau of Investigation* (2002) 4 SCC 713.
[77] Convention of International Trade on Endangered Species of Wild Fauna and Flora signed on 3 March 1973 at Washington DC. Entered into force 1 July 1975. India signed 9 July 1974; ratified 20 July 1976.
[78] The leopard is listed in Appendix I of CITES that enumerates the most endangered species.

of a severe man–animal conflict because of expanding agricultural practices and development projects, its habitat has depleted to mostly sub-Saharan Africa and fragmented populations in Asia. As one of South Africa's 'Big Five', the leopard forms a lucrative part of South Africa's economy being a favourite to both the tourist and hunting industries. The ecological importance of this animal lies in its position at the top of the food chain in most ecosystems. The shooting of wild game purely for sport and trophies is no longer compatible with our commitment to preserve local fauna as a national treasure....

Because the trade in wild animals and plants crosses borders between countries, the effort to regulate it requires international cooperation to safeguard certain species from over-exploitation. CITES was conceived in the spirit of such cooperation.

In order to perform its task, namely, to regulate the animal species mentioned in Appendix-I, Scientific as well as Management Authority are also contemplated in this convention which have to perform some designated function as mentioned therein. Clauses (f) and (g) of Article I defines these authorities as below:

(f) 'Scientific Authority' means a national scientific authority designated in accordance with Article IX;

(g) 'Management Authority' means a national management authority designated in accordance with Article IX.

Article II which deals with the fundamental principles, *inter alia*, mentions that it shall include all species threatened with extinction which are or may be effected by trade. It also stipulates that trade in specimens of these species must be subject to particularly strict regulation in order not to endanger further their survival and must be in authorization in exceptional circumstances.

Next Article which is of relevance to this case is Article III (iii) as it stipulates the role of Scientific as well as Management Authority. In order to understand the importance of these authorities we reproduce clause (iii) of Article III as under:

> The import of any specimen of species included in Appendix-I shall require the prior grant and presentation of an import permit and either an export permit or a re-export certificate etc. An import shall only be granted when the following conditions have been met:
>
> (a) a Scientific Authority of the State of import advised that the import will be for the purposes which are not detrimental to survival of the species involved;
>
> (b) a Scientific authority of the State of import is satisfied that the proposed recipient of a living specimen is suitably equipped to house and care for it; and
>
> (c) a Management Authority of the State of import is satisfied that the specimen is not to be used for primarily commercial purposes.

We may also point out at this stage that under Article IX, the functions of Management and Scientific Authorities are mentioned.

What flows from the conjoint reading from the aforesaid provisions is that before import of any specimen of species included in appendix I, prior import permit of Scientific Authority and Management Authority is required and before such a permit is given, the opinion of Scientific Authority as well as the Management Authority on particular aspects is required. Insofar as the Scientific Authority is concerned, it would look into the matter from two angles, namely, that the import is not detrimental to the survival of the species involved and further the proposed recipient is suitably equipped of house and care for it. Insofar as the Management Authority is concerned, it is to satisfy itself that the specimen is not to be used for primary commercial purposes.

The High Court while observing that the only function of the Management Authority was to ensure that 'specimen' is not to be used for commercial purpose looked into the function of Management Authority alone. Error is committed by glossing over the function of the Scientific Authority. This resulted in passing the impugned directions which are clearly erroneous.... It is stated at the cost of repetition that that matter is to be placed before the Scientific Authority and it is this Authority which has to form an opinion as to whether the import will or will not be detrimental to the survival of the species involved. This becomes extremely important to carry out the objects of the aforesaid conventions read with the fundamental principles stipulated in Article II thereof.

The judgment of the High Court, therefore, is not sustainable....

NOTES AND QUESTIONS

1. The Supreme Court is spot on in emphasizing the importance of eco-system services. But is its construction of Article 3(iii) correct? On what basis may the Scientific Authority in India advise that the import is for purposes 'which are not detrimental to survival of the species involved'? Remember, Zambia had issued requisite hunting permits and export licences.

2. Since Poonawala was in possession of the trophy after he succeeded in the High Court, the Supreme Court permitted him to apply to the Scientific Authority for necessary permission in light of the observations made by the court. However, in a part of the judgment that is not excerpted, the Supreme Court observed that in relation to species enumerated in Appendix-I of CITES:

> Their import and export is to be restricted inasmuch as the spirit of the prohibition against import/export/trade of trophies of prohibited and protected animals is that it is reprehensible to hunt and display endangered species which are fast vanishing from the earth. Such animals and trophies should not be made objects of aggrandizement and display in homes and commercial establishments.

With these observations, did the court leave any discretion to the authority? Has the Supreme Court legislated a complete prohibition on import of Appendix-I species, in opposition to the text of the convention which seeks strict regulation, not prohibition?

D. FOREST DWELLERS AND PARKS

The provisions to eliminate human intervention within national parks and sanctuaries operate harshly against forest communities, one of the poorest and politically weakest constituencies in India. Tribal activists argue against protected areas because they deprive forest dwellers of access to common property resources, uproot communities, halt development activities and heighten tensions between local residents and the wildlife bureaucracy. Severing forest dwellers from their traditional access to forest produce 'criminalizes' honest citizens who have little choice but to tap the forests for fodder, fuel, food and minor forest produce. Conservationists sympathize with this view, but justify the extension of the national park and sanctuary network because of the degraded condition of our forests. They argue that the best preserved wildernesses in India are within the national parks and sanctuaries. Imperfect as the Wild Life Act is, it offers a proven legal framework to preserve our vanishing natural heritage.

I. PRE-FOREST RIGHTS ACT

The passage of the Forest Rights Act of 2006 (FRA) marks a watershed in the legal relationship between forest dwellers and protected areas. The *Pradeep Krishen* and the *Animal & Environment Legal Defence Fund* cases, excerpted below, are pre-FRA decisions. The impact of the FRA is discussed later in this section.

PRADEEP KRISHEN v UNION OF INDIA
AIR 1996 SC 2040

Ahmadi, C J: The petitioner, an environmentalist actuated by public interest, has filed this petition under Article 32 of the Constitution of India challenging the legality and constitutional validity of an order issued by the state of Madhya Pradesh, Department of Forest, No. F.14/154/91/10/2 dated 28 March 1995, permitting collection of tendu leaves from Sanctuaries and National Parks by villagers living around the boundaries thereof with the avowed object of maintenance of their traditional rights. The petitioner contends that this act of the state government is *ultra vires* the provisions of the Wild Life (Protection) Act, 1972, as well as the petitioner's fundamental rights guaranteed by Article 14 and 21 of the Constitution and is even otherwise inconsistent with the Directive Principle contained in Article 48A and the Fundamental Duty cast on every citizen under clause (g) of Article 51A of the Constitution of India. The petitioner further contends that the said order is *mala fide* and against public interest. The order complained of [in pertinent part reads:]

1. Keeping in view the traditional rights of the villagers around the boundaries of those National Parks and Sanctuaries in respect of which the final notification U/s 26-A and 35 have not been issued, the blocks/areas earmarked for collection of tendu leaves would be reopened as done in the past.
2. In order to provide sufficient wages to the villagers living in these areas, labour intensive works should be provided to them to the maximum extent possible.

According to the petitioner, in the state of Madhya Pradesh, 11 areas have been declared as National Parks and 33 areas as Sanctuaries covering a total area of nearly 16,790 sq kms i.e. 12.4% of the total forest area of the state admeasuring 1,35,396 sq kms. He refers to a news item published in 'The Sunday Times' dated 16 April 1995, headlined 'Forest cover shrinking in MP' and further refers to the report of the Comptroller and Auditor General of India stating that excessive grazing, reckless felling of trees and forest fires are responsible for the depletion of the forest area by 145 sq kms between 1991 and 1993. He further contends that indiscriminate felling of trees has resulted in a depletion of the forest area in the entire country including Madhya Pradesh, causing concern to not only environmentalists, but also referred to the criticism appearing in the media in regard to the issuance of the order dated 28 March 1995. . . .

The petitioner contends that while the impugned order dated 28 March 1995 permitting collection of tendu leaves has been issued ostensibly with a view to providing employment living in the vicinity of the National Parks and Sanctuaries, it has ignored the need to protect the flora and the fauna as well as wild life which are, so to say, nature's laboratory where evolutionary process of life in all forms takes place and which ought not to be interfered with. The presence of human beings, albeit in earmarked Parks, will not only adversely affect the flora and the fauna but will also scare away wild life. That is because, contends the petitioner, the collection of tendu leaves is a destructive process and can cause extensive damage to ecology and regeneration of trees etc. Besides, the destruction of organic matter is bound to affect the structure of the soil and there is the real apprehension of forest fires. The petitioner has, therefore, filed this petition with a view to preserving the National Parks and Sanctuaries which are likely to be adversely affected by the implementation of the impugned order. On the above pleadings and contentions, the petitioner has raised two contentions which have been formulated as under:

(i) Whether an area declared as a Sanctuary and National Park under section 18 and section 35, respectively, of the Wild Life (Protection) Act, 1972 can be exploited for the collection of minor forest produce in violation of the restrictions contained in the said Act? and

(ii) Whether the state government has the right to exploit minor forest produce from the Sanctuaries and National Parks which have been so declared for the protection and preservation of ecology, flora, fauna, geomorphological, natural or zoological significance?

* * *

Dealing with the apprehension of the petition that setting fire to tendu bushes may set the forest on fire, the deponent states that the practice of setting fire to tendu bushes has been completely stopped and only pruning operations are permitted under strict supervision and no pruning is done by setting fire to bushes or trees in the forest.... With a view to protecting the wild life and curbing poaching activities in the forest area, a special cell comprising police and forest officials under the control of the Inspector General of Police had been set up to supervise the forest area. There is, therefore, no real danger to the flora, fauna, trees and wild life in the National Parks and Sanctuaries. It is, therefore, contended that the entire petition is based on suspicion and misconceived apprehension.

In his rejoinder ... the petitioner ... clarified that the petitioner does not challenge the right of the tribals living in and around the National Parks and the Sanctuaries to collect minor produce for their personal *bona fide* use, but only challenges the commercial exploitation thereof, in particular, the tendu leaves through contractors, since it is inconsistent with the object and spirit of the Act.... According to the petitioner, Sanctuaries which were declared as such under Section 18 of the Act prior to its amendment would continue as such even after the amendment and their status does not get affected by the amendment and therefore, in respect thereof, a second notification under section 26A is unnecessary and non-issuance of a fresh notification cannot take way the protection extended by sections 27 to 34 of the Act. This, in brief, is the stand taken in the rejoinder.

In the present proceedings, three persons (i) Bali Ram (ii) Shyam Lal and (iii) Munshi Lal, have filed I.A. No. 3 of 1995 seeking permission to intervene. These three persons, who claim to be tribals, contend that they are vitally interested in the present proceedings as they largely depend on minor forest produce for their survival. They contend that they collect tendu leaves during the forty-day season on a token payment to the state government and if the prayer sought in the writ petition is granted, their interest will be greatly prejudiced. They deny the allegation that during the process of collection of tendu leaves, they disturb the eco-system of the sanctuaries. They also deny that their presence is the prime cause for fires in the forest area. This, they say, is the handiwork of racketeers and contractors. According to them, what they earn from the tendu leaves is barely enough for their sustenance and is not a big commercial venture as is sought to be made out by the petitioner. They lastly contend that they have been enjoying this privilege for generations and the denial of this privilege to the small tribal population located around the sanctuaries would result in ruination of the entire tribal population since their survival is on minor forest produce only.... They, therefore, contend that no fundamental right of the petitioner, for the matter of environmentalists, is violated and the Court should refuse to entertain the petition. [The court set out the provisions of the Act and in the absence of reliable evidence, rejected the petitioner's apprehension in respect of forest fires.]

It is evident from the above pleadings that since neither the traditional rights of those living in the vicinity of these parks and sanctuaries have been acquired, nor have provisions been made to either compensate or rehabilitate them, the final declaration under sections 26A and 35 has not been possible. That is the reason why the state government had to permit collection of tendu leaves by the impugned notification dated 28.3.1995. [The court referred to the constitutional and statutory provisions relating to the declaration and the settlement of rights in national parks and sanctuaries.]

On a plain reading of these provisions, it is. therefore, obvious that the procedure in regard to acquisition of rights in and over the land to be included in a Sanctuary or National Park has to be followed before a final notification under section 26A or section 35(1)) is issued by the state government. In the instant case, it is not the contention of the petitioner that the procedure for the acquisition of rights in or over the land of those living in the vicinity of the areas proposed to be declared as Sanctuaries and National Parks under section 26A and 35 of the Act has been undertaken. It was for this reason that the order of 28.3.1995 in terms stated that since no final notification was issued under the said provisions, the state government was not in a position to bar the entry of villagers living in and around the Sanctuaries and the National Parks so long as their rights were not acquired and final notifications under the aforesaid provisions were issued. It is, therefore, not possible to conclude that the state government had violated any provision of law in issuing the notification dated 28.3.1995 in question.

The matter, however, does not rest there. The petitioner contends that the forest cover in the state of Madhya Pradesh is gradually shrinking. As pointed out earlier, there is a shrinkage to the extent of 145 sq kms between 1991 and 1993. In our country, the total forest cover is far less than the ideal minimum of one-third of the total land. We cannot, therefore, afford any further shrinkage in the forest cover in our country. If one of the reasons for this shrinkage is the entry of villagers and tribals living in and around the Sanctuaries and the National Parks, there can be no doubt that urgent steps must be taken to prevent any destruction or damage to the environment, the flora and fauna and wildlife in those areas. If the only reason which compels the state government to permit entry and collection of tendu leaves is it not having acquired the rights of villagers/tribals and having failed to locate any area for their rehabilitation, we think that inertia in this behalf cannot be tolerated. We are, therefore, of the opinion that while we do not quash the order of 28.3.1995, we think that the state government must be directed to decide on the question of completing the process for issuing final notifications and then take urgent steps to complete the procedure for declaring/notifying the areas as Sanctuaries and National Parks under sections 26A and 35 of the Act. We, therefore, direct that the state government shall take immediate action under Chapter IV of the Act and institute an inquiry, acquire the rights of those who claim any right in or over any land proposed to be included in the Sanctuary/National Park and thereafter proceed to issue a final notification under sections 26A and 35 of the Act declaring such areas as Sanctuaries/National Parks. We direct the state government to initiate action in this behalf within a period of 6 months from today and expeditiously conclude the same showing that sense of urgency as is expected of a state government in such matters as enjoined by Article 48A of the Constitution and at the same time keeping in view the duty enshrined in Article 51A (g) of the Constitution. We are sure, and we have no reason to doubt, that the state government would show the required zeal to expeditiously declare and notify the areas as Sanctuaries/National Parks.

We dispose of the writ petition with these directions. We make the rule absolute as per the conditions given above with no order as to costs.

NOTES AND QUESTIONS

1. What is likely to happen to the tribals after their rights are acquired and the final notification is issued?

2. The directions requiring Madhya Pradesh to complete the procedure for finally declaring sanctuaries and national parks was extended by the Supreme Court to cover all the states, in a petition filed by the WWF.[79] Why were so many states dragging their feet?

[79] *Centre for Environmental Law, WWF v Union of India* 1997 (6) SCALE 8 (SP) and AIR 1999 SC 354. In *Kunapuraju Rangaraju v Government of AP* 1998(3) ANDH L T 215, the Andhra Pradesh High Court directed

3. How does the FRA impact this case?

4. *Niyamavedi v State of Kerala*[80] is an unusual case where a well-known environmental group of Kochi petitioned the High Court to prevent a biological park from being established in 'Agasthayavanam', an extraordinarily rich evergreen forest, having 150 species of plants. Niyamavedi feared that the project would denude the forests and would oust the Adivasis from six ancient settlements. The court declined to interfere, accepting the respondents' case that the park would promote the conservation of flora and fauna of the Western Ghats.

5. Where the government of Mizoram was unable to produce the Official Gazette proving publication of the areas of Dampa Wildlife Sanctuary, the Guwahati High Court quashed government orders for shifting the villages which fell within the sanctuary. The court held that eviction proceedings must strictly accord to the requirements of the law.[81]

ANIMAL & ENVT LEGAL DEFENCE FUND v UNION OF INDIA
AIR 1997 SC 1071

SUJATA V MANOHAR, J: The petitioner is an association of lawyers and other persons who are concerned with protection of the environment. They have filed the present petition in public interest challenging the order of the Chief Wildlife Warden, Forest Department, Government of Madhya Pradesh (second respondent) granting 305 fishing permits to the tribals formerly residing within the Pench National Park area for fishing in the Totladoh reservoir situated in the heart of the Pench National Park Tiger Reserve....

Under S.26(1)(i) of the Indian Forest Act, 1927, any person who in contravention of any rules made in this behalf by the state government hunts, shoots, fishes, poisons water or sets traps or snares, shall be punishable in the manner provided in that section. According to the petitioner, in view of these provisions, the ancestors of the present tribals could not have acquired any fishing right in the Pench River. The present permits which are issued in lieu of this traditional right, therefore, are unwarranted and must be cancelled or set aside.

[The court reviewed the provisions of the Wild Life Act in respect of the declaration of sanctuaries and national parks. On 1 March 1983, the government of Madhya Pradesh notified its intention under section 35(1) to constitute the Pench National Park. Thereafter, claims were invited by the District Collectors under sections 19 and 21 of the Act, but no claims were received. In the absence of any claim, final orders were issued under section 24. However, no final notification under section 35(4) was issued by the Madhya Pradesh government.]

As per the counter-affidavit filed on behalf of the second respondent it has been stated that although the necessary proclamations were issued earlier nobody came forward to claim their rights on account of illiteracy and unawareness. However, recently three applications regarding claims had been received pertaining to the traditional rights of villagers residing in 8 villages within the notified area which have now relocated outside the National Park area. These villagers are tribals. The villagers claim that they had a traditional right of fishing for their livelihood in the Pench river. They have claimed that their traditional right of fishing should be preserved as this is their only source of livelihood. Most of these tribals have been displaced from their original villages and have been resettled in villages outside the National Park area. Under an order dated 30-5-1996 these tribals have now been given permits to fish in the Totladoh reservoir which came into existence in 1986–87 on construction of a dam across the Pench river as a part of Pench Hydro Electric Project. The reservoir is in the center

---

the state to issue a final notification under section 26A within six months and permitted fishing operations in the meantime. The proposed sanctuary was in the Kolleru Lake area.

[80] AIR 1993 KER 262.

[81] *Jaladhar Chakma v The Deputy Commissioner, Aizawl, Mizoram* AIR 1983 GAU 18.

of the National Park area which partly falls in Maharashtra and partly in Madhya Pradesh. Apparently, fishing activity had been started in this reservoir by the Fisheries Development Corporation of the State of Madhya Pradesh despite protests from the forest department.

The petitioner as well as the state of Maharashtra have pointed out that if fishing is permitted in the heart of the National Park and as many as 305 fishing permits are issued, the bio-diversity and ecology of the area will be seriously affected. Fishing activity is a potential source of danger to the National Park because it may also lead to illegal felling of trees or poaching. It will be humanly impossible to monitor 305 licensees, their ingress and egress and to ensure that these licensees do not indulge in poaching and other ecologically harmful activities.... The National Park is also a tiger reserve and all these other activities have a direct bearing on the protection of wildlife in the National Park area.

The petitioner is undoubtedly justified in expressing his apprehensions and in pointing out the dangers of permitting 305 licensees to fish in the Totladoh reservoir. The fishing permits, however, have been granted to the tribals in lieu of their traditional fishing rights. Although the petitioner relies upon the provisions of the Indian Forest Act in support of the contention that the tribals cannot have any rights in a Reserved Forest which has subsequently become a National Park, the Collector of Chhindwara, in his report has pointed out that in fact that there were four villages of tribals in Chhindwara District falling within the Reserved Forest-cum-National Park area where these tribals resided and fishing was their main source of livelihood....

[W]hile every attempt must be made to preserve the fragile ecology of the forest area, and protect the Tiger Reserve, the right of the tribals formerly living in the area to keep body and soul together must also receive proper consideration. Undoubtedly, every effort should be made to ensure that the tribals, when resettled, are in a position to earn their livelihood....

[The court issued detailed directions for the proper implementation of the licence condition. The directions included the issue of photo identity cards for permit holders; restrictions on the route travelled while entering and leaving the Park; a prohibition on lighting fires for cooking or for any other purpose; and strict monitoring by the state government, to ensure that there was no poaching.]

The intervenor organization which has intervened in this petition, namely, Jan Van Andolan Samiti, Totladoh shall explain to the concerned fishermen, the conditions, subject to which they are allowed to fish in the Totladoh reservoir and shall impress upon these fishermen their obligation to carry on the fishing activity in a manner which does not damage the ecology of the National Park or disturb its environment.

Since all the claims in respect of the National Park area in the state of Madhya Pradesh as notified under S.35(1) have been taken care of, it is necessary that a final notification under S.35(4) is issued by the state government as expeditiously as possible. In the case of *Pradeep Krishen v Union of India* AIR 1996 SC 2040, this Court had pointed out that the total forest cover in our country is far less than the ideal minimum of 1/3rd of the total land. We cannot, therefore, afford any further shrinkage in the forest cover in our country. If one of the reasons for this shrinkage is the entry of villagers and tribals living in and around the sanctuaries and the National Park there can be no doubt that urgent steps must be taken to prevent any destruction or damage to the environment, the flora and fauna and wildlife in those areas. The state government is, therefore, expected to act with a sense of urgency in matters enjoined by Art. 48A of the Constitution keeping in mind the duty enshrined in Art. 51A(g). We, therefore, direct that the state government of the state of Madhya Pradesh shall expeditiously issue the final notification under S.35(4) of the Wild Life (Protection) Act, 1972 in respect of the area of the Pench National Park falling within the state of Madhya Pradesh.

The petition is disposed of with these directions.

NOTES AND QUESTIONS

1. How persuasive is the reasoning of the court? Did the court have an answer to the petitioner's case that the tribals could not have acquired any rights since the land was a reserved forest before conversion into a national park? Looked at differently, are not all statutory provisions subordinate to the right to life? If so, the court was justified in protecting the life and livelihood of the tribals.

2. Apart from tribals residing in wilderness reserves, park administrators must confront encroachers who have settled on protected lands. The Guwahati High Court turned down the claims of villagers who sought protection against eviction when the state notified that the Burachapari Reserve Forest was to be a wildlife sanctuary. The petitioners claimed to represent two thousand graziers engaged in cattle rearing and the supply of milk. Justice Sharma found no infirmity in the procedure adopted by the government. Her judgment records: '[The] learned ... government advocate has submitted that these petitioners are not actual inhabitants of the area in question and they are recent encroachers through the unprotected border. I find sufficient merit in the submissions of the learned government advocate and prefer to take judicial notice of it as large scale influx of encroachers in such a forest land is a common phenomena, putting the forest authority in innumerable and unsolvable problems at the cost of the protection of precious endangered wildlife.'[82]

3. When judicial orders to relocate thousands of squatters from Borivali National Park in Bombay met with resistance, the Bombay High Court called in platoons of the state reserve police to assist in forcibly evicting the encroachers.[83]

II. FOREST RIGHTS ACT

Forest dwellers achieved an important milestone with the passage of the Scheduled Tribes and Other Traditional Forest Dwellers (Recognition of Forest Rights) Act of 2006 (FRA). The FRA seeks to resolve the conflict in favour of forest dwellers by conferring on them individual and community rights over forest lands irrespective of whether the lands fall within or outside protected areas. Acknowledging the historical injustice in failing to recognize the rights of forest dwelling tribal people, the FRA seeks to correct this wrong. The Statement of Objects and Reasons of the Bill explains the reasons for the law:

> Forest dwelling tribal people and forests are inseparable. One cannot survive without the other. The conservation of ecological resources by forest dwelling tribal communities have been referred to in ancient manuscripts and scriptures. The colonial rule somehow ignored this reality for greater economic gains and probably for good reasons prevalent at that time. After independence, in our enthusiasm to protect natural resources we continued with colonial legislation and adopted more internationally accepted notions of conservation rather than learning from the rich traditions of the country where conservation is imbedded in the ethos of tribal life. The reservation process for creating wilderness and forest areas for production forestry somehow ignored the bona fide interests of the tribal community from legislative framework in the regions where tribal communities primarily inhabit.... There is a recognition of the fact that forests have the best chance to survive if communities participate

[82] *Chandamari Tea Co v State of Assam* AIR 2000 Gau 13, 21. The judgment disposed of a group of petitions some of which challenged the extension of the Kaziranga National Park. The state justified the extension on the ground that some poachers used the encroachments to sneak into Kaziranga.

[83] *Bombay Environmental Action Group v A R Bharati, Deputy Conservator of Forests*, Writ Petition No. 305 of 1995, orders dated 2 March 2000 and 13 March 2000. For a softer approach to forest encroachers see *Nature Lovers Movement v State of Kerala* AIR 2000 Ker 131.

> in the conservation and regeneration measures. Insecurity of tenure and fear of eviction from these lands where they have lived and thrived for generations are perhaps the biggest reasons why the tribal communities feel emotionally as well as physically alienated from forests and forest lands.

Section 3 of the FRA lists individual and community forest rights. Section 4 opens with words that give overriding effect to the FRA: '*Notwithstanding anything contained in any other law for the time being in force*, and subject to the provisions of this Act, the Central Government hereby recognizes and vests forest rights in' forest dwelling Scheduled Tribes and other traditional forest dwellers. The effect of these provisions is that the rights conferred under the FRA defeat any obligation under the Wild Life Act for resident communities to shift out from national parks and sanctuaries or for forest dwellers to refrain from carrying on economic activities recognized by the FRA. As a consequence of the FRA, a range of new economic activities are now carried out by forest dwellers without conflict with the department.

The FRA seeks to balance the interests of wildlife conservation by creating inviolate areas known as critical wildlife habitat. Section 2(b) of the FRA provides this definition:

> 2(b) 'critical wildlife habitat' means such area of National Parks and Sanctuaries where it has been specifically and clearly established, case by case, on the basis of scientific and objective criteria, that such areas are required to be kept as inviolate for the purposes of wildlife conservation as may be determined and notified by the Central Government in the Ministry of Environment and Forests after open process of consultation by an Expert Committee, which includes experts from the locality appointed by that Government wherein a representative of the Ministry of Tribal Affairs shall also be included, in determining such areas according to the procedural requirements arising from sub-sections (1) and (2) of section 4 ...

Fourteen years after the FRA was enforced, the Central Government had yet to notify a single critical wildlife habitat.

E. COMMERCIAL INTERESTS AND PROTECTED AREAS

I. SARISKA

The Tarun Bharat Singh is a non-governmental organization engaged in rural development in Rajasthan. One of the critical needs in Rajasthan's villages is water. The Aravalli range and its forests trap rain water during the brief monsoons and release the water over the dry months, like a soaked sponge being gently squeezed.

Widespread open-cast mining for limestone and marble in the Alwar District was disturbing the aquifers, springs and the water-holding capacity of the Aravalli. The use of dynamite had scarred and devastated the hills. Rajinder Singh, the secretary of the Tarun Bharat Sangh, was troubled by the impact of unregulated mining on the water resources in the region. These common property and development concerns prompted him to launch the *Sariska* case. The area, now popularly known as the 'Sariska Tiger Sanctuary' was an exclusive hunting reserve of the former Rulers of Alwar.

At the admission stage, the Supreme Court noted the apparent contradictions in the Rajasthan government's policy:

> The purpose of the notification declaring the area as a Game Reserve under the Rajasthan Wild Animals and Birds Protection Act, 1951; or the declaration of the area as a sanctuary under the Wild Life (Protection) Act, 1972 and the notification dated 1-1-1975 declaring the area as a protected forest under the Rajasthan Forest Act, 1953 is to protect the forest wealth and wild life of the area. It is, indeed, odd that the state government while professing

to protect the environment by means of these notifications and declarations should, at the same time, permit degradation of the environment by authorizing mining operations in the protected area.[84]

On 14 May 1992, the court framed the issues before it and set the tone for deliberations:

This litigation concerns environment.... The issues and concerns in this case far transcend the trivialities and inhibitions of an adversarial litigation.... The issues of environment must and shall receive the highest attention from this Court.

The primary issue in the case is the protection of the forest-wealth and wild life in Alwar district in the state of Rajasthan. The area in question has been declared a 'protected forest' by virtue of the notification dated 1st January, 1975 issued under sections 29 and 30 of the Rajasthan Forest Act, 1953. Some areas are also declared as 'Reserved Areas, Sariska' under the Rajasthan Wild Animals & Birds Protection Act, 1951. Some parks have also been declared as 'National Park' under section 35 of the Wild Life (Protection) Act, 1972. The question that requires to be solved is whether in these areas which are covered by the various statutory notifications illegal mining activities are carried on and if so whether such activities require to be stopped by the intervention of the Court.[85]

TARUN BHARAT SANGH, ALWAR v UNION OF INDIA
(1993) SUPP (3) SCC 115

B P Jeevan Reddy, J: Tarun Bharat Sangh, a voluntary organization interested *inter alia* in protection of environment, approached this Court complaining that widespread illegal mining activity was going on in the area declared as tiger reserve in Alwar district of Rajasthan. In the interest of ecology, environment and rule of law, it said, the activity should stop.

The petitioner's case is that the area wherein the illegal mining is going on has been declared as a tiger reserve under Rajasthan Wild Animal and Birds Protection Act, 1951, as a Sanctuary and a National Park under Wild Life (Protection) Act, 1972, and as protected forest under the Rajasthan Forest Act, 1953. These various notifications, said the petitioner, prohibit all or any mining activity and yet the Government of Rajasthan had granted hundreds of licenses for mining marble, dolomite and other minerals in late 1980s, contrary to law....

Petitioner's case was that no mining lease/license can be granted within the protected forest except with the prior permission of the Government of India—section 2 of the Forest (Conservation) Act, 1980 and rule 4(6) of Rajasthan Minor Mineral Concession Rules—and that no such permission was obtained in fact.

By its order dated 26 November 1991, the court clarified that the order dated 11 October 1991 was not intended to permit the mine-owners to carry on their mining activity where such activity was prohibited by any Act, rule or notification having the force of law. In effect, the order said, it meant to prohibit—and not to permit—the mining activity.

In its order dated 14 May 1992, the court clarified the meaning of the expression 'protected area' used in the order dated 11 October 1991. The expression, it was clarified, was intended to and does refer to all the areas which have had legal protection against non-forest activities that devastated the environment including poaching, mining, felling of trees etc. It was further clarified that once an area is declared as protected forest, it becomes a protected forest notwithstanding the fact that a part of that area is waste. The idea behind declaring an area as protected forest, it was pointed out, is not merely the protection of the existing forest but also afforestation.

---

[84] *Tarun Bharat Sangh, Alwar v Union of India* AIR 1992 SC 514, 516.

[85] *Tarun Bharat Sangh, Alwar v Union of India*, Writ Petition (Civil) No. 509 of 1991, Supreme Court, 14 May 1992 (M N Venkatachaliah and B P Jeevan Reddy, JJ).

The committee submitted its report dated 28 September 1992. The report states that the committee verified and cross-checked the tracing maps furnished by the Revenue Department and found that both of them matched. After looking into the khasra numbers mentioned in the notification dated 1 January 1975 and all other material placed before it by the parties including the mine-owners, the report states, the committee identified the areas declared as protected forest. The report indicates that the area declared as protected forest under the said notification was not in one contiguous block but was comprised in several blocks or areas, as it may be called.

As per the said report, 215 mines mentioned in Appendix 'A' to the report fall completely within the areas declared as protected forest while 47 mines mentioned in Appendix 'B' to the report fall partly inside and partly outside the areas declared as protected forest. (These 262 mines are referred to hereinafter as 'listed mines'). To this extent, there is no difference of opinion among the members of the committee. Differing opinions have, however, been expressed when it came to making of recommendations for the consideration of this Court. The Chairman, Shri Justice M L Jain recommended that the mining operations in all the 215 mines listed in Appendix 'A' should be stopped forthwith to the extent they fell within the area declared as protected forest. Three other members of the committee (Collector, Alwar, the Chief Conservator of Forest and Chief Wildlife Warden, Rajasthan and the Additional Director of Mines) differed from the Chairman. They suggested that this Court be pleased to accept the representation of the State Government (appended as Appendix 'C' to the report) wherein it was prayed that the area covered by the mines should be allowed to be excluded from the protected forest, in lieu of which the Government of Rajasthan will provide an equal extent of area for being included in the protected forest. An application has also been filed by the State of Rajasthan to the same effect. It is stated therein that the protected forest area measures about 800 sq kms, whereas the 262 mines mentioned in Appendices 'A' and 'B' cover only an area of 2.08 sq kms including the area covered by the said mines to be allowed deleted from the protected forest. In lieu thereof, the Government of Rajasthan offered to place an equal extent for the purpose being declared as protected forest. It is submitted further that when the mining leases with respect to the said 262 mines were granted, the Government of Rajasthan was under the impression that the said mines did not fall within the protected forest area. Indeed, it was so clarified by the Forest Department. This happened because of want of clarity about the precise boundaries of the areas declared as protected forest.

[The court recorded the submissions made by the parties. The Central Government submitted that the Forest (Conservation) Act extended not only to reserve and protected forests but all areas recorded as forests in government records. No mining could be permitted in the absence of prior approval of the Central Government. On 7 May 1992, the Central Government had issued a notification under section 3 of the Environment (Protection) Act prohibiting mining in the Sariska National Park, Sariska Sanctuary and areas under Project Tiger. The petitioner argued that the government of Rajasthan was colluding with the mine-owners. The mining leases granted were illegal. Counsel for the state of Rajasthan urged the court to delete 5 sq kms from the protected areas to enable mining to continue in the public interest. The mine-owners disputed the demarcation by the committee and the maps put forward by the state. They disputed the claim that the mines fell in the tiger reserve and pointed to the unemployment and economic loss that would result from closure.]

At the outset, we may be permitted to clarify an aspect. This is not a case where we are called upon to shut down an activity being carried on lawfully, in the name of higher considerations of ecology and environment. This is a simple case where we are called upon to ensure observance of enacted laws made by the state to protect the environment and ecology of the area. In such a case, we need not be oppressed by considerations of balancing the interests of economy and ecology. That has already been done by the Legislature and Parliament. The grievance of the petitioner is against the executive. Charged with the delegation of implementing the laws of the land, the executive is yet failing to do its duty by law and by people, when faced with the might of money; respect for law is dissolving into respect for

Mammon, says the petitioner. Let us therefore first find out which laws are violated, if any, and then decide, what are the proper directions to make.

(A) Section 2 of the Forest (Conservation) Act read with section 29 of the Rajasthan Forest Act and rule 4(6) of the Rajasthan Minor Mineral Concessions Rules:

* * *

Once an area is declared as a protected forest, it comes within the purview of the Forest (Conservation) Act, 1980. It becomes a forest land within the meaning of section 2. The effect of this position is that no non-forest activity can be carried on in the said area except with the prior approval of the Central Government. Even the state government cannot carry on such non-forest activity in the said area without prior approval. That the mining activity amounts to non-forest purpose is beyond dispute. Thus, the grant of mining leases/ licenses and their renewal by the state government, without obtaining the prior approval of the Central Government, in respect of the mines situated within the protected forest, after 1 January 1975 is contrary to law. All the mines listed in Appendix 'A' to the committee's report do fall within the areas declared as protected forest while the mines listed in Appendix 'B' fall partly within and partly outside such areas. According to rule 4(6) of the Rajasthan Minor Mineral Concession Rules, 1986, too, no mining lease could have been granted or renewed within the forest 'without clearance from the Central Government in accordance with the Forest (Conservation) Act, 1980 and the rules made thereunder.' Admittedly no such prior approval or clearance of Central Government was obtained. The Chairman of the committee, Shri Justice M L Jain has recommended that 215 mines mentioned in Appendix 'A' to his report, which are situated wholly within the protected forest should be closed forthwith. There can hardly be any valid objection in law to the said recommendation. Similarly, with respect to 47 mines mentioned in Appendix 'B' to the report, the learned Chairman has recommended that they should be closed forthwith insofar as they fall within the protected forest. To this recommendation also, there can be no valid objection in law.

At this stage, it would be appropriate to consider the application filed by state of Rajasthan for permission to delete an extent of 5.02 sq kms from out of the protected forest. The application is confined only to 208 mines out of 262 listed mines. Fifty-four mines mentioned in para (9) of the application are proposed to be closed; indeed, according to the counsel for the state, they have already been closed. Reliance is placed upon the order dated 14 May 1992 in this behalf. It is pointed out that the said order does contemplate such modification, of course, with the permission of this Court and for valid reasons. It is pointed out that for such deletion or modification, the prior approval of the Central Government is not required. No such requirement is prescribed either in the Forest (Conservation) Act or Rajasthan Forest Act, it is submitted in this context, the submission of [counsel for the mine-owners] may also be considered. He says that there are a number of mines around and outside the area declared as protected forests and that no purpose would be served by merely closing the mines within the protected forest and leaving those outside unhindered. He says that all these mines within and outside, are outside the sanctuary. Maybe so. But it cannot be forgotten that purpose of Forest Acts and purpose of Environmental Protection Acts may not always be the same. Such closure may not serve the environmental purpose—assuming that the factual situation asserted by the learned counsel is true, upon which aspect we need not and do not make any pronouncement—but it may serve the forest purpose. Be that as it may, both the purposes appear to be intertwined in this case. In this situation, we think it appropriate that the merits of the said proposal be examined by the Ministry of Environment and Forests, Government of India and a report submitted to this Court, within three months from today. Orders will be passed on the application for directions filed by the state of Rajasthan after considering the said report.

(B) Notification issued by the Central Government under section 3 of the Environment (Protection) Act, 1986 on 7 May 1992

This notification expressly prohibits the carrying on of the mining operations, except with the Central Government's prior permission, in the 'areas covered under project tiger.' The prohibition extends to existing mining leases in sanctuaries/National Park. All mining operations are prohibited therein. The table appended to the notification particularises the areas where carrying on of the processes and operations aforesaid is prohibited without the permission of the Central Government. They include all reserve forest, protected forest or any other area shown as forest in the land records maintained by the state government as on the date of the issuance of the said notification in relation to *inter alia* Alwar district of the state of Rajasthan. The table also includes all areas of Sariska National Park and Sariska Sanctuary notified under the Wild Life (Protection) Act, 1972. We cannot agree with the learned counsel for mine-owners that the area declared as project tiger in the Alwar district has not been identified or that it is not properly identifiable. Both the state government and Central Government have demarcated them in exactly identical manner. The map produced before us by the state government is a detailed plan, prepared with great care. There is no reason to presume that it is not prepared by competent persons on the basis of the relevant material. The map delineates the area declared as sanctuary within the area declared as tiger reserve—though outside the sanctuary. A publication by the Forest Survey of India, Dehradun, Ministry of Environment and Forest, Government of India, entitled 'Status of Forest Covering in Project Tiger Reserve' has been placed before us. At pages 92–94, we find the map of Sariska Tiger Reserve, Rajasthan. The boundaries, shape and dimensions of the said map tally fully and perfectly with the map prepared by the state of Rajasthan. Thus, there can be no legitimate dispute with respect to the correctness of map produced by Government of Rajasthan or with respect to the area declared as tiger reserve. Both the state government and Central Government have delineated it. Maybe that the declaration as tiger reserve was without any statutory authority and is relatable to the executive power of the Union of India—but the notification issued under section 3 of the Environment (Protection) Act puts the stamp of statutory authority over it. The Central Government has specifically stated in its affidavit that no 'prior permission' was obtained with respect to the mines located within the tiger reserve. On this ground, the mining operations being carried on in the tiger reserve, including the listed mines also appears to be contrary to law. Of course, this notification has come only in May 1992.

[The court directed the listed mines (those listed in Appendices 'A' and 'B') to stop forthwith. The Central Government was directed to submit a report within three months on the state government's proposal to delete 5.02 sq kms from the protected area. Mines situated outside the protected forests within the tiger reserve were permitted to continue for four months, within which period they were permitted to approach the Central Government for permission to continue their operations. If no permission was obtained, they were directed to cease mining activity.]

NOTES AND QUESTIONS

1. In November 1991, the mine-owners turned violent. Rajinder Singh, secretary of the petitioners, was attacked and beaten by a crowd of mine-owners when he accompanied the court-appointed committee on a site inspection. Ashok Agarwal, one of the mine-owners, was convicted of criminal contempt and was sentenced by the court to imprisonment for seven days and a fine of Rs. 500. 'The atmosphere of show of force said to have been displayed by the mine-owners ... is really disturbing. We should make this case one which will unmistakably tell those like-minded with the contemner that this kind of crime against the course of justice and process of law does not pay....'[86]

2. Since its action in permitting mining was illegal, the state proposed to 'move the forest' by de-reserving about 5.02 sq kms of protected forest and offering compensatory reservation

[86] *Tarun Bharat Sangh, Alwar v Union of India* (1992) Supp (2) SCC 750, 754.

of an equal area. Should the court have encouraged the forest swap proposed by Rajasthan? Does it set a dangerous precedent?

3. The Justice Jain committee submitted its report on 28 September 1992. The report was not signed by the environmentalist, Anil Agarwal, who submitted his dissent in November, 1992. Surprisingly, the principal judgment makes no reference to Agarwal's dissent. Agarwal was dissatisfied with the committee's obsession with the boundary disputes rather than the main environmental concerns.

4. Why did the court not provide for the rehabilitation of the mine-owners elsewhere in the state, following the precedent of the *Dehradun Quarrying* litigation?[87]

5. An administrative directive establishing the Project Tiger Reserve, by itself, affords no protection. To prevent mining activity, the prohibition must have statutory backing. In the *Sariska* case, the backing was eventually provided by the 1992 notification under the Environment (Protection) Act of 1986.

6. On 12 April 1994, the Supreme Court rejected review applications filed by some of the aggrieved miners.[88]

II. KOLLERU

Kolleru is a large, shallow, freshwater lake and marshland between the Krishna and Godavari rivers. It was declared a Ramsar site in November 2002 and supports more than 50,000 waterfowl. Kolleru is threatened by encroachments, overfishing, industrial effluents and increasing salinity due to bunding for pisciculture.[89] On 25 September 1995, Andhra Pradesh issued a *preliminary* notification under section 18 of the Wild Life (Protection) Act of 1972 declaring its intention to constitute a wildlife sanctuary at Kolleru. The collectors of the West Godavari and Krishna districts began deciding the claims of persons having rights over the land falling within the proposed sanctuary. The preliminary notification and the collectors' actions were challenged before the Andhra Pradesh High Court which disposed of the case, holding that private rights could not be curtailed without a *final* notification under section 26A of the Act.[90] The state was directed to take steps to issue such a notification. After hearing citizens' objections, on 4 October 1999 Andhra Pradesh issued a final notification under section 26A. This notification restricted commercial activity by preventing construction of tanks for aquaculture, limiting pisciculture to traditional methods, prohibiting the use of pesticides and chemicals for agriculture and requiring the removal of encroachments.

The restrictions in the final notification were necessary because encroachers had blocked the free flow of water into Kolleru Lake. Huge tracts of land stood converted into fish tanks, disrupting the natural drainage. Scores of encroachers had raised bunds up to a height of 20–25 feet above the ground level, impounding water in artificial tanks and lakes. Designed to boost pisciculture, the bunds resulted in submergence of crops upstream.

The Andhra Pradesh High Court repelled a challenge to the final notification on 30 July 2001.[91] Moreover, the Central Empowered Committee (CEC)[92] on 20 March 2006

---

87 *Rural Litigation and Entitlement Kendra, Dehradun v State of Uttar Pradesh* AIR 1988 SC 2187.

88 *Tarun Bharat Sangh Alwar v Union of India* 1994 (2) SCALE 68.

89 M Z Islam & A R Rahmani, *Important Bird Areas in India* 147 (2004).

90 *Kunapuraju Rangaraju v Government of Andhra Pradesh* (1998) 3 ANDH L T 215.

91 *D Patanjali Sastri (Dr) v Chairman, A P Pollution Control Board* (2001) 5 ANDH L T 315.

92 The CEC at the time was a statutory committee constituted under section 3(3) of the Environment (Protection) Act of 1986. It has rendered invaluable assistance by filing reports based on site visits in a number of environmental cases before the Supreme Court. When the Union Government declined to extend the term of the CEC, the Supreme Court in the exercise of its jurisdiction (presumably under Articles 21, 32, 136 and

recommended demolition of all fish tanks constructed inside Kolleru Wildlife Sanctuary within a specified time. The objectors assailed the final notification claiming that as owners of private lands they were entitled to construct bunds on their own land. For more than two decades prior to the final notification, huge investments were made in the business of pisciculture and thousands of employees earned a livelihood from the fish tanks. The bunds had been put up after securing the requisite permissions. Examine how the Supreme Court balances private rights and environmental concerns.

T N GODAVARMAN THIRUMULPAD v UNION OF INDIA
(2006) 5 SCC 47

S H Kapadia, J: Development needs of the present without compromising the ability of the future generations to meet their own needs is called 'sustainable development', a concept based on the principle of inter-generational equity....

Kolleru lake is one of the largest shallow freshwater lakes in Asia located between the delta of Krishna and Godavari rivers in the State of Andhra Pradesh. It serves as a natural flood balancing reservoir for the two rivers. It receives water from 67 inflowing drains and channels. It sustains flora and fauna and people living around it. The area of the lake at various contour levels is as under:

Contour level at mean sea level (MSL)	*Area*
At + 10 feet MSL	901 sq km (2.25 lakh acres)
At + 7 feet MSL	675 sq km (1.69 lakh acres)
At + 5 feet MSL	308 sq km (0.77 lakh acres)

It is found between the alluvial plains of River Godavari and River Krishna due to natural geological formation covering 2 mandals in West Godavari district and 7 mandals in Krishna district. Ecologically it is a wetland ecosystem.... The lake supports biodiversity and high biomass of fish plankton which constitute the source of food for birds.

Kolleru lake extends over 901 sq km at plus 10 contour. However, only 308 sq km out of 901 sq km have been declared as wildlife sanctuary. This has been done in order to strike a balance between the rights of the people living in and around the lake on one hand and to protect the ecosystem on the other hand.

Government of India is the signatory to 1971 Convention of Ramsar (Iran) where it is declared that Kolleru is a wetland ecosystem of international importance. In the said convention it is decided that encroachments in the lake would not be tolerated. The said convention is also known as Wetland Convention. [The court recorded the rationale for the final notification, the objections from the landowners, the relevant statutory provisions and the restrictions imposed on commercial activity.]

From the above, it is clear that the right of the local fishermen to do fishing by traditional methods is not taken away, but aquaculture in the form of any tank is prohibited. Further, wherever pisciculture existed in private land, as on the date of the notification, fishing by traditional method is permitted without causing environmental hazard, till the Government acquires such private lands under the said 1972 Act. The right to do traditional agriculture without using pesticides and chemicals is also permitted under the notification. Lastly, the encroachment activities are directed to be stopped, forthwith. The final notification, therefore, seeks to regulate, in public interest and in the interest of ecology, activities, such as aquaculture, pisciculture, prawn culture and shrimp culture, basically to preserve the identity of the lake which otherwise is likely to become extinct within 12 years....

142 of the Constitution of India) continued the CEC by order dated 14 December 2007, *T N Godavarman Thirumulpad v Union of India* (2013) 8 SCC 204.

Before us it has been repeatedly urged that the objectors have made huge investments over the years, that they were permitted to put up bunds under permissions given by the Collector and that equity demands that a balance be struck down between preservation of the lake and the livelihood of persons surviving on aquaculture and pisciculture. It is further argued that mud bunds constituted a part of traditional fishing practice and consequently this Court should not direct demolition of these bunds.

We do not find any merit in the above arguments for the following reasons. Firstly, section 29 specifically prohibits commercial activity inside the Sanctuary. It prohibits commercial activity which diverts, stops or increases the flow of water into or outside the Sanctuary. With the issuance of the final notification formation of fish tanks for aquaculture or for any other purpose is prohibited as they obstruct free flow of water both into or outside the Sanctuary. Secondly, the notification dated 4-10-1999 provides a limited right to carry on fishing inasmuch as it permits fishing with traditional methods using mavus and nets. It expressly, however, prohibits the objectors from forming any fish tank(s) for aquaculture or for any other purpose. It also expressly provides that whenever pisciculture was existing on the date of the notification in private lands, fishing by traditional methods shall be permitted, without causing environmental hazard, till the Government acquires such private lands. It also cancels the pattas granted in the past. In our view, therefore, the notification regulates aquaculture, pisciculture, prawn culture, shrimp culture, etc. Thirdly, the argument advanced on behalf of the objectors that mud bund formation is compatible with traditional fishing practice, and therefore, should be allowed to continue to exist, has no merit. When a bund is formed in a sanctuary or a lake it seeks to encapsulate an area which in turn obstructs free flow of water in the lake bed area. As stated above, formation of bund reduces the retention capacity of the lake. These formations, if allowed, would destroy the lake. In view of the provisions of section 26-A read with section 29 all commercial activities which seek to destroy the ecology, stands prohibited. Compatibility of mud bunds with the traditional fishing practice in a lake is a concept different from formation of the entire area of the lake. Out of 901 sq km of Kolleru lake, an area of 308 sq km alone is notified as Sanctuary. [The court banned the transport of inputs for pisciculture and ordered the demolition of fish tanks in the sanctuary.]

NOTE AND QUESTION

The statutory framework to test the legality of state action in the *Kolleru Lake* case was provided by the Wild Life (Protection) Act of 1972. Given the importance of Kolleru and other threats to the larger ecosystem from industrial effluents and non-degradable garbage, should the Union Government have issued suitable directions under section 5 of the EPA or, indeed, framed regulations under section 3(2)(v) of the EPA read with rule 5 of the Environment (Protection) Rules of 1986?

III. JAMNAGAR

In *Essar Oil Ltd v Halar Utkarsh Samiti*,[93] the Supreme Court salvaged from the doldrums a giant refinery project located in Gujarat off the west coast of India. The refinery depended on crude oil from West Asia and needed a single buoy mooring at sea from where an underwater pipeline would transport the imported crude for refining. Without this umbilical link the refinery was a worthless asset. The CRZ notification expressly permitted such pipelines. The challenging feature of this case was that the pipeline was required to traverse through the Jamnagar Marine National Park and Sanctuary. The expert opinion of the National Institute

[93] (2004) 2 SCC 392.

of Oceanography (NIO) supported the project since in NIO's view, the pipeline could be laid without permanently damaging the wildlife and ecological system. While the judgment navigates past a minefield of legal impediments and allows the project to proceed, the excerpt below focuses on the interpretation of section 29 of the Wild Life (Protection) Act of 1972 (WPA).

ESSAR OIL LTD v HALAR UTKARSH SAMITI

(2004) 2 SCC 392

* * *

RUMA PAL, J:

Jamnagar Marine National Park and Sanctuary lie along the lower lip of the Gulf of Katchch in the State of Gujarat covering reserve forests and territorial waters. Essar Oil Ltd, Bharat Oman Refineries Ltd (BORL) and Gujarat Positra Port Co Ltd, seek to lay pipelines to pump crude oil from a single buoy mooring in the Gulf across a portion of the Marine National Park and Marine Sanctuary to their oil refineries in Jamnagar district. On the basis of separate public interest litigation petitions filed by Halar Utkarsh Samiti and Jansangharsh Manch, the High Court, by the impugned judgment, has held that BORL may lay its pipelines but the others may not and has restrained the State Government from granting any more authorizations and permissions for laying down any pipeline in any part of the sanctuary or national park. BORL was allowed to lay its pipelines by the High Court, since permission to do so had already been granted to it by the State Government and since no such permission had, according to the High Court, been granted to Essar Oil, its application together with all pending applications were to be decided in accordance with what had been decided by the Court....

What we are really concerned with is section 29 of the WPA and its interpretation. This can be said to be the core issue in all the appeals. Section 29 reads:

> 29.*Destruction etc. in a sanctuary prohibited without a permit* — No person shall destroy, exploit or remove any wildlife from a sanctuary or destroy or damage the habitat of any wild animal or deprive any wild animal of its habitat within such sanctuary except under and in accordance with a permit granted by the Chief Wildlife Warden and no such permit shall be granted unless the State Government, being satisfied that such destruction, exploitation or removal of wildlife from the sanctuary is necessary for the improvement and better management of wildlife therein, authorises the issue of such permit.
>
> *Explanation* — For the purposes of this section, grazing or movement of livestock permitted under clause (d) of section 33 shall not be deemed to be an act prohibited under this section.

The corresponding provision relating to national parks is section 35 sub-section (6)....

The challenge by the respondent-writ petitioners before the High Court which was accepted, rested on an interpretation of sections 29 and 35 of the WPA. Construing section 29, the High Court held that the Marine Sanctuary and Marine National Park were not to be utilized for any purpose other than the purposes prescribed under the Wild Life (Protection) Act and except in accordance with sections 26-A(3), 30 and section 35(6) thereof. The High Court said that:

> The Government could arrive at the satisfaction that it is necessary to grant such permission for destruction of wildlife, as otherwise in case such permission for destruction, exploitation or removal is not granted, the same would adversely affect the improvement and better management of the wildlife.

The word 'necessary' was construed to mean indispensable, needful or essential. It was held that unless the Government was satisfied 'beyond reasonable doubt' that the laying of the pipeline was indispensable for the better management of the wildlife, no permission could be granted under section 29. The High Court found that it could not be said that the laying of crude oil pipeline was necessary or indispensable for the purpose of improvement and better management of the wildlife. The reports given by the Institute of Oceanography and NEERI were held not to be binding on the Court. It was further held that neither of the expert bodies had reported that the laying of the crude pipeline in the sanctuary area was necessary for the better health, improvement and management of the wildlife therein. The High Court was also of the view that it was not open to the executive to interfere with the power of the legislature under section 26-A(3) by granting permission to lay pipelines thus 'directly or indirectly' affecting the alteration of the boundaries of the sanctuary. Summing up, the High Court's view was that the State Government can accord permission under section 29 of the Wild Life (Protection) Act only if it is necessary for improvement and better management of wildlife and since the laying of pipeline through the sanctuary was not for the improvement and better management of the wildlife, no permit could be granted under section 29.

[The judgment summarizes the rival submissions and then turns to the Stockholm Declaration of 1972 which it describes as the 'Magna Carta of our environment'. Referring to Principles 2, 8 and 11 of the Stockholm Declaration, the court emphasized the need to balance economic and social needs with environmental considerations. The court held: 'The objective of all laws on environment should be to create harmony between the two since neither one can be sacrificed at the altar of the other.']

Section 29 must be construed with this background in mind. The section has been quoted verbatim earlier. Analysed, it provides for three prohibitions: (a) destruction, exploitation or removal of any wildlife from a sanctuary; (b) destruction or damage to the habitat of any wildlife; and (c) deprivation of any wild animal of its habitat within such sanctuary. Prohibition '(a)' is concerned with wildlife and its protection. Wildlife, which includes any animal, bees, butterflies, crustacea, fish and moths and aquatic or land *vegetation* which form part of any habitat under sub-section (37) of section 2, cannot be destroyed, removed or exploited.

Prohibitions '(b)' and '(c)' relate to the habitat of 'wild animals'. The word 'habitat' has been defined in section 2(15) as including 'land, water or *vegetation* which is the natural home of any wild animal'. Therefore, while some habitats may fall within the definition of wildlife, namely, vegetation, habitats which do not consist of vegetation would not. The difference in the definition is of significance and reflects the varying standards of protection afforded under the provisions of the WPA. The protection afforded to wildlife is more rigorous, but in no case is the prohibition absolute in the sense that the prohibited activities may not be allowed under any circumstances whatsoever. Thus wildlife may be destroyed, exploited or removed from a sanctuary under and in accordance with a permit granted by the Chief Wildlife Warden. Similarly, the habitat of the wild animals within the sanctuary may be destroyed or damaged and a wild animal can be deprived of its habitat within such sanctuary under and in accordance with a permit granted by the Chief Wildlife Warden.

The power of the Chief Wildlife Warden to grant a permit is generally controlled under section 4(2) which requires him to perform his duties and exercise his powers under the directions of the State Government. But the State Government is itself statutorily restrained from directing the grant of a permit in respect of the destruction, exploitation or removal of wildlife from the sanctuary unless it is satisfied that 'such destruction, exploitation or removal ... is necessary for the improvement and better management of wildlife therein'. The phrase does not, as has been rightly contended by the appellant, relate to prohibitions (b) and (c). The particular satisfaction regarding betterment of wildlife is a precondition to be fulfilled only when there is destruction, exploitation or removal of wildlife prohibited under (a). Plainly stated, when wildlife is to be bettered, its destruction, exploitation or removal may be permitted. The example of 'culling' given by the Manch is apt.

To destroy means to deprive of life, kill, wipe out or annihilate.... In other words, section 29 bars anyone from completely, irreparably and irreversibly putting an end to wildlife or to the habitat in a sanctuary. The word 'removal' would have a similar connotation. However, 'exploitation' or using the wildlife for any purpose, although it may not lead to extinction of wildlife, or 'damage' which may not cause any irreparable injury to the habitat, are forbidden nevertheless. It is necessary to note at this stage, that there is no allegation in the present case that the proposed activity will remove or exploit wildlife within the sanctuary or national park.

In view of the plain language of the statute, we are not prepared to accept the submission on behalf of the private respondents that permits allowing activities relating to the *habitat* and covered by '(b)' and '(c)' also require the State Government to come to the conclusion that the proposed activities should result in the betterment of wildlife before it can be allowed. This is not to say that permits can ever be given indiscriminately. The State must, while directing the grant of a permit in any case, see that the habitat of the wildlife is at least sustained and that the damage to the habitat does not result in the destruction of the wildlife. That is the underlying assumption and is the implicit major premise which is contained in the definition of the word 'sanctuary' in section 2(26) and the declaration under section 18 of the WPA—that it is an area which is of particular ecological, faunal, floral, geomorphological, natural or zoological significance which is demarcated for protecting, propagating or developing wildlife.

The next question is whether it can be stated that the laying of pipelines through a sanctuary necessarily results in the destruction of the wildlife. That is, is it an activity falling under prohibition (a) .... The CRZ notifications issued under the EPA in 1991 and 2001 clearly allowed the laying of pipelines across ecologically sensitive areas such as national parks/ marine parks and sanctuaries. The laying of pipelines is one of the exceptions to the general bar against any construction in CRZ I areas.

It cannot therefore be said, as the High Court seems to have held, that the invariable consequence of laying pipelines through ecologically sensitive areas has been the destruction or removal of the wildlife. It would ultimately be a question of fact to be determined by experts in each case. We will have occasion to consider the opinion of the expert bodies on this when we take up the facts of the appellant's case. Suffice it to say at this stage that there is no a priori presumption of destruction of wildlife in the laying of pipelines. Cases of oil spills have undoubtedly been ecologically disastrous and have drawn the attention of the world but our attention was not drawn to any instance of leakage resulting from the laying of pipelines.

These observations, however, are not meant and should not be read as a general licence to lay a network of pipelines across sanctuaries and national parks. Every application must be dealt with on its own merits keeping in view the need to sustain the environment. Before according its approval to the grant of any permit under section 29 or 35, the State Government should consider whether the damage in respect of the proposed activity is reversible or not. If it is irreversible, it amounts to destruction and no permission may be granted unless there is positive proof of the betterment of the lot of the wildlife. Where activities are covered by '(a)', mitigation of damages would not do. There must be betterment of the wildlife by the proposed activity. Mitigation of damages would be relevant to proposed projects under '(b)' and '(c)'....

As far as the appellant is concerned, however, the way is now clear to proceed with the project in accordance with the permissions granted to it under the WPA, FCA and EPA. The State Government will issue the authorization in the requisite format under section 29 and 35 within a fortnight. We, therefore, allow the appeals to the extent stated with no order as to costs....

NOTES AND QUESTIONS

1. Do you agree with the Supreme Court's reading of 'the plain language' of section 29? Was the High Court's reading more 'plain' and the Supreme Court's reading more pragmatic?

2. Reliance Petroleum Ltd faced a similar challenge relating to its pipelines cutting across the Jamnagar Marine National Park and Sanctuary. The challenge was rejected by the Gujarat High Court[94] and the Supreme Court dismissed the petition for special leave to appeal under Article 136. Oddly, in *Essar's* case, the High Court declined to follow the *Reliance Petroleum* judgment.

3. Had the Supreme Court rejected the appeal, the only option available to Essar might have been to persuade the authorities to alter the boundary of the national park and sanctuary and permit a corridor for the pipeline. Essar claimed that it has invested Rs. 5,388.41 crores in setting up the project on 4,500 acres of land in Jamnagar District. Construction was well under way when the Supreme Court heard the case and the project was substantially financed through public funds from financial institutions and banks.

IV. KUDREMUKH

Kudremukh, which translates as 'horse face', is a region in Karnataka that draws its name from the mountainous Western Ghats. The Kudremukh Iron Ore Company Ltd (KIOCL) was established in 1976 and worked iron ore mines for decades. The forests in the area are among the 18 internationally recognized 'hotspots' for biodiversity conservation. Apart from its deposits of iron ore, the rivers Thunga, Bhadra and Netravathi rise from Kudremukh. Unsurprisingly, the region's Shola forests were damaged by the mining.[95]

The Kudremukh Iron Ore Company sought renewal of its mining lease which expired in July 1999. By this time, a new township came up at Kudremukh, a port called 'New Mangalore Port' was established and, during the 1970s, Kudremukh came to symbolize the modernity of the region.[96] The company's operations were export oriented with 82% of its production leaving Indian shores.

While the mining activities were continuing, the reserved forests in the region were constituted into the Kudremukh National Park. Concerned about the threat to the flora and fauna, K M Chinappa, a trustee of Wildlife First, applied to the Supreme Court seeking to stop the mining activities. The Supreme Court sought a report from the Central Empowered Committee and recorded:

> After hearing the parties and taking note of the materials placed before it the Committee has recommended as follows:
>
> > After carefully considering all the views and suggestions, the exceedingly rich biodiversity of the area and investment made by KIOCL, suggestion made by the learned *amicus curiae*, the Committee is of the view that KIOCL be asked to wind up its operations within a period of five years or on the exhaustion of the oxidized weathered secondary ore, whichever is earlier, in the already broken-up area. It is clarified that the period of 5 years would commence from 25-7-1999, when its lease had expired.

---

[94] *Gujarat Navodaya Mandal v State of Gujarat* AIR 1998 GUJ 141.
[95] Muzaffar Assadi, *Kudremukh: Of Mining and Environment*, 37 ECONOMIC & POLITICAL WEEKLY 4898 (2002).
[96] *Id.* at 4899.

The winding-up period of five years shall be subject to the following conditions:

(i) MoEF should prepare or get a rehabilitation and reclamation and a proper eco-restoration plan prepared for the mined area and project impact area through appropriate agency at the cost of KIOCL;
(ii) KIOCL shall undertake to make available funds necessary for implementing the aforesaid plans. The plans would be implemented by the agencies selected by MoEF and under the supervision of MoEF;
(iii) a monetary compensation of Rs 25 crores @ Rs 5 crores per year will have to be deposited by KIOCL with MoEF in a separate bank account which would be utilized for the purposes of research, monitoring and strengthening protection of Kudremukh National Park and for other protected areas in the State of Karnataka;
(iv) a Monitoring Committee shall be constituted by MoEF comprising representative of MoEF, representative of the State of Karnataka, two NGO experts preferably from Karnataka, which shall monitor the implementation of the rehabilitation plans; and
(v) after the winding-up operations are complete, KIOCL will transfer all the buildings and other infrastructure to the Forest Department of the State of Karnataka at book value....[97]

The Kudremukh Iron Ore Company, a profit-making public sector enterprise, resisted the application asserting that it had made enormous capital investments and the land under mining stood excluded from the final notification of the National Park published on 16 June 2001. The company had subsisting contracts operative till 2006 and shutting down the unit would deprive the country of valuable foreign exchange as well as render nearly 2,500 employees jobless.

According to the Supreme Court: 'The seminal issue involved is whether the approach should be "dollar-friendly" or "eco-friendly".' Invoking the principles of sustainable development, the precautionary principle and the Convention on Biological Diversity, the court held that KIOCL had no vested right to seek renewal of the mining lease. The court concluded:

> It is of significance that in the present case the Forest Advisory Committee under the Conservation Act on 11-7-2001 examined the renewal proposal in respect of the Company's mining lease. It recommended that the mining may be allowed for a period of four years i.e. up to the year 2005 by which time the weathered secondary ore available in the already broken-up area would be exhausted. The Ministry of Environment and Forests deferred a formal decision on the said recommendation as the matter was pending before this Court.
>
> On consideration of the materials on record we find no reason to vary the majority view of the Committee, a statutory one when its findings and conclusions are based on assessments of the factual aspects and after duly considering the materials and reports placed before it by the parties. We have also taken note of the period indicated by the Forest Advisory Committee, which is also a statutory committee.
>
> Taking note of the factual background and the legal position highlighted above, we think it proper to accept the time period fixed by the Forest Advisory Committee constituted under section 3 of the Conservation Act. That means mining should be allowed till the end of 2005 by which time the weathered secondary ore available in the already broken area should

[97] *T N Godavarman Thirumalpad v Union of India* (*Kudremukh Iron Ore Company* case) (2002) 10 SCC 606, 614. One of the members of the Committee, Valmik Thapar dissented and recommended an immediate stop to all mine operations.

be exhausted. This is, however, subject to fulfilment of the recommendations made by the Committee on ecological and other aspects.[98]

NOTES AND QUESTIONS

1. On 16 December 2005, the Supreme Court recorded KIOCL's undertaking that it would stop mining operations from 1 January 2006.[99]

2. The company, however, persisted in its endeavour to resume mining operations. It proposed a scheme under which 50% of its net profit would be utilized for rehabilitation and eco-restoration of the Kudremukh National Park and forests. In KIOCL's estimation, this would yield between Rs. 150 and Rs. 225 crores over a three-year period necessary for excavating 33.81 ha of already broken-up area. KIOCL claimed that about 20 million tons of weathered secondary ore was still available in the area and that the principal judgment had not envisaged that such a large amount of weathered secondary ore would remain at the end of 2005. On 15 December 2006, the Supreme Court declined the request and required appropriate measures to close the mines and to stabilize the slopes created by mining operations.[100]

3. Did the Supreme Court miss out on a win-win resolution? What was the danger in yielding to KIOCL's request?

V. SUKHNA

At times, development activity occurs beyond the boundaries of a protected area. This raises conflicts between those operating on the periphery and the wildlife which recognizes natural features, not formal boundaries set out in a statutory notification. Peripheral activity may also cause pollution that may disrupt the protected habitat and disturb the wildlife. To reduce these conflicts, the MoEF, at the urging of the Supreme Court,[101] has worked to limit activities around the protected areas by declaring Eco Sensitive Zones (ESZ). As of 25 June 2019, Eco Sensitive Zone notifications covering 316 protected areas across the country were issued. In addition, the process was underway for 199 protected areas where objections and suggestions were being examined in response to draft notifications. Out of the 316 protected areas 100 were in the Andaman and Nicobar islands, 29 in Maharashtra, 23 in Madhya Pradesh and 21 in Gujarat.[102]

While the breadth of the ESZ varies depending on local factors, the maximum extent of the zone is 10 kms from the boundary of the park. In certain cases, the band of the zone is just 100 metres wide. While agriculture and horticulture are permitted in these zones, commercial mining, saw mills and industries causing pollution are prohibited.

Tata Housing secured permissions from the Nagar Panchayat, Naya Gaon to develop a large housing project covering 52.66 acres on the outskirts of Chandigarh. Naya Gaon is located within the State of Punjab and is adjacent to Sukhna Wildlife Sanctuary. The village also falls within the catchment area of Sukhna Lake, an artificial lake in Chandigarh.

[98] *T N Godavarman Thirumulpad v Union of India* (*Kudremukh Iron Ore Company* case) (2002) 10 SCC 606, 636.
[99] *T N Godavarman Thirumulpad v Union of India* (2006) 5 SCC 23, 24.
[100] *T N Godavarman Thirumulpad v Union of India* (2009) 17 SCC 169.
[101] See *Goa Foundation v Union of India* (2011) 15 SCC 791.
[102] Lok Sabha, Unstarred question No. 1311 in respect of Eco Sensitive Zones answered 28 June 2019.

The high rise buildings envisaged under the project were cleared by the State Expert Appraisal Committee under the EIA process but were denounced by Chandigarh residents, who complained that the project would sully the city's skyline. The Delhi High Court (to which the case was transferred by the Supreme Court) found that the project site was within the catchment of Sukhna Lake and consequently set aside permissions which had failed to consider this dimension.

In an appeal filed by Tata Housing, the Supreme Court primarily examined whether the establishment of a housing project within a short distance of Sukhna Wildlife Sanctuary could be permitted. Sukhna sanctuary bordered both the Union territory of Chandigarh as well as the state of Punjab. While the buffer zone around the sanctuary with respect to Chandigarh varied between 2 kms and 2.75 kms, Punjab recommended a narrow buffer zone of just 100 metres within its territory.

Dismissing Tata Housing's appeal, the Supreme Court held:

> In the aforesaid facts and circumstances of the case, considering the distance of 123 meters from the Northern side and 183 meters from the Eastern side of the project in question from wildlife sanctuary, in our opinion, no such project can be allowed to come up in the area in question. The State of Punjab was required to act on the basis of Doctrine of Public Trust. It has failed to do so. The origination of the project itself indicates that State of Punjab was not acting in furtherance of Doctrine of Public Trust as 95 MLAs were to be the recipients of the flats. It is clear why Government has not been able to protect the eco-sensitive zone around a wildlife sanctuary and has permitted setting up of high-rise buildings up to 92 meters in the area in question, which is not at all permissible.
>
> Resultantly, we hold that such projects cannot be permitted to come up within such a short distance from the wildlife sanctuary. More so, in view of the Notification issued with respect to the Sukhna wildlife sanctuary towards the side of Chandigarh Union Territory and also considering the fact that proposal made by the Punjab Government, confining the Buffer Zone to 100 meters, has rightly not been accepted by MoEF, as the Government of Punjab as well as the MoEF, cannot be the final arbiter in the matter. The Court has to perform its duty in such a scenario when the authorities have failed to protect the wildlife sanctuary eco-sensitive zone. The entire exercise of obtaining clearance relating to the project is quashed. We regret that such a scenario has emerged in the matter and that it involved a large number of MLAs of Punjab Legislative Assembly. The entire exercise smacks of arbitrariness on the part of Government including functionaries.[103]

VI. THE *ELEPHANT CORRIDOR* CASE

Between November 2001 and April 2004, the Wildlife Trust of India, a non-profit conservation organization, carried out field surveys to identify biological corridors used by elephants to move between two habitats. The exercise identified 88 elephant corridors of which 20 were in southern India.[104] In 2008, In Defence of Environment and Animals (IDEA) petitioned the Madras High Court seeking directions to keep the elephant corridors free from encroachment. The High Court issued several protective interim directions and constituted an Expert Committee to identify the elephant corridor in the Sigur Plateau of the Nilgiris region. On 31 August 2010, the state issued a government order notifying the elephant corridor map that was prepared by the Expert Committee.

This prompted an association of resort and guest house owners to challenge the government order in a writ petition before the Madras High Court. The High Court upheld the order and

103 *Tata Housing Development Company Ltd v Aalok Jagga* (2020) 15 SCC 784.

104 *Right of Passage: Elephant Corridors of India* 11, 12 (Ed. Vivek Menon, *et al*, 2005).

directed the resort owners and other private landowners to vacate and hand over possession of the land falling within the notified elephant corridor to the District Collector, Nilgiris.

Responding to interim directions passed by the Supreme Court, the District Collector identified 309 buildings within 39 resort complexes. Since the owners failed to produce valid documents to run their resorts, she implemented the court's interim directions and sealed 38 resorts. She also removed electric fences and barbed wire installed by the resort owners. We next turn to the final judgment.

HOSPITALITY ASSN OF MUDUMALAI v IDEA
(2020) 10 SCC 589

S Abdul Nazeer, J: ***

Despite being a figure of traditional cultural reverence, today the elephant species is severally threatened in India. The crux of the problem is one that affects all wildlife in the country: land. As India's human population has grown exponentially in the past several decades, so has its demand for resources. At its essence, that demand boils down to the requirement for more land—for agriculture to grow more food and for construction of roads, dams, mines, railways and housing. This demand for land has led to the degradation and fragmentation of the country's forest cover. The elephant ... may weigh up to 4–5 tons and requires about 200–300 kg of fodder comprising of various plant species daily. It, therefore, needs large areas, which it uses by rotation, so that it may not overgraze an area and in the process destruct it altogether. This allows the natural vegetation of the habitats a chance to regenerate....

Increasingly, elephants have to move farther and farther afield, even from one forest area to another, often through small patches of forests called corridors. As forest lands continue to be lost, these relatively narrow and linear patches of vegetation form vital natural habitat linkages between larger forest patches. They allow elephants to move between secure habitats freely, without being disturbed by humans. Further, elephants are genetically programmed by nature to never inbreed within their birth family and thus need to move around between gene pools to reproduce. These corridors aid this process by helping different elephant populations to intermingle, which is essential for retaining the vigour of the species and ensuring its long-term survival. By identifying and nurturing such corridors, deadly confrontations between humans and elephants can be avoided, in addition to safeguarding the welfare of the wildlife....

At the very outset, it must be noted that the Wildlife Trust of India terms elephants as a 'keystone species' because their nomadic behavior is immensely important to the environment. Herds of roaming elephants play several important roles in the ecosystem:

(i) Landscape architects: Elephants create clearings in the forest as they move about, preventing the overgrowth of certain plant species and allowing space for the regeneration of others, which in turn provide sustenance to other herbivorous animals.
(ii) Seed dispersal: Elephants eat plants, fruits and seeds, releasing the seeds when they defecate in other places as they travel. This allows for the distribution of various plant species, which benefits biodiversity.
(iii) Nutrition: Elephant dung provides nourishment to plants and animals and acts as a breeding ground for insects.
(iv) Food chain: Apex predators like tigers will sometimes hunt young elephants. Further, elephant carcasses provide food for other animals.
(v) The umbrella effect: By preserving a large area for elephants to roam freely, one provides a suitable habitat for many other animal and plant species of an ecosystem.

Elephant corridors allow elephants to continue their nomadic mode of survival, despite shrinking forest cover, by facilitating travel between distinct forest habitats. Corridors are narrow and linear patches of forest which establish and facilitate connectivity across habitats. In the context of today's world, where habitat fragmentation has become increasingly common, these corridors play a crucial role in sustaining wildlife by reducing the impact of habitat isolations. In their absence, elephants would be unable to move freely, which would in turn affect many other animal species and the ecosystem balance of several wild habitats would be unalterably upset. It would also eventually lead to the local extinction of elephants, a species which is widely revered in our country and across the world. To secure wild elephants' future, it is essential that we ensure their uninterrupted movement between different forest habitats. For this, elephant corridors must be protected.

Legal intervention in preservation of these corridors has been necessitated because wildlife corridors are threatened by various social, economic and anthropogenic factors, as noted above. Commercial activities such as running of private resorts and construction of new buildings with barbed and electric fences within elephant corridors pose a serious threat of fragmentation and destruction of habitats. The long-term survival of the species depends on maintaining viable habitats and connecting corridors which maintain variance in the species' gene pool and avoid other risks associated with habitat fragmentation and isolation of species.

Over time, several environmental legislations including the Forest Act, 1927 and the Wild Life Act have been enacted to provide for the protection of forests and wild animals, with a view to ensuring ecological balance and preserving natural habitats including such corridors. [The court explained the object of the Wild Life Act by relying on *State of Bihar v Murad Ali Khan* (1988) 4 SCC 655.]

Specifically, in issue before us, is the corridor in the Sigur Plateau of Tamil Nadu. It connects the Western and the Eastern Ghats and sustains elephant populations and their genetic diversity. The Sigur Plateau has the Nilgiri Hills on its south-western side and the Moyar River Valley on its north-eastern side. Depending on the monsoon, the elephants migrate in search of food and water and during the course of their migration, they have to cross the Sigur Plateau. This migratory path is considered to be very crucial as it connects several contiguous forest areas forming the Nilgiri Biosphere Reserve in the States of Tamil Nadu, Karnataka and Kerala, the largest protected forest area in India.

Conflicting maps of this corridor were presented before the Madras High Court, which thus directed the State Government to choose between: (i) the elephant corridors identified in the Wildlife Trust of India's book titled *Right of Passage: Elephant Corridors of India* which were referred to by the Central Government in its letter dated 11-8-2006 to the State Government; or (ii) the single elephant corridor identified by the Expert Committee appointed by the High Court. As per the aforesaid book titled *Right of Passage*, the following 4 corridors lie in the Sigur Plateau region: (i) Avarahalla—Sigur, (ii) Kalhatti—Sigur at Glencorin, (iii) Moyar—Avarahalla and (iv) Kalmalai—Singara and Avarahalla. The Expert Committee examined all the elephant corridors in the area and identified a single elephant corridor comprising of various elephant corridors in the Sigur Plateau region. The State Government, vide the impugned G.O., notified this single elephant corridor, along the lines of the recommendations made by the Expert Committee.

The first limb of the appellants' contentions before us is that there is no statutory power for creating/recognition of new corridors by the State Government. We do not find merit in this argument and, in principle, are in agreement with the findings of the High Court regarding the power of the State Government to take measures, including issuance of the impugned G.O., for protection of wildlife in Tamil Nadu. It is undeniable that the State Government is empowered to take measures to protect forests and wildlife falling within its territory in light of Entries 17-A 'Forest' and 17-B 'Protection of wild animals and birds' in the Concurrent List and the power of the State Government under the Wild Life Act to notify sanctuaries and other protected areas. It is an admitted position that the land of the appellants has also been notified as private forest in 1991 under the Tamil Nadu Preservation of Private Forests Act, 1949, which prohibits cutting of trees in private forests.... [G]iven that the classification of the appellants' land as private forest land is not in dispute here, we find no difficulty in holding that the State Government was empowered to protect the habitats situated on the appellants' land by notifying an elephant corridor thereupon.

Furthermore, since the impugned decision of the High Court, the Ministry of Environment, Forest and Climate Change vide its Notification S.O. 4498(E) dated 13-12-2019 has declared the entire area in question and adjoining areas around the Mudumalai Tiger Reserve as an eco-sensitive zone. Under this Notification, the State Government of Tamil Nadu has been expressly directed to regulate land use generally, as well commercial establishment of hotels/resorts specifically, in the eco-sensitive zone so established. [The court found that the government order was an appropriate application of the precautionary principle.]

The second limb of the appellants' submissions comprises of questions about the scientific accuracy of the Expert Committee's Report and contentions that the dimensions as well as the location of the single corridor identified therein are at odds with authoritative scientific publications. [The court rejected this submission having regard to the factual findings by the High Court and since the notified location was based on an Expert Committee Report.]

This brings us to the last limb of the submissions of the appellants, which is comprised of factual objections to the acreage of the elephant corridor as notified by the impugned G.O. and the actions taken by the District Collector, Nilgiris in pursuance thereof. [The court appointed a three-member inquiry committee consisting of (i) Justice K Venkatraman, Former Judge of the Madras High Court (Chairman); (ii) Mr Ajay Desai, Consultant to World Wide Fund for Nature-India and (iii) Mr Praveen Bhargava, Trustee of Wildlife First to decide the objections of the appellants regarding the acreage, removal of fencing beyond the designated corridor and other similar issues.]

NOTES AND QUESTIONS

1. One of the important state laws that tilted the case against the appellants was the Tamil Nadu Preservation of Private Forests Act of 1949 (TNPPFA). Large tracts of land in the Nilgiris were notified as 'private forests' in 1991. These notified areas fell within and outside the elephant corridor identified in the government order. The object of the TNPPFA is:

> to prevent the indiscriminate destruction of private forests and interference with customary and prescriptive rights therein and for certain other purposes.

Considering the long and continuous use of the corridor by successive generations of elephants, do the elephants enjoy a prescriptive 'right of passage'?

2. The TNPPFA prohibits the sale or transfer of notified private forests without the permission of a committee headed by the District Collector and declares that any transfer contravening the embargo is void. Although, an amendment to the Act in 2015 allowed *post facto* sanction where no permission was obtained, several resorts and guest houses were established in violation of the embargo.

3. Section 2(16) of the Wild Life Act, in pertinent part, reads:

> 'hunting', with its grammatical variations and cognate expressions, includes, …
> (b) capturing, coursing, snaring, trapping, driving or baiting any wild or captive animal and every attempt to do so;

Can electric fences be fixed on private land without permission of the forest department in forests and wildlife habitat? Would it amount to 'hunting'?

12

URBAN PROBLEMS

Well planned cities and towns greatly enhance the quality of life of the citizenry. A well-managed city has good public transport, public spaces in the shape of parks and recreational areas, often separate zones for residential and commercial activity and an effective waste disposal system. Conversely, residents in poorly planned cities suffer noise, traffic congestion, poor sanitation and haphazard development which add to community stress, impact health and reduce productivity. This is why the Supreme Court has emphasized strict enforcement of planning laws. Planning laws are usually self-contained codes which govern all aspects of the planning process.

In many respects the citizens of eighteenth-century Jaipur enjoyed civic facilities far superior to the contemporary urban Indian. The reasons for the slide in the quality of urban life are complex, involving an interplay of demographic factors, obsolete land-holding and rental laws, the failure of administrators to anticipate and plan for future needs and economic constraints. In addition, the model of urban development adopted by our planners ignores local, regional and cultural needs.

As the edifice of many of our smaller towns deteriorates and the larger cities suffer from intolerable levels of air, water and noise pollution and a strain on the housing, energy and transport infrastructure, citizen groups have sprung up across the country to spur the civic administration into action. In this chapter, we analyse the judicial response to citizens' complaints. Many of these cases underscore the limitations of the judicial process and the need for even greater citizen participation to secure better civic governance.

A. RIGHT TO THE CITY

Indians move. The most common reason for rural folk to move to cities is economic survival and advancement. More than in villages and small town India, cities enable citizens to access water, power, education and jobs. The right to the city is integral to the right to life and livelihood. The right to migrate for survival or for a better living would embrace: (a) the right to access community spaces to enable a migrant to trade or sell her wares; (b) the right to shelter and affordable housing; (c) the right to basic education; (d) the right to community services that facilitate working, including safe and affordable public transport, crèches and health support.

Our city planning remains unresponsive to these concerns especially the need to invest in community spaces and community infrastructure. Some of these themes are explored in the following reading and judgment.

Environmental Law & Policy in India. Shyam Divan and Armin Rosencranz, Oxford University Press.
 DOI: 1093/oso/9780192865458.003.0012

R B BHAGAT; MIGRATION, GENDER AND RIGHT TO THE CITY 52
Economic & Political Weekly 35 (2017)

While it is true that cities have evolved through migration, cityward migration, and interstate migration in particular, has been sensitive issue in India. India is a federal country and states are organised along linguistic lines. Linguistic differences are essentially cultural differences, which are pronounced in the event of migration. Though the Constitution guarantees freedom of movement and freedom to settle within India as a fundamental right of all citizens (Article 19), migrants face several barriers in their ability to access civic amenities, housing, and employment. They also encounter restrictions on their political and cultural rights because of linguistic and cultural differences. Discrimination against migrants is articulated in various parts of India under the 'sons of the soil' political ideology, which simultaneously justifies the natives' lay to claim on local jobs while blaming migrants for snatching them away. This ideology has evoked sharp anti-migrant sentiments, leading to occasional violence against migrants. Migrants are also vulnerable to discrimination and exploitation as many of them are poor, illiterate, and live in slums and hazardous locations that are prone to disasters and natural calamities. Women migrants are likely to suffer more in such situations.

Migration raises the central issue of the right to the city: the right of everyone, including migrants (men and women), minorities, and the marginalised to access the benefits that a city offers. This perspective also seeks to identify how best to promote awareness and representation of these groups within the city. The right to the city perspective ultimately seeks to achieve urban transformation that is just and equitable in contrast to urbanisation based on neo-liberal policies, which promotes exclusion, deprivation, and discrimination. Right to the city is also expected to unite disparate categories of deprived people under the common vision of building our future by building cities. . . .

Exclusion and deprivation are ubiquitous in cities as every fifth urban dweller lives in a slum and about 90% work in the socially unprotected informal sector with very low wages and salaries. Cities pose many challenges to women in general and migrant women in particular. For example, the built environment in cities and urban planning in India are not women-friendly, which is glaringly evident in the case of public transport in Indian cities. For example, a lack of bus services at non-peak hours, roads designed without taking into account women's safety needs, and a lack of streetlights that increases crimes against women are major issues. . . . Women's access to safe public transport when they travel alone or walk around poses powerful restrictions on their mobility and right to the city. In many cities in India, women also face the risk of violence during the night, when toilet facilities are not available within the residential premises or are located far outside the home. A lack of water supply in the residential premises also forces women to spend more time on water collection. The availability of schools, hospitals, and crèches in the neighbourhood, or within walking distance, matters to women in particular. Urban infrastructure and services are usually not gender-neutral, as men and women do not have equal access. In general, Indian cities do not show gender sensitivity in urban planning and policies.

It is important to mention that women are not a homogeneous group, and some are more vulnerable than others. There are poor migrant women who live in slums and work as domestic and construction workers—these women face greater disadvantages as compared to middle- and upper-class urban women. There are also female-headed households, single women and professional women who migrate to the city and who encounter different types of vulnerability in the workplace, at home and in transit. There is an appalling shortage of basic amenities in Indian cities such as access to water, sanitation, cooking fuel, and a supply of electricity. As many women have to take care of household and workplace duties, the lack of such basic services represents a failure of the state and reinforces the patriarchal structure of society and denies them their right to the city. . . .

The democratisation of city governance, and the political inclusion of men and women migrants in decision-making processes, are important steps to ensuring the right to the city for all, for promoting alternative urbanisation, and building cities based on the principles of freedom, human development and gender equality. In this light, the constitutional provisions under the 74th amendment to reserve one-third of seats for women in urban local bodies should be implemented in letter, spirit and practice. Women should be given responsibility in planning and decision-making processes in municipal administration bodies. Any approach remains incomplete until the right to the city philosophy occupies a central position in planning, and women participate in making decisions that are sensitive to gender and the rights of migrants, minorities and the poor.

NOTES AND QUESTIONS

1. Is the right to the city an enforceable right or a notional construct for academics?

2. Bhagat urges gender sensitivity when drawing up city plans: gender-sensitive investments in public amenities would greatly improve the quality of life for city dwellers living on the margins. Should master plans and regional plans go through a gender impact assessment or social impact assessment similar to an environmental impact assessment?

3. An enormous divide persists between urban and rural India with respect to the quality of life enjoyed by citizens. Economic, social and cultural opportunities available in urban India are absent in villages and small towns. The migration from rural to urban India is a continuous tide of families and individuals searching for economic betterment or opportunities to escape the harsh social landscape of rural community life. Does every Indian have a 'right to the city' which takes in its fold access to education, electricity, economic opportunity, food and several other benefits that cities provide? Should constitutional courts recognize the 'right to the city'? What might be the demographic and social impact of such recognition?

4. With India's increasing population and the large migrations into cities, can any plan realistically provide for such a large influx of citizens exercising their right to the city? Until population growth stabilizes, is there any escape from chaotic urban life in India?

5. Referring to the Seventy-Fourth Constitutional Amendment, Bhagat argues that reservations of seats for women in urban local bodies would improve the decision-making process.

6. In *Rajendra Shankar Shukla v State of Chhattisgarh*,[1] the Supreme Court drew on Parts IX and IX-A of the Constitution to recognize the high status conferred on local authorities in rural and urban areas after the Seventy-Third and Seventy-Fourth Constitutional Amendments. The Constitution now mandates that local authorities (panchayats and municipalities) must participate and be involved in the planning process. The statutory plans that determine land use and chart the manner in which a city or region develops have to be framed by democratic institutions. While panchayats and municipalities comprise elected representatives, the Raipur Development Authority (RDA) was a statutory authority lacking representative character. The court held that the RDA's town planning scheme failed to take into consideration the opinion and suggestions of elected local bodies. This process of an unelected authority imposing a town planning scheme on the public violated the provisions of the Madhya Pradesh Nagar Tatha Gram Nivesh Adhiniyam of 1973 and Parts IX and IX-A of the Constitution. The RDA could not usurp the power of local authorities by first framing a scheme defining land use and then seek changes in the master plan.

---

[1] (2015) 10 SCC 400.

Ajay Maken, a former parliamentarian and legislator, filed a public interest petition before the Delhi High Court seeking relief in respect of the forced eviction of around 5,000 dwellers who lived in 1,200 shanties at Shakur Basti (West). He moved the petition on 13 December 2015, a day after the eviction. A division bench of the Delhi High Court examined the international law with respect to the right to adequate housing and drew support from South African jurisprudence as well as Indian judgments. We carry a short excerpt discussing the right to the city. The shanties are referred to as *jhuggis* and the settlement is called *jhuggi jhopri basti* (JJ basti).

AJAY MAKEN v UNION OF INDIA
(2019) SCC ONLINE DEL 7618

DR S MURALIDHAR, J: * * *

Right to the City

In the context of the right to shelter and its sub-species, the right to adequate housing, it is necessary to acknowledge that there is an increasing recognition in the international sphere of what is termed as the 'right to the city' (RTTC), which in the context of the case on hand, is an important element in the policy for rehabilitation of slum dwellers. According to Professor Upendra Baxi:

> 'The idea that the RTTC is a right to "change ourselves by changing the city" needs close consideration. It is a right not in the sense of liberty but in the sense of power; it is an individual as well as collective or common right; it is a right to call for, or achieve, change in our living spaces and ourselves. However, the "we-ness" for transformation is not a given but has to be constructed, forged, or fabricated if only because those who wield economic, social, and political domination aspire always towards fragmentation of the emergent "we-ness". In this sense, then the RTTC is a "right" to struggle for maintaining critical social solidarities.
>
> And, accordingly, such a right presupposes the respect for freedom of speech and expression, advocacy and dissent, movement and assembly, or the popular capacity to struggle to attain these. In sum, the moral RTTC assumes legal duties of respect for the conventionally called civil and political human rights.'

The Court at this juncture seeks to trace the background to the recognition of RTTC in international law, as an integral part of the right to adequate housing. The Istanbul Declaration on Human Settlements was adopted by heads of Governments and the official delegations of countries assembled at the United Nation's Conference on Human Settlements (Habitat II) in Istanbul, Turkey from 3rd to 14th June 1996. It endorsed 'the universal goals of ensuring adequate shelter for all and making human settlements safer, healthier and more reliable, equitable, sustainable and productive.' There were two major themes at that conference: adequate shelter for all and 'sustainable human settlement development' in an urbanising unit. The conference recognised with a sense of urgency the continuing deterioration of conditions and shelter of human settlements. It reaffirmed its commitment to better the standards of living 'in larger freedom of all human right.' The conference also reaffirmed the commitment to 'the full and progressive realization of the right to adequate housing as provided for in international instruments' and to that end sought the active participation of public, private and non-governmental partners at all levels 'to ensure legal security of tenure, protection from discrimination and equal access to affordable, adequate housing for all persons and their families.'

Two decades later, a 'New Urban Agenda' was unanimously adopted at the United Nations Conference on Housing and Sustainable Urban Development (Habitat III) in Quito, Ecuador on 20 October 2016. In December 2016, during the 68th plenary session of the 71st General Assembly, all United Nations Member States endorsed the New Urban Agenda and committed to work together towards a paradigm shift in the way cities are planned, built, and managed.

Preceding the adoption of the New Urban Agenda, a Habitat III Policy Unit 'Right to the City, and Cities for All', consisting of experts from Member States, was formed to provide inputs into formulation of the Agenda. The aforesaid policy paper defined the RTTC as under:

> '10. The right to the city is . . . defined as the right of all inhabitants present and future, to occupy, use and produce just, inclusive and sustainable cities, defined as a common good essential to the quality of life. The right to the city further implies responsibilities on governments and people to claim, defend, and promote this right.'

The policy paper also sets out a non-exhaustive list of components that ensure the 'city as a common good': (a) a city free of discrimination; (b) a city of inclusive citizenship; (c) a city with enhanced political participation in all aspects of urban planning; (d) a city ensuring equitable access for all to shelter, goods and services; (e) a city with quality public spaces for enhancing social interaction; (f) a city of gender equality; (g) a city with cultural diversity; (h) a city with inclusive economies; and, (i) a city respecting urban-rural linkages, biodiversity and natural habitats.

The aforementioned components of the 'city as a common good' have been ultimately incorporated in the New Urban Agenda as a 'shared vision' for 'the equal use and enjoyment of cities and human settlements, seeking to promote inclusivity and ensure that all inhabitants, of present and future generations, without discrimination of any kind are able to inhabit and produce just, safe, healthy, accessible, affordable, resilient and sustainable cities and human settlements to foster prosperity and quality of life for all'. Formulated thus, what the New Urban Agenda has acknowledged is a RTTC.

The RTTC acknowledges that those living in JJ clusters in *jhuggis*/slums continue to contribute to the social and economic life of a city. These could include those catering to the basic amenities of an urban population, and in the context of Delhi, it would include sanitation workers, garbage collectors, domestic help, rickshaw pullers, labourers and a wide range of service providers indispensable to a healthy urban life. Many of them travel long distances to reach the city to provide services, and many continue to live in deplorable conditions, suffering indignities just to make sure that the rest of the population is able to live a comfortable life. Prioritising the housing needs of such population should be imperative for a state committed to social welfare and to its obligations flowing from the International Covenant on Economic, Social and Cultural Rights [adopted in 1966, ratified by India in 1976] and the Indian Constitution. The RTTC is an extension and an elaboration of the core elements of the right to shelter and helps understand the broad contours of that right. As will be seen hereafter, the 2015 Policy implicitly acknowledges the RTTC and seeks to expand and deepen the right to shelter in more meaningful ways. . . .

Concluding observations

The right to housing is a bundle of rights not limited to a bare shelter over one's head. It includes the right to livelihood, right to health, right to education and right to food, including right to clean drinking water, sewerage and transport facilities.

The law [discourages] a narrow view of the dweller in a JJ *basti* or *jhuggi* as an illegal occupant without rights. [The decisions] acknowledge that the right to adequate housing is a right to access several facets that preserve the capability of a person to enjoy the freedom to live in the city. They recognise such persons as rights bearers whose full panoply of constitutional guarantees require recognition, protection and enforcement. . . .

Once a JJ *basti/cluster* is eligible for rehabilitation, the agencies should cease viewing the JJ dwellers therein as 'illegal encroachers'. The decisions of the Supreme Court of India on the right to shelter and the decision of this Court . . . require a Court approached by persons complaining against forced eviction not to view them as 'encroachers' and illegal occupants of land, whether public or private, but to require the agencies to first determine if the dwellers are eligible for rehabilitation in terms of the extant law and policy. Forced eviction of *jhuggi* dwellers, unannounced, in co-ordination with the other agencies, and without compliance with the above steps, would be contrary to the law explained in the above decisions....

NOTES AND QUESTIONS

1. In *Ajay Maken*, the Delhi High Court required a survey of JJ basti dwellers. The court ordered that if no rehabilitation at the site was feasible, then as and when the authorities are in a position to rehabilitate eligible dwellers, those eligible for rehabilitation under the extant policy must be given adequate time to make arrangements to move to the relocation site.

2. The judgment views cities as a common good or common property resource available to all citizens, present and future. Does the inclusive and equitable character of a common good entitle citizens to live and ply their trade on *every* community space such as pavements and open grounds? Is the constitutional mandate met where city administrators keep clear pavements and public grounds but also provide community spaces for street trade and zones for affordable shelter? Where should a court strike the balance?

3. Across India the process of urbanization is characterized by large migration from rural to urban areas. Migrants arriving in the city find that they do not possess the skills valued in the urban, industrial sector. Inevitably, most migrants are absorbed in low income occupations in the 'informal sector',[2] which is distinctive in the use of traditional technology, an unprotected labour market, ease of entry, low economic returns and the tendency for activity to operate on pavements and other public spaces. The informal sector makes a significant contribution to urban economies in the Third World.

The conflict between hawkers and vendors who comprise the most visible segment of the informal sector and municipalities as well as citizens' groups anxious to protect public spaces from encroachment, is among the most vexing questions to reach the courts. Who is entitled to use the pavement: the pedestrian or the hawker? Both competing claims may be considered facets of the right to the city.

In progressive legislation enacted in 2014, Parliament passed the Street Vendor (Protection of Livelihood and Regulation of Street Vending) Act. This law recognizes street vending as an important source of self-employment and implements the National Policy on Urban Street Vendors of 2009. The law requires compulsory registration of street vendors and confers a statutory right on every street vendor to carry on her business in areas other than 'no vending zones'.

Prior to the 2014 law, the principal judgments of the Supreme Court balancing competing claims over pavements and community spaces are *Bombay Hawkers' Union v Bombay Municipal Corporation*,[3] *Municipal Corporation of Delhi v Gurnam Kaur*,[4] *Sodan Singh v New Delhi Municipal Committee*,[5] *Maharashtra Ekta Hawkers' Union v Municipal Corporation, Greater Mumbai*,[6] *Gainda Ram v Municipal Corporation of Delhi*[7] and *Maharashtra Ekta Hawkers' Union v Municipal Corporation, Greater Mumbai*.[8]

[2] The segment of the labour force outside the organized labour market.
[3] AIR 1985 SC 1206.
[4] AIR 1989 SC 38.
[5] AIR 1989 SC 1988.
[6] (2004) 1 SCC 625; (2009) 17 SCC 151.
[7] (2010) 10 SCC 715.
[8] (2014) 1 SCC 419.

THE *MUMBAI MILL LANDS* CASE

Community rights, community spaces and city planning in the larger public interest are at the heart of the right to the city. The *Mumbai Mill Lands* case was a contest between two competing visions of urban renewal.

For much of the nineteenth century, Mumbai's economic engine was its textile mills spreading over 600 acres of a central section of the city known as Girangaon. By the 1970s, most of the mills were making losses. A crippling 18-month strike in the early 1980s devastated the industry.

Across the world, several industrial cities have reinvented themselves by transforming their economy and recycling the industrial land. Such an opportunity presented itself to Mumbai in the mid-1980s. Highly congested and lacking civic amenities, this is how Jamsheed Kanga, former Municipal Commissioner viewed the city:

> Because of its peculiar geography and burgeoning population of 15 million, Greater Mumbai can claim to have the lowest per capita open space in the world, now probably a miserable 0.015 acres (0.006 hectares) per 1000 population, while even Delhi and Chennai have 4 acres (1.6 hectares).... The increase in open space created by DCR 58 promised to provide some relief in the most crowded parts of the city—in central Mumbai—which had long been neglected. It also presented an opportunity to improve the transport network as this part of the city was criss-crossed by roads and also served by railway lines. It would enable roads to be widened and address, to a limited extent, the shortage of housing.[9]

On 29 April 1985, the architect and planner Charles Correa wrote to the chair of the Mumbai Metropolitan Region Development Authority proposing a formula that would rejuvenate the city. The mills, steeped in debt to lenders and workmen, needed to sell their land. Correa suggested that one-third of the land be surrendered to the municipal corporation for parks, schools or other social amenities; another third be used for low income housing; and the remaining third be sold by the mill owners (including development rights relating to the lands surrendered to the corporation). This concept would help increase the amenities, augment the stock of affordable housing and provide substantial monetary benefits, since two-thirds of the development potential would enure to the textile companies.[10] The proposal was structured on the notion of incentive zoning, where the owner is encouraged to surrender land for a public amenity conditional on being able to raise additional construction on the retained portion.

Mumbai eventually adopted Development Control Regulations in 1991 where DCR 58 sought to strike a balance between the interests of the mill landowners and the city. DCR 58 was amended in 2001 and the government issued a clarification on 28 March 2003 regarding interpretation of the amended provision.

The Bombay Environmental Action Group (BEAG) petitioned the Bombay High Court on 18 February 2005, questioning the validity of DCR 58. According to BEAG, the quality of life in Mumbai had drastically deteriorated and DCR 58 failed to ensure that adequate open spaces and public housing plots were unlocked in the course of developing the mill lands. BEAG amended the writ petition to challenge the pro-landowner clarification.

The Bombay High Court allowed the writ petition, interpreting DCR 58 in a manner it considered just and reasonable. On its interpretation, the High Court found that the regulation

---

[9] Jamsheed Kanga, *Public vs Private: The Legal Battle in Mills for Sale: The Way Ahead* 29 (Ed. Darryl D'Monte, 2006).

[10] *Mills for Sale: The Way Ahead* 133 (Ed. Darryl D'Monte, 2006).

did not violate the Constitution. The High Court held that the term 'open lands' used in DCR 58 should be given its natural, unrestricted meaning to cover lands which are presently vacant and lands which become vacant at any time by demolishing the structures on the land. Simply put, the High Court read '33%' in DCR 58 to apply to the entire mill and not just the open-to-sky, unbuilt portions. In this way a larger chunk of land would be available for public amenities. According to the High Court, this interpretation was in consonance with the constitutional mandate under Article 48A of the Constitution. The High Court set aside the government's clarification since it amounted to an amendment of the regulation which could not be done without following the prescribed procedure.

By an extremely lengthy judgment, the Supreme Court reversed the Bombay High Court. We carry a very short excerpt focusing on some facets of DCR 58.

BOMBAY DYEING & MFG CO LTD v BEAG
(2006) 3 SCC 434

S B Sinha, J:

* * *

The writ petition questioning the validity of DCR 58 by the first and second respondents was filed allegedly to protect the interests of the residents of Mumbai and to improve the quality of life in the town of Mumbai which is said to have drastically deteriorated during the last fifteen years as also for preventing further serious damage to town planning and ecology so as to avoid an irretrievable breakdown of the city. The main thrust of the writ petitioners was to ensure 'open spaces' for the city and to provide for the crying need of space for public housing.

In the said writ petition, apart from the State of Maharashtra, the Municipal Corporation of Greater Mumbai (MCGM), the Maharashtra Housing and Area Development Authority (MHADA), the National Textile Corporation (NTC) North Maharashtra and South Maharashtra were impleaded as respondents. Before the High Court, a large number of mill-owners and others who allegedly have invested huge sums on the lands of the mill-owners or otherwise interested in implementation of DCR 58 of 2001 filed applications for their impleadment as parties therein which were opposed by the writ petitioner-respondents. The said applicants were, however, allowed to intervene in the matter.

* * *

The aforementioned writ petition was allowed by the Bombay High Court on 18-2-2005. By its judgment, the Division Bench of the High Court, *inter alia*, held:

(i) DCR 58 should be construed having regard to the importance of open space and public space;
(ii) By reason of the 2001 Amendment, no substantial change had been made and the amendments carried out therein must be construed having regard to the expression 'development' which included 'demolition of structures'.
(iii) DCR 58 as amended must be harmoniously construed so as to uphold the constitutionality thereof. The expression 'open space' would take within its ambit the same space as was obtaining after demolition.
(iv) DCR 58, if not construed in the manner as contended by the writ petitioners would render it *ultra vires* Articles 14, 21 and 48-A of the Constitution. . . .
(ix) It concluded:
 '(a) In amended DCR 58(1)(b), 'open lands' would include lands after demolition of structures.
 (b) Clarification dated 28-3-2003 is clearly violative of Section 37 of the MRTP Act and Article 21 of the Constitution.
 (c) The issue whether the amended DCR 58 is contrary to Section 37 of the MRTP Act or Article 21 of the Constitution, is kept open.

(d) All the constructions carried out by various developers are clearly in violation of EIA notification as amended on 7-7-2004 as admittedly none of them have obtained clearance from the Ministry of Environment and Forests.

(e) All sales of mill lands carried out by NTC are clearly contrary to the Supreme Court orders dated 11-5-2005 and 27-9-2002 and contrary to the sanctioned BIFR Schemes.'

* * *

In 2001, DCR 58 was amended/modified. DCR 58 as amended in the year 2001 reads as under:

58. *Development or redevelopment of lands of cotton textile mills.*—

(1) *Lands of sick and/or closed cotton textile mills.*—With the previous approval of the Commissioner to a layout prepared for development or redevelopment of the entire open land built-up area of the premises of a sick and/or closed cotton textile mill, and on such conditions deemed appropriate and specified by him, and as a part of a package of measures recommended by the Financial Institutions and Commissionerate of Industries for the revival/rehabilitation of a potentially viable sick and/or closed mill, the Commissioner may allow;

(a) The existing built-up areas to be utilised—

(i) for the same cotton textile or related user subject to observance of all other Regulations;

(ii) for diversified industrial users in accordance with the industrial location policy, with office space only ancillary to and required for such users, subject to and observance of all other Regulations;

(iii) for commercial purposes, as permitted under these Regulations:
Provided that in the island city, the area used for office purposes shall not exceed that used earlier for the same purpose.

(b) Open lands and balance FSI shall be used as in the table below:

Sl. No.	*Extent*	*Percentage to be earmarked for recreation ground/garden, playground or any other open user as specified by the Commissioner*	*Percentage to be earmarked and handed over for development by MHADA for public housing/for mill workers' housing (as per guidelines approved by the government to be shared equally)*	*Percentage to be earmarked and to be developed for residential or commercial user (including users permissible in residential or commercial zone as per these Regulations or diversified industrial users as per industrial location policy) to be developed by the owner*
(1)	(2)	(3)	(4)	(5)
1.	Up to and inclusive of 5 Ha	33	27	40
2.	Between 5 Ha and up to 10 Ha	33	34	33
3.	Over 10 Ha	33	37	30

[Rest of DCR 58 omitted. The court laid out a table comparing DCR 58 as it stood before and after the 2001 amendment to the Development Control Regulations of 1991.]

Old DCR 58	New DCR 58
58. *Development or redevelopment of lands of cotton textile mills*.—(1) Lands of sick and/or closed cotton textile mills.—With the previous approval of the Commissioner to a layout prepared for development or redevelopment of the entire open land built-up area of the premises of a sick and/or closed cotton textile mill, and on such conditions deemed appropriate and specified by him, and as a part of a package of measures recommended by the Board of Industrial and Financial Reconstruction (BIFR), Financial Institutions and Commissionerate of Industries for the revival/rehabilitation of a potentially viable sick mill, the Commissioner may allow:	58. *Development or redevelopment of lands of cotton textile mills*.—(1) Lands of sick and/or closed cotton textile mills.—With the previous approval of the Commissioner to a layout prepared for development or redevelopment of the entire open land built-up area of the premises of a sick and/or closed cotton textile mill, and on such conditions deemed appropriate and specified by him, and as a part of a package of measures recommended by the Financial Institutions and Commissionerate of Industries for the revival/rehabilitation of a potentially viable sick and/or closed mill, the Commissioner may allow:
(a) The existing or newly built-up areas to be utilised—	(a) The existing built-up areas to be utilised—
(*i*) for the same cotton textile or related user subject to permissible FSI and observance of all other Regulations;	(*i*) for the same cotton textile or related user subject to observance of all other Regulations;
(*ii*) for diversified industrial users in accordance with the industrial location policy, with office space only ancillary to and required for such users, subject to FSI of 1.00 and observance of all other Regulations;	(*ii*) for diversified industrial users in accordance with the industrial location policy, with office space only ancillary to and required for such users, subject to and observance of all other Regulations;
(*iii*) for commercial purposes, as permitted under these Regulations:	(*iii*) for commercial purposes, as permitted under these Regulations:
Provided that in the island city, the area used for office purposes shall not exceed that used earlier for the same purpose.	Provided that in the island city, the area used for office purposes shall not exceed that used earlier for the same purpose.
(b) Open lands and lands after demolition of existing structures in case of a redevelopment scheme to be used as in the table below . . .	(b) Open lands and balance FSI shall be used as in the table below. . . .

A bare comparison of the said provisions would show that in sub-regulation (1) of DCR 58, the language remains the same. However, in clause (a) thereof the words 'or newly' have been omitted in the 2001 Regulations. Clause (a) of sub-regulation (1) provides for change of user in relation to the existing built-up area, subject to the recommendations of Board of Industrial and Financial Reconstruction (BIFR) as a package. . . .

The drastic changes have, however, been made in clause (b) of sub-regulation (1) of DCR 58. It refers to a case of redevelopment. In clause (b) the words 'after demolition of existing structures in case of a redevelopment scheme' have been deleted.

DCR 58 as made in 1991 consisted of four different concepts:

(1) existing built-up areas;
(2) newly built-up areas in DCR 58(1)(a);
(3) open land; and

(4) lands after demolition of existing structures in the case of a redevelopment scheme in DCR 58(1)(b).

It is not in dispute that the scheme framed thereunder did not work or in any event did not work to the satisfaction of all the mill-owners and other players including the State.

In view of the limited options contained therein and the consequences flowing therefrom in terms of the old Regulations a mill-owner could:

(i) continue to use the existing cotton textile mill;

(ii) redevelop the existing structure without changing its shell and without touching the open land, in which event no sharing of land or structure was necessary;

(iii) retain existing structure and develop the open land in which event the mill-owners were required to share 2/3rd of the open land used;

(iv) demolish the existing structures and develop the entire land, meaning thereby, the open land as also the land available after demolition of the existing structure in which event sharing of entire land was contemplated.

We have noticed that only five mills opted in terms of the old regulation. Hardly any development took place. Thus, most textile mills continued with status quo. Closed mills remained closed, workers were not paid their wages, banks and financial institutions did not receive back their dues. Even the statutory dues and taxes continued to mount. The structures might have become more dilapidated, and ten years went down the line in the aforementioned scenario. Even otherwise, mills like Phoenix Mills retained more than 100 years' old shell and glassed it up and even in the said shell, malls, supermarkets, night clubs and restaurants were constructed. Thus, it resulted in unplanned and unregulated development. It is in that situation, the State might have thought that workable changes are necessary wherefore, after taking into consideration some reports, they had come out with a draft. When the draft was published in terms of Section 37(1-AA) of the Maharashtra Regional and Town Planning (MRTP) Act, 24 objections were received. The writ petitioners admittedly were not amongst them. The said objections were placed before the planning authorities. The Bombay Municipal Corporation had also put inputs as a planning authority. Only thereafter the matter went back to the State.

The effect of amendment in clause (b) must be seen from the table appended thereto. In terms of the old regulation in respect of land covering more than 10 hectares, for green area 33% land was to be set apart, and for MHADA 37% thereof, whereas the owner retained 30%. Under the new DCR 58, admittedly the owner of the mill at least obtains construction rights over 63% of the land as the land in terms of column (3) gets loaded in column (5). The mill-owner furthermore even according to the writ petitioners gets TDR of 37%. Open land in clause (b) is what is not covered by the built-up area. The balance FSI, indisputably, is not open area.

The meaning of 'open land' must be construed as land other than land required to sustain the built-up area. We may now attempt to understand the effect of FSI having regard to a concrete example. If the area of a plot is 1000 sq m, applying FSI of 1.33, a person will be entitled to construct a built-up area of 1330 sq m. If he intends to build a two-storeyed building, he will utilise 665 sq m of land whereas in a case of ground plus four-storeyed building, he will be using 266 sq m of land and in case of nine-storeyed structure, he will be using only 133 sq m.

The greater the height of the building, the more lands will be available either by way of public greens or private greens as also for MHADA. However, in such a case, the plinth area will vary significantly. Whereas in the first case, it would be 665 sq m, in the third case, it would only be 133 sq m although the built-up area remains the same.

Taking the illustration as mentioned hereinbefore, the open land in each case shall vary. Thus, open land would not mean land occupied by the plinth but would mean land other than that is necessary to sustain the built-up area.

We do not accept the contention of [counsel for BEAG] that clause (b) applies to open land as also lands after demolition of existing structure in case of a redevelopment scheme and only because the words 'and lands after demolition of existing structures' had been deleted, the same may not be of much significance inasmuch as clause (b) of the new Regulations will have to be construed in the light of clause (a). It will bear repetition to state that whereas clause (a) refers to change of user in relation to the existing built-up area, clause (b) provides for open lands. The manner in which the development and/or redevelopment should take place has been clubbed in sub-regulation (1) of DCR 58 read with sub-regulation (6) thereof. For proper interpretation, all the relevant provisions are required to be read harmoniously.

DCR 58(1)(a) deals with a case of non-sharing of a land as is evident from the fact that no sharing percentage is provided therein. It, therefore, envisages change of user for the three purposes mentioned therein, in the event the existing built-up area is utilised. In terms of the said provision, the internal area of such structure remains the same although it can be re-designated or reconstructed. The only benefit conferred by reason thereof is grant of change of user indicated therein. The State while making this regulation contemplated that the change of user would enable earning of additional sums of money from the assets which were unproductive. Clause (b), however, expressly provides for sharing of land as specified in the table therein. The question, however, is as to what would be the extent of open land available on the spot.

Existing built-up area, in our view, would not be open land. We have also to take note of the fact that the newly built-up area, as existing in the old clause (a) of sub-regulation (1) of DCR 58 has been omitted....

The contention of BEAG is that the implementation of DCR 58 would lead to a disastrous result and in this behalf our attention was drawn to a sanctioned plan in respect of Mill No. 4 to show that the consequences thereof would be that the share of MCGM and MHADA would come to 662.61 sq m and 542.13 sq m respectively, although the plot area of Mill No. 4 is 58,458.36 sq m. We do not find any merit in the said contention.... [computation omitted.]

We do not furthermore agree with the approach of the High Court in interpreting the aforementioned provisions having regard to certain other factors, namely, deluge in Bombay in the year 2005 as also the requirements of the entire population of Bombay from environmental aspect. Such factors cannot be taken into consideration for interpretation of a statute. We cannot look to a statute with a coloured glass, we have to consider the provisions as the legislature thought. The same should be subject, of course, to the constitutional and other limitations....

Ecological factors indisputably are very relevant considerations in construing a town planning statute. The court normally would lean in favour of environmental protection in view of the creative interpretation made by this Court in finding a right of environmental protection including the right to clean water, air, etc. under Article 21 of the Constitution. But, in this case, we are not dealing with a similar problem. It must be borne in mind while interpreting DCR 58 that there exists a stark distinction between the interpretation of planning and zoning statutes enforcing ecology *vis-à-vis* industrial effluents and hazardous industries and those relating to concerted efforts at rehabilitating the industry. It is around this pivot that interpretation must revolve. It is also interesting to note that in *American Jurisprudence* 2d, wherein at p. 496 of Vol. 82, it is stated that zoning laws should be construed strictly in favour of the property owners and that they should not be extended by implication to include restrictions not clearly prescribed. Ecology in terms of DCR 58 has not been marginalised. The statute does not prescribe any fixed norm. It provides for guidelines. It has not been shown that the said guidelines have been violated. The environmental aspect considered in DCR 58 may not be to everybody's satisfaction but the regulation in question has to be interpreted having regard to the purport and object for which the same was enacted, meaning thereby, a holistic approach to a large number of problems....

In a case of this nature, an endeavour should be made in giving effect to the intention of the legislature. For the said purpose, it is necessary to ascertain the object the legislature seeks to achieve. It may also be necessary to address questions as regards the nature of the statute. Does the statute *ex facie* point out degradation of the environment? Would by change of user envisaged by the legislature, the existing open space be decreased? Would it be necessary in view of the legislative scheme to invoke the precautionary principles?

* * *

The upshot of our aforementioned discussions is:

(i) The public interest litigation was maintainable.

(ii) DCR 58 is valid in law. DCR 58(1) applies also to closed mills but sub-regulation (6) of DCR 58 does not apply to sick industries which have not been referred to BIFR.

(iii) The clarification made by the State is neither *ultra vires* Section 37 of the MRTP Act nor is it violative of the constitutional provisions.

(iv) DCR 58, as inserted in 2001 and as clarified in 2003, is not contrary to the principles governing environmental aspects including the principles of sustainable and planned development *vis-à-vis* Article 21 of the Constitution....

(vii) Although, delay and laches play an important role, as we have considered the merit of the matter, the writ petition filed by Respondents 1 and 2 is not being dismissed on that ground alone....

For the reasons aforementioned, these appeals are allowed, the impugned judgment of the High Court is set aside. However, in the facts and circumstances of the cases, there shall be no order as to costs.

NOTES AND QUESTIONS

1. It is difficult to conceive a greater disservice to the city of Mumbai than the Supreme Court judgment in the *Mill Lands* case. A once in a lifetime opportunity to transform the city for millions of its residents and future generations was lost. The localities once occupied by textile mills have since transformed into a gridlocked urban nightmare. The Supreme Court's grant to Mumbai: shrunken open public spaces, fewer civic amenities and miniscule affordable housing.

2. In cases like *Mill Lands*, judges have preferred outcomes which shade their approach. This is how the High Court viewed the case:

> It is vital to note that we are neglecting the importance of these open spaces both from the environmental angle and ecological angle, and the importance has been grossly underestimated and unvalued.... As a direct result, Mumbai had already lost a large number of fresh water reservoirs, tanks, etc., and even the existing ones are under perennial threat. This has been one of the major causes for heavy flooding in Mumbai during the last week of July, 2005.... Today no one can dispute that all cities and towns need green spaces as much as other amenities like hospitals, educational institutions, roads, public chowks etc. That is the reason these green and open spaces are called lungs of the cities.... In view of lack of proper outdoor recreation facilities, the social behaviour patterns get seriously affected ...
>
> Both the un-amended regulations (DCR 58) are framed to fulfil the purpose of achieving revival and rehabilitation of the textile mills and curbing uncontrolled and unregulated

development of their lands. In this view of the matter, it is not permissible to hold that there is no obligation to revive, rehabilitate or modernise the mills.... The intention is not [to] allow mill owners to trade in property.... There is no question of allowing a contention that the scheme is unworkable and the regulation does not allow enough free play to meet the obligations towards workers and financial institutions.[11]

3. The Supreme Court is especially concerned about the environment in New Delhi. Vast amounts of the court's judicial time and resources are spent on air pollution in Delhi caused by vehicles,[12] industry,[13] firecrackers,[14] stubble burning[15] and dust;[16] strict enforcement of the Delhi Development Plan;[17] diversion of heavy vehicular traffic to bypass Delhi;[18] cleaning up the Yamuna[19] and several other aspects of the environment in the National Capital Region (NCR). In most of these cases, the Supreme Court exercised its original jurisdiction under Article 32. These judgments are also final since there is no higher forum. Had there been an appeal, many of the Supreme Court's environmental decisions in the context of the NCR might have been overturned.

By adopting a narrow and technical approach in *Mill Lands* did the Supreme Court miss the wood for the trees? Should the Supreme Court have been more deferential to the Bombay High Court which was alive to the city's history and evolution?

4. The history of Mumbai is intertwined with commerce and mercantile pragmatism—qualities that inform the Supreme Court judgment. The High Court judgment, with its emphasis on public spaces, public amenities and public housing may have been out of step with Mumbai's commercial ethos.

5. Assuming the Supreme Court upheld the Bombay High Court judgment, what might have happened next? Would developers in Mumbai have lobbied for a further amendment to DCR 58?

6. Do you agree with the Supreme Court dismissing the High Court's concern regarding the deluge in Mumbai in July 2005? Among the factors contributing to the deluge were poor planning, cheek by jowl development and inadequate storm water drainage.

7. Revisit DCR 58 and assess whether the High Court's view was a possible view? If it were plausible, should the Supreme Court have overturned the interpretation under Article 136 of the Constitution?

8. Considering that the interpretation of DCR 58 impacted the metropolis of Mumbai and unborn generations of Mumbaikars, was the Supreme Court correct in holding that the writ petition filed in 2005 was hit by the doctrine of delay and laches?

9. The Supreme Court relied on a statement from *American Jurisprudence* that zoning laws should be construed strictly in favour of the property owners and that restrictions should

---

11 *Bombay Environmental Action Group v State of Maharashtra* (2005) 6 Bom C R 574. Judgment dated 17 October 2005.

12 *M C Mehta v Union of India* (2002) 4 SCC 356.

13 *M C Mehta v Union of India* AIR 1996 SC 2231.

14 *Arjun Gopal v Union of India* (2017) 10 SCC 701.

15 *M C Mehta v Union of India* 2019 (14) Scale 602.

16 *M C Mehta v Union of India* (2004) 12 SCC 188; (2016) 4 SCC 269.

17 *M C Mehta v Union of India* (2004) 6 SCC 588.

18 *M C Mehta v Union of India* (2016) 2 SCC 33.

19 News Item Published in Hindustan Times Titled "And Quiet Flows The Maily Yamuna", In re (2009) 17 SCC 708.

not be extended by implication. Does this principle apply here? The table appended to DCR 58(1)(b) clearly requires that 33% 'open lands' be earmarked for recreation ground, garden, playground, etc. The High Court's interpretation of 'open land' intended to advance the community interest by applying 33% to the whole of the textile mill plot and not just to 33% of open compounds, parking lots and yards.

10. Which judgment—the High Court or the Supreme Court—comports to 'right to the city' values?

B. PRINCIPLES OF PLANNING LAW

This section explains the basic principles underlying planning law. In essence, these rules are: (a) new buildings must conform to the zoning or land use prescribed in a statutory land use map; (b) the extent of construction should be within the upper limit of the buildable area defined in terms of FAR/FSI (Floor Area Ratio/Floor Space Index); (c) the construction must be preceded by a building plan that is approved by the authorities; (d) the developer must obey special provisions due to the location (e.g. near the coast or abutting an airport) and heritage preservation requirements (if applicable); and (e) for large development projects follow environmental impact assessment procedures. The following cases explain and apply some of these principles.

I. PUNE

Manohar Joshi of the Shiv Sena party became the Chief Minister of Maharashtra in March 1995 and held office until January 1999. His government was elected in the wake of the Enron power project scandal that had sullied the image of the previous Congress administration. In 1998, when he was Chief Minister, two writ petitions were filed in the Bombay High Court complaining that the provisions of the Maharashtra Regional and Town Planning Act of 1966 ('MRTP Act') and the Development Control Rules ('D C Rules') framed under the MRTP Act were breached to favour Girish Vyas, the Chief Minister's son-in-law. Vyas developed real estate. His company constructed a ten-storeyed residential building on a plot in Pune that was reserved for a primary school. According to him, the municipal authorities had sanctioned the building plans in a fair exercise of power and in the final analysis all that had happened was that a residential building had been erected in a residential zone that already had a surfeit of neighbourhood schools.

Given the involvement of a sitting Chief Minister, the marathon High Court hearing was political theatre and newspapers carried detailed reports. The case was also closely watched by Joshi's political rivals, some of whom may have sponsored this well-funded public interest litigation. 'It is unusual for PIL counsel to be flown in from Delhi and lodged at Mumbai's finest hotel.'[20]

By the time the High Court rendered judgment in March 1999, Joshi had resigned as the Chief Minister (for unconnected reasons) and was replaced by his political rival, Narayan Rane. Though the case had by then lost much of its political bite, the division bench comprising B N Srikrishna and S S Parkar, JJ delved deep into government records and delivered a strong rebuke to the ministers and officers. The building permissions were illegal and tainted with favouritism. The High Court quashed the planning permissions and directed demolition of the residential building that had been erected on the plot designated in the Pune development plan for a primary school.

[20] Interview with Deepak Nargolkar, the lawyer for Manohar Joshi. Conducted by S Divan on 12 September 2016.

In 2000, the Supreme Court admitted the appeals from the High Court judgment and stayed the demolition. There the case remained for over a decade, awaiting its turn for disposal. Meanwhile, on 10 May 2002, the tides of fortune lifted Manohar Joshi to the high office of Speaker of the Lok Sabha, a post he held for more than two years.

When the case was taken up for final hearing, the Supreme Court first examined whether a settlement between the parties could be reached that would advance the public interest and prevent waste, since the building was complete. The suggested terms involved the developer constructing a government primary school in another part of Pune and ceding some of the flats in the tainted building to the Pune Municipal Corporation to ensure that Vyas did not gain from his enterprise and was sufficiently deterred. When the parties failed to settle, the Supreme Court revisited the record and upheld the High Court judgment. The Supreme Court found that the inference of *mala fide* conduct on the part of the concerned ministers and officers was justified. The judgment underscores the importance of town planning, the role of municipalities and the duty of courts where public amenities are diverted for private gain.

MANOHAR JOSHI v STATE OF MAHARASHTRA

(2012) 3 SCC 619

H L Gokhale, J:

* * *

What is the nature and significance of the planning process for a large municipal town area? In that process, what is the role of the municipal corporation, which is the statutory planning authority? Can the state government interfere in its decisions in that behalf and if so, to what extent? Does the State Government have the power to issue instructions to the Municipal Corporation to act in a particular manner contrary to the development plan sanctioned by the state government, and that too a number of years after the municipal corporation having taken the necessary steps in consonance with the plan? Can the state government instruct a municipal corporation to shift the reservation for a public amenity such as the primary school on a plot of land, and also instruct it to grant a development permission for residential purposes thereon without modifying the development plan? . . . Is it permissible for the landowner and developer to explain and justify such a favourable government decision by relying upon the authority of the government under another section of the statute which is not even invoked by the government? What inference is expected to be drawn in such a situation with respect to the role played by the ministers or the municipal officers? What orders are expected to be passed when such facts are brought to the notice of the High Court in a public interest litigation? These are some of the issues which arise in this group of Civil Appeals in the context of the provisions of the MRTP Act concerning a property situated in Pune Municipal area. [The court reconstructed the events that led to the planning permission being granted and held that the statutory process had been subverted.]

As stated above, we adopted the model of democratic planning which involves the participation of the citizens, planners, administrators, municipal bodies and the government as is also seen throughout the MRTP Act. Thus when it comes to the development plan for a city, at the initial stage itself there is the consideration of the present and future requirements of the city. Suggestions and objections of the citizens are invited with respect to the proposed plan, and then the planners apply their mind to arrive at the plan which is prepared after a scientific study, and which will be implemented during the next 10 to 20 years as laid down under section 38 of the MRTP Act. The plan is prepared after going through the entire gamut under sections 21 to 30 of the Act, and then only the sanction is obtained thereto from the state government. That is why the powers to modify the provisions of the plan are restricted. . . . If the plan is to be tinkered for the benefit of the interested persons, or for those who can approach the persons in authority, then there is no use in having planned development. Therefore, section 37 which permits the minor modifications provides that even that should not result into changing the character of the development plan, prior whereto also a notice in the gazette is required to be issued to invite suggestions and objections. Where the modification is of a substantial nature, then the procedure under section 29 of the Act requiring a notice in the local newspapers inviting objections and suggestions from the citizens is to be resorted to. Even the deletion of reservation under section 50 is at the instance of the appropriate authority only when it does not want the land for the designated purpose. The idea is that once the plan is formulated, one has to implement it as it is, and it is only in the rarest of the rare cases that you can depart therefrom. There is no exclusive power given to the state government, or to the planning authority, or to the Chief Minister to bring about any modification, deletion or de-reservation, and certainly not by a resort to any of the D C Rules. All these constituents of the planning process have to follow the mandate under section 37 or 22A as the case may be if any modification becomes necessary. That is why this court observed in *Chairman, Indore Vikas Pradhikaran v Pure Industrial Coke & Chemicals Ltd* (2007) 8 SCC 705 as follows:–

> Town and country planning involving land development of the cities which are sought to be achieved through the process of land use, zoning plan and regulating building activities must receive due attention of all concerned. We are furthermore not oblivious of the fact that such *planning involving highly complex cities depends upon scientific research, study and experience and, thus, deserves due reverence.* (emphasis supplied)

* * *

People of a state look up to the Chief Minister and those who occupy the high positions in the government and the administration for redressal of their grievances. Citizens are facing so many problems and it is expected of those in such positions to resolve them. Children are particularly facing for their education and sports, quality of teaching, their health and nutrition. It is the duty of those in high positions to ensure that their conduct should not let down the people of the country, and particularly the younger generation. The ministers, corporators and the administrators must zealously guard the spaces reserved for public amenities from the preying hands of the builders. What will happen, if the protectors themselves become poachers? Their decisions and conduct must be above board. Institutional trust is of utmost importance. In the case of *Bangalore Medical Trust v B S Muddapa* (1991) 4 SCC 54, this court observed that 'the directions of the Chief Minister, the apex public functionary of the State, was in breach of public trust, more like a person dealing with his private trust, more like a person dealing with his private property than discharging his obligation as head of the state administration in accordance with law and rules.' Same is the case in the present matter where Shri Manohar Joshi, the then Chief Minister and Shri Ravindra Mane, the Minister of state have failed in this test, and in discharge of their duties. Nay, they have let down the people of the city and the state, and the children.

Importance of the spaces for public amenities

As we have seen, the MRTP Act gives a place of prominence to the spaces meant for public amenities. An appropriately planned city requires good roads, parks, playgrounds, markets, primary and secondary schools, clinics, dispensaries and hospitals and sewerage facilities amongst other public amenities which are essential for a good civic life. If all the spaces in the cities are covered only by the construction for residential houses, the cities will become concrete jungles which is what they have started becoming. That is how there is need to protect the spaces meant for public amenities which cannot be sacrificed for the greed of a few landowners and builders to make more money on the ground of creating large number of houses. The MRTP Act does give importance to the spaces reserved for public amenities, and makes the deletion thereof difficult after the planning process is gone through, and the plan is finalized. Similar are the provisions in different State Acts. Yet, as we have seen from the earlier judgments concerning the public amenities in Bangalore and Lucknow (*M I Builders Pvt Ltd v Radhey Shyam Sahu* (1999) 6 SCC 464) and now as is seen in this case in Pune, the spaces for the public amenities are under a systematic attack and are shrinking all over the cities in India, only for the benefit of the landowners and the builders. Time has therefore come to take a serious stock of the situation. Undoubtedly, the competing interest of the landowner is also to be taken into account, but that is already done when the plan is finalized, and the landowner is compensated as per the law. Ultimately when the land is reserved for a public purpose after following the due process of law, the interest of the individual must yield to the public interest....

The government and the municipal corporations are trustees of the citizens for the purposes of retention of the plots meant for public amenities. As the Act has indicated, the citizens are vitally concerned with the retention of the public amenities, and, therefore deletion or modification should be resorted to only in the rarest of rare case, and after fully examining as to why the concerned plot was originally reserved for a public amenity, and as to how its deletion is necessary....

The development permission was wholly illegal and unjustified. As far as the building meant for the tenants is concerned, the developer as well as PMC have indicated that they have no objection to the building being retained. As far as the ten storied building meant for private sale is concerned, the developer had offered to hand over half the number of floors to PMC, provided it permits the remaining floors to be retained by the developer. PMC has rejected that offer since the plot was reserved for a primary school. The building must therefore be either demolished or put to a permissible use. The illegal development carried out by the developer has resulted into a legitimate primary school not coming up on the disputed plot of land. Thousands of children would have attended the school on this plot during last 15 years. The loss suffered by the children and the cause of education is difficult to assess in terms of money, and in a way than the cost of construction of this building. Removal of this building is however not going to be very easy. It will cause serious nuisance to the occupants of the adjoining buildings due to noise and air pollution. The citizens may as well initiate actions against the PMC for appropriate reliefs. It is also possible that the developer may not be able to remove the disputed building within a specified time, in which case the PMC will have to incur the expenditure on removal. It will, therefore, be open to the developer to redeem himself by offering the entire building to PMC for being used as a primary school or for the earmarked purpose, free of cost. If he is so inclined, he may inform PMC that he is giving up his claim on this building also in favour of PMC....

The spaces for public amenities such as roads, playgrounds, markets, water supply and sewerage facilities, hospitals and particularly educational institutions are essential for a decent urban life. The planning process therefore assumes significance in this behalf. The parcels of land reserved for public amenities under the urban plans cannot be permitted to be tinkered with. The greed for making more money is leading to all sorts of construction for housing in prime city areas usurping the lands meant for public amenities wherever possible and in utter disregard for the quality of life. Large number of areas in big cities have already become concrete jungles bereft of adequate public amenities. It is therefore, that we have laid down the guidelines in this behalf which flow from the scheme of the MRTP Act itself so that this menace of grabbing public spaces for private ends stops completely. We are also clear that any unauthorized construction particularly on the lands meant for public amenities must be removed forthwith. We expect the guidelines laid down in this behalf to be followed scrupulously....

NOTES AND QUESTIONS

1. Development plans are publicly accessible documents reflecting existing and future patterns of land use. The Supreme Court in *Manohar Joshi* interprets the provision of the MRTP Act to give primacy to the development plan sanctioned under the Act. The court's approach is sensible. It promotes transparency and certainty in the planning process.

2. Planning statutes generally adopt a threefold strategy to enforce planned development. First, there is a regional plan covering one or more districts. Second, there is a detailed development plan for a city or town which demarcates industrial, commercial and residential zones. Public amenities like hospitals, schools, parks, etc. are designated on the plan and are called 'reservations'. All future development must conform to the land use specified in the development plan as well as the broader patterns of use in the regional plan. The third tool employed is the regulation of buildings with detailed provisions regarding construction parameters such as height of buildings, the extent of building coverage on a plot, amenities like elevators, car parks and so on.

3. Although the judgment asserts that the urban planning process is the result of scientific research and study, this observation in the Indian context is more aspirational than accurate. Indian cities rarely employ any qualified planners. There is neither any political nor administrative vision that informs the planning process, resulting in a dismal quality of urban life. Indeed, the planning process in India ignores even the obvious. For example, despite the pervasiveness of street vending and street food, cities make no provision for hawking zones, or the regulation of street food. This fosters a continuous tension between petty traders anxious to eke out a living and city officials willing to turn a Nelson's eye for a price.

4. In a part of the judgment that is not excerpted the Supreme Court emphasized the 12th Schedule and Part IX-A of the Constitution introduced by the Seventy-Fourth Amendment.[21] These constitutional provisions enumerate the functions of municipalities: urban planning, land use regulation, construction of roads and bridges, water supply, public health, sanitation, solid waste management, slum improvement, provision of parks, gardens, playgrounds, public conveniences, etc. The court held that proper planning was essential for the discharge of these essential obligations.

5. When the original development plan itself is weak at anticipating the needs of citizens, is the 'rarest of rare' standard a correct test for altering a reservation?

6. To ensure that public amenities are not diverted in the future, the Supreme Court passed guidelines requiring proposed deletions to be given wide publicity in newspapers so that concerned citizens may comment on them. The court also suggested that where a municipality is faced with a paucity of funds to acquire land for the amenity, it may invite contributions from philanthropists and corporate bodies or individuals to support the public project. Is this a pragmatic or realistic approach? Will it result in abuse?

7. The endorsement by Manohar Joshi on the government file read, 'All action be taken in accordance with law. No objection.' The Supreme Court found this to convey the Chief Minister's approval to a change in the reservation. Were the High Court and Supreme Court justified in their interpretation when the Chief Minister had expressly required that further action 'be taken in accordance with law'? Conversely, should the Chief Minister have dealt with the file at all, considering that his son-in-law had a stake in the project?

8. Municipalities in India are afflicted by a culture of graft at every tier of administration. The process of granting building permissions is no exception. The culture of corruption is so deeply entrenched that bribes are demanded regardless of whether or not the project is fully compliant with the law. Officers charged with processing building applications and ministers overseeing the bureaucracy frequently withhold building clearances until a substantial percentage of the project outlay is paid as bribe. So deep is the rot that architects who refuse to engage in unethical practices are forced to restrict their work to designing, leaving the messy

[21] The Constitution (Seventy-Fourth Amendment) Act came into force on 1 June 1993.

part of liaising with municipal departments to less squeamish colleagues. What reforms may eliminate institutional graft in our cities?

II. INDORE

The broad frame of town planning legislation with minor variations across states is outlined in the *Indore* judgment. In *Indore*, the Supreme Court was concerned with the Madhya Pradesh Nagar Tatha Gram Nivesh Adhiniyam of 1973—the state's town and country planning law. The respondent's lands were in Bicholi and Kanadia villages, falling within the respective jurisdictions of gram panchayats constituted under the Madhya Pradesh Gram Panchayat Act. The panchayats were the local authorities and they approved building plans on 5 April 1991. Although it is unclear what happened during the next 13 years, the judgment records that the Joint Director, Town and Country Planning, refused to sanction the plans on 14 December 2004. This was because, in the meanwhile, the planning area around Indore extended to the two villages and the land was affected by a proposed 70 ft wide bypass road. The landowner petitioned the High Court seeking a writ, directing the authorities to sanction the site plan which was submitted. Although the petition was dismissed by the single judge, the division bench of the High Court allowed the appeal on 6 March 2007, nearly 16 years after the gram panchayat's sanction.

CHAIRMAN, INDORE VIKAS PRADHIKARAN v PURE INDUSTRIAL COKE & CHEMICALS LTD

(2007) 8 SCC 705

S B Sinha, J:

* * *

There are two competing interests viz. one, the interest of the State *vis-à-vis* the general public and, two, to have better living conditions and the right of property of an individual which although is not a fundamental right but is a constitutional and human right....

Town and country planning involving land development of the cities which are sought to be achieved through the process of land use, zoning plan and regulating building activities must receive due attention of all concerned. We are furthermore not oblivious of the fact that such planning involving highly complex cities depends upon scientific research, study and experience and, thus, deserves due reverence.

Where, however, a scheme comes into force, although it may cause hardship to the individual owners as they may be prevented from making the most profitable use of their rights over property, having regard to the drastic consequences envisaged thereunder, the statute should be considered in such a manner as a result whereof greater hardship is not caused to the citizens than actually contemplated thereby. Whereas an attempt should be made to prevent unplanned and haphazard development but the same would not mean that the court would close its eyes to the blatant illegalities committed by the State and/or the statutory authorities in implementation thereof. Implementation of such land development as also building laws should be in consonance with public welfare and convenience. In United States of America zoning ordinances are enacted pursuant to the police power delegated by the State. Although in India the source of such power is not police power but if a zoning classification imposes unreasonable restrictions, it cannot be sustained. The public authority may have general considerations, safety or general welfare in mind, but the same would become irrelevant, as thereby statutory rights of a party cannot be taken away. The courts must make an endeavour to strike a balance between public interest on the one hand and protection of a constitutional right to hold property, on the other.

For the aforementioned purpose, an endeavour should be made to find out as to whether the statute takes care of public interest in the matter *vis-à-vis* the private interest, on the one hand, and the effect of lapse and/or positive inaction on the part of the State and other planning authorities, on the other.

The courts cannot also be oblivious of the fact that the owners who are subject to the embargos placed under the statute are deprived of their valuable rightful use of the property for a long time. Although ordinarily when a public authority is asked to perform statutory duties within the time stipulated it is directory in nature but when it involves valuable rights of the citizens and provides for the consequences therefor it would be construed to be mandatory in character. . . .

While determining the questions involved in these appeals, we are not unmindful that the purpose and object of the town development scheme is a laudable one insofar as it purports to allocate areas covered by Scheme No. 164 for residential purposes and a bypass road 70 ft wide is to be built along the eastern periphery of the area covered by the scheme. The question, however, would be as to whether the development can be said to be a haphazard one or would completely destroy the purpose for which the land was to be reserved for planned development of the residential area.

The process started in the year 1974. Only 37 villages were included within the planning area [and not the two subject villages]. It may be that with the passage of time the requirements for a better planned city were felt, but it is difficult to conceive that the State of Madhya Pradesh while constituting the appellant Authority in terms of section 38(1) of the Act by reason of its Notification dated 9-5-1977 was wholly oblivious thereto. When the Act came into force the existing land use was determined. The area for which, thus, land could be put to use was fixed. No land could be used for a purpose which is not envisaged by land use. . . .

The respondents obtained permission for development from the competent authority for diversion of land use as far back as on 12-1-1989. They had applied for and were granted sanction of building plan by the Gram Panchayat in the year 1991. No step was taken by the statutory authorities or the appellant herein to notify a draft development plan. It was not notified till [2004]. No further step was taken pursuant thereto or in furtherance thereof. The respondents filed an application before the Director for grant of permission only on 2-12-2004 which was rejected by reason of an order dated 14-12-2004 purported to be for the following reason:

> subjected land of Village Bicholi Hapsi has been included in the proposed Development Scheme No. 164 of Indore Development Authority.

We may notice two precise submissions of [counsel for the appellant] at this stage:

(i) The development plan includes draft development plan;

(ii) Existence of any draft development plan would authorise the appellant Authority to declare its intention to prepare a town development scheme at any time. The draft development plan was published on 27-6-2003 although it was sent for consideration of the State in terms of section 19 of the Act on 9-10-2003. The same was returned to the appellant Authority stating that plan to be prepared for the projected population in the year 2021 on or about 4-1-2005. A Draft Development Plan, 2021 was published only on 13-7-2006 whereas the declaration by the appellant Authority was notified on 20-8-2004. Submission of [counsel] that a development plan would include a draft development plan is sought to be made as the statute has interchangeably used draft development plan, sanctioned development plan as development plan and, secondly, on the strength of Clause (iv) of sub-section (1) of section 18 of the Act laying down that a notice shall be issued thereunder containing inter alia the particulars viz. the provisions for enforcing the draft development plan and stating the manner in which permission for development may be obtained.

We do not see any force in the said argument. It is possible to enforce a draft development plan in a given case, but the statute must specifically provide for the same. But, a draft development plan which has not attained finality cannot be held to be determinative of the rights and obligations of the parties and, thus, it can never be implemented. Section 50 of the Act explicitly states that the authority may declare its intention to prepare a town development scheme which having regard to section 2(u) of the Act must be read to mean declaration of its [intention] to prepare a scheme for the implementation of the provisions of a development plan.

[The court dismissed the appeal.]

NOTES AND QUESTIONS

1. The Supreme Court held that the Indore Development Plan did not extend the jurisdiction of the appellant authority because the two villages were excluded from the statutory notification constituting the authority in 1974. It was only on 28 October 2005 that the villages were included in the territorial jurisdiction of the appellant. The owners succeeded on this vital technicality.

Moreover, construing the provisions of the Act, the court found that a proposed road and residential layout in a scheme would not impact the property owner's rights. Under the Madhya Pradesh statute, a prerequisite for enforcing a town development scheme was the existence of a *final* development plan, and there was none in existence when the Joint Director refused sanction. Under the Madhya Pradesh law, existence of a *draft* development plan was not enough to impact property owner's rights.

Notice how long the planning process took with consultation and inputs at every level. Was the Supreme Court correct in dismissing the appellant's plea to rely on the draft and thereby save the alignment of the proposed road? What weighed with the court was the lengthy freeze on use of private property, were the court to accept the appellant's plea regarding draft plans.

2. The respondent may have won the battle, but it lost the war. Although, there was no cross appeal from the division bench judgment, the respondent complained to the Supreme Court that the High Court committed a manifest error by limiting its direction to quashing the refusal by the Joint Director. The respondent asked the Supreme Court to issue a mandamus to the Director 'to consider the respondents' application in accordance with the law *as it existed at the relevant point of time*'. The Supreme Court declined the mandamus observing:

> [W]here a statute provides for a right, but enforcement thereof is in several stages, unless and until the conditions precedent laid down therein are satisfied, no right can be said to have been vested in the person concerned.... The question ... came up for consideration in *Howrah Municipal Corpn v Ganges Rope Co Ltd*, (2004) 1 SCC 663 wherein this Court categorically held:
>
> > '... The claim based on the alleged "vested right" or "settled expectation" cannot be set up against statutory provisions which were brought into force by the State Government by amending the Building Rules and not by the Corporation against whom such "vested right" or "settled expectation" is being sought to be enforced. The "vested right" or "settled expectation" has been nullified not only by the Corporation but also by the State by amending the Building Rules. Besides this, such a "settled expectation" or the so-called "vested right" cannot be countenanced against public interest and convenience which are sought to be served by amendment of the Building Rules and the resolution of the Corporation issued thereupon.'

The Supreme Court arrived at the same conclusion in *Usman Khatri v Cantonment Board*,[22] albeit by a slightly different process of reasoning.

[22] (1992) 3 SCC 455.

III. DELHI

Parliament introduced the Delhi Law (Special Provisions) Act of 2006 to overcome orders issued by the Supreme Court in respect of unauthorized development.

A set of writ petitions challenging the Act were brought at the Supreme Court. The Supreme Court sent the petitions to the Delhi High Court in April 2013 to be disposed within a year. However, the High Court was unable to dispose the cases expeditiously. Finally, in December 2017, after a hiatus of over four years, the Supreme Court transferred the petitions back to itself.

The judgment traces the history of the case and the efforts by the Supreme Court to introduce a compliance culture in relation to land use in Delhi. The judgment dealt with industries and commercial users operating from residential zones. The short excerpt below highlights how the Rule of Law stands undermined when the Master Plan for Delhi is continuously breached with the authorities looking the other way.

M C MEHTA v UNION OF INDIA

(2018) 2 SCC 144

MADAN B LOKUR, J: ***

Way back in the 1990s it was brought to the notice of this Court that a variety of illegal activities were being carried on in the capital city of Delhi with reference to industries established in residential or non-conforming areas as well as misuse of residential premises for other commercial purposes. On an application having been moved, this Court realised that those in authority and power were not at all keen to take steps to remove hazardous and noxious industries and heavy and large industries out of Delhi, prohibit or prevent the continuing illegalities or even otherwise stop the misuse of residential premises for a commercial purpose. Since the attitude of the powers that be raised an issue of misgovernance or non-governance affecting the well-being of the citizens of Delhi, this Court felt that it could no longer be a mute spectator to the whims and fancies of those in power and authority. It was also felt that it would be necessary to direct those in authority and power to implement the law for the sake of the citizens of Delhi. This Court faced a situation where there was little or no support to the rule of law by the officials concerned and today the citizens of Delhi are faced with and are witnessing, among other issues, outrageous levels of pollution in Delhi entirely due to the lack of concern for the rule of law—the citizens of Delhi are paying a heavy price with hopelessly polluted air to breathe and consequent damage to their lungs, respiratory problems and possible damage to the brain of infants and children.

M C Mehta, an environmental activist, had already moved this Court with an application to find a remedy for the air pollution in Delhi in a pending writ petition. Although he sought several reliefs, this Court first concentrated on use of residential areas for industrial purposes and later, the misuse of residential premises for other commercial activities. For the present, we are concerned with the misuse of residential premises for other commercial activities. These issues first arose when preliminary orders were passed by this Court on his application on 30-9-2002 and 19-8-2003. Thereafter, this Court addressed the issue of residential areas being used for industrial purposes by a judgment and order dated 7-5-2004 in *M C Mehta v Union of India* (2004) 6 SCC 588.

A reading of the judgment and order dated 7-5-2004 makes it apparent that this Court expected all those concerned with governance of Delhi to adhere to the rule of law and ensure its implementation. Unfortunately, this Court was anguished by the events that demonstrated that the trust reposed was belied in terms of action for implementation of the law and that industrial activity continued in areas despite the Master Plan for Delhi, meaning thereby that impermissible industrial activity continued in residential areas in Delhi.

This Court also noted that no dispute was raised by the Government of India or the Delhi Government or by any statutory authority that unauthorised and illegal industrial activity had commenced and continued in Delhi in blatant breach of the provisions of the Master

Plan and no action, or ineffective action, had been taken by the authorities concerned. Rather than put their respective houses in order, it was noted that a blame game had begun with the responsibility of taking action being shifted with each authority blaming one another—be it the Government of India or the Delhi Government or the statutory authorities. Tragically, the situation continues even today and those who are suffering are the citizens of Delhi, the sufferance being not only confined to breathing hazardous and noxious air but also the health of thousands of people including children and infants residing in Delhi. In other words, the consequences of the failure to implement the rule of law in Delhi were having a generational impact, which cannot be anything but disastrous.

This Court noted that according to the Delhi Government it is not the function of the State Government to implement the Master Plan. According to the Government of India it is not the implementing agency and this Court noted that the Government of India had taken a somersault in this regard. According to other statutory authorities in Delhi, they too avoided shouldering any responsibility for inaction. Each of these authorities of the State was shifting their stands, as convenient, without any regard for statutory provisions and in blatant breach of the rule of law. This Court darkly hinted that in all this there was connivance with industry for extraneous considerations....

This Court also considered an extremely pertinent issue: what would happen when those entrusted by law to protect the rights of the citizens are themselves violators and/or abettors of the violations? The difficult task faced in such a situation was noted where, as a part of its constitutional duty, this Court is required to preserve the rule of law so that people may not lose faith in it and also point out violations of the rule of law by those who are supposed to implement the law. It was observed that the issue is not one of an absence of law but of its implementation....

NOTES AND QUESTIONS

1. The judgment traces a cat and mouse game between the court repeatedly mandating adherence to land use plans and the executive and legislature attempting to 'cure' violations by converting residential zones into 'mixed-use' zones.

2. At the time of writing, the challenge to the Delhi Laws (Special Provisions) Act of 2006 was pending. Examine the provisions extracted below and a statutory notification issued by the Government of India on 20 May 2006, a day after the 2006 law was passed.

A. Section 2. (1)(i) 'unauthorised development' means use of land or use of building or construction of building carried out in contravention of the sanctioned plans or without obtaining the sanction of plans, or in contravention of the land use as permitted under the Master Plan or Zonal Plan or layout plan, as the case may be, and includes encroachment.

B. Section 3. *Enforcement to be kept in abeyance.* – (1) Notwithstanding anything contained in any relevant law or any rules, regulations or bye-laws made thereunder, the Central Government shall within a period of one year of the coming into effect of this Act, take all possible measures to finalise norms, policy guidelines and feasible strategies to deal with the problem of unauthorised development with regard to the undermentioned categories, namely –
   (a) mixed land use not conforming to the Master Plan;
   (b) construction beyond sanctioned plans; and
   (c) encroachment by slum and Jhuggi-Jhompri dwellers and hawkers and street vendors, so that the development of Delhi takes place in a sustainable and planned manner.

(2) Subject to the provisions contained in sub-section (1) and notwithstanding any judgment, decree or order of any court, status quo as on the 1st day of January, 2006 shall

be maintained in respect of the categories of unauthorised development mentioned in sub-section (1).

(3) All notices issued by any local authority for initiating action against the categories of unauthorised development referred to in sub-section (1), shall be deemed to have been suspended and no punitive action shall be taken during the said period of one year.

(4) Notwithstanding any other provision contained in this Act, the Central Government may, at any time before the expiry of one year, withdraw the exemption by notification in the Official Gazette in respect of one or more of the categories of unauthorised development mentioned in sub-section (2) or sub-section (3), as the case may be.

C. Excerpt from notification dated 20 May 2006:

(1) The premises sealed by any local authority in pursuance of a judgment, order or decree of any court after the 1st day of January 2006 shall be eligible to be restored, for a period of one year, with effect from the 19th day of May 2006 to the position as was obtaining as on the 1st day of January 2006.

(2) All commercial establishments which are required to cease carrying out commercial activities at their premises by the 30th day of June 2006 may continue such activities, as they were being carried out on the 1st day of January 2006 for a period of one year, with effect from the 19th day of May 2006.

Are the statutory provisions and the notification constitutional? Do they advance or subvert the Rule of Law?

3. In a part of the judgment that is not excerpted, the court records that 40,812 commercial establishments filed affidavits before the court-appointed Monitoring committee assuring the committee that they would conform to the residential land use requirement. While the court is correct in upholding the Rule of Law by insisting on statutory compliance, is the Delhi Master Plan itself fundamentally defective? Where those responsible for planning have failed to anticipate and provide for new commercial zones, can citizens be blamed for setting up enterprises in residential localities? Should the court have redirected its focus at requiring those entrusted with preparing the Master Plan to explain how they propose to address the deficit in commercial space?

4. In 2006, the Supreme Court constituted a Monitoring committee to prevent misuse of residential premises for commercial use. In 2019, the Monitoring committee sealed numerous residential premises which, according to the committee, were unauthorized. The Supreme Court quashed the orders and required de-sealing since the committee had exceeded its authority:

> It is apparent from the various orders passed by this Court from time to time and from the various reports of the Monitoring Committee that it was never authorized by this Court to take action against the residential premises that were not being used for commercial purposes. It was appointed only to check the misuser of the residential properties for commercial purposes. After that, this Court directed that the Monitoring Committee should also look into the matter of 'encroachment on the public land' and 'unauthorized colonies' that have come up on the public land and were wholly unauthorized without sanction. At no point in time, this Court had empowered the Monitoring Committee to act *vis-à-vis* to the purely residential premises.
>
> The power of sealing of property carries civil consequences. A person can be deprived of the property by following a procedure in accordance with law. The Monitoring Committee is not authorized to take action concerning the residential premises situated on the private land. If there is unauthorized construction or in case of deviation, the requisite provisions are under the [Delhi Municipal Corporation Act of 1957]. The mode of action and adjudication under the Act is provided including appellate provisions and that of the Tribunal. It would not be appropriate to the Monitoring Committee to usurp statutory powers and act beyond

authority conferred upon it by the Court. The Monitoring Committee could not have sealed the residential premises, which were not misused for the commercial purpose ... nor it could have directed the demolition of those residential properties.

Article 300A of the Constitution provides that nobody can be deprived of the property and right of residence otherwise in the manner prescribed by law. When the statute prescribes a mode, the property's deprivation cannot be done in other modes since this Court did not authorize the Committee to take action in the matter. An action could have been taken in no other manner except in accordance with the procedure prescribed by law. . . [23]

5. While the contests that reach court frequently relate to the violations of a city development plan, occasionally the judgment exposes the poor quality of the plan itself. The Master Plan of Delhi 2021 (MPD 2021), enforced from 7 February 2007, fails to recognize many of the requirements of a rapidly growing metropolitan region. MPD 2021 is silent on climate change impacts and makes no provision to adapt the city to it, to reduce carbon emissions and prepare the region for the potential disruptions from soaring temperatures. Strangely, Delhi's planners did not anticipate the need for office and commercial space to house businesses and professions. The result is that MPD 2021 allows for 'mixed use' of residential areas, to accommodate the requirements of burgeoning businesses. Inevitably, this leads to conflicts amongst neighbours.

Anirudh Kumar, after being rebuffed by the Delhi High Court, turned the tables on Dr Dang's Diagnostic Centre. Beginning in 1995, Dr Dang's pathological laboratory expanded upwards from the basement and ground floor to occupy a mezzanine floor and the first floor. This annoyed Anirudh Kumar in his second-floor residence, but his complaints were ignored by the municipal corporation (MCD) as well as the Delhi Pollution Control Committee (DPCC). The Supreme Court judgment sets out the Byzantine complexity of Delhi's building regulations and holds MCD and DPCC guilty of having abdicated their statutory duties. The court minutely examined the relevant regulations and held that the diagnostic centre required statutory consents under the Water Act as well as the Air Act.[24]

IV. SURAT

Bhikubhai Patel's case is testament to the misery and harassment that vindictive government departments may inflict on the citizen. Here, the cunning device used was successive reservations in a development plan to block the owner from enjoying his property.

BHIKUBHAI VITHALBHAI PATEL v STATE OF GUJARAT

(2008) 4 SCC 144

B SUDERSHAN REDDY, J:

***

The Gujarat Town Planning and Urban Development Act, 1976 (for short 'the said Act') came into force with effect from 1-2-1978. The State Government in exercise of its power conferred under the provisions of the Act constituted Surat Urban Development Authority (SUDA) which prepared a draft development plan whereby the lands belonging to the appellants were proposed for designating the use of the lands for residential purposes. The State Government having considered the draft development plan submitted by SUDA sanctioned the plan in the modified form on 31-1-1986 whereby the appellants' lands in question were reserved for 'education complex of South Gujarat University'. The final development plan was accordingly brought into force with effect from 31-3-1986. Neither

23 *M C Mehta v Union of India* (2020) SCC Online SC 648.
24 *Anirudh Kumar v Municipal Corporation of Delhi* (2015) 7 SCC 779.

the Area Development Authority nor the authority for whose purpose land has been designated in the final development plan initiated any steps to acquire the lands of the appellants. The appellants having waited for a period of 10 years from the date of coming into force of the final development plan got served a notice on the authority concerned requiring it to acquire the land within six months from the date of the service of such notice. However, no steps were taken by any of the authorities proposing to acquire the lands. Instead SUDA, in purported exercise of its power under section 21 of the Act sought to revise the development plan by reserving the lands in question once again for education complex of South Gujarat University.

The appellants challenged re-reservation of the lands for South Gujarat University on various grounds which ultimately culminated in the judgment of this Court in *Bhavnagar University v Palitana Sugar Mill (P) Ltd.*, (2003) 2 SCC 101. This Court in clear and categorical terms laid down that section 21 of the Act may impose statutory obligations on the part of the State and the appropriate authority to revise the development plan but under the garb of exercising the power to revise the development plan 'the substantial right conferred upon the owner of the land or the person interested therein' cannot be taken away. It is observed:

> 38. Section 21 does not envisage that despite the fact that in terms of sub-section (2) of section 20, the designation of land shall lapse, the same, only because a draft revised plan is made, would automatically give rise to revival thereof. Section 20 does not manifest a legislative intent to curtail or *take away the right acquired by a landowner under section 22 of getting the land defreezed.*

The revised development plan submitted by SUDA was awaiting the sanction of the State Government. The State Government in exercise of powers conferred by the proviso to sub-clause (ii) of Clause (a) of section 17(1) of the Act proposed modifications in the draft revised development plan submitted by SUDA and proposed to designate the land under section 12(2)(o) for 'educational use'. The appellants challenged the action on the part of the State Government in issuing Notification dated 22-7-2004 on various grounds. During the pendency of the writ petition the State Government came out with final Notification dated 28-9-2004 designating the land in question for educational use under section 12(2)(o) of the Act. The appellants sought the leave of the Court to challenge the said notification also. The final notification was set aside on the ground that there was no material before the Government on the basis of which the decision to designate the lands for educational purposes could have been arrived at. The matter was remitted for fresh consideration in the light of the observations and the directions issued by the High Court. . . .

Before we address ourselves to the questions for their determination it would be appropriate to notice [section 17 which is as under:]

> 17. *Power of State Government to sanction draft development plan.–*
>
> (i)(a) On receipt of the draft development plan under section 16, the State Government may, by notification,– . . .
>
> (ii) return the draft development plan and the regulations to the area development authority or, as the case may be, to the authorised officer, for modifying the plan and the regulations in such manner as it may direct:
> Provided that, where the State Government is of opinion that substantial modifications in the draft development plan and regulations are necessary, the State Government may, instead of returning them to the area development authority or, as the case may be, the authorised officer under this sub-clause, publish the modifications as considered necessary in the Official Gazette along with a notice in the prescribed manner inviting suggestions or objections from any person with respect to the proposed modifications within a period of two months from the date of publication of such notice; or

(iii) refuse to accord sanction to the draft development plan and the regulations and direct the area development authority or the authorised officer to prepare a fresh development plan under the provisions of this Act.

* * *

On consideration of the facts and the material available on record, it is established that the State Government took the action proposing to make substantial modifications to the plan without forming of any opinion, which is a condition precedent for the use of power under proviso to Section 17(1)(a)(ii). The power, to restrict the use of land by the owners thereof, is a drastic power. The designation or reservation of the land and its use results in severe abridgment of the right to property. Statutory provisions enabling the State or its authorities to impose restrictions on the right to use one's own land are required to be construed strictly. The legislature has, it seems to us, prescribed certain conditions to prevent the abuse of power and to ensure just exercise of power. Section 17 and more particularly the proviso to Section 17(1)(a)(ii) prescribes some of the conditions precedent for the exercise of power. The order proposing to make substantial modifications, in breach of any one of those conditions, will undoubtedly be void. On a successful showing the order proposing substantial modifications and designating the land of the appellants for educational use under section 12(2)(o) of the Act has been made without the State Government applying its mind to the aspect of necessity or without forming an honest opinion on that aspect, it will, we have no doubt, be void.

For the view we have taken to strike down both the notifications and declare them *ultra vires* it is unnecessary to go into various other contentions urged before us.

The appellants are deprived of their right to use the land for residential purposes for over a period of more than a quarter century. The Authority included the land in the residential zone but the State Government reserved the land for the purposes of South Gujarat University but the authority for whose benefit it was required failed to acquire the land leading to re-reservation of the land for the very same purpose which was ultimately struck down by this Court in *Bhavnagar University*.

The present move of the State Government to designate the land for the educational use under section 12(2)(o) of the Act is declared *ultra vires* and void and this shall put an end to the controversy enabling the appellants to utilise the land for residential purposes. The authorities including the State Government shall accordingly do the needful, without creating any further hurdle in the matter.

The appeal is, accordingly, allowed with costs.

NOTES

1. Smarting from defeat in the first round of litigation which commenced in 1992 and concluded with the Supreme Court judgment rendered on 3 December 2002 in *Bhavnagar University v Palitana Sugar Mill Pvt Ltd*,[25] SUDA revised the development plan interposing 'educational use' for the earlier reservation in favour of a university. This trickery nearly paid off when the Gujarat High Court dismissed the landowners' petition in the second round. But for the Supreme Court's intervention, the state would have been able to indefinitely block the owners from using their property for residential housing.

2. In many parts of the country, city administrations do not have funds to acquire land reserved for public purposes such as parks, playgrounds and schools. Consequently, reservations

[25] (2003) 2 SCC 101.

lapse and districts develop without the proposed public amenity. To overcome the financial constraint, some town planning legislation empowers the planning authority to grant development rights to the owner in lieu of monetary compensation to acquire reserved land. These development rights may be used by the property owner at some buildable location elsewhere within the city or may be traded.

There being no free lunch, the notion of transferable development rights (TDR) translates into more intense building activity in some other part of the city and inevitably increases stress on the city infrastructure there. In the context of Mumbai, TDR was introduced without any environmental impact assessment in disregard of the congestion consequences in the recipient zone. TDR certificates are a handy tool to overcome the municipal corporation's inability to print currency notes.

C. UNEVEN IMPLEMENTATION

Despite the rhetoric commending strict enforcement of town planning laws, the results in the Supreme Court are occasionally unexpected. Notice how background factors, unconnected to black letter law, may influence the eventual outcome.

I. SHANTI SPORTS CLUB

Deep anguish runs through the Supreme Court's judgment in the *Shanti Sports Club* case. The facts testify to a feeble regard for planning laws and a culture of official complicity.

Delhi's Master Plan of 1962 designated land use for residential, commercial, institutional and industrial activities. To implement planned development, the state commenced acquiring vast tracts of land under the Land Acquisition Act of 1894 (Act). The land holders challenged the acquisition, but to no avail. In the early 1990s, Satish Khosla a sports enthusiast, entered into some arrangements with the owner and commenced constructing a sports complex for a club. The Delhi Lands (Restrictions on Transfer) Act of 1972 (1972 Act) prohibits transfers once land acquisition proceedings have commenced. Realizing that sanctions for building plans may be difficult in view of the restrictions imposed by the 1972 Act, Khosla developed a cricket ground, tennis stadium, badminton courts, billiards room, swimming pool, table tennis room, squash court—all without securing approval for construction from the authorities. The club had plush lawns and gardens with two cottages that were hired out for a handy sum to diplomats and for parties and celebrations. Over time, around 1,500 members enjoyed recreational and sports facilities offered by the club.

Through a series of writ petitions, interim protective orders and legal maneuvering, the club managed to fend off efforts by the Delhi Development Authority (DDA) to take possession of the property and implement the Master Plan. On 8 June 1999, Ram Jethmalani, the Union Urban Development Minister (whose portfolio was about to change), recorded the following note in the file:

> Extensive construction has taken place. This must be with full co-operation of the public servants concerned.
>
> In accordance with the settled policy, no demolition can or will be ordered. At the last meeting, I indicated that suitable terms of regularisation be settled by negotiations. I would leave this now to my successor.

The succeeding Minister declined to release the club land since it was needed for the Vasant Kunj residential project and the construction was done after the award was passed under the

Act. The club challenged the decision claiming that the succeeding Minister could not have overturned the 8 June 1999 decision; demolishing the huge sports complex would be a waste of national resources; a sports complex was consistent with planned development; and that the residential neighbourhood greatly benefited from the recreational facilities. Since a few neighbourhood schools had secured release of their land from the acquisition process, the club land too should be spared.

SHANTI SPORTS CLUB v UNION OF INDIA
(2009) 15 SCC 705

G S Singhvi, J: These appeals filed against order dated 21.8.2001 of the Division Bench of Delhi High Court whereby it refused to interfere with the Central Government's decision not to exercise discretion under section 48(1) of the Land Acquisition Act, 1894 (for short 'the Act') to withdraw from the acquisition of land comprised in khasra Nos.35, 369/36, 37, 38, 367/21 and 365/33 of Village Masudpur, Tehsil Mehrauli, Delhi are illustrative of how the litigants use the court process for frustrating the acquisition of land for a public purpose for years together and seek equity after raising illegal construction over the acquired land under the cloak of interim order(s) passed by one or the other court....

The appellants' plea that the Government ought to have de-notified the land covered by the sports complex because the same has been built by spending crores of rupees and is being used by a large section of people sounds attractive, but, after having given serious thought to the entire matter, we are convinced that the Government rightly refused to exercise discretion under section 48(1) of the Act for de-notifying the acquired land and the High Court did not commit any error whatsoever by refusing to fall in the trap of alluring argument that demolition of the sports complex built by spending substantial amount will be a waste of national wealth and nobody will be benefitted by it. The appellants have not denied that fact that the land on which the sports complex has been constructed was acquired by the Government by issuing notification dated 23.1.1965 under Section 4(1) of the Act, which culminated in the making of award dated 22.12.1980. It is also not their case that the construction activity was started prior to initiation of acquisition proceedings. Rather, their admitted stance is that they came in possession of the land between 1990–1993, i.e. more than 10 years after finalization of the acquisition proceedings. This being the position, the appellants cannot plead equity and seek court's intervention for protection of the unauthorised constructions raised by them. It is trite to say that once the land is acquired by following due process of law, the same cannot be transferred by the land owner to another person and that any such transfer is void and is not binding on the State. A transferee of the acquired land can, at best, step into the shoes of the land owner and lodge claim for compensation....

Although, the then Minister for Urban Development, who recorded note dated 8.6.1999, was extremely magnanimous to the appellants when he wrote that the extensive construction must have been made with full cooperation of public servants concerned, but having carefully examined the entire record, we have no hesitation to observe that the construction of this magnitude could not have been possible, but for the active connivance of the concerned public servants who turned blind eye to the huge structure being built on the acquired land without any sanctioned plan. We are amazed to note that after having secured some sort of transfer of the acquired land in stark violation of the prohibition contained in Section 3 of the 1972 Act, the appellants could raise massive structure comprising cricket ground, tennis stadium, badminton courts, swimming pool, table tennis room, squash court, etc. and cottages with modern facilities without even submitting building plans for sanction by any competent authority and without being noticed by any of the authorities entrusted with the duty of checking illegal/unauthorised construction. This mystery may perhaps never be solved because the officers responsible for ignoring the blatant violation of Section 3 of the 1972 Act, Delhi Development Authority Act and Building Rules, Regulations and By-laws must have either retired or moved to higher positions in the administration where they will be able to block any inquiry in the matter. Be that as it may, such illegal constructions cannot be protected by the court by nullifying the decision taken by the Government not to withdraw from the acquisition of the land in question. . . .

At this stage, we may also take cognizance of the commercial activities being undertaken in what has been described by the appellants as sports complex simpliciter. [Referring to the income from hiring out the cottages, garden and other amenities, the court concluded that the appellants' 'so-called love for sports has substantial flavour of commerce.']

Before concluding, we consider it necessary to enter a caveat. In all developed countries, great emphasis has been laid on the planned development of cities and urban areas. The object of planned development has been achieved by rigorous enforcement of master plans prepared after careful study of complex issues, scientific research and rationalisation of laws. The people of those countries have greatly contributed to the concept of planned development of cities by strictly adhering to the planning laws, the master plan, etc. They respect the laws enacted by the legislature for regulating planned development of the cities and seldom there is a complaint of violation of master plan, etc. in the construction of buildings, residential, institutional or commercial. In contrast, scenario in the developing countries like ours is substantially different. Though, the competent legislatures have, from time to time, enacted laws for ensuring planned development of the cities and urban areas, enforcement thereof has been extremely poor and the people have violated the master plans, zoning plans and building regulations and bye-laws with impunity. In last four decades, almost all cities, big or small, have seen unplanned growth. In the 21st century, the menace of illegal and unauthorised constructions and encroachments has acquired monstrous proportions and everyone has been paying heavy price for the same. Economically affluent people and those having support of the political and executive apparatus of the State have constructed buildings, commercial complexes, multiplexes, malls, etc. in blatant violation of the municipal and town planning laws, master plans, zonal development plans and even the sanctioned building plans. In most of the cases of illegal or unauthorised constructions, the officers of the municipal and other regulatory bodies turn blind eye either due to the influence of higher functionaries of the State or other extraneous reasons. Those who construct buildings in violation of the relevant statutory provisions, master plan, etc. and those who directly or indirectly abet such violations are totally unmindful of the grave consequences of their actions and/or omissions on the present as well as future generations of the country which will be forced to live in unplanned cities and urban areas. The people belonging to this class do not realize that the constructions made in violation of the relevant laws, master plan or zonal development plan or sanctioned building plan or the building is used for a purpose other than the one specified in the relevant statute or the master plan, etc., such constructions put unbearable burden on the public facilities/amenities like water, electricity, sewerage, etc. apart from creating chaos on the roads. The pollution caused due to traffic congestion affects the health of the road users. The pedestrians and people belonging to weaker sections of the society, who cannot afford the luxury of air-conditioned cars, are the worst victims of pollution. They suffer from skin diseases of different types, asthma, allergies and even more dreaded diseases like cancer. It can only be a matter of imagination how much the government has to spend on the treatment of such persons and also for controlling pollution and adverse impact on the environment due to traffic congestion on the roads and chaotic conditions created due to illegal and unauthorised constructions. This Court has, from time to time, taken cognizance of buildings constructed in violation of municipal and other laws and emphasized that no compromise should be made with the town planning scheme and no relief should be given to the violator of the town planning scheme etc. on the ground that he has spent substantial amount on construction of the buildings, etc. [Citations omitted.]

> Unfortunately, despite repeated judgments by this Court and High Courts, the builders and other affluent people engaged in the construction activities, who have, over the years shown scant respect for regulatory mechanism envisaged in the municipal and other similar laws, as also the master plans, zonal development plans, sanctioned plans, etc. have received encouragement and support from the State apparatus. As and when the courts have passed orders or the officers of local and other bodies have taken action for ensuring rigorous compliance of laws relating to planned development of the cities and urban areas and issued directions for demolition of the illegal/unauthorized constructions, those in power have come forward to protect the wrong doers either by issuing administrative orders or enacting laws for regularization of illegal and unauthorised constructions in the name of compassion and hardship. Such actions have done irreparable harm to the concept of planned development of the cities and urban areas. It is high time that the executive and political apparatus of the State take serious view of the menace of illegal and unauthorized constructions and stop their support to the lobbies of affluent class of builders and others, else even the rural areas of the country will soon witness similar chaotic conditions. [The court dismissed the appeals and gave the appellants three months to hand over possession of the land to the DDA.]

NOTES AND QUESTIONS

1. What does this case tell you about the Rule of Law? Who is responsible for ingraining a respect for the law? Schools? Parents? Law colleges?

2. Can you fault the court's tough line? Could the court have crafted a better solution that might have saved the sports complex while penalizing the wrongdoer? For instance, forfeiture of the sports complex to the DDA which could thereafter operate the facility as a municipal club. Would such a direction encourage unplanned building activity?

3. Picture the size of the sports complex. It was created over several years in full sight of the city engineers charged with authorizing new development. What does that tell you about the venality of the planning authority's officers? If the rot runs deep, can any number of judicial interventions reverse the tide of illegal constructions?

As the judgment notes, in several large cities, entire townships rise without permission. What systemic changes may bring about an improvement? Do we need new legislation, more stringent penalties or greater responsibility amongst citizens, real estate developers and government departments? What might motivate society to move towards greater compliance to our planning laws?

4. The judgment records a succession of litigations in respect of the land, both before and after Satish Khosla set up a sports club. Khosla filed two injunction suits in 1991 and 1993, writ petitions in 1993 and 2000 and also applications in proceedings filed by landowners. By indulging Khosla, was the judiciary responsible for prolonging the non-implementation of the Master Plan?

II. CAMPA COLA COMPOUND

Campa Cola, a popular soft drink in the 1980s, is now associated with a troubling saga of unplanned development, manipulation and brazen disregard of the law. The Campa Cola compound located at Worli in Mumbai gets its name from the adjacent drinks factory. On 8 June 1981, the developer received approval for six buildings each comprising a ground and five upper floors. Over the next several years, employing formidable persuasion, seven buildings were built, two of them stretching as high as 17 and 20 storeys. More than 200 families moved into the apartments that were organized into seven housing societies. The municipal corporation, for most part, turned a blind eye to the soaring construction and illegal occupation of the flats.

In 1999 and 2000, believing that their occupation was by now inviolable, the societies separately petitioned the High Court to restrain the authorities from turning off the water supply. The manoeuvre boomeranged. The water supply petitions triggered an enquiry into the residential towers and culminated in a direction for demolition. The Bombay High Court refused relief to the societies, and the Supreme Court yet again lamented the disregard of town planning laws. The excerpt[26] focuses on the case from a flat owner's perspective.

ESHA EKTA APART COOP HSG LTD v MUN CORP OF MUMBAI
(2013) 5 SCC 357

G S Singhvi, J: In the last five decades, the provisions contained in various municipal laws for planned development of the areas to which such laws are applicable have been violated with impunity in all the cities, big or small, and those entrusted with the task of ensuring implementation of the master plan, etc. have miserably failed to perform their duties. It is highly regrettable that this is so despite the fact that this Court has, keeping in view the imperatives of preserving the ecology and environment of the area and protecting the rights of the citizens, repeatedly cautioned the authorities concerned against arbitrary regularisation of illegal constructions by way of compounding and otherwise.

* * *

At the outset, we would like to observe that by rejecting the prayer for regularisation of the floors constructed in wanton violation of the sanctioned plan, the Deputy Chief Engineer and the appellate authority have demonstrated their determination to ensure planned development of the commercial capital of the country and the orders passed by them have given a hope to the law-abiding citizens that someone in the hierarchy of administration will not allow unscrupulous developers/builders to take law into their hands and get away with it.

Although the members of the Housing Societies knew that the construction had been raised in violation of the sanctioned plan and permission for occupation of the buildings had not been issued by the competent authority, a large number of them occupied the illegally constructed buildings. After this, the Housing Societies started litigation in one form or the other.

When the writ petitions filed by the Housing Societies and their members for issue of direction to the Corporation to supply water to their buildings were taken up for hearing, the Division Bench of the High Court noted that even though the buildings were constructed in violation of the sanctioned plan, the Corporation had not taken action against those responsible for such construction and passed the order dated 11-10-2005 for appearance of the Additional Commissioner of the Corporation.

On the next date of hearing, the Commissioner of the Corporation appeared before the High Court and gave an assurance that necessary steps will be taken in accordance with law within a period of two months. Thereafter, the Corporation issued notices dated 11-11-2005, 19-11-2005 and 5-12-2005 under section 351 of the [Municipal Corporation] Act giving details of the illegal structures proposed to be demolished. The Housing Societies submitted their respective replies which were rejected by the Corporation vide order dated 3-12-2005/ 8-12-2005.

The first question which arises for consideration … is: whether the writ petitioners are entitled to seek regularisation of the illegal and unauthorised construction made by the developers/builders?

---

[26] To retain the flow, we take an editorial liberty in the second of the four segments and join discontinuous paragraphs.

* * *

The argument of [counsel] that the flat buyers should not be penalised for the illegality committed by the lessee and the developers/builders in raising construction in violation of the sanctioned plan sounds attractive in the first blush but on a closer scrutiny, we do not find any merit in the same. Admittedly, the flat buyers had entered into agreements with the developers/builders much before the commencement of the construction. They were aware of the fact that the revised plans submitted by the architect had not been approved by the Planning Authority and the developers/builders had foretold them about the consequence of rejection of the revised plans. Therefore, there is no escape from the conclusion that the flat buyers had consciously occupied the flats illegally constructed by the developers/builders. In this scenario, the only remedy available to them is to sue the lessee and the developer/builder for return of the money and/or for damages and they cannot seek a direction for regularisation of the illegal and unauthorised construction made by the developers/builders.

* * *

An analysis of the above reproduced provisions makes it clear that any person who undertakes or carries out development or changes the use of land without permission of the Planning Authority is liable to be punished with imprisonment. At the same time, the Planning Authority is empowered to require the owner to restore the land to its original condition as it existed before the development work was undertaken. The scheme of these provisions does not mandate regularisation of construction made without obtaining the required permission or in violation thereof.

The Circular dated 4-2-2011, on which reliance was placed by [counsel], cannot be invoked for entertaining the prayer for regularisation. That circular only contains the procedure for regularisation of unauthorised works/structures. It neither deals with the issues relating to entitlement of the applicant to seek regularisation nor lays down that the Planning Authority can regularise illegal construction even after dismissal of the appeal filed under section 47 of the [Town Planning] Act. Therefore, the procedure laid down in the Circular dated 4-2-2011 is of no avail to the flat buyers.

Though the argument of [counsel] that the developers/builders/promoters are responsible for the illegal construction finds support from the provisions of the [Maharashtra Ownership Flats] Act, 1963 but that does not help the Housing Societies and their members because there is no provision under that Act for condonation of illegal/unauthorised construction by the developers/builders and promoters or for regularisation of such construction.

It is thus evident that the 1963 Act obligates the promoter to obtain sanctions and approvals from the authority concerned and disclose the same to the flat buyers. The Act also provides for imposition of penalty on the promoters. However, the provisions contained therein do not entitle the flat buyers to seek a mandamus for regularisation of the unauthorised/illegal construction.

In view of the above discussion, we hold that the petitioners in the transferred case have failed to make out a case for directing the respondents to regularise the construction made in violation of the sanctioned plan. Rather, the ratio of the abovenoted judgments and, in particular, *Royal Paradise Hotel (P) Ltd v State of Haryana*, (2006) 7 SCC 597 is clearly attracted in the present case. We would like to reiterate that no authority administering municipal laws and other similar laws can encourage violation of the sanctioned plan. The courts are also expected to refrain from exercising equitable jurisdiction for regularisation of illegal and unauthorised constructions else it would encourage violators of the planning laws and destroy the very idea and concept of planned development of urban as well as rural areas.

In the result, the appeals and the transferred case are dismissed and it is declared that there is no impediment in the implementation of notices issued by the Corporation under section 351 of the [Municipal Corporation] Act and order dated 3-12-2005/8-12-2005 passed by the competent authority. The Corporation is expected to take action in the matter at the earliest.

> We also direct that the State Government and its functionaries/officers as also the officers/employees of the Corporation shall not put any hurdle or obstacle in the implementation of notices issued under section 351 of the [Municipal Corporation] Act.
>
> It is needless to say that the flat buyers shall be free to avail appropriate remedy against the developers/builders.

NOTES AND QUESTIONS

1. For more than three decades, the High Courts and the Supreme Court have underscored the importance of adhering to building regulations. When so many developers across the country consider town planning laws ornamental, is something the matter with builders as a class or is something the matter with the law? Should building laws be simpler—easy to comprehend and comply with? Should less discretion be conferred on planning authorities? Should the response to widespread violations be less regulation or more regulation? Should town planning laws be made by a more participative and transparent process to improve compliance? Might all this be a waste considering the get-rich-quick motive behind many real estate developments?

Experience reveals an enormous chasm between the letter of these laws and the construction in our cities. Systemic violation of the law over decades weakens societal respect for the Rule of Law with far-reaching consequences.

2. Were an audit conducted of all buildings in a city, say Mumbai, how many buildings do you think would pass muster?

3. What legislative changes might reduce situations like *Campa Cola compound*? Consider a law that established a building regulator who is required to certify every real estate transfer. No transfer of property would be recognized in law unless that premises conformed to all town planning laws. Would such a law improve compliance or would the regulator swiftly degenerate into yet another rent-seeking agency?

4. Who should bear the loss? Flat purchasers, the builder, the municipal corporation or negligent officers of the corporation? What legal and practical difficulties might the affected residents face when suing the others? What about the impact of demolition on residents living in the lower 'legal' floors of the buildings?

5. The Campa Cola compound saga continued long after the principal judgment was rendered by Justice G S Singhvi on 27 February 2013. Two months later, a fresh writ petition was filed before the High Court by Rajesh Parekh seeking to restrain demolition. The High Court dismissed the petition on 29 April 2013 and the Supreme Court rejected the subsequent special leave petition on 2 May 2013.[27] A period of five months was granted to the petitioner and other occupants of the illegal portions of the building to vacate the premises. This was subject to conditions laid down by the court:

> Within four weeks from today they shall file affidavits in this Court and give unequivocal undertaking that at the end of five months' period all of them will voluntarily vacate the disputed portions of the buildings and will not cause any hindrance in the action which may be taken by the Corporation in the light of the observations made by this Court in judgment dated 27-2-2013 in *Esha Ekta Apartments Coop Housing Society Ltd v Municipal Corpn of Mumbai* (2013) 5 SCC 357.

[27] *Rajesh S Parekh v State of Maharashtra* (2014) 14 SCC 565.

During the period of five months, the petitioners and other occupiers shall not induct any other person in the disputed premises. They shall also not file litigation of any kind in the Bombay High Court or the courts subordinate to the High Court for frustrating the action already taken by the Corporation or which may be taken hereinafter.

On 16 September 2013, as the end of the fifth month approached, the residents applied to the municipal corporation seeking approval of amended plans for the buildings. When the corporation refused to entertain the application because of the final orders passed by the Supreme Court, yet another writ petition was filed before the Bombay High Court. A Division Bench of the High Court dismissed the petition on 26 September 2013 observing that the application was an abuse of process. With the deadline approaching, the Campa Cola Residents' Association moved the Supreme Court yet again. On 1 October 2013, the special leave petition was dismissed, with the Supreme Court frowning upon the petitioner's effort to create 'an artificial dispute [to] frustrate implementation of the notices issued by the Corporation under section 351 of the 1888 Act'.[28] However, the court added:

Having considered the rival submissions and keeping in view the forthcoming Dussehra and Diwali festivals, we deem it proper to accept the prayer made by [petitioner's counsel] and allow time to the members of the house building societies up to 11-11-2013 to vacate the premises in their occupation. This would be subject to the condition that they shall not file any litigation in any court in the State of Maharashtra including the Bombay High Court except for recovery of the amount paid to the developers/builders. At the same time, it is clarified that this liberty shall not entitle the petitioners or anyone else to file any case and seek injunction against demolition of the illegally constructed portions of the building.

As the new deadline of 11 November 2013 approached, the residents of Campa Cola compound changed tack. With the last seconds of a final 48-hour eviction notice ticking to a close, the residents employed a public relations firm, Concept PR, to stave off the municipal corporation's heavy machinery. Concept PR detailed its campaign, introducing a few boasts:[29]

Agency Brief

After months of fighting losing court battles and faced with a 48-hour eviction notice from the BMC, residents of over 25 years at the Compound, approached one of India's leading Public Relations firm, Concept PR, for support.

Generate heightened media focus to carry their voice across the length and breadth of Mumbai and later the Nation and impact influencers.

Focus attention on the plight of the residents while the BMC officials and developers went scot-free.

The Action

Concept PR's newly established Concept Community relations team given the mandate.

- Created a war room like set-up that enabled 24x7 monitoring.
- Dedicated senior resources operated as thought leaders.
- Young team put together for round the clock monitoring and to manage media across platforms—Electronic, Print, Social, Radio, Outdoor and Cinema Halls.

[28] *Campa Cola Residents' Association v State of Maharashtra* (2014) 14 SCC 568.

[29] Campa Cola Compound, http://www.conceptpr.com/campa-cola.html, accessed on 21 April 2020. (The authors were unable to access these pages on 3 June 2021.) Also see https://timesofindia.indiatimes.com/blogs/in-conversation/despite-a-well-orchestrated-pr-stint-campa-cola-campaign-loses-fizz/?source=app&frmapp=yes, accessed on 3 June 2021.

- Relevant and impactful content had to be developed on regular basis.
- Ensure quick turnaround for all media queries....

The PR Plan

- Summon entire city media to the Compound for a first hand feel of the situation
- Plan and action impromptu press conferences by office bearers and harassed residents.
- Appeal to all authorities.
- Encourage voluntary participation of elected representatives
- Continuous feed of content/headlines to media
- Regular alerts to FM Radio Stations
- An active and engaging Social Media campaign
- Ensuring media spotlight at all critical junctures
  - Residents move Supreme Court seeking more time.
  - Resident Groups seeking legal remedies.
- Design content focused on emotional stories of senior citizens and school going children.
- Highlighting residents' activities from prayer meets to fasts held within the compound.

October Impact

- Massive media response, across local, regional and national channels (print and electronic).
- The continuous live coverage of the demolition deadline resulted in Supreme Court giving further reprieve till Nov. 12th, 2013.
- Senior leaders from across parties, both National and Regional, became the face of the residents' cause and added their weight behind them.

Intensified Action

- With the new demolition deadline closing in media coverage was intensified and content focused on
  Residents being cheated by Officials and Developers
  BMC sparing errant builders while hapless residents/home buyers suffer
  The step-motherly treatment being meted to Campa Cola Compound while illegal buildings in Thane allowed to begin cluster development.
- Top news channels run debates with all stake holders.

The media blitz paid off. On 13 November 2013, the Supreme Court passed an unprecedented *suo moto* order after noting the residents' counsel's earlier statement that 75% of the residents had vacated the illegally constructed portions:

> In the early morning today, we read reports in the newspaper *The Hindu* about the proposed demolition of the unauthorised and illegal constructions in the Campa Cola compounds and found that majority of the members of the house building societies have so far not vacated the disputed constructions. Some of them could not vacate the disputed constructions on account of non-availability of alternative place.... Accordingly, an oral order was passed in the pre-lunch session that the Corporation shall not carry out demolition....
>
> The learned Attorney General made some suggestions for finding a permanent solution to the problem faced by the residents of the cooperative housing societies. He [stated] that a specific proposal would be submitted to the Court....
>
> Till further orders, the Corporation shall not carry out demolition in furtherance of the action initiated by notices issued under Section 351 of the Mumbai Municipal Corporation Act, 1888....[30]

[30] *Campa Cola Residents' Association v State of Maharashtra* (2014) 14 SCC 561.

On 19 November 2013, the court issued these directions:

> Having considered the entirety of the matter, we deem it proper to extend the time fixed in the earlier orders up to 31-5-2014. This order has been passed on purely humanitarian considerations and will not, in any manner, dilute the judgment and orders passed by the Court earlier and the occupants of the flats will have to vacate the premises in their occupation on or before 31-5-2014. The benefit of the aforesaid direction would be available subject to the filing undertakings by all the occupants before this Court within a period of six weeks from today. It is made clear that if all the occupants fail to file the required undertakings within the time specified, then the Municipal Corporation shall be entitled to take action in accordance with the judgment dated 27-2-2013.[31]

In December 2013, Justice G S Singhvi who had authored the principal judgment dated 27 February 2013 and was the presiding judge in the subsequent rounds, retired.

On 30 January 2015, nearly two years after its main judgment, the Supreme Court passed this order:

> The applicants-appellants want clarification of the judgment and orders dated 27.02.2013 and 01.10.2013 to the extent that the State Government may consider the representation in accordance with law.
>
> Learned counsel appearing for the respondents have no objection to that clarification.
>
> In the aforesaid premises, we clarify the order by observing that in the event the applicants-appellants approach the State Government by filing representation, the latter shall consider the representation in accordance with law and the State Government may pass a reasoned order.
>
> With the aforesaid clarification/directions, these applications stand disposed of.[32]

6. In its principal judgment, the Supreme Court complimented the authorities for having 'given a hope to the law-abiding citizens' that unscrupulous builders cannot 'take law into their hands and get away with it'. The municipal corporation was asked to proceed with its demolition notice 'at the earliest' and the state government along with its agencies was specifically told not to 'put any hurdle or obstacle in the implementation of notices issued under section 351'.

Thereafter, while maintaining a stern facade, the court extended time till October 2013 and then up to June 2014. Finally, the court diluted its own go-ahead to the municipal corporation by allowing a representation to the state which was required to pass a 'reasoned order'.

As media coverage mounted, the court simply did not have the stomach to dishouse the residents.

7. The court repeatedly extended the deadline, entertained fresh rounds of litigation on the very same issue, acted *suo moto* in response to the choreographed media campaign and refrained from enforcing undertakings it insisted the residents supply. Did the Supreme Court severely dent its own prestige? If final Supreme Court judgments are not so *final* after all, what is the message this sends to society at large? Is there no sanctity in undertakings furnished to the Supreme Court of India?

---

[31] *Campa Cola Residents' Association v State of Maharashtra* (2014) 14 SCC 557.

[32] *Midtown Apartments Coop Housing Society Ltd v Municipal Corporation of Greater Mumbai*, IA No. 3 of 2014 in Civil Appeal No. 7938 of 2012, order dated 30 January 2015.

Were you the municipal officer who had mobilized the machinery and coordinated with the police to maintain law and order at the site during the demolition operation, how would you view the successive reprieves?

8. What does the judicial flip-flop in this case tell you about media impact on the supposedly impervious judiciary? Who holds the trumps?

Destroying homes will hardly ever be a popular move, regardless of how lawful it may be. Are courts the 'planned development' police? Should they be?

9. What is the lesson: 'Never-say-die' and engage an effective public relations agency? For all the high-sounding principles in the judgments, did the judicial process at the highest level eventually condone dishonesty? Quite apart from what the builder did, the residents were fairly economical with the truth when they obtained an extension on the representation that 75% of the residents had vacated on 10 October 2013.

10. Would the Supreme Court have been as indulgent if 200 families living in a slum were about to be dishoused? Assume they lacked the cunning to engage public opinion-moulding professionals.

11. There were four distinct rounds before the Supreme Court: (1) Esha Ekta Apartments, (2) Rajesh Parekh, (3) Campa Cola Residents' Association and (4) Mid-Town Apartments. By tucking in a requirement for the state to pass a 'reasoned order' in the fourth round, the Supreme Court opened a gateway for a fifth round.

12. What is expected of the state government should it receive a representation like the one contemplated in the *Mid-Town Apartments* order? Is it required to follow the main judgment with its express mandate not to obstruct implementation of the demolition notices or should it adhere to the clarification on 30 January 2015 that the state government shall 'consider the representation in accordance with law'? Can the state government *allow* a representation and thereby nullify the final Supreme Court judgment?

13. In an earlier case dealing with the regularization of an illegal structure,[33] Justice B N Srikrishna (then in the Bombay High Court) opened his judgment with a reference to a parable from the Mahabharata. In the judge's telling, during the Great War, Sanjaya counsels King Dritharashtra that Shalya would defeat the Pandavs, though all the veterans like Bhisma, Drona and Karna were disabled from combat. The aphorism, 'hope springs eternal in the human breast' is apposite to the *Campa Cola* case.

III. SURESH ESTATES

Suresh Estates Pvt Ltd v Municipal Corporation of Greater Mumbai[34] is a curious case decided with commendable dispatch. The case began in the Bombay High Court in 2007 and ended within the calendar year with a detailed (and from the appellant's standpoint, favourable) Supreme Court judgment. The case concerned an important issue—the interplay between the CRZ notification of 1991 and the Development Control *Regulations* (DCR) enacted for Mumbai in that year. As we shall see, to decide the case, the Supreme Court ignores the DCR that came into force one day after the CRZ notification, and resurrects a long dead statute that was replaced nearly 17 years prior to the *Suresh Estates* judgment.

[33] *Overseas Chinese Cuisine (India) Pvt Ltd v Municipal Corporation* (2000) 1 Bom C R 341. Unlike *Campa Cola*, this petition failed.

[34] (2007) 14 SCC 439.

Interfering in an innocuous Bombay High Court order,[35] the Supreme Court decision turns on their head elementary notions of town planning and interpretation of statutes. Using tortuous reasoning, the court sided with Suresh Estates, stopping just short of approving its building plans.

In 1967, the Development Control *Rules* (DC Rules) were framed to manage building activity in Mumbai. Since these rules were not in tune with the requirements of a rapidly growing metropolis, draft DCR were published in 1989 inviting suggestions and objections from the public. (These draft DCR, together with the draft land use map, comprised the draft development plan for Mumbai.) Section 46 of the Maharashtra Regional and Town Planning Act of 1966, the umbrella statute for the DCR reads:

> The Planning Authority in considering application for permission, shall have due regard to the provisions of any draft or final plan or proposal published by means of notice submitted or sanctioned under this Act.

On 19 February 1991, the CRZ notification was published. A day later, on 20 February 1991, the final DC Regulations for Greater Bombay were enforced, replacing the DC Rules.

The appellant owned a plot in Bhuleshwar, an extremely congested part of the city. The plot was reserved for the playground of a municipal school as well as a proposed road but when a notice was served on the municipal corporation on 16 June 2005 asking the corporation to purchase the plot, the corporation declined. It found the purchase price of Rs. 13.6 crores very high and consequently the reservation lapsed.

Although the plot fell on the landward side of two major arterial roads and a railway corridor, the property, being within 500 metres of the high-tide line, was in the control zone of the CRZ. The broad norm for the FSI available for development was 1.33 both under rule 10(1) of the DC Rules as well as the DCR. However, in terms of the DC Rules, there were certain exceptions and discretion reserved to government in terms of rule 10(2):

> 10(2). With the previous approval of Government the Floor Space Indices specified above, may be permitted to be exceeded in respect of buildings of Educational and Medical Relief Institutions and Government and Semi-Government Offices and Luxury Hotels and in respect of any building on the top of which any revolving structure is to be constructed as a place of public entertainment or amusement.

Suresh Estates decided to construct a luxury hotel and claimed an additional FSI of 3.73 beyond the permissible 1.33. It relied on the examples of the Taj and Oberoi hotels which had been granted an FSI of 5.32 when they put up towers much prior to 1991. Applying for permission on 26 December 2005, Suresh Estates claimed that with respect to FSI it was not governed by the extant 1991 DCR but by the DC Rules of 1967. This was because the CRZ Regulations (having entered the statute book one day prior to the DCR) provided:

> Buildings permitted ... shall be subject to the existing local Town and Country Planning Regulations including the existing norms of Floor Space Index/Floor Area Ratio.

Since the existing norms of FSI on 19 February 1991 were under the DC Rules, Suresh Estates claimed that it was these rules alone that were applicable.

---

[35] The High Court merely asked the state to decide within six weeks an application by the builder for additional FSI (floor space index).

The state government resisted Suresh Estates' submissions contending: (a) the DCR of 1991 applied, not the dead letter of the DC Rules of 1967; (b) the DCR had no provision for the grant of higher FSI for the hotel projects; (c) on the date the CRZ Regulations were enacted the planning authority was bound to have regard to the draft DCR of 1989 in terms of section 46 of the MRTP Act which did not recognize higher FSI for hotels; and (d) granting additional FSI was a matter of discretion and the state could not be compelled to exercise its discretion in favour of Suresh Estates.

Rendering judgment on 14 December 2007, the Supreme Court bought the appellant's primary submissions. It first resurrected the long extinct DC Rules of 1967. Then, by a feat of nimble jurisprudence, it declared Suresh Estates to be entitled to the discretionary FSI beyond 1.33 in terms of rule 10(2).

This is how the Supreme Court dealt with the state's objections regarding section 46 of the MRTP Act and the FSI norm of 1.33 prescribed in rule 10(1) of the DC Rules:

> (a) The draft regulations of 1989 were not in force as on 19-2-1991 and, therefore, would not apply to the plot in question. What is emphasised in section 46 of the MRTP Act, 1966 is that the Planning Authority should have due regard to the draft regulations. The legislature has not used the phrase 'must have regard' or 'shall have regard'. Municipal Corporation of Greater Mumbai which is the Planning Authority had given due regard to the draft DC Regulations of 1989 in the light of CRZ notification and recommended to the Government to grant additional FSI of 3.73 times permissible as per the Development Control Rules, 1967 over and above 1.33 permissible, to the appellants. Having regard to the facts of the case this Court is of the opinion that the contention that the Planning Authority has to take into consideration the draft regulations of 1989 and, therefore, the appellants would not be entitled to additional FSI, cannot be accepted and is hereby rejected.
>
> (b) The norm of FSI specified in rule 10(1) of the Rules of 1967 would be subject to the discretion to be exercised by the Government under rule 10(2) of the Rules. The norm as set out regarding FSI in the DC Rules of 1967 will have to be construed to mean also the norm of FSI which can be granted by the Government in exercise of discretion vested in it under rule 10(2) of the Rules of 1967. The case of the appellants is that normally all luxury hotels which had applied for additional FSI under rule 10(2) of the DC Rules, 1967 were allowed additional FSI. Having regard to the intention of the legislature the prevalent norm of FSI under rule 10(1) of the Rules, 1967 will have to be construed to mean also the norm of FSI which can be granted in exercise of discretion under rule 10(2) of the Rules. Therefore, the stand taken by the respondents that the appellants would not be entitled to more than 1.33 FSI in view of norm set out in the DC Rules of 1967 cannot be upheld and it is held that the question of grant of FSI would be subject to the discretion to be exercised by the competent authority under rule 10(2) of the Rules on analysis of objective facts placed before it.

Suresh Estates is a deeply flawed and disquieting judgment that potentially could drive a tank through Mumbai's DCR. The CRZ Regulations apply across the country and their clear intent is to ensure that buildings in this zone conform to local building regulations. The interpretation adopted by the Supreme Court suggests that all planning regulations 'existing' on 19 February 1991 stand frozen and cannot be altered. Thus, the Supreme Court resurrected the repealed DC Rules of 1967 that had outlived their utility and were replaced by the DCR of 1991.

At its narrowest, *Suresh Estates* implies that in the CRZ zone, the 1967 *FSI rules* continue to operate even though replaced by Mumbai's 1991 Development Plan prepared after an elaborate notice and comment process. And if this were not enough, a broader interpretation of *Suresh Estates* may mean that in the CRZ zone, *all aspects* of building regulation also continue to be governed by the 1967 DC Rules, notwithstanding the subsequent DCR. Consider the huge disruptive impact of the court's interpretation on planning and property rights. Could it ever have been the intention of the CRZ Regulations to disable thousands of towns and cities along the Indian coast from framing new regulations in response to changing times? What is a law-abiding citizen or administrator to do? Exhume long-buried laws?

The Supreme Court is startlingly wrong when it ignores the plain language of the expression 'existing norms of' FSI/FAR. The existing norm was obviously 1.33 specified in rule 10(1) and not the FSI granted to two hotels in exercise of the government's discretion. Besides, the effect of the Supreme Court judgment is exactly the opposite of what the CRZ notification intended. The CRZ Regulations intended to cap FSI to what obtained on 19 February 1991 but the Supreme Court's judgment removes the limit, leaving matters to the government's discretion.

How convincing is the Supreme Court's reasoning on section 46 of the MRTP Act? In making a distinction between the expressions 'shall have due regard to' 'must have regard' or 'shall have regard', is the court splitting hairs?

Bhuleshwar is a congested locality even by Mumbai's dense standard. Was it correct for the Supreme Court to virtually force the hand of government in a discretionary matter with regard to allowing a high rise luxury hotel to be built in a district already crammed with citizens and buildings?

Suresh Estates challenges our notion of common sense. CRZ Regulations framed under section 3(2)(v) the Environment (Protection) Act of 1986 are by their very nature restrictive. Here, Suresh Estates ingeniously utilized the CRZ Regulations to catapult to a higher FSI entitlement than otherwise available.

The judgment calls in question the utility of the CRZ Regulations in fully developed urban centres like Mumbai. How does regulating a plot separated from the sea by two major roads and a railway corridor protect the coast?

IV. LUTYENS' BUNGALOW ZONE

Named after the British architect Edwin Lutyens who designed the Imperial Capital, the Lutyens' Bungalow Zone (LBZ) comprises over 25 sq kms of stately avenues and lush residences, home to Independent India's political, administrative and judicial elite. Tanvi Trading and its co-purchasers bought a 5,000 sq yard plot on Amrita Shergil Marg on 28 October 1994. To make the most of this coveted address, the new owners asked the New Delhi Municipal Council (NDMC) to sanction a building plan for constructing a two-and-a-half-storey building with 15 dwelling units. NDMC rejected the plan on 17 June 1998 principally because it breached the LBZ Guidelines. The LBZ Guidelines issued on 8 February 1988 provided numerous restrictions including this norm:

> The new construction of dwelling on a plot must have the same plinth area as the existing bungalow and must have a height not exceeding the height of the bungalow in place, or if the plot is vacant, the height of the bungalow which is the lowest of those on the adjoining plots.

When administrative appeals failed, Tanvi Trading petitioned the Delhi High Court which rendered judgment in its favour. The division bench of the High Court quashed the rejection as being illegal and declared that the building plans submitted were deemed to have been sanctioned under the NDMC Act. NDMC was directed to return the building plans with an endorsement 'sanctioned' within the period specified in the order.

The Supreme Court justices, all denizens of LBZ, allowed NDMC's appeal.[36] They traced the source of power to issue the guidelines to Article 73 of the Constitution which recognizes that the executive power of the Union extends to matters with respect to which Parliament has power to make laws. This, however, would not be enough because an administrative direction (unless backed by statute) cannot impinge upon the constitutional property rights of the owner.

The Supreme Court attempted to overcome this gap with this abysmal reasoning:

> The record further shows that Zonal Development Plan ... was approved by [Delhi Development Authority] on 27-7-1993. During the pendency of the petition before the High Court, the Zonal Development Plan was approved by the Central Government on 1-10-1999 *excluding LBZ area* as contained in the Ministry's guidelines dated 8-2-1988. It means that the Central Government while approving the Zonal Development Plan *has approved* the Ministry's guidelines dated 8-2-1988 under the Act and therefore, in terms of section 12 of the Act neither the Authority nor the local authority could have sanctioned the plans submitted by the respondents, which were contrary to the Ministry's guidelines dated 8-2-1988. [Emphasis supplied]

This too may not be enough since Tanvi Trading had made its application on 20 April 1998, 17 months before the statutory approval in October 1999. The Supreme Court blocked this escape by shifting the goalposts from NDMC's initial rejection date (17 June 1998) to the date of an appellate order passed on 1 December 1999 which was challenged in the High Court. Having moved the date beyond 1 October 1999, the Supreme Court concluded:

> It is well settled that the law for approval of the building plan would be the date on which the approval is granted and not the date on which the plans are submitted. This is so in view of para 24 of the decision of this Court in *Usman Gani J Khatri v Cantonment Board* (1992) 3 SCC 455. It would not be out of place to mention that on 7-2-2007, the Master Plan, 2021 has been approved in which the LBZ guidelines have been incorporated and since the plan submitted by the respondents was not approved up to the date of coming into force of Master Plan of 2021, the LBZ guidelines will apply with full force to the plan submitted by the respondents and the plan which is contrary to the LBZ guidelines could not have been directed to be sanctioned.

Might the outcome of this case have been different had the locality in question been in a distant corner of the country unfamiliar to the judges of the Supreme Court?

V. DELHI BUS DEPOT

In 2011, Anand Arya approached the Delhi High Court in a public interest litigation challenging the construction of a bus depot by the Delhi government for use by the Delhi Transport Corporation (DTC). The depot was being built on a site described as a river flood plain in the Master Plan for Delhi 2021 (MPD 2021). The writ petitioner assailed the construction since it was contrary to the Master Plan, would adversely impact the ecology and the environment of the area and violate principles such as the public trust doctrine. DTC successfully resisted the grant of a temporary injunction, completed the depot and began operating 900 buses from the terminal. It spent near Rs. 100 crores to develop the infrastructure. DTC

[36] *NDMC v Tanvi Trading and Credit Pvt Ltd* (2008) 8 SCC 765.

acknowledged that the land was allotted for use as a bus depot during the Commonwealth Games held around October, 2010.

The High Court found that since the depot violated MPD 2021, construction carried out by DTC was impermissible. It granted DTC six months to have the Master Plan changed, failing which DTC would have to relocate the bus depot to an alternate site.

The MPD 2021 was not amended to reflect a bus depot and when six months had expired, contempt proceedings were initiated against the chairman and managing director (CMD) of DTC. The CMD filed an affidavit undertaking to the High Court that the site would be vacated on or before 31 October 2014. The undertaking was not adhered to and instead DTC applied to extend time.

The High Court would have none of this. It dismissed the application.

The government of the National Capital Territory (NCT) of Delhi and DTC petitioned the Supreme Court seeking special leave to appeal under Article 136 of the Constitution. DTC and NCT projected that there was a reasonable possibility of an amendment to MPD 2021. The Supreme Court noted the material placed by Arya:

> The Delhi Urban Art Commission (DUAC) after its inspection carried out on 2-11-2010 had directed both Delhi Development Authority (DDA) and DTC to vacate the riverbed and to ensure the removal of all the constructions carried out in the past.... Even the Shunglu Committee which was set up to go into the conduct of Commonwealth Games 2010 had adversely commented upon the construction of the said structure and in its report by observing as under:
>
> > All clearances were provided by the Lieutenant Governor for construction of a 'temporary' structure which was ostensibly to be dismantled after the conclusion of the Games. But this Project was implemented by the Transport Department, GNCTD and DTC right from the beginning as a 'permanent' structure. It appears as if the hosting of Commonwealth Games provided a pretext for 'land grab' by various government agencies after short-circuiting the established rules and procedures.
>
> In its affidavit filed by the DUAC, it also categorically mentioned that no proposal regarding the alleged construction was ever referred to the DUAC at any time and no sanction or approval was thus obtained.

The court concluded:

> Another significant development which was pointed out was the order dated 13-1-2015 of the National Green Tribunal passed in *Manoj Mishra v Union of India*.[37] That case pertains to cleaning of River Yamuna. In the aforesaid order, after comprehensively reviewing the situation in the light of various technical reports, etc. the Tribunal has given some directions which, *inter alia*, include the direction to all authorities concerned, including DDA, Municipal Corporations and the Government of NCT of Delhi, to take immediate and effective steps for identification of flood plain. The Tribunal has directed preparation of a map in this regard and physically demarcate the entire flood plain. There is also a direction to the Principal Committee to identify which structures were to be demolished and which ones were to be retained, in the interest of ecology and environment. The public interest in retaining the said bus depot was again emphasized and it was submitted that once the aforesaid exercise of demarcation of the entire flood plain is carried out by the Principal Committee, the

[37] *Manoj Misra v Union of India* OA No. 6 of 2012 and MAs Nos. 967 of 2013 and 275 of 2014, order dated 13 January 2015, (2015) SCC Online NGT 840.

stand of the appellants would be vindicated that the area in question where the bus depot has been constructed does not fall within the flood plain thereby paving way for the amendment of the Master Plan.

We have considered the respected submissions of the learned counsel for the parties on either side. As is clear from the tenure and spirit behind the orders dated 13-9-2012 passed by the High Court, the chance was given to the appellants to have the MPD 2021 amended if it was permissible in law and the period of six months was given for this purpose. This was done by the High Court keeping in view the submission of the appellants herein that the bus depot in question was constructed to serve greater public purpose; the area in question was, as a matter of fact, was not falling on the riverbed; and there was no threat to environment or ecology in having the bus depot at the given site. Exercise to consider the aforesaid aspect has not taken place, or for some reason or the other, whether it was because of dispute … on the issue of land ownership or otherwise. However, the development which have taken place in recent times, particularly the orders of the National Green Tribunal, point out to the fact that things have started moving and it would be known in near future as a result of study conducted by the Expert Committee, whether area in question where the bus depot stands, is viable for this purpose or not, directing DTC to demolish the bus depot at this juncture may not be appropriate and the decision in this regard can be deferred for some time to await the outcome of the report of the identification of flood plain.

Accordingly, we dispose of these appeals by granting one year's time to DTC during which period DTC shall either get the MPD 2021 amended, failing which it shall shift the depot in question. We make it clear that no further time on any ground whatsoever shall be granted in this behalf.

NOTES AND QUESTIONS

1. Was the Supreme Court justified in exercising its discretionary jurisdiction under Article 136? Did the case involve a substantial question of law? The appellant had breached the undertaking to the High Court to vacate the site before 31 October 2014. By granting an additional year's time (till 4 February 2017) did the Supreme Court weaken the administration of justice? Will this not encourage high government officials (here it was the CMD, DTC) to furnish undertakings to fob off contempt and after breaching the timeline hand the case to a legal wizard to pursue an appeal?

2. The conduct of DTC was brazen at every stage. It treated the temporary allotment of land for the Commonwealth Games as a licence to establish a permanent bus depot, it constructed the depot contrary to MPD 2021 and it failed to abide by an undertaking. While this conduct reflects poorly on DTC's and NCT's regard for town planning and environmental protection, it also sanctifies the age-old advice that Supreme Court lawyers give their clients: 'Take a chance and file a special leave petition.'

VI. CALCUTTA TAJ HOTEL

Obviously, each case is different. The judges involved have different inclinations and values; the quantum of public benefit varies from one development project to the next and the court may sometimes be influenced—favourably or unfavourably—by the political status of the parties. While judges are seldom wholly 'pro-environment' or wholly 'pro-development', their preference for certain outcomes undoubtedly influences their response to particular arguments of the parties before them. It is hard to imagine how the judicial system can operate differently, and still enable judges to respond flexibly and creatively to grievances and disputes that reach the courts.

Sachidanand Pandey v State of West Bengal is not merely another town planning case but a ringing endorsement of the courts' duty to protect the environment. Here, the duly authorized construction of a medium-rise five-star hotel was alleged to interfere with the flight path of migratory birds, and the Supreme Court inquired extensively into this question. If migratory birds are worthy of the court's attention, *a fortiori* the court's protection would extend to environmental issues of more direct impact on human beings.

The land on which the hotel was to be constructed formerly belonged to the Alipore Zoological Garden and was put to important zoo-related uses. The zoo directors had withdrawn their objections to the hotel after the government promised them adjacent lands and relocation grants, and the hoteliers agreed to reconstruct all displaced facilities on the adjacent lands, at no expense to the zoo.

SACHIDANAND PANDEY v STATE OF WEST BENGAL

AIR 1987 SC 1109

Chinnappa Reddy, J: * * *

Today society's interaction with nature is so extensive that the environmental question has assumed proportions affecting all humanity....

In India, as elsewhere in the world, uncontrolled growth and the consequent environmental deterioration are fast assuming menacing proportions and all Indian cities are afflicted with this problem. The once Imperial City of Calcutta is no exception. The question raised in the present case is whether the Government of West Bengal has shown such lack of awareness of the problem of environment in making an allotment of land for the construction of a Five Star Hotel at the expense of the zoological garden that it warrants interference by this Court. Obviously, if the Government is alive to the various considerations requiring thought and deliberation and has arrived at a conscious decision after taking them into account, it may not be for this Court to interfere in the absence of mala fides. On the other hand, if relevant considerations are not borne in mind and irrelevant considerations influence the decision, the Court may interfere in order to prevent a likelihood of prejudice to the public. Whenever a problem of ecology is brought before the Court, the Court is bound to bear in mind Art. 48-A of the Constitution, Directive Principle which enjoins that 'The State shall endeavour to protect and improve the environment and to safeguard the forests and wild life of the country,' and Art. 51-A(g) which proclaims it to be the fundamental duty of every citizen of India 'to protect and improve the natural environment including forests, lakes, rivers and wild life, and to have compassion for living creatures.' When the Court is called upon to give effect to the Directive Principle and fundamental duty, the Court is not to shrug its shoulders and say that priorities are a matter of policy and so it is a matter for the policy-making authority. The least that the Court may do is to examine whether appropriate considerations are borne in mind and irrelevancies are excluded. In appropriate cases, the Court may go further, but how much further must depend on the circumstances of the case. The Court may always give necessary directions. However the Court will not attempt to nicely balance relevant considerations. When the question involves the nice balancing of relevant considerations, the Court may feel justified in resigning itself to acceptance of the decision of the concerned authority....

Bearing in mind the proper approach that we have to make when questions of ecology and environment are raised, an approach which we have mentioned at the outset, we are satisfied that the facts and circumstances brought out by the appellants do not justify an inference that the construction of the proposed hotel in the Begumbari land would interfere in any manner with the animals in the Zoo and the birds arriving at the Zoo or otherwise disturb the ecology: The proposed hotel is a garden-hotel and there is perhaps every chance of the ecology and environment improving as a result of planting numerous trees all around the proposed hotel and the removal of the burial ground and dumping ground for rubbish....

On a consideration of all the facts and circumstances of the case, we are satisfied that the Government of West Bengal acted perfectly bona fide in granting the lease of Begumbari land to the Taj Group of Hotels for the construction of a Five Star Hotel in Calcutta. The Government of West Bengal did not fail to take into account any relevant consideration. Its action was not against the interests of the Zoological Garden or not in the best interests of the animal inmates of the zoo or migrant birds visiting the zoo. The financial interests of the State were in no way sacrificed either by not inviting tenders or holding a public auction or by adopting the 'net sales' method. In the result, the judgments of the learned single Judge and the Division Bench of the Calcutta High Court are affirmed and the appeal is dismissed. In the circumstances of the case, we do not desire to award any costs.

NOTES AND QUESTIONS

1. Sachidanand Pandey is an exceptionally long and detailed case, a product of much pains-taking effort by the court. Each major point is gone into several times. Was it worth all this effort? Most of the issues had already been resolved in negotiations among the zoo directors, the hoteliers and the state government. Was this a wise use of judicial time, especially when the courts have such a large backload of cases?

2. The proposed five-star hotel in question was to be a medium-rise six-storey structure within an area containing several much taller structures. Should not the court have taken judicial notice of the areas' architectural configuration and dismissed the ornithological concerns on that count alone?

3. In a concurring opinion, Khalid, J deplores the time, energy and expense involved in this public interest litigation, and suggests that a flood of rash or ill-conceived public interest litigations may abuse the judicial process and unduly impose on the hospitality and patience of the judiciary. He worries that instead of dispensing justice, the courts will be pushed by public interest litigants to assume administrative and executive functions.

D. PUBLIC PARKS

Among the strongest town planning judgments rendered by the Supreme Court is the *Bangalore Medical Trust* case. It has two important pro-citizen dimensions. It lays down that power exercised under an environmental statute must further the legislative object of the Act. Further, it invalidates a favour by the Karnataka Chief Minister on the ground that it was in breach of public trust since it deprived Bangalore residents of a public park. We excerpt from Justice Sahai's opinion disapproving the intended change of user to enable a private nursing home to be built.

BANGALORE MEDICAL TRUST v B S MUDDAPPA

AIR 1991 SC 1902

R M Sahai, J:

***

Public park as a place reserved for beauty and recreation was developed in 19th and 20th century and is associated with growth of the concept of equality and recognition of importance of common man. Earlier it was a prerogative of the aristocracy and the affluent either as a result of royal grant or as a place reserved for private pleasure. Free and healthy air in beautiful surroundings was privilege of few. But now it is a 'gift from people to themselves'. Its importance has multiplied with emphasis on environment and pollution. In modern planning and development, it occupies an important place in social ecology. A private nursing home on the other hand is essentially a commercial venture, a profit oriented industry. Service may be its motto but earning is the objective. Its utility may not be undermined but a park is a necessity, not a mere amenity. A private nursing home cannot be a substitute for a public park. No town planner would prepare a blueprint without reserving space for it. Emphasis on open air and greenery has multiplied and the city or town planning or development Acts of different states require even private house owners to leave open space in front and back for lawn and fresh air. In 1984 the [Bangalore Development Authority Act of 1976 as amended] itself provided for reservation of not less than 15 per cent of the total area of the layout in a development scheme for public parks and playgrounds the sale and disposition of which is prohibited under section 38-A of the Act. Absence of open space and public park, in present day when urbanization is on increase, rural exodus is on large scale and congested areas are coming up rapidly, may give rise to health hazard. May be that it may be taken care of by a nursing home. But it is axiomatic that prevention is better than cure. What is lost by removal of a park cannot be gained by establishment of a nursing home. To say, therefore, that by conversion of a site reserved for low lying park into a private nursing home social welfare was being promoted was being oblivious of true character of the two and their utility....

Did the Division Bench commit any error of law? Was the conversion of site in accordance with law? Were any of the authorities aware or apprised of the provisions under which they could convert a site reserved for public park into a nursing home? Did the authorities care to ascertain the provisions of law or rules under which they could act? Was any precaution taken by the Chief Executive of the state to adhere to legislative requirement of altering any scheme? Not in the least. The direction of the Chief Minister, the apex public functionary of the state, was in breach of public trust, more like a person dealing with his private property than discharging his obligation as head of the state administration in accordance with law and rules. The government record depicted an even more distressing picture. The role of the administration was highly disappointing. This culture of public functionary, adorning highest office in the state of being law to himself and the administration acting on dictate, for whatever reason disturbs the balance of rule of law. What is more shocking is that this happened in 1976 and not even one out of various departments from which the papers were routed through raised any objection. And the statutory body like [The Bangalore Development Authority, (BDA)] with impressive members too succumbed under the pressure without, even, a murmur.

Financial gain by a local authority at the cost of public welfare has never been considered as legitimate purpose even if the objective is laudable. Sadly, the law was thrown to winds for a private purpose. The extract of the Chief Minister's order quoted in the letter of Chairman of the BDA leaves no doubt that the end result having been decided by the highest executive in the state the lower in order of hierarchy only followed with 'ifs' and 'buts' ending finally with resolution of BDA which was more or less a formality. Between 21 April and 14 July 1976, that is less than ninety days, the machinery in BDA and government moved so swiftly that the initiation of the proposal by the appellant, a rich trust with 90,000 dollars in foreign deposits, query on it by the Chief Minister of the state, guidance of way out by the Chairman, direction on it by the Chief Minister, orders of Government resolution by the BDA and allotment were all completed and the site for public park stood converted into site for private nursing home without any intimation direct or indirect to those who were being deprived of it. Speedy or quick action in public institutions call for appreciation but our democratic system shuns exercise of individualized discretion in public matters requiring participatory decision by rules and regulations. No one howsoever high can arrogate to himself or assume without any authorization, express or implied in law, a discretion to ignore the rules and deviate from rationality by adopting a strained or distorted interpretation as it renders the action ultra vires and bad in law. Where the law requires an authority to act or decide, 'if it appears to it necessary' or if he is 'of opinion that a particular act should be done' then it is implicit that it should be done objectively, fairly and reasonably. Decisions affecting public interest or the necessity of doing it in the light of guidance provided by the Act and rules may not require intimation to person affected yet the exercise of discretion is vitiated if the action is bereft of rationality, lacks objective and purposive approach. The action and decision must not only be reached reasonably and intelligibly but it must be related to the purpose for which power is exercised. The purpose for which the Act was enacted is spelt out from the Preamble itself which provides for establishment of the Authority for development of the city of Bangalore and areas adjacent thereto. To carry out this purpose the development scheme framed by the Improvement Trust was adopted by the Development Authority. Any alteration in this scheme could have been made as provided in sub-section (4) of section 19 only if it resulted in improvement in any part of the scheme. As stated earlier a private nursing home could neither be considered to be an amenity nor it could be considered improvement over necessity like a public park. The exercise of power, therefore, was contrary to the purpose for which it is conferred under the statute....

NOTES AND QUESTIONS

1. Justice Thommen in his concurring opinion emphasized the importance of public spaces. Referring to Indian and foreign statutes as well as English and American case law, he held that the reservation of open spaces for parks and playgrounds was a legislative attempt to eliminate the ill-effects of urbanization. Open spaces for recreation and fresh air, playgrounds for children and promenades for residents were vital to any urban development scheme. These public spaces could not be privatized to the detriment of the citizenry.

2. Both Justice Thommen and Justice Sahai recognized the *locus standi* of residents to challenge government decisions destructive of the environment in their locality. The residents of a locality were the persons directly affected by an adverse town planning decision and could not be termed busybodies or interlopers.[38]

3. Section 65 of the BDA Act empowered the Karnataka government to give such directions to the BDA as were, in its opinion, necessary or expedient for carrying out the purposes of the Act. The BDA was bound by such directions. The state government argued that even if the BDA had not followed the statutory procedure for changing the user, the result was lawful since the Chief Minister's directions were protected by section 65. The Supreme Court rejected the plea. It was not open to the state government to give directions to the BDA that defied the very object of the Act. What was not permitted to be done by the BDA could not be legitimized by the state under section 65. For a direction issued under section 65 to be valid, it must advance the object of the Act.

4. Discretionary power under environmental statutes is sometimes exercised for ends that apparently conflict with the object of the law. For example, the power of government to alter the boundary of a sanctuary under the Wild Life Protection Act of 1972 has on occasion been exercised to de-notify large tracts and deprive wildlife and its habitat of protection. This may not be permissible under the *Bangalore Medical Trust* judgment.[39] The court held that the exercise of discretionary power must be related to the purpose of the statute. In Justice Thommen's words, 'Any repository of power—be it the government or the BDA—must act reasonably and rationally and in accordance with law and with due regard to the legislative intent.'

---

[38] A similar view was expressed in *K Ramdas Shenoy v The Chief Officers, Town Municipal Council, Udipi* AIR 1974 SC 2177.

[39] In *Indian Council for Enviro-Legal Action v Union of India* (*CRZ Notification* case) (1996) 5 SCC 281, the Supreme Court went further and held that amendments to delegated legislation would be *ultra vires* where they were contrary to the object of the Environment (Protection) Act of 1986 or were likely to result in ecological degradation.

5. What might have been the outcome of the case if a site reserved for a private hospital had been converted on the diktat of the Chief Minister into a public park?

6. The principles laid down in *Bangalore Medical Trust* are regularly applied by the Supreme Court. One such case is *Purushottam v State of Karnataka*,[40] where the facts as narrated in the judgment are confusing.[41] The writ petitioners before the Karnataka High Court were keen on a park or playground in the vicinity of their residential layout. They urged the court to quash an allotment made on 4 August 2005 by the Bangalore Development Authority (BDA) in favour of Bharat Petroleum Corporation Ltd (BPCL) for establishing a petrol station. The allotment was followed by a 30-year lease and BPCL, a public sector undertaking, began operating the petrol station through its dealer.

Earlier in 1984, the site was earmarked in the Bangalore Development Plan for a park or playground. The plan was revised to accommodate reservoirs needed for city water supply and residential sites. Apart from this site, the only other nearby land designated for a park was used as a cemetery. After the carve-outs, all that remained of the park envisioned in 1984 was a plot earmarked for a bank.

The expression 'amenity', as defined in section 2(bb) of the Bangalore Development Authority Act, 1976, covered both banks and petrol retail outlets. Both the BDA and BPCL contended that the designation or re-designation of an amenity was the planning authority's prerogative and there was no illegality as long as *some* public amenity existed at the site. The recognized need for a petrol station in the locality was the reason for the BPCL allocation.

The High Court found that since the subject site at the time of its allotment to BPCL was expressly earmarked for use as a 'bank', the allotment amounted to a transgression of section 38A of the BDA Act. Section 38A reads:

> 38-A. *Grant of area reserved for civic amenities, etc.* — (1) The Authority shall have the power to lease, sell or otherwise transfer any area reserved for civic amenities for the purpose for which such area is reserved.
>
> (2) The Authority shall not sell or otherwise dispose off any area reserved for public parks and playgrounds and civic amenities, for any other purpose and any disposition so made shall be null and void:
>
> Provided that where the allottee commits breach of any of the conditions of allotment, the Authority shall have right to resume such site after affording an opportunity of being heard to such allottee.

The Supreme Court agreed with the High Court and held that even though both bank and petrol pump were civic amenities, BDA could not change the reservation from one particular user to another without a necessary amendment in the development plan.[42]

Though the writ petitioners clearly triumphed, their gain is unclear: the allotment in favour of the petrol pump was set aside, but there was no direction to develop a park. Perhaps the Supreme Court's observations in *Purushottam* stressing the importance of parks and playgrounds may encourage residents to lobby BDA to restore the 1984 reservation on the patch of open space that remained.

---

[40] (2014) 3 SCC 721.

[41] The reader may reconstruct the facts from the report. The authors' summary is at best one manner of reconciling the inconsistencies.

[42] It is unclear from the judgment whether the *zoning map* showed 'amenity' generally or 'bank' specifically. (The earmarking of 'bank', 'petrol pump', etc. was probably done administratively by BDA resolution.)

7.*Suresh Mehta v State of Rajasthan*[43] provides a startling contrast to *Bangalore Medical Trust*. Mehta petitioned the Rajasthan High Court to quash the allotment of open land to the Jodhpur Medical Research Centre Trust, which proposed to establish a hospital on the plot. The petitioner asked that the open land be used as a public park since in a previous litigation in respect of the same site the government had assured the High Court that the land would be maintained as a park. On this assurance, the previous petition was dismissed. This time, in the absence of a land use map designating the site as a park, the High Court declined to hold the government to its assurance. 'The land was described as open land and could not be held to be meant for use of park.' The division bench made light of the *Bangalore Medical Trust* precedent: 'Each decision is an authority [for] what it decides.' One might expect greater deference to a Supreme Court judgment also dealing with the diversion of an open plot for a private hospital. Among the factors that may have persuaded the High Court to a different view were the doubt in respect of the petitioner's motive, the completion of the hospital during the pendency of the case and an 'unjustified outburst' by counsel for the petitioner against the judges constituting the bench.

8. Justice N L Tibrewal of the Rajasthan High Court was more vigorous in applying the *Bangalore Medical Trust* ratio to save a park in Jaipur from being changed to a school.[44] Declaring the allotment in favour of the school illegal, the court held that the residents of a locality have a right to be heard before being deprived of a public space. The High Court also directed the respondent to list all open spaces in Jaipur and to prepare a scheme for preserving these spaces.

Contrast the outcomes of the *Suresh Mehta* and *Nizam* cases. Both are judgments of the Rajasthan High Court. Is the law relating to public parks and open spaces certain? Is it predictable?

9. M C Mehta, the public-spirited advocate and environmentalist, successfully obtained directions restricting the use of public parks for marriages or commercial purposes;[45] prohibiting the Delhi Chief Minister from running a camp office in a public park;[46] clearing the Delhi Ridge area from unauthorized encroachments,[47] including eleven places of worship;[48] and protecting Asola Wildlife Sanctuary within the National Capital Territory from degradation.[49]

10. In the case of *C R Dalvi v Municipal Corporation of Greater Bombay*,[50] a few Bombay residents brought an action to stop all commercial uses of a particular playground, claiming that those commercial uses illegally interfered with the enjoyment of the playground by the neighbourhood children. The court, on its own initiative, widened the scope of the case to include all playgrounds in Bombay. The court recognized both the importance and the scarcity of open recreational space within the city. It crafted a sensible and fair ruling, viz., that smaller playgrounds (less than 5,000 sq m) are not to be hired out at all. Larger playgrounds (more than 5,000 sq m) are to be divided into halves—one half to be reserved exclusively for recreation and the other half available for hire (but not for circuses, film shoots or fairs) for a

43 AIR 1993 Raj 61.
44 *Nizam v Jaipur Development Authority* AIR 1994 Raj 87.
45 1997 (6) Scale 13 (SP).
46 1997 (6) Scale 14 (SP).
47 1996 (1) Scale 22 and 1996 (3) Scale 51 (SP).
48 1996 (2) Scale 55 (SP) and 1996 (3) Scale 37 (SP).
49 1996 (2) Scale 55 (SP); 1996 (2) Scale 81 (SP); 1996 (3) Scale 20 (SP) and 1996 (3) Scale 37 (SP).
50 1987 Mah L J 373.

period not exceeding one day. The *C R Dalvi* case held the field for a decade until negated by an amendment to the Maharashtra Regional and Town Planning Act in 1997. The amendment empowered the state government or the planning authority to permit playgrounds to be used for up to 30 days in a year for 'national events and religious functions'. To overcome the *C R Dalvi* judgment, the new provision declares, 'Notwithstanding anything contained in ... any judgment, order or direction of any court ... such use shall not be deemed to be a change of user.' Is the new provision constitutional? On what grounds might you assail it?

11. The Borivali National Park is a unique preserve of wilderness within the densely populated Mumbai metropolitan region. The park supports several species of birds, reptiles and large mammals including the leopard. The city exerts a constant pressure on the fringes of the reserve and according to the park authorities illegal quarrying and extensive encroachments by thousands of poor squatters are degrading the forest. Remote sensing imagery reveals that around 772 hectares of park land are encroached, mainly by hutments (512 ha) and quarries (111 ha). The continuous human intervention—vehicles, commercial shops and stores, slums, quarries—disturbs the wildlife and damages the natural habitat.

In 1995, the Bombay Environmental Action Group filed a writ petition in the Bombay High Court seeking effective measures by the government to protect the National Park.[51] Through a series of orders, the High Court attempted to strengthen the protective framework. On 12 February 1997, the court constituted a committee to recommend measures for preventing further encroachment of the forest and curbing illegal activities within the park. Based on the recommendations of the committee, on 7 May 1997, the High Court restricted public transport within the National Park area, ordered the disconnection of telephone lines, restrained the authorities from permitting any commercial or industrial activity within the park and directed the prosecution of persons refusing to vacate forest land. The state government was directed to increase the strength of the forest staff and to provide adequate infrastructure and equipment to enable effective policing of the region. The state government was also given 18 months to relocate thousands of slum dwellers outside the park boundary and to demolish the illegal structures.

Implementation of the court's directions was resisted by stallholders who catered food and beverages to visitors. Several of them claimed that they had been running their business for more than three decades and that the High Court's directions would deprive them of their livelihood. The Bombay High Court declined to modify its 7 May 1997 order since unauthorized non-forest activities were not permissible within a National Park and the court's previous directions allowed sufficient time to the unauthorized occupants to vacate their premises.[52]

On 23 March 1998, the Bombay High Court issued further directions requiring a factory located within the park to shift out, directing the state to appoint two public prosecutors to deal exclusively with forest cases and ordering the electricity utility to disconnect illegal power connections provided in the National Park.

Reviewing implementation measures, in March 2000 the High Court found that several encroachers had refused to move away from the park and avail of alternative pitches under the court-approved relocation scheme. Finding that the time had come 'to send a clear message',

---

[51] *Bombay Environmental Action Group v A R Bharati, Deputy Conservator of Forests*, Writ Petition No. 305 of 1995.

[52] *Anil Kumar K. Parekh v Municipal Corporation for Greater Mumbai*, Writ Petition No. 803 of 1997, 12 June 1997. The Supreme Court dismissed SLP (Civil) No. 19050/97 on 20 October 1997.

the High Court gave a final opportunity to the squatters to shift out or else face forcible eviction.[53]

12. In *Almitra H Patel v Union of India*, the Supreme Court issued a warning against the encroachment of public lands.

> Establishment or creating of slums, it seems, appears to be good business and is well organised.... Large areas of public land, in this way, are usurped for private use free of cost. It is difficult to believe that this can happen in the capital without passive or active connivance of the land owning agencies and/or the municipal authorities.... Rewarding an encroacher on public land with free alternate site is like giving a reward to a pickpocket. The department of slum clearance does not appear to have cleared any slum despite its being in existence for decades.[54]

As a first step, the court directed the authorities to prevent fresh encroachments. How effective is this direction likely to be? Can slums be banished without addressing the underlying social and economic causes? What about the right to the city? Was it fair on the part of the court to equate citizens forced to migrate to cities and live in slums, to pickpockets?

In July 1999, the Supreme Court delivered a strong judgment against the illegal development of an underground market below a public park in Lucknow. The petitioners in the High Court were city corporators who challenged the agreement between the municipal corporation and the builder on the grounds that it was contrary to statute and was executed with doubtful motives.

M I BUILDERS PVT LTD v RADHEY SHYAM SAHU

AIR 1999 SC 2468

D P Wadhwa, J: These appeals are directed against the judgment dated 23 August 1994 of a Division Bench of the High Court of Judicature at Allahabad, (Lucknow Bench). By a common judgment in three writ petitions, the High Court speaking through Shobha Dixit, J held that the decision of the Lucknow Nagar Mahapalika ('Mahapalika' for short) (is now called Nagar Nigam or Corporation) permitting M I Builders Pvt Ltd (the appellant herein) to construct underground shopping complex in the Jhandewala Park ... situated at Aminabad Market, Lucknow, was illegal, arbitrary and unconstitutional. High Court set aside and quashed the relevant resolution of the Mahapalika permitting such construction and also the agreement dated 4 November 1993 entered into between the Mahapalika and the appellant for the purpose. Writ of mandamus was issued to the Mahapalika to restore back the park in its original position within a period of three months from the date of the judgment and till that was done, to take adequate safety measures and to provide necessary safeguard and protection to the public users of the park. High Court had noticed that the fact that the park was of historical importance was not denied by the Mahapalika and also the fact that (preservation) or maintenance of the park was necessary from the environmental angle and that only reason advanced by the Mahapalika for construction of the underground commercial complex was to ease the congestion in area. High Court, however, took judicial notice of the conditions prevailing at the Aminabad market. It said it was so crowded that it was bursting from all its seams. Construction of the underground shopping complex in question would only complicate the situation and that the present scheme would further congest the area. It said that the public purpose, which is alleged to be served by construction of the underground commercial complex, seemed totally illusory.

---

[53] *Bombay Environmental Action Group v A R Bharati, Deputy Conservator of Forests*, Writ Petition No. 305 of 1995, orders dated 2 March 2000 and 13 March 2000.

[54] (2000) 2 SCC 679, 685.

Aggrieved by the impugned judgment of the High Court, appellant has come to this Court....

Jhandewala Park, the park in question, has been in existence for a great number of years. It is situated in the heart of Aminabad a bustling commercial-cum-residential locality in the city of Lucknow. The park is of historical importance. Because of the construction of underground shopping complex and parking it may still have the appearance of a park with grass grown and path laid but it has lost the ingredients of a park inasmuch as no plantation now can be grown. Trees cannot be planted and rather while making underground construction many trees have been cut. Now it is more like a terrace park. Qualitatively it may still be a park but it is certainly a park of different nature. By construction of underground shopping complex irreversible changes have been made. It was submitted that the park was acquired by the state Government in the year 1913 and was given to the Mahapalika for its management. This has not been controverted. Under section 114 of the [Municipal Corporation Act] it is the obligatory duty of the Mahapalika to maintain public places, parks and plant trees. By allowing underground construction Mahapalika has deprived itself of its obligatory duties to maintain the park which cannot be permitted. But then one of the obligatory functions of the Mahapalika under section 114 is also to construct and maintain parking lots. To that extent some area of the park could be used for the purpose of constructing underground parking lot. But that can only be done after proper study has been made of the locality, including density of the population living in the area, the floating population and other certain relevant considerations. This study was never done. Mahapalika is the trustee for the proper management of the park. When true nature of the park, as it existed, is destroyed it would be violative of the doctrine of public trust as expounded by this Court in *Span Resort Case* (1997) 1 SCC 388. Public Trust doctrine is part of Indian law....

It is not disputed that there is a Master Plan applicable to city of Lucknow. This Master Plan is prepared under the Development Act. It was submitted by the builder that the park could be exploited for commercial purposes as Aminabad has been shown to be a commercial area. No doubt Aminabad is a commercial area but that does not mean that the park can be utilized for commercial purposes. Rather using the park for commercial purposes would be against the Master Plan....

The facts and circumstances when examined point to only one conclusion that the purpose of constructing the underground shopping complex was a mere pretext and the dominant purpose was to favour the M I Builders to earn huge profits. In depriving the citizens of Lucknow of their amenity of an old historical park in the congested area on the specious plea of decongesting the area, Mahapalika and its officers forgot their duty towards the citizens and acted in a most brazen manner....

Now construction of shops will bring in more congestion and with that the area will get more polluted. Any commercial activity now in this unauthorized construction will put additional burden on the locality. Primary concern of the Court is to eliminate the negative impact the underground shopping complex will have on environment conditions in the area and the congestion that will aggravate on account of increased traffic and people visiting the complex. There is no alternative to this except to dismantle the whole structure and restore the park to its original condition leaving a portion constructed for parking. We are aware that it may not be possible to restore the park fully to its original condition as many trees have been chopped off and it will take years for the trees now to be planted to grow. But beginning has to be made....

NOTES

1. The bench noticed that a number of cases were reaching the court, pointing to unauthorized constructions at many places in the country. The Supreme Court held that in such

cases, in addition to directing demolition, the court ought to direct an inquiry to bring the offenders to book.

2. Before the High Court, the municipal corporation resisted the petitions and in 1994 appealed to the Supreme Court against the High Court judgment. In August 1996, the corporation resolved to withdraw the appeals and resist the developer. At the final hearing in the Supreme Court, M I Builders invoked the principle of estoppel by pleading to tie down the corporation to its original stand. The Supreme Court rejected this plea, holding that the contract violated the statute and there could be no estoppel against a statute.

3. Though 80% of the market was complete and 50 prospective allottees had paid the builder for their shops, the court directed demolition. The bench held: 'Unauthorized construction, if it is illegal and cannot be compounded, has to be demolished. There is no way out. Judicial discretion cannot be guided by expediency.'

When a municipality seeks to demolish an illegal structure, it must provide adequate notice and furnish an opportunity to the occupant. To discourage municipalities from riding roughshod over citizens' rights, the Bombay High Court allowed reconstruction where the demolition was in breach of the procedure. The Supreme Court considered this issue in *Sunbeam* and further directed municipal corporations in Maharashtra to employ modern technologies to detect and discourage illegal constructions.

MUN CORP OF GR MUMBAI v SUNBEAM HIGH TECH DEV PVT LTD
(2019) 20 SCC 781

Deepak Gupta, J: The issue involved in these appeals is whether if a municipal corporation demolishes a structure in exercise of powers vested in it but in violation of the procedure prescribed, can the High Court direct the 'owner/occupier' of the building to reconstruct the demolished structure?

The municipal corporations in the State of Maharashtra like in any other part of the country are vested with the power to demolish structures which violate the laws and have been built without any building plans or in violation of the laws. The exercise of the power of demolition which affects the property of the citizens of this country must be exercised in an absolutely fair and transparent manner. Rules in this regard must be followed. At the same time, the Court has to balance the private interest with the larger public interest. Cities and towns must be well planned and illegal structures must be demolished. Rule of law comprises not only of the principles of natural justice but also provides that the procedure prescribed by law must be followed. Rule of law also envisages that illegal constructions which are constructed in violation of law must be demolished and there can be no sympathy towards those who violate law....

We are constrained to observe that we cannot approve of such directions [issued by Bombay High Court permitting reconstruction of the structure using the same material and of the same dimensions]. The High Court itself is aware that some of these structures may have been constructed without permission. If that be so, even if the demolition was carried out without giving the second notice, why should the party who has violated the law by raising the construction without obtaining permission be permitted to raise another illegal structure which only has to be razed to the ground, after following the procedure prescribed by law? Why should the Nation's wealth be misutilised and misused for raising an illegal construction which eventually has to be demolished?

We make it clear that we do not approve the action of the Municipal Corporation or its officials in demolishing the structures without following the procedure prescribed by law, but the relief which has to be given must be in accordance with law and not violative of the law. If a structure is an illegal structure, even though it has been demolished illegally, such a structure should not be permitted to come up again. If the Municipal Corporation violates the procedure while demolishing the building but the structure is totally illegal, some compensation can be awarded and, in all cases where such compensation is awarded the same should invariably be recovered from the officers who have acted in violation of law. However, we again reiterate that the illegal structure cannot be permitted to be re-erected....

[Referring to modern technologies and the need for amending laws, the Court issued directions.] Till the State frames any laws in this regard, we direct that before any construction/reconstruction, or repair not being a tenantable repair is carried out, the owner/occupier/builder/contractor/architect, in fact all of them should be required to furnish a plan of the structure as it exists. This map can be taken on record and, thereafter, the construction can be permitted. In such an eventuality even if the demolition is illegal it will be easy to know what were the dimensions of the building. This information should not only be in paper form in the nature of a plan, but should also be in the form of 3D visual information, in the nature of photographs, videos etc.

All over the country we find that when people raise illegal constructions it is claimed that the said construction has been existing for long. The answer is to get Geomapping done. The relevant technology is Geographic Information System (GIS). If on Google Maps one can get a road view, we see no reason as to why this technology cannot be used by the municipal corporations. At the first stage we direct that all the cities in Maharashtra where the population is 50 lakhs or more the municipal authorities will get Geomapping done not only of the municipal areas but also of areas 10 kms from the outer boundary. This can be done by satellite, drones or vehicles. Once one has the whole city geomapped it would be easy to control illegal constructions. We further direct the State of Maharashtra to ensure that sufficient funds are made available to the municipal corporations concerned and this exercise should be completed within a period of one year from the date of this order....

NOTES AND QUESTIONS

1. Across the country, the poor and those living on the margins often live and work from structures where there are no sanctioned building plans. Has the Supreme Court taken away an important safeguard available to the disadvantaged? Previously, occupants were secure in the belief that should their structures be demolished without following the proper procedure, they would get back their structure through a vigilant High Court.

2. Another pervasive problem is that municipal officials engage in rent seeking before sanctioning building plans and issuing completion certificates, leaving the citizen with few choices.

3. Are the directions practical?

E. SOLID WASTE MANAGEMENT

Municipal solid waste (MSW) management or garbage disposal is a neglected area of urban development. Most cities are unable to fully treat the MSW generated. The urban poor bear the immediate impact of the resulting unhygienic conditions but few city dwellers escape the periodic outbreaks of diseases that spread in unhealthy urban environments. Municipal waste is generally carried to the city periphery where it is dumped in open landfills on neighbouring village lands. These dump sites are poorly managed and are swarmed by vermin and mosquitoes. Composting is seldom practised and the groundwater in some areas is contaminated by leachate.

The magnitude of the problem prompted Almitra Patel of Bangalore to file an Article 32 writ petition before the Supreme Court, seeking writs against the states and principal municipalities to implement 'cradle to grave' MSW management. In the wake of the Surat plague of 1994, Patel campaigned across the country urging municipalities to clean up their act. Though many of the municipal officers were receptive to her suggestions, few displayed the initiative to secure budgetary support and political backing to implement comprehensive MSW management measures.

On 3 March 1997, the Supreme Court directed the respondents to furnish details in respect of existing MSW practices adopted by them.[55] Since the affidavits filed by some municipalities and states were inadequate, in April 1997 they were asked to report whether the recommendations made by the High Power Committee set up by the Planning Commission in 1995 and the 1994 report of the Central Pollution Control Board (CPCB) on the management of municipal wastes, had been implemented.[56] On 28 July 1997, the respondents were told to frame time-bound schemes for the disposal of MSW in a scientific and hygienic manner. In framing the schemes, the local bodies were directed to seek expert advice on vector control and were urged 'immediately to take steps to phase out the routine use of insecticides like DDT and BHC and similar dangerous insecticides on garbage heaps and dump sites'. Nearly a quarter century after the Water Act was passed, the Central and state pollution control boards were directed to ensure that local bodies complied with the provisions of the Act.[57]

In January 1998, the Supreme Court constituted an Expert Committee to examine all aspects of MSW management in Class I cities (having a population over one lakh). The committee's charter extended to reviewing municipal laws, formulating standards and regulations for the management of MSW and suggesting suitable practices and proven technologies for the sorting, collection, transport, disposal, recycling and reuse of MSW in an eco-friendly manner.[58]

On 20 July 1998, the Supreme Court considered the interim report of the committee and approved its proposal to conduct regional workshops to sensitize and inform municipal officials about good MSW disposal practices.[59] On 12 April 1999, the court appreciated the work by the committee and directed the states to respond to the recommendations made in the final report.[60] On 13 August 1999,[61] the Supreme Court noted that the CPCB had formulated draft MSW (Management and Handling) Rules, which were notified in the following month for inviting suggestions and objections. In subsequent proceedings, the court decided to take up the problems facing the four metropolises and Bangalore. Since a large proportion of the municipal revenue in the metros was being spent on wages for an inefficient staff, the court mooted the idea of privatizing garbage disposal services.[62] On 15 February 2000 the court issued directions specific to Delhi, ordering the authorities to identify landfill and composting sites, to recover fines for littering and to appoint magistrates to try offences in relation to littering, public nuisance and public health.[63]

In October 2000, the Municipal Solid Waste (Management and Handling) Rules were issued under the Environment (Protection) Act of 1986 and these rules prescribed timelines for municipalities to put in place procedures for segregation, collection, processing and disposal of MSW. Subsequent orders of the Supreme Court sought to ensure compliance with the new rules[64] and decided ancillary issues.[65]

---

55 *Almitra H Patel v Union of India* 1997 (6) SCALE 10 (SP).
56 *Almitra H Patel v Union of India* 1997 (6) SCALE 11 (SP).
57 *Almitra H Patel v Union of India* 1997 (6) SCALE 12 (SP).
58 *Almitra H Patel v Union of India* AIR 1998 SC 993.
59 *Almitra H Patel v Union of India* 1998 (4) SCALE 9 (SP).
60 *Almitra H Patel v Union of India* 1999 (2) SCALE 685.
61 *Almitra H Patel v Union of India* 1999 (5) SCALE 154.
62 *Almitra H Patel v Union of India* 1999 (7) SCALE 1 and (2000) 2 SCC 166.
63 *Almitra H Patel v Union of India* (2000) 2 SCC 679.
64 *Almitra H Patel v Union of India* (2004) 13 SCC 536; (2004) 13 SCC 538; (2010) 15 SCC 619.
65 *Almitra H Patel v Union of India* (2003) 12 SCC 254.

On 2 September 2014, after 18 years of monitoring the case, the Supreme Court transferred the public interest litigation to the National Green Tribunal (NGT).[66] The transferred case was disposed of by the NGT on 22 December 2016. The Tribunal referred to a report of the CPCB which estimated that merely 27% of the municipal solid waste generated in the country was treated. Recording that in 2012–13, the country was generating 133,760 MT of waste per day, a figure that had increased with the passage of time, the Tribunal noticed the nationwide failure to create sufficient landfill sites. The NGT required the states and Union territories to implement the 2016 Rules without delay and specifically prohibited the burning of waste on landfill sites.[67]

In *Almitra Patel*, the directions passed by the court had an impact on the informal recycling sector. The Asim Burman Committee set up in *Almitra Patel* held four regional workshops where municipal administrators participated and which allowed for limited NGO participation. Professor Rajamani's research with respect to these workshops reveals:

> One NGO observer noted that NGOs were not invited, and that she had to 'force' her way in, and another that he had to 'ask to be invited'. Once they got past the door they realized that events were 'not structured to be participative,' and the process was 'neither consultative nor democratic'. In addition to the non-participative process, NGOs were also alienated by the 'technology focus' of the agenda. The solutions devised and recommended by the Committee are driven by the notion that 'leaner municipalities and greater efficiency' would solve the problem of MSW management. Most of the NGOs working in the area, on the other hand, are focused on the rights of rag-pickers, social implications of policy changes and 'zero waste and waste minimization' as elements of the solution. The technology focus of the agenda revealed that the 'understanding of waste as perceived by the mover of the PIL is very narrow.' It is perhaps not surprising, given the lack of public participation in the process leading up to the MSW Rules, that the Rules do not create any avenues for public participation.[68]

The Supreme Court left it to the Asim Burman Committee to decide on its procedure and whom to consult. Is this hybrid, judiciary-driven legislative process, desirable? The exclusion of an important perspective during the legislative drafting—that of the poor involved in the informal recycling sector—brings in focus the 'undemocratic' procedure of such law-making. The drafting stage is crucial because it is at this point that the framework and policy perspective is set. Here, the draft MSW Rules were published by the MoEF for public comment in October 1999, diluting the criticism against the method of rule-making.

In 2016, the MSW Rules of 2000 were replaced by the Solid Waste Management Rules. Simultaneously, the Central Government also issued Construction and Demolition Waste Management Rules.

Shortly before taking up the *Almitra Patel* case, the Supreme Court had already directed its attention to garbage clearance in Delhi. Chastising the authorities for permitting the Capital to become 'an open dust bin' with 'garbage strewn all over', the court issued a range of directions for the proper disposal of hospital wastes, public education of residents and the management of sanitary landfills. The court found that the municipal authorities had failed in their duties despite employing 40,000 workers to keep the city clean. In an echo of the *Ratlam* case,[69] the court held:

> It is clear from various provisions of the [Delhi Municipal Corporation Act of 1957 and the New Delhi Municipal Council Act of 1994] that the Municipal Corporation of Delhi (MCD) and

[66] *Almitra H Patel v Union of India*, Writ Petition (Civil) No. 888 of 1996.

[67] *Almitra H Patel v Union of India*, order dated 22 December 2016, Original Application No. 199 of 2014, (2016) SCC Online NGT 2981.

[68] Lavanya Rajamani; *Public Interest Environmental Litigation in India: Exploring Issues of Access, Participation, Equity, Effectiveness and Sustainability* 19 JR OF ENVIR LAW 1, 12 (2007).

[69] *Municipal Council, Ratlam v Vardhichand* AIR 1980 SC 1622.

> the New Delhi Municipal Council (NDMC) are under a statutory obligation to scavenge and clean the city of Delhi. It is mandatory for these authorities to collect and dispose of the garbage/waste generated from various sources in the city. We have no hesitation in observing that the MCD and the NDMC have been wholly remiss in the performance of their statutory bodies. Apart from the rights guaranteed under the Constitution the residents of Delhi have a statutory right to live in a clean city. The Courts are justified in directing the MCD and NDMC to perform their duties under the law. Non-availability of funds, inadequacy or inefficiency of staff, cannot be pleaded as grounds for non-performance of their statutory obligations.[70]

Despite the MSW Rules of 2000 and their replacement in 2016, city administrations have been slow to rise to the challenge and upgrade capacities to dispose MSW in an environmentally acceptable manner. Typical of this sloth is the case of the Mumbai Municipal Corporation which over decades has displayed an inability to manage its existing landfills and create new ones. Initially, the Bombay High Court issued directions in 1997 to stop the burning of garbage at the municipal dumping site at Deonar.[71] When the problem persisted, a fresh set of petitions were moved before the Bombay High Court which were disposed of by a consent arrangement on 2 April 2013. This arrangement envisaged an action plan for treating the MSW generated by the city through upgraded facilities, the establishment of processing plants and the acquisition of new landfill sites. The court estimated that the municipal corporation continued to illegally dump between 5,000 and 6,000 MT of solid waste every day. With the municipal corporation displaying masterly inactivity, the Bombay High Court took a drastic step: it restrained the municipal corporation from granting new development permissions.[72] A city that cannot treat its existing waste cannot grow indefinitely.

In 2014, the government of India launched a countrywide mission to eliminate open defecation under the banner Swachh Bharat Abhiyan. Within five years, the government constructed 110 million toilets in an extraordinary campaign that improved sanitation and health as well as lent dignity to millions of citizens.

Nevertheless, an enormous sanitation deficit remains with inadequate treatment of sewage by municipalities. The leading case on sanitation and the duty of a municipality to dispose of human waste is the *Ratlam* case,[73] discussed in the public nuisance section of the Judicial Remedies and Procedures chapter. Several High Courts have attempted to compel municipalities to do their job by providing suitable sanitation infrastructure.[74]

---

70 *B L Wadehra v Union of India* AIR 1996 SC 2969.

71 *Shanti Park 'Sorento' Co-op Society Ltd v Municipal Corporation of Greater Mumbai*, Writ Petition No. 1138 of 1996; 6 August 1996, 14 March 1997, 1 July 1997.

72 *Pandurang Patil v Municipal Corporation of Greater Mumbai*, Public Interest Litigation No. 217 of 2019, orders dated 2 April 2013, 29 February 2016 & 3 August 2018.

73 *Municipal Council, Ratlam v Vardhichand* AIR 1980 SC 1622.

74 *L K Koolwal v State of Rajasthan* AIR 1988 RAJ 2 (Jaipur); *Dr K C Malhotra v State of MP* AIR 1994 MP 48 (Gwalior); *M C Mehta v State of Orissa* AIR 1992 ORI 225 (Cuttack); *Ambala Urban Estate Welfare Society v Haryana Urban Development Authority* AIR 1994 P&H 288 (Ambala); *S K Garg v State of UP* AIR 1999 ALL 41 (Allahabad); *Vinod Chandra Varma v State of UP* AIR 1999 ALL 108 (Allahabad); *Dhanjirao Jivarao Jadhav v State of Maharashtra* 1998 (2) MAH L J 462 (Kolhapur); *Siromani Mittasala v President, Brindavanam Colony* (2002) 2 ANDH L T 356 (Kavali, Nellore); *Suo Motu v State of Rajasthan* AIR 2005 RAJ 82 (Jaipur); *Citizens Forum, Maharashtra v State of Maharashtra* (2006) 3 MAH L J 133 (Nagpur); *Ilaben Pathak v State of Gujarat* (2011) SCC Online GUJ 7560 (Ahmedabad); *Rythu Seva Sangam v Bhimavaram Municipality* (2012) 5 ANDH L D 551 (Bhimavaram, West Godavari); *Vimal Chaudhary v State of Rajasthan* (2013) 3 RAJ L W 2734 (Jaipur); *Nazmaben Saddambhai Shakarayani v State of Gujarat* (2014) SCC Online GUJ 299 (Dhoraji);

F. TRANSLOCATION OF INDUSTRIES

With few exceptions, Indian cities throb with industrial activity. Factories provide employment, pay taxes and, more generally, vitalize the urban economy. Factories also pollute, despoiling the environment. Economic and political constraints prevent local bodies from vigorously pursuing an industrial location policy that would require factories to shift away from urban centres. As cities extend into the countryside and surround industrial plants that hitherto were located at a great distance from the urban population, the conflict between industry and neighbouring communities grows. In this section, we examine the initiative by the Supreme Court, compelling hazardous industrial units to relocate beyond Delhi or shut down. Labour unions and a few non-governmental organizations have criticized the court for pursuing an elite agenda and depriving workers of their livelihood. Is the criticism justified?

M C MEHTA v UNION OF INDIA
AIR 1996 SC 2231

Order: The Master Plan for Delhi 1962 (MPD-62) was prepared and enforced under the Delhi Development Act, 1957 (the Act). At that point of time it was realized that the solution of the impending problems of the National Capital could only be found in regional context and as such the MPD-62 recommended that a statutory National Capital Region Planning Board should be set up for ensuring balanced and harmonised development of the region. The National Capital Region Planning Board Act, 1985 (Capital Region Act) came into force on 11 February 1985. The National Capital Region Plan 2001 (the Regional Plan) was published as a statutory document. In the words of the then chairperson, National Capital Region Planning Board, the purpose sought to be achieved by the Regional Plan was as under:

> The two important goals to be achieved by the Regional Plan are a balanced and harmoniously developed region, leading to dispersal of economic activities and immigrants to Delhi, thereby leading to a manageable Delhi. This is to be achieved by the progressive de-concentration of population and economic activities in the Region and their judicious dispersal to various priority towns as identified in the plan. The plan is a framework of policies relating to population distribution, settlement system, transport and communications, physical and social infrastructure, regional land use, environment and ecodevelopment, management structure for plan implementation and counter magnet areas for development. The focus of the plan is Delhi whose extraordinary growth has put great pressure on its essential services and civic facilities. It is expected that a vigorous implementation of the policies contained in the plan would help maintain the quality of life of our National Capital.

* * *

Delhi is recording heavy population growth since 1951. As the city grows, its problems of land, housing, transportation and management of essential infrastructure like water supply and sewage have become more acute. Delhi is one of the most polluted cities in the world. The quality of ambient air is so hazardous that lung and respiratory diseases are on the increase. The city has become a vast and unmanageable conglomeration of commercial, industrial, unauthorized colonies, resettlement colonies and unplanned housing. There is total lack of open spaces and green areas. Once beautiful city, Delhi now presents a chaotic picture. The only way to relieve the capital city from the huge additional burden and pressures, is to deconcentrate the population, industries and

---

Vipan Kumar v State of Punjab (2017) SCC Online P & H 3420 (Mukerian, District Hoshiarpur); *Court on its own Motion v State of H P* (2018) SCC Online H P 2117 (Shimla).

economic activities in the city and relocate the same in various priority towns in the National Capital Region (NCR).

The Master Plan for Delhi-perspective 2001 (the Master Plan) as approved by the Central Government under S.11A(2) of the Act was published in the Gazette of India on 1 August 1990. The question for consideration, before us, is whether the hazardous/noxious/heavy/large industries operating in Delhi are liable to be shifted/relocated to other towns in the NCR?

The relevant part of the Master Plan is as under:

> '*Hazardous and Noxious Industries: Refer Annexure III, H(a).*
> (a) The hazardous and noxious industrial units are not permitted in Delhi.
> (b) The existing industrial units of this type shall be shifted on priority within a maximum time period of three years. Project report to effectuate shifting shall be prepared by the concerned units and submitted to the authority within a maximum period of one year....
> (d) Action shall be taken by Delhi Administration to prepare a list of individual noxious and hazardous industrial units to be shifted and depending on the pollution/hazard, administration may force these industrial units to shift within a maximum prescribed period of three years.
>
> *Heavy and Large Industries: Refer Annexure III, H (b).*
> (a) No new heavy and large industrial units shall be permitted in Delhi.
> (b) The existing heavy and large scale industrial units shall shift to Delhi Metropolitan Area and the National Capital Region keeping in view the National Capital Region plan and National Industrial Policy of the Government of India....
> (d) Modernization of heavy and large scale industrial units shall be permitted subject to the following conditions:
> (i) It will reduce pollution and traffic congestion.
> (ii) Whenever the unit is asked to shift according to the policies of the plan, no compensation shall be paid for assets attained because of modernization.'

It is thus obvious that under the mandatory provisions of the Master Plan the hazardous and noxious industrial units (H(a) industries) are not permitted to operate in Delhi. So far as the existing H(a) industries are concerned, they were required to be shifted within a maximum prescribed period of three years. The Master Plan came into force in August, 1990. H(a) industries should have been shifted by the end of 1993. It is unfortunate that no action in this respect was taken by the authorities concerned. The industries were required to prepare and submit the project reports to effectuate shifting. This was to be done within one year of the coming into force of the Master Plan. None of the H(a) industries submitted the required project reports within the statutory period of one year. We have no hesitation in holding that the H(a) industries are operating in Delhi illegally and in utter violation of the mandatory provisions of the Master Plan. Delhi Administration was under a statutory obligation to prepare a list of H(a) industries. No such list was prepared within the statutory period of three years. It was only under the directions of this Court that the necessary lists were prepared.

There is no doubt that the H(a) industries have been operating in Delhi illegally during the last about three years. They must stop operating in Delhi and relocate themselves to some other industrial estate in the NCR. We are further of the view that the concerned officers of the Delhi Administration are equally responsible for continuous illegal operation of the H(a) industries in the city of Delhi. The Chief Secretary, Delhi Administration shall hold an inquiry and fix the responsibility of the officers/officials who have been wholly remiss and negligent in the performance of the statutory duties entrusted to them under the Master Plan.

The Master Plan provides that 'no new heavy and large industrial units shall be permitted in Delhi'. Heavy and large industries have been categorized as H(b) under the Master Plan. It is further provided that the existing H(b) industries shall shift to Delhi Metropolitan Area (DMA) and the NCR keeping in view the Regional Plan and the National Industrial Policy of the Government of India. Although no period has been prescribed for the shifting of these industries ... in the absence of any such provision the shifting has to be done within a reasonable time period of six years from August 1990 when the Master Plan came into force.... Some of these industries have, during the course of arguments, offered for modernization and also for conversion from polluting to non-polluting industries. The offers are simple ipse-dixit with no material. We are not impressed by the offers made by these industries at this late stage. They should have modernized or changed the process of manufacture during the six years they have been operating in violation of the Master Plan. We, therefore, reject these offers....

NOTES AND QUESTIONS

1. This order was passed on 8 July 1996. Earlier, under the supervision of the court, the polluting units were classified in the H(a) and H(b) categories. In the concluding portion of the order, the court directed 168 listed units in the 'H' categories to stop operating in Delhi from 30 November 1996. The authorities were directed to render all assistance in the process of relocating the units within permitted industrial zones.

Apart from the designated units, the court also directed the Delhi pollution control committee (DPCC) to identify additional units that would fall within the 'H' categories. In February, 1998, the DPCC confirmed the closure of 1,328 industries.

2. The Supreme Court created entitlements for the workers employed in the 168 industries ordered for closure and relocation. They were guaranteed continuity of employment during the period of closure and shifting, assured equivalent terms of employment at the new site, assured full wages during the transition, granted one year's wages as 'shifting bonus' and granted an option to claim retrenchment compensation if they chose not to move to the new site. In December 1996, the court enhanced the compensation for workers opting for retrenchment. They were now entitled to six years' wages as additional compensation, over the statutory compensation under the Industrial Disputes Act of 1947. The court also made special provision for the residential accommodation of the workers.[75] Was this enough? What more might the court have done?

3. In February 1996, the court directed the authorities and industry to construct common effluent treatment plants (CETPs) in all the industrial areas of Delhi. The CETPs were to be funded by government and industry with financial institutions assisting industry to meet the costs.[76]

4. The court's sweeping closure order appears to have improved the local ambient air quality in parts of Delhi and, more significantly, reduced the risk to public health and safety.

The impact of the shutdown on labour was harsh. According to one report published nearly two years after the November 1996 deadline, none of the workers, except those in a government textile mill, had been paid their compensation.[77] Recourse to the courts to enforce the entitlements was a slow process, forcing most industrial workers to take up irregular, part-time, low-paying jobs.

---

[75] *M C Mehta v Union of India* (1997) 11 SCC 327, 329. The Supreme Court's decisions in the *Calcutta Tanneries* case (1997) 2 SCC 411 and *the Taj Trapezium* case AIR 1997 SC 734 also contain directions to compensate and protect labour.

[76] *M C Mehta v Union of India* 1996 (2) SCALE 89 (SP).

[77] N Dasgupta, *Tall Blunders*, DOWN TO EARTH, 30 September 1998, 22 at 24.

Some managements used the court order as an excuse to shut down ailing industry—a near-impossible task under India's existing industrial law and policy.[78] Others avoided the compensation obligations, until the July and December 1996 directions were clarified by the Supreme Court in December 1998, on the application of workmen.[79]

The excerpt below is an offshoot of Mehta's 1996 effort, demonstrating the tenacity of industry and its audacious recourse to the review jurisdiction multiple times.

SEIL FOODS AND FERTILIZERS INDUSTRIES v UNION OF INDIA
(2010) 5 SCC 169

K G Balakrishnan, C J: In the city of Delhi, there were several hazardous and noxious industries, as also several large and heavy industries, causing extensive pollution. The Master Plan for Delhi—Perspective 2001, which was published in the Gazette of India on 1-8-1990, did not permit any of these industries to operate in Delhi.

In a public interest litigation i.e. *M C Mehta v Union of India*, the question of shifting these polluting industries from Delhi and relocating them outside the city of Delhi and other related issues were considered and a series of orders were passed regarding shifting and relocating the industries. The polluting industries were notified through individual notices, public notices in newspapers and electronic media. This Court monitored the matter from January 1995 and all stakeholders, including the Union of India, Delhi Administration, Central Pollution Control Board, National Capital Region Planning Board, Delhi Development Authority, and the polluting industries were heard/consulted during several hearings. The Delhi Development Authority (for short 'DDA') was also directed to frame suitable schemes regarding the utilisation of land which would become available after the relocation of the hazardous/noxious/heavy/large industries from Delhi. DDA constituted a Committee with Mr K J Alphons, Commissioner, Land Management, DDA, as Chairman for this purpose. The said Committee examined the question regarding the utilisation of land made available as a result of the relocation/shifting of the industries and submitted detailed proposals. Views of other experts were also considered.

[The Supreme Court extensively quoted from its previous orders in the case including the following passage from its order dated 10 May 1996:

> The Master Plan indicates that 'approximately 34% of recreational areas have been lost to other uses'. We are aware that the housing, the sports activity and the recreational areas are also part of the 'community need' but the most important community need which is wholly deficient and needed urgently is to provide for the 'lung spaces' in the city of Delhi in the shape of green belts and open spaces. *We are, therefore, of the view that totality of the land which is surrendered and dedicated to the community by the owners/occupiers of the relocated/shifted industries should be used for the development of green belts and open spaces.*']

We have carefully considered the various review petitions and other applications filed in this regard. We have extracted the relevant portions of the orders dated 10-5-1996 *M C Mehta v Union of India* (1996) 4 SCC 351, 8-7-1996 *M C Mehta v Union of India* (1996) 4 SCC 750, 4-12-1996 *M C Mehta v Union of India* (1997) 11 SCC 327 and 28-4-2000 *M C Mehta v Union of India* (2000) 5 SCC 525 which clearly demonstrate that the owners of land/industries were given a fair hearing before passing the order on 10-5-1996. The petitioners have now raised these very contentions that their lands will have to be acquired and that they are entitled to get reasonable compensation when their land was taken over. All these pleas have been repeatedly rejected by this Court.

---

[78] *Id.*
[79] *M C Mehta v Union of India* (1999) 2 SCC 91.

The scheme evolved by this Court in its order dated 10-5-1996 is clear:

(i) The land which becomes available on account of an industry being shifted out of Delhi would be divided equitably into two portions. The one portion to be retained by the landowner for development for his own benefit and the other portion to be surrendered to DDA for community use for development of green belts, open/lung spaces. The land to be surrendered and dedicated for community use was 57% (where the size of the plot was 0.2 ha to 5 ha), 65% (where the size of the plot was 5 ha to 10 ha) and 68% (where the plot was over 10 ha). The balance was to be retained by the landowner. The percentage was to be calculated after deducting first 2000 sq m for development by the owner.

(ii) In consideration of the landowners surrendering and dedicating a part of the land for community use, they (landowners) will be entitled to an additional 50% FAR [floor area ratio] in regard to the land permitted to be retained by them for their benefit. That is, FAR would stand increased to one-and-a-half times of the admissible FAR under the Master Plan. The landowners will not be entitled to any other consideration/compensation for the land surrendered and dedicated to the community.

(iii) The portions of land surrendered to DDA and dedicated for community purposes, that is, only for being used as green belt or open 'lung spaces' for the city, such dedicated land will be used only for such dedicated purpose and not any other purpose.

(iv) The land will be at the disposal of the community at large and DDA shall not exploit it for either commercial use or construction of residential flats. As DDA is not going to derive any benefit by exploitation thereof, and was to only hold it in trust for and on behalf of the community, there was no question of DDA paying any compensation therefore to the landowners.

It, therefore, follows that such land dedicated by private owners to the community, if acquired for any other purpose, or is diverted to any other use by DDA (as, for example, for putting up constructions or for sale or lease for development or construction), the landowner will be entitled to compensation. But so long as the land remained as lung space/green area, there is no question of any payment to the owner, as compensation or otherwise.

The order dated 10-5-1996 was passed to give effect to the Master Plan, to save the city and in public interest. Therefore, by surrendering a part of the land, the owners were not only benefiting the community but themselves. The records clearly show that before the order dated 10-5-1996 was passed, the question what should be the compensation for the surrendered lands was specifically raised and considered. It was made clear that additional FAR will be in lieu of any monetary compensation for the land to be surrendered and dedicated to DDA for community use, for development of green belts and lung spaces. Therefore, it is evident that the order dated 10-5-1996 clearly intended that the land to be surrendered would vest in trust in DDA for the benefit of the community and the additional FAR was the only compensation for such surrendered land for community benefit and there would be no further compensation. Contentions similar to the contentions now raised were rejected by this Court by order dated 28-4-2000. Therefore, it is not possible for this Court to again review all these orders or take a different view. Therefore, all these review petitions, applications for directions and clarifications are without any merit.

We may note that some of these review petitions have been filed after dismissal or withdrawal of the earlier petition by the very same petitioners seeking almost the very same reliefs. Therefore, such petitions are prima facie not maintainable and the pleas raised by these petitioners to review the earlier order passed by this Court cannot be considered. Be that as it may. As the contentions raised by others have been considered, this issue loses relevance.

One aspect requires clarification, particularly in view of some of the surrendered land being acquired or taken on perpetual lease by Delhi Metro Rail Corporation [DMRC] from DDA. The landowners surrendered and dedicated portions of the land as ... contained in para 9 of the order dated 10-5-1996 exclusively for the purpose of development of green belt and open spaces. Therefore, wherever such open lung space is created, it shall be shown in the municipal/DDA records as 'DDA land—dedicated by....' DDA shall maintain a trust account of such surrendered lands. This would mean that DDA which holds the surrendered and dedicated land in trust cannot use it for any purpose other than as green belt or other spaces for the benefit of the community. This will be necessary to identify if the land held by DDA in trust for the community is not lost and is not treated as DDA owned land which can be dealt with by DDA as absolute owner. In the event of any acquisition or development of such surrendered land, the owner/dedicator will have the benefit of compensation on account of land ceasing to be 'land dedicated to the community purpose of lung/open space'. As the owner has already received some consideration in the form of 50% additional FAR, we are of the view that when such acquisition/alienation takes place, DDA and the landowner will be entitled to share the compensation at 50% each.

The second aspect is where the land surrendered is very small (say on account of 57% of 0.2 ha, that is, 1140 sq m being surrendered) or being of an irregular shape, and DDA finds that it is not feasible or practical to maintain any small areas as independent green belt or park or playground or lung space or to safeguard any such area from encroachers, DDA can take steps to consolidate several smaller areas into larger blocks in the same locality so that they can be used effectively. For that purpose, DDA may also enter into suitable arrangements by way of exchange or otherwise. But any such consolidation or exchange shall be only with the sanction of the District Court, Delhi, after notice to the landowners/dedicators. Any change in use of such surrendered land held in trust by DDA or any transfer by DDA shall be only after securing prior permission from the High Court of Delhi.

M/s SIEL Ltd, the applicant in IA No. 1914 of 2006 and IA No. 2205 of 2007 (SIEL Ltd) submitted that DDA, out of 18.854 ha surrendered by it though it did not have either ownership or right of commercial exploitation had transferred 7.5 ha plus 1.21 ha to DMRC on payment of a premium of Rs 1,55,33,213 plus other amounts. It is contended that such transfer was impermissible and the monetary gain should be paid over to the owner of the land. It is also contended that the land should be used only in accordance with the order dated 10-5-1996.

The land surrendered by SIEL Ltd as per the order dated 10-5-1996 to DDA could be used only for community purposes and cannot be used for any private purpose. In circumstances where the land is acquired or used (other than as green belt and open lung space) for any other purpose under extreme necessity, the landowner would be entitled to get 50% of the compensation or consideration for the use of such land. We make it clear that the owner of such land would be entitled to get 50% of the amount received by DDA as consideration/compensation. If DDA fails to pay the same, such persons would be entitled to take appropriate legal action. We again reiterate that any such diversion of use by DDA shall henceforth be only with the permission of the District Court, Delhi, after notice to the landowners concerned....

NOTES AND QUESTIONS

1. Long after a final judgment was rendered in *M C Mehta*'s case on 10 May 1996, industries repeatedly applied to the Supreme Court seeking review, clarifications, modifications and what-have-you to somehow vary the directions and secure value for their land. Why was the Supreme Court so indulgent 14 years after its original verdict? Were the judges overawed by the eminence of counsel representing the companies or simply poor managers of time?

Whatever the reason, having regard to the huge pendency in the Supreme Court, repeat review petitions ought to have been dismissed summarily without such a lengthy judgment.

2. The original petition was filed by M C Mehta under Article 32 of the Constitution. Since such petitions are directly filed before the highest judicial forum, the decision of the Supreme Court in this original jurisdiction is final and parties have no recourse by way of appeal. Fundamental rights enforceable under Article 32 were traditionally exercised against the state. Now, with the right to life receiving an expansive interpretation, other private parties are also impacted by judgments rendered under Article 32, most often in the PIL jurisdiction. Should the Supreme Court, as a matter of judicial policy, be more liberal in entertaining and deciding review petitions arising from Article 32 cases to make up for the absence of an appeal?

3. At the end of the day, a Master Plan framed under a town planning statute is legislative in character. Does the business of a court extend to prescribing green zones and lung spaces where the Master Plan itself makes no provision? Should the Supreme Court have left this exercise to expert town planners? Where are these experts? Most planning authorities in India do not employ any qualified town planners and this may explain the poor design elements and aesthetics of Indian cities.

4. The 10 May 1996 order draws attention to Delhi being one of the most polluted cities in the world. Decades later, air quality data confirms that Delhi's air is hazardous to health, causing acute respiratory diseases and death. Children are particularly vulnerable to the harmful air. This state of affairs persists despite several interventions by the Supreme Court. In this bleak milieu should the court resign to a traditional hands-off approach leaving matters to the sub-competent pollution control boards and the NGT or continue its activist role in pollution cases?

5. SEIL's application succeeded, with the Supreme Court directing DDA to hand over 50% of the compensation it received from Delhi Metro. Considering that SEIL had long surrendered its land to the DDA pursuant to the Supreme Court directions and DDA was the subsequent owner, was SEIL entitled to this windfall?

6. Revisit the *Mumbai Mill Lands* case[80] discussed earlier in this chapter and contrast the approaches of the court in securing industrial land for the community in Mumbai and Delhi.

7. In *Oswal Agro Mills Limited v HPCL*,[81] the two junior judges[82] crowded out the presiding judge[83] whose opinion was reduced to a dissent. In 1989, nearly five years after the Bhopal gas leak, Oswal purchased tracts of land at Chembur, Mumbai from Union Carbide Ltd and, in March 2006, initiated the process for changing land use. In 2009, Oswal obtained permission from the municipal corporation to alter the land use from industrial to residential/commercial. Meanwhile, in 2008, the MoEF granted environmental clearance under category 8(b) of the EIA notification of 2006 to Oswal, enabling construction of commercial, office and residential buildings. From 2010 onwards, the corporation issued various planning permissions including a commencement certificate.

---

[80] *Bombay Dyeing & Mfg Co Ltd v Bombay Environmental Action Group* (2006) 3 SCC 434.

[81] (2014) 2 SCC 491.

[82] Justice H L Gokhale and Justice Ranjana P Desai were both residents of Mumbai and earlier in their judicial career were judges of the Bombay High Court.

[83] Justice G S Singhvi's judicial career began in the Rajasthan High Court.

Meanwhile HPCL, a public sector oil company which operated its refinery and had a number of storage tanks for oil and petroleum products in the vicinity of Oswal's land, unsuccessfully urged the municipal corporation and the state government to block Oswal's plans. HPCL insisted that the project would imperil the safety and security of the refinery, apart from the adverse health impact on occupants of the new premises. HPCL then petitioned the Bombay High Court, this time successfully. The High Court quashed the sanction accorded by the corporation for change of user and the construction permissions. It directed the municipal commissioner to reconsider Oswal's applications, keeping in view objections raised by the police department, the Union Ministry of Petroleum and the intelligence bureau.

In his minority judgment, Justice G S Singhvi accepted Oswal's contention. He found that although when the refinery was established in the 1950s, its location was remote, with the passage of time, there were 3,50,000 persons residing in villages and slums in the immediate vicinity of the refinery. In many cases, multi-storied buildings and residential towers had been built near the refinery. He found that the High Court had 'not considered the issue of security and possible impact on the health of those who may occupy the building to be constructed by [Oswal] due to the existence of the refineries and industries in the area in a correct perspective' and remitted the matter on these issues back to the High Court.

The majority opinion authored by Justice Gokhale upheld the High Court judgment, emphasizing Development Control Regulation 16 the relevant portion of which reads:

16. *Requirements of sites.* — No land shall be used as a site for the construction of buildings –

(a) if the Commissioner considers that the site is insanitary *or that it is dangerous to construct a building on it* or no water supply is likely to be available within a reasonable period of time;

...

(e) *if the use of the said site is for a purpose which in the Commissioner's opinion may be a source of danger to the health and safety of the inhabitants of the neighbourhood*;

...

(n) if the proposed development is likely to involve damage to or have deleterious impact on or is against urban aesthetics or environment or ecology and/or on historical/architectural/aesthetical buildings and precincts *or is not in the public interest.* [emphasis supplied]

In the majority view, the Municipal Commissioner was under a duty to give paramount importance to safety.

For junior judges to out-vote their senior colleague is rare. Might their personal knowledge of Mumbai and its environs have played a role in the outcome? Was HPCL's claim just and equitable? Is it fair for a hazardous industry to render sterile or unbuildable neighbouring property without recompense? Should the court have compelled HPCL to buy out Oswal at a fair price? Considering that, in the vicinity of HPCL's refinery, there was another refinery as well as a fertilizer unit and the Bhabha Atomic Research Centre, should the neighbourhood be made a 'no-development' zone? How would this impact landowners? What about the slum dwellers residing on adjacent lands? Do not security and health issues apply to slum dwellers?

If you were a HPCL manager what long-term developments might concern you? What might happen if your refinery were ringed in by a curtain of concrete towers? Finally, considering that the project had an environmental clearance under the EIA notification, was the MoEF (and not the municipal commissioner) the appropriate authority to evaluate the probable safety and health impacts projected by HPCL?

8. The *Bayer* case illustrates the unpredictability of the judicial process. In the aftermath of the Bhopal tragedy and the principle of absolute liability laid down by the Supreme Court in the

Shriram Gas Leak case,[84] a number of pharmaceutical and chemical factories urged the Thane Municipal Corporation (TMC) not to permit residential buildings to be erected within a radius of one kilometre from the boundaries of these factories. The TMC was informed that the factories stored and used hazardous chemicals and that permitting multi-storeyed residential apartments in the industrial zone would increase the public risk posed by the units.

In January, 1990 the TMC issued an order rejecting building plans in the danger zone. In a writ petition filed by the developer assailing the TMC's refusal, the Bombay High Court quashed the TMC directive since, according to the court, TMC had acted on a mere complaint and its action was not backed by the development plan. The success of the developer spawned 29 writ petitions by other builders, all of which were allowed with a direction to the TMC to re-examine the building plans without regard to irrelevant considerations such as the complaint by industry regarding the risk to local residents.

Bayer (India) Ltd challenged the judgment before the Supreme Court, which permitted the company to approach the High Court in review. In a lengthy judgment rendered in Bayer's review petition, the High Court held that a safety zone with a radius of one kilometre was absolutely essential around the hazardous industrial units and that the TMC should not permit any new developments within the zone. The court found that the TMC was within its power to reject the building proposals in view of overriding public safety considerations. The High Court also rejected the contention of M C Mehta that the hazardous industries ought to move away.

> The units in question are not personal or proprietary businesses or small scale units, but are large industrial undertakings, shifting of which is hardly feasible. As of necessity, these chemical and pharmaceutical units have to be within the close proximity of area where the entire infrastructure is available and cannot be located at some isolated spot.... The consequence of thousands of persons being rendered jobless, if the industries were to move, is a consideration of much seriousness, particularly in view of the present level of unemployment. We, therefore, feel ... that the best in the present situation would be to at least maintain a safety distance around the [hazardous industry].[85]

In the Supreme Court, Bayer's initiative boomeranged. Back on his home turf, M C Mehta persuaded the court that the one kilometre prohibitory zone infringed on the right of the residents of Thane to reside in the locality, while leaving at the same time a large number of persons already living in the area exposed to the risk of an industrial accident. The Supreme Court observed: 'it was thought by us that if the industrialists wanted to safeguard their interest in the event of some accident happening in their factories, it was for them either to obtain the ownership of the area in question or to shift their factories to such places where the residential areas could be kept wide apart from their factory premises.'[86] Encountering resistance from the industry to relocate, the Supreme Court directed the Central Government to constitute an authority under section 3(3) of the Environment (Protection) Act of 1986 to examine the issues arising in the case and to make a report to the Central Government. The TMC was asked to await the report of the authority before finally sanctioning the plans.

Which approach would you consider best from an environmental viewpoint: the High Court's original decision, its judgment on Bayer's review petition or the Supreme Court's judgment? Which decision is the most equitable? Does the environmental and public health interest diverge from the social welfare interest in each of these approaches?

---

84 *M C Mehta v Union of India* AIR 1987 SC 1086.
85 *Bayer (India) Ltd v State of Maharashtra* 1994 (4) Bom C Rep 309, 353.
86 *F B Taraporawala v Bayer India Ltd* AIR 1997 SC 1846.

G. HERITAGE

India's rich and varied cultural heritage comprises a multitude of buildings and sites that link the present to the past. Due to their artistic or social significance these landmarks require special protection against the pressures of contemporary development and damage from the elements. Article 49 of the Constitution contains a directive principle obliging the state to protect every monument or place or object of artistic or historic interest declared by or under law enacted by Parliament to be of national importance from spoliation, destruction or removal. Parliament is conferred a corresponding legislative power under Entry 67 of List I, in the Schedule to the Constitution. The states have power to enact laws to preserve and protect lesser ancient and historical monuments.[87] The Union and the states have concurrent power to legislate on archaeological sites and remains other than those declared by Parliament to be of national importance.[88] The fundamental duty of every citizen under Article 51A(f) 'to value and preserve the rich heritage of our composite culture' may now be discharged by recourse to the writ courts, the Supreme Court having recognized that the right to life would extend to preserving 'the tradition and cultural heritage of the persons concerned.'[89]

These constitutional provisions have enabled Parliament to enact the Ancient Monuments and Archaeological Sites and Remains Act of 1958 covering monuments and sites of national importance, and the Antiquities and Art Treasures Act of 1972 to prevent the export and smuggling of art treasures. State-level laws such as the Maharashtra Ancient Monuments and Archaeological Sites and Remains Act of 1960 complement the national statutes. The Archaeological Survey of India (ASI) is the national agency responsible for preserving, protecting and restoring the nationally important sites. State departments of archaeology are supposed to protect the buildings, monuments and sites recognized under the state law.

Beyond this legislative framework but nevertheless worthy of conservation are a host of buildings, works, relics or places that are of historic, cultural, social, aesthetic or architectural significance. In a broad sense, these too are part of our environmental 'heritage'. In India, the notion of heritage would extend to natural features of cultural or social significance such as sacred groves, hills, hillocks, water bodies, open areas and wooded areas.

Since the 1980s, several NGOs have worked to protect heritage sites and sensitize planning authorities on the importance of conservation. The role of NGOs in the heritage movement is vital, largely because neither the ASI nor the town planning authorities display much initiative in the field. The Indian National Trust for Art and Cultural Heritage (INTACH) developed models to preserve historic precincts, among them Chanderi, a weaving town in Madhya Pradesh and the Varanasi Ghats. A G Krishna Menon, who worked on these projects for INTACH, argues: 'While in the West, traditional settlements have been more or less destroyed, in India the past is truly a living presence. Indeed, the paradox is that authenticity in the Indian context need not be preserved, it can be continually created today. It is this precious quality that characterizes our living environment and establishes its identity.'[90] The Bombay Environmental Action Group (BEAG) played a key role in introducing the first heritage regulations in India—The Heritage Regulations for Greater Mumbai framed in 1995 under the Maharashtra Regional and Town Planning Act of 1966. BEAG also lobbied to extend heritage protection to other cities in Maharashtra, notably Pune, Nashik and Nagpur and the hill

---

87 Entry 12, List II, Seventh Schedule.
88 Entry 40, List III, Seventh Schedule.
89 *Consumer Education and Research Centre v Union of India* AIR 1995 SC 922, 959.
90 A G Krishna Menon, *Cultural Identity and Urban Development* 4 (1989).

station of Mahabaleshwar.[91] The Indian Heritage Society (IHS) is best known for the annual awards it presents for heritage conservation efforts in Bombay. The IHS has assisted the government in identifying heritage buildings and precincts and has petitioned the courts for redress against the despoliation of the urban heritage.

The Mumbai Heritage Regulations grade heritage buildings and precincts into three categories based on their importance. Over 600 buildings and conservation areas are enumerated in a schedule appended to the Regulations. Heritage structures may be repaired or re-developed only after obtaining the prior written permission of the municipal commissioner, who, in turn, is required to consult the statutory Heritage Conservation Committee (HCC). The constitution of the HCC includes an environmentalist, a city historian as well as structural engineers and architects. Several incentives compensate the owner of a heritage property for the loss of development rights. Under the Regulations, heritage owners are entitled to 'transferable development rights'[92] as recompense for the impairment in the development potential at the site. Adopting the Mumbai model, in December 1995, heritage regulations were introduced to protect 151 buildings and six precincts in Hyderabad.[93]

The Union Ministry of Environment and Forests has encouraged the states and Union territories to adopt suitable local heritage regulations. In December, 1995, the MoEF circulated model heritage regulations and asked the regional governments to frame suitable laws. The MoEF followed this initiative with letters on 21 August 1998 and 8 April 1999 urging the states to frame regulations to conserve the natural and built heritage.

Responding to a petition filed by BEAG, the Bombay High Court directed the Maharashtra government to afford statutory heritage protection to designated buildings in the Mahabaleshwar region:

> With regard to the Heritage Committee constituted by the State Government *vide* the Government Resolution dated 21 July 1998, we are informed that a meeting of this Committee was held on 9 November 1998. The Heritage Committee is directed to finalize the list of heritage structures and sites (both natural and man-made), including scenic points, walks, rides, etc. within four months from today. The Heritage Committee shall also, within the said period, formulate and finalize the draft Heritage Regulations for Mahabaleshwar-Panchgani Region in conformity with the Draft Model Regulations for Conservation of Natural and Man-made Heritage formulated by the Union Government's Ministry of Environment & Forests and which has been circulated to all State Governments in 1995. Within one month of the receipt of the said list and draft Regulations, the State Government shall publish and notify the same following the procedure stipulated in Sections 37 and 20 of the Maharashtra Regional & Town Planning Act, 1966.[94]

The Supreme Court has issued directions to the ASI to protect the monuments in the Fatehpur Sikri area,[95] as well as the tomb of Mirza Ghalib.[96] In *Surendra Kumar Singh v State of Bihar*,[97] the Supreme Court considered a special leave petition against orders passed

---

[91] Shyam Chainani of BEAG recounts his efforts at conserving the built heritage in several cities and towns across India in *Heritage and Environment: An Indian Diary* (2007).

[92] A right to build elsewhere in the city ward where the heritage building stands. TDR may be encashed by sale to a developer.

[93] Shyam Chainani, *Heritage and Environment: An Indian Diary* 146 (2007).

[94] *Bombay Environmental Action Group v State of Maharashtra*, Writ Petition No. 2754 of 1997, 18 November 1998.

[95] *Wasim Ahmed Saeed v Union of India* 1997 (5) SCALE 451; 1999 (1) SCALE 683; and 1999 (1) SCALE 685.

[96] *M C Mehta v Archaeological Survey of India* 1996 (8) SCALE 11 (SP); 1997 (2) SCALE 25 (SP); and 1997 (5) SCALE 1 (SP).

[97] (1991) Supp (2) SCC 628.

by the Patna High Court preventing stone crushing operations within a distance of 500 m of three hills that had been declared as protected monuments. Dismissing the petitions, the court directed the state electricity board to aid the petitioners in shifting their operations away from the prohibited zone. In *Rajiv Mankotia v The Secretary to the President of India*,[98] the Supreme Court delved into the history and origins of the Viceregal Lodge at Shimla and issued directions to preserve the building and prevent its conversion into a hotel. In *Ram Sarup v State of Haryana*,[99] the Punjab and Haryana High Court examined the provisions of the Ancient Monuments and Archaeological Sites and Remains Act of 1958 and upheld the government notification under section 4 of the Act declaring an area around Brahm Sarovar at Kurukshetra to be a controlled area for the purpose of the Act.

THE *CENTRAL VISTA* CASE

Despite the enormous strides in creating statutory protection for heritage structures, the protection is only as strong as the willingness and ability of judges to stand up for heritage as a value. Heritage regulations, no matter how clearly worded, are rendered naught where the bench is unable or unwilling to recognize the importance of heritage and mandate strict compliance with the law. The majority judgment in the *Central Vista* case[100] is an example where lip service is paid to heritage but the command of the law diluted to accommodate a prestigious government project.

On 2 September 2019, the government invited bids to appoint a consultant for a comprehensive redevelopment of Parliament Building, Common Central Secretariat and Central Vista at New Delhi. The project proceeded apace without securing the mandatory permission being 'prior approval of the Heritage Conservation Committee' (HCC). The petitioners urged:

(a) The buildings and structures covered by the Central Vista Project are essential components of India's cultural, historical and built heritage meriting protection.
(b) The Central Vista precincts, the Parliament House and campus, Rashtrapati Bhavan, National Archives, and adjoining areas have been consistently recognized as having immense heritage value for their unique architectural design, historical importance and as symbols of lived heritage.
   i. All three editions of the Master Plan of Delhi acknowledge the importance of the Central Vista as the heritage and cultural centre of Delhi.
   ii. MPD 2021 notes that the built heritage of Delhi is 'an irreplaceable and non-renewable cultural resource … [that] … needs to be protected, nourished and nurtured by all citizens and passed on to the coming generations', and that the stretch from Rashtrapati Bhawan to India Gate 'has tremendous visual quality and is one of the finest examples of Urban Design and monumentality in planning in the world.'
   iii. The entire area of Central Vista is listed as a Grade 1 Heritage precinct, a unique status for any precinct in the country in view of its critical significance to the heritage of the country.
(c) The buildings in the Central Vista and the Central Vista precinct have heritage value in multiple respects.
   i. The Indo-classical fusion architecture and layout of the buildings have a distinctive and unique style (the 'Delhi Order') that has grown to be synonymous with Delhi all over the world.

[98] 1997 *(4)* SCALE 368.
[99] AIR 1993 P & H 204.
[100] *Rajeev Suri v Delhi Development Authority* (2021) SCC Online SC 7.

ii. The buildings and precincts are of historical importance and their preservation is an avenue to preserve India's history and its independence.
iii. Buildings such as Parliament and Rashtrapati Bhawan are also important symbols of India's living and continuing heritage because they have been transmitted from one generation to another and continue to be used for the same purpose.

Consequently, any interventions also have to be assessed from the perspective of whether the construction will impact the structure of the heritage buildings as well as the layout of a heritage precinct.

The majority judgment (authored by Justice A M Khanwilkar) ignored the national and international value of the heritage buildings and precincts, and overcame the petitioners' submissions by discovering an 'implicit' prior permission from the HCC (when in fact none existed):

> On change in land use, clause 1.12 is the guiding provision for the present enquiry which categorically states that listing does not *ipso facto* prohibit change of ownership or usage. However, it adds a caveat by stating that the change in land use of such listed heritage buildings/precincts is not permissible without a 'prior approval' of the HCC. It reads:
>
> > '1.12. ***Grading of the Listed Buildings/Listed Precincts:***
> >
> > … Listing does not prevent change of ownership or usage. However, change of use of such Listed Heritage Building/Listed Precincts is not permitted without the prior approval of the Heritage Conservation Committee. Use should be in harmony with the said listed heritage site….' (emphasis supplied)
>
> Therefore, it is urged that for the aforesaid two plots, the change in land use was contingent upon prior approval of HCC. In the first place this prior approval is required if the proposal for change in land use pertains to listed heritage building/listed precincts only. Not for other properties. In any case, the record reveals that this requirement has been substantially complied with by the respondents.
>
> Indisputably, the HCC is constituted as a part of the nodal Ministry i.e. [Ministry of Housing and Urban Affairs (MoHUA)] and Special Secretary/Additional Secretary of the Ministry is designated as the Chairman of the committee. Other members of the HCC include Additional D G (Architecture), CPWD, Chief Planner, Town and Country Planning Organisation, Commissioner (Planning), DDA, Secretary, [Delhi Urban Art Commission (DUAC)] among others. In the present case, both the meetings of the Authority wherein the proposal of change in land use was considered comprised of representatives of all the agencies which were required to give their approval to the project. The minutes of the DDA meeting dated 10.2.2020 wherein the project proposal was approved for final notification reveal that Shri Kamran Rizvi, Additional Secretary, MoHUA, Government of India, who is also the designated Chairman of the HCC, was present in the meeting and had unreservedly joined in the approval of the HCC to the proposed change in land use. Additionally, we note that various other members of the HCC had also participated in the meeting of the Technical Committee in December, 2019. In the participation of high officials of HCC including its Chairman, it can be safely accepted that those officials of HCC were fully informed and conscious about their role in approving the proposal regarding change in land use. In other words, the HCC was throughout a part of the process, represented by its Chairman and other members. Their approval to the proposal under consideration has been duly recorded in the said meetings. It must, therefore, follow that the approval of the HCC as regards the change in land use was implicit and understood in the approvals granted in the said meetings. Resultantly, there is substantial compliance of 'prior approval' under clause 1.12.
>
> This approval under clause 1.12, however, does not dispense with the requirement of a formal written 'prior permission' of HCC under clause 1.3. That would become essential before

> commencing the development work on listed heritage buildings/sites and that stage is yet to arrive, including in respect of construction on plot No. 118 likely to be affected by the expression 'Heritage building' to include such portion of land adjoining heritage building (existing Parliament building on plot No. 116) or part thereof as may be required for fencing or covering or in any manner preserving the historic and/or architectural and/or cultural value of such existing heritage building.

The minority judgment (authored by Justice Sanjiv Khanna) found that the HCC was bypassed. Justice Khanna required a fresh evaluation by the HCC, prior to allowing a modification or change in the land use within the Central Vista precinct. The minority reasoned:

> Paragraph 1.2 casts an obligation on the owner, including the government, municipal authorities, etc. to carry out regular repair and maintenance of the listed buildings. It also stipulates need for 'prior approval' for change of land use of the listed heritage building/precincts. Paragraph 1.3 is significant as it states that no development, re-development, engineering operations, additions/alterations, repairs or renovation, including painting of the building, replacement of special features or blasting or demolition of any part thereof, of the listed heritage buildings/listed precincts shall be carried out except with the permission of the authorities specified, which includes Vice Chairman, Authority and Chairman, NDMC. Further, before granting such permission, the agency shall consult the Heritage Conservation Committee and act in accordance with the advice of the Heritage Conservation Committee....
>
> For reasons stated above, on interpretation of Annexure II to the Unified Building Bye Laws it has to be held that prior approval/permission was necessary for land use change of the plots/area with the Listed Heritage Buildings and precincts. As observed above, Paragraph 1.3 states that redevelopment, engineering operations, or even additions/alterations etc. require prior permission of Heritage Conservation Committee. However for demolition, major repairs and alterations/additions to listed buildings or building precincts procedure of inviting objections and suggestions from the public shall be followed. Heritage Conservation Committee would consider the suggestions and objections. Decision of the Heritage Conservation Committee is final and binding....
>
> The Parliament House, National Archives, North Block, South Block, as well as the Central Vista precincts have been specifically graded as Grade-I buildings and, therefore, under different clauses of Annexure II several restrictions and bars apply. Whether or not the bars and restrictions apply again would be questions to be examined and decided by the Heritage Conservation Committee. Neither this Court nor government including local bodies can answer these questions. Compliance with Annexure II is mandatory and necessary, which essentially means that the proponent must approach the Heritage Conservation Committee. Central Government could not have notified the modified the land use changes, without following the procedure and without prior approval/permission from the Heritage Conservation Committee. Further, the local body is expressly interdicted from issuing building permits in respect of the listed heritage buildings/precincts. The local body i.e. NDMC should have approached the Heritage Conservation Committee for clarification/confirmation and proceed on their advice.

While the minority judgment exposed the cavalier approach of the majority to the express requirements of the heritage regulations, a broader lesson may be drawn. The constitutional courts including the Supreme Court of India, more often than not, will permit large government-backed projects, even where the breach of law appears apparent. Institutionally, as seen from this case, the majority preferred to ignore the unique and highest level of heritage significance of the Central Vista—which would have required the HCC to apply its mind before the project was initiated. It is but rarely that the Supreme Court summons the constitutional courage required to strike down large projects, preferring to articulate principles in less significant cases and thereafter distinguishing the very principles when a prestigious government-backed project is involved.[101] Even where the black letter law is clear, the court may abdicate its responsibility by asserting that the government's actions are a matter of policy where it lacks expertise.

[101] See *In Re: Construction of Park at NOIDA Near Okhla Bird Sanctuary* (*Okhla Bird Sanctuary* case) (2011) 1 SCC 744; and *Lafarge Umium Mining Pvt Ltd v Union of India* (*Lafarge* case) (2011) 7 SCC 338.

13

ENVIRONMENTAL IMPACT ASSESSMENT

The expression 'EIA', short for environmental impact assessment, is a common term that regularly appears in environmental campaigns, literature and cases. The EIA procedure culminates in an environmental clearance (EC) which is a permission allowing the project to proceed. Generally, the EC requires the applicant to fulfil dozens of conditions at the time of establishing and operating the project. When it comes to large projects, defects in the EIA procedure and the substance of the reports generated in the process are often the most tangible weapons used to challenge the project. On the other side, project proponents defending the EC rely on the layered decision-making EIA process to urge deference by the National Green Tribunal (NGT) and courts. The opening section of this chapter traces the evolution of EIA leading to the present statutory framework. We also examine the shortcomings that have limited the effectiveness of EIA. The next section explores some of the significant Supreme Court judgments on EIA and the patchy record of the judiciary in requiring meaningful implementation.

A. THE EIA REGIME

Responding to heightened public concern for the environment, the United States in the late 1960s and early 1970s framed new laws to clean up the air, the water and hazardous wastes.[1] Among this raft of legislation was the National Environmental Policy Act of 1969 (NEPA). The Act required federal actions, including large infrastructure projects, to conform to sound environmental policies. The machinery to implement the new legislative directives evolved into a formal exercise to predict probable changes to the environment and to mitigate environmental harm. The need for such an exercise was felt across several jurisdictions and amongst the early adopters were Canada, Australia and New Zealand.

Today, environmental impact assessment (EIA) is routinely employed across the globe to anticipate the negative effect of large projects, to justify the enterprise from a socio-ecological perspective and to tailor measures to minimize the harm. When applied sufficiently early in the decision-making process, an EIA may assist in choosing an optimal location, or, indeed, in judging whether a project is desirable at all.

At its broadest level, an EIA exercise is a facet of good governance; a tool to improve decision-making and, where accompanied by an effective public participation process, a means to deepen democracy and secure community inputs. That's the theory. As practised in India, EIA is a low obstacle for the project proponent to vault over; at best, a blunt instrument that helps mitigate the worst environmental excesses through a mix of bureaucratic conditions and an unreal expectation of corporate compliance.

---

[1] This section draws on and is a modified version of the chapter: Shyam Divan, *The Contours of EIA in India* in WATER AND THE LAWS IN INDIA 390 (Ed. Ramaswamy R Iyer, 2009).

Environmental Law & Policy in India. Shyam Divan and Armin Rosencranz, Oxford University Press.
 DOI: 1093/oso/9780192865458.003.0013

I. THE FRAMEWORK: 1994–2006

Until January 1994, EIA in India was carried out under a framework of administrative guidelines which required the proponents of major irrigation projects, river valley projects, power stations, ports and harbours to secure a clearance from the Union Ministry of Environment and Forests (MoEF). The project authority submitted information to the MoEF by filling out questionnaires or check lists. The environmental appraisal was carried out by the ministry's environmental appraisal committees. These committees discussed issues with the project officials and, on the basis of the deliberations, either approved or rejected the site. When approved, the project clearance was generally made conditional on specified safeguards.

The EIA Regulations were framed pursuant to the power conferred on the Central Government by Parliament under section 3 of the Environment (Protection) Act of 1986, which in pertinent part reads:

> 3. *Power of Central Government to take measures to protect and improve environment.* — (1) Subject to the provisions of this Act, the Central Government shall have the power to take all such measures as it deems necessary or expedient for the purpose of protecting and improving the quality of the environment and preventing, controlling and abating environmental pollution.
>
> (2) In particular and without prejudice to the generality of the provisions of sub-section (1), such measures may include measures with respect to all or of any of the following matters, namely:
>
> ...
>
> (v) restriction of areas in which any industries, operations or processes or class of industries, operations or processes shall not be carried out or shall be carried out subject to certain safeguards.

Rule 5(3) of the Environment (Protection) Rules of 1986 empowers the Central Government to impose prohibitions or restrictions on the location of any industry or the carrying on of processes and operations in an area. The EIA Regulations of 1994 and the successor EIA Regulations of 2006 were framed under these enabling powers.

On 27 January 1994, the MoEF notified mandatory EIAs for 29 designated projects.[2] The notification required an EIA, environment management plan (EMP) and a project report to be submitted to the impact assessment agency for clearance. The MoEF was designated as the impact assessment agency and was required to consult a multi-disciplinary committee of experts before taking a decision. The 1994 notification mandated public hearings and was India's first attempt at a comprehensive EIA scheme.

Barely three months later, on 4 May 1994, the MoEF diluted the January notification.[3] The MoEF dismantled some of the new safeguards, subordinating environmental concerns to economic objectives. The project proponent was no longer required to submit a detailed project report and the previous requirement of preparing both an EIA and EMP was changed to now only require either of these documents. The project authority was allowed to acquire land, fell trees, prepare the land, etc. even before receiving the EC. The project-related activities could proceed, so long as there was no construction at the site. Administrative guidelines in the form of an 'Explanatory Note' issued by the MoEF restricted public access to an executive summary of the documents filed and narrowed this entitlement to residents located around the project, the displacement site or where the environmental impact would fall. The

[2] Notification No. SO 60 (E) dated 27 January 1994.

[3] Notification No. SO 356 (E) dated 4 May 1994.

Explanatory Note scaled down the EIA report requirement, which was supposed to cover one year, to a single season report, termed as rapid EIA.

On 10 April 1997, some of the regressive changes introduced in May 1994 were undone by fresh amendments to the parent notification. The 1997 amendments restored public hearings and prescribed the procedure for these hearings. In a step towards decentralizing the process of granting ECs, the MoEF simultaneously notified an EIA procedure for clearance of certain types of thermal power plants, where the concerned state government was to vet the applications.[4] The procedures to be followed under this notification were similar to the amended procedure for central clearances.

The subsequent amendments to the parent EIA notification of 1994 chipped and chiselled at some provisions, retaining the essential framework that was in place by 1997. River valley projects including hydel power projects, major irrigation projects and flood control projects were covered by the EIA notification since its inception. The amendment introduced on 13 June 2002[5] obliged the project proponent to make copies of the EIA report available to members of the public. Previously, only the executive summary was available to the public and this had helped conceal inadequate or incomplete EIA reports. On 7 May 2003, an exception was carved out to enable improvement works to be undertaken without following the statutory EIA procedure. Where canals were widened and strengthened up to 20 metres (on both sides combined) along the existing alignment, there was no need to conduct an EIA unless the canals passed through ecologically sensitive areas such as national parks, sanctuaries, tiger reserves and reserve forests.[6] On 7 July 2004, responding to orders passed by the Supreme Court[7] and the Madras High Court,[8] the MoEF extended the EIA regulations to cover construction projects and industrial estates.[9]

Meanwhile, in 1997, Parliament enacted the National Environment Appellate Authority Act which constituted an authority headed by a retired Justice of the Supreme Court or Chief Justice of the High Court and comprising experts with technical knowledge on ecological matters. This authority (NEAA) was empowered to hear appeals filed by persons aggrieved by an order granting an EC. The validity of a project clearance granted by the impact assessment agency could now be tested before a statutory appellate forum.[10] The NGT replaced the NEAA and now hears appeals from decisions under the extant EIA notification.

In 2005, Kanchi Kohli and Manju Menon published a study analysing the working of the EIA process.[11] The report documented several structural weaknesses, amongst them: the exclusion of environmentally disruptive activities from the scope of the EIA process;[12] the poor quality of EIA reports, which frequently lacked information and candour;[13] ineffective public hearings;[14] frequent instances of ancillary activities at the project site before an EC of the

4 Notification No. SO 318 (E) dated 10 April 1997.

5 Notification No. SO 632 (E) dated13 June 2002.

6 Notification No. SO 506 (E) dated 7 May 2003.

7 *News Item 'Hindustan Times' A Q F M Yamuna v Central Pollution Control Board* (2004) 9 SCC 576.

8 *C S Kappuraj v State of Tamil Nadu* (2004) 2 Law Weekly 554; (2004) SCC Online Mad 366.

9 Notification No. SO 801 (E) dated 7 July 2004.

10 The National Environment Appellate Authority Act of 1997.

11 Kanchi Kohli & Manju Menon, *Eleven Years of the Environment Impact Assessment Notification, 1994: How Effective has it Been?* (2005).

12 *Id.* at 23.

13 *Id.* at 26.

14 *Id.* at 31.

core activity was received;[15] doubtful competence of personnel on the Expert Committees;[16] a failure of experts to assert environmental concerns;[17] poor compliance with post-operative conditions;[18] ineffective appellate oversight by the NEAA;[19] and limited institutional capacities to effectively work the EIA notification. Kohli and Menon wrote:

> After eleven years of the existence of this notification, citizens' experiences of the EIA notification and decision making process of development projects is still filled with disappointment, anger and frustration. There seems little political will to uphold the principles behind the notification or even the clauses of the notification. This is clear from the fact that though the MoEF has the powers to reject a project if it violates the notification, it has not done so in such cases brought to its notice by NGOs and community groups.[20]

Despite the recommendations designed to strengthen the EIA framework,[21] the shortcomings noticed in 2005 continue to dog the process.

II. THE 2006 FRAMEWORK

The need to stimulate economic growth by reforming existing legislation spurred the Union Government to review laws and streamline the process to establish new industry.[22] Propelled by the corporate perception that EIA clearances took far too long and, on the strength of its decade-long experience, on 15 September 2005 the MoEF invited public comments on a new EIA framework.[23] This process eventually culminated in a fresh EIA notification issued in September 2006.[24]

The current regime for EIA is contained in a statutory notification dated 14 September 2006 also framed under the EPA.[25] This notification replaced the previous regime introduced in January 1994. The September 2006 notification substantially alters and strengthens the EIA procedure. Thirty-nine projects[26] designated in the schedule to the notification are required to secure a prior EC from the MoEF in respect of category A projects, or from the State Environment Impact Assessment Authority (SEIAA) for matters covered by category B to the schedule. An EC from one of these regulatory authorities must be obtained before commencing construction or preparing the land by the project proponent. However, the land may be acquired before securing an EC. River valley projects, ports and harbours are listed in the schedule and require clearance from either the MoEF or the SEIAA, depending upon the project size. The SEIAA, comprising three persons, is required to be constituted by the Central Government.

Both the MoEF and SEIAA are required to decide on whether to grant environment clearance based on the recommendations of an Expert Appraisal Committee (EAC). The EACs are entrusted with the tasks of screening, scoping and appraising projects. Category B projects are

---

15 *Id.* at 26.
16 *Id.* at 28.
17 *Id.* at 29.
18 *Id.* at 27.
19 *Id.* at 47.
20 *Id.* at 9.
21 *Id.* at 73.
22 Government of India, *Report on Reforming Investment Approvals and Implementation Procedures* (2002). This report is popularly known as the 'Govindarajan Committee Report on Investment Reforms'.
23 Notification No. SO 1324 (E) dated 15 September 2005.
24 Notification No. SO 1533 (E) dated 14 September 2006.
25 At the time of writing, a draft EIA notification 2020 had been published by the MoEF on 12 March 2020 for comment. The draft notification dilutes the 2006 notification in significant ways.
26 The original notification covered 38 projects. A new category with respect to bio-medical waste treatment facilities was inserted by an amendment through Notification No. SO 1142 (E) dated 17 April 2015.

first screened by the state-level EAC for determining whether the project requires further environmental studies for preparation of an EIA. The projects requiring an EIA report (category B-1) are classified on the basis of guidelines framed by the MoEF. For all category A and B-1 projects, the EAC must determine detailed and comprehensive terms of reference addressing all environmental concerns. The terms of reference must be conveyed to the applicant within 60 days of receiving the application. Where this period is exceeded, the terms of reference suggested by the applicant are the basis for the EIA studies.

All category A and category B-1 projects are required to follow a public consultation process to address the concerns of local affected persons and others having a plausible stake in the environmental impact of the project. The public consultation involves a public hearing at the site and written responses from concerned stakeholders. The public hearing is organized by the state pollution control board (PCB) within 45 days of a request being made in this behalf by the applicant. For obtaining written responses from stakeholders, the state PCB is required to invite responses by placing on their website the summary EIA report prepared by the applicant. The authorities are also required to make available the draft EIA report for inspection. Once the public consultation process is complete, the project proponent is required to address all the material environmental concerns expressed during this process to make appropriate changes in the draft EIA and EMP. The final EIA report is then submitted to the MoEF or the SEIAA.

The first stage of the appraisal involves a detailed scrutiny by the EAC of the application and other documents such as the final EIA report, and the outcome of the public consultations. After interacting with the applicants and obtaining necessary clarifications, the EAC must make categorical recommendations to the MoEF or SEIAA, either for grant of an EC on stipulated terms and conditions or rejection of the application. The EAC must furnish reasons in support of its recommendations. This appraisal exercise must be completed within 60 days of receiving the final EIA report.

The MoEF or SEIAA is required to convey its decision to the applicants within 45 days of receiving the recommendations of the EAC. Generally, the decision for grant of the EC must be conveyed within 105 days of receiving the final EIA report. Normally, recommendations of the EAC must be accepted and when the regulatory authority disagrees with the recommendations, it may request reconsideration by the EAC within a period of 45 days. The decision of the regulatory authority, after considering the recommendations of the EAC following the remand, is final and must be conveyed to the applicant.

Environment clearance under the EIA notification of 2006 must be obtained prior to embarking on a project.[27] The EC granted for a project is valid for a period of seven years in most cases[28] and 10 years in the case of river valley projects. It is mandatory for the project management to submit half-yearly compliance reports in respect of terms and conditions mentioned in the EC. All such compliance reports are available to the public and the latest compliance report must be displayed on the website of the concerned regulatory authority.

In June 2007, nine months after the new EIA notification, Leo F Saldanha and his team published a vigorous critique on the new law.[29] The authors argued that the 2006 notification was formulated to appease the industrial lobby, ignoring the concerns of citizens' groups and

---

27 *The Secretary, Kerala State Coastal Management Authority v DLF Universal Ltd* (2018) 2 SCC 203.

28 The principal notification provided for five years as a general rule and this period was increased to seven years by notification No. SO 1141 (E) dated 29 April 2015.

29 Leo F Saldanha, Abhay Raj Naik, Arpita Joshi & Subramanya Sastry, *Green Tapism: A Review of the Environmental Impact Assessment Notification–2006* (2007).

NGOs working amongst affected communities.[30] The September 2006 notification did little to improve locational decisions or sensitize the project proponent to adverse environmental impacts. Indeed, the authors suggest that the MoEF had been captured by industrial lobbies, and that the new EIA regime was designed principally to facilitate economic growth.[31]

The EIA notification has a special significance to environmental activists and development workers. In a sub-continent mired in deep divisions between the empowered and the powerless, this law creates an entitlement amongst the politically and economically weak to influence the course of decision-making. The harmful impacts of large projects in an urban-centric political economy tend to fall on scattered rural communities. When sufficiently evolved, the public hearing process could enable affected communities to voice their concerns and cause the government and the project's corporate sponsors to re-evaluate the enterprise.

The principal EIA notification of September 2006 has undergone several amendments. Broadly, without disturbing the structure of the principal notification, the amendments have modified the entries in the schedule;[32] specified the qualifications of members of the EAC;[33] specified the qualifications of the chairperson of the SEIAA;[34] detailed the procedure for conducting public hearings;[35] clarified applicable conditions with respect to scheduled projects;[36] set out the appraisal procedure where public consultation is not mandatory;[37] refined the scoping process;[38] and streamlined the provisions relating to highway projects,[39] coal blocks[40] and situations where production technologies had changed after the grant of an EC.[41]

On 15 January 2016, the Central Government amended the principal notification to bring in a special EIA procedure with respect to river bed mining, sand mining and mining of minor minerals.[42] The amendment was in response to a Supreme Court judgment in *Deepak Kumar v State of Haryana*[43] concerning sand mining in river beds and directions issued by the NGT in January 2015,[44] where the government was asked to make an appropriate policy for mining leases operating in a cluster. The special regime with respect to the mining of minor minerals operates at the district level with a District Level Environment Impact Assessment Authority (DEIAA) chaired by the District Magistrate or the District Collector and three other members including the most senior divisional forest officer. The DEIAA is assisted by a District

30 *Id.* at 16.

31 *Id.* at 8.

32 Notification No. SO 1737 (E) dated 11 October 2007; Notification No. SO 3067 (E) dated 1 December 2009; Notification No. SO 696 (E) dated 4 April 2011; Notification No. SO 2896 (E) dated 13 December 2012; Notification No. SO 674 (E) dated 13 March 2013; Notification No. SO 2731 (E) dated 9 September 2013; Notification No. SO 1559 (E) dated 25 June 2014; Notification No. SO 2601 (E) dated 7 October 2014; Notification No. SO 3252 (E) dated 22 December 2014; Notification No. SO 1142 (E) dated 17 April 2015; Notification No. SO 1834 (E) dated 6 July 2015; Notification No. SO 246 (E) dated 25 January 2016 and Notification No. SO 236 (E) dated 16 January 2020.

33 Notification No. SO 1737 (E) dated 11 October 2007.

34 Notification No. SO 2600 (E) dated 9 October 2014.

35 Notification No. SO 3067 (E) dated 1 December 2009.

36 Notification No. SO 3067 (E) dated 1 December 2009.

37 Notification No. SO 696 (E) dated 4 April 2011.

38 Notification No. SO 2559 (E) dated 22 August 2013; Notification No. SO 996 (E) dated 10 April 2015 and Notification No. SO 751 (E) dated 17 February 2020.

39 Notification No. SO 382 (E) dated 3 February 2015 and Notification No. SO 996 (E) dated 10 April 2015.

40 Notification No. SO 811 (E) dated 23 March 2015.

41 Notification No. SO 246 (E) dated 25 January 2016.

42 Notification No. SO 147 (E) dated 15 January 2016.

43 (2012) 4 SCC 629.

44 *Himmat Singh Shekhawat v State of Rajasthan* MANU/GT/0008/2015. Original Application No. 123 of 2014, Principal Bench, National Green Tribunal, order dated 13 January 2015.

Level Expert Appraisal Committee (DEAC) with 11 members including a representative of the state PCB, forest department and remote sensing department or geology department. Apart from streamlining the provisions with respect to screening, scoping and appraisal generally, this amendment also prescribed the application procedures for permission to mine minor minerals where the lease was for an area of 5 hectares or less.

The EIA procedure in India draws on inputs from four sources. The primary burden is on the project proponent who must choose the site, identify the technology and employ suitable measures to mitigate the adverse environmental impact of the enterprise. This phase envisages a degree of corporate environmental responsibility and assumes that the project proponent will eliminate most of the adverse impacts by engaging competent experts to advise it on mitigation measures. The second source of inputs comes from the affected community and environmentalists who are expected to project the concerns of the people and the natural resources that are likely to be impacted by the project. This stream of inputs enters the process through the avenue of the public hearing. The third and most crucial intervention is provided by the EAC, the Expert Committee tasked to advise the impact assessment agency. This committee is supposed to evaluate the project from a multi-disciplinary perspective, drawing on the expertise of each specialist on the committee. Finally, the impact assessment agency is required to assimilate the information placed before it and take an informed decision on whether to grant the EC.

III. EIA AT GROUND LEVEL

Amongst the important water project proponents is the National Hydroelectric Power Corporation (NHPC), a government corporation that has been constructing irrigation and hydropower projects since 1975. Given its parentage, one would expect that the NHPC would set a high benchmark by conforming to EIA procedures. A study of NHPC projects suggests otherwise.[45] The corporation routinely commences construction prior to obtaining ECs and persistently breaches environmental norms without fear of being penalized.

The weak corporate ethic extends to environmental consultants engaged in preparing the EIA reports. In the case of the Dandeli mini hydel project, the concerned consultants were shown to have plagiarized material from another EIA report for a project in a neighbouring area.[46] In numerous cases, the EIA reports were so spare that a meaningful evaluation was not possible on the disclosed data.[47] At times, there was a concealment of vital information, or the cutting and pasting of material from other sources in order to create an aura of scientific rigour.[48] Recourse to rapid EIAs based on single season data has meant that even where reliable data was made available, the impact assessment was at best partial, since downstream impacts in water projects are apt to vary considerably from season to season.[49]

The public hearing process is the principal formal mechanism by which members of the affected community can voice their grievances. The effectiveness of public hearings has varied

---

[45] Kanchi Kohli & Manju Menon, *Eleven Years of the Environment Impact Assessment Notification, 1994: How Effective has it Been?* 26 (2005).

[46] *Id.* and Leo F Saldanha, Abhay Raj Naik, Arpita Joshi & Subramanya Sastry, *Green Tapism: A Review of the Environmental Impact Assessment Notification–2006* 35 (2007).

[47] Neeraj Vagholikar, *Undermining People's Participation* in Kanchi Kohli & Manju Menon, *supra* note 45 at 41; Aruna Murthy & Himanshu Sekhar Patra, *Environment Impact Assessment Process in India and the Drawbacks* 11 (2005), https://elibrarywcl.files.wordpress.com/2015/02/environment-impact-assessment-process-in-india-and-the-drawbacks-1.pdf, accessed 10 June 2021.

[48] Neeraj Vagholikar, *id.* and Kanchi Kohli & Manju Menon, *supra* note 45 at 26, 30 & 60.

[49] Kanchi Kohli & Manju Menon, *supra* note 45 at 26 and Aruna Murthy & Himanshu Sekhar Patra, *supra* note 47.

tremendously. In its most repressive form, as with some mining projects, the affected communities have been physically prevented from participating in the hearings through the deployment of the state police.[50] Frequently, the object of public hearings has been undermined by inadequate notice of the meeting, a refusal to publish and share essential information and an inaccurate communication to the MoEF of what transpired at the hearing.[51] In contrast, creative initiatives by NGOs and some government officials have enabled affected communities to genuinely understand the nature of the project and formulate responses to abate the potential impact. The best practices have involved distributing charts, diagrams and audio recordings describing the impact of the project so that the information spreads in the community; arranging advance meetings between the affected community and the project authority, where mitigation measures and concerns of the community are discussed before the formal public hearing; and uploading the EIA reports on websites to widen access to these core documents.[52]

Although the Expert Committees advising the MoEF are meant to comprise professionals from diverse disciplines, the reality has been different. Two studies found that the Expert Committees were not constituted as required.[53] There is a huge gap of expertise in the social sciences, with few qualified persons who can assess the project impact on local communities, women, children and socially disadvantaged groups.[54] Representatives of political parties to which the incumbent Minister of Environment and Forests belongs, but with little by way of expertise, roost on these committees. The composition of the committees is skewed in favour of engineers, with very few experts in wildlife conservation, social sciences, ecology, environment and health.[55] Although the chairpersons of these committees are supposed to hold outstanding credentials in the fields of environment and ecology, the posts have invariably been packed by former secretaries to the government.[56] The effectiveness of the Expert Committees was hobbled by the previous careers of the chairpersons and the continuing professional affiliations of the committee members. The chairpersons were frequently required to examine projects proposed by the ministries in which they had served.[57] Likewise, many of the committee members were drawn from government affiliated institutions or departments, undermining the independent character of the advice expected from experts. Moreover, the number of NGO representatives serving on the Expert Committees has been trimmed over the years,[58] and the regional diversity of representation has all but vanished, with the large chunk of the members being drawn from either Tamil Nadu or the Delhi region.[59]

A study that closely examined more than ten hydropower projects found that the project clearances were granted despite breaches of the EIA regulations. In the case of the Parbati project, the foundation stone was laid before the EC was granted, the impacts on biodiversity

---

[50] Kanchi Kohli & Manju Menon, *supra* note 45 at 31 and Leo F Saldanha, *et al*, *supra* note 46 at 94.

[51] Kanchi Kohli & Manju Menon, *supra* note 45 at 31–33; Leo F Saldanha, *et al*, *supra* note 46 at 44–61; Neeraj Vagholikar *supra* note 47; Aruna Murthy & Himanshu Sekhar Patra, *supra* note 47.

[52] Kanchi Kohli & Manju Menon, *supra* note 45 at 32.

[53] Kanchi Kohli & Manju Menon, *supra* note 45 at 28–30 and Leo F Saldanha, *et al*, *supra* note 46 at 31–6.

[54] Kanchi Kohli & Manju Menon, *supra* note 45 at 28.

[55] *Id.* at 28–9.

[56] *Id.* at 29.

[57] *Id.*

[58] *Id.*

[59] *Id.* at 30. In November 2004, the River Valley and Hydropower Projects Committee comprised of 14 members. Four of these persons including the chairperson and member secretary were directly from government ministries. One of the members was affiliated to a political party. There was no expert in flora and fauna conservation or in social sciences; and there was no representative from citizens' groups.

in the region were not studied adequately and the public hearing conducted was a charade.[60] The EIA report for the Karcham-Wangtoo project was not translated into the local language, undermining the purpose of the public hearings, which in this case were repeatedly boycotted by the local people.[61] The local community was not provided access to the EIA report and executive summary before the public hearing for the Chamera II hydroelectric project.[62] Similar shortcomings marred the EC procedure for Pala Maneri in Uttaranchal, Allain Duhangan in Himachal Pradesh, Athirampiplly in Kerala, Human Dam in Maharashtra, the Teesta Low Dam project in West Bengal, the lower Subansiri project in Arunachal Pradesh and the middle Siang hydropower project in Assam.[63]

The variable quality of inputs has resulted in numerous water projects being cleared by the MoEF without a satisfactory assessment of the costs and benefits. Indeed, the reluctance of the MoEF to reject project proposals on environmental grounds, and its inability to create a machinery by which post-clearance conditions are complied with, has resulted in most project authorities considering the EIA procedure as yet another 'administrative hassle'.[64] The clearances issued by the MoEF do not prescribe punitive pay-outs by the corporation or personal liabilities of senior managers where the conditions of the EC are breached. In the absence of any such strong deterrent it is improbable that the EIA procedure, as currently worked, will significantly improve environmental decision-making. It is only when the MoEF displays sufficient bite in the post-clearance phase by punishing deviating project executives that the self-regulatory regime will gain efficacy.

IV. APPELLATE AND JUDICIAL OVERSIGHT

The validity of an EC may be challenged before the National Green Tribunal under section 16(h) of the National Green Tribunal Act of 2010.[65] An appeal must be filed within a period of 30 days from the date of the EC. However, the NGT is conferred with discretion to entertain an appeal filed within 90 days where there is justification for the delay.

Where the appellant has genuine explanations for the delay such as securing 'expert as well as professional legal advice' and where the documentation is voluminous, the NGT ought to condone the delay. Applying this principle to a challenge to an EC for a greenfield international airport, the Supreme Court observed:

> An appeal to the NGT in such matters is no ordinary matter; it has the potential of irrevocably changing the environment with the possibility of likely injury. Application of judicial mind by an independent tribunal in such cases, at the first appellate stage, is almost a necessity.[66]

The NGT has a statutory responsibility to conduct a merit's review with respect to the EC and cannot abdicate its responsibility by simply claiming that the EAC had adequately examined relevant factors.[67] This principle laid down by the Supreme Court in March 2019 may

60 *Id.* at 34.
61 *Id.*
62 *Id.*
63 *Id.* at 34–40.
64 *Id.* at 25.
65 Previously, an EC could be challenged before the NGT's predecessor, the National Environment Appellate Authority constituted under the National Environment Appellate Authority Act of 1997. The decisions rendered by the NEAA displayed little environmental sensitivity and numerous appeals were rejected on narrow technical considerations. Kanchi Kohli & Manju Menon, *supra* note 45 at 47. The Law Commission of India in its 186th Report found that the NEAA had very little work and was largely non-functional. Law Commission of India, *186th Report on Proposal to Constitute Environment Courts* 6 (2003).
66 *Sridevi Datla v Union of India* (2021) SCC Online SC 235.
67 *Hanuman Laxman Aroskar v Union of India* (2019) 15 SCC 401.

pave the way for more meaningful appellate oversight by the Tribunal and may translate into more rigorous scrutiny by the EAC at the first level. For example, the Supreme Court upheld the decision of the NGT requiring a fresh rapid EIA for an eight-lane peripheral ring road around Bengaluru when it found that the clearance was based on stale data and the EIA consultant was not accredited for highway projects.[68]

The approach of the higher judiciary with respect to EIA is marked by great deference to the views of the impact assessment agency. In numerous judgments the Supreme Court of India has extolled the virtues of sustainable development and preservation of the environment. Nevertheless, when deciding upon the validity of the EC granted for the Sardar Sarovar Dam on the Narmada River, the court was content to adopt a hands-off approach. The Supreme Court examined the validity of the EC based upon the guidelines prevailing in 1987, the 1994 EIA notification being prospective in its operation. The *Narmada* court found that the conception and execution of a large dam were policy decisions and that courts ought not to transgress into the field of policy.[69] In effect, the court found that the present institutional mechanisms, supplemented by the grievance redressal agencies to examine displacement issues, were adequate to address the social and environmental impacts of large water projects.[70] Although the Sardar Sarovar Dam EC was granted when some studies were incomplete, the court declined to jeopardize the project since it was satisfied that further studies subsequent to the grant of the EC were being undertaken. This approach reinforces the general perception that EIA in India is a mitigation exercise rather than a tool to evaluate whether a project is societally worthwhile.

The other important large dam case that was decided by the Supreme Court concerned the Tehri Dam which impounds the Bhagirathi and Bhilangana rivers in the Garhwal Himalayas.[71] On both the occasions when the court examined environmental aspects of the project, particularly dam safety in view of the high seismicity in the region, the court declined to upset the decision granting an EC. Reiterating the *Narmada* case reasoning that construction of high dams was a policy matter, the *Tehri* court also held that it would not sit in judgment over the considered opinion of experts, such matters being best left to the government.

The Supreme Court again used the principle of agency deference to reject a challenge to raising the level of the Mullaperiyar Dam.[72] The court allowed an increase in the dam height since the Expert Committee had found that there would be no adverse impact on the flora and fauna and that the structural safety was not compromised by the project. The High Courts too have been reluctant to interfere in the execution of infrastructure projects on the ground that the EC was defective. Declining to overturn expert opinions, High Courts permitted the international airport project at Hyderabad to proceed[73] and also refused to quash an EC granted in favour of a power station.[74]

Confronted by the issue of whether or not to permit a ship breaker to dismantle a passenger liner at Alang, Gujarat, the Supreme Court appointed a technical committee of experts to

---

68 *Bengaluru Development Authority v Sudhakar Hegde* (2020) 15 SCC 63.

69 *Narmada Bachao Andolan v Union of India* (2000) 10 SCC 664.

70 John R Wood, *The Politics of Water Resource Development in India: The Narmada Dam Controversy* 192 (2007).

71 *Tehri Bandh Virodhi Sangharsh Samiti v State of U P* (1992) Supp (1) SCC 44 and *N D Jayal v Union of India* (2004) 9 SCC 362.

72 *Mullaperiyar Environmental Protection Forum v Union of India* (2006) 3 SCC 643.

73 *Forum for a Better Hyderabad (Confederation of Voluntary Organizations of Hyderabad) v Government of A P* 2004 (1) Andh L T 500.

74 *Indian Council for Enviro- Legal Action v Union of India* ILR 1997 Kar 2956.

guide the court. Upon receiving the report, the court held that the approach in such matters involved balancing developmental imperatives with environmental interests. Since all projects would have some adverse impact on the ecology and environment, a suitable balance must be struck between the competing interests of enterprise and environmental protection. The court permitted dismantling of the vessel in terms of the expert report.[75]

To facilitate the building of a research and development centre, the Karnataka Industrial Area Development Board acquired lands for the industry. Responding to a petition by the affected villagers that they would lose their cattle pastures, the High Court directed the board to maintain a green belt around the village limits where cattle could graze.[76] In its appeal before the Supreme Court, the board complained that any such norm would undermine its function to develop industrial areas within the state. Allowing the appeal, the Supreme Court set aside the green belt requirement but directed that in the future 'before acquisition of land for development, the consequences and adverse impact of development on environment must be properly comprehended and the land be acquired for development that do not gravely impair the ecology and environment'.[77]

The reluctance of courts to interfere in the correctness of decisions granting an EC has not prevented judges from strengthening the EIA procedure by fleshing out the provisions of the EIA Regulations. The Gujarat High Court has issued salutary directions pertaining to the conduct of public hearings, enabling citizens to receive information in the local language and thus effectively avail the opportunity afforded by the hearings.[78]

The Kerala High Court has insisted that the public hearing process be strictly complied with in respect of the dam at Athirampilly across the Chalakudy River.[79] The court also held that EIA studies could not be based on single season data gathered during the monsoon. In a second round of litigation challenging the EC granted for the same project, the Kerala High Court once again struck down the EC for procedural violations. This time the EIA report relied upon by the authorities was not released to the public before the public hearing.[80]

The Himachal Pradesh High Court restrained a pharmaceutical company from expanding its plant when it found that an EC under the EIA Regulations had not been obtained. The court held that where a project was likely to significantly impact the environment, a comprehensive EIA based on all season data was necessary.[81]

---

[75] *Research Foundation for Science Technology and Natural Resource Policy v Union of India* 2007 (11) Scale 75.

[76] *C Kenchappa v State of Karnataka* 2000 (4) Kar L J 1.

[77] *Karnataka Industrial Area Development Board v C Kenchappa* (2006) 6 SCC 371.

[78] *Centre for Social Justice v Union of India* AIR 2001 Guj 71. The High Court directed that (i) the venue of public hearing be as near as possible to the site of the proposed project and no further than the sub-district (taluka) headquarters; (ii) the state pollution control board public notice of the public hearing be placed in at least two newspapers widely circulated in the region (one in the vernacular language); (iii) the first public hearing be held at least 30 days after the newspaper notice; (iv) a summary of the EIA report in the local language and the EIA report be made available to concerned citizens; (v) the quorum of the committee conducting the public hearing would be half its membership and the representatives of the pollution control board, state department of environment and one of the three senior citizens nominated by the Collector, would have to be present for a valid public hearing; (vi) the minutes of the public hearing be supplied to citizens on demand; and (vii) the gist of the EC be published in the newspapers in which notice of the public hearing was given.

[79] *Chalakudy Puzha Samrakshna Samithy 'Chaithanya' v State of* Kerala High Court; OP 3581/2001 decided on 17 October 2001.

[80] *Athirappally Grama Panchayat v Union of India* Kerala High Court; W P (C) Nos. 9542, 11254 and 260763/2005 decided on 23 March 2006.

[81] *Baldev Singh v State of H P* 2006 (3) Shim LC 135.

All in all, the judiciary has stepped in where procedural deviations mar the environmental clearance. The fate of an EC is decided at the hands of the impact assessment agency, not a court. At best the courts may add environmental safeguards and require strict enforcement of the conditions appended to the EC.

V. RESETTLEMENT AND REHABILITATION

Where large projects displace communities, the resettlement and rehabilitation (R&R) component of the environment management plan is crucial since those impacted are generally economically and politically weak. India's poor record at R&R is poised to improve with the enactment of the transformative Right to Fair Compensation and Transparency in Land Acquisition, Rehabilitation and Resettlement Act of 2013 (RFCA). The RFCA is discussed in the Large Projects chapter. Here, we examine pre-RFCA cases which led to improvements in the R&R entitlements.

Prior to the RFCA, in the absence of any specific national statute recognizing the rights of those ousted by a large project, as a rule, the affected communities received nothing except small sums of monetary compensation under the erstwhile Land Acquisition Act of 1894 (LA Act). The money received was an illusion since it was never enough to replace the lost holding or to meaningfully resettle elsewhere. Rampant corruption nibbled at even the modest sums awarded.[82] Without a statutory counterweight that obliged the government to resettle communities elsewhere, in practice, the law operated to impoverish the weakest and most marginal segments of Indian society.

Campaigns by NGOs and media coverage contributed in influencing the R&R package.[83] These organs of an open society helped highlight the plight of the oustees and assisted in securing for them a better deal through sustained campaigns.[84] Pre-RFCA, in the absence of a statute codifying the entitlements of project affected persons, the struggle for a humane and just R&R package drew on more diffuse notions of equitable entitlements emanating from policy documents and the fundamental right to life.[85] Since the 1980s, particularly in the context of the struggle to secure a better R&R package for those affected by the Narmada Dams, there had been a gradual evolution of policy intended to soften the excesses of forced displacement.[86] The broad objectives of campaigners urging a humane R&R regime were to minimize displacement, introduce public consultation, introduce gender neutrality, provide land for all agricultural families, create job opportunities, provide a house for a house and provide basic amenities at the new site.[87]

Academic research as well as field experiences clearly indicated that relocated populations end up worse off than before. The principal impoverishment risks arising from forced displacement are landlessness, joblessness, homelessness, marginalization, increased morbidity, food insecurity, lack of access to common property and social disarticulation.[88] Recognizing that

---

[82] Hari Mohan Mathur, *New Livelihoods for Old* in MANAGING RESETTLEMENT IN INDIA: APPROACHES, ISSUES, EXPERIENCES 72 (Ed. Hari Mohan Mathur, 2006).

[83] Hari Mohan Mathur, *Introduction and Overview* in *id.* at 2.

[84] John R Wood, *supra* note 70 at 138.

[85] The fundamental right to life is guaranteed to every person under Article 21 of the Constitution of India. This right has been interpreted expansively to cover any action of the state that might adversely affect a person's livelihood, including forced displacements.

[86] Ramaswamy R Iyer, *Towards a Just Displacement and Rehabilitation Policy* 42 ECONOMIC & POLITICAL WEEKLY 3103 (2007); Sanjeev Khagram, *Dams and Development: Transnational Struggles for Water and Power* 90 (2004).

[87] N C Saxena, *The Resettlement and Rehabilitation Policy of India* in MANAGING RESETTLEMENT IN INDIA: APPROACHES, ISSUES, EXPERIENCES 99 (Ed. Hari Mohan Mathur, 2006).

[88] Ismail Serageldin, *Involuntary Resettlement in World Bank—Financed Projects* in *id.* at 52.

monetary compensation for acquisition of land was quite meaningless in the hands of marginal farmers and tribals, the Supreme Court in 1987 directed the state to provide alternative land or alternative employment so that members of the affected families were not deprived of subsistence.[89] However, no single solution appears perfect for the varied situational challenges faced in different projects. The land for land rehabilitation standard suggested by the Narmada Tribunal was found to be impracticable by the government and the judiciary.[90]

In the *Narmada* case, the Supreme Court primarily concerned itself with the resettlement and rehabilitation of the oustees. The court acknowledged that the packages in Gujarat, Maharashtra and Madhya Pradesh were different due to varying geographical, local and economic conditions and the availability of land in the states. While the *Narmada* case was pending before the Supreme Court, the riparian states set up grievance redressal authorities before whom the oustees could ventilate their grievances. To ensure that the rehabilitation programme was being carried out, the state governments appointed independent professional and academic institutions to monitor progress and identify difficulties in implementation so that corrective action could be taken.[91]

The Supreme Court has recognized that rehabilitation is not only about providing food, clothes and shelter but also extending support to help rebuild livelihoods by ensuring the availability of necessary amenities. The oustees ought to be in a better position to lead a decent life and earn a living in the new location. In the *Tehri Dam* case, the court found that the state government had a well-defined R&R policy and package.[92]

On 11 October 2007, the Union Cabinet approved the National Policy on Rehabilitation and Resettlement of 2007 which provided for the allotment of land in lieu of land and preferred employment opportunities for those displaced by projects. Eventually, the national R&R policy of 2007 was combined with a new land acquisition law and given a statutory basis in the RFRA.

To understand the grim impact of large projects that fail to provide adequately for R&R at inception and implementation, we carry a short excerpt from a piece written by Medha Patkar, who led the Narmada Bachao Andolan campaign. It was written shortly after the Prime Minister dedicated the Sardar Sarovar Dam to the nation on 7 September 2017.

MEDHA PATKAR, DROWNED BY THE DAM, Indian Express, 7 October 2017[93]

> Was the ceremonial dedication of the Sardar Sarovar Dam to the nation … a success or a failure? The answer to this question could vary.… For a project to be dedicated to the nation, shouldn't it be completed in the first place? When the project in question pertains to a dam, is it enough to raise a wall to its envisaged height or should canals be constructed as well? Only 33% of the canals in Gujarat have been constructed. Can the one dedicating the project and the one receiving the project—the nation—be satisfied if the enormous impacts of the 138.68 metre-high wall on communities upstream and the downstream, about 10 lakh people, and the ecosystem are not taken into account? The nation may not be aware of what has been gifted to it, but will soon realise the betrayal.…
>
> The present Sardar Sarovar Project, the 455-feet dam, is to be completed by filling a huge reservoir of 40,000 hectare, ousting 244 villages and one township—partly or fully.

---

89 *Karjan Jalasay Yojana Assagrasth Sahkar Ane Sangharsh Samiti v State of Gujarat* AIR 1987 SC 532.
90 John R Wood, *supra* note 70 at 251.
91 *Narmada Bachao Andolan v Union of India* (2000) 10 SCC 664.
92 *N D Jayal v Union of India* (2004) 9 SCC 362.
93 https://indianexpress.com/article/opinion/columns/drowned-by-the-dam-sardar-sarovar-narmada-narendra-modi-4878153/, accessed 11 June 2021.

> In an order on February 8, the Supreme Court ruled that those entitled to land should be paid a package of Rs 60 lakh. It also said that the others who had earlier received a meagre package be paid Rs 15 lakh. The Court also directed that all amenities, mandatory under law, should be in place at every resettlement site by June 2017, perhaps not realising the scale and unfeasibility of the task. The Grievance Redressal Authority was given the responsibility to receive complaints and pass orders that had to be implemented by the state authority.
>
> The state as well as the Grievance Redressal Authority have not fulfilled their duty but have been insistent that the 'oustees' should have left their lands by July 31. But how could they do so since all those eligible for compensation having not received the rehabilitation package and the rehabilitation sites are not ready—they do not have drinking water supply, there are no drainage facilities which has led to water logging and there is no grazing land for cattle. Their right to rehabilitation, to be completed at least six months before the submergence of their property—land, houses, trees or threshing ground—was upheld as part of their right to life by a three-member bench of the apex court. They stayed strong, in spite of the large battalions of police having moved in and braved threats by the government.... These are families of farmers who will lose prime agriculture land and at least a few thousand cattle in each village. They also include self-employed fisherpeople, potters, boatmen, traders, agricultural labourers.
>
> In response to the satyagraha by those threatened with displacement, the MP government declared packages that contain promises for cash, rights to fisherpeople, potters and boatmen. But these haven't materialised and the people continue to struggle non-violently against the violent path of development.
>
> In almost every project, be it related to infrastructure or 'smart-city', there is little concern for compensation and mitigation. People in the Narmada Valley have realised this over the past three decades. The larger question also remains: Who is this development for and at what cost? Dams may be dedicated, as are nuclear power plants, but it is only a resource transfer from nature-based communities to urban India at an unparalleled cost to not only those who lose but the country as a whole.

Writing in 2021, Medha Patkar draws attention to the continuing contributions by the Narmada Bachao Andolan. Nearly 6,000 adivasi children were educated through 8 Jeevanshalas (schools); corruption in the R&R process in Madhya Pradesh was exposed (including falsification of government registers); and due to a sustained campaign, around 50,000 families across Madhya Pradesh, Maharashtra and Gujarat received R&R benefits including land and house plots. Benefits to Madhya Pradesh and Maharashtra were primarily to take the form of cheap electricity. Since less power was delivered than assured, both states were seeking monetary compensation in lieu of the energy supply. Moreover, the Narmada water flowing into Gujarat was diverted to cities and for industrial use, at the cost of villages and agriculture.[94]

VI. EIA & SOMPETA THERMAL PLANT

Large infrastructure projects inevitably disrupt the local community, destroy rural lifestyles and impact the livelihood of traditional folk earning their living from agriculture, fishing and livestock-dependent activities. The prospect of displacement and the unknown fallout of industrial activity trigger protests that may grow into strong grassroots agitations. The project proponent, anxious to swiftly commence operations, usually discloses minimal information fearing that every additional disclosure may increase scrutiny. This atmosphere of mutual mistrust is evident in the following excerpt. The author, a former senior bureaucrat in the Ministry of Power was part of the community initiative opposing a coal-fired thermal power plant (TPP) located in coastal Andhra Pradesh. As you review the excerpt, remember that

[94] Correspondence between Medha Patkar and Shyam Divan in June 2021.

the narrative is from the perspective of the protestors. The project proponent and authorities would have a vastly different perception.

E A S SARMA; SAGA OF SOMPETA: PUBLIC DECEPTION, PRIVATE GAINS 45 Economic & Political Weekly 38 (2010)

The quiet town of Sompeta is located in the northern part of Srikakulam district of Andhra Pradesh (AP). It is 5–6 kilometres from the sea. The seaward terrain on the east of Sompeta constitutes a unique system of a coastal wetland or swamp known locally as the *beela* and the *tampara*. It supports a rich heritage of biodiversity. Rare migratory birds nest and feed in this area every year. The local fishing communities have enjoyed customary fishing rights here for generations. There are hundreds of marginal farmers, agricultural workers and shepherds who eke out their livelihoods from the swamp. This terrain personifies nature's tranquility.

On 14 July 2010, the swamp suddenly exploded with the fury of the local people, especially the fishing community, against the forcible entry by scores of security personnel employed by a private firm, Nagarjuna Construction Company (NCC), backed by hundreds of armed policemen.

The NCC was at the site to 'level' the ground for its proposed thermal power project. For more than a year, the villagers had tried every means at their behest to voice opposition to the project.

They resented the threat to their livelihoods and the pollution hazard posed by the project. They contended that NCC had not yet secured the mandatory Consent for Establishment (CFE) from the AP Pollution Control Board (APPCB). Their entreaties fell on the deaf ears of the officials. A minister, in fact, dared the people to stop the project, infuriating the villagers.

The local TV channels meticulously covered the events that followed. Against the lush green background of the swamp, hundreds of villagers, including panicking women and children, tried to ward off the blows and the bullets aimed at them. Hired employees of the company, in blue scarves and head bands were seen roughing up the villagers.

At the end of the day, two villagers lay shot dead, five persons sustained bullet injuries, scores of villagers, media persons and several policemen were injured. The central law, the Environment (Protection) Act, 1986 and the state law, the Water, Land and Trees Act, 2002 stood violated, apart from the large-scale violation of the human rights. . . .

The capacity of the project was originally planned to be 2,640 megawatts (MW), later trimmed down to 1,980 MW. The land required is 1,905 acres, located in Rushi Kudda, Gollangunda, Baruvapet and Benkili villages. In this, the extent of government land is 1046 acres, for which NCC had approached the government for alienation in their favour. The company hoped that once the government land was in its hands, the adjacent private owners could be forced to part with their lands for a distress price.

The project would burn 34,245 tonnes of coal, spew out about 14,380 tonnes of ash and deposit 226 tonnes of sulphur daily. In addition, it will also generate significant quantities of other toxic pollutants such as mercury, lead, zinc, cadmium, arsenic and chromium. Some pollutants could be radioactive. The plant will consume 250 million cubic metres of water drawn from the sea. . . .

The consultants who prepare EIA reports on industrial projects are required to evaluate objectively the impact of a given project on the people and the surrounding environment. The EIA manual published by the Ministry of Environment and Forests (MoEF) provided the necessary guidelines for this. The EIA report on Sompeta failed to conform to the format.

The report certified the non-existence of 'ecologically sensitive' areas within 15 km of the project site whereas, in the same breath, it also referred to the existence of seven protected forest blocks (Barua, Gollagundi, Mahendratanya, Erra Mukkum, Kalingapatnam,

Jalantrakota and Gaddur) within that zone, implying that the forest blocks were not ecologically sensitive.

The report described the land as 'uncultivable waste land' whereas the government lands included within the site were classified as Tampara Porampoke (249 acres in Gollagundi), Beela Gayalu (277 acres in Baruapeta), Beela Tampara (199 acres in Benkili) and Kaluva Porampoke (400 acres in Rushikudda) as per the official revenue records. This information was readily available in the government order in which land was given to NCC. As already explained, these are clearly swamps. Kaluva is a water course. Anyone with open eyes would have seen the site to be a lush green stretch of terrain, interspersed with patches of cultivation by small farmers and fishing activity going on. There are three lift irrigation (LI) projects set up by the Andhra Pradesh State Irrigation Development Corporation, located at Benkili, Rushikudda and Kuttuma villages, to pump the swamp waters and irrigate 750 acres. The EIA report was blissfully silent on this.

The report made no mention of the site being a part of the wetland system into which water accumulated continuously and drained into the sea. There was no mention of the Ramsar Convention on Wetlands that required India to identify and protect all wetlands, as degradation of wetlands would destroy the biodiversity and contribute significantly to greenhouse gas emissions. Year after year, India has reported compliance with the objectives of the convention. The union cabinet has approved the National Environment Policy that mandates the conservation of all wetlands. Had the EIA consultants cared to carry out a visual study of this wetland over different seasons of the year, they would not have missed the rare migratory birds nesting there. The report was also oblivious of the two other conventions, one on conservation of biodiversity and another on conservation of migratory birds, both relevant to Sompeta.

The socio-economic component of the report was sketchy. It failed to refer to the fact that a thousand families depended on the swamp for their livelihoods. It failed to evaluate the relative costs and benefits of continuing the wetlands in their present form, supporting the local community *vis-à-vis* diverting them for the power project. . . .

According to the replies received by the author in response to an application filed under Right to Information Act (RTI Act), the MoEF had no system in place to satisfy itself that those appointed as the members of the Expert Appraisal Committee (EAC) had no conflict of interest while appraising projects. Consequently, many industrial projects not strictly in conformity with the norms of environmental protection have found ready endorsement from the EACs dealing with the different sectors. Sompeta belonged to this category.

At its 42nd meeting held during 12–13 March 2009, the EAC constituted a subgroup of its own members to visit the site and report whether (i) there were any mudflats in the land, (ii) it was a marshy land, (iii) it was subject to any tidal action, and (iv) it had the CRZ characteristics. The subgroup visited the site on 4 April 2009 and submitted its report to the EAC. The report observed very clearly that the land, being marshy, was a wetland. However, they felt that it had no Coastal Regulation Zone (CRZ) characteristics. Since it was their own observation that the site was marshy, the subgroup should have straightaway recommended rejecting it for the proposed project because of the committed position of MoEF to conserve all wetlands in view of their ecological significance. Instead of making a recommendation on this, the subgroup conveniently skirted the issue and recommended exactly the opposite, saying that the power project should be permitted since the site was away from CRZ. It is doubtful whether the members of the subgroup had the expertise to pass a final judgment even on the CRZ issue. As a result, without awaiting any other professional input and without looking into the objections raised by some of us, the EAC went ahead and recommended the project for Environment Clearance (EC) for the first phase of 1,320 MW. On that basis, MoEF routinely issued the EC for the project, vide their letter no J13012/119/2008-IA II(T) dated 9 December 2009. . . .

NOTES AND QUESTIONS

1. Coastal locations like Sompeta are chosen for thermal plants because of the ease of importing coal though local jetties and the availability of sea water for cooling. The coast, by its very nature, is ecologically fragile and the wetlands at Sompeta support the protestors' view about the unsuitability of the site. Fishing and agricultural communities dwell throughout India's coastline. Someone is bound to be impacted by a coastal plant. Does the protestors' logic imply that no coastal power plants be built or should heightened scrutiny apply where additionally wetlands are liable to be damaged? The National Green Tribunal (NGT) attempts to resolve this dilemma in the next excerpt.

2. He who pays the piper calls the tune. The author questions the competence of the private expert who prepared the EIA report. The Supreme Court in *Lafarge*[95] was dissatisfied with the system under the EIA Regulations by which the project proponent engages a private organization to carry out the EIA study. The Supreme Court directed the Central Government to appoint a national regulator under section 3(3) of the Environment (Protection) Act of 1986 for appraising projects, enforcing environmental conditions for approvals and to impose penalties on polluters. Until such a regulatory body is constituted, the MoEF was directed to empanel accredited institutions (presumably of requisite competence) from which alone, EIA reports could be obtained. What further safeguards may improve the integrity of the EIA reports?

3. On 29 June 2010, the lone member of the National Environment Appellate Authority (NEAA) (predecessor of NGT) visited the site and posted the appeals challenging the EC dated 9 December 2009 for arguments on 13 July 2010. The local protestors apprehended that without securing its Consent for Establishment (CFE) from the Andhra Pradesh Pollution Control Board (APPCB), the company might commence activities at the site and this led to the violence at Sompeta on 14 July 2010, described in the opening part of Sarma's article. On 14 July 2010 itself,[96] the NEAA (with its seat at New Delhi) set aside the EC, accepting the contentions of the appellants that the EC was granted on a misrepresentation of fact and that the project was likely to destroy wetland systems of great ecological significance.

On 19 September 2011, the NGT allowed the review petition filed by NCC. The NGT recalled the order dated 14 July 2010, finding that the NEAA member breached cardinal principles of law by relying on his personal knowledge, by failing to observe the principles of natural justice and by failing to discuss the voluminous record of material before him. The NGT restored the appeals against the EC dated 9 December 2009 and directed consideration on merits.

4. The next excerpt is from the NGT decision on the restored appeals.

National Green Tribunal, New Delhi[97]

T MOHANA RAO v THE DIRECTOR, MoEF

JUDGMENT:

* * *

The controversy in the present six appeals centres around … three issues:

i. The Project Site, being Wetland and would cause environment hazards apart from ecological imbalance, and hence not proper to set up TPP.

[95] *Lafarge Umium Mining Pvt Ltd v Union of India* (2011) 7 SCC 338, 382.

[96] Sarma's article refers to this date as 15 July 2010. However, we use 14 July 2010 since this is the date mentioned in subsequent orders passed by the NGT.

[97] Appeal No. 23/2011 (NEAA Appeal No. 1/2010) Principal Bench; Judgment dated 23 May 2012.

ii. The Environment Assessment Committee (EAC) has not properly dealt with the proposal submitted by the Project Proponent and has violated and/or by passed certain mandatory requirements stipulated under the EIA Notification, 2006 basing on false data submitted by the Project Proponent.
iii. The Public Hearing was not conducted in proper manner. Consequently, the entire procedure culminating in grant of EC has become vitiated and a nullity in the eye of law.

Now, we propose to deal with the issues one by one.

So far as issue no. 1 is concerned, the grievance of the appellants is that the proposed project site is Poramboke Wetlands and Swampy land which is not fit for setting up of a Thermal Power Plant. The said submission has been strongly repudiated by the [Respondents].

In course of hearing we called upon ... Learned Counsel for the appellant to produce a copy of the environmental guidelines and/or siting criteria framed by the MoEF for setting up of a Thermal Power Plant. In response a set of guidelines framed by the MoEF way back in the year 1987 [were produced]. According to the guidelines, the location of the Thermal Power Plant should be avoided within 25 km of outer peripheries of metropolitan cities, national parks and wild life sanctuaries, ecological sensitive areas like tropical forests, bio-sphere reserves, national parks and sanctuaries, important lakes and coastal areas rich in coral formation etc. The guidelines do not create any embargo with regard to setting up Coal Based Power Plant in/or around Wetland.

After going through the guidelines, we feel that the same are not exhaustive nor has taken care of many factors affecting environment and ecology prevailing as on date. It is pertinent to note that the siting criteria produced before us, were framed 25 years ago (1987). By afflux of time number of further studies have been undertaken, new concept and theories in the field of environment and ecology have developed. The changed scenario, scientific developments and change in technology mandates that the siting criteria as well as guidelines for setting up Thermal Power Stations (TPPs) should be revised to bring it in par with the modern techniques to suit the present environmental condition and to protect the ecologically sensitive areas. All these eventualities have not been kept in mind by the MoEF, which is still guided by the siting criteria formulated way back in the year 1987. We, therefore, direct the MoEF to take cognizance of the present day scenario and revise the siting criteria, guidelines for setting up of Thermal Power Projects to match with the present day requirements as early as possible so as to avoid future controversies. In course of hearing, this Tribunal was informed that an exercise in this respect was initiated in the year 2009 but then till date MoEF has not arrived at a logical conclusion. It should be kept in mind that the updated guidelines for setting up TPPs would not only avoid unnecessary litigation but would also go a long way in providing proper selection of environmentally compatible sites. Further, the principles of sustainable development and precautionary principles mandate that the guidelines should clearly spell out 'Go' and 'No Go' areas for locating Thermal Power Plant so that the environmental issues can be internalised right from the beginning of project formation stage. We, therefore, direct the MoEF to frame new guidelines and siting criteria with the observations made in this paragraph for TPPs and file a copy thereof before this Tribunal within a period of three months hence.

However, it is made clear that the proposal of the present Project Proponent has rightly been dealt with in view of the siting criteria guidelines which were prevailing at the relevant time.

[On the second issue, the NGT found that the EIA report relied on data collected prior to the Terms of Reference [ToR] being fixed. Moreover, the methodology adopted by the consultant was flawed.]

As the EIA report is the key on which the EIA process revolves, it is important that EIA report prepared should be scientific and trustworthy and without any mistakes or ambiguity.

MoEF may ensure that the quality of the EIA report remains fool proof and any consultants whose EIA reports are not found satisfactory, should be blacklisted.

The third and most important issue which remains to be addressed is public hearing. Importance of public hearing is very much wider and has to be sacrosanct emphasised and followed:

Public hearing/consultation is based on the principles of participatory democracy and ensures community participation and is aimed to ensure that the affected persons have a say and their voice is heard and respected. The legislature in its wisdom has given people a right of meaningful participation in decisions affecting their lives and livelihood. In order to have a proper and effective Public Hearing the common man is to be provided access to the executive summary of EIA report and the relevant studies carried out.

To appreciate the entire procedure of public hearing better, it would be necessary to refer to some of the provisions of EIA Notification, 2006. [Provisions omitted.]

The purpose of the above clauses is to make the public hearing a meaningful one with full participation of all interested persons who may have a point of view to state. The above clauses operationalize the de-centralised decision making in a democratic set up where the views of those who are likely to be affected by a decision are given a say and an opportunity to voice their concerns. This procedure is intended to render the decision fair and participative and not to thrust it on people, who may be unaware of the implications of the decision.... In the above background, it is not possible to agree with the stand of the Project Proponent and MoEF that there is no requirement in terms of the above clauses to make available the Executive Summary of the EIA Report of the Project, to the persons likely to be affected at least 30 days in advance of the public hearing. If their participation has to be meaningful, then they must have full information of the *pros* and *cons* of the proposed project and the impact it is likely to have on the environment in the area.

[The NGT ordered a fresh public hearing, directed the MoEF to take a fresh decision regarding the grant of an EC based on the updated EIA report and the views of the public, and ordered that the 2009 EC would remain suspended until the fresh decision was taken. Further, the MoEF was directed to notify the important wetlands in the country so that such controversies could be avoided in the future. The MoEF was also asked to finalize guidelines for siting TPPs in three months.]

NOTES AND QUESTIONS

1. Was the NGT correct in faulting the environmental consultant for relying on baseline data collected prior to finalizing the ToR? Most of the requirements in the ToR for a TPP are standard and are known to experts working in the field. Having regard to the lengthy period of gestation for a TPP, is there anything legally or ethically objectionable in collecting baseline data such as water and air quality samples *prior* to the formal issue of the ToR?

2. The NGT directions should help reduce conflict and improve decision-making for locating future TPPs. But what about the community around Sompeta? Regardless of the extant 1987 Guidelines, was it not the duty of the NGT to satisfy itself about the project's impact on the wetlands? Why should the appellants suffer adverse consequences due to the MoEF's failure to update the guidelines for two and a half decades? The appellants' case was independent of the siting criteria guidelines, an aspect the NGT ignored in its analysis. Is the role of the NGT confined to requiring the government to set standards or is it also under a duty to test environmental decision-making where no administrative guidelines exist?

3. In August 2015, the state government cancelled the land allocation in favour of the power station, conceding to the demands of the protestors.

4. Kanchi Kohli and Manju Menon found that under the 2006 EIA notification every project is green signalled, regardless of its harm to the environment. Their study showed that the emphasis had shifted away from evaluating whether a project was beneficial or not to a defensive regime concerned less with environmental protection and more with 'managing' impacts. The emphasis on economic development and administrative efficiency had all but reduced the EIA process to an exercise in mitigation.[98] EIA was no longer a decision-making tool to secure public inputs and thereafter evaluate whether a project should be allowed in societal interest. Go ahead, it must. The emphasis now was on granting clearance and managing adverse impacts 'by short–sighted compensatory clauses'.[99]

Writing in 2008, this is their insight into the public hearing process:

> In the initial years of the EIA notification 1994, the public hearing process held much promise as it was the first formal space where citizens could rightfully participate in environmental decision-making. This euphoria quickly vanished with the stories of how power and social dynamics were playing up in public hearings. Today, the platform has become a space for project proponents to prove their popularity and support at any cost. They resort to corrupt practices of bribing influential elders and politicians; providing faulty information about the project and obstructing the presentation of opinions that may be critical to the project. The use of violence by the state machinery is a feature in almost every public hearing that is taking place today.[100]

The authors lament that the EIA process under pressure for speedy clearances of infrastructure and development projects was 'more than ever before ... marked by violence'. The state machinery is marshalled to stifle protest, divide communities and generally rush through projects notwithstanding irreversible impacts to forests, wetlands and the coast.[101]

B. THE SUPREME COURT ON EIA

I. THE *OKHLA BIRD SANCTUARY* CASE

The EIA notification of 2006 was carefully examined by the Supreme Court in the *Okhla Bird Sanctuary* case. The citizens petitioning the Supreme Court contended that the memorial park project was covered by the schedule to the EIA notification of 2006 which read:

[98] Kanchi Kohli & Manju Menon, *Re-Engineering the Legal and Policy Regimes on Environment* 43 Economic & Political Weekly 14, 16 (2008).

[99] Kanchi Kohli & Manju Menon, *Environmental Decision-Making: Whose Agenda?* 42 Economic & Political Weekly 2490, 2493 (2007).

[100] Kanchi Kohli & Manju Menon, *supra* note 98 at 17.

[101] Kanchi Kohli & Manju Menon, *id.* at 16. Also see Kanchi Kohli & Manju Menon, *From Impact Assessment to Clearance Manufacture* 44 Economic & Political Weekly 20 (2009).

SCHEDULE

(See Paras 2 and 7)

List of Projects or Activities Requiring Prior Environmental Clearance

Project or Activity		*Category with threshold limit* A	B	*Conditions if any*
8		*Building/Construction projects/Area development projects and Townships*		
(1)	(2)	(3)	(4)	(5)
8(a)	Building and construction projects		>20,000 sqm and <1,50,000 sq m of built-up area*	* (built-up area for covered construction; in the case of facilities open to the sky, it will be the activity area)
8(b)	Townships and area development projects.		Covering an area >50 ha and or built-up area >1,50,000 sq m**	** All projects under Item 8(b) shall be appraised as Category B1

The Supreme Court found that the project was not covered by the notification and consequently no EC was necessary. It also rejected the challenge on the grounds that a forest was illegally cleared to accommodate the park and the project's proximity to the bird sanctuary would adversely impact avian life. The following excerpt deals with the EIA issue.[102]

IN RE: CONSTRUCTION OF PARK AT NOIDA NEAR OKHLA BIRD SANCTUARY

(2011) 1 SCC 744

Aftab Alam, J:

* * *

The CEC in its report to this Court dated 4-9-2009 held and found that the project was covered by the EIA Notification, 2006 and it required prior environmental clearance in terms of the notification. In its report, the CEC observed as follows:

> 30. The CEC does not agree with the stand taken by the State Government as well as the MoEF that the project does not require environmental clearance in terms of the MoEF Notification dated 14-9-2006. The MoEF, as well as the State of Uttar Pradesh have taken this view primarily on the ground that the built-up area of the project is less than 20,000 sq m and therefore the project does not require environmental clearance. The built-up area has been calculated by the State of Uttar Pradesh on the basis of its building bye-laws. The CEC is of the view that for the purpose of environmental clearance, the building bye-laws of the State Government have no relevance at all. As per the details provided by the State Government itself, out of 33.43 ha of the project area, 3499.50 sq m is being used for memorial building and toilet blocks, 3500 sq m is being used for utilities and facilities, 1,29,140.80 sq m area is being used for hard landscape including for platforms, plinth, sculptures and surrounded paved area, path, etc. Another 34,850 sq m area is to be used for vehicular movement. The above comes to more than 50% of the project area which in CEC's view qualify to be included in the activity area. The project cost is about Rs. 685 crores. As per the MoEF Notification dated 14-9-2006, for building/construction project, in the case of facilities open to the sky, the activity area is to be included in the built-up area. In the present case, after including the activity area the total built-up area, for the purpose of environmental clearance, far exceeds the threshold limit of 20,000 sq m of built-up area provided in the notification. The MoEF, on its own admission, has merely relied on the details of the built-up area as provided by the State Government without independently verifying

102 For a fuller understanding of the case examine the discussion on this case in the Forests chapter.

> it and has not included the area falling in the category of activity area. In any case, even if there was any doubt in the MoEF regarding the applicability of the environmental clearance in the present case, in view of precautionary principle it should have erred on the side of the caution and should have insisted for the environmental clearance.

* * *

It is extremely difficult to accept the contention that the categorisation under Items 8(a) and 8(b) has no bearing on the nature and character of the project and is based purely on the built-up area. A building and construction project is nothing but addition of structures over the land. A township project is the development of a new area for residential, commercial or industrial use. A township project is different *both quantitatively and qualitatively* from a mere building and construction project. Further, an area development project may be connected with the township development project and may be its first stage when grounds are cleared, roads and pathways are laid out and provisions are made for drainage, sewage, electricity and telephone lines and the whole range of other civic infrastructure. Or an area development project may be completely independent of any township development project as in case of creating an artificial lake, or an urban forest or setting up a zoological or botanical park or a recreational, amusement or a theme park.

The illustration given by [counsel for the petitioner] may be correct to an extent. Constructions with built-up area in excess of 1,50,000 would be huge by any standard and in that case the project by virtue of sheer magnitude would qualify as township development project. To that limited extent there may be a quantitative correlation between Items 8(a) and 8(b). But it must be realised that the converse of the illustration given by [counsel] may not be true. For example, a project which is by its nature and character an 'area development project' would not become a 'building and construction project' simply because it falls short of the threshold mark under Item 8(b) but comes within the area specified in Item 8(a). The essential difference between Items 8(a) and 8(b) lies not only in the different magnitudes but in the difference in the nature and character of the projects enumerated thereunder.

In light of the above discussion, it is difficult to see the project in question as a 'building and construction project'. Applying the test of 'dominant purpose or dominant nature' of the project or the 'common parlance' test i.e. how a common person using it and enjoying its facilities would view it, the project can only be categorised under Item 8(b) of the schedule as a 'township and area development project'. But under that category it does not come up to the threshold marker inasmuch as the total area of the project (33.43 ha) is less than 50 ha and its built-up area even if the hard landscaped area and the covered areas are put together comes to 1,05,544.49 sq m i.e. much below the threshold marker of 1,50,000 sq m. The inescapable conclusion, therefore, is that the project does not fall within the ambit of the EIA Notification S.O. 1533(E) dated 14-9-2006. This is not to say that this is the ideal or a very happy outcome but that is how the notification is framed and taking any other view would be doing gross violence to the scheme of the notification....

Before putting down the records of the case a few observations may not be out of place. The EIA Notification dated 14-9-2006 urgently calls for a close second look by the authorities concerned. The projects/activities under Items 8(a) and 8(b) of the schedule to the notification need to be described with greater precision and clarity and the definition of built-up area with facilities open to the sky needs to be freed from its present ambiguity and vagueness. The question of application of the general condition to the projects/activities listed in the schedule also needs to be put beyond any debate or dispute. We would also like to point out that the environmental impact studies in this case were not conducted either by the MoEF or any organisation under it or even by any agencies appointed by it. All the three studies that were finally placed before the Expert Appraisal Committee and which this Court has also taken into consideration, were made at the behest of the project proponents and by agencies of their choice. This Court would have been more comfortable if the environment impact studies were made by the MoEF or by any organisation under it or at least by agencies appointed and recommended by it.

NOTES AND QUESTIONS

1. In a part of the judgment (not excerpted), the court records that the sanctuary is a haven for birds with an annual population/visits estimated at 21,272 in 2008–09. The sanctuary is home to about 302 species of birds of which, according to the Bombay Natural History Society, two are critically endangered, 11 are vulnerable and seven are threatened. If, as the judgment notes, two bird species are *critically* endangered and therefore facing extinction, should the EIA process *a fortiori* apply? Should not decision-makers, including the court, be aware of the possible impact that the project would have on all the endangered species?

2. In the *Wild Buffalo* case[103] and the *Sandalwood* case[104] (rendered after the *Okhla Bird Sanctuary* judgment), the Supreme Court commends an eco-centric approach that recognizes every species' right to live. Is the *Okhla Bird Sanctuary* decision consistent with an eco-centric approach?

3. Cut to the bone, EIA is an exercise to locate a project at an optimal site from an environmental standpoint. Should the court have asked the state to shift the memorial park to some other tract of vacant land available in Noida? By engaging in a hair-splitting analysis of the EIA notification, did the court miss the wood for the trees in terms of the underlying objective of the EIA process? Was this a case where the court, in the exercise of its powers under Articles 21, 32 and 142 of the Constitution, ought to have asked the memorial to be shifted to a more benign site?

4. If you were the Chief Minister of Uttar Pradesh and wanted to set up a memorial park (with or without your statue), why would you insist on this site alone, regardless of the 6,000 trees to be felled? Viewing the location of the park on a map may provide the answer.

5. In the operative directions, the Supreme Court engaged in a landscaping exercise: '[W]e feel that the extent of stone and concrete constructions in the name of 'hard landscaping' is highly out of proportion.' The court required the hard surfaces to be reduced from 35.54% of the total project area to 25%. In the remaining 75%, it ordered that '25% should be used for soft/green landscaping and the remaining, preferably 50% must have a thick cover of trees of the native variety'. It ordered also that the plantation of trees be especially dense towards the Okhla Bird Sanctuary and that an Expert Committee be established to oversee the project.

6. Applying the 'common parlance' test, the court found that the project would *not* fall under Item 8(a). Had the project fallen under this category, an EC would have been mandatory. Revisit the schedule extracted earlier in this section and work out for yourself whether the court's reasoning and analysis is correct.

7. Did the court stretch the law to green flag the project?

II. THE *RIVERBED SAND MINING* CASES

An EC under the EIA notification of 2006 is required with respect to specified projects and activities listed in the schedule to the notification. Conversely, projects that do not fall within the ambit of the specified categories may be implemented without any environmental scrutiny. The call on whether to include a particular project or activity in the EIA schedule is a techno-economic decision by the Union Government. Certain projects that have a significant environmental impact are intentionally excluded from the schedule. For example, while dams and barrages used for the generation of hydroelectricity or irrigation require an EC, an identical dam or barrage used for supplying drinking water is excluded. What might be

[103] *T N Godavarman Thirumulpad v Union of India* (2012) 3 SCC 277.
[104] *T N Godavarman Thirumulpad v Union of India* (2012) 4 SCC 362.

the reasons for keeping certain projects outside EIA purview? Do citizens have a remedy in respect of excluded projects?

In *Deepak Kumar v State of Haryana*,[105] the Supreme Court confronted a situation where the EIA notification did not cover the disruptive activity. Sand mining in riverbeds and other ecologically sensitive areas was damaging the environment in Haryana, Rajasthan and Uttar Pradesh. Sand is a 'minor mineral' falling under the regulatory control of the states. It is the states who may frame suitable regulations with respect to mining such minerals under section 15 of the Mines and Minerals (Development and Regulation) Act of 1957 (MMDRA). While the predecessor 1994 EIA notification excluded from its purview the mining of minor minerals, the EIA notification of 2006 covers mineral leases where the area of the lease is a minimum of 5 hectares. Haryana decided to promote the development of sand quarries that had an area which was 4.5 hectares or less, thereby slipping below the statutory EIA threshold. The Supreme Court thought dimly of this ploy. It directed Haryana (and other states) to implement a set of recommendations of the Union Ministry of Environment and Forests (MoEF). One of these recommendations was that the minimum size of a mine lease should be 5 hectares. Until these recommendations were implemented by the states, the Supreme Court ordered that fresh leases of minor minerals in respect of an area of less than 5 hectares be granted only after obtaining an EC from the MoEF. In effect, the Supreme Court *extended* operation of the 2006 notification to leases that were less than 5 hectares. Was this a legitimate exercise of judicial power? What are the pitfalls in such an approach?

Responding to complaints about environmentally disruptive large-scale sand mining, the Supreme Court directed the Central Empowered Committee (CEC) to conduct an inspection with respect to the allegations of illegal mining. The CEC was also asked to examine whether Haryana's action was an attempt to flout the EIA notification by breaking homogeneous areas into pieces of less than 5 hectares. The Supreme Court found the CEC report inadequate, but nevertheless investigated the issues.

DEEPAK KUMAR v STATE OF HARYANA

(2012) 4 SCC 629

K S P RADHAKRISHNAN, J:

* * *

We have no materials before us to come to the conclusion that the removal of minor minerals, boulders, gravel, sand quarries, etc. covered by the auction notices dated 3-6-2011 and 8-8-2011, in the places notified therein and also in the riverbeds of Yamuna, Ghaggar, Tangri, Markanda, Krishnavati River basin, Dohan River basin, etc. would not cause environmental degradation or threat to the biodiversity, destroy riverine vegetation, cause erosion, pollute water sources, etc. Sand mining on either side of the rivers, upstream and instream, is one of the causes for environmental degradation and also a threat to the biodiversity. Over the years, India's rivers and riparian ecology have been badly affected by the alarming rate of unrestricted sand mining which damages the ecosystem of rivers and the safety of bridges, weakening of riverbeds, destruction of natural habitats of organisms living on the riverbeds, affects fish breeding and migration, spells disaster for the conservation of many bird species, increases saline water in the rivers, etc.

Extraction of alluvial material from within or near a streambed has a direct impact on the stream's physical habitat characteristics. These characteristics include bed elevation, substrate composition and stability, instream roughness elements, depth, velocity, turbidity, sediment transport, stream discharge and temperature. Altering these habitat characteristics can have deleterious impacts on both instream biota and the associated riparian habitat. The demand for sand continues to increase day by day as building and construction of new infrastructures

[105] (2012) 4 SCC 629.

and expansion of existing ones is continuous thereby placing immense pressure on the supply of the sand resource and hence mining activities are going on legally and illegally without any restrictions. Lack of proper planning and sand management cause disturbance of marine eco-system and also upset the ability of natural marine processes to replenish the sand.

We are expressing our deep concern since we are faced with a situation where the auction notices dated 3-6-2011 and 8-8-2011 have permitted quarrying, mining and removal of sand from instream and upstream of several rivers, which may have serious environmental impact on ephemeral, seasonal and perennial rivers and riverbeds and sand extraction may have an adverse effect on biodiversity as well. Further, it may also lead to bed degradation and sedimentation having a negative effect on the aquatic life. The rivers mentioned in the auction notices are on the foothills of the fragile Shivalik Hills. Shivalik Hills are the source of rivers like Ghaggar, Tangri, Markanda, etc. River Ghaggar is a seasonal river which rises up in the outer Himalayas between Yamuna and Satluj and enters Haryana near Pinjore, District Panchkula, which passes through Ambala and Hissar and reaches Bikaner in Rajasthan. River Markanda is also a seasonal river like Ghaggar, which also originates from the lower Shivalik Hills and enters Haryana near Ambala. During monsoon, this stream swells up into a raging torrent, notorious for its devastating power, as also, River Yamuna.

We find that it is without conducting any study on the possible environmental impact on/in the riverbeds and elsewhere the auction notices have been issued. We are of the considered view that when we are faced with a situation where extraction of alluvial material within or near a riverbed has an impact on the river's physical habitat characteristics, like river stability, flood risk, environmental degradation, loss of habitat, decline in biodiversity, it is not an answer to say that the extraction is in blocks of less than 5 ha, separated by 1 km, because their collective impact may be significant, hence the necessity of a proper environmental assessment plan.

Possibly this may be the reason that in the affidavit filed by MoEF on 23-11-2011 along with Annexure 2, report, the following stand has been taken:

> 'The Ministry is of the opinion that where the mining area is homogenous, physically proximate and on identifiable piece of land of 5 ha or more, it should not be broken into smaller sizes to circumvent the EIA Notification, 2006 as the EIA Notification, 2006 is not applicable to the mining projects having lease area of less than 5 ha. The report of the Committee on Minor Minerals, under the Chairmanship of the Secretary (Environment & Forests) with representatives of various State Governments as members including the States of Haryana and Rajasthan recommended a minimum lease size of 5 ha for minor minerals for undertaking scientific mining for the purpose of integrating and addressing environmental concerns. Only in cases of isolated discontinued mineral deposits in less than 5 ha, such mining leases may be considered keeping in view the mineral conservation.'

Situations referred to earlier prevail not only in the State of Haryana but also in the neighbouring and other States of the country as well and those issues had come up for serious deliberations before the Government of India, on various occasions.

The Government of India was receiving various reports regarding the adverse impacts on riverbeds and groundwater due to quarrying/mining of minerals. The Mines and Minerals (Development and Regulation) Act, 1957 empowers the State Governments to make rules in respect of minor minerals. It was noticed that proposals for mining of major minerals typically undergo environmental impact assessment and environmental clearance procedure, but due attention has not been given to environmental aspects of mining of minor minerals. . . .

We are of the view that all State Governments/Union Territories have to give due weight to the abovementioned recommendations of MoEF which are made in consultation with all the State Governments and Union Territories. The Model Rules of 2010 issued by the Ministry of Mines are very vital from the environmental, ecological and biodiversity point of view and therefore the State Governments have to frame proper rules in accordance with the recommendations, under section 15 of the Mines and Minerals (Development and Regulation) Act, 1957.

Quarrying of river sand, it is true, is an important economic activity in the country with river sand forming a crucial raw material for the infrastructural development and for the construction industry but excessive instream sand and gravel mining causes the degradation of rivers. Instream mining lowers the stream bottom of rivers which may lead to bank erosion. Depletion of sand in the streambed and along coastal areas causes the deepening of rivers which may result in destruction of aquatic and riparian habitats as well. Extraction of alluvial material as already mentioned from within or near a streambed has a direct impact on the stream's physical habitat characteristics.

We are of the considered view that it is highly necessary to have an effective framework of mining plan which will take care of all environmental issues and also evolve a long-term rational and sustainable use of natural resource base and also the bio-assessment protocol. Sand mining, it may be noted, may have an adverse effect on biodiversity as loss of habitat caused by sand mining will affect various species, flora and fauna and it may also destabilise the soil structure of river banks and often leaves isolated islands. We find that, taking note of those technical, scientific and environmental matters, MoEF, Government of India, issued various recommendations in March 2010 followed by the Model Rules, 2010 framed by the Ministry of Mines which have to be given effect to, inculcating the spirit of Article 48-A and Article 51-A(*g*) read with Article 21 of the Constitution.

The State of Haryana and various other States have not so far implemented the above recommendations of MoEF or the guidelines issued by the Ministry of Mines before issuing auction notices granting short-term permits by way of auction of minor minerals boulders, gravel, sand, etc., in the riverbeds and elsewhere of less than 5 ha. We, therefore, direct all the States, Union Territories, MoEF and the Ministry of Mines to give effect to the recommendations made by MoEF in its Report of March 2010 and the model guidelines framed by the Ministry of Mines, within a period of six months from today and submit their compliance reports.

The Central Government also should take steps to bring into force the Minor Minerals Conservation and Development Rules, 2010 at the earliest. The State Governments and UTs also should take immediate steps to frame necessary rules under section 15 of the Mines and Minerals (Development and Regulation) Act, 1957 taking into consideration the recommendations of MoEF in its Report of March 2010 and model guidelines framed by the Ministry of Mines, Government of India. Communicate the copy of this order to MoEF, Secretary, Ministry of Mines, New Delhi; Ministry of Water Resources, Central Government Water Authority; the Chief Secretaries of the respective States and Union Territories, who would circulate this order to the Departments concerned.

We, in the meanwhile, order that leases of minor minerals including their renewal for an area of less than five hectares be granted by the States/Union Territories only after getting environmental clearance from MoEF. Ordered accordingly.

The ripples from *Deepak Kumar* periodically reach the Supreme Court. The following excerpt concerns Rajasthan, where the problem of illegal mining persists.

BAJRI LEASE LOI HOLDERS WELFARE SOCIETY v RAJASTHAN
(2021) SCC ONLINE 1043

L Nageswara Rao, J:

* * *

The CEC, in its report, has highlighted the delay in the grant of EC by the MoEFCC to the [Letter of Intent/LoI] holders as the cause for widening the gap in demand and supply of sand, which has resulted in proliferation of illegal sand mining activities to meet the shortfall in supply. The recommendation made by the CEC is that the MoEFCC will issue EC in respect of all the valid LoI holders recommended by the [Expert Appraisal Committee/EAC], within a period of three months, without insisting on submission of the scientific replenishment study report as a pre-condition for the grant of EC, with the replenishment study due to be undertaken during the course of mining.

In spite of the order passed by this Court on 16.11.2017 that no river sand shall be permitted unless a scientific replenishment study is completed and EC is granted, 194 mining leases of *Khatedari* lands have been granted in the State of Rajasthan, with most of these lands being in close proximity of the river banks of the State. 114 *Khatedari* leases are within a distance of 100 metres or less from the river bank and only 23 *Khatedari* leases have been granted beyond a distance of 5 km from the river bank. The CEC has stated in its report that the agricultural lands do not have deposits of quality sand suitable for construction, being a mixture of sand, silt and clay. The *Khatedars* have been exploiting the locational proximity to the river banks by excavating sand from the river bed, instead of restricting the mining to their leasehold areas, completely in violation of the mining plan. The quantity of sand is in excess of the permissible limit which is transported by being shown as having been mined in the *Khatedari* lands. The CEC has commented upon the involvement of sand *mafia* in the trade of sand illegally mined by the *Khatedars* as well as the involvement of authorities in the State of Rajasthan. Therefore, the CEC has recommended the cancellation of all *Khatedari* leases located within 5 km from the river banks as well as those leases where violation of lease conditions including misuse of e-ravannas are detected. The CEC further recommended that no fresh *Khatedari* leases shall be granted, except for Palaeo deposits, without the approval of this Court....

The damage caused to the environment due to rampant unscientific illegal mining needs no reiteration. Unabated illegal mining has resulted in the emergence of sand *mafia* who have been conducting illegal mining in the manner of organized criminal activities and have been involved in brutal attacks against members of local communities, enforcement officials, reporters and social activists for objecting to unlawful sand excavation. The statistics provided by the State Government highlights the magnitude of the problem as about 2411 FIRs have been registered in relation to illegal mining in the State of Rajasthan, between 16.11.2017 and 30.01.2020. When this Court has restrained 82 mining lease/quarry holders from carrying on mining of sand and *bajri* unless a scientific replenishment study is completed and EC is issued by the MoEFCC, the State of Rajasthan ought not to have issued mining leases in favour of the *Khatedars*. It is clear from the report of the CEC that the majority of the *Khatedari* leases are within 100 metres from the river bed. The 2020 Sand Mining Guidelines prescribe that mining plan for mining leases on *Khatedari* lands shall only be approved if there is a possibility of replenishment of the mineral or when there is no possibility of river bed mining within 5 km of the patta land/*Khatedari* land. Agreeing with the CEC's conclusions on the issue of mining leases in *Khatedari* lands facilitating legalisation of transportation and sale of illegally extracted sand, we approve the recommendation of the CEC that all *Khatedari* leases which are located within 5 km from the river bed and those leases where lease conditions have been violated have to be terminated forthwith and that *Khatedari* leases shall be granted only with the permission of this Court....

The scale of compensation by those who are involved in illegal mining has been dealt with by the NGT in *National Green Tribunal Bar Association v Virender Singh*. In its order dated 26.02.2021, the NGT considered and approved the Report submitted by the Central Pollution Control Board dated 30.01.2020, in pursuance of its earlier orders, on scale of compensation to be recovered for violation of norms for mining on 'Polluter Pays' principle. Additionally, para 9.2 of the 2020 Sand Mining Guidelines provides as follows:

> 'The environmental damages incurred or resulting due to illegal mining shall be assessed by a committee constituted by District Administration having expertise from relevant fields, and also having independent representation of locals and State Pollution Control Board. Guidelines for assessment of ecological damages prescribed by the State Government or Concerned Pollution Control Boards or any other authority shall be applicable and compensation as fixed shall be paid by the project proponent, in light of Hon'ble National Green Tribunal orders.'

... The CEC is directed to follow the directions given by the NGT in respect of imposition of penalty/determining scale of compensation for illegal mining and the provisions of the

2020 Sand Mining Guidelines and determine the penalty/compensation afresh and submit a report to this Court within a period of eight weeks from today….

NOTES AND QUESTIONS

1. Clearly, the court was gravely concerned about widespread sand mining. It may have liked to rely on the CEC's findings, but to the disappointment of the judges, the CEC report was silent on the extent of illegalities. To overcome this factual gap and to justify judicial intervention, the court reversed the burden for showing harm: 'We have no materials before us to come to the conclusion that [sand mining] would not cause environmental degradation or threat to the biodiversity, destroy riverine vegetation, cause erosion, pollute water sources, etc.' Generally, a court will insist that the complainant produce some material showing the extent of environmental degradation. Here, the court virtually took judicial notice of the environmental harm occurring across several states and implicitly applied the precautionary principle. The precautionary principle requires the project proponent to show the absence of any environmental harm.

2. Haryana insisted that its actions were perfectly legal. There was no need for an EC because the EIA notification of 2006 applied only where the leased area was more than 5 hectares and, in these cases, the plots were smaller than 5 hectares and were separated by a distance of 1 km. Haryana argued that the auction notices were valid and sand mining in terms of these notices should be allowed. The Supreme Court trumped these submissions by reaching to the spirit of Article 48A and Article 51A(g) read with Article 21 of the Constitution. The constitutional mandate was to protect the environment and both the states as well as the Union Government were under a duty to follow the EIA process regardless of the 5-hectare limit. Moreover, the Supreme Court recognized the important notion of cumulative environmental harm from the working of several small leases, though individually each project would slip below the EIA radar.

3. The EIA notification of 2006 is subordinate legislation framed by the Central Government pursuant to authority conferred on it by Parliament under section 3 of the Environment (Protection) Act of 1986. Likewise, Parliament has empowered the states to frame appropriate subordinate legislation under the MMDRA with respect to minor minerals such as sand. The court found that the existing framework of subordinate legislation was inadequate to effectively curb the menace of excessive sand mining of riverbeds. Does any court have the power to direct the government to frame legislation—plenary or subordinate? If not, were the directions passed by the court justified?

4. The stand of the MoEF before the court was curious and limp. The MoEF which issued the EIA notification of 2006 is empowered to amend the notification. It can always alter the categories of activities covered by the EIA process. In so far as mining of minerals is concerned, the 2006 notification itself restricts the EIA process to mining projects where the area leased is more than 5 hectares. If the MoEF felt that its notification was deficient or was being circumvented by states leasing out small plots, the correct response was an amendment to the notification. Was the Central Government justified in shifting the responsibility to the court when it could have removed the 5-hectare limit or could have added a statutory explanation that homogenous mining areas should not be broken into smaller plots?

5. *Deepak Kumar* illustrates the challenges in framing a comprehensive legal regime in a federal polity where legislative powers are divided between the Union Government and the states. Here, to curb rampant abuse of riverbeds, it was necessary for coordinated initiatives

to be taken by the states and the Centre. The Supreme Court's judgment in *Deepak Kumar* facilitates the creation of a consistent national regime for the use of riverine sand in a sustainable manner.

6. Sand is an essential material for most construction activity in India. The Supreme Court judgment in *Deepak Kumar* disrupted the economy. It brought to a standstill building activity in several parts of the country.

7. Responding to *Deepak Kumar* the Central Government amended the principal EIA notification of 2006. The 2016 amendment established a special procedure for riverbed sand mining. The new provisions required the establishment of a District Level Environment Impact Assessment Authority (DEIAA) chaired by the District Magistrate or District Collector and the constitution of a District Level Expert Appraisal Committee. To carry out riverbed sand mining, the lessee must now secure an EC from the DEIAA.[106]

8. Punjab's Department of Mines and Geology was granted an EC for mining sand over a stretch of 12.96 hectares from the riverbed of Satluj River. Thereafter, the department auctioned 102 sites and applied to transfer the EC to the successful bidders. At this stage, the SEIAA revoked the EC since many of the sites were in the stream or active channel of the river and other sites were located on agricultural land. A spot inspection by an Expert Committee confirmed that the ground reality was different from what was projected by the department when it applied for the EC. The NGT and the Supreme Court upheld the action of the SEIAA.[107]

Without repeated judicial interventions by the Supreme Court and the High Court, the 'sand mafia' rules the roost. The commercial interests and the state government interests are so closely aligned that preventing illegal riverbed sand mining appears beyond the executive's capacity.

III. THE *STERLITE* CASE

In the *Sterlite* case, the appellant impugned a division bench judgment of the Madras High Court, rendered in a batch of writ petitions challenging environmental permissions granted to the company. The High Court directed Sterlite to close down its copper smelter at Tuticorin and issued ameliorative directions to protect the employees. Tuticorin, a port city in southern Tamil Nadu, was not the company's first choice—its previous efforts to establish a smelter elsewhere were thwarted by stiff local resistance in Gujarat, Goa and Maharashtra. The Supreme Court reversed the High Court judgment, allowed the smelter to operate and required the appellant to deposit Rs. 100 crores with the District Collector for having polluted the environment. Examine carefully three facets of the case: (a) the standard of judicial review applied by the court; (b) the discussion regarding monetary compensation; and (c) the court's approach to the misrepresentation and suppression of material facts by the appellant. Keep in mind that the EC in *Sterlite* was issued under the erstwhile 1994 EIA notification.

STERLITE INDUSTRIES (INDIA) LTD v UNION OF INDIA

(2013) 4 SCC 575

***

A K PATNAIK, J:

The relevant facts very briefly are that the appellant Company applied and obtained 'no-objection certificate' on 1-8-1994 from the Tamil Nadu Pollution Control Board (for short

106 Notification No. SO 147 (E) dated 15 January 2016.

107 *Department of Mines & Geology, State of Punjab v State Level Environment Impact Assessment Authority* (2019) 16 SCALE 504; (2019) SCC Online SC 1485.

'the TNPCB') for setting up a copper smelter plant (for short 'the plant') in Melavittan Village, Tuticorin. On 16-1-1995, the Ministry of Environment and Forests, Government of India, granted environmental clearance to the setting up of the plant of the appellants at Tuticorin subject to certain conditions including those laid down by the TNPCB and the Government of Tamil Nadu. On 17-5-1995, the Government of Tamil Nadu granted clearance subject to certain conditions and requested the TNPCB to issue consent to the proposed plant of the appellants. Accordingly, on 22-5-1995, the TNPCB granted its consent under section 21 of the Air (Prevention and Control of Pollution) Act, 1981 (for short 'the Air Act') and under section 25 of the Water (Prevention and Control of Pollution) Act, 1974 (for short 'the Water Act') to the appellants to establish the plant in the SIPCOT Industrial Complex, Melavittan Village, Tuticorin Taluk.

The environmental clearance granted by the Ministry of Environment and Forests, Government of India, and the consent orders under the Air Act and the Water Act granted by the TNPCB were challenged before the Madras High Court in WPs Nos. 15501–503 of 1996 by the National Trust for Clean Environment. While these writ petitions were pending, the appellants set up the plant and commenced production on 1-1-1997. Writ Petition No. 5769 of 1997 was then filed by V Gopalsamy, General Secretary, MDMK Political Party, Thayagam, praying for, *inter alia*, a direction to the appellants to stop forthwith the operation of the plant. Writ Petition No. 16861 of 1998 was also filed by Shri K Kanagaraj, Secretary, CITU District Committee, District Thoothukudi, for directions to the State of Tamil Nadu, the TNPCB and the Union of India to take suitable action against the appellant Company for its failure to take safety measures due to which there were pollution and industrial accidents in the plant.

A Division Bench of the High Court heard Writ Petitions Nos. 15501–503 of 1996, Writ Petition No. 5769 of 1997 and Writ Petition No. 16861 of 1998 and by the common judgment dated 28-9-2010 allowed and disposed of the writ petitions with the direction to the appellant Company to close down its plant at Tuticorin. By the common judgment, the High Court also declared that the employees of the appellant Company would be entitled to compensation under Section 25-FFF of the Industrial Disputes Act, 1947 and directed the District Collector, Tuticorin, to take all necessary and immediate steps for the re-employment of the workforce of the appellant Company in some other companies/factories/organisations so as to protect their livelihood and to the extent possible take into consideration their educational and technical qualifications and also the experience in the field.

Aggrieved, the appellant has filed these appeals against the common judgment dated 28-9-2010 and on 1-10-2010, this Court passed an interim order staying the impugned judgment of the High Court....

The first question which we will have to decide is whether the High Court could have interfered with the environmental clearances granted by the Ministry of Environment and Forests, Government of India, and the Government of Tamil Nadu, Department of Environment?

The environmental clearance for setting up the plant was granted to the appellants under [the EIA notification dated 27-1-1994].

Para 2 of the Notification dated 27-1-1994 lays down the requirements and procedure for seeking environmental clearance of projects, and clause (c) of Para 2 provides that the Impact Assessment Agency could solicit comments of the public within thirty days of receipt of proposal, in public hearings, arranged for the purpose, after giving thirty days' notice of such hearings in at least two newspapers, and after completion of public hearing, where required, convey its decision. The language of this notification did not lay down that the public hearing was a must. The impact assessment was done by Tata Consultancy Services as per the requirements then existing and the Government of India has granted the environmental clearance on 16-1-1995. The Notification dated 27-1-1994, however, was amended by Notification dated 10-4-1997 and it was provided in clause (c) of Para 2 of the notification that the Impact Assessment Agency shall conduct a public hearing and the procedure for public hearing was detailed in Schedule IV to the notification by the amendment Notification dated 10-4-1997. Admittedly, in this case, the environmental clearance was granted by the Ministry of Environment, Government of India, on 16-1-1995 in accordance with the procedure laid down by the Notification dated 27-1-1994 well before the Notification dated 10-4-1997 providing for mandatory public hearing in accordance with the procedure laid down in Schedule IV. As there was no mandatory requirement in the procedure laid down under the Environment (Protection) Act, 1986 and the Environment (Protection) Rules, 1986 and the Notification dated 27-1-1994 as amended by the Notification dated 4-5-1994 that a public hearing has to be conducted before grant of environmental clearance, the High Court could not have allowed the writ petitions challenging the environmental clearances on the ground that no public hearing was conducted before grant of the environmental clearances.

An explanatory note regarding the EIA Notification dated 27-1-1994 was also issued by the Central Government and Para 5 of the explanatory note clarified that project proponents could furnish rapid EIA report to the Impact Assessment Agency based on one season data, for examination of the project and comprehensive EIA report may be submitted later, if so asked for by the Impact Assessment Agency and this was permitted where comprehensive EIA report would take at least one year for its preparation. In Para 5 of the affidavit filed by the Union of India before the High Court in Writ Petitions Nos. 15501–503 of 1996, the allegation of the writ petitioner that the Ministry of Environment and Forests have accorded environmental clearance without applying its mind and without making any analysis of the adverse impacts on the marine ecological system has been denied and it has been further stated that after detailed examination of rapid EIA/EMP, filled-in questionnaire for industrial projects, NOC from the State Pollution Control Board and risk analysis, the project was examined as per the procedure laid down in the EIA Notification dated 27-1-1994 (as amended on 4-5-1994) and the project was accorded approval on 16-1-1995 subject to specific conditions. As the procedure laid down under the Environment (Protection) Act, 1986 and the Environment (Protection) Rules, 1986 and the Notification dated 27-1-1994 as amended by the Notification dated 4-5-1994 and as explained by the explanatory note issued by the Government of India permitted rapid EIA in certain circumstances, the High Court could not have allowed the writ petitions on the ground that environmental clearance was issued to the appellant Company on the basis of inadequate rapid EIA, particularly when the Union of India in its affidavit had clearly averred that the environmental clearance was granted after detailed examination of rapid EIA/EMP, filled-in questionnaire for industrial projects, NOC from the State Pollution Control Board and risk analysis in accordance with the procedure laid down in EIA Notification dated 27-1-1994 (as amended on 4-5-1994).

The High Court has noticed some decisions of this Court on sustainable development, precautionary and polluter pays principles and public trust doctrine, but has failed to appreciate that the decision of the Central Government to grant environmental clearance to the plant of the appellants could only be tested on the anvil of well-recognised principles of judicial review as has been held by a three-Judge Bench of this Court in *Lafarge Umiam Mining (P) Ltd v Union of India* (2011) 7 SCC 338. To quote *Environmental Law* edited by David Woolley, QC, *et al*,

> 'The specific grounds upon which a public authority can be challenged by way of judicial review are the same for environmental law as for any other branch of judicial review, namely, on the grounds of illegality, irrationality, and procedural impropriety.'

Thus, if the environmental clearance granted by the competent authority is clearly outside the powers given to it by the Environment (Protection) Act, 1986, the Environment (Protection) Rules, 1986 or the notifications issued thereunder, the High Court could quash the environmental clearance on the ground of illegality. If the environmental clearance is based on a conclusion so unreasonable that no reasonable authority could ever have come to the decision, the environmental clearance would suffer from *Wednesbury* unreasonableness and the High Court could interfere on the ground of irrationality [*Associated Provincial Picture Houses Ltd v Wednesbury Corpn* (1947) 2 All ER 680 (CA)]. And, if the environmental clearance is granted in breach of proper procedure, the High Court could review the decision of the authority on the ground of procedural impropriety.

Where, however, the challenge to the environmental clearance is on the ground of procedural impropriety, the High Court could quash the environmental clearance only if it is satisfied that the breach was of a mandatory requirement in the procedure. As stated in *Environmental Law* edited by David Woolley, QC, *et al*,

> 'It will often not be enough to show that there has been a procedural breach. Most of the procedural requirements are found in the regulations made under primary legislation. There has been much debate in the courts about whether a breach of regulations is mandatory or directory, but in the end the crucial point which has to be considered in any given case is what the particular provision was designed to achieve.'

As we have noticed, when the plant of the appellant Company was granted environmental clearance, the Notification dated 27-1-1994 did not provide for mandatory public hearing. The explanatory note issued by the Central Government on the Notification dated 27-1-1994 also made it clear that the project proponents may furnish rapid EIA report to the IAA based on one season data (other than monsoon), for examination of the project comprehensive EIA report was not a must. In the absence of a mandatory requirement in the procedure laid down under the scheme under the Environment (Protection) Act, 1986 at the relevant time requiring a mandatory public hearing and a mandatory comprehensive EIA report, the High Court could not have interfered with the decision of the Central Government granting environmental clearance on the ground of procedural impropriety.

Coming now to the ground of irrationality argued so vehemently . . . we find that no materials have been produced before us to take a view that the decision of the Central Government to grant the environmental clearance to the plant of the appellants was so unreasonable that no reasonable authority could ever have taken the decision. . . .

In *Belize Alliance of Conservation Non-Governmental Organisations v Dept of the Environment* (2003) 1 WLR 2839, the Lords of the Judicial Committee of the Privy Council have quoted with approval the following words of Linden, JA with reference to the Canadian legislation in *Bow Valley Naturalists Society v Canada (Minister of Canadian Heritage)* (2001) 2 FC 461 (Can), FC at p 494:

> 'The Court must ensure that the steps in the Act are followed, but it must defer to the responsible authorities in their substantive determinations as to the scope of the project, the extent of the screening and the assessment of the cumulative effects in the light of the mitigating factors proposed. It is not for the Judges to decide what projects are to be authorised but, as long as they follow the statutory process, it is for the responsible authorities.'

The aforesaid passage will make it clear that it is for the authorities under the Environment (Protection) Act, 1986, the Environment (Protection) Rules, 1986 and the notifications issued thereunder to determine the scope of the project, the extent of the screening and the assessment of the cumulative effects and so long as the statutory process is followed and the EIA made by the authorities is not found to be irrational so as to frustrate the very purpose of EIA, the Court will not interfere with the decision of the authorities in exercise of its powers of judicial review.

The next question that we have to decide is whether the High Court was right in directing closure of the plant of the appellants on the ground that the plant of the appellants is located at Tuticorin within 25 km of four of the twenty-one islands in the Gulf of Mannar, namely, Vanthivu, Kasuwar, Karaichalli and Villanguchalli. The reason given by the High Court in coming to this conclusion is that the TNPCB had stipulated in the consent order dated 22-5-1995 that the appellant Company has to ensure that the location of the unit should be 25 km away from ecologically sensitive area and as per the report of NEERI, the plant of the appellants was situated at a distance of 6 km of Vanthivu, 7 km of Kasuwar and 15 km of Karaichalli and Villanguchalli and these four villages are part of the twenty-one islands in the Gulf of Mannar. Hence, the High Court directed closure of the plant because the appellant Company has violated the condition of the consent order dated 22-5-1995 issued by the TNPCB under the Water Act.

The consent order dated 22-5-1995 issued by the TNPCB under Section 25 of the Water Act states as follows: [Quote omitted]

The aforesaid extract from the consent order dated 22-5-1995 of the TNPCB issued under the Water Act makes it clear that the appellant Company was given consent to establish its plant in the SIPCOT Industrial Complex, Meelavittam Village, Tuticorin Taluk. Along with the consent order under the Water Act, special conditions were annexed and Clause 20 of the special conditions reads as follows:

> '20. (i) 1 km away from the water resources specified in GOMs No. 213 E&P Deptt, dt. 30-3-1989.
> (ii) 25 km away from ecological/sensitive areas.
> (iii) 500 metres away from high tide line.'

On the one hand, therefore, the appellants were given consent to establish their plant in the SIPCOT Industrial Complex, which as per the NEERI report is within 25 km of four of the twenty-one islands in the Gulf of Mannar. On the other hand, a condition was stipulated in the consent order that the appellants have to ensure that the location of the unit is 25 km away from ecologically sensitive area. It thus appears that the TNPCB while granting the consent under the Water Act for establishment of the plant of the appellants in the SIPCOT Industrial Complex added the above requirement without noting that the SIPCOT Industrial Complex was within 25 km from ecologically sensitive area. Since, however, the consent order was granted to the appellant Company to establish its plant in the SIPCOT Industrial Complex and the plant has in fact been established in the SIPCOT Industrial Complex, the High Court could not have come to the conclusion that the appellant Company had violated the consent order and directed closure of the plant on this ground.

This is not to say that in case it becomes necessary for preservation of ecology of the aforesaid four islands which form part of the Gulf of Mannar, the plant of the appellants cannot be directed to be shifted in future. We find from the affidavit filed on behalf of the State of Tamil Nadu on 29-10-2012 that the Gulf of Mannar consisting of 21 islands including the aforesaid four islands have been notified under section 35(1) of the Wild Life (Protection) Act, 1972 on 10-9-1986 and a declaration may also be made under section 35(4) of the said Act declaring the Gulf of Mannar as a marine national park. We have, therefore, no doubt that the Gulf of Mannar is an ecologically sensitive area and the Central Government may in exercise of its powers under clause (v) of sub-rule (1) of rule 5 of the Environment (Protection) Rules, 1986 prohibit or restrict the location of industries and carrying on processes and operations to preserve the biological diversity of the Gulf of Mannar. As and when the Central Government issues an order under rule 5 of the Environment (Protection) Rules, 1986 prohibiting or restricting the location of industries within and around the Gulf of Mannar marine national park, then appropriate steps may have to be taken by all concerned for shifting the industry of the appellants from the SIPCOT Industrial Complex depending upon the content of the order or notification issued by the Central Government under the aforesaid rule 5 of the Environment (Protection) Rules, 1986, subject to the legal challenge by the industries.

***

If ... after the environmental clearance is granted under the Environment (Protection) Act, 1986, and the Rules and the notifications issued thereunder and after the consents granted under the Air Act and the Water Act, the industry continues to pollute the environment so as to affect the fundamental right to life under Article 21 of the Constitution, the High Court could still direct the closure of the industry by virtue of its powers under Article 21 of the Constitution if it came to the conclusion that there were no other remedial measures to ensure that the industry maintains the standards of emission and effluent as laid down by law for safe environment (see *M C Mehta v Union of India* (1987) 4 SCC 463 in which this court directed closure of tanneries polluting the waters of River Ganga).

We have, therefore, to examine whether there were materials before the High Court to show that the plant of the appellants did not maintain the standards of emission and effluent as laid down by the TNPCB and whether there were no remedial measures other than the closure of the industry of the appellants to protect the environment. We find on a reading of the impugned judgment [*National Trust for Clean Environment v Union of India*, WPs Nos. 15501–503 of 1996, decided on 28-9-2010 (Mad)] of the High Court that it has relied on the report of NEERI of 2005 to hold that the plant site itself is severely polluted and the ground samples level of arsenic justified classifying the whole site of the plant of the appellant as hazardous waste. [The court set out extracts from NEERI Report of 2005.]

It will be clear from the extracts from the Executive Summary of NEERI in its report of 2005, that while some of the emissions from the plant of the appellants were within the limits stipulated by the TNPCB, some of the emissions did not conform to the standards stipulated by TNPCB. It will also be clear from the extracts from the executive summary relating to water environment that the surface water samples were found to be within the prescribed limits of drinking water (IS:10500-1995) whereas groundwater samples showed high mineral contents in terms of dissolved solids as compared to the drinking water standards, but concentrations of nutrient demand parameters revealed that the phosphate and nitrate contents were within the limits stipulated under drinking water standards and levels of chromium, copper and lead were found to be higher in comparison to the parameters stipulated under drinking water standards, whereas the heavy metal concentrations, namely, iron, manganese, zinc and arsenic were within the drinking water standards. Soil samples also revealed heavy metals. Regarding the solid waste out of slag in the plant site, the CPCB has taken a view in its communication dated 17-11-2003 to TNPCB that the slag is non-hazardous. Thus, the NEERI report of 2005 did show that the emission and effluent discharged affected the environment but the report read as whole does not warrant a conclusion that the plant of the appellants could not possibly take remedial steps to improve the environment and that the only remedy to protect the environment was to direct closure of the plant of the appellants.

* * *

The conclusion in the joint inspection report of CPCB and TNPCB [prepared pursuant to directions by the court] is extracted herein below:

> 'Out of the 30 directions issued by the Tamil Nadu Pollution Control Board, the industry has complied with 29 directions. The remaining Direction 1(3) under the Air Act on installation of bag filter to converter is at the final stage of erection, which will require further 15 working days to fully comply as per the industry's revised schedule.'

From the aforesaid conclusion of the joint inspection report, it is clear that out of the 30 directions issued by the TNPCB, the appellant Company has complied with 29 directions and only one more direction under the Air Act was to be complied with. As the deficiencies in the plant of the appellants which affected the environment as pointed out by NEERI have now been removed, the impugned order of the High Court directing closure of the plant of the appellants is liable to be set aside.

We may now consider the contention on behalf of the intervenors that the appellants were liable to pay compensation for the damage caused by the plant to the environment. The NEERI reports of 1998, 1999, 2003 and 2005 show that the plant of the appellant did pollute the environment through emissions which did not conform to the standards laid down by the TNPCB under the Air Act and through discharge of effluent which did not conform to the standards laid down by the TNPCB under the Water Act. As pointed out, ... on account of some of these deficiencies, TNPCB also did not renew the consent to operate for some periods and yet the appellants continued to operate its plant without such renewal.

* * *

For such damages caused to the environment from 1997 to 2012 and for operating the plant without a valid renewal for a fairly long period, the appellant Company obviously is liable to compensate by paying damages.

In *M C Mehta v Union of India* (1987) 1 SCC 395, a Constitution Bench of this Court held:

> '... The enterprise must be held to be under an obligation to provide that the hazardous or inherently dangerous activity in which it is engaged must be conducted with

> the highest standards of safety and if any harm results on account of such activity, the enterprise must be absolutely liable to compensate for such harm and it should be no answer to the enterprise to say that it had taken all reasonable care and that the harm occurred without any negligence on its part.'

The Constitution Bench in the aforesaid case further observed that the quantum of compensation must be co-related to the magnitude and capacity of the enterprise because such compensation must have a deterrent effect and the larger and more prosperous the enterprise, the greater must be the amount of compensation payable by it.

In the Annual Report 2011 of the appellant Company, at pp. 20 and 21, the performance of its copper project is given. We extract hereinbelow the paragraph titled 'Financial Performance':

> 'PBDIT [Profit before deduction of income tax] for the financial year 2010–2011 was Rs 1043 crores, 40% higher than PBDIT of Rs 744 crores for the financial year 2009–2010. This was primarily due to higher LME prices and lower unit costs at Copper India and with the improved by-product realisation.'

Considering the magnitude, capacity and prosperity of the appellant Company, we are of the view that the appellant Company should be held liable for a compensation of Rs 100 crores for having polluted the environment in the vicinity of its plant and for having operated the plant without a renewal of the consents by the TNPCB for a fairly long period and according to us, any less amount, would not have the desired deterrent effect on the appellant Company. The aforesaid amount will be deposited with the Collector of Thoothukudi District, who will invest it in a fixed deposit with a nationalised bank for a period of five years. The interest there from will be spent for improving the environment, including water and soil, of the vicinity of the plant after consultation with TNPCB and approval of the Secretary, Environment, Government of Tamil Nadu.

We now come to the submission ... that we should not grant relief to the appellants because of the misrepresentation and suppression of material facts made in the special leave petition that the appellants have always been running their plant with statutory consents and approvals and misrepresentation and suppression of material facts made in the special leave petition that the plant was closed at the time the special leave petition was moved and a stay order was obtained from this Court on 1-10-2010. There is no doubt that there has been misrepresentation and suppression of material facts made in the special leave petition but to decline relief to the appellants in this case would mean closure of the plant of the appellants. The plant of the appellants contributes substantially to the copper production in India and copper is used in defence, electricity, automobile, construction and infrastructure, etc. The plant of the appellants has about 1300 employees and it also provides employment to a large number of people through contractors. A number of ancillary industries are also dependent on the plant. Through its various transactions, the plant generates a huge revenue to the Central and State Governments in terms of excise, custom duties, income tax and VAT. It also contributes to 10% of the total cargo volume of Tuticorin Port. For these considerations of public interest, we do not think it will be a proper exercise of our discretion under Article 136 of the Constitution to refuse relief on the grounds of misrepresentation and suppression of material facts in the special leave petition.

Before we part with this case, we would like to put on record our appreciation for the writ petitioners before the High Court and the intervenor before this Court for having taken up the cause of the environment both before the High Court and this Court and for having assisted this Court on all dates of hearing with utmost sincerity and hard work.... Very few would venture to litigate for the cause of environment, particularly against the mighty and the resourceful, but the writ petitioners before the High Court and the intervenor before this Court not only ventured but also put in their best for the cause of the general public.

In the result, the appeals are allowed and the impugned common judgment of the High Court is set aside. The appellants, however, are directed to deposit within three months from today a compensation of Rs 100 crores with the Collector of Thoothukudi District, which will be kept in a fixed deposit in a nationalised bank for a minimum of five years, renewable as and when it expires, and the interest there from will be spent on suitable measures for improvement of the environment, including water and soil, of the vicinity of the plant of the appellants after consultation with TNPCB and approval of the Secretary, Environment, Government of Tamil Nadu. In case the Collector of Thoothukudi District, after consultation with TNPCB, finds the interest amount inadequate, he may also utilise the principal amount or part thereof for the aforesaid purpose after approval from the Secretary, Environment, Government of Tamil Nadu. By this judgment, we have only set aside the directions of the High Court in the impugned common judgment and we make it clear that this judgment will not stand in the way of the TNPCB issuing directions to the appellant Company, including a direction for closure of the plant, for the protection of environment in accordance with law.

We also make it clear that the award of damages of Rs 100 crores by this judgment against the appellant Company for the period from 1997 to 2012 will not stand in the way of any claim for damages for the aforesaid period or any other period in a civil court or any other forum in accordance with law.

NOTES AND QUESTIONS

1. The legislative history shows that both before 4 May 1994 and after 10 April 1997, public hearings were mandatory under the statutory EIA procedure. Sterlite received its EC on 16 January 1995 when the mandatory public hearing requirement stood eclipsed by the 4 May 1994 amendment. When the Supreme Court decided the case in 2013, a mandatory public hearing was required by law for the past 16 out of 19 years. Should the court, with the advantage of hindsight, have held that the three-year gap when public hearings were not mandatory, was an aberration? Even if public hearings were not mandatory in January 1995, having regard to the highly polluting nature of a copper smelter and the history of protests that plagued this project in Gujarat, Goa and Maharashtra, was not the MoEF duty bound to require a public hearing in this case?

What is a public hearing designed to achieve? Clause 4 of the Explanatory Note provided: 'Public hearings could be called for in case of projects involving large displacement or having severe environmental ramification.' Did the Sterlite copper smelter meet the criteria?

2. To justify the adequacy of a rapid EIA report (in place of a comprehensive EIA report covering one year), the Supreme Court reached out to the Explanatory Note issued by the MoEF together with the 4 May 1994 amendment. This Explanatory Note is a curious document. It is certainly not subordinate legislation since it was not issued in the formal manner required by law. Could the MoEF through an 'Explanatory Note' dilute the mandate of an environmental law which the ministry is meant to vigorously enforce? Remember, the Explanatory Note also diluted several other beneficial provisions regarding public access to documents and the standing of citizens to obtain the documents. On the other hand, it is always open to a ministry to issue clarifications and guidelines for a better understanding of its rules and regulations; and courts do rely on such clarifications to interpret ambiguous provisions.

3. Notice the structure of analysis in *Sterlite*. First, the court lays down the appropriate standard for judicial review. It is for the authorities to determine the scope of the project, the extent of the screening and the assessment of cumulative impacts. A court should not strike down an EC unless a mandatory procedural requirement is breached or the decision of the authority is so irrational that no reasonable person could ever have taken the decision.

Second, the court applies this standard of review to the facts and rejects each of the specific grounds urged to invalidate the EC (i.e. no public hearing held; no comprehensive EIA). Third, the court finds that there was no breach of the consent issued under the Water Act since the plant was established in the SIPCOT Industrial Complex in terms of the statutory consent. Fourth, the court inquires whether ongoing pollution justified the extreme step of closure or whether remedial measures could bring the industry to compliance. Here, the court found that in course of the litigation, the industry had complied with almost all the pollution parameters and the directions issued by the authorities, obviating the necessity for closure. Fifth, the court finds that for nearly 15 years the industry continued breaching pollution norms and was liable to make compensatory payments. Sixth, the court assesses damages on the principle that it must have a deterrent effect. Seventh, the court considers the issue whether it ought to entertain Sterlite's appeal at all, having regard to misrepresentation and suppression of material facts by the company. Finally, the court confines its determination to the case before it, leaving it open to the authorities to take suitable action against Sterlite in the future, should circumstances warrant.

4. Rather than shut down a functioning industry, the Supreme Court adopts a pragmatic middle path that balances economic considerations with environmental requirements. However, while the industry is given time to meet the norms, it escapes without censure despite an incorrect statement in its petition for special leave to appeal. Was this a case of 'too big to fail'? The 1,300 employees, the need for copper in diverse industries and the economic contribution made by Sterlite appear to have weighed heavily in the court deciding to keep the copper smelter running.

5. The court praises the public interest writ petitioners and the intervenors as well as their teams of lawyers for having done a commendable job. Should the court have awarded more realistic costs for this enormous effort? Are public interest litigants whose campaign yields wide societal benefits entitled to full recompense for legal costs incurred? Did the Supreme Court lose an opportunity to develop costs jurisprudence?

6. In arriving at a ballpark figure of Rs. 100 crores, the court felt that this seemingly large amount would act as a deterrent. Do you think so? Whether it be banks, pharmaceutical manufacturers or polluting industry, most large enterprises would gladly 'pay and play'. In the Indian corporate sector and even globally, large fines seldom discipline violators in the long term. Can you design a more effective strategy that would ensure future compliance? In the Indian context, where some of the largest publicly held corporations are family controlled, would it be better if a court were to target the promoters in control of the enterprise? In what manner and on what principle would this be justified?

7. Sterlite's problems did not end with this judgment. In March 2013, complaints by the residents of nearby areas that emissions were causing breathing problems triggered a spiral of regulatory actions and contests. Sterlite secured interim orders of protection from the NGT and continued to operate its plant. On 9 April 2018, TNPCB refused to renew Sterlite's consent to operate due to non-compliance with certain conditions that were laid down under the Air Act and the Water Act. On 12 April 2018, TNPCB passed an order under section 33A of the Water Act and section 31A of the Air Act, directing that the unit shall not resume production without obtaining prior approval or the renewal of consent from the board. On 22 and 23 May 2018, street protests against Sterlite in Thoothukudi town turned violent leaving over a dozen dead when the police opened fire. On 23 May 2018, TNPCB again invoked sections 33A and 31A to close down the unit and disconnect the power supply to it. On 28 May 2018, the state government issued an order under section 18(1)(b) of the Water Act requiring the TNPCB 'to seal the unit and close the plant permanently'.

Sterlite filed appeals to the NGT which appointed an Expert Committee headed by Justice Tarun Agarwala, former Chief Justice of the Meghalaya High Court, together with representatives of the CPCB and the MoEF. The NGT accepted the recommendations of the committee and by an order dated 15 December 2018 it set aside various orders that were challenged by Sterlite.[108]

On 22 January 2019, the TNPCB again rejected Sterlite's application seeking renewal of consent to operate, stating that conditions of various previous consents issued over the past two decades had not been followed.

The Supreme Court by its judgment dated 18 February 2019 allowed the appeals filed by TNPCB and set aside the orders passed by the NGT on a jurisdictional ground that Sterlite's appeals were not maintainable.[109] As a result, Sterlite approached the Madras High Court seeking to quash the orders passed by the TNPCB and the state government.

On 18 August 2020, the Madras High Court rejected Sterlite's petitions,[110] compelling the company to approach the Supreme Court. When the COVID-19 pandemic caused a huge upsurge in demand for medical grade oxygen, the Supreme Court allowed the company to reopen its oxygen plant as an interim measure.[111]

IV. THE *TALAULICAR & SONS* CASE

Talaulicar and Sons Pvt Ltd,[112] posed a knotty issue of interpretation concerning the EIA notification of 1994. Yet, the Supreme Court chose to sidestep this point, crafting a solution that limited the wrecking ball impact of the Bombay High Court judgment under challenge.[113]

Shankar Jog, an activist and serial public interest petitioner, moved the Bombay High Court against the MoEF and Talaulicar and Sons Pvt Ltd. The foundation of Jog's case was built on the language in paragraph 2(III)(c) of the 1994 notification which read:

> 2. (III)(c) The Impact Assessment Agency shall prepare a set of recommendations based on technical assessment of documents and data, furnished by the project authorities, supplemented by data collected during visits to sites or factories, if undertaken, and interaction with affected population and environmental groups, if necessary. Summary of the reports, the recommendation and the conditions, subject to which environmental clearance is given, shall be made available subject to the public interest to the parties concerned or environmental groups on request. Comments of the public may be solicited, if so decided by the Impact Assessment Agency, within thirty days of receipt of proposal, in public hearings arranged for the purpose after giving thirty days' notice of such hearings in at least two newspapers. Public shall be provided access, subject to the public interest, to the summary of the reports/environmental management plans at the headquarters of the Impact Assessment Agency.
>
> The assessment shall be completed within a period of ninety days from receipt of the requisite documents and data from the project authorities and completion of public hearing, where required, and decision conveyed within thirty days thereafter.

[108] *Vedanta Ltd v State of Tamil Nadu* (2018) SCC Online NGT 1239.

[109] *Tamil Nadu Pollution Control Board v Sterlite Industries (I) Ltd* (2019) 19 SCC 479.

[110] *Vedanta Ltd v State of Tamil Nadu* (2020) SCC Online MAD 14684; (2021) 1 MAD L J 331.

[111] *Vedanta Ltd v State of Tamil Nadu* Supreme Court, Special Leave to Appeal (C) Nos. 10159–10168/2020, order dated 27 April 2021. At the time of writing, the special leave petitions were pending before the Supreme Court.

[112] *Talaulicar and Sons Pvt Ltd v Union of India* (2016) 8 SCC 299.

[113] *Shankar Raghunath Jog v Talaulicar & Sons (P) Ltd* 2011 (5) ALL M R 803; 2012 (1) BOM C R 658.

> The clearance granted shall be valid *for* a period of five years *for* commencement of the construction or operation. [Italics supplied]

The Bombay High Court in its judgment rendered on 12 August 2011, accepted Jog's submission that an EC under the 1994 notification was *'for a term of five years'*, which meant that at the end of every five years, the project proponent was required to go through the entire process again—including technical assessments and a public hearing—and obtain a fresh EC. The High Court applied the rule of strict interpretation and rejected the alternative interpretation that the last clause of the quoted paragraph meant that a person must *commence* construction or operations within five years of the grant of the clearance. This alternative approach is obvious to anyone with a basic understanding of EIA and who is aware of the reality that several large projects such as industrial plants, dams, etc. may take more than five years to begin operations. An EC, by its very nature, is a one-time permission. Should the project proponent deviate or breach the conditions in the EC, the wrongdoer may be penalized or, in extreme cases, the EC could be withdrawn.

Apart from Talaulicar who operated an iron ore mine, the MoEF too appealed to the Supreme Court, because the High Court interpretation, if correct, jeopardized several thousand ECs issued under the 1994 notification on the common understanding that an EC for a project was required just once before commencement.

Having succeeded before the Bombay High Court, Jog approached the NGT and asked for a direction (based on the High Court judgment) to close all iron ore mines in the state of Goa. Confident of sustaining the High Court judgment, Jog asked the Supreme Court to transfer and decide his NGT petition along with Talaulicar's appeal.

The Supreme Court noted that the EIA notification of 1994 had since been replaced and superseded by a subsequent EIA notification issued on 14 September 2006 and which did not contain the ambiguous language of its predecessor. Turning to the facts, the Supreme Court held that Talaulicar was initially granted a conditional EC requiring the miner to conduct detailed hydrogeological studies within two years. The Supreme Court found that after Talaulicar submitted hydrogeological reports, the final clearance issued by the MoEF on 18 October 2007 'was a cryptic one without giving due regard to the various salient features concerning the environment protection and the interest of the public at large'. The court went on to hold:

> In that perspective we are convinced that the order dated 18-10-2007 is liable to be set aside with necessary direction to the [MoEF] to look into the application of [Talaulicar] afresh after the submission of the hydrogeological report and after giving an opportunity of hearing to [Talaulicar] as well as [Jog] or such other bodies to whom such hearing is to be offered as per the subsequent Notification dated 14-9-2006, permit them to file the required material documents in support of their respective stand and pass a reasoned order in accordance with the procedure prescribed under the said notification.
>
> With that view, we set aside the order dated 18-10-2007, and consequently, the impugned order [of the Bombay High Court] cannot also stand.[114]

The Supreme Court thereafter transferred Jog's NGT petition to itself and dismissed the case 'as having become infructuous', since it was based upon the Bombay High Court judgment that had been set aside.[115]

---

114 *Talaulicar and Sons Pvt Ltd v Union of India* (2016) 8 SCC 299 at 304. Unusually, the 18 October 2007 final clearance was *not* challenged by Jog before any court, but was nevertheless set aside by the Supreme Court.

115 *Id.* at 306.

In *Talaulicar*, the Supreme Court indirectly sustained the interpretation that requires a one-time EC, without saying so. Perhaps the Supreme Court did not want to be seen as accepting a purposive interpretation of an environmental regulation that would favour project proponents.

V. THE *ELECTROTHERM* CASE

After receiving a no-objection certificate from the Gujarat Pollution Control Board on 25 February 2005 and a statutory consent on 10 November 2005, Electrotherm (India) Limited (EIL) set up a steel plant. The plant commenced operations in 2005, albeit without an EC required under the EIA notification of 1994.

On 30 November 2007, EIL applied to the MoEF under the extant EIA notification of 14 September 2006[116] requesting permission to expand its pig iron plant. On 20 February 2008, the MoEF granted an EC, noting that a public hearing/consultation was held on 12 June 2007. (The MoEF ignored the lapse on the part of EIL in failing to obtain a prior EC before commencing operations in 2005.)

A couple of years later, EIL again sought an EC, this time for a much bigger expansion. The Expert Appraisal Committee exempted EIL from the requirement of conducting a public hearing in terms of paragraph 7(ii) of the EIA notification, 2006. On 27 January 2010, the MoEF granted an EC, dispensing with the public hearing in respect of the second expansion in view of the hearing held at the stage of the first expansion.

Patel Vipulkumar Ramjibhai petitioned the Gujarat High Court in the public interest seeking revocation of the EC permitting the second expansion. The company resisted the attack, claiming that Patel was put up by its business rivals. The MoEF defended its actions. The High Court was unimpressed by the defence. It set aside the EC granted on 27 January 2010, primarily because the public hearing was wrongly dispensed with. The court shut the plant and permitted resumption of operations subject to a fresh EC being issued.[117]

Electrotherm (India) Ltd appealed to the Supreme Court which granted an interim stay of the High Court judgment (thereby allowing the plant to operate) and directed a field inspection to ascertain whether or not EIL was complying with pollution standards. Upon being satisfied that EIL was generally compliant, the Supreme Court disposed of EIL's appeal.

ELECTROTHERM (INDIA) LIMITED v PATEL VIPULKUMAR RAMJIBHAI

(2016) 9 SCC 300

UDAY U LALIT, J:

* * *

The facts on record are clear that while granting environmental clearance on 20-2-2008, public consultation/public hearing was undertaken on 12-6-2007. As on that date the status of the project was that the capacity of pig iron plant was to be 350 TPD, power plant to be 24 MW, the total cost of the project was Rs 90.00 crores and the total water requirement was 650 m^3/day. The High Court was absolutely right that after expansion the capacity of the plant was to increase threefold. The tabular chart given in environmental clearance dated 27-1-2010 itself shows the tremendous increase in the capacity. Consequently, the pollution load would naturally be of greater order than the one which was contemplated when the earlier public consultation/public hearing was undertaken on 12-8-2007. Further, the water requirement had also risen from 650 m^3/day to 2165 m^3/day. The increase in pollution load and water requirement were certainly matters where public in general and those living in the vicinity in particular had and continue to have a stake.

---

[116] The EIA notification of 2006 had by then replaced the 1994 notification.

[117] *Patel Vipulkumar Ramjibhai v Union of India* 2012 (3) GUJ L R 2312.

Public consultation/Public hearing is one of the important stages while considering the matter for grant of environmental clearance. The minutes of the meetings held on 9-2-2009 to 11-2-2009 show that the request of the appellant for exemption from the requirement of public hearing was accepted by the [Expert Appraisal] Committee. The observations of the Committee suggest that there would be no additional land requirement, groundwater drawal and certain other features. However, the water requirement, which is a community resource, was definitely going to be of greater order in addition to the fact that the expansion of the project would have entailed additional pollution load.

It must be stated here that after the EIA Notification of 2006, a draft Notification was issued on 9-1-2009 wherein an amendment was suggested in Para 7(ii) of the EIA Notification dated 14-9-2006 to the effect that in cases of expansion of projects involving enhancement by more than 50% holding of public consultation/public hearing was essential; implying thereby that in cases where expansion was less than 50% public consultation/public hearing could be exempted. Without going into the question whether public consultation/public hearing could be so exempted, it is relevant to note that this idea in the draft Notification was not accepted, after a Committee constituted to advise in the matter had given its report on 30-10-2009 to the contrary. As a result, the final Notification dated 1-12-2009 did not carry or contain the amendment that was suggested by way of draft notification. Consequently, no exemption on that count could be given when the environmental clearance came to be issued on 27-1-2010.

In *Lafarge Umiam Mining (P) Ltd v Union of India* (2011) 7 SCC 338 public consultation/public hearing was considered and found to be mandatory requirement of the environmental clearance process by this Court. In its conclusions culled out in para 122(xiv) as regards public consultation/public hearing, it was observed by this Court:

> The public consultation or public hearing as it is commonly known, is a mandatory requirement of the environment clearance process and provides an effective forum for any person aggrieved by any aspect of any project to register and seek redressal of his/her grievances.

At the same time, the observations by this Court while summing up the discussion in para 119 are quite eloquent:

> It cannot be gainsaid that utilisation of the environment and its natural resources has to be in a way that is consistent with principles of sustainable development and intergenerational equity, but balancing of these equities may entail policy choices. In the circumstances, barring exceptions, decisions relating to utilisation of natural resources have to be tested on the anvil of the well-recognised principles of judicial review. Have all the relevant factors been taken into account? Have any extraneous factors influenced the decision? Is the decision strictly in accordance with the legislative policy underlying the law (if any) that governs the field? Is the decision consistent with the principles of sustainable development in the sense that has the decision-maker taken into account the said principle and, on the basis of relevant considerations, arrived at a balanced decision? Thus, the Court should review the decision-making process to ensure that the decision of MoEF is fair and fully informed, based on the correct principles, and free from any bias or restraint.

In terms of the principles as laid down by this Court in *Lafarge*, we find that the decision-making process in doing away with or in granting exemption from public consultation/public hearing, was not based on correct principles and as such the decision was invalid and improper.

At the same time, we cannot lose sight of the fact that in pursuance of environmental clearance dated 27-1-2010, the expansion of the project has been undertaken and as reported by Central Pollution Control Board in its affidavit filed on 7-7-2014, most of the recommendations made by CPCB are complied with. In our considered view, the interest of justice would be subserved if that part of the decision exempting public consultation/public hearing is set aside and the matter is relegated back to the authorities concerned to effectuate public consultation/public hearing. However, since the expansion has been undertaken and the industry has been functioning, we do not deem it appropriate to order closure of the entire plant as directed by the High Court. If the public consultation/public hearing results in a negative mandate against the expansion of the project, the authorities would do well to direct and ensure scaling down of the activities to the level that was permitted by environmental clearance dated 20-2-2008. If public consultation/public hearing reflects in favour of the expansion of the project, environmental clearance dated 27-1-2010 would hold good and be fully operative. In other words, at this length of time when the expansion has already been undertaken, in the peculiar facts of this case and in order to meet ends of justice, we deem it appropriate to change the nature of requirement of public consultation/public hearing from pre-decisional to post-decisional. The public consultation/public hearing shall be organised by the authorities concerned in three months from today.

This appeal, therefore, stands disposed of with the aforesaid modifications. No order as to costs.

NOTES AND QUESTIONS

1. Both the Supreme Court and the High Court were correct in emphasizing the importance of a public hearing/consultation. This is an extremely important stage in the EIA procedure which allows local communities to express their concerns.

2. The language of the Supreme Court in the penultimate paragraph is perplexing. By using the expression 'negative mandate', the court appears to treat public hearings as a validating process without which the project cannot proceed. If this is what the judgment holds, it is plainly erroneous. The purpose of a public hearing or consultation is *not* to secure local consent, but to understand and recognize legitimate community concerns pertaining to the environment. The concerns of residents must be faithfully recorded and communicated to the Expert Appraisal Committee as well as the authority granting the EC, so that an informed decision is made. Generally, the EC will contain special conditions that will address local community concerns and reduce negative impacts. Very rarely, where the grievances are legitimate and weighty, the clearance itself may be withheld.

3. Was the court justified in advising the authorities 'to scale down' the operations to the 2008 level, in the event of a negative public hearing mandate? What is a negative mandate? Should those attending the public hearing be asked to vote? Where is the requirement in law for such a referendum?

If the public hearing is to be regarded as a 'mandate' it may result in the project proponent and its business rivals resorting to dubious means to garner support, diminishing the purpose of this exercise.

4. Did EIL get off lightly? Remember, the original project had no EC.

VI. THE *GOEL GANGA* CASE

The *Goel Ganga* case illustrates the enormous costs that society must bear due to poor legislative drafting and the misalignment of building regulations framed by two sets of regulators. Town and country planning laws are framed by the states under the Constitution.[118] These laws are enforced by municipalities and other local authorities. The MoEF has the power under the central Environment (Protection) Act of 1986[119] to frame subordinate legislation

---

[118] See entries 5, 6, 10, List II, Schedule VII, Constitution of India.

[119] The Centre enacted the EPA under Article 253 of the Constitution.

directly impacting town and country planning across the nation. Two examples of central environmental regulations that illustrate this layering are the Coastal Regulatory Zone (CRZ) Regulations and the EIA Regulations. However, when it comes to implementation, the EPA does not have its own enforcement agency and relies on the same local authorities.

Ideally, from a citizen's standpoint, the local town planning authorities should amend their regional and town plans to align them to the central regulations. This would make it easier for citizens and developers who would like to be guided by a single set of consistent laws on matters as commonplace as putting up a building. Unfortunately, this is not the case. The following judgment shows how a building that comports with local town planning regulations can still be 'noncompliant' and liable to be demolished. There are few other jurisdictions that task and tax the citizen so greatly.

GOEL GANGA DEVELOPERS INDIA PVT LTD v UNION OF INDIA

(2018) 18 SCC 257

DEEPAK GUPTA, J:

* * *

These matters are being decided by one judgment since they all arise out of one original application filed by Shri Tanaji Balasaheb Gambhire (hereinafter referred to as 'the original applicant') before the National Green Tribunal ('NGT', for short) being Application No. 184 of 2015.

The original applicant filed an application before NGT claiming that the project proponent i.e. M/s Goel Ganga Developers India Pvt Ltd, had raised construction in violation of the environmental clearance ('EC', for short) granted for the project and also in violation of the various municipal laws. It was prayed that the illegal structures be demolished; the State Level Environment Impact Assessment Authority (SEIAA) and the Maharashtra State Pollution Control Board be directed to initiate appropriate action against the project proponent for violation of the Environment Impact Assessment (EIA) Notification, 2006; the Union of India be directed to take action against SEIAA; and lastly, it was prayed that the project proponent be directed to pay/deposit a heavy amount of compensation in the environment relief fund. NGT vide its order dated 27-9-2016 [*Tanaji Balasaheb Gambhire v Union of India* 2016 SCC Online NGT 4213] allowed the application in the following terms:

> For the aforesaid reasons, the applicant succeeds in his legal pursuit to challenge the non-compliance of EC conditions by Respondent 9 [Goel Ganga] and obtain certain directions. Hence the Application is allowed and we issue following directions:
>
> 1. Respondent 9 shall pay environmental compensation cost of Rs 100 crores or 5% (five per cent) of the total cost of project to be assessed by SEAC whichever is less for restoration and restitution of environment damages and degradation caused by the project proponent by carrying out the construction activities without the necessary prior environmental clearance within a period of one month. In addition to this, it shall also pay a sum of Rs 5 crores for contravening mandatory provision of several Environmental Laws in carrying out the construction activities in addition to and exceeding limit of the available environment clearance and for not obtaining the consent from the Board.
> 2. In view of our finding that there has been manifest, deliberate or otherwise suppression of facts of illegality in the project activity of Respondent 9 by the officers of [Pune Municipal Corporation], we impose fine of Rs 5 lakhs upon the PMC and direct Commissioner PMC to take appropriate action against the erring officers. The amount of Rs 5 lakhs shall be paid within one month.

3. We direct the Chief Secretary, State of Maharashtra and the competent authority to take notice of the conduct of the officers concerned who have misled the Department of Environment in the matter relating to interpretation of [Floor Space Index and Built Up Area] in terms of which order dated 31-5-2016 has been issued in particular the Principal Secretary, Department of Environment who has authored the order dated 31-5-2016.
4. PMC, DoE and SEIAA are directed to pay cost of Rs 1 lakh each to the applicant within 4 weeks.

***

On 12-3-2007, the project proponent applied for sanction of layout and building proposal plan on an area of 15,141.70 sq m, originally depicted as Plot No.3 and the sanctioned FSI was 15,313.16 sq m. Thereafter, on 5-9-2007, revised layout plan was submitted for an area measuring 28,233.23 sq m and the sanctioned FSI was 39,526.54 sq m. The project proponent applied for EC for the project and in the proposal dated 27-6-2007, he had shown that he would be erecting/constructing 12 buildings having 552 flats, 50 shops and 34 offices. The 12 buildings were to have stilts with basement and 11 floors. The total built-up area was indicated as 57,658.42 sq m. The EC was granted to the project proponent on 4-4-2008. Paras 2 and 3 of the communication granting EC read as under:

> 2. The project proponent is proposing for construction of group housing project at Sl. Nos. 35 to 40, Village Vadgaon Budruk, Singhad Road, Pune, Maharashtra at a cost of Rs 10,737.14 lakhs. The project involves construction of 12 buildings with stilt, basement plus 11 floors for 552 flats, 50 shops and 34 offices. The total plot area is 79,100.00 sq m. Total built-up area as indicated is 57,658.42 sq m. Total water requirement will be 745 KLD and 400 KLD of waste water will be generated from the buildings which will be treated in sewage treatment plant. The treated waste water will be used for landscaping, DG set cooling and horticulture purpose. The solid waste generated from the buildings will be 1500 kg/day and disposed as per the MSW Rules, 2000. The parking space is proposed for parking of 1072 cars.
> 3. EAC after due consideration of the relevant documents submitted by the project proponent and additional clarifications furnished in response to its observations have recommended the grant of environmental clearance for the project mentioned above subject to compliance with EMP and other stipulated conditions. Accordingly, the Ministry hereby accords necessary environmental clearance for the project under Category 8(a) of the EIA Notification, 2006 subject to the strict compliance with the specific and general conditions mentioned below....

It is not disputed that EC was granted for built-up area of 57,658.42 sq m. The main dispute is with regard to the interpretation of the term 'built-up area'. The case of the project proponent is that the term 'built-up area' is synonymous with 'floor space index' or FSI and that the constructed area, which is exempted from FSI area or is a non-FSI area is not a part of the 'built-up area'. On the other hand, the submission made by the original applicant as well as by the learned Additional Solicitor General appearing for the Ministry of Environment, Forests and Climate Change is that the built-up area will cover all constructed area and the concept of FSI area or non-FSI area is totally alien to environmental laws.

The learned Senior Counsel for the project proponent has drawn our attention to the Development Control Rules for Pune Municipal Corporation, Pune, 1982 ('DCR', for short). Under DCR, no building can be constructed without grant of building permission/commencement certificate by Pune Municipal Corporation. There is a detailed procedure for obtaining the building permission/commencement certificate wherein layout plans, building plans, etc. have to be submitted. The main emphasis was on Rule 2.13 of DCR, which defines 'built-up area' as follows:

> 2.13. *Built-up area.* — Area covered immediately above the plinth level by the building or external area of any upper floor whichever is more excepting the areas covered by Rule 15.4.2.'

Rule 2.39 defines 'floor area ratio' as follows:

> '2.39. *Floor area ratio (FAR).* — The quotient obtained by dividing the total covered area (plinth area) on all floors excluding exempted areas as given in Rule 15.4.2 by the area of the plot.
>
> $$\text{FAR} = \frac{\text{Total converted area on all floors}}{\text{Plot area}}$$

Note. — The term FAR is synonymous with floor space index (FSI).

Strong reliance is placed on Rule 15.4.2, which reads as under:

> 15.4.2. In addition to Rules 15.4.1.1(a), (b) and (c) and 17.7.3, the following shall not be included in covered area or FAR and built-up area calculations:
>
> (a) A basement or cellar space under a building constructed on stilts and used as parking space, and air conditioning plant rooms used as accessory to the principal use;
>
> (b) Electric cabin or substation, watchman's booth of maximum size of 1.6 sq m with minimum width or diameter of 1.2 m, pump house, garage shaft, space required for location of fire hydrants, electric fittings and water tanks;
>
> (c) Projection as specifically exempted under these Rules;
>
> (d) Staircase room and/or lift rooms above the topmost storey, architectural features, chimneys, elevated tanks of dimensions as permissible under these Rules;
>
> *Note.* — The shaft provided for lift shall be taken for covered area calculations only on one floor up to the minimum required as per these Rules;
>
> (e) One room admeasuring 2 m × 3 m on the ground floor of cooperative housing societies or apartment owners/cooperative societies buildings and other multi-storeyed buildings as office-cum-letter box room;
>
> (f) Rockery, well and well structures, plant, nursery, water pool, swimming pool, (if uncovered) platform round a tree, tank fountain, bench, chabutra with open top and unenclosed sides by walls, ramps, compound wall, gate, slide, swing, overhead water tank on top buildings;
>
> (g) (*Deleted*);
>
> (h) Sanitary block subject to provision of Rule 15.4.1(a) and built-up area not more than 4 sq m

The contention of the learned Senior Counsel appearing for the project proponent is that while calculating the built-up area the constructions mentioned in Rules 15.4.1.1(a), (b) and (c) and Rule 17.7.3 in addition to the areas specifically exempted under Rule 15.4.2 are to be excluded. He submits that if the built-up area is calculated in accordance with DCR then the project proponent has till date not constructed the built-up area of 57,658.42 sq m, which it was permitted to construct under the EC granted to it on 4-4-2008.

On the other hand, the stand of the Union of India and the original applicant is that built-up area means all area which is covered regardless of the area being FSI or non-FSI in terms of the EIA Notification of 2006. The building/construction projects are covered by Item 8 of the schedule to the EIA Notification dated 14-9-2006. Construction of a project which is covered under the schedule can be commenced only after obtaining EC in terms of Para 2 of the said notification. The schedule itself categorises the various projects and activities into two categories being 'Category A' and 'Category B'. 'Category A' projects require clearance by the Central Government in the Ministry of Environment, Forests and Climate Change on the recommendation of the Expert Appraisal Committee to be constituted by the Central Government whereas those activities which form 'Category B' of the schedule including modernisation and expansion of such projects require EC from the State/Union Territory Environment Impact Assessment Authority (SEIAA) and such authority is required to base its decision on the recommendation of the State/Union Territory Level Expert Appraisal Committee (SEAC). There is further division of 'Category B' into B-1 and B-2. B-1 projects require Environmental Impact Assessment (EIA) Report to be prepared and scoping to be done whereas B-2 projects do not require any Environmental Impact Assessment Report. Item 8 of the schedule, with which we are concerned, reads as follows:

Project or Activity		*Category with threshold limit*		*Conditions if any*
		A	*B*	
8		*Building/Construction projects/Area development projects and Townships*		
(1)	(2)	(3)	(4)	(5)
8(a)	Building and construction projects		>20,000 sqm and <1,50,000 sq m of built-up area*	* (built-up area for covered construction; in the case of facilities open to the sky, it will be the activity area)
8(b)	Townships and area development projects.		Covering an area >50 ha and or built-up area >1,50,000 sq m**	** All projects under Item 8(b) shall be appraised as Category B1

From a bare perusal of the two hashtags (#) in Columns 4 and 5 of Item 8(a), it is apparent that what is shown under Column 5 is actually a continuation of Column 4 and basically it describes or defines 'built-up area' to mean covered construction and if the facilities are open to the sky, it will be taken to be the activity area. This by itself clearly shows that under the notification of 2006, all constructed area, which is covered and not open to the sky has to be treated as 'built-up area'. There is no exception for non-FSI area.

Indeed, the concept of FSI or non-FSI has no concern or connection with grant of EC. The same may be relevant for the purposes of building plans under municipal laws and regulations but it has no linkage or connectivity with the grant of EC. When EC is to be granted, the authority which has to grant such clearance is only required to ensure that the project does not violate environmental norms. While projects and activities, as mentioned in the notification, may be allowed to go on, the authority while granting permission should ensure that the adverse impact on the environment is kept to the minimum. Therefore, the authority granting EC may lay down conditions which the project proponent must comply with. While doing so, such authority is not concerned whether the area to be constructed is FSI area or non-FSI area. Both will have an equally deleterious effect on the environment. Construction implies usage of a lot of materials like sand, gravel, steel, glass, marble, etc., all of which will impact the environment. Merely because under the municipal laws some of this construction is excluded while calculating the FSI is no ground to exclude it while granting the EC. Therefore, when EC is granted for a particular construction it includes both FSI and non-FSI areas. As far as environmental laws are concerned, all covered construction, which is not open to the sky is to be treated as built-up area in terms of the EIA Notification dated 14-9-2006....

Our attention has been drawn to the Notification dated 4-4-2011 issued by the Ministry of Environment and Forests. By means of this notification, the words of Column 5 against Item 8(a) have been replaced and substituted as under:

> The built-up area for the purpose of this Notification is defined as 'the built-up or covered area on all the floors put together including basement(s) and other service areas, which are proposed in the building/construction projects'.

This notification clearly defines 'built-up area' as all constructed area including basement and service areas without any exception.

[The court quoted an office memorandum dated 7-7-2017 issued by Dr Ashish Kumar, Joint Director, Ministry of Environment, Forests and Climate Change.

OFFICE MEMORANDUM

Sub.: Clarification on the date of applicability of Notification No. S O(E) 695 dated 4-4-2011 issued by MoEF & CC defining 'built-up area' of the project.

...

4. The definition provided in the Ministry's notification [dated 4-4-2011] will have its effect from the prospective date of the notification only. The projects which are not covered in the period of above notifications should be assessed as per the definition of built-up area provided in the building bye-laws or Development Control Regulation (DCR) of the local authorities in the States.]

[W]e are clearly of the view that such an office memorandum could not and should not have been issued. The Notification dated 14-9-2006 is a statutory notification issued in terms of Rule 5(3) of the Environment (Protection) Rules, 1986 which provides that before such a notification is issued, the Central Government has to give notice of its intention of issuing a notification and objections to the same are invited. No doubt the Central Government is empowered in public interest to dispense with the requirement of notice but this obviously has to be done in exceptional cases. The Notification dated 14-9-2006 was issued by the Central Government and published in the gazette after inviting objections from the public. The first clarification with regard to this notification was issued on 4-4-2011 to which we have adverted above. These two decisions of the Central Government which were notified as per the provisions of law could not have been set at naught by the Joint Director even if it was issued with the approval of a higher authority. We are of the view that since such decision has not been notified in the gazette, the statutory Notification dated 14-9-2006 and its subsequent clarification dated 4-4-2011 could not have been virtually set aside by this office memorandum.

[The court upheld the NGT order which had found that the construction raised by the project proponent was in violation of the EC dated 4-4-2008. The court imposed damages of Rs. 100 crores or 10% of the project cost, whichever is higher, on the project proponent in addition to Rs. 5 crores levied by NGT. The project proponent was restrained from raising construction of two buildings having 454 tenements and was allowed to complete construction of 807 flats, 107 being shops/offices and a cultural centre including a clubhouse.]

NOTES AND QUESTIONS

1. When the EC was issued on 4 April 2008 the EIA notification did not have a definition of 'built-up area'. At this time, PMC's building regulations defined 'built-up area' and this definition excluded certain construction. In this situation, was it reasonable for Goel Ganga, PMC and the SEIAA to be guided by the only available statutory definition, albeit in the DCR? If the DCR definition is accepted for understanding the EIA notification provisions, then the project and the EC would be valid.

2. Often administrators notice gaps in subordinate legislation and respond by clarifying the position through an amendment. The concerned ministry may always issue a clarification to prevent a provision from operating harshly. This is what the MoEF did when it amended the notification by introducing a definition of 'built-up area' on 4 April 2011 and clarifying its prospective operation through a memorandum on 7 July 2017. Was the Supreme Court justified in criticizing the ministry's conduct?

3. In the *Okhla Bird Sanctuary* case[120] the Supreme Court when construing the same entries in the schedule to the EIA notification observed that Items 8(a) and 8(b):

> need to be described with greater precision and clarity and the definition of built-up area with facilities open to the sky needs to be freed from its present ambiguity and vagueness.

If the three-judge bench hearing the *Okhla Bird Sanctuary* case found the provision ambiguous and vague, was it fair and just on the part of the two-judge bench in *Goel Ganga* to fault the developer and the local authorities for construing the provisions in a particular manner? Recall that the amendment of 4 April 2011 was issued after the *Okhla Bird Sanctuary* judgment.

When the *Okhla Bird Sanctuary* case was pointed out to the court in *Goel Ganga*, the Supreme Court found that the earlier judgment 'will have no impact on the present case'.[121]

4. The Supreme Court in *Goel Ganga* held that 'the officials of PMC have given an interpretation which was tailor-made to suit the project proponent'. However, the Chief Secretary to the government of Maharashtra made a report on 7 January 2019 concluding that *all* ECs issued prior to 4 April 2011 were in terms of the 'built-up area' as defined in the DCR. If this was the uniform understanding of the bureaucracy, does *Goel Ganga* require reconsideration?

Consider the nationwide implications of the judgment. Should all development projects where the EC was issued based on the local authorities' understanding of 'built-up area' be treated as illegal? What consequences should visit the occupants, developers and officials of the buildings that have been erected based upon a faulty understanding?

5. Keystone Realtors received permission to erect a residential building at Bandra (East), Mumbai with a total construction area of 8720.32 sq m. When the ambit of the project expanded to 32,395.17 sq m, Keystone obtained an EC since the total construction exceeded the threshold of 20,000 sq m under the EIA notification. In the course of development, the builder decided on 16 more flats, pushing up the construction to 40,480.88 sq m. Without going through the process for securing a fresh EC, Keystone sought and was granted an 'amendment' premised on the second expansion being a 'marginal increase'. Both the NGT and the Supreme Court held that the second expansion obliged Keystone to reapply for a fresh EC and that the 'amendment' route was impermissible. The Supreme Court held:

> In a case where the text of the provisions requires interpretation, this Court must adopt an interpretation which is in consonance with the object and purpose of the legislation or delegated legislation as a whole. The EIA Notification was adopted with the intention of restricting new projects and the expansion of new projects until their environmental impact could be evaluated and understood. It cannot be disputed that as the size of the project increases, so does the magnitude of the project's environmental impact. This Court cannot adopt an interpretation of the EIA Notification which would permit, incrementally or otherwise, project proponents to increase the construction area of a project without any oversight from the Expert Appraisal Committee or SEAC, as applicable. It is true that there may exist certain situations where the expansion sought by a project proponent is truly marginal or the environmental impact of such expansion is non-existent. However, it is not for this Court to lay down a bright-line test as to what constitutes a 'marginal' increase and what constitutes a material increase warranting a fresh Form 1 and scrutiny by the Expert Appraisal Committee. If the Government in its wisdom were to prescribe that a one-time 'marginal' increase (e.g. 5% or 10%) in project size, within the threshold limit stipulated in the Schedule, could be subject to a lower standard of scrutiny without diluting the urgent need for environmental

[120] *In Re: Construction of Park at Noida Near Okhla Bird Sanctuary* (2011) 1 SCC 744.
[121] *Goel Ganga Developers India Pvt Ltd v Union of India* (2019) 9 SCC 288, 291.

> protection, conceivably this Court may give effect to such a provision. This would be subject to any challenge on the ground of there being a violation of the precautionary principle. However, as the EIA Notification currently stands, an expansion within the limits prescribed by the Schedules would be subject to the procedure set out in Para 7(ii).[122]

The court held that for a residential project covered by the EIA Regulations a holistic evaluation of water availability, management of solid and wet waste and the urban carrying capacity of the area were imperative.

VII. THE *GOA AIRPORT* CASES

Mopa – 1

Mopa village nestles on an elevated plateau in North Goa. Since the Naval airbase at Dabolim could not handle the projected air traffic, in 1997 Goa initiated the process of identifying a site and soon zeroed in on Mopa.

On 1 May 2000, the Union Government approved setting up a greenfield international airport at Mopa. The process to acquire land commenced in 2008. In March 2011, the state government, as project proponent, commenced the process for securing an EC under the EIA notification of 2006. On 1 June 2011, MoEF issued Terms of Reference (ToR) for preparing the EIA report. The ToR, initially valid for two years, was periodically extended. A public hearing was conducted at the project site on 1 February 2015 and, on 20 May 2015, the state submitted a final EIA report. On 20 October 2015, the Expert Appraisal Committee (EAC) recommended the grant of an EC for the project. On 28 October 2015, the MoEF granted an EC.

Meanwhile, in October 2014 the state government floated a tender to develop the project on a public private partnership (PPP) basis. The tender process culminated in an award of the contract to a private company, GMR, with the state receiving a revenue share of 36.99% over the life of the 40-year concession. The concessionaire was granted three years from 4 September 2017 to commission the first phase of the airport.

The EC was challenged before the NGT by the Federation of Rainbow Warriors and Hanuman Aroskar. On 21 August 2018, the NGT rejected the challenge, upholding the EC and imposing certain additional conditions to safeguard the environment. The analysis by the NGT was confined to one paragraph:

> We find that the Expert Appraisal Committee had before it point wise reply of the project proponent which we have already quoted above. Therein delay in land acquisition process and collection of fresh baseline data are mentioned. It is also mentioned that data for Maharashtra was also considered. Other issues duly explained are hydro-geological features and data with regard to flora and fauna, socioeconomic profile, topography, vegetation, observance of due procedure in public hearing, relevance of study with regard to eco-sensitive areas of Western Ghats, feasibility of proposed airport in terms of cost benefit analysis as well as environmental cost benefit analysis. EAC also considered the data compiled by various offices. Mere fact that different opinions have been expressed by other experts is not enough to hold that EAC did not apply its mind. The rehabilitation programme was also produced before the EAC.

In appeals against the NGT order, the Supreme Court delivered an elaborate judgment on 29 March 2019. By this time the project had progressed substantially: 54,676 trees were felled between 3 September 2018 and 14 January 2019; the state had spent Rs. 240 crores for acquiring land, widening roads and other related expenses; and the concessionaire had

122 *Keystone Realtors Pvt Ltd v Anil V Tharthare* (2020) 2 SCC 66.

incurred Rs. 230 crores on developing the site. According to GMR, around 14% of the project work was complete and 1,500 persons were working at the site to meet the deadline.

The appellants raised several issues touching on the integrity of the process. They complained that the project proponent concealed vital facts; the EIA report was flawed since essential studies were not carried out; the public hearing process was negated by a failure to consider the objections; the EAC had abdicated its duty to carefully examine the issues; and finally that the NGT had failed to conduct a merits review.

After examining the EIA process under the 2006 notification, the Supreme Court found that the authorities had indeed committed procedural as well as substantive violations. Refraining from striking down the EC, the Supreme Court remitted the matter back to the EAC for a relook. It suspended the EC until the EAC completed a fresh exercise. We carry a short excerpt, focusing on the court's effort to enhance the integrity of the process with a view to strengthening environmental Rule of Law.

HANUMAN LAXMAN AROSKAR v UNION OF INDIA

(2019) 15 SCC 401

Dr Dhananjaya Y Chandrachud, J: * * *

The 2006 notification embodies the notion that the development agenda of the nation must be carried out in compliance with norms stipulated for the protection of the environment and its complexities. It serves as a balance between development and protection of the environment: there is no trade-off between the two. The protection of the environment is an essential facet of development. It cannot be reduced to a technical formula. The notification demonstrates an increasing awareness of the complexities of the environment and the heightened scrutiny required to ensure its continued sustenance, for today and for generations to come. It embodies a commitment to sustainable development. In laying down a detailed procedure for the grant of an EC, the 2006 notification attempts to bridge the perceived gap between the environment and development.

It is for this reason that the EAC and SEAC comprise experts in the field of environmental law. The Chairperson of the EAC shall be a person who is an 'outstanding and experienced environmental policy expert or expert in management or public administration with wide experience in the relevant development sector'. Appendix VI to the 2006 notification stipulates that the EAC and the SEAC comprise 15 members who are either 'experts' or 'professionals'. Experts must have at least 15 years of relevant experience in the field or an advanced degree (PhD) with 10 years of relevant experience. Where experts are not available, professionals may be appointed to the EAC.

The EAC and the SEAC are charged with evaluating the information submitted by the applicant in Form 1/Form 1A and preparing comprehensive ToR which guide the preparation of the EIA reports. Given that these bodies comprise experts in the field of environmental law, the recommendation of the EAC or the SEAC to grant EC to an applicant or reject the application is normally accepted by the regulatory authority.

The regulatory authority at the state level (SEIAA) which is charged with the approval or rejection of an application for EC comprises three members who possess the qualifications in the field as prescribed in Appendix VI. Significantly, sub clause (7) of paragraph 3 of the 2006 notification stipulates that all decisions of the SEIAA shall be unanimous and taken in a meeting. Given the environmental consequences of a proposed project, no difference of opinion is provided for in the grant of an EC at the state level. It is further mandated that the project management submit half-yearly compliance reports to the regulatory authority in respect of the EC and conditions....

We cannot gloss over the patent and abject failure of the State of Goa as the project proponent in failing to disclose wet lands, water sources, water bodies, biospheres, mountains and forests within an aerial distance of 15 kilometres as required by Form 1. The disclosure in Form 1 constitutes the very foundation of the process which is initiated on the basis of the information supplied by the project proponent. Following the disclosure in Form 1, ToR are formulated, and this leads to the preparation of the EIA report. A duty is cast upon the project proponent to make a full, complete and candid disclosure of all aspects bearing upon the environment in the area of study. The project proponent cannot profess an ignorance about the environment in the study area. The project proponent is bound by the highest duty of transparency and rectitude in making the disclosures in Form 1....

We are unable to accept the submission that the disclosure required was of reserved forests comprehended within a notification under sub-section (2) of section 20 of the Indian Forest Act 1927. Form 1 requires a disclosure of areas which are important or sensitive for ecological reasons, among them, being 'forests'. The expression 'forests' is used without reference to a statutory or artificial definition and must hence incorporate a meaning which bears upon the ordinary description of the term. The expression 'forests', means a forest as commonly understood, without reference to a notification under the Indian Forest Act 1927 or any other statutory enactment. Such an interpretation will sub-serve the purpose of an EIA. The purpose is to ensure that all relevant facets of the environment are noticed, that base-lines are documented, and that the potential impact of a project or activity on the environment is assessed. Forests are forests without reference to recognition in a statutory form devised for a specific purpose....

Though the EIA report adverts to the presence of forests within the study area in Goa and Maharashtra, we have to consider whether this by itself warrants the grant of an EC inspite of the fact that there has been a patent failure on part of the project proponent to make a transparent and candid disclosure of material facts in Form 1.... The ToR guide the preparation of the EIA report. A failure to disclose information in Form 1 impairs the functioning of the EAC in the preparation of the ToR and in consequence, leads to preparation of a deficient EIA report....

The failure on part of a project proponent to disclose material information in Form 1 as stipulated under the 2006 notification has a cascading effect on the salient objective which underlies the 2006 notification. The 2006 notification represents an independent code with the avowed objective of balancing the development agenda with the protection of the environment. An applicant cannot claim an EC, under the 2006 notification, based on substantial or proportionate compliance with the terms stipulated in the notification. The terms of the notification lay down strict standards that must be complied with by an applicant seeking an EC for a proposed project. The burden of establishing environmental compliance rests on a project proponent who intends to bring about a change in the existing state of the environment. Whereas, in the present case, there has thus been a patent failure on part of the project proponent to make mandatory disclosures stipulated in Form 1 under the 2006 notification, that must have consequences in law. There can be no gambles with the environment: a 'heads I win, tails you lose' approach is simply unacceptable; unacceptable if we are to preserve environmental governance under the rule of law.... The EIA report fails to meet a classical requirement of administrative law: to take into account a relevant consideration namely, that within the study area which has to be considered, there is the presence of Ecologically Sensitive Zones (ESZs).

In deducing the impact of a proposed activity on an ESZ, it is not sufficient to take recourse to a generic assessment of a proposed activity on the ecology of the study area. The EIA report must factor in those specific features which make an area ecologically sensitive. These would encompass all aspects of environmental concern which render the area ecologically sensitive. This would include wet lands, water sources, water bodies, costal zones, biospheres, mountains and forests. The vulnerabilities of each of them must be studied as distinctive components together with a holistic analysis of their existence in a chain of bio-diversity. Where an area is ecologically sensitive because of the presence of flora or fauna requiring protection, that must be specifically adverted to and studied. The deficiency of the EIA report emanates from its failure to notice that the purpose of the study was not only to determine whether the project site is ecologically sensitive. Confining itself to this aspect, the EIA report failed to consider a crucial and relevant consideration....

We express our serious displeasure with the manner in which the EIA report made an attempt to gloss over the existence of trees. The EIA report prevaricated by recording that the area required for the proposed airport has only a few trees, mostly bushes. The EIA report states that vegetation and trees are sparse at the site. A photograph and a google map image are put forth as illustrations in figure 2.3 of Chapter II. To realize later that the project involved the felling of 54,676 trees is indicative of the cavalier approach to the issue and a process of fact finding which is parsimonious with the truth. Post facto explanations are inadequate to deal with a failure of due process in the field of environmental governance. The State of Goa would have us gloss over the felling of trees by submitting that 54,676 trees over a project area of 2,133 acres averages out to 25 trees per acre or one tree over an area of 160 square metres. This is a fallacious approach to the issue. Mathematical averages cannot displace factual data about the actual number of trees which were affected by the project. The EIA report ought to have scrutinized the number of trees, their nature and longevity. Issues such as the extent to which the trees or some of them were capable of being transplanted had to be considered in the EIA report. The location of the trees is also significant. In a given case, if the trees appear in clusters or in a dense formation in segments of the project site, it would be necessary to determine whether felling all of them was necessary for the project to be implemented.

* * *

The 2006 notification postulates:

(i) A public hearing at or in close proximity to the project site to ascertain the views of 'locally affected persons';

(ii) Obtaining written responses from 'other concerned' individuals having a 'plausible stake' in the environmental aspects of the project or the activity;

(iii) The duty of the SPCB to conduct hearings and to forward the proceedings to the regulatory authority within the stipulated time;

(iv) Placing on the website of the Pollution Control Board a summary of the EIA report in the prescribed format and the making available of the draft EIA report by the regulatory authority on a written request by any person concerned, for inspection;

(v) The duty of the applicant to address all material concerns expressed during the process of public consultation;

(vi) The making of appropriate changes in the draft EIA and EMP; and

(vii) The submission of the final EIA report by the applicant to the regulatory authority for appraisal.

Each of these features is crucial to the success of a public consultation process. Public consultation cannot be reduced to a mere incantation or a procedural formality which has to be completed to move on to the next stage. Underlying public consultation is the important constitutional value that decisions which affect the lives of individuals must, in a system of democratic governance, factor in their concerns which have been expressed after obtaining full knowledge of a project and its potential environmental effects....

Fundamental to the outcome of this case is a quest for environmental governance within a rule of law paradigm. Environmental governance is founded on the need to promote environmental sustainability as a crucial enabling factor which ensures the health of our eco system.

Since the Stockholm Conference, there has been a dramatic expansion in environmental laws and institutions across the globe. In many instances, these laws and institutions have helped to slow down or reverse environmental degradation. However, this progress is also accompanied, by a growing understanding that there is a considerable implementation gap between the requirements of environmental laws and their implementation and enforcement—both in developed and developing countries alike. The environmental rule of law seeks to address this gap.

The environmental rule of law provides an essential platform underpinning the four pillars of sustainable development—economic, social, environmental, and peace. It imbues environmental objectives with the essentials of rule of law and underpins the reform of environmental law and governance. The environmental rule of law becomes a priority particularly when we acknowledge that the benefits of environmental rule of law extend far beyond the environmental sector. While the most direct effects are on protection of the environment, it also strengthens rule of law more broadly, supports sustainable economic and social development, protects public health, contributes to peace and security by avoiding and defusing conflict, and protects human and constitutional rights. Similarly, the rule of law in environmental matters is indispensable 'for equity in terms of the advancement of the Sustainable Development Goals, the provision of fair access by assuring a rights-based approach, and the promotion and protection of environmental and other socio-economic rights.'

* * *

The 2006 notification must hence be construed as a significant link in India's quest to pursue the SDGs. Many of those goals, besides being accepted by the international community of which India is a part, constitute a basic expression of our own constitutional value system. Our interface with the norms which the international community has adopted in the sphere of environmental governance is hence as much a reflection of our own responsibility in a context which travels beyond our borders as much as it is a reflection of the aspirations of our own Constitution. The fundamental principle which emerges from our interpretation of the 2006 notification is that in the area of environmental governance, the means are as significant as the ends. The processes of decision are as crucial as the ultimate decision. The basic postulate of the 2006 notification is that the path which is prescribed for disclosures, studies, gathering data, consultation and appraisal is designed in a manner that would secure decision making which is transparent, responsive and inclusive. . . .

NOTES AND QUESTIONS

1. The *Goa Airport* case significantly advances environmental jurisprudence. It is a powerful pro-environment judgment. A strong current commending integrity and responsibility courses through the reasoning: 'A regulatory regime for environmental governance is based on the hypothesis that all stakeholders will act with rectitude.'

2. To bolster environmental decision-making, the court closely examined the EIA procedure and fixed responsibility at every stage. The project proponent is obliged to make a full and comprehensive disclosure of all anticipated environmental impacts, the agency preparing the EIA report must study all aspects of the environment and the EAC must employ its expertise to carefully scrutinize the proposals before it. Finally, the NGT has a statutory responsibility to conduct a merits review. It cannot abdicate that responsibility by recording a cryptic finding (as in this case), that all aspects were adequately examined by the lower authorities.

3. The judgment examines the qualifications of experts both in the EAC as well as on the NGT. Admirably, instead of adopting a hands-off approach to the EAC assessment, the judgment exposes how the EAC failed to exercise its expertise. The experts ignored significant gaps in the studies though these issues were raised during the public hearing.

4. The court relies on the principle of environmental Rule of Law. Since environmental problems are frequently polycentric with numerous social, economic, scientific and ecological dimensions—a good way to improve environmental governance is to strictly follow the procedure mandated. Where the process is followed in a responsible, meaningful and transparent manner the eventual decision is likely to comport with sustainable development goals.

5. Despite having concluded that the process for granting the EC was deeply flawed, the court declined to set aside the clearance. Instead, it required the EAC to re-examine its recommendation based on the issues highlighted in the judgment. Acting promptly, in April 2019, the EAC added further safeguards and again recommended an EC.

6. Recall the *Lafarge* case,[123] where the Supreme Court allowed the project to resume despite the misdescription of forest lands as 'barren'. In the *Goa Airport* case, the EC survived despite false representations regarding the proximity of the site to wetlands, water bodies, mountains and forests.

Due to the perceived public interest and the large investment of resources, often public funds, courts find it difficult to stall large projects even where the project proponent was 'parsimonious with the truth'.

7. What was gained by the appellants? Considering the huge expenditure incurred and the progress of the project, was it realistic to expect the court to stop the airport from being built?

8. Should Goa have to wait for over two decades for an international airport? Who gains from the delay? Who loses?

9. In *Lafarge*,[124] the Supreme Court issued specific directions to strengthen the EIA process. The court held that the Central Government should appoint a national regulator for appraising projects, enforcing environmental conditions contained in approvals and to impose penalties on polluters. This direction was passed in the backdrop of Lafarge having relied on certificates by authorities and on EIA reports by private consultants that did not accurately reflect the position on the ground. To reduce disputes regarding the status of the land and its non-forest character, the court required site inspections by the regional office of the MoEF and state forest department and also directed government to increase the number of regional offices of the MoEF across the country. The judgment also set out guidelines and safeguards for strengthening transparency and improving the public hearing process.

10. In September 2013, two years after *Lafarge*, the Supreme Court required the Solicitor General to obtain instructions and apprise the court as to when the directions would be complied with. The Central Government submitted that it was not necessary to appoint a national regulator and that the observations in *Lafarge* were merely suggestions. In January 2014, the court rejected the government's stand:

> It will be clear ... that this Court on an interpretation of section 3(3) of the Environment (Protection) Act, 1986 has taken a view that it confers a power coupled with duty to appoint an appropriate authority in the form of a Regulator at the State and at the Central level ... [Therefore, it is] not right [that] this Court has merely suggested that a National Regulator should be appointed and has not issued any mandamus to appoint a National Regulator.
>
> We further find ... that this Court has not found the mechanism of making the EIA appraisals of projects by the MoEF to be satisfactory.
>
> [T]he present mechanism under the EIA Notification dated 14-9-2006, issued by the Government with regard to processing, appraisals and approval of the projects for environmental clearance is deficient in many respects and what is required is a Regulator at the national level having its offices in all the States which can carry out an independent, objective and transparent appraisal and approval of the projects for environmental clearances and

123 *Lafarge Umium Mining Pvt Ltd v Union of India* (2011) 7 SCC 338. The *Lafarge* case is discussed in the Forests chapter.

124 *Id.*

which can also monitor the implementation of the conditions laid down in the environmental clearances.[125]

The Supreme Court directed the Union of India to appoint the regulator and file an affidavit of compliance by 31 March 2014.[126]

Mopa – 2

The MoEF asked the Supreme Court to take on record the fresh decision of the EAC dated 23 April 2019 and urged the court to lift the embargo placed by its judgment. The project proponent, whose lack of candour had irked the Supreme Court, had by now furnished supplementary information which revealed significant environmental features:

(a) There are seven reserved forests within 15 km of the proposed Airport in the Goa region (under Section-20) and six proposed reserved forests (under section-4) of Indian Forest Act, 1927. (Survey of India Toposheet and Forest Working Plan of North Goa).
(b) There are twenty-nine proposed reserve forests within 15 km. of the proposed Airport in Maharashtra region under Section-4 of Indian Forest Act, 1927 (Survey of India Toposheet & Forest Department, Sawantwadi Division).
(c) There are four rivers in Goa viz. Terekhol river, Kalna river, Chapora river, Moide river and one river viz. Tilari river in Maharashtra (source: Survey of India Toposheet).
(d) There are few patches of mangroves observed near Moide river, Terekhol river, Chapora river.
(e) Western Ghat Mountain range falls within the study area.
(f) There are two wetlands, of which one i.e. Anjuna reservoir has been identified in National Wetland Atlas of Goa.
(g) There are no coastal areas and declared biospheres in the vicinity of the proposed airport site.

Despite the breadth of these fresh disclosures, no new studies were called for and in less than a month of the Supreme Court judgment, the EAC expressed its satisfaction at the project proponent's explanations, management plan and mitigation measures. The EAC again recommended the grant of an EC with additional safeguards and conditions.

In the second round, the Supreme Court repelled the challenges advanced by the appellant with respect to the adverse impact of the project on forests, the Western Ghats, ecologically sensitive areas and the flora and fauna.[127] The court also turned down preliminary points raised by the appellant regarding the lack of expertise on the EAC and a conflict of interest on the part of EIA consultant who also acted as an independent engineer on the project. The Supreme Court held:

> The EAC has accounted for the relevant factors outlined by this Court in its previous judgment in the assessment leading to the grant of the EC.
>
> The evaluation of merits is a matter which primarily rests with an expert authority. The court can certainly supervise procedural compliance and ensure that all necessary inputs which are required to be factored into the decision-making process have been duly borne in mind. Once this has been done, the court must be circumspect in micro-managing the decision-making process by the EAC by substituting its own opinion for that of the EAC. Undoubtedly, no process can be perfect or free from studied criticism. . . .

125 *T N Godavarman Thirumulpad v Union of India* (2014) 4 SCC 61.

126 At the time of writing, a national regulator had not been notified. On the need for a national regulator see Sharadchandra Lele, Navroz K Dubash & Shantanu Dixit, *A Structure for Environment Governance: A Perspective* 45 Economic & Political Weekly 13 (2010) and Shibani Ghosh, *Is There a Case for an Environmental Regulator?* 49 Economic & Political Weekly 19 (2014).

127 *Hanuman Laxman Aroskar v Union of India* (2020) 12 SCC 1.

We have also taken note of the assurance which has been tendered on behalf of the concessionaire that it will adopt a Zero Carbon Programme both in the construction and operational phases of the airport. We accept the undertaking of the concessionaire and issue a direction for compliance.

The earlier judgment of this Court highlighted numerous deficiencies by the project proponent leading to the grant of the EC. This Court highlighted numerous concerns including the preservation of forests, the existence of [Ecologically Sensitive Areas] with their attendant features and the impact of the proposed project on natural water channels. The Court also noted the abject failure of the project proponent to provide complete information on the existence of reserved forests. In the proceedings that followed the judgment of this Court, the project proponent sought to remedy its failure by taking into account additional information on significant aspects of the environment. In the process leading to the grant of the EC as well as the lifting of its suspension by this Court, numerous mitigatory conditions have been imposed on the project proponent. We deem it appropriate to ensure the oversight of the project by a specialized body to ensure compliance with the directions cumulatively issued by this Court. We direct the National Environmental Engineering Research Institute to be appointed to oversee compliance with the directions cumulatively issued by this Court. The project proponent shall bear the costs, expenses and fees of NEERI.

The suspension on the EC shall accordingly stand lifted. The Miscellaneous Application is accordingly disposed of.[128]

Consider this critique of the second *Goa Airport* case judgment:

RITWICK DUTTA; THE MANY ABSURDITIES OF THE SUPREME COURT JUDGMENT ON GOA'S NEW AIRPORT, The Wire, 8 April 2020[129]

The second judgment (Mopa 2), delivered by the same bench of Justice Chandrachud and Justice Hemant Gupta, reiterated the 'necessity to balance' the need for an airport and the environment. This is where almost all judicial decision making ends up—the 'environment versus development' debate. Preserving livelihoods, forest, water sources, culture and countless species of flora and fauna comes under the category of 'environment'—viewed as a luxury by the decision-makers. 'Development' on the other hand is viewed as a basic human need—for shopping malls, convention centres, bullet trains, international airports, casinos, tourism infrastructure, five-star hotels and resorts, urban redevelopment, etc.

In the case of Mopa airport, the chief minister of Goa announced in 2019 that a casino will be an integral part of the airport complex. At the end of the day, it is not really 'development' but more 'lifestyle', and the courts balance environment and lifestyle, and often that comes down to livelihoods versus lifestyle. It may not be out of place to state that the job of the court is not to 'balance' but only to interpret the law and ensure environmental laws and processes such as the EIA are followed in letter and spirit. The principle of balance provides an escape route for violators. . . .

The Mopa 1 judgment had the potential to change the way EIAs were done in the country and could have led to the overhaul of the environmental governance system. It became a precedent with respect to other projects but it also failed to impact the EAC's subsequent appraisal of the Mopa airport, carried out within a few weeks of the judgment. In January 2020, the same bench of the Supreme Court lifted the suspension and allowed the work on the project to proceed on the ground that the EAC had completed its task to the court's satisfaction.

The records however show the contrary. Despite specific direction by the court that 'a careful avi-faunal study was necessary', no such study was undertaken. The Supreme Court in the

---

128 *Id.*

129 https://science.thewire.in/environment/supreme-court-mopa-airport-moefcc-eac-environment-development-eia/, accessed 12 June 2021.

2020 (Mopa 2) judgment accepted the statement of the EIA consultant (Engineers India Ltd), that 'no set routes of flyways were observed near the airport site'. Clearly no one can ever 'observe' set routes of flyway in the sky or going to the airport site. The fact is that the whole of Goa is part of the Central Asia Flyway, and the MoEF&CC has an action plan under implementation from 2018 to 2023 with respect to flyways, and no party pointed this out.

A detailed report on the avifauna was crucial since the court, in the Mopa 1 judgment, had categorically stated that the 'report must deal with the impact of the airport on birds and likewise the impact of birds on aircraft operations'. It is worth pointing out that the court did not find it objectionable that the EIA consultant for the project—Engineers India Ltd.—is also the independent engineering firm contracted to oversee the construction of the airport.

The state of Goa and the MoEF&CC, which had earlier stated that there were no wetland, forest, rivers, mountains, etc., suddenly discovered that the Western Ghats, a world heritage site, is within the study area (10 km radius). In addition, it discovered four rivers, 42 reserve forests, two wetlands, mangroves and 10 ecologically sensitive areas notified by the MoEF&CC, as per the Kasturirangan Committee. These were not instances of minor omission, and this is not specific to Mopa either.

After analysing 75 different EIA reports of mining projects in Goa, Madhav Gadgil had concluded that every single report described Goa as a treeless, waterless, barren land with no hills and plateaus. The EAC in Mopa concluded that the failures to disclose were 'inadvertent'. The Supreme Court did not consider it necessary to either blacklist the EIA consultant or direct action against the officers who made the wrong disclosure. This sets an unhealthy precedent: that there will be no punitive action for false declarations. And despite such new disclosures, neither the EAC/MoEF&CC nor the Supreme Court directed any fresh EIAs. The revisit was based on the old EIA report, with no new studies.

Disturbingly, the Government of Goa admitted before the EAC that details of wild animals were collected only from the 'nearest village' and not from any of the 42 reserve forests. It is incomprehensible, and absurd, that a study of wild animals will be conducted in villages but not in forest areas, which—as we all know—is the preferred habitat for wild animals. The Supreme Court refused to question the improper collection of data on the grounds that 'the court should be circumspect in micromanaging the decision making process by the EAC' and that 'no process can be perfect or free from studied criticism'.

The manner in which the issue of deforestation was dealt [with] is a cause for greater concern. The felling of over 55,000 trees was justified on the grounds that for every tree felled, 10 trees would be planted. This is three-times the existing norm of three trees for every one felled. The court accepted this as proof that the project has been subject to stringent conditions.

But what the state of Goa and the MoEF&CC failed to inform the court was the state's dismal performance with respect to compensatory afforestation. In the last 10 years, Goa has failed to meet any of the targets for compensatory afforestation—so much so that the MoEF&CC has stopped allocating funds to Goa under the Compensatory Afforestation Management and Planning Authority. Thus, like all other projects, trees were felled without any assurance of afforestation....

The answer to 55,000 trees being cut for the Mopa airport is not planting 10-times the number of trees (even if the trees are actually planted) but studying the impact due to felling before the decision to fell them is taken. The answer to the destruction of livelihoods, ways of life and sacred forests is not a 'zero carbon' airport. At a time when the world is reeling from a pandemic caused by a zoonotic virus, the public health impact of deforestation has to be at the top of our minds ...

The Mopa 1 judgment of 2019 marked a significant advance in promoting the environmental rule of law. The Mopa 2 judgment of 2020 turned the tide back. Lifestyle triumphed over livelihoods—as always.

NOTES AND QUESTIONS

1. Videh Upadhyay argued that the expansion of judicial power in the sphere of environmental law is characterized by a curious dichotomy. In matters relating to pollution, the courts are proactive to the point of being 'aggressive' in ensuring compliance. Polluting units that breach environmental norms must shut down. When it comes to large infrastructure projects, the approach of the same judiciary is 'defensive'.[130] Infrastructure projects should be allowed regardless of whether the government's decision to allow the project is right or wrong; the limited question to be considered by the court is whether the decision-making process was satisfactory. What might explain the contrasting approach?

2. Upadhyay's analysis predated appellate review and was in the context of judicial review exercised by the High Courts and the Supreme Court. Will appellate review by the NGT increase judicial intervention? Is this good or bad?

VIII. THE *CENTRAL VISTA* CASE

In September 2019, the Central Public Works Department (CPWD) announced a plan to redevelop the Central Vista area of New Delhi. The notice inviting bids, issued out of the blue, envisioned a large-scale, transformative project based on a new 'visionary master plan'.

The Central Vista has as its main axis Rajpath, which runs east–west originating from the Rashtrapati Bhawan on Raisina Hill, flanked by the Secretariat Buildings (North Block and South Block), the Parliament House (adjacent to the North Block), various Bhavans of Ministries like the Krishi Bhavan and Shastri Bhavan, the Indira Gandhi National Centre for the Arts, the National Archives and the National Museum, finally leading to India Gate.

The notice inviting bids issued by CPWD, described as the Consultation Services NIT, stated:

> 3. *Objectives of Bid Documents*
>
> The objective of this bid document is to re-plan the entire Central Vista area from the gates of Rashtrapati Bhavan up to India Gate, an area of approximately 4 square kilometres. A new Master Plan is to be drawn up for the entire Central Vista area that represents the values and aspirations of a New India—Good Governance, Efficiency, Transparency, Accountability and Equity and is rooted in the Indian Culture and social milieu. The Master Plan shall entail concept, plan, detailed design and strategies development/redevelopment works, refurbishment works, demolition of existing buildings as well as related infrastructure and site development works. These new iconic structures shall be a legacy for 150 to 200 years at the very least.

The Consultation Services NIT was the only notice inviting bids for the redevelopment of the Central Vista area, including the Parliament Building. There was no separate plan with respect to the Parliament Building.

Moreover, the technical evaluation criteria specified: '[t]he Bidder shall make an [Approach and Methodology (A&M)] submission of the Vision Master Plan of the Central Vista area including Parliament Building, Common Central Secretariat and Central Vista.' The document envisaged the development/redevelopment of: Parliament Building by July 2022; Common Central Secretariat to be developed in the Central Vista area by March 2024; and an upgrade of the public facilities, amenities, parking and green space in Central Vista to make it a world class tourist destination by November 2020.

[130] Videh Upadhyay, *Changing Judicial Power: Courts on Infrastructure Projects and Environment* 35 ECONOMIC & POLITICAL WEEKLY 3789 (2000).

On 25 October 2019, the Central Government issued a press release stating:

> 'CPWD has awarded the consultancy work to M/s HCP Design, Planning & Management Pvt Ltd on 18.10.2019 and now the firm is on board for development of the Master Plan of Central Vista area and design of buildings as per new requirements. The Govt. has set stringent timelines to complete the development/redevelopment of Parliament building, Common Central Secretariat and Central Vista. While the timelines given to CPWD to complete the Central Vista project is November, 2021, the work on Parliament building is to be completed by March, 2022 and the common Central Secretariat by March 2024.'

The documents and actions of the Central Government clearly show that there was a single Central Vista project which included the Parliament Building.

From an EIA perspective, where a project is comprehensive in its conception and design, it cannot be sliced into smaller components because cumulative environmental impacts may be missed through such an exercise. The notion of cumulative impact assessments was introduced in 2006 by the National Environment Policy which states: 'Encourage regulatory authorities, Central and State, to institutionalize regional and cumulative environmental impact assessments … to ensure that environmental concerns are identified and addressed at the planning stage itself.'[131]

The requirement for a comprehensive EIA examining cumulative impacts is evident from the statutory application form which obliges a party to disclose all interlinked projects and whether separate applications for interlinked projects have been submitted. Further, this principle requiring cumulative impact assessment is established by a series of judgments of the NGT[132] and the Supreme Court.[133]

Cumulative assessment of environmental impacts is a widely recognized global norm and is explained by an office memorandum issued by the MoEF. Captioned, 'Consideration of integrated and inter-related projects', the memorandum states that integrated and inter-related projects shall be appraised collectively, covering the impact of each of the components in a comprehensive manner. Further, the memorandum records:

> (v) The respective EACs will consider the sector specific proposals based on the common EIA report and will make their recommendations relating to that particular component. However, in doing so, the overall impact of the project as a whole will also be considered.[134]

In February 2020, CPWD disaggregated the Central Vista project and applied for an EC only with respect to the Parliament Building. In the statutory application form, CPWD represented:

S No	Item	Details
17	Interlinked Projects	No
18	Whether separate application of interlinked project has been submitted?	No

131 Ministry of Environment & Forests, Government of India, *National Environment Policy* 18 (2006).

132 *Krishi Vigyan Arogya Sanstha v MoEF* (2011) SCC Online NGT 18 (Appeal No. 7 of 2011(T), order dated 20 September 2011); *Ossie Fernandes v MoEF* (2012) SCC Online NGT 7 (Appeal No. 12/2011, order dated 30 May 2012); *Jeet Singh Kanwar v Union of India* (2013) SCC Online NGT 1 (Appeal No. 10 of 2011 (T), order dated 16 April 2013) and *T Muruganandam v MoEF* (Appeal No. 50 of 2012, order dated 10 November 2014), (2014) SCC Online NGT 7161.

133 *Alaknanda Hydropower Co Ltd v Anuj Joshi* (2014) 1 SCC 769 and *Deepak Kumar v State of Haryana* (2012) 4 SCC 629.

134 Ministry of Environment & Forests, Government of India, OM No. J-11013/41/2006-IA. II (I) dated 24 December 2010.

The application was taken up for consideration by the Expert Appraisal Committee at its 49th meeting held on 25–26 February 2020. Many representations were received by the MoEF as well as the EAC expressing concerns on the following issues:

- The Indian Parliament is structurally a part of the composite notified heritage precinct, the Central Vista. The application completely disregards the historical, cultural and social importance of the existing Parliament by treating its 'expansion and renovation' any other regular construction project.
- The application treats the expansion of the Parliament as a stand-alone project when it is only one part of the proposed redevelopment of the Central Vista heritage precinct.
- The treatment of the Parliament expansion as a separate project violates the MoEFCC's OM dated (No. J-11013/41/2006-IA. II (I)) for 'consideration of integrated and inter related projects for grant of environmental clearance'. The current application is in complete disregard of the requirements of this OM.
- The application contains false and misleading information stating that the project will have no 'cumulative effects due to proximity to other existing or planned projects with similar effects', that there will be no significant impacts on ecology and public space, and on areas protected under conventions or legislations for their ecological, landscape, cultural or other values.
- The application is full of subjective responses to questions of scale and duration of various impacts that are likely to be caused by the proposed construction. These can only be treated as opinions because there are no studies or detailed assessments to support the application.
- The application for environment clearance must be set aside due to pending litigation on the land use change for the project. The land use change notification for Central Vista, which includes plot 118 is under litigation before the High Court of Delhi i.e. W P C 1575/2020 and W P (C) 1568/2020.[135]

The EAC required the CPWD to submit a revised application, since there was a mistake in calculating the total built-up area, and asked the project proponent to respond to the representations.

The revised application was considered at the 50th Meeting of the EAC held on 20 April 2020. The project proponent claimed that integrated and interrelated projects are those where there is a functional unity. Since Parliament's functions were distinct from executive functions, the expansion of Parliament was distinct from the rest of the Central Vista project, justifying segregation. The EAC recorded its conclusions and findings in a single sentence paragraph:

> 50.3.7.5. Based on the information and clarifications provided by the proponent *vis-à-vis* mitigation measures for likely environmental impacts proposed by the proponent, the EAC appraised environmental aspects of the project and recommended for grant of Environmental Clearance with following specific conditions along with other Standard EC Conditions as specified by the Ministry *vide* OM dated 4th January, 2019 for the said project/activity ... while considering for accord of environmental clearance.

The EC granted to the project was challenged on several grounds, including the patent illegality in slicing a comprehensive project and since the CPWD falsely represented that there were no interlinked projects. We carry a short excerpt from the majority opinion.

---

[135] *Rajeev Suri v Delhi Development Authority* (*Central Vista* case) (2021) SCC Online SC 7, para 704.

RAJEEV SURI v DELHI DEVELOPMENT AUTHORITY
(2021) SCC ONLINE SC 7

***

A M Khanwilkar, J:

Principally speaking, in a matter of planning and development activity, the Government has the sole prerogative to decide the nature, expanse and timeline of development work. The Government may choose to begin the development of an entire region at once or do it in a phased manner. We hasten to add that this prerogative of the Government is subject to due observance of rules, regulations and other procedures. The scrutiny of the Court is to ensure that the Government does not transgress its boundaries in the task of governance. For the purpose of inviting a consultant and changing use of land involved in the project, it is understandable, rather desirable, that the entire project is treated as one. It would be absurd to invite different consultants for different components of a project, the very idea behind which is to ensure uniformity of design and efficiency. It would be a never-ending spiral. The job of consultant herein was to present a vision document for the whole project at once so that the Government is in a position to plan further course of action as per the approved design. It could not have been expected to seek such consultancy services in a piecemeal manner. Therefore, merely because the project was presented as a cumulative one for the aforesaid purposes, it cannot be inferred that the Government intended or is legally obliged to treat it as such from the stage of conception to the stage of execution....

It is true that the 2006 Notification prescribes for a cumulative impact assessment. We are in agreement with the proposition that the basic purpose of an environmental impact assessment is to determine and mitigate the cumulative impact of a project—if the project proponent intends to commence development together or within reasonable time space. However, the meaning of the expression 'cumulative impact/effect' is not to be understood as an expression of art. It does not shun segregating an independent project. In an examination of this nature, the foremost requirement is to identify the precise expanse of a project. For this purpose, the first source is the information supplied by the project proponent in Form I as it expressly requires information on any interlinked projects. Upon the receipt of that information, it falls upon the EAC to check and scrutinize whether there is more to the project which has been left out of its scrutiny. This latter scrutiny is dependent upon the nature of the project as it would involve collective consideration of all operational aspects of a project. It does not mean connecting independent projects upon a subjective notion that it is necessary to do so for a collective appraisal merely because such projects fall in the same region. The word 'cumulative' is to be read in conjunction with the word 'project' and idea behind examination of cumulative impact is to assess the impact of the project including all its functional components, and not of all development activities going on in a region.

In the light of 2006 Notification read with Office Memorandum dated 7.10.2014 issued by MoEF, it is settled that environmental clearance is always site specific and is required to be obtained only before the actual commencement of work on the project and not before that. Thus, there is no sound basis for the argument that the Central Secretariat project must be assessed with the Parliament project. For, the stage of commencement of work in respect of the former Project has not [been] reached yet and indisputably the same will be on a different site altogether....

The petitioners' reliance upon O M dated 24.12.2010 titled 'Consideration *of Integrated and Inter-linked projects—Procedure Regarding*' is misplaced. The real purport of this O M is to ensure that projects which entail multi-sectoral components are not dissected by the project proponent in a sectoral manner, thereby rendering the EAC incapable of assessing the multi-dimensional aspects of a project. The first and foremost requirement for the applicability of this O M is that the subject project should involve multi-sectoral components. The case on hand does not involve multi-sectoral components to it as it is a simpliciter construction project. If a project does not involve multi-sectoral components, there is no occasion for the EAC to examine this aspect. The words 'integrated' and 'inter-linked' offer guidance on this count. Any two activities/projects could be said to be integrated or inter-linked when they are functionally connected in the manner that operability of one is intrinsically dependent on the operability of another. It is a scientific and functional connection, not a hypothetical or theoretical connection. The above discussion on cumulative impact supplements this position....

Irrefutably, any exposition on what could amount to an integrated project, thereby calling for a cumulative assessment, has to be done with circumspection. For, the 2006 Notification would apply equally to other public projects including private projects without variation in the legal standard. The question here is whether a common builder/developer undertaking construction work on ten different plots totalling upto thousand acres scattered in different areas of a region/state/country and not adjoining or contiguous could be subjected to the rigours of cumulative assessment equivalent to an integrated project merely because the total area across which the projects are spread, when added up, turns out to be beyond permissible limits warranting such assessment. That is not the dispensation prescribed by law as of now. In our considered opinion, this interpretation would be counter-productive to the very idea of sustainable development. To be considered as integrated, the plots must involve multi-sectoral components in close proximity if not contiguous and fulfil other specifications under the notification....

We find merits in the plea taken by the respondents that the Parliament project cannot be regarded as inter-linked or interdependent with the central secretariat project. The differences relating to functionality, budgeting, timelines and purpose are glaring and substantial.

Notably, the argument of the petitioners alleging fraud in segregation of the project is also devoid of merit. For, it completely blurs the line between a conscious policy decision to separate the development project need-based and concealment, misrepresentation or fraud. Fraud stands on the foundation of a fraudulent mental intent and culling out that specific intent is a pre-requisite for establishing the ground of fraud in a court of law. The petitioners' argument of fraud lacks a judicial sustainable basis....

Upon a close scrutiny of the information supplied in Form I and I-A, documents supplied by the project proponent and appraisal made by the EAC, we are of the view that the grant of EC is in conformity with the mandate of the competent authority and is just and proper. The project proponent has undertaken various expert studies to prepare a comprehensive traffic management plan, solid waste management plan, water management plan and waste disposal plan. There is ample information on record to show that the project proponent has adequately addressed various facets of the project including source of water, disposal of water, generation of concrete, disposal of concrete, power availability, concerns relating to landscape etc. and the petitioners have outrightly failed to substantiate their apprehensions by placing material on record to the contrary....

The minutes of the two meetings of EAC are self-explanatory and reveal due application of mind, in light of the principles relating to application of mind enunciated above. We do not wish to repeat the same to avoid prolixity. EAC is an expert body and it is amply clear that it has been made aware of all relevant information relating to the project and it has applied its mind to the proposal. Even on settled principles of judicial review, it is clear that relevant material has been considered by the committee and no reliance has been pointed out on any irrelevant material. The specific recommendations given by the committee do indicate that the committee was aware of the need for precautionary measures in environmental matters and accordingly, it suggested requirement of further permissions on certain counts....

NOTES AND QUESTIONS

1. How persuasive is the reasoning employed by the Supreme Court? Is there any doubt that the Central Vista project is a single project and could not in law be sliced to separate the Parliament Building component? Revisit the Approach and Methodology (A&M) stipulations in the bid document and the press release of 25 October 2019.

2. The reasoning adopted by the majority judgment is superficial, shallow and wrong. Having accepted that the 2006 EIA notification requires cumulative impact assessment, and considering that the Central Vista project was a single conception with tight deadlines to be achieved between November 2021 and March 2024, it follows that the principle of cumulative impact applied.

3. The majority judgment is on a weak footing when it draws on functional independence of components within the Central Vista project. The project was required to obtain a prior EC since the activity was covered by serial number 8 of the EIA notification. Serial number 8 reads: 'Building/Construction projects/Area Development projects and Townships'. The Central Vista project was clearly a single comprehensive area development project. Consequently, from the standpoint of EIA, the function that a particular building served was a wholly irrelevant consideration. On this reasoning, project proponents of townships and area development projects will slice their projects into separate components like schools, hospitals, shopping areas, offices, residential units, club houses, etc. and claim that each one has a distinct function and may be separated from the larger project.

4. The majority opinion accepts that the project is indeed a single project for conception and design, holding that it 'would be absurd to invite different consultants for different components of a project'. Having acknowledged multiple components in a single project covering a single area known as the Central Vista, was it not elementary that the environmental impacts of all the components on air quality, water extraction and use, traffic, heritage, noise—ought to be studied and mitigated as part of one exercise? Considering the compact time frame for all the components, does the adjective 'absurd' more aptly apply to the strained reasoning of the court?

5. The EAC provided no discernable reasons, but this too was accepted by the majority. The minority judgment authored by Justice Sanjiv Khanna dissented:

> What is of concern is lack of discussion, reasons or even the conclusion or finding on the aspect of slicing or inclusion. On the matter of 'appraisal' in *Bengaluru Development Authority v Sudhakar Hegde* (2020) 15 SCC 63, this court has elucidated:
>
>> 'Appraisal by the SEAC is structured and defined by the 2006 Notification. At this stage, the SEAC is required to conduct "detailed scrutiny" of the application and other documents including the EIA report submitted by the applicant for the grant of an EC. Upon the completion of the appraisal process, the SEAC makes "categorical recommendations" to the SEIAA either for: (i) the grant of a prior EC on stipulated terms and conditions; or (ii) the rejection of the application. Significantly, the recommendations made by the SEAC for the grant of EC, are normally accepted by the SEIAA and must be based on "reasons"....'

> Proceedings before the EAC are not adversarial in nature. EAC acts both as a fair investigator and an independent objective adjudicator when deciding whether or not to grant environmental clearance. There must be application of mind which is reflected when reasons justifying the conclusion are recorded. Mere reproduction of the contesting stands is not sufficient. On the contrary it would reflect mechanical grant without application of mind. Further, it is not for the court/appellate forum to assume what weighed, whether the conclusion relies on material which is relevant, irrelevant or partly relevant, or whether the decision is partly based on surmises and conjectures and partly on evidence. Some reasons at least in brief to understand what had weighed and persuaded the authority is mandated and required. One issue certainly raised that required an answer was the question of slicing or inclusion. We are unable to fathom and ascertain reasons or the findings recorded on this aspect....
>
> We set aside the order of the EAC dated 22nd April, 2020 and the environment clearance by the Ministry of Environment and Forest dated 17th June, 2020, and would pass an order of remit to the EAC with a request that they may decide the question on environment clearance within a period of 30 days from the date copy of this order received, without awaiting the decision on the question of change/modification of land use. Speaking and reasoned order would be passed.

Re-examine the sole paragraph containing reasons reproduced in the introduction to this case. If the majority opinion is correct and this is all that is required to be provided by the EAC, can the EAC not simply 'block and copy' paragraph 50.3.7.5 in every case? Does the endorsement by the majority opinion gut the principle of merit review and the administrative law principle requiring the furnishing of reasons? Which judgment is correct: the majority or the minority?

6. The CPWD in its application declared that there were no interlinked projects. Had you been responsible for filling in the basic information for the Parliament Building EC application, what would you have stated? The majority judgment did not find any misdeclaration on the part of the project proponent.

7. By disaggregating the composite Central Vista project and truncating the application to cover the Parliament Building alone, the CPWD skirted the scoping stage and the requirement for an EIA report at the appraisal stage. In this manner, the project proponent avoided a higher degree of scrutiny under the EIA notification.

8. The fragile reasoning in the majority judgment is a reminder that environmental rights and more generally liberty quickly perish when judges are unable or unwilling to stand up for the citizen against the executive.

IX. THE *ALEMBIC* CASE

Though the 27 January 1994 EIA notification mandated a prior EC, industry was remiss in following these regulations and the pollution control boards were lax in implementation. The MoEF periodically extended the deadline for obtaining an EC, culminating in a circular dated 14 May 2002 which stated:

> Keeping the foregoing in view, it has been decided to extend the deadline up to 31 March 2003 so that defaulting units could avail of this last and final opportunity to obtain ex-post-facto environmental clearance. This would apply to all such units, which had commenced construction activities/operations without obtaining prior environmental clearance in violation of the EIA Notification of 27 January 1994.

The circular provided that the defaulting units seeking an expansion were to earmark a separate fund for 'eco-development measures including community development measures' in project areas linked to the investment in the project. The contributions to the fund were indicated in a table:

A	Projects with investment upto Rs. 100 crores	1% of the project cost with a minimum of Rs. 50,000
B	Projects with investment beyond Rs. 100 crores and upto Rs. 1,000 crores	0.5% of the project cost subject to a minimum of Rs. 1 crore and a maximum of Rs. 2.5 crores
C	Projects with investment exceeding Rs. 1,000 crores	0.25% of the project cost subject to a maximum of Rs. 5 crores

The validity of the circular was challenged successfully before the NGT, leading to a set of appeals in the Supreme Court.

ALEMBIC PHARMACEUTICALS LTD v ROHIT PRAJAPATI
(2020) SCC ONLINE SC 347

Dr Dhananjaya Y Chandrachud, J: By a judgment dated 8 January 2016, the Bench of the National Green Tribunal for the Western Zone held that a circular issued by the Union Ministry of Environment and Forests on 14 May 2002 is contrary to law. The circular envisaged the grant of *ex post facto* environmental clearances. The NGT issued a slew of directions including the revocation of environmental clearances and for closing down industrial units operating without valid consents. On 17 May 2016, the NGT dismissed an application for review filed by one of the affected industrial units. The industrial units and MoEF are in appeal.…

Having held that the concept of an 'ex *post facto* environmental clearance' was not sustainable with reference to any provision of law, the NGT issued the following directions:

(i) The authorities of the Union of India, including the MoEF, State of Gujarat, Gujarat Pollution Control Board and District Collectors shall not grant consent for an industrial activity covered by the EIA notification of 1994 without the steps mandated by the notification such as screening, scoping, public hearing and decision being fulfilled;
(ii) The ECs granted to the industrial units of the sixth to ninth respondents shall be revoked;
(iii) All the industrial activities which were being operated without a valid EC and consent to operate shall be closed down within one month;
(iv) Each of the units shall deposit a compensation of Rs.10 lakhs for having caused environmental degradation; and
(v) The amount deposited shall be used for the restoration of the environment in and around the industrial area of Ankleshwar in the State of Gujarat.

* * *

[L]earned Additional Solicitor General made an attempt to demonstrate that the power to issue the circular dated 14 May 2002 that extended the deadline for defaulting units to avail of an *ex post facto* clearance until 30 March 2003 could well be traceable to section 3 of the Environment (Protection) Act, 1986. Section 3, to the extent relevant, provides thus:

> Section 3. *Power of central government to take measures to protect and improve environment* (1) Subject to the provisions of this Act, the Central Government, shall have the power to take all such measures as it deems necessary or expedient for the purpose of protecting and improving the quality of the environment and preventing controlling and abating environmental pollution.

Section 3(1) is an enabling provision for the Central Government to undertake all such measures as it deems necessary or expedient for the purpose of protecting and improving the quality of the environment and preventing, controlling and abating environmental pollution. This limb of the submission of the Additional Solicitor General is crucial to the issue as to whether the NGT has exceeded its jurisdiction since the decision in *Sterlite*, [(2019) SCC Online SC 221] holds that the NGT, while exercising its appellate jurisdiction, 'cannot strike down rules or regulations made *under this Act*'. In the present case, to demonstrate that the NGT did not have the jurisdiction to strike down the circular dated 14 May 2002, it was urged that the circular was issued by the MoEF pursuant to its powers under section 3 of the Environment (Protection) Act, 1986. There is an inherent difficulty in accepting the submission. Before this Court, the Union of India has not pleaded the case that the circular dated 14 May 2002 is a measure which is traceable to the provisions of section 3. On the contrary, in its pleadings the Union of India construed it as a 'purely administrative decision'. Ground (iii) in paragraph 3 of the memo of appeal states the position of the Union government:

> Because the Hon'ble Tribunal failed to appreciate that after the EIA, Notification 1994 the opportunity to seek ex-post facto environmental clearance was given to industries in background of far reaching impact in terms of direct loss of livelihood in the employees working in the units which also supply inputs to other units and their indirect employment. *It was submitted to the Hon'ble High Court of Gujarat that issuance of circular dated 14/05/2002, based on which environmental clearance was given, was purely an administrative decision before taking stringent action.* (Emphasis supplied)

The omission in the appeal to make any attempt to sustain the circular dated 14 May 2002 with reference to the provisions of section 3 of the Environment (Protection) Act, 1986 is significant. For an action of the Central government to be treated as a measure referable to section 3 it must satisfy the statutory requirement of being necessary or expedient 'for the purpose of protecting and improving the quality of the environment and preventing, controlling and abating environment pollution'. The circular dated 14 May 2002 in fact does quite the contrary. It purported to allow an extension of time for industrial units to comply with the requirement of an EC. The EIA notification dated 27 January 1994 mandated that an EC has to be obtained before embarking on a new project or expanding or modernising an existing one. The EIA notification of 1994 has been issued under the provisions of the Environment (Protection) Act, 1986 and the Environment (Protection) Rules, 1986, with the object of imposing restrictions and prohibitions on setting up of new projects or expansion or modernisation of existing project. The measures are based on the precautionary principle and aim to protect the interests of the environment. The circular dated 14 May 2002 allowed defaulting industrial units who had commenced activities without an EC to cure the default by an *ex post facto* clearance. Being an administrative decision, it is beyond the scope of section 3 and cannot be said to be a measure for the purpose of protecting and improving the quality of the environment. The circular notes that there were defaulting units which had failed to comply with the requirement of obtaining an EC as mandated. The circular provided for an extension of time and inexplicably introduced the notion of an *ex post facto* clearance. In effect, it impacted the obligation of the industrial units to be in compliance with the law. The concept of *ex post facto* clearance is fundamentally at odds with the EIA notification dated 27 January 1994. The EIA notification of 1994 contained a stipulation that any expansion or modernisation of an activity or setting up of a new project listed in Schedule–I 'shall not be undertaken in any part of India unless it has been accorded environmental clearance'. The language of the notification is as clear as it can be to indicate that the requirement is of a prior EC. A mandatory provision requires complete compliance. The words 'shall not be undertaken' read in conjunction with the expression 'unless' can only have one meaning: before undertaking a new project or expanding or modernising an existing one, an EC must be obtained. When the EIA notification of 1994 mandates a prior EC, it proscribes a post activity approval or an *ex post facto* permission. What is sought to be achieved by the administrative circular dated 14 May 2002 is contrary to the statutory notification dated 27 January 1994. The circular dated 14 May 2002 does not stipulate how the detrimental effects on the environment would be taken care of if the project proponent is granted an *ex post facto* EC. The EIA notification of 1994 mandates a prior environmental clearance. The circular substantially amends or alters the application of the EIA notification of 1994. The mandate of not commencing a new project or expanding or modernising an existing one unless an environmental clearance has been obtained stands diluted and is rendered ineffective by the issuance of the administrative circular dated 14 May 2002. This discussion leads us to the conclusion that the administrative circular is not a measure protected by section 3. Hence there was no jurisdictional bar on the NGT to enquire into its legitimacy or vires. Moreover, the administrative circular is contrary to the EIA Notification 1994 which has a statutory character. The circular is unsustainable in law....

The concept of an *ex post facto* EC is in derogation of the fundamental principles of environmental jurisprudence and is an anathema to the EIA notification dated 27 January 1994. It is, as the judgment in *Common Cause* (2017) 9 SCC 499 holds, detrimental to the environment and could lead to irreparable degradation. The reason why a retrospective EC or an *ex post facto* clearance is alien to environmental jurisprudence is that before the issuance of an EC, the statutory notification warrants a careful application of mind, besides a study into the likely consequences of a proposed activity on the environment. An EC can be issued only after various stages of the decision-making process have been completed. Requirements such as conducting a public hearing, screening, scoping and appraisal are components of the decision-making process which ensure that the likely impacts of the industrial activity or the expansion of an existing industrial activity are considered in the decision-making calculus. Allowing for an *ex post facto* clearance would essentially condone the operation of industrial activities without the grant of an EC. In the absence of an EC, there would be no conditions that would safeguard the environment. Moreover, if the EC was to be ultimately refused, irreparable harm would have been caused to the environment. In either view of the matter, environment law cannot countenance the notion of an *ex post facto* clearance. This would be contrary to both the precautionary principle as well as the need for sustainable development....

Learned counsel for the three industries urged that the EIA notification of 1994 did not apply to their manufacturing units as they were covered by the exemption in terms of Clause 8 of the explanatory note. The issue which needs to be considered is whether the industries were covered by the exemption and were not required to obtain ECs. Clause 8 to the explanatory note to the EIA notification of 1994 states thus:

> 8. *Exemption for projects already initiated*
>
> For projects listed in Schedule–I to the notification in respect of which the required land has been acquired and all relevant clearances of the State Government including NOC from the respective State Pollution Control Board have been obtained before 27th January 1994, a project proponent will not be required to seek environmental clearance from the [Impact Assessment Agency]. However, those units who have not as yet commenced production will inform the IAA.

* * *

From the material placed on the record by the industries, it becomes evident that there has been a gross abdication of responsibility by all the three industries in terms of obtaining timely consents and authorisations from the GPCB. There exists a distinction between obtaining relevant clearances and consents from the State Pollution Control Board and obtaining an environmental clearance in accordance with the procedure laid down under the EIA notification of 1994. A consent order issued by the State Pollution Control Board allows an industry to operate within the prescribed emission norms. However, the consent orders do not account for the social cost and impact of undertaking an industrial activity on the environment and its surroundings. A holistic analysis of the environmental impact of an industrial activity is only accounted for once all the steps listed out in EIA notification of 1994 are followed. The purpose of setting in place specific requirements such as public hearing, screening, scoping and appraisal is to foster deliberative decisions and protect environmental concerns. The detailed process listed out in the EIA notification of 1994 for obtaining an EC allows for minimising the adverse environmental impact of any industrial activity and improving the quality of the environment. One must adopt an ecologically rational outlook towards development. Given the social and environmental impacts of an industrial activity, environment compliance must not be seen as an obstacle to development but as a measure towards achieving sustainable development and inter-generational equity.

We have therefore come to the conclusion that none of the three industries were entitled to the benefit of the exemption contained in Clause 8 of the explanatory note to the EIA notification of 1994....

Guided by the precepts that emerge from the above decisions, this Court has taken note of the fact that though the three industries operated without an EC for several years after the EIA notification of 1994, each of them had subsequently received ECs including amended ECs for expansion of existing capacities. These ECs have been operational since 14 May 2003 (in the case of Alembic Pharmaceuticals Limited), 17 July 2003 (in the case of United Phosphorous Limited), and 23 December 2002 (in the case of Unique Chemicals Limited). In addition, all the three units have made infrastructural investments and employed significant numbers of workers in their industrial units.

In this backdrop, this Court must take a balanced approach which holds the industries to account for having operated without environmental clearances in the past without ordering a closure of operations. The directions of the NGT for the revocation of the ECs and for closure of the units do not accord with the principle of proportionality. At the same time, the Court cannot be oblivious to the environmental degradation caused by all three industries units that operated without valid ECs. The three industries have evaded the legally binding regime of obtaining ECs. They cannot escape the liability incurred on account of such noncompliance. Penalties must be imposed for the disobedience with a binding legal regime. The breach by the industries cannot be left unattended by legal consequences. The amount should be used for the purpose of restitution and restoration of the environment. Instead and in place of the directions issued by the NGT, we are of the view that it would be in the interests of justice to direct the three industries to deposit compensation quantified at Rs.10 crores each. The amount shall be deposited with GPCB and it shall be duly utilised for restoration and remedial measures to improve the quality of the environment in the industrial area in which the industries operate. Though we have come to the conclusion, for the reasons indicated, that the direction for the revocation of the ECs and the closure of the industries was not warranted, we have issued the order for payment of compensation as a facet of preserving the environment in accordance with the precautionary principle. These directions are issued under Article 142 of the Constitution. Alembic Pharmaceuticals Limited, United Phosphorous Limited and Unique Chemicals Limited shall deposit the amount of compensation with GPCB within a period of four months from the date of receipt of the certified copy of this judgment. This deposit shall be in addition to the amount directed by the NGT. Subject to the deposit of the aforesaid amount and for the reasons indicated, we allow the appeals and set aside the impugned judgment of the NGT dated 8 January 2016 in so far as it directed the revocation of the ECs and closure of the industries as well as the order in review dated 17 May 2016.

NOTES AND QUESTIONS

1. Do you agree with the reasoning adopted by the Supreme Court regarding the NGT's power of judicial review? According to *Alembic*, the NGT has no power to invalidate rules

and regulations but can invalidate administrative directions and circulars. Is this a case of judicial hair-splitting?

2. One of the points urged by the industries was that the MoEF had issued subsequent ECs for expansion of industrial activity. In view of the subsequent ECs there was no necessity for an EC with respect to the original project. The Supreme Court rejected the submission upholding the requirement of a prior EC both at the stage of setting up an industrial project and expansion.

14

LARGE PROJECTS

A. INTRODUCTION

In this chapter, we look at large development projects: dams, the river interlinking project, power stations and large real estate development, and efforts to reduce their environmental impact.

India ranks among the most important dam-building nations. It began building large dams shortly after Independence. Large-scale river development began in 1930 with the Mettur Dam on the Cauvery and accelerated after Independence with the Bhakra Nangal and Hirakud projects. Currently, India has tapped only 33% of its total hydroelectric potential, estimated at 148 gigawatts.[1]

These dams are the cornerstones of large-scale multi-purpose river valley projects intended to meet regional needs for irrigation, hydroelectric power and flood control. Since the 1950s, the governments, both state and national, have vigorously promoted dam building as a means to economic progress. Today, all major rivers in India are either dammed or in the process of being dammed.

Since the 1970s, citizen protests and international human rights and environmental pressures have increasingly been brought to bear against these projects. The central issue in the citizen campaigns is the problem of mass displacement: the backwaters of a large dam generally displace many thousands of people, often tribals and forest dwellers who are the poorest and most powerless members of society. There are no reliable official figures on the number of people displaced but some estimates put this figure as high as 50 million. To compound this problem, the Indian Government's often extreme reaction to protests by potentially and actually displaced people has drawn unfavourable attention from the international human rights community. In addition, the structural design of dams built in seismically unstable areas has drawn even more attention to the potential loss of life and displacement that might result from a dam that fails.

To whom do the benefits of large dams accrue? Often the benefits go to large urban populations far downstream and not to the people who pay for the dam with their land and even their lives. In addition, funding for dams, often in the form of loans from other countries or multilateral development banks, raises international issues of responsibility and fault for human and environmental damage.

[1] Ramesh Raja, *Time to Tap Hydropower*, Governance Today, 11 December 2014, http://www.governancetoday.co.in/time-tap-hydropower/, accessed on 24 April 2020.

Environmental Law & Policy in India. Shyam Divan and Armin Rosencranz, Oxford University Press.
 DOI: 1093/oso/9780192865458.003.0014

Large dams are often ecologically unsound and economically unjustified if environmental and health costs are fully accounted for. These costs include the loss of forests and wildlife, waterlogging, siltation, loss of arable land and increases in water-borne diseases. Finally, the religious significance that many Indians attribute to the free-flowing rivers and the communities endangered by faulty dam construction may not be adequately accounted for.

As we have seen in the previous chapter, the environmental harm from a large project could be reduced if the probable environmental impacts are explored before the project's inception. In this chapter we examine the new land acquisition regime and important elements of this law that seek to dispel the harsh consequences that previously destroyed lives through displacement. We thereafter review the legal dimensions of important environmental campaigns and cases which ran their course in parallel to the evolving EIA regime.

B. LAND ACQUISITION

Large projects require large tracts of land. To acquire the land, the state resorts to the Right to Fair Compensation and Transparency in Land Acquisition, Rehabilitation and Resettlement Act of 2013 (RFCA). The RFCA replaced the colonial Land Acquisition Act of 1894 (LA Act). The RFCA (like its predecessor) empowers the Union Government and state governments to take land for public purposes. The theory underlying this Act is the doctrine of eminent domain, which permits the state to reassert its right over a portion of the land for the public good. The exercise of eminent domain under the LA Act operated extremely harshly on the persons displaced, dishoused and uprooted, as explained in this pre-RFCA piece.

USHA RAMANATHAN; A WORD ON EMINENT DOMAIN IN DISPLACED BY DEVELOPMENT—CONFRONTING MARGINALISATION AND GENDER INJUSTICE 133 (Ed. Lyla Mehta, 2009)[2]

An inquiry into eminent domain demonstrates that the power of eminent domain has been interpreted as being close to absolute power of the State over all land and interests in land within its territory. The effect of this has been that those without access to land and rights over land (including the landless, artisans, women as a composite group), those who may have use rights but no titles, communities holding common rights and others with inchoate interests, have had to bear the burden heaved on to them by eminent domain. Simultaneously, the plenitude of powers presumed to arise from the doctrine of eminent domain has allowed for an engorgement of state power over land.

In relatively recent times, the policies of the State, ruggedly supported by legislation, have reintroduced the power of the 'sovereign' to use its discretion in facilitating the concentration of land in corporations. This is not a replication of the *zamindari* system of wealth transfer by the use of state power, but a neo-liberal version of it. Mining and Special Economic Zones (SEZs) have been added to the arenas of contest, wherein the contestants are made even more unequal by law and state force, which are deployed in effecting the transfer. There are nuances that have begun to enter state practice, wherein, for instance, corporations are being advised to buy land in the 'open market'. In such cases, the need for the State to intervene to secure the interests of the land holders is being recognised, even as the potential of a fair transaction of sale is not discounted. Other arrangements, including shareholding and leasing as opposed to outright sale require the State to step in to conceive and implement alternative arrangements that will allow for varied, but responsible, uses of land, without dispossession being a necessary consequence.

[2] http://www.ielrc.org/content/a0902.pdf, accessed 15 June 2021.

While these changes are occurring with remarkable swiftness, the status of the recognised property interests of women, the landless and the marginal farming and artisan communities does not even feature in the discourse. It is the zone of neglect that these communities inhabit. Dislodging the current appreciation of the doctrine of eminent domain is a necessary first step in the route to a return to equity, distributive justice and the limiting of the extraordinary and absolute power that the doctrine has allowed to be vested in the State.

The RFCA is a unified legislation combining two distinct strands of the government policy: (1) The acquisition of land in exercise of eminent domain powers (previously under the LA Act); and (2) rehabilitation and resettlement (R&R) under *ad hoc* policies. The broad definition of 'public purpose' under the erstwhile LA Act, the failure of the state to respond to genuine grievances of landowners, the abuse of the LA Act process to favour real estate developers and the meagre compensation along with the delays in disbursing the amounts, invited criticism from the Supreme Court and commentators. Further, a long record of poor implementation of R&R led to resistance against large projects through ground-level mobilization that highlighted human rights violations, caused project delays and resulted in cost overruns.

The Statement of Objects and Reasons (SOR) accompanying the RFCA Bill recognized that the new law would provide for just and fair compensation and cushion the impact of displacement which had the effect of 'depriving [people] of their land, livelihood and shelter, restricting their access to traditional resource base and uprooting them from their socio-cultural environment'. Indeed, the SOR recognized that displacement had 'traumatic psychological and socio-cultural consequences on the affected population which call for protecting their rights, particularly in case of weaker sections of the society including members of the Scheduled Castes, Scheduled Tribes, marginal farmers and their families'.

Underscoring a break from the past, the full title of the RFCA captures a range of objectives that the new law is designed to meet:

> An Act to ensure, in consultation with institutions of local self-government and Gram Sabhas established under the Constitution, a humane, participative, informed and transparent process for land acquisition for industrialisation, development of essential infrastructural facilities and urbanisation with the least disturbance to owners of the land and other affected families and provide just and fair compensation to the affected families whose land has been acquired or proposed to be acquired or are affected by such acquisition and make adequate provisions for such affected persons for their rehabilitation and resettlement and to ensuring that the cumulative outcome of compulsory acquisition should be that affected persons become partners in development leading to an improvement in their post-acquisition social and economic status and for matters connected therewith or incidental thereto.

The provisions of the RFCA relating to land acquisition compensation, rehabilitation and resettlement apply where the government acquires land for its own use or for public sector undertakings for a public purpose including infrastructure projects. The law also applies where land is acquired by the government for projects being executed by private companies. However, in the case of acquisition for a private company or public private partnership projects it is necessary to secure prior consent of a super-majority of affected families.[3]

[3] Section 2. Where land acquisition is for private companies 80% of the affected families must give prior consent and in the case of public-private partnership projects the threshold is 70%.

Chapter II of the Act lays out the detailed procedure for carrying out a social impact assessment study which must cover an assessment of whether the proposed acquisition serves a public purpose; an estimate of the affected families, including how many are likely to be displaced; the extent of land likely to be affected; and an examination of the social impact of the project. The social impact assessment study must cover the likely impact of the project on the livelihood of affected families; public and community properties; assets and infrastructure, particularly road, public transport, drainage, sanitation, sources of drinking water and healthcare facilities. The authority carrying out the study is required to prepare a social impact management plan listing the ameliorative measures required.[4] A public hearing must be held in the affected area after giving due notice to ascertain the view of the affected families.[5] Where an environmental impact assessment is required, a copy of the social impact assessment report must be made available to the impact assessment agency.[6]

An Expert Group comprising two social scientists, two local representatives, two experts on rehabilitation and a technical expert in the subject relating to the project are required to appraise the social impact assessment report and make their recommendation to the government.[7] The appropriate government after examining reports, plan and recommendations may 'recommend such area for acquisition which would ensure minimum displacement of people, minimum disturbance to the infrastructure, ecology and minimum adverse impact on the individuals affected'.[8]

Chapter III contains special provisions to safeguard food security and prescribes a general rule that no irrigated multi-crop land shall be acquired under the RFCA. In exceptional circumstances, and as a demonstrable last resort, the acquisition may be made within prescribed limits.[9] Where acquisition proceeds, the Administrator for R&R must initiate a survey and undertake a census of the affected families.[10]

Chapter V requires the Collector to pass R&R awards for each affected family in terms of the entitlements provided in the Second Schedule to the Act.[11] Moreover, the Collector must ensure the provision for all infrastructural facilities and basic minimum amenities in every resettlement area.[12] As a general rule, in order to protect Schedule Castes and Scheduled Tribes, no acquisition of land is to be made in Scheduled areas except as a demonstrable last resort.[13]

Chapter VI provides for the appointment of an Administrator,[14] Commissioner[15] and Rehabilitation and Resettlement Committee[16] for smooth implementation of R&R. Chapter VIII provides for the establishment of an authority to settle disputes relating to land acquisition or R&R.

[4] Section 4.
[5] Section 5.
[6] Section 6(2).
[7] Section 7.
[8] Section 8(2).
[9] Section 10.
[10] Section 16.
[11] Section 31.
[12] Section 32.
[13] Section 41.
[14] Section 43.
[15] Section 44.
[16] Section 45.

NOTES AND QUESTIONS

1. In a deliberate departure from the erstwhile LA Act, the RFCA injects a strong dose of constitutional values to temper the operation of eminent domain. The RFCA makes affected citizens 'more equal' under law by engrafting principles to minimize the impact of compulsory displacement. The policies, statutory checks and balances in the RFCA should reduce the impoverishment and unjust displacement that the old regime foisted upon citizens.

2. With its growing population and infrastructure deficit, India requires large infrastructure projects to improve communications and the quality of life. Post RFCA, are large projects possible? Or is the new regime more equitable with the real project costs, previously invisible and borne by the oustees, now being paid for by the general public for whose benefit the projects are undertaken?

3. In this chapter you will encounter a number of large projects such as Narmada and Tehri which uprooted settled communities. The acquisitions for these projects were under the LA Act. When you review these sections consider whether these projects would have at all fructified under the RFCA regime.

4. Will commercial interests fight back by seeking amendments and dilutions to the RFCA?

C. THE SILENT VALLEY PROJECT

The campaign against the Silent Valley project in the late 1970s was the earliest struggle against a large project on environmental grounds. It led to a pioneering public interest petition to protect the environment.

The proposed project, now abandoned, was to dam the Kuntipuzha River in Kerala's Palghat District. As it flows through the Valley, the Kuntipuzha drops 857 m, making the Valley an attractive site for generating electricity. Those promoting the project claimed that it would produce 240 MW of power, irrigate 10,000 hectares of land and provide over 2,000 jobs. Environmentalists, on the other hand, asserted that as home to one of the few remaining rain forests in the Western Ghats, the Valley ought to remain pristine. They further contended that with over 900 species of flowering plants and ferns and several endangered species of animals and birds, the Valley was one of the world's richest biological and genetic heritage sites.

In the campaign to save Silent Valley, legal strategies played a peripheral role. The environmentalists' success was due to a combination of several other factors, including the grassroots campaign led by the Kerala Sastra Sahitya Parishad (KSSP), intense lobbying by several non-governmental organizations and influential environmentalists within and outside government and international pressure exerted on Prime Minister Indira Gandhi. Examine the judgment of the Kerala High Court in the *Silent Valley* case (appended to the Prasad article, later in this section), in the backdrop of the larger campaign described in D'Monte's account.

D'MONTE; STORM OVER SILENT VALLEY, 9 India International Centre Quarterly 288 (1982)

No other environmental issue has raised more heat and dust in the country than Silent Valley—a small and hitherto almost unheard of strip of dense forest in Kerala's western ghats. One reason is the very elemental nature of the controversy: whether or not to preserve this tropical forest belt, one of the few uninhabited areas in the entire country, for the future benefit of mankind....

It all started with a slim green report of the Task Force of the National Committee on Environmental Planning and Coordination (NCEPC), on the ecological planning of the western ghats. The group, appointed in 1976, was headed by the prominent environmentalist, Zafar Futehally. In the brief section on Silent Valley, it concluded: 'The task force feels very strongly that the project should be abandoned and the area declared a Biosphere Reserve.' However, Futehally and his team were apparently under the impression that the Silent Valley multi-purpose project, then expected to cost Rupees twenty-five crores, was practically a *fait accompli* (though not as much as the Kudremukh iron-mines in Karnataka, which it also studied). This is why it laid down several safeguards 'if the government feels the project cannot be abandoned for any reason'.

This triggered off an enormous row, the echoes of which have by no means died down, even five long years later. The two main opponents of the scheme in Kerala itself were the Kerala Sastra Sahitya Parishad (KSSP), a science-for-the-people organization which is to date the most effective grassroots environmental body in the country; and the Friends of the Trees, or more specifically, its indefatigable guiding spirit, Joseph John. They were given moral and material support from a 'Save Silent Valley' committee in Bombay, backed by individuals from the World Wildlife Fund, Bombay Natural History Society, and the Save Bombay Committee.

Pitted against these environmentalists were the Kerala government—irrespective of the particular party or the front in power at the time, the Kerala State Electricity Board (KSEB), which was to implement the project, and a group of scientists who banded together under the title, Parisara Asoothrana Samrakshana Samithy (PASS) which in Malayalam means Environmental Planning and Conservation Society.

Various international bodies jumped into the fray. Most were contacted to lend their considerable weight by environmentalists here. The most prominent of them was the International Union for Conservation of Nature and Natural Resources in Switzerland, which at its conference in Ashkabad in the USSR in September 1978, called upon the Kerala government to abandon the project. A few other foreign scientists also provided data in support of conservation; these were either experts in tropical rain forests, or zoologists who had studied the lion-tailed macaque. The IUCN, in fact, made its intentions quite clear from the very outset by offering the Futehally task force ten thousand dollars to help in its work, as part of its international campaign to save rain forests.

Before the NCEPC could even pronounce judgment on the task force recommendations, the Kerala government rushed to Delhi and convinced the Prime Minister, then Morarji Desai, that the scheme should be given the go-ahead. It did this armed with a unanimous resolution passed in the Kerala Assembly—in itself no mean feat, given the plethora of parties in that highly politicized state—accepting the task force report, together with all the safeguards. In fact, the only previous occasion when such unanimity was displayed was a resolution sanctioning pay rises for MLAs!

Belatedly, environmentalists realized that the seventeen safeguards listed by the task force wouldn't stop the forests from irretrievable damage. Futehally and the other members disowned their recommendations regarding safeguards and refused to serve on the Kerala government's Silent Valley Monitoring Committee. The debate grew really hot—on public platforms, where both KSSP and KSEB members spoke, and in the press. The furore at home, and its unexpected echoes at international forums, was sufficient to persuade the next Prime Minister, Charan Singh, to tell the Kerala government to stop further work on the project in late 1979.

In October that year, Central government, as much confused as anyone else by the charges and counter charges being traded in the dispute, decided to send the country's most reputed agricultural scientist to look at it. Dr M S Swaminathan, who was then Secretary to the Union Agricultural Ministry, also endorsed the task force's opinion, recommending that the project be scrapped and that the entire area of Silent Valley and its environs—a total of

30,000 hectares—be converted into a rain forest Biosphere Reserve. The NCEPC was able to endorse these findings wholeheartedly on this occasion.

The Kerala authorities held a controversial seminar in April 1980 in Trivandrum, ostensibly with a view to clearing the air by allowing scientists and experts from either side to voice their opinion....

While genuflecting to the need for preserving the environment, the state sponsored seminar concluded that 'a small disturbance in nature must be taken as a part of the game, when it comes to the question of prosperity of a region. Industries, projects and other developmental activities should not be stopped because of the fear of impending pollution'. It was believed that any threat to the environment could be contained, because of the great leaps made in pollution control technology.

Since the seminar in no way resolved the controversy, Mrs. Gandhi called a meeting in August 1980 with Chief Minister Nayanar. There it was decided to conclusively come to a decision on the fate of Silent Valley, by appointing yet another committee, this time headed by Prof M G K Menon, then Secretary of the Department of Science and Technology in Delhi. It was to consist of four members ... nominated by the Kerala government, and an equal number by the Centre.

The Menon Committee Report, originally due in three months, was finally submitted in the summer of 1983. Although the report's conclusions were ambiguous, a personal note appended by Menon made it clear that as chairperson he was in favour of preserving the Valley. Ultimately, in November 1983, Kerala's Electricity Minister announced that his government had scrapped the Silent Valley project in deference to the wishes of Prime Minister Indira Gandhi.

In his book, *Temples or Tombs?*, Darryl D'Monte offers a retrospective analysis of the decisive factors in the struggle to save Silent Valley. We carry a brief excerpt.

D'MONTE; TEMPLES OR TOMBS? INDUSTRY VERSUS ENVIRONMENT: THREE CONTROVERSIES 57 (1985)

It was a fascinating *pot pourri* of factors that went into the halting of the Silent Valley project, of which attitudes of the Prime Ministers concerned were perhaps the most important. At each stage, different scientific arguments were advanced: first, the loss of one of the last remaining tropical rain forests, then the lion-tailed macaque, then the question of it being a 'gene pool'. Correspondingly, the protagonists of the project tried to adduce their own facts to disprove each of these arguments. The weight of the national institutions which voted against the project was plainly far more impressive than that of local scientists whose command performance was orchestrated by the KSEB. When I asked Prof M G K Menon how the public was to choose between the two apparently contradictory sets of scientific data, he answered with a twinkle in his eye: 'Look at the credentials of the scientists.' Undeniably, the rallying force of the KSSP made Silent Valley a unique environmental campaign in the entire Third World because it took the issue out of lecture rooms and the columns of the press to the people. If many people in Kerala today are aware of the meaning of 'ecology', it is solely due to Silent Valley. This interplay of international pressure, lobbying in Delhi and counter-lobbying in the state, local agitation for the project, press campaigns and scientific deliberation, is witnessed, in varying proportions, in each of the three cases in this book. It bears testimony to the genuinely democratic process at work in this country, which will be hard to find anywhere else, in the Third World. In general, it can be concluded that the access of environmentalists to the highest echelons of power in Delhi turned the tables decisively in Silent Valley ... while scientific opinion took a back seat.

NOTES

1. Dilnavaz Variava, coordinator of the Save Silent Valley Committee at Mumbai, describes her learning from the campaign:

> A major requirement of such a campaign is a constant sensitivity to what is the most appropriate message, to whom it should be addressed, and by whom. Lion-tailed macaques were useful in obtaining support from international and national conservation bodies, but counterproductive at the local level. The 'genetic treasure house' concept was effective both for decision-makers and the general public. The Silent Valley name was deeply evocative, and if such an advantage does not exist in other cases, it would be useful to search for some element that could create it. Above all, however, the environmental education effort must start with an effort to understand the needs of the local people and project how the proposed conservation movement is directly beneficial to them.[17]

2. Sanjeev Khagram argues that the Silent Valley victory inspired big dam opponents across India.[18] In his view, the deceleration in the rate of completing big dam projects in India may be attributed in part to emerging environmental consciousness and the development of institutional mechanisms that respond to environmental and human rights concerns.[19]

3. Silent Valley was declared a National Park in 1980. It is a part of the Western Ghats World Heritage Site, recognized by UNESCO in 2007.

M K PRASAD; SILENT VALLEY CASE: AN ECOLOGICAL ASSESSMENT,
8 Cochin University Law Review 128 (1984)

Lack of proper appreciation of environmental information may often lead to decisions going against the interest of the general public. Consequently, priority is given to developmental activities aimed at short term benefits over conservation oriented actions with a long term perspective of sustainable benefits. It is this unfortunate position that prompted the author to evaluate the judgment pronounced by the Kerala High Court on 2 January 1980 in *Society for Protection of Silent Valley v Union of India and others*.[20] The judgment was not reported. Hence I have given an extract in the appendix. Petitions were filed seeking a writ forbidding the state of Kerala from proceeding to construct a hydroelectric project at Silent Valley.[21] This venture was represented as fraught with adverse consequences deleterious to the environment. Experts including scientists attached to the Department of Science and Technology, Government of India had warned against the proposed construction. Environmentalists, scientists and conservation societies in India and abroad expressed great concern and joined the chorus of denunciation of the Silent Valley Hydro-Electric Project called SVHEP.

---

[17] Dilnavaz S Variava, *The Saving of the Silent Valley: A Case Study of Environmental Education in Action* in THE ENVIRONMENT AND SCIENCE AND TECHNOLOGY EDUCATION (Ed. A V Baez, *et al*, 1987).

[18] Sanjeev Khagram, *Dams and Development: Transnational Struggles for Water and Power* 49 (2004).

[19] *Id.* at 41.

[20] OP Nos. 2949 and 3025 of 1979.

[21] The petition pointed out that Silent Valley in the district of Palghat contained one of India's largest tropical evergreen forests and is the only vestige of virgin forest of the Western Ghats. It is estimated to have a continuous record of not less than 50 million years of evolutionary history, with diverse and complex flora and fauna. It is a unique vegetable food resource which contains mammals and birds in the Valley. A number of endangered plants and animals live there. The forests perform very many important functions. They regulate water supply to the plains by retaining rain water in the soil and releasing it slowly down, maintaining the hydrological balance, averting floods and droughts in the plains. Soil erosion is prevented and the climatic condition of the whole area is regulated by the forests.

APPENDIX

EXTRACT FROM THE JUDGEMENT BY HON'BLE MR JUSTICE V P GOPALAN NAMBIAR IN THE SILENT VALLEY CASE

There is, in the Palghat District of this state, 45 kilometres to the north of Mannarghadu, a stretch of forest, nearly 8952 hectares in extent, known as the 'Silent Valley'. The name is apparently derived from the peace, quiet and serenity of the place. But, paradoxically enough, as was once remarked in the far past in the Madras Legislature, the valley has been creaking and squeaking loudly on many occasions. The present noise and bustle are over the hydroelectric project sought to be built in this valley. These writ petitions, broadly stated, seek to forbid the state from proceeding with the project. As representatives of the arguments advanced, we may refer to O P No. 2949 of 1979. The government of Kerala is proposing to deforest the Silent Valley and to construct a dam for … a hydroelectric project for power generation and supply of electricity. It is said that the dam is to generate 120 M Watts of power by 1985. (The learned Advocate General rated the power generation much higher, viz., at 240 M Watts). This venture has been represented as fraught with adverse consequences deleterious to the public. Experts have warned against the proposed construction of the dam and processing of the project. Scientists and technologists have joined the chorus of denunciation of the project.

The adverse effects from the conversion of the Silent Valley into a hydroelectric project were listed thus: first, the deforestation was bound to affect the climatic conditions in the state and even outside, by depriving the state of its legitimate share of rain during the Monsoon; second, that the preservation of the forests was needed for conducting research in medicine, pest control, breeding of economic plants and a variety of purposes, and third that deforestation was bound to interfere with the balance of nature, as between the forest land on the one side and arable and other types of lands on the other.

The argument stressed that a project like the hydroelectric project, if sanctioned and set up would have its impact on environment, and this has to be carefully considered. Copious citations were made from various treatises, reports, and publications, to show the importance of the environmental factor in industrial planning. [The court referred to some of these treatises and reports]. It is pointed out that the Legislature of Kerala was of the unanimous view that the project was of crucial importance to the state. A resolution was unanimously adopted on 22-8-1978 expressing anxiety on the continuing delay. An all-party delegation from Kerala visited the Prime Minister on 7-4-1978. The various steps and developments of a similar nature are detailed in paragraph 20. They show clearly that the Government's mind was addressed to the question of the ecological aspects involved in the execution of the project and its impact upon the same. We were taken through copious extracts from various works, reports and other materials regarding the technical feasibility of the project and the importance of ecological considerations in assessing the worth and utility of a proposed project. But in this region we cannot substitute our judgment for that of the Government, on the question as to whether a national asset is to be more conveniently utilized as a hydroelectric project with prospects of greater power generation, or retained in its pristine glory for preservation of forests and wildlife, prevention of soil erosion, and avoidance of other deleterious effects on the community. The scope for interference with such policy decision of the Government, should, in the nature of things be limited. A wealth of material was cited and placed before us on the technical feasibility of the project and the impolitic decision to destroy the forest....

Counsel for the petitioner stressed the national importance of forests as having been responsible for certain amendments in the Constitution. Reference was made to Article 48A of the Constitution where by the preservation of forests and wildlife is one of the directive principles of state policy. Article 49 was also stressed giving obligation to protect every monument or place or object of artistic or historic interest, declared by Parliament to be of national importance from destruction, removal etc.

Rich and worthy material of a variegated nature was placed before us in regard to the national policy and environmental considerations. We are by no means satisfied that these aspects have not been borne in mind by the Government in planning and processing the project. We are also not satisfied that the assessment of these considerations made by the Government and the policy decisions taken thereafter are liable to be reviewed by this Court in these proceedings. Even if they be open to review no grounds for such review have been disclosed....

As for the danger of extinction of the lion-tailed monkey, the matter is dealt with in paragraph 8 of the counter-affidavit. We do not think it necessary to cover the entire gamut of the material—whether scientific, technical, technological or ecological placed before us in great detail. It is not for us to evaluate these considerations again as against the evaluation already done by the Government. It is enough to state that we are satisfied that the relevant matters have received attention before the Government decided to launch the project. There has been no non-advertence of the mind to the salient aspects of the project. We are not to substitute our opinion and notions on these matters for those of the Government.

We find no reason to interfere. We dismiss these applications with no order as to costs.

NOTES AND QUESTIONS

1. Although the High Court eventually rejected the petitions, the legal action may have had a beneficial effect: a two-week interim stay on the construction of the dam in August 1979 boosted the environmentalists' morale. The interim order might also have emboldened the NCEPC to record, at its meeting in September 1979, that it did not favour the hydel project and that the Valley should be preserved in its natural state.

2. Shouldn't the clear directive in Article 48A of the Constitution that 'the State shall endeavour to protect and improve the environment and to safeguard the forests and wild life of the country' have persuaded the Kerala High Court to subject the state government's decision to a more searching scrutiny?

3. In its 1987 judgment in the *Calcutta Taj Hotel* case,[22] the Supreme Court inquired extensively into the government permission for the construction of a medium rise hotel on the allegation that the building would interfere with the flight path of migratory birds. The Kerala High Court's deferential approach to the government in the *Silent Valley* case—involving, as it did, the submergence of a pristine valley with its extraordinary wealth of flora and fauna—seems hard to reconcile with the Supreme Court's searching inquiry for what appears to have been a less momentous issue. What factors may account for this discrepancy?

4. Has any government the authority to order the extinction of an endangered species in this case the rare lion-tailed macaque? How could this issue be raised in a legal action? What constitutional provisions could be cited?

5. In 1979–80, when the case was argued and decided, there was no statutory EIA in India. Since 1994 we have had a statutory regime. Has this helped preserve the environment? Or does the statutory mantle simply shield weak scientific and technical opinions, like the ones used to advocate the Silent Valley project?

[22] AIR 1987 SC 1109.

D. THE TEHRI DAM PROJECT

The rivers Bhagirathi and Bhilangana rise in the Garhwal Himalayas in northwestern Uttar Pradesh and flow south to the plains as the Ganga. As part of a larger plan to trap the waters of the Upper Ganga Basin, a clay core, rock fill dam was constructed at the confluence of the Bhagirathi and Bhilangana, close to the Garhwal town of Tehri. The 260.5 m high dam was commissioned in 2006. The lake created by the dam extends up to 45 kms in the Bhagirathi Valley and 25 kms in the Bhilangana Valley with a water spread area of 42 sq kms. It submerged nearly 100 villages, including Tehri, a historical capital. Over 10,000 families were relocated as a result. On the benefits side of the equation, the project generates 1,000 MW of electricity (eventually, 2,400 MW), creates and supplies irrigation facilities for 270,000 hectares of land, and supplies 500 cusecs of water to New Delhi and villages and towns along the way.

The Tehri Dam Project provoked controversy focused on three issues. The completed project will displace many people and submerge several towns, among them the town of Tehri; the region is vulnerable to earthquakes and the dam may be structurally incapable of withstanding them or may perhaps even cause them;[23] and the possible failure of the dam could kill hundreds of thousands of people and destroy downstream towns of immense religious significance. Of particular concern are the inhabitants of the downstream Hindu holy towns of Hardwar and Rishikesh. Both the resettlement policies and the structural flaws of the dam provoked civil protests, lawsuits and international attention.

The Tehri project was unsuccessfully challenged in the Supreme Court in a writ petition filed by the Tehri Bandh Virodhi Sangharsh Samiti (TBVSS) in 1985. In April 1987, the Indian National Trust for Art and Cultural Heritage (INTACH), an 'intervenor' in this petition and a leading non-governmental organization in the field of conservation, sponsored an independent assessment of the economic feasibility of the dam. The principal finding of the multi-disciplinary team that conducted the appraisal was that the benefit to cost ratio of the Tehri Dam, after calculating social and environmental costs and benefits, works out to 0.56:1, well short of the 1.5:1 ratio adopted by the Planning Commission to sanction such projects.

In addition, in 1986, the Soviet Union agreed to help fund the project with loans at extremely concessional terms. As a part of the agreement with the Indian Government, Soviet experts conducted a review of the proposed project and made several ominous findings, the most frightening of which was that the high seismicity of the Tehri area had not been adequately taken into consideration by Indian planners. The INTACH team, under the leadership of Vijay Paranjpye, also found that while the Indian Government projected a useful life of 100 years, the actual siltation rate would render the dam useless in 62 years or less. Finally, while the authorities put the number of displaced people, or oustees, at 46,000, the INTACH team found that 85,600 people would be displaced by the project.[24]

The Supreme Court dismissed the petition in 1990 after a very limited enquiry. Although the Environmental Appraisal Committee had unanimously concluded that the Tehri project should not be approved, the Central Government relied instead on an opinion of the Department of Mines to convince itself and the court that the project was sound.

---

[23] Dams cause earthquakes if the weight of the water activates unnoticed faults in the earth, as was the case in Koyna, Maharashtra in 1967 when 200 people were killed and 1,500 were injured.

[24] Vijay Paranjpye, *Evaluating the Tehri Dam: An Extended Cost Benefit Appraisal* 31 (1988).

TEHRI BANDH VIRODHI SANGHARSH SAMITI v STATE OF UTTAR PRADESH 1992 SUPP (1) SCC 44

Order: This petition under Article 32 of the Constitution of India has been filed in public interest by Tehri Bandh Virodhi Sangarsh Samiti and others. The petitioners have prayed that the Union of India, State of Uttar Pradesh and the Tehri Hydro Development Corporation be restrained from constructing and implementing the Tehri Hydro Power Project and the Tehri Dam.

The main grievance of the petitioners is that in preparing the plan for the Tehri Dam project the safety aspect has not been taken into consideration. It is asserted that the dam if allowed to be constructed poses a serious threat to the life, ecology and the environment of the entire northern India as the site of the dam is prone to earthquake. After this petition was filed a number of persons have intervened and the parties have filed affidavits and counter affidavits. The matter was heard by this Court at various stages. The controversy relating to the project has not only been debated in this Court but has also taken a good deal of Parliament's time.

[Counsel] appearing for the petitioners has argued that the seismic experts in India and abroad are of the view that past records of earthquake show that the likely length of fracture along the convergence boundary is of the order of 200–300 kilometers. According to him, it is thus possible that segment of such a length along the Himalayan belt covering the region from approximately Dehradun on the west and India-Nepal border in the east, could be the fracture area of a future large earthquake of magnitude 8 or so. According to him, the Government of India has not applied its mind to this very important aspect in preparing the project.

Shri V K Khanna, Joint Secretary, Ministry of Energy, Department of Power, New Delhi has filed an affidavit dated 5 November 1990 wherein relevant material has been placed before this Court showing that the Government of India, through its various departments and ministries has at every stage considered all relevant data and fully applied its mind to the safety and various other aspects of the project.

The project was initially considered by the Environmental Appraisal Committee of the Ministry of Environment and Forests and the said Committee, taking into consideration the geological and seismic setting, the consequent risks, and hazards, ecological and social impacts accompanying the project and the costs and benefits expected, came to the unanimous conclusion that the Tehri Dam Project did not merit environmental clearance and should be dropped.

The report submitted by the Environmental Appraisal Committee was considered and discussed in the meeting of the Committee of Secretaries held on 20 March 1990. The Committee of Secretaries came to the conclusion that the Environmental Appraisal Committee ought to have concerned itself with the environmental parameters within which the opinion of the said Committee was relevant. It was also opined by the Committee of Secretaries that the safety aspect of the design and earthquake engineering could be best looked into by the scientific and specialized organizations such as Geological Survey of India, National Geological Research Institute, Central Water Commission and Earthquake Engineering Department of the Roorkee University. In this context the Committee of Secretaries further observed that the safety aspect relating to the project ought to be resolved and in this regard directed the constitution of a High Level Committee of Experts to examine the issues relating to the safety aspects of Tehri Dam Project....

The High Level Committee of Experts under the Chairmanship of Shri D P Dhoundial, Director General, Geological Survey of India rendered its report on 6 April 1990. The affidavit filed by the Government of India stated as under regarding the said report:

The said Committee considered all safety aspects of the Tehri Dam and opined with reference to all the issues that were to be decided upon. The said Committee assumed the worst scenario of the possible occurrence of a large magnitude earthquake in the area and rendered an opinion to the effect that the design of the Tehri Dam incorporated adequate defensive measures in accordance with the recommendations of the International Congress of Large Dams on seismic design of dams made from time to time and that additional safety measures had been inbuilt to ensure an adequate and well evolved seismic design for this high dam.

The affidavit further gave details of the report of the High Level Committee in the following words:

> The conclusions culled out from the said report of the High Level Committee are set out hereunder for the purpose of convenience:
>
> 'CONCLUSIONS OF HIGH LEVEL COMMITTEE
>
> I. Whether the earthquake potential of the zone in which the dam is being located has been fully taken into account in designing the dam:
>   a. Modern researches are being directed towards refining models of seismic potential in seismically active belts of the world. Different models suggesting probable source potentials in the Himalayan geotectonic setting around Tehri have been examined. In the absence of any definitive model the worst scenario of a Mag 8+ earthquake has been considered. The probable locale of such earthquake has been considered to be at a depth of 15 km below the dam site;
>   b. The seismic potential at a project site is characterized by the maximum intensity of ground motion due to earthquake occurrence on the likely seismic sources surrounding the site. The effective peak ground acceleration, considering earthquake events up to Mag 8+ has been evaluated at the dam site to be 0.22g.
>   c. The effective peak ground acceleration for which the design of the dam has been checked for stability is 0.25g. Thus, the seismic potential of the dam site has been fully taken into account in the design.
>
> II. Whether the proposed dam would be safe as designed *vis-à-vis* earthquake potential of the area:
>   a. Cross section of the proposed dam would be safe *vis-à-vis* the maximum earthquake potential as indicated by the estimated effective peak ground acceleration (EPA) of 0.22g. on the following counts:
>   b. The design side slopes are stable with adequate factor of safety.
>   c. Settlement likely to occur in the height of dam, when subjected to an EPA of 0.25g will be within permissible limits and is taken care of by way of liberal free board provided in the design.
>   d. The shell material proposed to be used in the construction of the dam when subjected to an EPA of 0.25g does not show potential for liquefaction.
>
> III. Whether there would be any threat posed by Reservoir Induced Seismicity (RIS) to the dam or civilian structures in the vicinity:
>   a. Seismicity induced by a large artificial reservoir can only act as a trigger to initiate a natural earthquake that would have occurred otherwise. Therefore, the presence of a reservoir does not increase the size of an earthquake event.
>   b. Since the design is considered safe for the worst case earthquake no additional consideration for RIS is necessary.
>   c. Earthquake vulnerability of the existing civil structures would depend upon the earthquake resistance built in the same. The construction of the dam would not in any way add to the vulnerability of the existing structures or affect the design requirements for the future constructions.
>
> IV. Have all potential dangers arising out of seismicity been taken note of and adequate precautions taken in planning all aspects of the Project? If there are any lacunae in these respects, the same may be elaborated upon and action required in this regard spelt out.
>
> All dangers arising out of seismicity have been taken note of and taken care of in the planning of the Tehri Dam Project.'

* * *

The report of the High Level Committee was again considered by the Committee of Secretaries in its meeting dated 23 April 1990. The Committee of Secretaries found on a consideration of the report of the High Level Committee that the Tehri Dam as designed was safe and seismic potential of the site was taken into consideration by the experts. Meanwhile Dr V K Gaur, a member of the High Level Committee of Experts, who had earlier agreed with the unanimous report, later on sent a note of dissent of 12 May 1990 wherein he questioned the conclusion of the High Level Committee of Experts in respect of the safety aspects of the project.

In the light of the letter of dissent sent by Dr Gaur the Government of India decided to revive the High Level Committee of experts and referred the points raised by Dr Gaur for further consideration of the Committee. The High Level Committee thereafter on 20 July 1990 rendered a supplementary report endorsing its earlier views rendered unanimously on 6 April 1990. This endorsement, however, was a majority view since Dr V K Gaur this time issued a note of dissent stating that the opinion of the High Level Expert Committee was based on questionable grounds and formulations and that because of his dissent the entire matter ought to be referred to an independent seismological expert of international repute.

The Committee of Secretaries met again on 10 August 1990 and considered the recommendations of the High Level Committee along with the dissent of Dr V K Gaur and in the circumstances requested the Department of Mines to refer the matter to an independent expert seismologist whose opinion should be taken as final. Pursuant to the said decision Prof Jai Krishna a renowned expert of international repute examined the reports of the High Level Committee dated 6 April 1990, 20 July 1990 and also the dissenting note of Dr V K Gaur. Prof Jai Krishna submitted his report to the Department of Mines, Government of India on 8 September 1990 wherein he concurred with the conclusions arrived at by the High Level Committee of Experts. He did not agree with the view expressed by Dr V K Gaur in his dissenting note. Prof Jai Krishna confirmed that the recommendations of the High Level Committee of Experts were in accord with international experience and practice. He also opined that the design of the Tehri Dam as suggested by Indian and Russian experts was quite safe against the strongest expected earthquake in the region.

The aforesaid facts clearly show that the Union of India considered the question of safety of the project in various details more than once. It satisfied itself by obtaining the reports of experts and also took into consideration the dissenting view of Dr V K Gaur. The project has been finalized after obtaining the expert report of Prof Jai Krishna. In the circumstances, it is not possible to hold that the Union of India has not applied its mind or has not considered the relevant aspects of safety of the dam.

Learned counsel for the petitioners [has] urged that the report submitted by Prof Jai Krishna should not have been relied upon, instead the matter should have been referred to a seismologist and that the safety of the dam is still in danger. In this connection he referred to the opinion given by Prof James N Brune to Dr V K Gaur as well as to his dissenting opinion. The questions relating to the design of the dam, the seismic potential of the site where the dam is proposed to be constructed and the various steps which have been taken for ensuring the safety of the dam are a highly intricate question relating to science and engineering. This Court does not possess the requisite expertise to render any final opinion on the rival contentions of the experts. In our opinion the Court can only investigate and adjudicate the question as to whether the Government was conscious to the inherent danger as pointed out by the petitioners and applied its mind to the safety of the dam. We have already given facts in detail which show that the Government has considered the question on several occasions in the light of the opinions expressed by the experts. The Government was satisfied with the report of the experts and only thereafter clearance has been given to the project. The petitioners contend that the project has not as yet been cleared.

Mr N D Jayal appearing for the intervenor—INTACH also referred to the various technical aspects of the matter and urged that the safety of the dam is still in danger having regard to the seismological aspects of the area where the dam is to be constructed. We need not discuss this matter any further, as in our opinion, the Government has already fully considered every aspect of the project including its safety.

We appreciate the petitioners' concern for the safety of the project which is of prime importance to the general public, however, in view of the material on the record we do not find any good reason to issue a direction restraining the respondents from proceeding ahead with the implementation of the project. The petition, therefore, fails and is accordingly dismissed with no order as to costs.

NOTES AND QUESTIONS

1. The campaign against the Tehri Dam began in the mid-1970s. The TBVSS initially enjoyed the support of all political parties. As the construction progressed the opposition weakened. With the freeze on government spending in old Tehri town due to its impending submergence, many local residents gave up active opposition. The struggle continued, inspired by Sunderlal Bahuguna, whose non-violent protests to save the Garhwal from environmental degradation have earned him recognition the world over.

2. The Tehri Dam Project was a hot potato for the Supreme Court. Expert opinion on the safety of the project was divided, more than 70,000 persons were going to be uprooted and the local people were opposed to the dam. At the same time, over Rs. 3 billion had already been spent on the project and powerful interests in the state and Centre were intent on seeing it through.

The court took an easy way out. It quite rightly disclaimed expertise to render any final opinion on the rival contentions of the experts, defining its narrow role thus: 'In our opinion the court can only investigate and adjudicate the question as to whether the government was conscious to the inherent danger as pointed out by the petitioners and applied its mind to the safety of the dam.' The court found that the government had indeed considered the question of safety, and hence rejected the petitioners' challenge.

3. While it is difficult to fault this broad approach, vigorous application by the court of its own standard would have made for more meaningful judicial review. For example, the court might have insisted on an affidavit by the Secretary, Ministry of Environment and Forests on the environmental aspects of the project. Under the present administrative framework, it is the MoEF that is charged with environmental impact appraisal. In particular, it is this ministry's job to assess and advise on environmental risks of the type created by the Tehri Dam Project. Nevertheless, the court did not seek the Environment Ministry's opinion, and instead relied on an affidavit filed by the Joint Secretary, Ministry of Energy, Department of Power. Considering that the Department of Power's primary task is to boost power generation (and the Tehri project would supply power to the Uttar Pradesh grid), was it not more than likely that the department would play down the risks involved? In this situation, was it wise for the court to rely exclusively on an affidavit from the Ministry of Energy?

4. The members of the Environmental Appraisal Committee (EAC)—an expert body within the Ministry of Environment and Forests—unanimously concluded that the Tehri project did not merit environmental clearance and should be dropped. Ordinarily, the government should adhere to the recommendations of its own expert agency or cogently explain any departure from the course of action suggested by its experts. Here, the committee of secretaries brushed aside the EAC's recommendations and the court did not seek a detailed explanation from the government for departing from the EAC's report.

5. It appears that the Central Government took a political decision to proceed with the Tehri project and then structured an *ad hoc* administrative framework that would secure expert opinion to support that decision. Review of the safety aspect of the project was abruptly removed from the province of the MoEF and entrusted to the committee of secretaries, even though this committee had no expertise in environmental matters. Besides, by the nature of its composition, that is, secretaries representing ministries that were committed to achieve developmental targets, not protect the environment—the committee was apt to discount environmental and safety factors. Note well that when it came to obtaining an additional opinion, in view of the note of dissent submitted by Dr V K Gaur, the committee of secretaries assigned this task to the Department of Mines. The Department of Mines is an aggressive, 'pro-development' agency with a none-too-happy environmental record.

6. The Department of Mines' 'independent expert seismologist' Prof Jai Krishna, was neither independent nor a seismologist. Professor Jai Krishna was an earthquake engineer who had previously filed an affidavit in this case supporting the project.[25]

7. The only seismologist who gave an opinion on the project was Prof James N Brune. Based on the Brune opinion, Dr V K Gaur's dissenting report disputed the High Level Committee's conclusions. Ordinary good judgment suggests that a seismologist's opinion ought to be verified or disputed by another seismologist not an engineer. For reasons best known to it, however, the Supreme Court considered the opinion of an earthquake engineer, Prof Jai Krishna, to be an adequate affirmation of the High Level Committee report.

8. In the language of the judgment, Prof Jai Krishna 'opined that the design of the Tehri Dam as suggested by Indian and [Soviet] experts was quite safe against the strongest expected earthquake in the region'. The project being 'quite safe', the court declined to intervene.

Given the potentially catastrophic effect of a dam burst at Tehri, was it reasonable to accord approval on a 'quite safe' opinion? Should the standard for such project approvals not be far more stringent? Would not an 'insignificant risk' standard be more appropriate? Is the project consistent with the precautionary principle?

9. Keeping in view that the expenditure incurred on the project exceeded Rs. 3 billion when the case was heard by the court, was the court ever likely to stop the project?

10. The fundamental right to freedom of religion is guaranteed under Articles 25 to 28 of the Constitution. Located downstream from the proposed Tehri reservoir are the towns of Rishikesh and Hardwar—considered by Hindus to be among the holiest of pilgrim centres. Both towns would probably be devastated in the event of a dam burst at Tehri. Is the project a threat to the right of Hindus to 'profess, practice and propagate religion'? Would the siting of a nuclear power project near Rishikesh and Hardwar threaten the community's fundamental right to freedom of religion?

11. There is a temporal dimension to Article 21 and the right to equality guaranteed in Article 14, which recognize 'intergenerational equity'. Consider this argument: all members of each generation of human beings, as a species, inherit a natural and cultural patrimony from past generations, both as beneficiaries and as custodians who are under a duty to pass on this heritage to future generations. Therefore, the right of each generation to benefit from and develop this natural and cultural heritage is inseparably coupled with the obligation to use this heritage in such a manner that it can be transmitted to future generations in no worse

[25] Interview with N D Dayal, Director (Natural Heritage), INTACH, 10 December 1990. Conducted by S Divan.

condition than it was received from past generations. Do you agree with this argument? Is the Tehri Dam Project consistent with this argument?

In October 1991, about a year after the Supreme Court judgment, an earthquake measuring 6.1 on the Richter scale hit the Garhwal region, flattening villages in Uttarkashi and Chamoli, killing 2,000 people and causing some damage in the town of Tehri itself. Although the Power Ministry maintained that the dam works were not damaged in any way by the quake, its occurrence reignited the debate over the safety of the plans for a dam in such an earthquake-prone region, as well as the more specific controversy over exactly how great a quake the completed dam is designed to withstand.[26]

While project authorities have consistently maintained that the dam is designed to withstand quakes of up to 8 on the Richter scale, other experts disagree. In 1993, INTACH organized a workshop concerning the dam, which was attended by James Brune of the seismological laboratory at the University of Nevada, whose formula to determine quake resistance was relied upon by the Indian Government. Brune contended that the Indian Government misapplied his formula and consequently exaggerated the quake resistance potential of the dam and overestimated the dam's life. Moreover, he charged that the data concerning geological studies, silt load in the river and earthquake measurements were all incomplete.

In protest, on 14 December 1991, 5,000 people led by environmental activist Sunderlal Bahuguna brought work on the project to a complete halt through 'direct action' protests. They, in fact, placed their bodies on and around the site and the machinery, making any further work impossible. They maintained their 'sit in' for a full two months until finally Bahuguna and 14 others were arrested on 29 February 1992. Following the arrests, Bahuguna went on a hunger strike that lasted for 45 days. Fearing more unrest in the event of the death of the popular activist, Prime Minister P V Narasimha Rao called a halt to all blasting and construction at the Tehri site, pending yet another review of the project. Despite these promises, dam construction work continued.

In April 1995, Bahuguna went on another hunger strike. He was arrested and forcibly hospitalized, only to be released following a court order. Two thousand protesters then marched on the dam site, only to be beaten back by police, who reportedly injured at least 150 of the protesters. After 49 days of fasting, the government again capitulated to Bahuguna's demands for review.

The government promised that this time, as opposed to the 1992 review, a panel of independent experts would be convened to consider the project. The government invited activists to select their own representative to work with officials on the review panel. In addition, the government promised that the panel would consider the ecological, economic, social and cultural impacts of the Tehri project, all of which the 1992 panel had ignored. However, as the 1992 panel and the two prior reviews had considered the seismic safety of the project, that subject was, according to the Prime Minister, a dead issue.

In August, 1995 the government again broke its word. The Minister of State for Water Resources told the Rajya Sabha that there was no going back on the Tehri Dam, on which

---

[26] The material in this part of the Tehri Dam section is drawn from wire service reports; M Kishwar, *A Himalayan Catastrophe: The Controversial Tehri Dam in the Himalayas*, 91 Manushi 5 (1995), http://manushi-india.org/test/pdfs_issues/PDF%20files%2091/a_himalayan_catastrophe.pdf, accessed 19 June 2021; and P McCully, *Silenced Rivers: The Ecology and Politics of Large Dams* 336 (1996).

huge amounts had already been spent. He claimed that the government was willing to look into new and substantial issues.

NOTES AND QUESTIONS

1. Who pays for the Tehri Dam and who benefits?

2. One of the driving forces behind the continuation of the Tehri project was the vast amounts of money that had already been spent. The Indian Government's intractable stand based on money already spent raises economic questions. When, for example, is the cost of stopping construction greater than the cost of reassessing or abandoning the project? Does this take into account the cost of disaster relief if the dam does fail, as many predict that it will?

3. Another issue raised in any EIA cost-benefit analysis is the cost assigned to human life, both in terms of resettlement and rehabilitation (R&R) and lives lost in the event of dam failure. Is it possible, as it appears from the disjointed nature of reviews of the Tehri project, that these costs have simply been ignored? If not, who assigns value to them? Should anyone?

4. Why, in a region as prone to earthquakes as the Tehri site, would the government reject the idea of several smaller hydroelectric projects, as opposed to the one gargantuan dam? Are lots of little projects perhaps not as conspicuous and therefore politically less appealing?

5. In the context of the Tehri project, how complete does an EIA or review need to be? How many things must the project planners take into account? The Supreme Court relied on a review from the Department of Mines, that the government submitted in lieu of the review by the EAC. Who decides which report is the most accurate? And should accuracy be measured in terms of irrigation and energy benefits or in terms of R&R and potential disaster? Where do environmental effects figure in the equation? Is it more important to preserve the environment or provide drinking water? How many 'experts' are needed and what if their opinions differ?

6. Finally, what is the role of popular protest in development and planning? While protestors did successfully catalyse further reviews, and probably delayed construction, they were unable to halt the project. Does this imply that their efforts have been futile? Has there been any sort of beneficial community empowerment as a result? If so, is that valuable in and of itself, despite the failure to halt the project?

The first *Tehri* case[27] arose from a writ petition filed before the Supreme Court under Article 32 of the Constitution and the final judgment was rendered on 7 November 1990. In 1992, a second petition was filed before the Supreme Court by N D Jayal, who had intervened in the first case on behalf of INTACH. In addition to safety concerns, Jayal claimed that the authorities had failed to comply with the conditions attached to the environmental clearance of 19 July 1990 and also that rehabilitation was unsatisfactory.

By the time the Supreme Court decided *N D Jayal v Union of India (Tehri-II)*,[28] the Supreme Court judgment in the *Narmada* case[29] was available. Like *Narmada*, the verdict in *Tehri-II* was split 2:1 with the majority declining judicial review since the decision to construct a large

---

[27] *Tehri Bandh Virodhi Sangharsh Samiti v State of U P* (1992) Supp 1 SCC 44.
[28] (2004) 9 SCC 362.
[29] *Narmada Bachao Andolan v Union of India* (2000) 10 SCC 664.

dam was a policy decision. The *Tehri-II* court re-examined safety aspects and held that the court cannot sit in judgment over cutting edge scientific analysis—'such matters must be left to the mature wisdom of government or the implementing agency. It is their forte.'[30]

With respect to the environmental clearance, the court found that the conditions attached pertained to (1) catchment area treatment; (2) command area development; (3) flora and fauna; (4) establishment of the Bhagirathi Basin Management Authority; (5) disaster management; and (6) rehabilitation. Reiterating the principles of sustainable development, the fundamental right to a clean environment and the principles for rehabilitation of the oustees, the Supreme Court concluded:

> In this background, we find that the petitioners have not established nor is there any material to conclude that the project work is being carried on without complying with the conditions of clearance. Though there were certain lapses at certain stages, they were taken care of by monitoring agencies.
>
> To ensure that all the conditions for environmental clearance are fulfilled and for proper monitoring, we transfer all these cases to the High Court of Uttaranchal to be dealt with by a Division Bench. The High Court shall deal with these matters as if filed before it and shall be at liberty to pass any orders. However, it is made clear that it shall not be open to re-examine the matters such as safety of the dam and other aspects relating to implementation of conditions contained in the government orders which have been decided in this case.[31]

Justice D M Dharmadhikari dissented. On safety, he held:

> The precautionary principle accepted by India being a party and signatory to international agreements and understandings in the field of environment has become part of domestic law i.e. the Environment (Protection) Act. The governmental authorities in India cannot be permitted to set up the plea of scientific uncertainty of 3-D non-linear analysis of the dam. On the safety aspect pleas like *res judicata* based on earlier decisions of this Court cannot be allowed to be raised when further developments and events in the course of the project require further precautions to be taken before filling the dam to the optimum capacity. It is not the case of the respondents that 3-D non-linear analysis of the dam cannot be undertaken with the assistance of foreign experts on the subject. To take care of all eventualities of damage to the dam by an earthquake, 3-D non-linear analysis of the dam suggested by four experts as a matter of abundant caution must be undertaken. It is only after 3-D non-linear analysis of the dam is completed and the opinion of the experts on the safety aspects is again sought that further impoundment of the dam should be allowed.[32]

Moreover, the dissenting opinion required the establishment of a committee of experts with NGO representatives to assess whether the conditions of the environmental clearance were indeed being complied with and also to report on progress of resettlement and rehabilitation (R&R) measures. The minority view (of no legal effect) restrained impoundment of the reservoir until R&R work is complete in all respects and until the 3-D non-linear analysis and dam-break analysis are completed and the results assessed by experts.

While the government claims that the Tehri R&R policy was adequate, the situation on the ground, particularly for women, was far from satisfactory.

[30] *N D Jayal v Union of India* (2004) 9 SCC 362, 380.
[31] *Id.* at 403.
[32] *Id.* at 414.

VANDANA ASTHANA; FORCED DISPLACEMENT: A GENDERED ANALYSIS OF THE TEHRI DAM PROJECT, 57 Economic & Political Weekly 96 (2012)

Women form an integral part of the hill ecosystem. Despite their illiteracy, lack of exposure and drudgery, they have exhibited great potential as leaders. Women in Uttarakhand have spearheaded several movements across the state and played a pivotal role in the formation of the state. These hill women are bound together by the common bond of their tremendous work burden. However, though they remain an invisible workforce, they are the (unacknowledged) backbone of the family-economy....

In this subsistence or survival economy, women were responsible for collecting water, food, fuel, fodder, habitat, etc. for sustaining their families. Collection of minor forest produce and herbs not only provided extra income to the women but valuable nutrition and medicinal support as well. Animal husbandry was also an important supplemental activity that contributed to household income. Family members normally shared a single roof and lived under a single patrilineal unit. The families were mostly subsistence farming communities that provided enough for survival as the topography did not allow them to market or reap surplus produce. Importantly, the women had free access to these resources, which they claimed by traditional rights under common property resources. To ensure a more adequate livelihood, the men migrated to cities in search of employment, sending money home to the women who took care of the household.

After relocation, the women in resettlement sites complained of lack of access to common property resources that not only constituted a major portion of their survival strategies but also led to loss of supplemental income....

Displacement compensation for the dam-affected initially began in 1976 under the department of irrigation, Uttar Pradesh. Later, with the formation of Tehri Hydro Development Corporation (THDC) in 1990, a resettlement and rehabilitation policy was drafted that became effective in 1995. Two types of compensation were provided to the displaced population: land and cash. The displaced people were offered either two acres of land in rural settlement areas or half an acre of land within the periphery of urban municipal centres. A 200 sq m plot to build a new house and compensation for the old house was calculated on the age and type of house in existence at the pre-displacement site. The resettlers were given a land possession certificate but that did not give them the legal title to the land. In some cases, constructed houses were provided after a fixed sum varying from Rs.1.3 lakh was deposited. In many cases, corrupt government officials also demanded bribes in the absence of which many men and women lost their allotted shops or houses....

The Tehri Dam case study applied a culture-based understanding of the dam displacement processes in Uttarakhand in north India through the lens of the affected women. The question asked was: 'How do women experience displacement and relocation in the dam project?' In a region where women and children make up the majority of the displaced population, insensitivity to the needs of women has shaped post-rehabilitation programmes in a way where women face impoverishment, income decline and destitution. The eight interlinked potential risks intrinsic to displacement ... manifest themselves in the daily lives of these displaced women. They suffer from loss of land, joblessness and homelessness. Many of them live in tin sheds as they have lost their traditional houses and cannot afford to build new ones. They also suffer from a loss of access to commons, which creates a fodder and fuelwood shortage and decline in income and food diversity. The women face further hardships when community support structures disintegrate and family and kinship networks break down. Systems of care, protection, compensation, and R & R remain largely insensitive to women's needs leading to a fundamentally disenfranchising experience.

In this patriarchal set-up, the women have been denied compensation for the land they had cultivated for years but did not have a patta (land deed) in their name. Cases of ineligibility have been identified in many households headed by women and widows have been excluded from compensations in the resettlement package. Since only men are recognised as heads of households, the compensation is often paid only to them. The resettlement process is fraught with impoverishment risks and the reconstruction remains incomplete. Women are forced into adopting a culture they have never known, and limitations in their social space have prevented them from rebutting their daily practices in a new environment. Thus, the women remain marginalised at the community level as well as at the national level policy-framework because of their disadvantageous position ascribed by patriarchal gender relations.

The narrative of women clearly brought out the insensitivity of state discourses to the needs of women. Although the national R&R policy acknowledges gender as a category in the resettlement process, the implementing agency is the state government. That is why state government policies should consider these problems to enable the participation of women and move towards gender justice. This narrative-based approach highlights the concerns of women affected by displacement processes for consideration by policy planners whose decisions in the name of 'development and public purpose' have far-reaching implications for women.

NOTES AND QUESTIONS

1. While shifting to New Tehri, a city designed for the displaced residents from the submerged settlements brought better access to education, the overall package was harsh:

> Unfortunately for the thousands of displaced people, the negative results of the Tehri Dam and its byproducts far outweigh the positive progress that has been achieved. The dam's environmental effects have altered the lives of the relocated people, and brought about significant negative economic impacts, urban problems, and religious and cultural change.... The relocation of the thousands of people that took place in Tehri and the resulting effects it had on the community has been described by the leader of the opposition Chipko movement, Sunderlal Bahuguna, as 'the end of a civilization.'[33]

2. Between 1981 and 1983, Sunderlal Bahuguna carried out a Himalaya *padyatra*, a foot march where he covered 4,870 kms of the mountain range to assess the environmental problems being faced by citizens and to increase awareness against deforestation. The Tehri Dam protest which he led was but a part of a larger commitment to save the Himalayas from degradation. What challenges did the protest movement face?

> Bahuguna himself analysed the causes of decline of the movement as follows. Firstly, the local people yielded to the power of fear and greed, which were the major two weapons of the government. People were provided with compensation money, and threatened with the example of the 'killing' of 16 ordinary people, who had just participated in the demonstration meeting, in the bus accident in 1992. Secondly, the movement could not make itself heard above the 'democratic' preferential for the vested interests around Delhi, the main consumer of the Tehri water.
>
> It seems that the main reason why the movement had declined was the failure in organising or institutionalising a stronghold of the movement. The base of the [protest movement] had been Bahuguna's small hut which was situated at the side of one end of the entrance bridge to Tehri town. However, there were no full-time staff at the hut, and this hut was submerged under water earlier than any other places in the town when the two of the four diversion tunnels were closed in 2001.[34]

---

[33] Jason Newton, *Displacement and Development: The Paradoxes of India's Tehri Dam*, 49 The Geographical Bulletin 19 (2008).

[34] Shinya Ishizaka, *The Anti Tehri Dam Movement as a New Social Movement and Gandhism* 18 Jr Of The Japanese Assn For South Asian Studies 76 (2006).

E. THE NARMADA VALLEY PROJECT

The Narmada River springs from a holy pool amidst Hindu temples on the Amarkantak plateau in the forested Shahdol District of Madhya Pradesh, and then winds westward along a 1,300 kilometre course to drain into the Arabian Sea. The Narmada is one of India's most sacred rivers. A verse in the ancient Matsya Purana commends those who wish to wash away their sins to bathe three times in the Saraswati River, seven times in the Yamuna or once in the Ganga, but, if it is the Narmada that one visits, the mere sight of the river is cleansing enough.

The Narmada Basin drains an area of 98,796 square kilometres. About a quarter of the basin is covered in moist and dry deciduous forests and about 60% of it has black soils composed of silty clay with low permeability.

Although the Narmada Valley Project was conceived in 1946, final planning and work on it commenced only after the Narmada Water Disputes Tribunal passed its final orders in 1978. This tribunal was established in 1969 under the Interstate Water Disputes Act of 1956 to resolve the dispute on river water sharing among the riparian states of Madhya Pradesh, Gujarat and Maharashtra. The tribunal also laid down conditions regarding resettlement and rehabilitation of the people to be displaced by the submergence—the 'oustees'.

The Narmada Valley roject, when completed, will rank as the largest irrigation project ever planned and implemented as a single unit anywhere in the world. By the year 2040, the project authorities hope to complete 31 major dams (11 on the Narmada and 20 on its tributaries), 135 medium dams and 3,000 minor dams. Out of the 31 major dams, the most controversial are the Sardar Sarovar project (SSP) in Gujarat and the Narmada (Indira) Sagar project (NSP) in Madhya Pradesh. The NSP, commissioned in 2005, has the largest submergence zone and creates the biggest artificial reservoir in India. The Sardar Sarovar Dam has a height of 138.98 m and was commissioned in 2017. The SSP became the rallying cry of international and Indian NGOs as a symbol of everything that is wrong with the way big dams are built, from international funding to environmental impacts to displacement and abuse of human rights.

The SSP brings drinking water to Kutch and other drought-ridden regions of Gujarat. The dam will eventually impound water in a 535-foot-high reservoir that will submerge 375 sq kms in the three states of Gujarat, Maharashtra and Madhya Pradesh. It will also divert 9.5 million acre feet (MAF) of water into a canal and irrigation system. The canal is the biggest in the world—450 kms long. The aggregate length of the distribution network is 750 kms and it extends into Rajasthan.

Because the Narmada Valley Project is such an enormous endeavour that has spanned such a significant length of time, it is impossible to cover every legal nuance of every step of the project, the protest and the plans. Narmada was plagued by many of the same problems discussed in the Tehri project section, namely inadequate EIAs, funding setbacks and faulty R&R. This section opens with an excerpt outlining the agitation against the SSP followed by an analysis of the principal judgments delivered by the Supreme Court. We focus on human rights violations in the course of the campaign and project implementation.

PATRICK McCULLY; SILENCED RIVERS: THE ECOLOGY AND POLITICS OF LARGE DAMS 301 (1996)

Medha Patkar was a 30-year-old social activist and researcher when she first came to the Narmada Valley in 1985 to work in the villages to be submerged by the Sardar Sarovar

Dam. Over the next few years, Patkar travelled by foot, bus and boat throughout the nearly 200-kilometre-long submergence zone, which includes parts of three states and people speaking five different languages. Patkar lived with the villagers to be displaced, listened to their fears for the future, and urged them to organize to force the government to respect their rights.

Patkar spent most of her time among the adivasis in the remote and rugged Satpura hills of Maharashtra state. Her oratorical and organizing skills helped build the trust of many local people and also attracted a committed coterie of young outside activists to come to the valley. These activists, who included engineers, social workers and journalists, were to play a vital role in the Narmada movement. Early in 1986, Patkar and other activists and the Maharashtra villagers set up the Narmada Dharangrast Samiti (Committee for Narmada Dam-Affected People). The NDS villagers refused to be moved out or to cooperate with dam officials in any way until their demands for fair compensation and information about the impacts of the project were met.

The NDS also began to investigate the official claims of the benefits the project would provide. Among their findings were that crucial environmental studies had not been conducted, that the number of people to be displaced was not known, that estimates of the amount of land to get irrigation water were wildly optimistic, and that while the supply of drinking water to some 40 million people was supposed to be one of the project's main benefits, the massive sums needed to build the pipes and pumps to deliver this water had been left out of the estimated project costs. These findings led the NDS and two other oustees' groups they had helped to set up in Gujarat (the state where the dam is located) and Madhya Pradesh (the state where most of the reservoir would lie) to conclude that the claims of project benefits were fraudulent and just resettlement impossible. At six rallies held simultaneously in the three affected states on 18 August 1988 the NDS and their allies announced their total—but strictly nonviolent—opposition to the dam.

National press coverage and awareness of the anti-Sardar Sarovar campaign burgeoned in the late 1980s and support for the Narmada activists mounted among environmental, human rights, religious, landless and adivasi organizations around the country. Within the valley, the activists built alliances across class and caste boundaries between adivasi and 'caste Hindu' areas, and between the reservoir oustees and people affected by the project in other ways—in particular, families losing land to the massive canal network. In 1989, this growing network of local and international groups was formally named the Save the Narmada Movement, or Narmada Bachao Andolan (NBA).

The International Front

Interest in the growing Narmada controversy within the international environmental community was boosted by two trips Medha Patkar made to Washington in 1987 and 1989. Lori Udall from the Environmental Defense Fund (EDF) in Washington was inspired by Patkar to take the lead role in raising the NBA's concerns with the World Bank. Udall also helped build a network of committed and informed activists in North America, Europe, Japan and Australia who become known as the Narmada Action Committee.

Medha Patkar met with some World Bank executive directors during her 1989 visit. 'When I hear what NGOs say about this project and then what the operations staff say,' one director remarked afterwards, 'it sounds like they are talking about two different projects.' Patkar also gave testimony at a congressional subcommittee hearing into the World Bank's performance on Sardar Sarovar. Congressional staff, journalists and environmentalists broke into spontaneous applause after her impassioned, hour-long presentation. A number of Congressmen later wrote to Bank President Barber Conable urging that the project be suspended.

The next foreign success for the NBA was a symposium in Tokyo in April, 1990. Influencing opinion in Japan was vital for the Narmada campaign as the Japanese government was lending some $200 million for the turbines for Sardar Sarovar. NBA and international activists joined Japanese NGOs, academics and politicians at the Tokyo symposium, which received considerable national press coverage. The activists later met with Japanese government officials. Within a month of the symposium, the Japanese withdrew all further funding for the dam. This was the first time that a Japanese aid loan had been withdrawn for environmental and human rights reasons.

The Long Road to the Indian Review

Back in India, the NBA had changed its straight forward 'no dam' position in March 1990, and, seeking a way of breaking the stalemate between pro- and anti-dam forces proposed the project be suspended pending a comprehensive and open review. In an attempt to pressure the government into holding the review, the NBA organized the most spectacular action of its long campaign. On Christmas Day 1990, 5,000 oustees and NBA supporters, including the widely respected veteran social activists Baba Amte, set off for the dam site from the town of Rajghat in Madhya Pradesh on a Struggle March Towards People's Development—to become known as the 'Long March'. Eight days later the marchers reached the village of Ferkuwa on the border with Gujarat and found their way blocked by the police and a counter-demonstration organised by the Gujarat government. An angry month-long stand-off ensued.

At first the NBA attempted to break through by sending forward groups of volunteers, their hands tied in front of them to symbolize their commitment to nonviolence. The police repeatedly forced back the volunteers. Some were beaten and around 140 detained. Patkar and six others then began a fast by the side of the road. The days passed but the government remained unresponsive. Then, on 29 January, the twenty-first day of the fast, news came from Washington DC that the World Bank would commission a review of the project. The following day, the press coverage throughout India, greatly increased country-wide support for the NBA, and made Medha Patkar a national celebrity.

By 1991, full-scale construction on the dam had been under way for four years. Submergence was clearly possible during the upcoming monsoon, which hits the Narmada Valley between June and September every year. At a ceremony in Manibeli, the Maharashtra village closest to the dam, a group of oustees and activists vowed to be the first to face the waters rising behind the part-built dam. An NBA compound was set up at one of the lowest parts of Manibeli with a house where the *Samarpit Dal*, or 'Save or Drown Squad', would sit and wait to be engulfed by the new reservoir. In response, the government banned Patkar and other activists from the villages during the monsoon, and prohibited the villagers from holding anti-dam protests.

The NBA defied the bans, and hundreds of their supporters were arrested during the monsoon months. Members of the *Samarpit Dal* went into hiding to avoid detention and so be able to carry out their vow. A weak monsoon, however, meant that the water stayed several metres below Manibeli in 1991.

The following year the Narmada rose during one monsoon storm to within a metre of the lowest house behind the dam, Patkar was among 11 people in the house at the time. Also in 1992, police shot dead an *adivasi* woman while evicting her community from forest land which was to be given to resettled oustees.

The fiercely critical report of the World Bank-funded Independent Review team, headed by Bradford Morse, was released in June 1992, after nine months of research and writing. The NBA and its international supporters were delighted that the Review vindicated so many of their claims and they used it to step up pressure on the World Bank. Environmentalists wrote an open letter to World Bank President Lewis Preston which they published as a full-page advertisement in the London Financial Times. It warned that if the Bank refused to withdraw funding for Sardar Sarovar then NGOs would launch a campaign to cut government funding of the Bank. The letter was endorsed by 250 NGOs and coalitions from 37 countries. Full page advertisements placed in the *Washington Post* and *New York Times* by US environmental groups made similar demands.

After the Bank

The Bank finally announced its withdrawal in March 1993. The Indian authorities' initial reaction was to step up the use of violence and intimidation. In November, police shot dead an *adivasi* boy. Street demonstrations against the killing were met with *lathi* charges and yet more arrests.

Without World Bank funds, work on the canal system soon all but ground to a halt. Available financial resources were poured into raising the dam wall—most visible symbol of the project and the most intimidating to the people refusing resettlement. Large-scale submergence began during the 1993 monsoon with the dam wall 44 metres high. The lands of hundreds of villagers were inundated and the homes and possessions of 40 families washed away. Police arrested the occupants of the lowest houses and dragged them to higher ground to prevent them carrying out their pledge to drown. Similar scenes were repeated during the 1994 and 1995 monsoons. In 1995 some villagers braved water which rose to chest height before receding.

With the World Bank out of the way, the NBA stepped up pressure on the Indian government to commission a comprehensive review, one which would look at all aspects of Sardar Sarovar—the terms of reference for the Morse Commission had covered only resettlement and the environment. In June 1993, Medha Patkar and Devram Kanera, a farmer from Madhya Pradesh, began a fast in downtown Bombay. After 14 days the government agreed to start the review process—but once the fast was called off it reneged on its promise.

Ever more frustrated with the government's duplicity, the continuing arrests and beatings of activists, and the submergence of homes in the valley, the NBA decided once again to use the strongest weapon at its disposal—the lives of its own members. In July 1993, the NBA announced that unless the review process began by 6 August, seven activists would throw themselves into the monsoon-swollen Narmada. Less than 24 hours before the deadline, the central government announced that it would establish a five-member group of experts nominated by both the NBA and dam supporters to 'look into all aspects of SSP'. The group met within hours of the announcement and called on the NBA to halt their action, while assuring them that they were committed to an unbiased and comprehensive review of SSP. The *jal samarpan*—'self-sacrifice by drowning'—was called off.

The review committee heard submissions from the NBA, affected people, central government ministries and the relevant state governments except that of Gujarat, which boycotted the review. Scientists and engineers presented detailed suggestions for alternative methods of supplying water and power. The release of the report, however, was delayed indefinitely by legal action from the Gujarat government.

In May 1994, the NBA opened another front in its campaign by filing a comprehensive case against the project with the New Delhi Supreme Court. The case moved forward at a painfully slow pace with numerous postponements, delays and cancellations.

New hope for the campaign came in late 1994 when the Madhya Pradesh government announced that it had neither the land nor resources to resettle the state's huge numbers of oustees and that it wanted the planned dam height to be reduced. In an effort to pressure the upstream government to force Gujarat to halt the dam, the NBA decided the muster its resources for yet another round of fasts, this time to be held in Bhopal, the Madhya Pradesh capital. On 21 November 1994, Patkar and three men from the valley stopped eating. Twenty-six days later, the Madhya Pradesh government agreed to demand a halt to construction pending progress on resettlement. The NBA called off the fasts.

Three days before the end of the Bhopal fasts the Supreme Court ordered the government-commissioned review to be made public. The report questioned the basic data used to design the project and criticized the resettlement effort. The court asked the review team to investigate further the viability of the project.

The NBA received a significant boost in January 1995 when the central government in New Delhi forced Gujarat to suspend raising the dam wall with its lowest point 63 metres above the riverbed, just under half the planned final height. The suspension order came because the project was violating a court ruling that oustees must be resettled six months before their land is submerged....

Whatever the final outcome, the long struggle of the people of the valley and their supporters within India and around the world has left deep scars on the World Bank and the Indian and International dam industry. It is unlikely that the Bank will ever fund another river development project on such a scale in a democratic country. It is also unlikely for the foreseeable future that the Indian dam lobby will succeed in pushing through any projects involving such large-scale displacement. 'We are not going in for large dams anymore,' Indian power minister N K P Salve told International Water Power & Dam Construction in late 1993. 'We want run of the river projects and to have smaller dams, if they are necessary at all, which will not cause any impediment whatsoever to the environmental needs.'

The NBA sees its role as much more than challenging a single dam or even dam building in general. Patkar and other NBA leaders have travelled throughout India supporting other struggles against destructive state and corporate development projects which strip the poor of their right to livelihood. Together with other leading environmental, women's lower-caste and Gandhian groups, the NBA has helped establish a National Alliance of People's Movements (NAPM). In March 1996, representatives from around 100 groups in 17 states drew up a 'People's Resolve', a common ideological platform for the NAPM around which it is hoped India's many thousands of diverse people's organizations can unite in a 'strong social, political force.'

On 18 October 2000, the Supreme Court delivered a split verdict in the *Narmada* case. The majority comprising Chief Justice A S Anand and Justice B N Kirpal traced the history of the project from early studies in the 1940s and rejected the petition. The minority authored by Justice S P Bharucha allowed the writ petition, finding that there was no proper environmental clearance. The first excerpt is from the majority opinion, followed by a short extract from the dissent.

NARMADA BACHAO ANDOLAN v UNION OF INDIA
(2000) 10 SCC 664

KIRPAL, J:

* * *

Laches

As far as the petitioner is concerned, it is an anti-dam organisation and is opposed to the construction of the high dam. It has been in existence since 1986 but has chosen to challenge the clearance given in 1987 by filing a writ petition in 1994. It has sought to contend that there was lack of study available regarding the environmental aspects and also because of the seismicity, the clearance should not have been granted. The rehabilitation packages are dissimilar and there has been no independent study or survey done before decision to undertake the project was taken and construction started.

The project, in principle, was cleared more than 25 years ago when the foundation stone was laid by late Pandit Jawaharlal Nehru. Thereafter, there was an agreement of the four Chief Ministers in 1974, namely, the Chief Ministers of Madhya Pradesh, Gujarat, Maharashtra and Rajasthan for the project to be undertaken. Then dispute arose with regard to the height of the dam which was settled with the award of the Tribunal being given in 1978. For a number of years, thereafter, final clearance was still not given. In the meantime, some environmental studies were conducted. The final clearance was not given because of the environmental concern which is quite evident. Even though complete data with regard to the environment was not available, the Government did in 1987 finally give environmental clearance. It is thereafter that the construction of the dam was undertaken and hundreds of crores have been invested before the petitioner chose to file a writ petition in 1994 challenging the decision to construct the dam and the clearance as was given. In our opinion, the petitioner which had been agitating against the dam since 1986 is guilty of laches in not approaching the Court at an earlier point of time.

When such projects are undertaken and hundreds of crores of public money is spent, any individual or organisations in the garb of PIL cannot be permitted to challenge the policy decision taken after a lapse of time. It is against the national interest and contrary to the established principles of law that decisions to undertake developmental projects are permitted to be challenged after a number of years during which period public money has been spent in the execution of the project....

This Court has entertained this petition with a view to satisfy itself that there is proper implementation of the relief and rehabilitation measures at least to the extent they have been ordered by the Tribunal's award. In short, it was only the concern of this Court for the protection of the fundamental rights of the oustees under Article 21 of the Constitution of India which led to the entertaining of this petition. It is the relief and rehabilitation measures that this Court is really concerned with and the petition in regard to the other issues raised is highly belated. Though it is, therefore, not necessary to do so, we however presently propose to deal with some of the other issues raised....

The displacement of the tribals and other persons would not per se result in the violation of their fundamental or other rights. The effect is to see that on their rehabilitation at new locations they are better off than what they were. At the rehabilitation sites they will have more and better amenities than those they enjoyed in their tribal hamlets. The gradual assimilation in the mainstream of the society will lead to betterment and progress.

Environmental issues

The four issues raised under this head by [petitioner's counsel] are as under:

I. Whether the execution of a large project, having diverse and far-reaching environmental impact, without the proper study and understanding of its environmental impact and without proper planning of mitigative measures is a violation of fundamental rights of the affected people guaranteed under Article 21 of the Constitution of India?

II. Whether the diverse environmental impacts of the Sardar Sarovar Project have been properly studied and understood?

III. Whether any independent authority has examined the environmental costs and mitigative measures to be undertaken in order to decide whether the environmental costs are acceptable and mitigative measures practical?

IV. Whether the environmental conditions imposed by the Ministry of Environment have been violated and if so, what is the legal effect of the violations?

* * *

Dam serves a number of purposes. It stores water, generates electricity and releases water throughout the year and at times of scarcity. Its storage capacity is meant to control floods and the canal system which emanates therefrom is meant to convey and provide water for drinking, agriculture and industry. In addition thereto, it can also be a source of generating hydropower. Dam has, therefore, necessarily to be regarded as an infrastructural project.

There are three stages with regard to the undertaking of an infrastructural project. One is conception or planning, second is decision to undertake the project and the third is the execution of the project. The conception and the decision to undertake a project is to be regarded as a policy decision. While there is always a need for such projects not being unduly delayed, it is at the same time expected that a thorough possible study will be undertaken before a decision is taken to start a project. Once such a considered decision is taken, the proper execution of the same should be undertaken expeditiously. It is for the Government to decide how to do its job. When it has put a system in place for the execution of a project and such a system cannot be said to be arbitrary, then the only role which a court may have to play is to see that the system works in the manner it was envisaged....

Any delay in the execution of the project means overrun in costs and the decision to undertake a project, if challenged after its execution has commenced, should be thrown out at the very threshold on the ground of laches if the petitioner had the knowledge of such a decision and could have approached the court at that time. Just because a petition is termed as a PIL does not mean that ordinary principles applicable to litigation will not apply. Laches is one of them.

Public interest litigation (PIL) was an innovation essentially to safeguard and protect the human rights of those people who were unable to protect themselves. With the passage of time PIL jurisdiction has been ballooning so as to encompass within its ambit subjects such as probity in public life, granting of largesse in the form of licences, protecting environment and the like. But the balloon should not be inflated so much that it bursts. Public interest litigation should not be allowed to degenerate to becoming publicity interest litigation or private inquisitiveness litigation....

Displacement of people living on the proposed project sites and the areas to be submerged is an important issue. Most of the hydrology projects are located in remote and inaccessible areas, where local population is, like in the present case, either illiterate or having marginal means of employment and the per capita income of the families is low. It is a fact that people are displaced by projects from their ancestral homes. Displacement of these people would undoubtedly disconnect them from their past, culture, custom and traditions, but then it becomes necessary to harvest a river for the larger good. A natural river is not only meant for the people close by but it should be for the benefit of those who can make use of it, being away from it or nearby. Realising the fact that displacement of these people would disconnect them from their past, culture, custom and traditions, the moment any village is earmarked for takeover for dam or any other developmental activity, the project-implementing authorities have to implement R&R programmes. The R&R plans are required to be specially drafted and implemented to mitigate problems whatsoever relating to all, whether rich or poor, landowner or encroacher, farmer or tenant, employee or employer, tribal or non-tribal. A properly drafted R&R plan would improve the living standards of displaced persons after displacement. For example residents of villages around Bhakra Nangal Dam, Nagarjuna Sagar Dam, Tehri, Bhilai Steel Plant, Bokaro and Bala Iron and Steel Plant and numerous other developmental sites are better off than people living in villages in whose vicinity no development project came in. It is not fair that tribals and the people in undeveloped villages should continue in the same condition without ever enjoying the fruits of science and technology for better health and have a higher quality of lifestyle. Should they not be encouraged to seek greener pastures elsewhere, if they can have access to it, either through their own efforts due to information exchange or due to outside compulsions. It is with this object in view that the R&R plans which are developed are meant to ensure that those who move must be better off in the new locations at government cost. In the present case, the R&R packages of the States, specially of Gujarat, are such that the living conditions of the oustees will be much better than what they had in their tribal hamlets.

The loss of forest because of any activity is undoubtedly harmful. Without going into the question as to whether the loss of forest due to river valley project because of submergence is negligible, compared to deforestation due to other reasons like cutting of trees for fuel, it is true that large dams cause submergence leading to loss of forest areas. But it cannot be ignored and it is important to note that these large dams also cause conversion of wasteland into agricultural land and make the area greener. Large dams can also become instruments in improving the environment, as has been the case in western Rajasthan, which transformed into a green area because of Indira Gandhi Canal which draws water from Bhakra Nangal Dam. This project not only allows the farmers to grow crops in deserts but also checks the spread of Thar Desert in the adjoining areas of Punjab and Haryana.

The environmental and ecological consideration must, of course, be given due consideration but with proper channelisation of developmental activities ecology and environment can be enhanced. For example, Periyar Dam Reservoir has become an elephant sanctuary with thick green forests all around while at the same time it wiped out famines that used to haunt the district of Madurai in Tamil Nadu before its construction. Similarly Krishnaraja Sagar Dam which has turned Mandya District which was once covered with shrub forests with wild beasts into a prosperous one with green paddy and sugarcane fields all around.

So far a number of such river valley projects have been undertaken in all parts of India. The petitioner has not been able to point out a single instance where the construction of a dam has, on the whole, had an adverse environmental impact. On the contrary the environment has improved. That being so, there is no reason to suspect, with all the experience gained so far, that the position here will be any different and there will not be overall improvement and prosperity. It should not be forgotten that poverty is regarded as one of the causes of degradation of environment. With improved irrigation system the people will prosper. The construction of Bhakra Dam is a shining example for all to see how the backward area of erstwhile undivided Punjab has now become the granary of India with improved environment than what was there before the completion of the Bhakra Nangal Project.

* * *

One of the indicators of the living standard of people is the per capita consumption of electricity. There is, however, perennial shortage of power in India and, therefore, it is necessary that the generation increases. The world over countries having rich water and river systems have effectively exploited these for hydel-power generation. In India, the share of hydel power in the total power generated was as high as 50% in the year 1962–63 but the share of hydel power started declining rapidly after 1980. There is more reliance now on thermal-power projects. But these thermal-power projects use fossil fuels, which are not only depleting fast but also contribute towards environmental pollution. Global warming due to the greenhouse effect has become a major cause of concern. One of the various factors responsible for this is the burning of fossil fuel in thermal-power plants. There is, therefore, international concern for reduction of greenhouse gases which is shared by World Bank resulting in the restriction of sanction of funds for thermal-power projects. On the other hand, the hydel power's contribution to the greenhouse effect is negligible and it can be termed ecology-friendly. Not only this but the cost of generation of electricity in hydel projects is significantly less. The award of the Tribunal has taken all these factors into consideration while determining the height of the dam at 455 ft. Giving the option of generating eco-friendly electricity and substituting it by thermal power may not, therefore, be the best option. Perhaps the setting up of a thermal plant may not displace as many families as a hydel project may but at the same time the pollution caused by the thermal plant and the adverse effect on the neighbourhood could be far greater than the inconvenience caused in shifting and rehabilitating the oustees of a reservoir.

There is and has been in the recent past protests and agitations not only against hydel projects but also against the setting up of nuclear or thermal power plants. In each case reasons are put forth against the execution of the proposed project either as being dangerous (in case of nuclear) or causing pollution and ecological degradation (in the case of thermal) or rendering people homeless and posing adverse environment impacts as has been argued in the present case. But then electricity has to be generated and one or more of these options exercised. What option to exercise, in our constitutional framework, is for the Government to decide keeping various factors in mind. In the present case, a considered decision has been taken and an award made, whereby a high dam having an [full reservoir level (FRL)] of 455 ft with capability of developing hydel power is to be constructed. In the facts and circumstances enumerated hereinabove, even if this Court could go into the question, the decision so taken cannot be faulted....

S P Bharucha, J (*dissenting*): I have read the judgment proposed to be delivered by my learned brother, the Hon'ble Mr Justice B N Kirpal. Respectfully, I regret my inability to agree therewith....

The contemporaneous notes prepared by the Ministry of Water Resources and the Ministry of Environment and Forests, also referred to above, leave no manner of doubt that the requisite data for assessment of the environmental impact of the project was not available when the environmental clearance thereof was granted. In the words of one of the notes:

While some plans have been made, studies undertaken and action initiated, it will be clear from the preceding paragraphs that much still remains to be done. Indeed, it is the view of the Ministry of Environment, Forests and Wildlife that what has been done so far whether by way of action or by way of studies does not amount to much and that many matters are yet in the early and preliminary stages.

The notes make clear that the studies, censuses, mapping of areas and field surveys for the collection of data for assessment of the environmental impact of the project were likely to take a further 2 to 3 years. An environmental clearance based on next to no data in regard to the environmental impact of the project was contrary to the terms of the then policy of the Union of India in regard to environmental clearances and, therefore, no clearance at all.

The environmental clearance of 24-6-1987 stated that details had been sought from the project authorities in respect of the rehabilitation master plan, phased catchment area treatment scheme, compensatory afforestation plan, command area development, survey of flora and fauna, carrying capacity of surrounding area, seismicity and health aspects; field surveys had yet to be completed and complete details had been assured by 1989. Clearly, therefore, the necessary particulars in regard to the environmental impact of the project, as required by the Guidelines, were not available when the environmental clearance was given, and it, therefore, could not have been given....

When the writ petition was filed the process of relief and rehabilitation, such as it was, was going on. The writ petitioners were not guilty of any laches in that regard. In the writ petition they raised other issues, one among them being related to the environmental clearance of the project. Given what has been held in respect of the environmental clearance, when the public interest is so demonstrably involved, it would be against public interest to decline relief only on the ground that the Court was approached belatedly.

I should not be deemed to have agreed to anything stated in brother Kirpal's judgment for the reason that I have not traversed it in the course of what I have stated....

NOTES AND QUESTIONS

1. On the issue of laches, do you prefer the reasoning of the majority or the dissent?

2. Was it a good strategy for NBA to petition the Supreme Court? In terms of power, politics and policy do constitutional courts have the capacity to prevent the implementation of such a large project? Should NBA have continued its agitation at the field level without recourse to the Supreme Court? What constraints bind a party once it petitions a court and the case is *sub judice*?

3. The majority bought the engineering arguments: big is beautiful; water flowing into the seas is a waste; dams are essential for irrigation, drinking water, hydroelectricity and also for national development. The minority view is more sensitive to the ecological imperative: no matter how beneficial, environmentally disruptive projects must undergo a rigorous environmental impact assessment before implementation. Without EIA, it is not possible to identify and thereafter implement mitigation measures.

4. With climate change altering precipitation patterns, it is crucial for decision-makers to correctly project precipitation patterns before selecting the sites for new dams. The logic of a tribunal award (in the case of an interstate river) or an agreement amongst state governments may not be sufficient justification for building a large dam where the projected rainfall in the catchment shows a decline in the coming decades. A well-prepared environmental study anticipates such trends and eventually improves the quality of the decision.

5. The operative directions by the majority related to relief and rehabilitation (R&R) measures. The court allowed construction of the dam as per the tribunal award, provided that R&R measures kept pace with the increased height of the dam. 'We direct the States of Madhya Pradesh, Maharashtra and Gujarat to implement the award and give relief and rehabilitation to the oustees in terms of the packages offered by them and these States shall comply with the directions in this regard which is given either by Narmada Control Authority or the Review Committee or the Grievance Redressal Authorities.'

6. The operative directions in the minority judgment required an environmental impact assessment exercise to be carried out under the EIA notification of 1994. Moreover, until the environmental clearance was accorded, the minority directed further construction to cease. What use is a minority judgment in a final court?

7. Do you agree with the majority opinion regarding the displacement of tribals and their assimilation in mainstream society? Is the view patronizing and contrary to numerous provisions in the Constitution that specially protect members of Scheduled Tribes?

Professor Philippe Cullet, an international authority on water law, was disappointed by the Supreme Court's failure to adequately address the human rights violations of the Sardar Sarovar oustees.

> PHILIPPE CULLET; HUMAN RIGHTS AND DISPLACEMENT: THE INDIAN SUPREME COURT DECISION ON SARDAR SAROVAR IN INTERNATIONAL PERSPECTIVE, 50 International and Comparative Law Quarterly 973 (2001)
>
> The majority judgment statement that the oustees' fundamental rights are its main preoccupation is significant since it highlights the importance of human rights in this context. However, while the majority judgment accepts in theory the importance of the fundamental rights of the oustees and indicates that it should not deal with any other issue but the problems arising from the displacement of human beings by the dam, the actual reasoning gives a completely different picture. Indeed, it focuses largely on administrative procedures and arrangements but does not analyse the fundamental rights of the oustees. This is reinforced by the fact that the judgment tends to quote extensively from government affidavits.
>
> One of the dimensions highlighted in the petition which is not fully addressed in the judgments is that of project affected people's participation in decision-making. Significantly, even the old ILO Convention 107 does not stop at requiring countries not to displace tribal people unless it is in the interest of national economic development. It also requires governments to involve tribal people or their representatives in taking decisions concerning them.

Since then, there have been sweeping changes in the perception of participation as a human right. This covers a number of dimensions from political participation recognised, for instance, under the Covenant on Civil and Political Rights to participation in environmental decision-making. The latter is, for instance, embodied in Principle 10 of the Rio Declaration which states that '[e]nvironmental issues are best handled with the participation of all concerned citizens.'

While disposing of the NBA petition, the majority judgment notes that a challenge should have been brought before the project was started. It notes earlier in the same paragraph that the Court has 'a duty to see that in the undertaking of a decision, no law is violated and people's fundamental rights are not transgressed upon except to the extent permissible under the Constitution. The judgment indirectly implies that a decision which cannot be challenged after a certain point has been taken with the full participation and knowledge of the people from whom a sacrifice is demanded for the good of the country at large. In the present case, the Narmada Water Disputes Tribunal (NWDT) never attempted to foster the participation of oustees in its proceedings. Merely, reiterating that the NWDT Award is final and binding does not answer the central question of the oustees' right to participate in the proceeding.

Participation in decision-making is more than a formal requirement meant to give an opportunity to hear the views of the people who are not promoters of the project. It constitutes one of the avenues for making sure that displaced people share in the benefits of the project. Indeed, everybody seems to agree that displaced people should not be worse off following their displacement. There are, however, widely divergent views concerning the rationale and process for relief and rehabilitation. On the one hand, the majority judgment takes the view that tribal people are in indigent circumstances and have been deprived of the modern fruits of development. The judges feel that 'it is not fair that tribals and the people in un-developed villages should continue in the same condition without ever enjoying the fruits of science and technology for better health and have a higher quality of life style.' In other words, the state is doing tribal people a favour by displacing them and bringing them into the mainstream society. On the other hand, human rights related instruments or the World Bank draft resettlement policy recognise that displacement can be a traumatic experience and that significant efforts must be made to ensure that displaced people do not adversely suffer and do not lose out overall. It is noteworthy that the World Commission on Dams (WCD) report's answer to this problem is to argue that adversely affected people are entitled to benefit from some of the project benefits. These can take the form of irrigated land, access to irrigation water or provision of electricity supply. If this were to be put in practice, it would constitute a sound basis for making sure that displacement does not appear to constitute the denial of existing amenities to some for increasing the amenities of others.

While the judgment never fully addresses fundamental rights issues, it surprisingly goes much beyond the scope of the petition to discuss the usefulness of dams as a whole in India. Indeed, the majority judgment clearly brings out its liking of big dams despite having specifically requested the petitioners not to comment on the usefulness of dams in general....

One of the major shortcomings of an approach focusing on a broad notion of well-being of the nation at large is that it completely sidelines the fundamental rights of people affected by large development projects. In the present case, the acknowledgement by the states that they do not have land to resettle oustees makes the general policy statement appear even more unbalanced and dismissive of oustees' fundamental rights. The policy statements of the majority judgment are also surprising since they contradict nationally and internationally accepted opinions concerning the contribution of dams to national well being. Thus, while the majority judgment opines that large scale river valley projects *per se* all over the country have made India more than self-sufficient in food, the WCD report notes much more cautiously that the actual extent of the contribution of large dams to these improvements is difficult to determine. The India study for the WCD does not arrive at an estimated figure and stops at declaring that dams have made a contribution to the development of irrigation and therefore to food production....

The question of the 'human cost' of development cannot be dealt with in a technical manner but must necessarily refer to the fundamental rights of people whose lives and/or livelihoods are threatened by development projects. The judgment that was delivered last October fails to grasp this fundamental dimension of the development process.

NOTES AND QUESTIONS

1. The petitioners argued that the involuntary displacement of tribals violated Article 21 of the Constitution read with India's international obligation with respect to the rights of those affected to participate in decision-making. The emergence of these community rights may be traced to ILO Convention 107. This Convention was adopted by the International Labour Organization and is entitled 'Convention concerning the Protection and Integration of Indigenous and Other Tribal and Semi-Tribal Populations in Independent Countries, 1957'. India is a contracting party to Convention 107 and ratified the Convention on 29 September 1958.

2. As Professor Cullet notes, the majority judgment in *Narmada* treats the project as *fait accompli* since the NWDT award of 1978 could not be reopened and the 1994 petition challenging the conditional environmental clearance granted in 1987 was barred by the long delay. The Narmada Bachao Andolan (NBA) commenced its struggle in 1989 and initially resorted to a non-violent campaign to force reconsideration of the project. In the backdrop of this legitimate campaign and given the magnitude of the displacement, could the petitioners be faulted for the delay in approaching the court? What might be the reasons—legal, political and strategic—for NBA to have delayed the challenge?

3. In the public eye, a Supreme Court or High Court judgment rejecting a challenge lends legitimacy to the enterprise that it may not otherwise enjoy. Approaching a Constitutional court is a double-edged weapon requiring careful evaluation of the downside, should the petition fail. Where a large community is affected by the incipient PIL, a broad consensus to file the case is desirable. Frequently, slapdash and poorly researched PILs are filed by publicity-seeking lawyers and litigants who end up doing a disservice to the cause.

4. Ramaswamy Iyer, a leading authority on water resources, was critical of the *Narmada* judgment. He too was disappointed at the failure of the court to protect the interest of the project-affected persons and the ill-informed 'Ode to Dams by Their Lordships'.[35]

5. Note how so many of the demands of the NBA—participatory decision-making before displacement, a social impact study before embarking on a project and strong R&R procedures—are now engrafted into the RFCA 2013.[36] In a parallel development, the EIA regime has also strengthened to address the concerns projected by NBA and expressed in the dissent.

In March 2005, the Supreme Court disposed of a set of interim applications by extending relief to project-affected families (PAFs). The court held that the benefit of the rehabilitation

[35] Ramaswamy R Iyer, *A Judgment of Grave Import*, 35 ECONOMIC & POLITICAL WEEKLY 3913 (2000).

[36] Right to Fair Compensation and Transparency in Land Acquisition, Rehabilitation and Resettlement Act of 2013.

package would extend to all oustees regardless of whether they were permanently or temporarily affected by submergence by reason of raising the height of the dam. The court also held that sons who had attained majority would be entitled to an allotment of two hectares of land as they constitute a separate family.[37] The court made no similar provision for daughters who had attained majority. Why?[38]

The R&R problems persisted. On 8 February 2017, the Supreme Court examined the difficulties faced by 4,998 PAFs in Madhya Pradesh. Since suitable land was difficult to locate, Madhya Pradesh introduced a special rehabilitation package (SRP) in June 2005, under which cash was offered in lieu of land. The families could then purchase land out of the payment received from the government. To settle matters the Supreme Court directed payment of Rs. 60 lakhs per family to 681 PAFs who had yet to receive compensation. The court also directed a payment of Rs. 15 lakhs to families who had received compensation under the package but were duped:

> It is also apparent, that a large number of families, out of the 4264 families which had received both installments, under the 'Special Rehabilitation Package', were duped. The number of duped 'project affected families', indicated in the Justice S S Jha Commission's Report, is 1358. This number is affirmed by the learned Attorney General for India, and confirmed by the respective State counsel. Referring to these 1358 families, the Jha Commission in its report of January, 2016, had observed as under:
>
> > (29) Poor oustees particularly tribals have been looted by middlemen. They have lost their livelihood and are not daily wagers. Their installments have been siphoned off by the middlemen. When oustees appeared before the Commission were not even having clothes to wear. They have wrapped small cloth or towel round their waist when they appeared before the Commission.
>
> It is in the above circumstances, that the Jha Commission recorded the following conclusions, in its report:
>
> > 'CONCLUSION
> >
> > 1. The reason for fake sale deeds is a faulty SRP policy of the Government. The Government was not having sufficient irrigated agricultural lands in their Land Banks near the R&R sites. The Policy itself is against Narmada Award, and the judgment of the Supreme Court. Supreme Court has observed that the PAFs and Project Affected Persons (PAPs) should live better life has been frustrated by this Policy.
> >   (i) By not allowing any scrutiny of the sale deeds and free hand has been given to the Rehabilitation Officers and Land Acquisition Officers in disbursing the compensation which resulted into large number of fake sale deeds.
> >   (ii) The free access to middlemen in the Office of [Narmada Valley Development Authority] (NVDA) in getting the money withdrawn of the oustees also reflects about the interest of middlemen and nexus with NVDA officials. Though evidence is not received against the NVDA officials all the oustees have stated that they were made to sit outside the NVDA office and their work was done by the middlemen and they were made to sign on the papers without explaining the contents discloses that NVDA officials had obtained signatures or thumb impressions of the oustees without explaining the contents demonstrate irregularity on their part and they are prima facie responsible for large number of fake registries.

---

[37] *Narmada Bachao Andolan v Union of India* (2005) 4 SCC 32.

[38] The Narmada Water Disputes Tribunal made an award on 16 August 1978. The award defined a 'family' for the purpose of relief and rehabilitation. This definition specified 'every major son will be treated as a separate family'. The State of Gujarat with respect to its R&R packages extended the facility of land allotment to unmarried daughters. *Narmada Bachao Andolan v Union of India* (2005) 4 SCC 32, 41, 50.

2. The quality of construction was very poor without any planning. No geographical mapping was done before selecting the R&R sites whereby cultivable good black cotton soil is converted into house building sites for residential plots. There was a faulty policy of not establishing a laboratory to test the soil for carrying out constructions on the black cotton soil. The construction was done on the R&R sites on common maps and designs of the building. Superior officers had never cared to visit R&R sites to examine the construction work. The Government has found 40 engineers responsible for substandard quality of construction, but has not cared to rectify the defect after finding the substandard construction. Most of the places the expenditure on construction has gone waste as the R&R sites are not occupied by the oustees or they are occupied by very few PAPs and PAFs. Thus, the expenditure on these sites is waste of money.
3. The NVDA has not maintained proper records relating to livelihood grants and alternative livelihood which itself demonstrate that there was large scale corruption in the livelihood grants and alternative livelihood.
   The officers of NVDA involved in allotment of house plot sites have not followed the Rules framed by the Government in allotting the plots. They have allotted the plots in an arbitrary matter and usurp the power of changing the allotment which was not vested with them. Thus, this shows their corrupt intention. Any arbitrary action attracts the vice of mala fide. The officers involved in allotment of plots are wholly responsible for irregularities and corruption in allotment and change of plots.'

We are of the considered view, that even though the above-mentioned 1358 project affected families were paid both installments, they need to be further compensated, so as to alleviate their hardship, as they have not been able to purchase land in lieu of land, not because of their own fault or lapse, but because they were duped. This would enable them to purchase alternative land at the lesser rate suggested by the learned counsel for the applicants. It is in the above view of the matter, that we hereby direct the concerned authorities, to pay these 1358 project affected families, a sum of rupees fifteen lakhs per family.[39]

In May 2011, the Supreme Court heard a set of appeals from interim orders that were passed by the Madhya Pradesh High Court in a challenge to another dam, Omkareshwar Dam, also on the Narmada. This project and its submergence zone fell entirely in Madhya Pradesh. The following excerpt is critical of NBA's role.

STATE OF MADHYA PRADESH v NARMADA BACHAO ANDOLAN
(2011) 7 SCC 639

DR B S CHAUHAN, J:

* * *

The facts and circumstances giving rise to these cases are as follows:

(A) Narmada River starts at Amarkantak. It flows through Madhya Pradesh for 1077 km, then forms a common boundary in Maharashtra for 74 km (35 km with Madhya Pradesh and 39 km with Maharashtra) and then passes through Gujarat for 161 km before meeting the Arabian Sea after a total length of 1312 km. The Narmada Water Disputes Tribunal apportioned the water in Narmada between Madhya Pradesh, Gujarat, Maharashtra and Rajasthan, subject to review after 45 years.

(B) The State of Madhya Pradesh conducted a survey in 1955 for the establishment of hydropower projects in the Narmada basin at different sites including Barwaha (Omkareshwar Project). In 1983, the Narmada Valley Development (Irrigation) Department (hereinafter called 'NVD') was set up and further studies were conducted for the establishment of hydropower projects.

---

39 *Narmada Bachao Andolan v Union of India* (2018) 14 SCC 507.

(C) Omkareshwar Dam, an intra-State project for generating 520 MW of power, which also involved the irrigation of 1.47 lakh hectares of agricultural land, was approved by the State Government, with an assessment that on the completion of the project, 30 villages would be submerged at the full reservoir level i.e. 196.60 m.

(D) The Government of Madhya Pradesh framed a rehabilitation and resettlement policy in 1985 (hereinafter called 'the R&R Policy') for the oustees of all the Narmada projects in the State. The said policy was amended from time to time as is evident from the R&R Policies dated 9-6-1987; 5-9-1989; 7-6-1991 and 27-8-1993. The said policy provided for the allotment of a minimum of 2 ha of agricultural land; irrigation facilities at government cost; grant-in-aid for small and marginal farmers and SC/ST families and to meet the entire cost of the allotted land. The policy further provided that the allotment of agricultural land would be carried out much in advance, before the dam construction reached the crest level. The land required for allotment would be procured in the common area from the farmers having holdings of more than 4 ha of land.

The State authorities obtained environmental clearance for the Omkareshwar Project from the Ministry of Environment and Forests on 13-10-1993. The Ministry of Welfare granted clearance on 8-10-1993. The Planning Commission also granted clearance on condition of compliance with welfare and environmental clearances vide Order dated 25-5-2001. The Central Electricity Authority accorded techno-economic clearance under the provisions of the Electricity (Supply) Act, 1948 on 24-7-2001. The Government of India approved and granted financial concurrence from the Public Investment Board of the Planning Commission for this project on 17-5-2002. Forest clearance was granted on 20-8-2004 under the provisions of Section 2 of the Forest (Conservation) Act, 1980 for the diversion of 5829 ha of forest lands. Therefore, there had been various statutory and non-statutory clearances from the authorities.

(E) The R&R Policy further stood amended on 3-7-2003, to the effect that agricultural land would be offered to the oustees 'as far as possible', and not to those who would make application in writing to receive compensation for their acquired land.

(F) The construction of Omkareshwar Dam began in 2002 and stood completed in October 2006. A large number of families had been uprooted on construction of the dam up to its 190 m height. For the dam site, a huge area of land had been acquired under the provisions of the Land Acquisition Act, 1894 (hereinafter called as 'the 1894 Act'). The displaced persons were allegedly not offered the land under the R&R Policy, as amended on 3-7-2003, rather compensation for their land was deposited in their accounts.

(G) Narmada Bachao Andolan, Respondent 1 (hereinafter referred to as 'NBA'), an action group, had been espousing the grievances of displaced persons by filing public interest litigations (hereinafter called 'PILs') before the High Court/further to this Court from time to time and a large number of orders had been passed by the courts to redress the grievances of the oustees. When the decision was taken to raise the height of the dam, NBA filed Writ Petition No. 4457 of 2007 before the High Court seeking a number of reliefs, inter alia, to stop all eviction; directions for serving of life supplies such as drinking water and electricity; not to take any other coercive measures; to stop closure of the radial gates of Omkareshwar Dam above the crest level of EL 179.60 m and to stop the blocking of the sluice gates below the crest level, until all project affected families (hereinafter called 'PAFs') were rehabilitated as per the R&R Policy. Further reliefs sought included the issuance of appropriate directions for an assessment by the Grievance Redressal Authority (hereinafter called 'GRA') for Omkareshwar Project of the status of relief and rehabilitation of the oustees affected at full reservoir level (hereinafter called 'FRL') and backwater level (hereinafter called 'BWL') within a stipulated period.

(H) During the pendency of the writ petition in pursuance of the orders passed by the High Court from time to time, a large number of reports/interim reports were

> furnished by the authorities concerned. The High Court after considering the said reports and submissions advanced on behalf of the parties passed the impugned judgment and order dated 21-2-2008. The High Court issued a large number of directions as interim measures, including the direction for allotment of land in lieu of land acquired and to treat the major sons of the family, as independent families for the purpose of allotment of agricultural land. Hence, these appeals.
>
> * * *

The matter was argued by [NBA's counsel] at great length to impress upon the Court that the tenure-holders had been actually dispossessed long ago. This fact was denied by the State. It was only after considering the rival submissions on behalf of the parties that this Court thought it fit and appropriate to have a spot inspection report and then the District Judge, Indore, was asked to make a local inspection and submit the report. The report has been made after making an inspection of the area and recording statements of the tenure-holders in the presence of Shri Alok Agrawal, chief activist of NBA and thus, we accept the same. It is evident from the said report that statements made by the said respondent applicant in the Court, in this regard are factually incorrect and false. The Court has been entertaining this petition under the bona fide belief that NBA was espousing the grievance of inarticulate and illiterate poor farmers with all sincerity and thus, would not make any misleading statement. However, our belief stands fully belied. The respondent applicant made pleadings and advanced arguments without any basis only to secure unwarranted benefits to those tenure-holders. In the instant case it stands discredited totally in the eyes of this Court. This Court had been a little careful and cautious in this regard, which has exposed the true picture....

In view of the above, we reach the inescapable conclusion that NBA has not acted with a sense of responsibility and so far succeeded in securing favourable orders by misleading the Court. Such conduct cannot be approved. However, in a PIL, the Court has to strike a balance between the interests of the parties. The Court has to take into consideration the pitiable condition of the oustees, their poverty, inarticulateness, illiteracy, extent of backwardness, unawareness also. It is desirable that in future the Court must view any presentation by NBA with caution and care, insisting on proper pleadings, disclosure of full facts truly and fairly and in case it has any doubt, refuse to entertain NBA. However, considering the interests of the oustees, it may be desirable that the Court may appoint an *amicus curiae* to present their cause, if such a contingency arises....

We have been given to understand that on Narmada River, in the State of Madhya Pradesh, in all 29 major and minor projects are contemplated. Some of them have already been completed, but on account of stay order by the court/authority some projects could not be completed. It is unfortunate that in spite of the fact that a huge amount has been spent, yet no one is able to reap the fruits of investment. The State should take immediate steps to get the final verdict in such cases or stay vacated and start the project at the earliest....

NOTES AND QUESTIONS

1. As the last paragraph of the excerpt suggests, the Supreme Court continues to see dams as essential for economic progress with little room for debate.

2. In a part of the judgment that is not excerpted, the Supreme Court found that its May 2005 judgment[40] was incorrect in treating major sons as being separately entitled to allotment of land. The High Court decision directing allotment of land to every major son was consequently reversed. Examine the 2005 judgment and decide for yourself if the Supreme Court was justified in 2011 to label its previous decision '*per incuriam*'.

[40] *Narmada Bachao Andolan v Union of India* (2005) 4 SCC 32.

3. The Supreme Court's attack on the NBA was excessive and probably unjustified. Remember the great service rendered by NBA in conducting post-Independence India's largest non-violent protest movement that mobilized thousands of the most disadvantaged citizens who were seeking to exercise their constitutional rights. Contrast this movement with the extreme violence embraced by certain other groups also agitating for the marginalized and dispossessed.

4. The 'incorrect' statements by NBA that so troubled the court were in the context of the state having taken 'possession' of certain lands. The state appears to have taken 'symbolic' possession of the land and changed the name of the land holders in the revenue records to show NVDA. The oustees, with little choice, continued to occupy their lands and grow crops until they were physically ousted. The court faulted NBA for giving an impression that the oustees were physically removed from their lands, when they were in fact cultivating them.

5. In *State of Madhya Pradesh v Bheru Singh*,[41] the Supreme Court heard complaints of PAFs impacted by the Man Dam on a tributary of the Narmada River. Madhya Pradesh had a Grievance Redressal Authority (GRA) to resolve disputes and complaints with respect to implementation of the rehabilitation and resettlement (R&R) policy. Recognizing that the GRA may at times fall into error or overlook legitimate grievances, the court directed the state to constitute an appellate forum comprising a District Judge, an administrative member and a retired judge of the High Court as chair.

F. RIVER INTERLINKING

On 18 July 1994, the *Hindustan Times* carried a report on the severe pollution of the Yamuna as it passes Delhi. Noticing this report titled 'And Quiet Flows the *Maili* Yamuna',[42] the Supreme Court registered a *suo motu* Writ Petition No. 725 of 1994.[43] Eight years later, on the eve of Independence Day in 2002, President Dr A P J Abdul Kalam spoke of floods and droughts in different regions in the country and wondered whether this disparity could be reduced by joining India's rivers through a network of canals. The *amicus curiae* in the *Yamuna* case drew the Supreme Court's attention to the President's speech and received an encouraging judicial response on 16 September 2002:

> Based on the speech of the President on the Independence Day eve relating to the need of networking of the rivers because of the paradoxical phenomenon of flood in one part of the country while some other parts face drought at the same time, the present application is filed. It will be more appropriate to treat it as an independent public interest litigation with the cause-title—'*In re: Networking of Rivers v*—'. Amended cause-title be filed within a week.
>
> Issue notice returnable on 30-9-2002 to the respondents as well as to the Attorney General. Serve notice on the Standing Counsel of the respective States.[44]

At the next hearing, the court recorded a short submission with respect to Parliament's power to enact laws concerning: 'Regulation and development of inter-State rivers and river valleys to the extent to which such regulation and development under the control of the Union is

---

[41] (2012) 3 SCC 287.

[42] *Maili'* in the Hindi language means sullied.

[43] We deal with this case in the Water Pollution Control chapter. It bears an ungainly name: *News Item: 'Hindustan Times' A Q F M Yamuna* with reports at 1999 (5) SCALE 418, 2000 (1) SCALE 134, 2000 (1) SCALE 657, 2000 (3) SCALE 122 and 2009 (10) SCALE 464 and 2012 (3) SCALE 1. This case was transferred by the Supreme Court to the National Green Tribunal on 24 April 2017.

[44] *Networking of Rivers, In Re* (2012) 4 SCC 78.

declared by Parliament by law to be expedient in the public interest.'[45] The 30 September 2002 order reads:

> Learned *amicus curiae* has drawn our attention to Entry 56 List I of the Seventh Schedule to the Constitution and contends that the interlinking of the inter-State rivers can be done by Parliament and he further contends that even some of the States are now concerned about the phenomenon of drought in one part of the country, while there is flood in the other parts and disputes are arising amongst the egalitarian States relating to sharing of water. He submits that not only these disputes would come to an end but also the pollution levels in the rivers will be drastically decreased, once there is sufficient water in different rivers because of their interlinking.[46]

On 31 October 2002, the court gave the project a mighty heave through the order excerpted below:

NETWORKING OF RIVERS, IN RE

(2004) 11 SCC 360

> ORDER: Pursuant to the notice issued by this Court to all the States and the Union Territories in relation to the interlinking of the rivers, an affidavit has been filed by the Union of India and also by the State of Tamil Nadu. No other State or Union Territory has filed any affidavit and the presumption, therefore, clearly is that they do not oppose the prayer made in this writ petition and it must be regarded that there is a consensus amongst all of them that there should be interlinking of rivers in India....
>
> Along with [Tamil Nadu's] affidavit the perspective plan for implementation of inter-basin water transfer proposals prepared by the National Water Development Agency in May 2000 has been placed on record. We are distressed to note that milestone for the perspective plan indicated in the report of the agency shows that even though the pre-feasibility reports regarding the Peninsular and Himalayan Projects are already completed, the completion of the link projects ultimately will be by the year 2035 in respect of Peninsular Link Project and 2043 regarding Himalayan Link Project.
>
> It is difficult to appreciate that in this country with all the resources available to it, there will be a further delay of 43 years for completion of the project to which no State has any objection and whose necessity and desirability is recognised and acknowledged by the Union of India. The project will not only give relief to the drought-prone areas but will also be an effective flood-control measure and would be a form of water harvesting which is being rightly propagated by the Union of India and all the States.
>
> Learned Attorney General states that a more realistic view will be taken and a revised programme on completion would be drawn up and be presented to the Court. We do expect that the programme when drawn up would try and ensure that the link projects are completed within a reasonable time of not more than ten years. We say so because recently the National Highways Projects have been undertaken and the same are nearing completion and the interlinking of the rivers is complementary to the said project and the waterways which are so constructed will be of immense benefit to the country as a whole....

Displaying considerable prescience, the water resources expert Ramaswamy R Iyer conveyed his despair at this judicial initiative:

45 Entry 56, List I, Schedule VII, Constitution of India.

46 *Networking of Rivers, In Re* (2004) 11 SCC 363.

> The Supreme Court has decreed that the rivers of India shall be linked within 10 years. The usual response 'one does not know whether to laugh or to cry' would be inappropriate in this case, as one is not permitted to laugh at anything that the judges say except at their jokes if they make any; but presumably one is not precluded from crying in despair. An almost abandoned idea has been given fresh currency; a dubious idea has been given legitimacy; and a wild-goose chase has been not merely sanctioned but mandated.[47]

On 5 May 2003, the court was placated by the fresh timetable offered by the Union Government. With regard to the environmental impact assessment process, the court seemed to consider it a peripheral inconvenience, not a substantive input required to decide on whether the project should be undertaken at all:

> It seems that in the last about four months three meetings of the Task Force have been held on 6-1-2003, 27-3-2003 and 28-4-2003. In the last meeting the first action plan as per the government resolution was considered and adopted. Now as per Action Plan I the schedule for implementation is 10 years from the start. It stipulates that the work on the links can be started from 2007. It is envisaged to be completed by, say, end of 2016. Further, it envisages that the group of Task Force for interlinking rivers will examine the two schedules and is expected to arrive at a reasonable and predicable implementation schedule in due course. According to Action Plan I the said Task Force has laid emphasis on demonstrative value of starting work on a link or two, as soon as possible.
>
> The process of preparation of a detailed project report for an inter-basin link needs to cover also, detailed environmental impact assessment, environmental management plan and R&R plan for project-affected persons. We find no substance in the apprehension that the Task Force will not implement the law. We have also no doubt that in case the other experts in the field provide necessary inputs to the Task Force, it will give it due consideration if the same deserves.[48]

On 6 January 2004, the Supreme Court noted the progress:

> The Task Force for Interlinking of Rivers has filed a progress report which deals with various aspects. It, *inter alia*, mentions that interlinking of rivers has two major components i.e. Himalayan component (14 links) and Peninsular component (16 links). It further mentions that the former component i.e. Himalayan links require an understanding with neighbouring countries like Bhutan and Nepal. We hope that steps are being taken to have requisite discussions with the said countries. Regarding Peninsular link, the progress report records that in respect of two links: (1) Ken-Betwa link (U P and M P), and (2) Parbati-Kalisindh-Chambal link (M P and Rajasthan), quick implementation is feasible in respect of the first link. In respect of the first link, feasibility report is stated to be complete and the Central Water Commission has been asked to initiate steps for preparation of detailed project report. It is, however, not indicated as to when the said DPR is likely to be prepared. In respect of the second, the report notes that the National Water Development Agency has been directed to take necessary steps to prepare feasibility report by March 2004 so as to take action for preparation of DPR thereafter. It is stated by learned counsel appearing for the Union of India that in respect of these two links the State of Madhya Pradesh and the State of Rajasthan have given their consent and the discussions with the State of Uttar Pradesh are at an advanced stage and the feasibility report shall be prepared once the consent is received from the State of Uttar Pradesh.[49]

On 26 April 2004, the Supreme Court noted that negotiations were continuing between various States, that the detailed project report for the Ken-Betwa link would take 30 months

---

[47] Ramaswamy R Iyer, *Linking of Rivers: Judicial Activism or Error?* 37 Economic & Political Weekly 4595 (2002).

[48] *Networking of Rivers, In Re* (2012) 4 SCC 77.

[49] *Networking of Rivers, In Re* (2004) 11 SCC 359.

to complete and then asked the Union Government to file an affidavit on central legislation to cover the project.[50] On 30 August 2004, the court deferred consideration of the case and sought a progress report.[51] On 8 April 2005, the court directed that feasibility reports be put up on the government website so as to elicit views from environmentalists.[52] Finally, on 27 February 2012, close to a decade after it embarked on the enterprise, the Supreme Court rendered a lengthy final judgment. The short excerpt below captures a few of the themes and the notes that follow highlight other aspects of this extraordinary judicial foray.

NETWORKING OF RIVERS, IN RE
(2012) 4 SCC 51

SWATANTER KUMAR, J: [The judgment traces the history of the case and then turns to the responses of ten states that filed affidavits.]

While the States of Rajasthan, Gujarat and Tamil Nadu have supported the concept of interlinking of rivers, the State of Madhya Pradesh had stated that networking of rivers is a subject falling under the jurisdiction of the Central Government and the Central Government should consider the matter. The States of Karnataka, Bihar, Punjab, Assam and Sikkim have given their approval to the concept in principle, but with definite reservations i.e. a kind of qualified approval, arguing that the matters with regard to the environmental and financial implications, socio-economic and international aspects, such as inter-basin water transfer, need to be properly examined at the appropriate levels of the Government. For example, all the rivers in Bihar originate from Nepal and it may be necessary or desirable to take the consent of neighbouring countries, is a matter which would require consideration of the appropriate authority in the Central Government.

According to the State of Punjab, interlinking of rivers should be started only from water-surplus States to the States facing water deficit. The States of Assam, Sikkim and Kerala had raised their protests on the grounds that they should have exclusive right to use their water resources and that such transfer should not affect any rights of these States. The State of Sikkim was concerned with particular reference to tapping of the hydropower potential in the State and the State of Kerala entirely objected to long-distance, inter-basin, water transfer.

The Union of India filed three different affidavits dated 25-10-2002, 5-5-2003 and 24-12-2003. From these affidavits, the stand of the Union of India appears to be that networking of rivers had been considered with great seriousness even after the 1972 Rao Committee Report. Surveys and studies were underway. The 1980 National Perspective Plan of the erstwhile Ministry of Irrigation, presently the Ministry for Water Resources, envisaged inter-basin transfer from water-surplus to deficit areas. It would have direct benefits, like the irrigation of 35 million hectares (Mha), full exploitation of existing irrigation projects of 140 Mha, power generation of 34 million kilowatt (KW); besides the indirect benefits like flood control, navigation, water supply, fisheries, pollution control, recreation facilities, employment generation, infrastructure and socio-economic development, etc.

With regard to the approvals required, it is submitted that the Ministry of Environment and Forests, Union of India had given some clearances, while refusing the same in other cases. The consent of some of the States had not been received. The expected financial implication as far back as in 2002 was Rs 5,60,000 crores.

However, the Union of India has submitted that there is no necessity for formation of a High-Powered Committee as prayed for in the petitions. [The judgment referred to the stand of the Union Government and noted that various bodies such as a High-Level Task Force,

50 *Id.* at 358.
51 *Networking of Rivers, In Re* (2012) 4 SCC 76.
52 *Id.* at 874.

the National Water Development Agency (NWDA), Standing Committee of Parliament had examined aspects of the interlinking project and prepared reports.]

One aspect that needs to be noticed is that, till today, no minor or major project has been actually implemented at the ground level despite the fact that this case has been pending before this Court for more than ten years. Only the DPR of the Ken-Betwa link has been prepared and its implementation is awaiting the approval of the State Governments as well as the allocation of funds, even to begin the work. This does not speak well of the desire on the part of any of the Governments concerned to implement these projects, despite the fact that there is unanimity of views among all that this project is in the national interest.

The Committee of Environmentalists, Social Scientists and Other Experts on interlinking of rivers had met after the submission of the status report dated 5-3-2010. They discussed various aspects of different projects. In the Himalayan region, FRs [Feasibility Reports] of two remaining links were completed i.e. the Sarda-Yamuna link and the Ghagra-Yamuna link. The field survey and investigation for Sone Dam on the southern tributaries of the Ganga link, was still in progress. The Ministry of Environment and Forests had refused permission for survey and investigation of the Manas-Sankosh-Tista-Ganga link, but the toposheet study for the alternative Jogigopa-Tista-Farakka link has been completed. In the peninsular region, the projects relating to Bedti-Varada and Netravati-Hemavati-Tapi are awaiting Karnataka Government's consent. In Netravati-Hemavati-Tapi link, the Karnataka Government has refused to consent even to the preparation of FR until the decision of related cases, pending in the courts.

[The court surveyed various implementation challenges but remarked: 'From the above, it is not difficult to visualise the difficulties in preparation, execution, financing and consensus building, still, it is the need of the hour to carry out these projects more effectively and with greater sensitivity.' The judgment thereafter sets out economic aspects of the project, drawing on reports of the National Council for Applied Economic Research (NCAER). The judgment cites the benefits of the Bhakra Dam in boosting the economy of the states of Punjab and Haryana relative to rest of the country.]

From the above-narrated facts, stated recommendations and principles, it is clear that primarily there is unanimity between all authorities concerned including the Centre and a majority of the State Governments, with the exception of one or two, that implementation of river linking will be very beneficial. In fact, the expert opinions convincingly dispel all other impressions. There shall be greater growth in agricultural and allied sectors, prosperity and stimulus to the economy potentially causing increase in per capita income, in addition to the short and long-term benefits likely to accrue by such implementation. These would accrue if the expert recommendations are implemented properly and within a time-frame. Then there shall be hardly any financial strain on the economy. On the contrary, such implementation would help advancement of India's GDP and bring greater wealth and prosperity to the nation as a whole. Besides actual benefits accruing to the common man, the Governments also benefit from the definite possibility of saving the States from drought on the one hand and floods on the other. This project, when it becomes a reality, will provide immeasurable benefits.

We see no reason as to why the Governments should not take appropriate and timely interest in the execution of this project, particularly when, in the various affidavits filed by the Central and the State Governments, it has been affirmed that the Governments are very keen to implement this project with great sincerity and effectiveness. [The court thereafter noted the objections of certain states to inter-basin water transfers and had this to say: 'Be that as it may, we have no hesitation in observing that the national interest must take precedence over the interest of the individual States. The State Governments are expected to view national problems with a greater objectivity, rationality and spirit of service to the nation and ill-founded objections may result in greater harm, not only to the neighbouring States but also to the nation at large.' The court then turned to certain constitutional provisions.]

The above-stated principles clearly show that a greater element of mutuality and consensus needs to be built between the States and the Centre on the one hand, and the States inter se on the other. It will be very difficult for the courts to undertake such an exercise within the limited scope of its power of judicial review and even on the basis of expanded principles of public interest litigation. A public interest litigation before this Court has to fall within the contours of constitutional law, as no jurisdiction is wider than this Court's constitutional jurisdiction under Article 32 of the Constitution. The Court can hardly take unto itself tasks of making of a policy decision or planning for the country or determining economic factors or other crucial aspects like need for acquisition and construction of river linking channels under that programme. The Court is not equipped to take such expert decisions and they essentially should be left for the Central Government and the State concerned. Such an attempt by the Court may amount to the Court sitting in judgment over the opinions of the experts in the respective fields, without any tools and expertise at its disposal.

The requirements in the present case have different dimensions. The planning, acquisition, financing, pricing, civil construction and environmental issues involved are policy decisions affecting the legislative competence and would squarely fall in the domain of the Government of States and Centre. We certainly should not be understood to even imply that the proposed projects of interlinking of rivers should not be completed.

We would recommend, with all the judicial authority at our command, that these projects are in the national interest, as is the unanimous view of all experts, most State Governments and particularly, the Central Government. But this Court may not be a very appropriate forum for planning and implementation of such a programme having wide national dimensions and ramifications. It will not only be desirable, but also inevitable that an appropriate body should be created to plan, construct and implement this Interlinking of Rivers Programme for the benefit of the nation as a whole.

Realising our limitations, we would finally dispose of this public interest litigation with the following directions:

1. We direct the Union of India and particularly the Ministry of Water Resources, Government of India, to forthwith constitute a committee to be called 'Special Committee for Interlinking of Rivers' (hereinafter referred as 'the Committee') of which, the following shall be the members:
   (a) The Hon'ble Minister for Water Resources.
   (b) Secretary, Ministry for Water Resources.
   (c) Secretary, Ministry of Environment and Forests.
   (d) Chairman, Central Water Commission.
   (e) Member-Secretary, National Water Development Authority.
   (f) Four experts to be nominated, one each from the following Ministries/bodies:
      (i) One expert from the Ministry of Water Resources.
      (ii) One expert from the Ministry of Finance.
      (iii) One expert from the Planning Commission.
      (iv) One expert from the Ministry of Environment and Forests.
   (g) Minister for Water and/or Irrigation from each of the concurring States, with the Principal Secretary of the Department concerned of the same State.
   (h) The Chief Secretary or his nominee not below the rank of the Principal Secretary of the Department concerned in case of any other State involved directly or indirectly in the river water linking project.
   (i) Two social activists to be nominated by each of the Ministries concerned.
   (j) [The *Amicus Curiae*].

[The court issued further directions on the periodicity of committee meetings, a requirement for the committee to submit biannual reports to the Cabinet, a direction to the committee to take up for implementation the Ken-Betwa project 'at the first instance itself'.]

2. There are projects where the paper work has been going on for the last ten years and at substantial cost to the public exchequer. Therefore, we direct the Central and the State

Governments to participate in the programme and render all financial, administrative and executive help to complete these projects more effectively.
3. It is evident from the record that the reports submitted by the Task Force have not been acted upon. Thus, the entire effort put in by the Task Force has practically been of no use to the Governments concerned, much less the public. The Task Force has now been wound up. Let the reports of the Task Force also be placed before the Committee which shall, without fail, take due note of the suggestions made therein and take decisions as to how the same are to be implemented for the benefit of the public at large.
4. The Committee constituted under this order shall be responsible for carrying out the interlinking programme. Its decisions shall take precedence over all administrative bodies created under the orders of this Court or otherwise.
5. We grant liberty to the learned *amicus curiae* to file contempt petition in this Court, in the event of default or non-compliance with the directions contained in this order....

We not only express a pious hope of speedy implementation but also do hereby issue a mandamus to the Central and the State Governments concerned to comply with the directions contained in this judgment effectively and expeditiously and without default. This is a matter of national benefit and progress. We see no reason why any State should lag behind in contributing its bit to bring the Interlinking of Rivers Programme to a success, thus saving the people living in drought-prone zones from hunger and people living in flood-prone areas from the destruction caused by floods....

NOTES AND QUESTIONS

1. The judgment excerpted above was rendered in the *suo moto* case as well as in a writ petition filed in 2002 by K S Radhakrishnan, a lawyer activist. Radhakrishnan's previous efforts on similar issues failed before the Madras High Court in 1983 and the Supreme Court in 1998. Nevertheless, he persisted and asked for the following relief in his 2002 case:

(a) Issue an appropriate writ, order or direction, more particularly a writ in the nature of mandamus directing Respondent No. 1[53] to take appropriate steps/action to nationalise all the rivers in the country.
(b) Issue an appropriate writ, order or direction, more particularly a writ in the nature of mandamus, directing Respondent No. 1 to take appropriate steps/action to interlink the rivers in the southern peninsula, namely, Ganga, Kaveri, Vaigai and Thamirabarani.
(c) Issue an appropriate writ, order or direction in the nature of mandamus directing the respondents to formulate a scheme whereby the water from the west-flowing rivers could be channelised and equitably distributed.

Are any of these prayers capable of being granted? Should the petition have been dismissed at the threshold? Would any conventionally trained lawyer draft such a petition? Is it time we discarded orthodox notions of what a party may seek from a writ court?

2. In constituting an oversight committee with the Union Minister for Water Resources at the helm and by strongly endorsing the project, did the Supreme Court step beyond its realm of expertise? Notice that the judgment does pay lip service to judicial restraint, but thereafter virtually mandates the river interlinking project. Given the tone of the judgment and the

53 Respondent No. 1 was the Union of India.

obvious preference of the Supreme Court, will any authority be able to independently and objectively evaluate the project on environmental, technical and sociological grounds?

3. When it came to exercising judicial review over the Sardar Sarovar project on the Narmada River, the court in the year 2000 held that construction of a dam was a policy decision and the court would not investigate those areas which are the function of the executive.[54] The interlinking of rivers project (though still on the drawing board) is far bigger and more complex in every respect than the project in the *Narmada* case. Can you reconcile the two judgments? Is there any factor that explains the divergence—apart from the Supreme Court itself having kick-started one enterprise?

4. Inter-basin transfers of water generally involve more than one state. Was it correct on the part of the Supreme Court to discount objections by states such as Kerala? Does the judgment dilute state sovereignty under the Constitution and the principle of federalism?

5. This Supreme Court judgment is by some measures the worst in the court's history. It could severely compromise the ecological integrity of the sub-continent, disrupt wildlife habitats, displace tens of thousands of families residing along the alignment of the link canals and reservoirs and stifle objective appraisals of costs and benefits. With the Supreme Court's advance ruling, the project must be implemented, come what may. Hereafter, will any subordinate authority such as the National Green Tribunal rule against the project?

How environmentally myopic can the Supreme Court get?

6. The judgment ignores climate change impacts that are projected to alter precipitation patterns and raise temperatures across the sub-continent. How might climate change destroy the premise of the project?

7. Do you agree with the court's decision to constitute an oversight committee? Revisit its composition: what is the *amicus curiae* doing on the committee? Note that the committee's decisions take precedence over all administrative bodies, upending the doctrine of separation of powers.

In a devastating critique, Ramaswamy R Iyer punctured the judgment: 'This is a deeply disquieting judgment because it (1) is a clear encroachment into the executive domain, (2) shows an inadequate awareness of the extensive debate on the project, and (3) provides a strong backing to a 'project' that many hold to be fundamentally flawed and potentially disastrous.'[55] In 2014, he renewed his call for a rational debate in the article excerpted below:

RAMASWAMY R IYER: INTERLINKING OF RIVERS: A PLEA TO THE GOVERNMENT, 49 Economic & Political Weekly 16 (2014)

Rationale of the Project

There are some basic flaws in the very idea of interlinking of rivers:

(a) Instead of exploring local and intra basin answers to the needs of water-scarce areas in Rajasthan, Madhya Pradesh, Maharashtra, Karnataka, Andhra Pradesh and Tamil Nadu, and considering whether there is a need for bringing in water from outside, the project inverts that logical sequence, looks at a map of India, decides a priori that the rivers of

---

[54] *Narmada Bachao Andolan v Union of India* (2000) 10 SCC 664.

[55] Ramaswamy R Iyer, *River Linking Project: A Disquieting Judgment* 47 Economic & Political Weekly 33 (2012).

India can and should be linked, and then proceeds to consider the modalities of doing so. In other words, instead of proceeding from felt needs upwards the project proceeds from a macro concept downwards.

(b) References are made to a 'national water grid' on the analogy of a power grid or the linking of highways. The analogy is inapt and misleading. In a power grid or a highway-link, the movement can be in both directions, but that is not the case with a river-link; water will flow only in one direction. Moreover, highways and power lines are human creations and can be manipulated by humans. Rivers are not human artefacts; they are natural phenomena, integral components of ecological systems, and inextricable parts of the cultural, social, economic and spiritual lives of the communities concerned. They are not pipelines to be cut, turned around, welded and rejoined. Further, the project is in essence an attempt to redesign the geography of the country.

(c) The idea of transferring flood waters from flood-prone areas to drought-prone or arid areas, thus moderating floods in the former areas and providing some water to the latter, is fallacious. A significant moderation of floods will call for a massive diversion of flood waters which may not be feasible at all, or if technically feasible, it may have serious impacts. On the other hand, if only small fractions of the flood flows are to be diverted (as seems to be the intention), there will be hardly any flood moderation. Even if all the river-linking proposals are implemented, the contribution that this will make to the mitigation of the flood problem will not be substantial. The late Bharat Singh, former vice chancellor of the University of Roorkee, and member of the National Commission for Integrated Water Resources Development Plan (1996–99), had observed in an article in 2003 categorically that 'any water resources engineer will immediately discard the idea of the inter-linking of rivers as a flood control measure'.

(d) As for the provision of water to drought-prone areas, the proposed river links (reportedly mainly by gravity, with a few modest lifts) are no answer to drought-prone areas. Linking a river to another will merely provide additional water to areas already served by rivers. Most of the uplands and dry lands of this country are distant from rivers, and at elevations of 300 m to 1,000 m above mean sea level. The ILR will serve very few such areas. Fortunately, no such long distance transfer is necessary. There are several well-known examples of the transformation that can be brought about through local rainwater-harvesting and watershed development even in low rainfall areas. In brief, the primary answer to drought has to be local; it is only thereafter, and in some very unpromising places where rainwater-harvesting may not be feasible or may yield meagre results, that the bringing in of some external water may need to be considered.

(e) Another fallacious idea behind the project is that of transfers from surplus to deficit basins. Scholars have pointed out the highly problematic nature of the notions of 'surplus' and 'deficit' rivers.... We cannot determine the surplus in a basin by comparing the flow in the river with the aggregate of requirements for domestic, municipal, industrial and agricultural uses. The river also serves many other purposes as it flows. For instance it supports aquatic life and vegetation; provides drinking water to human beings, their livestock and wildlife; influences the micro-climate; recharges groundwater; dilutes pollutants and purifies itself; sustains a wide range of livelihoods; transports silt and enriches the soil; maintains the estuary in a good state; provides the necessary freshwater to the sea to keep its salinity at the right level; prevents the incursion of salinity from the sea; provides nutrients to marine life; and so on. The river is also an integral part of human settlements, their lives, landscape, society, culture, history and religion. It follows that any diversion of waters from a river, however small, is bound to have some consequences, major or minor. This makes it very difficult to estimate the 'surplus', if any, in the river. In fact, the term surplus is meaningless in the hydrological/ecological context (surplus over what?) and must be abandoned. The term deficit is equally inappropriate. The flow in the river is what it is, neither surplus nor deficit; we, with our excessive 'demand', call it 'deficit'. Leaving that aside, it will be necessary to examine whether a projected deficit is in fact the result of bad water management and unsustainable demands. If it is, the deficit will disappear with better water management. Careful, economical and sustainable intra-basin management should come first, and bringing water from elsewhere should be the last recourse. Moreover, even in the states that are presumed to be water-rich (eg, Bihar, Odisha, Andhra Pradesh) there are problem areas, and their needs should be met before sending the water to distant places.

(f) Turning to water transfer for irrigation, which is in fact the main driving force behind the project, difficult questions arise. In irrigated areas, the question is whether large demands for additional irrigation water should be unquestioningly accepted and met through supply-side solutions such as large dams or inter-basin transfers. Should not serious attempts be made to improve water use efficiency in irrigated agriculture, get more value out of a given quantum of water, reduce the water-demand, and minimise the need for supply-side projects? In the context of the prevailing low efficiency of water-conveyance in canal systems and water-use in irrigated agriculture, bringing in more water from another basin would really amount to the provision of more water to be wasted. In arid or drought-prone areas, the introduction of irrigated agriculture of a kind appropriate to wet areas may be unwise. Development in arid areas should perhaps take other, less water-intensive forms.

(g) It must also be remembered that long-distance water transfers will entail losses en route, and also make the delivered cost of water at the destination so high as to render it irrecoverable from any category of user.

(h) A supplementary justification offered for the project is that there will be a net generation of electric power (of upwards of 30,000 MW). This seems very questionable and in need of careful examination, but it is a secondary aspect that need not be gone into here. Thus, the rationale of the project is extremely weak. To put it bluntly, it does not have a leg to stand on.

Features and Implications

Let us consider next the features and implications of the project.

(a) It has been claimed that the flows will be largely by gravity with lifts (not exceeding 120 m) at a few selected points, and that the need for a transfer of water through natural barriers between basins will be obviated. If indeed the links are to be largely by gravity with a few modest lifts, will not such an approach limit the extent of water transfers and the scope of the project? Can large claims still be made for the project? There seems to be a dilemma here: if we want an ambitious project we must go in for massive lifts and incur the related costs and risks of gigantism; alternatively, we must content ourselves with a modest project, in which case, the tall claims made for it will have to be abandoned.

(b) The project (i.e. the grand design consisting of 30 projects) will be a major intervention in nature and is potentially fraught with serious consequences. It will necessarily involve a large number of dams (upwards of 80), reservoirs, diversion of waters, canal systems, and so on. What a dam does to a river is a familiar story, and it is not necessary to repeat it here. However, one point must be mentioned, namely, that before diverting waters and reducing downstream flows we must make sure that disaster will not follow. It is well known that river-diversions by the former Soviet Union led to the virtual death of the Aral Sea. That cautionary example should not be forgotten. It is surely not necessary for India to relearn that lesson by actual experience.

(c) Each of the 80+ dams will have environmental and ecological consequences, and many of them may involve significant social impacts, such as the displacement of people and their livestock, necessitating elaborate resettlement and rehabilitation programmes. In each case, financial/economic analyses, and environmental, ecological, and social impact assessments will have to be undertaken. We cannot know in advance how many will pass muster and how many will fail, and we cannot know the total cost of the project and the budgetary implications. In advance of such a dam-by-dam examination and appraisal, how can a decision about the total project be taken, and implementation begun? After an advance announcement of the grand design at the highest levels, is it likely that the individual components of that grand design will be subjected to rigorous examination?

(d) Consider the potential for conflicts. We have not so far been notably successful in persuading states *within* a basin to share river waters without disputes; instead of resolving such *intra-basin* disputes through the better, more economical and more cooperative management of the resources of the basin, should we try to bring water from another and more distant basin? Further, even if we assume that the conflict within a 'watershort' river-basin will be eased by the importation of external water, such an effort may initiate new conflicts *between* basins. Is it a good idea to resolve an intra-basin inter-state dispute by creating an inter-basin dispute?

(e) Incidentally, there is already much concern in the north-east about the large number of hydroelectric projects that are proposed to be undertaken on the rivers in that area. The ILR project will accentuate the anxiety of the people there. The sensitivities of the north-eastern states must be kept in mind. It seems hardly necessary to add one more element of discord in an already difficult situation.

International Aspects

(a) When the project was initially announced, there were serious apprehensions in Nepal and Bangladesh about its implications for them. Those anxieties were muted by the Government of India's assurance that for the time being only the peninsular rivers would be considered, and that before taking up the Himalayan component, there will be consultations with Nepal and Bangladesh. In any case, the project seemed to be in the doldrums, and Nepal and Bangladesh ceased to worry too much about it. However, the Supreme Court's judgment of February 2012 has revived their anxieties.

(b) It must also be noted that the Ganges Water-Sharing Treaty (1996) with Bangladesh lays upon India the obligation of ensuring that the flows arriving at Farakka (the sharing point) are not diminished (on a 40-year average basis). The consistency of the ILR project with that treaty obligation needs to be examined. Further, it is common ground between India and Bangladesh that the Ganga is water-short and that its flows need to be augmented in some manner. Is a proposal to divert water from the Ganga consistent with that understanding? … One knows that the Supreme Court has, in an act of judicial error and excess, directed the Government of India to implement the project. However, if the government is convinced that it would be wrong to do so, it can and must say so to the Supreme Court.

Disaster beckons: let us pull back from the brink.

NOTES AND QUESTIONS

1. The international dimensions of the river interlinking project are examined in the Transboundary Environmental Issues chapter.

2. Are the following observations of Justice Jasti Chelameswar, in his dissent in the *NJAC* case,[56] relevant to the approach of the court in *Networking of Rivers* case?

> We the members of the judiciary exult and frolic in our emancipation from the other two organs of the State. But have we developed an alternate constitutional morality to emancipate us from the theory of checks and balances, robust enough to keep us in control from abusing such independence? Have we acquired independence greater than our intelligence, maturity and nature could digest?[57]

[56] *Supreme Court Advocates-on-Record Association v Union of India* (2016) 5 SCC 1. In the *NJAC* case, a Constitution bench by a majority struck down the Constitution (Ninety-Ninth Amendment) Act of 2014 regarding the establishment of a National Judicial Appointments Commission.

[57] *Id.* at 740.

G. POWER PROJECTS

I. NUCLEAR

Located close to the southern tip of the Indian peninsula, Kudankulam lies at the edge of the Gulf of Mannar, which separates India from the western shores of Sri Lanka. The Gulf of Mannar is rich in marine life with over a hundred species of coral. It is home to sea turtles, sharks, dugongs and dolphins.[58] Kudankulam was the subject of a vigorous contest between local communities and India's nuclear establishment that culminated in a Supreme Court judgment.

As part of its national policy to harness nuclear energy for development needs, India passed the Atomic Energy Act in 1962. Thereafter in 1983, the government constituted the Atomic Energy Regulatory Board (AERB) to ensure public safety. Keen to establish a nuclear power plant (NPP) in the southern part of the country, a site selection committee constituted by the Department of Atomic Energy (DAE) picked Kudankulam as the most suitable location. The nuclear power plant at Kudankulam (KKNPP) was initially to be comprised of two units. On 25 February 1988, the Committee on Conservation of Seashore, State of Tamil Nadu approved the site and, in December of that year, the Tamil Nadu State Environmental Committee also cleared the project. Meanwhile, in November 1988, India and the erstwhile USSR entered into an agreement to establish KKNPP. This agreement was followed by a supplementary agreement on 21 June 1998 between India and Russia with respect to the same project.

On 19 April 1989, Prime Minister Rajiv Gandhi exempted the project from the 500 m 'no construction' administrative norm prevalent at that time in respect of coastal development. On 9 May 1989, the MoEF granted an environmental clearance. Land for the project was acquired between 1991 and 1993 and pre-project activities such as construction of boundary walls, roads and certain buildings commenced. By August 2001, over Rs. 377 crores had been spent for KKNPP on various activities.

On 31 August 2001, the Director of MoEF found that the land acquisition was completed and the township, environment and health research centre and other facilities were being put up. Construction of the NPP began on 31 March 2002. On 23 September 2008 and 31 December 2012, environmental clearances were issued for units 3–4 and 5–6, respectively, under the EIA notification of 2006. On 28 August 2012, the Tamil Nadu Pollution Control Board accorded consent to operate KKNPP units 1 and 2.

Meanwhile, catastrophe hit Japan. On 11 March 2011, following the undersea Tohoku earthquake, a series of tsunamis hit Japan's eastern shores. The Fukushima NPP was impacted by the tidal waves and went through a series of nuclear meltdowns, triggering massive discharges of radioactive material affecting several thousand people. For a society with a long track record for nuclear safety, Fukushima was a colossal calamity. Not only Japan, but the world was reminded about the enormous dangers and risks posed by NPPs.

Immediately after the Fukushima accident, the AERB constituted a high level committee of specialists to review all safety aspects. The Expert Committee in its final report dated 1 August 2011, made 17 safety recommendations.

---

[58] In recognition of the high diversity of marine life, India has established the Gulf of Mannar Marine National Park (560 sq kms) within a much larger Biosphere Reserve covering 10,500 sq kms.

The disaster sparked a wave of anti-nuclear power protests around the world. The similarities between Kudankulam and Fukushima, including the coastal location, proximity to fault lines and the possibility of tsunami or other extreme weather disruptions became the focal points of a challenge to the KKNPP. Long troubled by the prospect of a gigantic NPP in their backyard, the Fukushima tragedy galvanized the fishing community and local residents to organize protests in the field and to challenge the project in writ petitions before the Madras High Court.

A division bench of the Madras High Court was satisfied that the safety standards employed at Kudankulam were at par with global standards and cleared the way for the operation of KKNPP.[59] Relying on a Japanese report that attributed the meltdown to human error and inadequate safety measures, the High Court distinguished the Fukushima disaster. The writ petitioners appealed to the Supreme Court. The petitioners claimed that NPPs violated the fundamental right to life guaranteed under Article 21 of the Constitution of India. In so far as KKNPP was concerned, the project deserved to be scrapped because its coastal location was unsuitable; the project violated the provisions of the EIA notifications as well as the coastal regulation zone (CRZ) notifications. Moreover, the project would have a devastating impact on the ecology in the Gulf of Mannar.

The Supreme Court rendered an extremely long and detailed judgment, carefully reviewing the safety aspects. We carry a short excerpt from the judgment.

G SUNDARRAJAN v UNION OF INDIA

(2013) 6 SCC 620

K S P RADHAKRISHNAN, J: Leave granted. We are in these appeals concerned with an issue of considerable national and international importance, pertaining to the setting up of a nuclear power plant in the south-eastern tip of India, at Kudankulam in the State of Tamil Nadu. The incidents occurred in Three Mile Island Power Plant, USA; Chernobyl, Ukraine, USSR; Fukushima, Japan; Union Carbide, Bhopal might be haunting the memory of the people living in and around Kudankulam, leading to large-scale agitation and emotional reaction to the setting up of the Nuclear Power Plant (NPP) and its commissioning. The nature of potential adverse effects of ionising radiation, adds to fears and unrest which might not have been even thought of by Enrico Fermi, a Nobel Laureate in Physics in 1938, who was responsible for the setting up of the first nuclear reactor in a doubles squash court at Stagg Field, at Chicago University, USA. Since then, it is history, India has now 20 nuclear reactors, in place, and the world over about 439, but people still react emotionally, for more reasons than one, when a new one is being established. . . .

As a sequel to that national policy [to develop, control and use atomic energy for the welfare of the people of India], the Central Government, with the active cooperation of Atomic Energy Commission (AEC), Bhaba Atomic Research Centre (BARC), Nuclear Power Corporation of India Limited (NPCIL), AERB, etc., have already set up about twenty operating power reactors in the country with installed nuclear capacity of 4780 MWe, which have been commissioned over the last four decades from the years 1969 to 2011. Seven more units with a capacity of 5300 MWe are under construction (commissioning). The latest one to be commissioned is at Kudankulam in the State of Tamil Nadu. The first Nuclear Power Plant (NPP) in the country, Tarapur Atomic Power Station (TAPS) Units 1 and 2, based on boiling water reactors (BWR), was supplied by General Electric USA and became operational in the year 1969. Rajasthan Atomic Power Stations (RAPS) 1 and 2 with two units of 200 MWe were established in 1970s at Rawatbhata in Rajasthan with the technical cooperation of AECL (Canada). Later, in 1980s two units of 220 MWe Pressurised Heavy Water

[59] *G Sundarrajan v Union of India* (2012) 6 MAD L J 529.

Reactors (PHWRs), Madras Atomic Power Stations 1 and 2 were constructed at Kalpakkam in Tamil Nadu. Later, India developed a standardised design of 220 MWe PHWRs. Four reactors of that standardised design were built, two each at Narora in Uttar Pradesh (Narora Atomic Power Stations 1 and 2) and Kakrapar in Gujarat (Kakrapar Atomic Power Project 1 and 2). Those plants became operational in 1990s. Later eight more units of standardised 220 MWe PHWRs were built, four each at Kaiga in Karnataka (Kaiga Generating Station Units 1–4) and Rawatbhata in Rajasthan (RAPS Units 3–6). India in 1990s undertook the design and development of 540 MWe PHWR. Two reactors based on that design became operational in 2005–2006 at Tarapur. India has also developed 700 MWe design with limited boiling in the coolant channels. The construction of four such units was almost completed at Kakrapar and Rawatbhata sites. Currently, 500 MWe Prototype Fast Breeder Reactor (PFBR) is under construction at Kalpakkam. PFBR is built with the design and technology developed at Indira Gandhi Centre for Atomic Research (IGCAR). Over and above, India has now set up two PHWRs of Water-Water Energetic Reactor (VVER) based NPPs (2 × 1000 MWe) at Kudankulam in Tamil Nadu with the cooperation of Russian Federation which is the subject-matter of this litigation.

India draws bulk of its electricity, above 64%, from thermal sources, especially coal. Hydropower comes second at 18% and then renewable sources provide small share at about 15%. We are informed that, at present, the share of nuclear energy is hardly 3% of India's total electricity production, while France accounts for 74.6% as in 2008. NPPs provide about 6% of the world's energy and 13%–14% of the world's electricity with US, France and Japan together accounting for about 50% of nuclear generated electricity. USA has 104 nuclear reactors and more than 1,00,000 MWe of electricity is produced by nuclear generation. International Atomic Energy Agency (IAEA) has reported that in the year 2007, there were 439 nuclear power reactors in operation in the world operating in thirty-one countries. DAE, it is reported, plans to increase its nuclear energy production to 20,000 MWe by 2020 and 63,000 by 2030.

The policy-makers consider that the nuclear energy remains as an important element in India's energy mix for sustaining economic growth of natural and domestic use. One of the reasons for preferring nuclear energy as an alternative source of energy is that it is a clean, safe, reliable and competitive energy source which can replace a significant part of the fossil fuels like coal, oil, gas, etc. Oil and natural gas resources might exhaust themselves. Coal is also not an effective substitution since forests are also no longer able to satisfy the energy requirements. Major source of electricity generation, about 66%, is still contributed by fossil thermal powers, like coal. To put into practice the national policy, India has already entered into various collaborations with most of the developed countries which have proved expertise and experience in the field of establishment and production of nuclear energy.

Economic growth and energy support have to go hand in hand, for the country's development for which India has entered into various collaboration agreements with USA, Canada, Russia, etc. and several NPPs have already been set up in the country. The Government of India, in implementation of its national policy, had made a joint statement with USA, called Indo-US Joint Statement, 2005, for a renewed global civil nuclear energy cooperation. A cooperation agreement called the 2007 Cooperation Agreement was also entered into between India and USA for the peaceful uses of nuclear energy. This was later followed by the Indo-France Joint Statement in September 2008. A joint statement was made in February 2010 with the United Kingdom. Above facts would indicate that in order to give effect to the national policy for development, control and use of atomic energy, India has entered into various bilateral treaties and arrangements with countries which have considerable expertise and experience. For establishing NPP at Kudankulam, India had entered into an inter-Governmental agreement with the erstwhile USSR in November 1988 followed by a supplementary agreement on 21-6-1998 signed by India and Russia which is in tune with India's national policy.

* * *

The Government of India's decision to establish NPP at Kudankulam, as already stated, cannot be questioned before this Court being part of a national policy. Lot of scientific literatures, expert opinions, etc. have been produced before us to show its dangers, harm it may cause to human health, environment, marine life and so on not only on the present generation but on future generation as well. Further, it was also pointed out that due to growing nuclear accidents and the resultant ecological and other dangers, many countries have started retreating from their forward nuclear programmes.

We have already indicated that these issues are to be addressed to the policy-makers and not to the courts because the destiny of a nation is shaped by the people's representatives and not by a handful of Judges, unless there is an attempt to tamper with the fundamental constitutional principles or basic structure of the Constitution.

We are, however, deeply concerned with the safety and security of the people of this country, its environment, its flora and fauna, its marine life, ecology, biodiversity and so on which the policy-makers cannot, in the guise of national policy, mutilate or rob: in such an event the courts can unveil the mask and find out the truth for the safety, security and welfare of the people and the mother earth....

We are convinced that KKNPP design incorporates advanced safety features complying with the current standards of redundancy, reliability, independence and prevention of common cause failures in its safety systems. Design also takes care of anticipated operational occurrences (AOO), design basis accidents (DBA) and beyond design basis accidents (BDBA) like station blackout (SBO), anticipated transients without scram (ATWS), metal water reaction in the water core and provision of core-catcher to take care of core degradation. The design also includes the provisions for withstanding external events like earthquake, tsunami/storm, tidal waves, cyclones, shock waves, aircraft impact on main buildings and fire. The 17 recommendations were made after the Fukushima accident, the cause of which is a natural phenomenon. The facts would indicate that tsunamigenic zone along the east coast of India is more than 1300 km away from the nearest NPP site (Madras/Kalpakkam) and about 1000 km away from Kudankulam. The possibility of hitting tsunami at Kudankulam, as the one that hit Fukushima, seems to be very remote....

Much hue and cry has been raised by some sections of the people about the possible impact of radiation from KKNPP Units 1 and 2, a point which has been addressed by AERB, NPCIL, MoEF and all the Expert Committees constituted to go into the impact and effect of radiation from the units not only on humans but also on ecology. The Experts Committees are of the unanimous opinion that there will not be any deleterious effects due to radiation from the operation of KKNPP, and that adequate safety measures have already been taken. We cannot forget that there are many potential areas of radiation reflected in many uses of radioactive materials. Radioactive materials are used in hospitals, surgeries and so on. Mobile phone use, though minor, also causes radiation. In a report of the Department of Telecommunication 'Mobile Communication—Radio Wave and Safety' released in October 2012, it has been stated that a human body is exposed to more electromagnetic field radiation in case of a call from mobile phone in comparison to the radiation from a mobile tower.

We have, therefore, to balance 'economic scientific benefits' with that of 'minor radiological detriments' on the touchstone of our national nuclear policy. Economic benefit, we have already indicated has to be viewed on a larger canvas which not only augment our economic growth but alleviate poverty and generate more employment. NPCIL, while setting up the NPP at Kudankulam, have satisfied the environmental principles like sustainable development, corporate social responsibility, precautionary principle, inter-/intra-generational equity and so on to implement our National Policy to develop, control and use of atomic energy for the welfare of the people and for economic growth of the country. Larger public interest of the community should give way to individual apprehension of violation of human rights and right to life guaranteed under Article 21.

Public money running into crores and crores of rupees have already been spent for the development, control and use of atomic energy for the welfare of the people and hence, we have to put up with such 'minor inconveniences', 'minor radiological detriments' and 'minor environmental detriments' in our lives because the benefits we reap from KKNPP are enormous since nuclear energy remains as an important element in India's energy mix which can replace a significant part of fossil fuels like coal, gas oil, etc.

* * *

KKNPP has, therefore, been set up as part of India's national policy so as to develop, control and use of atomic energy for the welfare of the people of India. Policy-makers consider nuclear energy as an important element in India's energy mix for sustaining economic growth of natural and domestic use. For setting up the project, the project proponent has taken all safety requirements in site and off site and has followed the code of practices laid down by AERB, based on nationally and internationally recognised safety methods. Safeguarding the nuclear plants, radioactive materials and ensuring its physical security have become a central part of nuclear law. Adequate measures have, therefore, to be taken for storage of Nuclear Spent Fuel (NSF) at site, and also for the physical safety of stored NSF. Of the seventeen suggested safety measures, by AERB, ... twelve have already been implemented and the rest, in a phased manner have to be implemented which the experts say, are meant for extra security. DMP is already in place, so also the emergency preparedness plan, off site and on site and all programmes under Corporate Social Responsibility (CSR) are progressing in the right direction with the cooperation and assistance of the District Administration.

NPCIL, has also received necessary environmental clearance from MoEF, TNPCB, etc. for Units 1 to 6. No violation of CRZ is also noticed. Desalination plant is also established after following rules and regulations and there is no violation of CRZ. Experts say that there will be no impact on the marine ecosystem due to discharge of +7°C Condenser Cooling Water (CCW) over and above the ambient temperature of the sea. Radiation impact on the ecosystem is also within the standard set by AERB, MoEF, EAC, Pollution Control Board, etc., so opined by the experts. In other words, all the expert teams are unanimous in their opinion of the safety and security of KKNPP both to life and property of the people and the environment which includes marine life. The Court has to respect national nuclear policy of the country reflected in the Atomic Energy Act and the same has to be given effect to for the welfare of the people and the country's economic growth and it is with these objectives in mind that KKNPP has been set up.

* * *

We, therefore, fully endorse the view ... taken by the Division Bench of the High Court, however, in the facts and circumstances of the case, we are inclined to give the following directions:

(1) The plant should not be made operational unless AERB, NPCIL, DAE accord final clearance for commissioning of the plant ensuring the quality of various components and systems because their reliability is of vital importance.

(2) MoEF should oversee and monitor whether NPCIL is complying with the conditions laid down, while granting clearance vide its communication dated 23-9-2008 under the provisions of the EIA Notification of 2006, so also the conditions laid down in the environmental clearance granted by MoEF vide its communication dated 31-12-2009. AERB and MoEF will see that all the conditions stipulated by them are duly complied with before the plant is made operational.

(3) Maintaining safety is an ongoing process not only at the design level, but also during the operation for the nuclear plant. Safeguarding NPP, radioactive materials, ensuring physical security of NSF are of paramount importance. NPCIL, AERB, the regulatory authority, should maintain constant vigil and make periodical inspection of the plant at least once in three months and if any defect is noticed, the same has to be rectified forthwith.

(4) NPCIL shall send periodical reports to AERB and AERB shall take prompt action on those reports, if any fallacy is noticed in the reports.

(5) SNF generated needs to be managed in a safe manner to ensure protection of human health and environment from the undue effect of ionising radiation now and future,

for which sufficient surveillance and monitoring programme have to be evolved and implemented.

(6) AERB should periodically review the design-safety aspects of AFR feasibly at KKNPP so that there will be no adverse impact on the environment due to such storage which may also allay the fears and apprehensions expressed by the people.

(7) Deep Geological Repository (DGR) has to be set up at the earliest so that SNF could be transported from the nuclear plant to DGR. NPCIL says the same would be done within a period of five years. Effective steps should be taken by the Union of India, NPCIL, AERB, AEC, DAE, etc. to have a permanent DGR at the earliest so that apprehension voiced by the people of keeping NSF at the site of Kudankulam NPP could be dispelled.

(8) NPCIL should ensure that the radioactive discharges to the environmental aquatic atmosphere and terrestrial route shall not cross the limits prescribed by the regulatory body.

(9) The Union of India, AERB and NPCIL should take steps at the earliest to comply with rest of the seventeen recommendations, within the time stipulated in the affidavit filed by NPCIL on 3-12-2012.

(10) SNF is not being reprocessed at the site, which has to be transported to a reprocessing facility. Therefore, the management and transportation of SNF be carried out strictly by the Code of Practices laid down by AERB, following the norms and regulations laid down by IAEA.

(11) NPCIL, AERB and the State of Tamil Nadu should take adequate steps to implement the National Disaster Management Guidelines, 2009 and also carry out the periodical emergency exercises on and off site, with the support of the Ministries of the Government of India, Officials of the State Government and local authorities concerned.

(12) NPCIL, in association with the District Collector, Tiruneveli should take steps to discharge NPCIL corporate social responsibilities in accordance with the Department of Public Enterprises (DPE) Guidelines and there must be effective and proper monitoring and supervision of the various projects undertaken under CSR to the fullest benefit of the people who are residing in and around KKNPP.

(13) NPCIL and the State of Tamil Nadu, based on the comprehensive emergency preparedness plan should conduct training courses on site and off site, administer personnel, including the State Government officials and other stakeholders, including police, fire service, medicos, emergency services, etc.

(14) Endeavour should be made to withdraw all the criminal cases filed against the agitators so that peace and normalcy be restored at Kudankulam and nearby places and steps should be taken to educate the people of the necessity of the plant which is in the largest interest of the nation particularly the State of Tamil Nadu.

(15) AERB, NPCIL, MoEF and TNPCB would oversee each and every aspect of the matter, including the safety of the plant, impact on environment, quality of various components and systems in the plant before commissioning of the plant. A report to that effect be filed before this Court before commissioning of the plant....

NOTES AND QUESTIONS

1. In his concurring judgment, Justice Dipak Misra writes:

At the very inception, I may state that in the cases at hand, we are faced with a situation whether to interfere in the establishment, operation and functionalism of a nuclear plant coming up at Kudankulam and interdict its operation because of numerous grounds assiduously urged in voluminous pleadings encompassing the broad canvas, namely, statutory violations of the entire gamut of environmental law, exhibition of nonchalant attitude towards

> public opinion, show of total disrespect towards nature's inconsistencies, keeping at bay the constant apprehension and threat of the known and the unknown, absolute contempt for predictable danger that has surfaced on certain parts of the globe and the unpredictable disaster that may be faced by the populace of the locality and, most importantly, the public safety in *praesenti* and in *futuro*, or take cognizance of the needs and necessities of the public at large, the concept of public policy and the scope of judicial review, the precautions already undertaken and further assured to be taken within a specific time span, the opinion of the experts, the impossible avoidance of certain facets of existence in today's world, the global phenomena of requirement of electricity as a source of energy and various innovative methods to meet the same, the safety measures carried out and the steps undertaken to manage the disaster in case it occurs and finally to march ahead with life allaying all apprehensions with a scientific mindset accepting the nature's unpredictability to survive on the planet earth on the bedrock of the doctrine—survival of the fittest.[60]

Elsewhere, the judge records:

> The present generation has no right to enjoy by eating away the time of the future generation. The protection of the environment and the safety for the present generation in its connotative sense covers the posterity.[61]

Can you make sense of what is said? Should courts express themselves simply for the benefit of the public? Perhaps, as the judge later remarks in his judgment: 'The grammar has to be totally different.'[62]

2. Broadly, the court's analysis was in three parts. First, the court surveyed domestic and international safety standards regarding NPPs, and found that Kudankulam was meeting or exceeding the norms. Second, while acknowledging the danger inherent in NPPs despite precautionary measures, the court held that community apprehensions must yield to government policy. Third, the court used a balancing test to hold that the greater good of energy security for the whole of India outweighed the health and environmental concerns of the local community.

3. The KKNPP when fully operational will be the largest nuclear power station in India. It is set to have six VVER-1000 reactors with a total installed capacity of 6000 MWe. Units 1 and 2 were commissioned in 2013 and 2016 and the four remaining units were under construction at the time of writing.

Practically, what options did the Supreme Court have? The government having spent a massive amount, having worked in concert with the USSR, later Russia, and finally having nearly reached the completion of a 25-year long project in respect of units 1 and 2, could the court realistically have shut down the entire project? Would such a decision have been an example of judicial overreach?

4. The location of the KKNPP in some ways makes a lot of sense. The plant is next to the Gulf of Mannar, which will supply the water necessary for cooling the NPP. In addition, rural Kudankulam is not densely populated. On the other hand, the Gulf of Mannar is one of the richest coastal areas in all of Asia, with fragile coral reefs and other habitats home to over 3,500 species.

5. The location of KKNPP, close to Sri Lanka puts the population of that country at risk from radiation and fallout in the event of a serious mishap at Kudankulam. Is it fair for a country

---

60 *G Sundarrajan v Union of India* (2013) 6 SCC 620, 720.
61 *Id.* at 734.
62 *Id.* at 737.

to locate an NPP near another country, potentially endangering populations who have no say in choosing the site? Should India have consulted Sri Lanka before establishing such a large nuclear facility close to its shores?

6. The Supreme Court painstakingly examined and eventually repelled every legal objection. It found that the site selection decisions were taken before both the CRZ notification of 1991 and the EIA notification of 1994 came into force after Units 1 and 2 were granted clearance by the MoEF under the extant administrative procedures. The Supreme Court found that the authorities were alive to the special problems relating to the treatment and disposal of radioactive waste and closed the case by issuing specific directions that reinforced the safety regime.

7. Do you agree with the balancing test formulated by the Supreme Court weighing 'economic scientific benefits' against the 'minor radiological detriments'?

8. Are you convinced by the court's rather cursory discussion of 'apprehension of harm'? Is it really true that so long as a project is justified, any apprehension of future harm from the project is insignificant? Apprehension of harm is central to environmental law and is embedded in the precautionary principle.

9. While a mishap at an NPP could be devastating, nuclear energy provides an alternative to fossil fuels and thereby contributes to reducing carbon emissions. Viewed from this perspective, a safe nuclear power programme would help India attain its climate change goals by reducing carbon emissions.

10. While the concerns of the local fishing community were perfectly legitimate, the government of India projected the protests against KKNPP as being orchestrated or encouraged by foreign elements.[63] The agitation by local fishermen delayed the project and resulted in the arrest and detention of local leaders. The Supreme Court endeavoured to soothe the confrontation by suggesting that the criminal cases be withdrawn.

11. It was no accident that India's contract was with the USSR/Russia rather than with a US company. Private companies, such as Westinghouse in the USA, are reticent to enter into the NPP industry in India due to the lack of certainty with respect to statutory caps on financial liability.

12. Should the Madras High Court and Supreme Court have declined to examine the merits of the case considering the delay in filing the writ petitions? While construction of NPP began in 2002, the petitions were filed a decade later in 2012.

13. The legal case was preceded by civil society agitations on the ground. From the perspective of those against the project, was it wise to approach the court? Did the petitioners stand a chance?

[63] Prime Minister Manmohan Singh blamed 'foreign money', specifically from the United States and Scandinavian countries, as the impetus behind domestic NGOs responsible for the anti-nuclear demonstrations against the KKNPP. Critics of the Prime Minister's statement pointed out that demonstrations over the KKNPP had been going on for over 25 years, and also questioned why the United States would be against NPPs in India when many US companies want to sell nuclear reactors to India. NDTV, *PM blames American NGOs for Kudankulam Power Plant Protests*, 24 February 2012, https://www.ndtv.com/tamil-nadu-news/pm-blames-american-ngos-for-kudankulam-power-plant-protests-569436, accessed 19 June 2021; Dinesh C Sharma, *Foreign Hand Nuking Tamil Nadu Nuclear Power Project, says Prime Minister Manmohan Singh*, https://www.indiatoday.in/india/north/story/kudankulam-row-prime-minister-blames-foreign-countries-94032-2012-02-24, accessed 19 June 2021.

14. Protesters against KKNPP have been slapped with multiple prosecutions for sedition, waging war on the state and damage to public property. Thousands of protesters are arraigned as accused, effectively disrupting their regular lives.[64]

II. HYDRO

Alaknanda Hydropower is a lengthy judgment that examines the hurdles encountered by a run-of-the-river project initiated in 1982. It finally passed muster when the Supreme Court rendered its judgment three decades later in August 2013. Meanwhile, a statutory EIA regime was introduced on 27 January 1994 under the Environment (Protection) Act of 1986 and was replaced by another EIA notification on 14 September 2006. The judgment in most part narrates facts and the reasoning is at best thin. Notice how the court shifts the focus of the judicial exercise in the final paragraphs of the judgment.

ALAKNANDA HYDROPOWER COMPANY LIMITED v ANUJ JOSHI

(2014) 1 SCC 769

K S P RADHAKRISHNAN, J: Leave granted. Srinagar Hydroelectric Project (SHEP) located in Tehri/Pauri Garhwal District of Uttar Pradesh was a project envisaged by the then Uttar Pradesh State Electricity Board (UPSEB) on River Alaknanda, which was basically run-of-the-river scheme.

The techno-economic approval of the scheme was granted for 200 MW by the Central Electricity Authority (CEA), a competent authority exercising powers under section 29 of the Electricity (Supply) Act, 1948, in its meeting held on 6-11-1982, subject to the environmental clearance from the Ministry of Environment. SHEP was later segregated from twenty-two other Ganga Valley projects. A separate environment impact assessment (EIA) was made on SHEP on 9-2-1985. No adverse effect had been noticed on the environment in that assessment on setting up of the Project. On the contrary, it was felt that such a scheme would add to the richness of the scenic beauty by creation of beautiful lakes attracting more tourists and also meet the energy requirements of the State and could be completed within a short span of five years. Dhari Devi Temple, it was noticed, was likely to be submerged in water, therefore was also considered while considering the environmental impact assessment (EIA). It was suggested that the temple would be raised and created with a pleasing architecture suiting the surroundings.

The Ministry of Environment and Forests (MoEF) granted environmental clearance for the Project to UPSEB vide its letter dated 3-5-1985 subject to certain safeguards. The Project involved diversion of forest land to the extent of 338.38 ha which was cleared by the Forest Department vide Proceeding No. 8-227/86-PC dated 15-4-1987, in accordance with section 2 of the Forest (Conservation) Act, 1980. The Project involved construction of concrete gravity dam affording a gross storage of 8 Mcum water conductor system designed for 660 cumecs and a powerhouse with an installation of six units of 55 MW each. UPSEB later carried out a detailed study and submitted a report stating that taking into consideration the peaking capacity, the installed capacity of the Project would be increased from 200 MW to 330 MW. CEA approved and granted the techno-economic clearance in the enhanced capacity of 330 MW vide its letter dated 18-12-1987. The Planning Commission vide its letter dated 29-1-1988 accorded the investment approval. UPSEB started the work but due to the paucity of funds the Project could not make any effective progress.

---

[64] Ramesh Babu, *Kudankulam Nuclear Plant Row: Protesters Live Under the Shadow of Sedition*, HINDUSTAN TIMES, 6 December 2016, https://www.hindustantimes.com/india-news/kudankulam-nuclear-plant-row-protesters-live-under-the-shadow-of-sedition/story-pRw5tO3AiF2Neh1rZrRI4I.html, accessed 19 June 2021; Sweta Daga, *The Women Protesting the Kudankulam Nuclear Plant*, THE CARAVAN, 2 July 2019, https://caravanmagazine.in/communities/women-protest-kudankulam-nuclear-plant, accessed 19 June 2021.

[Under a liberalized policy that encouraged private sector participation in power development, the state government entered into a memorandum of understanding with Duncan Industries Ltd in 1994. The MoEF transferred the environmental clearance to Duncan on 27-7-1999 and the CEA also issued a techno-economic clearance to Duncan on 14-6-2000. Upon Duncan giving up the project, the appellant (AHPCL) took over and on 27-3-2006 the MoEF transferred the environmental clearance to AHPCL.

Anuj Joshi filed a PIL before the High Court of Uttarakhand at Nainital in 2009 asking that the environmental clearances issued on 27-7-1999 and 27-3-2006 be quashed and that the Central Bureau of Investigation (CBI) inquire into the enhanced project capacity from 200 MW to 330 MW. The High Court rejected Joshi's request for an injunction, allowing construction up to the height of 63 m which was envisaged for generation of the original project capacity of 200 MW. To proceed beyond this height, the High Court required clearance from the MoEF.

On 3-8-2011, the MoEF clarified that the project stood approved for a dam height of 90 m. This prompted Joshi to file a second PIL challenging the MoEF clarification. The High Court disposed of the petition on 3-11-2011 directing AHPCL to submit documents in terms of the EIA notification dated 27-1-1994 before the MoEF and asked the MoEF to conduct a public hearing at the Dhari Devi Temple premises. AHPCL challenged the order in this appeal and questioned the applicability of the EIA notification since the permissions of the MoEF, CEA and the Planning Commission to the 330 MW project were all accorded before 27-1-1994.]

We may indicate that while going through the averments made in the writ petition as well as the impugned judgment and the pleadings of the parties, it is seen that the question that was primarily raised before the High Court was with regard to the necessity of a public hearing and also whether the sanction had been accorded to construct the Project with the capacity of 330 MW. This Court in *Narmada Bachao Andolan v Union of India* (2000) 10 SCC 664 has held that the 1994 Notification applies only prospectively, in any view so far as this case is concerned the environmental clearance cannot be an issue in view of the specific stand taken by MoEF and the Order dated 3-8-2011 passed by MoEF which can also be considered as an ex post facto approval. SHEP, it may be noted, is an ongoing project for which environmental clearance was granted as early as in the year 1985 and forest clearance in the year 1987. Further, about 95% of the work is already over and nearly Rs 4000 crores have been spent. If public hearing is found necessary, then the same should have been held before granting environmental clearance. The purpose of public hearing, it may be noted, is to know the concerns of the affected people and to incorporate their concerns appropriately into Environment Management Plan (EMP) and it is after incorporation of the concerns and revision/modifying plan, the final EMP would be submitted to MoEF for granting environmental clearance. Environmental clearance, in the instant case, had been granted in the year 1985 and the Project is an ongoing project which is now nearing completion and, therefore, no purpose would be achieved by way of a public hearing at this stage. We also notice from the various committees' reports and the report dated 3-5-2013 that they had met the temple trustees, priests and residents of the locality, and they had not raised any objection for not holding a public hearing. Further, the State of Uttarakhand has also never canvassed for a public hearing nor was any complaint received by the temple authorities or the worshippers raised any complaint of not holding any public hearing there. We, therefore, set aside the direction given by the High Court directing MoEF to hold a public hearing.

[A new dimension was added to the litigation by fresh proceedings against the project before the National Green Tribunal (NGT) and the NGT requiring the MoEF to take a suitable decision. The MoEF was required to take a final decision in the backdrop of a stop work order the MoEF had issued to AHPCL under section 5 of the EPA. MoEF directed AHPCL to address specific issues such as:

(i) mounting Dhari Devi Temple at a higher elevation as per the plan prepared by INTACH,
(ii) maintain and manage muck at the various muck disposal sites by providing retention wall, slopes, compacting and terracing, etc.,

(iii) develop green belt,
(iv) catchment area treatment,
(v) undertaking Supana quarry restoration,
(vi) maintain minimum environmental flow, etc.

The judgment thereafter narrates the establishment of numerous committees by the MoEF as well as the Supreme Court and reproduces extracts from the committee reports. By and large, the committees (which inspected the site and interviewed the temple management) found that AHPCL had complied with the conditions of the environmental clearance and the directions issued by the MoEF on 30-6-2011.]

The final report was submitted by B K Chaturvedi Committee on April 2013 (Vol 1) before MoEF, *inter alia*, reiterating its interim report on Dhari Devi Temple. Das Committee, Chaturvedi Committee and joint team constituted on the basis of direction of this Court have, therefore, fully endorsed the views [of the Architectural Heritage Division of the Indian National Trust for Art and Cultural Heritage (INTACH)] on Dhari Devi Temple. We find no reason to differ from the views expressed by the Expert Committee, which was submitted after hearing all the affected parties, including the trustees of the Temple, devotees, pujaris, etc. The Committee reports to that extent stand accepted.

We are also not impressed by the argument that by accepting the suggestions of all the expert committees to raise the Temple as such to a higher place, would wound the religious feelings of the devotees or violate the rights guaranteed under Article 25 of the Constitution. The sacred rock on which the Temple exists is still kept intact and only the height of the Temple is increased so that the Temple would not be submerged in the water.

[The court discussed issues of dam safety, muck management and disposal, catchment area treatment, green belt development, etc. and then turned its attention to proliferation of hydroelectric projects in the state of Uttarakhand and its impact on Alaknanda and Bhaghirathi River Basins. The court found that the Wildlife Institute of India in a report in December 2012 had found that 24 of 39 proposed projects would significantly impact biodiversity in the region and endanger the habitat of rare, endangered and threatened species of flora and fauna.]

The abovementioned reports would indicate the adverse impact of the various hydroelectric power projects on the ecology and environment of Alaknanda and Bhagirathi River Basins. The cumulative impact of the various projects in place and which are under construction on the River Basins have not been properly examined or assessed, which requires a detailed technical and scientific study.

We are also deeply concerned with the recent tragedy, which has affected the Char Dham area of Uttarakhand. Wadia Institute of Himalayan Geology (WIG) recorded 350 mm of rain on 15-6-2013/16-6-2013. Snowfall ahead of the cloudburst also had contributed to the floods resulting in the burst on the banks of Chorabari Lake near Kedarnath, leading to a large-scale calamity leading to loss of human lives and property. The adverse effect of the existing projects, projects under construction and proposed, on the environment and ecology calls for a detailed scientific study. Proper Disaster Management Plan, it is seen, is also not in place, resulting in loss of lives and property. In view of the abovementioned circumstances, we are inclined to give following directions:

(a) We direct MoEF as well as the State of Uttarakhand not to grant any further environmental clearance or forest clearance for any hydroelectric power project in the State of Uttarakhand, until further orders.
(b) MoEF is directed to constitute an expert body consisting of representatives of the State Government, WII, Central Electricity Authority, Central Water Commission and other expert bodies to make a detailed study as to whether hydroelectric power projects existing and under construction have contributed to the environmental degradation, if so, to what extent and also whether it has contributed to the present tragedy which occurred at Uttarakhand in the month of June 2013.

(c) MoEF is directed to examine, as noticed by WII in its report, as to whether the proposed 24 projects are causing significant impact on the biodiversity of Alaknanda and Bhagirathi River Basins.
(d) The Disaster Management Authority, Uttarakhand would submit a report to this Court as to whether they had any disaster management plan in place in the State of Uttarakhand and how effective that plan was for combating the present unprecedented tragedy at Uttarakhand.
(e) Reports would be submitted within a period of three months....

In view of above, civil appeals and transferred cases are disposed of.

NOTES AND QUESTIONS

1. Run-of-the-river projects utilize the natural drop in the height of the river as it cuts through a mountain to generate electricity. These projects are environmentally less disruptive since they do not require large reservoirs for water storage. Nevertheless, as this case shows, there are distinct environmental challenges that remain and, where a large number of projects are clustered in a river basin, the cumulative impacts of all these projects may escape the notice of the EIA agency.

2. The court allows the project on three principles: (a) the EIA notification operates prospectively and a public hearing is not necessary where the clearance is issued before the notification; (b) in appropriate cases, the court may consider *ex post facto* approval by the MoEF, such as where large funds are expended; and (c) the right to freedom of religion guaranteed under Articles 25 and 26 of the Constitution of India was not violated. The court held: 'We are of the view that none of the rights of the devotees of the Dhari Devi Temple has been affected by raising the level of the Temple, which remains attached to the sacred rock.'

3. Submergence of the Dhari Devi Temple in the reservoir created by the project posed a delicate issue. Eventually, the INTACH plan to raise the temple at its current location but to a level above the highest water level, and to instal the idol on the raised platform, was accepted by the court. The MoEF, possibly to fend off criticism, filed written submissions objecting to the INTACH plan of lifting the temple on columns and claimed this 'would wound the religious feelings of large sections of Hindus'. Why then did MoEF grant permissions and clear the project? What factors might have persuaded the ministry to belatedly raise this objection?

4. When the initial permissions were issued in the 1980s, the project was to be completed within five years. Three decades after conception and the expenditure of nearly Rs. 4,000 crores, uncertainty dogged the project. What does this say about the ease of doing business in India and the risks an entrepreneur must take? Does the judicial system reduce or increase business risk?

5. The writ petitioner before the High Court asked for a CBI inquiry. Why? Was this a cunning strategy or careless drafting?

III. THERMAL

North of Mumbai, on the west coast of India lies Dahanu, an ecologically sensitive region with a thriving agrarian economy.[65] Dahanu is best known for its chikoo fruit. Its orchards also grow vast quantities of guava and coconut. It supplies fodder, rice, milk and poultry to

[65] This section has benefited from the insights shared by Kerban Anklesaria.

the surrounding regions and the Mumbai metropolitan area. Fishermen reap a rich harvest of fish, crabs and shrimp. According to the Dahanu Taluka Environment Welfare Association (DTEWA) nearly half of the sub-district is under forest cover. About 65% of the Dahanu population is comprised of tribals who are engaged in cultivating their land and working on orchards.

The DTEWA vigorously campaigned against the despoliation of this area. The campaign began in the late 1980s when the Bombay Suburban Electric Supply Company (BSES) decided to establish a 500 MW coal-fired thermal power station at Dahanu. BSES engaged a consulting firm to locate a suitable site for the power station to supply electricity to Mumbai. Out of the nine sites investigated, only one—Bassein—was found to be technically viable. However, this site was discarded because it fell within the Mumbai metropolitan region and would add to the existing high level of pollution in the area. Eventually, Dahanu was approved by the authorities.

The location of any thermal power station which draws on sea water to cool its turbines is bound to impact the marine environment. The warm water discharged by the plant alters the local ecology. Some species thrive in the warm water whilst others perish in the changed environment. Environmentalists feared that emissions from the proposed coal-fired plant, particularly sulphur dioxide, would adversely affect the chikoo crop. Another concern related to environmental harm from the disposal of ash in wetlands and reclaimed creek areas. The complex web of ecological issues and social impacts posed by the Dahanu siting were reduced to three easy-to-explain contentions before the Bombay High Court. The Bombay Environmental Action Group (BEAG) and DTEWA urged the court to stall the project since (i) the Central Government had issued environmental clearance contrary to the opinion of its Appraisal Committee of the MoEF; (ii) the project was being set up within 500 m of the high-tide line (HTL) mark, contrary to the guideline and condition imposed by the MoEF; and (iii) the discharge of water would increase the sea temperature and adversely affect marine life.

A division bench of the Bombay High Court rejected the petitions, finding that the site offered several advantages. The land was barren, no tree would be felled, there was no habitation at the site and consequently no relocation of villagers, and the use of marine water for cooling would help conserve scarce freshwater resources. Accepting the stand of the state government and BSES that the 500 m distance from the HTL would be maintained, the court found that the concerned authorities had considered all the relevant factors, had imposed stringent safeguards and hence there was no justification for interfering with the project under Article 226 of the Constitution.[66]

The environmental groups petitioned the Supreme Court for special leave to appeal under Article 136 of the Constitution of India. We carry an excerpt from the Supreme Court judgment.

DAHANU TALUKA ENVIRONMENT PROTECTION GROUP v BSES

(1991) 2 SCC 539

RANGANATHAN, J: The two petitioners, who are 'Environment Protection Groups' objected to the clearance, by the State of Maharashtra and the Union of India, of a proposal of the Bombay Suburban Electricity Supply Company Limited (hereinafter referred to as 'BSES') for the construction of a thermal power plant over an area of 800 hectares or thereabouts in Dahanu, Maharashtra. They filed writ petitions in the Bombay High Court challenging

[66] *Bombay Environmental Action Group v State of Maharashtra* AIR 1991 BOM 301.

the decision of the Central Government to that effect dated 29 March 1989. After some hearing the Bombay High Court passed an order dated 30 March 1990 adjourning the hearing to enable the Government of India to consider the representations made by the two petitioners. Government of India did this and reaffirmed its decision to clear the project. A detailed affidavit was filed on behalf of the Union on 29 June 1990. To this was enclosed a memorandum dealing in seriatim with the various objections raised by the petitioners and setting out the government's findings thereon. After considering the same and hearing the counsel at length, the High Court, by a detailed order, dismissed the writ petitions by its order dated 12 December 1990. The objectors have thereupon filed these two petitions for leave to appeal before us.

***

We have come to the conclusion that there are no grounds to grant leave to appeal from the order passed by the High Court. We shall briefly deal with the contentions urged before us:

(1) The BSES undertook surveys some time in 1976 and selected about ten sites where its thermal power station could be located and Dahanu was not one of them. After consideration, a site at Bassein was cleared in 1985. But the state government objected to this site later on the ground that Bassein was located within a distance of one kilometer from the sea shore and 500 meters from the river banks. This region was reserved in a plan for extending Bombay metropolitan region and no construction activity could be permitted therein. When this happened, the company has manoeuvred to get approval for the plant location at Dahanu although even the company had not found it suitable earlier and although the objections raised about Bassein equally apply to Dahanu. This criticism is unfounded. The Bassein site fell within the extended Bombay metropolitan region; Dahanu falls outside this region. That apart, there were also other reasons to discard the Bassein site which do not apply to the Dahanu site. If the Bassein site having been rejected, an alternate site in Western Maharashtra had to be chosen and Dahanu being close to Bombay after Bassein and beyond the metropolitan development region has been chosen, there is nothing wrong in this.

(2) The principal objection on behalf of the petitioners is that the clearance is in the teeth of the findings of an expert body appointed by the government itself to examine all the aspects of the proposed location at Dahanu. It is contended that this Appraisal Committee for Thermal Power Stations (EAC) held its meetings on 27 October 1988 and 29 December 1988. The meetings were attended by the members of the EAC, concerned officers of the state of Maharashtra, the representatives of the company and representatives of various public bodies and groups. The Committee, after examining the various aspects, considered the site at Dahanu unsuitable and listed nine reasons for this conclusion. It is pointed out that this conclusion of the EAC was arrived at on 29 December 1988. Surprisingly, counsel say, despite the opinion of the EAC, the Government of India cleared the proposal on 29 March 1989 without any reasons disclosed for rejecting the expert body's report. This, it is urged, shows absence of application of mind on the part of the government to the dimensions of the problem.

Prima facie, this appears to be very forceful objection. But it proceeds on the misapprehension that the views of the EAC represent a decision of the government and that the approval of the project is in the nature of a volte face. This is not correct. [Counsel for BSES] sought to brush aside the EAC papers relied upon as nothing but 'minutes' and as ex cathedra pronouncements. This may be going too far. But we are in agreement with counsel that the findings of the EAC cannot be treated as conclusive or binding on the Central Government. We find that the Central Government had before it not only this 'report' but also the findings of a State Expert Committee which had gone into the matter in detail and recommended the Dahanu site. The state government in turn had before it several reports of expert bodies. The details are fully explained in the affidavit ... on behalf of the Government of Maharashtra which has been referred to in the judgment by the High Court. It is also seen that a comparative study of the two sites on all aspects such as pollution, contamination of fresh water resources, effect on fisheries, effect on plantation, agriculture and forests and effect on the tribal population living in the affected areas was looked into.

After examining all the aspects, the state government approved the proposal subject to several stringent conditions. There were also a couple of reports received after 29 December 1988 but before 29 June 1990 when the final decision of the Central Government, after the reconsideration directed by this Court, was taken. The several expert reports expressed the view that the pollution of water on account of the hot water discharge from the cooling plant and the atmospheric pollution due to outlet of gases would be well within permissible limits. Though the EAC had pronounced against the location of the thermal station at Dahanu, the Government of India had before it the strong recommendations of the state of Maharashtra and the several reports referred to above. If, after considering all the material, the Central Government chose to accept the recommendations of the state government, its action cannot be said to be arbitrary....

(3) Another grievance of the petitioners is that the clearance in respect of the site in question had been issued contrary to the 'Environmental Guidelines for Thermal Power Plants' issued by the Government of India in 1987. The guidelines lay down various criteria, two of which, according to the petitioners, are very important. These are: (1) that thermal power plants should not be located within 25 km of the outer peripheries of metropolitan cities, national parks, and wildlife sanctuaries and ecologically sensitive areas like tropical forests; and (2) that, in order to protect coastal areas, a distance of 500 meters from the high tide line (HTL) and a further buffer zone of 5 km from the seashore should be kept free of any thermal power station.

It is pointed out that the EAC had decided against the Dahanu location as it is the only green belt left in the region having about 40 to 60% of forest cover located in Thane district and also as Dahanu town has chikoo gardens and forest areas located at about 3 to 7 kms from the power station. It opined that the emissions of pollutants and the coal and fly ash contaminants are likely to have an adverse effect on the chikoo plant and forest. In the memorandum dated 29 June 1989, it is said, the Government of India has waived away this important objection with a very brief comment that there are no ecologically sensitive areas within 25 kms of the project site....

The distances mentioned in the guidelines are only intended as a safeguard against possible pollution effects; it cannot be treated as rigid and inflexible irrespective of local conditions. It is, therefore, quite natural for the Government of India to decide that the site could be cleared subject to stringent conditions to prevent danger of pollution. They have insisted on the installation of a multi-fuel boiler making possible the utilisation of not merely coal but also oil, gas or LSHS to the maximum extent possible. They have insisted upon a tall stack of not less than 275 meters, electrostatic precipitators and a Flue Gas Desulphurisation Plant (FGD). Continuous monitoring of stock emissions and ambient air quality have been insisted upon. Taking into account the Expert Committees' reports, which have been referred to earlier, the Central Government was satisfied that if these conditions are adhered to there will be no significant impact on the environment either due to atmospheric or water pollution.

(4) The second objection based on the guidelines is that the present plant cannot be located in such a way as to ensure being away from HTL (high tide line) by more than 500 meters not to speak of its being beyond 5 kms from the coastline. Here again attention is drawn to the EAC's report which says that 'the site falls within high tide line in Dahanu creek' and that 'the site is low-lying land virtually in the creek which gets submerged during high tide'. It is true that the plant is located within 5 kms of the sea but, for the reasons already pointed out, it is impossible to rigidly apply this standard in the context of the present project. The second part of the objection regarding its being within 500 meters of the HTL is, however, based on a misconception. In the first place the restriction in the guidelines is only for the buildings of the thermal station and, for obvious reasons pointed out by [BSES], cannot be read so as to mean that no part of the site of the thermal station of about 800 hectares should at all fall within the distance of 500 meters....

> We would, however, like to place the matter beyond doubt by directing the Central and the state governments to monitor the construction of the buildings under the scheme to ensure that no building of the thermal power station comes up within a distance of 500 meters from the HTL.
>
> * * *
>
> For the reasons discussed above, we are satisfied that the clearance to the thermal power station was granted by the Central Government after fully considering all relevant aspects and in particular the aspects of the environmental pollution. Sufficient safeguards against pollution of air, water and environment have been insisted upon in the conditions of grant. However, in order to allay the apprehensions on the part of the petitioners that the company may seek and obtain relaxations or modifications of the conditions that may prove detrimental to environment, we direct that the condition requiring the installation of a FGD plant should not be relaxed without a full consideration of the consequences and that, if there is any proposal from the company to relax this or any other condition subject to which the plant has been cleared, neither the state government nor the Union Government should permit such relaxation without giving notice of the proposed changes to the petitioner groups and giving them an opportunity of being heard....

NOTES AND QUESTIONS

1. The Bombay High Court relied on the Supreme Court judgment in the *Calcutta Taj Hotel* case.[67] There, the Supreme Court held that while it was the duty of the court to examine whether appropriate considerations had been borne in mind and irrelevancies excluded, the court should not attempt 'to nicely balance relevant considerations. When the question involves the nice balancing of relevant considerations, the court may feel justified in resigning itself to accepting the decision of the concerned authority.'[68]

2. Environmentalists complain that the conditions imposed by the MoEF and state governments at the time of granting clearance are meaningless since there is no effective post-clearance machinery to monitor compliance. Once the project is cleared, the implementation of the conditions depends entirely on the good faith of the project proponent. The material in the following notes justifies the apprehensions of the DTEWA and BEAG in respect of the conditions that were imposed on BSES.

3. The High Court judgment was delivered on 12 December 1990. The Supreme Court's decision on the special leave petitions was rendered on 19 March 1991. On 21 May 1991, Dr Maudgal, scientific advisor to the MoEF, filed a report in his ministry after conducting a site visit. His report notes diverse breaches by BSES and confirms that, contrary to the assurances given by the company to the courts, the site was located within the high-tide submergence zone and was within a distance of 500 m from the HTL. BSES had pushed back the natural HTL by constructing artificial bunds. Dr Maudgal notes:

> Considering the elaborate arrangements being made through creation of bunds and for the blocking of criss-crossing streams and inlets of the creeks and raising of the site level through dumping ... one has to come to the unmistakable conclusion that the proposed site is lying within the High Tide Line. This is further confirmed by aerial photographs as well as hydrographic maps of the area.

---

67 *Sachidanand Pandey v State of West Bengal* AIR 1987 SC 1109.
68 *Id.* at 1115.

4. In view of the breaches noticed in this report, BEAG once again moved the Bombay High Court by filing Writ Petition No. 428 of 1992. The High Court summarily rejected the petition, observing that it was not open to a public interest group to re-agitate the same issue over and over again:

> The Petitioners cannot consider themselves to be the super monitors of the two Governments. The Supreme Court has expressed confidence by directing the two Governments to monitor the progress ... and we do not see any reason to doubt that the two Governments will ... discharge their duties.[69]

Was it strategically sound to move the Bombay High Court after the special leave petitions were rejected by the Supreme Court? Would it have been wiser for the environmental groups to directly approach the Supreme Court by an interim application in view of that court's direction that all the conditions including the 500 m distance from the HTL be strictly observed? Should the High Court have stalled the project in view of the incorrect statements by BSES and the state government in respect of the distance from the HTL?

5. On 20 June 1991, the MoEF declared Dahanu as 'an ecologically fragile area' and imposed restrictions on the establishment of industries under section 3(2)(v) of the EPA. This notification lists the industries that are permitted and prohibited in Dahanu and also required the state government to prepare within a year a regional plan based on the existing land use in the region. The state was asked to clearly demarcate on the plan the existing green areas, orchards, tribal areas and other environmentally sensitive areas. The Dahanu notification prohibited a change in land use and confined industrial activity in the Taluka to a maximum of 500 acres within designated industrial estates. The notification was a triumph for the environmental groups which had long campaigned to preserve Dahanu's natural heritage.

6. Predictably, local businessmen as well as the state lobbied the MoEF to dilute or repeal the notification. To thwart the challenge, in 1994, the environmental groups filed a writ petition under Article 32 of the Constitution before the Supreme Court complaining that, despite the June 1991 notification, the state government and local authorities were permitting unchecked industrial growth which was irreversibly harming Dahanu.[70] The principal grievance was that the state government had failed to prepare a regional plan within a year under the terms of the notification.

In March 1996, the MoEF approved the regional plan for Dahanu submitted belatedly by the state government. According to the environmentalists, this plan violated the Dahanu notification and at their request on 24 September 1996, the Supreme Court directed the National Environmental Engineering Research Institute, Nagpur (NEERI) to study the plan and report on whether it conformed to the Dahanu notification and the Coastal Regulatory Zone (CRZ) notification of 1991. In its report of 19 October 1996, NEERI found that the plan breached the notifications and 'is also ecologically and environmentally unviable'. Turning specifically to the BSES plant, the report observed that the thermal power station was located on wetlands in violation of the Coastal Zone Regulations. The report recommended that BSES should use natural gas as fuel in place of coal; that all obstructions to the free flow of sea water into the creeks should be removed by BSES; and that the company should improve the monitoring of hot water discharges as well as air quality and emissions. NEERI suggested that BSES should study the effect of gaseous emissions on horticulture, particularly chikoo and mango trees.

---

[69] Order dated 12 March 1992.

[70] *Bittu Sehgal v Union of India*, Writ Petition (Civil) No. 231 of 1994.

7. By an order dated 31 October 1996, the Supreme Court directed the state government to implement the regional plan subject to the conditions imposed by the MoEF. The state was also asked to implement 'all the recommendations of NEERI' as reproduced in the Supreme Court order. The court directed the Central Government to constitute an authority under section 3(3) of the EPA to protect the ecologically fragile Dahanu Taluka and to control pollution in the area. The Supreme Court also transferred the petition to the High Court with a request to the Chief Justice of the Bombay High Court to constitute a 'Green Bench' for the purpose of adjudicating public interest environmental cases.[71]

8. In its report to the Supreme Court, NEERI found that between October 1991 and October 1996, the ecology of Dahanu Creek, where the BSES hot water discharges occurred, had dramatically altered. There was a steep decline in the biomass at all hierarchical levels contributing to the instability of the ecological pyramid. The number of fish and prawn varieties had decreased within five years of commissioning the thermal power plant. There was a drastic variation in the salinity within the creek due to the incomplete mixing of creek and sea waters. The drop in salinity was the principal reason for the sudden change in the aquatic fauna. NEERI observed that the power plant's operations had decreased the wetlands and caused disappearance of criss-crossing creeks and natural drains which functioned as the breeding ground for aquatic fauna and which aided nutrient recycling and erosion control.

9. On 19 December 1996, a day before the deadline, the MoEF constituted the Dahanu Taluka Environment Protection Authority (DTEPA) chaired by Justice C S Dharmadhikari, a retired judge of the Bombay High Court. The Authority was charged with protecting the ecologically fragile areas of Dahanu whilst having regard to the 'precautionary principle' and 'the polluter pays principle' as enunciated by the Supreme Court. Justice Dharmadhikari discharged his role as chairperson till his passing in January 2019. Throughout his tenure he worked steadfastly to protect Dahanu against environmental harm.[72]

10. BSES worked hard to waive its obligation to install an FGD plant claiming that the sulphur dioxide emissions were well within the prescribed limits and that the large quantity of gypsum generated in the form of sludge would create disposal problems. When the DTEPA rejected the request applying the precautionary principle, BSES petitioned the Bombay High Court. Recognizing the special status of Dahanu and the importance of an FGD plant as a preventive measure, the High Court rejected the petition.[73] Despite the DTEPA's direction to initiate installation of the plant, the company prevaricated. Over several years, it mulled the appropriate technology while attempting to have a review of the requirement through pollution control board committees. The FGD plant was eventually commissioned in 2007, but only after the DTEPA had seen through the company's stratagems and required a bank guarantee of Rs. 300 crores to be issued in favour of MoEF.

11. Another challenge to the DTEWA came with the state government issuing a letter of intent on 17 February 1997 to the Indian subsidiary of P&O Ports, Australia for establishing a giant port at Vadhavan, Dahanu. The state was anxious to build a major port facility in North Maharashtra for the purpose of handling coal, hazardous chemicals and other international cargo. The special geological feature of Vadhavan that attracted P&O Ports was the natural rock strata in the harbour that could save the company substantial costs when building the port facilities.

---

[71] *Bittu Seghal v Union of India* (2001) 9 SCC 181.

[72] At the time of writing, the Union of India had applied to the Supreme Court requesting the disbanding of DTEPA.

[73] *BSES Ltd v Union of India* AIR 2001 BOM 128.

The DTEWA along with other local groups campaigned against the proposed port. Unlike the previous protest against BSES, this campaign enjoyed mass political support, with fishermen, agriculturists and tribals joining hands with the environmentalists. All of them feared that a major port would disrupt the community and deplete the natural resources on which they were dependent. On 13 April 1998, the Dahanu Authority restrained the government and P&O Ports from proceeding further in the matter until the Authority finally decided the question relating to the feasibility of the Vadhavan Port.

On 19 September 1998, the Dahanu Authority ruled that the proposed port would breach the CRZ Regulations of 1991, the Dahanu notification dated 20 June 1991 and the regional plan for Dahanu. In February 2020, the Union Cabinet revived the Vadhavan Port project, intending the new container port to be among the largest in the country.

H. OTHER PROJECTS

In July 2009, the Supreme Court faced a dilemma regarding the soon to be hosted XIX Commonwealth Games, 2010 at New Delhi. The organizers envisaged a posh village to host athletes, coaches and officials from the visiting nations. And no site appeared better than a flat plain across the Yamuna, close to the recently built Akshardham temple. The writ petitioners included renowned water resource and heritage experts. They claimed that the village was being built on the Yamuna riverbed or the flood plain and that this would irreversibly damage an ecologically sensitive zone. They asked that the environmental clearances granted on 14 December 2006 and subsequently between January and April 2007 be struck down. In short, the petitioners asked the High Court to throw out the village (and by necessary implication, scrap the games).

The Delhi High Court was unconvinced about the ecological wisdom in locating the games village on a tract close to the Yamuna. The High Court allowed construction but frowned at the government officials' conduct and required a committee to inquire whether the Commonwealth Games Village (CGV) complex was indeed situated on the Yamuna 'riverbed' or 'floodplain'. Construction was permitted at the risk and peril of the organizers.

With the games a little over a year away, the Supreme Court cleared the decks and dismissed the challenge both on the merits as well as on the issue of delay.

DELHI DEVELOPMENT AUTHORITY v RAJENDRA SINGH
(2009) 8 SCC 582

P SATHASIVAM, J: All these special leave petitions are directed against the common judgment and order dated 3-11-2008 of the High Court of Delhi in WPs (C) Nos. 6729 and 7506 of 2007 which, inter alia, issued certain directions for setting up of a committee to enquire as to whether the Commonwealth Games Village (CGV) site complex is situated on Yamuna 'riverbed' or 'flood plain' and further observed that any construction made or third-party rights created are at the peril and risk of the organisers/Government.

Aggrieved by the said judgment, Delhi Development Authority (in short 'DDA') has filed SLPs (C) Nos. 29055-56 of 2008, Ministry of Urban Development and Poverty Alleviation has filed SLP (C) No. 30075 of 2008 and Ministry of Youth Affairs and Sports has filed SLPs (C) Nos. 4408-09 of 2009 as well as SLPs (C) Nos. 6029-30 of 2009 and the Organising Committee, Commonwealth Games has filed SLPs (C) Nos. 31123-24 of 2008....

On 13-9-2003, Commonwealth Games Federation selected Delhi as the venue for Commonwealth Games scheduled to be held from 3-10-2010 to 14-10-2010. After due deliberations, XIXth Commonwealth Games, 2010 are being hosted in Delhi pursuant to a commitment made by the Indian Olympic Association in the form of an agreement in which it agreed to host the games in India with the approved standards and requirements of the Commonwealth Games Federation.

Complaining that the governmental agencies and DDA are effecting various steps including massive construction on the periphery of Yamuna River, apprehending that the action being taken would not only destroy River Yamuna but also pose severe threat to Delhi City as well and in order to stop the entire proceedings, the said petitioners moved the High Court of Delhi. The main claim of the petitioners before the High Court was to the effect that the ongoing construction would affect the ecological integrity of the 'riverbed' besides causing irreversible damage to the 'flood plain'....

Though in NEERI Report, 2005, it was observed that no residential or industrial facilities requiring permanent structure should be provided on the riverbed, the learned Solicitor General of India pointed out that NEERI Report of 2008 clearly takes note of the fact that the final report submitted by it in October 2005 did not assess the embankment within Akshardham bund which had come into existence later as it was not part of the original study carried out by NEERI in the year 1999.

It is relevant to mention that after taking note of embankment, NEERI Report clearly observed that the area does not form part of the 'flood plain'. The same reads as under:

(a) Given the definition of the project area, as considered by MoEF in its clearance letter dated 29-3-2007, the boundaries of Yamuna River, which were considered in the earlier NEERI Report, were demarcated by east and west bank bunds, whereas now the river, post 2002, has new boundaries in the project region i.e. 45 m wide and about 1 km long (stretching between New Railway Bridge and Nizamuddin Road Bridge) newly constructed bund in east and original bund in west. *The reclaimed area, Pocket III is deemed to be no more a part of the flood plain zone by the Akshardham bund and MoEF has in principle approved the bund* ... .

(b) The mitigation measures prescribed by MoEF in its clearance letter dated 14-12-2006, if implemented, should be adequate for environmental safeguards. The concern about groundwater recharge in this region can be addressed by creating an appropriate water body in the project area. Therefore, a detailed action plan including artificial recharge for the same should be formulated to avoid depletion in the groundwater level.

(c) A Monitoring Committee should be constituted to review periodically the post-project environmental quality. The committee should guide DDA on mitigation measures.

* * *

It is brought to our notice that during the course of hearing in view of certain doubts raised by the counsel for the petitioner before the High Court, NEERI, filed an affidavit dated 29-1-2008 wherein it clarified the entire aspects and asserted that the site in question is not even 'flood plain' much less a 'riverbed'. It is also pointed out in its report that 85% of the land at the present site is being used for recreational purposes and 15% for development purposes (including residential and commercial). We have already pointed out that the present site falls within Pocket III, NEERI and Yamuna Standing Committee gave clearance only for development of Pocket III.

Though there is no statutory definition for 'riverbed' and 'flood plain' from the statute, the dictionary meaning of the same is as under:

> '*Riverbed*' has been defined as the area over which the river flows. In *Thames Conservators case* [*Thames Conservators v Smeed, Dean & Co*, (1897) 2 QB 334 (CA)], QB 334 at p 337 it was held that the word riverbed denotes that portion of the river which in the ordinary or regular course of nature is covered by the waters of the river.
>
> The '*bed of the river*' was defined as the area covered by the river and is the space subadjacent to the river over which it flows between the banks. It is the space between the banks occupied by the river at its fullest flow. [Additional definitions omitted.]

Flood plain. — Land adjacent to rivers, which, because of its level topography, floods when river overflows. (*Black's Law Dictionary*, 6th Edn, p 641)

It is also being defined as 'a low, flat area in either side of a river that can accommodate large amounts of water during a flood, lessening flood damage further downstream.' (*Fredd Michaels, Dictionary of Environment Studies*)

In view of the literal meaning and in the light of the clarification by NEERI in their affidavit dated 29-1-2008, the site in question is neither a 'flood plain' nor a 'riverbed', hence contrary arguments of the writ petitioners before the High Court and in this Court and the ultimate conclusion of the Division Bench for appointment of a fresh committee cannot be sustained. We have already pointed out and in fact it is not in dispute that the present CGV site is situated adjoining to Akshardham Temple. When land was allotted for construction of Akshardham Temple, UP State Employees Confederation and another filed Writ Petition No. 353 of 2004 before this Court under Article 32 of the Constitution of India. At the relevant time, the land was in the hands of the State of UP. The petitioners therein also challenged the allotment of the said land by DDA to the third respondent (Akshardham) on the ground that the same would adversely affect recharging of underground water and the allotment is contrary to the land user as declared in the development plan.... On behalf of DDA, it was stated that the construction that was being put up by the third respondent is in accordance with the sanctioned plan and the same is nearly 1700 m away from Yamuna river bank. It was also placed before this Court that the construction thereon was permitted after obtaining the opinion of the Central Water Commission and NEERI which is an autonomous body.... Now, let us consider whether the writ petitions filed in the High Court in the year 2007 are justifiable and ought to have been dismissed on the ground of delay/laches. Though an objection was raised by all the official respondents before the High Court about the inordinate delay in filing the writ petitions by the petitioners, the said aspect was not either adverted to or considered by the Division Bench.

We have already referred to the fact that the site in question was changed to 'public and semi-public' way back on 21-9-1999. Before reclassifying the site, DDA and the authorities concerned issued public notice calling for objections/suggestions. The particulars furnished by the official bodies clearly show that after getting the suggestions from the public change of land use for the site falling in Zone O was changed on 21-9-1999 from 'agricultural and water body' to 'public and semi-public' purpose. Apart from this, the decision of hosting the Commonwealth Games at Commonwealth Games Village site was taken in 2003. The Department also issued a global tender process for public-private partnership ('PPP') participation in the residential portion of the Commonwealth Games Project which was floated in December 2006 and was completed in June 2007....

We reiterate that the delay rules apply to PILs also and if there is no proper explanation for the delay, PILs are liable to be summarily dismissed on account of delay. In the case on hand, it is not in dispute that both the petitioners though claiming that they are very much conversant with environment and ecology, approached the High Court only in the middle of 2007, hence on the ground of delay and laches, the writ petitions were liable to be dismissed.

***

In the light of the above discussion, the following conclusions would emerge:

(a) In view of the Notification in the Gazette of the Government of India dated 21-9-1999 relating to change of land use and to the fact that the site in question for the construction of CGV had been chosen and widely published way back in the year 2003 itself, the writ petitions which were filed before the High Court of Delhi only in the year 2007, in the absence of proper explanation, the High Court ought not to have probed the matter at this juncture.

(b) On a conjoint reading of NEERI Reports of 1999, 2005 and January 2008 coupled with its assertion in the form of an affidavit dated 29-1-2008 clearly show that the CGV site is not either on a 'riverbed' or on the 'flood plain' of Yamuna River.

(c) The decision of an expert and autonomous body, NEERI supported by materials placed by other bodies such as CWPRS and MoEF, the same cannot be lightly interfered with by the Court without adequate contra materials.
(d) After due deliberations by DDA with other Departments including Yamuna Committee and pursuant to the elaborate discussion on 10-11-1997 itself, 35 ha of land were recommended for change of land use and the same was approved (Pocket III) on 21-9-1999 for 'public and semi-public purpose'.
(e) Before change of the land use, the authority concerned issued public notice, heard objections/suggestions and in consultation with expert bodies such as NEERI, CWPRS and MoEF, approved the said proposal and permitted DDA to use the area covered under Pocket III for 'public and semi-public purpose'.
(f) The observation and conclusion of the High Court that the site in question is on a 'riverbed' cannot be sustained. The High Court disregarded and ignored material scientific literature and the opinion of experts and scientific bodies which have categorically held that CGV site is neither located on a 'riverbed' nor on the 'flood plain'. Further, in view of the change of the land use which was approved way back in 1997 by the Yamuna Committee and by NEERI permitting DDA to use Pocket III for 'public and semi-public purpose', the contrary conclusion arrived at by the High Court is liable to be set aside.
(g) Inasmuch as Akshardham Temple site is adjacent to CGV site, the decision of this Court dated 12-1-2005 [*UP State Employees Confederation v Principal Secy* (2009) 8 SCC 604] in Writ Petition (C) No. 353 of 2004 has a bearing on the issue and it is a binding precedent for all purposes.
(h) The direction of the Division Bench for formation of a fresh committee by the Government to examine and monitor the construction carried out by DMRC is also liable to be set aside. However, as assured by the Attorney General for India, the Committee approved by the Prime Minister of India consisting of Lt Governor of Delhi as Chairperson, Chief Minister of Delhi as Vice-Chairperson and other members who are all representing various Departments should monitor the entire activities in association with Dr R K Pachauri.
(i) In view of our conclusion, DDA and other authorities are free to proceed with the work at CGV site.

NOTES AND QUESTIONS

1. The XIX Commonwealth Games was an extremely prestigious international sport meet. Should the Delhi High Court have entertained the writ petition at all and put the entire event in jeopardy?

Viewed differently, does the High Court's searching scrutiny speak well of its independent judges who are not cowed by grand enterprises when the ecological integrity of a great river is at stake?

2. Great cities, the engines of civilization, grew on sea coasts and river banks. Delhi rose on the banks of the Yamuna whose course altered over the centuries. Throughout history, cities have built protective embankments, channelled river waters and developed riverfronts. What was so unusual or environmentally disruptive in building the CGV complex at a distance of 1.7 kms from the Yamuna channel?

3. Did the Supreme Court have a choice? Assume that the court declined to interfere in the High Court ruling and the committee eventually found that the project was on the Yamuna flood plain. What directions might the High Court have then issued?

4. Mocking the Supreme Court's finding (and NEERI's report) that the construction was *not* in the flood plain, weeks before the onset of the games, the Yamuna rose to the perimeter of the CGV complex and flooded the building basements.[74]

5. Was the court correct in holding the writ petitioners' guilty of unexplained delay and laches? The writ petitions were filed in the High Court in mid-2007 and the earliest of the environmental clearances challenged was of 14 December 2006. Subsequent environmental clearances under the EIA notification were issued between January and April 2007. In terms of the EIA notification, construction cannot commence until the clearance is granted. Where was the question of delay dating back to 1999 when the project had no environmental clearance till December 2006? Disregarding the court's feeble reasoning on the issue of delay, would it have made a difference to the outcome?

6. Examine a satellite image and a topography sheet of the CGV complex and judge for yourself whether these lands constitute 'a low, flat area on either side of a river that can accommodate large amounts of water during a flood, lessening flood damage further downstream'? Keep in mind that the original land use map showed this area as 'agricultural and water body'; and NEERI's position was that the land was 'no more a part of the flood plain zone' because of a bund constructed in 2002 as part of the Akshardham Temple project.

7. Are courts ever entitled to condone relatively minor statutory breaches when large economic costs are involved? Or is that only the province of the legislature? Consider the *Snail Darter* case,[75] where the US Supreme Court stopped the construction of a large and nearly completed hydroelectric dam whose construction had cost over 100 million dollars. The court found that the subsequent flooding could harm the tiny snail darter, which was protected under the Endangered Species Act. Shortly afterward, the US Congress amended the Endangered Species Act to allow the dam to be completed.

[74] Kanchi Kohli, *Where does the Yamuna Flow?* INDIA TOGETHER 31 October 2010, http://www.indiatogether.org/yamuna-environment, accessed 20 June 2021.

[75] *TVA v Hill* 437 US 153; 57 L Ed. 2d 117.

15

THE COAST, WETLANDS AND SENSITIVE AREAS

In this omnibus chapter we examine three topics: the coast, wetlands and ecologically sensitive areas (ESAs). The regulations that preserve the Indian coast seek to balance the needs of diverse interests that use coastal resources. The cases in this chapter illustrate the conflicts between hoteliers and environmentalists, real estate developers and planning authorities, the shrimp industry and fisherfolk and between those who seek coastal development *vis-à-vis* citizen groups who urge protecting coastal areas. The importance of these contests is elevated by the impending rise in sea levels consequent to global warming and climate change. Current global estimates project that a global mean temperature increase of 1°C translates into a sea level rise by 2.5 metres. In India, the states of West Bengal and Gujarat are most vulnerable to rising sea levels. An increase of 1 metre in the sea level will inundate 6,000 kms^2 of coastal lands. In the case of neighbouring Bangladesh, a 1-metre rise in sea level will cause 17% of the land to be inundated.[1]

The section on wetlands dwells on the ecological importance of inhospitable bogs and swamps and the growing realization about the range of 'nature services' that these regions provide. The Calcutta High Court has been at the forefront of developing wetland conservation jurisprudence. We use this platform to explore whether courts ought to take in their stride critiques of their procedures and personnel. We finally look at initiatives to preserve ecologically sensitive areas through a framework of customized restrictions imposed under the Environment (Protection) Act of 1986. But for the ESA notifications, developmental pressures would by now have denuded the natural heritage of the notified areas.

A. PROTECTING THE COASTAL REGION

India's lengthy coast stretches over 7,516 kilometres,[2] supporting numerous fishing communities and driving the economies of coastal villages, towns and cities. The importance of coastal ecology and the linkages between community life, economic development and the environment are explored in a report prepared by Claude Alvares of the Goa Foundation, titled *Fish Curry and Rice*.[3] The report argues that overfishing in the near shore waters, marine pollution, excessive sand extraction, shore-line development and destruction of the *khazans*[4]

---

[1] J Srinivasan, *Impacts of Climate Change on India* in HANDBOOK OF CLIMATE CHANGE AND INDIA: DEVELOPMENT, POLITICS AND GOVERNANCE 29, 34 (Ed. Navroz K Dubash, 2012).

[2] This measurement of the sea coast includes 5,422 kms of the mainland, 962 kms of the Andaman and Nicobar Islands and 132 kms of the Lakshadweep Islands. Shyam Chainani, *Heritage and Environment: An Indian Diary* 205 (2007).

[3] Claude Alvares, *Fish Curry and Rice:* A *Citizens' Report on the Goan Environment* 52–95 (1993). The chapter on the coastal region is authored by N Dantas and V Gadgil.

[4] *Khazans* are saline flood plains in Goa's tidal estuaries.

Environmental Law & Policy in India. Shyam Divan and Armin Rosencranz, Oxford University Press.
 DOI: 1093/oso/9780192865458.003.0015

are endangering Goa's 'fish-curry-and-rice' ethos, which had evolved over the centuries in harmony with the environment. Many of these problems confront other coastal communities as well.

Three broad classes of human intervention threaten India's marine environment: maritime trade, the exploitation of ocean resources and on-land coastal development. Although we briefly review developments relating to the former two categories, this section mainly focuses on efforts to regulate land use along the ecologically sensitive coastline.

I. MARINE POLLUTION

India's ocean resources are primarily threatened by terrestrial sources of pollution, seemingly regulated under the Water Act of 1974 and the Environment (Protection) Act of 1986. Several Indian coastal cities such as Mumbai directly discharge untreated city sewage into the sea.[5] Industrial wastes and pesticide runoff contaminate the ocean through rivers and creeks. Studies conducted since the 1970s confirm the presence of high levels of heavy metals such as mercury in the coastal waters around Bombay and Gujarat.[6]

The legislative framework for controlling marine pollution is provided by the Territorial Waters, Continental Shelf, Exclusive Economic Zone and Other Maritime Zones Act of 1976. The Territorial Waters (TW) extend 12 nautical miles from the defined base line; the Continental Shelf (CS) is the natural prolongation of India's land territory to the outer edge of the continental margin, or 200 nautical miles, where the continental margin does not extend up to that distance. The Exclusive Economic Zone (EEZ) extends beyond the TW, over a distance of 200 nautical miles. The Act asserts India's sovereignty over the natural resources in the CS[7] and EEZ.[8] Sections 6(3)(d) and 7(4)(d) confer exclusive jurisdiction on the Central Government to preserve and protect the marine environment and to prevent and control marine pollution within the CS and EEZ.

Apart from these general provisions, there are no specific regulations framed under the Territorial Waters Act to regulate the dumping of substances in the sea or other causes of marine pollution. The Indian Coast Guard patrols the maritime zones and is responsible for 'taking such measures as are necessary to preserve and protect that maritime environment and to prevent and control marine pollution'.[9]

Specific provisions under the Merchant Shipping Act of 1958 (MSA) govern the civil and criminal liability regimes in respect of oil spills. Part X-B of the MSA deals with the civil liability of the owner of an Indian or foreign vessel that damages the environment in the TW or the EEZ. Part XI-A of the Act contains provisions for preventing and controlling oil pollution. Both parts were inserted in the parent Act in 1983, to give effect to international

---

[5] *Citizen Circle for Social Welfare and Education v State of Maharashtra* Bombay High Court; PIL No. 3 of 2018, order dated 11 July 2019.

[6] A Velusamy, *et al*, *Bioaccumulation of Heavy Metals in Commercially Important Marine Fishes from Mumbai Harbour, India*, 81 MARINE POLLUTION BULLETIN 218 (2014), https://www.sciencedirect.com/science/article/abs/pii/S0025326X14000502?via%3Dihub, accessed 21 June 2021; M Srinivasa Reddy, *et al*, *Distribution, Enrichment and Accumulation of Heavy Metals in Coastal Sediments of Alang-Sosiya Ship Scrapping Yard, India*, 48 MARINE POLLUTION BULLETIN 1055 (2004), https://www.sciencedirect.com/science/article/abs/pii/S0025326X03005526?via%3Dihub, accessed 21 June 2021.

[7] Section 6(3)(a).

[8] Section 7(3)(a).

[9] Section 14(2)(c), The Coast Guard Act of 1978.

conventions.[10] Taken together, they provide a comprehensive code for dealing with the civil liability arising from oil pollution damage, and being a special law, would prevail over general pollution control statutes. The quantum of the owner's liability is limited under section 352J of the MSA where the damage occurs without fault of the owner. Conversely, limitation does not apply where the damage is caused by negligence. Section 436 of the MSA prescribes penalties for wrongful oil discharges into Indian coastal waters.

The leading Indian decision on marine pollution is *Samir Mehta v Union of India*[11] decided by the National Green Tribunal. The case concerned pollution from an oil spill that occurred when the vessel *MV Rak* sank 20 nautical miles from the coast of South Mumbai.[12]

II. OCEAN RESOURCES

Until the 1950s, the coastal waters were fished by traditional fisherfolk, employing rowing and sailing boats. The catch was consumed mostly in neighbouring coastal communities. Fishery development in the post-Independence era received a boost from governmental support to mechanized craft, development of refrigeration and canning facilities and the promotion of marine product exports. These changes threatened the lifestyles and livelihood of traditional fishing communities.

In the 1960s big business entered the fishery sector. The introduction of mechanized trawlers initially increased the fish catch by permitting trawling further off the coast, but gradually the fish landings plateaued and even declined. While some of the fisherfolk were able to adjust to the new capital and resource intensive fishery culture, the majority were threatened by depleting returns. The ensuing clashes between fisherfolk and mechanized trawlers were most intense in Kerala, where the agitation led to strikes, protest marches and violent clashes between the traditional fishermen and trawler owners. The campaign resulted in restrictions on trawling, including a ban during the monsoon months which is the breeding season for several important species of fish. The ban imposed in 1988 and 1989 resulted in a better harvest in the aftermath of the monsoons.[13]

The clash between the fishermen and mechanized trawler owners in Kerala has reached the courts. In 1980 the Kerala government enacted the Kerala Marine Fishing Regulation Act. The operators of mechanized vessels challenged notifications issued under the Act that prohibited mechanized vessels from trawling within the territorial waters and banned the use of certain types of gear by the mechanized craft. In a detailed judgment reviewing the history of the conflict, the Supreme Court upheld the notifications. The court found that the ban was a reasonable restriction on the freedom to trade since it was necessary for protecting the source of livelihood of traditional fisherfolk and also to save the pelagic fish wealth within the territorial waters from depletion.[14]

III. COASTAL DEVELOPMENT

The Indian coastline is protected by two primary sets of regulations framed in 2019 under the Environment (Protection) Act of 1986. The mainland coast is regulated by the Coastal

---

10 Part X-B gave effect to the provisions of the International Convention on Civil Liability for Oil Pollution Damage (1969); and Part XI-A gave effect to amendments to the International Convention for the Prevention of Pollution of Sea by Oil (1954).

11 (2016) SCC Online NGT 479 and (2017) SCC Online NGT 7.

12 The case is discussed in the National Green Tribunal chapter.

13 Madhav Gadgil & Ramachandra Guha, *Ecology and Equity* 16, 81–3 (1995).

14 *State of Kerala v Joseph Antony* AIR 1994 SC 721.

Regulation Zone (CRZ) notification of 18 January 2019.[15] Coastal stretches of the Andaman and Nicobar Islands and the Lakshadweep Islands are protected by the Island Coastal Regulation Zone (ICRZ) notification issued on 8 March 2019.[16]

The regime evolved in four stages. The first stage comprised administrative directions issued by the Prime Minister in 1981. The second step came a decade later with the framing of the first national regime under the EPA—the CRZ notification of 1991. This was followed in 2011 by the MoEF splitting the coastal regulations into two sets: one set for the mainland and the other for islands. Finally, we have two notifications in 2019 which continue the dual regime.

Since 1991, development along coastal stretches has been severely restricted. The broad structure of the CRZ regime comprises: (i) defining the regulated zone; (ii) classifying coastal areas based on ecological importance and the existing level of development; (iii) enumerating permissible activity; (iv) listing prohibited activity; (v) prescribing limits and rules for coastal development where permissible; (vi) preparing coastal zone management plans intended to identify the regulated zone on a map so that citizens are aware whether a particular location is impacted by the regulations; and (vii) constituting coastal zone management authorities. There is no special enforcement agency and the task of implementing coastal regulations primarily falls on the municipality or the collector in rural areas. Development along the coast must meet the twin requirements of local town and country planning laws as well as the overriding provisions of the CRZ Regulations.

Pre-1991

Foreshore development was initially regulated by building rules under local planning laws or the land revenue code. The first federal initiative came on 27 November 1981 when Prime Minister Indira Gandhi wrote to the state Chief Ministers:

> I have received a number of reports about the degradation and mis-utilisation of beaches in our coastal states by building and other activity. This is worrying as the beaches have aesthetic and environmental value as well as other uses. They have to be kept clear of all activities at least upto 500 m from the water at the maximum high tide. If the area is vulnerable to erosion, suitable trees and plants have to be planted on the beach sands without marring their beauty.
>
> Beaches must be kept free from all kinds of artificial development. Pollution from industrial and town wastes must be also avoided totally.
>
> Please give thought to this matter and insure that our lively coastline and its beaches remain unsullied.[17]

Several coastal states urged the Centre to reduce the restriction to a distance of 200 m from the high-tide line (HTL) since the prohibition discouraged tourism. In 1986, the Union Government set up an inter-ministerial committee to scrutinize proposals for setting up tourist resorts in Goa, Thiruvananthapuram, Mahabalipuram and Puri. In respect of these specific beaches, the limit of 500 m was relaxed to 200 m from the HTL. An early public interest litigation seeking to enforce the Prime Minister's directive against a hotel resort in

---

[15] Notification No. GSR 37 (E) dated 18 January 2019. The CRZ notification must be read with Notification No. SO 2502 (E) dated 12 July 2019 regarding permissible structures such as container-based toilet blocks, changing rooms, shower panels, drinking water kiosks, portable seating, etc. for the purpose of improving 12 popular beaches for Blue Flag certification. A 'Blue Flag' beach provides clean bathing water and essential infrastructure for tourists.

[16] Notification No. SO 1242 (E) dated 8 March 2019 as amended by Notification No. SO 3840 (E) dated 3 August 2018.

[17] Quoted in Shyam Chainani, *Heritage and Environment: An Indian Diary* 205 (2007).

Goa was rejected by the Bombay High Court in 1988. The court held that the directive was no more than an executive fiat, without the authority of law.[18] Nevertheless, the diktat was beneficial. Several large government projects relocated away from the coastal zone in view of the directive.[19]

In July 1983, the Union Department of Environment[20] issued administrative guidelines to regulate the development of beaches.[21] Beaches were defined to cover the entire coast as well as the waterfront along rivers and lakes. These guidelines laid the foundation for the statutory regulations that followed in the next decade.

Gulf Goans examines the informal regime that preceded the 1991 Regulations and concluded that it lacked bite. Neither the judgment's compact analysis nor the eventual outcome offered much solace to the harried hoteliers who constructed according to plans and yet found their project mired in litigation for nearly a quarter of a century.

GULF GOANS HOTELS COMPANY LIMITED v UNION OF INDIA
(2014) 10 SCC 673

RANJAN GOGOI, J:

* * *

The appellants are the owners of hotels, beach resorts and beach bungalows in Goa who have been facing the prospect of demolition of their properties for the last several decades. The respondent Goa Foundation is a non-governmental body which claims to be dedicated to the cause of environmental and ecological well being of the State of Goa. The respondent Goa Foundation had filed parallel writ petitions before the High Court for demolition of the allegedly illegal constructions raised by the appellants. Both sets of writ petitions i.e. those filed by the appellants against the orders of demolition by the State authorities and the writ petitions filed by the Goa Foundation seeking demolition of constructions raised by each of the appellants were heard together by the Bombay High Court. The High Court, by separate impugned orders dated 13-7-2000, had upheld the orders passed by the authorities requiring the appellants to demolish the existing structures. It is against the aforesaid orders passed by the High Court that the present group of appeals have been filed upon grant of leave by this Court under Article 136 of the Constitution of India.

The constructions raised by the appellants are not *per se* illegal in the conventional sense. They are not without permission and sanction of the competent authority. What has been alleged by the State and has been approved by the High Court is that such constructions are in derogation of the environmental guidelines in force warranting demolition of the same as a step to safeguard the environment of the beaches in Goa. Specifically, it is the case of the State that the constructions in question are between 90 to 200 m from the high tide line (HTL) despite the fact that under the guidelines in force, which partake the character of law, constructions within 500 m of HTL are prohibited except in rare situations where construction activity between 200 to 500 m from HTL is permitted subject to observance of strict conditions. Admittedly, all constructions, though completed on different dates and in different phases, were so completed before the Coastal Regulation Zone (CRZ) [Regulations] were enacted (w.e.f. 19-2-1991) in exercise of the powers under the Environment (Protection) Act, 1986.

The above basis on which the impugned action of the State is founded has been sought to be answered by the appellants by contending that at the relevant point of time when building permissions and sanctions were granted in respect of the constructions undertaken,

18 *Sergio Carvalho v State of Goa* 1989 (1) GOA LAW TIMES 276, 289.

19 Shyam Chainani, *supra* note 17 at 206.

20 Predecessor to the Union Ministry of Environment and Forests.

21 Department of Environment, Government of India, *Environmental Guidelines for Development of Beaches* (1983).

the prohibition was with regard to construction within 90 m from HTL. Admittedly, none of the constructions are within the said divide. The guidelines, detailed reference to which are made in the succeeding paragraphs of the present order, are not 'law' so as to constitute activities contrary thereto as acts of infringement of the law and hence illegal. Such guidelines do not confer the power of enforcement and lack the authority to bring about any penal consequences....

The question 'what is "law"?' has perplexed many a jurisprude; yet, the search for the elusive definition continues. It may be unwise to posit an answer to the question; rather, one may proceed by examining the points of consensus in jurisprudential theories. What appears to be common to all these theories is the notion that law must possess a certain *form*; contain a clear mandate/explicit command which may be prescriptive, permissive or penal and the law must also seek to achieve a clearly identifiable purpose. While the form itself or absence thereof will not be determinative and its impact has to be considered as a lending or supporting force, the disclosure of a clear mandate and purpose is indispensable.

It may, therefore, be understood that a government policy may acquire the 'force of "law"' if it conforms to a certain form possessed by other laws in force and encapsulates a mandate and discloses a specific purpose. It is from the aforesaid prescription that the guidelines relied upon by the Union of India in this case, will have to be examined to determine whether the same satisfies the minimum elements of law. The said guidelines are:

1. Directives to the State Governments in Letter dated 27-11-1981 of the then Prime Minister;
2. Notification dated 22-7-1982 of the Governor setting up the Ecological Development Council for Goa, *inter alia*, for scrutiny of beach construction within 500 m of HTL;
3. Environmental Guidelines for Development of Beaches of July 1983;
4. Order dated 11-6-1986 of the Under-Secretary, Ministry of Tourism, also addressed to Chief Secretary, Government of Goa, constituting an Inter-Ministerial Committee for considering tourist projects within 500 m.

The genesis of the Executive's decision to restrict construction activity within 500 m of HTL can be traced to the Stockholm Conference. It is India's participation in the Conference that led to the introduction of Articles 48-A and 51-A(g) in the Constitution and the enactment of several legislations like the Air (Prevention and Control of Pollution) Act, 1981; the Forest (Conservation) Act, 1980; the Environment (Protection) Act, 1986, etc. all of which seek to protect, preserve and safeguard the environment. It may be possible to view the aforesaid guidelines as 'affirmative action', aimed at implementation of Articles 21 and 48-A of the Constitution and, therefore, outlining a visible purpose. The search for a clear, unambiguous and unequivocal command to regulate the conduct of the citizens in the said guidelines must also be equally fruitful. However, we are unable to find in the said guidelines any expressed or clearly defined dicta. In fact, having read and considered the guidelines, we are left with a reasonable doubt as to whether what has been spelt out therein are not mere suggestions or opinions expressed in the process of a continuing exploration to identify the correct parameters that would effectuate the purpose i.e. safeguarding and protecting the environment (sea beaches) from human exploitation and degradation. The above is particularly significant in view of the fact that the Stockholm Declaration in its core resolutions, merely enunciates very broad propositions and commitments including those concerning the sea beaches as distinguished from specific parameters that could have application, without variation or exception, to all the signatories to the declaration. The Stockholm Conference having nowhere expressed any internationally approved parameters of acceptable distance from HTL, incorporation of any such feature of international values in the municipal laws of the country cannot arise even on the principle enunciated in *Gramophone Co of India v Birendra Bahadur Pandey* (1984) 2 SCC 534.

The position is best highlighted by noticing in a little detail the objectives sought to be achieved in the Stockholm Conference and the core principles adopted therein so far as they are relevant to the issues in hand:

'The United Nations Conference on the Human Environment, having met at Stockholm from 5 to 16 June 1972, having considered the need for a common outlook and for common principles to inspire and guide the peoples of the world in the preservation and enhancement of the human environment....

The Conference calls upon Governments and peoples to exert common efforts for the preservation and improvement of the human environment, for the benefit of all the people and for their posterity.' (emphasis supplied)

Extract of the relevant principles —

'*Principle 7*

States shall take all possible steps to prevent pollution of the seas by substances that are liable to create hazards to human health, to harm living resources and marine life, to damage amenities or to interfere with other legitimate uses of the sea....

Principle 11

The environmental policies of all States should enhance and not adversely affect the present or future development potential of developing countries, nor should they hamper the attainment of better living conditions for all, and appropriate steps should be taken by States and international organisations with a view to reaching agreement on meeting the possible national and international economic consequences resulting from the application of environmental measures....

Principle 14

Rational planning constitutes an essential tool for reconciling any conflict between the needs of development and the need to protect and improve the environment....'

Article 77 of the Constitution provides the form in which the Executive must make and authenticate its orders and decisions. Clause (1) of Article 77 provides that all executive action of the Government must be expressed to be taken in the name of the President.... Clause (2) of Article 77 also provides for the authentication of orders and instruments in a manner as may be prescribed by the Rules. In this regard, vide S.O. No. 2297 dated 3-11-1958 published in the Gazette of India, the President has issued the Authentication (Orders and Other Instruments) Rules, 1958. The said Rules have been superseded subsequently in 2002. Admittedly, the provisions of the said 1958 Rules had not been followed in the present case insofar as the promulgation of the guidelines is concerned.

In the absence of due authentication and promulgation of the guidelines, the contents thereof cannot be treated as an order of the Government and would really represent an expression of opinion. In law, the said guidelines and their binding effect would be no more than what was expressed by this Court in *State of Uttaranchal v Sunil Kumar Vaish* (2011) 8 SCC 670 in the following paragraph of the report:

'It is settled law that all executive actions of the Government of India and the Government of a State are required to be taken in the name of the President or the Governor of the State concerned, as the case may be [Articles 77(1) and 166(1)]. Orders and other instruments made and executed in the name of the President or the Governor of a State, as the case may be, are required to be authenticated in the manner specified in the rules made by the President or the Governor, as the case may be [Articles 77(2) and 166(2)]. In other words, unless an order is expressed in the name of the President or the Governor and is authenticated in the manner prescribed by the rules, the same cannot be treated as an order on behalf of the Government.

A noting recorded in the file is merely a noting simpliciter and nothing more. It merely represents expression of opinion by the particular individual. By no stretch of imagination, can such noting be treated as a decision of the Government. Even if the competent authority records its opinion in the file on the merits of the matter under consideration, the same cannot be termed as a decision of the Government unless it is sanctified and acted upon by issuing an order in accordance with Articles 77(1) and (2) or Articles 166(1) and (2). The noting in the file or even a decision gets culminated into an order affecting right of the parties only when it is expressed in the name of the President or the Governor, as the case may be, and authenticated in the manner provided in Article 77(2) or Article 166(2). A noting or even a decision recorded in the file can always be reviewed/reversed/overruled or overturned and the court cannot take cognizance of the earlier noting or decision for exercise of the power of judicial review.'

It is also essential that what is claimed to be a law must be notified or made public in order to bind the citizen. In *Harla v State of Rajasthan* AIR 1951 SC 467, while dealing with the vires of the Jaipur Opium Act, which was enacted by a resolution passed by the Council of Ministers, though never published in the Gazette, this Court had observed:

'Natural justice requires that before a law can become operative it must be promulgated or published. It must be broadcast in some recognisable way so that all men may know what it is, or, at the very least, there must be some special rule or regulation or customary channel by or through which such knowledge can be acquired with the exercise of due and reasonable diligence. The thought that a decision reached in the secret recesses of a chamber to which the public have no access and to which even their accredited representatives have no access and of which they can normally know nothing, can nevertheless affect their lives, liberty and property by the mere passing of a resolution without anything more, is abhorrent to civilised man. . . .'

If the guidelines relied upon by the Union of India in the present case fail to satisfy the essential and vital parameters/requirements of law as the trend of the above discussion would go to show, the same cannot be enforced to the prejudice of the appellants as has been done in the present case. For the same reason, the issue raised with regard to the authority of the Union to enforce the guidelines on the coming into force of the provisions of the Environment (Protection) Act so as to bring into effect the impugned consequences, adverse to the appellants, will not require any consideration.

An argument had been offered by learned counsel appearing for the respondent, Goa Foundation, that while dealing with issues concerning ecology and environment, a strict view of environmental degradation, which counsel would contend has occurred in the present case, should be adopted having regard to the rights of a large number of citizens to enjoy a pristine and pollution free environment by virtue of Article 21 of the Constitution. We cannot appreciate the above view. Violation of Article 21 on account of alleged environmental violation cannot be subjectively and individually determined when parameters of permissible/impermissible conduct are required to be legislatively or statutorily determined under sections 3 and 6 of the Environment (Protection) Act, 1986 which has been so done by bringing into force the Coastal Regulation Zone (CRZ) Notification w.e.f. 19-2-1991.

In view of the foregoing discussion, the orders impugned in the writ petitions filed by the appellants cannot be sustained. Consequently, the said orders as well as each of the orders dated 13-7-2000 passed by the High Court of Bombay will have to be set aside which we hereby do while allowing the appeals.

NOTES AND QUESTIONS

1. Was there an alternative approach to deciding this case? For instance, if a person builds in terms of a sanctioned plan, short of fraud, demolition ought not to be directed, since a citizen is entitled to assume that the planning authority knows the law when it sanctions plans. Would this simple approach strengthen the Rule of Law and reduce the protracted uncertainty of litigation?

2. In 1991, when the cases began in the Bombay High Court at Goa, the CRZ Regulations were freshly minted and required judicial interpretation. The petitions remained in the High Court for nine years, culminating in demolition orders which the Supreme Court took 14 years to overturn. Prolonged legal risk smothers enterprise. What can courts do to reduce the wait? Perhaps, limit the length of pleadings and oral arguments? How can lawyers enhance efficiency? Is there a role and responsibility for Bar associations to foster legal reform?

3. The Supreme Court judgment is sound as it is anchored on a foundational principle: impinging on citizens' rights is a serious business. To do so, government must show the sanction of law. Executive guidelines to streamline administration and create policy are fine, so long as they do not violate individual rights. Hence the enquiry—'what is law?' and when do administrative directives qualify as law?

4. The Union Government and the Goa Foundation reached out to the Stockholm Declaration of 1972 to justify demolition. Was this a bit of a stretch? How well informed should hoteliers be? Is the study of international conference deliberations part of a hotelier's curriculum?

CRZ 1991

In February, 1991 the Union Ministry of Environment and Forests (MoEF) framed regulations under the Environment (Protection) Act of 1986 (EPA), and the Environment (Protection) Rules of 1986, to preserve a coastal zone extending over a strip of land up to 500 m from the HTL along the entire Indian coast.

The 1991 CRZ Regulations were poorly drafted, leading to a great deal of uncertainty. The non-standard format of these Regulations contributed to the confusion. The opening clause of the 1991 CRZ Regulations defined the regulatory zone:

> [T]he coastal stretches of seas, bays, estuaries, creeks, rivers and backwaters which are influenced by tidal action (in the landward side) upto 500 meters from the High Tide Line (HTL) and the land between the Low Tide Line (LTL) and the HTL.

When originally issued, the paragraph continued:

> For purposes of this Notification, the High Tide Line (HTL) will be defined as the line up to which the highest high tide reaches at spring tides.
>
> Note: The distance from the High Tide Line (HTL) to which the proposed regulations will apply in the case of rivers, creeks and backwaters may be modified on a case by case basis for reasons to be recorded while preparing the Coastal Zone Management Plans (referred to below); however this distance shall not be less than 100 meters or the width of the creek, river or backwater whichever is less.

On 18 August 1994, an amending notification was issued substituting the clause quoted above, with the words:

> For the purposes of this notification, the High Tide Line means the line on the land upto which the highest water line reaches during the spring tide and shall be demarcated uniformly in all parts of the country by the demarcating authority so authorised by the Central Government in consultation with the Surveyor General of India.
>
> Note: The distance from the High Tide Line shall apply to both sides in the case of rivers, creeks and backwaters and may be modified on a case by case basis for reasons to be recorded while preparing the Coastal Zone Management Plans. However, this distance shall not be less than 50 meters or the width of the creek, river or backwater, whichever is less. The distance upto which development along rivers, creeks and backwaters is to be regulated shall be governed by the distance upto which the tidal effect of sea is experienced in rivers, creeks or backwaters, as the case may be, and should be clearly identified in the Coastal Zone Management Plans.

In *Indian Council for Enviro-Legal Action v Union of India*,[22] the Supreme Court held that the amendment reducing the width of the zone from 100 m to 50 m in respect of rivers, creeks and backwaters was contrary to the object of the EPA and was illegal. While the intention of the order to restore the 100 m zone is clear, the effect of the judicial declaration is uncertain. The judgment does not in clear words restore the original 100 m zone. It appears to strike down the words '50 meters', leaving a gap in the Regulations.[23]

Hoteliers were quick to criticize the new 1991 regime, claiming that the CRZ Regulations would stifle beach tourism. Responding to this lobby, the MoEF constituted an Expert Committee headed by B B Vohra to examine whether the 1991 notification needed amendment. The Vohra Committee submitted its report on 31 December 1991 which was followed by the MoEF diluting the parent CRZ notification on 18 August 1994.

The relaxation of norms was assailed by the Indian Council for Enviro-Legal Action (ICELA) led by M C Mehta, in an Article 32 petition before the Supreme Court. The court struck down portions of the amendment that may have adversely affected coastal ecology and modified others to conform with the object of the CRZ Regulations.[24]

Meanwhile, in interlocutory proceedings in ICELA's case, the Supreme Court took notice of widespread breaches of the law and issued a general moratorium on *all* development within 500 m of the HTL.[25] Several projects, big and small, were halted. Four months later, the Supreme Court lifted the ban, but required strict enforcement of the CRZ Regulations: 'The activities that have been declared as prohibited within the Coastal Regulation Zone shall not be undertaken by any of the Respondent-States. The regulation of permissible activities shall also be meticulously followed.'[26] In a similar vein, in May 1995 the Supreme Court issued an interim injunction in the *Shrimp Culture* case, prohibiting the setting up of new shrimp farms or the conversion of agricultural lands for aquaculture purposes in the coastal stretches of Andhra Pradesh, Tamil Nadu and Pondicherry.[27] This injunction was extended to all the coastal states in August 1995.[28]

On 18 April 1996, the Supreme Court rendered judgment in the petition filed by ICELA.[29] Amongst the directions issued by the court was a deadline to all coastal states to file their CZMPs (Coastal Zone Management Plans) with the MoEF by 30 June 1996. The MoEF was directed to approve the plans by September 1996. A flurry of activity ensued, culminating in the MoEF issuing separate letters to each state on 27 September 1996 approving the CZMPs with modifications.[30] The conditions imposed by the MoEF in each letter are part of the CZMP and are integral to the coastal regime in each state.[31]

On 31 January 1997, the CRZ Regulations were amended a second time to overcome the practical difficulties faced by the islanders of Andaman and Nicobar. A third set of amendments

---

22 *CRZ Notification* case (1996) 5 SCC 281.

23 The Supreme Court order assumes that apart from having the power to strike down the invalid portion of the regulations, the court may also *modify* the wording to cure the provision of the *ultra vires* effect.

24 *CRZ Notification* case (1996) 5 SCC 281.

25 *Indian Council for Enviro-Legal Action v Union of India* 1995 (2) SCALE 120, order dated 12 December 1994.

26 AIR 1995 SC 2252, 2253, order dated 9 March 1995.

27 *S. Jagannath v Union of India* 1995 (3) SCALE 126.

28 1995 (5) SCALE 66.

29 *Supra* note 24.

30 The approval letters for all the states and Union territories are published by the Goa Foundation in *The Coastal Regulation Zone Notification in India* (1997).

31 The approval letters were in a standard format. Part 'A' enumerates general conditions applicable to all states. Part 'B' mentions specific conditions, modifications and clarifications particular to each state.

were introduced on 9 July 1997 to reduce the difficulties being faced by the local people and also for construction of essential facilities in the coastal zone.

Apart from the statutory modifications, the MoEF issued letters explaining the scope of the Regulations. On 27 March 1998 the MoEF wrote to the Chief Secretary, government of Maharashtra: 'In the areas categorized as CRZ-II, construction of buildings can be permitted on the landward side of the imaginary line drawn along the existing authorized structures.' On 8 September 1998, the MoEF clarified that the imaginary line would run parallel to the HTL and connect authorized structures on adjoining plots. The ministry also explained the ambit of the expression 'existing authorized buildings' to cover buildings of a permanent nature that were constructed in accordance with building regulations prior to the coming in force of the 1991 notification.[32]

In terms of clause 4 of the 1991 CRZ Regulations, the MoEF constituted a National Coastal Zone Management Committee (NCC) in August 1998. The NCC comprised eight officials and four representatives of fisherfolk and coastal communities. Its functions were chiefly to advise the MoEF on matters relating to coastal policy, planning and enforcement of the Regulations. The NCC was stillborn, yielding to a National Coastal Zone Management Authority (NCZMA) which was notified on 26 November 1998.[33]

The constitution of the NCZMA was identical to the NCC, with the same proportion of official and community representation. However, the NCZMA was conferred greater power to effectively protect the coast. The functions of the Authority include coordinating the actions by State Coastal Zone Management Authorities (SCZMAs), examining proposals for changes in the classification of coastal areas or in CZMPs, recommending suitable changes to the MoEF and ensuring strict compliance with the CRZ Regulations. For effective implementation, the NCZMA was empowered to review cases of CRZ violations and, where necessary, to issue remedial directions under section 5 of the EPA. The Authority was also empowered to file complaints under section 19 of the EPA (to initiate prosecutions) and, in terms of section 10 of the EPA, could enter and inspect any place with a view to ascertaining the facts. Moreover, the NCZMA was required to provide technical assistance to state governments, institutions and authorities that seek its guidance in matters relating to the coastal environment.

Simultaneously with the constitution of the NCZMA, the MoEF issued a series of orders constituting separate SCZMAs for each coastal state and Union territory. The SCZMAs comprised six or seven persons, who were either officials in government departments or experts on coastal issues. Unlike the NCZMA, the SCZMAs did not when originally constituted have any community or NGO representation. The functions and powers of the SCZMAs were similar to those of the NCZMA.

The battle to save India's coast from destruction has several foot soldiers. Shyam Chainani, a pioneering environmentalist, was at the forefront of efforts by citizens to frame a law. He recounts the saga in *Heritage and Environment: An Indian Diary*.[34] In a separate volume, Chainani recalls the arduous battle to save the island of Nhava from development pressures. His account shows the importance of engaging with the bureaucracy at the stage of preparing the CZMP and how much can be achieved in this way.

---

[32] See *Ameeta Shah v State of Maharashtra* 2003 (5) Bom C Rep 95 and Annexure II of the document at, shorturl.at/gxSW9, accessed 22 June 2021.

[33] The NCZMA notification superseded the NCC notification and came to be issued after the Supreme Court expressed its dissatisfaction on 21 August 1998 regarding the designation and powers of the NCC. *Indian Council for Enviro-Legal Action v Union of India* 1998 (5) Scale 5 (SP).

[34] Shyam Chainani, *supra* note 17.

SHYAM CHAINANI; NHAVA & SHEVA, BATTLING FOR THE ENVIRONMENT: OIL, PORTS AND THE COASTLINE 188 (2012)

In conservation it is necessary to have as many layers of protection as possible. With Nhava being on the waterfront, the CRZ Notification is an obvious instrument for environmental protection.

The CRZ Notification divides coastlines (which include all waters such as rivers, creeks and backwaters which are subject to tidal action) into three categories of areas. CRZ I includes ecologically sensitive areas in which hardly any development is permitted within 500 meters of the High Tide Line. In CRZ II (areas which are substantially built up within municipal limits), by and large normal urban development is permitted with some restrictions. In CRZ III (areas which are not substantially built up), very restricted development is allowed.

In the Coastal Zone Management Plan of Greater Bombay which was to go to the Environment Ministry for approval, the Maharashtra Government had classified the whole of Greater Bombay and New Bombay as CRZ II. When I bumped into D T Joseph in the High Court in July 1993, I pointed out that the whole of Bombay could by no means be classified as 'substantially built up', specially the very large green areas of Madh, Erangal, Marve, Manori, Gorai and the huge stretches of mangroves on the north-eastern coast of Bombay. I was a member of the Environment Ministry Coastal Zone Task Force and suggested to D T Joseph that rather than fighting in Delhi, we should settle matters amongst ourselves in Bombay. Even though he had already signed the file, he accepted the logic and over the next two-and-a-half years discussions took place. Eventually in November 1995, a point of view was accepted.

Once agreement had been reached for Greater Bombay, I asked that the same logic be applied to New Bombay and that the area which had been classified in New Bombay's Development Plan as 'Regional Park' be classified as CRZ III or CRZ I. D T Joseph eventually agreed that (except for the villages in Uran), Regional Park lands abutting the sea and also the creeks could be classified as CRZ III or CRZ I. This was a huge step forward and would protect all of Nhava. However, after D T Joseph was transferred, R.C. Sinha, his successor as Urban Development Secretary, tried hard to get this decision reversed but failed.

The Coastal Zone Management Plan (CZMP) for Maharashtra, as approved by the Environment Ministry on 27th September 1996, stipulated: 'All areas marked in the development plan of New Bombay as Regional Parks are classified as CRZ III. These include Nerul and Nhava. In case of Nhava, the areas mentioned in the environmental clearance issued by this Ministry vide letter No. J-11013/21/88-IA, dated 16.9.1988. For Nhava Sheva Port project, viz., the green area of 500 meters all along the periphery of the port; *800 ha. Afforestation land inside the port and low-lying areas for mangrove plantation, along with mudflats and mangroves on the shoreline around Nhava, are classified as CRZ-I.*' (Emphasis mine). In addition to protecting Nhava, this stipulation would also apply to the coastline of Uran which we had fought for long and arduously.

However, CIDCO[35] once again tried very hard to get the whole of New Bombay declared as CRZ II. My colleague, Samir Mehta and I protested furiously over several years pointing out that these areas were not substantially built up and could not be classified as CRZ II and gave a large number of photographs to prove our point.

Eventually on 29 May 2000 the Environment Ministry constituted a committee to look into the issue. I was one of the committee members. The only NGO member, and had a very difficult time....

The reason CIDCO gave for wanting Nhava classified as CRZ II, was that they wished to develop roadside amenities and facilities along the 15-metre-wide stretch on the south side of the Nhava-mainland *bundh*. This proposal would involve the destruction of dense mangroves on both sides of the *bundh*. Another reason CIDCO gave was that Sewri-Nhava road bridge would land there and attract illegal development. It was not clear how destruction of

[35] The authority developing New Bombay (Navi Mumbai).

mangroves and construction of roadside amenities would stop illegal encroachment. One of the Committee members had missed this discussion and did not believe me when I told him of the proposal. CIDCO pressed for this proposal several times, especially after the Committee visited this area. This was turned down.

Perhaps more importantly, the classification of CRZ II and CRZ I for Nhava was not disturbed.

NOTES AND QUESTIONS

1. Are the CRZ Regulations consistent with India's federal system of government? Is it sound legislative policy to enable a ministry in Delhi to impose nationwide restrictions affecting 3,000 sq kms of coastal stretches through subordinate legislation? Remember, 'land', 'fisheries' and local authority administration are subjects in the State List (List II) of the Seventh Schedule to the Constitution of India. Do the CRZ Regulations encroach upon the powers of municipalities, local communities and the state governments to regulate and develop coastal stretches within their territory?

2. Are the CRZ Regulations 'democratic'? Do they allow local communities to participate in decisions relating to the nature of the development in their neighbourhood? Is it wise to impose a single set of regulations for the entire length of the Indian coast, without regard to regional factors such as population density, geography, social and community needs and aesthetic features?

3. Like forests, rivers and the air we breathe, the coast is a common property resource. Do the CRZ Regulations preserve the common property for the benefit of the community at large or do they operate as a 'fencing regime' similar to the Forest (Conservation) Act of 1980 and the Wild Life (Protection) Act of 1972? Are fencing regimes that alienate local communities from the immediate environment a sustainable solution for the medium and long-term management of natural resources?

4. The CRZ Regulations are framed under section 3(2)(v) of the EPA which enables the Central Government to impose restrictions on areas where any industry, operation or process or class of industries, operations or processes may be carried out. Considering the power under which the CRZ Regulations are framed, it is hardly surprising that the framework of these regulations is exclusionary rather than participative. What changes might you introduce in the CRZ Regulations to allow community inputs in planning and development decisions?

5. There is no provision in the notifications constituting the NCZMA and SCZMAs for budgetary support. One of the principal constraints that impede the proper functioning of the pollution control boards is a lack of resources. In the absence of dedicated personnel, adequate resources and proper budgets the coastal zone management authorities have functioned ineffectively. Is it worthwhile setting up environmental authorities without guaranteeing funds for the effective implementation of environmental laws?

Diluting CRZ 1991

The Indian Council for Enviro-Legal Action filed a petition under Article 32 of the Constitution complaining that the Central Government was remiss in implementing the CRZ notification of 1991. The petitioner submitted that non-implementation had led to continued degradation of the coast. In ICELA's petition, Goa Foundation filed an application challenging the validity of the notification dated 16 August 1994 by which the main notification dated 19 February 1991 was amended.

INDIAN COUNCIL FOR ENVIRO-LEGAL ACTION v UNION OF INDIA
(1996) 5 SCC 281

ORDER:

* * *

According to clause [3(3)(i)] of the main Notification, the coastal States and Union Territory Administrations were required to prepare the Management Plans within one year from the date of the main Notification. This was essential for the implementation of the said Notification. The lack of commitment on the part of these States and Administrations, towards the protection and regulation of the coastal stretches, is evident from their inaction in complying with the aforesaid statutory directive requiring the preparation of Management Plans within the specified period. In view of the fact that there had been a non-compliance with this provision, this Court on 3.4.1995 directed all the coastal States and Union Territory Administrations to frame their plans within a further period of six weeks thereof.

A status report was filed in court by the Union of India which shows non compliance of clause [3(3)(i)] by practically everyone concerned.... Explanations for the delay in preparation of the Management Plans and their approval have been offered, but they are far from satisfactory. If the mere enactment of the laws relating to the protection of environment was to ensure a clean and pollution free environment, then India would, perhaps, be the least polluted country in the world. But, this is not so. There are stated to be over 200 Central and state statutes which have at least some concern with environment protection, either directly or indirectly. The plethora of such enactments has, unfortunately, not resulted in preventing environmental degradation which, on the contrary, has increased over the years. Enactment of a law, relating to protection of environment, usually provides for what activity can or cannot be done by people. If the people were to voluntarily respect such a law, and abide by it, then it would result in law being able to achieve the object for which it was enacted. Where, however, there is a conflict between the provision of law and personal interest, then it often happens that self-discipline and respect for law disappear.

Enactment of a law, but tolerating its infringement is worse than not enacting law at all. The continued infringement of law, over a period of time, is made possible by adoption of such means which are best known to the violators of law. Continued tolerance of such violations of law not only renders legal provisions nugatory but such tolerance by the Enforcement Authorities encourages lawlessness and adoption of means which cannot, or ought not to be tolerated in any civilized society.... When a law is enacted containing some provisions which prohibit certain types of activities, then, it is of utmost importance that such legal provisions are effectively enforced. If a law is enacted but is not being voluntarily obeyed, then, it has to be enforced. Otherwise infringement of law, which is actively or passively condoned for personal gain, will be encouraged which will in turn lead to a lawless society. Violation of anti-pollution laws not only adversely affects the existing quality of life but the non-enforcement of the legal provisions often results in ecological imbalance and degradation of environment, the adverse effect of which will have to be borne by the future generations.

The present case also shows that having issued the main Notification, no follow up action was taken either by the coastal states and union territories or by the Central Government. The provisions of the main Notification appear to have been ignored and, possibly, violated with impunity....

The Notification dated 18.8.1994 made six amendments in the main Notification. These amendments were made after the receipt of the report of a Committee, headed by Mr B B Vohra, which had been set up by the Central Government. The validity of amended Notification was also challenged in I A 19/1995 which was filed by three environment protection groups, namely, the Goa Foundation, Nirmal Vishwa and Indian Heritage Society (Goa Chapter). In the said application, the applicants gave a table containing the main points of the main Notification, the recommendations made by the Vohra Committee and the amendments made by amended Notification of 1994. The said particulars are as follows:

Main CRZ Notification dated 19.2.1991	Vohra Committee recommendations	Amending Notification dated 18.8.94
1. 200 meters from HTL is no-development zone.	Relaxation allowed [for] rocky and hilly areas; No limit specified.	Blanket relaxation for all areas up to HTL if Central Government so desires.
2. No-development zone for rivers, creeks and backwaters: 100 meters.	Clarification demanded about limits; no relaxation suggested.	No-development zone relaxed to 50 meters.
3. No leveling or digging or sand dunes or sand.	Allows destruction of sand dunes.	No destruction of sand dunes allowed. However, goal posts, net posts, lamp posts allowed.
4. No-development zone area cannot be used for FSI calculations.	Recommends no-development zone area be permitted for FSI calculations.	Relevant section not amended but explanation added as an after-thought in the Notification permitting no-development zone area to be included for FSI Calculations.
5. No basements allowed; area not to be included in FSI.	Basement permitted.	Basement allowed.
6. No fencing permitted within 300 meters zone from HTL.	Only green fencing permitted, no barbed wire fencing allowed.	Allows green and barbed wire fencing.

* * *

According to the Union of India, while implementing the main Notification, certain practical difficulties were faced by the concerned authorities. There was a need for having sustainable development of tourism in coastal areas and that amendments were effected after giving due consideration to all relevant issues pertaining to environment protection and balancing of the same with the requirement of development. It has been specifically averred that a Committee headed by Mr B B Vohra was set-up by the Government in response to the need for examining the issues relating to development of tourism and hotel industry in coastal areas and to regulate the same keeping in view the requirements of sustainable development and the fragile coastal ecology. According to the Union of India, the Committee also included three environmentalist members who had expressed their views and that the Government had accepted the recommendations of the Vohra Committee with slight modifications. According to it, there has been no blanket relaxation in any area as alleged and adequate environmental safeguards have been provided in the 1994 Notification. . . .

The relaxation with regard to [No Development Zone (NDZ)] was sought by the Hotel and Tourism Industry and they desired concession only with regard to 20–30 kms of coastline. By the amended Notification, power had been given to the Central Government to make such relaxation with regard to any part of the 6,000 kms long coastline of India. The Central Government, has, thus, retained the absolute power of relaxation of the entire 6,000 kms long coastline and this, in effect, may lead to the causing of serious ecological damage as the said provision gives unbridled power and does not contain any guidelines as to how or when the power is to be exercised. The said provision is capable of abuse. The Central Government also did not confine the relaxation to the extent as specified by the Vohra Committee. No satisfactory reason has been given by the Union of India as to why it departed from the opinion of the expert Committee and that too in such a manner that the concession which has now been given is far in excess of what was demanded by the Hotel and Tourism Industry.

We, accordingly, hold that the newly added proviso in Annexure III in paragraph 7 sub-paragraph (1) (item i) which gives the Central Government arbitrary, uncanalized and unguided power, the exercise of which may result in serious ecological degradation and may make the NDZ ineffective is ultra vires and is hereby quashed. No suitable reason has been given which can persuade us to hold that the enactment of such a proviso was necessary, in the larger public interest, and the exercise of power under the said proviso will not result in large scale ecological degradation and violation of Article 21 of the citizens living in those areas....

Even the Vohra Committee which had been set-up to look into the demands of Hotel and Tourism Industry had not made such a proposal and, therefore, it appears to us that ... a reduction [to 50 meters] does not appear to [have] been made for any valid reason and is arbitrary. This is more so when it has been alleged that in some areas like Goa, there are mangrove forests that need protection and which stretch to more than 100 meters from the river bank and this contention has not been denied. In the absence of any justification for this reduction being given the only conclusion which can be arrived at is that the relaxation to 50 meters has been done for some extraneous reason.... In the absence of a categorical statement being made in an affidavit that such reduction will not be harmful or result in serious ecological imbalance, we are unable to conclude that the said amendment has been made in the larger public interest and is valid. This amendment is, therefore, contrary to the object of the Environment Act and has not been made for any valid reason and is, therefore, held to be illegal.... We do not see any illegality having been committed by allowing the goal posts, net posts and lamp posts to be erected. In fact the erection of these would facilitate or lead to more enjoyment of the beaches. Therefore, the challenge to this amendment fails....

> We, therefore, modify the amendment and direct that a private owner of land in NDZ shall be entitled to take into account half of such land for the purpose of permissible-FSI in respect of the construction undertaken by him outside the NDZ.

The primary effort of the Court, while dealing with the environmental related issues, is to see that the enforcement agencies, whether it be the state or any other authority, take effective steps for the enforcement of the laws. The Courts, in a way, act as the guardian of the people's fundamental rights but in regard to many technical matters, the Courts may not be fully equipped. Perforce, it has to rely on outside agencies for reports and recommendations whereupon orders have been passed from time to time. Even though, it is not the function of the Court to see the day to day enforcement of the law, that being the function of the Executive, but because of the non-functioning of the enforcement agencies, the Courts as of necessity have had to pass orders directing the enforcement agencies to implement the law.

With the increasing threat to the environmental degradation taking place in different parts of the country, it may not be possible for any single authority to effectively control the same. Environmental degradation is best protected by the people themselves. In this connection, some of the non-governmental organisations (NGOs) and other environmentalists are doing singular service. Time has perhaps come when the Government can usefully draw upon the resources of such NGOs to help and assist in the implementation of the laws relating to protection of environment. Under section 3 of the Act, the Central Government has the power to constitute one or more authorities for the purposes of exercising and performing such powers and functions, including the power to issue directions under section 5 of the Act of the Central Government as may be delegated to them....

NOTES AND QUESTIONS

1. In the two final paragraphs excerpted above, the court seems to sense that it is on the horns of a dilemma: it does not want to intrude on executive functions, and, indeed, recognizes that it lacks the resources to do so. At the same time, as 'the guardian of the people's fundamental rights', it needs 'to pass orders directing the enforcement agencies to implement the law'. But

what can courts do when enforcement agencies flout court orders? Can NGOs be expected to step into this breach?

2. Conventionally, the role of the High Courts and the Supreme Court was limited to striking down invalid portions of delegated legislation. In this case, the Supreme Court went further, and where it considered appropriate, it modified the subordinate legislation by introducing beneficial provisions. Merely striking down the illegal amendments would have left a gap in the CRZ Regulations. What are the limits to this jurisdiction? What may happen if the High Court went about 'modifying' regulations to cure the offending provision of the *ultra vires* effect?

3. In November 1998, more than two and a half years after the judgment, the MoEF constituted National and State Coastal Zone Management Authorities, in response to the suggestion made by the Supreme Court. In one significant respect the suggestion of the court was ignored. In constituting the state authorities, the MoEF did not draw on the expertise of NGOs and environmentalists.

4. The CRZ Regulations extend along rivers, creeks and backwaters that are affected by tidal action. In Goa, tidal action affects all the principal rivers, including the Zuari, the Mandovi and their tributaries. Tidal influence extends several kilometres upstream from the mouth of these rivers. As a result, waterfront development is severely restricted on extensive stretches of riparian property. A similar situation arises along the backwaters of Kerala. Should these regions be exempted from the rigours of the CRZ notification?

5. A laterite stone and concrete beach house on Colva beach, Goa built without approved plans on sand dunes in the CRZ prohibited zone was termed a 'misadventure'. Sunbathers and visitors who earlier enjoyed a thatched roof shack had to now do with the old charm. Upholding the Bombay High Court's demolition order passed at the request of an aggrieved neighbour, the Supreme Court held: 'Construction raised in violation of such regulations cannot be lightly condoned.'[36]

6. The Supreme Court in *Anil Hoble v Kashinath Jairam Shetye*[37] declined to review the evidence produced before the National Green Tribunal and upheld a direction to demolish all structures including a restaurant and pub. The NGT found that when the appellant purchased the property on 3 August 1992, the CRZ notification was in force. At the time of acquisition, the plot had a small structure used as a garage for motor car repair. The NGT refused to buy the appellant's story that the new enterprise was the outcome of permissible repairs and renovations to the old garage.

The Zuari river rises in the Western Ghats and flows west through Sanguem, Quepem, Ponda and Mormugao before meeting the Arabian Sea. Adding to this musical geography, on the north bank of the Zuari, is Bambolim Beach where guests at the Grand Hyatt Hotel enjoy fine views of the tidal river. Because the Bambolim stretch of the river is affected by sea tides, the CRZ Regulations apply. The 1994 amendment to the 1991 Regulations led to a tangle of disputes between the developer and the People's Movement for Civil Action (PMCA). The bone of contention was constructions put up in the 50 m–100 m zone.

[36] *Piedade Filomena Gonsalves v State of Goa* (2004) 3 SCC 445, 447.
[37] (2016) 10 SCC 701.

There are two sets of litigations. In the first set are five decisions of the Supreme Court with the title *Goan Real Estate and Construction Limited.*[38] The Supreme Court decisions are a jumble of confusion worse confounded.[39] The upshot of this quintet is that the Supreme Court framed the question:

> Whether the constructions made or ongoing pursuant to the plans sanctioned on the basis of the notification dated 16 August 1994 would be affected or not[40] by the *ICELA* judgment?

And answered the issue declaring:

> The judgment dated 18 April 1996 rendered in *Indian Council For Enviro-Legal Action* will not affect the ongoing constructions or completed constructions pursuant to the plans sanctioned under the amending Notification of 1994 till two clauses of the same were set aside by this Court.... [The *ICELA* judgment] will not affect the completed or the ongoing constructions being undertaken pursuant to the said notification.[41]

Goan Real Estate (GRE) lucked out before the Supreme Court. In 1993, GRE submitted plans for construction of a hotel and residential complex. At this time, the area up to 100 m from the high-tide line (HTL) was earmarked as 'no development zone' and no construction was permitted within this zone except for repairs. The plans as originally sanctioned contemplated constructions beyond 100 m. With the 1994 amendment, the prohibited zone was relaxed to just 50 m and consequently GRE submitted an additional proposal for constructing 18 blocks in the 50–100 m zone. Approvals were issued and plans revalidated. During a site inspection on 25 September 1996, a village official found that GRE had completed foundation work up to the plinth and in some parts of the property, buildings were complete. Between 1997 until 2005, economic factors impaired construction.

Meanwhile, the Supreme Court rendered its decision in the *ICELA* case on 18 April 1996, where it found that reduction of the no development zone from 100 m to 50 m was illegal. Since constructions in this twilight zone had been built or were ongoing at a time when the 1994 amendment held sway, the MoEF clarified that development activity between 16 August 1994 and 18 April 1996 might be completed but no new development would be allowed after the date of the Supreme Court judgment.

Despite work having stalled for over seven years, the Supreme Court sided with GRE holding its project to be an ongoing one. The court held that the purpose of *ICELA* decision was not to prejudice citizens who had assumed the 1994 amendment to be valid.

After 2010, the stage shifted to the Goa bench of the Bombay High Court where GRE's run of luck continued. PMCA's principal complaint before the High Court was that regardless of GRE's Supreme Court success, all that the developer could lawfully complete in the twilight zone was the buildings envisaged in the sanctioned development plans that were obtained on the date of the *ICELA* judgment. After *ICELA*, GRE could not come up with entirely new plans and layouts in the prohibited zone restored by the Supreme Court. This was because the Supreme Court had held the relaxation illegal and, as a matter of law, any development within 100 m of the HTL was illegal. The only concession to the rigour of the embargo was

38 (2008) 8 SCC 645; (2008) 12 SCC 574; (2010) 5 SCC 388; (2010) 5 SCC 440 and (2010) 5 SCC 441. The first two judgments are dated 28 August 2008 and the three that follow were all delivered on 31 March 2010.

39 This includes 'recall' of the decision reported at (2008) 12 SCC 574 by the judgment reported at (2010) 5 SCC 441 because of a 'mistake' acknowledged by the court.

40 *Goan Real Estate and Construction Ltd v Union of India* (2010) 5 SCC 388, 397.

41 *Id.* at 400.

with respect to ongoing projects but that too would not allow GRE to alter its plans with respect to the 50–100 m zone.

The Bombay High Court rendered a split verdict on 23 January 2014. Justice Roshan Dalvi, after a detailed analysis of the documents, concluded that the construction erected at what is now the Grand Hyatt was at complete variance from the sanctioned plan of 31 May 1995 and the 'alternative' plan relied upon by the developer (mysteriously unavailable in the record of the authorities) was doubtful. Justice Dalvi found that GRE had put up the constructions in a wholly illegal and brazen manner. She ordered removal of the offending construction.

Justice F M Reis agreed with his senior colleague that the plan proffered by the developer was not the approved plan of 1995 but tempered his verdict by allowing the developer to approach the development authorities for securing approval to *revised* plans. Justice Reis understood the Supreme Court's judgment to allow revisions to plans sanctioned on or before 18 April 1996, provided the planning authorities agreed.

Justice U V Bakre, to whom the matter was referred to resolve the conflict, agreed with Justice Reis. Consequently, the developer was allowed to approach the planning authorities and explain why the constructions put up were tolerable deviations. The authorities would then examine the revised plans and decide whether they were approvable. As regards the dubious plan (bearing the endorsement of the statutory authorities) relied upon by the developer, the majority fixed the blame on the developer and awarded 'exemplary and punitive costs' of Rs. 25 lakhs.

Examine all three judgments rendered by the High Court.[42] With whose view do you agree? The majority having found that the plan relied on by the developer was not genuine, it must follow that the constructions put up were unrelated to any statutory approval. In the circumstances, considering the luxury hotel operating at the site, were the costs imposed a flea bite?

IV. THE *SHRIMP CULTURE* CASE

The *Shrimp Culture* case is the second important Supreme Court judgment on coastal ecology during the CRZ 1991 regime. The decision was controversial and an array of political and economic interests joined hands to thwart effective implementation of the judicial orders. The case raised several complicated questions of fact and law, and involved intricate technical issues mixed with policy considerations. Shrimp farms along the coast were causing severe environmental degradation. The farms depleted drinking water supplies, caused salinization, resulted in mangrove destruction, infringed the rights of traditional fisherfolk and damaged wetlands. Shrimp farming also earned foreign exchange for the country from the export of marine products and received strong government backing due to the economic benefits. Aquaculture projects appear to have benefited poor coastal communities that had invested in the shrimp farms by providing employment and income.

On 27 March 1995, the Supreme Court directed the National Environment Engineering Research Institute (NEERI) to visit coastal areas of Andhra Pradesh and Tamil Nadu and report on the prawn farms being set up. NEERI's assignment was later expanded to cover the other coastal states. Concerned at the severe degradation described in NEERI's reports, on 9 May 1995 the Supreme Court directed 'no part of agricultural lands and salt farms be converted into commercial aquaculture farms' and 'no groundwater withdrawal be allowed

[42] The judgments of Justice Dalvi and Justice Reis are reported at *People's Movement for Civil Action v Goa Coastal Zone Management Authority* 2014 (3) BOM C REP 12 and Justice Bakre's judgment is reported at (2015) SCC Online BOM 228.

for aquaculture purposes'. The authorities were restrained from permitting new aquaculture farms from being set up and the local collectors and police superintendents were told to ensure strict enforcement of the interim directions. In August 1995, the Supreme Court directed the coastal states and Union territories as well as the Marine Products Export Development Authority (MPEDA) to issue individual notices of the case to the aqua-farms, to enable them to appear before the court.

In the judgment, the court relied on a paper prepared by Dr Alagarswami, Director of the Central Institute of Brackishwater Aquaculture, Madras (Alagarswami Report), the NEERI Reports and a report prepared by the Justice Suresh Committee which had visited several shrimp farms in Tamil Nadu and Pondicherry in July 1995. We carry a short excerpt from this lengthy judgment.

S JAGANNATH v UNION OF INDIA

AIR 1997 SC 811

KULDIP SINGH, J: Shrimp (Prawn) Culture Industry is taking roots in India. Since long the fishermen in India have been following the traditional rice/shrimp rotating aquaculture system. Rice is grown during part of the year and shrimp and other fish species are cultured during the rest of the year. However, during the last decade the traditional system which, apart from producing rice, produced 140 kgs of shrimp per hectare of land began to give way to more intensive methods of shrimp culture which could produce thousands of kilograms per hectare. A large number of private companies and multinational corporations have started investing in shrimp farms. In the last few years more than eighty thousand hectares of land have been converted to shrimp farming. India's marine export weighed in at 70,000 tonnes in 1993 and these exports are projected to reach 200 thousand tonnes by the year 2000. The shrimp farming advocates regard aquaculture as potential saviour of developing countries because it is a short duration crop that provides a high investment return and enjoys an expanding market. The said expectation is sought to be achieved by replacing the environmentally benign traditional mode of culture by semi-intensive and intensive methods. More and more areas are being brought under semi-intensive and intensive modes of shrimp farming. The environmental impact of shrimp culture essentially depends on the mode of culture adopted in the shrimp farming. Indeed, the new trend of more intensified shrimp farming in certain parts of the country—without much control of feeds, seeds and other inputs and water management practices—has brought to the fore a serious threat to the environment and ecology which has been highlighted before us.

This petition under Art 32 of the Constitution of India—in public interest has been filed by S Jagannathan, Chairman, Gram Swaraj Movement, a voluntary organisation working for the upliftment of the weaker section of society. The petitioner has sought the enforcement of Coastal Zone Regulation Notification dated 19 February 1991 issued by the Government of India, stoppage of intensive and semi-intensive types of prawn farming in the ecologically fragile coastal areas, prohibition from using the waste lands/wetlands for prawn farming and the constitution of National Coastal Management Authority to safeguard the marine life and coastal areas....

Shri M C Mehta, learned counsel for the petitioner has taken us through the NEERI reports and other voluminous material on the record. He has vehemently contended that the modern—other than traditional techniques of shrimp farming are highly polluting and are detrimental to the coastal environment and marine ecology. According to him only the traditional and improved traditional systems of shrimp farming which are environmentally friendly should be permitted. Mr Mehta has taken us through the Notification dated 19 February 1991 issued by the Government of India under S 3 of the Environment (Protection) Act, 1986 (the Act) (CRZ Notification) and has vehemently contended that setting up of shrimp farms on the coastal stretches of seas, bays, estuaries, creeks, rivers and backwaters up to 500 meters from the High Tide Line (HTL) and the HTL is totally prohibited under Para 2 of the said notification. The relevant part of the notification is as under:

'Prohibited Activities:

The following activities are declared as prohibited within the Coastal Regulations Zone, namely:

(i) Setting up of new industries and expansion of existing industries, except those directly related to water front or directly needing foreshore facilities;

(ii) Manufacture or handling or storage or disposal of hazardous substances as specified in the Notifications of the Government of India in the Ministry of Environment and Forests No. 9.0.594 (E) dated 28 July 1989, S O 966(E) dated 27 November 1989 and GSR 1037 (E) dated 5 December 1989;

(iii) Setting up and expansion of fish processing units including warehousing (excluding hatchery and natural fish drying in permitted areas); ...

(v) Discharge of untreated wastes and effluent from industries, cities or towns and other settlements. Schemes shall be implemented by the concerned authorities phasing out the existing practices, if any, within a reasonable time period not exceeding three years from the date of this notification; ...

(viii) Land reclamation, bunding or disturbing natural course of sea water with similar obstructions, except those required for control of coastal erosion and maintenance or clearing of waterways, channels and ports and for prevention of sandbars and also except for tidal regulators, storm water drains and structures for prevention of salinity increase and for sweet water recharge; ...

(x) Harvesting or drawal of ground water and construction of mechanisms therefor within 200 m of HTL; in the 200 m to 500 m zone it shall be permitted only when done manually through ordinary wells for drinkng, horticulture, agriculture and fisheries.'

According to Mr Mehta the shrimp culture industry is neither 'directly related to water front' nor 'directly needing foreshore facility' and as such is a prohibited activity under Para 2(i) of the CRZ Notification. [Counsel for some of the respondents] on the other hand has argued that a shrimp farm is an industry which is directly related to water front and cannot exist without foreshore facilities. Relying upon Oxford English Dictionary, [he] contended that 'water front' means land abutting on the sea, that part of a town which fronts on a body of water. According to him 'foreshore' in terms of the said dictionary means the part of the shore that lies between the High Tide and the Low Tide. According to Webster Comprehensive Dictionary, International Edition the expression 'foreshore' means 'that part of a shore uncovered at low tide'.

It is, thus, clear that the part of the shore which remains covered with water at the High Tide and gets uncovered and become visible at the Low Tide is called 'foreshore'. It is not possible to set up a shrimp culture farm in the said area because it would completely submerge in water at the High Tide. It is, therefore, obvious that foreshore facilities are neither directly nor indirectly needed in the setting up of a shrimp farm. So far as 'water front' is concerned it is no doubt correct that a shrimp farm may have some relation to the water front in the sense that the farm is dependent on brackish water which can be drawn from the sea. But on a close scrutiny, we are of the view that shrimp culture farming has no relation or connection with the 'water front' though it has relation with brackish water which is available from various water bodies including sea. What is required is the 'brackish water' and not the 'water front'. The material on record shows that the shrimp ponds constructed by the farm draw water from the sea by pipes, etc. It is not the 'water front' which is needed by the industry, what is required is the brackish water which can be drawn from any source including sea and carried to any distance by pipes etc. The purpose of CRZ Notification is to protect the ecologically fragile coastal areas and to safeguard the aesthetic qualities and uses of the sea coast. The setting up of modern shrimp aquaculture farms right on the sea coast and construction of ponds and other infrastructure thereon is per se hazardous and is bound to degrade the marine ecology, coastal environment and the aesthetic uses of the sea coast.

* * *

It is thus obvious that an industry dependent on sea water cannot by itself be an industry 'directly related to water front' or 'directly needing foreshore facilities'. The shrimp culture industry, therefore, cannot be permitted to be set up anywhere in the coastal regulation zone under the CRZ Notification.

We may examine the issue from another angle. Sea coast and beaches are a gift of nature to mankind. The aesthetic qualities and recreational utility of the said area has to be maintained. Any activity which has the effect of degrading the environment cannot be permitted. Apart from that the right of the fishermen and farmers living in the coastal areas to eke their living by way of fishing and farming cannot be denied to them. Alagarswami report states that 'the shrimp farms do not provide access to the beach for traditional fishermen who have to reach the sea from their villages. As farms are located and entry is restricted the fishermen have to take a longer route to the sea for their operation. This is being objected by traditional fishermen.'

The Alagarswami report further highlights the drinking water problem, salinization and destruction of mangrove by the shrimp culture industry. The relevant paragraphs have already been quoted above. The increase of stocking densities, heavy inputs of high energy feeds, use of drugs and chemicals result in the discharge of highly polluted effluent into the sea, creeks etc. and on the sea coast by the shrimp farms. It is, therefore, not possible to agree with (counsel for the respondents) that commercial shrimp farming has no adverse effect on environment and coastal ecology. . . .

Under Para 2 of the CRZ notification, the activities listed thereunder are declared as prohibited activities. Various state governments have enacted coastal acquaculture legislations regulating the industries set up in the coastal areas. It was argued before us that certain provisions of the State legislations including that of the state of Tamil Nadu are not in consonance with the CRZ notification issued by the Government of India under section 3(3) of the Act. Assuming that is so, we are of the view that the Act being a Central legislation has the overriding effect. The Act (the Environment Protection Act, 1986) has been enacted under Entry 13 of List I Schedule VII of the Constitution of India. The said entry is as under:

> Participation in international conferences, associations and other bodies and implementing of decisions made thereat.

The preamble to the Act clearly states that it was enacted to implement the decisions taken at the United Nations Conference on the Human Environment held at Stockholm in June 1972. The Parliament has enacted the Act under Entry 13 of List 1 Schedule VII read with Article 253 of the Constitution of India. The CRZ notification having been issued under the Act shall have overriding effect and shall prevail over the law made by the legislatures of the states. . . .

We are of the view that before any shrimp industry or shrimp pond is permitted to be installed in the . . . fragile coastal area it must pass through a strict environmental test. There had to be a high powered 'Authority' under the Act to scrutinize each and every case from the environmental point on view. There must be an environmental impact assessment before permission is granted to install commercial shrimp farms. The conceptual framework of the assessment must be broad-based primarily concerning environmental degradation linked with shrimp farming. The assessment must also include the social impact on different population strata in the area. The quality of the assessment must be analytically based on superior technology. It must take into consideration the inter-generational equity and the compensation for those who are affected and prejudiced.

Before parting with this judgment we may notice the 'Dollar' based argument advanced before us. It was contended before us by the learned counsel appearing for the shrimp aquaculture industry that the industry has achieved singular distinction by earning maximum foreign exchange in the country. Almost 100% of the produce is exported to America, Europe and Japan and as such the industry has a large potential to earn 'Dollars'. That may be so but the farm-raised production of shrimp is much lesser than the wild caught production. . . .

> It is obvious from the [United Nations] figures quoted above that farm raised production of shrimp is of very small quantity as compared to wild-caught. Even if some of the shrimp culture farms which are polluting the environment, are closed, the production of shrimp by environmentally friendly techniques would not be affected and there may not be any loss to the economy specially, in view of the finding given by NEERI that the damage caused to ecology and economies by the aquaculture farming is higher than the earnings from the same of coastal aquaculture produce. That may be the reason for the European and American countries for not permitting their sea coasts to be exploited for shrimp-culture farming. The UN report shows that 80% of the farm cultured shrimp comes from the developing countries of Asia....

NOTES AND QUESTIONS

1. The Supreme Court Bench headed by Justice Kuldip Singh issued a range of mandatory injunctions and remedial directions. The Union Government was directed to establish a coastal authority under section 3(3) of the EPA, to be headed by a retired judge of a High Court. The authority was required to 'deal with the situation created by the shrimp culture industry', with power to issue remedial directions consistent with the precautionary principle and the polluter pays principle. The shrimp culture industry was prohibited in the coastal zone and existing farms were directed to be demolished. Special protective and remedial orders were issued in respect of Chilka Lake, Orissa and Pulicat Lake, Tamil Nadu. The workers rendered unemployed by the order of the court were awarded compensation, payable by the aqua-farm owners. Farmers operating traditional systems of shrimp cultivation were permitted to adopt improved technology to increase their yield.

2. Shortly after Justice Kuldip Singh retired, review petitions were filed before the court. On 30 July 1997, a bench comprising Justices S C Sen and S Saghir Ahmad referred the matter to a large bench, directed that the matter be heard 'with utmost expedition' and in the meanwhile stayed demolition of the aqua-farms.[43] In August 1997, Justice A S Anand joined the other two judges and heard the matters in part. They directed the court registry to list the case on an appropriate day. The stay on the demolition was continued.[44] In December 1997 Justice Sen retired, leaving the review cases unfinished.

3. One of the review petitions filed before the Supreme Court alleged that the NEERI Reports were unreliable. They questioned NEERI's competence, since the institute had earlier submitted a detailed report to a government undertaking where it encouraged the setting up of shrimp farms.[45]

Since the pollution control boards have proved unreliable, the Supreme Court has turned to NEERI on numerous occasions. What standards of disclosure apply to NEERI before accepting such assignments? So long as NEERI continues to act as a consultant to industry, should it accept these assignments? Is it time to look for other expert bodies in the field? Will they not suffer from a similar institutional bias?

4. In a part of the judgment which is not excerpted, the Supreme Court prohibited 'extensive, modified-extensive, semi-intensive and intensive' shrimp farm technologies. Were the

---

[43] 1997 (5) SCALE 406.

[44] 1997 (6) SCALE 7 (SP).

[45] A K Ganguli, *In Public Interest: A Review of PIL in the Supreme Court* in SUPREME COURT ON PUBLIC INTEREST LITIGATION A1, A15 (Ed. J Kapur, Vol I, 1998).

respondents justified in resisting judicial intervention on the ground that the case involved difficult technical and economic policy issues apart from raising disputed questions of fact on the impact of aqua-farms?

5. There is a tradition in common law countries to construe laws strictly, and to base their violation on the narrowest possible grounds. In the above case, the court could have followed that tradition by holding that the CRZ notification was violated by the shrimp culture industry. Instead, the court went far afield, delving into intergenerational equity, the Stockholm Conference on the Human Environment (1972), the economies of shrimp farming and its impact on the country's foreign exchange. Is this good judicial reasoning? Is it sound jurisprudence?

6. In concluding that aquaculture was prohibited in the CRZ, the court interpreted the expression 'foreshore' to mean that part of a shore uncovered at low tide. Another popular meaning of foreshore is the part of the shore that lies just above the high-water mark. Would this interpretation have affected the outcome of the case?

7. The judgment met with stiff resistance from the Centre and the states. To blunt the decision, Parliament enacted the Coastal Aquaculture Authority Act of 2005 'to provide for the establishment of a Coastal Aquaculture Authority for regulating the activities connected with coastal aquaculture in the coastal areas....'

8. On 18 July 2006, with the Act allowing coastal aquaculture in place, the review petitions resurfaced.[46] On 8 February 2007, a decade after the Supreme Court had stayed demolition of the aqua-farms in the review proceedings, the review petitions were disposed of by a short order: 'All the parties agree that the review petitions have become infructuous in view of the enactment of subsequent legislation by the Parliament.'[47]

Notice the fortuitous timing of the review petitions reappearing from the bowels of the Supreme Court registry. What might have been the fate of the coastal shrimp farms had the review petitions surfaced before the 2005 Act?

9. The disputes between traditional fisherfolk, non-fishermen and the prawn culture industry around Chilka Lake were the subject of a division bench judgment of the Orissa High Court.[48] The court held that the state could not encourage intensive prawn culture to earn 'prawn-dollars' at the cost of the environment. The High Court modified the government policy on Chilka in an attempt to curb the 'mafia raj' that had gripped Chilka after the advent of the aquaculture industry.

10. Shortly after the principal judgment in the *Shrimp Culture* case, three shrimp farm owners petitioned the Supreme Court under Article 32 of the Constitution, claiming that the decision rendered was not binding upon them. The petitioners submitted that since they were neither parties nor had the procedure under Order I, Rule 8 of the Code of Civil Procedure (relating to class actions) been followed, the directions issued by the court would not apply to their farms. The Supreme Court dismissed the petitions at the threshold, holding that the *Shrimp Culture* case had received very wide publicity over a span of two years during which it was heard. The judges found it difficult to accept the petitioners' claim that they were unaware of the proceedings or the investigations and reports made by various authorities. The court held that the principles of Order I, Rule 8 would not apply to public interest litigations

---

[46] *Orissa Shrimp Farmers Association v Union of India* Review Petition (C) 872 of 1997 in Writ Petition No. 561 of 1994.

[47] *Id.*

[48] *Kholamuhana Primary Fisherman Co-op Soc v State of Orissa* AIR 1994 Ori 191.

since that would enable a few persons to rob the judgment of its efficacy by claiming that they were not parties and that the case should be heard again. The Supreme Court also refused to examine the merits of the petitioners' contention that the CRZ notification was *ultra vires* the Environment (Protection) Act of 1986 and the fundamental rights guaranteed under the Constitution.[49]

CRZ 2011 & IPZ 2011

Drawing on two decades of experience, the MoEF introduced a new regime in 2011. The first important feature of this framework was that there were now two notifications that protected the coast. The CRZ notification of 2011[50] applied to the mainland coast and the Island Protection Zone (IPZ) notification of 2011 governed coastal development in the Andaman and Nicobar and Lakshadweep Islands.[51] A second feature of the 2011 CRZ regime was that the regulated zone now extended over the water and the bed area between the low-tide line (LTL) to the territorial water limit of 12 nautical miles in the case of the sea. This region was unregulated under CRZ 1991. The 2011 notification also introduced the notion of a hazard line within the CRZ which was required to be demarcated by the Survey of India. The hazard line recognizes the dangers of natural hazards in the coastal areas and sea level rise due to global warming. It is intended to discourage development in the coastal zone that would be impacted by tides, waves, and sea level rise and shoreline changes.

While continuing with the broad categorization of the coast into CRZ I, CRZ II and CRZ III areas, the 2011 CRZ notification responded to the criticism that a 'one size fits all' regimen operated harshly for certain regions with peculiar needs. Consequently, the 2011 notification had special provisions for slum rehabilitation and for the redevelopment of old and dilapidated buildings in Greater Mumbai, CRZ for Kerala, CRZ of Goa and for Critical Vulnerable Coastal Areas (CVCA) including the Sunderbans mangrove area.[52]

The 2011 notification was carelessly drafted and was soon followed by a corrigendum correcting more than two dozen errors in the original gazette.[53] Moreover, the parent notification was amended 15 times before it was replaced in 2019.[54] Curiously, a 16th amendment was made in May 2020 after the supersession in 2019.[55] Most of these amendments carried out small repairs or were made to accommodate specific projects such as a memorial for Dr B R Ambedkar[56] and a sewage treatment plant in Greater Mumbai.[57] The parent CRZ notification 2011 required draft Coastal Zone Management Plans (CZMPs) to be submitted

---

[49] *Gopi Aqua Farms v Union of India* AIR 1997 SC 3519.

[50] Notification No. SO 19 (E) 6 January 2011.

[51] Notification No. SO 20 (E) 6 January 2011.

[52] The notification lists certain other ecologically important areas to be designated as CVCA, such as the Gulf of Khambat and Gulf of Kutch in Gujarat; Malvan and Achra in Maharashtra; Karwar and Coondapur in Karnataka; Vembanad in Kerala; Gulf of Mannar in Tamil Nadu; Bhaitarkanika in Orissa; Coringa, East Godavari and Krishna in Andhra Pradesh.

[53] Corrigendum No. SO 651 (E) dated 29 March 2011. The changes introduced by the corrigendum are so numerous that the original notification and corrigendum must be read together.

[54] Notification Nos. SO 2557 (E) dated 22 August 2013; SO 1244 (E) dated 30 April 2014; SO 3085 (E) dated 28 November 2014; SO 383 (E) dated 4 February 2015; SO 556 (E) dated 17 February 2015; SO 938 (E) dated 31 March 2015; SO 1599 (E) dated 16 June 2015; SO 3552 (E) dated 30 December 2015; SO 1212 (E) dated 22 March 2016; SO 4162 (E) dated 23 December 2016; SO 621 (E) dated 23 February 2017; SO 1393 (E) dated 3 May 2017; SO 2444 (E) dated 31 July 2017; GSR 1227 (E) dated 6 October 2017; and SO 1022 (E) dated 6 March 2018.

[55] Notification No. SO 1422 (E) dated 1 May 2020.

[56] Notification No. SO 4162 (E) dated 23 December 2016.

[57] Notification No. SO 1393 (E) dated 3 May 2017.

within six months and the MoEF was required to approve CZMPs within a further period of four months. To accommodate the failure of coastal states to meet this deadline, time was repeatedly extended by amending clause 5(xii) and pushing forward the date for submission and approval.[58] The effect of these extensions was that CZMPs approved under the 1991 notification continued to remain valid, diluting the obligation of coastal states to prepare fresh CZMPs consistent with the 2011 notification.

The Island Protection Zone 2011 notification set out a detailed regime for island shorelines. For regulatory purposes the IPZ classified islands based on their geographic size. The coastal stretches of large islands in the Andaman and Nicobar[59] were categorized into four Island Coastal Regulation Zones (ICRZs). Depending upon ecological factors and the existing level of development, each zone allowed varying levels of development. In all the remaining islands including the Lakshadweep Islands, development was required to comport to Integrated Islands Management Plans (IIMPs).[60] Annexure 1 to the IPZ 2011 notification provided guidelines for the preparation of ICRZ plans and IIMPs.

CRZ 2019 & ICRZ 2019

In 2014, the Central Government constituted a committee with a remit to examine specific issues raised by Maharashtra, Karnataka and Kerala and to generally suggest improvements to the CRZ notification of 2011.[61] Noting the recommendations of the committee, on 18 January 2019, the MoEF issued a new CRZ notification for the mainland coast, superseding the previous Notification of 2011.[62]

The opening clause of the 2019 notification defines the CRZ to cover:

(i) The land area from High Tide Line (hereinafter referred to as the HTL) to 500 meters on the landward side along the sea front.

Explanation—For the purposes of this notification, the HTL means the line on the land upto which the highest water line reaches during the spring tide, as demarcated by the National Centre for Sustainable Coastal Management (NCSCM) in accordance with the laid down procedures and made available to various coastal States and Union territories.

(ii) CRZ shall apply to the land area between HTL to 50 meters or width of the creek, whichever is less on the landward side along the tidal influenced water bodies that are connected to the sea and the distance upto which development along such tidal influenced water bodies is to be regulated shall be governed by the distance upto which the tidal effects are experienced which shall be determined based on salinity concentration of five parts per thousand (ppt) measured during the driest period of the year and distance up to which tidal effects are experienced shall be clearly identified and demarcated accordingly in the Coastal Zone Management Plan (hereinafter referred to as the CZMP):

---

[58] Notification Nos. SO 2557 (E) dated 22 August 2013; SO 1244 (E) dated 30 April 2014; SO 938 (E) dated 31 March 2015; SO 1212 (E) dated 22 March 2016; SO 621 (E) dated 23 February 2017; and SO 2444 (E) dated 31 July 2017.

[59] Four large islands were covered by the ICRZ: Middle Andaman, North Andaman, South Andaman and Greater Nicobar.

[60] The parent IPZ Notification No. S(E) dated 6 January 2011 has been amended by Notifications No. SO 2558 (E) dated 22 August 2013; SO 2445 (E) dated 31 July 2017; and SO 3840 (E) dated 3 August 2018.

[61] After consulting stakeholders, the committee, chaired by Dr Shailesh Nayak, made its report in 2015 containing a set of recommendations and a draft CRZ law, https://www.indiaspend.com/wp-content/uploads/2020/06/Shailesh-Nayak-Committee.pdf, accessed 21 June 2021.

[62] Notification No. GSR 37 (E) dated 18 January 2019.

Provided that the CRZ limit of 50 meters or width of the creek whichever is less, shall be subject to the revision and final approval of the respective CZMPs as per this notification, framed with due consultative process, public hearing etc. and environmental safeguards enlisted therein, and till such time the CZMP to this notification is approved, the limit of 100 meters or width of the creek whichever is less, shall continue to apply.

Explanation—For the purposes of this sub-paragraph the expression 'tidal influenced water bodies' means the water bodies influenced by tidal effects from the sea in the bays, estuaries, rivers, creeks, backwaters, lagoons, ponds that are connected to the sea.

(iii) The 'intertidal zone' means land area between the HTL and the Low Tide Line (hereinafter referred to as the LTL).

(iv) The water and the bed area between the LTL to the territorial water limit (12 Nm) in case of sea and the water and the bed area between LTL at the bank to the LTL on the opposite side of the bank, of tidal influenced water bodies.

Clause 2 classifies the CRZ into four zones. CRZ-I areas are environmentally the most critical and are further subdivided. CRZ-IA covers ecologically sensitive areas having mangroves, corals and coral reefs, sand dunes, national parks, marine parks, etc., salt marshes, turtle nesting grounds, horse shoe crabs' habitats, sea grass beds, nesting grounds of birds and areas or structures of archaeological importance and heritage sites. The intertidal zone between the LTL and HTL falls under CRZ-IB.

Developed areas up to or close to the shoreline within municipal limits are classified as CRZ-II. Land areas that are relatively undisturbed such as rural areas fall under CRZ-III. CRZ-III areas are subdivided into CRZ-IIIA and CRZ-IIIB, depending on the population density. Within CRZ-III, a strip of land ranging between 50 m and 200 m from the HTL is designated as a 'No Development Zone' (NDZ). CRZ-IV is the water area and is also subdivided. CRZ-IVA comprises the water area and the sea bed area between the LTL up to 12 nautical miles. CRZ-IVB applies to the water area and the bed area of tidal influenced water bodies such as creeks, estuaries and bays.

Clause 3 identifies areas requiring special consideration 'for the purpose of protecting the critical coastal environment and difficulties faced by local communities'. This includes the Critical Vulnerable Coastal Areas (CVCAs) recognized since 2011, the CRZ for inland backwater islands and islands along the mainland coast and the CRZ falling within Greater Mumbai.

Continuing the framework adopted in 1991, the restrictions imposed are of two types. Clause 4 prohibits 11 designated activities including establishing new industries and expanding existing units. The prohibition extends to land reclamation, bunding or disturbing the natural course of seawater; the mining of sand and rocks; and the drawing of groundwater. Clause 5 provides for the regulation of permissible activities. The nature and extent of permissible development is specific to each subcategory of the CRZ.

Clause 6 deals with CZMPs. All coastal states and Union territories must revise and update existing CZMPs under the 2011 notification and submit them to the MoEF 'for approval at the earliest'.[63] The MoEF is tasked with approving the CZMPs which should generally be revised by the coastal government after five years.

Clause 7 mandates that all permitted or regulated project activities are required to obtain CRZ clearance prior to their commencement. For projects in CRZ-I and CRZ-IV areas, the

63 The 2019 Notification does away with the specific timeline mandated in 2011 for submission and approval of CZMPs. The older, less elastic provision, when coupled with the failure to prepare CZMPs within time, had required periodic amendments extending the deadline.

MoEF grants clearance based on the recommendation of the CZMA. In CRZ-II and CRZ-III areas, the concerned CZMA is required to grant the CRZ clearance. Clause 8 prescribes the procedure to be followed for obtaining a CRZ clearance. The project proponent must furnish information to the CZMA as required in Annexure V and the CZMA must decide the application within 60 days of receiving the proposal. Where the MoEF is required to grant the clearance based on the recommendations of the CZMA, it must do so within an additional 60 days. A CRZ clearance is valid for a period of seven years for completing construction and commencing operations. This term may be extended for three more years.

Clause 9 titled 'Enforcement of this notification' provides in sub-clause (iii):

> The State Government or the Union territory Coastal Zone Management Authority shall primarily be responsible for enforcing and monitoring of this notification and to assist in this task, the State Government and the Union territory shall constitute district level Committees under the Chairmanship of the District Magistrate concerned comprising at least three representatives of local traditional coastal communities including from fishermen, and the State Government may consider the enforcement of this notification to the level of respective District Magistrates.

Clause 10 prescribes specific provisions for CVCAs and other areas requiring special attention. Annexure I outlines a conservation, protection and management framework for ecologically sensitive areas with specific prescriptions and embargos for each class of ESAs. Guidelines for the development of beach resorts, hotels and tourism development projects in CRZ-II and CRZ-III areas are set out at Annexure III. Guidelines for preparing CZMPs including specifications with respect to CRZ maps and the demarcation of the HTL, LTL and the Hazard Line are provided for in Annexure IV. Before CZMPs are finalized, a public hearing of the draft CZMP must be held at the district level by the concerned CZMA.

In a parallel development, the IPZ notification of 2011 was replaced by the Island Coastal Regulation Zone (ICRZ) notification of 2019.[64] The ICRZ notification classifies islands into two sets: (i) ICRZ islands comprising the eight bigger oceanic islands in Andaman and Nicobar and (ii) small islands of the Andaman and Nicobar and Lakshadweep. The ICRZ islands are grouped into islands having a geographical area greater than 1,000 sq kms such as South Andaman, Middle Andaman, North Andaman and Great Nicobar (Group-I) and islands with geographical areas ranging between 100 sq kms and 1,000 sq kms such as Baratang, Little Andaman, Havelock and Car Nicobar (Group-II).

The ICRZ notification follows the pattern of the CRZ 2019 by classifying the ICRZ into sub-categories,[65] listing prohibited activities,[66] regulating permissible activities in each zone,[67] requiring preparation of ICRZ plans,[68] requiring prior ICRZ clearance for permitted and regulated projects,[69] prescribing the procedure for securing clearance[70] and by providing for enforcement of the ICRZ notification.[71] Small islands are treated as areas requiring special consideration and are managed through Integrated Island Management Plans.[72]

64 Notification No. SO 1242 (E) dated 8 March 2019.
65 Clause 2.
66 Clause 3.
67 Clause 4.
68 Clause 5.
69 Clause 7.
70 Clause 8.
71 Clause 9.
72 Clause 6.

V. KERALA CASES

Vembanad Backwaters

The Green Lagoon Resort found its plan to develop 5 acres on an island in Kerala's picturesque backwaters thwarted by restrictions under the CRZ Regulations. Having secured building permission from the village panchayat, the resort filed a petition in the High Court challenging classification of its lands within the regulatory zone and continued to build in the optimistic belief that it would eventually succeed. A cross petition by an NGO challenged the building permit issued by the panchayat and asked for removal of all encroachments and illegal constructions. The High Court ruled against Green Lagoon which brought the matter to the Supreme Court.

VAAMIKA ISLAND (GREEN LAGOON RESORT) v UNION OF INDIA
(2013) 8 SCC 760

K S P Radhakrishnan, J: Vembanad Backwaters is a critically vulnerable coastal area (for short 'Cvca'), which supports exceptionally large biological diversity and constitutes the second largest wetlands in India. There are several islands in and around Vembanad Backwaters of which Vettila Thuruthu is one amongst them.

The special leave petitioner preferred Writ Petition (Civil) No. 2947 of 2013 before the High Court of Kerala seeking a declaration that few items of its properties, described therein, approximately 5.21 acres were wrongly included in Map No. 32-A of the Coastal Zone Management Plan (for short 'Czmp') prepared by the Kerala Coastal Zone Management Authority (for short 'Kczma') and hence ultra vires the Coastal Regulation Zone (CRZ) Notification, 1991 (for short 'the 1991 Notification') and CRZ Notification, 2011 (for short 'the 2011 Notification'). The petitioner has also sought for a declaration that classification of its properties situated in Vettila Thuruthu Island as filtration pond (for short 'FP') and the consequent categorisation of the same under CRZ I is unconstitutional, being *ultra vires* CRZ 1991 as well as CRZ 2011.

Kczma took up the stand that Czmp for the State of Kerala was prepared based on the guidelines issued by the Ministry of Environment and Forests (for short 'MoEF'), Government of India. Czmp (1995) of the State indicates the entire Vettila Thuruthu as FP. The 1991 Notification, therefore, shows the entire Vettila Thuruthu as CRZ I, and as per CRZ 2011, it is either CRZ I, CRZ III or CRZ IV. The 2011 Notification has defined Vembanad Backwaters as Cvca.

MoEF also filed a statement before the High Court wherein it was stated that Czmp for Kerala was prepared by MoEF on 27-9-1996 and that the construction of beach resorts within CRZ area requires prior clearance from MoEF, based on the recommendation of Kczma. Further, it was also pointed out, that Category I (CRZ I) includes the areas that are ecologically sensitive and important and that the Government of India, in exercise of the powers conferred under sub-sections (1) and (3) of section 3 of the Environment (Protection) Act, 1986, has notified Kczma as the authority for the implementation of the provisions of both the 1991 Notification as well as 2011 Notification....

We are, in this case, concerned with an island named Vettila Thuruthu in Vembanad Lake in the State of Kerala. Vembanad Lake plays an important role in the ecology and economy of the south-west coast of India. Vembanad Lake, along with adjacent Kol lands, wetlands, is a complex system of backwaters, marshes, lagoons, mangrove forests, reclaimed land and an intricate network of natural, manmade canals, etc. The Lake is fed by six rivers falling from Western Ghats: Achankovil, Pampa, Meenachil, Manimala, Muvattupuzha and Periyar. Vembanad Lake was declared as a Ramsar site in the year 2002. Ramsar list was published in response to Article 2.1 of the Convention on Wetlands (Ramsar, Iran, 1971). The wetlands included in the list acquire a new status at the national and international level and the Convention mission is the conservation and wise use of such wetlands, through local, regional and national actions and international cooperation as a contribution towards achieving sustainable development. India is a signatory to the Ramsar Convention.

Vembanad Backwaters has been defined as a CVCA as per 2011 Notification. The Lake has immense conservation importance as it supports a large aquatic biodiversity and the most important migrating birds' habitat. Vembanad Lake conserves as a habitat to a variety of fin and shell fish and a nursery of several species of aquatic life. Considering the fragile ecosystem of the wetland, deterioration of water quality and consequent damage to aquatic organisms and the shrinkage of Vembanad Lake, this wetland system was included in the National Lake Conservation Programme (for short 'NLCP') by the National River Conservation Authority under MoEF. The State of Kerala has also decided to establish Vembanad Eco-Development Authority towards implementation of project for restoration and regeneration of Vembanad Lake. The shrinkage of Vembanad Lake as a result of land reclamation has been the most damaging environmental consequence of various human interventions. Vembanad Lake, it is well known, is undergoing severe environmental degradation due to increased human interventions which is of serious concern for the State of Kerala as well as the country at large. [The court narrowed the issues 'to the legality or otherwise of Map No. 32-A of CZMP and the inclusion of the petitioner's property in the island of Vettila Thuruthu in the map and the question as to whether there is any illegality in the preparation of map and whether the same is ultra vires the 1991 and 2011 Notifications'.]

CZMP 1995 of the State shows the entire Vettila Thuruthu as FP. CZMP described FP as: another fish spawning/breeding ground and these are shallow water bodies adjoining the backwater system where certain species of fish are grown in large numbers. The 50 m belt adjoining it is also demarcated as CRZ I, since this area is low lying, it is likely to be inundated due to sea level rise (SLR). Hence, the entire Vettila Thuruthu is described as CRZ I as per 1991 Notification and, as per 2011 Notification, it is described as either CRZ I, CRZ III or CRZ IV. New constructions are not permitted in CRZ I, the no-development zone of CRZ III and in CRZ IV. Repairs of existing structures can be permitted in no-development zone of CRZ III subject to conditions for permissible activities as per the notification. Tourism activity is also not permitted in the no-development zone of CRZ III or CRZ I.

CRZ for Kerala in CRZ 2011 also prohibits new construction within 50 m from high tide line and only dwelling units of local communities could be repaired or reconstructed.

KCZMA was prepared, as already indicated, based on the guidelines of MoEF, taking care of the maps prepared by the Survey of India (Government of India) and cadastral maps prepared by the Survey Department of Kerala Government were used as base map for preparation of CZMP of the State. The area between low tide line and high tide line is also CRZ I. The FPs, as already indicated, are shallow water bodies which are spawning/breeding area of fishes and hence, as per notification, they are CRZ I.

CRZ 2011 has been made applicable with effect from 6-1-2011. CZMP is being prepared on CRZ 2011, at that time the plan prepared on the basis of the 1991 Notification would be 'in force'. Coastal plan prepared on the basis of the 1991 Notification clearly shows Vettila Thuruthu as 'FP'. We do concur with the view of the High Court that islands could be coastal stretches of river or backwater or backwater islands in Kerala are clearly covered by CRZ I. It cannot fall under either CRZ III or CRZ IV. We also fully endorse the view of the High Court that even before the salinity test was incorporated in the year 2002, reliance was placed on that test, on the basis of 5 ppt, which was made as per standard measurements technique in parts per thousand. Satellite imagery also, in our view, is one of the best scientific indicators to know, when was the construction effected in violation of CRZ which, in our view, has been correctly applied in this case.

We, therefore, find no illegality in the map prepared by KCZMA as well as the techniques employed to ascertain that works/constructions have been made in violation of CRZ 1991 as well as 2011.

The petitioner had effected the construction in violation of the provisions of 1991 and 2011 Notifications as well as Map No. 32-A, so found by the High Court. The factual details of the same and where actually the portion of some of the properties of the petitioner in Vettila Thuruthu will fall, has been elaborately dealt with by the High Court in its judgment in paras 109 to 119. We notice that the High Court has dealt with the issue pointing out that so far as buildings which have been constructed by the petitioner during the currency of the Notification issued in 1991 are concerned, they are clearly in violation of this notification, hence, action has to be taken for the removal of the same. The Director of Panchayat also vide letters dated 7-3-1995, 17-7-1996 directed all the panchayats to strictly follow the provisions of CRZ notification which it was found not followed by granting permission. The High Court has also found on facts that reconstruction work appeared to have been done during the currency of the 2011 Notification and two buildings were also constructed illegally. The High Court has also noticed another new construction underway. [The court declined to re-examine factual controversies.]

We are of the considered view that the above direction was issued by the High Court taking into consideration the larger public interest and to save Vembanad Lake which is an ecologically sensitive area, so proclaimed nationally and internationally. Vembanad Lake is presently undergoing severe environmental degradation due to increased human intervention and, as already indicated, recognising the socio-economic importance of this water body, it has recently been scheduled under 'vulnerable wetlands to be protected' and declared as CVCA. We are of the view that the directions given by the High Court are perfectly in order in the abovementioned perspective.

Further, the directions given by the High Court in directing demolition of illegal construction effected during the currency of the 1991 and 2011 CRZ Notifications are perfectly in tune with the decision of this Court in *Piedade Filomena Gonsalves v State of Goa* (2004) 3 SCC 445, wherein this Court has held that such notifications have been issued in the interest of protecting environment and ecology in the coastal area and the construction raised in violation of such regulations cannot be lightly condoned....

NOTES AND QUESTIONS

1. When a petition under Article 136 of the Constitution is filed before the Supreme Court seeking permission ('special leave') to appeal the judgment of the lower court or tribunal, the court at the initial stage decides *ex parte* on whether to hear the appeal or to dismiss the petition. Where petitions are dismissed, it is generally by a very short order. Where the court decides to entertain a special leave petition, it will either issue a notice to the respondent and seek its response on the question of admission of the appeal or grant leave and hear all parties at the stage of final hearing.

Here, the Supreme Court dismissed the special leave petition with an elaborate judgment at the admission stage without notifying the respondents. What might explain this departure from the near-universal practice of one-line dismissal orders?

2. Article 141 of the Constitution provides: 'The law declared by the Supreme Court shall be binding on all courts within the territory of India.' Is the *ex parte* dismissal order in *Vaamika* entitled to Article 141 deference?

The Supreme Court provided an answer in *Kapico Kerala Resorts*,[73] a case arising from the same Kerala High Court judgment that was challenged in *Vaamika Island*:

> [T]here is a distinction between the dismissal of a special leave petition by a non-speaking order where no reasons are recorded and the dismissal of a special leave petition by a speaking or reasoned order. In both cases, the doctrine of merger would not apply. But in cases falling under the latter category, the reasons stated by the Court would attract the applicability of Article 141 of the Constitution, if a point of law has been declared therein. If what is stated in

[73] *Kapico Kerala Resorts Pvt Ltd v State of Kerala* (2020) 3 SCC 18.

the order of the Supreme Court (before the grant of leave) happen to be findings recorded by the Supreme Court, not amounting to a declaration of law, the findings so recorded would bind only the parties thereto.

3. Green Lagoon Resort presented three sharp arguments: (1) there were no FPs on the island; (2) the categorization based on satellite imagery was unreliable, absent a ground study after notice to the affected parties; and (3) no salinity test was conducted to establish that the threshold of 5 ppt (parts per thousand) was crossed. Each of these contentions, if accepted, would have helped the resort escape the tight restrictions imposed in the CRZ. Did the Supreme Court consider these points sufficiently? As a principle, should satellite images without a corresponding ground study be allowed to severely undermine property rights? Conversely, is an exhaustive ground survey feasible?

4. Green Lagoon's strategy to obtain permission from the village panchayat and then swiftly proceed with the construction in breach of the CRZ is fairly typical of beach resorts which find India's coastal regulations very restrictive. At one point in the 1990s, the Bombay Environmental Action Group stopped complaining to the Alibaug Collector about brazen violations of the CRZ, when its activists discovered that their complaints were being misused by unscrupulous officials to extract illicit payments.

5. *Vaamika Island* arose from a batch of cases decided by the Kerala High Court on 25 July 2013. Broadly, the High Court disposed of petitions dealing with resorts and development on two islands: Vettila Thuruthu and Nediyathuruthu. While *Vaamika Island* dealt with the construction of a resort on Vettila Thuruthu, the resort on Nediyathuruthu (named Kapico) filed review petitions before the High Court and filed special leave petitions in the Supreme Court only after judgment was reserved in the *Vaamika Island* case. When Kapico approached the Supreme Court seeking reversal of the Kerala High Court judgments, the court held:

> Once we find that the main issues arising in common for both the islands and dealt with in common by the High Court, had received a seal of approval from this Court by a reasoned order, there is no scope for revisiting the same on the basis of certain minor ancillary issues not specifically dealt with, in the judgment. Therefore, we hold that the distinctions sought to be made out by the appellants are not substantial and hence, we are not inclined to revisit the issues already clinched by this Court....
>
> Hence, in the light of our finding: (i) that the substantial issues that arose in common for both the islands have already been answered in *Vaamika Island* and (ii) that the distinguishing features sought to be projected, are not so material as to take a different view than the one taken therein, the appeals are liable to be dismissed.[74]

VI. THE *DLF* CASE

The *DLF* case[75] brings to the fore the poor enforcement of coastal waterfront regulations and the inability of authorities to respond to violations. DLF purchased 5.12 acres of waterfront property in 2006 for a residential complex of 185 units on the eastern bank of Chilavannur Kayal (backwaters) in Kerala. The area fell within the jurisdiction of the Kochi Corporation and was within the CRZ. After the structure was complete, on 21 July 2014 a sub-committee of the Kerala Coastal Zone Management Authority (KCZMA) discovered major breaches. The sub-committee found that since the CRZ notification was brought into force on 19 February 1991 there were massive reclamations on the property and it estimated that the high-tide line (HTL) had been shifted towards the backwater in the range of 60–130 m through

[74] *Id.*

[75] *The Secretary, Kerala State Coastal Management Authority v DLF Universal Ltd* (2018) 2 SCC 203.

reclamation of water bodies during 2005–06. The report of the sub-committee mapped the reclaimed portion on the statutory Coastal Zone Management Plan (CZMP) prepared in 1996, to show how the entire structure had come up in a prohibited zone.

The Supreme Court chose to downplay these findings, highlighting instead the neglect on the part of the authority to enforce regulations at the time when the project was being executed:

> On the Court query about the silence of this important authority for such a long period of time, the only answer available was that it did not have an enforcement mechanism and is dependent on the [Kochi] Corporation for the same. That, in our view, could hardly be an answer for such inaction if there were violations. Enforcement is different from detection of violations. There can hardly be any doubt about the bounden duty of this authority to play a crucial role in preserving the environment in the coastal area and it cannot wash its hands off by giving an explanation for inaction as the alleged absence of an enforcement force. Had this authority kept an eye open right from the beginning and played the role which it was required to play, the situation which has come to pass would not have so occurred and the identification of the violations, if any, would have been made at the threshold stage itself. This did not happen here.[76]

Examine the CRZ notification and the notification that establishes the KCZMA. Is there any prospect of improved compliance when the authorities operate without any staff, budget or other resources?

Reversing findings by the single judge and division bench of the Kerala High Court which found serious breaches on the part of DLF, the Supreme Court disapproved the stand of the MoEF which 'indulged in a complete flip-flop-flip without even explaining the reasons':

> On the conclusion of the hearing, when crystallised written synopsis had to be filed, an affidavit is sought to be slipped in by one Mr Ritesh Kumar Singh, Joint Secretary of MoEF, stating that this affidavit is in 'continuation' of the earlier affidavit dated 6-11-2017 filed on 7-11-2017. For the first time, it is sought to be now pleaded that CRZ Notification, 1991; CRZ Notification, 2011 and EIA Notification, 2006 have been violated and that prior clearance under the Notifications before the commencement of construction activity was mandatory. It is also sought to be alleged that reclaimed water bodies and land falling under CRZ for housing projects is prohibited under CRZ Notification. The post-construction environment clearance is stated to have been granted to the project by SEIAA without appraisal and recommendations of Seac and in the absence of approval of KCZMA.... We fail to appreciate the contradictory stands of the authority and the endeavour to set up a different case after the conclusion of the hearing. Such conduct is unacceptable.[77]

VII. THE *MARADU MUNICIPALITY* CASE

The KCZMA was more persuasive in the *Maradu Municipality* case.[78] Maradu is a suburb of Kochi abutting backwaters that garland the region. Until it was upgraded to a municipality in 2010, Maradu was a panchayat. The panchayat issued numerous building permits under the Kerala Municipality Building Rules without securing clearance from the KCZMA.

The vigilance section of the Maradu panchayat noticed the anomaly, prompting the state to direct revocation of 31 building permits. Meanwhile, several multi-storeyed apartment buildings were built and families moved in.

---

[76] *Id.* at 213.

[77] *Id.* at 216.

[78] *The Kerala State Coastal Zone Management Authority v State of Kerala, Maradu Municipality* (2019) 7 SCC 248.

In a batch of writ petitions filed by the affected developers, the High Court quashed the notices holding that statutory building permissions could not be withdrawn except in limited circumstances such as a mistake, fraud or patent error.[79] No such situation existed since the building permits were issued in a regular manner. Citizens could not be faulted where Maradu failed to notify KCZMA. The division bench of the High Court was also concerned about scores of innocent flat purchasers who had occupied the buildings.

By an interim direction, the Supreme Court constituted a committee to determine whether the area was CRZ-III (as asserted by KCZMA) or CRZ-II as claimed by the developers. The report concluded that Maradu fell in the CRZ-III category under the CZMP approved in 1996. The 1996 CZMP remained valid until the *draft* CZMP under the CRZ notification of 2011 was approved by the MoEF. (The draft CZMP reclassified the area as CRZ-II. Upon approval by MoEF, this would have the effect of lifting the 200 m 'no development zone' embargo applicable to CRZ-III areas. However, on the date of Supreme Court judgment, there was no certainty whether MoEF would accept the reclassification in the draft CZMP forwarded by the state.)

The Supreme Court deplored construction activities on the shores of the backwater, recognizing that the backwater 'supports exceptionally large biological diversity and constitutes one of the largest wetlands in India'. The court held:

> It is necessary for the local authority to follow the restrictions imposed by the notification, as amended from time to time. Thus, it was not open to the local authority, i.e., Panchayat, in view of the notification of 1991 to grant any kind of permission without concurrence of KCZMA. Admittedly, Panchayat has not forwarded any such application for building permissions and there is no concurrence or permission granted by the KCZMA. As such, we find that once due inquiry has been held by the Committee, there is no escape from the conclusion that the area fell within CRZ-III, it was wholly impermissible and unauthorised construction within the prohibited area. We take judicial notice of recent devastation in Kerala which had taken place due to such unbridled construction activities resulting into colossal loss of human life and property.

Consequently, the building permits issued by Maradu panchayat were declared void and the authorities were directed to remove the structures within a month.

NOTES AND QUESTIONS

1. While the court was correct in holding that building permissions cannot violate the CRZ notification, where is the requirement for 'concurrence' of KCZMA? Who applies for permission: the municipality or the property owner? Under which law? Does the KCZMA or any other Coastal Zone Management Authority have the wherewithal to review thousands of applications for building permission?

2. After efforts to persuade the Supreme Court to reconsider its order failed, in January 2020 four apartment buildings were demolished through implosion.

3. Amita Singh argues that the CRZ law suffers from inconsistent judicial approaches and consequently unpredictable outcomes. She attributes failure of implementation to 'too many cooks' with multiple administrative authorities exercising oversight and none willing to take

79 *Maradu Municipality v State of Kerala* (2015) SCC Online KER 16228.

responsibility. In the case of Kerala, the authorities involved included the KCZMA, SEIAA, SEAC, the Port Trust, Kerala Fisheries Department and the Municipal Corporation.

> The urban local body as part of district administration and town and country planning failed to enforce land use and municipal laws, building structural plans and floor-size regulations. The Vigilance and Anticorruption Bureau made surprise raids at the construction sites of 10 municipalities only after the Comptroller and Auditor General reported violations in its report. When the corporation sent notices to some of them it was more a ritual administrative exercise to be on the right side of law rather than any commitment to stop illegal construction....
>
> In most of the violations it was found that the municipal corporation gave permission for construction without addressing and insisting on the need for obtaining even the required mandatory approvals from the KCZMA and the MoEF. The KCZMA later informed the corporation about the ongoing construction in 13 buildings, but the corporation sent notices to only one construction company to stop work. The role of the corporation secretary also vacillated between different options. The electricity board overlooked the mandatory requirement of possessing occupancy certificates from municipal corporations for obtaining electricity connections for the buildings....
>
> The law of conservation is not weak. What makes it weak is the combination of the failure of state leadership, administrative and judicial corruption and ecological awareness.[80]

VIII. MANGROVES

Krishnadevi Kamathia worked salt pans, trapping and evaporating sea water to manufacture salt at Dahisar village. The tide washed past a thicket of mangroves and was captured by an earthen bund at one edge of her land. This tranquil enterprise attracted little attention for more than three decades after it commenced in 1959. In the 1990s the tempo altered. As Mumbai stretched northwards, real estate developers began nibbling away at vacant spaces to fulfil the city's appetite for housing. Mangroves thrive in the inter-tidal zone and are nourished by nutrients in the tidal wash. Block the sea water, the mangroves desiccate and die, opening up land for development.

The Bombay Environmental Action Group (BEAG) petitioned the High Court to thwart the stealthy decimation of mangroves at the metropolis fringes and secured this order on 6 October 2005:

> (xi) From the list of 'mangrove areas' so identified government-owned lands will automatically be declared/notified as 'protected forest'. Likewise, privately-owned lands from the list of 'mangrove areas' so identified, the same will be declared/notified as 'forest'.

The government then issued a notification on 18 February 2009, covering Krishnadevi's land. Consequently, she could not restart salt manufacture which had continued up to 1990 and was permissible under the CRZ Regulations of 1991.

Krishnadevi complained to the Supreme Court that she needed to repair the damaged bund and that the High Court order was passed without hearing her. The Supreme Court permitted her to approach the District Collector, the official primarily responsible to oversee repairs. On 27 January 2010, the Collector passed a lengthy order tracing the history of the land including an ownership dispute between the government and Krishnadevi and eventually allowed repair of the bund without destroying the mangroves or vegetation on the land.

On 7 May 2010, the Supreme Court disposed of Krishnadevi's appeal with these directions:

---

80 Amita Singh, *Coastal Ballads and Conservation Ironic: Understanding Implementation Slippages of the CRZ Law*, 51 ECONOMIC & POLITICAL WEEKLY 70, 74 (2016).

By an interim order passed by this Court on 22-3-2010, this Court permitted the petitioners to repair the bund. This interim order is made absolute and the petitioners are permitted to maintain and upkeep the bund till final adjudication regarding Notifications dated 18-2-2009 and 15-6-2009 is made and violation of these orders by the parties or other authorities could be brought to the notice of this Court for appropriate directions.

Krishnadevi then filed a suit in the Bombay High Court challenging the notification dated 18 February 2009 and commenced repairs with exceptional zeal.

This raised the hackles of BEAG who initiated contempt proceedings before the Supreme Court claiming Krishnadevi was willfully destroying mangroves under the guise of repairing the bund. The Collector, separately, asked the Supreme Court to initiate contempt proceedings against Krishnadevi for violating the order dated 7 May 2010. The Collector sought directions against the contemnors to remove the newly constructed bund and allow sea water ingress to save the mangrove forest. Krishnadevi counter-attacked, accusing the Collector of contempt and claimed that the Collector was impeding repairs allowed by the Supreme Court. The contemptuous action of the Collector, according to Krishandevi, was in appointing a committee to assess whether the bund construction had destroyed the mangroves in breach of the Collector's order dated 27 January 2010. We excerpt from the Supreme Court judgment deciding the three contempt applications. The extract begins with a report filed pursuant to the Supreme Court order appointing the Principal Judge, City Civil Court, Mumbai to inspect the bund.

KRISHNADEVI KAMATHIA v BOMBAY ENVIRONMENTAL ACTION GROUP
(2011) 3 SCC 363

DR B S CHAUHAN, J:

***

The learned Principal Judge, City Civil Court submitted the report dated 10-12-2010 along with a large number of photographs to substantiate the contents of the report. Relevant part thereof reads as under:

> 'At the outset it may be briefly stated that during the course of visit it was noticed that the debris and boulders including big broken pieces of RCC slabs were found lying at various places on the bund. The debris and boulders were found used for pitching or reinforcement of the bund because of the dumping of debris and boulders on a large scale.... Apart from dumping of debris and boulders in large quantities, what was noticed was that there were about 12 to 13 places where big platforms were found made of debris and boulders. The length of those platforms was something between 25 m to 35 m each and width was on an average 16 m to 20 m each.... That debris was being dumped beyond the area of the platform in property Survey No. 344 and there was an attempt to increase the width of the platforms. In the process the mangroves obviously were being destroyed.... [T]he mangroves were destroyed at a considerable length from the bund in Survey No. 344 ... the destruction was at considerably large scale.... a large number of mangroves were found cut manually. It was possible that the mangroves were cut to increase width of the bund. The cut mangroves were found to have been used in increasing the height of the bund. Breathing roots and branches of mangroves were found stuck in the muddy area of the bund.... The said bund appeared to have been erected after excavation of mud from both sides of the bund.... Mangroves were found cut at many places. The mangroves were found to have died because of removal of mud and stagnation of water.... There were 3-4 patches where mangroves appeared to have been destroyed manually.'

The CRZ Regulations define for regulating developmental activities, coastal stretches within 500 m of the landward side of the high tide line into four categories. Category I (CRZ-I) is defined as under:

'(i) Areas that are ecologically sensitive and important, such as, national parks/marine parks, sanctuaries, reserved forests, wildlife habitats, mangroves, corals/coral reefs, areas close to breeding and spawning grounds of fish and other marine life, areas of outstanding natural beauty/historical/heritage areas, areas rich in genetic diversity, areas likely to be inundated due to rise in sea level consequent upon global warming and other such areas as may be declared by the Central Government or the authorities concerned at the State/Union Territory level from time to time.'

The regulation of development or construction activities in CRZ-I areas is to be in accordance with the following norms:

'CRZ-I

...

Between LTL and HTL in areas which are not ecologically sensitive and important, the following may be permitted: (a) exploration and extraction of natural gas; (b) activities as specified under proviso of sub-paras (i) and (ii) of Para 2; (c) construction of dispensaries, schools, public rain shelters, community toilets, bridges, roads, jetties, water supply, drainage, sewerage which are required for traditional inhabitants of the Sunderbans Biosphere Reserve Area, West Bengal, on a case-to-case basis, by the West Bengal State Coastal Zone Management Authority; (d) *salt harvesting by solar evaporation of seawater*; (e) desalination plants; (f) storage of non-hazardous cargo such as edible oil, fertilisers and foodgrain within notified ports; (g) construction of trans-harbour sea links.' (Emphasis added)

From the above, it is evident that mangroves fall squarely within the ambit of CRZ-I. The Regulations allow for salt harvesting by solar evaporation of seawater in CRZ-I areas *only* where such area is not ecologically sensitive and important. In the instant case it has been established that mangrove forests are of great ecological importance and are also ecologically sensitive. Thus, salt harvesting by solar evaporation of seawater cannot be permitted in an area that is home to mangrove forests.

In view of the aforesaid discussion, we reach the following inescapable conclusions:

(1) The land in dispute has not been used for manufacturing of salt for more than two decades.
(2) The land in dispute stands notified as a reserve forest, though it may be a private land and requires to be protected.
(3) The High Court while disposing of the writ petition filed by the BEAG has issued several directions including the direction to identify mangrove area and declare/notify it as a forest.
(4) The Coastal Regulatory Zone Regulations, 1991 impose certain restrictions on the land in dispute.
(5) The District Collector while deciding the application of the applicants for according permission to repair the bund has explicitly incorporated the conditions that the appellants would only repair the old bund without raising its height and ensure full protection of mangroves.
(6) This Court while disposing of the appeal filed by the appellants has directed to ensure compliance with the order of the District Collector and in case of any kind of violation to bring the matter to the notice of the Court.
(7) In respect of the repairing of the bund, a large number of complaints had been made to the authorities concerned, by the public, representatives of the people and various officials and statutory authorities alleging that the appellants have violated the conditional order passed by the District Collector for permitting the appellants to repair the bund.
(8) Various reports submitted to the authorities concerned make it clear that there have been flagrant violations of the conditional order and that included:
    (i) Closing the natural flow of water which has adverse effect on existing mangroves;

(ii) A large number of mangroves had been cut/destroyed while repairing the bund and a large number of mangroves were found cut manually;
(iii) Height and width of the bund had been increased to an unwarranted extent. The reports reveal that width of the bund had been extended by 12 ft to 15 ft while the old bund was not beyond 6 ft width;
(iv) Instead of mud, big boulders, concrete, debris had been used. Several platforms of 25 m to 30 m with the width of 16 m to 20 m have been constructed;
(v) Debris was being dumped beyond the area of platform in the land in dispute making an attempt to increase the width of the platform;
(vi) The cut mangroves have been used to increase the height of the bund;
(vii) Breathing roots and branches of mangroves were found sticking out of the muddy area of the bund; and
(viii) A large number of mangroves died because of removal of mud and stagnation of water.

In view of the above, we have no hesitation to hold that the appellants are guilty of wilful defiance of the orders passed by this Court as well as by the District Collector and they have filed the contempt petitions using it as a legal thumbscrew to enforce their claims, though totally unwarranted and unfounded on facts. It is a crystal clear case of contumacious conduct, as the conduct of the appellants is not explainable otherwise, for the reason that disobedience is deliberate. The appellants cannot be permitted to make allegations against the authorities and drag them to the court alleging disobedience of the orders of this Court without realising that contempt proceedings are quasi-criminal in nature. They have knowingly and purposely damaged the mangroves and other vegetation of the wetland of the CRZ-I area, which could not have been disturbed. Under the garb of repairing the old bund, a sort of pukka bund using boulders and debris has been constructed along with a huge platform, violating the norms of environmental law and in flagrant violation and utter disregard of orders passed by the courts and the District Collector. No court can validate an action which is not lawful at its inception.

It is often reiterated that justice is only blind or blindfolded to the extent necessary to hold its scales evenly. It is not, and must never be allowed, to become blind to the reality of the situation, lamentable though that situation may be.

In view of the above, the contempt proceedings filed by the District Collector and the BEAG are allowed and the contempt petition filed by the appellants is hereby dismissed with the following directions:

(1) The appellants are directed to restore the height and width of the bund as it was existing prior to the order passed by the District Collector dated 27-1-2010 within a period of 60 days from today by removing all debris, grit, boulders, etc., dismantling of platforms and reducing the height and width of the bund.
(2) All culverts and drains which existed prior to 27-1-2010 which could facilitate the natural flow of seawater into the land, shall be restored.
(3) In case the appellants fail to carry out the aforesaid directions within the stipulated period, the District Collector, Suburban District shall carry out the aforesaid directions and recover the cost from the appellants as arrears of land revenue and shall ensure in future that the appellants would not act in a manner detrimental to the ecology of the area and ensure the preservation of mangroves and other vegetation....

NOTES AND QUESTIONS

1. Krishnadevi retained top-tier lawyers and seemingly expended resources beyond the capacity of traditional salt works. Might Krishnadevi have harboured dreams different from manufacturing salt on 175 hectares of Survey No. 344? What might those be?

2. Disputes on the extent of forest cover have narrowed with public access to remote sensing imagery. In this case, the Collector was fortified by a Maharashtra Remote Sensing Application Centre map that used satellite images to show the extent of mangrove destruction.

3. Krishnadevi's lawyers attacked the very basis of the Collector's actions by claiming that the government's notification dated 18 February 2009, declaring her lands as mangrove forest, was illegal. The Supreme Court refused to be drawn into the controversy since this issue was the subject of Krishnadevi's suit pending before the High Court. Instead, the court applied an important principle of administrative law: Even where a government order or notification is void or voidable, the aggrieved person cannot ignore the order by deciding for herself that the order is invalid. She must approach a court and seek an appropriate declaration of invalidity.

4. The civil contempt jurisdiction of the Supreme Court is a limited jurisdiction intended to be exercised sparingly to punish persons who wilfully disobey court orders. In contempt cases the court examines its order and verifies compliance, generally on the basis of affidavits. Was interpretation of the CRZ notification and the massive fact-finding exercise which involved deputing the Principal Judge of the City Civil Court to carry out a field inspection a legitimate exercise of contempt jurisdiction? Was the Supreme Court justified in reducing the Principal Judge to a court commissioner? Are the directions in the final paragraph of *Krishnadevi* reconcilable with these observations in a subsequent judgment?

> The power vested in the High Courts as well this Court to punish for contempt is a special and rare power available both under the Constitution as well the Contempt of Courts Act, 1971.... The Courts must also ensure that while considering a contempt plea the power available to the Court in other corrective jurisdictions like review or appeal is not trenched upon. No order of directions supplemental to what has been already expressed should be issued by the Court while exercising jurisdiction in the domain of the contempt law. Such an exercise is more appropriate in other jurisdictions vested in the court, as noticed above.[81]

Assuming that the contempt jurisdiction was not appropriate, what jurisdictions might the parties have invoked?

5. Having found Krishnadevi guilty, should the court have imprisoned or fined the wrongdoers in strict exercise of its contempt powers?

IX. COASTAL INDUSTRY

The case excerpted in what follows reveals the enormous challenge in establishing a large industrial project, particularly PIL-related legal risk. The petitioners went for the jugular, and this is how.

Chemplast Sanmar Ltd explored putting up a polyvinyl chloride (PVC) manufacturing unit in an industrial complex at Cuddalore District, Tamil Nadu. The case arose from a batch of writ petitions filed before the Madras High Court as well as a petition directly to the Supreme Court under Article 32 of the Constitution. The petitions questioned a short but vital length of Chemplast's pipelines that lay below the Uppanar River. Chemplast commissioned an EIA report and risk analysis report in 2002, secured environmental clearance from the MoEF in 2005 and obtained consents and permissions under the Water Act, the Air Act, the Hazardous Chemicals Rules and other applicable statutes.

One of the raw materials used for manufacturing PVC is vinyl chloride monomer (VCM), a hazardous substance. Since VCM is not available indigenously, Chemplast planned to import the raw material from international suppliers. For this it installed a marine terminal

[81] *Sudhir Vasudeva v M George Ravi Shekaran* (2014) 3 SCC 373, 381.

facility where ships carrying VCM would berth and it proposed an underground pipeline to transfer the VCM from the ships to the PVC plant. Since the transport of hazardous chemicals was involved, Chemplast obtained permissions from the District Coastal Zone Management Committee; the Tamil Nadu State Coastal Zone Management Authority; the Navigational Safety and Ports Committee, Goa; the Tamil Nadu Pollution Control Board; and the National Coastal Zone Management Authority and eventually the MoEF issued a second environmental clearance on 19 December 2005 under the CRZ notification. This clearance covered the subsea pipelines as well as the onshore piping from the landfall point to the plant.

Finally, with all permissions from the experts in hand, Chemplast applied to the executive engineer of the local public works department for permission to carry sea water and raw materials through pipelines laid 3.5 metres below the river bed. The engineer granted permission on 27 February 2008 but inexplicably changed his mind on 19 March 2008, observing that VCM may cause pollution and pose a health hazard to the public. The Madras High Court on Chemplast's petition quashed the engineer's cancellation order, thereby restoring the permission initially granted. At this stage, M Nizamudeen filed a PIL in the High Court challenging the executive engineer's order passed on 27 February 2008 and sought an injunction restraining Chemplast from laying pipelines that would draw VCM from the jetty to its manufacturing plant. The High Court dismissed the petition on 31 October 2008 and by the time the Supreme Court delivered judgment on 10 March 2010 several other good Samaritans joined the fray.

M NIZAMUDEEN v CHEMPLAST SANMAR LIMITED

(2010) 4 SCC 240

R M Lodha, J:

* * *

In view of the contentions advanced by the ... counsel for the parties, the first question which we have to look to is, whether Uppanar River and its banks at the point where pipelines pass, fall in the CRZ III area. If the answer to this is in the affirmative, obviously, the pipelines crossing underneath Uppanar River would require environmental clearance. The other main question we have to consider in connection with these matters is, whether Para 2(ii) of the 1991 Notification restricts transfer of VCM (hazardous substance) beyond port area to the PVC plant through pipelines. Other considerations would depend on answer to these two core issues.

In considering the first question, we need to look to the 1991 Notification which came to be issued by the MoEF declaring the coastal stretches as coastal regulation zone (CRZ) and regulating activities in such area. The 1991 Notification has been amended from time to time. To the extent it is relevant, it reads:

> 'Now, therefore, in exercise of the powers conferred by clause (d) of sub-rule (3) of rule 5 of the Environment (Protection) Rules, 1986, and all other powers vesting in its behalf, the Central Government hereby declares the coastal stretches of seas, bays, estuaries, creeks, rivers and backwaters which are influenced by tidal action (in the landward side) up to 500 meters from the high tide line (HTL) and the land between the low tide line (LTL) and HTL as coastal regulation zone; and imposes with effect from the date of this notification, the following restrictions on the setting up and expansion of industries, operations or processes, etc. in the said coastal regulation zone (CRZ).
>
> (i) For the purposes of this notification, the high tide line means the line on the land up to which the highest waterline reaches during the spring tide. The high tide line shall be demarcated uniformly in all parts of the country by the demarcating authority or authorities so authorised by the Central Government, in accordance with the general guidelines issued in this regard.

(ii) The distance from the high tide line shall apply to both sides in the case of rivers, creeks and backwaters and may be modified on a case-by-case basis for reasons to be recorded in writing while preparing the coastal zone management plans provided that this distance shall not be less than 100 meters or the width of the creek, river or backwaters, whichever is less. The distance up to which development along rivers, creeks and backwaters is to be regulated shall be governed by the distance up to which the tidal effects are experienced which shall be determined based on salinity concentration of 5 parts per thousand (ppt). For the purpose of this notification, the salinity measurements shall be made during the driest period of the year and the distance up to which tidal effects are experienced shall be clearly identified and demarcated accordingly in the coastal zone management plans.

2. *Prohibited activities.* — The following activities are declared as prohibited within the coastal regulation zone, namely: ...

(ii) manufacture or handling or storage or disposal of hazardous substances as specified in the Notifications of the Government of India in the Ministry of Environment and Forests, Nos. S O 594(E) dated 28-7-1989, S O 966(E) dated 27-11-1989 and GSR 1037(E) dated 5-12-1989; except transfer of hazardous substances from ships to ports, terminals and refineries and *vice versa,* in the port areas....

3. *Regulation of permissible activities.* — All other activities, except those prohibited in Para 2 above, will be regulated as under: ...

(2) The following activities will require environmental clearance from the Ministry of Environment and Forests, Government of India, namely: ...

(ii) Operational constructions for ports, harbours and lighthouses and construction activities of jetties, wharves, slipways, pipelines and conveying systems including transmission lines provided that environmental clearance in case of constructions or modernisation or expansion of jetties and wharves in the Union Territory of Lakshadweep for providing embarkation and disembarkation facilities shall be on the basis of a report of scientific study conducted by the Central Government or any agency authorised or recognised by it suggesting environmental safeguard measures required to be taken for minimising damage to corals and associated biodiversity....

(3)(i) The coastal States and Union Territory Administrations shall prepare, within a period of one year from the date of this notification, coastal zone management plans identifying and classifying the CRZ areas within their respective territories in accordance with the guidelines given in Annexures I and II of the notification and obtain approval (with or without modifications) of the Central Government in the Ministry of Environment and Forests;

(ii) Within the framework of such approved plans, all development and activities within the CRZ other than those covered in Para 2 and Para 3(2) above shall be regulated by the State Government, Union Territory Administration or the local authority as the case may be in accordance with the guidelines given in Annexures I and II of the notification; and

(iii) In the interim period till the coastal zone management plans mentioned in Para 3(3)(i) above are prepared and approved, all developments and activities within the CRZ shall not violate the provisions of this notification. State Governments and Union Territory Administrations shall ensure adherence to these regulations and violations, if any, shall be subject to the provisions of the Environment (Protection) Act, 1986.'

[The court referred to its judgment in the *CRZ Notification* case and the directions issued to finalize the Coastal Zone Management Plans across the country.]

[C]onsequent upon directions of this Court, the State of Tamil Nadu submitted its Coastal Zone Management Plan to the MoEF on 23-8-1996 which was approved on 27-9-1996 (the 1996 Plan) containing 31 sheets corresponding to maps for different stretches of the coastline of the State of Tamil Nadu with certain conditions/modifications/classifications. Sheet No. 10 pertains to the coastal stretch of Cuddalore District. The MoEF, based on Sheet No. 10 (the 1996 Plan) have stated in their affidavit that the land portion of the banks of Uppanar River adjacent to the plant in Thiyagavalli Village where the pipeline crosses Uppanar River does not come under the CRZ area. This position is reiterated by TNCZMA in their affidavit filed before this Court:

> '... as per the approved Coastal Zone Management Plan, the banks of Uppanar River adjacent to the plant in Thiyagavalli Village where the pipeline crosses River Uppanar does not come under CRZ area....'

We were also shown a copy of Sheet No. 10 from which it did not transpire that Uppanar River and its banks where the pipelines pass have tidal influence and come under the CRZ area. That the 1996 Plan does not reflect the area on both sides of Uppanar River through which the pipelines pass as CRZ area is not in dispute. The contention of the Senior Counsel for the appellant-petitioner is that the 1996 Plan has become redundant and obsolete in view of change in the CRZ regime due to amendments in the 1991 Notification, first on 29-12-1998 and then on 21-5-2002.

By the 1998 amendment, it has been provided in the 1991 Notification that HTL shall be demarcated uniformly in all parts of the country by the demarcating authority or authorities so authorised by the Central Government in accordance with the general guidelines issued in this regard. By further amendment on 21-5-2002, sub-para (ii) was inserted in the first para of the 1991 Notification providing therein that the distance from HTL shall apply to both sides in the case of rivers, creeks and backwaters. The said amendment provides that the distance up to which development along rivers, creeks and backwaters is to be regulated shall be governed by the distance up to which the tidal effects are experienced which shall be determined based on salinity concentration of 5 ppt. It further provides that salinity measurements shall be made during the driest period of the year and distance up to which tidal effects are experienced shall be clearly identified and demarcated in the Coastal Zone Management Plans.

It is perfectly true that at the time of preparation and approval of the 1996 Plan, the amendments of 29-12-1998 and 21-5-2002 in the 1991 Notification had not seen the light of the day and the declaration made in first para that the coastal stretches of seas, bays, estuaries, creeks, rivers and backwaters which are influenced by tidal action (in the landward side) up to 500 meters from HTL and the land between LTL and HTL are CRZ was kept in view but in the absence of any modification carried out thereafter, the 1996 Plan remains operative. The authorities authorised to demarcate HTL, we are afraid, cannot override the plan prepared and approved under Para 3(3)(i) as the said paragraph leaves no manner of doubt that Coastal Zone Management Plan prepared by the coastal State (or for that matter the State Coastal Zone Management Authority) and duly approved by the MoEF is the relevant plan for identification and classification of CRZ areas. The plan prepared by NIO, thus, cannot be said to have superseded the 1996 Plan for the Cuddalore coastal stretch.

More so, while giving approval on 27-9-1996 to the 1996 Plan, the MoEF appended, inter alia, a condition that the Government of Tamil Nadu would not make any change in the approved categorisation of CRZ area without its prior approval. Seen thus, the 1996 Plan for the purposes of demarcation and classification of CRZ area in the State of Tamil Nadu has to be treated as final and conclusive and has been rightly treated as such by the MoEF. We hold, as it must be, that Uppanar River and its banks at the relevant place where the pipelines laid by Chemplast pass do not fall under CRZ III area as per the 1996 Plan and no environmental clearance is needed for such pipelines. The stand of the MoEF is, which seems to us to be correct, that they have granted permission to the onshore pipelines insofar as these pass through CRZ abutting the sea i.e. 500 meters from HTL and no clearance has been granted as it was not required for laying of pipelines under Uppanar River.

* * *

Now, we advert to the other main issue concerning Para 2(ii) of the 1991 Notification. This paragraph prohibits manufacture or handling or storage or disposal of hazardous substances, as specified in the Notifications issued by the MoEF (dated 28-7-1989, 27-11-1989 and 5-12-1989), except transfer of hazardous substances from ships to ports, terminals and refineries and vice versa, in the port areas. That VCM is a hazardous substance notified vide Notification dated 27-11-1989 is not in dispute. There is also no dispute, rather it is an admitted position, that handling of a substance includes transfer as per section 2(d) of the Environment (Protection) Act, 1986.

It was contended by the Senior Counsel for the appellant-petitioner that transfer of VCM in CRZ area is completely prohibited and VCM cannot be carried through the CRZ except in the port area. Their argument is that VCM can be brought onshore by pipeline to the port area but not in the CRZ area. The arguments of learned Senior Counsel have put in issue the scope of expression, 'except transfer of hazardous substances from ships to ports, terminals and refineries and vice versa in the port areas' which was added in Para 2(ii) on 9-7-1997. We are called upon to ascertain the true meaning and intention of the executive in bringing this exception.

In the original 1991 Notification there was no exception clause. It appears to have been added for the purpose of enabling transfer of hazardous substances from ships to ports, ships to terminals and ships to refineries and vice versa. Is such transfer of hazardous substances confined to terminals and refineries located in the port areas? The answer in the affirmative may make the said provision unworkable and would also result in absurdity inasmuch as the hazardous substance would be brought into the port, refinery or terminal in the port area from the ship and would remain there and could not be taken beyond the port area because of the prohibition. This surely could not have been the intention of the executive in adding the exception clause.

It is well settled that if exception has been added to remedy the mischief or defect, it should be so construed that it remedies the mischief and not in a manner which frustrates the very purpose. Purposive construction has often been employed to avoid a lacuna and to suppress the mischief and advance the remedy. It is again a settled rule that if the language used is capable of bearing more than one construction and if construction is employed that results in absurdity or anomaly, such construction has to be rejected and preference should be given to such a construction that brings it into harmony with its purpose and avoids absurdity or anomaly as it may always be presumed that while employing a particular language in the provision absurdity or anomaly was never intended.

Notwithstanding imperfection of expression and that exception clause is not happily worded, we are of the view that by applying purposive construction, the expression, 'in the port areas' should be read as 'in or through the port areas'. The exception in Para 2(ii) then would achieve its objective and read, 'except transfer of hazardous substances from ships to ports, ships to terminals and ships to refineries and vice versa, in or through the port areas'. This construction will be harmonious with Para 3(2)(ii) which permits the activity of laying pipelines in the CRZ area.

As a matter of fact, the MoEF in their affidavit before this Court have clearly stated that the permission granted to Chemplast on 19-12-2005 is in exercise of the powers conferred under Para 3(2)(ii) of the 1991 Notification. We do not find any infirmity in the permission granted by the MoEF on 19-12-2005. Having held that, there is no illegality in the permission granted by the Executive Engineer on 27-2-2008 either....

NOTES AND QUESTIONS

1. The Supreme Court rendered judgment in 2010 nearly eight years after Chemplast initiated the process of seeking environmental permissions. Is this an acceptable time frame for entrepreneurs and investors seeking to expand industry and manufacturing in India? Had an

investor known about the legal risk posed by the PILs and such a long gestation, would she have put down the money?

Remember, in order to compete globally businesses must be efficient. Delays in commissioning projects add costs and reduce efficiency. Courts are alive to disruptions caused by injunctions and also to the cloud of uncertainty brought by pending litigations. PILs dampen investor confidence because they are potentially disruptive of projects and pose huge legal risks that are difficult to anticipate because of the *ad hoc* nature of these adjudications.

2. Was it necessary for the Supreme Court to examine the issues in intricate detail considering the extensive scrutiny by numerous expert bodies? Moreover, Nizamudeen did not challenge the environmental clearances granted by MoEF in 2005 and a grossly belated challenge was made in the Article 32 petition filed in 2009. Considering that Rs. 600 crores was invested by Chemplast and the plant was operating by the time the Supreme Court decided the matter, should the Supreme Court have rejected the PILs on the principle of delay and laches?

3. The Supreme Court declined to examine Chemplast's contention that the PIL was instigated by a corporate rival, Cuddalore Powergen Corporation Ltd. Since a PIL petitioner must observe an *uberrimae fidei* (utmost good faith) standard, should the Supreme Court have required Nizamudeen and friends to disclose their sources of funding? Should the lawyers appearing in the PILs be required to disclose whether they are earning a fee and if so how much and from whom? Unless the courts require such disclosure, the abuse of the PIL jurisdiction will continue with unverified allegations of corporate sponsorship sullying genuine cases.

4. Was the Supreme Court correct in ignoring amendments to the CRZ notification and adhering to the CZMP as if it were cast in stone? Was it not the duty of the public authorities to rework the CZMP approved in 1996, incorporating changes required by subsequent amendments? How were the complaining citizens at fault? If the Uppanar River was indeed part of the CRZ in terms of the amended notification, should the court have directed the MoEF to suggest appropriate safeguards for the subsoil stretch below the river and put an end to the controversy?

5. The rule of purposive interpretation was applied sensibly. Was it reasonable for the PIL petitioner to suggest an interpretation that would allow the VCM to reach the port but not be transported out to the plant?

X. LAKSHADWEEP

Union Territory of Lakshadweep v Seashells Beach Resorts[82] arose from an interim order passed by the Kerala High Court permitting the respondent to operate its resort at Agatti, the principal island in the Lakshadweep archipelago. The respondent asserted that it had numerous permissions from the authorities and that the administration was discriminating against the respondent while permitting other resorts to operate. The High Court allowed the resort, which employed 47 persons, to operate until a decision was taken by the authorities on certain pending applications. The Supreme Court set aside the interim order of the High Court holding that in such a case, equitable considerations were subordinate to statutory requirements. The court held:

> The High Court obviously failed to appreciate that equitable considerations were wholly misplaced in a situation where the very erection of the building to be used as a resort violated the CRZ requirements or the conditions of land use diversion. No one could in the teeth of those requirements claim equity or present the administration with a *fait accompli*. The

[82] (2012) 6 SCC 136.

resort could not be commissioned under a judicial order in disregard of serious objections that were raised by the Administration, which objections had to be answered before any direction could issue from a writ court.

The court noticed that the Integrated Island Management Plan (IIMP) contemplated under the 6 January 2011 notification was under preparation with scientific inputs being received from the Centre for Earth Science Studies (CESS), Trivandrum. The IIMP for Agatti was expected to be final by 6 January 2013 within the time frame prescribed for its preparation. Nevertheless, the Supreme Court recorded that neither of the parties before it was 'averse to the constitution of an expert committee' that could assist the Lakshadweep administration in finalizing the IIMP 'so that the same is submitted to the Government of India for approval at the earliest'. The Supreme Court thereafter constituted an Expert Committee presided over by a recently retired justice of the Supreme Court and comprising four other members with expertise in earth sciences, coastal management, engineering and planning. The chairman of the committee was empowered to co-opt or associate any other expert member from any field considered relevant or to take the assistance of any scientific or expert body for completing the assignment. The remit of the Expert Committee was outlined in the judgment:

> The Committee shall endeavour to work on the following broad terms of reference:
>
> (i) The Committee shall use its expertise for evaluation of the draft IIMPs received from CESS or others that may be received in due course, and make such additions or alterations in the same as it may consider proper having regard, inter alia, to the following:
>
> (a) The development already in existence and the future developments, conservation and preservation of the entire area keeping in view the statutory Notification dated 6-1-2011 issued by the Government of India under the provisions of the Environment (Protection) Act, 1986.
>
> (b) The impact of the proposed development on the livelihood of indigenous population and the various vulnerability issues.
>
> (c) Reservation/identification of suitable locations and areas for creation of public and semi-public facilities for development of tourism in the Islands.
>
> (d) Redevelopment/sustainable development of inhabited and/or uninhabited areas of each island as independent and self-contained units or as part of a larger development plan along scientific lines.
>
> (ii) The Committee may consider and recommend incorporation in the IIMP, Development Control Regulations governing the developmental activity in accordance with the final proposals on the IIMP for the purpose of islanders seeking clearances for permissible development activities on the Islands. Such regulations may also include setting up of an appellate authority for the grievance redressal of the islanders with respect to such clearances. The Committee may suggest an outer time-frame within which the Authority may have to respond to the applications of the islanders seeking permission for development activities.
>
> (iii) The Committee may examine the desirability and the feasibility of running 'home stays' for tourism purpose in the Islands and may suggest the same to be incorporated in the IIMPs. The Committee may examine and suggest necessary guidelines keeping in mind environmental, economic and security considerations for running of such home stays including norms/rules for such 'home stays' and the number of 'home stays' to be permitted, the number of permits to be granted, the norms for identification of houses for home stays, and the facilities to be offered, etc.
>
> (iv) The Committee may in its wisdom and discretion make suggestions on any other issue concerning the Islands which it may deem fit.
>
> The Committee shall examine allegations regarding violation of CRZ and other irregularities committed by the respondent or by other individuals/entities in relation to establishment and/or running resorts and 'home stays' in the Islands. Allegations regarding irregularities in the matter of grant of permits to the tourists visiting the Islands as also in regard to

> permissions granted to the resort owners/home stays to operate on the Islands shall also be examined by the Committee. So, also the Committee shall be free to examine whether any official of the Lakshadweep Administration has been guilty of any act of omission or commission in the discharge of his official duties and if considered necessary recommend action against such officials.

This was not public interest litigation. There was no complaint about the authorities under the IPZ notification being dysfunctional. Did the Supreme Court have any business then, in private litigation, to appoint a committee when *neither* party sought its appointment? The standard applied by the court was the absence of any objection by counsel for the parties. Is it realistic to expect a counsel to oppose a suggestion from the bench when it could boomerang on her client's fortune? Will the creation of such an extra-statutory body help or harm the working of the IPZ Regulations? Could the High Court, whose interim order was upset, have constituted an Expert Committee to look into third-party irregularities and official conduct, when all this was beyond the scope of the petition? If the High Court could not, how could the Supreme Court do so in appeal?

What do you make of the following direction of the court?

> The remuneration payable to the Chairman and the members of the Committee is not being determined by us. We deem it fit to leave that matter to be decided by the Committee keeping in view the nature of work to be undertaken by it and the time required to accomplish the same.

XI. SAND MINING

Sandy beaches protect coastal land from the impact of waves and also prevent the sea water from entering into freshwater sources such as wells and ponds. Unregulated sand mining is a problem in coastal areas as well as inland, along riverbeds. Rampant sand mining is devastating rivers in several regions, causing a steep fall in groundwater levels. River sand acts as a sponge holding the water till it percolates into the ground.[83] *State v Sanjay* required the Supreme Court to clarify the law and mend the cleavage amongst different High Court opinions. The moot issue was whether a person accused of illegally mining sand from a natural source could be proceeded against under the general law applicable to theft (sections 378 and 379 of the Indian Penal Code) or whether the offence committed was exclusively with respect to violating the Mines and Minerals (Development and Regulation) Act, 1957 (MMDR Act), as amended, which regulates sand mining. Remember, sand mining from river beds and beaches is a low investment enterprise capable of swift re-location should the authorities detect mischief.

STATE (NCT OF DELHI) v SANJAY
(2014) 9 SCC 772

> M YUSUF EQBAL, J: The principal question which arises for consideration in these appeals is whether the provisions contained in sections 21, 22 and other sections of the Mines and Minerals (Development and Regulation) Act, 1957 operate as bar against prosecution of a person who has been charged with allegation which constitutes offences under sections 379/114 and other provisions of the Penal Code, 1860. In other words, whether the provisions of the Mines and Minerals Act explicitly or impliedly exclude the provisions of the Penal Code when the act of an accused is an offence both under the Penal

[83] M Rajshekhar, *Think Sand Mining Damages the Ecology? It Ruins Politics as Well*, SCROLL.IN, 20 September 2016, https://scroll.in/article/815139/think-sand-mining-damages-the-ecology-it-ruins-politics-as-well, accessed on 22 June 2021.

Code (in short 'IPC') and under the provisions of the Mines and Minerals (Development and Regulation) Act....

Before answering the question, we shall first refer in brief the relevant provisions of the Mines and Minerals (Development and Regulation) Act, 1957 and the Code of Criminal Procedure. Section 4 of the Act puts a restriction on mining operation or prospecting mining operation by any person except under a lease or licence.

Section 4 reads as under:

> '4. *Prospecting or mining operations to be under licence or lease* — (1) No person shall undertake any reconnaissance, prospecting or mining operations in any area, except under and in accordance with the terms and conditions of a reconnaissance permit or of a prospecting licence or, as the case may be, of a mining lease, granted under this Act and the Rules made thereunder: ...
>
> (1-A) No person shall transport or store or cause to be transported or stored any mineral otherwise than in accordance with the provisions of this Act and the Rules made thereunder....'

A bare perusal of section 4, particularly Section 4(1-A), would show that there is a total restriction on transportation or search of minerals otherwise than in accordance with the provisions of the Act and the Rules made thereunder. The next relevant provisions are sections 21 and 22 of the Act:

> '21. *Penalties* — (1) Whoever contravenes the provisions of sub-section (1) or sub-section (1-A) of section 4 shall be punished with imprisonment for a term which may extend to two years, or with fine which may extend to twenty-five thousand rupees, or with both....'
>
> '22. *Cognizance of offences* — No court shall take cognizance of any offence punishable under this Act or any Rules made thereunder except upon complaint in writing made by a person authorised in this behalf by the Central Government or the State Government.'

Reading the aforesaid provision would show that cognizance of any offence punishable under the Act or the Rules made thereunder shall be taken only upon a written complaint made by a person authorised in this behalf by the Central Government or the State Government. [The court thereafter quoted sections 149–152 of the Code of Criminal Procedure which casts a duty upon a police officer to prevent the commission of offences, report a design to commit any offence to her superior and confers power on the police to arrest and prevent harm to public property.]

A perusal of the aforementioned provisions would show that a police officer of his own authority has the duty to prevent any injury attempted to be committed to any public property or national assets and to prosecute such person in accordance with law.

The policy and object of the Mines and Minerals Act and Rules have a long history and are the result of an increasing awareness of the compelling need to restore the serious ecological imbalance and to stop the damages being caused to the nature. The Court cannot lose sight of the fact that adverse and destructive environmental impact of sand mining has been discussed in the UNEP Global Environmental Alert Service Report. As per the contents of the Report, lack of proper scientific methodology for river sand mining has led to indiscriminate sand mining, while weak governance and corruption have led to widespread illegal mining. While referring to the proposition in India, it was stated that sand trading is a lucrative business, and there is evidence of illegal trading such as the case of the influential mafias in our country.

The mining of aggregates in rivers has led to severe damage to rivers, including pollution and changes in levels of pH. Removing sediment from rivers causes the river to cut its channel through the bed of the valley floor, or channel incision, both upstream and downstream of the extraction site. This leads to coarsening of bed material and lateral channel instability. It can change the riverbed itself. The removal of more than 12 million tonnes of sand a year from Vembanad Lake catchment in India has led to the lowering of the riverbed by 7 to 15 cm a year. Incision can also cause the alluvial aquifer to drain to a lower level, resulting in a loss of aquifer storage. It can also increase flood frequency and intensity by reducing flood regulation capacity. However, lowering the water table is most threatening to water supply exacerbating drought occurrence and severity as tributaries of major rivers dry up when sand mining reaches certain thresholds. Illegal sand mining also causes erosion. Damming and mining have reduced sediment delivery from rivers to many coastal areas, leading to accelerated beach erosion.

The Report also dealt with the astonishing impact of sand mining on the economy. It states that tourism may be affected through beach erosion. Fishing, both traditional and commercial, can be affected through destruction of benthic fauna. Agriculture could be affected through loss of agricultural land from river erosion and the lowering of the water table. The insurance sector is affected through exacerbation of the impact of extreme events such as floods, droughts and storm surges through decreased protection of beach fronts. The erosion of coastal areas and beaches affects houses and infrastructure. A decrease in bed load or channel shortening can cause downstream erosion including bank erosion and the undercutting or undermining of engineering structures such as bridges, side protection walls and structures for water supply.

Sand is often removed from beaches to build hotels, roads and other tourism-related infrastructure. In some locations, continued construction is likely to lead to an unsustainable situation and destruction of the main natural attraction for visitors—beaches themselves. Mining from, within or near a riverbed has a direct impact on the stream's physical characteristics, such as channel geometry, bed elevation, substratum composition and stability, instream roughness of the bed, flow velocity, discharge capacity, sediment transportation capacity, turbidity, temperature, etc. Alteration or modification of the above attributes may cause hazardous impact on ecological equilibrium of riverine regime. This may also cause adverse impact on instream biota and riparian habitats. This disturbance may also cause changes in channel configuration and flow paths....

Reading the provisions of the Act minutely and carefully, *prima facie* we are of the view that there is no complete and absolute bar in prosecuting persons under the Penal Code where the offences committed by persons are penal and cognizable offence.

Sub-section (1-A) of Section 4 of the MMDR Act puts a restriction in transporting and storing any mineral otherwise than in accordance with the provisions of the Act and the Rules made thereunder. In other words no person will do mining activity without a valid lease or licence. Section 21 is a penal provision according to which if a person contravenes the provisions of sub-section (1-A) of Section 4, he shall be prosecuted and punished in the manner and procedure provided in the Act. Sub-section (6) has been inserted in section 4 by amendment making the offence cognizable notwithstanding anything contained in the Code of Criminal Procedure, 1973. Section 22 of the Act puts a restriction on the court to take cognizance of any offence punishable under the Act or any Rule made thereunder except upon a complaint made by a person authorised in this behalf. It is very important to note that section 21 does not begin with a *non obstante* clause. Instead of the words 'notwithstanding anything contained in any law for the time being in force no court shall take cognizance....', the section begins with the words 'no court shall take cognizance of any offence.'

It is well known that a *non obstante* clause is a legislative device which is usually employed to give overriding effect to certain provisions over some contrary provisions that may be found either in the same enactment or some other enactment, that is to say, to avoid the operation and effect of all contrary provisions.

***

Considering the principles of interpretation and the wordings used in Section 22, in our considered opinion, the provision is not a complete and absolute bar for taking action by the police for illegal and dishonestly committing theft of minerals including sand from the riverbed. The Court shall take judicial notice of the fact that over the years, rivers in India have been affected by the alarming rate of unrestricted sand mining which is damaging the ecosystem of the rivers and safety of bridges. It also weakens riverbeds, fish breeding and destroys the natural habitat of many organisms. If these illegal activities are not stopped by the State and the police authorities of the State, it will cause serious repercussions as mentioned hereinabove. It will not only change the river hydrology but also will deplete the groundwater levels.

There cannot be any dispute with regard to restrictions imposed under the MMDR Act and remedy provided therein. In any case, where there is a mining activity by any person in contravention of the provisions of section 4 and other sections of the Act, the officer empowered and authorised under the Act shall exercise all the powers including making a complaint before the Jurisdictional Magistrate. It is also not in dispute that the Magistrate shall in such cases take cognizance on the basis of the complaint filed before it by a duly authorised officer. In case of breach and violation of section 4 and other provisions of the Act, the police officer cannot insist the Magistrate for taking cognizance under the Act on the basis of the record submitted by the police alleging contravention of the said Act. In other words, the prohibition contained in section 22 of the Act against prosecution of a person except on a complaint made by the officer is attracted only when such person is sought to be prosecuted for contravention of Section 4 of the Act and not for any act or omission which constitutes an offence under the Penal Code.

However, there may be a situation where a person without any lease or licence or any authority enters into river and extracts sand, gravel and other minerals and remove or transport those minerals in a clandestine manner with an intent to remove dishonestly those minerals from the possession of the State, is liable to be punished for committing such offence under sections 378 and 379 of the Penal Code.

From a close reading of the provisions of the MMDR Act and the offence defined under section 378 IPC, it is manifest that the ingredients constituting the offence are different. The contravention of terms and conditions of mining lease or doing mining activity in violation of Section 4 of the Act is an offence punishable under section 21 of the MMDR Act, whereas dishonestly removing sand, gravel and other minerals from the river, which is the property of the State, out of the State's possession without the consent, constitute an offence of theft. Hence, merely because initiation of proceeding for commission of an offence under the MMDR Act on the basis of complaint cannot and shall not debar the police from taking action against persons for committing theft of sand and minerals in the manner mentioned above by exercising power under the Code of Criminal Procedure and submit a report before the Magistrate for taking cognizance against such persons. In other words, in a case where there is a theft of sand and gravel from the government land, the police can register a case, investigate the same and submit a final report under section 173 CrPC before a Magistrate having jurisdiction for the purpose of taking cognizance as provided in section 190(1)(d) of the Code of Criminal Procedure.

After giving our thoughtful consideration in the matter, in the light of the relevant provisions of the Act *vis-à-vis* the Code of Criminal Procedure and the Penal Code, we are of the definite opinion that the ingredients constituting the offence under the MMDR Act and the ingredients of dishonestly removing sand and gravel from the riverbeds without consent, which is the property of the State, is a distinct offence under IPC. Hence, for the commission of offence under section 378 IPC, on receipt of the police report, the Magistrate having jurisdiction can take cognizance of the said offence without awaiting the receipt of complaint that may be filed by the authorised officer for taking cognizance in respect of violation of various provisions of the MMDR Act. Consequently, the contrary view taken by the different High Courts cannot be sustained in law and, therefore, [is] overruled. Consequently, these criminal appeals are disposed of with a direction to the Magistrates concerned to proceed accordingly.

NOTES AND QUESTIONS

1. Alive to widespread illegal sand mining often involving organized sand mafias with political links, the Supreme Court strengthened the criminal response and investigation machinery. Before

this decision, the sand mafia shielded itself behind certain High Court judgments that required the criminal process to be initiated *only* by a specifically authorized officer under the MMDR Act. Previously, the accused argued that a police officer must remain a bystander. By recognizing the undiminished power of a police officer, the Supreme Court enabled a quick response to illegal sand mining detected in the field. The police may now immediately respond to illegal sand mining brought to their notice by taking recourse to the general criminal law on theft.

2. Do you agree with the reasoning in this case?

3. In *State of Gujarat v Jayesh Kanjibhai Kalathiya*,[84] the Supreme Court considered the validity of a rule which had been struck down by the Gujarat High Court. The rule read:

> No movement of sand shall be allowed beyond the border of the State. In case, any vehicle is found transporting sand to the neighbouring State even with authorised royalty pass or delivery challan, it shall be treated as violation of the Act and the rules made thereunder and the penal provisions, except compounding, as specified therein shall be applicable.

The state sought to defend the rule on environmental grounds, claiming that excessive extraction of sand was having adverse impact by destroying Gujarat's riverbeds. The Supreme Court dismissed the appeals holding that it was constitutionally impermissible to restrict interstate movement of sand. If the state was serious about the environmental issue, it could restrict the quantum of sand being excavated.

B. WETLANDS

Wetlands are bogs, swamps and marshes. They provide numerous eco-system services including water purification, maintaining surface moisture, curbing soil erosion, reducing the impact of floods and droughts and re-charging wells. Wetlands support a host of wildlife such as birds, fish, reptiles, amphibians and insects.

An international treaty to protect wetlands was signed in the city of Ramsar, Iran in 1971. Commonly referred to as the Ramsar Convention, the full title of the Treaty captures its focus: Convention on Wetlands of International Importance, Especially as Waterfowl Habitat. India acceded to the Convention on 1 October 1981 and the Convention entered into force in India on 1 February 1982.

India has designated 49 sites as being wetlands of international importance (Ramsar sites).[85] Cases to protect some of the Ramsar sites have reached the courts, including efforts to protect Bhitarkanika,[86] Chilika Lake,[87] the East Kolkata Wetlands,[88] Kolleru Lake[89] and the Vembanad Wetland.[90] The largest Ramsar site in India is the Sunderban Wetland admeasuring 423,000 ha designated in January 2019. The total surface area of the 49 sites adds up to 1,093,636 ha.[91]

---

[84] (2019) 16 SCC 513.

[85] https://www.ramsar.org/wetland/india, accessed on 30 April 2022.

[86] *Centre for Environmental Law, World Wide Fund for Nature v State of Orissa* AIR 1999 Ori 15.

[87] *Kholamuhana Primary Fisherman Co-op Soc v State of Orissa* AIR 1994 Ori 191; *Jogendranath Tarai v State of Orissa* 111 (2011) Cuttack L T 868, (2011) SCC Online Ori 102.

[88] *People United for Better Living in Calcutta v State of West Bengal* AIR 1993 Cal 215; *People United for Better Living in Calcutta v East Kolkata Wetlands Management Authority* (2009) ILR (2) Cal 37; *State of West Bengal v Sanjeevani Projects (P) Ltd* (2006) 1 CHN 241.

[89] *T N Godavarman Thirumulpad v Union of India* (2006) 5 SCC 47.

[90] *Vaamika Island (Green Lagoon Resort) v Union of India* (2013) 8 SCC 760.

[91] *Supra* note 85.

National regulations for wetlands were framed in 2010[92] under the Environment (Protection) Act of 1986 and were replaced by the Wetlands (Conservation and Management) Rules of 2017. The object of the 2017 Rules and the threats they seek to address are captured in the preamble:

> Whereas the wetlands, vital parts of the hydrological cycle, are highly productive ecosystems which support rich biodiversity and provide a wide range of ecosystem services such as water storage, water purification, flood mitigation, erosion control, aquifer recharge, microclimate regulation, aesthetic enhancement of landscapes while simultaneously supporting many significant recreational, social and cultural activities, being part of our rich cultural heritage;
>
> And whereas many wetlands are threatened by reclamation and degradation through drainage and landfill, pollution (discharge of domestic and industrial effluents, disposal of solid waste), hydrological alteration (water withdrawal and changes in inflow and outflow), over-exploitation of their natural resources resulting in loss of biodiversity and disruption in ecosystem services provided by wetlands.

The 2017 Rules apply to Ramsar sites and to wetlands notified by the state or Union territory administration. Wetlands that fall within protected forests or protected areas under the Wildlife Act or covered by the CRZ notification are excluded from the purview of the rules.

Rule 5 constitutes Wetland Authorities in each state and Union territory. The state authorities are chaired by the Minister holding the environment portfolio and comprise 16 bureaucrats from designated departments and five experts drawn from the fields of wetland ecology, hydrology, fisheries, landscape planning and socio-economics. The Union territory authorities are chaired by the chief secretary and have a similar composition. The main task of these authorities is to identify and recommend wetlands for regulations under the rules. The authorities are required to frame strategies for conservation and 'wise use' of wetlands within their jurisdiction. The 'wise use' principle for managing eco-systems is one which 'incorporates sustainable uses (such as capture fisheries at subsistence level or harvest of aquatic plants) as being compatible with conservation, if ecosystem functions (such as water storage, ground water recharge, flood buffering) and values (such as recreation and cultural) are maintained or enhanced'.[93]

Rule 4(1) requires wetlands to 'be conserved and managed in accordance with the principle of "wise use" as determined by the Wetlands Authority'. Rule 4(2) lists activities that are prohibited within wetlands including conversion of the wetland, setting up or expanding industries, handling or storing construction and demolition waste or hazardous substances, dumping solid waste, discharging untreated waste and effluents, construction activity and poaching.

A National Wetlands Committee is required to advise the Central Government on appropriate conservation policies and programmes and evolve norms and guidelines for integrated management of wetlands based on the 'wise use' principle.[94]

I. EAST KOLKATA WETLANDS

Since 1992, a Kolkata-based organization, PUBLIC, has campaigned hard to preserve the wetlands near the metropolis and protect them from reclamation and encroachment. Decided

---

[92] Wetlands (Conservation and Management) Rules of 2010.

[93] Rule 5(3)(g).

[94] Rule 6.

well before the first wetlands conservation statutes, PUBLIC's first notable success remains the cornerstone of wetland jurisprudence in India.

PEOPLE UNITED FOR BETTER LIVING IN CALCUTTA v STATE OF WEST BENGAL

AIR 1993 CAL 215

ORDER: * * *

Turning attention on to the Calcutta wetlands we find that there are 40 species of algae and 2 species of fern, 7 species of monocods and 21 species of dicods. Latest datas suggest the presence of about 155 species of summer birds of which 64 species are resident birds and 91 are migratory. There are 90 species of winter birds of which 44 are residents and 46 are migratory. These migratory birds are mainly from Siberia and East Europe and they arrive at the city through Trans-Asia Migration Route. Admittedly, Calcutta has had around 20,000 acres approximately of wetland area, of which 10,000 acres have already been reclaimed and the sprawling metropolis under the name of Salt Lake City being a satellite township area of Calcutta exists, and the East Calcutta wetlands now therefore comprises of around 9,000 and odd hundred acres approximately on the eastern fringe of the city with a natural slope from the west to the east. The entire area comprises of low lands characterized by marshes and ponds etc. As regards the soil, there is no manner of doubt that it has very high moisture content of a mixed clay and alluvium type. On the issue of hydrology, the entire waste and drainage (sewer) water of Calcutta runs through a system of main and ancillary channels going through the wetlands; these flows are channelised into the sewage-fed fisheries for pisciculture and the wetlands purify the entire waste water through a natural process of oxidation, radiation, biological breakdown of organic wastes and pisciculture....

Calcutta wetlands presents a unique eco-system apart from the material benefit to the society at large. Within the Calcutta Metropolitan area, the Calcutta wetlands can be easily identified as the most outstanding wetland cluster. As already mentioned, these wetlands bear the oldest tradition in the world of resource recovery from city's waste besides being the largest of such systems in the world. They have now become a subject of international interest. Since the beginning of this century, various forms of agriculture and pisciculture have been practised in the region. These wetlands are interdistributory marshes lying between the levee of the river Hugli to the west and of Bidyadhari to the east. The Bidyadhari can now be traced only by its aggraded bed presently under paddy cultivation. It was a tidal channel and the shallow marshes acted as spill basins. Gradually with diversion of city sewage, premature reclamation by building embankments for the then existing salt water fisheries and with silting up of the river, these marshes became stagnant and ceased to be saline. Since then they have become sewage receptacles for the city and with innovative enterprise of local people they have been used as waste water fisheries producing more than 10 quintals of fish per acre per year for the city. These wetlands also store run off from the adjacent areas during the rains, and are traversed by the sewage outfall channels of the city. These channels carry the wastewater eastwards to the Kulti River which eventually falls into the Raimangal which drains into the Bay of Bengal. These wetlands recycle waste water for efficient nutrient recovery, provide fresh fish to the market of Calcutta and employ thousands of rural people over an area of about 7,500 acres....

Before proceeding further, however, it is to be noted that India is a contracting party to the Ramsar Convention, an Inter Governmental Treaty on Wetlands under which she is obliged to promote the conservation of wetlands habitat in her territory. The Salt Lake Swamp is acknowledged as an important wetland by virtue of its socio economic and ecological values. As a matter of fact, it is in the Directory of Asian Wetlands and a wetland of international importance—it meets all accepted criteria for identification of an internationally important wetland....

When considered as an ecosystem, the wetlands are useful for nutrient recovery and cycling, releasing excess nitrogen, inactivation of phosphates, removing toxins, chemicals, heavy metals through absorption by plants, and also in treating waste water. Removal of suspended solids from flowing water by reducing the flow also benefits the retention of water for sometime whereby biological, physical and chemical changes are made possible (Mitsch & Gosselink, 1986). Retention of sediments by wetlands also reduces siltation in the rivers. Wetlands also help in mitigating floods, recharging acquifers and in reducing surface run off and consequent erosion. Mangrove wetlands on India and Bangladesh act as buffers against devastating storms of the Bay of Bengal. Wetlands also influence microclimate of a locality. Besides these, they are also valued for their aesthetic qualities and recreational opportunities. A fresh water wetland checks underground salt water intrusion of an adjacent brackish water environment through interface pressure (US, EPA, 1985).

On a global scale the wetlands function significantly in maintaining air and water quality including nitrogen, sulphur, methane and carbon dioxide cycles....

There is no manner of doubt, therefore, that wetlands being a bounty of nature do have a significant role to play in the proper development of the society—be it from environmental perspective or from economic perspective. Pollutionwise this metropolitan city of Calcutta tops the list in the country—can we in this city further endanger the environment by reclaiming the nature's gift to mankind when, in fact, such a reclamation is only for the purpose of expansion of the satellite township on the Eastern fringe of the city of Calcutta[?] The only developmental project spoken of is the World Trade Centre along with the Public Exhibition Centre which [has] already been dealt with in this order as above and apart therefrom no other developmental project has been spoken of during the course of submission in the matter. If, however, it is said that the reclamation is not for developmental projects, then and in that event, I am of the view that question of further consideration of the matter does not and cannot arise since wetland is precious, wetland ensures the benefit of the society at large and assists mankind to live in a cleaner and purer environment—which in my view, one cannot afford to lose neither the Court of Law can lend assistance to contra-belief or contra action of a State Agency. Wetland acts as a benefactor to the society and there cannot be any manner of doubt in regard thereto and as such encroachment thereof would be detrimental to the society which the Law Courts cannot permit. This benefit to the society cannot be weighed on mathematical nicety so as to take note of the requirement of the society—what is required today may not be a relevant consideration in the immediate future. Therefore, it cannot really be assessed to what amount nature's bounty is required for the proper maintenance of environmental equilibrium. It cannot be measured in terms of requirement and as such, the Court of Law cannot, in fact, decry the opinion of the environmentalist in that direction. Law Courts exist for the benefit of the society. Law Courts exist for the purpose of giving redress to the society when called for and it must rise above all levels so that justice is meted out and the society thrives thereunder. I do not find any justiciable reason to disagree with the opinion expressed by the environmentalists that wetland should be preserved and no interference or reclamation should be permitted.

It is, however, placed on record that no issue as regards the maintainability of the writ petition or that of *locus standi* was raised before the Court during the entire course of hearing of the matter and as such I need not delve into the issue.

In that view of the matter, there shall be an order of injunction restraining the State Respondents from reclaiming any further wetland. There shall also be an order of injunction prohibiting the respondents from granting any permission to any person whatsoever for the purpose of changing the use of the land from agricultural to residential or commercial in the area as indicated in the map annexed to the petition and marked with letter 'C'. The State Respondents are further directed to take steps so as to stop private alienation and, if required, by extending the statutory provisions in regard thereto....

NOTES AND QUESTIONS

1. The court seems to take notice of the importance of wetlands and relies on that notion to restrain the state from reclaiming any further wetland. Is there any statutory or common

law basis for the judgment? Should a court simply nullify executive action based on its own notion of what is best for society?

2. Does the court's citing of the Ramsar Convention justify its nullification of executive action?

3. On 30 November 1994, the High Court modified its previous order on an application by the promoters of the World Trade Center. Reiterating the importance of wetlands and the need to balance development with environment, the court permitted the project.

4. In 2007, PUBLIC returned to court, this time challenging a water treatment plant being put up by the Kolkata Municipal Corporation.[95] In the intervening years, due to the efforts of PUBLIC, the East Kolkata Wetlands (EKW) were declared as a protected site under the Ramsar Convention. Moreover, West Bengal enacted the East Kolkata Wetlands (Conservation and Management) Act of 2006 establishing a Wetlands Management Authority (WMA). In the *EKW* case, PUBLIC urged the Calcutta High Court to quash the sanction granted by the WMA. PUBLIC argued that since the Authority's function was to preserve the character of the wetlands and any change allowed could only be for improvement and upkeep of the local environment and surroundings, the impugned sanction was bad. The proposed plant would irreversibly alter the wetlands and disrupt the fragile ecosystem by construction of facilities, laying pipelines and building access roads.

The High Court repelled the challenge, finding that the plant was in the interest of the public at large and was essential because the clean water supply would help citizens threatened by arsenic poisoning from contaminated groundwater. The High Court noted that the plant was to come up at the western edge of the wetland area and abutted a major road. Besides, the Municipal Corporation had no alternative plot extending over 20 acres that was required for the project. Against this backdrop, the High Court allowed the project, directing the WMA to keep a close watch over the work. As an additional safeguard, the division bench appointed an independent Monitoring committee to periodically report to the court and ensure that implementation was done in an ecologically friendly manner with minimal damage to the water body.

5. What is the status of the WMA constituted under the State Act of 2006 upon the State Authority being constituted under the Central Rules of 2017? Do both authorities continue side by side? Is there a mechanism in the Constitution to resolve such issues?

The 2017 Rules acknowledge the potential overlap in the preamble:

> And whereas the State Governments and Union Territory Administrations need to take into account wetland ecosystem services and biodiversity values likewise within their developmental programming and economic well-being, also taking into cognizance that land and water, two major ecological constituents of wetland ecosystems, are enlisted as State subjects as per the Constitution; . . .

6. In *State of West Bengal v Sanjeevani Projects (P) Ltd*,[96] a division bench of the Calcutta High Court repelled the claims by developers to allow housing projects on lands proposed to be added to the EKW. The court found that construction had proceeded without securing permissions for a change in the land use under local laws and was evidently illegal. The division bench reiterated the crucial importance of the EKW 'being the lifeline of the drainage system of the city of Kolkata for discharge of effluent and drainage of excess rainwater' and

[95] *PUBLIC v East Kolkata Wetlands Management Authority* (2009) ILR (2) CAL 37.
[96] (2006) 1 CHN 241.

the necessity to preserve the wetlands for the eco-system services provided. The court held that it was the duty of the state to ensure that the wetland was preserved and the illegal constructions removed.

II. CRITIQUING THE COURT

The German scholar Hans Dembowski studied the Calcutta High Court's response to the city's environmental problems, including the depletion of the East Kolkata Wetlands.

> HANS DEMBOWSKI; COURTS, CIVIL SOCIETY AND PUBLIC SPHERE: ENVIRONMENTAL LITIGATION IN CALCUTTA 34 Economic & Political Weekly 49 (1999)
>
> The case studies suggest that the judiciary as a whole is muddling through rather than applying an overarching, consistent body of law. This is exacerbated by the fact (not elaborated on here) that changes of judges may radically change the course of proceedings. Individual bench members dealt thoroughly with some issues and seemed eager to dispose of other questions quickly. . . .
>
> It would be wrong to simply blame individual judges for this state of affairs. Their task of setting administrative shortcomings straight is daunting. As has been scholarly discussed, environmental legislation is often not realistic in India, consisting more of propagandist promises than of pragmatically implementable programmes.
>
> In this context, it is worth keeping in mind that environmental challenges are always among the most difficult any polity faces. This is the reason why they are good test cases to investigate questions of governance in general. Environmental matters affect economy, culture, social habits and security, traditions and the distribution of incomes. Even in countries much richer than India (Germany for instance), the policy arenas are haunted by fancy rhetoric followed up by merely symbolical, ineffective measures. . . .
>
> Just as legislations or policy statements are not always followed up by action, so court rulings are not necessarily implemented. This is again not simply the consequence of personal wrong-doing or incompetence. Many government agencies are inadequately staffed, equipped and organised to do their jobs properly.
>
> For instance, the West Bengal Pollution Control Board only has a technical staff of 25 to check pollution in a state with almost as many people as reunited Germany and with the oldest industrial base in Asia. Nevertheless, the green bench relies on this agency's reports. By trying to make the state Pollution Control Board its investigating agency, the high court judges have increased its workload and added to its already overburdened agenda. Consequently, Pollution Control Board reports are often of a rather dubious quality. . . .
>
> The judiciary cannot solve all technical, economic, social and other questions related to environmental problems. But it has scope to provide more transparency and more responsibility—in the very literal sense of making those in charge respond. If successful, this might over the long run not only inspire hope but also encourage trust in the democratic state.

In 2001 Dembowski published his book titled *Taking the State to Court: Public Interest Litigation in Metropolitan India.* The study is a pioneering work deserving wide readership but was withdrawn by the publisher because the Calcutta High Court initiated contempt of court proceedings which remain pending for nearly two decades. While the book recognizes the sincerity of the High Court in its pro-environment initiative, as a mark of independent scholarship it also comments on the milieu in which society operates, including reports on some of the High Court's personnel.

HANS DEMBOWSKI; TAKING THE STATE TO COURT, PUBLIC INTEREST LITIGATION AND THE PUBLIC SPHERE IN METROPOLITAN INDIA 188 (2001)[97]

Court sessions are held in public, but it is difficult to follow them concisely. Unless one was exceptionally well placed, it was very difficult to hear the discussion in courtroom number 17, where the Green Bench would sit every Friday. The room was crammed with up to 140 persons. Some twenty cases might be listed. It was unclear exactly at what time individual matters would come up. Most parties involved in any item on the agenda were represented in the court room. At most, a quarter of the attending persons were seated. The air was stuffy. Very often, the noise of rotating fans made it difficult to follow the proceedings. There was constant agitation in the room. People would go out to have a cigarette or come in to see whether their matter was coming up....

The High Court, moreover, before the establishment of the Green Bench, had not had a good reputation, particularly as far as public interest litigation was concerned. Its speed in dealing with the wetlands case was not considered typical. PUBLIC and its lawyers had been surprised by their own success. They attributed the initial speed of proceedings to the originally keen interest of the state government to have the matter disposed of quickly as it did not doubt that the court would rule in favour of the World Trade Centre. For me, the German sociologist, it appeared to be a collusion suspicion, articulated subtly, that PUBLIC would attempt to link court actions with the government's wishes....

Apparently, delay was no isolated experience. On 24 November 1997, the local page of the *Asian Age* ran an article by Kinsuk Basu under the headline 'High Court officer files PIL against corrupt practices'. The clipping stated that the Supreme Court had appointed someone to report on the state of affairs in the High Court. This person had filed a writ petition in the Supreme Court to set matters straight in Calcutta. The *Asian Age* listed the following findings:

- The judicial process in Calcutta High Court is marred by rampant corruption prevalent in the system of listing out cases.
- Thousands of pending case files are missing from the record department and there is no system of recording movement of pending record....
- PIL cases are affected due to administrative mismanagement.
- In contempt cases, the contemnors never appear on time rendering the judicial process futile.

The article also stated:

> Unless litigants pay 'speed money', officials ensure that the files lie untouched for decades. Only the rich litigants or the hard pressed ones, who are aware of the system, get the privilege of superseding those who have waited for months to see their case on the list....

Indeed, accusations of corruption were made not only against the court administration, but also against individual judges. [References to individual judges removed. The author refers to a judge who was arrested after retirement and also to certain judges who were allotted 'attractive real estate in Salt Lake City by the chief minister'. The author relies on newspaper and magazine reports to support the narrative.]

Advocates also told me that the High Court had ruled that such allotment of plots was within the personal discretion of the chief minister. There had been no legal consequence. To my surprise, this did not seem to even raise an eyebrow among the legal community.... Among Calcutta's legal community, it was taken for granted that judges wanted to maintain good relations with governments in general. After all, they would want to be eligible for various appointments to well-paid positions in committees as consultants after retirement.

[97] Asia House's online version of the book originally published in 2001, https://www.asienhaus.de/public/archiv/taking_the_state_to_court.pdf, accessed 22 June 2021.

NOTE

On 19 November 2004, the Supreme Court rendered judgment in a PIL challenging the allotment of government land in Salt Lake City, Kolkata from the discretionary quota of the Chief Minister (CM).[98] The judgment records that Justice B P Banerjee (respondent 24) applied to the CM for a plot of land in Salt Lake City and a plot was allotted from the CM's discretionary quota. At the time when he applied for and was allotted the plot, Justice Banerjee was hearing a case in the Calcutta High Court relating to the violation of the master plan in Salt Lake City. The Supreme Court held: 'The facts speak volumes that the learned Judge has misused his judicial function as liveries to obtain personal interest ...'[99] Striking down the allotment, this is how the Supreme Court dealt with one of the submissions made by counsel for Justice Banerjee:

> It is also contended ... that a large number of Judges of the High Court and the Supreme Court have also been allotted plots in Salt Lake City under the discretionary quota of the Chief Minister and it will be unfair to single out respondent 24 for meting out a different treatment. At the time of hearing of this writ petition, we requested the learned Senior Counsel to inform us whether any other Judge or Judges obtained the allotment order from the discretionary quota of the Chief Minister by compromising his judicial duties, we would also proceed against such allottee. He, however, was unable to receive any instructions in this behalf. It is trite, unequals cannot be treated equally.[100]

Writing in 2016, 15 years after the book was withdrawn, Dembowski critiqued the system:

> At this point, you will probably wonder why such a favourable assessment might have irritated the high court to the point of starting contempt proceedings. The problem was that my book included sections that dealt with the public reputation of the judiciary and the Calcutta high court in particular. These sections were necessary. It is impossible to assess the socio-political relevance of an institution without considering its public image.
>
> In the 1990s, the higher judiciary's reputation was good in the sense of being better that that of most other institutions of the Indian state, but it was nonetheless tarnished. The truth is that most Indians did not trust state institutions, and that included judicial ones.
>
> I never intended to scandalise or irritate the court in any way. To this day, I am convinced that my book is fair and balanced. My duty as a social scientist was to offer a comprehensive assessment of the socio-political role of the courts in PIL cases. To put it very crudely, even gossip, if it spreads widely enough, has a bearing on an institution's reputation and is therefore relevant in sociological terms.
>
> The contempt petition was filed against myself and several other parties, including most prominently [Oxford University Press] OUP. The petition was based almost entirely on sections of one single chapter that concern the public image of the court. To a considerable extent, this chapter is based on references to the Indian media's coverage of court affairs. At the time, it was quite obvious that the courts did not enjoy unquestioning public trust.
>
> Friends and colleagues tell me I have become the victim of a human rights abuse, as my freedom of expression and my freedom to pursue academic work have been limited by the high court without a final judgment. They also tell me that human rights violations in India are normally more traumatic in terms of broken limbs and unending detention or even lost

---

98 *Tarak Singh v Jyoti Basu* (2005) 1 SCC 201.
99 *Id.* at 207.
100 *Id.* at 209.

lives, whereas I was able to pursue a journalistic career quite successfully in Germany thanks to my academic work. They have a point.

However, I believe the Indian public is the real victim. They have been denied insights into the merits as well as the limits of PILs—not in the context of legal principles but in the context of empirical social life....

Freedom of speech, freedom of the press and academic freedom serve a socio-political function. They are not primarily about allowing individuals to do whatever they please; they are about facilitating meaningful public discourse. The fate of my book proves that such discourse cannot be taken for granted in contemporary India. The case has been kept pending for 15 years—and I have not even been notified by the high court. This state of affairs sends a dire warning to any Indian scholar who is interested in the kind of studies I have done. Though studying the empirical reality of PILs would be a service to the nation, it may easily ruin an aspiring Indian sociologist's career—especially, if the research results are interesting.

The conclusion of my book was that the courts were fostering reasoned discourse in India in the 1990s. Its fate, unfortunately, proves that the conclusion may have been too optimistic.[101]

NOTES AND QUESTIONS

1. Dembowski's book is a deep study of environmental litigation in West Bengal. A system that prevents scholarship and analysis from reaching a wide readership ranks low on any freedom index.

2. What does it say about the efficiency of the Calcutta High Court when contempt applications remain on its docket for over a decade?

3. Do citizens have a right to know about the integrity of judges in the High Courts and the Supreme Court of India? Unless we discuss issues relating to the integrity of judges, how will the system improve?

III. CHENNAI WETLANDS

In late 2015, the city of Chennai was severely flooded over several days. Contributing to the devastation was the lack of drainage caused by the reclamation of wetlands. R Seenivasan recalls how the Madras High Court was warned about the destructive potential of projects that drained waterbodies but failed to heed these warnings.

R SEENIVASAN; JUDICIARY AND THE DESTRUCTION OF CHENNAI'S WETLANDS 51 Economic & Political Weekly 17 (2016)

The loss and damages to wet-lands (tanks, ponds, channels, canals, rivers, marshes and backwaters) led to the floods of November–December 2015. Most news items focused on encroachment of waterbodies and rivers. They blamed the flood on unplanned urban development—especially the housing boom—and saw it as an instance of administrative failure. However, most critics are silent on the judiciary's role....

Before proceeding, some simple facts need to be told about Chennai and its waterbodies. Present-day Chennai is a city made out of several villages that were once thriving paddy fields fed by a series of tanks. This means, that just as in paddy fields, every bit of excess water could easily be drained without causing much damage. The tanks (estimated to be in the

[101] Hans Dembowski, *How an Unresolved Contempt Case Has Kept a Scholarly Book off the Shelves for 15 Years*, THE WIRE, 21 February 2016, https://thewire.in/law/how-an-unresolved-contempt-case-has-buried-a-scholarly-book-for-15-years, accessed 22 June 2021.

order of hundreds) in and around the present city as well as surrounding watersheds from Tamil Nadu and Andhra Pradesh are entirely man-made—over the last two millennia. . . .

Buckingham Canal Case

Exnora International v The Government of Tamil Nadu (2006) was an early case that demonstrated the need to use the writs of the high court to prevent partial obliteration of the Buckingham Canal. The canal was originally laid for navigation in early 19th century. It had an average width of 25 m with aide bunds and integrated many local streams, backwaters, artificial and natural river channels. Since the 1960s, the canal ceased to be used for transportation, but carried water during floods. The Chennai Mass Rapid Transit System or MRTS train line is laid on tracks that were carried on huge pillars erected inside the canal. Eleven train stations were built on the edges and embankments of the canal. . . .

Exnora argued in the court that: first, the pillars and stations for the train line obstructed water flow and created flooding within the city; second, the government did not follow the time-tested BSO, town planning laws, and coastal zone regulations; and third, the project would destroy the Pallikaranai tank—a large water body at the edge of the city—by not allowing enough water to reach it. The essence of the government replies were: first, the floods are not created by the obstructions that ensued as a result of the train line but by the excessive rainfall; second, the train line project was done for the larger 'public interest' to provide a rapid transport and hence the laws protecting the waterbodies and channels need not be followed; and third, the Pallikaranai tank lands and marshes linked by the canal could not be preserved anymore because of rapid urbanisation.

The High Court quoted the Supreme Court's understanding in *Susetha v State of Tamil Nadu* 2006 on the tanks in support of their decision. Para 22 of the *Buckingham Canal* judgment reads:

> Water bodies are required to be retained. Such requirement is envisaged not only in view of the fact that the right to water as also quality life are envisaged under Art 21 of the Constitution of India, but also in view of the fact that the same has been recognised in Arts 47 and 45–A of the Constitution of India. Art 51–A of the Constitution of India . . . furthermore makes a fundamental duty of every citizen to protect and improve the natural environment including forests, lakes, rivers and wildlife. But this principle applies only to natural water storage resources. *The same principle cannot be applied in relation to artificial tanks* (*Exnora International v The Government of Tamil Nadu* 2006; emphasis added).

Protecting a Tank Bed

Susetha v The Union of India 2010 is another case about preventing the conversion of a defunct wetland. [Susetha Kumaradev—the then ward councillor of Thoraipakkam who since then has become a crusader for wetlands] challenged the reclassification of a wetland and its subsequent conversion into a site for building tenements. Most of these tenements were constructed by the Tamil Nadu Slum Clearance Board for those evicted from slums including those from the banks of the Buckingham Canal. The government argued that the place was not a proper wetland but an 'assessed waste wetland,' and it has powers to change the classification. It is true that the [Revenue Board Standing Orders] (BSO) gives such powers to the government; however, a due process has to be followed. Susetha's argument was that such a process was not followed.

Leaving the legal arguments aside, understanding the logic behind the numerous land revenue classifications becomes necessary. In Tamil Nadu, all useful lands, according to BSO, are categorised into wet and dry. 'Wet' are those that get irrigated by tanks or rivers or canals. Some of them are categorised 'waste wetlands.' This bizarre classification is a product of colonial revenue authorities aimed to collect graded land revenue from every bit of land. The court appointed an expert committee to verify Susetha's claims.

The experts, beyond verifying the simple facts about the disputed land's status as a wetland, described the government actions responsible for floods, water scarcity, salinity and sea water ingression. They warned about the impending eco-logical disaster to the natural environment including floods and water shortages. The court found fault with this committee of experts comprising two professors in ecology and water resources, and a civil servant for 'overstretching' their mandate. The judges felt the committee needlessly used ecology, environment, hydrological sciences and Tamil literature.

Eventually, the court preferred a dictionary understanding of a 'marshy land' and concluded the area is not worthy of revival or protection as a wetland. As in earlier occasions, it recognised the powers of the government and considered the 'larger public interest' the case presented. That public interest was to resettle the slum dwellers in a chronically flood-affected area.

NOTES

1. In *Consumer Action Group v Union of India*,[102] the Madras High Court prevented the destruction of wetlands in the Adyar estuary which were being reclaimed to erect a memorial to Dr Ambedkar. The petitioners complained that while they had no objection to the construction of a memorial, they objected to the wetlands being converted into an auditorium and car park. Allowing the petition, the High Court directed the respondents to restrict construction to the eastern end of the 5-acre plot, restore the rest of the plot to its original condition and refrain from constructing an auditorium. The Madras Metropolitan Development Authority was told to preserve about 45 acres of low-lying wetlands and not permit any construction in the area.

2. In 2001, M K Balakrishnan petitioned the Supreme Court under Article 32 of the Constitution seeking protection for wetlands and water bodies that were being neglected by the state or lost to projects that ignored their ecological importance. Nothing significant happened in the case until 2009, when the Supreme Court *suo motu* expanded the scope of the matter in an effort to solve the nation's acute water resource problem.[103] In 2014, the case was brought back on track with the government being directed to respond to issues pertaining to wetland conservation. On 3 April 2017, nearly 16 years after the petition was filed, the Supreme Court noted:

> We have also been shown a statement of expenditure that has been filed by the Union of India along with an affidavit dated 28 March 2017. While huge amounts appear to have been spent to the extent of Rs. 945.95 crores, it appears from the reading of the affidavit that not much improvement seems to have been made at least on the ground. That apart, the activities or the steps undertaken and the expenditure incurred in respect of those activities are extremely general in nature.[104]

The court thereafter segregated the case. The Ramsar Convention sites being of international significance were ordered to be monitored by the respective High Courts with a request to the High Courts to take assistance of an *amicus curiae*. The case with respect to other wetlands continued before the Supreme Court.

IV. TANKS

Across India, communities have long depended on tanks and lakes as a source of fresh water. Frequently, these traditional means of water conservation and supply fall into disuse because

---

[102] 1994 (1) Mad L J Rep 481.

[103] This phase of the case is discussed in the Public Interest Litigation chapter.

[104] *M K Balakrishnan v Union of India* (2017) 7 SCC 813.

development in the catchment diverts feeder streams or disrupts springs and aquifers that replenish the water bodies. Neglected storage structures attract encroachers and once built upon, the tanks are forever lost to the community. Recognizing the crucial role of tanks and lakes in augmenting water supply, the courts have intervened to protect them.

Intellectuals Forum, a society whose environmental vigour considerably surpassed its modesty, petitioned the Andhra Pradesh High Court in 1994 seeking restoration of two tanks located in the suburbs of Tirupathi, a pilgrimage centre and home to the Sri Venkateswara Swami Temple. The petitioners claimed that the Avilala and Peruru tanks which had existed for centuries served as sources of irrigation and replenishment of the groundwater table. These tanks were vital in a drought-prone region; Rayalaseema and the government's action in permitting housing to be built on the tank beds was illegal. Each of the tank beds covered more than 150 acres.

The respondents persuaded the High Court to reject the public interest litigation.[105] They argued that both the tanks had dried up and were abandoned; the feeder sources were disrupted and there was hardly any prospect of bringing back water; substantial public funds were spent on constructing houses; Tirupathi was growing rapidly and with it, the demand for housing; and there were other tanks and water sources identified for conservation which could meet future needs.

In the appeal, on 5 December 2003, the Supreme Court directed the Union Government to constitute an Expert Committee to report on whether the tanks could be utilized for water harvesting. After inspecting the area, the committee found that it was not feasible to restore the tanks to their original size since the construction of check dams, percolation tanks and other structures for trapping rain water had disrupted the re-charge potential. The Supreme Court in a lengthy exercise examined aspects of the local hydrology and then applied the principles of sustainable development, the public trust doctrine as well as intergenerational equity to balance the rival claims.

INTELLECTUALS FORUM v STATE OF ANDHRA PRADESH

(2006) 3 SCC 549

A R Lakshmanan, J:

* * *

The set of facts in the present case relates to the preservation of and restoration of *status quo ante* of two tanks, historical in nature being in existence since the time of Shrikrishnadevaraya, The Great, 1500 A D where the cry of socially spirited citizens calling for judicial remedy was not considered in the right perspective by the Division Bench of the High Court of Andhra Pradesh despite there being overwhelming evidence of the tanks being in existence and were being put to use not only for irrigation purpose but also as lakes which were furthering percolation to improve the groundwater table, thus serving the needs of the people in and around these tanks. The Division Bench of the High Court, in the impugned order, has given precedence to the economic growth by completely ignoring the importance and primacy attached to the protection of environment and protection of valuable and most cherished fresh water resources.

No doubt, the wishful thinking and the desire of the appellant forum, that the tanks should be there, and the old glory of the tanks should be continued, is laudable. But the ground realities are otherwise. We have already noticed the ground realities as pointed out by the Government of Andhra Pradesh, (Tuda) Tirupathi Urban Development Authority and Tirumala Tirupathi Devasthanam (TTD) in their reply to the civil appeals by furnishing details, datas and particulars. Nowadays because of poverty and lack of employment avenues,

105 *Intellectuals Forum v State of A P* AIR 2001 AP 118.

migration of people from rural areas to urban areas is a common phenomenon. Because of the limited infrastructure of the towns, the towns are becoming slums. We, therefore, cannot countenance the submissions made by the appellant in regard to the complete restoration and revival of two tanks in the peculiar facts and circumstances of this case. We cannot, at the same time, prevent the Government from proceeding with the proper development of Tirupathi town. The two government orders which are impugned have been issued long before and pursuant to the issuance of the government orders, several other developments have taken place. Constructions and improvements have been made in a vast measure. Because of spending crores and crores of rupees by various authorities, the only option now left to the appellant and the respondents is to see that the report submitted by the Expert Committee is implemented in its letter and spirit and all the respondents shall cooperate in giving effect to the Committee's report.

It is true that the tank is a communal property and the State authorities are trustees to hold and manage such property for the benefits of the community and they cannot be allowed to commit any act or omission which will infringe the right of the community and alienate the property to any other person or body.

Taking into account all these principles of law, and after considering the competing claims of environment and the need for housing, this Court holds the following as per the facts of this case.

The respondents have claimed that the valuable right to shelter will be violated if the impugned government orders are revoked. On the facts of the present case, it seems that the respondents intend to build residential blocks of flats for high and middle income families, institutions as well as infrastructure for TTD. If the proposed constructions are not carried on, it seems unlikely that anyone will be left homeless or without their basic need for shelter. Therefore, one feels that the right to shelter does not seem to be so pressing under the present circumstances so as to outweigh all environmental considerations.

Another plea repeatedly taken by the respondents corresponds to the money already spent on developing the land. However, the decision of this case cannot be based solely upon the investments committed by any party. Since, otherwise, it would seem that once any party makes certain investment in a project, it would be a *fait accompli* and this Court will not have any option but to deem it legal.

Therefore, under the present circumstances, the Court should do the most it can, to safeguard the two tanks in question. However, due to the persistent developmental activities over a long time, much of the natural resources of the lakes have been lost, and considered irreparable. This, though regrettable, is beyond the power of this Court to rectify.

One particular feature of this case was the competing nature of claims by both the parties on the present state of the two tanks and the feasibility of their revival. We thought that it would be best, therefore, if we place reliance on the findings of the Expert Committee appointed by us which has considered the factual situation and the feasibility of revival of the two tanks. Thus, in pursuance of a study of that Committee, this Court passes the following orders.

The appeals are disposed of with the following directions:

With regard to Peruru tank

(i) No further constructions to be made.

(ii) The supply channel of Bodeddulu vanka needs to be cleared and revitalized. A small check dam at Malapalli to be removed to ensure the free flow and supply to the tank.

(iii) Percolation tank to be constructed and artificial recharge to be done to ensure the revival of the tank, keeping in mind its advantage at being situated at the foothills.

(iv) The area allotted by the Mandal Revenue Office for construction of the tank to be increased to a minimum of 50 acres. Percolation tank with sufficient number of recharge shafts to be developed to recharge the unsaturated horizons up to 20 m. The design of the shafts, etc. to be prepared in consultation with the Central Ground Water Board (CGWB). The proposed percolation tank to be suitably located along the bund keeping in view the inlets, irrigation sluices and surplus water.

(v) Feasibility and cost estimation for the revival of the old feeder channel for Swarnamukhi river should be carried and a report to be submitted to the Court.
(vi) Each house already constructed by TTD must provide for rooftop rain water harvesting. Abstraction from groundwater to be completely banned. No borewell/tubewell for any purpose to be allowed in the area.
(vii) Piezometers[106] to be set up at selected locations, in consultation with CGWB to observe the impact of rain water harvesting in the area on groundwater regime.

With regard to Avilala tank

(i) No further construction to be allowed in the area.
(ii) Each house already constructed by A P Housing Board/TUDA must provide structure for rooftop rain water harvesting. All the storm water in the already built colonies to be recharged to groundwater. Structures for such purposes to be designed in consultation with CGWB.
(iii) No borewell/tubewell for any purpose to be allowed in the area.
(iv) An area of 40 acres presently reserved for the Government should not be developed in any way that may lead to concretization of the ground surface. Recharge structures to be constructed for rain water harvesting.
(v) Piezometers to be set up at selected locations, in consultation with CGWB to observe the impact of rain water harvesting in the area on groundwater regime.

NOTES AND QUESTIONS

1. The Supreme Court found that the tanks were an important part of the environment of the area and it was the responsibility of the government to protect and preserve them. Moreover, the conversion of the tank beds for housing violated two principles of the public trust doctrine: (1) the property subject to the trust must be used for a public purpose and it must be held available for use by the general public; and (2) the property must be maintained for particular types of uses, either traditional uses or some uses particular to that form of resource. The court then attempted to rectify these violations by issuing the directions excerpted above.

2. The operative directions issued by the Supreme Court expose the limits of a judicial solution. Here, as evident from the painstaking exercise it undertook, the court was anxious to restore the tanks but found that it had little room to maneuver beyond stopping further construction and directing implementation of the Expert Committee report. Absent a clear violation of law or procedural infraction, partial gains are the best that a public interest litigation can realistically achieve. Notions of sustainable development inevitably require balancing and where public funds are expended the court's effort is generally directed towards preventing further damage. Though Intellectuals Forum was unable to fully attain its goals, carrying the contest to the Supreme Court provided significant gains: close to a third of the area was saved, and there is now a Supreme Court judgment applying the public trust doctrine to tanks. The court's strong judicial endorsement of the value of freshwater resources may help save and rejuvenate other tanks imperilled by development. Moreover, the court laid down a strict scrutiny standard of judicial review:

> [W]hen the State holds a resource that is freely available for the use of the public, it provides for a high degree of judicial scrutiny upon any action of the Government, no matter how consistent with the existing legislations, that attempts to restrict such free use. To properly scrutinise such actions of the Government, the Courts must make a distinction between

106 A piezometer is an instrument to measure water pressure and helps gauge the groundwater table.

the Government's general obligation to act for the public benefit, and the special, more demanding obligation which it may have as a trustee of certain public resources.[107]

3. This case illustrates how well intentioned but inadequately planned projects can destroy cisterns. The Expert Committee found that Peruru tank suffered from a reduced inflow because 22 check dams, eight percolation tanks, 437 rock fill dams and contour trenches trapped the rain water before it reached the tank. These public works spanned half a century. A comprehensive environmental impact assessment, undertaken before the Peruru catchment was fragmented, might have saved public expenditure and pointed the authorities towards repairing and strengthening the ancient tank. Who gains and who loses from ill-conceived public works?

4. Interpreting the provisions of the UP Zamindari Abolition and Lands Reforms Act of 1950, the Supreme Court found that the revenue authorities were wrong in allotting portions of a pond (that had fallen in disuse) for building houses. The court also supported its conclusion on a wider principle.

> It is important to notice that the material resources of the community like forests, tanks, ponds, hillock, mountain, etc. are nature's bounty. They maintain delicate ecological balance. They need to be protected for a proper and healthy environment which enables people to enjoy a quality life which is the essence of the guaranteed right under Article 21 of the Constitution. The government, including the Revenue Authorities, i.e. Respondents 11 to 13, having noticed that a pond is falling in disuse, should have bestowed their attention to develop the same which would, on one hand, have prevented ecological disaster and on the other provided better environment for the benefit of the public at large. Such vigil is the best protection against knavish attempts to seek allotment in non-abadi sites.[108]

Applying this judgment, the Supreme Court refused to allow a students' hostel to be built on a dry pond bed.[109]

5. Despite noticing *Intellectuals Forum*, the Supreme Court in *Susetha*[110] found no fault in a panchayat resettling shopkeepers, displaced by a highway project, on a disused temple tank. Absent any water shortage in the village, since the tank was in a dilapidated condition for a long time and was reduced to a dumping yard, the court declined to 'direct its resurrection'.[111] *Susetha*'s reluctance to vigorously apply the public trust doctrine demonstrates the difficulty in predicting the outcome of public interest litigation. Discretionary factors matter under Articles 32, 136 and 226 of the Constitution and occasionally trump principle. Cases like *Susetha* erode the precedential value of *Intellectuals Forum* and are apt to confuse lower courts. For instance, *Susetha* obliquely suggests that the public trust doctrine may not apply because 'The tank in question is not a natural tank'. But then, what is a natural tank? The *Intellectuals Forum* decision describes the two tanks as 'historical in nature being in existence since the time of Srikrishnadevaraya, 1500 AD'. Presumably, some man-made works are needed to channel and bund rainwater. Where a freshwater resource is long used by the community, should the 'man-made' *vis-à-vis* 'natural' divide make any difference to application of the public trust doctrine?

---

[107] The court drew on the analysis of Prof Joseph Sax in *The Public Trust Doctrine in Natural Resource Law: Effective Judicial Intervention*, 68 Michigan Law Review 471 (1970).

[108] *Hinch Lal Tiwari v Kamladevi* (2001) 6 SCC 496, 501.

[109] *Meghwal Samaj Shiksha Samiti v Lakh Singh* (2011) 11 SCC 800.

[110] *Susetha v State of Tamil Nadu* (2006) 6 SCC 543.

[111] *Id.* at 548.

6. A division bench of the Gujarat High Court clubbed together numerous petitions seeking to protect water bodies in different parts of the state. Justice R K Abhichandani's judgment in *Shailesh R Shah v State of Gujarat*[112] provides a template for measured judicial intervention and illustrates how the High Court may use PILs to improve governance. We quote the operative order:

To sum up, we issue the following directions:–

[A] The State Government will notify all the lakes and ponds as may have been shown in the areas covered by the Town Planning Schemes and the Development Plans, as also those in the areas not so covered throughout the State, in short, all the water-bodies in the territory of the State that vest in the State and/or the Area Development Authorities or the Local Bodies including Panchayats, in the Official Gazette within three months from the date of this order.

[B] The State Government and all Area Development Authorities and Local Bodies will protect, maintain and preserve all the water-bodies in the State which are identified as per the development plans, town planning schemes and the Government records and which will be notified in the Official Gazette, as water-bodies and they will not be alienated or transferred or put to any use other than as water-bodies.

[C] The respondents-authorities should take steps to get the standards of quality of water of the lakes and ponds prescribed by the concerned authority under the law, and devise mechanism for periodic monitoring of the quality of water in these lakes and ponds.

[D] The State Government, the Area Development Authorities and the Local Authorities should take urgent measures to rejuvenate the water-bodies which are to be notified in the Gazette by undertaking a declared phased programme of desiltation and make adequate provisions for recharging them by appropriate storm water drains and other feasible means and to take measures against pollution of such water-bodies.

[E] The State Government shall expeditiously take steps to constitute Water Resources Council as contemplated in the Draft Water Policy of-the State, headed by the Hon'ble the Chief Minister with other Ministers, including the Ministers in charge of Environment and Urban Development Departments to oversee the programme for protection, preservation and improvement of the water-bodies. The State Government will also constitute the Water Resources Committee headed by the Chief Secretary which may include the Secretaries of Environment, Urban Development and Agriculture Departments, for monitoring the implementation of the programme in a time-bound manner with periodic review of its success. This Committee shall place the particulars of the targets achieved and the causes of non-fulfilment of the targets periodically before the Water Resources Council, for its consideration.

[F] The State Government, the Area Development Authorities and the Local Bodies are directed to prepare an authenticated record in form of videography, photography and panchnamas of the existing encroachments and take urgent steps to remove them in accordance with law and the rehabilitation policies of the Government. Responsibilities of the officers/staff concerned should be fixed in respect of non-removal of encroachments and fresh encroachments. The Water Resources Committee will closely monitor the removal of encroachments by the concerned authorities, and the Area Development Authorities and the Local Bodies shall furnish, quarterly, particulars of such encroachments and their removal to the Water Resources Committee.

[G] The question of determining the peripheral area surrounding a lake or pond on which construction may be prohibited will be taken up by the concerned authorities for consideration in the context of the development of individual lakes and ponds

[112] 2002 (3) Guj L R 447.

> and the authorities will take decisions thereon having regard to the relevant factors which may have a bearing on the protection, preservation and improvement of lakes, ponds and other water-bodies, and once the peripheral area, around a lake or pond, in which there will be no construction allowed is determined, the same shall be notified. All the applications for building permissions which may be pending, may accordingly be decided as per the regulations and keeping in view the requirement of individual water-bodies.

Rule is made absolute in all these petitions accordingly with no order as to costs.

7. Several other High Courts have endeavoured to protect individual water bodies.[113] Amongst the most painstaking efforts is the case brought by Rajendra Kumar Razdan to protect the lakes of Rajasthan. The writ petition, filed in 1999, was periodically heard by the Rajasthan High Court and culminated in a final judgment rendered on 6 February 2007. The judgment tracks how the court constituted an Expert Committee and worked to revive major lakes by overseeing the establishment of sewerage systems and monitoring progress with respect to de-silting, control of water hyacinths, solid waste management, removal of encroachments and restoration of water channels that fed the lakes.[114]

C. ECOLOGICALLY SENSITIVE AREAS

Conservation strategies range from creating 'No Go' areas where human activity is severely restricted to a light touch approach. The core areas of National Parks notified under the Wildlife Act and CRZ-IA areas under the Coastal Regulations of 2019 are efforts to protect certain regions by keeping them pristine. At the other end of the spectrum are regulations such as the Noise Rules which lay down parameters that are met through small adjustments to social behaviour. Falling between these extremes is a set of tailor-made regulations for what are termed Ecologically Sensitive Areas (ESAs).

In several parts of the world, the natural and built heritage is protected by town and country planning laws. Local interests and pressures in India make it very difficult to introduce district-level environmental regulations that curtail economic development. Environmentalists seeking to protect small regions have found an easier route in ESA notifications issued by the Central Government under the enabling provisions of the Environment (Protection) Act of 1986. This process appears relatively insulated from local political pressures.

The Bombay Environmental Action Group and its foremost campaigner Shyam Chainani balanced court battles against authorities with personal lobbying to introduce environmental regulations. Amongst Chainani's successes are the earliest urban heritage regulations in India, the Coastal Regulations of 1991, and securing ESA status for Murud-Janjira, Mahabaleshwar–Panchgani, Matheran and Pachmarhi. At one point, the Union Law Ministry was reluctant to notify ESAs, apprehending constitutional impediments. Here is an account about how that hurdle was crossed.

---

[113] *Forum for a Better Hyderabad v Government of AP* 2001 (4) Andh L T 275; *L Krishnan v State of Tamil Nadu* AIR 2005 Mad 311; *Abdul Rehman v State of Rajasthan* 2004 (4) Western Law Cases (Raj) 435.

[114] *Rajendra Kumar Razdan v State of Rajasthan*, DB Civil Writ Petition No. 4271/1999 decided on 6 February 2007 (N N Mathur and Manak Mohta, JJ); 2007 (2) WLN 351.

SHYAM CHAINANI: NHAVA & SHEVA, BATTLING FOR THE ENVIRONMENT: OIL, PORTS AND THE COASTLINE 178 (2012)

The best way to protect Nhava would be to get Nhava declared as an environmentally sensitive area under The Environment (Protection) Act, 1986 (EP Act). We had been able to get similar notification issued, first in January 1989 protecting the Dighi-Murud-Janjira area, and much more recently in June 1991 for Dahanu Taluka. Subsequently, in May 1992, a Notification had also been issued for the Aravallis. The Dahanu and Aravalli Notifications had both been issued during Rajamani's tenure as Secretary.

I took up the Nhava matter with Rajamani in December 1993, at the same time that I took up the question of the ship repair yard. I pointed out that in the Development Plan (Master Plan) for New Bombay, except for the area occupied by ONGC, the rest of Nhava had been designated as a Regional Park. In the light of many proposals for setting up units in and around Nhava, of which the ship repair yard was only one, the only sure way to provide protection was to declare the Regional Park area of Nhava an ecologically sensitive area under the EP Act.

With difficulty, I was able to get the Maharashtra Government to give their concurrence. However, a serious and unexpected glitch occurred when Dr N Bagchi, a Joint Secretary level officer of the Environment Ministry, wrote to the Maharashtra Urban Development Secretary D T Joseph on 12 August 1994 on the subject of Nhava and the EP Act. His letter said that it had been reported to the Environment Ministry that some private parties were approaching the Maharashtra Government for establishment of ship repair facilities on Nhava Island in violation of the Development Plan of New Bombay in which parts of Nhava Island had been classified as a 'Regional Park'. He added that the Environment Ministry had been requested to declare the area of the notified Regional Park on Nhava Island an environmentally sensitive area under the EP Act. He went on to say that as the Maharashtra Government had declared certain areas of Nhava Island a Regional Park, declaring Nhava an environmentally sensitive area would be a duplicating exercise.

This was an amazing communication, the like of which I have never seen before or after. Firstly, Dr Bagchi had himself pointed out that violations of the Regional Park notification were likely to occur. Secondly, normally it is the state governments which resist Central Government Notifications on the grounds that they are infringements of their powers; here it was the Centre resisting an addition to their own powers. Another important point was that Dr Bagchi kept referring to Nhava as an island; actually the original island was only a small portion of the total village of Nhava.

It took several months and several reminders from me for D T Joseph to reply. His reply of January 1995 was well worth waiting for and was the only one of its kind that I have seen from any state government to the Centre. He said that it was true that no development could be permitted on Nhava contrary to Regional Park uses. However, it was always possible that by an act of 'minor modification', the Master Plan could easily be changed. Hence 'if there is a second line of protection through the operation of the Environment Protection Act, 1986, it would ensure greater protection.'

Matters progressed and in March 1995 I gave two alternative drafts of the Notification to the Ministry.

On 17 May 1995, I got a very pleasant surprise when Kamal Nath [Minister of Environment] came up to me during the tea break of a seminar at Nirman Bhavan in Delhi. He told me that he had agreed to declare Nhava as environmentally sensitive areas. Clearly the file had been processed and he had given his approval without even waiting for the Review Committee's report, which had yet to be finalised. Immediately after the tea break I went to Paryavaran Bhavan, the Environment Ministry headquarters. When I mentioned Kamal Nath's statement to one of the officers, he smiled. He said that Kamal Nath did so many things which did not please us that he had to do some that did.... I was jubilant. However, the best laid plans of mice and men often go awry.

While following up on this, I was told the Law Ministry, while vetting the draft Notification relating to Pachmarhi, had held up current pending notifications on the grounds that 'Land and

Land Use' is a State subject under the Constitution, on which the Centre has no powers to legislate. This was a severe disappointment. It was also extremely surprising as the Ministry had, at least since 1988, issued a series of notifications covering different parts of India—Murud-Janjira, Doon Valley, Dahanu and the Aravallis—not to speak of the famous CRZ notification which covers the entire coastline of India. All these notifications had been vetted and cleared by the Law Ministry. Since the Constitution had not been amended in this respect, what had suddenly caused them to do an about–turn? I told the Minister's Private Secretary that we would seek legal opinion from our Senior Counsel, but he replied that there would not be much point in doing that, since the Government would be bound by their own Ministry's advice.

I did not know till years later that what had apparently transpired in March 1995, while examining the draft notification for Pachmarhi, the Law Ministry had excised from it the provisions relating to the Zonal Development Plan, tourism, natural heritage and built heritage. In May 1995 the Environment Ministry asked the Law Ministry to reconsider these deletions. The previous Notifications were also shown to them. However, the Law Ministry stuck to its position. The matter was therefore closed and it seemed that the process of declaring areas as environmentally sensitive—a far bigger issue than just Nhava—was dead....

I was sufficiently upset to once again approach Senior Counsel Atul Setalvad who said that those who talked about the Constitution should first read the Constitution. His legal opinion stated that as per Article 253 of the Constitution, Parliament does have the powers to legislate on any subject whatever, regardless of whether such subject is in the Union, Concurrent or State List, provided that such legislation is required to implement an international treaty, convention, or a decision taken at an international conference. The Statement of Objects and Reasons and the Preamble to The Environment (Protection) Act 1986 said that the EP Act had been enacted to implement to the Stockholm Declaration of 1972—which had been issued after the Stockholm Conference in which India had participated. Hence the EP Act, together with the rules and notifications framed under it, would be valid even if they related to subjects on the State List.

I knew Union Environment Secretary Vishwanath Anand very well. I do not now remember how the subject came up but during one of our periodic meetings, I mentioned this opinion to him and gave it to him in March 1997. I thought that he would just file it without taking action. However, to his credit, he did not follow the normal bureaucratic path of saying that he was bound by the Law Ministry's stand but passed Atul Setalvad's opinion to the Ministry staff of processing. The Environment Ministry took a long time to process the file and it was not till March 1998 that they wrote to the Law Ministry. In May 1998 the Law Ministry accepted the points made by Atul Setalvad. The way was now open to declare areas as environmentally sensitive. In July 1998 during one of my periodic visits to Delhi, both Vishwanath Anand and Additional Secretary Roy Paul informed me about the Law Ministry's concurrence. I was told that issuing of Notifications, starting with Pachmarhi, was under process. This was one of the most far-reaching environmental decisions ever....

Though Nhava did not benefit from Atul Setalvad's opinion, other places did. The hill stations of Mahableshwar and Panchgani together with more than 200 square kilometers around them, the hill station of Matheran along with the surrounding hills, and the hill station of Mount Abu along with surrounding areas have been declared as eco-sensitive zones under the EP Act, giving them the sort of protection we had tried to obtain for Nhava. Several other areas have also been given EP Act protection, declared as eco-sensitive zones, and more such Notifications are on the anvil.

NOTES

1. Ecologically sensitive areas are notified by the MoEF under section 3(2)(v) of the EPA read with rule 5 of the Environment (Protection) Rules. Section 3(2)(v) empowers the Central Government to take measures in respect of:

(v) restriction of areas in which any industries, operations or processes or class of industries, operations or processes shall not be carried out or shall be carried out subject to certain safeguards.

Rule 5 enumerates specific factors that the Central Government may consider when imposing prohibitions and restrictions, including the topographic and climatic features of an area; the biodiversity of the area; proximity to archaeological sites; sanctuaries or National Parks or:

(x) Any other factors as may be considered by the Central Government to be relevant to the protection of the environment in an area.[115]

2. A fine study, *India's Notified Ecologically Sensitive Areas: The Story So Far*,[116] explains the manner in which ESAs were notified in different regions. At times, the ESA notification responded to environmental concerns highlighted in public interest litigations.[117] In other cases, the persistence of local groups and environmentalists led to the MoEF acknowledging that the special character of the region would be lost without special restrictions. Occasionally, as in the case of Dahanu, when a pushback seeking dilution of the notification occurs, environmentalists must engage in protracted battles to retain ESA status.

3. While each ESA notification has special features, the framework broadly identifies geographical location, indicates the ecological significance of the region, imposes restrictions on development and lists activities permitted in the zone.

4. Ecologically sensitive area notifications have been issued to create buffer zones around protected areas under the Wild Life Act. These notifications were issued after the National Board of Wildlife resolved on 21 January 2002 to notify lands falling within 10 kms of boundaries of National Parks and Sanctuaries as ESAs.[118] The final notifications issued in consultation with the states designate buffer zones of varying depth, dependent on local conditions.

5. An illustrative list of ESA notifications together with their purpose are set out in the Legislative Provisions chapter.

---

115 Rule 5(1)(x).

116 Meenakshi Kapoor, Kanchi Kohli & Manju Menon, *India's Notified Ecologically Sensitive Areas: The Story So Far* (2009).

117 E.g., the Doon Valley Notification dated 1 February 1989, the Dahanu Notification dated 20 June 1991 and the Taj Trapezium Zone Notification dated 13 May 1998.

118 Ministry of Environment and Forests, Government of India, *Guidelines for Declaration of Eco-sensitive Zones Around National Parks and Wildlife Sanctuaries* 3 (2011).

16

REGULATION OF HAZARDOUS SUBSTANCES

This chapter traverses two broad areas. In the first part, we examine the general regulatory regime covering hazardous substances and the case law. In the second part, we look at the legal fallout from the Bhopal Gas Leak disaster which occurred on 3 December 1984 and remains the worst industrial accident in history. The ripples of that tragedy continue to affect victims and scar the community after three and a half decades.

A. LEGISLATIVE FRAMEWORK

Hazardous substances pervade modern industrialized societies. Indian industry generates, uses and discards toxic substances. Increasing numbers of farmers—encouraged by government agricultural policies—spray highly toxic chemical pesticides to protect their crops. Hazardous substances include flammables, explosives, heavy metals such as lead, arsenic and mercury, nuclear and petroleum fuel byproducts, dangerous micro-organisms, and scores of synthetic chemical compounds like DDT and dioxins.

Section 2(e) of the Environment (Protection) Act of 1986 (EPA) defines a 'hazardous substance' to mean 'any substance or preparation which, by reason of its chemical or physico-chemical properties or handling, is liable to cause harm to human beings, other living creatures, plants, micro-organisms, property or the environment'.

Exposure to toxic substances may cause acute or chronic health effects. Acute effects occur soon after a high-level exposure and range in severity from temporary rashes to death. Chronic effects frequently result from long-term, low-level exposure and include cancers, birth defects, miscarriages and damage to the lungs, liver, kidneys and nervous system.

Toxic substances are extensively regulated in India. The primary rules are the Manufacture, Storage and Import of Hazardous Chemicals Rules of 1989 which were introduced in November 1989 and have been periodically amended in 1994 and 2000.

These Rules apply to industries that use or store specified hazardous chemicals. Rule 3 prescribes the duties of various governmental authorities. For example, the Central and state pollution control boards (PCBs) are required to enforce governmental directives and procedures pertaining to the isolated storage of hazardous chemicals, and the District Collector (or other designated authority) is required to prepare off-site emergency plans to contain major chemical accidents. The responsibility of preparing and upgrading on-site emergency plans rests with the 'occupier' who controls the industrial activity. Rule 3 was amended in October 1994 requiring each of the designated authorities to inspect the industrial activity at least once in a calendar year and report annually to the Union Ministry of Environment and Forests (MoEF) on the occupier's compliance with the Rules. Under rule 4, an occupier must identify the major hazards posed by his industry, take steps to prevent and limit the consequences of an accident, and inform and train workers in occupational safety. The 1994 amendments

Environmental Law & Policy in India. Shyam Divan and Armin Rosencranz, Oxford University Press.
 DOI: 1093/oso/9780192865458.003.0016

strengthened the safeguards to prevent chemical accidents by requiring the authorities to inform the occupier about any lacunae in its systems needing rectification,[1] obliging the occupier to obtain site approval prior to commencing the industrial activity,[2] and mandating an independent annual safety audit of the industrial activity.[3]

Under rule 18, an importer of hazardous chemicals into India must disclose complete product safety information. Where the imported chemical is likely to cause a major accident, the designated governmental authorities are empowered to issue directions, including an order to stop the import. The importer must also ensure that the transport of the chemicals from the port of entry accords with the central Motor Vehicles Rules of 1989. On 19 January 2000, the Central Government amended the Rules. The amendment redefined 'major accident', introduced fresh parameters to identify toxic chemicals, flammable chemicals and explosives, and altered the schedules, including the insertion of a revised list of hazardous chemicals in Schedule I.

Apart from hazardous chemicals used and stored in industrial processes, toxic waste generated during industrial activity poses an enormous regulatory challenge. The Hazardous and Other Wastes (Management and Transboundary Movement) Rules of 2016 are designed to address these concerns, including the import and export of hazardous wastes. Chapter 2 of the rules covers the procedure for managing hazardous wastes. The occupier of the industrial facility is obliged to prevent, minimize, reuse, recycle, recover and safely dispose of the hazardous and other wastes. In addition to adopting safe and environmentally sound practices at its site, the occupier is required to transport the waste to an authorized actual user or to an authorized disposal facility.[4] State governments are responsible for ensuring that hazardous industries are located at proper locations within industrial areas.[5] Facilities generating, transporting and disposing of hazardous waste are required to be authorized by the state PCBs.[6]

Chapter 3 covers transboundary movement and prohibits the import of hazardous waste and other waste for disposal. However, hazardous and other waste may be imported for recycling, recovery, reuse and processing.[7] Chapter 4 covers facilities where hazardous waste is treated, stored or disposed of.[8] Chapter 5 provides for the packaging, labelling[9] and transport of hazardous and other wastes.[10] Schedule I to the Rules identifies hazardous waste generated in respect of listed industries. Schedule II specifies concentration limits or thresholds for chemicals in wastes, which when exceeded require the waste to be treated as being hazardous. Schedule III to the 2016 Rules implements the Basel Convention on the Control of Transboundary Movements of Hazardous Wastes and Their Disposal of 1989.[11] Part A of Schedule III lists hazardous wastes which may be imported or exported with prior informed consent as recognized in Annexure VIII of the Basel Convention. Parts B and D of Schedule

[1] Rule 5(5).
[2] Rule 7.
[3] Rule 10(4)–(7).
[4] Rule 4.
[5] Rule 5.
[6] Rule 6.
[7] Rule 12.
[8] Rule 16.
[9] Rule 17.
[10] Rule 18.
[11] The Basel Convention was signed on 22 March 1989 and came into effect on 5 May 1992. India signed on 15 March 1990 and ratified the treaty on 24 June 1992; the instrument entered into force for India on 22 September 1992.

III list other wastes that may be imported or exported and that do not require to follow the prior informed consent procedure in terms of Annexure IX of the Basel Convention.

The hazardous waste disposal regime has two other sets of rules. The Bio-Medical Waste Management Rules of 2016 apply to hospitals, clinics, blood banks and other organizations generating bio-medical wastes. These rules replaced an earlier set of rules[12] and provide a regimen for waste generators as well as for the treatment, disposal, segregation, packaging, transport and storage of bio-medical wastes through a licensing system. The E-Waste (Management) Rules of 2016 define 'e-waste' to cover electrical and electronic equipment discarded as waste by the consumer as well as rejects from the manufacturing and repair processes. The Rules cast a responsibility on the manufacturer to collect e-waste generated during manufacture and to channelize it for recycling or disposal.[13] The producer of electrical and electronic equipment is under an extended producer's responsibility to collect a specified percentage of e-waste.[14]

Since lead is harmful to humans but nevertheless essential in certain common products, special rules regulate lead acid batteries[15] and the contents of lead in paints.[16]

As we shall see later in this chapter, toxic substance regulation in India was largely a response to the Bhopal tragedy that occurred in December 1984. Among the judicial responses to Bhopal was the Supreme Court judgment in the *Shriram Gas Leak* case,[17] where the court articulated a new standard of absolute liability. The plight of the victims in the aftermath of Bhopal also underscored the need for a simple compensation regime that would assure subsistence for chemical accident victims and their dependents. Parliament addressed these issues by enacting the Public Liability Insurance Act of 1991 (PLIA). The Statement of Objects and Reasons that accompanied the Bill recognizes that industry is seldom willing to compensate the victims of accidents, compelling the victims to engage in prolonged litigation. The PLIA gives statutory recognition to 'no-fault' liability and provides that where death or injury to any person or damage to property has resulted from a hazardous substance accident, the owner of the hazardous substance will be liable to give relief in the sum prescribed in the Schedule to the Act.[18] Section 3(2) provides that in any claim for relief under the Act, 'the claimant shall not be required to plead and establish that the death, injury or damage in respect of which the claim has been made was due to any wrongful act, neglect or default of any person'. The compensation figures mentioned in the Schedule are very low, with fatal accidents and cases of permanent disability entitling the maximum award of Rs. 25,000. Section 8 of the Act clarifies that any relief under the PLIA would be in addition to the right to recover compensation under any other law.

To ensure that the victims receive compensation quickly, the Act requires every owner to obtain mandatory insurance cover[19] and provides an independent machinery administered by the District Collector for the filing and adjudication of claims.[20] The Collector is empowered to award relief under the Act after conducting an inquiry for which he may adopt a summary procedure.[21] The Act also contemplates the establishment of an Environment Relief Fund,[22]

---

[12] Bio-Medical Waste (Management and Handling) Rules of 1998.
[13] Rule 4.
[14] Rule 5, 13 and Schedule III (A).
[15] The Batteries (Management and Handling) Rules of 2001.
[16] The Regulation of Lead Contents in Household and Decorative Paints Rules of 2016.
[17] *M C Mehta v Union of India* AIR 1987 SC 1086.
[18] Section 3(1).
[19] Section 4.
[20] Sections 5 and 6.
[21] Rule 5, Public Liability Insurance Rules of 1991.
[22] Section 7A.

to which every owner must make a contribution.[23] The Rules framed under the PLIA limit the liability of an insurer to Rs. 5 crores for every accident.[24]

The 'no-fault' liability regime received further legislative endorsement in the National Environment Tribunal Act of 1995 as well as the successor National Green Tribunal Act of 2010 (NGT Act). Section 17 of the NGT Act provides that where death or injury to any person or damage to any property or the environment has resulted from an accident, the owner shall be liable to pay compensation under the heads specified in Schedule II to the Act on the principle of no-fault liability. Schedule II enumerates various heads including death; permanent, temporary, total or partial disability; loss of wages; medical expenses; damage to private property; expenses incurred by government in providing relief to victims or in coping with damage to the environment; damage to draught animals; claims arising from damage to flora and fauna; and loss of business or employment. The quantum of compensation is required to be determined by the NGT.

In addition to the EPA, NGT Act and the PLIA, provisions touching on certain other aspects of storage, transportation and regulation of hazardous substances are contained in the Motor Vehicles Rules of 1989, the Insecticides Act of 1968, the Explosive Substances Act of 1908, the Inflammable Substances Act of 1952 and the Atomic Energy Act of 1962.

B. THE *SHRIRAM GAS LEAK* CASE

This case originated in a writ petition (No. 12739 of 1985) filed in the Supreme Court by the environmentalist and lawyer M C Mehta, as a public interest litigation. The petition sought to close and relocate Shriram's caustic chlorine and sulphuric acid plants located in a thickly populated section of Delhi. One month after the filing of this petition, oleum leaked from the sulphuric acid plant located in the same 76-acre industrial complex as the chlorine plant, affecting several people. The leak took place on 4 December 1985—a day after the first anniversary of the Bhopal gas leak—and caused widespread panic in the surrounding community.

The Inspector of Factories and the Assistant Commissioner (Factories) issued separate orders on 7 and 24 December 1985 shutting down both plants. Aggrieved, Shriram filed a writ petition (No. 26 of 1986) challenging the two prohibitory orders issued under the Factories Act of 1948 and sought interim permission to reopen the caustic *chlorine* plant.

On behalf of those affected by the *oleum* leak, the Delhi Legal Aid and Advice Board and the Delhi Bar Association filed applications for compensation in the original petition by M C Mehta. (Neither the claimants nor the legal aid bodies were parties in the original petition.)

The *Shriram Gas Leak* case pitted the Supreme Court against one of India's large corporations. But it was an unusual confrontation because Shriram invariably bowed to the court's directions and willingly complied with its often unprecedented orders. Several of these orders required Shriram to deposit significant sums of money to finance the court's exercise of seemingly executive and legislative functions in the process of adducing evidence in the case.

Chief Justice Bhagwati, who presided over the Supreme Court bench, was deeply concerned for the safety of Delhi's citizens and was anxious to improve plant safety at the caustic chlorine unit—a task which the statutory agencies seemed incapable of performing. Moreover, the Chief Justice, who was a year away from retirement age at the time of the oleum gas leak, saw

[23] Section 4(2C).
[24] Rule 10.

in the Shriram oleum leak a way of influencing the pending and far more important *Bhopal Gas Leak* case.

Reviewers of this case should focus on:

(a) instances of the judicial assumption of functions normally performed by executive and legislative bodies;
(b) the stringent standards that the court imposes before permitting Shriram to operate its caustic chlorine unit;
(c) the court's laudable contribution in introducing a new 'no-fault' liability standard ('absolute liability') for industries engaged in hazardous activities;
(d) the anomaly of making major reforms in the Indian law of liability and compensation without first deciding whether the court has jurisdiction over the company to which such liability attaches; and
(e) the court's creative approach to fact-finding and to securing scientific and technical advice regarding an industry whose government regulators were lax and ineffective.

There are six reported orders in the *Shriram* case.[25] We excerpt from the three principal orders of 17 February, 10 March and 20 December 1986.

M C MEHTA v UNION OF INDIA
AIR 1987 SC 965

Bhagwati, C J: Writ Petition No. 12739 of 1985 which has been brought by way of public interest litigation raises some seminal questions concerning the true scope and ambit of Articles 21 and 32 of the Constitution, the principles and norms of determining the liability of large enterprises engaged in manufacture and sale of hazardous products, the basis on which damages in case of such liability should be quantified and whether such large enterprises should be allowed to continue to function in thickly populated areas, and, if they are permitted so to function, what measures must be taken for the purpose of reducing to a minimum the hazard to the workmen and the community living in the neighbourhood. These questions which have been raised by the petitioner are questions of the greatest importance particularly since, following upon the leakage of MIC gas from the Union Carbide Plant in Bhopal, lawyers, judges and jurists are considerably exercised as to what controls, whether by way of relocation or by way of installation of adequate safety devices, need to be imposed on Corporations employing hazardous technology and producing toxic or dangerous substances and if any liquid or gas escapes which is injurious to the workmen and the people living in the surrounding areas, on account of negligence or otherwise, what is the extent of liability of such Corporations and what remedies can be devised for enforcing such liability with a view to securing payment of damages to the persons affected by such leakage of liquid or gas. These questions arise in the present case since on 4 and 6 December 1985, there was admittedly leakage of oleum gas from one of the units of Shriram Foods and Fertiliser Industries and as a result of such leakage, several persons were affected and according to the petitioner and the Delhi Bar Association, one advocate practising in the Tis Hazari Courts died. We propose to hear detailed arguments on these questions at a later date. But one pressing issue which has to be decided by us immediately is whether we should allow the caustic chlorine plant of Shriram Foods and Fertilisers Industries to be restarted and that is the question which we are proceeding to decide in this judgment....

Since there were conflicting opinions put forward before us in regard to the question whether the caustic chlorine plant should be allowed to be restarted without any real hazard or risk

[25] 31 January 1986, 1986 (1) Scale 153; 17 February 1986, AIR 1987 SC 965; 24 February 1986, 1986 (1) Scale 341; 10 March 1986, AIR 1987 SC 982; 20 December 1986, AIR 1987 SC 1086; and 24 March 1987, 1987 (1) Scale 1271 *(2)*.

to the workmen and the public at large, we thought it desirable to appoint an independent team of experts to assist us in this task. We accordingly by an order dated 18 December 1985 constituted a Committee of Experts consisting of Dr Nilay Choudhary as Chairman and Dr Aghoramurty and Mr R K Garg as members to inspect the caustic chlorine plant and submit a report to the court on the following three points:

1. Whether the plant can be allowed to recommence the operations in its present state and condition?
2. If not, what are the measures required to be adopted against the hazard or possibility of leaks, explosion, pollution of air and water etc., for this purpose?
3. How many of the safety devices against the above hazards and possibility exist in the plant at present and which of them, though necessary, are not installed in the plant?

* * *

We have thus two major reports, one of Manmohan Singh Committee and the other of Nilay Choudhary Committee, setting out the recommendations which must be complied with by the management of Shriram in order to minimize the hazard or risk which the caustic chlorine plant poses to the workmen and the public. The question is whether these recommendations have been complied with by the management of Shriram, for it is only if these recommendations have been carried out that we can possibly consider whether the caustic chlorine plant should be allowed to be restarted....

There can ... be no doubt that there would be hazard to the life and health of the community, if there is escape of chlorine gas from the caustic chlorine plant, whether by reason of negligence of the management or due to accidental release... We cannot therefore ignore the possible hazards to the health and well-being of the workmen and the people living in the vicinity on account of escape of chlorine gas. We also cannot overlook the old and worn out state of machinery and equipment, the negligence of the management in the maintenance and operation of the caustic chlorine plant and the indifference shown by the management in installing proper safety devices and safety instruments and taking proper and adequate measures for ensuring safety of the workmen and the people living in the vicinity. These are considerations which are very relevant in deciding whether the caustic chlorine plant should be allowed to be restarted. But as against these considerations, we must also take into account the proven fact that all the recommendations made in the reports of Manmohan Singh Committee and Nilay Choudhary Committee have been carried out by the management of Shriram and it is the opinion of not only Manmohan Singh Committee and Nilay Choudhary Committee but also of the last Committee appointed by us on January 31, 1986 that since all these recommendations have been complied with by the management in satisfactory manner, Shriram may be allowed to restart the caustic chlorine plant. There can be no doubt, particularly having regard to the opinion of Manmohan Singh Committee, Nilay Choudhary Committee and the last Committee appointed by us, that the possibility of hazard or risk to the community is considerably minimised and there is now no appreciable risk of danger to the community if the caustic chlorine plant is allowed to be restarted. We cannot also ignore the interests of the workmen while deciding this delicate and complex question. It could not be disputed either by the Government of India or by the Delhi Administration or even by the petitioner that the effect of permanently closing down the caustic chlorine plant would be to throw about 4000 workmen out of employment and that such closure would lead to their utter impoverishment. The Delhi Water Supply Undertaking which gets its supply of chlorine from Shriram would also have to find alternative sources of supply and it was common ground between the parties that such sources may be quite distant from Delhi....

We have ... decided to permit Shriram to restart its power plant as also plants for manufacture of caustic chlorine including by-products like sodium sulphate, hydrochloric acid, stable bleaching powder, superchlor, and sodium hypochlorite, vanaspati refined oil including its by-products and recovery plants like soap, glycerine and technical hard oil and container works.... But we are laying down certain conditions which shall be strictly and scrupulously followed by Shriram and if at any time it is found that any one or more of these conditions are violated, the permission granted by us will be liable to be withdrawn. We formulate these conditions as follows:

[(1) The court constituted an Expert Committee to monitor Shriram's compliance with the recommendations of the Manmohan Singh and the Nilay Choudhary Committees. Shriram was asked to deposit Rs. 30,000 to meet the travelling, boarding and lodging expenses of the Expert Committee.

(2) The court stipulated that one operator be designated as personally responsible for each safety device in the caustic chlorine plant.

(3) The Chief Factory Inspector was directed to inspect the caustic chlorine plant at least once a week.

(4) The Central pollution control board was asked to depute an inspector to visit the Shriram plants at least once in a week to ascertain Shriram's compliance with the effluent discharge and emission standards prescribed in the consent orders under the Water Act and the Air Act.]

(5) The management of Shriram will obtain an undertaking from the Chairman and Managing Director of the Delhi Cloth Mills Ltd which is the owner of the various units of Shriram as also from the officer or officers who are in actual management of the caustic chlorine plant that in case there is any escape of chlorine gas resulting in death or injury to the workmen or to the people living in the vicinity, they will be personality responsible for payment of compensation for such death or injury and such undertakings shall be filed in court within one week from today.

[(6) The court constituted a workers' safety committee.

(7) Shriram was asked to publicize the effects of chlorine and the appropriate post-exposure treatment through charts placed at the gate of the premises and within the plant.

(8) Shriram was directed to instruct and train its workers in plant safety through special audio-visual programmes.

(9) Shriram was directed to install loudspeakers to alert neighbours in the event of a chlorine leak.

(10) Shriram was asked to ensure that the workers use safety devices like gas masks, safety belts, etc., and was directed to provide regular medical check-ups to the workers.]

(11) The management of Shriram will deposit in this court a sum of Rs. 20 lakhs as and by way of security for payment of compensation claims made by or on behalf of the victims of oleum gas, if and to the extent to which such compensation claims are held to be well founded. This amount deposited by the management of Shriram will be invested by the Registrar of this Court in fixed deposit with a nationalised Bank so that it earns interest and it will abide further directions of this Court. The management of Shriram will also furnish a bank guarantee to the satisfaction of the Registrar of this Court for a sum of Rs. 15 lakhs which bank guarantee shall be encashed by the Registrar, wholly or in part, in case there is any escape of chlorine gas within a period of three years from today resulting in death or injury to any workman or to any person or persons living in the vicinity. The amount of the bank guarantee when encashed shall be utilised in or towards payment of compensation to the victims of chlorine gas, the quantum of compensation being determinable by the District Judge, Delhi on applications for recompensations being made to him by the victims of chlorine gas. The amount of Rs. 20 lakhs shall be deposited and the bank guarantee for Rs. 15 lakhs shall be furnished within a period of two weeks from today and on failure of the management of Shriram to do so, the permission granted by us by this judgment to restart the caustic chlorine plant and other plants shall stand withdrawn.

* * *

It is ... necessary to point [out] that when science and technology are increasingly employed in producing goods and services calculated to improve the quality of life, there is a certain element of hazard or risk inherent in the very use of science and technology and it is not possible to totally eliminate such hazard or risk altogether. We cannot possibly adopt a policy of not having any chemical or other hazardous industries merely because they pose hazard or risk to the community. If such a policy were adopted, it would mean the end of all progress and development. Such industries, even if hazardous, have to be set up since they are essential for economic development and advancement of well-being of the people. We can only hope to reduce the element of hazard or risk to the community by taking all necessary steps for locating such industries in a manner which would pose least risk of danger to the community and maximising safety requirements in such industries. We would therefore like to impress upon the Government of India to evolve a national policy for location of chemical and other hazardous industries in areas where population is scarce and there is little hazard or risk to the community, and when hazardous industries are located in such areas, every care must be taken to see that large human habitation does not grow around them. There should preferably be a green belt of 1 to 5 km. width around such hazardous industries....

NOTES AND QUESTIONS

1. The court's order of 17 February 1986 makes clear in its first paragraph that the court is interested in a prospective application of its *Shriram* rulings to impose liability on Carbide in the pending *Bhopal Gas Leak* case. Is the court's clear intention to affect the *Bhopal* case objectionable?

2. Put yourself for a moment in Chief Justice Bhagwati's shoes: all government agencies with any responsibility over Shriram's operations have apparently been lax, and have made no move to change Shriram's operations, until the oleum leak. The Chief Justice wants to discover and remedy any problems that exist at the Shriram complex and the only person offering any assistance is M C Mehta—a single lawyer without substantial resources. In these circumstances, did he not act creatively and resourcefully in setting up an effective fact-finding and safeguard-implementing process?

3. Note that in its order of 17 February 1986, the court engages in an *ad hoc* balancing of economic and health considerations (4,000 jobs are at stake in the chlorine plant, and chlorine is needed to purify Delhi's water supply) with environmental and safety considerations (chlorine is hazardous and could harm Shriram's employees and the surrounding community). Ultimately, the court decides to reopen the chlorine plant 'temporarily'. Is not this balancing more properly the province of executive organs?

4. The court deserves praise for minimizing the danger to workers and the surrounding community by requiring Shriram to take stringent safety measures before restarting its hazardous caustic chlorine unit. Apart from compliance with the recommendations of the Manmohan Singh and Nilay Choudhary Committees, Shriram was required to 'strictly and scrupulously' follow 11 further conditions. Some of these conditions, viz., making senior-level management responsible for hazardous industrial operations, introducing workers' participation in safety management, publicizing preventive measures in the case of an emergency and requiring trained and experienced personnel to handle hazardous substances—have been codified into the Factories Act by the 1987 amendment.

5. Viewed from the court's perspective, the court's exercise of quasi-executive functions in creating agencies, appointing a safeguard committee, appointing a committee of inspectors, recruiting experts from all over India and paying for their air travel to and from Delhi and so on helps the court ascertain the facts of the case and secure objective scientific advice. The court's creativity in marshalling these resources may deserve commendation rather than criticism. Similarly, the court manifests creativity in attempting to ensure compliance with its

orders—by appointing Monitoring committees that must report back to the court regarding the measures taken to remedy Shriram's unsafe procedures and conditions.

6. Commendably, in its 17 February 1986 order, the court requires Shriram to present a bank guarantee of Rs. 15 lakhs to ensure compensation for any future chlorine victims. The court also requires Shriram to deposit Rs. 20 lakhs as a condition to reopening the *chlorine* plant, with the money to be used to compensate the *oleum* leak claimants. Isn't this a bit of a Robin Hood-type remedy? If so, did the court exceed its authority?

7. In any case, when the court determined on 20 December 1986 that it would not assert jurisdiction over Shriram, should it not have returned to Shriram the Rs. 20 lakhs it had earlier ordered to be deposited? By normal standards of orderly judicial procedure, liability cannot be imposed on a company over which a court has no jurisdiction. Is there any justification for the court retaining Shriram's Rs. 20 lakhs?

8. In a part of the judgment that is not excerpted, the court suggested the creation of environmental courts. This suggestion has taken shape in the National Green Tribunal. To be responsive and effective, should there not be a bench of the NGT in every state?

9. The court awarded Rs. 10,000 to be paid (by Shriram) to the petitioner M C Mehta. Considering the time, effort and resources expended by M C Mehta in this public interest litigation, what amount might you have awarded?

M C MEHTA v UNION OF INDIA
AIR 1987 SC 982

Order: This application has been made by Shriram Foods and Fertiliser Industries (hereinafter referred to as 'Shriram') for clarification in respect of certain conditions set out in the Order passed by us on 17 February 1986 in Writ Petns. Nos. 12739 of 1985 and 26 of 1986 (AIR 1987 SC 965). Though the application has been styled as an application for clarification, it is really and in substance, an application for modification of some of the conditions contained in the Order. . . .

[The court turned to condition No. 5 pertaining to the personal liability of the Chairman and Managing Director.] The contention of Shriram is that it is not clear as to who can be described as officer in actual management of the caustic chlorine plant and that this particular direction requires clarification so that the management can obtain the necessary undertaking from such officer. So far as this difficulty pointed out on behalf of Shriram is concerned, we would like to clarify that the officer whose undertaking is required to be taken under the directions given in our Order dated 17 February 1986, is the officer who is the 'occupier' under the Factories Act, 1948 because he is the person who has actual control over the affairs of the factory and/or the officer who is in charge of the actual operation of the caustic chlorine plant and who is responsible to the management for the operation of the plant. But it was urged on behalf of Shriram that if we insist upon an undertaking to be given by any such officer or officers it would be impossible to secure the services of any competent officers because they would not be willing to accept employment in a situation where they are made responsible not only for their own acts or omissions but also for the acts or omissions of others over whom they have no control.

[W]e are not unmindful of the fact that if absolute unlimited liability were to be imposed on any officer or officers in the employ of Shriram for death or injury arising on account of possible escape of chlorine gas many competent persons would shy away from accepting employment in Shriram and that would make it difficult for Shriram to have really competent and professionally qualified persons to manage and operate the caustic chlorine plant. We would therefore modify the condition prescribed by us by providing that undertaking shall be obtained from the officer who is 'occupier' of the caustic chlorine plant under the Factories Act, 1948, and/or the officer who is responsible to the management for the actual operation of the caustic chlorine plant as its head and such undertaking shall stipulate that in case there is any escape of chlorine gas resulting in death or injury to the workmen or to the people living in the vicinity the officer concerned will be personally responsible, to the extent of his annual salary with allowances, for payment of compensation for such death or injury but if he shows that such escape of gas took place as a result of Act of God or vis major or sabotage or that he had exercised all due diligence to prevent such escape of gas, he shall be entitled to be indemnified by Shriram.

So far as the undertaking to be obtained from the Chairman and Managing Director of Shriram is concerned it was pointed out by Shriram that Delhi Cloth Mills Ltd which is the owner of Shriram has several units manufacturing different products and each of these units is headed and managed by competent and professionally qualified persons who are responsible for the day to day management of its affairs and the Chairman and Managing Director is not concerned with day to day functioning of the units and it would not therefore be fair and just to require the Chairman and Managing Director to give an undertaking that in case of death or injury resulting on account of escape of chlorine gas, the Chairman and Managing Director would be personally liable to pay compensation. We find it difficult to accept this contention urged on behalf of Shriram. We do not see any reason why the Chairman and/or Managing Director should not be required to give an undertaking to be personally liable for payment of compensation in case of death or injury resulting on account of escape of chlorine gas, particularly when we find that according to the reports of various expert committees which examined the working of caustic chlorine plant, there was considerable negligence in looking after its safety requirements and in fact considerable repair and renovation with and installation of safety devices had to be carried out at a fairly heavy cost in order to reduce the element of risk or hazard to the community....

NOTES AND QUESTIONS

1. Recognizing that many companies have named low-level officials as 'occupier' and 'manager'—posts liable for prosecution under the Factories Act of 1948—section 2(n) of that Act was amended in 1987 to specify that the 'occupier' of a factory 'means the person who has ultimate control over the affairs of the factory: Provided that ... in the case of a company, any one of the directors shall be deemed to be the occupier ...'. The last clause was somewhat ambiguous, leading to a divergence of opinion among the High Courts in respect of who might be an occupier. In *J K Industries Ltd v Chief Inspector of Factories & Boilers*,[26] the Supreme Court resolved the issue, holding that after the 1987 amendment, a company could only nominate a director as an occupier and not any other employee or officer. The amended provision was constitutional and did not confer unguided power on the Inspector of Factories. It was for the board of directors of a company to notify the particular director who was to be treated as an occupier and only where the board failed was it left to the Inspector of Factories to choose one among the directors as a deemed occupier.

2. Shriram pursued an entirely different litigation strategy than Union Carbide did in the *Bhopal Gas Leak* case. Shriram complied with all orders, including those requiring them to subsidize the court's fact-finding, without complaint or demur. Carbide seemed inclined to contest virtually every order of every court. What might account for the difference? The nationality of the company? The fact that Shriram was a going concern keen to continue its business in India, while the Union Carbide Corporation had no future stake in Indian

[26] (1996) 6 SCC 665.

business? The fact that feelings were running high against Carbide, and Shriram did not want to be tarred with the same brush? Other factors?

M C MEHTA v UNION OF INDIA

AIR 1987 SC 1086*

BHAGWATI, C J: This writ petition under Article 32 of the Constitution has come before us on a reference made by a Bench of three Judges. The reference was made because certain questions of seminal importance and high constitutional significance were raised in the course of arguments when the writ petition was originally heard.... When applications for compensation came up for hearing it was felt that since the issues raised involved substantial questions of law relating to the interpretation of Articles 21 and 32 of the Constitution, the case should be referred to a larger Bench of five Judges and this is how the case has now come before us.

[The court then considered Shriram's preliminary objection. Shriram urged the court not to decide the issues arising from the compensation claims since no such claim was made in the original petition and the petitioner had not amended the pleadings to incorporate a compensation plea. The court, however, dismissed the objection, stating that a hyper-technical approach would defeat the ends of justice.

Thereafter, the court examined the ambit of Article 32 of the Constitution and concluded that under that article the Supreme Court may award compensation in appropriate cases.]

The next question which arises for consideration on these applications for compensation is whether Article 21 is available against Shriram which is owned by Delhi Cloth Mills Limited, a public company limited by shares and which is engaged in an industry vital to public interest and with potential to affect the life and health of the people.... [W]e do not propose to decide finally at the present stage whether a private corporation like Shriram would fall within the scope and ambit of Article 12, because we have not had sufficient time to consider and reflect on this question in depth. The hearing of this case before us concluded only on 15 December 1986 and we are called upon to deliver our judgment within a period of four days, on 19 December 1986. We are therefore, of the view that this is not a question on which we must make any definite pronouncement at this stage. But we would leave it for a proper and detailed consideration at a later stage if it becomes necessary to do so.

We must also deal with one other question which was seriously debated before us and that question is as to what is the measure of liability of an enterprise which is engaged in an hazardous or inherently dangerous industry, if by reason of an accident occurring in such industry, persons die or are injured. Does the rule in *Rylands v Fletcher* (1868 LR 3 HL 330) apply or is there any other principle on which the liability can be determined. The rule in *Rylands v Fletcher* was evolved in the year 1868 and it provides that a person who for his own purposes brings on to his land and collects and keeps there anything likely to do mischief if it escapes must keep it at his peril and, if he fails to do so, is prima facie liable for the damage which is the natural consequence of its escape. The liability under this rule is strict and it is no defence that the thing escaped without that person's wilful act, default or neglect or even that he had no knowledge of its existence. This rule laid down a principle of liability that if a person who brings on to his land and collects and keeps there anything likely to do harm and such thing escapes and does damage to another, he is liable to compensate for the damage caused. Of course, this rule applies only to non-natural user of the land and it does not apply to things naturally on the land or where the escape is due to an act of God and an act of a stranger or the default of the person injured or where the thing which escapes is present by the consent of the person injured or in certain cases where there is statutory authority.... We are of the view that an enterprise which is engaged in a hazardous or

* The report of the judgment in the All India Reporter is slightly different from the report carried in the Supreme Court Cases reporter. These differences are not material. In a few places we have departed from the AIR report since the SCC report appeared to be more accurate.

inherently dangerous industry which poses a potential threat to the health and safety of the persons working in the factory and residing in the surrounding areas owes an absolute and non delegable duty to the community to ensure that no harm results to anyone on account of hazardous or inherently dangerous nature of the activity which it has undertaken. The enterprise must be held to be under an obligation to provide that the hazardous or inherently dangerous activity in which it is engaged must be conducted with the highest standards of safety and if any harm results on account of such activity, the enterprise must be absolutely liable to compensate for such harm and it should be no answer to the enterprise to say that it had taken all reasonable care and that the harm occurred without any negligence on its part. Since the persons harmed on account of the hazardous or inherently dangerous activity carried on by the enterprise would not be in a position to isolate the process of operation from the hazardous preparation of substance or any other related element that caused the harm the enterprise must be held strictly liable for causing such harm as a part of the social cost of carrying on the hazardous or inherently dangerous activity.... This principle is also sustainable on the ground that the enterprise alone has the resource to discover and guard against hazards or dangers and to provide warnings against potential hazards. We would therefore hold that where an enterprise is engaged in a hazardous or inherently dangerous activity and harm results to anyone on account of an accident in the operation of such hazardous and inherently dangerous activity resulting, for example, the escape of toxic gas the enterprise is strictly and absolutely liable to compensate all those who are affected by the accident and such liability is not subject to any of the exceptions which operate *vis-à-vis* the tortious principle of strict liability under the rule in *Rylands v Fletcher*.

We would also like to point out that the measure of compensation in the kind of cases referred to in the preceding paragraph must be correlated to the magnitude and capacity of the enterprise because such compensation must have a deterrent effect. The larger and more prosperous the enterprise, the greater must be the amount of compensation payable by it for the harm caused on account of an accident in the carrying on of the hazardous or inherently dangerous activity by the enterprise....

NOTES AND QUESTIONS

1. The Article 32 writ petition process is designed to alter the behaviour of government officials. *Shriram* is the first case in which an Article 32 petition was used to seek compensation from a private company, viz., Shriram. The court attempted to cope with this dilemma by drawing on American cases where private companies acting under the colour of state law (i.e., with the sanction and cooperation of state officials) are deemed to be engaging in *state action* (and hence subject to the US Constitution's 14th Amendment, regulating the conduct of the states).

Does this imply that Shriram, and other private companies whose activities, like Shriram's, have a 'public character'[27] should be treated as an instrumentality of the state for purposes of an Article 32 writ petition? If so, it could result in a deluge of writ petitions, and would expose countless private enterprises to writ proceedings asserting infringements of fundamental rights.

The court could undoubtedly counter this 'flood of litigation' argument by observing that it seeks only a very narrow expansion, namely those private corporations affected with a

[27] We use the term 'public character' to summarize the court's description of Shriram as 'a private corporation under the functional control of the State, engaged in an activity which is hazardous to the health and safety of the community and is imbued with public interest and which the State ... proposes to exclusively run under its industrial policy....' (AIR 1987 SC 1086, 1097).

public purpose that allegedly deprive citizens of their right to life under Article 21. Is it likely that such a 'narrow' expansion would be maintained? This deluge was held back by the Chief Justice's failure to assemble a majority of his bench behind the 'state action' doctrine. Accordingly, if Shriram is not a state instrumentality under Article 12 of the Constitution then it must be a private party, and not capable of receiving a writ of mandamus. The court does not say that Shriram is not a state instrumentality, but clearly there is no majority for the view that it is, and so the court does not decide whether it has Article 32 jurisdiction over Shriram.

2. Do you believe that the court's response was a reaction to the *Bhopal* case?

3. If the *Shriram* court was inclined to exercise judicial self-restraint, the case would have ended here: no affirmative holding on the threshold issue of jurisdiction means that the court will not decide the questions of liability and compensation. But the court, having come this far, and having a great desire to prospectively reach the *Bhopal Gas Leak* case, does not let its lack of jurisdiction inhibit it from articulating a new absolute liability standard and a new standard also for determining the quantum of damages.

4. In its 20 December 1986 judgment, the court did not decide whether Shriram could be characterized as the 'state' within the meaning of Article 12. The court observed:

> [W]e have not had sufficient time to consider and reflect on this question in depth. The hearing of this case before us concluded only on 15 December 1986, and we are called upon to deliver our judgment within a period of four days.... We are, therefore, of the view that this is not a question on which we must make any definite pronouncement at this stage....

If four days were not sufficient time to reflect in depth on the Article 12 ('state action') question, how could it have been sufficient to radically change the liability and compensation laws of India, as the court then proceeded to do?

5. The final portion of Chief Justice Bhagwati's 20 December 1986 order makes two quantum leaps in the law, viz., the articulation of a new standard of a hazardous industry's *absolute liability* for the harm resulting from its activities—a standard which admits of no defences—and the declaration that damages are to be commensurate with the tortfeasor's ability to pay. Can one argue that these policies fall within the normal function of a common law judge to refine and extend reasoned principles articulated in earlier cases? Or are they simply judge-made laws?

6. Judge-made law can be far more potent than an Act of Parliament: in the *Shriram* case, for example, the court declares a new *absolute liability* standard and applies this standard to the instant case. If a legislature attempted to articulate a liability standard and to apply it to a gas leak that happened a year earlier, such action would very likely be challenged. It could be attacked as unreasonable and arbitrary, and violative of Article 14 of the Constitution. But a court encounters no such impediments: it merely announces that the newly revealed standard has *always* implicitly been the law of the land. The court has simply found the standard embedded in the common law and has interpreted it to apply to the instant case.

7. Note that the court justifies its formulation of a 'no exceptions' strict liability rule by observing:

> [I]n part, as new situations arise the law has to be evolved in order to meet the challenge of such new situations.... We have to evolve new principles and lay down new norms which would adequately deal with the new problems which arise in a highly industrialised economy.

Is the articulation of new principles and norms not the quintessential legislative function?

8. There is nothing in the reported orders in the *Shriram* case that justifies the expansion of the *Rylands v Fletcher* strict liability rule. It appears that Shriram offered none of the defences recognized as exceptions to *Rylands v Fletcher* (such as an act of God, the act of a third party and statutory authority). Hence, there seems to have been no reason for the court to announce a new rule of absolute liability allowing no exceptions. This adds support to the supposition that the court's agenda was to anticipate and nullify the third-party 'saboteur' defence in the *Bhopal* case.

9. Cost internalization and loss-spreading arguments suggest that, regardless of negligence, hazardous industries rather than innocent victims should bear the cost of injuries caused by hazardous substances. These two arguments support the court's articulation of a new 'absolute liability' standard.

Imposing absolute liability ensures that the cost of injuries from toxics are borne by the manufacturers who use, market and profit from these products. Cost internalization is intuitively just, in that victims obtain compensation from those who profit from their harmful activity. Moreover, cost internalization deters future tortious conduct.

Absolute liability guarantees that hazardous industries become insurers against risk of injury arising from their activity and, through higher prices, the cost of injuries caused by the toxic substance is then distributed among the public as part of business costs rather than borne in entirety by the injured individual. Loss spreading is fair because everyone in society benefits from the products that the hazardous industries manufacture and, therefore, everyone should pay for a portion of the harm associated with these products.

10. But is an absolute liability standard that makes no allowances for war, a terrorist attack or an act of God (storms, cyclones, lightning, tidal waves, etc.) consistent with notions of fundamental fairness and justice?

11. Each of the major new principles in the *Shriram* case—absolute liability and the quantum of damages determined by the respondent's ability to pay—seems defensible, standing alone. They are much harder to defend together: absolute liability admitting no defences amounts to a 'no-fault' system. In a no-fault system, the person or company made liable needs to know in advance what the quantum of liability will be, so that he or she can obtain liability insurance. An *indeterminate sliding scale* seems unconstitutionally vague, as well as bad public policy.

12. Over the years, the *Shriram* principles have waxed and waned. In December 1989 (three years after the *Shriram* judgment) a five-judge bench of the Supreme Court upheld the validity of Bhopal Gas Leak Disaster (Processing of Claims) Act of 1985.[28] Certain observations in the opinions delivered in the *Bhopal Act* case appear to weaken the *Shriram* court's standard that the quantum of damages should be on the basis of the monetary capacity of the delinquent. Referring to this standard, Chief Justice Mukharji (for himself and Saikia, J) stated:

> This is an uncertain promise of law. On the basis of evidence available and on the basis of the principles so far established, it is difficult to see any reasonable possibility of acceptance of this yardstick. And even if it is accepted, there are numerous difficulties of getting that view accepted internationally as a just basis in accordance with law.[29]

Justice Ranganathan (for himself and Ahmadi, J) concurred:

[28] *Charan Lal Sahu v Union of India* AIR 1990 SC 1480.
[29] *Id.* at 1545.

> Whether the [*Bhopal* case] settlement should have taken into account (the Shriram standard of punitive liability) is, in the first place a moot question. Mukharji, C J has pointed out-and we are inclined to agree that this is an 'uncertain province of the law' and it is premature to say whether this yardstick has been, or will be, accepted in this country, not to speak of its international acceptance which may be necessary should occasion arise for executing a decree based on such a yardstick in another country.[30]

Justice K N Singh (who was also a member of the *Shriram* court) did not express any opinion on the quantum of damages issue.

13. The absolute liability theory was examined by the Supreme Court when deciding the Bhopal Settlement review petitions,[31] the *Bichhri* case[32] as well as *Research Foundation.*[33]

In an industrial pollution case involving several polluters in Gujarat the Supreme Court remitted the matter back to the High Court observing: 'compensation to be awarded must have some broad correlation not only with the magnitude and capacity of the enterprise but also with the harm caused by it.'[34]

14. In its petition for review of the 20 December 1986 order, Shriram stated that it did not argue the question of exemplary damages since the court declared that it would not be considering the question. If this is correct, was it proper for the court to create a new standard for compensation without giving an opportunity to be heard to the party newly made liable?

15. The Supreme Court directed that the oleum gas leak claimants should file their claims in the Tis Hazari Courts (the trial courts in Delhi, located quite close to the Shriram complex). After the Delhi High Court designated five judges to hear these claims, most other judges of the Tis Hazari Courts immediately filed claims against Shriram, claiming personal injury in the oleum gas leak!

16. In the 1990s, Shriram relocated some of its units at Patiala in Punjab. Several other polluting industries in Delhi were also directed by the Supreme Court to move operations away from the National Capital Region.[35]

Eventually, Shriram settled with the claimants. Although Shriram considered many claims to be bogus, the company decided to pay reasonable amounts to every claimant, rather than risk a contest and an award in a few genuine cases that was linked to the company's 'ability to pay'. The settlement also involved a payout by Shriram's insurers.

C. HAZARDOUS SUBSTANCE CASES

I. THE *FACT* CASE

Rarely does the judicial system stall a large project on environmental grounds. When the Kerala High Court elevated safety concerns over economic interests to safeguard Cochin, the decision did not survive appellate scrutiny by the Supreme Court. The Law Society of India urged the Kerala High Court to restrain a giant public sector fertilizer company from operating its 10,000-ton ammonia storage tank in Cochin. The petitioners claimed that an

30 *Id.* at 1557.
31 *Union Carbide Corporation v Union of India (Bhopal Review)* AIR 1992 SC 248.
32 *Indian Council for Enviro-Legal Action v Union of India* AIR 1996 SC 1446.
33 *Research Foundation for Science v Union of India* (2005) 13 SCC 186, 201.
34 *Deepak Nitrite Ltd v State of Gujarat* (2004) 6 SCC 402, 407.
35 *M C Mehta v Union of India* AIR 1996 SC 2231.

accidental leakage of ammonia could devastate the entire city and its environs. A division bench of the High Court embarked on a detailed evaluation of the technical and legal aspects of the case and delivered a lengthy judgment requiring the ammonia storage tank to be decommissioned. Contrast the reasoning of the High Court and the Supreme Court.

LAW SOCIETY OF INDIA v FERTILIZERS & CHEMICALS TRAVANCORE LTD
AIR 1994 KER 308

***

VARGHESE KALLIATH, J:

The ammonia stored in the storage tank is imported in special refrigerated ships and is pumped from the ships to the refrigerated storage tank at atmospheric pressure. Since the first respondent required ammonia for the purpose of production of fertilizers and caprolactum, it is importing ammonia after obtaining the required governmental sanction. The tank, which was designed in March, 1973 was commissioned in August, 1976 to receive liquid ammonia from ship. The ammonia stored in this tank is transferred into rail tank wagons and transported to first respondent's Cochin Division, where it is stored in a 5000 tonne capacity ammonia storage tank before being pumped to the consuming plants. Part of the ammonia that is stored in the tank is transported to Udyogmandal through barges specially made for the purpose of refrigeration....

We have to investigate two broad questions in this case. The first question is the possibility of the operational failure of 10,000 tonnes of ammonia storage tank and the consequent leak of ammonia and the degree of pollution of air and the resultant ecological imbalance they may cause thereby and as a result of this environmental pollution the hazards that have to be faced by the people of Willingdon Island and the city of Cochin. The second question that we have to answer is as to whether there is any reasonable possibility of catastrophic failure, of the tank resulting in a crack or break or a rupture which would result in an uncontrollable major leak of ammonia with its resultant devastation of the entire population in Willingdon Island and the city of Cochin and surrounding places on account of the seminal sensitive and [strategic site] of the tank in the port area very close to the runway of the airport and very near to the Southern Naval Command....

Certain important facts and circumstances unfolded in the case and the findings.

(i) In case of a catastrophic accident to the storage tank resulting in a major crack or rupture, it would lead to disastrous and devastating consequences of annihilating all living beings, inverting the city of Cochin into a city of the dead and nearby places, a morbid grave-yard.
(ii) The catastrophic failure of the tank is not an unreal or remote possibility, but a credible and contingent possibility to be reasonably anticipated on the facts unfolded in the case.
(iii) Though the catastrophic event is only a possibility and when it would happen is unpredictable, it is unwise to forget or slur it. Once it happens, it is irreversible, so prudence dictates not complaisance, but positive action.

[The court concluded that the location of the tank endangered public safety.]

On the findings and conclusions, we have decocted from the mass of materials placed before us, we have to make our own final decision in the matter. We are fully aware of the fact that directing the first respondent to decommission the ammonia tank would certainly involve very far reaching and serious economic issues as well as issues relating to loss of employment to large number of persons. Certainly these issues involve vital and serious consequences. But we have to balance these issues with the real and intelligible potential possibility of a catastrophic accident to the ammonia tank resulting in extermination of all living beings in Willingdon Island, City of Cochin and nearby places. We have found that the catastrophic failure of the tank not a remote possibility, but a credible and contingent possibility to be reasonably anticipated on the facts unfolded in the case. We feel that we have to discharge our obligation informed of the fact that the human population of the Cochin City and Willingdon Island should not be compelled to remain under the dark shadow of a genocide.

> Life on earth can never be peaceful if it is shrouded in perpetual anxiety and fear of extermination on account of an avoidable human activity. It is the plain and clear negation of the most basic human right and gross violation of the fundamental right guaranteed under Article 21 of the Constitution of India....
>
> In the result, on an anxious consideration of the rival claims and competing concerns, we order the first respondent to de-commission and empty the ammonia storage tank at Willingdon Island within 3 months from today. Further we direct that the storage tank at Willingdon island should not be used for storing liquid ammonia after decommissioning the tank....

NOTES

1. Fertilizers & Chemicals Travancore (FACT) employed more than 8,500 persons, some of whom were directly concerned with the operation of the storage tank. The company staff perceived the petition as a threat to their livelihood and filed a strong affidavit opposing relief. The trade unions and workers' associations alleged that the petitioners were instigated by foreign multinationals interested in retarding India's development. The High Court, however, rejected the conspiracy theory out of hand.

2. A better point raised by the workmen was that several other ports in India and elsewhere in the world had similar storage installations and the petitioners' apprehensions were unjustified. This argument was turned down by the High Court after considering the special features at the Cochin facility, expert opinions on safety and after balancing the rival interests.

3. In a significant development, the High Court implicitly laid down the standard which project proponents must adopt when introducing hazardous technologies capable of causing catastrophic damage. Three solutions were recommended by Dr Kurt Mager to strengthen the defective foundation work. FACT selected the most economical and least time-consuming method, although this was not the safest option. In paragraph 88 of the judgment (not excerpted), the High Court disapproved the selection in view of the high risk involved and held that the safest solution, albeit more expensive and time consuming, ought to have been adopted. This is the first reported case in India where the court required the *best available technology* to be employed, irrespective of the financial costs.

4. As with the *Tehri Dam*[36] and *Irish Butter*[37] cases, expert opinion was divided on the question of safety. The Central Building Research Institute gave a clean bill of safety to FACT with regard to repaired foundation work. The Indian Institute of Technology, Madras was more ambivalent, reporting that the foundation was not in an 'alarming condition'. As against this, the Port Trust, the Southern Naval Command, the Kerala PCB and the MoEF emphasized the need to immediately shift the tank. Dr Campbell, the court-appointed Commissioner, pointed out that the proximity of the tank to the airport increased the risk of a catastrophe.

5. In the *Bayer* case,[38] the company was concerned that an accident at its chemical factory near Thane city in Maharashtra might endanger persons who came to live in the locality. The case boomeranged on Bayer when the Supreme Court suggested that the industry should move, not the residents.

---

36 *Tehri Bandh Virodhi Sangharsh Samiti v State of UP* (1992) Supp (1) SCC 44.

37 *Dr Shivarao Shantaram Wagle v Union of India* AIR 1988 SC 952.

38 *Bayer (India) Ltd v State of Maharashtra* 1994 (4) BOM C REP 309 and *F B Taraporawala v Bayer India Ltd* (1996) 6 SCC 58.

6. Risk-taking is inherent to our species and the story of civilization. Complex technologies pervade modern life. Developing new technologies and applying them inevitably involves risks. Entrepreneurs and businesses have an appetite for risk. Environmentalists seek to temper this appetite with critical environmental considerations. Decision-makers and courts must balance the risk and, consistent with the precautionary principle, take a call on whether a particular project may proceed.

FERTILIZERS AND CHEMICAL TRAVANCORE LTD EMPLOYEES ASSOCIATION v LAW SOCIETY OF INDIA

(2000) 4 SCC 420

***

S H Kapadia, J:

By a voluminous judgment dated 14-2-1994 in a public interest litigation instituted by the Law Society of India, a Division Bench of the Kerala High Court directed Fertilizers and Chemicals Travancore Ltd to decommission and empty the ammonia storage tank at Willingdon Island within three months as the said tank was vulnerable to major leaks in the event of an air crash, sabotage and earthquake.

Fertilizers and Chemicals Travancore Ltd is a public sector undertaking which manufactures chemicals and fertilizers to the extent of 4% of total fertilizer production in the country. Ammonia is the chemical used as raw material in production of fertilizers like urea, ammonium sulphate and ammonium chloride. Ammonia imported in special refrigerated ships is stored in the storage tank located in Willingdon Island. It is pumped from the ships into the storage tank at an atmospheric pressure. The tank was designed in March 1973 and it was commissioned in August 1976 to receive liquid ammonia from special refrigerated ships. The ammonia stored in this tank is transferred into railway wagons which carry liquid ammonia to the Cochin Division of the Company where it is stored in a bigger ammonia storage tank before it is pumped to various consuming plants. The complaint of the original petitioner was of massive environmental pollution caused by the existence of the tank. The original petitioner anticipates devastating catastrophe of exterminating large population of Willingdon Island and the city of Cochin in the event of a major leak in the said ammonia tank. In this connection the original petitioner relied upon accidents which have taken place in Soviet Union and Pakistan where leakages developed in the plants injuring thousands of persons. According to the original petitioner, in Willingdon Island there is an airport which is in the vicinity of the tank and if by chance an air crash takes place it would lead to human tragedy. It was further stated that such leakage in existing ammonia storage tank cannot be ruled out and in which event the fire force, police, navy and district health authorities were not capable to provide adequate safety measures.

The High Court came to the conclusion that the environmental imperative is ultimately a matter of public rights and duties. That effective environmental protection and improvement is a matter of legal rights and duties. The High Court examined two questions viz. possibility of operational failure of the tank which weighs 10,000 tonnes and leakage of ammonia on account of rupture in the tank which would result in an uncontrollable devastation of the entire living population in Willingdon Island, city of Cochin and surrounding places. The High Court further observed that major leak could be caused by air crash in the vicinity of the tank as there was an airport in the vicinity or by an act of sabotage or by earthquake which would lead to loss of human life on a tragic scale. Consequently, it directed the Company to close down the tank and not to operate the tank in Willingdon Island. Being aggrieved, the Association has come by way of civil appeal to this Court.

Two questions arise for determination in these civil appeals viz. location of the tank and structural integrity of the tank. Since the matter is of a technical nature this Court appointed M/s Engineers India Limited (in short 'EIL'), New Delhi to re-examine all the issues and submit its report. The report dated 24-12-2003 has now been submitted. It is ordered to be taken on record. In the said report EIL has given technical details of the foundation of the tank at Annexure II. Clause 4.1 deals with adequacy of foundation. EIL carried out a hydrostatic test under which the foundation was progressively loaded and readings were accordingly recorded. After carrying out the test EIL has opined that the tank can continue in service in its present condition subject to certain measures being taken by the Company as suggested in the report to further enhance the safety in the operation of the tank. Similarly, EIL also examined structural integrity of the tank, soundness of accessories and connected systems. It also took assistance of specialized agencies in this regard. EIL also examined risk factors including the location of the tank and in this connection EIL has also considered the nature of operations and the handling of the toxicity of ammonia. Based on the results of various studies carried out on the above items EIL has opined that the tank can continue in service in its present condition subject to certain measures suggested in the report. EIL further examined chronology of leak history collected from the Company from January 1985 till December 2003 and has opined that all such leaks had developed outside the storage tank at the time of loading and unloading and not on account of failure of structural integrity. It further found that most of the leaks during the above period were on account of maintenance-related problems and such leakages can be contained to a minimum with systematic planning, monitoring and improvement in system. EIL further examined the possibility of operational failure from connected systems viz. safety valves, pipes and fittings. EIL has suggested steps and measures to be taken to contain such operational failures. EIL has further commented about steps taken by the Company to implement recommendations given by experts in the past to contain corrosion of components. EIL has further stated that the Company has undertaken safety audits from time to time. The original petitioner has relied upon observations of Dr Campbell who has made a detailed study on the subject. However, his study has been confined to the documents on record. Dr Campbell has not visited the site at any time. However, he is an expert and we respect his opinion. Dr Campbell has opined that worst cases like tank rupture, terrorist attack and earthquake could occur. However, he has also opined that containment of small leakage by proper operational procedure and maintenance practices is possible. In fact, Dr Campbell has opined that relocation of tank to a new site will not solve the perceived major hazard. He considered the location of the airport as a significant risk factor. In the light of the opinion expressed by Dr Campbell, EIL carried out a separate study on risk assessment and has made suggestions as contained in the report to contain the risk factor.

Taking into account the report in its entirety, the conclusion of EIL is that the tank can continue in service in its present condition subject to certain measures being taken by the Company as suggested in the report to further enhance the safety in operations.

We may deal with the arguments advanced on behalf of the original petitioner. It was contended that in the event of earthquake or terrorist attack or sabotage or an air crash into the tank from the nearby airport, there would be human tragedy caused on account of leakage of ammonia from the storage tank and, therefore, the said tank should be relocated. We do not find any merit in this argument as stated in this case. As stated by Dr Campbell, relocation is not the solution. We are mainly concerned with two issues viz. structural integrity of the tank and its operations. On both these issues EIL has recommended continuance of the tank in its present condition subject to certain measures being taken by the Company. The Company has taken those steps. Sabotage, attack by terrorists, earthquake, etc. are all unenforceable (*sic* unforeseeable) events. We have to strike a balance between existing utilities which exist in public interest on the one hand and human safety conditions on the other hand. It is not in dispute that such plants are needed for the welfare of the society. In modern times we have nuclear plants which generate electricity. Their structural integrity and their operations are vulnerable to certain risks. However, generation of electricity is equally important and within the prescribed limits society will have to tolerate existence of such plants. It is for this reason that we called for a report from EIL so that they can examine the structural integrity of the tank, its operations and the measures which are required to be taken to minimize the risk factors. If the arguments of the original petitioner are accepted then no such utility can exist, no power plant can exist, no reservoir can exist, no nuclear reactor can exist. We do not discount such risks but we have to live with such risks which are counterbalanced by services and amenities provided by these utilities.

Accordingly, we dispose of these appeals in terms of the report of EIL dated 24-12-2003. There shall be no order as to costs.

NOTES AND QUESTIONS

1. Interpreting Article 21 of the Constitution, the High Court held that locating a dangerous industrial facility with potentially catastrophic effects in a city would violate the right to life of the citizens put at risk. The Supreme Court found the standard unreal, emphasizing technological risks inherent in the contemporary world.

2. Was the Supreme Court's approach to the safety of Cochin's citizens considerably laxer than when it required polluting industries to shift away from Delhi?[39]

3. Recall the devastating explosions on 4 August 2020 in Beirut which were linked to ammonium nitrate confiscated by the Lebanese government and stored in the port without adequate safety measures.

Considering that expert opinion was divided, should the courts have asked FACT to propose a schedule for shifting the storage tank to a safer location away from densely populated Cochin? Would this have been a more sensible application of judicial balancing? A clear time marker defined in consultation with the company would have ensured that the risk to the city would diminish from that point.

II. THE *BICHHRI* CASE

In the *Bichhri* case, the Supreme Court rendered two judgments 15 years apart. The first judgment arose from a public interest litigation and culminated in the Supreme Court directing closure of the chemical units in question and requiring MoEF to assess the amount required for environmental restoration and to recover the amount from the companies.[40] *Bichhri-2* arose from two applications filed by Hindustan Agro Chemicals Ltd (HACL), one of the offending industries. HACL presented expert evidence after a lapse of 15 years claiming that no remediation was required. It asked that the attachment levied by *Bichhri-1* be raised. In the second application, HACL challenged the assessment by which it was asked to pay Rs. 37.385 crores since the basis of the evaluation was flawed.

The judgment in *Bichhri-1* is excerpted in the Absolute Liability section of the Judicial Remedies and Procedures chapter. Here, we excerpt from *Bichhri-2*.

INDIAN COUNCIL FOR ENVIRO-LEGAL ACTION v UNION OF INDIA
(2011) 8 SCC 161

DR DALVEER BHANDARI, J: This is a very unusual and extraordinary litigation where even after fifteen years of the final judgment of this Court (dated 13-2-1996) the litigation has been deliberately kept alive by filing one interlocutory application or the other in order to avoid compliance with the judgment. The said judgment of this Court has not been permitted to acquire finality till date. This is a classic example how by abuse of the process of law even the final judgment of the Apex Court can be circumvented for more than a decade-and-a-half. This is indeed a very serious matter concerning the sanctity and credibility of the judicial system in general and of the Apex Court in particular.

[39] *M C Mehta v Union of India* AIR 1996 SC 2231.
[40] *Indian Council for Enviro-Legal Action v Union of India (Bichhri-1)* (1996) 3 SCC 212.

An environmentalist organisation brought to light the sufferings and woes of people living in the vicinity of chemical industrial plants in India. This petition relates to the suffering of people of Village Bichhri in Udaipur District of Rajasthan. In Writ Petition No. 967 of 1989, it was demonstrated how the conditions of a peaceful, nice and small village of Rajasthan were dramatically changed after Respondent No.4, Hindustan Agro Chemicals Ltd started producing certain chemicals like oleum (concentrated form of sulphuric acid) and single super phosphate. Respondents 4 to 8 are controlled by the same group and they were known as chemical industries. The entire chemical industrial complex is located within the limits of Bichhri Village, Udaipur, Rajasthan. Pursuit of profit of entrepreneurs has absolutely drained them of any feeling for fellow human beings living in that village.

The basic facts of this case are taken from the judgment delivered in *Indian Council for Enviro-Legal Action v Union of India.*[41] In the beginning of the judgment of this Court delivered on 13-2-1996, it is observed as under:

> It highlights the disregard, nay, contempt of law and lawful authorities on the part of some among the emerging breed of entrepreneurs, taking advantage, as they do, of the country's need for industrialisation and export earnings. Pursuit of profit has absolutely drained them of any feeling for fellow human beings—for that matter, for anything else. And the law seems to have been helpless. Systemic defects? It is such instances which have led many people in this country to believe that disregard of law pays and that the consequences of such disregard will never be visited upon them—particularly, if they are men with means. Strong words indeed—but nothing less would reflect the deep sense of hurt, the hearing of this case has instilled in us.

It seems that the Court was prophetic when it made observation that at times men with means are successful in avoiding compliance with the orders of this Court. This case is a classic illustration where even after a decade and a half of the pronouncement of the judgment by this Court based on the principle of 'polluter pays', till date the polluters (industries concerned in this case) have taken no steps to ecologically restore the entire village and its surrounding areas or complied with the directions of this Court at all. The orders of this Court were not implemented by keeping the litigation alive by filing interlocutory and interim application even after dismissal of the writ petition, the review petition and the curative petition by this Court....

It is settled principle of law that no one can take advantage of his own wrong. Unless courts disgorge all benefits that a party availed by obstruction or delays or non-compliance, there will always be incentive for non-compliance, and parties are ingenious enough to come up with all kinds of pleas and other tactics to achieve their end because they know that in the end the benefit will remain with them.

Whatever benefits a person has had or could have had by not complying with the judgment must be disgorged and paid to the judgment-creditor and not allowed to be retained by the judgment-debtor. This is the bounden duty and obligation of the court. In fact, it has to be looked at from the position of the creditor. Unless the deprivation by reason of delay is fully restituted, the creditor as a beneficiary remains a loser to the extent of the unrestituted amount....

The Court in its order dated 4-11-1997 while accepting the report of MoEF directed the applicant M/s Hindustan Agro Chemicals Ltd to pay a sum of Rs 37.385 crores towards the costs of remediation. The amount which ought to have been deposited way back in 1997 has yet not been deposited by keeping the litigation alive.

[41] *Id.*

We have carefully considered the facts and circumstances of this case. We have also considered the law declared by this Court and by other countries in a number of cases. We are clearly of the opinion that the applicant industry concerned must deposit the amount as directed by this Court vide order dated 4-11-1997 with compound interest. The applicant industry has deliberately not complied with the orders of this Court since 4-11-1997. Thousands of villagers have been adversely affected because no effective remedial steps have been taken so far. The applicant industry has succeeded in their design in not complying with the Court's order by keeping the litigation alive.

Both these interlocutory applications being totally devoid of any merit are accordingly dismissed with costs. Consequently, the applicant industry is directed pay Rs.37.385 crores along with compound interest @ 12% per annum from 4-11-1997 till the amount is paid or recovered. The applicant industry is also directed to pay costs of litigation. Even after final judgment of this Court, the litigation has been kept alive for almost 15 years. The respondents have been compelled to defend this litigation for all these years. Enormous Court's time has been wasted for all these years.

On consideration of the totality of the facts and circumstances of this case, we direct the applicant industry to pay costs of Rs 10 lakhs in both the interlocutory applications. The amount of costs would also be utilised for carrying out remedial measures in Village Bichhri and surrounding areas in Udaipur District of Rajasthan on the direction of the authorities concerned.

In case the amount as directed by this Court and costs imposed by this Court are not paid within two months, the same would be recovered as arrears of land revenue. Both these interlocutory applications are accordingly disposed of.

NOTES AND QUESTIONS

1. In *Bichhri-1*, the court underscored the importance of the absolute liability principle laid down in the *Shriram* case.[42] This was because a subsequent concurring opinion by Chief Justice Ranganath Misra, in the *Bhopal Review* case,[43] cast a doubt on the absolute liability standard by suggesting that the departure from the *Rylands v Fletcher* rule 'was essentially obiter'.[44]

2. In its operative directions in *Bichhri-1*, the court relegated the Bichhri villagers to the remedy of individual suits for compensation. Should the court, in exercise of its expansive jurisdiction under Article 21, have awarded compensation in the writ proceedings? What are the pitfalls in adopting a summary procedure?

3.*Bichhri-2* is an extraordinarily long-winded judgment excavating deep into issues concluded 15 years earlier and adding little to jurisprudence. The bench cites 84 judgments and visits the law of Australia, England, Canada and Fiji to draw support for a rather obvious conclusion: once the Supreme Court has finally disposed of a case and the review is dismissed, there is virtually no scope to maintain an application to reopen the matter.

Judgments of Indian courts are frequently criticized for being short on analysis and long on quotations from previous authority. In common law jurisdictions, the stature of a court

---

42 *M C Mehta v Union of India* AIR 1987 SC 1086.

43 *Union Carbide Corporation v Union of India (Bhopal Review)* AIR 1992 SC 248.

44 *Id.* at 261. Obiter dicta are words of a judgment unnecessary for the decision of the case. *Rylands v Fletcher* (1868) LR 3 HL 330 laid down a rule of strict liability. This is discussed in the Judicial Remedies and Procedures chapter.

grows on the strength of its analysis, not the length of its judgments. Far too often, lengthy Supreme Court judgments are described by lawyers appearing in that court as 'landmark', 'path breaking' or 'seminal'. Does this fawning culture contribute to prolix judgments? What else contributes to lengthy judgments?

4. Why was the Supreme Court so indulgent to HACL? On 4 November 1997,[45] the Supreme Court considered applications filed by respondents 4 to 8 requesting a fresh assessment of the remedial measures required. By this time, the MoEF had quantified the cost of remedial measures at Rs. 37.385 crores based on a report prepared by NEERI.[46] Before fixing this assessment, the MoEF sought the views of the polluters who furnished their expert reports. The industries' experts did not furnish any cost estimates. The Supreme Court rejected industries' application holding 'remedial measures taken on the basis of the NEERI report *shall be treated as final*'. On 18 July 2002, the Supreme Court rejected a curative petition filed by HACL.[47] Was the elaborate and tedious judicial exercise undertaken in 2011 a waste of judicial resources? Should not the judges have summarily dismissed the new applications at the first hearing?

5. Despite the Supreme Court judgment, this summary from a field report from Bichhri suggests that little had changed on the ground as a result of the court's intervention.

> On February 13, 1996, the Supreme Court, the highest seat of justice in the country ruled that five units of a particular company, producing toxic chemicals in Bichhri village in Rajasthan's Udaipur district, be shut down. In reality, the main errant units had already been closed for the last five years.... People's protests and NGO action had forced them to scoot. But not before they had completely poisoned the aquifer. Today, there is no drinking water from natural sources for either the humans or the animals of Bichhri. Agriculture has touched rock bottom. Every monsoon, rainwater rushes over the sludge, and more toxic chemicals seep into the aquifer. The water has become carcinogenic. The villagers had been waiting for the last seven years for compensation. But none is coming forth.... The Court has told them that they will have to file [actions] once again in local courts. There is confusion. There is also anger. And there seems to be no one, anywhere, to turn to. Meanwhile, the same company has shifted base and is merrily doing an encore in Vapi, Gujarat, arrogantly confident that no one can touch it.[48]

What may be done to ensure better compliance with court orders?

III. THE *RESEARCH FOUNDATION* CASE

In 1995, the Research Foundation for Science, Technology and Natural Resource Policy directly petitioned the Supreme Court under Article 32 of the Constitution. The case spanned over one and a half decades, drawing the Supreme Court into complex science and policy issues more suited to the executive and legislature. We carry an excerpt from one amongst a

[45] *Indian Council for Enviro-Legal Action v Union of India* (2011) 12 SCC 752.

[46] National Environmental Engineering Research Institute. NEERI, a research institute, occasionally assists the Supreme Court by providing reports in environmental cases.

[47] *Hindustan Agro Chemicals Ltd v Union of India* (2011) 12 SCC 751. After the Supreme Court decides a case, parties may request the court to review its decision under Article 137 of the Constitution of India. As a practical matter, review petitions are seldom entertained and are usually dismissed in chambers. In *Rupa Ashok Hurra v Ashok Hurra* (2002) 4 SCC 388, the Supreme Court created a new channel to cure a grave miscarriage of justice. 'Curative petitions' are entertained by the Supreme Court in extremely rare cases where the review is rejected.

[48] Anju Sharma & Rajat Banerji, *The Blind Court* in DOWN TO EARTH (last updated 7 June 2015), https://www.downtoearth.org.in/coverage/the-blind-court-25812, accessed on 23 June 2021.

series of judgments tracking the enormous effort by successive benches of the Supreme Court to prevent toxic waste dumping in India.[49]

RESEARCH FOUNDATION FOR SCIENCE TECHNOLOGY AND NATURAL RESOURCE POLICY v UNION OF INDIA
(2012) 7 SCC 769

ALTAMAS KABIR, J: This writ petition has been filed by the Research Foundation for Science, Technology and Natural Resource Policy, through its Director Ms Vandana Shiva, for the following reliefs:

(1) direct the Union of India banning all imports of all hazardous/toxic wastes;
(2) direct amendment of the Rules in conformity with the Basel Convention and Articles 21, 47 and 48-A of the Constitution as interpreted by this Court;
(3) declare that without adequate protection to the workers and public and without any provision of sound environment management of disposal of hazardous/toxic wastes, the Hazardous Wastes (Management and Handling) Rules, 1989 are violative of the fundamental rights and, therefore, unconstitutional;

On 29-10-1995, this Court directed notice to issue on the writ petition and also on the application for stay.

The basic grievance of the writ petitioner was with regard to the import of toxic wastes from industrialised countries to India, despite such wastes being hazardous to the environment and life of the people of this country. The writ petitioner sought to challenge the decision of the Ministry of Environment and Forests permitting import of toxic wastes in India under the cover of recycling, which, according to the petitioner, made India a dumping ground for toxic wastes. It was alleged that these decisions were contrary to the provisions of Articles 14 and 21 of the Constitution and also Article 47, which enjoins a duty on the State to raise the standards of living and to improve public health. [The court also quoted Article 48A.]

In the writ petition, Ms Vandana Shiva, the Director of the petitioner Foundation, who is a well-known environmentalist and journalist, while highlighting some of the tragedies which had occurred on account of either dumping or release of hazardous and toxic wastes into the atmosphere, such as the tragedy which took place in the Union Carbide Factory at Bhopal in 1984, referred to the Basel Convention on the Control of Transboundary Movements of Hazardous Wastes and their Disposal. It was submitted that an international awareness had been created under the Basel Convention against the movement of hazardous wastes and their disposal in respect whereof the United Nations Environment Programme (UNEP) had convened a Conference on the Global Convention on the Control of Transboundary Movements of Hazardous Wastes pursuant to the decision adopted by the Governing Council of UNEP on 17-6-1987. The said Conference met at the European World Trade and Convention Centre, Basel, from 20-3-1989 to 22-3-1989. India also participated in the Conference. On the basis of the deliberations of the Committee, the Basel Convention on the Control of Transboundary Movements of Hazardous Wastes and their Disposal was adopted on 22-3-1989.

It was the grievance of the writ petitioner that since India became a signatory to the Basel Convention on 22-9-1992, it should have amended the definition of 'hazardous wastes', as provided in Article 3 read with Articles 4.1 and 13 of the said Convention. It was the further grievance of the writ petitioner that India should have enacted laws in regard to the transboundary movement procedures with regard to hazardous wastes. [The judgment sets out Article 4 and refers to Article 6 of the Basel Convention.]

[49] Several substantive interim orders were passed in this case, amongst them: (2005) 13 SCC 655 dated 5 May 1997; (1999) 1 SCC 223 dated 13 October 1997; (2000) 9 SCC 41 dated 10 December 1999; (2005) 13 SCC 657(2) dated 14 September 2001; (2005) 13 SCC 658 dated 3 December 2001; (2005) 13 SCC 659 dated 4 February 2002; (2005) 13 SCC 661 dated 24 September 2003; (2005) 10 SCC 510 dated 14 October 2003; (2005) 13 SCC 186 dated 5 January 2005; (2005) 13 SCC 671 dated 9 May 2005.

In the writ petition various instances were provided of the type of toxic wastes imported into the country under the garb of recycling. The writ petitioner has also drawn the attention of the Court to the provisions of the Hazardous Wastes (Management and Handling) Rules, 1989 (hereinafter referred as 'the HWMH Rules, 1989'), and complained of the fact that the same had not been implemented both by the Central Government and the State Governments and Union Territories and their respective Pollution Control Boards.

Based on the said allegations, this Court initially asked all the State Governments and Union Territories and their respective Pollution Control Boards to submit affidavits as to how far the provisions of the aforesaid Rules had been implemented. The Central Government was asked to file a comprehensive affidavit in respect thereof. From the affidavits filed, this Court appears to have come to the conclusion that the States and their respective authorities did not seem to appreciate the gravity of the matter and the need for taking prompt measures to prevent the adverse consequences of such neglect.

In the said background, this Court by its order dated 13-10-1997 [(1999) 1 SCC 223], appointed a High-Powered Committee, with Prof M G K Menon as its Chairman, and referred 14 issues to the Committee on which it was required to give its report and recommendations. Since the said 14 terms of reference are of great relevance in the matter of disposal of the writ petition, the same are reproduced hereinbelow:

'(1) Whether and to what extent the hazardous wastes listed in the Basel Convention have been banned by the Government and to examine which other hazardous wastes, other than listed in the Basel Convention and the Hazardous Wastes (Management and Handling) Rules, 1989, require banning.

(2) To verify the present status of the units handling hazardous wastes imported for recycling or generating/recycling indigenous hazardous wastes on the basis of information provided by the respective States/UTs and determine the status of implementation of the Hazardous Wastes (Management and Handling) Rules, 1989 by the various States/UTs and in the light of the directions issued by the Hon'ble Supreme Court.

(3) What safeguards have been put in place to ensure that banned toxic/hazardous wastes are not allowed to be imported?

(4) What are the changes required in the existing laws to regulate the functioning of units handling hazardous wastes and for protecting the people (including workers in the factory) from environmental hazards?

(5) To assess the adequacy of the existing facilities for disposal of hazardous wastes in an environmentally sound manner and to make recommendations about the most suitable manner for disposal of hazardous wastes.

(6) What is further required to be done to effectively prohibit, monitor and regulate the functioning of units handling hazardous wastes keeping in view the existing body of laws?

(7) To make recommendations as to what should be the prerequisites for issuance of authorisation/permission under Rule 5 and Rule 11 of the Hazardous Wastes (Management and Handling) Rules, 1989.

(8) To identify the criteria for designation of areas for locating units handling hazardous wastes and waste disposal sites.

(9) To determine as to whether the authorisations/permissions given by the State Boards for handling hazardous wastes are in accordance with Rule 5(4) and Rule 11 of the Hazardous Wastes (Management and Handling) Rules, 1989 and whether the decision of the State Pollution Control Boards is based on any prescribed procedure of checklist.

(10) To recommend a mechanism for publication of inventory at regular intervals giving area wise information about the level and nature of hazardous wastes.

(11) What should be the framework for reducing risks to environment and public health by stronger regulation and by promoting production methods and products which are ecologically friendly and thus reduce the production of toxics?

(12) To consider any other related area as the Committee may deem fit.
(13) To examine the quantum and nature of hazardous waste stock lying at the docks/ports/ICDs and recommend a mechanism for its safe disposal or re-export to the original exporters.
(14) Decontamination of ships before they are exported to India for breaking.'

Each one of the said terms of reference are of special significance as far as the reliefs prayed for in the writ petition are concerned. The said High-Powered Committee, comprised of experts from different fields, submitted its report after making a thorough examination of all matters relating to hazardous wastes.

[The judgment records the shift in the court's priorities as the case developed. The deliberations of the committee were initially in respect of identifying different toxic materials and then shifted to imported waste oil lying in ports as well as ship-breaking. Another issue concerned disappearance of hazardous waste from ports and container depots. Detailed orders were passed for the disposal of imported hazardous substances. A Monitoring committee was appointed to oversee the disposal process. The court referred to the MARPOL Convention[50] which was designed to preserve the marine environment by eliminating the dumping of oil in the sea. The court turned to the disposal of sludge oil.]

However, during the course of hearing in regard to the import of waste oil purportedly in violation of the HWMH Rules, 1989, the two dominating principles relating to pollution, namely, the polluter pays principle and the precautionary principle, were examined at length. The report of the Committee indicated that the hazardous waste oil was imported into the country in the garb of furnace oil and, in fact, the containers and the vessels in which they were being transported, were also highly polluted, causing a tremendous risk to the environment and to human existence. Ultimately, by the said order of 14-10-2003 [(2005) 10 SCC 510], certain directions were given regarding the procedure to be adopted, with regard to ship-breaking, to the Central Pollution Control Board, to prepare a national inventory for rehabilitation of hazardous waste dump sites. The State Pollution Control Boards were directed to ensure that all parties dealing in hazardous chemicals which generated hazardous wastes, displayed online data in that regard outside their respective factories, on the pattern of Andhra Pradesh. The Ministry of Environment and Forests was also directed to consider making provision for bank guarantees. Certain recommendations were also made with regard to legislation in order to destroy any transboundary movement of hazardous wastes or other wastes and to punish such illegal trafficking stringently.

[The court set out how 133 containers of 'lubricating oil' lying at Nhava Sheva port after laboratory tests were found to be hazardous waste. This waste was ordered to be destroyed by incineration at the cost of the importers.]

Since the proceedings became a continuing mandamus, this Court from time to time took up several issues emanating from the first prayer in the writ petition to ban imports of all hazardous/toxic wastes. However, in the process, one of the Conventions, namely, the impact of the MARPOL Convention, though referred to, was not decided and left for decision at the final hearing. Accordingly, that aspect of the matter has to be decided also in these proceedings.

[The court summarized the evolution and framework of the MARPOL Convention.]

India is a signatory, both to the Basel Convention as also the MARPOL Convention, and is, therefore, under an obligation to ensure that the same are duly implemented in relation to import of hazardous wastes into the country. As we have noticed earlier, the Basel Convention prohibited the import of certain hazardous substances on which there was a total ban. However, some of the other pollutants, which have been identified, are yet to be notified and, on the other hand, in order to prevent pollution of the seas, under the MARPOL

50 MARPOL is an acronym for 'Marine Pollution'. The Convention was signed on 17 February 1973 and subsequently, in combination with the 1978 Protocol, the Convention was brought into force on 2 October 1983.

Convention the signatory countries are under an obligation to accept the discharge of oil wastes from ships. What is, therefore, important is for the authorities concerned to ensure that such waste oil is not allowed to contaminate the surrounding areas and also, if suitable, for the purposes of recycling, to allow recycling of the same under strict supervision with entrusted units and, thereafter, to oversee its distribution for reuse.

As far as the first two prayers in the writ petition are concerned, the same have already been taken care of by the orders dated 13-10-1997 [(1999) 1 SCC 223 and 14-10-2003 [(2005) 10 SCC 510]. By the first of the two orders, this Court appointed the High-Powered Committee with Prof M G K Menon as its Chairman and 14 issues were referred to the said Committee. After the said Committee submitted its report, another Committee under the Chairmanship of Mr A C Wadhawan was appointed to enquire into the disappearance of hazardous wastes from various ports and container depots, and the question relating to the working conditions of the workmen who handle such wastes. After the Wadhawan Committee submitted its report, various directions were given with regard to the handling of such hazardous wastes. Furthermore, the contamination risks involved in ship-breaking also came into focus in the light of the provisions of the Hazardous Wastes (Management and Handling) Rules, 1989, and directions were given as to how ships, which were carrying wastes, were to be dealt with before entering into Indian waters, which included the prohibition on the exporting country to export such oil or substance without the concurrence and clearance from the importing country.

* * *

The directions contained in the second order are based on the polluter pays principle, which is duly recognised as one of the accepted principles for dealing with violation of the Basel Convention and the HWMH Rules, 1989, and the same will be applicable whenever such violations occur. However, till such time as a particular product is identified as being hazardous, no ban can be imposed on its import on the ground that it was hazardous. Such import will, however, be subject to all other statutory conditions and restrictions, as may be prevailing on the date of import. Accordingly, the general prayer made in the writ petition that the Government of India should put a total ban on all hazardous wastes, can be applied in respect of such hazardous wastes as have been identified by the Basel Convention and its Protocols over the years and/or where import into the country has been restricted by the municipal laws of India. In respect of such banned items, directions have already been given in the order dated 13-10-1997 to issue a notification to ban the import of such identified hazardous substances. In the event any other items have since been identified, the Central Government is directed to issue appropriate notifications for banning the import of such hazardous substances as well.

The third prayer, that in the event of non-compliance, the provisions of the Hazardous Wastes (Management and Handling) Rules, 1989, should be declared as unconstitutional, cannot be granted, since the same are in aid and not in derogation of the provisions of Articles 21, 39(e), 47 and 48-A of the Constitution. In fact, as mentioned hereinabove, even at the interim stage, directions were given for compliance with the said Rules, particularly in the matter of destruction of the waste oil contained in 170 containers by incineration at the cost of the importer.

The writ petition has been entertained and has also been treated by all concerned not as any kind of adversarial litigation, but litigation to protect the environment from contamination on account of attempts made to dump hazardous wastes in the country, which would ultimately result in the destruction, not only of the environment, but also the ecology as well and, in particular, the fragile marine biodiversity along the Indian coastline. The petitioner Foundation has played a very significant role in bringing into focus some very serious questions involving the introduction of hazardous substances into the country, which needed the Court's attention to be drawn having regard to the Basel Convention, aimed at protecting marine biology and countries having coastlines alongside seas and oceans.

The writ petition is, therefore, disposed of by reasserting the interim directions given with regard to the handling of hazardous wastes and ship-breaking in the various orders passed in the writ petition from time to time and, in particular, the orders dated 13-10-1997 [(1999) 1 SCC 223] and 14-10-2003 [(2005) 10 SCC 510]. The Central Government is also directed to ban import of all hazardous/toxic wastes which had been identified and declared to be so under the Basel Convention and its different protocols. The Central Government is also directed to bring the Hazardous Wastes (Management and Handling) Rules, 1989, in line with the Basel Convention and Articles 21, 47 and 48-A of the Constitution. The further declaration sought for that without adequate protection to the workers and public, the aforesaid Rules are violative of the fundamental rights of the citizens and are, therefore, unconstitutional, is, however, rejected in view of what has been discussed hereinabove.

In the peculiar facts of the case, there will be no order as to costs.

NOTES AND QUESTIONS

1. Re-examine the relief sought. Could a court grant the second and third prayers? Should the petition have been dismissed at the threshold for misdirected relief? How would you re-cast the prayers?

Unlike a traditional suit where the relief sought must be clearly indicated, the rules of pleadings in a PIL are flexible. In a PIL, where the main issue merits consideration, the judge will overlook technical objections with respect to the wording of relief. Often the nature of the relief itself alters as the case progresses and new challenges vie for judicial attention.

2. The Supreme Court monitored the case for over 16 years. How long should a continuing mandamus continue?

3. Had the Supreme Court not engaged in this massive administrative and supervisory exercise, what might have happened? Is there no alternative to judicial policing of India's ports and other entry points? How might a less judge-dependent society respond to the challenge? What factors may have persuaded the petitioner to adopt judicial recourse in preference to lobbying the MoEF? Had Research Foundation known in 1995 that its case would have lingered till 2012, might it have preferred an alternative avenue to prevent the dumping of toxic substances?

4. Early in this case, the court required affidavits from the states and PCBs to gauge the administrative capacity of the executive to deal with the issues. The agencies lacked even basic knowledge with regard to the total quantity of hazardous waste generated in the country.[51] The court found that the HWMH Rules remained only on paper and were not being implemented. The MoEF had failed to make a 'concerted or consistent effort' to build local regulatory capacities. 'There seems to be a uniform lack of concern at all levels in the Government about the serious implications of the import, generation, build up, transport and disposal of hazardous waste in the country.'[52] Recognizing the magnitude of the problem, the potential impact on human life and the administrative shortcoming, the court moved in to fill the gap.

The enormous effort put in by the Supreme Court to curb the dumping of toxic wastes, follows on similar efforts to clean the River Ganga and to protect national forests. Having regard to the endemic sub-competence of the PCBs to deal with pollution issues over a period of four decades, is it time Parliament recognized the obvious and disbanded the PCBs? Do we

---

[51] *Research Foundation for Science Technology and Natural Resource Policy v Union of India* (2005) 10 SCC 510.

[52] *Id.* at 524.

require a stronger national environment protection agency to replace the state PCBs? What counter-currents might oppose a new administrative architecture?

Throughout the duration of this case, the respondent government agencies meekly abided by judicial orders and, indeed, appear to have welcomed them. At no stage did any of the agencies press the court to withdraw its oversight by claiming enhanced capacities. Does this suggest that the judicial intervention is infantilizing the bureaucracy? What is better from the perspective of citizen welfare and governance—judicial non-interference leaving matters to the political process or agencies that remain stultified because judges do the job? Is there a better way for courts addressing PILs to strengthen the long-term competence of the PCBs?

5. The lack of coordination amongst government departments extended to a mismatch between the HWMH Rules and the Customs Act. The Supreme Court required the Central Government to issue a suitable prohibition in terms of Section 11 of the Customs Act of 1962, aligning the law followed by customs officers with the 29 items banned for import under Schedule 8 of the HWMH Rules.[53]

6. In a previous judgment in the same case, the Supreme Court (a) ordered state PCBs to implement MoEF directions; (b) directed PCBs to report on hazardous waste dump sites in their jurisdiction along with rehabilitation plans; (c) framed special guidelines to regulate the ship-breaking industry; and (d) prescribed a time-bound programme comprising 29 action points for the MoEF, Central and state PCBs.[54]

The Supreme Court drew heavily on the recommendations of the HPC while framing its order and also constituted a Monitoring committee to ensure implementation of its directions. The Monitoring committee was asked to submit quarterly reports to the court.

7. Alang in Gujarat is a preferred destination for ships condemned to the scrapyard. In 2007, when considering the grant of permission for dismantling the ship 'Blue Lady', the Supreme Court noticed that ship-breaking activity over the last decade had provided 23 million tonnes of steel.[55] Ship-breaking is a messy business not least because embedded in the vessel may be large quantities of hazardous substances such as asbestos as well as radioactive contaminants in the case of nuclear-powered ships. These toxic substances pose a grave risk to workers at Alang and to society at large along the trail the hazardous waste moves from the ship till its secure disposal.

8. The French Navy's decommissioned aircraft carrier Clemenceau sailed into a storm of protest when it arrived in Indian waters. The Supreme Court initially restrained entry into Alang but the controversy dissipated when the vessel sailed away. Nevertheless, since the problem of ship dismantling was a recurring one, the Supreme Court directed the Union Government to constitute a technical committee of experts to recommend a framework and remedial measures to upgrade the Alang infrastructure. The Expert Committee consulted various stakeholders including representatives of workers and ship-breakers and prepared a comprehensive report. Quoting from the report with respect to the recommended procedure for the grant of statutory clearances as well as for anchoring, beaching and breaking vessels, the Supreme Court issued the following directions:

[53] *Research Foundation for Science Technology and Natural Resource Policy v Union of India* (2005) 13 SCC 661.

[54] *Research Foundation for Science Technology and Natural Resource Policy v Union of India* (2005) 10 SCC 510, 536–42.

[55] *Research Foundation for Science Technology and Natural Resource Policy v Union of India* 2007 (11) SCALE 75 (11 September 2007).

> It is desirable that the Government of India shall formulate a comprehensive Code incorporating the recommendations and the same has to be operative until the concerned Statutes are amended to be in line with the recommendations. Until the Code comes into play, the recommendations shall be operative by virtue of this order.[56]

The Supreme Court directed the Gujarat Maritime Board, the Gujarat State Pollution Control Board, the National Institute of Occupational Health and the Atomic Energy Regulatory Board to oversee implementation.

The following week, the court permitted the Blue Lady to be dismantled consistent with the recommendation of the technical Expert Committee. The court emphasized the notion of 'balance' between economic development and environmental protection:

> India after globalization is an emergent economy along with Brazil, Russia and China. India has economic growth of above 9%. However, that growth is lop-sided. A large section of the population lives below poverty line. India has largest number of youth in the world. Unemployment is endemic. Article 21/14 is the heart of the Chapter of fundamental rights. Equality of opportunity is the basic theme of Article 14. In an emergent economy, the principle of proportionality based on the concept of balance is important. It provides level playing field to different stakeholders. Ship breaking is an industry. When we apply the principle of sustainable development, we need to keep in mind the concept of development on one hand and the concepts like generation of revenue, employment and public interest on the other hand. This is where the principle of proportionality comes in. Even in the case of Blue Lady, the figures indicate that 700 workers would be employed in ship breaking. Further, 41000 MT of steel would be made available. To that extent, there will be less pressure on mining activity elsewhere.... Today ship-breaking provides resources not only in terms of steel but also in terms of employment, skill and capability. Competition exists in the said business of ship-breaking amongst Bangladesh, Pakistan and India. In our view, if 'capability' is a resource with our skilled workers it needs to be protected by strict implementation of Health Hazard Preventive Measures suggested in the report of TEC [Technical Expert Committee] and implementation of Recycling Plans, generation of pollutants like asbestos to the extent of 20% can be almost eliminated. As stated, 85% of asbestos is ... in panels which is reusable. Therefore, the report provides State-of-the-Art mechanism which is the key element of 'sustainable development'.[57]

9. In 2012, Alang received and dismantled the Exxon Valdez,[58] a notorious oil tanker that ran aground in 1989 spilling thousands of barrels of crude oil along the Alaskan coast. The owner of the tanker, Best Oasis Ltd, navigated the gauntlet of a Supreme Court application and scrutiny by each of the overseeing agencies before being allowed to beach the vessel.[59]

D. PESTICIDE AND RADIATION CASES

I. PESTICIDE CASES

Several cases have arisen involving the manufacture and use of pesticides, but most have involved issues of procedure rather than substance, and are not reproduced here. In *Dr Ashok*

[56] *Research Foundation for Science Technology and Natural Resource Policy v Union of India* (2007) 10 Scale 594 (6 September 2007).

[57] *Research Foundation for Science Technology and Natural Resource Policy v Union of India* 2007 (11) Scale 75 (11 September 2007).

[58] The Exxon Valdez was rechristened Oriental Nicety.

[59] *Research Foundation for Science Technology and Natural Resource Policy v Union of India* (2012) 7 SCC 764.

v Union of India,[60] the Supreme Court treated a letter addressed to the Chief Justice of India as a public interest petition. Dr Ashok complained that several widely used insecticides, colour additives and food additives ought to be banned since they were carcinogenic. Most of the 40 chemicals complained of were banned in the USA. The Union Government filed a detailed affidavit explaining the measures it had taken to prohibit these chemicals or restrict their use. In the judgment, the court acknowledged that broad spectrum pesticides upset the eco-system and possibly caused cancer. The court was satisfied with the measures taken by the government in respect of the impugned items, but directed an inter-ministerial committee to review the cases of other chemicals and recommend additional measures in the future.

The campaign to ban endosulfan was long and arduous, involving a range of strategies employed by activists and victims as well as aggressive responses by industry. India was a big producer and consumer of endosulfan. Private and government enterprises lobbied hard to preserve their market share and profits. Although there is no definitive judgment in the endosulfan case, a crucial interim order by the Supreme Court on 13 May 2011 tipped the scale against industry.[61] The following article traces the journey to the judicial embargo.

D DILEEP KUMAR & C JAYAKUMAR; FROM PRECAUTIONARY PRINCIPLE TO NATIONWIDE BAN ON ENDOSULFAN IN INDIA 4 Business and Human Rights Journal 343 (2019)

Endosulfan, a highly hazardous organochlorine pesticide became a topic of burning discussion on the Indian subcontinent during the 1990s after stories of individuals and communities suffering from a vast array of hitherto unknown health impacts were widely reported from Kasaragod, the northernmost district of Kerala. The main actor responsible for spraying of endosulfan was the Plantation Corporation of Kerala (PCK), owned by the Kerala Government. PCK had been spraying endosulfan aerially to control tea mosquito bugs in its 4,696 hectares of cashew plantations spread across 11 villages in Kasaragod without ensuring adequate safety precautions, until a lower court stopped it in 2001. From the late 1970s to 2001, PCK sprayed endosulfan two to three times a year without any investigation into its impacts....

Multiple ... studies and assessments indicated that endosulfan was the probable causal factor for the peculiar and complex health implications noted among the community in Kasaragod, such as congenital anomalies, physical deformities, neurological disorders, impaired mental health, disorders related to hormonal irregularities, defective reproductive health, developmental health disorders, different types of cancers and respiratory and immune systems disorders.

After long-pending demands from the community, the government initiated a process to identify victims of endosulfan poisoning. As per a 2017 government record, 6,212 victims enlisted in this process, although unofficial records suggest that more than twice this number suffered harmful effects from endosulfan exposure. Fact-finding teams and studies could not find any other factors that could possibly cause similar health problems, such as exposure to other environmental or industrial contaminants. A committee appointed by the Kerala Government in 2001 concluded that 'the undulating nature of land, presence of large number of water bodies and human inhabitation in and near the plantations make the area unsuitable for aerial spraying of pesticides.' ...

Neither existing government institutions nor the Insecticides Act of 1968, which was adopted to 'regulate pesticides with a view to prevent risk to human beings or animals', did anything to protect the community in Kasaragod from being poisoned. A government committee known as the Dr Banerjee Committee, which was constituted in 1981 to review the

60 AIR 1997 SC 2298.

61 *Democratic Youth Federation of India v Union of India* (2011) 15 SCC 530.

use of certain pesticides, looked into the matter and, in 1991, permitted the continued use of endosulfan with the recommendation that 'the Registration Committee should not allow the use of endosulfan near rivers, lakes, ponds and sea, which are expected to be polluted.' Yet, PCK kept spraying endosulfan near bodies of water and their catchment areas in Kasaragod. In 1999, another government committee found that the recommendations for restrictions on endosulfan issued by the Dr Banerjee Committee had never been implemented....

Although villagers and local journalists complained about illnesses and the impact of endosulfan in the region during 1979–1980, an organized protest was only initiated in the 1990s. In 1984, two panchayats passed resolutions banning the aerial spraying of endosulfan, but PCK and government agencies failed to take measures to control or stop the use of this toxic chemical. In the late 1990s, isolated villager protests started against the spraying of endosulfan. Only then did local arts and sports clubs as well as village libraries and community organizations start to realize the severity of the issue and began taking it seriously.

Many local environmental groups ... got involved in and supported the struggle of villagers. The Pesticide Action Network Asia Pacific, CSE and Thanal also supported the struggle by providing technical and scientific information and assessments establishing the link between endosulfan and health issues. The Endosulfan Spray Protest Action Committee led by local doctors, farmers, teachers and journalists was formed in 2000. Following this, the Ban Endosulfan District Coordination Action Committee and Endosulfan Virudha Samithi were also formed, and joined forces to demand a ban on the pesticide. Despite the presence of these strong movements, the government did not react and the company continued its business under the cover of law. That was when litigation strategies started in earnest.

The very first legal intervention was initiated in 1998 with a petition filed by Leelakumari, a mother of two children who were suffering various health effects linked to endosulfan exposure. This petition was filed in the Munsif Court of Hosdurg (a lower court) demanding legal intervention to stop endosulfan spraying on the basis of Article 21 of the Indian Constitution (Right to Life and Personal Liberty). Leelakumari decided to approach the court after her appeals for intervention to the district authority for the Agriculture Department and the Kerala State Pollution Control Board (KSPCB) failed.

After hearing the matter, the lower court issued an order to temporarily stop the aerial spraying of endosulfan in Periya Panchayat in 1999. The court also restricted PCK from using other methods that might cause harm to private properties. PCK appealed to the High Court of Kerala, which sent the case back to the Munsif Court, asking it to re-hear the case and reach a decision. The Munsif Court passed final orders in 2001, upholding the right to life and property and restricting PCK from using endosulfan. Both in response to the legal battle and public demand, the District Collector of the area formally banned the aerial spraying of endosulfan in 2001.

Following the endosulfan ban in PCK plantations in Kasaragod, further campaigns and legal actions were launched to achieve a statewide ban in Kerala. Responding to public demand, the Kerala Government suspended use of endosulfan in 2001. This move is considered to be the first response by a State Government in the country to protect public health from exposure to a pesticide. It was also the first instance of state-level action on pesticide regulation in India. Accordingly, the Pesticide Manufacturers and Formulators Association of India (PMFAI) immediately challenged it.

In response to the challenge by PMFAI, the Thiruvamkulam Nature Lovers Movement decided once again to use the law to achieve its objectives. It filed a Public Interest Litigation case in the High Court of Kerala, demanding a state-level ban on endosulfan. The High Court directed the government to issue a decision based on certain provisions of section 27 of the Insecticides Act, which pertains to the prohibition of selling insecticides for reasons of public safety. Following this, the Kerala Government issued an order that continued the prohibition of aerial spraying of endosulfan in the state. Although the prohibition was challenged again by PMFAI, the High Court decided to impose a temporary statewide ban on endosulfan use as a precautionary measure....

In 2006, for the first time, the State Government acknowledged the suffering of endosulfan victims and offered them nominal compensation. Most, however, considered it far from adequate. Therefore, the same year, the Kerala Government decided to go ahead with a Bhopal-model litigation to demand compensation for the victims. In November 2011, the Kerala Government announced a comprehensive package for relief and rehabilitation for the victims and sought about US$15.35 million in assistance from the Union Government of India. . . .

Following a writ petition filed by the Democratic Youth Federation of India on 25 April 2011, the Supreme Court of India passed an interim order on 13 May 2011 to ban the use, sale, production and export of endosulfan throughout the country. The judgment specifically mentioned that the order to ban the pesticide was passed in consideration of various prior judgements under Article 21 of the Constitution of India (Right to Life and Personal Liberty) and particularly with the precautionary principle in mind. In another remarkable development, five and a half years after the ban order, the Supreme Court issued another order on 10 January 2017, directing the State Governments to release the entire payment of compensation, amounting to half a million Indian rupees for each of the affected persons, within three months from the date on which the order was issued. . . .

Although the endosulfan mass poisoning happened in extremely rural areas of the Kasaragod district in Kerala in peninsular India, the protest triggered locally in response to it paved the way for taking the issue to both the state and national levels. Eventually, it even reached international forums like the Persistent Organic Pollutants (POPs) Review Committee of the Stockholm Convention and led to the launch of a successful campaign for a global ban and phase-out of endosulfan in 2011, the same year that the Supreme Court of India ordered a national ban on the deadly chemical. . . .

Demanding that compensation be disbursed to all victims yet to receive it, inclusion of newly identified victims to the official list, and demanding that any new victims discovered in the future also be added to the list, the victims group is organizing struggles and protests before the State government. Thus, the endosulfan issue is far from being fully settled. Victims still have to stage hunger strikes and protests to achieve comprehensive inclusion of all victims on the list of those eligible for compensation, as well as for the compensation's disbursement. Although challenging, the technical complexity of identifying victims must be resolved to make the list inclusive, with all those harmed by endosulfan to be compensated. In addition, efforts to prosecute the actors responsible for the endosulfan mass poisoning must be initiated to enforce their liability and accountability for such serious crimes.

NOTES AND QUESTIONS

1. 'Highly disturb[ed]' by the photographs in a report published by the government of Kerala, the Supreme Court expressed its concern about the health hazards posed by endosulfan. Noting that the right to life 'is the most fundamental of all human rights, and any decision affecting human life or which may put an individual's life at risk, must call for the most anxious scrutiny',[62] the court appointed a committee. The remit of the committee was to conduct a scientific study on whether the use of endosulfan was hazardous to human health and the environment. The committee was required to make an interim report in eight weeks that would suggest alternatives to endosulfan. Most important, the 13 May 2011 order directed:

[62] *Id.* at 531.

> Till the report is submitted, keeping in mind the various judgments of this Court under Article 21 of the Constitution of India, particularly keeping in mind the precautionary principle, we hereby pass an ad interim order to immediately ban the production, use and sale of Endosulfan all over India and we further direct the statutory authorities to seize the permit given to the manufacturers of Endosulfan till further orders.[63]

On 30 September 2011, the Supreme Court referred to the interim report of the committee and allowed manufacturers to fulfil their contractual obligations by exporting existing stocks of endosulfan.[64]

2. On 9 October 2012, the court found that the committee had not furnished specific answers to the questions posed. The court expanded the composition of the committee and framed a further set of questions to be reported on within six weeks.[65] On 12 December 2012, the court fixed the calendar for receiving responses to the report of the committee and listed the case in January 2013 for disposal.[66] The case remained dormant for several years until 26 February 2016,[67] after which it again disappeared from the active business of the court until it was disposed of on 10 January 2017:

> Having heard learned counsel for the rival parties, we are of the view, that the remaining aspects, which emerge out of the controversy raised in the instant petition, can be disposed of by directing the respondents—State Governments, to release the entire undisbursed payment of compensation, quantified as Rs. 5 lakhs each, to all the affected persons, within three months from today.
>
> Needless to mention, that it shall be open to the State Governments to recover the aforestated compensation either from the concerned industry or from the Government of India, in case it is open to the State Governments to make such recovery, in consonance with law.
>
> We also hereby direct the State Governments, to take into consideration the feasibility of providing medical facilities/treatment for life-long health issues, arising out of the effects of endosulfan, keeping in mind, that there seems to be a large number of such affected persons.[68]

Although the court does not examine the expert report, implicit in the final directions is a recognition of the harmful impacts of endosulfan.

3. What became of the interim direction? Technically, the interim embargo imposed on 13 May 2011 merged in the final order of the Supreme Court and ceased to exist. However, by 2014 the government of India had changed its policy and had decided to phase out endosulfan by 2017.

4. Nearly a decade before the Supreme Court's interim order, a division bench of the Kerala High Court on 8 December 2002 imposed a temporary ban on the use of endosulfan within the state. The High Court justified its injunction as a necessary precautionary measure pending a decision by the Central Government.[69]

5. Industry employed hardball tactics to fend off the campaign. This included legal notices to the Centre for Science and Environment (CSE), defamation actions against CSE and its

---

63 *Id.*
64 *Democratic Youth Federation of India v Union of India* (2011) 15 SCC 528.
65 *Democratic Youth Federation of India v Union of India* (2014) 14 SCC 549.
66 *Democratic Youth Federation of India v Union of India* MANU/SCOR/73664/2012.
67 *Democratic Youth Federation of India v Union of India* MANU/SCOR/36195/2016.
68 *Democratic Youth Federation of India v Union of India* (2017) SCC Online SC 1901.
69 *Thiruvamkulam Nature Lovers Movement v Plantation Corporation of Kerala* OP No. 20716/2002.

Director General, Sunita Narain, the picketing of the offices of campaign groups and the harassment of scientists aligned to the campaign.[70]

II. RADIATION CASES

Exposure to radioactive substances can occur in a variety of ways, most commonly through leaks from nuclear power plants, mining of radioactive compounds such as uranium and improper disposal or transportation of radioactive wastes. India is plagued by all these threats.

In 1996, a series of newspaper reports and editorials criticizing the safety record of the atomic energy programme appeared in the Indian press. The articles referred to a report prepared by the Atomic Energy Regulatory Board (AERB) listing about 130 safety violations and defects in various nuclear power plants in India and the statements of Dr A Gopalkrishnan, former chair of AERB, expressing his concern at safety features in the nuclear establishment. The People's Union for Civil Liberties petitioned the Bombay High Court demanding disclosure of the AERB Report and also seeking appropriate directions against the respondents to rectify each of the defects. The petitioners asked for an expert body to investigate whether there were any incidents of negligence in respect of the nuclear installations. The respondents resisted disclosure, citing the secrecy provisions under the Atomic Energy Act of 1962. A division bench of the Bombay High Court held for the respondents. The court upheld the government's claim of privilege in respect of the report; upheld the constitutional validity of section 18 of the Atomic Energy Act which enabled the government to withhold information from the public; and found that the authorities were sufficiently alive to the safety concerns expressed by the petitioners, having themselves constituted a committee to review the regulatory framework.[71]

One widely publicized case decided by the Supreme Court involved imported Irish butter, which was alleged to have been contaminated by the radioactive fallout from the Chernobyl (USSR) nuclear disaster. Following the example of *Shriram*, the court in the *Irish Butter* case[72] appointed a three-person committee of experts to determine whether the butter was safe for human consumption. The Expert Committee concluded that the butter was indeed safe. On the basis of the committee's report, the Supreme Court rejected the petitioners' challenge and permitted distribution of the imported butter.

The Expert Committee seemed to rely heavily on the fact that India's AERB has stricter standards than most other countries for permissible radioactivity in dairy products. But no one really knows whether low levels of radioactivity are in fact harmless, and there will always be some reputable scientists advising against taking any risk. The court, its experts, the AERB and the entire scientific community must simply do the best they can within the limits of scientific uncertainty.

Those advocating the view that all exposure to low-level radioactivity should be avoided are undoubtedly frustrated by the difficulty in finding respected scientists in India with no ties to the government and, by implication, no axe to grind. Hence, the petitioner in the *Irish Butter* case had to resort to the supposedly more objective views of Nobel Laureates from abroad.

---

[70] Centre for Science and Environment, *Endosulfan Industry's Dirty War—A Chronology of Events*, https://www.cseindia.org/endosulfan-industrys-dirty-war-a-chronology-of-events– 1927, accessed 23 June 2021.

[71] *People's Union for Civil Liberties v Union of India*, Writ Petition No. 1785 of 1996, order dated 30 January 1997.

[72] *Dr Shivrao Shantaram Wagle v Union of India* AIR 1988 SC 952.

But was not the Supreme Court correct in associating these Nobel Laureates with a particular school of thought, and thus no more authoritative than the Indian scientists?

The leading case on safety at a nuclear power plant is *G Sundarrajan v Union of India*,[73] where the court held that despite the inherent danger of such plants, nuclear energy was necessary as a matter of energy security.[74]

M K Sharma v Bharat Electronics[75] involved a petition brought by a union representing employees at Bharat Electronics Ltd, a public sector company, some of whom were exposed to X-ray radiation in the course of their work. They alleged that the company's failure to adequately protect their health and safety had deprived the exposed workers of their fundamental rights and entitled them to compensation. The Supreme Court found no proof of injury and, therefore, no entitlement to compensation, but recorded the employers' assumption of responsibility to compensate workers in the event of future proof of injury resulting from present and continuing employment. This is a significant gain for the workers and their union.

The *Bharat Electronics* court evolved two important occupational health and safety policies, viz., that the workers' health status shall be periodically evaluated and publicized, and that this company—and presumably all others similarly involved in hazardous activities exposing workers to long-term health damage—must carry and pay for insurance for each exposed worker and officer.

E. THE LEGAL HISTORY AND IMPLICATIONS OF THE BHOPAL GAS TRAGEDY

I. INTRODUCTION

Bhopal, the capital city of the Indian state Madhya Pradesh, is widely known around the world for the worst industrial disaster in history. Even to this day, the exact number of people that were killed remains unclear. Approximations range from 5,200 to 25,000.[76] Over a half million people continue to live with various types of injuries as a consequence of the disaster.[77]

On closer inspection, Bhopal was not just a single disaster but in fact three disasters, the first being the toxic leak of poisonous gases; the second was the response to the leak, demonstrating the incompetence of the Indian state and the liable corporation; and the final catastrophe was the ongoing water contamination from waste jettisoned by the original factory and the chemicals that were abandoned on site.[78] Toxicological studies conducted by the Indian Council for Medical Research (ICMR) confirmed that Bhopal victims inhaled aerosols

---

73 (2013) 6 SCC 620.

74 This case is discussed in the Large Projects chapter.

75 1987 (1) SCALE 1049.

76 Neeraj Santoshi, *Bhopal Disaster: So How Many Died? 32 Years On, No One Sure*, HINDUSTAN TIMES, 3 December 2016, https://www.hindustantimes.com/bhopal/bhopal-disaster-so-how-many-died-32-years-on-no-one-sure/story-luLN0QaTxHlu05RTGNHOoI.html, accessed 24 June 2021. The disaster occurred on the night of 2 December 1984.

77 The Supreme Court records the deaths at 5,295 and the injured at 568,292 in its 11 May 2011 judgment rejecting curative petitions that sought to revive criminal proceedings. *CBI v Keshub Mahindra* (2011) 6 SCC 216, 218.

78 Tomas Mac Sheoin & Frank Pearce, *Introduction: Bhopal and After*, 41 SOCIAL JUSTICE 1 (2014). [Special Issue: *Bhopal and After: The Chemical Industry as Toxic Capitalism* (2014).]

laced with methyl isocyanate as well as hydrogen cyanide.[79] This confirms the agony faced by the victims as they slowly died.

The Indian state displayed extreme callousness while responding to the environmental degradation at the plant. Even after 36 years of the disaster there is no remediation for the contaminated soil and water at the Bhopal site.[80]

The judicial system failed to deliver justice to the victims of Bhopal. India was viewed, at the time, as a crusader intent on protecting nations against abuse by multinational corporations. But soon the hidden agendas and intentions came out.

India's imperfect response led to various important legal developments such as absolute liability, interim monetary relief and the *parens patriae* doctrine, among others.[81] However, these small victories were meaningless to the victims, who witnessed a legal system that denied them their rightful compensation and allowed the guilty American and Indian parties to walk away. It was an 'unholy alliance' of the state of Madhya Pradesh, the Union of India and the corporation Union Carbide (UCC) that sabotaged the efforts of thousands of victims to obtain compensation (which were in all respects comparable to the tortious actions in other US cases) for the wrongs they suffered. Subsequently, the accused corporation was prosecuted in India.[82]

In this section, we will chart out the various legal issues discussed by the Indian and American courts on the Bhopal gas leak disaster. Arguments for imposition of liability on the state and the corporation are discussed in detail, following which some judicial innovations by the Indian courts are also considered.

II. THE DISASTER

Operated by a company called Union Carbide of India Ltd (UCIL), the Bhopal facility was initiated in 1969. Through negotiations, it was settled that UCC would own 50.9% of UCIL and the Indian Government through its financial institutions would own approximately 20%. Originally the plant strictly manufactured pesticides containing methyl isocyanate (MIC), but from 1980 the plant also started manufacturing the raw MIC.

Methyl isocyanate is an extremely dangerous and volatile toxin which can cause blindness, spleen and liver damage, gynecological disorders, tuberculosis, emphysema and birth defects.[83] Post-mortem reports of the victims who died during the disaster discuss the cherry-red discoloration of blood and lung tissues. Early phase autopsies revealed generalized oedema and marked congestion in the respiratory tract and the brain. Medical examiners at the time reported that the lung, which was the most damaged organ, weighed over twice the normal amount in most of the victims, indicating the gruesome pain encountered during their last hour of life.[84]

---

[79] S Sriramachari, *Bhopal Gas Tragedy: Scientific Challenges and Lessons for Future*, 18 JR OF LOSS PREVENTION IN THE PROCESS INDUSTRIES 264 (2005).

[80] N D Jayaprakash, *Bhopal: A Toxic Tragedy Continues*, THE LEAFLET, 11 September 2020, https://www.theleaflet.in/bhopal-a-toxic-tragedy-continues/#, accessed 24 June 2021.

[81] Armin Rosencranz, Shyam Divan & Antony Scott, *Legal and Political Repercussions in India* in LEARNING FROM DISASTER: RISK MANAGEMENT AFTER BHOPAL 44, 62 (Ed. Sheila Jasanoff, 1994).

[82] Colin Gonsalves, *The Bhopal Catastrophe: Politics, Conspiracy and Betrayal*, 45 ECONOMIC & POLITICAL WEEKLY 68 (2010).

[83] S Sriramachari, *The Bhopal Gas Tragedy: An Environmental Disaster*, 86 CURRENT SCIENCE 905 (2004), http://indiaenvironmentportal.org.in/files/The%20Bhopal%20gas%20tragedy.pdf, accessed 24 June 2021. Also see generally, Jamie Cassels, *The Uncertain Promise of Law: Lessons from Bhopal*, 29 OSGOODE HALL LAW JR 1, 4 (1991).

[84] S Sriramachari, *id.*

On the night of 2 December 1984, there was a chemical reaction which burst open the MIC storage facility and discharged about 50 tons of the toxic gas all across the city of Bhopal. The immediate cause of the catastrophe was linked to the seepage of water into the MIC tank. Union Carbide vehemently proposed theories for the disaster, ranging from it being a direct result of sabotage by extremists to a single discontented saboteur. The company argued that an accidental introduction of water into the tank was impossible owing to its design. However, another theory which came to be more widely accepted was that the disaster was a result of a human and accidental failure to maintain a system of valves which controlled the flushing operations. This ultimately resulted in an overflow of water into the MIC storage tank.[85]

There were several warning signs leading up to the disaster, with a local journalist even warning of a possible catastrophe almost two years prior to the disaster.[86] There were other minor leaks which had injured and killed various workers earlier.[87] The Bhopal plant had been operating at a loss for years, resulting in the departure of skilled employees. This led to poor management of the plant and few safety measures. For over a decade till the disaster, process wastes, by-products, sub-standard products, and polluted water were disposed of by the company at dump sites, both outside and inside the plant. Even now, tonnes of waste continue to be stored in a shed at the site.[88]

Moreover, the plant was located close to a very densely populated area whose populace had no idea about the potential dangers of the hazardous chemicals nearby. The medical and legal fallout was also impossible to deal with, as India's health and safety regulations were still in their nascent stages. The plant was orphaned by the original corporation and in effect unregulated by Indian law. Therefore, the Bhopal gas leak was not a result of unexpected events but a series of predictable failures.[89]

III. ENVIRONMENTAL DEGRADATION AND GENETIC DAMAGE

Union Carbide of India mainly produced three pesticides at the Bhopal plant. Even prior to the accident, toxic waste was being dumped inside the premises of the plant and in its solar evaporation pond. After the plant was shut down, the toxic waste was lying in the plant premises untouched for more than 35 years.

The waste has been a continuous source of serious groundwater contamination and is a primary health concern for the neighbouring areas. Many of the chemicals degrade slowly and are likely to remain in the neighbouring environment for long amounts of time. Unless taken out and a process of decontamination takes place, these will keep spreading.

---

[85] Ashok Bhargava, *The Bhopal Incident and Union Carbide: Ramifications of an Industrial Accident*, 18 Bulletin Of Concerned Asian Scholars 2 (1986),https://www.tandfonline.com/doi/pdf/10.1080/14672715.1986.1040976, accessed 24 June 2021.

[86] Rajkumar Keswani, *Bhopal On the Edge of a Volcano*, Jansatta 26 September 1982. Also see Sanjoy Hazarika, *Indian Journalist Offered Warning*, New York Times, 11 December 1984, https://www.nytimes.com/1984/12/11/world/indian-journalist-offered-warning.html, accessed 24 June 2021.

[87] Ingrid Eckerman, *The Bhopal Saga – Causes and Consequences of the World's Largest Industrial Disaster* 38–40 (2005).

[88] Malavika Vyawahare, *Over 300 Tonnes of Toxic Waste Still Lying At The Bhopal Gas Tragedy Site*, Hindustan Times, 29 March 2017, https://www.hindustantimes.com/india-news/over-300-tonnes-of-toxic-waste-still-lying-at-the-bhopal-gas-tragedy-site/story-gEnRYdmEfNsbSKRDrZ7AuL.html, accessed 24 June 2021.

[89] Jamie Cassels, *Outlaws: Multinational Corporations and Catastrophic Law*, 31 Cumb Law Review 311, 315 (2001). Also see generally, Ingrid Eckerman, *supra* note 87.

In recent years another worrying aspect has emerged: that the contaminations have spread through the groundwater. Most studies did find the groundwater located near the plant site to be contaminated. All the contamination can be linked to the wastes that were being continuously dumped by the UCIL plant while it was operating.[90]

Union Carbide Corporation has shed any form of liability for the disaster by its Indian subsidiary or any responsibility for remediation of the site. After a disappointing and fruitless series of litigations, in July 2004 one of the victims' organizations filed proceedings in the Madhya Pradesh High Court seeking environmental remediation.[91] Both Dow Chemical, UCC's successor, and the former UCIL company denied responsibility. The High Court ordered in 2005 that remediation be carried out irrespective of imposition of liability. In the meantime, the government of India decided to bear the cost of the remediation pending restitution from the polluter.[92] However, authorities have struggled to decide on a place to dump the hazardous material. From Germany to neighbouring villages, ministries have offered and then rejected numerous sites. Remediation is yet to be taken by the authorities. The site is still being polluted by the original pesticide toxins.

Methyl isocyanate has been proven to cause damage to human DNA and this was detailed in various ICMR studies following the disaster. In 2017, a new study found that even if people who had been exposed to the toxin had few remaining abnormal cells, the aberrations that occurred within these cells had increased a lot with time.[93] Chromosomal aberrations also increased in people who were moderately exposed to the gases. The researchers also pointed to the continuous contamination that the soil had absorbed from the chemical wastes and the possibility of it having caused genetic damage. However, till date no accurate understanding of the health impacts has been made available to the victims or their hospitals.[94]

IV. UNION CARBIDE'S LIABILITY

In September 1986, the Union of India filed a suit against Union Carbide seeking a compensation amount of US$ 3.3 billion. The claim was centred on strict and absolute liability. UCC had stored an extremely harmful chemical in an unsafe facility.

In response, UCC gave its own sabotage theory. They argued that the government had been negligent for failing to enforce safeguards and by allowing slum settlements near the plant. To prove liability, it had to be shown that UCC had a duty to oversee the Bhopal operation, and that it had failed to use reasonable care.

The liability of Union Carbide under the doctrine of strict liability is limited. To escape liability, UCC argued that it was at arm's length with the Indian facility and that it would be unjust to hold it responsible for the damage caused. India proposed a theory of multinational enterprise liability, arguing that in some cases a parent company ought to be held responsible. UCC was under contract to supervise, maintain standards and warn of hazards.

---

[90] Center for Science and Environment, *Action Plan: Environmental Remediation in and around UCIL, Bhopal* (2013).

[91] *Alok Pratap Singh v Union of India*, Writ Petition No. 2802 of 2004.

[92] Department of Chemicals & Petro-chemicals, Government of India, ANNUAL REPORT 2011–2012, 35 (2013), https://chemicals.nic.in/sites/default/files/Annual%20Report%202011-2012.pdf, accessed 24 June 2021.

[93] Sarah Iqbal, *Victims of Bhopal Gas Tragedy Continue To Suffer Damage in their DNA: New Study*, DOWN TO EARTH, 6 December 2017, https://www.downtoearth.org.in/news/science-technology/dna-damage-continues-in-mic-exposed-in-bhopal-study-59291, accessed 24 June 2021.

[94] Sunita Narain & Chandra Bhushan, *Bhopal Must Never Be Forgotten, Indeed Must be Fixed*, DOWN TO EARTH, 2 December 2016, https://www.downtoearth.org.in/news/environment/bhopal-must-never-be-forgotten-indeed-must-be-fixed-56496, accessed 24 June 2021.

Both US District Judge John Keenan and the US Court of Appeals in the eventual American litigation decided that the Bhopal operation was indeed autonomous.[95] However, after the forum shifted to India, Justice Seth of the High Court of Madhya Pradesh held that the parent company was the majority shareholder and controlled the composition of the board of directors and management of the Indian company. Even the technology and information were entirely dependent on UCC.

Warren Anderson, UCC's CEO, admitted: '[W]e have 100,000 Carbide workers and half of them reside outside of the USA.'[96] UCC's corporate policy documents clearly showed that it was the general policy of the corporation to secure and maintain the effective management of an affiliate. Further, the corporate charter even said that the UCC management system would be designed to show centralized and integrated corporate planning and control.

The UCIL board was made up of members from overseas Union Carbide companies. In fact, UCIL's budgets, policy decisions, company reports and even expenditures above 10,000 dollars had to be approved by UCC. Lastly, various documents from the US litigation revealed that, according to a 1973 budget plan, UCC was to provide the technology and process design for the project. This responsibility was to continue for life. After the disaster, even Warren Anderson said that the Indian plant was built using the design criteria and safety features as their other pesticide plants.[97]

In response to the failure of Indian and American courts to redress the damage arising from the Bhopal gas tragedy, the Indian courts in the *Shriram Gas Leak* case[98] created the standard of 'absolute liability'. This new standard cast liability on the proponent of an activity without making available the possible defences under strict liability.

V. THE BHOPAL ACT

Through a Presidential Ordinance followed by a statute, the Indian Government made itself the exclusive representative of all Bhopal victims. The Bhopal Gas Leak Disaster Act[99] was to be applied retrospectively. It authorized a claims scheme which was to be the only mode of redress for the sufferers. Using the *parens patriae* doctrine, the Indian Government eliminated all individual pursuits of claims against Carbide. It also allowed the government to take control of the US litigation, perhaps to extract large amounts of money from Carbide as 'damages'.[100]

The distrust towards the Bhopal Act was similar to the problems of general class action suits. To achieve administrative efficiency, the interests of individuals are subordinated as a whole. Moreover, the use of *parens patriae* is also problematic in the Bhopal tragedy because the state was itself implicated as being partly responsible for the disaster. There was a considerable conflict of interest as the state was a major owner of the plant and hence this could be seen as an attempt to shield its own liability.[101]

---

95 *In Re: Union Carbide Corp Gas Plant Disaster*, 634 F Supp 842 (SDNY 1986). Also see, Julie M Bunck & Michael R Fowler, *Law, Politics, and the Bhopal Tragedy: Contrasting American Perspectives after 35 Years*, 13 NUALS LAW JR 1, 6–7 (2019).

96 Julie M Bunck & Michael R Fowler, *id.* Also see, *In the Aftermath of Bhopal, Anderson Speaks*, HARTFORD COURANT, 16 January 1985.

97 Julie M Bunck & Michael R Fowler, *id.* Also see, Tim Edwards, *Criminal Failure and 'The Chilling Effect': A Short History of the Bhopal Criminal Prosecutions*, 41 SOCIAL JUSTICE 53 (2014). [Special Issue: *Bhopal and After: The Chemical Industry as Toxic Capitalism* (2014).]

98 *M C Mehta v Union of India* AIR 1987 SC 965.

99 Bhopal Gas Leak Disaster (Processing of Claims) Act of 1985.

100 Upendra Baxi & Amita Dhanda, *Valiant Victims and Lethal Litigation: The Bhopal Case* page v (1990).

101 Jamie Cassels, *supra* note 89. Also see generally, Ingrid Eckerman, *supra* note 87 and L F Butler, *Parens Patriae Representation in Transnational Crises: The Bhopal Tragedy*, 17 CAL WESTERN INT'L LAW JR 175 (1987).

But as serious as the problems were, most victims were poor and had no means of legal redress. The government simply substituted itself as a prospective lawyer for the victims. The government could have adopted a superfund model,[102] through which victims could have received a minimum level of compensation irrespective of what the outcome of the case might have been later. Through it, the government could have had a more complete role in ensuring the victims' well-being.[103]

VI. AMERICAN LITIGATION

In 1986, the government of India and the UCC argued in an American court over whether the case ought to be heard in the US or in India. India argued that the US courts were the appropriate forum because the corporation was headquartered in the US and several executives were American citizens residing in the US. But UCC contended that the dispute could be best adjudicated in Bhopal as that was the region where the gas leak had occurred and where the victims lived.

Judge Keenan based his ruling on the US Supreme Court *Piper Aircraft* judgment,[104] holding that the rule for a *forum non conveniens* petition was whether the balancing of public and private interests would serve the ends of justice. He further questioned whether the Indian courts were equipped to handle the case. The government of India argued that India's tort law system was underdeveloped. Large case backlogs made the courts slow to deliver remedies. Expert Marc Galanter argued for the government's position, citing various Indian legal professionals who described the limitations of India's legal system. But Judge Keenan disregarded these arguments as Professor Galanter had not practised in India. Instead, he found merit in Nani Palkhivala and J B Dadachanji's expert testimony put forward by UCC. They stated that India had the necessary infrastructure and the technological capacity to do justice. Since both experts arguing for Carbide had extensive practice in the Indian courts, Judge Keenan found them to be more convincing.[105]

Secondly, Judge Keenan questioned whether the Indian courts were an appropriate forum to investigate all the different pieces of evidence. He held that nearly all of the plant's facilities, records and personnel were in India and it was the Indian employees and other managerial staff that were central to the investigation. They had to be held accountable because the plant was managed by Indian nationals who were employed by UCIL. Judge Keenan believed that the logistical costs of hosting the litigation in India were far lower than they would be in the US. He reasoned that the victims were from India and India had a larger stake in the case. Judge Keenan required that UCC would waive any statute of limitations defence it might make and agree to abide by any judgment of the Indian court. Lastly, he ruled that UCC would be subject to discovery under the US model Rules of Civil Procedure.[106]

Not satisfied, UCC filed an appeal against conditions contained within the ruling. The US Court of Appeals for the Second Circuit struck down the requirement that UCC would

[102] The United States adopted this model to clean up toxic sites through the Comprehensive Environmental Response, Compensation and Liability Act, 42 Uscs, CH 103 (1982 & Supp IV, 1986).

[103] Jamie Cassels, *The Uncertain Promise of Law: Lessons from Bhopal*, 29 OSGOODE HALL LAW JR 1, 16 (1991).

[104] *Piper Aircraft Co v Reyno* 454 US 235 (1981).

[105] Jayanth K Krishnan, *Bhopal in the Federal Courts: How Indian Victims Failed to Get Justice in the United States*, 72 RUTGERS UNIV LAW REVIEW 101, 113–14 (2020).

[106] The principal pleadings, judgments and orders in the *Bhopal* case are reprinted in three volumes compiled by the Indian Law Institute: *Mass Disaster and Multi-National Liability: The Bhopal Case* (1986); *Inconvenient Forum and Convenient Catastrophe: The Bhopal Case* (1986) and Upendra Baxi & Amita Dhanda, *Valiant Victims and Lethal Litigation: The Bhopal Case* (1990).

abide by any Indian judgment and it also struck down the allowance of broader US-style discovery rules. This discovery limitation restricted India's access to evidentiary material held by UCC.[107]

Judge Keenan's approach seemed to trivialize the disaster. He believed that the blame must be localized. UCC could not be held liable for its international operations. Judge Keenan failed to take into account the fact that the government of India claim was against the multinational corporation. His judgment supported the principle that home states were not responsible for the overseas actions of their corporations. The judgment encourages corporate irresponsibility: corporations can get away with weak safety standards where hazardous technology is exported to a developing country and there is no accountability for subsequent disasters.[108]

VII. INTERIM COMPENSATION

The disaster victims were extremely poor and the local and national welfare mechanisms were inadequate to provide assistance. For the first three years after the disaster, the case was held up in pre-trial proceedings and the sufferers received no interim assistance. UCC maintained that the question of interim compensation could only arise after the state had determined the extent and nature of injuries suffered by the victims. Such a determination was unlikely in this case owing to the lack of resources and insufficient knowledge about the damage caused by MIC poisoning. However, the Madhya Pradesh High Court held that the District Court ought to 'examine what interim relief could be granted to minimize the human tragedy'.

Judge Deo of the District Court, Bhopal had been in favour of an urgent out of court settlement for the case. When the parties failed to reach one in late 1987, he ordered Carbide to pay US$ 270 million as interim compensation.

Union Carbide retaliated and vehemently argued that as the gas leak was a result of sabotage by a disgruntled employee of UCIL, this court order awarded damages without a trial. UCC maintained that Judge Deo's reasoning was not one based in law but an emotional response to the tragedy.

Justice Seth of the Madhya Pradesh High Court upheld the order but reduced the amount (US$ 192 million) and relied on section 20 of the English Administration of Justice Act which mentions interim compensation. He reasoned that it was not hard to accept that the intervening period between the offence and trial was indeed a hardship in a developing nation like India. Hence, this foreign statutory rule, with modifications, could be assimilated into Indian common law. Moreover, relying on the absolute liability argument of the *Shriram* judgment and the control of UCIL by UCC, there was a *prima facie* case to provide interim relief.

Carbide intimated that they would not comply with the order since it failed to comply with 'due process'. But courts in other cases, like the ones where the Mareva injunction[109] and Anton Piller[110] orders are passed, have crafted pre-trial remedies to protect plaintiffs from a

---

[107] *In Re: Union Carbide Corp Gas Plant Disaster*, 634 F Supp 842 (SDNY 1986), *aff'd*, 809 F 2d 195 (2d Cir 1986), *cert denied*, 484 US 871 (1987).

[108] Gunther Handl, *Environmental Protection and Development in Third World Countries: Common Destiny—Common Responsibility*, 20 NYU JR INT'L LAW & POLICY 603 (1988). Also see Jamie Cassels, *supra* note 103.

[109] *Mareva Compania Naviera SA v International Bulkcarriers SA* (1975) 2 Lloyd's Rep 509 (CA).

[110] *Anton Piller KG v Manufacturing Processes Ltd* (1976) Ch 55 (CA).

long trial.[111] The only legally sound argument against the order would be that it envisaged no mechanism for Carbide to claim reimbursement if it were successful at trial.

VIII. THE SETTLEMENT

After Justice Seth pronounced his judgment ordering interim compensation, UCC immediately appealed the decision. UCC believed the Madhya Pradesh High Court had virtually decided the liability question and had violated the company's right to due process. The case reached the Supreme Court where the Union Government argued that regardless of the causes of the accident and irrespective of UCC and UCIL's relationship with each other, the corporation was legally responsible for the tragedy. Surprisingly, on 14 February 1989, the Supreme Court bench presided over by Chief Justice R S Pathak facilitated a settlement under which UCC was required to pay US$ 470 million in damages.[112] The Supreme Court held that this case was fit for an overall settlement considering the 'enormity of the human suffering' brought to the victims by the Bhopal Gas Disaster. The amount of the award was much lower than the government's original claim of US$ 3.3 billion.

There were supposedly good reasons to settle according to the Supreme Court, as litigation could drag on indefinitely. Even if the government were successful in imposing liability, it was unclear what damages it could receive. Further, since UCC had no assets in India, enforcement of a decree in the United States may have posed special challenges with the possibility that US judges might seek to protect the assets of a US corporation.

The settlement decision was heavily critiqued by civil society bodies: former Supreme Court Chief Justice P N Bhagwati gave a scathing condemnation that 'the people of India had lost'. Further, the quantification process of the harms caused by the accident was not yet completed. The calculation of compensation to be paid was likely underestimated owing to the multi-generational effects of the gas leak on victims' families. The only clear reason for the acceptance of such a low amount was perhaps to maintain India as an attractive destination for foreign capital.[113]

Defending its actions in a public statement, the government of India declared that non-acceptance and going to American courts for a larger sum would be akin to a vote of no confidence in the country's own judicial system. The Supreme Court also justified its decisions and explained the settlement by arguing that the primary consideration behind it was the immediate relief for the victims. The expected length of the litigation period could not be justified. The Supreme Court reasoned that the total figure would provide just compensation for the victims, higher than any conventional sums awarded in fatal accidents or other injury cases.

However, the calculation accepted by the court to determine the compensation amount was based on data which concluded that the tragedy caused death to 3,000 people and injured 100,000. Scholars and researchers suggest that this data radically underestimated the true numbers.[114]

---

[111] In cases where there is a huge financial loss due to a civil wrong, there exist two powerful civil remedies. A Mareva injunction allows freezing of the suspect's assets, including a compulsory asset disclosure term which can help the plaintiff to find the suspect's assets and uncover the fraud. In such cases, where there is a risk that the defendant will destroy or conceal it, an Anton Piller order grants the right to search a suspect's premises and seize evidence without prior notice, before the trial.

[112] *Union Carbide Corporation v Union of India* AIR 1990 SC 273.

[113] Upendra Baxi, *Revictimizing the Bhopal Victims*, 34 LEX ET JURIS 38 (1989).

[114] Ingrid Eckerman, *supra* note 87.

Moreover, the court failed to hear the victims at each stage of the trial and did not account for their views before giving its judgment.

In December 1989, the Supreme Court, in a long-winded judgment, upheld the constitutional validity of the Bhopal Act under which the Indian Government gave itself the exclusive right to represent all Bhopal victims in civil litigation against Carbide.[115] The court acknowledged that the Bhopal Act entitled the victims to notice and an opportunity to be heard on any proposed settlement, and the February 1989 settlement of US$ 470 million failed to give such notice and hearing. Nevertheless, the court concluded that in the special facts and circumstances of the case, 'a post-decisional hearing would not be in the ultimate interest of justice'. The court noted that the hearings to be held during the review of the settlement (in review petitions filed by some of the victims in the Supreme Court) afforded a 'sufficient opportunity' to the victims. The court rationalized its view by declaring: '"To do a great right" after all, it is permissible sometimes "to do a little wrong".'[116]

IX. THE CRIMINAL PROCEEDINGS

In the Hanumanganj Police Station on 3 December 1984, less than 24 hours after disaster struck, a First Information Report (FIR) was registered under section 304A of the Indian Penal Code.[117] Following this, some junior UCIL employees became the first and till then the only Carbide representatives to serve time in custody. They were released after 12 days.[118] Twenty-five years later, seven Carbide officials were convicted but were granted immediate bail. Currently, various appeals are still pending.

In the FIR, the only foreign official charged was UCC Chairman Warren Anderson. He arrived in Bhopal on the morning of 7 December, five days after the gas leak. He was arrested by Superintendent Swaraj Puri and kept under house arrest for the next two hours until criminal charges were filed in the presence of a magistrate. Six hours later, Anderson was released on bail of Rs. 25,000 (approximately US$ 407 at the time). The bail bond contained several strictly non-bailable offences including section 304.[119] It has been reported that his release was enabled by then Prime Minister Rajiv Gandhi.[120] Anderson's bail bond required him to be present whenever he was directed to be. He never returned to India and died in the US in 2014. For the Indian directors Keshub Mahindra and V P Gokhale the treatment was different: they were kept in custody and their oral plea for bail was rejected on the grounds that the charges on the accused were non-bailable.

After three years of investigation and through careful collection of evidence, the Central Bureau of Investigation filed a charge sheet which contained charges against 12 accused under sections 304, Part II, 324, 326 and 429 read with section 35 of the Indian Penal Code.[121] The charge sheet determined that the major source of responsibility fell on Carbide. Summons were issued repeatedly but for months were not delivered to the accused. Even when they

---

115 *Charanlal Sahu v Union of India* AIR 1990 SC 1480.

116 The court drew on William Shakespeare, *The Merchant of Venice*, Act 4, Scene 1.

117 The section relates to the offence of causing death by negligence.

118 Dan Kruzman, *A Killing Wind: Inside Union Carbide and the Bhopal Catastrophe* (1987).

119 The section provides for punishment for culpable homicide not amounting to murder.

120 *Bhopal Gas Tragedy: How Warren Anderson Got Away From Our Grasp*, INDIA TODAY, 1 November 2014, https://www.indiatoday.in/india/north/story/bhopal-gas-tragedy-warren-anderson-union-carbide-dow-chemicals-rajiv-gandhi-congress-arjun-singh-225398-2014-11-01, accessed 26 February 2022.

121 The charges covered voluntarily causing hurt/grievous hurt by dangerous weapons or means (sections 324/326) and mischief by killing or maiming cattle (section 429).

were, these were unanswered. A bailable warrant was issued against Warren Anderson and other officials in 1988.[122]

By the beginning of 1989, reports started to appear regarding a possible settlement agreement between the Indian Government and the UCC.[123] Then, on 9 February 1989, Warren Anderson and other officials were declared 'absconders' and non-bailable arrest warrants were issued.[124]

On 14 February 1989, the Supreme Court endorsed a full and final settlement where it also directed that all criminal proceedings related to and arising out of the disaster shall stand quashed wherever these may be pending. In October 1991, the Supreme Court reinstated criminal charges against top executives at Union Carbide, including Warren Anderson, while upholding the rest of the settlement.[125]

By March 1992, the Chief Judicial Magistrate (CJM) threatened to impose fugitive status and asset seizure. To escape attachment of its assets, UCC made a failed attempt to endow assets to a newly registered trust in London. The CJM declared this transfer as *mala fide* and ordered the immediate attachment of all UCC's movable property in India. Two years later, due to a special plea by UCC's counsel, the Supreme Court modified the attachment order to allow the sale of UCC shares to construct a hospital for the victims. All attempts by activist groups to recall this order proved futile.

Union Carbide Corporation had exited the Indian markets for good by October 1994 after the sale of its shares. The criminal charges against Indians accused were moved to the local sessions court. Subsequently, on an appeal heard in 1996 by the Supreme Court, a bench presided over by Chief Justice Ahmadi, despite incriminatory material being available on record, asserted that there was no *prima facie* evidence to suggest that any Indian accused had knowledge of the dangers. He diluted the main charge to that of 'rash and negligent act'. A review filed by Bhopal Gas Peedith Sangharsh Sahyog Samiti was dismissed without any explanation in March 1997. After retirement, Justice Ahmadi was appointed the chairman of the Bhopal Memorial Hospital Trust that had received the proceeds of the sale of UCC's shares.[126]

In the criminal case against UCC personnel, the former director of the CBI revealed in 2010 that the ministry had consistently pushed for him to not pursue the case. It was finally in 2003, 16 years after the inception of criminal proceedings, that the extradition request reached the US authorities. Initially, the extradition requests were rejected by the US Department of State as they did not meet the requirements of the extradition treaty.[127]

Union Carbide Corporation remains protected by the multinational corporation Dow Chemical which has owned it since 2001. Attempts to summon Dow have been largely futile because of a system in which elected Indian officials and ministries aim to make India an attractive destination for foreign capital.

---

[122] Reuters, *India Acts in Carbide Case*, 17 May 1988.

[123] The Sunday Observer, 7 January 1989.

[124] Tim Edwards, *supra* note 97 at 66.

[125] This judgment was rendered in petitions seeking review of the settlement. *Union Carbide Corporation v Union of India* AIR 1992 SC 248.

[126] Tim Edwards, *supra* note 97 at 69. Justice Ahmadi resigned as the chairman in 2009. His resignation was accepted by the Supreme Court in 2010 when the Central Government took over management of the hospital. Anup Dutta, *SC Lets Bhopal Trust Chief Quit Amid Cries for Investigation*, India Today, 20 July 2010, https://www.indiatoday.in/india/north/story/sc-lets-bhopal-trust-chief-quit-amid-cries-for-investigation-78969-2010-07-20, accessed 24 June 2021.

[127] Tim Edwards, *supra* note 97 at 70–2.

X. THE ROLE OF THE STATE

While it is important to remember Carbide's liability in the case, it is also important to recognize the role of other actors in the creation of the disaster. Both the Central and the state governments were aware of the extent of contamination at the project site. The callous reaction to the disaster from the government might have been different if the wind had blown the toxic gases towards the northern richer areas of Bhopal, instead of the poor residing in the nearby slums. Three reasons can be attributed to this reaction of the state, namely an effort to cover up regulatory failure, the desire not to frighten off foreign capital and to avoid a public examination of the connections between the political elite and the corporation.

The responsibility of the Indian state can also be looked at through the design and manufacture of the plant. A 1972 letter of intent between UCIL and UOI reveals that only the purchase of those design and consultancy services were intended which were not available in the country. Ranjit Dutta, who was the general manager at UCIL (Agricultural Products division), testified that the Indian Government in a process of indigenization of the plant had restricted the amount of foreign materials and mandated the use of Indian experts wherever possible.[128] The American litigation at the US Second Circuit Court of Appeals agreed and stated that India had considered the plant to be an Indian one and the disaster to be an Indian problem.

Even though UCC had delivered the original plans for the site, a group of engineers working for the government out of Mumbai had modified and changed the design of the plant in a number of ways. On comparison with the American MIC plant in West Virginia, it was clear that the difference in features caused Bhopal to be more prone to an accident. Other safety mechanisms such as training of the staff to inform the police after a disaster were also missing. Most staff was underprepared and UCC seldom communicated with the plant. Moreover, the site of the Bhopal plant was not zoned for hazardous industry. It was only later in 1974 that the government of India acknowledged that UCIL manufactured pesticides at the plant. Indeed, the government of India encouraged manufacture of pesticides and licensed the plant. UCIL opted to respond to enhanced competition by manufacturing pesticides rather than simply mixing stable substances. Lastly, the hazardous wastes were being dumped on site.[129]

XI. THE PANDEMIC AND THE VICTIMS

The COVID-19 pandemic was particularly harsh for the survivors of the Bhopal gas tragedy and adversely impacted their economic and physical well-being.

The economic slowdown brought on by the pandemic affected the entire nation. Its impact on the victims of the Bhopal gas tragedy was especially severe. The pension provided to the survivors, including widows of the victims, has been suspended since December 2019.[130] Coupled with the suspension of economic activities during the nationwide lockdown, this meant severe financial crisis for them. According to Balkrishna Namdeo, President, *Gas*

---

[128] *In Re: Union Carbide Corp Gas Plant Disaster*, 634 F Supp 842 (SDNY 1986), *aff'd*, 809 F 2d 195 (2d Cir 1986), *cert denied*, 484 US 871 (1987).

[129] Julie M Bunck & Michael R Fowler, *supra* note 95 at 6–8.

[130] Sidharth Yadav, *Bhopal Gas Tragedy Victims Launch Fast to Demand Resumption of Pension*, THE HINDU, 14 September 2020, https://www.thehindu.com/news/national/other-states/bhopal-gas-tragedy-victims-launch-fast-to-demand-resumption-of-pension/article32601420.ece, accessed 24 June 2021.

Peedit Nirashrit Pension Bhogi Sangharsh Morcha, the 2011–12 Annual Report of the Bhopal Gas Tragedy Relief and Rehabilitation Department had reported that the victims would receive a lifelong pension. However, the pension has been erratic, and was stopped earlier too, from April 2016 to November 2017.[131] On 1 October 2020, the survivors staged a protest with *Khali Thali* (an empty plate), showcasing their financial distress.[132]

In terms of their susceptibility to Covid-19, over half a million people in Bhopal are five times more susceptible to the novel coronavirus infection because of the multi-systemic damage from their exposure to Union Carbide's toxic gases.[133] Data collected between 1998 and 2016, from eight units of the Bhopal Memorial Hospital and Research Centre (BMHRC), records that 50.4% of gas-affected patients suffered from cardiovascular problems; 59.6% from pulmonary problems and 15.6% were diabetic.

Despite these numbers, the BMHRC has been grossly inadequate in dealing with the pandemic. A non-profit advocacy group has filed a writ petition in the Madhya Pradesh High Court, suing the BMHRC for criminal negligence.[134] According to the writ petition, six patients allegedly died in the Covid-19 isolation wards, which did not have a dedicated supervisor and lacked basic patient facilities such as oxygen and ventilators.[135] Furthermore, data collected by the Bhopal Group for Information and Action through a right to information (RTI) requisition filed on 2 September 2020, alleges a downward trend in the admission rates of BMHRC, despite an increase in the number of cases.

Higher susceptibility of the Bhopal victims to the novel coronavirus infection, coupled with inadequate healthcare services, has obviously threatened the physical well-being of these victims.

XII. CONCLUSION

The Bhopal story is one that clearly shows us the limits and collective failures of the legal system. India invited foreign companies with hopes of providing jobs and economic growth. The failure and neglect on the part of UCC decimated an entire community of people in a small city.

The storied and tragic legal history of the incident is ripe with contradictions such as the Indian Government preferring to litigate in a foreign land and a foreign company refusing to admit any responsibility toward its affiliate. The legal battle arising from the Bhopal gas tragedy favoured Union Carbide rather than the victims. The death and horror associated with this tragedy is still fresh in the minds of the victims and their families. But this narrative of suffering seems to be overlooked by the courts. Dow Chemical Company, the successor of Union Carbide, is the second-largest chemical company in the world. With their enormous financial capability and assets, Dow could easily take the necessary steps to clean the Bhopal site and help the Bhopal gas tragedy victims in these difficult economic times.

---

131 *Widows of Gas Tragedy Victims Stage Protest for Pension*, The Hitvada, 2 October 2020, https://www.thehitavada.com/Encyc/2020/10/2/Widows-of-gas-tragedy-victims-stage-protest-for-pension.html, accessed 24 June 2021.

132 *Id.*

133 Swagata Dey, *Covid-19: Deaths of 6 Bhopal Gas Survivors Turn Spotlight on Healthcare Malady*, Down To Earth, 21 September 2020, https://www.downtoearth.org.in/news/health/covid-19-deaths-of-6-bhopal-gas-survivors-turn-spotlight-on-healthcare-malady-73463, accessed 24 June 2021.

134 *Id.*

135 *Id.*

While the Bhopal gas leak victims and their families bore the brunt of the industrial disaster, the event triggered enactment of the Environment (Protection) Act of 1986, which provides the framework of modern Indian environmental law. If the nation is better prepared today to prevent what Justice Krishna Iyer described as 'Bhoposhima',[136] it is largely due to the extensive regulations framed under the EPA and cognate statutes such as the NGT Act. Nevertheless, as we have seen throughout this book, new laws without competent administrators do not translate into better air, water and safety for the citizen.

[136] V R Krishna Iyer, *Bhoposhima: Crime Without Punishment – Case for Crisis Management Jurisprudence*, 26 Economical & Political Weekly 2705 (1991).

17

INTERNATIONAL ENVIRONMENTAL LAW AND GLOBAL ISSUES

A. INTRODUCTION

In international law, a distinction is often made between hard and soft law. Hard international law generally refers to agreements or principles that are directly enforceable by a national or international body. Soft international law refers to agreements or principles that are meant to influence individual nations to respect certain norms or incorporate them into national law. Although these agreements sometimes oblige countries to adopt implementing legislation, they are not usually enforceable on their own in a court.

If a treaty or convention does not specify an international forum that has subject-matter jurisdiction, such as the World Trade Organization (WTO), often the only place to bring a suit with respect to that treaty is in the member state's domestic court system. This presents at least two additional hurdles. If the member state being sued does not have domestic implementing legislation in place to hear the dispute, there will be no forum available. Even in the event that the domestic legislation provides for such suits, since the judges who decide the case are residents of the country against which it is brought, potential conflicts of interest arise.

Only nations are bound by treaties and conventions. In international forums, such as the International Court of Justice (ICJ), countries must consent to being sued. Thus, it is often impossible to sue a country. The final question in the international jurisdictional arena is who may bring a suit. Typically, only countries may sue countries. Individual citizens and non-governmental organizations (NGOs) cannot. This has huge repercussions. First, the environmental harm must be large and notorious for a country to notice. Second, for a country to have a stake in the outcome of the subject matter, some harm may have to cross the borders of the violating country into the country that is suing. Finally, even if transboundary harm does exist, the issue of causation, especially in the environmental field, is often impossible to prove with any certainty.

The enforcement issue is one where advocates for a safer environment most often find themselves stymied. Even if a treaty or convention provides for specific substantive measures to be taken by a country (many treaties merely provide 'frameworks'), specifies a forum for dispute resolution and authorizes sanctions for non-compliance, international law remains largely unenforceable. A country cannot be forced to do what it is not willing to do. One can sanction the country, order damages, restrict trade or, most frequently, publicize non-compliance. But beyond that, if a country will not comply, there is very little to be done.

Environmental Law & Policy in India. Shyam Divan and Armin Rosencranz, Oxford University Press.
 DOI: 1093/oso/9780192865458.003.0017

NOTES AND QUESTIONS

1. Consider for a moment why any law is enacted—domestically or internationally. Some would maintain that it is a moral statement about behaviour that a society cannot tolerate. Others would argue that certain conduct is outlawed to deter that conduct, which is why we also attach a penalty. Some would argue, especially in light of the inefficiencies in enforcement, that laws socialize society's members to behave in a certain way by defining a code.

What is the purpose of international environmental law—is it a moral statement, a deterrent or a socializing tool? If it is a moral statement, which many of the framework conventions seem to be, is it merely aspirational? Do we honestly believe that all nations will achieve all the goals expressed in all the agreements? Or do we, as a global community, simply like to think of ourselves as the kind of people who believe in these things? If these are intended to deter, why are there not more international forums for dispute resolution, more international bodies empowered to enforce agreements, more substantive requirements and more 'hard law' self-executing agreements? If there were, would any nation sign them? If it is intended as a socialization technique, is it working? Are nations more environmentally aware?

2. If ultimately all international environmental law is unenforceable, what good is it? Does it accomplish anything to find a country out of compliance with a treaty? What about publicity? What if the economic benefits of a project, such as the Narmada Valley Project, are believed by government officials to outweigh the negative effects of the publicity?

The fact is that true enforcement of international law can only be achieved through domestic law. One good example of this is the Dispute Settlement Understanding of the WTO which is one of the only forms of international law where the United States of America has been willing to accept multilateral rules.[1] The United States is bound by the dispute-resolution system (it has sued and been sued at the Dispute Settlement Body) due to its Congress having passed implementing legislation,[2] the Uruguay Round Agreements Act of 1994 and associated Statements of Administrative Action.

3. Notwithstanding the limited enforceability of international environmental law *per se*, international environmental law issues often come up before international courts in other matters. For instance, one of the seminal judgments of the International Court of Justice in relation to international environmental law was the *Gabcíkovo-Nagymaros* case,[3] which arose from a dispute between Hungary and Slovakia in relation to the construction of dams on the river Danube. Similarly, the advisory opinion of the International Court of Justice on the legality of the use of nuclear weapons addressed the environmental impact of the use of nuclear weapons.[4]

4. Three cases decided by the International Court of Justice have featured prominent environmental issues—the decision in the *Pulp Mills on the River Uruguay* case between Argentina

---

[1] Robert Z Lawrence, *The United States and the WTO Dispute Resolution System*, The Bernard and Irene Schwartz Series on American Competitiveness, Council on Foreign Relations, CSR No. 25 (March 2007).

[2] Jeanne J Grimmett, *WTO Dispute Settlement: Status of US Compliance in Pending Cases*, 7-5700 Congressional Research Service, RL32014 (23 April 2012).

[3] International Court of Justice, Judgment dated 25 September 1997 *Gabčíkovo-Nagymaros Project (Hungary/Slovakia)*, https://www.icj-cij.org/en/case/92/judgments, accessed 24 June 2021.

[4] International Court of Justice, Advisory Opinion dated 8 July 1996 *Legality of the Threat or Use of Nuclear Weapons*, https://www.icj-cij.org/en/case/95/advisory-opinions, accessed 24 June 2021.

and Uruguay,[5] the *Aerial Herbicide Spraying* case between Ecuador and Colombia[6] and the *Whaling in the Antarctic* case between Australia and Japan.[7] Similarly, the *Southern Bluefin Tuna* case[8] at the International Tribunal for the Law of the Sea, and the *Shrimp-Turtle*[9] and *Rare Earths*[10] cases at the WTO have all involved significant environmental issues. Interestingly, the ICJ established a dedicated chamber for environmental law cases between 1993 and 2006, but this was never used and was discontinued in 2006.[11]

5. The *Whaling* case[12] at the ICJ is one example of a case arising out of an international environmental treaty and being litigated to force adherence to the environmental objectives of the Treaty (as opposed to the private interests of the claimant state). The case considered the International Convention for the Regulation of Whaling which imposes restrictions on the killing of whales and allows limited exceptions for the killing of whales for scientific research. Australia initiated proceedings against Japan, alleging that Japan was abusing the scientific activity exception to permit large-scale whaling. One of the issues that has excited commentary is that Australia did not actually suffer from Japan's alleged violation of its treaty obligations. Australia's claim was founded on Japan's violation of a treaty obligation owed to all state parties to the Whaling Convention.

6. The practice of relying on domestic implementing legislation to enforce international environmental agreements leaves state parties in the position of having different obligations under the same treaty, depending on how their own legislative, executive and judicial bodies interpret and implement the Treaty. Is this fair? What about the costs and administrative burdens that are associated with creating and enforcing legislation? Does this put richer countries in a better position to comply with treaties? Does this not mean that poorer countries, who may wish to comply, will often be unable to? Should they be held to the same standards? Is it patronizing to hold them to *lower* standards?

7. What is the purpose of the informational roles of international institutions? Will more knowledge about the global environment and our impacts on it lead to better compliance? Or will so many new issues lead to non-compliance due to uncertainty? If it appears to the average citizen that virtually everything she does has a negative environmental impact, will she not cease to try to change her behaviour?

8. What are the difficulties with the monitoring role of international institutions? If information gathered by monitoring bodies is generated by governmental institutions, how accurate may it be? Is it better to have inaccurate information or no information? How much of a

---

[5] International Court of Justice, Judgment dated 20 April 2010, paragraph 204, *Pulp Mills on the River Uruguay (Argentina v Uruguay)*, https://www.icj-cij.org/en/case/135/judgments, accessed 24 June 2021.

[6] International Court of Justice, Judgment dated 13 September 2013, https://www.icj-cij.org/public/files/case-related/138/138-20130913-ORD-01-00-EN.pdf, accessed 24 June 2021.

[7] International Court of Justice, Judgment dated 31 March 2014 *Whaling in the Antarctic (Australia v Japan)*, https://www.icj-cij.org/en/case/148, accessed 24 June 2021.

[8] Office of Legal Affairs, United Nations, Reports of International Arbitral Awards *Southern Bluefin Tuna (New Zealand-Japan, Australia-Japan)* 4 August 2000, https://legal.un.org/riaa/cases/vol_XXIII/1-57.pdf, accessed 24 June 2021.

[9] The WTO Dispute Settlement Archive Reports List, *United States—Import Prohibition on Certain Shrimp and Shrimp Products*, https://www.wto.org/english/tratop_e/dispu_e/distab_e.htm#r58, accessed 24 June 2021.

[10] The WTO Dispute Settlement, *China—Measures Related to the Exportation of Rare Earths, Tungsten and Molybdenum*, https://www.wto.org/english/tratop_e/dispu_e/cases_e/ds431_e.htm, accessed 24 June 2021.

[11] International Court of Justice, *Chambers and Committees*, https://www.icj-cij.org/en/chambers-and-committees, accessed 24 June 2021.

[12] International Court of Justice, Judgment dated 31 March 2014 *Whaling in the Antarctic (Australia v Japan)*, https://www.icj-cij.org/en/case/148, accessed 24 June 2021.

threat to a nation's sovereign status is an international monitoring institution? When should a nation's sovereignty have to be compromised for the greater global good? Who is to say?

B. INDIA'S INTERNATIONAL OBLIGATIONS

India has obligations under numerous international treaties and agreements that relate to environmental issues. To be bound as a contracting party, India must have ratified a treaty, that is, adopted it as national law before it came into force, or acceded to it after it has come into force. For a treaty to enter into force, the requisite number of countries must ratify the Treaty, which then has the force of international law.

Specific obligations under any treaty vary. The nature and degree of compliance and implementation depend on a number of factors, among them: (1) the capabilities and staff of an international institution charged with coordinating national compliance efforts; (2) the willingness of other state parties to enforce or comply with the Treaty; (3) the political agenda of the domestic government and popular support; (4) trade and diplomatic pressures brought to bear by other countries; and (5) sometimes, judicial or NGO involvement through court cases and publicity.

INDIA'S TREATY OBLIGATIONS

While India is party to a host of international conventions relating to environmental matters, it does not necessarily approach them all with the same assiduousness in terms of implementation. Some of the agreements to which it has demonstrated stronger adherence include:

- The Antarctic Treaty (Washington, 1959). Entered into force 23 June 1961. India ratified with qualifications, 19 August 1983.
- Protocol on Environmental Protection to the Antarctica Treaty (Madrid, 1991). Entered into force 15 January 1998. India ratified, 1997.
- Convention on Wetlands of International Importance, Especially as Waterfowl Habitat (Ramsar, 1971). Entered into force 21 December 1975. India acceded, 1 October 1981.
- Convention Concerning the Protection of the World Cultural and Natural Heritage (Paris, 1972). Entered into force 17 December 1975. India signed, 16 November 1972.
- Convention on International Trade in Endangered Species of Wild Fauna and Flora (Washington, 1973). Entered into force 1 July 1975. India signed, 9 July 1974; ratified 20 July 1976.
- United Nations Convention on the Law of the Sea (Montego Bay, 1982). Entered into force 16 November 1994. India signed, 10 December 1982.
- Convention for the Protection of the Ozone Layer (Vienna, 1985). Entered into force 22 September 1988. India ratified, 18 March 1991.
- Protocol on Substances that Deplete the Ozone Layer (Montreal, 1987). Entered into force 1 January 1989. India acceded, 19 June 1992.
- Amendments to the Montreal Protocol on Substances that Deplete the Ozone Layer (London, 1990). Entered into force 10 August 1992. India acceded, 19 June 1992.
- Convention on the Control of Transboundary Movements of Hazardous Wastes and their Disposal (Basel, 1989). Entered into force 5 May 1992. India signed, 5 March 1990; ratified, 24 June 1992.
- Convention on Biological Diversity (Rio de Janeiro, 1992). Entered into force 29 December 1993. India signed, 5 June 1992; ratified, 18 February 1994.
- Convention on Persistent Organic Pollutants (Stockholm, 2001). Entered into force 17 May 2004. India signed, 14 May 2002; ratified, 13 January 2006.

Examples of domestic implementation include India's National Implementation Plan for Persistent Organic Pollutants (POPs), to meet its obligations under the Stockholm Convention on POPs.[13] India has also put in place an extensive domestic institutional framework to meet its obligations under the Convention on Biodiversity. Through the Biodiversity Act of 2002, India set up a National Biodiversity Authority, State Biodiversity Boards and local Biodiversity Management Committees.[14]

C. ESTABLISHED NORMS OF INTERNATIONAL ENVIRONMENTAL LAW

Norms are general legal principles that are widely accepted. This acceptance is evidenced in a number of ways, such as international agreements, national legislation, domestic and international judicial decisions, and scholarly writings. The leading norms in the field of international environmental law are addressed below:

(1) *Principle 21 and Sic Utere Tuo*: Foremost among these norms is Principle 21 of the 1972 Stockholm Declaration on the Human Environment. Principle 21 declares:

> 'States have, in accordance with the Charter of the United Nations and the principles of international law, the sovereign right to exploit their own resources pursuant to their own environmental policies, and the responsibility to ensure that activities within their jurisdiction or control do not cause damage to the environment of other States or of areas beyond the limits of national jurisdiction.'[15]

This approach is reflective of the roman maxim, *sic utere tuo ut alienum non laedas*, which means to use your property so that the property of others is not damaged. In customary international environmental law, this rule translates to the *no-harm rule*, which precludes transboundary environmental damage. In the *Trail Smelter* case, the International Arbitral Tribunal held:

> '[N]o state has the right to use or permit the use of its territory in such a manner as to cause injury by fumes in or to the territory of another state or the properties or persons therein, when the case is of serious consequence and the injury is established by clear and convincing evidence.'[16]

The no-harm rule now protects all states, however distantly located from the polluting state.[17]

(2) *Polluter Pays Principle*: Most industrialized countries subscribe to the 'polluter pays principle'. This means polluters should internalize the costs of their pollution, control it at its source and pay for its effects, including remedial or clean-up costs, rather than forcing

---

[13] Project Management Cell, Stockholm Convention on Persistent Organic Pollutants, 'National Implementation Plan', http://chm.pops.int/Implementation/NationalImplementationPlans/NIPTransmission/tabid/253/ctl/Download/mid/13657/Default.aspx?id=80&ObjID=11745, accessed 24 June 2021.

[14] National Biodiversity Authority, India, 'FAQs', http://nbaindia.org/content/19/16/1/faq.html, accessed 24 June 2021.

[15] Declaration of the United Nations Conference on the Human Environment (Stockholm, 1972), https://www.ipcc.ch/apps/njlite/srex/njlite_download.php?id=6471#:~:text=Principle%2021%20Page%204%20States,jurisdiction%20or%20control%20do%20not, accessed 24 June 2021.

[16] *Trail Smelter Arbitration (United States v Canada)* 1941 UN Rep Int'l Arb Awards 1905 (1941).

[17] Christina Voigt, *State Responsibility for Climate Change Damages*, 77 Nordic Jr Of Int'l Law 1 (2008).

other states or future generations to bear such costs. The principle first emerged at the international level through the work of the OECD,[18] and has been formally incorporated into the laws of the European Union.[19] It has been recognized by the Indian Supreme Court as a 'universal' rule to be applied to domestic polluters as well.[20] Moreover, it has been accepted as a fundamental objective of government policy to abate pollution[21] and is engrafted in the National Green Tribunal Act of 2010.[22]

(3) *Precautionary Principle*: Another pivotal norm in international environment law is the 'precautionary principle'. This is a duty to foresee and assess environmental risks, to warn potential victims of such risks and to behave in ways that prevent or mitigate such risks. It is captured in Principle 15 of the Rio Declaration 1992.[23] In the context of municipal law, Justice Kuldip Singh of the Indian Supreme Court has explained the meaning of this principle in the *Vellore Citizens' Welfare Forum* case,[24] which is excerpted later in this section. In *Alembic Pharmaceuticals Ltd v Rohit Prajapati*,[25] the Supreme Court applied the principle to disallow *ex post facto* environmental clearances.

While some often equate the principle to simply being cautious, the principle is more proactive in nature; it requires the taking of precautionary action, either preventive or anticipatory, before scientific certainty of cause and effect is established. For instance, in the area of climate change, we may not be able to measure with certainty exactly how devastating the consequences will be in a particular place or region. However, especially given what we already know to be true including the broader ramifications of inaction, that should not prevent us from taking preventive action, such as reducing fossil fuel consumption, before the suspected harm occurs. The principle does not specify how much anticipatory or preventive action one needs to take, but it does suggest that one must foresee and assess environmental risks, warn potential victims of these risks and behave in ways that mitigate the risks.

The precautionary principle has been recognized in several international instruments, including the United Nations Framework Convention on Climate Change 1992, the

---

18 Organisation for Economic Co-operation and Development, *Guiding Principles Concerning the International Economic Aspects of Environmental Policies*, Doc. C(72)128 (26 May 1972), https://legalinstruments.oecd.org/en/instruments/OECD-LEGAL-0102, accessed 24 June 2021.

19 European Commission, 'Environment', https://ec.europa.eu/environment/legal/law/5/e_learning/module_4_7.htm, accessed 24 June 2021.

20 *Indian Council for Enviro-Legal Action v Union of India* (*Bichhri* case) AIR 1996 SC 1446, 1466; *Vellore Citizens' Welfare Forum v Union of India*, AIR 1996 SC 2715, 2721; *S Jagannath v Union of India* (*Shrimp Culture* case) AIR 1997 SC 811, 846, 850; *Karnataka Industrial Area Development Board v C Kenchappa* (2006) 6 SCC 371, 387; *Bittu Sehgal v Union of India* (2001) 9 SCC 181, 193; *M C Mehta v Kamal Nath* (2002) 3 SCC 653, 660, 661; *Research Foundation for Science (18) v Union of India* (2005) 13 SCC 186, 200; *Lal Bahadur v State of U P* (2017) SCC Online SC 1558, para 21; and *M C Mehta v Union of India* (*Kant Enclave* case) (2018) SCC Online SC 1426, para 141.

21 Ministry of Environment, Forest and Climate Change, 'Policy Statement for Abatement of Pollution' (26 February 1992), para 3.3, https://www.iitr.ac.in/wfw/web_ua_water_for_welfare/environment/Pollution_Policy_Statement_1992.pdf, accessed 24 June 2021.

22 Section 20 reads: 'The Tribunal shall, while passing any order or decision or award, apply the principles of sustainable development, the precautionary principle and the polluter pays principle.'

23 United Nations Environment Program, Rio Declaration on Environment and Development (1992), https://www.un.org/en/development/desa/population/migration/generalassembly/docs/globalcompact/A_CONF.151_26_Vol.I_Declaration.pdf, accessed 24 June 2021.

24 *Vellore Citizens' Welfare Forum v Union of India* AIR 1996 SC 2715, 2721. In *A P Pollution Control Board v Prof M V Nayudu* AIR 1999 SC 812, the Supreme Court traced the development of the precautionary principle. Also see *Karnataka Industrial Area Development Board v C Kenchappa* (2006) 6 SCC 371, 386; *Bittu Sehgal v Union of India* (2001) 9 SCC 181, 193, 196; *Research Foundation for Science (18) v Union of India* (2005) 13 SCC 186, 200; *Amarnath Shrine, In Re* (2013) 3 SCC 247; and *Arjun Gopal v Union of India* (2017) 16 SCC 267, 269.

25 *Alembic Pharmaceuticals Ltd v Rohit Prajapati* (2020) SCC Online SC 347.

Convention on Biological Diversity 1992, the Fish Stocks Agreement 1995 and the Persistent Organic Pollutants Convention 2001. Its legal status is still evolving. Thus far, it has not been declared as a customary principle of international environmental law. In the *Hormones* case,[26] WTO's Appellate Body categorically declared that the principle is not yet a part of customary international law. However, in its 2011 advisory opinion, the Seabed Disputes Chamber of the International Tribunal for the Law of the Sea deliberately moved towards making the precautionary principle a part of customary international law.[27]

(4) *Sustainable Development*: In October 1982, the United Nations General Assembly adopted the World Charter for Nature.[28] The agreement expressly recognized the principle of 'sustainable development', defined as using living resources in a manner that 'does not exceed their natural capacity for regeneration' and using 'natural resources in a manner that ensures the preservation of the species and ecosystems for the benefit of future generations'. The principle of sustainable development was also acknowledged in the 1987 report 'Our Common Future', published by the United Nations World Commission on Environment and Development.[29] This report defined sustainable development as 'humanity's ability to ensure that (development) meets the need of the present generation without compromising the ability of future generations to meet their needs'. The Supreme Court[30] and the Indian Government have recognized the principle of sustainable development as a basis for balancing ecological imperatives with developmental goals.[31]

(5) *Intergenerational Equity*: 'Intergenerational equity' is among the newest norms of international environmental law. John Rawls' *A Theory of Justice*, published in 1971, brought the concept of intergenerational equity into common parlance. It can best be understood not so much as a principle in isolation, but rather as an argument in favour of sustainable economic development and natural resource use. If present generations continue to consume and deplete resources at unsustainable rates, future generations will suffer the environmental (and economic) consequences. It is our children and grandchildren who will be left without forests (and their carbon retention capacities), without vital and productive agricultural land and without water suitable for drinking or for sustaining cultivation or aquatic life. Therefore, we must all undertake to pass on to future generations an environment as intact as the one we inherited from the previous generation, and not cause damage to common property that belongs to all generations.

Proponents of intergenerational equity maintain that the present generation has a moral obligation to manage the earth in a manner that will not jeopardize the aesthetic and economic welfare of the generations that follow. From this moral premise flow certain ecological commandments: 'Do not cut down trees faster than they grow back. Do not

---

[26] *EC Measures Concerning Meat and Meat Products (Hormones)*, WTO Appellate Body, Judgment dated 16 January 1998.

[27] *Responsibilities and Obligations of States Sponsoring Person and Entities with Respect to Activities in the Area* (Advisory Opinion, order dated 1 February 2011) ITLOS Reports 2011, 10 (Advisory Opinion) para 135.

[28] World Charter for Nature, 28 October 1982, GA Res 37/7, UN GAOR, 37th Sess., UN Doc A/RES/37/7, 1982 WL 184343.

[29] United Nations Commission on Environment, *Our Common Future* (1987), http://www.un-documents.net/our-common-future.pdf, accessed 24 June 2021.

[30] *Vellore Citizens' Welfare Forum v Union of India* AIR 1996 SC 2715; *M C Mehta v Union of India* (2001) 4 SCC 577, 580; *N D Jayal v Union of India* (2004) 9 SCC 362, 381–3; *Amarnath Shrine, In Re* (2013) 3 SCC 247; *Alembic Pharmaceuticals Ltd v Rohit Prajapati* (2020) SCC Online SC 347; and *State of Meghalaya v All Dimasa Students Union* (2019) 8 SCC 177, 196.

[31] Ministry of Environment, Forest and Climate Change, *National Conservation Strategy and Policy Statement on Environment and Development*, paras 1.1 and 1.3 (1992), http://moef.gov.in/wp-content/uploads/2017/07/introduction-csps.pdf, accessed 24 June 2021. Also see *supra* note 20.

farm land at levels, or in a manner, that reduce the land's regenerative capacity. Do not pollute water at levels that exceed its natural purification capacity.'

In *State of Himachal Pradesh v Ganesh Wood Products*, the Supreme Court recognized the significance of intergenerational equity and held a government department's approval to establish forest-based industry to be invalid because 'it is contrary to public interest involved in preserving forest wealth, maintenance of environment and ecology and considerations of sustainable growth and intergenerational equity. After all, the present generation has no right to deplete all the existing forests and leave nothing for the next and future generations.'[32]

(6) *Common Heritage of Mankind*: The concept of 'Common Heritage of Mankind' can be first read into the Antarctic Treaty of 1959.[33] It is derived from the notion of *res communis*, in furtherance of which certain geographical spaces fall under the common ownership of humankind. In 1972, the idea of protecting the 'global commons' was further articulated in Principles 21 and 22 of the Stockholm Declaration.[34] At the 1982 United Nations Conference on the Law of the Sea (UNCLOS), the 'Group of 77' developing countries, led by India, articulated the norm that certain resources, such as the deep seabed, are part of the common heritage of mankind and the economic benefits must be shared by all nations, that is, no country can claim exclusive right to exploit such resources. This was adopted into the final Law of the Sea Convention.[35] By extension, this also means that these common resources must be safeguarded and protected by all.

(7) *Common But Differentiated Responsibilities*: The 1992 Rio de Janeiro Earth Summit articulated the norm of 'common but different responsibilities', in Principle 7 of the Rio Declaration.[36] With regard to global environmental concerns such as global climate change or stratospheric ozone layer depletion, all nations have a shared responsibility, but richer nations are better able than poorer nations to take the financial and technological measures necessary to shoulder the responsibility, and thus must demonstrate this leadership by paying for preventive and remedial action. Examples of this approach can be seen in the Montreal Protocol on Substances that Deplete the Ozone Layer,[37] and the Convention on Biological Diversity.[38]

One of the most visible areas of international environmental law where the principle is embodied (and oft-debated), is under the United Nations Framework Convention on Climate Change.[39] Article 3 stipulates that state parties are to undertake protective action

---

[32] (1995) 6 SCC 363, 389. Also see *Indian Council for Enviro-Legal Action v Union of India* (*CRZ Notification* case) (1996) 5 SCC 281 (where the court expressed its concern at the adverse ecological effects which will have to be borne by future generations); *Glanrock Estate Pvt Ltd v State of Tamil Nadu* (2010) 10 SCC 96, 109; *Amarnath Shrine, In Re* (2013) 3 SCC 247; *Alembic Pharmaceuticals Ltd v Rohit Prajapati* (2020) SCC Online SC 347; and *State of Meghalaya v All Dimasa Students Union* (2019) 8 SCC 177, 196.

[33] The Antarctic Treaty, 1 December 1959, 402 UNTS 71, https://treaties.un.org/doc/Publication/UNTS/Volume%20402/volume-402-I-5778-English.pdf, accessed 24 June 2021.

[34] *Supra* note 15.

[35] UN Convention on the Law of the Sea, 10 December 1982, GA Res A/RES/37/7, 48th Sess., UN Doc A/CONF 62/122 (1982), https://www.un.org/depts/los/convention_agreements/texts/unclos/unclos_e.pdf, accessed 24 June 2021.

[36] *Supra* note 23.

[37] The Montreal Protocol on Substances that Deplete the Ozone Layer, 16 September 1987, https://treaties.un.org/doc/Treaties/1989/01/19890101%2003-25%20AM/Ch_XXVII_02_ap.pdf, accessed 24 June 2021.

[38] The Convention on Biological Diversity, 1760 UNTS 79, https://www.cbd.int/doc/legal/cbd-en.pdf, accessed 24 June 2021.

[39] 1771 UNTS 107, https://unfccc.int/files/essential_background/background_publications_htmlpdf/application/pdf/conveng.pdf, accessed 24 June 2021.

against climate change, on the basis of equity and in accordance with the principle of 'common but differentiated responsibilities and respective capabilities'. To that end, primary mandatory mitigation responsibilities were placed on developed countries owing to their disproportionate historical contribution to climate change.

However, with the Bali Action Plan in 2007, there was an evident shift in the interpretation of the principle. In conferences leading up to the Paris Agreement 2015, a more nuanced version of the principle was being negotiated. To that end, the Durban Platform for Enhanced Action Plan categorically stipulated that *all* parties had an obligation to undertake the highest level of mitigation obligations. Ultimately, in the Paris Agreement 2015, a qualifier was added to the principle. Consequently, under the Paris Agreement, the principle has been reiterated as 'common but differentiated responsibilities and respective capabilities, *in the light of national circumstances*'. In furtherance of this, *all* parties have mitigation and adaptation responsibilities.

(8) *The Public Trust Doctrine*: This principle establishes that the state, in exercise of its sovereign functions, holds certain shared resources—like air, water, rivers and coastlines—in permanent trusteeship for the uninterrupted use of the public. In performance of its duties as a trustee, a government must prevent the diversion of such trust 'property' into private hands, and must maintain the trust in good condition. The doctrine is reflected in the Stockholm Declaration of 1972, and was highlighted by the Indian Supreme Court in *M C Mehta v Kamal Nath*.[40]

(9) *State Sovereignty*: Principle 21 of the Stockholm Declaration establishes the norm of 'State Sovereignty'. In keeping with broader principles of international law, this tenet establishes that nation states and their governments have the sovereign right, within their territory, of exploiting their own natural resources in any manner they choose to do.[41] Principle 21 phrases this as 'States have, in accordance with the Charter of the United Nations and the principles of international law, the sovereign right to exploit their own resources pursuant to their own environmental policies. . . .'[42]

(10) *Right to a Decent or Healthful Environment*: Another emerging norm is the guarantee in the domestic constitutions, laws or executive pronouncements of several states, including India,[43] South Africa, Malaysia, Thailand, Indonesia, Singapore and the Philippines, that all 'citizens have a right to a decent and healthful environment'. The precise phrasing of the right may differ from jurisdiction to jurisdiction. However, the common underlying principle is that citizens are entitled to enjoy a clean environment that is not damaging to their health at the individual or collective level. The framing as a right allows people to seek recourse from the government when the environment is damaged, degraded, polluted, or hazardous.

(11) *Notification and Consultation*: Another widely shared norm is the duty of a state to notify and consult with other states when it undertakes an operation that is likely to harm neighbouring countries' environments, such as the construction of a power plant that

---

[40] (1997)1 SCC 388. Also see *M I Builders v Radhey Shyam Saahu* AIR 1999 SC 2468, 2498; *Karnataka Industrial Area Development Board v C Kenchappa* (2006) 6 SCC 371, 388; *Intellectuals Forum v State of AP* (2006) 3 SCC 549, 574; *Fomento Resorts and Hotels Ltd v Minguel Martins* (2009) 3 SCC 571, 614; *Centre for Public Interest Litigation v Union of India* (2012) 3 SCC 1; *Association for Environment Protection v State of Kerala* (2013) 7 SCC 226, 229; and *Tata Housing Development Company Ltd v Aalok Jagga* (2020) 15 SCC 784.

[41] See *Centre for Public Interest Litigation v Union of India* (2012) 3 SCC 1 excerpted in the Environmental Policy in India chapter.

[42] *Supra* note 15.

[43] The fundamental right to life guaranteed under Article 21 of the Indian Constitution has been interpreted by the Supreme Court to include the right to a wholesome environment. *Subhash Kumar v State of Bihar* AIR 1991 SC 420, 424.

may impair air or water quality in downwind or downstream states. This norm emerged from the Organisation for Economic Cooperation and Development (OECD)[44] and has also evolved into the principle of 'prior informed consent' enshrined in the Basel Convention on Hazardous Waste.[45]

(12) *Monitoring, Reporting and Disclosure*: Over and above the duty to notify and consult, a relatively new norm has emerged whereby states are expected to monitor and assess specific environmental conditions domestically, and disclose these conditions through some agreed form of reporting mechanism to an international agency or international executive body created by an international agreement, and authorized by the parties to the agreement to collect and publicize such information. Parties bound by the Kyoto Protocol under the United Nations Framework Convention on Climate Change (UNFCCC), for instance, have had to report their annual greenhouse gas (GHG) emissions to the Convention secretariat, which makes them publicly available.

(13) *Environmental Impact Assessment*: Environmental impact assessment is another widely accepted norm of international environmental law. Typically, such an assessment balances economic benefits with environmental costs. The logic of such an assessment dictates that before a project is undertaken, its economic benefits must substantially exceed its environmental costs. In its judgment in the *Pulp Mills on the River Uruguay* case between Argentina and Uruguay in 2010, the International Court of Justice found environmental impact assessments to be required by general international law when the proposed activity might be expected to have significant adverse transboundary impacts.[46] The European Union's member states are parties to the Convention on Environmental Impact Assessment in a Transboundary Context (Espoo Convention).[47] India adopted this norm for select projects that are covered under the Environmental Impact Assessment (EIA) regulations introduced in January 1994.[48] Currently, EIA notification 2006 is in operation. Under the 2006 notification, the environmental clearance process is divided into four stages, namely screening, scoping, public consultation and the final appraisal. Expert Appraisal Committees (EACs) are formed at both the Union and state levels. Depending on the nature of the project in question, it is decided whether it will be assessed by the Union EAC or a state's EAC. Projects like nuclear power plants, hydel power and airports are mostly within the jurisdiction of the Union EAC.[49]

In March 2020, the government of India issued the draft EIA notification 2020, which seeks to replace the 2006 notification. The draft notification has invited widespread public criticism on several grounds, especially dilution of the public consultation process.[50]

---

[44] Procedure for Notification and Consultation on Measures for Control of Substances Affecting Man and His Environment, Doc C(71)73 (18 May 1971). Also see OECD, Recommendation of the Council concerning Information Exchange related to Export of Banned or Severely Restricted Chemicals, OECD/LEGAL/0210, https://legalinstruments.oecd.org/public/doc/33/33.en.pdf, accessed 24 June 2021.

[45] Convention on the Control of Transboundary Movements of Hazardous Wastes and their Disposal, U N Doc EP/IG.80/3, shorturl.at/oCQZ2, accessed 24 June 2021.

[46] International Court of Justice, Judgment dated 20 April 2010, para 204 *Pulp Mills on the River Uruguay (Argentina v Uruguay)*, https://www.icj-cij.org/en/case/135/judgments, accessed 24 June 2021.

[47] Convention on Environmental Impact Assessment in a Transboundary Context, Espoo, Finland, 25 February 1991, https://treaties.un.org/pages/ViewDetails.aspx?src=IND&mtdsg_no=XXVII-4&chapter=27&clang=_en, accessed 24 June 2021.

[48] The EIA Regulations are dealt with in the chapter on Environmental Impact Assessment.

[49] Shibani Ghosh, *Demystifying the Environmental Clearance Process in India*, 6 NUJS LAW REVIEW 433 (2013).

[50] Express News Service, *Over 50 Youth Groups Write to Environment Ministry to Put on Hold Draft EIA Notification*, THE INDIAN EXPRESS, 25 June 2020, https://indianexpress.com/article/india/50-youth-groups-envrionment-ministry-hold-draft-eia-notification-covid-6475555/, accessed 24 June 2021.

(14) *Civil Society and NGO Input*: Another recent norm is to invite the input of civil society groups and NGOs, especially those representing grassroots or community-based interests. This is part of a larger effort to integrate stakeholder consultation into key environmental decision-making. NGOs' participation ensures that the people who are likely to be most directly affected by environmental accords will have a major role in monitoring and otherwise implementing those accords. This principle is mirrored in the 'public participation' element of the Indian Government's domestic pollution control policy[51] and the national conservation policy,[52] and is given statutory recognition in the EIA Regulations of 2006. The Supreme Court has also urged the government to draw upon the resources of NGOs to prevent environmental degradation.[53]

(15) *Subsidiarity*: Subsidiarity dictates that whatever decisions can be undertaken locally, should be, whether it involves local ownership, local political authority or local economic self-reliance. Subsidiarity does not necessarily advocate local action but the lowest appropriate level of action. For example, subsidiarity would dictate local control of urban air pollution; regional control of transboundary air pollution, as in the Acid Rain Convention;[54] and global control of global atmospheric pollution as in the Global Climate Change Regime and the Stratospheric Ozone Layer Regime.

(16) *Environmental Rule of Law*: In the *Goa Airport* case excerpted below,[55] the Supreme Court traced the development of environmental Rule of Law as an international norm to secure better enforcement of environmental legislation.

HANUMAN LAXMAN AROSKAR v UNION OF INDIA
(2019) 15 SCC 401

Dr Dhananjaya Y Chandrachud, J: * * *

Fundamental to the outcome of this case is a quest for environmental governance within a rule of law paradigm. Environmental governance is founded on the need to promote environmental sustainability as a crucial enabling factor which ensures the health of our ecosystem.

Since the Stockholm Conference, there has been a dramatic expansion in environmental laws and institutions across the globe. In many instances, these laws and institutions have helped to slow down or reverse environmental degradation. However, this progress is also accompanied, by a growing understanding that there is a considerable implementation gap between the requirements of environmental laws and their implementation and enforcement—both in developed and developing countries alike. The environmental rule of law seeks to address this gap.

The environmental rule of law provides an essential platform underpinning the four pillars of sustainable development—economic, social, environmental and peace. It imbues environmental objectives with the essentials of rule of law and underpins the reform of environmental law and governance. The environmental rule of law becomes a priority particularly

51 Ministry of Environment and Forests, Government of India, *Policy Statement for Abatement of Pollution* (February 1992), para 11, https://www.iitr.ac.in/wfw/web_ua_water_for_welfare/environment/Pollution_Policy_Statement_1992.pdf, accessed 24 June 2021.

52 Ministry of Environment and Forests, Government of India, *National Conservation Strategy and Policy Statement on Environment and Development* (June 1992), para 8.7, http://indiaenvironmentportal.org.in/files/introduction-csps.pdf, accessed 24 June 2021.

53 *Indian Council for Enviro-Legal Action v Union of India* (*CRZ Notification* case) (1996) 5 SCC 281.

54 Convention on Long Range Transboundary Air Pollution, 13 November 1979, 1302 UNTS 217, https://treaties.un.org/Pages/ViewDetails.aspx?src=IND&mtdsg_no=XXVII-1&chapter=7&clang=_en#:~:text=217.&text=The%20Convention%20was%20adopted%20on,United%20Nations%20Office%20in%20Geneva, accessed 24 June 2021.

55 This case is also discussed in the Environmental Impact Assessment chapter.

when we acknowledge that the benefits of environmental rule of law extend far beyond the environmental sector. While the most direct effects are on protection of the environment, it also strengthens rule of law more broadly, supports sustainable economic and social development, protects public health, contributes to peace and security by avoiding and defusing conflict, and protects human and constitutional rights. Similarly, the rule of law in environmental matters is indispensable 'for equity in terms of the advancement of the Sustainable Development Goals (SDGs), the provision of fair access by assuring a rights-based approach, and the promotion and protection of environmental and other socioeconomic rights.'... The intertwined concepts of environmental rule of law thus further intragenerational as well as intergenerational equity.

Decision 27/9 which was adopted by the United Nations Environment Programme's (UNEP's) Governing Body at its first universal session in 2013 on 'Advancing Justice, Governance and Law for Environmental Sustainability' was the first internationally negotiated document to establish the term 'environmental rule of law.' It declared that 'the violation of environmental law has the potential to undermine sustainable development and the implementation of agreed environmental goals and objectives at all levels and that the rule of law and good governance play an essential role in reducing such violations'. It thus urged governments and organisations to reinforce cooperation to combat non-compliance with environmental laws towards achieving sustainable development. It also called upon the Executive Director to assist with the 'development and implementation of environmental rule of law with attention at all levels to mutually supporting governance features, including information disclosure, public participation, implementable and enforceable laws, and implementation and accountability mechanisms including coordination of roles as well as environmental auditing and criminal, civil and administrative enforcement with timely, impartial and independent dispute resolution'. Similarly, the first United Nations Environment Assembly in 2014 adopted Resolution 1/13, which calls upon countries 'to work for the strengthening of environmental rule of law at the international, regional and national levels'.

In 2016, the First World Environmental Law Congress, co-sponsored by the International Union for Conservation of Nature and UN Environment, adopted the IUCN World Declaration on the Environmental Rule of Law which outlines 13 principles for developing and implementing solutions for ecologically sustainable development:

(i) Obligation to Protect Nature
(ii) Right to Nature and Rights of Nature
(iii) Right to Environment.
(iv) Ecological Sustainability and Resilience
(v) *In Dubio Pro Natura*
(vi) Ecological Functions of Property
(vii) Intragenerational Equity
(viii) Intergenerational Equity
(ix) Gender Equality
(x) Participation of Minority and Vulnerable Groups
(xi) Indigenous and Tribal Peoples
(xii) Non-regression
(xiii) Progression

In 2015, the International Community adopted the 2030 Agenda for Sustainable Development and its 17 SDGs. These [goals include: (xiii) Climate action; (xiv) Protecting life below water; (xv) Life on land].

Each of these goals has a vital connection to the others. Together, they provide an agenda for human development: development in a manner which accords adequate protection to the environment. UNEP recognises that the natural environment—forests, soils and wetlands—contributes to the management and regulation of water availability and water quality, strengthening the resilience of watersheds and complements investments in physical infrastructure and institutional and regulatory arrangements for water access and disaster preparedness.

SDG 13 emphasises the urgent action required to combat climate change and its impacts. This is based on the recognition that extreme weather events such as heat waves, droughts, floods and tropical cyclones have aggravated the need for water management, pose a threat to food security, increase health risks, damage critical infrastructure and interrupt the provision of basic civil services....

NOTES AND QUESTIONS

1. As mentioned, norms of customary international law evolve through custom and usage. Not all norms are of equal importance however, some being accorded the status of fundamental norms. The category of fundamental norms comes under the doctrine of *jus cogens*, or the doctrine of peremptory norms. The 1969 Vienna Convention on the Law of Treaties[56] serves to clarify the concept in Article 53, stating:

> A treaty is void if, at the time of its conclusion, it conflicts with a peremptory norm of general international law. For the purposes of the present Convention, a peremptory norm of general international law is a norm accepted and recognized by the international community of States as a whole as a norm from which no derogation is permitted and which can be modified only by a subsequent norm of general international law having the same character.

The doctrine of *jus cogens* is extremely limited and extends to only a handful of norms, the most long-standing of which are the prohibitions against the slave trade, piracy and genocide. Many scholars also believe that the norm expressed in Principle 21 of the Stockholm Convention has risen to *jus cogens* status. However, again the question arises, what good does an international peremptory norm, like an international agreement, achieve?

2. Consider some of the other norms addressed earlier, such as the right to a healthful environment. Is there to be one standard by which all environments are judged, or is it a relative concept? If cutting down trees for firewood destroys the environment, but provides life-sustaining fuel, which right will prevail? Which right *should* prevail? How much weight does each of the two rights carry when the concept of intergenerational equity is introduced?

When considering moral ideals such as the principles of a common heritage and intergenerational equity, what incentives do countries have to try to mould their practices to achieve these ideals? How can countries be better motivated? Is saving the environment for its own sake going to appeal to the majority of people?

3. What exactly is sustainable development? What is 'sustainable'? Could not intelligent and informed people differ over whether producing more minerals or preserving a landscape is sustainable? If so, which is more important? And what is 'development'? Factories that employ thousands, may give a country more industry with which to compete in the world market, but discharge effluents into the water and produce piles of hazardous waste. Do some countries have more of a right to development and less of an obligation to ensure sustainability and vice versa? How much more do industrialized nations need to develop? Have they not gone far enough? Who is to judge?

4. In *Himachal Pradesh Bus Stand Management & Development Authority v Central Empowered Committee*,[57] Justice D Y Chandrachud explained the inter-relationship between environmental Rule of Law, Rule of Law and constitutional democracy.

---

[56] 1155 UNTS 331, https://legal.un.org/ilc/texts/instruments/english/conventions/1_1_1969.pdf, accessed 24 June 2021.

[57] (2021) SCC Online SC 15.

In a constitutional framework which is intended to create, foster and protect a democracy committed to liberal values, the rule of law provides the cornerstone. The rule of law is to be distinguished from rule by the law. The former comprehends the setting up of a legal regime with clearly defined rules and principles of even application, a regime of law which maintains the fundamental postulates of liberty, equality and due process. The rule of law postulates a law which is answerable to constitutional norms. The law in that sense is accountable as much as it is capable of exacting compliance. Rule by the law on the other hand can mean rule by a despotic law. It is to maintain the just quality of the law and its observance of reason that rule of law precepts in constitutional democracies rest on constitutional foundations. A rule of law framework encompasses rules of law but it does much more than that. It embodies matters of substance and process. It dwells on the institutions which provide the arc of governance. By focussing on the structural norms which guide institutional decision making, rule of law frameworks recognise the vital role played by institutions and the serious consequences of leaving undefined the norms and processes by which they are constituted, composed and governed. A modern rule of law framework is hence comprehensive in its sweep and ambit. It recognises that liberty and equality are the focal point of a just system of governance and without which human dignity can be subverted by administrative discretion and absolute power. Rule of law then dwells beyond a compendium which sanctifies rules of law. Its elements comprise of substantive principles, processual guarantees and institutional safeguards that are designed to ensure responsive, accountable and sensitive governance.

The environmental rule of law, at a certain level, is a facet of the concept of the rule of law. But it includes specific features that are unique to environmental governance, features which are *sui generis*. The environmental rule of law seeks to create essential tools—conceptual, procedural and institutional to bring structure to the discourse on environmental protection. It does so to enhance our understanding of environmental challenges—of how they have been shaped by humanity's interface with nature in the past, how they continue to be affected by its engagement with nature in the present and the prospects for the future, if we were not to radically alter the course of destruction which humanity's actions have charted. The environmental rule of law seeks to facilitate a multi-disciplinary analysis of the nature and consequences of carbon footprints and in doing so it brings a shared understanding between science, regulatory decisions and policy perspectives in the field of environmental protection. It recognises that the 'law' element in the environmental rule of law does not make the concept peculiarly the preserve of lawyers and judges. On the contrary, it seeks to draw within the fold all stakeholders in formulating strategies to deal with current challenges posed by environmental degradation, climate change and the destruction of habitats. The environmental rule of law seeks a unified understanding of these concepts. There are significant linkages between concepts such as sustainable development, the polluter pays principle and the trust doctrine. The universe of nature is indivisible and integrated. The state of the environment in one part of the earth affects and is fundamentally affected by what occurs in another part. Every element of the environment shares a symbiotic relationship with the others. It is this inseparable bond and connect which the environmental rule of law seeks to explore and understand in order to find solutions to the pressing problems which threaten the existence of humanity. The environmental rule of law is founded on the need to understand the consequences of our actions going beyond local, state and national boundaries. The rise in the oceans threatens not just maritime communities. The rise in temperatures, dilution of glaciers and growing desertification have consequences which go beyond the communities and creatures whose habitats are threatened. They affect the future survival of the entire eco-system. The environmental rule of law attempts to weave an understanding of the connections in the natural environment which make the issue of survival a unified challenge which confronts human societies everywhere. It seeks to build on experiential learnings of the past to formulate principles which must become the building pillars of environmental regulation in the present and future. The environmental rule of law recognises the overlap between and seeks to amalgamate scientific learning, legal principle and policy intervention. Significantly, it brings attention to the rules, processes and norms followed by institutions which provide regulatory governance on the environment. In doing so, it fosters a regime of open, accountable and transparent decision making on concerns of the environment. It fosters the importance of participatory governance—of the value in giving a voice to those who are most affected by environmental policies and public projects. The structural design of the environmental rule of law composes of substantive, procedural and institutional elements. The tools of analysis go beyond legal concepts. The result of the framework is more than just the sum total of its parts. Together, the elements which it embodies aspire to safeguard the bounties of nature against existential threats. For it is founded on the universal recognition that the future of human existence depends on how we conserve, protect and regenerate the environment today....

The need to adjudicate disputes over environmental harm within a rule of law framework is rooted in a principled commitment to ensure fidelity to the legal framework regulating environmental protection in a manner that transcends a case-by-case adjudication. Before this mode of analysis gained acceptance, we faced a situation in which, despite the existence of environmental legislation on the statute books, there was an absence of a set of overarching judicially recognized principles that could inform environmental adjudication in a manner that was stable, certain and predictable. In an article in the Asia-Pacific Journal of Environmental Law (2014), Bruce Pardy describes this conundrum in the following terms:

> 'Environmental regulations and standards typically identify specific limits or prohibitions on detrimental activities or substances. They are created to reflect the principles and prohibitions contained in the statute under which they are promulgated. However, where the contents of the statute are themselves indeterminate, there is no concrete rule or set of criteria to apply to formulate the standards. Their development can therefore be highly political and potentially arbitrary.
>
> ...
>
> Instead of serving to protect citizens' environmental welfare, an indeterminate environmental law facilitates a utilitarian calculus that allows diffuse interests to be placed aside when they are judged to be less valuable than competing considerations.'

However, even while using the framework of an environmental rule of law, the difficulty we face is this—when adjudicating bodies are called on to adjudicate on environmental infractions, the precise harm that has taken place is often not susceptible to concrete quantification. While the framework provides valuable guidance in relation to the principles to be kept in mind while adjudicating upon environmental disputes, it does not provide clear pathways to determine the harm caused in multifarious factual situations that fall for judicial consideration. The determination of such harm requires access to scientific data which is often times difficult to come by in individual situations.

In an article in the Georgetown Environmental Law Review (2020), Arnold Kreilhuber and Angela Kariuki explain the manner in which the environmental rule of law seeks to resolve this imbroglio:

> 'One of the main distinctions between environmental rule of law and other areas of law is the need to make decisions to protect human health and the environment in the face of uncertainty and data gaps. Instead of being paralyzed into inaction, careful documentation of the state of knowledge and uncertainties allows the regulated community, stakeholders, and other institutions to more fully understand why certain decisions were made.'

The point, therefore, is simply this—the environmental rule of law calls on us, as judges, to marshal the knowledge emerging from the record, limited though it may sometimes be, to respond in a stern and decisive fashion to violations of environmental law. We cannot be stupefied into inaction by not having access to complete details about the manner in which an environmental law violation has occurred or its full implications. Instead, the framework, acknowledging the imperfect world that we inhabit, provides a roadmap to deal with environmental law violations, an absence of clear evidence of consequences notwithstanding.

5. In *Citizens for Green Doon v Union of India* [(2021) SCC Online SC 1074], the Supreme Court reiterated the importance of transparency in securing environmental Rule of Law:

> The grievance of the appellant before this Court is that the permission for tree felling dated 27 August 2021 was not placed in the public domain, as mandated by the circular dated 28 August 2015. On the contrary, when an application for disclosure of information was moved under the [Right to Information Act, 2005/RTI Act] to the [Divisional Forest Officer/DFO] on 11 September 2021, the response on 11 October 2021 was that no order had been passed for permitting the felling of trees. Yet the same officer, namely, the DFO Dehradun, had passed an order on 27 August 2021 granting the permission for the felling of trees, which was annexed to an application for additional documents filed by the respondents for the first time in this Court. The DFO has misled the appellants by furnishing incorrect information in response to the RTI query. The permission for felling trees has to be placed in the public domain, which again, according to the appellant, was not done. The purpose of placing the permission in the public domain is to ensure that persons aggrieved would have a right to challenge it. There is no rebuttal to this grievance of the appellant. A veil of secrecy does not portend well for environmental clearances, since it takes away the right from individuals to challenge them using legal remedies. In the meantime, tree felling proceeded apace. This lack of transparency, leading to a lack of accountability, is in stark contrast to the 'environmental rule of law', which is crucial for good governance.

At the end of a judicial career which earned him the sobriquet 'Green Judge', Justice Kuldip Singh of the Supreme Court issued comprehensive directions to clean up the mess created by the leather tanneries of Tamil Nadu. In the following excerpt from this leading case, Justice Singh borrows international law norms and applies them to the local milieu.

VELLORE CITIZENS' WELFARE FORUM v UNION OF INDIA
AIR 1996 SC 2715

KULDIP SINGH, J:

* * *

> The traditional concept that development and ecology are opposed to each other, is no longer acceptable. 'Sustainable Development' is the answer. In the International sphere 'Sustainable Development' as a concept came to be known for the first time in the Stockholm Declaration of 1972. Thereafter, in 1987 the concept was given a definite shape by the World Commission on Environment and Development in its report called 'Our Common Future'. The Commission was chaired by the then Prime Minister of Norway Ms G H Brundtland and as such the report is popularly known as 'Brundtland Report'. In 1991 the World Conservation Union, United Nations Environment Programme and World Wide Fund for Nature, jointly came out with a document called 'Caring for the Earth' which is a strategy for sustainable living. Finally, came the Earth Summit held in June, 1992 at Rio which saw the largest gathering of world leaders ever in the history—deliberating and chalking out a blue print for the survival of the planet. Among the tangible achievements of the Rio Conference was the signing of two conventions, one on biological diversity and another on climate change. These conventions were signed by 153 nations. The delegates also approved by consensus three non-binding documents namely, a Statement on Forestry Principles, a declaration of principles on environmental policy and development initiatives and Agenda 21, a programme of action into the next century in areas like poverty, population and pollution. During the two decades from Stockholm to Rio 'Sustainable Development' has come to be accepted as a viable concept to eradicate poverty and improve the quality of human life while living within the carrying capacity of the supporting eco-systems. 'Sustainable Development' as defined by the Brundtland Report means 'development that meets the needs of the present without compromising the ability of the future generations to meet their own needs'. We have no hesitation in holding that 'Sustainable Development' as a

balancing concept between ecology and development has been accepted as a part of the Customary International Law though its salient features have yet to be finalized by the International Law Jurists.

Some of the salient principles of 'Sustainable Development', culled-out from Brundtland Report and other international documents, are inter-generational equity; use and conservation of natural resources; environmental protection; the precautionary principle; polluter pays principle; obligation to assist and cooperate; eradication of poverty and financial assistance to the developing countries. We are, however, of the view that 'the precautionary principle' and 'the polluter pays' principle are essential features of 'Sustainable Development'. The 'precautionary principle'—in the context of the municipal law—means:

(i) Environmental measures—by the State Government and the statutory authorities—must anticipate, prevent and attack the causes of environmental degradation.
(ii) Where there are threats of serious and irreversible damage, lack of scientific certainty should not be used as a reason for postponing measures to prevent environmental degradation.
(iii) The 'Onus of proof' is on the actor or the developer/industrialist to show that his action is environmentally benign.

'The polluter pays' principle has been held to be a sound principle by this Court in *Indian Council for Enviro-Legal Action vs Union of India (The Bichhri case),* (1996) 3 SCC 212. The Court observed, 'We are of the opinion that any principle evolved in this behalf should be simple, practical and suited to the conditions obtaining in this country'. The Court ruled that 'Once the activity carried on is hazardous or inherently dangerous, the person carrying on such activity is liable to make good the loss caused to any other person by his activity irrespective of the fact whether he took reasonable care while carrying on his activity. The rule is premised upon the very nature of the activity carried on'. Consequently, the polluting industries are 'Absolutely liable to compensate for the harm caused by them to villagers in the affected area, to the soil and to the underground water and hence, they are bound to take all necessary measures to remove sludge and other pollutants lying in the affected areas'. The 'polluter pays' principle as interpreted by this Court means that the absolute liability for harm to the environment extends not only to compensate the victims of pollution but also the cost of restoring the environmental degradation. [Remedying] the damaged environment is part of the process of 'Sustainable Development' and as such [the] polluter is liable to pay the cost to the individual [who] suffers as well as the cost of reversing the damaged ecology.

[The court then set out the provision of the Constitution as well as the Water Act, Air Act and Environment (Protection) Act.] In view of the above mentioned constitutional and statutory provisions we have no hesitation in holding that the precautionary principle and the polluter pays principle are part of the environmental law of the country.

Even otherwise once these principles are accepted as part of the Customary International Law there would be no difficulty in accepting them as part of the domestic law. It is almost accepted proposition of law that the rules of Customary International Law which are not contrary to the municipal law shall be deemed to have been incorporated in the domestic law and shall be followed by the Courts of Law. For support we may refer to Justice H R Khanna's opinion in *Addl Distt Magistrate Jabalpur v Shivakant Shukla* (AIR 1976 SC 1207), *Jolly George Verghese's* case (AIR 1980 SC 470) and *Gramophone Company's* case (AIR 1984 SC 667).

The Constitutional and statutory provisions protect a person's right to fresh air, clean water and pollution free environment, but the source of the right is the inalienable common law right of clean environment. [The court proceeded to quote a paragraph from Blackstone's commentaries on the Laws of England (1876) in respect of 'nuisance'.] Our legal system having been founded on the British Common Law the right of a person to pollution free environment is a part of the basic jurisprudence of the land. . . .

NOTES AND QUESTIONS

1. In the concluding part of the *Vellore* judgment (not reproduced above), the Supreme Court issued a wide range of directions. The Central Government was required to establish an authority under section 3(3) of the Environment (Protection) Act of 1986 headed by a retired High Court judge, to deal with the situation created by the tanneries and other polluting industries in Tamil Nadu. The authority so constituted was asked to apply the precautionary principle and the polluter pays principle whilst identifying the individuals who had suffered due to the pollution, assessing the loss incurred and determining the compensation payable by the polluters. The authority was conferred wide powers by the court, including the power to direct the closure of industry and the relocation of units. The court also imposed a pollution fine of Rs. 10,000 on each of the tanneries in five districts of the state.

2. The discussion in the judgment relating to the polluter pays principle is unsatisfactory. In *Indian Council for Enviro-Legal Action* (the *Bichhri* case) the Supreme Court recognized the distinction between the principle of 'absolute liability' applicable only to hazardous industries, and the wider 'polluter pays' principle which applies whenever an industry pollutes the air, water or land, irrespective of whether it is a hazardous unit or not. The court in the *Vellore* case appears to have mixed up these two distinct principles and rolled them into one. Would you interpret the *Vellore* judgment to mean that the 'no-fault' liability principle extends to all situations where the damage is caused by pollution, and is no longer restricted in India to damage caused by hazardous industries? Does this mean that in India a polluter is no longer entitled to the defences that are available to him under the law of torts?

D. CONFLICTS BETWEEN THE ENVIRONMENT AND FREE TRADE

To help promote responsible environmental practices at home and abroad, many countries have enacted legislation that contains certain trade restrictions preventing the free flow of goods across borders. Such environmental restrictions often conflict with the terms of international free trade agreements, primarily with the WTO's rules and agreements, which seek to discourage or prohibit the use of import restrictions.

The WTO was established in 1995 and subsumes the earlier trade rules created by the General Agreement on Tariffs and Trade (GATT). GATT was formed in 1947 in the aftermath of World War II, primarily to encourage global economic development by limiting the use of tariffs and import restrictions. The GATT agreement comprised the initial 1947 document and its periodic 'rounds' of amendment. The WTO Secretariat is the administrative body that sits in Geneva, Switzerland. Its purpose is to implement the terms and requirements of a host of negotiated agreements under the aegis of the WTO, including on issues like agriculture, intellectual property and tariffs. The WTO also has a dispute resolution mechanism where member states can reconcile conflicting interpretations of WTO provisions.

The General Agreement on Tariffs and Trade allows nations to restrict the import of products from other member nations, so long as these restrictions do not discriminate between foreign and domestic products. For instance, under GATT the United States may ban the import of a dangerous pesticide so long as the use of the pesticide is also banned in the United States. Article 20 lists the exceptions that justify a deviation from GATT's general free trade requirements. Among these exceptions are trade restrictions 'necessary to protect human, animal or plant life and health'[58] and those 'relating to the conservation of exhaustible natural resources'.[59] Most of the controversy regarding WTO's impact on environmental protection has centered on the dispute resolution panel's interpretations of the Article 20 exceptions which allow member states to take necessary and proportionate trade-restrictive measures to protect larger interests, including health, environmental and security concerns.

THE *SHRIMP TURTLE* CASE: GATT ARTICLE 20

The *Shrimp Turtle* case[60] is pivotal in this context. Briefly, the dispute related to a ban placed by the United States on the import of shrimp from India, Pakistan, Malaysia and Thailand.

According to the United States, the four countries' process of shrimp harvesting was detrimental to sea turtles, an endangered species. The United States argued that shrimp harvesting should be carried out using turtle excluder devices (TEDs). Furthermore, it argued that under section 609 of the US Endangered Species Act, the US government needed to ensure that all shrimp imported were harvested in a manner that protected marine turtles from incidental drowning. The countries in question filed a claim under the dispute resolution mechanism with the WTO, on several grounds, *inter alia*, that the ban is discriminatory in nature and allows differential treatments to countries producing the same end-product.[61] Specifically, with regards to Article 20, which allows necessary trade-restrictive measures for protecting larger health and environmental interests even if they are discriminatory, the claimants argued that such discriminatory measures should not be arbitrary. They claimed that the ban was not 'necessary' and other means, such as bilateral/multilateral agreements, could have been used to protect sea turtles. They also contended that exceptions under Article 20 could not be applied extraterritorially. In this context, the United States argued that sea turtles are a common, shared global resource and thus the ban was not extraterritorial. Moreover, it argued that Article 20 protects animals regardless of their 'location'.

The WTO Panel held that the US ban could not be justified under the exceptions of Article 20 because the ban was arbitrary. Upholding the decision of the panel, WTO's Appellate Body clarified that while the ban was allowed under Article 20(g), it violated the preamble provision of Article 20, as it arbitrarily discriminated between Western economies and eastern economies, and gave the former more transition time and financial support to supplement their harvesting process.

NOTES AND QUESTIONS

1. The General Agreement on Tariffs and Trade is one of the most powerful international agreements in the world and often supersedes environmental treaties. Why is this? Is it because the WTO, unlike most environmental law regimes, has an institutional dispute resolution mechanism and enforcement procedures? Or is it because the global community puts greater emphasis on commodities and trade than on the environment and conservation?

2. Many treaties, recognizing the power of market-based incentives, have tried to turn environmental issues into commodity issues. Is the market the proper mechanism for saving

[58] Article 20(b).
[59] Article 20(g).
[60] The WTO Dispute Settlement Archive Reports List, *United States—Import Prohibition on Certain Shrimp and Shrimp Products*, https://www.wto.org/english/tratop_e/dispu_e/distab_e.htm#r58, accessed 25 June 2021.
[61] They claimed it violated Articles 1, 11 and 13 of the GATT.

the environment? Would not the unfettered operation of free trade, as pictured under GATT, lead to the eventual destruction of the environment? Has it not brought us perilously close to that point already? Why, then, are economic approaches and GATT so powerful? Is economic self-interest the only true motivator for people and states? If so, is there a way to give greater economic value to the environment? Is there an economic theory or accounting mechanism that can take true environmental costs into account in the face of a project's touted economic benefits?

E. HUMAN RIGHTS, INDIGENOUS PEOPLE AND THE ENVIRONMENT

Although environmental protection and human rights are often treated as separate legal topics, there are many situations where the two fields overlap. First, many governments and international bodies have recognized the right of citizens to live in a clean and healthful environment. Second, environmental and natural resource policies may disproportionately affect poor and minority communities.

The rights of indigenous people are a 'cross-over' issue in that they may be protected under both international human rights law and international environmental law. (Any environmental right can theoretically be couched in terms of a human right, so this is not the only area where the two bodies of law dovetail.)

The rights of indigenous people may be seen in two basic lights: (1) the right to protect and manage natural resources located on traditional indigenous lands; (2) the right of citizens to live in a healthful environment. Many environmentally destructive development practices severely impact the traditional lands and lifestyles of indigenous communities. Therefore, their rights often provide another tool in the fight against such projects.

With respect to the protection of indigenous people as a means to conserve biodiversity, international environmental law can play an important role. Many native and indigenous people have opposed government policies that permit resource exploitation on traditional lands. Because this exploitation threatens to undermine the economic and spiritual fabric of their cultures, and often results in forced migration and resettlement, the struggle to protect the environment is often a part of the struggle to protect the cultures of indigenous people.

At the Earth Summit in 1992, three documents emerged, one of which was the Rio Declaration on Environment and Development.[62] In Principle 22, the Declaration states that '[i]ndigenous people and their communities and other local communities have a vital role in environmental management and development because of their knowledge and traditional practices. States should recognize and duly support their identity, culture and interests and enable their effective participation in the achievement of sustainable development.'

The same principle is echoed in the Convention on Biodiversity in Article 8(j). However, as discussed later in the section on Protecting Endangered Species, both the Declaration and the Convention lack substantive obligations and enforcement mechanisms. Thus, both are regarded as 'framework' conventions upon which truly binding rights and responsibilities can only be built through further agreements.

---

[62] *Supra* note 23. The Supreme Court referred to Principle 13 of the Declaration requiring states to develop national laws to compensate the victims of pollution and other environmental damage in *Indian Council for Enviro-Legal Action v Union of India* (*CRZ Notification* case) (1996) 5 SCC 281.

The combination of human rights and environmental obligations can provide a powerful tool to protect land and eco-systems where indigenous people reside. This protection is evidenced by the reservation of lands for indigenous peoples, such as the Yanomami lands in Brazil, that incidentally also contain some of the world's precious rain forests. As the conservation expertise of indigenous peoples becomes more widely acknowledged, indigenous rights are likely to play an increased role in national and international environmental protection efforts.

A case significant to the environmental rights of indigenous communities is *Africa Commission of Human Rights v Kenya*.[63] The dispute related to the appropriation of the Mau forest which is key to the survival of the Ogiek community. The appropriation, carried without any consultation with the Ogiek community, disrupted, *inter alia*, their hunting and gathering lifestyle and misappropriated several religious sites located in the forest. A 30-day eviction notice was served by the government to the Ogieks, following which an application was made to the African Commission on Human Rights (ACHR) in 2009. Given the indifference of the government, and evidence of serious and massive human rights violation of the Ogieks, the ACHR referred the case to the Africa Court of Human Rights (ACtHR), which gave its final ruling in 2017.

The Ogieks argued that the misappropriation of the Mau forest and the eviction notice violated several provisions of the African Charter of Human Rights, including freedom of religion (Article 8), the right to culture (Article 17(2) and (3)), the right to freely dispose of wealth and natural resources (Article 21) and the right to development (Article 22). At their end, the government argued that the Ogieks were not a unique indigenous community but rather an amalgamation of several ethnic communities. On merits, they argued that the government followed the appropriate consultation process and the Ogieks consented to the appropriation. They alleged that the community had abandoned their religion. They argued that there was no evidence substantiating the location of the religious sites in question. Moreover, the government indicated that the community's access has not been altogether suspended; they might access the forest except at night, and needed licences for some practices. Ultimately, the government argued that there is a need to balance between the cultural rights of the Ogieks and the interest of maintaining ecological balance. Since the Ogieks' practices are not environmentally sustainable, the government's notice did not violate the Charter.

Declaring the Ogiek as an indigenous community, the ACtHR held that while there is no straitjacket formula to make the said determination, there are certain determinant factors, namely, the priority in time with respect to the occupation and use of a specific territory; a voluntary perception of cultural distinctiveness; self-identification as well as recognition by other groups, or by state authorities that they are a distinct collectivity; and an experience of subjugation, marginalization, dispossession, exclusion or discrimination, whether or not these conditions persist.

With regard to the religious identity of the Ogieks, the court held that not all Ogieks had abandoned their religion, that is, converted to Christianity. A significant number were still non-Christians; in the absence of religious institutions in tribal societies, religion is inextricably tied to land. Therefore, denying them access to land and forest was denying their right to practise religion.

[63] *African Commission on Human and Peoples' Rights v Republic of Kenya*, ACtHPR, Application No. 006/2012 (2017), https://www.escr-net.org/caselaw/2017/african-commission-human-and-peoples-rights-v-republic-kenya-acthpr-application-no, accessed 25 June 2021.

Significantly, addressing the government's argument about maintaining ecological balance, the court held that preservation of forest did not allow removal of the Ogieks, because their lifestyle cannot be said to be harming the forest.

Just as protecting the rights of indigenous communities has increasingly become a visible strand of international environmental law, it has also been increasingly manifested within recent developments in Indian environmental law. In 2006, India passed the Scheduled Tribes and Other Traditional Forest Dwellers (Recognition of Forest Rights) Act of 2006, which gives certain tribal populations and forest-dwelling communities rights over the management and use of a range of forest resources. The Act gives forest-dependent beneficiaries community rights over common property resources in forest areas (including water bodies), and also gives them the right to protect, regenerate, conserve or manage any community forest resource which they have traditionally protected and conserved for sustainable use.

A noteworthy development that has implications for international environmental law, in relation to the environmental rights of indigenous groups, is the 'environmental referendum' that took place in India at the behest of the Supreme Court. In *Orissa Mining Corporation Ltd v Ministry of Environment and Forests*,[64] the Supreme Court held that a bauxite (precursor to aluminum) mine in the state of Odisha could not receive clearance until it was evident that the affected local communities were in favour of the project. Since the project entailed diversion of forest land where tribal groups reside, the court ordered that the Ministry of Environment and Forests conduct a referendum of the *gram sabhas* (village local government units) of 12 villages in the region. After a unanimous vote by the tribal communities rejecting the project, the ministry had to deny the mine developer clearance.

QUESTIONS

1. Why and how can indigenous communities and indigenous practices be preserved, protected and promoted? While we preserve biodiversity, how do we conserve human diversity—the diversity of culture, livelihoods and ways of being? How should constitutional values of equality, inclusion and conservation be balanced?

2. What if a community that suffers from an environmental threat or hazard is not indigenous? Do they therefore deserve less protection? What if indigenous people inhabit fragile lands that ought to remain pristine? What if indigenous people are engaged in environmentally destructive practices? When does the protection of indigenous people, and their common property lands, conflict with their right to development and self-determination?

3. How can the state ensure that environmental laws do not violate essential human rights and that conservation actions do not exclude indigenous communities?

In the late 1990s, Lafarge, a multinational cement manufacturer, initiated a cross-border project that straddled the India-Bangladesh boundary near the state of Meghalaya. Cement was manufactured in Bangladesh but the crucial raw material, limestone, was imported by a conveyor system from a mine located in the vicinity of Nongtrai village in the East Khasi Hills District, Meghalaya. Lafarge depended on Indian limestone because Bangladesh had no proximate limestone deposits. According to the company, there was no forest in the limestone

[64] (2013) 6 SCC 476, commonly called the *Vedanta* case. Vedanta was the UK-based aluminum company seeking to exploit the bauxite in the Nyamgiri Hills.

mine area in India and various authorities concurred. In the Supreme Court, the focus was on Lafarge's failure to recognize the forest and obtain prior permission before mining under the Forest (Conservation) Act of 1980. The Supreme Court permitted Lafarge to operate, rejecting the contention that the company had secured initial environmental clearances on an incorrect representation about the character of the land. The main analysis of the *Lafarge* case is in the Forests chapter, but here we examine an important ancillary issue concerning tribal rights and the participation of tribal citizens in the decision-making process.

LAFARGE UMIAM MINING (P) LTD v UNION OF INDIA

(2011) 7 SCC 338

S H Kapadia, C J: * * *

Apart from the above circumstances, on 22-4-1998, a Notification was issued by the State Pollution Control Board constituting an Environmental Public Hearing Panel to evaluate and assess the documents submitted by [Lafarge]. A public notice was also issued in the local newspapers on 25-5-1998. The State Pollution Control Board also sent a letter to the Secretary, Shella Village informing him of the date and time of public hearing and accordingly on 3-6-1998, a public hearing did take place. According to the minutes of the meeting, 31 citizens of Shella, Nongtrai and Pyrkan attended the hearing.

In the hearing, the purpose, objective, composition and procedure of environmental public hearing was discussed. The Headman of Nongtrai was also present. He gave reasons as to why the village durbar had agreed to the proposed project. The main reason being that the limestone was abundantly available in the area but the same remained unutilised by local villagers themselves due to lack of infrastructure. That, for economic development of the local population, the village durbar had decided to lease the area required for the project to Lafarge. In the meeting, the economic benefits of the local people from the project proponent were also discussed. The environmental implications were also discussed. The mitigating measures to be adopted by the project proponent were also discussed to maintain the ecology and environmental balance of the area. The objections of certain persons were also noted and discussed. The durbar came to the conclusion that there was no destruction of any caves. The complainant was not even present during the hearing. Thus, a public hearing did take place on 3-6-1998.

One more aspect at this stage needs to be mentioned. Public participation provides a valuable input in the process of identification of forest. Today, amongst the tribals of the North-East, there is a growing awareness of the close relationship between poverty and environmental pollution....

In our view, the natives and indigenous people are fully aware and they have knowledge as to what constitutes conservation of forests and development. They equally know the concept of forest degradation. They are equally aware of systematic scientific exploitation of limestone mining without causing of 'environment degradation'. However, they do not have the requisite wherewithal to exploit limestone mining in a scientific manner. These natives and indigenous people know how to keep the balance between economic and environment sustainability....

The manner and method of allocation, use and occupation of the community lands are decided by the village durbar. The village durbar has granted lease of 100 ha of community land out of 900 ha which as stated above is limestone bearing land. It is important to note that apart from the minutes of the meeting held on 3-6-1998 which was attended by the Headman of Nongtrai Village, a detailed written submission has been filed on 13-5-2011 by the Nongtrai village durbar fully supporting the impugned project. Thus, this is a unique case from the North-East. We are fully satisfied that the natives and the indigenous people of Nongtrai Village are fully conscious of their rights and obligations towards clean environment and economic development. There is ample material on record which bears testimony to the fact of their awareness of ecological concerns which has been taken into account by MoEF. In the circumstances, it cannot be said that the impugned project should be discarded and that the decision of MoEF granting ex post facto clearances stands vitiated for non-application of mind as alleged by Shella Action Committee....

NOTES

The *Lafarge* case illustrates how large projects may divide a community. As the excerpt shows, a significant number of villagers of Nongtrai village supported the project and were keen on the economic development that would accompany a working limestone mine. The project was opposed by the Shella Action Committee (SAC), a society of villagers whose object was to protect and safeguard the rights and interests of the tribal residents of Shella village. Shella village, like Nongtrai, was close to the mine site.

Shella has a population of around 7,500 and the village economy is primarily dependent on agriculture. The villagers grow paddy, oranges, pineapples and areca nut. The residents of Shella belong to the Khasi tribe which is a Scheduled Tribe under Part XI of the Constitution (Scheduled Tribes) Order of 1950. Shella villagers believed that the mine site was on land over which they exercised traditional rights. Nongtrai claimed that the mine site was in its area. The SAC urged that before the forest clearance was granted by the MoEF on 22 April 2010 it should have insisted upon the rights of tribals being settled in terms of the Scheduled Tribes and Traditional Forest Dwellers (Recognition of Forest Rights) Act of 2006. It is only after these forest rights are recognized and registered that the issue of third-party rights such as those claimed by Lafarge could be considered. The Supreme Court took an overall view of the project and was satisfied about local support for economic development.

F. ENVIRONMENTAL JUSTICE

I. ENVIRONMENT AND POVERTY

There is a growing awareness of the close relationship between poverty and environmental pollution. It is broadly recognized that poorer citizens are more likely to suffer the consequences of environmental pollution than other citizens, on both the national and international levels. It has also given rise to environmental poverty law, or environmental justice, which seeks legal remedies to the disproportionate environmental abuse suffered by poorer citizens.

Internationally, less affluent nations tend to have more severe environmental problems than wealthier nations. Examples of these problems are easy to identify. Air pollution in Mexico and China is generally more severe than in France or Australia. Hazardous waste is treated less safely in Eastern Europe and Africa than in Western Europe and Canada. The reasons for this situation are frustrating but not difficult to understand. Less affluent nations lack the financial resources to purchase modern pollution control or energy-efficient technologies, or to implement environmental protection policies.

At the 1992 Earth Summit in Rio, developing countries asked for increased technology transfers. These countries pointed out that if the developed world is truly concerned with stemming the environmental deterioration in developing countries, new technologies for environmental protection need to be made available at little or no cost to developing countries.

On the national level, there have also been important developments. In India, for example, judicial decisions have held that the urban poor must be treated fairly and that government policies must respect their human rights.[65] Moreover, legislative recognition of the right of slum dwellers to decent housing, the Scheduled Tribes and Other Traditional Forest Dwellers (Recognition of Forest Rights) Act of 2006 and the Street Vendors (Protection of Livelihood and Regulation of Street Vending) Act of 2014 entitle poor citizens to utilize common property resources for essential livelihood requirements.

II. NORTH–SOUTH TENSIONS

Tensions between the developed and developing world are found at the international level. Many transnational corporations headquartered in the developed world have chosen to move environmentally dangerous industrial activities to the developing world.

Why do transnational corporations relocate to these poorer nations? First, labour costs are much cheaper. Second, taxes are substantially lower. Finally, environmental standards in the developing world are generally lower (and therefore less expensive) than in the developed world. This means, of course, that workers are often exposed to hazardous materials or unsafe conditions.

The export of environmental harm to the world's poorer nations has resulted in many instances of severe health and environmental problems. Two widely publicized examples are the lethal 1984 Union Carbide gas leak in Bhopal, and the continuing logging of tropical rain forests by timber companies headquartered in rich Western nations.

NOTES AND QUESTIONS

1. Environmental justice has become one of the most sensitive issues within the environmental movement. It underlies almost all of the negotiating sessions and the disputes leading up to international environmental agreements. Poorer, less developed countries (LDCs) feel strongly that developed countries exercise 'eco-imperialism' in all arenas. Is this correct? Why? Does it help powerful nations stay powerful? By not transferring technology, do the rich get richer? At whose expense? Is it not in the best interests of the developed countries, who after all share the planet with the LDCs, to ensure that LDCs have the technologies and economic resources to invest in sustainable development projects and industries, in order to preserve the global commons (the deep sea, the atmosphere, Antarctica)? Keep in mind that global environmental degradation, like global climate change and stratospheric ozone depletion, recognizes no boundaries.

2. The United States' initial refusal under President Bush to sign the 1992 Convention on Biological Diversity was based on one of the most controversial environmental justice issues, namely intellectual property rights over plant genetic resources. The privatization of biotechnology and plant genetic resources, primarily derived from LDCs but patented in developed countries, has led to wide-scale protests and civil unrest, resulting in what has become known as 'seed wars'. Are not seeds, as well as all plant genetic resources, humankind's 'common heritage'? Should they be allowed to be patented? If so, should they be patented in their countries of origin? Would allowing countries of origin to patent, thereby obtaining royalties, provide an economic incentive to conserve them?[66]

---

[65] An early case was *Olga Tellis v Bombay Municipal Corporation* AIR 1986 SC 180.

[66] India does not recognize plant patents: section 3(j), Patents Act of 1970. The Protection of Plant Varieties and Farmers' Rights Act of 2001 envisages a benefit-sharing scheme amongst registered plant breeders and farmers.

G. AIR POLLUTION AND PROTECTION OF THE ATMOSPHERE

During the 1980s, international environmental efforts shifted from transboundary or regional air pollution concerns, such as acid rain, to threats to the global atmosphere. This shift was prompted by scientific evidence that emerged in the mid-1970s. The evidence linked the release of chlorofluorocarbons (CFCs) and other chlorine-based aerosols with the destruction of the stratospheric ozone layer. The ozone layer shields human beings and plant life from the harmful effects of solar radiation. CFCs are used in refrigeration, air conditioning and foam furniture among other applications. To reduce the use of these substances, and protect the global atmosphere, the 1985 Vienna Convention for the Protection of the Ozone Layer[67] and the 1987 Montreal Protocol on Substances that Deplete the Ozone Layer[68] were adopted. Because the 1987 Protocol incorporated the 1985 Convention's basic aims, the international regime to protect the ozone layer is usually referred to as the Montreal Protocol.

In the 1970s, evidence also started building about another environmental threat—climate change. Public and political debate on the issue gained traction in the 1990s, as the ramifications of climate change became clearer. The issue of global climate change encompasses many underlying environmental concerns, including air pollution, energy consumption, deforestation and management of the global commons. For the purposes of this chapter, the issue will be discussed in the present section on air pollution and protection of the atmosphere. The primary international agreements relating to global warming and climate change are the United Nations Framework Convention of Climate Change (UNFCCC) signed at the Rio de Janeiro Earth Summit in 1992;[69] the Kyoto Protocol to the UNFCCC, signed at Kyoto, Japan in 1997;[70] and the Paris Agreement of 2015 under the UNFCCC.[71]

I. 1987 MONTREAL PROTOCOL ON SUBSTANCES THAT DEPLETE THE OZONE LAYER

The 1987 Montreal Protocol on Substances that Deplete the Ozone Layer (Montreal Protocol) sets firm targets for reducing consumption and production of a range of ozone-depleting substances—chiefly chlorofluorocarbons (CFCs). The standards set forth in the 1987 Protocol were strengthened and expanded to cover additional ozone-depleting substances, through amendments adopted in 1990, 1992, 1997, 1999 and 2016. These amendments were prompted by the development of new technology and alternative 'ozone friendly' substances. The Protocol's ability to respond to and incorporate scientific/technological developments has been widely praised, and has provided a model of constructive flexibility for future international environmental agreements.

One of the major innovations of the Montreal Protocol is its recognition that all nations should not be treated equally. The agreement acknowledges that certain countries have

---

67 The Vienna Convention for the Protection of the Ozone Layer, https://ozone.unep.org/treaties/vienna-convention/vienna-convention-protection-ozone-layer, accessed 25 June 2021.

68 The Montreal Protocol on Substances that Deplete the Ozone Layer, https://ozone.unep.org/treaties/montreal-protocol-substances-deplete-ozone-layer/text, accessed 25 June 2021.

69 United Nations Framework Convention on Climate Change (UNFCCC), https://unfccc.int/resource/docs/convkp/conveng.pdf, accessed 25 June 2021.

70 The Kyoto Protocol, https://unfccc.int/sites/default/files/resource/docs/cop3/l07a01.pdf, accessed 25 June 2021.

71 The Paris Agreement, https://unfccc.int/sites/default/files/english_paris_agreement.pdf, accessed 25 June 2021.

contributed greatly to ozone depletion while other countries have made very small contributions. The agreement also recognizes that a nation's obligation to reduce current emissions should reflect its technological and financial ability to abate CFC pollution. Because of this situation, the agreement applies more stringent standards, and a more accelerated phase-out timetable, to the countries that have contributed the most to ozone depletion. Such countries had to eliminate all CFCs by the year 1995. Developing countries had a 15-year 'grace period' and were obligated to phase out CFC use by 2010. The Kigali Amendment of 2016 extended the phase-out to hydrofluorocarbons (HFCs). Some industries adopted HFCs as substitutes for ozone-depleting substances though HFCs are potent greenhouse gases that contribute to global warming.

The Montreal Protocol also includes innovative funding provisions providing less affluent member countries financial and technical incentives (such as the transfer of technology and patents) to encourage a rapid switch to non-ozone-depleting substances and production methods. Specifically, Article 10 of the Protocol established a fund to facilitate technical cooperation and technology transfer to assist developing states.

This Multilateral Ozone Fund, administered by the Global Environment Facility (GEF),[72] depends on the support of the developed countries. While this system seems fair, it also creates a loophole in the Protocol through which many less developed countries (LDCs) would have been able to avoid meeting the standards set out in the Protocol if the developed countries did not meet their financial obligations. However, the obligations were met successfully.

Finally, the Protocol also contains provisions to deal with the problem of the few nations that have not signed the Protocol and continue to produce and consume ozone-depleting substances, by banning trade in these substances with non-member states. Thus, parties to the Protocol are prohibited from importing such substances, or exporting CFC production technology and equipment. This comprehensive trade ban places both economic and diplomatic pressure on all nations to join the Protocol.

II. 1992 UNITED NATIONS FRAMEWORK CONVENTION ON CLIMATE CHANGE

A study on rising ocean temperatures found 2019 to be the hottest year for the oceans. How do rising ocean temperatures impact the global environment?

> Human-emitted greenhouse gases have resulted in a long-term and unequivocal warming of the planet. More than 90% of the excess heat is stored within the world's oceans, where it accumulates and causes increases in ocean temperature. Because the oceans are the main repository of the Earth's energy imbalance, measuring ocean heat content (OHC) is one of the best ways to quantify the rate of global warming.... New OHC data for the year 2019 reveals that the world's oceans ... were the warmest in recorded human history....
> Increased ocean temperatures lead to rising sea levels (thermal expansion of the ocean and added mass from melting land ice). According to the altimetry satellite record, the past 10 years are also the highest in global mean sea level since 1900.... The increasing heat increases evaporation, and the extra moisture in the warmer atmosphere nourishes heavy rains and promotes flooding, leading to a more extreme hydrological cycle and more extreme weather (in particular hurricanes and typhoons). It is one of the key reasons why the Earth has

[72] GEF was initially established in 1991 as a pilot programme of the World Bank, UNEP and the UN Development Programme. It was restructured in 1994 following the decisions taken at the Rio Conference.

experienced increasing catastrophic fires in the Amazon, California, and Australia in 2019 (extending into 2020 for Australia).[73]

One hundred and fifty one million people across China, Bangladesh, India, Vietnam, Indonesia and Thailand are at risk of permanent inundation by the year 2100.[74] In India, West Bengal and coastal Odisha are predicted to be at a particularly higher risk. By 2050, much of Kolkata could be in the annual coastal flood risk zone. Global climatic disruptions are accelerating. They already pose an existential threat to island nations and coastal communities. The international response has been slow, despite scientists pointing out the urgency.[75]

The United Nations Framework Convention on Climate Change of 1992[76] was prompted by several scientific studies in the late 1970s and early 1980s, which indicated that increased levels of carbon dioxide (CO_2) in the atmosphere were causing global average temperatures to rise. This increase in temperatures is due to the 'greenhouse effect', where the sun's heat is trapped after radiating off the earth's surface, and is captured by the CO_2 in the earth's atmosphere (which prevents the heat from escaping). The Climate Change Convention was adopted to reduce the amount of CO_2 emitted into the atmosphere (as well as other greenhouse gases that were also contributing to the problem) and to preserve and increase the earth's carbon absorption capacities.

In addressing the global warming issue, the international community chose to model the process after the successful approach employed in the ozone/CFC context. Just as the general, aspirational 1985 Vienna Convention preceded the highly specific 1987 Montreal Protocol, the 1992 Framework Convention represented the first step in the international community's attempt to stop global warming (and was followed by the Kyoto Protocol). The Convention's purpose is to demonstrate and forge consensus, and to provide the diplomatic foundation for a more substantive agreement, while the Protocol provides the actual rules and procedures for reductions.

Article 2 of the Convention states that the 'ultimate objective' of the framework agreement is to stabilize the concentrations of greenhouse gases at a level which would prevent dangerous anthropogenic interference with the climate system. This broad and general phrasing provides participating countries with flexibility in implementation strategies. Member countries have interpreted this level to be a temperature rise of up to 2°C in the twenty-first century.

The Climate Change Convention was only a broad blueprint, but some significant principles and provisions were negotiated. Most of these provisions reflect North–South (developed–developing world) tensions. First, it was agreed that financial commitments should be based on the principles of 'common but different responsibilities and respective capabilities', and 'appropriate burden sharing' and 'equity', meaning that wealthier nations should be required to contribute more than poorer nations. Second, the Convention states that developed

---

[73] Cheng, L, *et al*, *Record-setting Ocean Warmth Continued in 2019* 37(2) Adv Atmos Sci 137 (2020), https://link.springer.com/content/pdf/10.1007/s00376-020-9283-7.pdf, accessed 25 June 2021.

[74] Climate Central, *Flooded Future: Global Vulnerability to Sea Level Rise Worse Than Previously Understood* (29 October 2019), https://www.climatecentral.org/pdfs/2019CoastalDEMReport.pdf, accessed 25 June 2021.

[75] See generally, *Climate Change Science and Policy* (Eds. Stephen Schneider, Armin Rosencranz, *et al*, 2010) and *Handbook of Climate Change and India* (Ed. Navroz K. Dubash, 2012). The Supreme Court recognized the adverse impact of climate change on India in *Municipal Corporation of Greater Mumbai v Ankita Sinha* (2021) SCC Online SC 897.

[76] 1771 Unts 107; S Treaty Doc No. 102-38; UN Doc A/AC.237/18 (Part II)/Add 1, https://unfccc.int/resource/docs/convkp/conveng.pdf, accessed 25 June 2021.

countries 'shall take all practical steps to promote, facilitate and finance, as appropriate, the transfer of, or access to, environmentally sound technologies'. In addition, the Framework Convention specifies that the Global Environmental Facility would act as the financial mechanism for allocating funding to developing countries.

In 1997, parties to the UN Climate Change Convention adopted the Kyoto Protocol.[77] The Protocol entered into force in 2005. It provided three specific mechanisms for reductions of global greenhouse gases, that is, emissions trading, the clean development mechanism (CDM) and joint implementation.[78] The most impactful is the CDM, where developed countries instal clean fuels and other technologies in developing countries and LDCs, in exchange for Certified Emission Reductions (CERs).[79] The emissions saved are credited to investing country/corporation, as the case may be. One CER unit is equivalent to 1 tonne of CO_2 emission.[80]

Recognizing that Western developed nations had both contributed more greenhouse pollution and had higher capacity to implement reductions, and in adherence to the principle of common but differentiated responsibilities and respective capabilities, the Protocol created a bifurcated system of obligations. Annex I countries (developed nations) were bound by emission reduction commitments that had to be achieved by 2012. Non-Annex I countries (developing and least developed nations) were not bound by such obligations, but would measure and provide data on their emissions to the UNFCCC for the purpose of record-keeping. The first phase of the Kyoto Protocol concluded in 2012, and after much fractious debate and controversy, the Protocol's second phase was formally adopted, to last through 2020. However, several countries that undertook obligations under the first phase declined to do so in the second.

One of the primary issues of contention in the realm of international climate law and policy is the absence of universal emissions reduction obligations. China, a developing country that was not bound by the Kyoto Protocol's emissions reduction obligations, is currently the world's biggest emitter. India, similarly situated, is the world's third biggest emitter (fourth if the EU is regarded as a single entity). Other big emitters from the developing world such as Indonesia are also not required to reduce emissions.[81] The result is a legal framework that does not cover the majority of the world's greenhouse gases, and one that has allowed global greenhouse gas emissions to rise by 35% between 1990 and 2010.[82] Radiative forcing, i.e., the warming effect on climate by long-lived greenhouse gases has also increased by 43% since 1990.[83]

---

77 UN Doc FCCC/CP/1997/7/Add.1, *supra* note 70.

78 UNFCCC, *The Kyoto Protocol Mechanisms* (2007), https://unfccc.int/resource/docs/publications/mechanisms.pdf, accessed 25 June 2021.

79 Armin Rosencranz & Kanika Jamwal, *Allowing Developed States To Get Away With Emissions*, THE STATESMAN, 27 February 2020, http://dspace.jgu.edu.in:8080/jspui/bitstream/10739/3348/1/Allowing%20developed%20states%20to%20get%20away%20with%20emissions.pdf, accessed 25 June 2021.

80 *Id.*

81 United States Environmental Protection Agency (EPA), Global greenhouse gas emissions data, https://www.epa.gov/ghgemissions/global-greenhouse-gas-emissions-data, accessed 25 June 2021.

82 United States Environmental Protection Agency, *Climate Change Indicators: Greenhouse Gases*, https://www.epa.gov/climate-indicators/greenhouse-gases#:~:text=From%201990%20to%202015%2C%20the,alone%20increased%20by%2030%20percent, accessed 25 June 2021.

83 World Meteorological Organization, *Greenhouse Gas Concentrations In Atmosphere Reach Yet Another High* (25 November 2019), https://public.wmo.int/en/media/press-release/greenhouse-gas-concentrations-atmosphere-reach-yet-another-high, accessed 25 June 2021.

In this context, the North–South divide became very evident. Focusing on the 'common responsibility' aspect of the principle of CBDRRC,[84] the developed countries, led by the United States, demanded that big emitters like India and China must have mandatory mitigation targets.[85] They argued emissions reductions by the developed world will be immaterial in curtailing climate change if the reductions are outweighed by the growth of emissions from the developing world. To that end, the United States' Senate passed the Byrd-Hagel Resolution, precluding the United States from undertaking any new mitigation targets, until developing country parties undertook similar commitments, starting at the same time, although varying in length and breadth.[86] The developing countries, spearheaded by India and China, while focusing on the 'differentiated responsibility' aspect of the principle of CBDRRC, pointed to the larger historical contribution of the West to cumulative historic emissions, justifying higher emission reduction targets for them. While both groups claimed adherence to the principle of CBDRRC, the different interpretations placed them at loggerheads for several years, until the Paris Agreement of 2015.

It is within this set of interests that nations were negotiating a new legal instrument that would replace the Kyoto Protocol in 2020. Countries adopted a new agreement in Paris, at the twenty-first Conference of Parties of the UNFCCC in 2015, which stipulates mitigation and adaptation obligations for *all Parties*.[87]

Developed country emitters believe this means that all countries—especially the world's worst emitters, developing and developed alike—will have to be bound by emissions reduction obligations. Developing country emitters like China and India suggest that the agreement may apply to all. That does not mean actual emissions reduction commitments will apply to all major emitters, and should still remain the obligation of Western nations. This distinction could be too wide a gulf to bridge and could lead to an impasse and potential failure of the multilateral climate negotiations process. In the absence of a strong, binding global treaty, countries may attempt to move towards plurilateral agreements and a network of voluntary, nationally adopted climate goals.

As countries engage in political debate, climate change impacts are already on the rise. Observed and projected impacts include the melting of glaciers; an increase in extreme weather events (such as wildfires, storms, hurricanes, more frequent and intense droughts, more episodes of heavy rainfall and flooding); the spread of vector-borne diseases (such as mosquito-borne malaria and dengue, and parasitic ailments like Lyme disease) due to the widening temperature range that makes elevated areas hospitable to disease-carrying agents; a rise in food and water-borne diseases; changes in agricultural growing seasons and ranges, affecting crop yields and food security; ocean acidification and ocean warming (leading to coral bleaching and threatening marine food chains); biodiversity loss; and a host of other consequences. Leaders have pledged to keep temperature rise in the twenty-first century to 2°C. If current emissions trajectories continue, it appears the world is on a path to a 3–5°C

---

[84] Short for 'Common but Differentiated Responsibilities and Respective Capabilities'. See *supra* notes 36–39 and the accompanying text.

[85] Lavanya Rajamani, *The Principle of Common but Differentiated Responsibilities and the Balance of Commitments Under the Climate Regime*, 9(2) REV OF EUROP COMM AND INT'L LAW 120 (2000).

[86] Lavanya Rajamani, *Ambition and Differentiation in the 2015 Paris Agreement: Interpretative Possibilities and Underlying Politics*, 65 INT'L & COMP LAW Q 493 (2016).

[87] In 2019, the United States expressed its intention to withdraw from the Paris Agreement, which took effect on 4 November 2020. While the newly elected President of the United States, Joe Biden, has expressed his intention to rejoin the Paris Agreement, it remains to be seen whether the Agreement will be able to prompt climate action or whether it will be yet another political compromise.

rise by 2100.[88] Countries need to start preparing for the damage from climate change (i.e. adaptation) just as much as they need to reduce the causal factors (mitigation).

III. THE PARIS AGREEMENT 2015

At the Conference of Parties in December 2015, state parties to the UNFCCC adopted a new, ambitious legal framework to address the global climate crisis, the Paris Agreement 2015. The Agreement aims to maintain the global temperature 'well below 2°C' above pre-industrial levels and strives towards a 1.5°C temperature limit. It revised Parties' commitments, and modelled them as per the principle of 'common but differentiated responsibilities and respective capabilities in light of national circumstances'. In what is ostensibly a slight departure from the UNFCCC's version of CBDRRC, the Paris Agreement introduced a more nuanced form of differentiation,[89] paving the way for universal adoption. The then UN Secretary General, Ban Ki Moon, declared it a monumental triumph.

Under the Paris Agreement, the principle of CBDRRC is operationalized across five categories of commitments, namely mitigation, adaptation, finance, technology and capacity building and transparency.[90] Furthering the idea of nuanced differentiation, there were mandatory commitments under the Paris Agreement for all parties. Effectively, it alienated itself from the stark differentiation that existed under the UNFCCC framework.

To that end, with regard to mitigation commitments under Article 4, the agreement introduces a form of self-differentiation, wherein all parties must undertake mitigation obligations, keeping in view their respective capabilities and prevailing national circumstances. These voluntary obligations are called Nationally Determined Contributions (NDCs). Each state will revise and submit a fresh set of NDCs every five years. Article 4(3) requires that each subsequent NDC must reflect a progression from the preceding one. However, what constitutes progression will be determined by the state party concerned, keeping in view its national circumstances. In a similar vein, each party must engage in adaptation planning and implementation of adaption related efforts,[91] and should submit and update adaptation communications; strengthen cooperation on adaptation; and enhance understanding, action and support with respect to loss and damage.[92]

The provisions relating to financial support under the Paris Agreement retain UNFCCC's differentiation. Developed countries are mandatorily obligated to continue providing financial support to developing countries, in furtherance of their commitments under the UNFCCC.[93] They will continue taking the lead in mobilizing climate finance.[94]

For developing countries, the Paris Agreement's obligations start from 2020 onwards. The fresh set of NDCs submitted in 2020 determine their commitments under the Paris Agreement for the next five years.[95] India committed to no absolute reductions in its carbon

---

[88] Reuters, *Global Temperatures On Track For 3–5 Degree Rise By 2100: UN* (29 November 2018), https://www.reuters.com/article/us-climate-change-un-idUSKCN1NY186, accessed 25 June 2021.

[89] Lavanya Rajamani, *supra* note 86.

[90] These key areas were recognized for the first time at the Durban Conference in 2011, and hence are commonly called the 'Durban Pillars'.

[91] Article 7.

[92] Lavanya Rajamani, *supra* note 86.

[93] Article 9(1).

[94] Article 9(3).

[95] For a survey of climate change litigation and its interface with human rights see Vidya Ann Jacob, Bhavna Mishra & Rishav Ambastha, *Climate Change Litigation and Human Rights* (22 March 2018), https://lawasia.asn.au/sites/default/files/2018-05/Academic-Paper-Climate-Change-Litigation-and-Human-Rights-22Mar2018.pdf, accessed 25 June 2021.

emissions under the Paris Agreement 2015. Although, in 2021, its per capita emissions have nearly doubled over 2005 levels, India with 17 per cent of the world's population emits only 5 per cent of the world's carbon.

At the Conference of Parties held in October and November 2021 at Glasgow, the following commitments were made by India. First, India will increase its 'non fossil fuel' energy capacity to 500 GW by 2030. Second, India will meet half its energy needs from renewables by 2030. Third, India will reduce its carbon emissions by one billion tons from business as usual projections by 2030. Fourth, India will reduce the carbon intensity of its GDP by 45 per cent. Finally, India will achieve net zero emissions by 2070.

The net zero target of 2070 in effect allows India to keep raising its emissions for a few more decades before it chooses to curb them.

NOTES AND QUESTIONS

1. Having gained the experience of moving from framework to substantive agreements in the case of the Montreal Protocol, why did the drafters of the Climate Change Convention seek to repeat the framework process? Now that we know it can be done, why not move directly to the implementing Protocol and skip the framework step altogether? Are there formalities involved in international negotiations that must be observed? Is this an efficient way to solve environmental problems? What if the problems are extremely urgent?

2. Since virtually all climate scientists agree on the likelihood of global climate change, why has collective action been so slow in coming? What happened to the precautionary principle, discussed earlier? How accurate and reliable does data have to be before we act on it? What if the effects of waiting cause irreparable harm?

3. How effectively can the Paris Agreement reduce global carbon pollution and greenhouse gases by the required levels in furtherance of the principle of 'common but differentiated responsibilities and respective capabilities (CBDRRC)'?

4. The disruptive impact of climate change is seen from our past. Research on the Indian sub-continent suggests that the vast cities of the Indus Valley Civilization too may have rapidly declined due to a sharp reduction in precipitation—it would appear the monsoons failed for 200 years. The clues for this catastrophic climate change were found in an ancient lakebed, Kotala Dahar in the State of Haryana, India. A team of paleoclimate scientists studied the isotopic values of calcium carbonate preserved in snails' shells. Oxygen-16 isotopes evaporate more quickly than oxygen-18 and consequently during droughts, the snails' shells become enriched with oxygen-18. Apparently, the drought in the Indus Basin occurred around 4,100 years ago, compelling its urban citizens to abandon the cities that had once flourished.[96]

5. There are several transboundary environmental issues between India and her neighbours. Most of them relate to international rivers and the very large populations that depend heavily on river water for basic sustenance. The transboundary river sharing arrangements are likely to come under stress with global climate change. Despite periodic posturing, the Indus Waters Treaty of 1960 between India and Pakistan, with its mechanism of intervention by a

[96] Yama Dixit, David A Hodell & Cameron A Petrie, *Abrupt Weakening of the Summer Monsoon in Northwest India ~ 4100 yr Ago*, 42 GEOLOGY 339 (2014), http://geology.gsapubs.org/content/early/2014/02/24/G35236.1.full.pdf, accessed 25 June 2021.

neutral mediator, is hailed across the world as a model for avoiding 'water war' type conflicts. The Treaty has survived over six decades despite three major armed conflicts and repeated spikes in hostilities and tension. The Indus river, which flows through India into Pakistan is experiencing a reduced flow because curiously, while glaciers across the world are receding, the Karakoram glacier which accounts almost for half of the flow of the Indus, is actually expanding.

6. The Ganga River flowing east and the Brahmaputra waters entering from Tibet in the north before flowing westward, join to create a massive delta that defines Bangladesh. The delta has enormous mangrove forests and wetlands that host a fishing industry upon which millions of people depend for livelihood. It is a major biodiversity hot spot but is threatened by pollution and salt water incursion from the rising sea level in the Bay of Bengal. Bangladesh's agrarian economy nourished by the low-lying delta is vulnerable to the rise in sea level as a consequence of climate change. Moreover, a river interlinking project planned by India to link 14 Himalayan rivers in North India and 16 peninsular rivers in South India may directly impact the Ganga–Brahmaputra river system in Bangladesh. Meanwhile, China has plans to develop the hydroelectric potential in Tibet. Major rivers flowing through India such as the Brahmaputra, Sutlej, Indus and two headwaters of the Ganga rise on the Tibetan plateau. Negotiations between the lower riparian states and China on the total available water are likely to be difficult and complicated.[97]

H. PROTECTING ENDANGERED SPECIES

I. 1973 CONVENTION ON INTERNATIONAL TRADE IN ENDANGERED SPECIES OF WILD FAUNA AND FLORA

By 1995, over 113 nations had signed the 1973 Convention on International Trade in Endangered Species (CITES).[98] CITES does not seek to directly protect endangered species or the development practices that destroy their habitats. Rather, it seeks to reduce the economic incentive to kill endangered species and destroy their habitat by closing off the international market. The sole aim of CITES is to control or prevent international commercial trade in endangered species or products derived from such species.

The Convention regulates by means of an international permit system. For plant and animal species threatened with extinction, international import or export is strictly forbidden. For plant and animal species suffering decline but not yet facing extinction, international import/export permits must be secured. These CITES permits enable the trade to be controlled and monitored so that it does not lead to species extinction or decline.[99]

Many environmentalists believe that CITES does not go far enough in protecting endangered species, and that it approaches protection from a philosophically questionable standpoint. The main animals that CITES protects are 'charismatic species'—so-called megafauna or animals whose parts and pelts have a market value. This prioritizing of species is objectionable to many. The only thing that CITES controls is trade, it does nothing to limit hunting or killing.

[97] Shyam Divan, *Through the Eye of an Elephant: An Indian Perspective on Climate Change*, 24(2) THE COMMONWEALTH LAWYER 33 (2015); Mohan V Katarki, *International Rivers: Challenges Posed by the Threat of Climate Change to India and Her Neighbours*, 9 BANGALORE UNIV LAW JR 17 (2019).

[98] 993 UNTS 243, https://cites.org/eng/disc/text.php, accessed 25 June 2021.

[99] The application of CITES was examined by the Supreme Court in *Regional Deputy Director v Zavary S Poonawala* (2015) 7 SCC 347 and is discussed in the Wildlife Protection chapter.

Theoretically, if a nation wanted to kill all of its species for domestic consumption, CITES could do nothing to prevent it.

One example in India where CITES appears to have no significant impact is in the context of tigers. In 2020, there were 3,000 tigers left in the wild in India.[100] Illegal trade in tiger parts is still rampant due to poor implementation and enforcement of the laws. The bulk of illegal tiger trade in India is channelled through the India-Nepal border. China is the main importer, where the use of tiger components in traditional medicine fuels demand.[101]

II. 1992 CONVENTION ON BIOLOGICAL DIVERSITY

At the 1992 United Nations Conference on Environment and Development (UNCED) meeting in Rio de Janeiro, an agreement was reached on the conservation and sustainable use of the world's biodiversity. The Convention on Biological Diversity (the Biodiversity Convention)[102] took effect on 29 December 1993, after it was ratified by the required minimum of 30 countries.

Although the Biodiversity Convention sets forth numerous obligations, most of these are aspirational; there are no specific standards or methods to ensure compliance. Article 8(c) requires that signatory nations 'regulate or manage biological resources important for the conservation of biological diversity whether within or outside protected areas, with a view to ensuring their conservation and sustainable use'. Article 8(d) obliges countries to 'promote the protection of ecosystems, natural habitats and the maintenance of viable populations of species in natural surroundings'. Under Article 9(b), nations agree to 'adopt measures relating to the use of biological resources to avoid or minimize adverse impacts on biological diversity'.

The environmentally progressive provisions listed above, however, are balanced against provisions that reaffirm each nation's sovereign right to manage and exploit its natural resources. Countries may adopt nature protection standards that are appropriate to their own economic needs and priorities. Taken as a whole, the Biodiversity Convention is broad and vague enough to be consistent with almost all natural resource policies, whether these policies are environmentally protective or destructive. The loose and contradictory language of the agreement has been criticized by many environmentalists, who maintain that an important opportunity was missed to create more sustainable international nature protection standards.

The Convention was supplemented by a protocol—the Cartagena Protocol on Biosafety, which was adopted in 2000 and entered into force in 2003.[103] It specifically regulates the transboundary movement, handling and trade of genetically engineered organisms. The precautionary principle is at the core of this Protocol, and it seeks to balance public health considerations against economic benefits. In 2010, another instrument—the Nagoya Protocol on Access and Benefit Sharing—was added to the Biodiversity Convention portfolio, and aims to ensure fair and equitable sharing of benefits arising out of the use of genetic resources. India signed it in 2011 and ratified it in 2012.

---

100 Wildlife Protection Society of India, *Current Status of Tiger in India*, http://www.wpsi-india.org/tiger/tiger_status.php, accessed 25 June 2021.

101 Brian Stallard, *Tracking Tiger Trade: Disturbing Trends*, NATURE WORLD NEWS, 26 September 2014, http://www.natureworldnews.com/articles/9204/20140926/tracking-tiger-trade-disturbing-trends.htm, accessed 25 June 2021. See *Sansar Chand v State of Rajasthan* (2010) 10 SCC 604, examined in the Wildlife Protection chapter.

102 1760 UNTS 79, https://www.cbd.int/convention/text/, accessed 25 June 2021.

103 2226 UNTS 208, https://www.cbd.int/doc/meetings/cop/excop-01/official/excop-01-03-en.pdf, accessed 25 June 2021.

Given India's rich biodiversity, it is natural that the Convention on Biological Diversity—relative to many other international agreements—has received attention from domestic policy-makers and government officials. A set of implementation mechanisms has been set up in India. After the passage of the Biological Diversity Act of 2002, the National Biodiversity Authority (NBA) was set up in 2003 to perform a facilitative, regulatory and advisory function for the Indian Government on the conservation and sustainable use of biological resources, and the fair equitable sharing of benefits of use. The NBA has helped 28 Indian states set up State Biodiversity Boards and facilitated the establishment of over 32,000 local-level Biodiversity Management Committees all over India.[104]

NOTES AND QUESTIONS

1. If Kenya decided to kill every elephant within its borders for purposes of internal domestic consumption, CITES would not prevent this policy from being carried out. What kind of environmental treaty is it, then? Is it not actually another commodities agreement in disguise? CITES is often mentioned as the environmental treaty most likely to be voidable under GATT. Why is this so?

2. Is it true, as many critics contend, that CITES is only good for the animals we humans find appealing? Do we not have a moral obligation to protect *all* animals?

The Biodiversity Convention is regarded by many as an unsuccessful attempt to please all the people all the time. Can its conservation principles truly coexist with its sovereignty principles? In fact, can inviolable sovereignty coexist with global environmental law in general?

While the Biodiversity Convention has been criticized for being only a framework, is it possible to create a treaty with more specific substantive obligations covering a topic as large as the planet's entire biodiversity? Is it more manageable to attempt to conserve different eco-systems individually, rather than impose guidelines that try to apply to all types in one instrument?

3. Amongst the great challenges confronting the sub-continent are the impacts of climate change and biodiversity loss. The loss of biodiversity covers several critically endangered species, amongst them the Great Indian Bustard (*Ardeotis nigriceps*), the Bengal Florican (*Houbaropsis bengalensis*), the Indian Wolf (*Canis lupus*), the Himalayan Brown Bear (*Ursus arctos isabellanus*) and the Snow Leopard (*Panthera uncia*). This short list of charismatic megafauna neglects dozens of other less flamboyant species that are tipping into extinction or are rapidly losing their share of the planet's space. The dramatic impacts of climate change will hasten the process of what is described as the Sixth Extinction.[105]

4. The estimated elephant range in India is 40,000 sq kms of which only 27% enjoys protected status. Out of the total range of tigers extending 53,000 sq kms, only 65% is protected. With climate impacts looming, the human pressure will likely increase on protected areas and zones we share with other species.

---

[104] National Biodiversity Authority, *About NBA—Introduction*, http://nbaindia.org/content/16/14/1/introduction.html, accessed 25 June 2021.

[105] Elizabeth Kolbert, *The Sixth Extinction* (2014).

I. PROTECTING THE GLOBAL COMMONS

There are some areas of sea, land and air that do not fall within recognized national boundaries. These areas are referred to as the 'global commons'. A primary example of global commons is international waters located outside each country's 200-mile exclusive economic zone.

I. 1982 UNITED NATIONS CONVENTION ON THE LAW OF THE SEA

The United Nations Law of the Sea Convention (UNCLOS)[106] established several duties regarding the marine environment. These obligations include (1) the duty of nations to protect and preserve the marine environment; (2) to take, individually or jointly, all measures necessary to prevent, reduce and control pollution of the marine environment from any source; (3) using the best practical means in accordance with the respective capabilities; (4) to take all measures necessary to ensure that activities under their jurisdiction or control do not cause damage by pollution.

The United Nations Law of the Sea Convention also obliges nations to: (1) cooperate on a global and regional basis with international organizations to formulate 'international rules, standards and recommended practices and procedures for the protection and preservation of the marine environment; (2) co-operate in the promotion of scientific research and data exchange programmes regarding marine pollution'; (3) cooperate in eliminating the effects of pollution and preventing or minimizing the damage; and (4) establish appropriate scientific criteria for the formulation of international environmental 'rules, standards and recommended practices and procedures for the prevention, reduction and control of marine pollution'.

Implementation and enforcement of UNCLOS is left to individual member nations. One national strategy to ensure compliance is to prohibit dumping or destructive fishing methods by all vessels registered in a particular country. Another strategy is to deny port privileges to vessels from nations that have failed to adopt national legislation implementing UNCLOS. Both of these strategies are means of controlling activity in international waters located outside national boundaries.

A major legacy of the Law of the Sea treaty process is the assertion by the so-called group of 77 developing nations that the deep seabed, and minerals contained there, are the 'common heritage of mankind'. It logically follows that the profits from any mining of the deep seabed must be shared with all countries. This was a key point that led the United States to not join the Convention. While this question remained in the theoretical realm until recently, the entry of Canadian companies into the deep-sea mining sector near Papua New Guinea,[107] and Japan's announcement that it will launch mining of methane hydrates,[108] have now made the question of the application of 'common heritage of mankind' to the deep sea a much more practical matter. This is thus an area of international environmental law that is continuing to evolve.

---

[106] 1833 UNTS 3, https://www.un.org/depts/los/convention_agreements/texts/unclos/unclos_e.pdf, accessed 25 June 2021.

[107] Meghan Miner, *Will Deep Sea Mining Yield and Underwater Gold Rush?* NATIONAL GEOGRAPHIC NEWS, 3 February 2013, https://www.nationalgeographic.com/news/2013/2/130201-underwater-mining-gold-precious-metals-oceans-environment/, accessed 25 June 2021.

[108] Hiroko Tabuchi, *An Energy Coup for Japan: 'Flammable Ice'*, THE NEW YORK TIMES, 12 March 2013, http://www.nytimes.com/2013/03/13/business/global/japan-says-it-is-first-to-tap-methane-hydrate-deposit.html?pagewanted=all, accessed 25 June 2021.

II. THE FISH STOCKS AGREEMENT

The United Nations Agreement for the Implementation of the Provisions of the United Nations Convention on the Law of the Sea of 10 December 1982 Relating to the Conservation and Management of Straddling Fish Stocks and Highly Migratory Fish Stocks of the Fish Stocks Agreement (FSA)[109] came into effect in 2001. The purpose of the Agreement is to secure the conservation and management of straddling fish stocks and highly migratory fish stocks, and adopt a precautionary approach in doing so.[110] It stipulates that the states must cooperate in conservation and optimum utilization of fisheries within and beyond their Exclusive Economic Zones (EEZs).

Interestingly, while the FSA uses the term straddling fish stocks, it does not specifically define it. A commonly accepted working definition may be, 'stocks occurring within the exclusive economic zones of two or more coastal States or both within the exclusive economic zone and in an area beyond and adjacent to it'.[111] Thus, the definition covers most of the fish inside the areas of the EEZs under national jurisdiction to most of the fish in an area beyond and adjacent to it, that is outside EEZs (in the high seas).

To meet its objectives, the agreement lays down detailed minimum international standards for the conservation and management of straddling and highly migratory fish stocks. The agreement seeks to ensure that measures taken for such conservation within and beyond the national jurisdiction are coherent, that there are effective mechanisms for compliance and enforcement of those measures on the high seas. It recognizes the special requirements of developing states in relation to conservation and management as well as the development and participation in fisheries for the straddling and highly migratory fish stocks.[112]

III. 1959 ANTARCTIC TREATY AND 1991 PROTOCOL ON ENVIRONMENTAL PROTECTION TO THE ANTARCTIC TREATY

The Antarctic Treaty[113] was the original application of the concept of 'common heritage of mankind'. It was signed in 1959 and came into effect in 1961, after 12 parties ratified it. India signed and ratified it in 1983. The Treaty remains in force indefinitely (i.e., for perpetuity), and has been successful thus far in its objective of preserving Antarctica for the benefit of all countries, for peaceful uses, and as a global hub of collaborative scientific research. The Treaty's other objectives include ensuring Antarctica will remain demilitarized, will be free of nuclear tests and the disposal of radioactive waste, and to prevent any disputes over territorial sovereignty of the area. The Treaty sets out certain areas as 'Specially Protected Areas' to preserve the 'unique natural ecological system' of the area.

Following the Treaty, in 1991, the Protocol on Environmental Protection to the Antarctic Treaty, also known as the Madrid Protocol, was adopted. In a novel move, the Protocol prioritized the conservation of living resources in the region, and set out the Antarctic Specially

---

[109] The United Nations Agreement for the Implementation of the Provisions of the United Nations Convention on the Law of the Sea of 10 December 1982 relating to the Conservation and Management of Straddling Fish Stocks and Highly Migratory Fish Stocks, https://www.un.org/Depts/los/convention_agreements/convention_overview_fish_stocks.htm, accessed 25 June 2021.

[110] United Nations Division for Ocean Affairs and Law of the Sea, *Overview to the Fish Stocks Agreement*, https://www.un.org/Depts/los/convention_agreements/convention_overview_fish_stocks.htm, accessed 25 June 2021.

[111] FAO Fisheries Department, *General Considerations*, http://www.fao.org/3/a0653e/a0653e04.htm, accessed 25 June 2021.

[112] *Overview to the Fish Stocks Agreement*, *supra* note 110.

[113] 402 UNTS 71, https://treaties.un.org/pages/showDetails.aspx?objid=0800000280136dbc, accessed 25 June 2021.

Managed Area and Antarctic Specially Protected Area and specified their scope and range. In addition, it laid down Multiple-use Planning Areas to assist and coordinate actions among parties and to reduce environmental impacts.[114]

Under Article 2 of the Protocol, Antarctica is designated as a 'natural reserve for peace and science'. Articles 2 and 3, in a sense, came to be recognized as the backbone of the Protocol and provided for the standard of appraisal of all activities conducted there, which was an unprecedented feat.[115] The Committee on Environmental Protection (CEP) provides Treaty parties with advice and recommendations, which considerably influence their respective national policies.[116]

Commercial exploitation of mineral resources for any activity other than scientific research is prohibited under Article 7. The Protocol stipulates that environmental impact assessment (EIA) is mandatory before conducting any activity. The six Annexes to the Protocol set out the requirements for EIA, flora-fauna conservation, waste disposal and management, prevention of marine pollution, liabilities for environmental emergencies and area conservation and management.[117]

India has been active in scientific expeditions and studies in Antarctica since 1981. Topics of study include atmospheric science, ozone depletion and adaptation of organisms to extreme environments. It established its first permanent scientific station at 'Dakshin Gangotri' in 1983 and the second station 'Maitri' in 1989.[118] Dakshin Gangotri had to be abandoned but India has since established another permanent scientific research station, 'Bharati', in 2012.[119]

IV. THE ARCTIC

The Arctic Circle is governed by a high-level intergovernmental body called the Arctic Council. The Council comprises of eight nations that have territory in the Arctic (Canada, Denmark representing Greenland and Faroe Islands, Finland, Iceland, Norway, Russia, Sweden and the United States), six permanent participants representing the indigenous peoples of the Arctic, six Working Groups and 33 Observers, India being one of them. The eight nations implement the policy in the region, and their work is supported by the Working Groups.

The Arctic ice is melting at a warp speed. In June 2020, temperature rise in Siberia affected the Arctic Ocean, triggering a record early sea ice melt in the Laptev Sea, and record low Arctic sea ice extent for this time of year.[120] The last three decades have witnessed a 95% decline in the older thick ice in the Arctic, and a warming rate twice the global rate of warming.[121]

---

114 Armin Rosencranz, D K Kaul & Aditya Vohra, *Internationally Cooperative Solutions to the Deteriorating Situation in Antarctica*, 1 Gnlu Law & Soc Review 134 (2019).

115 *Id.*

116 Donald R Rothwell, *Polar Environmental Protection and International Law: The 1991 Antarctic Protocol*, 11(3) Eur Jr Of Int'l Law 591 (2000).

117 The Protocol on Environmental Protection to the Antarctic Treaty, 1991, https://treaties.un.org/Pages/showDetails.aspx?objid=080000028006ab63&clang=_en, accessed 25 June 2021. See Kevin A Hughes, *et al*, *Antarctic Environmental Protection: Strengthening the Links Between Science and Governance*, 83 Env Sci & Pol 86, 88 (2018).

118 National Centre for Antarctic and Ocean Research, Ministry of Earth Sciences, *Antarctica Expeditions*, http://www.ncaor.gov.in/antarcticas, accessed 25 June 2021.

119 *Id.*

120 Gloria Dickie, *Siberian Heat Drives Arctic Ice Extent to Record Low For Early July*, Mongabay, 10 July 2020, https://news.mongabay.com/2020/07/siberian-heat-drives-arctic-ice-extent-to-record-low-for-early-july/, accessed 25 June 2021.

121 E Osborne, J Richter-Menge & M Jeffries, *Executive Summary, Arctic Report Card: Update for 2018 Arctic Program*, https://www.arctic.noaa.gov/Report-Card, accessed 25 June 2021.

If the current melting momentum continues, 2020 could be the lowest ice extent year, with unknown long-term ramifications for the Arctic and the global climate.[122]

Pivotal to this issue is The Northern Sea Route. It runs over 4,000 kms,[123] from Novaya Zemlya in Northern Russia, along Siberia to the Bering Strait. It lies entirely in Russia's Exclusive Economic Zone (EEZ). In 2018, for the first time in history, a vessel traversed this route, made possible by a record-breaking low volume of ice in Bering Strait. Opening of the Northern Sea Route could worsen the Arctic environment. An increase in shipping activity could damage the entire eco-system. It is likely to adversely impact marine life, increase local pollution levels and speed up the melting of ice sheets.

V. THE OUTER SPACE TREATY

The United Nations Treaty on Principles Governing the Activities of States in the Exploration and Use of Outer Space, Including the Moon and Other Celestial Bodies of 1967 (the Outer Space Treaty) (OST),[124] forms the keystone of the *corpus juris spatialis* or the body of law that regulates the activities of individuals and countries in space. The OST lays out general principles regarding the regulation of human conduct in outer space and on celestial bodies which are then developed in various other treaties and instruments. These principles include restrictions on the military use of space, the principle of non-appropriation of celestial resources, the common heritage of mankind, the allocation of jurisdiction over space objects and personnel, and the demarcation of responsibility and liability for conduct in space.

Article IX of the OST sets out obligations relating to environmental protection and enjoins state parties to the OST from the harmful contamination of outer space and celestial bodies as well as from causing 'adverse changes in the environment of the Earth resulting from the introduction of extraterrestrial matter'.

In 2017, a draft Space Law Bill was introduced in the Indian Parliament and is still pending. The Bill opens space activity to the private sector. It lays down a licensing procedure and precludes an unlicensed entity from engaging in space operations. Section 8 requires that the licence must contain the means and methods of conducting space activity. It stipulates that space activities must be conducted keeping in view India's international obligations and precluding the contamination of outer space. Since India is a party to OST 1967, it is obligated to conduct its space operations so that they do not cause pollution.

NOTES AND QUESTIONS

1. Why would the United States not accept the UNCLOS 'common heritage of mankind' principle? Is it because the US, as a richer, technically advanced nation, may be one of the first to mine the deep seabed?

2. One of the most difficult aspects of marine issues is the monitoring of behaviour on the open sea. How would any country know if another country observed the principles of

---

[122] Gloria Dickie, *supra* note 120.

[123] Protection of Arctic Marine Environment, *Northern Sea Route Shipping Statistics*, https://www.pame.is/index.php/projects/arctic-marine-shipping/older-projects/northern-sea-route-shipping-statistics, accessed 25 June 2021.

[124] The Treaty on Principles Governing the Activities of States in the Exploration and Use of Outer Space, including the Moon and Other Celestial Bodies, 610 UNTS 205, https://treaties.un.org/Pages/showDetails.aspx?objid=0800000280128cbd, accessed 25 June 2021.

international law on the high seas? Does this render all future international agreements with respect to oceans largely aspirational?

3. Given the difficult regulatory nature of the open sea, would it not make more sense to mandate design changes in ships, such as double hulling to insure against oil spills, that could be enforced in the port states or in the building process?

4. What might have been India's motivation for becoming party to the Antarctic Treaty in 1983?

5. A major environmental problem resulting from space exploration has been the issue of space debris in the Earth's atmosphere. The disintegration of space objects results in the creation of millions of tiny pieces of debris suspended in orbit around the Earth—any of which could be potentially fatal to other space objects.[125] The costs for cleaning up such debris in a limited gravity environment can be prohibitive.

[125] Brian Berger, *NASA's Terra Satellite Moved to Avoid Chinese ASAT Debris*, SPACE.COM, 6 July 2007, http://www.space.com/4038-nasa-terra-satellite-moved-avoid-chinese-asat-debris.html, accessed 25 June 2021.

18

TRANSBOUNDARY ENVIRONMENTAL ISSUES

A. WHAT ARE TRANSBOUNDARY ENVIRONMENTAL ISSUES?

Environmental resources often do not fit within man-made borders. They spill across the borders of nations. The sharing and common use of these resources constitute transboundary environmental issues. Simply put, these are issues relating to the international management of environmental resources and its impact. In this chapter, we consider transboundary water and air pollution from the Indian perspective.

Consider the Ganges River and its role in the relations between India and Bangladesh. The river passes through several states of India before flowing into Bangladesh, playing a major role in sustaining the Bangladeshi agricultural system. What would happen to Bangladesh's largely agriculture-fuelled economy if India were to construct a dam on the Ganges? Obviously, the flow of water to Bangladesh would diminish, negatively affecting its crop yields, in turn harming its economy. The Farakka Barrage to the north of Kolkata already diverts a substantial amount of the Ganges River water that would otherwise flow into Bangladesh.

Further east, the Brahmaputra or the Yarlung Tsangpo, as it is referred to in Tibet, is one of the widest rivers in the world. It enters India after originating in China and finally meets the Bay of Bengal after passing through Bangladesh. The river accounts for 44% of India's hydropower potential. The Chinese plans for dams and other diversion projects have been another point of tension between the two sparring nations.[1] A similar issue arises between India, China and Pakistan with the Indus River and its tributaries.

Often these resources are vital to the cultures, societies and economies of many nations. For example, the Ganges is of tremendous religious significance in both India and Bangladesh, in addition to its economic and agricultural importance. Thus, the issue fails to remain simply environmental. Religious, political and social overtones further complicate matters.

Transboundary air pollution in the Indian context is minimal. The Himalayas block much of the pollution moving across India and China. With sea on three sides, the only air movement worth noting is across India and Pakistan. Stubble burning, as will be discussed later, is the primary cause of transboundary air pollution.

---

[1] M M Rahaman & O Varis, *Integrated Water Management of the Brahmaputra Basin: Perspectives and Hope for Regional Development*, 33 National Resources Forum 1, 60–1 (2009).

Environmental Law & Policy in India. Shyam Divan and Armin Rosencranz, Oxford University Press.
 DOI: 1093/oso/9780192865458.003.0018

B. PLACING TRANSBOUNDARY ENVIRONMENTAL ISSUES IN CONTEXT

The transboundary implications of domestic decisions regarding environmental resources can be quite significant. Scarce environmental resources are already a major source of domestic and international conflict, and all evidence indicates that this will only increase. A prominent example is that of the Israel water wars—repeated and costly conflicts between Israel and its Arab neighbours over shared water resources.[2]

Transboundary environmental issues must be studied in the context of their ability to ignite conflict and their potential for resolving tension. Particularly in the context of South Asia, which is already a region rife with political and historical tension, transboundary environmental issues can spark conflict. In the sharing of freshwater resources, such as those of the Indus, Ganges and Brahmaputra rivers, these river-sharing agreements could serve as confidence-building measures, facilitating negotiation, progress and resolution of other contentious issues.[3]

This does not mean, however, that cooperation in the use of shared environmental resources should be viewed solely as a means of preventing and mitigating conflict. Such cooperation and agreement have the added advantage of responding to issues of degradation and depletion of environmental resources. In other words, the study of transboundary environmental issues is not just an exercise in preventing countries from fighting over environmental resources, but also in helping them to better use and preserve shared resources.

NOTES AND QUESTIONS

1. Do you think the presence of shared international rivers in the South Asian peninsula causes conflict in the region, exacerbates conflict in the region or is a result of pre-existing conflicts?

2. You will soon read about the Indus Waters Treaty (IWT) between India and Pakistan. Despite the successful conclusion of that Treaty as early as 1960, tensions between the two states have continued, and have, in fact, escalated. Why hasn't the IWT acted as a confidence-building measure in this context?

C. BACKGROUND TO TRANSBOUNDARY ENVIRONMENTAL ISSUES IN SOUTH ASIA

This section is intended to introduce the following ideas:

1. Large populations depend heavily for basic sustenance on diminishing environmental resources.
2. These environmental resources are often shared across borders.

---

[2] Meredith Giordano, Mark Giordano & Aaron Wolf, *The Geography of Water Conflict and Cooperation: Internal Pressures and International Manifestations*, 168(4) The Geographic Jr 293, 295 (2002).

[3] James Kraska, *Sustainable Development is Security: the Role of Transboundary River Agreements as a Confidence Building Measure in South Asia*, 28 Yale Jr Int'l Law 465 (2009).

3. The countries sharing these resources have a long history of military, political and cultural conflict.[4]
4. The limited success in terms of environmental cooperation has been in the area of river-sharing agreements. There is a noted absence of agreements regarding other environmental resources such as wildlife and forests. The focus of this chapter will be on river-sharing agreements.

D. THE LAW ON TRANSBOUNDARY ENVIRONMENTAL ISSUES

The law on transboundary international issues is well established. Its basic contours were laid out in the *Trail Smelter* arbitration discussed in what follows. As Oppenheim stated in 1905, it is now accepted customary international law that a state is not allowed to alter the use of its territory in a manner that disadvantages the territory of the neighbouring state.[5] This custom stems from the principle that all states are equal in international law, an idea also codified under the United Nations Charter.[6]

Widespread state practice supports this obligation for states to treat other states equally and thereby not use their natural resources in a manner that would adversely impact the other state. Judicial decisions too back this claim. Two decisions worth noting are the *Trail Smelter* case[7] and the *Corfu Channel* case.[8]

The *Trail Smelter* case was a dispute between the United States and Canada in the 1920s and 1930s. It is also known for being one of the foremost international arbitrations under environmental law. In this case, smoke and dust from a smelter in the town of Trail, British Columbia (Canada) crossed the border into the United States and affected the forests and farms in Washington State. An arbitration ensued which led to the foundation of the 'harm principle'. The principle suggests that no country should use its territory in a manner that causes environmental harm to another country.

The corollary of this principle is that the polluting country should pay damages to the harmed country. This principle, referred to as the 'polluter pays principle', is also extended domestically to compensate victims of environmental pollution. This decision supports the claim that any divergence or blockage of river flow to the detriment of a state's riparian neighbours is a harm caused to their crops, forests and soil, and therefore prohibited under international law.

The second decision worth noting is the *Corfu Channel* case. This was a decision by the International Court of Justice (ICJ) and does not directly relate to environmental pollution, but the principle is relevant. The dispute was between the United Kingdom and Albania. During the Greek Civil War, tensions between Albania and the United Kingdom were high. A Royal Navy flotilla entered the Corfu Channel that divides Albania and Greece and was hit by sea mines. The United Kingdom blamed Albania for installing sea mines without warning,

---

[4] For an overview of security aspects of river water disputes in the Indian sub-continent, see Paul Sullivan, *Glaciers, Monsoons, Rivers, and Conflict: China and South Asia*, 12 Georgetown Jr Int'l Affairs 107 (2011); Robert Wirsing, *Perilous Waters: The Changing Context of River Rivalry in South Asia*, 12 Whitehead Jr Of Diplomacy & Int'l Relations 39 (2011).

[5] L Oppenheim, *International Law* 175 (1905).

[6] Article 2, UN Charter.

[7] *Trail Smelter Arbitration* (*United States v Canada*) 1941 UN Rep Int'l Arb Awards 1905 (1941).

[8] *Corfu Channel* (*United Kingdom v Albania*) [1949] ICJ Rep 4.

a violation of international law. Albania denied having installed any mines and blamed it on Greece. The United Kingdom sued Albania in the ICJ. The court admitted that it could not be conclusively proven that Albania installed the mines. However, in deciding in favour of the United Kingdom, the court held that the mines were located in Albanian territory and thus it should be held responsible as it used its territory in a manner that caused injury to the United Kingdom. In a similar context, the use of territorial sovereignty of a state as a justification for diverting substantial portions of a river to the detriment of the riparian neighbour is not permissible under international law as it causes harm to that neighbour.

These two decisions were applied in the context of transboundary water resources in the *Gabčíkovo-Nagymaros* decision where the ICJ required 'equitable and reasonable' allocation of resources and held this to be a 'basic right'.[9] Hungary and Slovakia (erstwhile Czechoslovakia) signed a treaty to jointly construct a dam to share the resources of the Danube River. However, once disputes arose, Slovakia independently started constructing a dam on its territory cutting Hungary out. The ICJ ruled that Hungary was deprived of its right to use the resources of the Danube River in an equitable and reasonable manner, a right of Hungary under international law. Slovakia could not use its resources in a manner that would jeopardize the rights of Hungary.

These cases stem from customary international law and are not rights and obligations enshrined in a treaty. To remedy overreliance on vague and undefined principles of customary international law, the UN Watercourses Convention was adopted in 1997, though it entered into force only in 2014. The Convention governs all international watercourses for the purposes other than navigation.[10] China opposed the Convention in the UN and India abstained from voting, so any potential dispute between the two nations would be governed by customary international law as laid down in the above cases.

In the absence of a specific convention governing transboundary issues of South Asia, it would be pertinent to explore the state practice of India and China.

E. TRANSBOUNDARY RIVER ISSUES IN SOUTH ASIA

China's policy regarding sharing of international water resources with its riparian neighbours is that of bilateral 'dialogue and consultation'.[11] Paul Wouters argues that China's position is that of limited territorial sovereignty, suggesting that China is willing to abide by the applicable international law.[12]

However, its practice suggests that it far from accepts claims to sustainably share water resources when its national interests are involved. In its objection to the UN Watercourses Convention, China stated that it views sovereignty as a basic principle under international law. Accordingly, a state would have complete autonomy and sovereignty of the parts of the

9 International Court of Justice, Judgment dated 25 September 1997 *Gabčíkovo-Nagymaros Project (Hungary v Slovakia)* <https://www.icj-cij.org/en/case/92/judgments> accessed 23 January 2021.

10 Convention on the Law of the Non-navigational Uses of International Watercourses 1997. Adopted by the General Assembly of the United Nations on 21 May 1997. Entered into force on 17 August 2014. See General Assembly resolution 51/229, annex, Official Records of the General Assembly, Fifty-first Session, Supplement No. 49 (A/51/49) <https://legal.un.org/ilc/texts/instruments/english/conventions/8_3_1997.pdf> accessed 23 January 2021.

11 Paul Wouters, *The Yin and Yang of International Water Law: China's Transboundary Water Practice and the Changing Contours of State Sovereignty*, Special Issue: 23 Int'l Water Law 72 (2014).

12 *Id.*

watercourse that flows through that state. China observed: 'It is incomprehensible and regrettable that the draft Convention does not affirm this principle.'[13]

Eric Sievers has argued that China has violated international law when its interests are at stake.[14] It diverted substantial quantities of water from the Irtysh River into the Xinjiang Uighur Autonomous Region for irrigation and other uses. Uighur is a strategically important region for China where various human rights violations have been reported. China has exercised extensive influence, both political and economic, over the region. The downstream nations, Russia and especially Kazakhstan, have criticized this move. Kazakhstan has not only lost out on water for irrigation and other uses but also is unable to tap the full potential of the river as it operates hydroelectric plants whose power output is impacted by this divergence. This move by China seems to violate international law.[15] Additionally, China is also criticized for its opaqueness and lack of information-sharing and consultation with its neighbouring countries before diverting rivers.[16]

China shares its southern border with India. The two countries signed a Memorandum of Understanding (MoU) in 2013 to share information and data regarding the transboundary rivers (mainly the Indus and Brahmaputra, but also the Sutlej, Kosi and Ghaghara). The MoU also included a clause that requires China to consult with India if it plans to construct any dams on those rivers. China is required to share this information in the flood season (May–October) to enable India to better prepare.

The relations between the two nations have undoubtedly soured with constant and ever-escalating skirmishes across the Line of Actual Control in Kashmir and Arunachal Pradesh in the North and North-East, respectively. The example of the Doklam crises and China's reaction indicates the difficulty of the situation. China breached its obligation under the MoU citing the stand-off between the two armies. Chinese commentators justified this response stating: 'although China is a responsible country, we can't fulfil our obligations to India when it shows no respect to our sovereignty.'[17]

In summary, the UN Watercourses Convention does not apply to India and China as neither is a party. Further, the decisions of the ICJ that are considered to be a synthesis of customary international law do not seem to hold much weight with China. Sovereignty is something that China holds very dear, making progress on the environmental front difficult and extremely sensitive.

I. THE INDUS WATERS TREATY (IWT)

The Indus River Basin covers 930,000 sq kms in India and Pakistan. It consists of the Indus River, which rises from the Tibetan Plateau to travel 2,900 kms to the Arabian sea. Its major tributaries, ranging in length from 400 to 1,450 kms, are the Kabul, the Jhelum, the Chenab, the Beas, the Ravi and the Sutlej. Each year approximately 1,700 million acre feet of water

---

[13] UN Gaor, 51st Sess., 99th plen. mtg at 6, UN Doc. A/51/PV.99 (21 May 1997); Tarini Mehta, *India-China Transboundary River Governance: Pathways to Cooperation,* WIREs Water 2022 (Forthcoming); Eric Sievers, *Transboundary Jurisdiction and Watercourse Law: China, Kazakhstan, and the Irtysh*, 37 Texas Int'l Law Jr 1, 26 (2002).

[14] Eric Sievers, *id.* at 2.

[15] Selina Ho, *China's Transboundary River Policies towards Kazakhstan: Issue—Linkages and Incentives for Cooperation*, 42 Water Int'l 142 (2017).

[16] Tarini Mehta, *supra* note 13.

[17] Tarini Mehta, *supra* note 13; Claude Arpi, *China Plays the Water Card*, 21 August 2017 <http://claudearpi.blogspot.com/2017/08/china-plays-water-card.html> accessed 23 January 2021.

passes through the Indus system, 69% from India, 19% from Pakistan and 12% combined from Tibet and Afghanistan.[18]

Negotiated by the World Bank, India and Pakistan signed the Treaty at Karachi on 19 September 1960.[19] Six decades later, it is still in effect. Excerpts from this historic effort follow:

THE INDUS WATERS TREATY BETWEEN INDIA AND PAKISTAN;
19 September 1960

Preamble. The Government of India and the Government of Pakistan, being equally desirous of attaining the most complete and satisfactory utilization of the waters of the Indus system of rivers and recognising the need, therefore, of fixing and delimiting, in a spirit of goodwill and friendship, the rights and obligations of each in relation to the other concerning the use of these waters and of making provision for the settlement, in a cooperative spirit, of all such questions as may hereafter arise in regard to the interpretation or application of the provisions agreed upon herein, have resolved to conclude a Treaty in furtherance of these objectives * * *

ARTICLE I: *Definitions*

As used in this Treaty: * * *

(5) The term 'Eastern: Rivers' means The Sutlej, The Beas and The Ravi taken together.
(6) The term 'Western Rivers' means The Indus, The Jhelum and The Chenab taken together …
(8) The term 'Connecting Lake' means any lake which receives water from, or yields water to any of the Rivers; but any lake which occasionally or irregularly receives only the spill of any of the Rivers and returns only the whole or part of that spill is not a Connecting Lake.
(9) The term 'Agricultural Use' means the use of water for irrigation of household gardens and public recreational gardens.
(10) The term 'Domestic Use' means the use of water for:
  (a) Drinking, washing, bathing, recreation, sanitation (including the conveyance and dilution of sewage and of industrial and other wastes), stock and poultry, and other like purposes;
  (b) Household and municipal purposes (including use for household gardens and public recreational gardens); and
  (c) Industrial purposes (including mining, milling and other like purposes); but the term does not include Agricultural Use or use for the generation of hydroelectric power.
(11) The term 'Non-Consumptive Use' means any control or use of water for navigation, floating of timber or other property, flood protection or flood control, fishing or fish culture, wild life or other like beneficial purposes, provided that, exclusive of seepage and evaporation of water incidental to the control or use, the water (undiminished in volume within the practical range of measurement) remains in, or is returned to, the same river or its Tributaries; but the term does not include Agricultural Use or use for the generation of hydro-electric power. …
(13) The term 'Bank' means the International Bank for Reconstruction and Development. …

[18] Data for this section was drawn from Brian E Concannon, *The Indus Waters Treaty: Three Decades of Success, Yet, Will it Endure?* 2 Georgetown Int'l Law Rev 55 (1989).

[19] The full text of the treaty, with annexures, is available at <https://mea.gov.in/bilateral-documents.htm?dtl/6439/Indus> accessed 23 January 2021.

(15) The term 'interference with the waters' means:

(a) Any act of withdrawal therefrom; or

(b) Any man-made obstruction to their flow which causes a change in the volume (within the practical range of measurement) of the daily flow of the waters: Provided however that an obstruction which involves only an insignificant and incidental change in the volume of the daily flow, example, fluctuations due to afflux caused by bridge piers or a temporary by-pass, etc., shall not be deemed to be an interference with the waters....

ARTICLE II: *Provisions regarding Eastern Rivers*

(1) All the waters of the Eastern Rivers shall be available for the unrestricted use of India, except as otherwise expressly provided in this Article.

(2) Except for Domestic Use and Non-Consumptive Use, Pakistan shall be under an obligation to let flow, and shall not permit any interference with, the waters of the Sutlej Main and the Ravi Main in the reaches where these rivers flow in Pakistan and have not yet finally crossed into Pakistan....

(3) Except for Domestic Use, Non-Consumptive Use and Agricultural Use as specified in Annexure B, Pakistan shall be under an obligation to let flow, and shall not permit any interference with, the waters (while flowing in Pakistan) of any Tributary which in its natural course joins the Sutlej Main before these rivers have finally crossed into Pakistan.

(4) All the waters, while flowing in Pakistan, of any Tributary which, in its natural course, joins the Sutlej Main or the Ravi Main after these rivers have finally crossed into Pakistan shall be available for the unrestricted use of Pakistan: Provided however that this provision shall not be construed as giving Pakistan any claim or right to any releases by India in any such Tributary. If Pakistan should deliver any of the waters of any such Tributary, which on the Effective Date [1 April 1960] joins the Ravi Main after this river has finally crossed into Pakistan, into the reach of the Ravi Main upstream of this crossing, India shall not make use of these waters: each party agrees to establish such discharge observation stations and make such observations as may be necessary for the determination of the component of water available for the use of Pakistan on account of the aforesaid deliveries by Pakistan, and Pakistan agrees to meet the cost of establishing the aforesaid observations.

(5) There shall be a Transition Period (of 10–13 years) during which, to the extent specified in Annexure H, India shall:

(i) Limit its withdrawals for Agricultural Use,

(ii) Limit abstractions for storages, and

(iii) Make deliveries to Pakistan from the Eastern Rivers....

(9) During the Transition Period, Pakistan shall receive for unrestricted use the waters of the Eastern Rivers which are to be released by India in accordance with the Provisions of Annexure H. After the end of the Transition Period, Pakistan shall have no claim or right to releases by India of any of the waters of the Eastern Rivers. In case there are any releases, Pakistan shall enjoy the unrestricted use of the waters so released after they have finally crossed into Pakistan: Provided that in the event that Pakistan makes any use of these waters, Pakistan shall not acquire any right whatsoever, by prescription or otherwise, to a continuance of such releases or such use.

ARTICLE III: *Provisions regarding Western Rivers*

(1) Pakistan shall receive for unrestricted use all those waters of the Western Rivers which India is under obligation to let flow under the provisions of Paragraph (2).

(2) India is under an obligation to let flow all the waters of the Western Rivers, and shall not permit any interference with these waters, except for the following uses, restricted ... in

the case of each of the rivers, The Indus, The Jhelum and The Chenab, to the drainage basin thereof:

(a) Domestic Use;
(b) Non-Consumptive Use;
(c) Agricultural Use, as set out in Annexure C; and
(d) Generation of hydro-electric power, as set out in Annexure D....

(4) Except as provided in Annexure D and E, India shall not store water of, or construct any storage works on, the Western Rivers.

ARTICLE IV: *Provisions regarding the Eastern Rivers and the Western Rivers*

(1) Pakistan shall use its best endeavours to construct and bring into operation, with due regard to expedition and economy, that part of a system of works which will accomplish the replacement, from the Western Rivers and other sources, of water supplies for irrigation canals in Pakistan which, on 15 August 1947, were dependent on water supplies from the Eastern Rivers.

(2) Each Party agrees that any Non-Consumptive Uses made by it shall be so made as not to materially change, on account of such use, the flow in any channel to the prejudice of the uses on that channel by the other Party under the provisions of this Treaty. In executing any scheme of flood protection or flood control each Party will avoid, as far as practicable, any material damage to the other Party, and any such scheme carried out by India on the Western Rivers shall not involve any use of water or storage in addition to that provided under Article III.

(3) Nothing in this Treaty shall be construed as having the effect of preventing either Party from undertaking schemes of drainage, or from removal of stones, gravel or sand from the bed of the Rivers....

(6) Each Party will use its best endeavours to maintain the natural channels of the Rivers, as on the Effective Date, in such condition as will avoid, as far as practicable, any obstruction to the flow in these channels likely to cause material damage to the other Party....

(8) The use of the natural channels of the Rivers for the discharge of flood or other excess waters shall be free and not subject to limitation by either Party, and neither Party shall have any claim against the other in respect of any damage caused by such use. Each Party agrees to communicate to the other Party, as far in advance as practicable, any information it may have in regard to such extraordinary discharges of water from reservoirs and flood flows as may affect the other Party.

(9) Each Party declares its intention to operate its storage dams, barrages and irrigation canals in such manner, consistent with the normal operations of its hydraulic systems, as to avoid, as far as feasible, material damage to the other Party.

(10) Each Party declares its intention to prevent, as far as practicable, undue pollution of the waters of the Rivers which might affect adversely uses similar in nature to those to which the waters were put on the Effective Date, and agrees to take all reasonable measures to ensure that, before any sewage or industrial waste is allowed to flow into the rivers, it will be treated, where necessary, in such manner as not materially to affect those uses: Provided that the criterion of reasonableness shall be the customary practice in similar situations on the Rivers....

(12) The use of water for industrial purposes under Articles II (2), II (3), and III (2) shall not exceed:

(a) In the case of an industrial process known on the Effective Date, such quantum of use as was customary in that process on the Effective Date;
(b) In the case of an industrial process not known on the Effective Date:
  (i) Such quantum of use as was customary on the Effective Date in similar or in any way comparable industrial processes; or
  (ii) If there was no industrial process on the Effective Date similar or in any way comparable to the new process, such quantum of use as would not have a substantially adverse effect on the other Party....

ARTICLE V: *Financial provisions*

[Mandates India's payment to Pakistan of a contribution of Pounds Sterling 62,060,000 towards the cost of irrigation canals that will free Pakistan from its dependence on the supply of the Eastern Rivers. In the event that the transition period is extended from 10 to 13 years, the Bank will take over the payment of amounts deposited therein by India.]

ARTICLE VI: *Exchange of data*

[Mandates monthly exchange between the two countries of data on daily river discharges, daily extractions from and releases to reservoirs, daily withdrawals from the heads of canals, daily escapages from canals, and daily deliveries from link canals, plus any other information that might be available if requested.]

* * *

ARTICLE VII: *Future Co-operation*

[(1) The first section primarily reiterates the agreement to exchange data not specified by the Treaty at the request of a party, and encourages agreement and cooperation in building new drainage and engineering works involving the Rivers.]

(2) If either Party plans to construct any engineering work which would cause interference with the waters of any of the Rivers and which, in its opinion, would affect the other Party materially, it shall notify the other Party of its plans and shall supply such data relating to the work as may be available and as would enable the other Party to inform itself of the nature, magnitude and effect of the work. If a work would cause interference with the waters of any of the Rivers but would not in the opinion of the Party planning it affect the other Party materially, nevertheless the Party planning the work shall, on request, supply the other Party with such data regarding the nature, magnitude and effect, if any, of the work as may be available.

ARTICLE VIII: *Permanent Indus Commission*

(1) India and Pakistan shall each create a permanent post of Commissioner for Indus Waters, and shall appoint to this post, as often as a vacancy occurs, a person who should ordinarily be a high-ranking engineer competent in the field of hydrology and water-use. Unless either Government should decide to take up any particular question directly with the other Government, each Commissioner will be the representative of his Government for all matters arising out of this Treaty, and will serve as the regular channel of communication on all matters relating to the implementation of this Treaty....

(3) The two Commissioners shall together form the Permanent Indus Commission.

[The Commission's responsibilities include inspection tours of the River at least once every five years and annual meetings alternating from Pakistan to India. Each government shall grant the other's Commissioner the privileges and immunities that are granted to representatives of member states of the United Nations.]

ARTICLE IX: *Settlement of difference and disputes*

(1) Any question which arises between the Parties concerning the interpretation or application of this Treaty or the existence of any fact which, if established, might constitute a breach if this Treaty shall first be examined by the Commission, which will endeavour to resolve the question by agreement.

(2) If the Commission does not reach agreement on any of the questions mentioned in Paragraph (1), then a difference will be deemed to have arisen, which shall be dealt with as follows: [in most cases, first a neutral expert is consulted. If the neutral expert cannot

resolve the issue, then a dispute is deemed to have arisen. If the Commission cannot resolve the dispute, or one of the governments feels that there has been undue delay, the two governments may negotiate the dispute with mediators, finally resorting to a court of arbitration if necessary.]

* * *

ARTICLE XI: ***General Provisions***

(1) It is expressly understood that
  - (a) This Treaty governs the rights and obligations of each Party in relation to the other with respect only to the use of the waters of the Rivers and matters incidental thereto; and
  - (b) Nothing contained in this Treaty, and nothing arising out of the execution thereof, shall be construed as constituting a recognition or waiver (whether tacit, by implication or otherwise) of any rights or claims whatsoever of either of the Parties other than those rights or claims which are expressly recognised or waived by this Treaty.

Each of the Parties agrees that it will not invoke this Treaty, anything contained therein, or anything arising out of the execution thereof, in support of any of its own rights or claims whatsoever or in disputing any of the rights or claims whatsoever of the other Party, other than those rights or claims which are expressly recognized or waived in this Treaty.

(2) Nothing in this Treaty shall be construed by the Parties as in any way establishing any general principle of law or any precedent.
(3) The right and obligations of each Party under this Treaty shall remain unaffected by any provisions contained in, or anything arising out of the execution of, any agreement establishing the Indus Basin Development Fund....

The Indus is important for both India and Pakistan, with the agricultural systems in both relying heavily on the waters of the Indus river system. This is truer for Pakistan than India, which has the benefit of the waters of the Ganges and Brahmaputra river systems as well. Nevertheless, the importance of the waters of this major system for the western part of India and the eastern part of Pakistan is undeniable. This is of special importance in the context of the historically strained relations between the two states, which was a major hurdle to the negotiation of the Treaty. In fact, it was only through the intervention of the World Bank that the Treaty was finalized and adopted.[20]

Curiously, the IWT deviates from customary international legal practices concerning the sharing of freshwater resources, which tend to revolve around protecting the downstream state's right to traditional uses. In its place the IWT creates a geo-physical partition of the river.[21] The result of this has been that Pakistan has secured the lion's share of the waters of the Indus, securing 80% of the waters of the river system to India's 20%. This is better understood, however, in light of the particular interests of both states regarding the waters of the Indus. While Pakistan was primarily interested in agricultural and irrigational uses of the waters of the Indus, and thus needed the bulk of the waters, India was happy with using the water for generating hydroelectricity (depending more on location, quality and flow than

[20] Undala Z Alam, *Questioning the Water Wars Rationale: A Case Study of the Indus Waters Treaty*, 168 The Geographical Jr 341, 344 (2002).

[21] Manav Bhatnagar, *Reconsidering the Indus Waters Treaty*, 22 Tulane Envir Law Jr 271, 273–4 (2009).

quantity). India was especially happy to secure control over the eastern tributaries, which it intended to use to create irrigation canals in the dry state of Rajasthan.[22]

The IWT model—of intervention by a neutral mediator and concerted efforts to maintain long-term cooperation—has been hailed across the world as a model for avoiding potential 'water war' type conflicts. The treaty has survived over six decades, three major armed conflicts and repeated spikes in hostilities and tensions. In fact, a similar model, with similar substantive provisions (including the establishment of a river commission to facilitate long-term cooperation), is being considered for resolving water-sharing disputes involving the Tigris and Euphrates rivers in Turkey, Syria, Iran, Iraq, Saudi Arabia and Kuwait.[23]

The IWT is by no means free of criticism. The IWT has been faulted on a number of grounds—failure to adequately address the expanding water needs of both states, failure to allow India to fully harness its energy potential and failure to overcome hostilities with regard to Kashmir. The sharing agreement for the waters of the Mahakali river system between India and Nepal, which is based on integrated river basin development by both states, has been suggested as an effective model to replace the current IWT mechanism.[24]

NOTES AND QUESTIONS

1. For a while now, both India and Pakistan have been complaining about the IWT, alleging that it is unfair to them. How do you explain the continued survival of the Treaty?

2. The current stress on the IWT comes from the increasing demands for water from both sides. But there is only so much water in the Indus system. What is the solution?

3. Another challenge to the continued functioning of the IWT is its ability to respond to technological change. Recently there emerged a dispute between India and Pakistan with regard to the Baglihar Dam constructed by the Indian government on the River Chenab. The Pakistani Government objected to the design of the dam on the grounds that it contravened the provisions of the IWT. (The IWT goes into great detail on technical questions of dam design and construction.) The Indian Government defended the design on the grounds that it would facilitate more efficient usage of the collected water and would ensure that the dam survived longer. A neutral expert appointed under the auspices of the World Bank underscored the need to incorporate state of the art technology for projects built under the IWT for reasons of safety and optimum utilization of the waters.[25] He declared that 'the general rules of treaty interpretation allow him to have recourse to rules of science and technology and the state-of-the-art practices, in his assessment of the concept and design of the Baglihar Dam and Hydro Electric Plant'.[26]

4. The IWT assumes that the two states will remain hostile. Accordingly, it requires very little cooperation between the states for the continued functioning of the Treaty.

---

[22] Ramaswamy R Iyer, *Indus Treaty: A Different View*, 40 Economic & Political Weekly 3140 (2005).

[23] Neda A Zawahri, *Stabilising Iraq's Water Supply: What the Euphrates and Tigris Rivers Can Learn from the Indus*, 27(6) Third World Q 1041 (2006).

[24] *Supra* note 21.

[25] Ministry of External Affairs, Government of India, *Baligarh Dam Cleared by Neutral Expert* (12 February 2007) <https://www.mea.gov.in/press-releases.htm?dtl/2287/Baglihar+Dam+cleared+by+neutral+expert#:~:text=Raymond%20Lafitte%2C%20the%20Neutral%20Expert,representatives%20of%20India%20and%20Pakistan> accessed 23 January 2021.

[26] *Id.*

5. To settle a dispute between India and Pakistan regarding India's proposal to build a dam on the Jhelum River (the Kishenganga Dam), in 2010, Pakistan invoked the dispute resolution mechanism under the IWT for the first time ever. The dam aimed to divert water from the dam site on the Kishenganga/Neelum River to another river of the Indus system. Pakistan asked the Court of Arbitration[27] to determine whether such construction breached India's obligations under the IWT.[28] Pakistani concerns seemed to have been motivated at least partly by the fact that construction of the Kishenganga Dam would render it dependent on the Indian Government's willingness to release water as required by the IWT.[29] Through an interim order in 2011, the Court of Arbitration prohibited India from constructing any permanent obstructions on Kishenganga/Neelum riverbed which would prevent irreparable reduction in the water flow of the river.[30] In its partial award in February 2013, the court decided that while India had the right to divert the water under the IWT for the purpose of power generation by the Kishenganga Hydroelectric project, the same was not absolute: Pakistan's existing uses had to be taken into account in the operation of India's plants.[31] To that end, it held that India was obligated to construct and operate the project such that a minimum flow of water in the river was maintained. The rate of flow was determined in the Final Award in December 2013, where it was set at a minimum of 9 cubic metres/second.[32] In deciding the minimum rate of flow, the court took into account two major considerations: first, mitigating the adverse effects to Pakistan's agricultural and hydroelectric use, while preserving India's right to operate the project and maintaining the priority it acquired from having crystallized prior to Pakistan's Neelum-Jhelum Hydroelectric project. Second, 'the customary international law requirements of avoiding or mitigating trans-boundary harm and of reconciling economic development with the protection of the environment.'[33]

Do you think disputes with regard to the IWT are solely a result of competing demands for natural resources?

6. To appreciate the contribution of the IWT to resolving resource-related disputes between India and Pakistan, compare dispute resolution under the IWT with dispute resolution outside the IWT. An excellent example of the latter is the Rann of Kutch arbitration of 1962 which sparked tremendous controversy on both sides, and which continues to be a bone of contention with regard to the ownership of Sir Creek, which was left unresolved by the arbitral tribunal.[34]

---

27 The Court of Arbitration was constituted pursuant to the settlement machinery under Article IX of the Indus Waters Treaty.

28 Anupam Chakravarty, *Kishanganga Dam: Court at The Hague Seeks Details of its Environmental Impact*, Down To Earth, 19 February 2013 <https://www.downtoearth.org.in/news/kishanganga-dam-court-at-the-hague-seeks-details-of-its-environmental-impact-40401> accessed 23 January 2021.

29 See John Briscoe, *Troubled Waters: Can a Bridge be Built over the Indus?* 45 Economic & Political Weekly 28 (2010); Ramaswamy R Iyer, *Briscoe on the Indus Treaty: A Response*, 46 Economic & Political Weekly 68 (2011).

30 Centre for Borders Research, Durham University, *Tribunal Orders Interim Measures in Transboundary Water Arbitration Between India and Pakistan* (29 September 2011) <https://www.dur.ac.uk/ibru/news/boundary_news/?itemno=12866&rehref=%2Fibru%2Fnews%2F&resubj=Boundary+news+Headlines> accessed 23 January 2021.

31 Tamar Meshel, *The Indus Waters Kishenganga Arbitration—Reviving the Indus Waters Treaty and Arbitration of Interstate Water Disputes* (Kluwer Arbitration Blog, 21 January 2014) <http://arbitrationblog.kluwerarbitration.com/2014/01/21/the-indus-waters-kishenganga-arbitration-reviving-the-indus-waters-treaty-and-arbitration-of-interstate-water-disputes/> accessed 23 January 2021.

32 *Indus Waters Kishenganga Arbitration* (*Pakistan v India*), Final Award dated 20 December 2013 at 358 <https://legal.un.org/riaa/cases/vol_XXXI/1-358.pdf> accessed 23 January 2021.

33 *Id.* at 347.

34 See Sikander Ahmed Shah, *River Boundary Delimitation and the Resolution of the Sir Creek Dispute Between Pakistan and India*, 34 Vermont Law Review 357 (2009–10).

II. INDIA, BANGLADESH AND THE GANGES–BRAHMAPUTRA

This section examines two facets of the relationship between India and Bangladesh with regard to shared freshwater resources: the waters of the Ganges and the Farakka Barrage, and the interlinking of rivers project.

The Ganges–Brahmaputra Delta

This is a crisis created by the concerted efforts of both states. Untrammelled human activity and exploitation, including pollution, especially the dumping of waste into the rivers, is ruining the delta. This is having an immediate and undesirable effect on the mangrove forests and wetlands of the area. The delta hosts a massive fishing industry upon which many people depend for their livelihood. It is also a major biodiversity hotspot.

Further, increasing salinity of the rivers leading into the delta, largely caused by the Farakka Barrage, north of Kolkata, as well as saltwater intrusion from the rising sea level in the Bay of Bengal, is also adversely impacting both forests and delta cropland. Rice, a primary crop of Bangladesh, is particularly sensitive to salinity which has the potential to harm the agricultural economy.

This is a problem created by India, Bangladesh and climate change. There is an urgent need for both states to take cognizance of the problem and collaborate to solve it.

NOTES AND QUESTIONS

1. By all accounts, the attempt to revive the port of Kolkata through the Farakka Barrage is a failure. It has caused significant damage to the Bangladeshi economy and agriculture, and is destroying the Sunderbans Delta. It seems to have had *de minimis* benefits to India, and has exacerbated ethnic conflicts in eastern India. What prompts India to doggedly refuse to close the barrage?

2. If you were legal counsel advising Bangladesh on this matter, what would your advice be?

3. Do you think the religious significance of the Ganges in India in any way entitles India to lay claim to greater rights over it?

4. At the heart of the matter, this issue matches competing economic claims—agricultural on the one side, and trade-related on the other (assuming that the revival of the Kolkata port is essential for trade in the region, and that this is an effective way of achieving that result). How would you recommend resolution of this dispute?

5. The complexity of these issues is exacerbated by domestic political considerations. In 2011, efforts were made to negotiate a water-sharing agreement with Bangladesh with regard to the waters of the shared River Teesta; an interim deal was reached, giving India 42.5% of the Teesta's waters Bangladesh 37.5%.[35] However, Chief Minister Mamata Banerjee of West Bengal opposed the deal, and it was eventually shelved, saying that it would lead to water shortage in North Bengal.[36] The dispute has been an election issue for both Chief Minister

---

[35] *The Teesta River Dispute Explained in 10 Points*, Times Of India, 9 April 2017 <https://timesofindia.indiatimes.com/india/the-teesta-river-dispute-explained-in-10-points/articleshow/58091320.cms> accessed 23 January 2021.

[36] Geeta Mohan, *As Bangladesh Rakes Up Teesta Waters Issue in Modi-Hasina Talks, PM Sends Message To Mamata*, India Today, 18 December 2020 <https://www.indiatoday.in/india/story/modi-hasina-discuss-teesta-modi-message-to-mamata-1750653-2020-12-18> accessed 23 January 2021.

Mamata Banerjee and the Prime Minister of Bangladesh, Sheikh Hasina.[37] Bangladesh is now demanding 50% of Teesta's water for the period between December and March.[38]

River Interlinking Project

Another source of tension in the relations between India and Bangladesh is the proposed interlinking project planned by India. This project would link 14 Himalayan rivers in North India, as well as 16 peninsular rivers in South India, which will further be linked to the Ganges and Brahmaputra. The intended effect of this project is to improve water supply for agricultural and navigational purposes within India. Notwithstanding these alleged benefits for India, this project will definitely affect Bangladesh adversely.[39] An inevitable result of this plan will be the diminishing of water flows from the Ganges–Brahmaputra river system from India to Bangladesh, weakening the agricultural economy of the latter.

The legality of this project in international law is dubious.[40] As already noted, a basic principle of customary international environmental law is that a state has an undisputable sovereign right over its natural resources, subject to its non-interference in another state's use of its own natural resources. A corollary of this principle is the duty of an upper riparian state not to interfere with reasonable uses of shared rivers by lower riparian states. This principle seems to be violated in this case.

The need for a treaty to regulate the flow of the Ganges was felt before the creation of Bangladesh. East Pakistan, now Bangladesh, was concerned over India's move to create the Farakka Barrage. The construction of the barrage began in 1961. A treaty, the Ganges Water Treaty (GWT), with Bangladesh was finally inked in 1996, several years post the construction of the barrage. The GWT allows India to withdraw 40,000 cusecs from the barrage for the first five months of the year. However, if during that time the flow of the river drops below 70,000 cusecs, then the withdrawal must be equal. The determination of waterflow is at the barrage. This does not prevent India from withdrawing the water upstream. If the GWT be interpreted strictly to the letter, the interlinking project may be permissible.

III. INDIA AND TIBET/CHINA

Tibet is a major Asian watershed and is also the source for major rivers including the Brahmaputra, Sutlej and Indus.[41] China has significant plans to develop hydroelectric potential in Tibet and to divert some part of the waters of these transboundary rivers.[42] Tibet is also a strategically important region for China. Political tensions between India and China regarding the region have been high, especially with India giving sanctuary to the Dalai Lama.

These plans are still under development, but when they ripen,[43] a necessary result will be the reduction of total available water resources in the Indian sub-continent. This will significantly

---

[37] *Id.*

[38] *Teesta Water Dispute: Dhaka to Raise Issue With PM Modi in Virtual Summit on Dec 17*, The Sentinel, 15 December 2020 <https://www.sentinelassam.com/international/dhaka-to-raise-teesta-issue-with-pm-modi-in-virtual-summit-on-dec-17-516408> accessed 23 January 2021.

[39] Abu Raihan M Khalid, *The Interlinking of Rivers Project in India and International Water Law: An Overview*, 3 Chinese Jr Int'l Law 553, 555 (2004).

[40] Shawkat Alam, *An Examination of the International Environmental Law Governing the Proposed Indian River-Linking Project and an Appraisal of its Ecological and Socio-Economic Implications for Lower Riparian Countries*, 19 Georgetown Int'l Envir Law Review 209, 211 (2007).

[41] Thierry Mathou, *Tibet and its Neighbours: Moving Towards a New Chinese Strategy in the Himalayan Region*, 45 Asian Survey 503, 510 (2005).

[42] *Id.*

[43] David R Downes, *et al*, *International Environmental Law*, 45 The Int'l Lawyer 409, 416 (2011) <https://scholar.smu.edu/cgi/viewcontent.cgi?article=1418&context=til> accessed 23 January 2021.

complicate the tenuous cooperative agreements in place, which are already threatened by the lack of sufficient water availability. The difficulty of negotiating with an uncompromising Chinese state will be another significant problem.

NOTES AND QUESTIONS

1. Judge Weeramantry, in his separate opinion in the 1997 *Gabčíkovo-Nagymaros* case before the ICJ,[44] referred to an international obligation to conduct an environmental impact assessment (EIA) for any project that would ecologically affect other states. In its 2010 judgment in the case concerning *Pulp Mills on the River Uruguay*,[45] the ICJ held EIA to be a duty under international law. Do you think this in any way affects India's proposed interlinking of rivers, or China's plans to divert Tibetan rivers?

2. Now that India is in danger of suffering at the hands of China, as India has caused Bangladesh to suffer (in terms of an upper riparian state interfering with the rights of a lower riparian state), do you think this will lead to a reorientation of the Indian position? Or might it intensify the conflicts?

F. OTHER TRANSBOUNDARY ISSUES IN SOUTH ASIA

I. INDIA AND PAKISTAN—AIR POLLUTION

Stubble burning is a method used to clear the farm for the next crop. Once harvested, the stubble, that is the base, of the crop is unusable. Removing it is a demanding exercise as it is firmly embedded in the soil. The easy way out therefore is to burn the field and overturn the stubble on itself, which also serves as manure for the next crop. The downside, however, is air pollution from burning. With the onset of winter, in October–November, this stubble burning is at its peak, causing air purity levels to drop all over northern India. The Indian Government has banned stubble burning; however, the law is not strictly enforced as the farmers may need to adopt such a measure due to their financial difficulties. The government has aimed to provide financial assistance, though its adequacy and timeliness are questionable.

This stubble burning takes place primarily in Punjab and Haryana that are in close proximity with Pakistan and thus may cause transboundary air pollution.[46] Similar stubble burning occurs in the Pakistani state of Punjab. The Pakistani Government has in the past blamed India for smog in Lahore, which is only 20 kms (12 miles) from the international border.[47] Indian Ministers have countered this allegation and blamed the burning on the Pakistan side for polluting Indian cities. Cutting out the rhetoric, the air flow with the onset of winter months in October–November, when the burning is at its peak, is westerly. This also explains why Delhi is most affected by the burning. Because the burning happens so close to the border, undoubtedly some pollution could cross over.

---

[44] International Court of Justice, Judgment dated 25 September 1997 *Gabčíkovo-Nagymaros Project (Hungary v Slovakia)* <https://www.icj-cij.org/en/case/92/judgments> accessed 23 January 2021.

[45] International Court of Justice, Judgment dated 20 April 2010, paragraph 204 *Pulp Mills on the River Uruguay (Argentina v Uruguay)* <https://www.icj-cij.org/en/case/135/judgments> accessed 23 January 2021.

[46] BBC News, *Is India's Crop Burning Polluting Pakistan's Air?* 8 November 2019, <https://www.bbc.com/news/world-asia-india-50333985#:~:text=Pakistani%20ministers%20have%20blamed%20poor,polluting%20particles%20in%20the%20air> accessed 23 January 2021.

[47] *Id.*

II. INDIA, PAKISTAN AND SIACHEN

The Siachen glacier is one of the world's highest glaciers. It has also been the scene of continuing skirmishes between Indian and Pakistani forces. The continuation of this hostility, in this particular location, is undesirable for two reasons:[48]

(a) The land is of questionable strategic value, and taxes the economic and human resources of both sides.
(b) The area is home to a unique and fragile eco-system, which is harmed by the intermittent hostilities.

A suggestion that has gained currency is the conversion of the area into a peace park.[49] This would effectively mean the cessation of hostilities on the glacier, and allow concerted efforts from both sides to impose environmental management and preservation strategies over this shared natural resource.

III. INDIA, SRI LANKA AND THE SETHUSAMUDRAM CANAL PROJECT

This project proposes to widen the channel separating India from Sri Lanka and link the Palk Straits to the Gulf of Mannar, so as to facilitate maritime transportation between India's east and west coasts. The channel is currently too shallow, requiring vessels to go around Sri Lanka.

The project had earlier run into opposition within India, owing to the mythological bridge built by Lord Rama over the channel (Ram Setu). It was challenged in the Madras High Court[50] and then transferred to the Supreme Court of India in 2007.[51] In 2018, the government of India filed an affidavit before the court, stating that the bridge (Ram Setu) will not be damaged.[52]

The project has not, however, attracted sufficient attention in terms of its environmental fallout. Both the Palk Straits and the Gulf of Mannar are shallow eco-systems, where many varieties of aquatic flora and fauna flourish.[53] The dredging would disturb these fragile eco-systems as well as bring in external influences that would irreversibly change them. There is also a possibility that parts of northern Sri Lanka would be submerged by this project.[54]

In 2004, Coastal Action Network (CAN), filed a petition against the project's environmental impact assessment (EIA) at the Madras High Court, seeking an order to declare the public hearings for the project ineffective and not in compliance with the law. The court dismissed the petition as premature, since neither had the public hearings been completed when the

---

[48] Neal A Kemkar, *Environmental Peacemaking: Ending Conflict Between India and Pakistan on the Siachen Glacier through the Creation of a Transboundary Peace Park*, 25 Stanford Envir Law Jr 67 (2006) <http://www.uvm.edu/~shali/kemkar_siachen.pdf?&id=5> accessed 23 January 2021.

[49] *Id.*

[50] *Rama Gopalan v Union of India*, Writ Petition No. 18076 of 2007; *Dr Subramanian Swamy v Union of India*, Writ Petition No. 18223 of 2007; *Dr Subramanian Swamy v Union of India*, Writ Petition No. 18224 of 2007.

[51] Christian H Brill, *Holy Places in an Unholy World: Will Religious Beliefs Halt India's Suez of the East*, 35 North Carolina Jr Of Int'l Law & Commercial Regulation 447 (2009) <https://core.ac.uk/download/pdf/151516467.pdf > accessed 23 January 2021.

[52] Kumar Shakti Shekhar, *Affidavit on Ram Setu in Supreme Court: Modi Sarkar Fulfils 2014 Manifesto Promise*, India TodAY, 16 March 2018 <https://www.indiatoday.in/india/story/affidavit-on-ram-setu-in-supreme-court-modi-sarkar-fulfils-2014-manifesto-promise-1190821-2018-03-16> accessed 23 January 2021.

[53] Sudarshan Rodriguez, *Review of the Environmental Impacts of the Sethusamudram Ship Canal Project* 6 Indian Ocean Turtle Newsletter 16 (2007) <https://www.dakshin.org/wp-content/uploads/2013/04/sudarshan_sethu-iotn6_4.pdf> accessed 23 January 2021.

[54] Dr Lareef Zubair, *The Dangers Sri Lanka and Tamil Nadu Face From Sethusamudram* <http://www.tropicalclimate.org/docs/sethutsunamirev6.pdf> accessed 23 January 2021.

petition was filed nor had any adverse order been passed.[55] In March 2005, an environmental clearance was granted to the project on the basis of a rapid EIA report. This report was deemed questionable since it was based on insufficient and outdated data.[56] The EIA was challenged by CAN in the Madras High Court which dismissed the petition on the grounds that the petitioner should approach the National Environment Appellate Authority (NEAA).[57] Upon information that NEAA had not had a chairman since 2000, the court directed the Central Government to appoint a chairman within 30 days.[58] In July 2005, the project was inaugurated by Prime Minister Dr Manmohan Singh.[59]

The project was stayed by the Supreme Court in 2007, on environmental and religious grounds.[60] In 2010, the Supreme Court established the Pachauri Committee to carry out an extensive environmental impact assessment on the project.[61] The Committee deemed the project as economically and environmentally unfeasible, concluding that it posed a high risk to the biosphere reserve and eco-system of the region.[62] However, in 2013, the Union Government filed an affidavit before the court, rejecting the findings and conclusions of the Committee, deciding to continue with the project.[63]

Anti-Sethusamudram Canal Project activists fear that the project will lead to the loss of livelihood for approximately 15 lakh fishermen, along with the deterioration and destruction of the marine eco-system in the region.[64]

In late December 2020, the development of project had been dormant over the previous several years due to multiple litigations in the Supreme Court,[65] on ecological, religious and economic grounds.[66] The Sethusamudram Corporation has passed a resolution to end the

---

55 *O Fernandes v Tamil Nadu Pollution Control Board* MANU/TN/2411/2004.

56 *Ecological Reasons to Oppose Sethusamudram Project,* DOWN TO EARTH, 15 October 2007 <https://www.downtoearth.org.in/news/ecological-reasons-to-oppose-sethusamudram-project-6627> accessed 23 January 2021.

57 *O Fernandes, Co-convener, Coastal Action Network v Union of India* (2005)1 MAD L J 184.

58 T Rajaram & Ashutosh Das, *Need for Participatory and Sustainable Principles in India's EIA System: Lessons From the Sethusamudram Ship Channel Project*, 24 IMPACT ASSESSMENT AND PROJECT APPRAISAL 115 (2006) <https://www.tandfonline.com/doi/pdf/10.3152/147154606781765237> accessed 23 January 2021.

59 *Id.*

60 Centre for Science and Environment, India Environment Portal, *Sethusamudram Ship Canal Project* <http://www.indiaenvironmentportal.org.in/content/350820/sethusamudram-ship-canal-project/> accessed 23 January 2021; P Manoj, *Last Dredger Pulled Out, Work on Sethusamudram Grinds to a Halt*, MINT, 15 September 2009 <https://www.livemint.com/Politics/fc3gnf74bfLfPs2TopXsxJ/Last-dredger-pulled-out-work-on-Sethusamudram-grinds-to-a-h.html> accessed 23 January 2021.

61 Prakash Kamat, *Sethu Project: NIO to Carry Out Study for New Alignment*, THE HINDU, 16 January 2010 <https://www.thehindu.com/news/national/Sethu-project-NIO-to-carry-out-study-for-new-alignment/article16837747.ece> accessed 23 January 2021.

62 J Venkatesan, *'Alternative Alignment for Sethu Project Not Feasible'*, THE HINDU, 21 July 2016 <https://www.thehindu.com/news/national/alternative-alignment-for-sethu-project-not-feasible/article3594443.ece> accessed 23 January 2021.

63 Gyanant Singh, *Centre Junks Pachauri Report Will Go Ahead With Setusamudram Project*, INDIA TODAY, 23 February 2013 <https://www.indiatoday.in/mail-today/story/setusamudram-project-will-be-made-says-centre-154690-2013-02-23> accessed 23 January 2021.

64 Baibhav Mishra, *India's Sethusamudram Project: Not an Alternative for Convenient Shipping Down South*, SEANEWS, 22 May 2018 <https://seanews.co.uk/features/indias-sethusamudram-project-not-an-alternative-for-convenient-shipping-down-south/> accessed 23 January 2021.

65 C Shivakumar, *Is the Sethusamudram Project Being Laid to Rest by Litigations?* THE NEW INDIAN EXPRESS, 29 December 2020 <https://www.newindianexpress.com/cities/chennai/2020/dec/29/is-the-sethusamudram-project-being-laid-to-rest-by-litigations-2242435.html> accessed 23 January 2021.

66 P Manoj, *Sethusamudram Ship Channel Project Set To Be Beached*, THE HINDU BUSINESS LINE, 28 December 2020 <https://www.thehindubusinessline.com/economy/logistics/sethusamudram-ship-channel-project-likely-to-be-terminated/article33436612.ece> accessed 23 January 2021.

project, seeking an additional grant of Rs. 115.72 crore from the government of India to settle dues of the Dredging Corporation of India (DCI) for works it carried out at the project site along with a proposal to the Ministry of Ports, Shipping and Waterways for winding up the corporation.[67]

IV. CLIMATE CHANGE AND SOUTH ASIA

As the effects of climate change start to make themselves felt in the Indian sub-continent, the policies of individual states in the region with regard to climate change take on regional significance. For instance, increased and severe flooding in Pakistan has been linked to the effects of climate change. Similarly, Bangladesh, as a low-lying, densely populated state, is particularly vulnerable to the effects of climate change. Its territory is in great danger of being submerged or eroded by rising sea levels. In this context, India's role (along with China and the United States) in hindering the achievement of international consensus on binding emissions limits takes on added significance for India's neighbours in the sub-continent.

NOTES AND QUESTIONS

1. Do you think sub-continental environmental issues and disputes are best resolved in a South Asian regional forum or at the ICJ?

2. Do you think transboundary environmental disputes can be resolved in ordinary courts? Or is there a need for special courts qualified to judge environmental issues?

3. Do you think law and legal remedies can ever be truly effective for the resolution of disputes between states over essential natural resources?[68]

4. What is a fair basis for sharing common environmental resources by states—historical use, equality, present use, present need, future need? Consider the merits and demerits of each. Do you think efficiency of use should be a consideration in the allocation of shared resources?

5. This chapter has detailed several environmental conflicts between India and her neighbours. Despite the existence of these conflicts, on many other fronts, including trade, India maintains normal relations with all of these states except Pakistan. Why is this? Does it reflect the attachment of lower significance to environmental issues? If so, is this a desirable state of affairs?

6. Do you think transboundary environmental issues should be resolved at a bilateral level or at a regional level? Compare the river water disputes between India and Nepal with those between India and Pakistan, or India and Bangladesh. In which of these cases would you recommend a regional approach?[69]

7. How do you think climate change and its effects will impact existing disputes over the allocation of scarce and valuable natural resources?

---

[67] *Id.*

[68] See Anna Spain, *Beyond Adjudication: Resolving International Resource Disputes in an Era of Climate Change*, 30 Stanford Envir Law Jr 343 (2011) <https://scholar.law.colorado.edu/articles/190/> accessed 23 January 2021.

[69] See Bjørn-Oliver Magsig, *Overcoming State-Centrism in International Water Law: 'Regional Common Concern' as the Normative Foundation of Water Security*, 3 Goettingen Jr Of Int'l Law 317 (2011) <https://www.researchgate.net/publication/215610210_Overcoming_State-Centrism_in_International_Water_Law_%27Regional_Common_Concern%27_as_the_Normative_Foundation_of_Water_Security> accessed 23 January 2021.

INDEX

9 780192 86545